THE
BASKETBALL MANIAC'S ALMANAC

THE
BASKETBALL
MANIAC'S
ALMANAC

**The ABSOLUTELY, POSITIVELY, and WITHOUT
QUESTION GREATEST BOOK of FACTS,
FIGURES, and ASTONISHING LISTS
EVER COMPLIED**

**Compiled by the Editors of
Sports Publishing**

SPORTS
PUBLISHING

Visit our website at www.sportspubbooks.com.

10 9 8 7 6 5 4 3 2 1

Library of Congress Cataloging-in-Publication Data is available on file.

Compiled and edited by Jason Katzman

Copyedited and proofread by Ken Samelson

Cover design by David Ter-Avanesyan and Tom Lau
Cover photo credit: Getty Images

Print ISBN: 978-1-68358-439-1
Ebook ISBN: 978-1-68358-440-7

Printed in the United States of America

Found an error or typo? Please email basketballmaniacsalmanac@gmail.com so that we can correct and revise for future printings/editions.

CONTENTS

Scoring Average   29

Assists 88

Turnovers 108

Offensive Miscellany 115

2. Defense   127

Rebounds   127

Steals   160

7. **Coaches** 225

Awards 238

8. **Relatives** 242

10. **Playoffs/Finals**   257

Games/Minutes 276

Player Miscellany 280

Western Conference   440

American Basketball Association (ABA) Franchises   511

Franchises No Longer in Existence   526

INTRODUCTION

"Great players are willing to give up their own personal achievement for the achievement of the group. It enhances everybody."
—Kareem Abdul-Jabbar

"Not only is there more to life than basketball, there's a lot more to basketball than basketball."

—Phil Jackson

Throughout it's history, professional basketball has always been one thing: a team sport. While most who played growing up began by themselves—whether in their backyard or on a neighborhood hoop—a player's game must evolve to not think of just themselves, but the others that share the court. Their teammates.

While much has changed since Dr. James Naismith originally wrote the thirteen rules of "Basket Ball" in 1891, the fundamentals of the game still ring true: run, shoot, pass, defend. Without this, there is no game.

When looking at the game of baseball, statistics have been integral to the sport since the nineteenth century. It allows fans—and critics, for that matter—to compare players through the ages. While we must always take into account the evolution of the game, having the opportunity to visualize their accomplishments in the form of written statistics—especially when most were not alive when the first pioneers stepped onto the field for the first time—is a special opportunity. You know what a .300 hitter looks like, or a 20-game winner. It is something that keeps the national pastime relevant all these years later.

But the same can, and should, be said about the game of basketball.

The National Basketball League (NBL) began in 1937, and took strides that made the game available to those with the necessary skill set, no matter their race, creed, or relgion. In fact, during the 1942–43 season, with many men fighting overseas in World War II, two teams—the Toledo Jim White Chevrolets and the Chicago Studebakers—included rosters made up of numerous African American athletes, beating baseball (and Jackie Robinson) by five years.

On June 6, 1946, the Basketball Association of America (BAA) was founded, and in doing so absorbed most of the teams from the NBL.

Almost six months later, on November 1, 1946, the first game of the BAA was played between the New York Knickerbockers and Toronto Huskies, at Maple Leaf Gardens in Toronto, Canada. While the Knicks came out victorious, 68–64, it was the beginning of something special . . . even if it took several decades to rise in popularity.

After three seasons, the BAA rebranded itself as the National Basketball Association (NBA) and, since then, the game of basketball has gone on to become one of the most popular sports in the world.

Now, even though die-hard fans are able to look up the statistics of George Mikan, who was a member of the inaugural class of the Naismith Memorial Basketball Hall of Fame (located in Springfield, Massachusetts), his name is most certainly not one known in every household. But if you look at his stats, you'll find out that he averaged more than 20 points a game in five straight seasons for the Minnesota Lakers, and more than 13.5 rebounds in four straight seasons (beginning with when the NBA began keeping record). That also includes five championship rings.

The NBA celebrated its 75th Anniversary for the 2021–22 season. Per basketball-reference.com, that includes more than five thousand players and 370 coaches—not taking into account everyone else that has played a part in the league's evolution.

So . . . the question is, "How can we compare players and coaches over seventy-five years?" Well, *The Basketball Maniac's Almanac* hopes to fill that void.

Throughout these pages, the editors of Sports Publishing have worked to compile the most important, interesting, intriguing, insightful, and informative statistics we could find. From the obvious ones of who has scored the most points (Kareem Abdul-Jabbar, with 38,387) and which team has won the most championships (both the Boston Celtics and Minnesota-Los Angeles Lakers have 17), to the more obscure ones of who has the most games in which they played all 48 minutes (Wilt Chamberlain, a name you'll see often, with 539) and the team with the lowest field goal percentage to win a championship in the shot-clock era (the 1954–55 Syracuse Nationals, who shot .372 for the season).

In compiling *The Baseball Maniac's Almanac*—which this book has used a an integral source—iconic writer and statistician Bert Randolph Sugar stated the following, in his foreword:

> Statistics (or as they are known in their circumcised, smaller version of the word, "stats") have been a part of baseball—indeed, the very mortar of the sport—since the dawn of the game, even if in the beginning their number was so few they could be entered on a postcard with more than enough room left for an oversized one-cent stamp and a generous message. And those few reduced to paper could be called statistics only in the same way raisins could be called fruit—technically and only in a manner of speaking.

With baseball's popular moniker being "America's National Pastime," Sugar's goal was to give readers "a different perspective (call it a 'different view from the same pew,' if you will) on America's second most popular pastime: baseball statistics."

Our goal in compiling this almanac is to give fans of basketball the same thing: a source for all the incredible feats and moments that have taken place on the hardcourt, so that the game's history (and those who participated in helping the sport become what it is today) can be remembered and viewed in the same light as when someone tries to compare Babe Ruth to, well, anyone.

Today's fans and pundits love aguing over who is the GOAT. Is it Jordan or LeBron? But why stop there. Now, fans can add (if they haven't already) Kareem Abdul-Jabbar, Bill Russell, Wilt Chamberlain, Jerry West, Stephen Curry, Julius Erving, Elgin Baylor, Oscar Robertson, Kobe Bryant, Bob Pettit, Moses Malone, and numerous others to the conversation.

At the end of the day, we all love basketball (which is probably why you are reading this book). We hope that we have done as much of a service to the game as it has done for us. While most people have their allegiances, an appreciation for each and every player, coach, and team—whether they were members of the NBL, BAA, ABA, or NBA—is what helps the game grow.

We hope that you enjoy what you are about to read, and if even one person takes the time to look up a specific player they did not know about, watch a few videos on YouTube, or pick up a book on their life and career . . . well, then we will know that the time and effort in compiling the hundreds of different categories that appear in these pages will have all been worth it.

—Jason Katzman
Senior Editor, Sports Publishing
July 2022

SOURCES

This book would not be what it is today without the immense information available online.

Basketball-Reference.com was a large component for compiling much of the material you find in this book, especially their "Stathead" section, which allowed for the creation to some of the more quirky statistics you see herein.

The Association for Professional Basketball Research (APBR.org) was an immense help in filling in the blanks for attendance details for the early years of professional basketball.

Additional sources were used as well, including the Boxtop Box Score Project (michaelhamel.net/boxtop-aba) for detailed statistics/box scores/attendance of the ABA, and StatMuse (statmuse.com/nba) for various statistics.

ALMANAC KEY AND NOTES

Symbols

^—Player or coach is currently active, either in the league or with the team in question (where applicable).

a—Player or Team that was a member of the ABA (American Basketball Association) for the statistics in question.

*—Any additional footnotes to the statistics in question.

Statistic Dates
Not all statistics have been kept throughout the history of professional basketball. To avoid any confusion, below are the dates when such records became offical.

Offensive/Defensive Rebounds
Rebounds became an official statistic beginning in the 1950–51 NBA season, but the recording of offensive/defensive rebounds did not begin until the dates noted below.
> ABA: 1967–68 through 1975–76 (tenure of league)
> NBA: 1973–74 through present day

3-Pointers
> ABA: 1967–68 through 1975–76 (tenure of league)
> NBA: 1979–80 through present day

Steals
> 1973–74 through present day

Blocks
> 1973–74 through present day

Turnovers
> 1977–78 through present day

Additional Details

- Seasons are listed in their entirety, as opposed to a single year. We have chosen to use the 1996–97 season, as opposed to 1997. However, when a single year is listed (specifically when speaking about the playoffs), we use the year in which it took place. So if 1997 is listed as the year, it should be noted that it is from the 1996–97 season.
- A hyphen (-) used for a team name is to state that it is the same organization that has either changed cities or team names.
- A slash (/) used for a player's team entry is to state that the player changed teams mid-season.

The editors have chosen to include all rebounds—both offensive and defensive—under the "Defensive" section to avoid separating such information into two different categories.

Legend

2P%: Two Point Field Goal Percentage
2P: Two Point Field Goal
2PA: Two Point Field Goals Attempted
3P%: Three Point Field Goal Percentage
3P: Three Point Field Goal
3PA: Three Point Field Goals Attempted
3PAr: "Percentage of Field Goal Attempts from Three-Point Range"
3PM: Three Point Field Goals Made
ABA: American Basketball Association
APG: Assists Per Game
ASG: All-Star Game
AST: Assists
BAA: Basketball Association of America
BLK: Blocks
BPG: Blocks Per Game
BPM: Box Plus/Minus
COY: Coach of the Year
DIFF: Differential
DPOY: Defensive Player of the Year
DR: Defensive Rebounds
F: Fouls
FG%: Field Goal Percentage
FG: Field Goals
FGA: Field Goal Attempts
FGM: Field Goals Made
FPG: Fouls Per Game
FT%: Free Throw Percentage
FT: Free Throws
FTA: Free Throws Attempted

FTM: Free Throws Made
G: Game
GP: Games Played
HOF: Hall of Fame
Lg. Avg.: League Average
MP: Minutes Played
MPG: Minutes Per Game
MVP: Most Valuable Player
NBA: National Basketball Association
NCAA: National Collegiate Association of America
OR: Offensive Rebounds
OT: Overtime
OWS: Offensive Win Share
PER: Player Efficiency Rating
PF: Personal Fouls
PPG: Points Per Game
PTS: Points
ROY: Rookie of the Year
RPG: Rebounds Per Game
SPG: Steals Per Game
STL: Steals
TO: Turnovers
TS%: True Shooting Percentage
VORP: Value Over Replacement Player
W/L%: Win/Loss Percentage
Win%: Winning Percentage
WS: Win Share

PART 1
Individual Statistics

1

OFFENSE

Scoring

Most Points by Decade

4863	Joe Fulks
4196	Max Zaslofsky
3579	Ed Sadowski
3563	George Mikan
2987	Kenny Sailors
2972	John Logan
2936	Bob Feerick
2715	Fred Scolari
2560	Stan Miasek
2545	Belus Smawley

1950–51–1959–60

13,915	Dolph Shayes
13,399	Bob Cousy
12,728	Paul Arizin
11,689	Bill Sherman
10,776	Bob Pettit
10,153	Ed Macauley
10,093	Larry Foust
10,023	Neil Johnston
9272	Vern Mikkelsen
9063	George Yardley

1960–61–1969–70*

24,719	Wilt Chamberlain
22,009	Oscar Robertson
19,207	Elgin Baylor
19,144	Jerry West
17,228	Hal Greer
16,003	Walt Bellamy
15,560	Bailey Howell
13,512	Sam Jones
12,608	John Havlicek
12,236	Bob Boozer

1970–71–1979–80*

21,814	Kareem Abdul-Jabbar
18,525	Elvin Hayes
15,948	Pete Maravich
15,896	Bob Lanier
15,627	Bob McAdoo
15,212	Calvin Murphy
14,181	Bob Dandridge
13,787	John Havlicek
13,587	Jo Jo White
13,584	Randy Smith

1980–81–1989–90

21,133	Alex English
18,491	Moses Malone
17,974	Larry Bird
16,916	Adrian Dantley
16,695	Dominique Wilkins
15,587	Mark Aguirre
15,097	Tom Chambers
14,542	Kevin McHale
14,507	Reggie Theus
14,354	Isiah Thomas

1990–91–1999–00

20,925	Karl Malone
16,178	Mitch Richmond
16,149	David Robinson
15,773	Reggie Miller
15,595	Glen Rice
15,496	Patrick Ewing
15,261	Michael Jordan
14,944	Hakeem Olajuwon
14,687	Shaquille O'Neal
13,711	Scottie Pippen

2000–01–2009–10

21,550	Kobe Bryant
19,291	Dirk Nowitzki
17,681	Paul Pierce
17,550	Allen Iverson
16,478	Vince Carter
16,110	Tim Duncan
15,828	Antawn Jamison
15,771	Kevin Garnett
15,596	Ray Allen
15,412	Tracy McGrady

2010–11–2019–20

20,209	James Harden
18,990	LeBron James
17,834	Russell Westbrook
16,973	Kevin Durant
15,773	DeMar DeRozan
15,020	Stephen Curry
14,887	Damian Lillard
14,821	LaMarcus Aldridge
13,735	Carmelo Anthony
13,479	Blake Griffin

2020–21–2021–22

3902	Nikola Jokić
3749	Trae Young
3738	Jayson Tatum
3719	Giannis Antetokounmpo
3677	Luka Dončić
3645	Stephen Curry
3534	Devin Booker
3530	Joel Embiid
3434	DeMar DeRozan
3226	Zach LaVine

* Includes ABA.

Evolution of Scoring Record

1946–47 ... Joe Fulks, Phi. Warriors 1389	1958–59 ... Bob Pettit, St.L. Hawks 2105
1948–49 ... George Mikan, Min. Lakers 1698	1959–60 ... Wilt Chamberlain, Phi. Warriors 2707
1949–50 ... George Mikan, Min. Lakers 1865	1960–61 ... Wilt Chamberlain, Phi. Warriors 3033
1950–51 ... George Mikan, Min. Lakers 1932	1961–62 ... Wilt Chamberlain, Phi. Warriors 4029
1957–58 ... George Yardley, Det. Pistons 2001	

Most Points, Season

4029 ...... Wilt Chamberlain, Phi. Warriors, 1961–62	2649 .... Wilt Chamberlain, Phi. 76ers, 1965–66
3586 ...... Wilt Chamberlain, S.F. Warriors, 1962–63	2637 .... Charlie Scott, Vir. Squiresᵃ/Pho. Suns, 1971–72
3041 ...... Michael Jordan, Chi. Bulls, 1986–87	2633 .... Michael Jordan, Chi. Bulls, 1988–89
3033 ...... Wilt Chamberlain, Phi. Warriors, 1960–61	2596 .... Kareem Abdul-Jabbar, Mil. Bucks, 1970–71
2948 ...... Wilt Chamberlain, S.F. Warriors, 1963–64	2593 .... Kevin Durant, Ok.C. Thunder, 2013–14
2868 ...... Michael Jordan, Chi. Bulls, 1987–88	2551.......... George Gervin, S.A. Spurs, 1981–82
2832 ...... Kobe Bryant, L.A. Lakers, 2005–06	2541.......... Michael Jordan, Chi. Bulls, 1992–93
2831 ...... Bob McAdoo, Buf. Braves, 1974–75	2540.......... Karl Malone, Uta. Jazz, 1989–90
2822 ...... Kareem Abdul-Jabbar, Mil. Bucks, 1971–72	2538.......... Elgin Baylor, L.A. Lakers, 1960–61
2818 ...... James Harden, Hou. Rockets, 2018–19	2538.......... Dan Issel, Ken. Colonelsᵃ, 1971–72
2775 ...... Rick Barry, S.F. Warriors, 1966–67	2534.......... Wilt Chamberlain, S.F. Warriors/Phi. 76ers, 1964–65
2753 ...... Michael Jordan, Chi. Bulls, 1989–90	2520.......... Moses Malone, Hou. Rockets, 1981–82
2719 ...... Elgin Baylor, L.A. Lakers, 1962–63	2519.......... Spencer Haywood, Den. Rocketsᵃ, 1969–70
2719 ...... Tiny Archibald, K.C.-Oma. Kings, 1972–73	2518.......... Rick Barry, N.Y. Netsᵃ, 1971–72
2707 ...... Wilt Chamberlain, Phi. Warriors, 1959–60	

ᵃ ABA.

Most Points, Career·

38,387 .... Kareem Abdul-Jabbar	25,279 .... Rick Barry
36,928 .... Karl Malone	25,279 .... Reggie Miller
37,062 .... LeBron Jamesˆ	25,192 .... Jerry West
33,643 .... Kobe Bryant	24,941 .... Artis Gilmore
32,292 .... Michael Jordan	24,815 .... Patrick Ewing
31,560 .... Dirk Nowitzki	24,505 .... Ray Allen
31,419 .... Wilt Chamberlain	24,368 .... Allen Iverson
30,026 .... Julius Erving	23,757 .... Charles Barkley
29,580 .... Moses Malone	23,477 .... James Hardenˆ
28,596 .... Shaquille O'Neal	23,334 .... Robert Parish
28,289 .... Carmelo Anthonyˆ	23,298 .... Russell Westbrookˆ
27,482 .... Dan Issel	23,177 .... Adrian Dantley
27,313 .... Elvin Hayes	23,165 .... Dwyane Wade
26,946 .... Hakeem Olajuwon	23,149 .... Elgin Baylor
26,710 .... Oscar Robertson	22,195 .... Clyde Drexler
26,668 .... Dominique Wilkins	21,813 .... Gary Payton
26,595 .... George Gervin	21,791 .... Larry Bird
26,496 .... Tim Duncan	21,586 .... Hal Greer
26,397 .... Paul Pierce	20,941 .... Walt Bellamy
26,395 .... John Havlicek	20,936 .... Chris Paulˆ
26,071 .... Kevin Garnett	20,894 .... Pau Gasol
25,728 .... Vince Carter	20,880 .... Bob Pettit
25,613 .... Alex English	20,790 .... David Robinson
25,526 .... Kevin Durantˆ	20,558 .... LaMarcus Aldridgeˆ

continued on next page

20,497	Mitch Richmond
20,407	Joe Johnson^
20,064	Stephen Curry^

* Includes ABA.

^ Active.

Points Leaders by State of Birth

Alabama	Charles Barkley (Leeds)	23,757
Alaska	Mario Chalmers (Anchorage)	5743
Arizona	Sean Elliott (Tucson)	10,544
Arkansas	Joe Johnson^ (Little Rock)	20,405
California	Paul Pierce (Inglewood)	26,397
Colorado	Chauncey Billips (Denver)	15,802
Connecticut	Calvin Murphy (Norwalk)	17,949
Delaware	Walt Hazzard (Wilmington)	9087
Florida	Vince Carter (Daytona Beach)	25,728
Georgia	Dwight Howard^ (Atlanta)	19,485
Hawaii	Cedric Ceballos (Maui)	8693
Idaho	Luke Ridnour (Coeur d'Alene)	7740
Illinois	Dwyane Wade (Chicago)	23,165
Indiana	Larry Bird (West Baden)	21,791
Iowa	Harrison Barnes^ (Ames)	10,566
Kansas	Alvan Adams (Lawrence)	13,910
Kentucky	Allan Houston (Louisville)	14,551
Louisiana	Karl Malone (Summerfield)	36,928
Maine	Jeff Turner (Bangor)	3697
Maryland	Rudy Gay^ (Baltimore)	17,349
Massachusetts	Bill Laimbeer (Boston)	13,790
Michigan	George Gervin (Detroit)	20,708
Minnesota	Kevin McHale (Hibbing)	17,335
Mississippi	Chet Walker (Bethlehem)	18,831
Missouri	Jo Jo White (St. Louis)	14,399
Montana	Phil Jackson (Deer Lodge)	5428
Nebraska	Bob Boozer (Omaha)	12,964

Nevada	Ricky Davis (Las Vegas)	9912
New Hampshire	Matt Bonner (Concord)	4632
New Jersey	Shaquille O'Neal (Newark)	28,596
New Mexico	Bill Bridges (Hobbs)	11,012
New York	Kareem Abdul-Jabbar (New York)	38,387
North Carolina	Walt Bellamy (New Bern)	20,941
North Dakota	Doug McDermott^ (Grand Forks)	4846
Ohio	LeBron James^ (Akron)	37,062
Oklahoma	Blake Griffin^ (Oklahoma City)	14,343
Oregon	Mike Newlin (Portland)	12,507
Pennsylvania	Kobe Bryant (Philadelphia)	33,643
Rhode Island	Ernie DiGregorio (North Providence)	2997
South Carolina	Kevin Garnett (Greenville)	26,071
South Dakota	Mike Miller (Mitchell)	10,973
Tennessee	Oscar Robertson (Charlotte)	26,710
Texas	LaMarcus Aldridge^ (Dallas)	20,558
Utah	Tom Chambers (Ogden)	20,049
Vermont	N/A	N/A
Virginia	Moses Malone (Petersburg)	27,409
Washington	John Stockton (Spokane)	19,711
West Virginia	Jerry West (Chelyan)	25,192
Wisconsin	Latrell Sprewell (Milwaukee)	16,712
Wyoming	James Johnson^ (Cheyenne)	5763

District of Columbia	Kevin Durant^	25,526
Puerto Rico	J.J. Barea (Mayaguez)	7415
Virgin Islands	Tim Duncan (St. Croix)	26,496

^ Active.

All-Time Points Leaders by First Letter of Last Name

A	Abdul-Jabbar, Kareem	38,387
B	Bryant, Kobe	33,643
C	Chamberlain, Wilt	31,419
D	Duncan, Tim	26,496
E	Erving, Julius	30,026
F	Free, World B.	17,955
G	Gervin, George	26,595
H	Hayes, Elvin	27,313
I	Issel, Dan	27,482
J	James, LeBron^	37,062
K	King, Bernard	19,655
L	Lanier, Bob	19,248
M	Malone, Karl	36,928
N	Nowitzki, Dirk	31,560

O	O'Neal, Shaquille	28,596
P	Pierce, Paul	26,397
Q	Quinn, Chris	1092
R	Robertson, Oscar	26,710
S	Stockton, John	19,711
T	Theus, Reggie	19,015
U	Unseld, Wes	10,624
V	Vandeweghe, Kiki	15,980
W	Wilkins, Dominique	26,668
X	N/A	N/A
Y	Young, Thaddeus	13,473
Z	Zaslofsky, Max	7990

^ Active.

Most Points by Zodiac Sign*

Aquarius (Jan. 20–Feb. 18)	Kobe Bryant	33,643
Pisces (Feb. 19–Mar. 20)	Julius Erving	30,026
Aries (Mar. 21–Apr. 19)	Kareem Abdul-Jabbar	38,387
Taurus (Apr. 20–May 20)	George Gervin	26,595
Gemini May 21–Jun. 21)	Dirk Nowitzki	31,560
Cancer (Jun. 22–Jul.22)	Ray Allen	24,505
Leo (Jul. 23–Aug. 22)	Karl Malone	36,928
Virgo (Aug. 23–Sep. 22)	Reggie Miller	25,279
Libra (Sep. 23–Oct. 23)	Moses Malone	29,580
Scorpio (Oct. 24–Nov. 21)	Shaquille O'Neal	28,596
Sagittarius (Nov. 22–Dec. 21)	Oscar Robertson	26,710
Capricorn (Dec. 22–Jan. 19)	LeBron James^	37,062

* Includes ABA.

^ Active.

Most Times Leading League in Scoring

11	Michael Jordan	1984–85: 2313 (Chi. Bulls)
		1986–87: 3041 (Chi. Bulls)
		1987–88: 2868 (Chi. Bulls)
		1988–89: 2633 (Chi. Bulls)
		1989–90: 2753 (Chi. Bulls)
		1990–91: 2580 (Chi. Bulls)
		1991–92: 2404 (Chi. Bulls)
		1992–93: 2541 (Chi. Bulls)
		1995–96: 2491 (Chi. Bulls)
		1996–97: 2431 (Chi. Bulls)
		1997–98: 2357 (Chi. Bulls)
7	Wilt Chamberlain	1959–60: 2707 (Phi. Warriors)
		1960–61: 3033 (Phi. Warriors)
		1961–62: 4029 (Phi. Warriors)
		1962–63: 3586 (S.F. Warriors)
		1963–64: 2948 (S.F. Warriors)
		1964–65: 2534 (S.F. Warriors/Phi. 76ers)
		1965–66: 2649 (Phi. 76ers)
5	Kevin Durant	2009–10: 2472 (Ok.C. Thunder)
		2010–11: 2161 (Ok.C. Thunder)
		2011–12: 1850 (Ok.C. Thunder)
		2012–13: 2280 (Ok.C. Thunder)
		2013–14: 2593 (Ok.C. Thunder)
4	George Gervin	1977–78: 2232 (S.A. Spurs)
		1978–79: 2365 (S.A. Spurs)
		1979–80: 2585 (S.A. Spurs)
		1981–82: 2551 (S.A. Spurs)
4	Kobe Bryant	2002–03: 2461 (L.A. Lakers)
		2005–06: 2832 (L.A. Lakers)
		2006–07: 2430 (L.A. Lakers)
		2007–08: 2323 (L.A. Lakers)
4	James Harden	2014–15: 2217 (Hou. Rockets)
		2015–16: 2376 (Hou. Rockets)
		2018–19: 2818 (Hou. Rockets)
		2019–20: 2335 (Hou. Rockets)

continued on next page

3	George Mikan	1948–49: 1698 (Min. Lakers)
		1949–50: 1865 (Min. Lakers)
		1950–51: 1932 (Min. Lakers)
3	Neil Johnston	1952–53: 1564 (Phi. Warriors)
		1953–54: 1759 (Phi. Warriors)
		1954–55: 1631 (Phi. Warriors)
3	Kareem Abdul-Jabbar	1969–70: 2361 (Mil. Bucks)
		1970–71: 2596 (Mil. Bucks)
		1971–72: 2822 (Mil. Bucks)
3	Dan Issel	1970–71: 2480 (Ken. Colonels[a])
		1971–72: 2538 (Ken. Colonels[a])
		1972–73: 2292 (Ken. Colonels[a])
3	Bob McAdoo	1973–74: 2261 (Buf. Braves)
		1974–75: 2831 (Buf. Braves)
		1975–76: 2427 (Buf. Braves)
3	Shaquille O'Neal	1994–95: 2315 (Orl. Magic)
		1998–99: 1289 (L.A. Lakers)
		1999–00: 2344 (L.A. Lakers)
2	Paul Arizin	1951–52: 1674 (Phi. Warriors)
		1956–57: 1817 (Phi. Warriors)
2	Bob Pettit	1955–56: 1849 (St.L. Hawks)
		1958–59: 2105 (St.L. Hawks)
2	Julius Erving	1973–74: 2299 (N.Y. Nets[a])
		1975–76: 2462 (N.Y. Nets[a])
2	Adrian Dantley	1980–81: 2542 (Uta. Jazz)
		1983–84: 2418 (Uta. Jazz)
2	Alex English	1982–83: 2326 (Den. Nuggets)
		1985–86: 2452 (Den. Nuggets)

[a] ABA.

Consecutive Seasons Leading League in Scoring

7	Wilt Chamberlain	Phi. Warriors, 1959–60 (2707)
		Phi. Warriors, 1960–61 (3033)
		Phi. Warriors, 1961–62 (4029)
		S.F. Warriors, 1962–63 (3586)
		S.F. Warriors, 1963–64 (2948)
		S.F. Warriors/Phi. 76ers, 1964–65 (2534)
		Phi. 76ers, 1965–66 (2649)
7	Michael Jordan	Chi. Bulls, 1986–87 (3041)
		Chi. Bulls, 1987–88 (2868)
		Chi. Bulls, 1988–89 (2633)
		Chi. Bulls, 1989–90 (2753)
		Chi. Bulls, 1990–91 (2580)
		Chi. Bulls, 1991–92 (2404)
		Chi. Bulls, 1992–93 (2541)
5	Kevin Durant	Ok.C. Thunder, 2009–10 (2472)
		Ok.C. Thunder, 2010–11 (2161)
		Ok.C. Thunder, 2011–12 (1850)
		Ok.C. Thunder, 2012–13 (2280)
		Ok.C. Thunder, 2013–14 (2593)
3	George Mikan	Min. Lakers, 1948–49 (1698)
		Min. Lakers, 1949–50 (1865)
		Min. Lakers, 1950–51 (1932)

continued on next page

3	Neil Johnston	Phi. Warriors, 1952–53 (1564)
		Phi. Warriors, 1953–54 (1759)
		Phi. Warriors, 1954–55 (1631)
3	Kareem Abdul-Jabbar	Mil. Bucks, 1969–70 (2361)
		Mil. Bucks, 1970–71 (2596)
		Mil. Bucks, 1971–72 (2822)
3	Dan Issel	Ken. Colonels[a], 1970–71 (2480)
		Ken. Colonels[a], 1971–72 (2538)
		Ken. Colonels[a], 1972–73 (2292)
3	Bob McAdoo	Buf. Braves, 1973–74 (2261)
		Buf. Braves, 1974–75 (2831)
		Buf. Braves, 1975–76 (2427)
3	George Gervin	S.A. Spurs, 1977–78 (2232)
		S.A. Spurs, 1978–79 (2365)
		S.A. Spurs, 1979–80 (2585)
3	Michael Jordan	Chi. Bulls, 1995–96 (2491)
		Chi. Bulls, 1996–97 (2431)
		Chi. Bulls, 1997–98 (2357)
3	Kobe Bryant	L.A. Lakers, 2005–06 (2832)
		L.A. Lakers, 2006–07 (2430)
		L.A. Lakers, 2007–08 (2323)
2	Shaquille O'Neal	L.A. Lakers, 1998–99 (1289)
		L.A. Lakers, 1999–00 (2344)
2	James Harden	Hou. Rockets, 2014–15 (2217)
		Hou. Rockets, 2015–16 (2376)
		Hou. Rockets, 2018–19 (2818)
		Hou. Rockets, 2019–20 (2335)

[a] ABA.

Foreign-Born Players With More Than 10,000 Points, Career

31,560	Dirk Nowitzki	Germany (Würzburg)
26,946	Hakeem Olajuwon	Nigeria (Lagos)
26,668	Dominique Wilkins	France (Paris)
26,496	Tim Duncan	U.S. Virgin Islands (St. Croix)
24,815	Patrick Ewing	Jamaica (Kingston)
20,894	Pau Gasol	Spain (Barcelona)
19,473	Tony Parker	Belgium (Bruges)
17,623	Rolando Blackman	Panama (Panama City)
17,387	Steve Nash	South Africa (Johannesburg)
15,980	Kiki Vandeweghe	Germany (Wiesbaden)
15,761	Detlef Schrempf	Germany (Leverkusen)
14,321	Giannis Antetokounmpo^	Greece (Athens)
14,089	Kyrie Irving^	Australia (Melbourne)
14,043	Manu Ginóbili	Argentina (Bahía Blanca)
13,976	Carlos Boozer	Germany (Aschaffenburg)
13,647	Peja Stojaković	SR Croatia, SFR Yugoslavia (Slavonska Požega)
13,398	Vlade Divac	Serbia (Prijepolje)
13,361	Luol Deng	South Sudan (Wau)
12,989	Al Horford^	Dominican Republic (Puerto Plata)
12,871	Rik Smits	Netherlands (Eindhoven)
12,810	Mychal Thompson	Bahamas (Nassau)
12,553	Nikola Vučević^	Switzerland (Morges)

continued on next page

12,514	Marc Gasol	Spain (Barcelona)
12,203	Goran Dragić^	Slovenia (Ljubljana)
11,729	Dikembe Mutombo	Democratic Republic of the Congo (Kinshasa)
11,519	Andrew Wiggins^	Canada (Toronto)
11,327	Danilo Gallinari^	Italy (Sant'Angelo Lodigiano)
11,084	Ben Gordon	United Kingdom (London)
11,022	Hedo Türkoğlu	Turkey (Istanbul)
11,129	Zydrunas Ilgauskas	Lithuania (Kaunas)
10,962	Serge Ibaka^	Republic of the Congo (Brazzaville)
10,909	Nenê	Brazil (São Carlos)
10,364	Nikola Jokić^	Serbia (Sombor)
10,149	Nicolas Batum^	France (Lisieux)

^ Active.

Players with 5000 Points in Both ABA and NBA

	Points in ABA	Points in NBA
Rick Barry	6884	18,395
Zelmo Beaty	6100	9107
Ron Boone	12,153	5284
Joe Caldwell	5492	7127
Julius Erving	11,662	18,364
George Gervin	5887	20,708
Artis Gilmore	9362	15,579
Dan Issel	12,823	14,659
George McGinnis	7919	9090
Billy Paultz	7667	5432
James Silas	5978	5060

Playing in ABA, Scoring 10,000 Points in NBA

	Points in NBA	Points in ABA
Rick Barry	18,395	6884
Billy Cunningham	13,626	2684
Julius Erving	18,364	11,664
George Gervin	20,708	5887
Artis Gilmore	15,579	9362
Cliff Hagan	13,447	1423
Spencer Haywood	14,592	2519
Billy Knight	10,561	3340
Dan Issel	14,659	12,823
Maurice Lucas	12,339	2518
Charlie Scott	10,037	4800
Ray Scott	10,184	1445
David Thompson	11,264	282
Dan Roundfield	11,318	339

Players Scoring 1500 Points in Each of Their First Five Seasons

	Most Points in Season	Career Points
Kareem Abdul-Jabbar	2822* (1971–72, Mil. Bucks)	12,262
Carmelo Anthony^	2112 (2005–06, Den. Nuggets)	9264
Elgin Baylor	2538 (1960–61, L.A. Lakers)	10,909

continued on next page

	Most Points in Season	Career Points
Walt Bellamy	2495 (1961–62, Chi. Packers)	10,688
Dave Bing	2142* (1967–68, Det. Pistons)	9360
Larry Bird	1908 (1983–84, Bos. Celtics)	9022
Wilt Chamberlain	4029* (1961–62, Phi. Warriors)	16,303
Terry Cummings	1861 (1984–85, Mil. Bucks)	8709
Kevin Durant^	2472* (2009–10, Ok.C. Thunder)	9978
Darrell Griffith	1764 (1984–85, Uta. Jazz)	8362
Elvin Hayes	2350 (1970–71, S.D. Rockets[a])	10,713
LeBron James^	2478 (2005–06, Cle. Cavaliers)	10,689
Damian Lillard	2024 (2016–17, Por. Blazers)	8880
Hakeem Olajuwon	2034 (1988–89, Hou. Rockets)	8883
Oscar Robertson	2480 (1963–64, Cin. Royals)	11,620
David Robinson	2383* (1993–94, S.A. Spurs)	9971
Sidney Wicks	2009 (1971–72, Por. Blazers)	8882

* Led league.

^ Active.

[a] ABA.

Players Scoring 1500 Points in Rookie Season, Never Scoring 1500 Again in a Single Season

	Rookie Season	Pts	Next-Highest Point Total
Doug Moe	1967–68 (N.O. Buccaneers[a])	1884	1423 (Oak. Oaks[a], 1968–69)
Charlie Williams	1967–68 (Pit. Pipers[a])	1625	1295 (Mem. Pros[a], 1971–72)
Jim McDaniels	1971–72 (Car. Cougars[a]/Sea. Sonics)	1665	378 (Sea. Sonics, 1972–73)
Alvan Adams	1975–76 (Pho. Suns)	1519	1296 (Pho. Suns, 1976–77)
Willie Anderson	1988–89 (S.A. Spurs)	1508	1288 (S.A. Spurs, 1989–90)
O.J. Mayo	2008–09 (Mem. Grizzlies)	1516	1432 (Mem. Grizzlies, 2009–10)

[a] ABA.

Players Scoring 2000 Points in Rookie Season, Never Scoring 2000 Again in a Single Season

2031 .... Geoff Petrie*, Por. Blazers, 1970–71

2009 .... Sidney Wicks*, Por. Blazers, 1971–72

* Rookie of the Year.

Players Scoring 2000 Points in Most Consecutive Seasons

11 .... Karl Malone .... 2268 (Uta. Jazz, 1987–88)

2326 (Uta. Jazz, 1988–89)

2540 (Uta. Jazz, 1989–90)

2382 (Uta. Jazz, 1990–91)

2272 (Uta. Jazz, 1991–92)

2217 (Uta. Jazz, 1992–93)

2063 (Uta. Jazz, 1993–94)

2187 (Uta. Jazz, 1994–95)

2106 (Uta. Jazz, 1995–96)

2249 (Uta. Jazz, 1996–97)

2190 (Uta. Jazz, 1997–98)

7 .... Oscar Robertson .... 2165 (Cin. Royals, 1960–61)

2432 (Cin. Royals, 1961–62)

2264 (Cin. Royals, 1962–63)

2480 (Cin. Royals, 1963–64)

2279 (Cin. Royals, 1964–65)

continued on next page

		2378 (Cin. Royals, 1965–66)
		2412 (Cin. Royals, 1966–67)
7	Alex English	2082 (Den. Nuggets, 1981–82)
		2326 (Den. Nuggets, 1982–83)
		2167 (Den. Nuggets, 1983–84)
		2262 (Den. Nuggets, 1984–85)
		2414 (Den. Nuggets, 1985–86)
		2345 (Den. Nuggets, 1986–87)
		2000 (Den. Nuggets, 1987–88)
7	Dominique Wilkins	2217 (Atl. Hawks, 1984–85)
		2366 (Atl. Hawks, 1985–86)
		2294 (Atl. Hawks, 1986–87)
		2397 (Atl. Hawks, 1987–88)
		2099 (Atl. Hawks, 1988–89)
		2138 (Atl. Hawks, 1989–90)
		2101 (Atl. Hawks, 1990–91)
7	Michael Jordan	3041 (Chi. Bulls, 1986–87)
		2868 (Chi. Bulls, 1987–88)
		2633 (Chi. Bulls, 1988–89)
		2753 (Chi. Bulls, 1989–90)
		2580 (Chi. Bulls, 1990–91)
		2404 (Chi. Bulls, 1991–92)
		2541 (Chi. Bulls, 1992–93)
7	LeBron James	2175 (Cle. Cavaliers, 2004–05)
		2478 (Cle. Cavaliers, 2005–06)
		2132 (Cle. Cavaliers, 2006–07)
		2250 (Cle. Cavaliers, 2007–08)
		2304 (Cle. Cavaliers, 2008–09)
		2258 (Cle. Cavaliers, 2009–10)
		2111 (Mia. Heat, 2010–11)
6	Wilt Chamberlain	2707 (Phi. Warriors, 1959–60)
		3033 (Phi. Warriors, 1960–61)
		4029 (Phi. Warriors, 1961–62)
		3586 (S.F. Warriors, 1962–63)
		2948 (S.F. Warriors, 1963–64)
		2534 (S.F. Warriors/Phi. 76ers, 1964–65)
6	George Gervin	2232 (S.A. Spurs, 1977–78)
		2365 (S.A. Spurs, 1978–79)
		2585 (S.A. Spurs, 1979–80)
		2221 (S.A. Spurs, 1980–81)
		2551 (S.A. Spurs, 1981–82)
		2043 (S.A. Spurs, 1982–83)
6	James Harden	2217 (Hou. Rockets, 2014–15)
		2376 (Hou. Rockets, 2015–16)
		2356 (Hou. Rockets, 2016–17)
		2191 (Hou. Rockets, 2017–18)
		2818 (Hou. Rockets, 2018–19)
		2335 (Hou. Rockets, 2019–20)
5	Kareem Abdul-Jabbar	2361 (Mil. Bucks, 1969–70)
		2596 (Mil. Bucks, 1970–71)
		2822 (Mil. Bucks, 1971–72)
		2292 (Mil. Bucks, 1972–73)

continued on next page

		2191 (Mil. Bucks, 1973–74)
5	Kareem Abdul-Jabbar	2361 (Mil. Bucks, 1969–70)
		2596 (Mil. Bucks, 1970–71)
		2822 (Mil. Bucks, 1971–72)
		2292 (Mil. Bucks, 1972–73)
		2191 (Mil. Bucks, 1973–74)
5	Julius Erving	2290 (Vir. Squires^a, 1971–72)
		2268 (Vir. Squires^a, 1972–73)
		2299 (N.Y. Nets, 1973–74)
		2343 (N.Y. Nets, 1974–75)
		2462 (N.Y. Nets, 1975–76)
4	Bob Pettit	2120 (St.L. Hawks, 1960–61)
		2429 (St.L. Hawks, 1961–62)
		2241 (St.L. Hawks, 1962–63)
		2190 (St.L. Hawks, 1963–64)
4	Elvin Hayes	2327 (S.D. Rockets, 1968–69)
		2256 (S.D. Rockets, 1969–70)
		2350 (S.D. Rockets, 1970–71)
		2063 (Hou. Rockets, 1971–72)
4	Dan Issel	2480 (Ken. Colonels^a, 1970–71)
		2538 (Ken. Colonels^a, 1971–72)
		2292 (Ken. Colonels^a, 1972–73)
		2118 (Ken. Colonels^a, 1973–74)
4	Larry Bird	2295 (Bos. Celtics, 1984–85)
		2115 (Bos. Celtics, 1985–86)
		2076 (Bos. Celtics, 1986–87)
		2275 (Bos. Celtics, 1987–88)
4	Kobe Bryant	2832 (L.A. Lakers, 2005–06)
		2430 (L.A. Lakers, 2006–07)
		2323 (L.A. Lakers, 2007–08)
		2201 (L.A. Lakers, 2008–09)

^a ABA.

Scoring 2000 Points in a Season with Multiple Franchises

LeBron James^	Cle. Cavaliers	2175 (2004–05)
		2478 (2005–06)
		2132 (2006–07)
		2250 (2007–08)
		2304 (2008–09)
		2258 (2009–10)
		2251* (2017–18)
	Mia. Heat	2111 (2010–11)
		2036 (2012–13)
		2089 (2013–14)
Kareem Abdul-Jabbar	Mil. Bucks	2361* (1969–70)
		2596* (1970–71)
		2822* (1971–72)
		2292 (1972–73)
		2191 (1973–74)
	L.A. Lakers	2275 (1975–76)
		2152 (1976–77)
		2034 (1979–80)
		2095 (1980–81)

continued on next page

Wilt Chamberlain	Phi.-S.F. Warriors	2707* (1959–60)
		3033* (1960–61)
		4029* (1961–62)
		3586* (1962–63)
		2948* (1963–64)
	S.F. Warriors/Phi. 76ers	2534* (1964–65)
	Phi. 76ers	2649 (1965–66)
Kevin Durant^	Ok.C. Thunder	2472* (2009–10)
		2161* (2010–11)
		2280* (2011–12)
		2593* (2012–13)
		2029 (2015–16)
	G.S. Warriors	2027 (2018–19)
Allen Iverson	Phi. 76ers	2207 (2000–01)
		2262 (2002–03)
		2302* (2004–05)
		2377 (2005–06)
	Den. Nuggets	2164 (2007–08)
Rick Barry	S.F. Warriors	2059 (1965–66)
		2775* (1966–67)
	N.Y. Nets^a	2518 (1971–72)
	G.S. Warriors	2009 (1973–74)
		2450 (1974–75)
Bob McAdoo	Buf. Braves	2261* (1973–74)
		2831* (1974–75)
		2427* (1975–76)
	N.Y. Knicks	2097 (1977–78)
Shaquille O'Neal	Orl. Magic	2377 (1993–94)
		2315* (1994–95)
	L.A. Lakers	2344* (1999–00)
		2125 (2000–01)
Vince Carter	Tor. Raptors	2107 (1999–00)
		2070 (2000–01)
	N.J. Nets	2070 (2006–07)
Pete Maravich	Atl. Hawks	2063 (1972–73)
		2107 (1973–74)
	N.O. Jazz	2273* (1976–77)
Tracy McGrady	Orl. Magic	2065 (2000–01)
		2407 (2002–03)
	Hou. Rockets	2003 (2004–05)
Kiki Vandeweghe	Den. Nuggets	2186 (1982–83)
		2295 (1983–84)
	Por. Blazers	2122 (1986–87)
Carmelo Anthony^	Den. Nuggets	2122 (2005–06)
	N.Y. Knicks	2112 (2013–14)

* Led league.
^ Active.
a ABA.

Scoring 2500 Points, Season

4029 .... Wilt Chamberlain, Phi. Warriors, 1961–62
3586 .... Wilt Chamberlain, S.F. Warriors, 1962–63
3041 .... Michael Jordan, Chi. Bulls, 1986–87
3033 .... Wilt Chamberlain, Phi. Warriors, 1960–61
2948 .... Wilt Chamberlain, S.F. Warriors, 1963–64
2868 .... Michael Jordan, Chi. Bulls, 1987–88
2832 .... Kobe Bryant, L.A. Lakers, 2005–06
2831 .... Bob McAdoo, Buf. Braves, 1974–75
2822 .... Kareem Abdul-Jabbar, Mil. Bucks, 1971–72
2818 .... James Harden, Hou. Rockets, 2018–19
2775 .... Rick Barry, S.F. Warriors, 1966–67
2753 .... Michael Jordan, Chi. Bulls, 1989–90
2719 .... Tiny Archibald, K.C.-Oma. Kings, 1972–73
2719 .... Elgin Baylor, L.A. Lakers, 1962–63
2707 .... Wilt Chamberlain, Phi. Warriors, 1959–60
2649 .... Wilt Chamberlain, Phi. 76ers, 1965–66
2633 .... Michael Jordan, Chi. Bulls, 1988–89
2596 .... Kareem Abdul-Jabbar, Mil. Bucks, 1970–71
2593 .... Kevin Durant, Ok.C. Thunder, 2013–14
2585 .... George Gervin, S.A. Spurs, 1979–80
2580 .... Michael Jordan, Chi. Bulls, 1990–91
2558 .... Russell Westbrook, Ok.C. Thunder, 2016–17
2551 .... George Gervin, S.A. Spurs, 1981–82
2541 .... Michael Jordan, Chi. Bulls, 1992–93
2540 .... Karl Malone, Uta. Jazz, 1989–90
2538 .... Elgin Baylor, L.A. Lakers, 1960–61
2538 .... Dan Issel, Ken. Colonels[a], 1971–72
2534 .... Wilt Chamberlain, S.F. Warriors/Phi. 76ers, 1964–65
2520 .... Moses Malone, Hou. Rockets, 1981–82
2519 .... Spencer Haywood, Den. Rockets[a], 1969–70
[a] ABA.

Players with 5000 Total Points in First Three NBA Seasons

9769	Wilt Chamberlain	5599	Sidney Wicks
7779	Kareem Abdul-Jabbar	5543	Dave Bing
6933	Elvin Hayes	5495	George Mikan
6887	Walt Bellamy	5440	Walter Davis
6861	Oscar Robertson	5414	Bob Rule
6585	Shaquille O'Neal	5405	Carmelo Anthony
6533	Bob McAdoo	5401	Dominique Wilkins
6354	Elgin Baylor	5375	Terry Cummings
6307	LeBron James	5307	Karl-Anthony Towns
6172	Tiny Archibald	5301	Mitch Richmond
5978	Earl Monroe	5264	Bob Lanier
5967	Kevin Durant	5264	Mark Aguirre
5762	Michael Jordan	5250	Karl Malone
5672	David Robinson	5247	Larry Bird

continued on next page

5218	Pete Maravich	5100	Donovan Mitchell
5200	Marques Johnson	5090	Vince Carter
5188	Jerry West	5070	Bob Pettit
5133	Geoff Petrie	5044	Hakeem Olajuwon
5115	Luka Dončić	5020	Ralph Sampson
5104	Glenn Robinson	5006	Derrick Rose

Youngest Players to 5000 Points Scored

Age		Games
21 years, 22 days	LeBron James	197
21 years, 133 days	Kevin Durant	205
21 years, 292 days	Carmelo Anthony	223
22 years, 68 days	Luka Dončić	194
22 years, 81 days	Dwight Howard	306
22 years, 86 days	Devin Booker	245
22 years, 116 days	Kobe Bryant	292
22 years, 122 days	Karl-Anthony Towns	234
22 years, 191 days	Derrick Rose	240
22 years, 226 days	Tracy McGrady	301
22 years, 237 days	Andrew Wiggins	246
22 years, 292 days	Shaquille O'Neal	187
22 years, 332 days	Giannis Antetokounmpo	327
22 years, 337 days	Anthony Davis	246
22 years, 346 days	Kyrie Irving	239
22 years, 355 days	Chris Bosh	279
23 years, 12 days	Shareef Abdur-Rahim	237
23 years, 27 days	Stephon Marbury	262
23 years, 32 days	Jayson Tatum	269
23 years, 33 days	John Drew	235
23 years, 38 days	Trae Young	208
23 years, 93 days	Gilbert Arenas	258
23 years, 94 days	Russell Westbrook	274
23 years, 100 days	Josh Smith	361
23 years, 106 days	Bob McAdoo	194

Players Scoring 10,000 Points Before Their 25th Birthday

LeBron James	23 years, 59 days
Kevin Durant	24 years, 33 days
Kobe Bryant	24 years, 194 days
Carmelo Anthony	24 years, 251 days
Tracy McGracy	24 years, 272 days

Most Points Scored, Rookie Season

2707*	Wilt Chamberlain**, Phi. Warriors, 1959–60
2519*	Spencer Haywood**, Den. Rockets[a], 1969–70
2495	Walt Bellamy**, Chi. Packers, 1961–62
2480*	Dan Issel**, Ken. Colonels[a], 1970–71
2361*	Kareem Abdul-Jabbar**, Mil. Bucks, 1969–70
2327*	Elvin Hayes, S.D. Rockets, 1968–69
2313*	Michael Jordan**, Chi. Bulls, 1984–85
2290	Julius Erving, Vir. Squires[a], 1971–72

continued on next page

2276 .... Charlie Scott**, Vir. Squires[a], 1970–71
2165 .... Oscar Robertson**, Cin. Royals, 1960–61
2158 .... David Thompson**, Den. Nuggets[a], 1975–76
2059 .... Rick Barry**, S.F. Warriors, 1965–66
2031 .... Geoff Petrie**, Por. Blazers, 1970–71
2009 .... Sidney Wicks**, Por. Blazers, 1971–72
2003 .... Artis Gilmore**, Ken. Colonels[a], 1971–72
1993.................. David Robinson**, S.A. Spurs, 1989–90
1991 .... Earl Monroe**, Bal. Bullets, 1967–68
1959......................... Walter Davis*, Pho. Suns, 1977–78
1909.......................... Bernard King, N.J. Nets, 1977–78
1893................. Shaquille O'Neal**, Orl. Magic, 1992–93
1884* .... Doug Moe, N.O. Buccaneers[a], 1967–68
1880....................... Pete Maravich, Atl. Hawks, 1970–71
1875.................... Connie Hawkins, Pit. Pipers[a], 1967–68
1874...................... Ron Harper, Cle. Cavaliers, 1986–87
1849.............. Marvin Barnes**, Spirits of St.L.[a], 1974–75
1845.................... Blake Griffin**, L.A. Clippers, 2010–11
1787 .... Allen Iverson**, Phi. 76ers, 1996–97
1781 .... Bill Cartwright, N.Y. Knicks, 1979–80
1772...................... Kelly Tripucka, Det. Pistons, 1981–82
1765................... Darel Carrier, Ken. Colonels[a], 1967–68

* Led league.
** Rookie of the Year.
[a] ABA.

Players with 20,000 Points, Career*

38,387 .... Kareem Abdul-Jabbar	25,279 .... Reggie Miller
37,062 .... LeBron James^	25,279 .... Rick Barry
36,928 .... Karl Malone	25,192 .... Jerry West
33,643 .... Kobe Bryant	24,941 .... Artis Gilmore
32,292 .... Michael Jordan	24,815 .... Patrick Ewing
31,560 .... Dirk Nowitzki	24,505 .... Ray Allen
31,419 .... Wilt Chamberlain	24,368 .... Allen Iverson
30,026 .... Julius Erving	23,757 .... Charles Barkley
29,580 .... Moses Malone	23,477 .... James Harden^
28,596 .... Shaquille O'Neal	23,298 .... Russell Westbrook^
28,289 .... Carmelo Anthony^	23,334 .... Robert Parish
27,482 .... Dan Issel	23,177 .... Adrian Dantley
27,313 .... Elvin Hayes	23,165 .... Dwyane Wade
26,946 .... Hakeem Olajuwon	23,149 .... Elgin Baylor
26,710 .... Oscar Robertson	22,195 .... Clyde Drexler
26,668 .... Dominique Wilkins	21,813 .... Gary Payton
26,595 .... George Gervin	21,791 .... Larry Bird
26,496 .... Tim Duncan	21,586 .... Hal Greer
26,397 .... Paul Pierce	20,941 .... Walt Bellamy
26,395 .... John Havlicek	20,936 .... Chris Paul^
26,071 .... Kevin Garnett	20,894 .... Pau Gasol
25,728 .... Vince Carter	20,880 .... Bob Pettit
25,613 .... Alex English	20,790 .... David Robinson
25,526 .... Kevin Durant^	20,558 .... LaMarcus Aldridge^

continued on next page

20,497	Mitch Richmond	20,049	Tom Chambers
20,407	Joe Johnson^	20,042	Antawn Jamison
20,064	Stephen Curry^		

* Includes ABA.
^ Active.

Fewest Games Played to 20,000 Points

Games		Career Points
499	Wilt Chamberlain	31,419
620	Michael Jordan	32,292
671	Oscar Robertson	26,710
684	Kareem Abdul-Jabbar	38,387
711	Elgin Baylor	23,149
713	Allen Iverson	24,368
717	Jerry West	25,192
726	LeBron James^	37,062
727	Shaquille O'Neal	28,596
737	Kevin Durant^	25,526
747	George Gervin	26,595
753	Bob Pettit	20,880
763	Dominique Wilkins	26,668
772	Karl Malone	36,928
774	Adrian Dantley	23,177
793	Carmelo Anthony^	28,289
802	James Harden^	23,477
806	Larry Bird	21,791
811	Kobe Bryant	33,643
833	Hakeem Olajuwon	26,946

^ Active.

Players with 20,000 Career Points, Never Having a 2000-Point Season

Pts		Most Points in a Season
21,813	Gary Payton	1982 (Sea. Sonics, 1999–00)
20,833	Chris Paul^	1781 (N.O. Hornets, 2008–09)
23,334	Robert Parish	1590 (Bos. Celtics, 1981–82)
20,407	Joe Johnson^	1779 (Atl. Hawks, 2007–08)
21,586	Hal Greer	1976 (Phi. 76ers, 1967–68)
20,894	Pau Gasol	1628 (Mem. Grizzlies, 2005–06)
26,071	Kevin Garnett	1987* (Min. T'Wolves, 2003–04)
24,505	Ray Allen	1955 (Sea. Sonics, 2005–06)
20,454	LaMarcus Aldridge^	1769 (Por. Blazers, 2010–11)

^ Active.
* Led league.

Players Appearing in 500 Games, Not Scoring 2000 Points, Career

Pts		GP
1913	Ryan Hollins	518
1826	Charles Jones	726
1717	Greg Kite	680
1647	Scott Hastings	578
1599	Manute Bol	624
1594	Brian Scalabrine	520
1451	Ed Nealy	540

continued on next page

Pts		GP
1319	Ryan Bowen	507
1185	DeSagana Diop	601

Most Points by Age

Teens	Twenties	Thirties	Forties
1759 ... Kobe Bryant	21,539 .... LeBron James	19,387 ... Karl Malone	1941 .. Kareem Abdul-Jabbar
1725 ... Carmelo Anthony	21,522 .... Wilt Chamberlain	17,808 ... Kareem Abdul-Jabbar	1706 .. Robert Parish
1654 ... LeBron James	20,589 .... Michael Jordan	14,749 ... Alex English	1433 .. Vince Carter
1624 ... Kevin Durant	19,860 .... Kobe Bryant	14,197 ... Dirk Nowitzki	1088 .. John Stockton
1526 ... Luka Dončić	19,734 .... George Gervin	13,787 ... John Havlicek	671 .. Michael Jordan
1392 ... Anthony Edwards	19,289 .... Kevin Durant	13,161 .... LeBron James	576 .. Manu Ginóbili
1387 ... Andrew Wiggins	18,743 .... Oscar Robertson	12,812 ... Reggie Miller	560 .. Kevin Willis
1112 ... Jayson Tatum	18,638 .... Kareem Abdul-Jabbar	12,756 ... Elvin Hayes	554 .. Karl Malone
1057 ... Stephon Marbury	18,627 .... James Harden	12,729 ... Robert Parish	373 .. Dirk Nowitzki
1054 ... D'Angelo Russell	18,374 .... Julius Erving*	12,522 ... Patrick Ewing	364 .. Dikembe Mutombo

* 11,662 in ABA and 6712 in NBA.

Most Points, Not Playing College Basketball

Pts		Education
37,062	LeBron James^	High School (Saint Vincent-Saint Mary: Akron, OH)
33,643	Kobe Bryant	High School (Lower Merion: Philadelphia, PA)
31,560	Dirk Nowitzki	Overseas (Würzburg, Germany)
27,409	Moses Malone	High School (Petersburg: Petersburg, VA)
26,071	Kevin Garnett	High School (Mauldin: Mauldin, SC; Farragut Career Academy: Chicago, IL)
20,894	Pau Gasol	Overseas (Barcelona, Spain)
19,485	Dwight Howard^	High School (Southwest Atlanta Christian Academy: Atlanta, GA)
19,473	Tony Parker	Overseas (Paris, France)
18,381	Tracy McGrady	High School (Auburndale: Auburndale, FL; Mount Zio Christian Academy: Durham, NC)
15,994	Amar'e Stoudemire	High School (Lake Wales: Lake Wales, FL; Mount Zio Christian Academy: Durham, NC; Emmanuel Christian Academy: Durham, NC; West Orange*: Winter Garden, FL; Cypress Creek: Orlando, FL)
15,579	Rashard Lewis	High School (Alief Elsik: Houston, TX)
15,239	Lou Williams	High School (South Gwinnett: Snellville, GA)

^ Active.

* Attended school, but did not play basketball.

Most Points, Game

100	Wilt Chamberlain, Phi. Warriors	vs. N.Y. Knicks (Mar. 2, 1962)
81	Kobe Bryant, L.A. Lakers	vs. Tor. Raptors (Jan. 22, 2006)
78	Wilt Chamberlain, Phi. Warriors	vs. L.A. Lakers (Dec. 8, 1961)
73	Wilt Chamberlain, Phi. Warriors	vs. Chi. Packers (Jan. 13, 1962)
73	Wilt Chamberlain, S.F. Warriors	@ N.Y. Knicks (Nov. 16, 1962)
73	David Thompson, Den. Rockets	@ Det. Pistons (Apr. 9, 1978)
72	Wilt Chamberlain, S.F. Warriors	@ L.A. Lakers (Nov. 3, 1962)
71	Elgin Baylor, L.A. Lakers	@ N.Y. Knicks (Nov. 15, 1960)
71	David Robinson, S.A. Spurs	@ L.A. Clippers (Apr. 24, 1994)
70	Wilt Chamberlain, S.F. Warriors	@ Syr. Nationals (Mar. 10, 1963)
70	Devin Booker, Pho. Suns	@ Bos. Celtics (Mar. 24, 2017)

continued on next page

69	Michael Jordan, Chi. Bulls	@ Cle. Cavaliers (Mar. 28, 1990)
68	Wilt Chamberlain, Phi. 76ers	@ Chi. Bulls (Dec. 16, 1967)
68	Pete Maravich, N.O. Jazz	vs. N.Y. Knicks (Feb. 25, 1977)
67	Wilt Chamberlain, Phi. Warriors	vs. N.Y. Knicks (Mar. 9, 1961)
67	Wilt Chamberlain, Phi. Warriors	@ St.L. Hawks (Feb. 17, 1962)
67	Wilt Chamberlain, Phi. Warriors	vs. N.Y. Knicks (Feb. 25, 1962)
67	Wilt Chamberlain, S.F. Warriors	vs. L.A. Lakers (Jan. 11, 1963)
67	Larry Miller, Car. Cougars[a]	vs. Mem. Pros[a] (Mar. 18, 1972)
66	Wilt Chamberlain, L.A. Lakers	vs. Pho. Suns (Feb. 9, 1969)
65	Wilt Chamberlain, Phi. Warriors	@ St.L. Hawks (Feb. 27, 1962)
65	Wilt Chamberlain, Phi. Warriors	@ Cin. Royals (Feb. 13, 1962)
65	Wilt Chamberlain, Phi. 76ers	vs. L.A. Lakers (Feb. 7, 1966)
65	Kobe Bryant, L.A. Lakers	vs. Por. Blazers (Mar. 16, 2007)

[a] ABA.

Most Points Scored in First Career Game
NBA

			Age
43	Wilt Chamberlain, Phi. Warriors	@ N.Y. Knicks (Oct. 24, 1959)	23 years, 64 days
35	Frank Selvy, Mil. Hawks	vs. Bos. Celtics (Nov. 30, 1954)	22 years, 21 days
32	Maurice Stokes, Roc. Royals	vs. N.Y. Knicks (Nov. 5, 1955)	22 years, 141 days
32	John Drew, Atl. Hawks	@ Chi. Bulls (Oct. 18, 1974)	20 years, 18 days
31	Isiah Thomas, Det. Pistons	vs. Mil. Bucks (Oct. 30, 1981)	20 years, 183 days
30	Willie Anderson, S.A. Spurs	vs. L.A. Lakers (Nov. 5, 1988)	21 years, 302 days
30	Allen Iverson, Phi. 76ers	vs. Mil. Bucks (Nov. 1, 1996)	21 years, 147 days
30	Lamar Odom, L.A. Clippers	vs. Sea. Sonics (Nov. 2, 1999)	19 years, 361 days
29	Walt Bellamy, Chi. Packers	@ N.Y. Knicks (Oct. 19, 1961)	22 years, 87 days
29	Kareem Abdul-Jabbar, Mil. Bucks	vs. Det. Pistons (Oct. 18, 1969)	22 years, 185 days
29	Gordan Giriček, Mem. Grizzlies	vs. Dal. Mavericks (Oct. 30, 2002)	25 years, 132 days
28	Danny Finn, Phi. Warriors	vs. Mil. Hawks (Jan. 22, 1953)	24 years, 238 days
27	Ron Anderson, Cle. Cavaliers	@ Phi. 76ers (Oct. 26, 1984)	26 years, 11 days
27	Jerry Stackhouse, Phi. 76ers	vs. Was. Bullets (Nov. 3, 1995)	20 years, 363 days
27	Bobby Jackson, Den. Nuggets	vs. S.A. Spurs (Oct. 31, 1997)	24 years, 232 days
27	P.J. Washington, Cha. Hornets	vs. Chi. Bulls (Oct. 23, 2019)	21 years, 61 days
27	Chris Duarte, Ind. Pacers	@ Cha. Hornets (Oct. 20, 2021)	24 years, 129 days
26	Cleo Hill, St.L. Hawks	vs. Cin. Royals (Oct. 21, 1961)	23 years, 150 days
26	Magic Johnson, L.A. Lakers	@ S.D. Clippers (Oct. 12, 1979)	20 years, 59 days
26	Darrell Griffith, Uta. Jazz	vs. Por. Blazers (Oct. 10, 1980)	22 years, 116 days
26	Mitchell Wiggins, Chi. Bulls	vs. N.J. Nets (Oct. 29, 1983)	24 years, 31 days
26	Mahmoud Abdul-Rauf, Den. Nuggets	@ Pho. Suns (Nov. 10, 1990)	21 years, 246 days
26	Donyell Marshall, Min. T'Wolves	@ Den. Nuggets (Nov. 4, 1994)	21 years, 170 days
26	Jahlil Okafor, Phi. 76ers	@ Bos. Celtics (Oct. 28, 2015)	19 years, 317 days

ABA

			Age
41	Dan Anderson, N.J. Americans	vs. Pit. Pipers (Oct. 23, 1967)	24 years, 250 days
39	Willis Thomas, Den. Rockets	vs. Ana. Amigos (Oct. 15, 1967)	30 years, 287 days
34	Bob Verga, Dal. Chaparrals	vs. Ana. Amigos (Oct. 16, 1967)	22 years, 39 days
34	Connie Hawkins, Dal. Chaparrals	@ N.J. Americans (Oct. 23, 1967)	25 years, 98 days
33	Andrew Anderson, Oak. Oaks	vs. Ana. Amigos (Oct. 13, 1967)	22 years, 99 days
32	Charlie Williams, Pit. Pipers	@ N.J. Americans (Oct. 23, 1967)	24 years, 48 days
32	Jim McDaniels, Car. Cougars	vs. Vir. Squires (Oct. 15, 1971)	23 years, 196 days

continued on next page

			Age
30	Spencer Haywood, Den. Rockets	vs. N.O. Buccaneers (Oct. 19, 1969)	20 years, 180 days
30	Bo Lamar, S.D. Conquistadors	@ S.A. Spurs (Oct. 10, 1973)	22 years, 186 days
29	Charlie Scott, Vir. Squires	vs. Pit. Condors (Oct. 17, 1970)	21 years, 306 days
29	Artis Gilmore, Ken. Colonels	vs. N.Y. Nets (Oct. 16, 1971)	22 years, 25 days
28	Ralph Simpson, Den. Rockets	@ Uta. Stars (Oct. 14, 1970)	21 years, 65 days
28	David Thompson, Den. Nuggets	@ S.D. Sails (Oct. 24, 1975)	21 years, 103 days
27	Jimmy Jones, N.O. Buccaneers	vs. Hou. Mavericks (Oct. 19, 1967)	22 years, 291 days
25	John Beasley, Dal. Chaparrals	vs. Ana. Amigos (Oct. 16, 1967)	23 years, 253 days

Most Points in a Loss

			Score
78	Wilt Chamberlain, Phi. Warriors	vs L.A. Lakers, Dec. 12, 1961	151–147
73	David Thompson, Den. Nuggets	@ Det. Pistons, Apr. 9, 1978	139–137
72	Wilt Chamberlain, S.F. Warriors	@ L.A. Lakers, Nov. 3, 1962	127–115
70	Wilt Chamberlain, S.F. Warriors	@ Syr. Nationals, Mar. 10, 1963	163–148
70	Devin Booker, Pho. Suns	@ Bos. Celtics, Mar. 24, 2017	130–120
67	Wilt Chamberlain, Phi. Warriors	@ St.L. Hawks, Feb. 17, 1962	128–121
67	Wilt Chamberlain, Phi. Warriors	vs. N.Y. Knicks, Feb. 25, 1962	145–139
67	Wilt Chamberlain, S.F. Warriors	vs. L.A. Lakers, Jan. 11, 1963	134–129
65	Wilt Chamberlain, Phi. Warriors	@ Cin. Royals, Feb. 13, 1962	152–132
64	Michael Jordan, Chi. Bulls	vs. Orl. Magic, Jan. 16, 1993	128–124
63	Wilt Chamberlain, S.F. Warriors	vs. L.A. Lakers, Dec. 14, 1962	120–118
63	Wilt Chamberlain, S.F. Warriors	@ Phi. 76ers, Nov. 26, 1964	128–117
63	Julius Erving, N.Y. Nets[a]	@ S.D. Conquistadors[a], Feb. 14, 1975	176–166
63	George Gervin, S.A. Spurs	@ N.O. Jazz, April 9, 1978	153–132
62	Wilt Chamberlain, Phi. Warriors	@ Bos. Celtics, Jan. 14, 1962	145–136
61	Wilt Chamberlain, S.F. Warriors	vs. Cin. Royals, Nov. 21, 1962	145–139
61	Michael Jordan, Chi. Bulls	vs. Atl. Hawks, April 16, 1987	117–114
60	Bernard King, N.Y. Knicks	vs. N.J. Nets, Dec. 25, 1984	120–114
60	Kemba Walker, Cha. Hornets	vs. Phi. 76ers, Nov. 17, 2018	122–119
60	Damian Lillard, Por. Blazers	vs. Brk. Nets, Nov. 8, 2019	119–115
60	Bradley Beal, Was. Wizards	@ Phi. 76ers, Jan. 6, 2021	141–136

[a] ABA.

Most Consecutive Games Scoring 20 Points, Regular Season

		First Game of Streak	Last Game of Streak
126	Wilt Chamberlain	Oct. 19, 1961	Jan. 19, 1963
92	Wilt Chamberlain	Feb. 26, 1963	Mar. 18, 1964
79	Oscar Robertson	Oct. 22, 1963	Oct. 20, 1964
74	Connie Hawkins[a]	Dec. 31, 1967	Mar. 14, 1969
72	Michael Jordan	Dec. 29, 1987	Dec. 6, 1988
72	Kevin Durant	Nov. 23, 2015	Nov. 9, 2016
71	Kareem Abdul-Jabbar	Nov. 21, 1971	Nov. 8, 1972
70	Kareem Abdul-Jabbar	Feb. 6, 1970	Jan. 20, 1971
69	Michael Jordan	Nov. 24, 1990	Apr. 19, 1991
64	Elgin Baylor	Feb. 16, 1961	Oct. 23, 1962
63	Kobe Bryant	Dec. 9, 2005	Nov. 3, 2006
63	Dan Issel[a]	Oct. 25, 1972	Feb. 24, 1973
62	Wilt Chamberlain	Feb. 14, 1960	Jan. 22, 1961
57	James Harden	Dec. 8, 2018	Apr. 9, 2019

continued on next page

		First Game of Streak	Last Game of Streak
57	Allen Iverson	Dec. 10, 2004	Apr. 18, 2005
57	Bob McAdoo	Jan. 7, 1975	Nov. 21, 1975
56	Wilt Chamberlain	Oct. 24, 1959	Feb. 9, 1960
56	Kevin Durant	Dec. 22, 2013	Dec. 2, 2014
55	George Gervin	Mar. 10, 1981	Feb. 12, 1982
54	Elgin Baylor	Jan. 14, 1960	Nov. 25, 1960
52	Jerry West	Feb. 6, 1965	Dec. 7, 1965

ᵃ ABA.

Most Consecutive Games Scoring 30 Points, Regular Season

		First Game of Streak	Last Game of Streak
65	Wilt Chamberlain	Nov. 4, 1961	Feb. 22, 1962
32	James Harden	Dec. 13, 2018	Feb. 21, 2019
31	Wilt Chamberlain	Feb. 25, 1962	Dec. 8, 1962
25	Wilt Chamberlain	Nov. 11, 1960	Dec. 27, 1960
23	Larry Jonesᵃ	Feb. 1, 1969	Mar. 18, 1969
20	Wilt Chamberlain	Jan. 30, 1964	Mar. 1, 1964
18	Elgin Baylor	Dec. 20, 1961	Oct. 23, 1962
16	Kareem Abdul-Jabbar	Feb. 2, 1972	Mar. 1, 1972
16	Kobe Bryant	Jan. 29, 2003	Feb. 28, 2003
16	Wilt Chamberlain	Jan. 7, 1960	Jan. 31, 1960
16	Connie Hawkinsᵃ	Nov. 15, 1968	Dec. 20, 1968

ᵃ ABA.

Most 50-Point Games, Season

45	Wilt Chamberlain, Phi. Warriors, 1961–62
30	Wilt Chamberlain, S.F. Warriors, 1962–63
10	Kobe Bryant, L.A. Lakers, 2006–07
9	Wilt Chamberlain, S.F. Warriors, 1963–64
9	Wilt Chamberlain, S.F. Warriors/Phi. 76ers, 1964–65
9	James Harden, Hou. Rockets, 2018–19
8	Wilt Chamberlain, Phi. Warriors, 1960–61
8	Michael Jordan, Chi. Bulls, 1986–87
6	Rick Barry, S.F. Warriors, 1966–67
6	Kobe Bryant, L.A. Lakers, 2005–06
6	Damian Lillard, Por. Blazers, 2019–20

Most 50-Point Games, Career

118	Wilt Chamberlain
31	Michael Jordan
25	Kobe Bryant
23	James Harden^
19	Rick Barry
17	Elgin Baylor
14	LeBron James^
12	Damian Lillard^
11	Allen Iverson
10	Kareem Abdul-Jabbar
10	Stephen Curry^

^ Active

Youngest to Score 50 Points in a Game

Age		Pts
20 years, 52 days	Brandon Jennings, Mil. Bucks (vs. G.S. Warriors), Nov. 14, 2009	55
20 years, 80 days	LeBron James, Cle. Cavaliers (@ Tor. Raptors), Mar. 20, 2005	56
20 years, 145 days	Devin Booker, Pho. Suns (@ Bos. Celtics), Mar. 24, 2017	70
20 years, 345 days	LeBron James, Cle. Cavaliers (@ Mil. Bucks), Dec. 10, 2005	52
20 years, 358 days	Spencer Haywood, Den. Rocketsᵃ (vs. L.A. Starsᵃ), Apr. 15, 1970	59
20 years, 360 days	Kevin Porter, Hou. Rockets (vs. Mil. Bucks), Apr. 29, 2021	50
21 years, 22 days	LeBron James, Cle. Cavaliers (@ Uta. Jazz), Jan. 21, 2006	51
21 years, 154 days	Trae Young, Atl. Hawks (vs. Mia. Heat), Feb. 20, 2020	50
21 years, 229 days	David Thompson, Den. Nuggetsᵃ (vs. S.A. Spursᵃ), Feb. 27, 1976	50
21 years, 261 days	Rick Barry, S.F. Warriors (@ N.Y. Knicks), Dec. 14, 1965	57
21 years, 309 days	Allen Iverson, Phi. 76ers (@ Cle. Cavaliers), Apr. 12, 1997	50
21 years, 348 days	Jamal Mashburn, Dal. Mavericks (@ Chi. Bulls), Nov. 12, 1994	50

ᵃ ABA.

Oldest to Score 50 Points in a Game

Age		Pts
39 years, 20 days	Jamal Crawford, Pho. Suns (@ Dal. Mavericks), Apr. 9, 2019	51
38 years, 315 days	Michael Jordan, Was. Wizards (vs. Cha. Hornets), Dec. 29, 2001	51
37 years, 234 days	Kobe Bryant, L.A. Lakers (vs. Uta. Jazz), Apr. 13, 2016	60
37 years, 71 days	LeBron James, L.A. Lakers (vs. Was. Wizards), Mar. 11, 2022	50
37 years, 65 days	LeBron James, L.A. Lakers (vs. G.S. Warriors), Mar. 5, 2022	56
35 years, 64 days	Alex English, Den. Nuggets (@ Mia. Heat), Mar. 10, 1989	51
34 years, 257 days	Karl Malone, Uta. Jazz (@ G.S. Warriors), Apr. 7, 1998	56
34 years, 92 days	Bernard King, Was. Bullets (vs. Uta. Jazz), Mar. 6, 1991	50
34 years, 25 days	Bernard King, Was. Bullets (vs. Den. Nuggets), Dec. 29, 1990	52
33 years, 362 days	Rick Barry, G.S. Warriors (vs. N.Y. Knicks), Mar. 25, 1978	55
33 years, 339 days	Michael Jordan, Chi. Bulls (vs. N.Y. Knicks), Jan. 21, 1997	51
33 years, 323 days	LeBron James, L.A. Lakers (@ Mia. Heat), Nov. 18, 2018	51
33 years, 317 days	Andre Miller, Por. Blazers (@ Dal. Mavericks), Jan. 30, 2010	52
33 years, 263 days	Michael Jordan, Chi. Bulls (@ Mia. Heat), Nov. 6, 1996	50
33 years, 215 days	Rick Barry, G.S. Warriors (vs. Phi. 76ers), Oct. 29, 1977	51
33 years, 175 days	LaMarcus Aldridge, S.A. Spurs (vs. Ok.C. Thunder), Jan. 10, 2019	56
33 years, 185 days	Kevin Durant, Brk. Nets (vs. N.Y. Knicks), Mar. 13, 2022	53
33 years, 74 days	Kevin Durant, Brk. Nets (@ Det. Pistons), Dec. 12, 2021	51
33 years, 31 days	Clifford Robinson, Pho. Suns (vs. Den. Nuggets), Jan. 16, 2000	50
33 years, 29 days	Stephen Curry, G.S. Warriors (vs. Den. Nuggets), Apr. 12, 2021	53
33 years, 19 days	Michael Jordan, Chi. Bulls (vs. Det. Pistons), Mar. 7, 1996	53

Most Points, Last Season in League

1758....... Willie Somerset, Hou. Mavericks[a]/N.Y. Nets[a], 1968–69	1325....... George Gervin, Chi. Bulls, 1985–86
1706....... Paul Arizin, Phi. Warriors, 1961–62	1322....... John Havlicek, Bos. Celtics, 1977–78
1666....... Reggie Lewis, Bos. Celtics, 1992–93	1287....... Clyde Drexler, Hou. Rockets, 1997–98
1640....... Michael Jordan, Was. Wizards, 2002–03	1282....... Dave DeBusschere, N.Y. Knicks, 1973–74
1564....... Dražen Petrović, N.J. Nets, 1992–93	1161....... Kobe Bryant, L.A. Lakers, 2015–16
1550....... Rudy LaRusso, S.F. Warriors, 1968–69	1149....... Jimmy Walker, K.C. Kings, 1975–76
1510....... Reggie Theus, N.J. Nets, 1990–91	1140....... Sam Jones, Bos. Celtics, 1968–69
1473....... George Yardley, Syr. Nationals, 1959–60	1124....... Bob Pettit, St.L. Hawks, 1964–65
1461....... Chet Walker, Chi. Bulls, 1974–75	1111....... Ralph Beard, Ind. Olympians, 1950–51
1429....... Alex Groza, Ind. Olympians, 1950–51	1107....... Bill Keller, Ind. Pacers[a], 1975–76
1363....... Geoff Petrie, Por. Blazers, 1975–76	1105....... Dick Garmaker, N.Y. Knicks, 1960–61
1344....... Jim Hadnot, Oak. Oaks[a], 1967–68	

[a]ABA.

Scoring 50 Points in a Game, Playing Less Than 30 Minutes

	Pts	MP	
Klay Thompson, G.S. Warriors	60	29	vs. Ind. Pacers (Dec. 5, 2016)
C.J. McCollum, Por. Blazers	50	29	vs. Chi. Bulls (Jan. 31, 2018)
Damian Lillard, Por. Blazers	50	29	@ Sac. Kings (Feb. 9, 2018)
Klay Thompson, G.S. Warriors	52	27	@ Chi. Bulls (Oct. 29, 2018)
Joel Embiid, Phi. 76ers	50	27	vs. Orl. Magic (Jan. 19, 2022)

Fewest Field Goal Attempts in 50-Point Game

FG		Pts		FT	3P
12-for-17 (.706)	Adrian Dantley, Uta. Jazz	50	vs. Dal. Mavericks (Oct. 31, 1980)	26-for-29 (.900) .. 0-for-0 (.000)	
12-for-19 (.632)	Willie Burton, Phi. 76ers	53	vs. Mia. Heat (Dec. 13, 1994)	24-for-28 (.860) .. 5-for-8 (.625)	
13-for-20 (.650)	Damian Lillard, Por. Blazers	50	vs. N.O. Pelicans (Mar. 16, 2021)	18-for-18 (1.000) ... 6-for-13 (.462)	
17-for-21 (.650)	Giannis Antetokounmpo, Mil. Bucks	50	vs. Ind. Pacers (Feb. 15, 2022)	14-for-18 (.778) .. 2-for-3 (.667)	

continued on next page

FG		Pts		FT	3P
11-for-22 (.500)	Kevin Martin, Sac. Kings	50	@ G.S. Warriors (Apr. 1, 2009)	23-for-26 (.890)	5-for-11 (.455)
14-for-22 (.636)	Eric Gordon, Hou. Rockets	50	@ Uta. Jazz (Jan. 27, 2020)	16-for-20 (.800)	6-for-11 (.545)
20-for-23 (.870)	Wilt Chamberlain, Phi. 76ers	53	@ Sea. Sonics (Dec. 20, 1967)	13-for-26 (.500)	N/A
14-for-23 (.609)	Damian Lillard, Por. Blazers	50	vs. Ind. Pacers (Jan. 26, 2020)	14-for-16 (.880)	8-for-12 (.667)
19-for-23 (.826)	Kyrie Irving, Brk. Nets	54	vs. Chi. Bulls (Jan. 31, 2020)	9-for-10 (.900)	7-for-9 (.778)
17-for-23 (.739)	Fred VanVleet, Tor. Raptors	54	@ Orl. Magic (Feb. 2, 2021)	9-for-9 (1.000)	11-for-14 (.786)
17-for-23 (.739)	Joel Embiid, Phi. 76ers	50	vs. Orl. Magic (Jan. 19, 2022)	15-for-17 (.890)	1-for-4 (.250)
17-for-24 (.708)	Alonzo Mourning, Mia. Heat	50	vs. Was. Bullets (Mar. 29, 1996)	16-for-17 (.950)	0-for-0 (.000)
16-for-24 (.667)	Dirk Nowitzki, Dal. Mavericks	51	vs. G.S. Warriors (Mar. 23, 2006)	16-for-17 (.950)	3-for-4 (.750)
16-for-24 (.667)	Carmelo Anthony, Den. Nuggets	50	vs. Hou. Rockets (Feb. 7, 2011)	16-for-18 (.890)	2-for-3 (.667)
15-for-24 (.625)	Jimmy Butler, Chi. Bulls	52	vs. Cha. Hornets (Jan. 2, 2017)	21-for-22 (.960)	1-for-4 (.250)
15-for-24 (.625)	Stephen Curry, G.S. Warriors	51	vs. Was. Wizards (Oct. 24, 2018)	10-for-10 (1.000)	11-for-16 (.688)
16-for-24 (.667)	James Harden, Hou. Rockets	60	vs. Atl. Hawks (Nov. 30, 2019)	20-for-23 (.870)	8-for-14 (.571)
14-for-24 (.583)	Stephen Curry, G.S. Warriors	53	vs. Den. Nuggets (Apr. 12, 2021)	15-for-16 (.940)	10-for-18 (.556)

Least Amount of Games Played Before First 40-Point Game

Game #		Pts	
1	Wilt Chamberlain, Phi. Warriors	43	@ N.Y. Knicks (Oct. 24, 1959)
1	Dan Anderson, N.J. Americans[a]	41	vs. Pit. Pipers[a] (Oct. 23, 1967)
3	Frank Selvy, Mil. Hawks	42	vs. Min. Lakers (Dec. 2, 1954)
3	John Drew, Atl. Hawks	41	vs. Phi. 76ers (Oct. 22, 1974)
3	John Brisker, Pit. Pipers[a]	42	@ Ind. Pacers[a] (Oct. 29, 1969)
4	Alex Groza, Ind. Olympians	41	@ N.Y. Knicks (Nov. 10, 1949)
4	Dan Issel, Ken. Colonels[a]	43	@ The Floridians[a] (Oct. 20, 1970)
5	Stephen Chubin, Ana. Amigos[a]	42	@ Ken. Colonels[a] (Oct. 24, 1967)
6	Ticky Burden, Vir. Squires[a]	45	@ S.D. Sails[a] (Nov. 1, 1975)
7	Levern Tart, Oak. Oaks[a]	49	@ Ana. Amigos[a] (Oct. 31, 1967)
7	Kareem Abdul-Jabbar, Mil. Bucks[*]	43	vs. Bos. Celtics (Oct. 28, 1969)
7	Marvin Barnes, Spirits of St.L.[a]	48	vs. S.D. Conquistadors[a] (Oct. 29, 1974)
7	Bernard King, N.J. Nets[*]	41	vs. Phi. 76ers (Nov. 4, 1977)
7	Brandon Jennings, Mil. Bucks	55	vs. G.S. Warriors (Nov. 14, 2009)
9	Walt Bellamy, Chi. Packers[*]	45	vs. Cin. Royals (Nov. 11, 1961)
9	Mark Aguirre, Dal. Mavericks[*]	42	vs. G.S. Warriors (Nov. 14, 1981)
9	Michael Jordan, Chi. Bulls	45	vs. S.A. Spurs (Nov. 13, 1984)
10	Carl Braun, N.Y. Knicks	47	@ Pro. Steamrollers (Dec. 6, 1947)
10	Jim McDaniels, Car. Cougars[a]	45	@ Ind. Pacers[a] (Nov. 2, 1971)

[a] ABA.

[*] Team lost game.

Least Amount of Games Played Before First 50-Point Game

Game #		Pts	
7	Brandon Jennings, Mil. Bucks	55	vs. G.S. Warriors (Nov. 14, 2009)
8	Wilt Chamberlain, Phi. Warriors	55	@ Cin. Royals (Nov. 12, 1959)
13	Elvin Hayes, S.D. Rockets	54	vs. Det. Pistons (Nov. 13, 1968)
30	Rick Barry, S.F. Warriors[*]	57	@ N.Y. Knicks (Dec. 14, 1965)
43	Larry Jones, Den. Rockets[a]	52	vs. Oak. Oaks[a] (Nov. 28, 1967)
48	Bo Lamar, S.D. Conquistadors[a]	50	vs. Ind. Pacers (Jan. 13, 1974)
49	George Mikan, Min. Lakers	53	@ Bal. Bullets (Feb. 26, 1949)
58	David Thompson, Den. Nuggets[a]	50	vs. S.A. Spurs[a] (Feb. 27, 1976)
61	Elgin Baylor, Min. Lakers	55	vs. Cin. Royals (Feb. 25, 1959)
62	Earl Monroe, Bal. Bullets[*]	56	vs. L.A. Lakers (Feb. 13, 1968)
67	Kareem Abdul-Jabbar, Mil. Bucks	51	vs. Sea. Sonics (Feb. 21, 1970)

continued on next page

Game #		Pts	
68	Marvin Barnes, Spirits of St.L.[a]	54	vs. Mem. Sounds[a] (Mar. 16, 1975)
72	Louie Dampier, Ken. Colonels[a]	54	vs. Ind. Pacers[a] (Mar. 22, 1968)
72	Allen Iverson, Phi. 76ers*	50	@ Cle. Cavaliers (Apr. 12, 1997)
73	Kevin Porter, Hou. Rockets	50	vs. Mil. Bucks (Apr. 29, 2021)
82	Dan Issel, Ken. Colonels[a]	51	vs. Car. Cougars[a] (Mar. 28, 1971)

[a] ABA.

* Team lost game.

Players Scoring 49 Points in a Game, Never Scoring 50

Scoring 49

World B. Free	Dec. 2, 1979 (S.D. Clippers vs. Den. Rockets)
	Dec. 16, 1979 (S.D. Clippers vs. Det. Pistons)
Bob Love	Feb. 4, 1973 (Chi. Bulls vs. Mil. Bucks)
	Feb. 6, 1973 (Chi. Bulls vs. K.C.-Oma. Kings)
Mark Aguirre	Jan. 28, 1985 (Dal. Mavericks vs. Phi. 76ers)
Paul Arizin	Feb. 17, 1961 (Phi. Warriors vs. Bos. Celtics)
Otis Birdsong	Jan. 29, 1980 (K.C. Kings @ Den. Nuggets)
Larry Cannon	Dec. 26, 1970 (Den. Rockets[a] vs. Vir. Squires[a])
Terry Catledge	Jan. 13, 1990 (Orl. Magic vs. G.S. Warriors)
Brandon Ingram^	Jan. 16, 2020 (N.O. Pelicans vs. Uta. Jazz)
Willie Naulls	Feb. 7, 1961 (N.Y. Knicks vs. Det. Pistons)
Bob Rule	Nov. 15, 1969 (Sea. Sonics vs. Phi. 76ers)
Cazzie Russell	Dec. 11, 1973 (G.S. Warriors vs. Hou. Rockets)
Latrell Sprewell	Dec. 11, 2001 (N.Y. Knicks vs. Bos. Celtics)
Levern Tart	Oct. 31, 1967 (Oak. Oaks[a] vs. Ana. Amigos[a])
Bob Verga	Mar. 27, 1971 (Car. Cougars[a] @ Vir. Squires[a])
Antoine Walker	Jan. 7, 1998 (Bos. Celtics @ Was. Wizards)
Paul Westphal	Feb. 21, 1980 (Pho. Suns @ Det. Pistons)

[a] ABA.

^ Active.

Most Points Scored in a Game from Age 39 On

Age

51	Jamal Crawford, Pho. Suns	39 Years, 20 Days	Apr. 9, 2019 (vs. Dal. Mavericks), Loss
45	Michael Jordan, Was. Wizards	39 Years, 349 Days	Feb. 1, 2003 (vs. N.O. Hornets), Win
43	Michael Jordan, Was. Wizards	40 Years, 4 Days	Feb. 21, 2003 (vs. N.J. Nets), Win
41	Michael Jordan, Was. Wizards	39 Years, 321 Days	Jan. 4, 2003 (vs. Ind. Pacers), Win
40	Karl Malone, Uta. Jazz	39 Years, 231 Days	Mar. 12, 2003 (vs. Orl. Magic), Win
39	Michael Jordan, Was. Wizards	40 Years, 20 Days	Mar. 9, 2003 (vs. N.Y. Knicks), Loss
39	Reggie Miller, Ind. Pacers	39 Years, 206 Days	Mar. 18, 2005 (vs. L.A. Lakers), Win
37	Michael Jordan, Was. Wizards	39 Years, 6 Days	Feb. 23, 2002 (vs. Mia. Heat), Loss
36	Reggie Miller, Ind. Pacers	39 Years, 176 Days	Feb. 16, 2005 (vs. Por. Blazers), Win
35	Michael Jordan, Was. Wizards	40 Years, 10 Days	Feb. 27, 2003 (vs. Hou. Rockets), Win

Scoring 20 Points or More in a Loss, Career

LeBron James^	365
Karl Malone	361
Kareem Abdul-Jabbar	355
Kobe Bryant	343

Scoring 30 Points or More in a Loss, Career

Wilt Chamberlain	201
Michael Jordan	165
LeBron James^	160
Oscar Robertson	156

continued on next page

Carmelo Anthony^	326		Kobe Bryant	151
George Gervin	322		George Gervin	138
Elvin Hayes	319		Kareem Abdul-Jabbar	135
Dominique Wilkins	315		Rick Barry	135
Mitch Richmond	309		Allen Iverson	135
Antawn Jamison	304		Elgin Baylor	134
Allen Iverson	301		Adrian Dantley	130
Adrian Dantley	300		Dominique Wilkins	118
^ Active.			^Active.	

Scoring 40 Points or More In a Loss, Career

Wilt Chamberlain	107
Michael Jordan	52
Kobe Bryant	40
Elgin Baylor	31
Oscar Robertson	30
Rick Barry	29
Bob McAdoo	29
George Gervin	27
Allen Iverson	25
Russell Westbrook^	24
Bradley Beal^	22
James Harden^	22
Julius Erving	21
Bernard King	21
Kevin Durant^	20

^Active.

Scoring 50 Points or More in a Loss, Career

Wilt Chamberlain	37
Michael Jordan	8
Kobe Bryant	7
James Harden^	6
Allen Iverson	5
Rick Barry	4
Bernard King	4
Bob McAdoo	3
Dominique Wilkins	3
Kevin Durant^	3
Damian Lillard^	3
Bradley Beal^	3
Devin Booker^	3

^Active.

Most Points Scored in a Game without Committing a Foul

73	Wilt Chamberlain, S.F. Warriors	@ N.Y. Knicks	(Nov. 16, 1962)
72	Wilt Chamberlain, S.F. Warriors*	@ L.A. Lakers	(Nov. 3, 1962)
62	Stephen Curry, G.S. Warriors	vs. Por. Blazers	(Jan. 3, 2021)
61	Wilt Chamberlain, Phi. Warriors	vs. St.L. Hawks	(Feb. 22, 1962)
61	Wilt Chamberlain, S.F. Warriors	vs. Syr. Nationals	(Dec. 11, 1962)
61	Wilt Chamberlain, S.F. Warriors	vs. St.L. Hawks	(Dec. 18, 1962)
61	Michael Jordan, Chi. Bulls	@ Det. Pistons	(Mar. 4, 1987)
60	Klay Thompson, G.S. Warriors	vs. Ind. Pacers	(Dec. 5, 2016)
59	Wilt Chamberlain, Phi. Warriors	vs. N.Y. Knicks	(Feb. 8, 1962)
59	Wilt Chamberlain, S.F. Warriors	vs. N.Y. Knicks	(Oct. 30, 1962)
59	Damian Lillard, Por. Blazers	vs. Uta. Jazz	(Apr. 8, 2017)
58	Wilt Chamberlain, Phi. Warriors	@ Cin. Royals	(Feb. 25, 1961)
58	Wilt Chamberlain, Phi. Warriors	@ N.Y. Knicks	(Mar. 4, 1962)
57	Wilt Chamberlain, Phi. Warriors	@ Cin. Royals	(Dec. 19, 1961)
56	Wilt Chamberlain, Phi. Warriors*	@ Syr. Nationals	(Mar. 1, 1961)
56	Wilt Chamberlain, S.F. Warriors	vs. Det. Pistons	(Oct. 23, 1962)
56	LeBron James, Cle. Cavaliers*	@ Tor. Raptors	(Mar. 20, 2005)
56	LeBron James, L.A. Lakers	vs. G.S. Warriors	(Mar. 5, 2022)
55	Wilt Chamberlain, Phi. Warriors	@ Det. Pistons	(Dec. 20, 1961)
55	Wilt Chamberlain, S.F. Warriors	@ L.A. Lakers	(Mar. 14, 1964)
55	Tiny Archibald, Cin. Royals	vs. Por. Blazers	(Feb. 23, 1972)
55	Rick Barry, G.S. Warriors	vs. Phi. 76ers	(Jan. 23, 1975)
55	George Gervin, S.A. Spurs	@ Ind. Pacers	(Jan. 23, 1980)

continued on next page

55	Tony Parker, S.A. Spurs	@ Min. T'Wolves (Nov. 5, 2008)
55	Kyrie Irving, Cle. Cavaliers	vs. Por. Blazers (Jan. 28, 2015)
54	Allen Iverson, Phi. 76ers	@ Mil. Bucks (Dec. 18, 2004)
53	Wilt Chamberlain, Phi. Warriors	vs. N.Y. Knicks (Oct. 21, 1961)
53	Wilt Chamberlain, Phi. Warriors	vs. St.L. Hawks (Jan. 5, 1962)
53	Wilt Chamberlain, S.F. Warriors*	@ Bal. Bullets (Jan. 3, 1965)
53	Wilt Chamberlain, Phi. 76ers	vs. L.A. Lakers (Jan. 25, 1966)
53	Wilt Chamberlain, Phi. 76ers	vs. L.A. Lakers (Mar. 18, 1968)
53	Phil Chenier, Bal. Bullets	vs. Por. Blazers (Dec. 6, 1972)
53	Allen Iverson, Phi. 76ers*	@ Atl. Hawks (Dec. 23, 2005)
52	Wilt Chamberlain, Phi. Warriors*	@ Cin. Royals (Jan. 11, 1962)
52	Jimmy Butler, Chi. Bulls	vs. Cha. Hornets (Jan. 2, 2017)
52	D'Angelo Russell, G.S. Warriors*	@ Min. T'Wolves (Nov. 8, 2019)
51	Vernon Maxwell, Hou. Rockets	vs. Cle. Cavaliers (Jan. 26, 1991)
50	Wilt Chamberlain, Phi. Warriors	vs. Syr. Nationals (Feb. 4, 1962)
50	Wilt Chamberlain, S.F. Warriors	vs. Det. Pistons (Oct. 26, 1962)
50	Michael Jordan, Chi. Bulls	vs. Den. Nuggets (Mar. 24, 1992)
50	Lou Williams, L.A. Clippers	@ G.S. Warriors (Jan. 10, 2018)
50	Damian Lillard, Por. Blazers	vs. Ind. Pacers (Jan. 26, 2020)
50	Eric Gordon, Hou. Rockets	@ Uta. Jazz (Jan. 27, 2020)
50	Stephen Curry, G.S. Warriors	vs. Atl. Hawks (Nov. 8, 2021)

* Team lost game.

Most Games Scoring 20 Points without Committing a Foul, Career

161	LeBron James^	
105	Allen Iverson	
99	Kevin Durant^	
91	Wilt Chamberlain	
85	Dominique Wilkins	
84	Derrick Rose^	
77	Rolando Blackman	
74	Damian Lillard^	
74	Kemba Walker^	
67	Jeff Malone	
65	Latrell Sprewell	
63	Reggie Miller	
63	Steve Nash	
61	Jamal Crawford	
61	Tracy McGrady	
61	Tony Parker	

^ Active.

Most Points Scored in a Quarter (1996–97—Present)

Pts		Quarter	
37	Klay Thompson, G.S. Warriors	3rd	vs. Sac. Kings (Jan. 23, 2015)
34	Kevin Love, Cle. Cavaliers	1st	vs. Por. Blazers (Nov. 23, 2016)
33	Carmelo Anthony, Den. Nuggets	3rd	vs. Min. T'Wolves (Dec. 10, 2008)
32	Karl-Anthony Towns, Min. T'Wolves	3rd	@ S.A. Spurs (Mar. 14, 2022)
30	Kobe Bryant, L.A. Lakers	3rd	vs. Dal. Mavericks (Dec. 20, 2005)
30	Kobe Bryant, L.A. Lakers	3rd	vs. Uta. Jazz (Nov. 30, 2006)
29	James Harden, Hou. Rockets	3rd	vs. Atl. Hawks (Nov. 30, 2019)
29	Brandon Jennings, Mil. Bucks	3rd	vs. G.S. Warriors (Nov. 14, 2009)
29	Joe Johnson, Brk. Nets	3rd	vs. Phi. 76ers (Dec. 16, 2013)
29	Dirk Nowitzki, Dal. Mavericks	4th	vs. Uta. Jazz (Nov. 3, 2009)
29	Isaiah Thomas, Bos. Celtics	4th	vs. Mia. Heat (Dec. 30, 2016)

Most Points Scored in a Game without a Turnover

62	Carmelo Anthony, N.Y. Knicks	vs. Cha. Bobcats (Jan. 24, 2014)
60	Klay Thompson, G.S. Warriors	vs. Ind. Pacers (Dec. 5, 2016)
60	Jayson Tatum, Bos. Celtics	vs. S.A. Spurs (Apr. 30, 2021)

continued on next page

59	Damian Lillard, Por. Blazers	vs. Uta. Jazz (Apr. 8, 2017)
57	Reggie Miller, Ind. Pacers	@ Cha. Hornets (Nov. 28, 1992)
56	Kobe Bryant, L.A. Lakers	vs. Mem. Grizzlies (Jan. 14, 2002)
54	Michael Jordan, Chi. Bulls	vs. Cle. Cavaliers (Nov. 3, 1989)
54	Damon Stoudamire, Por. Blazers	@ N.O. Hornets (Jan. 14, 2005)
53	Allan Houston, N.Y. Knicks	@ L.A. Lakers (Feb. 16, 2003)
53	Allen Iverson, Phi. 76ers	@ Atl. Hawks (Dec. 23, 2005)
52	Michael Jordan, Chi. Bulls	vs. Cha. Hornets (Mar. 12, 1993)
52	Brandon Roy, Por. Blazers	vs. Pho. Suns (Dec. 18, 2008)
51	Michael Jordan, Chi. Bulls	@ Was. Bullets (Mar. 19, 1992)
51	Kobe Bryant, L.A. Lakers	@ Den. Nuggets (Feb. 12, 2003)
51	Damian Lillard, Por. Blazers	vs. G.S. Warriors (Feb. 19, 2016)
50	Moses Malone, Was. Bullets	@ N.J. Nets (Apr. 8, 1987)
50	Michael Jordan, Chi. Bulls	@ Mia. Heat (Nov. 6, 1996)
50	Clifford Robinson, Pho. Suns	vs. Den. Nuggets (Jan. 16, 2000)
50	Allan Houston, N.Y. Knicks	vs. Mil. Bucks (Mar. 16, 2003)
50	Rashard Lewis, Sea. Sonics	@ L.A. Clippers (Oct. 31, 2003)
50	Carmelo Anthony, N.Y. Knicks	@ Mia. Heat (Apr. 2, 2013)
50	Kyrie Irving, Brk. Nets	vs. Min. T'Wolves (Oct. 23, 2019)
50	Giannis Antetokounmpo, Mil. Bucks	vs. Uta. Jazz (Nov. 25, 2019)

Most Games Played without Scoring a Point (Min. 20 Minutes Played)

		Career	Career GP
57	Ben Wallace	1996–97—2011–12 (16 seasons)	1088
35	Dennis Rodman	1986–87—1999–00 (14 seasons)	911
29	Jason Kidd	1994–95—2012–13 (19 seasons)	1391
13	Gary Payton	1990–91—2006–07 (17 seasons)	1335
12	Wes Unseld	1968–69—1980–81 (13 seasons)	984
10	Nate Thurmond	1963–64—1976–77 (14 seasons)	964
8	Joe Dumars	1985–86—1998–99 (14 seasons)	1018
7	Dennis Johnson	1976–77—1989–90 (14 seasons)	1100
6	Grant Hill	1994–95—2002–03, 2004–05—2012–13 (18 seasons)	1026
5	K.C. Jones	1958–59—1966–67 (9 seasons)	676
5	Dikembe Mutombo	1991–92—2008–09 (18 seasons)	1196
5	Andy Phillip	1947–48—1957–58 (11 seasons)	701
5	Guy Rodgers	1958–59—1969–70 (12 seasons)	892

Most Starts without Scoring a Point, Career

Charles Jones	98	Ervin Johnson	65	Tree Rollins	50
Jason Collins	87	Mark Eaton	58	Jon Koncak	49
Ben Wallace	78	Caldwell Jones	52	Marc Iavaroni	45
Joel Przybilla	70	Kendrick Perkins	51		

Most Points Per Minute, Game

PPM		Pts	MP	
2.08	Wilt Chamberlain, Phi. Warriors	100	48	vs. N.Y. Knicks (Mar. 2, 1962)
2.07	Klay Thompson, G.S. Warriors	60	29	vs. Ind. Pacers (Dec. 5, 2016)
1.96	Klay Thompson, G.S. Warriors	52	27	@ Chi. Bulls (Oct. 29, 2018)
1.96	James Harden, Hou. Rockets	60	31	vs. Atl. Hawks (Nov. 30, 2019)
1.93	Kobe Bryant, L.A. Lakers	81	42	vs. Tor. Raptors (Jan. 22, 2006)

continued on next page

PPM		Pts	MP	
1.91	George Gervin, S.A. Spurs	63	33	@ N.O. Jazz (Apr. 9, 1978)
1.89	Kobe Bryant, L.A. Lakers	62	33	vs. Dal. Mavericks (Dec. 20, 2005)
1.85	Karl Malone, Uta. Jazz	61	33	vs. Mil. Bucks (Jan. 27, 1990)
1.85	Joel Embiid, Phi. 76ers	50	27	vs. Orl. Magic (Jan. 19, 2022)
1.72	Kyrie Irving, Brk. Nets	60	35	@ Orl. Magic (Mar. 15, 2022)
1.71	CJ McCollum, Por. Blazers	50	29	vs. Chi. Bulls (Jan. 31, 2018)
1.70	David Thompson, Den. Nuggets	73	43	@ Det. Pistons (Apr. 9, 1978)
1.70	Damian Lillard, Por. Blazers	50	29	@ Sac. Kings (Feb. 9, 2018)
1.70	Stephen Curry, G.S. Warriors	62	36	vs. Por. Blazers (Jan. 3, 2021)

Most Points Scored on Birthday

			Age
61	Shaquille O'Neal, L.A. Lakers*	@ L.A. Clippers (Mar. 6, 2000)	28
53	Dominique Wilkins, Atl. Hawks*	vs. L.A. Clippers (Jan. 12, 1987)	27
51	Rick Barry, N.Y. Nets°*	vs. Uta. Stars° (Mar. 28, 1971)	27
51	Julius Erving, N.Y. Nets°*	vs. S.D. Conquistadors° (Feb. 22, 1975)	25
48	LeBron James, Cle. Cavaliers*	vs. Atl. Hawks (Dec. 30, 2009)	25
47	Stephen Curry, G.S. Warriors*	vs. Was. Wizards (Mar. 14, 2022)	34
46	Michael Jordan, Chi. Bulls	vs. Cle. Cavaliers (Feb. 17, 1992)	29
46	Anthony Davis, N.O. Pelicans*	@ Cha. Hornets (Mar. 11, 2017)	24
45	Neil Johnston, Phi. Warriors*	vs. Roc. Royals (Feb. 4, 1955)	26
43	Elvin Hayes, Cap. Bullets*	@ Atl. Hawks (Nov. 17, 1973)	28
43	Kyrie Irving, Brk. Nets	@ Mem. Grizzlies (Mar. 23, 2022)	30
41	Charlie Scott, Pho. Suns*	vs. Bos. Celtics (Dec. 15, 1973)	25
41	Allen Crabbe, Brk. Nets*	vs. Chi. Bulls (Apr. 9, 2018)	26
40	Mark Aguirre, Dal. Mavericks*	@ G.S. Warriors (Dec. 10, 1983)	24
40	D'Angelo Russell, Brk. Nets*	@ Cha. Hornets (Feb. 23, 2019)	23
39	Dominique Wilkins, Atl. Hawks	vs. Bos. Celtics (Jan. 12, 1985)	25
39	Stephon Marbury, N.J. Nets*	@ Min. T'Wolves (Feb. 20, 2000)	23
39	Hedo Türkoğlu, Orl. Magic	vs. Was. Wizards (Mar. 19, 2008)	29
38	James Silas, S.A. Spurs°	vs. Den. Nuggets° (Feb. 11, 1976)	27
38	World B. Free, S.D. Clippers	@ N.J. Nets (Dec. 9, 1978)	25
38	Hakeem Olajuwon, Hou. Rockets*	vs. Det. Pistons (Jan. 21, 1993)	30
38	LeBron James, Cle. Cavaliers	@ Mia. Heat (Dec. 30, 2008)	24

* Team won game.
° ABA.

Most Points Scored Against Each Franchise, Career

Franchise	Pts		Franchise	Pts	
76ers-Nationals	2885	Wilt Chamberlain	Kings-Royals	3717	Wilt Chamberlain
Bucks	2129	Michael Jordan	Knicks	3878	Wilt Chamberlain
Bulls	1895	Kareem Abdul-Jabbar	Lakers	3393	Wilt Chamberlain
Cavaliers	2048	Michael Jordan	Magic	1577	LeBron James^
Celtics	3211	Wilt Chamberlain	Mavericks	2136	Karl Malone
Clippers-Braves	2150	Kareem Abdul-Jabbar	Nets**	2276	Dan Issel
Grizzlies	1636	Kobe Bryant	Nuggets**	2177	Karl Malone
Hawks	3071	Wilt Chamberlain	Pacers**	2475	Julius Erving
Heat	1205	Paul Pierce	Pelicans-Hornets***	1217	Dirk Nowitzki
Hornets-Bobcats*	1456	LeBron James^	Pistons	3659	Wilt Chamberlain
Jazz	1786	Hakeem Olajuwon	Raptors	1511	LeBron James^

continued on next page

Franchise	Pts			Franchise	Pts		
Rockets	2173	Kareem Abdul-Jabbar		Trail Blazers	2538	Kareem Abdul-Jabbar	
Spurs-Chaparrals**	2092	Dan Issel		Warriors	2881	Jerry West	
Suns	2558	Kareem Abdul-Jabbar		Wizards-Bullets-			
Thunder-SuperSonics	2639	Kareem Abdul-Jabbar		Zephrys-Packers	2818	Wilt Chamberlain	
Timberwolves	1677	Karl Malone					

^ Active.

* Cha. Hornets from 1988–2002; Cha. Bobcats-Hornets from 2004–present.

** Both as an ABA and NBA franchise.

*** Begins with N.O. Hornets in 2002–03 season.

Scoring Average

Highest Scoring Average by Decade* (Min. 200 Games Played)

1946–47–1949–50**		1950–51–1959–60		1960–61–1969–70**	
27.8	George Mikan	25.1	Bob Pettit	34.0	Wilt Chamberlain
23.4	Alex Groza	22.9	Paul Arizin	30.5	Rick Barry
21.1	Joe Fulks	21.2	George Mikan	29.3	Oscar Robertson
17.9	Max Zaslofsky	21.1	Jack Twyman	27.9	Jerry West
17.8	Frankie Brian	19.7	Dolph Schayes	27.8	Bob Pettit
16.8	Dolph Schayes	19.4	Neil Johnston	27.6	Elgin Baylor
16.1	Ed Macauley	19.4	Bob Cousy	24.5	Earl Monroe
15.6	Ed Sadowski	19.2	George Yardley	23.9	Louie Dampier
14.9	Ralph Beard	18.8	Cliff Hagan	23.6	Larry Jones
14.8	Jim Pollard	18.7	Tom Heinsohn	23.4	Dave Bing

1970–71–1979–80**		1980–81–1989–90		1990–91–1999–00	
28.2	Kareem Abdul-Jabbar	32.8	Michael Jordan	30.3	Michael Jordan
26.8	Bob McAdoo	26.1	Dominique Wilkins	27.5	Shaquille O'Neal
26.2	Julius Erving	26.0	Alex English	26.7	Karl Malone
25.3	David Thompson	25.6	Adrian Dantley	24.9	Allen Iverson
25.3	George Gervin	25.3	Larry Bird	23.6	David Robinson
24.6	Jerry West	24.9	Karl Malone	23.0	Hakeem Olajuwon
24.2	Pete Maravich	24.8	George Gervin	22.9	Dominique Wilkins
23.9	Dan Issel	23.8	Moses Malone	22.7	Patrick Ewing
23.1	Walter Davis	23.2	Hakeem Olajuwon	22.5	Mitch Richmond
23.0	Rick Barry	23.0	Bernard King	22.0	Tim Duncan

2000–01–2009–10		2010–11–2019–20		2020–21–2021–22**	
28.5	Kobe Bryant	27.7	Kevin Durant	29.7	Joel Embiid
27.8	LeBron James	26.7	James Harden	29.1	Giannis Antetokounmpo
27.4	Allen Iverson	26.5	LeBron James	28.7	Stephen Curry
25.4	Dwyane Wade	25.0	Russell Westbrook	28.7	Kevin Durant
25.3	Kevin Durant	24.3	Stephen Curry	28.1	Luka Dončić
24.8	Tracy McGrady	24.2	Damian Lillard	28.1	Bradley Beal
24.7	Carmelo Anthony	24.2	Kobe Bryant	27.9	LeBron James
24.4	Dirk Nowitzki	24.0	Anthony Davis	27.3	Damian Lillard
23.2	Paul Pierce	23.9	Joel Embiid	27.1	Kyrie Irving
22.9	Vince Carter	22.7	Karl-Anthony Towns	27.0	Trae Young
		22.7	Donovan Mitchell	27.0	Zion Williamson

* Includes ABA.

** Minimum 50 games played.

Evolution of Scoring Average Record

1946–47	Joe Fulks, Phi. Warriors	23.2
1948–49	George Mikan, Min. Lakers	28.3
1950–51	George Mikan, Min. Lakers	28.4
1958–59	Bob Pettit, St.L. Hawks	29.2
1959–60	Wilt Chamberlain, Phi. Warriors	37.6
1960–61	Wilt Chamberlain, Phi. Warriors	38.4
1961–62	Wilt Chamberlain, Phi. Warriors	50.4

Lifetime Scoring Average of 20-Year Players

Seasons

25.0	Kobe Bryant	20 (1996–97 – 2015–16)
24.6	Kareem Abdul-Jabbar	20 (1969–70 – 1988–89)
20.7	Vince Carter	22 (1998–99 – 2019–20)
20.3	Moses Malone	21 (1974–75 – 1994–95)
17.8	Kevin Garnett	21 (1995–96 – 2015–16)
16.7	Dirk Nowitzki	21 (1998–99 – 2018–19)
14.6	Jamal Crawford	20 (2000–01 – 2019–20)
14.5	Robert Parish	21 (1976–77 – 1996–97)
12.1	Kevin Willis	21 (1984–85 – 1987–88, 1989–90 – 2004–05, 2006–07)

Year-by-Year FG% and PPG

NBA

	FG%	PPG		FG%	PPG
1946–47	.279	67.8	1972–73	.456	107.6
1947–48	.284	72.7	1973–74	.459	105.7
1948–49	.327	80.0	1974–75	.457	102.6
1949–50	.340	80.0	1975–76	.458	104.3
1950–51	.357	84.1	1976–77	.465	106.5
1951–52	.367	83.7	1977–78	.469	108.5
1952–53	.370	82.7	1978–79	.485	110.3
1953–54	.372	79.5	1979–80	.481	109.3
1954–55	.385	93.1	1980–81	.486	108.1
1955–56	.387	99.0	1981–82	.491	108.6
1956–57	.380	99.6	1982–83	.485	108.5
1957–58	.383	106.6	1983–84	.492	110.1
1958–59	.395	108.2	1984–85	.491	110.8
1959–60	.410	115.3	1985–86	.487	110.2
1960–61	.415	118.1	1986–87	.480	109.9
1961–62	.426	118.8	1987–88	.480	108.2
1962–63	.441	115.3	1988–89	.477	109.2
1963–64	.433	111.0	1989–90	.476	107.0
1964–65	.426	110.6	1990–91	.474	106.3
1965–66	.433	115.5	1991–92	.472	105.3
1966–67	.441	117.4	1992–93	.473	105.3
1967–68	.446	116.6	1993–94	.466	101.5
1968–69	.441	112.3	1994–95	.466	101.4
1969–70	.460	116.7	1995–96	.462	99.5
1970–71	.449	112.4	1996–97	.455	96.9
1971–72	.455	110.2	1997–98	.450	95.6

continued on next page

	FG%	PPG			FG%	PPG
1998–99	.437	91.6		2010–11	.459	99.6
1999–00	.449	97.5		2011–12	.448	96.3
2000–01	.443	94.8		2012–13	.453	98.1
2001–02	.445	95.5		2013–14	.454	101.0
2002–03	.442	95.1		2014–15	.449	100.0
2003–04	.439	93.4		2015–16	.452	102.7
2004–05	.447	97.2		2016–17	.457	105.6
2005–06	.454	97.0		2017–18	.460	106.3
2006–07	.458	98.7		2018–19	.461	111.2
2007–08	.457	99.9		2019–20	.460	111.8
2008–09	.459	100.0		2020–21	.466	112.1
2009–10	.461	100.4		2021–22	.461	110.6

ABA

	FG%	PPG			FG%	PPG
1967–68	.420	109.0		1972–73	.470	111.6
1968–69	.436	114.8		1973–74	.460	106.4
1969–70	.445	113.0		1974–75	.473	108.8
1970–71	.455	117.5		1975–76	.466	112.5
1971–72	.461	113.5				

Most Seasons Averaging 20 PPG· (Qualifying for PPG Leaderboard)

18	LeBron James^	12	Hakeem Olajuwon	10	Elvin Hayes
17	Kareem Abdul-Jabbar	12	Shaquille O'Neal	10	Bernard King
17	Karl Malone	11	Wilt Chamberlain	10	Larry Bird
14	Julius Erving	11	Dan Issel	10	Dominique Wilkins
14	Kobe Bryant	11	Moses Malone	10	Patrick Ewing
13	Dirk Nowitzki	11	Charles Barkley	10	Russell Westbrook^
13	Carmelo Anthony^	11	Allen Iverson	10	DeMar DeRozan^
12	George Gervin	12	Kevin Durant^	10	James Harden^
12	Michael Jordan	10	Bob Pettit		

· Includes ABA.

^ Active.

Highest PPG, Not Leading League in Scoring Average

PPG	Runner-Up	Season	Leader	PPG
34.77	Elgin Baylor*, L.A. Lakers	1960–61	Wilt Chamberlain, Phi. Warriors	38.39
33.99	Elgin Baylor*, L.A. Lakers	1962–63	Wilt Chamberlain, S.F. Warriors	44.83
33.01	Allen Iverson*, Phi. 76ers	2005–06	Kobe Bryant, L.A. Lakers	35.40
31.58	Walt Bellamy*, Chi. Packers	1961–62	Wilt Chamberlain, Phi. Warriors	50.36
31.48	Rick Barry*, N.Y. Nets	1971–72	Charlie Scott, Vir. Squires*****	34.58
31.39	Oscar Robertson*, Cin. Royals	1963–64	Wilt Chamberlain, S.F. Warriors	36.85
31.37	LeBron James**, Cle. Cavaliers	2005–06	Kobe Bryant, L.A. Lakers	35.40
31.34	Jerry West*, L.A. Lakers	1965–66	Wilt Chamberlain, Phi. 76ers	33.53
31.30	Bradley Beal, Was. Wizards	2020–21	Stephen Curry, G.S. Warriors	31.98
31.29	Oscar Robertson**, Cin. Royals	1965–66	Wilt Chamberlain, Phi. 76ers	33.53
31.17	Jack Twyman*, Cin. Royals	1959–60	Wilt Chamberlain, Phi. Warriors	37.60
31.14	Bob Pettit**, St.L. Hawks	1961–62	Wilt Chamberlain, Phi. Warriors	50.36
31.11	Moses Malone*, Hou. Rockets	1981–82	George Gervin, S.A. Spurs	32.29
30.98	Karl Malone*, Uta. Jazz	1989–90	Michael Jordan, Chi. Bulls	33.57

continued on next page

PPG	Runner-Up	Season	Leader	PPG
30.97	Jerry West* , L.A. Lakers	1964–65	Wilt Chamberlain, S.F. Warriors/Phi. 76ers	34.71
30.80	Jerry West***, L.A. Lakers	1961–62	Wilt Chamberlain, Phi. Warriors	50.36
30.78	Oscar Robertson****, Cin. Royals	1961–62	Wilt Chamberlain, Phi. Warriors	50.36
30.73	Dominique Wilkins*, Atl. Hawks	1987–88	Michael Jordan, Chi. Bulls	34.98
30.62	Rick Barry*, G.S. Warriors	1974–75	Bob McAdoo, Buf. Braves	34.52
30.58	Dan Issel**, Ken. Colonels	1971–72	Charlie Scott, Vir. Squires*****	34.58
30.54	Bradley Beal, Was. Wizards	2019–20	James Harden, Hou. Rockets	34.34
30.53	Oscar Robertson*, Cin. Royals	1966–67	Rick Barry, S.F. Warriors	35.58
30.49	Oscar Robertson**, Cin. Royals	1960–61	Wilt Chamberlain, Phi. Warriors	38.39
30.39	Oscar Robertson**, Cin. Royals	1964–65	Wilt Chamberlain, Phi. 76ers	34.71
30.33	Adrian Dantley**, Uta. Jazz	1981–82	George Gervin, S.A. Spurs	32.29
30.22	World B. Free*, S.D. Clippers	1979–80	George Gervin, S.A. Spurs	33.14
30.16	Kareem Abdul-Jabbar*, Mil. Bucks	1972–73	Tiny Archibald, K.C.-Oma Kings	33.99
30.01	Kobe Bryant*, L.A. Lakers	2002–03	Tracy McGrady, Orl. Magic	32.09

* Second in scoring.

** Third in scoring.

*** Fourth in scoring.

**** Fifth in scoring.

***** Played 73 games with Vir. Squires (ABA) and 18 with Pho. Suns (NBA). Average is based soley on ABA stats.

Lowest Career PPG for Players Scoring 20,000 Points

Career PPG		Career Pts	Career PPG		Career Pts
14.5	Robert Parish	23,334	18.9	Ray Allen	24,505
16.0	Joe Johnson^	20,407	19.0	Tim Duncan	26,496
16.3	Gary Payton	21,813	19.1	LaMarcus Aldridge^	20,558
16.7	Vince Carter	25,728	19.2	Hal Greer	21,586
17.0	Pau Gasol	20,894	19.7	Paul Pierce	26,397
17.8	Kevin Garnett	26,071	20.1	Walt Bellamy	20,941
18.1	Tom Chambers	20,049	20.3	Moses Malone	29,580
18.2	Reggie Miller	25,279	20.4	Clyde Drexler	22,195
18.1	Chris Paul^	20,936	20.7	Dirk Nowitzki	31,560
18.5	Antawn Jamison	20,042	20.8	John Havlicek	26,395
18.8	Artis Gilmore	24,941			

^ Active.

Players Averaging 35 PPG, Season

Wilt Chamberlain, Phi. Warriors, 1959–60		37.6
Wilt Chamberlain, Phi. Warriors, 1960–61		38.4
Elgin Baylor, L.A. Lakers, 1961–62		38.3
Wilt Chamberlain, Phi. Warriors, 1961–62		50.4
Wilt Chamberlain, S.F. Warriors, 1962–63		44.8
Wilt Chamberlain, S.F. Warriors, 1963–64		36.9
Rick Barry, S.F. Warriors, 1966–67		35.6
Michael Jordan, Chi. Bulls, 1986–87		37.1
Kobe Bryant, L.A. Lakers, 2005–06		35.4
James Harden, Hou. Rockets, 2018–19		36.1

Youngest Player to Average 20 PPG, Season (Min. 1000 Minutes Played)

	Age (Birthdate)	PPG
LeBron James, Cle. Cavaliers, 2003–04	19 (Dec. 30)	20.9
Kevin Durant, Sea. Sonics, 2007–08	19 (Sep. 29)	20.3

continued on next page

	Age (Birthdate)	PPG
Carmelo Anthony, Den. Nuggets, 2003–04	19 (May 29)	21.0
Luka Dončić, Dal. Mavericks, 2018–19	19 (Feb. 28)	21.2
LeBron James, Cle. Cavaliers, 2004–05	20 (Dec. 30)	27.2
Devin Booker, Pho. Suns, 2016–17	20 (Oct. 30)	22.1
Kevin Durant, Ok.C. Thunder, 2008–09	20 (Sep. 29)	25.3
Tyreke Evans, Sac. Kings, 2009–10	20 (Sep. 19)	20.1
LaMelo Ball, Cha. Hornets, 2021–22	20 (Aug. 22)	20.1
Anthony Edwards, Min. T'Wolves, 2021–22	20 (Aug. 5)	21.3
Zion Williamson, N.O. Pelicans, 2020–21	20 (Jul. 6)	27.0
Carmelo Anthony, Den. Nuggets, 2004–05	20 (May 29)	20.8
Spencer Haywood, Den. Rockets°, 1969–70	20 (Apr. 22)	30.0
Kyrie Irving, Cle. Cavaliers, 2012–13	20 (Mar. 23)	22.5
Elton Brand, Chi. Bulls, 1999–00	20 (Mar. 11)	20.1
Anthony Davis, N.O. Pelicans, 2013–14	20 (Mar. 11)	20.8
Shaquille O'Neal, Orl. Magic, 1992–93	20 (Mar. 6)	23.4
Luka Dončić, Dal. Mavericks, 2019–20	20 (Feb. 28)	28.8
Andrew Wiggins, Min. T'Wolves, 2015–16	20 (Feb. 23)	20.7
LeBron James, Cle. Cavaliers, 2005–06	21 (Dec. 30)	31.4
Shareef Abdur-Rahim, Van. Grizzlies, 1997–98	21 (Dec. 11)	22.3
Bernard King, N.J. Nets, 1977–78	21 (Dec. 4)	24.2
Amar'e Stoudemire, Pho. Suns, 2003–04	21 (Nov. 16)	20.6
Karl-Anthony Towns, Min. T'Wolves, 2016–17	21 (Nov. 15)	25.1
Devin Booker, Pho. Suns, 2017–18	21 (Oct. 30)	24.9
Derrick Rose, Chi. Bulls, 2009–10	21 (Oct. 4)	20.8
John Drew, Atl. Hawks, 1975–76	21 (Sep. 30)	21.6
Kevin Durant, Ok.C. Thunder, 2009–10	21 (Sep. 29)	30.1
Trae Young, Atl. Hawks, 2019–20	21 (Sep. 19)	29.6
Donovan Mitchell, Uta. Jazz, 2017–18	21 (Sep. 7)	20.5
Kobe Bryant, L.A. Lakers, 1999–00	21 (Aug. 23)	22.5
Rudy Gay, Mem. Grizzlies, 2007–08	21 (Aug. 17)	20.1
Magic Johnson, L.A. Lakers, 1980–81	21 (Aug. 14)	21.6
Antoine Walker, Bos. Celtics, 1997–98	21 (Aug. 12)	22.4
David Thompson, Den. Nuggets°, 1975–76	21 (Jul. 13)	26.0
Clark Kellogg, Ind. Pacers, 1982–83	21 (Jul. 2)	20.1
RJ Barrett, N.Y. Knicks, 2021–22	21 (Jun. 14)	20.0
Allen Iverson, Phi. 76ers, 1996–97	21 (Jun. 7)	23.5
Carmelo Anthony, Den. Nuggets, 2005–06	21 (May 29)	26.5
Tracy McGrady, Orl. Magic, 2000–01	21 (May 24)	26.8
Isiah Thomas, Det. Pistons, 1982–83	21 (Apr. 30)	22.9
George Gervin, S.A. Spurs°/Vir. Squires°, 1973–74	21 (Apr. 27)	23.4
Tim Duncan, S.A. Spurs, 1997–98	21 (Apr. 25)	21.1
Spencer Haywood, Sea. Sonics, 1970–71	21 (Apr. 22)	20.6
Rick Barry, S.F. Warriors, 1965–66	21 (Mar. 28)	25.7
Chris Bosh, Tor. Raptors, 2005–06	21 (Mar. 24)	22.5
Kyrie Irving, Cle. Cavaliers, 2013–14	21 (Mar. 23)	20.8
Blake Griffin, L.A. Clippers, 2010–11	21 (Mar. 16)	22.5
Terry Cummings, S.D. Clippers, 1982–83	21 (Mar. 15)	23.7
Jabari Parker, Mil. Bucks, 2016–17	21 (Mar. 15)	20.1
Elton Brand, Chi. Bulls, 2000–01	21 (Mar. 11)	20.1
Anthony Davis, N.O. Pelicans, 2014–15	21 (Mar. 11)	24.4
Shaquille O'Neal, Orl. Magic, 1993–94	21 (Mar. 6)	29.3
Jayson Tatum, Bos. Celtics, 2019–20	21 (Mar. 3)	23.4

continued on next page

	Age (Birthdate)	PPG
Chris Webber, Was. Bullets, 1994–95	21 (Mar. 1)	20.1
Adrian Dantley, Buf. Braves, 1976–77	21 (Feb. 28)	20.3
Luka Dončić, Dal. Mavericks, 2020–21	21 (Feb. 28)	27.7
Andrew Wiggins, Min. T'Wolves, 2016–17	21 (Feb. 23)	23.6
Julius Erving, Vir. Squiresᵃ, 1971–72	21 (Feb. 22)	27.3
Stephon Marbury, Min. T'Wolves/N.J. Nets, 1998–99	21 (Feb. 20)	21.3
Michael Jordan, Chi. Bulls, 1984–85	21 (Feb. 17)	28.2
Collin Sexton, Cle. Cavaliers, 2019–20	21 (Jan. 4)	20.8

ᵃ ABA.

Rookies Averaging 25 PPG

Wilt Chamberlain*, Phi. Warriors, 1959–60	37.6
Walt Bellamy*, Chi. Packers, 1961–62	31.6
Oscar Robertson*, Cin. Royals, 1960–61	30.5
Spencer Haywood*, Den. Rocketsᵃ, 1969–70	30.0
Dan Issel**, Ken. Colonelsᵃ, 1970–71	29.9
Kareem Abdul-Jabbar*, Mil. Bucks, 1969–70	28.8
Elvin Hayes, S.D. Rockets, 1968–69	28.4
George Mikan, Min. Lakers, 1948–49	28.3
Michael Jordan*, Chi. Bulls, 1984–85	28.2
Julius Erving, Vir. Squiresᵃ, 1971–72	27.3
Charlie Scott**, Vir. Squiresᵃ, 1970–71	27.1
Connie Hawkins, Pit. Pipersᵃ, 1967–68	26.8
Jim McDaniels, Car. Cougarsᵃ, 1971–72	26.8
David Thompson*, Den. Nuggetsᵃ, 1975–76	26.0
Rick Barry*, S.F. Warriors, 1965–66	25.7
Terry Dischinger*, Chi. Zephyrs, 1962–63	25.5

* Rookie of the Year.

** Tied for Rookie of the Year.

ᵃ ABA.

Players Averaging 20 PPG in Rookie and Final Season of Career

	Rookie PPG			Final Season PPG	
Alex Groza	23.4	Ind. Olympians, 1949–50	21.7	Ind. Olympians, 1950–51	
Bob Pettit	20.4	Mil. Hawks, 1954–55	22.5	St.L. Hawks, 1964–65	
Larry Bird	21.3	Bos. Celtics, 1979–80	20.2	Bos. Celtics, 1991–92	
Michael Jordan	28.2	Chi. Bulls, 1984–85	20.0	Was. Wizards, 2002–03	

Highest Average PPG from Age 39 On, Season

			Age
20.6	Michael Jordan, Was. Wizards	2002–03	39
20.0	Karl Malone, Uta. Jazz	2002–03	39
17.5	Kareem Abdul-Jabbar, L.A. Lakers	1986–87	39
14.8	Reggie Miller, Ind. Pacers	2004–05	39
14.6	Kareem Abdul-Jabbar, L.A. Lakers	1987–88	40
13.4	John Stockton, Uta. Jazz	2001–02	39
13.2	Karl Malone, Uta. Jazz	2003–04	40
12.6	Robert Parish, Bos. Celtics	1992–93	39
12.0	Dirk Nowitzki, Dal. Mavericks	2017–18	39
11.7	Robert Parish, Bos. Celtics	1993–94	40

Most Points by Players Never Averaging 20 PPG

Career Pts		Highest PPG
23,334	Robert Parish	19.9 (Bos. Celtics, 1981–82)
19,711	John Stockton	17.2 (Uta. Jazz, 1989–90 and 1990–91)
18,881	Jason Terry	19.7 (Atl. Hawks, 2000–01)
17,529	Jason Kidd	18.7 (N.J. Nets, 2002–03)
17,387	Steve Nash	18.8 (Pho. Suns, 2005–06)
17,287	Jack Sikma	19.6 (Sea. Sonics, 1981–82)
17,253	Kevin Willis	19.1 (Atl. Hawks, 1993–94)
16,784	Buck Williams	18.3 (N.J. Nets, 1987–88)
16,278	Andre Miller	17.0 (Phi. 76ers, 2007–08)
16,006	Derek Harper	19.7 (Dal. Mavericks, 1990–91)
16,006	Rasheed Wallace	19.3 (Por. Blazers), 2001–02)
15,802	Chauncey Billups	19.5 (Den. Nuggets, 2009–10)
15,761	Detlef Schrempf	19.2 (Sea. Sonics, 1994–95)
15,635	Sam Cassell	19.8 (Min. T'Wolves, 2003–04)
15,586	Terry Porter	18.2 (Por. Blazers, 1992–93)
15,535	Dennis Johnson	19.5 (Pho. Suns, 1981–82)
15,324	Sam Perkins	16.5 (L.A. Lakers, 1991–92)
14,536	Paul Millsap^	18.1 (Atl. Hawks, 2016–17)
13,951	Andre Iguodala^	19.9 (Phi. 76ers, 2007–08)
13,848	Thaddeus Young^	17.9 (Phi. 76ers, 2013–14)
13,295	Jeff Green^	16.9 (Bos. Celtics, 2013–14)
12,989	Al Horford^	18.6 (Atl. Hawks, 2013–14)
11,593	Trevor Ariza^	14.9 (Hou. Rockets, 2009–10)

^ Active.

Players Averaging Higher PPG Than MPG, Season (Min. 20 MPG)

	PPG	MPG
Wilt Chamberlain, Phi. Warriors, 1961–62	50.4	48.5

Most FG Attempts, Game

FGA			Shooting
63	Wilt Chamberlain, Phi. Warriors*	vs. N.Y. Knicks (Mar. 2, 1962)	36-for-63 (.571)
62	Wilt Chamberlain, Phi. Warriors*	vs. L.A. Lakers (Dec. 8, 1961)	31-for-62 (.500)
60	Wilt Chamberlain, S.F. Warriors	@ Cin. Royals (Oct. 28, 1962)	23-for-60 (.383)
58	Wilt Chamberlain, S.F. Warriors	@ Phi. 76ers (Nov. 26, 1964)	27-for-58 (.466)
57	Wilt Chamberlain, S.F. Warriors*	vs. Syr. Nationals (Dec. 11, 1962)	27-for-57 (.474)
56	Joe Fulks, Phi. Warriors*	vs. Ind. Jets (Feb. 10, 1949)	27-for-56 (.482)
56	Wilt Chamberlain, Phi. Warriors*	vs. Chi. Packers (Jan. 24, 1962)	23-for-56 (.411)
55	Joe Fulks, Phi. Warriors*	vs. Pro. Steamrollers (Mar. 18, 1948)	13-for-55 (.236)
55	Elgin Baylor, L.A. Lakers*	@ Phi. Warriors (Dec. 8, 1961)	23-for-55 (.418)
53	Wilt Chamberlain, Phi. Warriors*	vs. Syr. Nationals (Dec. 26, 1961)	21-for-53 (.396)
53	Wilt Chamberlain, S.F. Warriors*	vs. St.L. Hawks (Dec. 18, 1962)	26-for-53 (.491)
52	Wilt Chamberlain, S.F. Warriors	vs. Cin. Royals (Nov. 21, 1962)	27-for-52 (.519)
51	Wilt Chamberlain, Phi. Warriors*	vs. Min. Lakers (Dec. 30, 1959)	19-for-51 (.373)
51	Wilt Chamberlain, S.F. Warriors*	vs. Chi. Zephyrs (Nov. 10, 1962)	24-for-51 (.471)
51	Wilt Chamberlain, S.F. Warriors	@ Cin. Royals (Nov. 18, 1962)	24-for-51 (.471)
51	Julius Erving, N.Y. Netsª	@ S.D. Conquistadorsª (Feb. 14, 1975)	25-for-51 (.490)
50	Joe Fulks, Phi. Warriors*	vs. Pro. Steamrollers (Dec. 3, 1946)	16-for-50 (.320)
50	Wilt Chamberlain, Phi. Warriors	vs. Cin. Royals (Jan. 18, 1962)	22-for-50 (.440)

continued on next page

FGA

FGA	Player	Game	Shooting
50	Wilt Chamberlain, S.F. Warriors*	@ Det. Pistons (Feb. 11, 1964)	25-for-50 (.500)
50	Rick Barry, S.F. Warriors*	@ Chi. Bulls (Feb. 5, 1967)	17-for-50 (.340)
50	Kobe Bryant, L.A. Lakers*	vs. Uta. Jazz (Apr. 13, 2016)	22-for-50 (.440)
49	Wilt Chamberlain, S.F. Warriors	@ L.A. Lakers (Jan. 26, 1964)	18-for-49 (.367)
49	Rick Barry, G.S. Warriors*	vs. Phi. 76ers (Jan. 23, 1975)	23-for-49 (.469)
49	George Gervin, S.A. Spurs	@ N.O. Jazz (Apr. 9, 1978)	23-for-49 (.469)
49	Michael Jordan, Chi. Bulls	vs. Orl. Magic (Jan. 16, 1993)	27-for-49 (.551)
48	Elgin Baylor, L.A. Lakers*	@ N.Y. Knicks (Nov. 15, 1960)	28-for-48 (.583)
48	Wilt Chamberlain, Phi. Warriors*	@ L.A. Lakers (Nov. 27, 1960)	16-for-48 (.333)
48	Wilt Chamberlain, Phi. Warriors*	vs. Det. Pistons (Nov. 4, 1961)	24-for-48 (.500)
48	Wilt Chamberlain, Phi. Warriors	vs. L.A. Lakers (Nov. 17, 1961)	24-for-48 (.500)
48	Wilt Chamberlain, Phi. Warriors*	vs. Chi. Packers (Dec. 9, 1961)	28-for-48 (.583)
48	Wilt Chamberlain, Phi. Warriors*	vs. Chi. Packers (Jan. 13, 1962)	29-for-48 (.604)
48	Wilt Chamberlain, Phi. Warriors*	vs. St.L. Hawks (Jan. 17, 1962)	24-for-48 (.500)
48	Wilt Chamberlain, S.F. Warriors	@ L.A. Lakers (Nov. 3, 1962)	29-for-48 (.604)
48	Wilt Chamberlain, S.F. Warriors*	vs. Bal. Bullets (Dec. 1, 1964)	22-for-48 (.458)
47	Joe Fulks, Phi. Warriors	@ Bos. Celtics (Dec. 30, 1947)	12-for-47 (.255)
47	Jack Twyman, Cin. Royals*	vs. St.L. Hawks (Feb. 28, 1959)	22-for-47 (.468)
47	Elgin Baylor, Min. Lakers*	vs. Bos. Celtics (Nov. 8, 1959)	25-for-47 (.532)
47	Wilt Chamberlain, Phi. Warriors*	@ N.Y. Knicks (Feb. 21, 1960)	26-for-47 (.553)
47	Wilt Chamberlain, Phi. Warriors*	@ Chi. Packers (Nov. 19, 1961)	24-for-47 (.511)
47	Wilt Chamberlain, Phi. Warriors*	@ L.A. Lakers (Dec. 1, 1961)	22-for-47 (.468)
47	Wilt Chamberlain, Phi. Warriors*	@ Cin. Royals (Dec. 19, 1961)	24-for-47 (.511)
47	Wilt Chamberlain, Phi. Warriors*	@ Det. Pistons (Dec. 20, 1961)	24-for-47 (.511)
47	Wilt Chamberlain, S.F. Warriors	vs. L.A. Lakers (Jan. 11, 1963)	28-for-47 (.596)
47	Wilt Chamberlain, S.F. Warriors*	@ L.A. Lakers (Feb. 16, 1963)	26-for-47 (.553)
47	Chris Webber, Sac. Kings	vs. Ind. Pacers (Jan. 5, 2001)	24-for-47 (.511)
47	Kobe Bryant, L.A. Lakers	@ Bos. Celtics (Nov. 7, 2002)	17-for-47 (.362)
46	Wilt Chamberlain, Phi. Warriors*	vs. L.A. Lakers (Jan. 21, 1961)	25-for-46 (.543)
46	Wilt Chamberlain, Phi. Warriors*	vs. L.A. Lakers (Oct. 20, 1961)	24-for-46 (.522)
46	Wilt Chamberlain, Phi. Warriors*	@ Det. Pistons (Nov. 8, 1961)	23-for-46 (.500)
46	Wilt Chamberlain, Phi. Warriors*	vs. Chi. Packers (Feb. 20, 1962)	21-for-46 (.457)
46	Wilt Chamberlain, Phi. Warriors*	@ Chi. Packers (Feb. 28, 1962)	24-for-46 (.522)
46	Wilt Chamberlain, S.F. Warriors	@ Det. Pistons (Dec. 7, 1962)	21-for-46 (.457)
46	Wilt Chamberlain, S.F. Warriors	@ Cin. Royals (Feb. 7, 1963)	23-for-46 (.500)
46	Wilt Chamberlain, S.F. Warriors*	@ L.A. Lakers (Mar. 7, 1964)	21-for-46 (.457)
46	Wilt Chamberlain, S.F. Warriors	@ Det. Pistons (Nov. 12, 1964)	22-for-46 (.478)
46	Rick Barry, S.F. Warriors*	vs. St.L. Hawks (Dec. 8, 1966)	19-for-46 (.413)
46	Bo Lamar, S.D. Conquistadors[a]*	vs. Ind. Pacers[a] (Jan. 13, 1974)	22-for-46 (.478)
46	Kobe Bryant, L.A. Lakers*	vs. Tor. Raptors (Jan. 22, 2006)	28-for-46 (.609)
45	George Mikan, Min. Lakers*	vs. Roc. Royals (Jan. 20, 1952)	22-for-45 (.489)
45	Wilt Chamberlain, Phi. Warriors*	vs. L.A. Lakers (Nov. 29, 1960)	21-for-45 (.467)
45	Elgin Baylor, L.A. Lakers*	@ Det. Pistons (Feb. 16, 1961)	23-for-45 (.511)
45	Wilt Chamberlain, Phi. Warriors	vs. Syr. Nationals (Oct. 27, 1961)	21-for-45 (.467)
45	Wilt Chamberlain, Phi. Warriors	@ Bos. Celtics (Jan. 14, 1962)	27-for-45 (.600)
45	Wilt Chamberlain, S.F. Warriors	vs. L.A. Lakers (Dec. 6, 1963)	22-for-45 (.489)
45	Wilt Chamberlain, S.F. Warriors*	@ N.Y. Knicks (Dec. 15, 1964)	25-for-45 (.556)
45	Elvin Hayes, S.D. Rockets*	vs. Det. Pistons (Nov. 13, 1968)	20-for-45 (.444)
45	Rick Barry, G.S. Warriors*	vs. Por. Blazers (Mar. 26, 1974)	30-for-45 (.667)
45	Kobe Bryant, L.A. Lakers	@ Cha. Bobcats (Dec. 29, 2006)	22-for-45 (.489)

[a] ABA.

* Team won game.

Multiple Seasons Averaging 25 FG Attempts Per Game, Career
(Qualifying for Field Goal Percent Leaderboard)

7.............................. Wilt Chamberlain	3.................................... Allen Iverson	2................................... Pete Maravich
5.................................... Elgin Baylor	2..................................... Rick Barry	2................................Michael Jordan
3...Joe Fulks	2..................................... Elvin Hayes	

^ Active.

Most FG Made, Game

FGM		Pts	Shooting
36..............	Wilt Chamberlain, Phi. Warriors...............vs. N.Y. Knicks (Mar. 2, 1962) 100		36-for-63 (.571)
31..............	Wilt Chamberlain, Phi. Warriors*...............vs. L.A. Lakers (Dec. 8, 1961)...............78		31-for-62 (.500)
30..............	Wilt Chamberlain, S.F. Warriors ....@ Chi. Bulls (Dec. 16, 1967)...............68		30-for-40 (.750)
30..............	Rick Barry, G.S. Warriors........................vs. Por. Blazers (Mar. 26, 1974).........64		30-for-45 (.667)
29..............	Wilt Chamberlain, Phi. Warriors ....vs. Chi. Packers (Jan. 13, 1962).........73		29-for-48 (.604)
29..............	Wilt Chamberlain, S.F. Warriors*...............@ L.A. Lakers (Nov. 3, 1962) 72		29-for-48 (.604)
29..............	Wilt Chamberlain, S.F. Warriors ....@ N.Y. Knicks (Nov. 16, 1962) 73		29-for-43 (.674)
29..............	Wilt Chamberlain, L.A. Lakers ....vs. Pho. Suns (Feb. 9, 1969) 66		29-for-35 (.829)
28..............	Elgin Baylor, L.A. Lakers...........................@ N.Y. Knicks (Nov. 15, 1960) 71		28-for-48 (.583)
28..............	Wilt Chamberlain, Phi. Warriors ....vs. Chi. Packers (Dec. 9, 1961) 61		28-for-48 (.583)
28..............	Wilt Chamberlain, S.F. Warriors*...............vs. L.A. Lakers (Jan. 11, 1963)...............67		28-for-47 (.596)
28..............	Wilt Chamberlain, Phi. 76ers ....vs. L.A. Lakers (Feb. 7, 1966)...............65		28-for-43 (.651)
28..............	David Thompson, Den. Nuggets*...............@ Det. Pistons (Apr. 9, 1978) 73		28-for-38 (.737)
28..............	Kobe Bryant, L.A. Lakers ....vs. Tor. Raptors (Jan. 22, 2006) 81		28-for-46 (.609)
27..............	Joe Fulks, Phi. Warriors.........................vs. Ind. Jets (Feb. 10, 1949)...............63		27-for-56 (.482)
27..............	Wilt Chamberlain, Phi. Warriors ....vs. N.Y. Knicks (Mar. 9, 1961)...............67		27-for-37 (.730)
27..............	Wilt Chamberlain, Phi. Warriors*...............@ Bos. Celtics (Jan. 14, 1962)...............62		27-for-45 (.600)
27..............	Wilt Chamberlain, S.F. Warriors*...............vs. Cin. Royals (Nov. 21, 1962)...............61		27-for-52 (.519)
27..............	Wilt Chamberlain, S.F. Warriors ....vs. Syr. Nationals (Dec. 11, 1962).......61		27-for-57 (.474)
27..............	Wilt Chamberlain, S.F. Warriors ....@ N.Y. Knicks (Jan. 29, 1963)...............62		27-for-44 (.614)
27..............	Wilt Chamberlain, S.F. Warriors*...............@ Syr. Nationals (Mar. 10, 1963)........70		27-for-38 (.711)
27..............	Wilt Chamberlain, S.F. Warriors*...............@ Phi. 76ers (Nov. 26, 1964)...............63		27-for-58 (.466)
27..............	Michael Jordan, Chi. Bulls*...................vs. Orl. Magic (Jan. 16, 1993)...........64		27-for-49 (.551)
26..............	Wilt Chamberlain, Phi. Warriors ....@ N.Y. Knicks (Feb. 21, 1960) 58		26-for-47 (.553)
26..............	Wilt Chamberlain, Phi. Warriors*...............@ St.L. Hawks (Feb. 17, 1962)...............67		26-for-44 (.591)
26..............	Wilt Chamberlain, S.F. Warriors ....vs. St.L. Hawks (Dec. 18, 1962) 61		26-for-53 (.491)
26..............	Wilt Chamberlain, S.F. Warriors ....@ L.A. Lakers (Feb. 16, 1963)...............56		26-for-47 (.553)
26..............	Wilt Chamberlain, S.F. Warriors ....@ Cin. Royals (Nov. 15, 1964)............62		26-for-44 (.591)
26..............	Wilt Chamberlain, Phi. 76ers ....vs. S.F. Warriors (Mar. 3, 1966).........62		26-for-39 (.667)
26..............	Wilt Chamberlain, Phi. 76ers ....vs. Cin. Royals (Feb. 13, 1967)...........58		26-for-34 (.765)
26..............	Pete Maravich, N.O. Jazz.....................vs. N.Y. Knicks (Feb. 25, 1977)...........68		26-for-43 (.605)
26..............	David Robinson, S.A. Spurs.....................@ L.A. Clippers (Apr. 24, 1994)...........71		26-for-41 (.634)
25..............	Elgin Baylor, Min. Lakers ....vs. Bos. Celtics (Nov. 8, 1959) 64		25-for-47 (.532)
25..............	Wilt Chamberlain, Phi. Warriors ....vs. Bos. Celtics (Feb. 23, 1960) 53		25-for-44 (.568)
25..............	Wilt Chamberlain, Phi. Warriors ....vs. L.A. Lakers (Jan. 21, 1961) 56		25-for-46 (.543)
25..............	Bob Pettit, St.L. Hawks ....@ Det. Pistons (Feb. 18, 1961) 57		25-for-42 (.595)
25..............	Wilt Chamberlain, Phi. Warriors ....@ Cin. Royals (Feb. 25, 1961) 58		25-for-38 (.658)
25..............	Wilt Chamberlain, Phi. Warriors ....vs. Syr. Nationals (Jan. 21, 1962).......62		25-for-42 (.595)
25..............	Wilt Chamberlain, Phi. Warriors*...............vs. N.Y. Knicks (Feb. 25, 1962)...........67		25-for-38 (.658)
25..............	Wilt Chamberlain, Phi. Warriors ....@ St.L. Hawks (Feb. 27, 1962)...........65		25-for-43 (.581)
25..............	Wilt Chamberlain, S.F. Warriors*...............vs. St.L. Hawks (Dec. 2, 1962)...........59		25-for-36 (.694)
25..............	Wilt Chamberlain, S.F. Warriors ....vs. Det. Pistons (Jan. 24, 1963)...........58		25-for-36 (.694)
25..............	Wilt Chamberlain, S.F. Warriors ....@ Det. Pistons (Feb. 11, 1964)...........59		25-for-50 (.500)

continued on next page

FGM | | **Pts** | **Shooting**

25	Wilt Chamberlain, S.F. Warriors	@ N.Y. Knicks (Dec. 15, 1964)	58	25-for-45 (.556)
25	Mel Daniels, Ind. Pacersª	vs. N.Y. Netsª (Mar. 18, 1969)	56	25-for-38 (.658)
25	Lou Hudson, Atl. Hawks	vs. Chi. Bulls (Nov. 10, 1969)	57	25-for-34 (.735)
25	Stew Johnson, Pit. Condorsª	vs. The Floridiansª (Mar. 6, 1971)	62	25-for-44 (.568)
25	Larry Miller, Car. Cougarsª	vs. Mem. Prosª (Mar. 18, 1972)	67	25-for-40 (.625)
25	Julius Erving, N.Y. Netsª*	@ S.D. Conquistadorsª (Feb. 14, 1975)	63	25-for-51 (.490)
25	Marvin Barnes, Spirits of St.L.ª	vs. Mem. Soundsª (Mar. 16, 1975)	54	25-for-34 (.424)

* Team lost game.

ª ABA.

Most FG Missed, Game

42	Joe Fulks, Phi. Warriors*	vs. Pro. Steamrollers (Mar. 18, 1948)		13-for-55 (.236)
37	Wilt Chamberlain, S.F. Warriors	@ Cin. Royals (Oct. 28, 1962)		23-for-60 (.383)
35	Joe Fulks, Phi. Warriors	@ Bos. Celtics (Dec. 30, 1947)		12-for-47 (.255)
35	George Mikan, Min. Lakers*	vs. Ft.W. Pistons (Nov. 17, 1951)		8-for-43 (.186)
34	Joe Fulks, Phi. Warriors*	vs. Pro. Steamrollers (Dec. 3, 1946)		16-for-50 (.320)
33	Joe Fulks, Phi. Warriors	vs. N.Y. Knicks (Nov. 27, 1947)		7-for-40 (.175)
33	Joe Fulks, Phi. Warriors	@ Roc. Royals (Feb. 22, 1949)		8-for-41 (.195)
33	Richie Guerin, N.Y. Knicks	@ Det. Pistons (Nov. 1, 1961)		7-for-40 (.175)
33	Wilt Chamberlain, Phi. Warriors*	vs. Chi. Packers (Jan. 24, 1962)		23-for-56 (.411)
33	Rick Barry, S.F. Warriors*	@ Chi. Bulls (Feb. 5, 1967)		17-for-50 (.340)
32	Wilt Chamberlain, Phi. Warriors*	vs. Min. Lakers (Dec. 30, 1959)		19-for-51 (.373)
32	Wilt Chamberlain, Phi. Warriors*	@ L.A. Lakers (Nov. 27, 1960)		16-for-48 (.333)
32	Elgin Baylor, L.A. Lakers*	@ Phi. Warriors (Dec. 8, 1961)		23-for-55 (.418)
32	Wilt Chamberlain, Phi. Warriors*	vs. Syr. Nationals (Dec. 26, 1961)		21-for-53 (.396)
31	Wilt Chamberlain, Phi. Warriors	vs. L.A. Lakers (Dec. 8, 1961)		31-for-62 (.500)
31	Wilt Chamberlain, S.F. Warriors	@ L.A. Lakers (Jan. 26, 1964)		18-for-49 (.367)
31	Wilt Chamberlain, S.F. Warriors	@ Phi. 76ers (Nov. 26, 1964)		27-for-58 (.466)
30	Wilt Chamberlain, S.F. Warriors*	vs. Syr. Nationals (Dec. 11, 1962)		27-for-57 (.474)
30	Kobe Bryant, L.A. Lakers	@ Bos. Celtics (Nov. 7, 2002)		17-for-47 (.362)
29	Joe Fulks, Phi. Warriors*	vs. Ind. Jets (Feb. 10, 1949)		27-for-56 (.482)
29	George Mikan, Min. Lakers*	@ Bos. Celtics (Feb. 18, 1949)		10-for-39 (.256)
29	George Mikan, Min. Lakers	@ And. Packers (Nov. 19, 1949)		7-for-36 (.194)
29	Wilt Chamberlain, Phi. Warriors*	@ N.Y. Knicks (Jan. 10, 1960)		13-for-42 (.310)
28	Joe Fulks, Phi. Warriors*	vs. Pit. Ironmen (Feb. 20, 1947)		13-for-41 (.317)
28	Joe Fulks, Phi. Warriors	vs. N.Y. Knicks (Dec. 18, 1947)		4-for-32 (.125)
28	Joe Fulks, Phi. Warriors*	@ N.Y. Knicks (Jan. 19, 1948)		8-for-36 (.222)
28	Joe Fulks, Phi. Warriors	vs. Bos. Celtics (Jan. 22, 1948)		5-for-33 (.152)
28	Joe Fulks, Phi. Warriors*	vs. Bos. Celtics (Mar. 4, 1948)		8-for-36 (.222)
28	George Mikan, Min. Lakers	@ Bos. Celtics (Nov. 9, 1948)		11-for-39 (.282)
28	Joe Fulks, Phi. Warriors	@ N.Y. Knicks (Jan. 1, 1949)		8-for-36 (.222)
28	Bob Cousy, Bos. Celtics	@ Phi. Warriors (Jan. 29, 1960)		11-for-39 (.282)
28	Elgin Baylor, L.A. Lakers*	vs. Cin. Royals (Oct. 24, 1961)		9-for-37 (.243)
28	Elgin Baylor, L.A. Lakers*	@ Phi. Warriors (Nov. 17, 1961)		15-for-43 (.349)
28	Wilt Chamberlain, Phi. Warriors	vs. Cin. Royals (Jan. 18, 1962)		22-for-50 (.440)
28	Kobe Bryant, L.A. Lakers*	vs. Uta. Jazz (Apr. 13, 2016)		22-for-50 (.440)

* Team won game.

Most FG Attempts without Hitting a Shot, Game

Shooting | | | **Pts**

0-for-17	Tim Hardaway, G.S. Warriors	@ Min. T'Wolves (Dec. 27, 1991)	2
0-for-15	Roy Hurley, Tor. Huskies	@ St.L. Bombers (Feb. 16, 1947)	1

continued on next page

Shooting   **Pts**

0-for-15	Howie Dallmar, Phi. Warriors	vs. N.Y. Knicks (Nov. 27, 1947)	5
0-for-15	Howie Dallmar, Phi. Warriors	vs. Was. Capitols (Nov. 25, 1948)	5
0-for-15	Dick Ricketts, Roc. Royals	vs. St.L. Hawks (Mar. 7, 1956)	2
0-for-15	Corky Devlin, Ft.W. Pistons	vs. Min. Lakers (Dec. 25, 1956)	3
0-for-15	Charlie Tyra, N.Y. Knicks	@ Phi. Warriors (Nov. 7, 1957)	1
0-for-15	Frank Ramsey, Bos. Celtics	vs. Cin. Royals (Dec. 8, 1960)	3
0-for-15	Les Hunter, Min. Muskies[a]	vs. Ken. Colonels[a] (Oct. 22, 1967)	6
0-for-15	Joe Hamilton, S.A. Spurs[a]	@ Vir. Squires[a] (Oct. 19, 1973)	0
0-for-15	Bob Love, Chi. Bulls	vs. K.C. Kings (Mar. 12, 1976)	1
0-for-15	Ray Williams, N.J. Nets	vs. Ind. Pacers (Dec. 28, 1981)	5
0-for-15	Rodney McCray, Sac. Kings	@ Uta. Jazz (Nov. 9, 1988)	4
0-for-14	Belus Smawley, St.L. Bombers	vs. Pro. Steamrollers (Nov. 20, 1947)	0
0-for-14	Ed Leede, Bos. Celtics	@ Was. Capitols (Dec. 13, 1950)	5
0-for-14	Jack George, Phi. Warriors	@ Syr. Nationals (Nov. 1, 1953)	2
0-for-14	Si Green, Chi. Packers	vs. Bos. Celtics (Dec. 14, 1961)	3
0-for-14	Bailey Howell, Det. Pistons	vs. St.L. Hawks (Jan. 4, 1963)	4
0-for-14	Bill Russell, Bos. Celtics	vs. Phi. 76ers (Jan. 23, 1965)	4
0-for-14	Adrian Smith, Cin. Royals	@ N.Y. Knicks (Dec. 18, 1965)	8
0-for-14	Joe Kennedy, Sea. Sonics	@ Atl. Hawks (Dec. 26, 1968)	2
0-for-14	Louie Dampier, Ken. Colonels[a]	@ Den. Rockets[a] (Apr. 1, 1969)	3
0-for-14	Connie Dierking, Cin. Royals	@ S.F. Warriors (Nov. 1, 1969)	2
0-for-14	Junior Bridgeman, Mil. Bucks	@ Was. Bullets (Jan. 24, 1984)	3
0-for-14	Dino Radja, Bos. Celtics	@ S.A. Spurs (Dec. 26, 1993)	0

[a] ABA.

Highest FG% for Players Attempting 150 Three Pointers, Season
(Min. 2000 Minutes Played)

.587	Charles Barkley, Phi. 76ers, 1987–88	.548	John Stockton, Uta. Jazz, 1996–97
.583	Nikola Jokić, Den. Nuggets, 2021–22	.548	LeBron James, Cle. Cavaliers, 2016–17
.579	Charles Barkley, Phi. 76ers, 1988–89	.545	Karl-Anthony Towns, Min. T'Wolves, 2017–18
.578	Giannis Antetokounmpo, Mil. Bucks, 2018–19	.544	Jonas Valančiūnas, N.O. Pelicans, 2021–22
.570	Charles Barkley, Phi. 76ers, 1990–91	.543	Mikal Bridges, Pho. Suns, 2020–21
.569	Giannis Antetokounmpo, Mil. Bucks, 2020–21	.542	John Stockton, Uta. Jazz, 1994–95
.567	LeBron James, Mia. Heat, 2013–14	.542	Karl-Anthony Towns, Min. T'Wolves, 2016–17
.566	Nikola Jokić, Den. Nuggets, 2020–21	.542	LeBron James, Cle. Cavaliers, 2017–18
.565	LeBron James, Mia. Heat, 2012–13	.538	John Stockton, Uta. Jazz, 1995–96
.553	Chris Mullin, G.S. Warriors, 1996–97	.537	Kevin Durant, G.S. Warriors, 2016–17
.553	Giannis Antetokounmpo, Mil. Bucks, 2021–22	.536	Chris Mullin, G.S. Warriors, 1989–90
.549	Pascal Siakam, Tor. Raptors, 2018–19	.536	T.J. Warren, Ind. Pacers, 2019–20

In Multiple Seasons, Playing All 82 Games of Season, Scoring 10 Points in Each Game

		PPG	High	Low
Hakeem Olajuwon	Hou. Rockets, 1989–90	24.3	52	11
	Hou. Rockets, 1992–93	26.1	45	10
Kareem Abdul-Jabbar	Mil. Bucks, 1969–70	28.8	51	13**
	Mil. Bucks, 1970–71	31.7	53*	15
	L.A. Lakers, 1979–80	24.8	42	10*
Karl Malone	Uta. Jazz, 1990–91	29.0	41*	14
	Uta. Jazz, 1992–93	27.0	42	13
	Uta. Jazz, 1993–94	25.2	38	13

continued on next page

	PPG	High	Low
Uta. Jazz, 1994–95	26.7	45	14
Uta. Jazz, 1995–96	25.7	51	12
Uta. Jazz, 1996–97	27.4	41**	11
Uta. Jazz, 1999–00	25.5	40	10
Kevin Garnett ... Min. T'Wolves, 1997–98	18.5	32	10
Min. T'Wolves, 2002–03	23.0	37	12*
Min. T'Wolves, 2003–04	24.2	35*	10
Min. T'Wolves, 2004–05	22.2	47	12**
Kobe Bryant ... L.A. Lakers, 2002–03	30.0	55	11
L.A. Lakers, 2008–09	26.8	61	10
Michael Jordan ... Chi. Bulls, 1984–85	28.2	49	13
Chi. Bulls, 1986–87	37.1	61*	11
Chi. Bulls, 1987–88	35.0	59	16*
Chi. Bulls, 1989–90	33.6	69	15
Chi. Bulls, 1990–91	31.5	46	14*
Chi. Bulls, 1995–96	30.4	53	12
Chi. Bulls, 1996–97	29.6	51	10
Chi. Bulls, 1997–98	28.7	49	11

* Accomplished twice.

** Accomplished three times.

Highest True Shooting Percentage* (TS%) for Players Scoring 50 Points

TS%		Pts	2P FG	3P FG	FT
1.011	Kyrie Irving, Brk. Nets @ Cha. Hornets (Mar. 8, 2022)	50	6-for-7 (.857)	9-for-12 (.750)	11-for-13 (.846)
1.001	Fred VanVleet, Tor. Raptors @ Orl. Magic (Feb. 2, 2021)	54	6-for-9 (.667)	11-for-14 (.786)	9-for-9 (1.000)
1.000	Jamal Murray, Den. Nuggets @ Cle. Cavaliers (Feb. 19, 2021)	50	13-for-15 (.867)	8-for-10 (.800)	0-for-0 (.000)
0.985	Kyrie Irving, Brk. Nets vs. Chi. Bulls (Jan. 31, 2020)	54	12-for-14 (.857)	7-for-9 (.778)	9-for-10 (.900)
0.930	Dana Barros, Phi. 76ers vs. Hou. Rockets (Mar. 14, 1995)	50	15-for-18 (.833)	6-for-8 (.750)	2-for-2 (1.000)
0.929	Stephen Curry, G.S. Warriors @ Orl. Magic (Feb. 25, 2016)	51	10-for-12 (.833)	10-for-15 (.667)	1-for-1 (1.000)
0.925	James Harden, Hou. Rockets vs. Uta. Jazz (Nov. 5, 2017)	56	12-for-17 (.706)	7-for-8 (.875)	11-for-12 (.917)
0.898	Stephen Curry, G.S. Warriors vs. Was. Wizards (Oct. 24, 2018)	51	4-for-8 (.500)	11-for-16 (.688)	10-for-10 (1.000)
0.895	Damian Lillard, Por. Blazers vs. N.O. Pelicans (Mar. 16, 2021)	50	7-for-7 (1.000)	6-for-13 (.462)	18-for-18 (1.000)
0.892	Glen Rice, Mia. Heat vs. Orl. Magic (Apr. 15, 1995)	56	13-for-19 (.684)	7-for-8 (.875)	9-for-10 (.900)
0.884	Klay Thompson, G.S. Warriors vs. Sac. Kings (Jan. 23, 2015)	52	5-for-10 (.500)	11-for-15 (.733)	9-for-10 (1.000)
0.879	James Harden, Hou. Rockets vs. Atl. Hawks (Nov. 30, 2019)	60	8-for-10 (.800)	8-for-14 (.571)	20-for-23 (.870)
0.877	CJ McCollum, Por. Blazers vs. Chi. Bulls (Jan. 31, 2018)	50	12-for-16 (.750)	6-for-9 (.667)	8-for-8 (1.000)
0.877	LeBron James, L.A. Lakers vs. Was. Wizards (Mar. 11, 2022)	50	12-for-16 (.750)	6-for-9 (.667)	8-for-8 (1.000)
0.870	Stephen Curry, G.S. Warriors @ Was. Wizards (Feb. 3, 2016)	51	8-for-13 (.615)	11-for-15 (.733)	2-for-3 (.667)
0.870	Klay Thompson, G.S. Warriors @ Chi. Bulls (Oct. 29, 2018)	52	4-for-5 (.800)	14-for-24 (.583)	2-for-2 (1.000)
0.869	Stephen Curry, G.S. Warriors @ N.Y. Knicks (Feb. 27, 2013)	54	7-for-15 (.467)	11-for-13 (.846)	7-for-7 (1.000)
0.864	Giannis Antetokounmpo, Mil. Bucks vs. Ind. Pacers (Feb. 15, 2022)	50	15-for-18 (.833)	2-for-3 (.667)	14-for-18 (.778)
0.862	T.J. Warren, Ind. Pacers vs. Phi. 76ers (Aug. 1, 2020)	53	11-for-17 (.647)	9-for-12 (.750)	4-for-4 (1.000)
0.859	Trae Young, Atl. Hawks @ Por. Blazers (Jan. 3, 2022)	56	10-for-14 (.714)	7-for-12 (.583)	15-for-15 (1.000)
0.855	Adrian Dantley, Uta. Jazz @ Den. Nuggets (Jan. 7, 1981)	51	20-for-25 (.800)	0-for-0 (.000)	11-for-11 (1.000)
0.854	Stephen Curry, G.S. Warriors vs. Den. Nuggets (Apr. 12, 2021)	53	4-for-6 (.667)	10-for-18 (.556)	15-for-16 (.938)

* True Shooting Percentage (TS%) is "A measure of shooting efficiency that takes into account 2-point field goals, 3-point field goals, and free throws."

(basketball-reference.com)

Highest TS%, Season (Min. 2000 Minutes Played)

.732	Rudy Gobert, Uta. Jazz, 2021–22	.697	Tyson Chandler, Dal. Mavericks, 2014–15
.708	Tyson Chandler, N.Y. Knicks, 2011–12	.697	Tyson Chandler, Dal. Mavericks, 2010–11
.702	Artis Gilmore, Chi. Bulls, 1981–82	.689	Wilt Chamberlain, L.A. Lakers, 1972–73
.699	Artis Gilmore, Chi. Bulls, 1980–81	.684	Duncan Robinson, Mia. Heat, 2019–20
.699	Kyle Korver, Atl. Hawks, 2014–15	.683	Rudy Gobert, Uta. Jazz, 2020–21
.699	Rudy Gobert, Uta. Jazz, 2019–20		

Scoring Title

Closest Scoring Title Races

Diff	Season		Pts
1	2015–16	James Harden, Hou. Rockets	2376
		Stephen Curry, G.S. Warriors	2375
5	1998–99	Shaquille O'Neal, L.A. Lakers	1289
		Allen Iverson, Phi. 76ers	1284
6	1993–94	David Robinson, S.A. Spurs	2383
		Shaquille O'Neal, Orl. Magic	2377
9	1967–68	Doug Moe, N.O. Buccaneers[a]	1884
		Connie Hawkins, Pit. Pipers[a]	1875
10	1974–75	George McGinnis, Ind. Pacers[a]	2353
		Julius Erving, N.Y. Nets[a]	2343
14	1971–72	Dan Issel, Ken. Colonels[a]	2538
		Charlie Scott[*], Vir. Squires[a]	2524
18	1984–85	Michael Jordan, Chi. Bulls	2313
		Larry Bird, Bos. Celtics	2295
23	2003–04	Kevin Garnett, Min. T'Wolves	1987
		Peja Stojaković, Sac. Kings	1964
24	1972–73	Dan Issel, Ken. Colonels[a]	2292
		Julius Erving, Vir. Squires[a]	2268
31	1981–82	George Gervin, S.A. Spurs	2551
		Moses Malone, Hou. Rockets	2520

[a] ABA.

[*] Played six games for the Pho. Suns (NBA), but point total was while a member of the Vir. Squires (ABA).

Largest Margin Between Points Champion and Runner-Up

Margin	Season	Leader (Points)	Runner-Up (Points)
+1534	1961–62	Wilt Chamberlain, Phi. Warriors (4029)	Walt Bellamy, Chi. Packers (2495)
+867	1962–63	Wilt Chamberlain, S.F. Warriors (3586)	Elgin Baylor, L.A. Lakers (2719)
+696	1986–87	Michael Jordan, Chi. Bulls (3041)	Alex English, Den. Nuggets (2345)
+659	2018–19	James Harden, Hou. Rockets (2818)	Paul George, Ok.C. Thunder (2159)
+570	1971–72	Kareem Abdul-Jabbar, Mil. Bucks (2822)	John Havlicek, Bos. Celtics (2252)
+503	1950–51	George Mikan, Min. Lakers (1932)	Alex Groza , Ind. Olympians (1429)
+495	1960–61	Wilt Chamberlain, Phi. Warriors (3033)	Elgin Baylor, L.A. Lakers (2538)
+481	2013–14	Kevin Durant, Ok.C. Thunder (2593)	Carmelo Anthony, N.Y. Knicks (2112)
+471	1987–88	Michael Jordan, Chi. Bulls (2868)	Dominique Wilkins, Atl. Hawks (2397)
+468	1963–64	Wilt Chamberlain, S.F. Warriors (2948)	Oscar Robertson, Cin. Royals (2480)
+466	1979–80	George Gervin, S.A. Spurs (2585)	Moses Malone, Hou. Rockets (2119)
+463	1946–47	Joe Fulks, Phi. Warriors (1389)	Bob Feerick, Was. Capitols (926)
+427	1972–73	Tiny Archibald, K.C.-Oma. Kings (2719)	Kareem Abdul-Jabbar, Mil. Bucks (2292)
+385	1995–96	Michael Jordan, Chi. Bulls (2491)	Karl Malone, Uta. Jazz (2106)
+381	1974–75	Bob McAdoo, Buf. Braves (2831)	Rick Barry, G.S. Warriors (2450)

continued on next page

Margin	Season	Leader (Points)	Runner-Up (Points)
+376	1953–54	Neil Johnston, Phi. Warriors (1759)	Bob Cousy, Bos. Celtics (1383)
+369	1949–50	George Mikan, Min. Lakers (1865)	Alex Groza, Ind. Olympians (1496)
+369	1959–60	Wilt Chamberlain, Phi. Warriors (2707)	Jack Twyman, Cin. Royals (2338)
+363	1966–67	Rick Barry, S.F. Warriors (2775)	Oscar Robertson, Cin. Royals (2412)
+357	2019–20	James Harden, Hou. Rockets (2335)	Damian Lillard, Por. Blazers (1978)
+354	2005–06	Kobe Bryant, L.A. Lakers (2832)	LeBron James, Cle. Cavaliers (2478)
+324	1992–93	Michael Jordan, Chi. Bulls (2541)	Karl Malone, Uta. Jazz (2217)
+317	2014–15	James Harden, Hou. Rockets (2217)	Stephen Curry, G.S. Warriors (1900)
+307	1988–89	Michael Jordan, Chi. Bulls (2633)	Karl Malone, Uta. Jazz (2326)
+304	1975–76	Julius Erving, N.Y. Nets[a] (2462)	David Thompson, Den. Nuggets[a] (2158)

[a] ABA.

Lowest Scoring Average to Lead League

22.1 .... Joe Fulks, Phi. Warriors, 1947–48
22.3 .... Neil Johnston, Phi. Warriors, 1952–53
22.7 .... Neil Johnston, Phi. Warriors, 1954–55
23.2 .... Joe Fulks, Phi. Warriors, 1946–47
24.4 .... Neil Johnston, Phi. Warriors, 1953–54
25.4 .... Paul Arizin, Phi. Warriors, 1951–52
25.6 .... Paul Arizin, Phi. Warriors, 1956–57
25.7 .... Bob Pettit, St.L. Hawks, 1955–56
26.8 .... Allen Iverson, Phi. 76ers, 1998–99
26.8 .... Connie Hawkins, Pit. Pipers[a], 1967–68
27.2 .... George Gervin, S.A. Spurs, 1977–78
27.4 .... Julius Erving, N.Y. Nets[a], 1973–74
27.4 .... George Mikan, Min. Lakers, 1949–50
27.7 .... Kevin Durant, Ok.C. Thunder, 2010–11
27.8 .... George Yardley, Det. Pistons, 1957–58

[a] ABA.

Lowest Lifetime Scoring Average for Players Who Led League

Career PPG		Led League
16.4	Joe Fulks	1946–47, Phi. Warriors (23.2); 1947–48, Phi. Warriors (22.1)
18.7	Connie Hawkins	1967–68, Pit. Pipers[a] (26.8)
18.8	Tiny Archibald	1972–73, K.C.-Oma. Kings (34.0)
19.1	Larry Jones	1968–69, Den. Rockets[a] (28.4)
19.2	George Yardley	1957–58, Det. Pistons (27.8)
19.4	Neil Johnston	1952–53, Phi. Warriors (22.3); 1953–54, Phi. Warriors (24.4); 1954–55, Phi. Warriors (22.7)
19.6	Tracy McGrady	2002–03, Orl. Magic (32.1); 2003–04, Orl. Magic (28.0)
20.2	George McGinnis	1974–75, Ind. Pacers (29.8)
20.3	Spencer Haywood	1969–70, Den. Rockets[a] (30.0)
20.7	Charlie Scott	1971–72, Vir. Squires[a] (34.6)
21.0	Elvin Hayes	1968–69, S.D. Rockets (28.4)
21.1	David Robinson	1993–94, S.A. Spurs (29.8)
21.5	Alex English	1982–83, Den. Nuggets (28.4)
22.0	Dwyane Wade	2008–09, Mia. Heat (30.2)
22.1	Bob McAdoo	1973–74, Buf. Braves (30.6); 1974–75, Buf. Braves (34.5); 1975–76, Buf. Braves (31.1)
22.5	Bernard King	1984–85, N.Y. Knicks (32.9)
22.5	Carmelo Anthony^	2012–13, N.Y. Knicks (28.7)
22.6	Dan Issel	1970–71, Ken. Colonels[a] (29.9)
22.8	Paul Arizin	1951–52, Phi. Warriors (25.4); 1956–57, Phi. Warriors (25.6)
22.8	Russell Westbrook^	2014–15, Ok.C. Thunder (28.2); 2016–17, Ok.C. Thunder (31.6)

[a] ABA.

^ Active.

Players Leading League in Scoring on Teams with Losing Records

	Pts	Record
Neil Johnston, Phi. Warriors, 1952–53	1564	12–57 (.174)
Neil Johnston, Phi. Warriors, 1953–54	1759	29–43 (.403)
Neil Johnston, Phi. Warriors, 1954–55	1631	33–39 (.458)
Bob Pettit, St.L. Hawks, 1955–56	1849	33–39 (.458)
George Yardley, Det. Pistons, 1957–58	2001	33–39 (.458)
Wilt Chamberlain, S.F. Warriors, 1962–63	3586	31–49 (.388)
Wilt Chamberlain, S.F. Warriors/Phi. 76ers, 1964–65	2534	17–63/40–40 (.213/.500)
Dave Bing, Det. Pistons, 1967–68	2142	40–42 (.488)
Elvin Hayes, S.D. Rockets, 1968–69	2327	37–45 (.451)
Tiny Archibald, K.C.-Oma. Kings, 1972–73	2719	36–46 (.439)
Pete Maravich, N.O. Jazz, 1976–77	2273	35–47 (.427)
Adrian Dantley, Uta. Jazz, 1980–81	2452	28–54 (.341)
Michael Jordan, Chi. Bulls, 1984–85	2313	38–44 (.463)
Michael Jordan, Chi. Bulls, 1986–87	3041	40–42 (.488)
Jerry Stackhouse, Det. Pistons, 2000–01	2380	32–50 (.390)

Points Guards Winning Scoring Title[*]

	Pts
Dave Bing, Det. Pistons, 1967–68	2142
Larry Jones, Den. Rockets[a], 1968–69	2133
Tiny Archibald, K.C.-Oma. Kings, 1972–73	2719
Allen Iverson, Phi. 76ers, 2004–05	2302
Russell Westbrook, Ok.C. Thunder, 2016–17	2558
James Harden, Hou. Rockets, 2018–19	2818
Stephen Curry, G.S. Warriors, 2020–21	2015
Trae Young, Atl. Hawks, 2021–22	2155

[*] Only includes players listed at the points guard position for that season.
[a] ABA.

Fewest Turnovers for Scoring Champion[*]

TO		Pts
122	Shaquille O'Neal, L.A. Lakers, 1998–99[**]	1289
166	Michael Jordan, Chi. Bulls, 1996–97	2431
185	Michael Jordan, Chi. Bulls, 1997–98	2357
197	Michael Jordan, Chi. Bulls, 1995–96	2491
199	Doug Moe, N.O. Buccaneers[a], 1967–68	1884
200	Michael Jordan, Chi. Bulls, 1991–92	2404
202	Michael Jordan, Chi. Bulls, 1990–91	2580
204	Shaquille O'Neal, Orl. Magic, 1994–95	2315
207	Michael Jordan, Chi. Bulls, 1992–93	2541
210	George Gervin, S.A. Spurs, 1981–82	2551
212	Kevin Garnett, Min. T'Wolves, 2003–04	1987
213	Stephen Curry, G.S. Warriors, 2020–21[***]	2015
216	Dan Issel, Ken. Colonels[a], 1972–73	2292
218	Kevin Durant, Ok.C. Thunder, 2010–11	2161
218	Larry Jones, Den. Rockets[a], 1968–69	2133
221	Dan Issel, Ken. Colonels[a], 1970–71	2480
223	Shaquille O'Neal, L.A. Lakers, 1999–00	2344
241	Paul Pierce, Bos. Celtics, 2001–02	2144
244	Dan Issel, Ken. Colonels[a], 1971–72	2538

continued on next page

TO		Pts
247	Michael Jordan, Chi. Bulls, 1989–90	2753
248	Kevin Durant, Ok.C. Thunder, 2011–12	1850
249	Alex English, Den. Nuggets, 1985–86	2414
250	Kobe Bryant, L.A. Lakers, 2005–06	2832

* Turnovers became an official stat in the ABA for the 1967–68 season and in the NBA for the 1977–78 season.

** Strike-shortened season.

*** Covid-shortened season.

ᵃ ABA.

Three Pointers

Most Three Pointers by Decade

NBA

1979–80 – 1989–90

568	Dale Ellis
520	Larry Bird
514	Danny Ainge
491	Michael Adams
483	Craig Hodges
482	Darrell Griffith
440	Trent Tucker
428	Michael Cooper
384	Sleepy Floyd
360	Derek Harper

1990–91 – 1999–00

1558	Reggie Miller
1336	Glen Rice
1214	Dennis Scott
1196	Tim Hardaway
1196	Mitch Richmond
1178	Dan Majerle
1177	Mookie Blaylock
1162	Vernon Maxwell
1151	Dale Ellis
1119	John Starks

2000–01 – 2009–10

1947	Ray Allen
1546	Rashard Lewis
1546	Peja Stojaković
1477	Jason Terry
1390	Chauncey Billups
1287	Paul Pierce
1271	Steve Nash
1255	Mike Miller
1245	Mike Bibby
1229	Jason Richardson

2010–11 – 2019–20

2329	Stephen Curry
2231	James Harden
1798	Klay Thompson
1776	Damian Lillard
1651	J.J. Redick
1600	Wesley Matthews
1595	Kyle Lowry
1590	Paul George
1554	Kyle Korver
1463	Kemba Walker

2020–21 – 2021–22

622	Stephen Curry
544	Buddy Hield
482	Duncan Robinson
444	Terry Rozier
417	Jayson Tatum
416	Fred VanVleet
410	Donovan Mitchell
398	Jordan Clarkson
393	Luka Dončić
388	Patty Mills

ABA

1967–68 – 1975–76

794	Louie Dampier
506	Bill Keller
503	Glen Combs
409	George Lehmann
398	Darel Carrier
322	Warren Jabali
312	Roger Brown
306	Chico Vaughn
275	Freddie Lewis
269	Stew Johnson

Evolution of Three-Point Record

NBA

1979–80 .... 90 .... Brian Taylor, S.D. Clippers
1983–84 .... 91 .... Darrell Griffith, Uta. Jazz
1984–85 .... 92 .... Darrell Griffith, Uta. Jazz
1987–88 .... 148 .... Danny Ainge, Bos. Celtics
1988–89 .... 166 .... Michael Adams, Den. Nuggets
1990–91 .... 172 .... Vernon Maxwell, Hou. Rockets
1993–94 .... 192 .... Dan Marjerle, Pho. Suns
1994–95 .... 217 .... John Starks, N.Y. Knicks
1995–96 .... 267 .... Dennis Scott, Orl. Magic
2005–06 .... 269 .... Ray Allen, Sea. Sonics
2012–13 .... 272 .... Stephen Curry, G.S. Warriors
2014–15 .... 286 .... Stephen Curry, G.S. Warriors
2015–16 .... 402 .... Stephen Curry, G.S. Warriors

ABA

1967–68 .... 147 .... Lester Selvage, Ana. Amigos
1968–69 .... 199 .... Louie Dampier, Ken. Colonels

Most 3P, Season

402 .... Stephen Curry, G.S. Warriors, 2015–16
378 .... James Harden, Hou. Rockets, 2018–19
354 .... Stephen Curry, G.S. Warriors, 2018–19
337 .... Stephen Curry, G.S. Warriors, 2020–21
324 .... Stephen Curry, G.S. Warriors, 2016–17
299 .... James Harden, Hou. Rockets, 2019–20
292 .... Paul George, Ok.C. Thunder, 2018–19
286 .... Stephen Curry, G.S. Warriors, 2014–15
285 .... Stephen Curry, G.S. Warriors, 2021–22
282 .... Buddy Hield, Sac. Kings, 2020–21
278 .... Buddy Hield, Sac. Kings, 2018–19
276 .... Klay Thompson, G.S. Warriors, 2015–16
275 .... Damian Lillard, Por. Blazers, 2020–21

Most 3P, Career

3117 .... Stephen Curry^
2973 .... Ray Allen
2593 .... James Harden^
2560 .... Reggie Miller
2450 .... Kyle Korver
2290 .... Vince Carter
2282 .... Jason Terry
2221 .... Jamal Crawford
2143 .... Paul Pierce
2143 .... Damian Lillard^
2140 .... LeBron James^

1988 .... Jason Kidd
1982 .... Dirk Nowitzki
1978 .... Joe Johnson^
1971 .... Kyle Lowry^
1950 .... J.J. Redick
1930 .... J.R. Smith
1912 .... Klay Thompson^
1852 .... Paul George
1830 .... Chauncey Billups
1827 .... Kobe Bryant

^Active.

Three-Point Leaders by State of Birth

Alabama	Chuck Person (Brantley)	1220
Alaska	Mario Chalmers (Anchorage)	755
Arizona	Sean Elliott (Tucson)	589
Arkansas	Joe Johnson^ (Little Rock)	1978
California	Ray Allen (Merced)	2973
Colorado	Chauncey Billups (Denver)	1830
Connecticut	Michael Adams (Hartford)	949
Delaware	Donte DiVincenzo^ (Wilmington)	310
Florida	Vince Carter (Daytona Beach)	2290
Georgia	Dale Ellis (Marietta)	1719
Hawaii	Cedric Ceballos (Maui)	235
Idaho	Luke Ridnour (Coeur d'Alene)	584
Illinois	Tim Hardaway (Chicago)	1542
Indiana	Eric Gordon^ (Indianapolis)	1746
Iowa	Kirk Hinrich (Sioux City)	1172
Kansas	Earl Watson (Kansas City)	502
Kentucky	Allan Houston (Louisville)	1305
Louisiana	Rashard Lewis (Pineville)	1787
Maine	Duncan Robinson^ (York)	762
Maryland	Dennis Scott (Hagerstown)	1214
Massachusetts	Dana Barros (Boston)	1090
Michigan	Jason Richardson (Saginaw)	1608
Minnesota	Devean George (Minneapolis)	427
Mississippi	Mo Williams (Jackson)	1094
Missouri	Bradley Beal^ (St. Louis)	1434
Montana	Adam Morrison (Glendive)	124
Nebraska	Fred Hoiberg (Lincoln)	373
Nevada	Pat Garrity (Las Vegas)	631
New Hampshire	Matt Bonner (Concord)	797
New Jersey	J.R. Smith (Freehold)	1930
New Mexico	Andre Roberson (Las Cruces)	112
New York	Carmelo Anthony^ (Brooklyn)	1731
North Carolina	Chris Paul^ (Winston-Salem)	1544
North Dakota	Doug McDermott^ (Grand Forks)	723
Ohio	Stephen Curry^ (Akron)	3117
Oklahoma	John Starks (Tulsa)	1222
Oregon	Damon Stoudamire (Portland)	1236
Pennsylvania	Kyle Lowry^ (Philadelphia)	1971
Rhode Island	Joe Hassett (Providence)	194
South Carolina	Khris Middleton^ (Charleston)	1216
South Dakota	Mike Miller (Mitchell)	1590
Tennessee	J.J. Redick (Cookeville)	1950
Texas	Wesley Matthews^ (San Antonio)	1782
Utah	Byron Scott (Ogden)	775
Vermont	N/A	N/A
Virginia	Dell Curry (Harrisonburg)	1245
Washington	Jason Terry (Seattle)	2282
West Virginia	Jason Williams (Belle)	1238
Wisconsin	Nick Van Exel (Kenosha)	1528
Wyoming	James Johnson (Cheyenne)	355
District of Columbia	Kevin Durant^	1770
Puerto Rico	J.J. Barea (Mayaguez)	819
Virgin Islands	Raja Bell (St. Croix)	956

^Active.

All-Time 3P Leaders by First Letter of Last Name

A	Allen, Ray	2973	N	Nowitzki, Dirk	1982
B	Billups, Chauncey	1830	O	Oladipo, Victor^	744
C	Curry, Stephen^	3117	P	Pierce, Paul	2143
D	Durant, Kevin^	1770	Q	Quickley, Immanuel^	255
E	Ellis, Dale	1719	R	Redick, J.J.	1950
F	Finley, Michael	1454	S	Smith, J.R.	1930
G	George, Paul^	1852	T	Terry, Jason	2282
H	Harden, James^	2593	U	Udrih, Beno	465
I	Irving, Kyrie^	1355	V	Van Exel, Nick	1528
J	James, LeBron^	2140	W	Walker, Kemba^	1663
K	Korver, Kyle	2450	X	N/A	N/A
L	Lillard, Damian^	2143	Y	Young, Nick	1039
M	Miller, Reggie	2560	Z	Zhizhi, Wang/Zipser, Paul	70

^ Active.

Most 3P, Month by Month (Regular Season)

October	55	Stephen Curry, G.S. Warriors
November	82	James Harden, Hou. Rockets
December	78	James Harden, Hou. Rockets
January	81	Stephen Curry, G.S. Warriors
February	75	Stephen Curry, G.S. Warriors
March	79	Klay Thompson, G.S. Warriors
April	96	Stephen Curry, G.S. Warriors
May	53	Stephen Curry, G.S. Warriors
July	8	Trey Burke, Dal. Mavericks
August	42	Damian Lillard, Por. Blazers

Most Times Leading League in 3P

7	Stephen Curry	2012–13, G.S. Warriors	272
		2013–14, G.S. Warriors	261
		2014–15, G.S. Warriors	286
		2015–16, G.S. Warriors	402
		2016–17, G.S. Warriors	324
		2020–21, G.S. Warriors	337
		2021–22, G.S. Warriors	285
3	Bill Keller	1972–73, Ind. Pacers[a]	71
		1974–75, Ind. Pacers[a]	80
		1975–76, Ind. Pacers[a]	123
3	Ray Allen	2001–02, Mil. Bucks	229
		2002–03, Mil. Bucks/Sea. Sonics	201
		2005–06, Sea. Sonics	269
3	James Harden	2017–18, Hou. Rockets	265
		2018–19, Hou. Rockets	378
		2019–20, Hou. Rockets	299
2	Louie Dampier	1968–69, Ken. Colonels[a]	199
		1969–70, Ken. Colonels[a]	198
2	Darrell Griffith	1983–84, Uta. Jazz	91
		1984–85, Uta. Jazz	92
2	Larry Bird	1985–86, Bos. Celtics	82
		1986–87, Bos. Celtics	90
2	Michael Adams	1988–89, Den. Nuggets	166
		1989–90, Den. Nuggets	158
2	Vernon Maxwell	1990–91, Hou. Rockets	172
		1991–92, Hou. Rockets	162
2	Dan Majerle	1992–93, Pho. Suns	167
		1993–94, Pho. Suns	192
2	Reggie Miller	1992–93, Ind. Pacers	167
		1996–97, Ind. Pacers	229

[a] ABA.

Consecutive Seasons Leading League in 3P

5	Stephen Curry	G.S. Warriors, 2012–13	272
		G.S. Warriors, 2013–14	261
		G.S. Warriors, 2014–15	286
		G.S. Warriors, 2015–16	402
		G.S. Warriors, 2016–17	324

continued on next page

3	James Harden	Hou. Rockets, 2017–18	265
		Hou. Rockets, 2018–19	378
		Hou. Rockets, 2019–20	299
2	Louie Dampier	Ken. Colonels[a], 1968–69	199
		Ken. Colonels[a], 1969–70	198
2	Bill Keller	Ind. Pacers[a], 1974–75	80
		Ind. Pacers[a], 1975–76	123
2	Darrell Griffith	Uta. Jazz, 1983–84	91
		Uta. Jazz, 1984–85	92
2	Larry Bird	Bos. Celtics, 1985–86	82
		Bos. Celtics, 1986–87	90
2	Michael Adams	Den. Nuggets, 1988–89	166
		Den. Nuggets, 1989–90	158
2	Vernon Maxwell	Hou. Rockets, 1990–91	172
		Hou. Rockets, 1991–92	162
2	Dan Majerle	Pho. Suns, 1992–93	167
		Pho. Suns, 1993–94	192
2	Ray Allen	Mil. Bucks, 2001–02	229
		Mil. Bucks/Sea. Sonics, 2002–03	201
2	Stephen Curry	G.S. Warriors, 2020–21	337
		G.S. Warriors, 2021–22	285

[a]ABA.

Former ABA Players to Lead NBA in 3P

1979–80	Brian Taylor, S.D. Clippers	90
1981–82	Don Buse, Ind. Pacers	73

Players Leading League in 3P for Multiple Teams

Ray Allen	Mil. Bucks, 2001–02	229
	Mil. Bucks/Sea. Sonics, 2002–03	201
	Sea. Sonics, 2005–06	269

Players with 300 Three Pointers on Three Different Teams

Ray Allen	1051	Mil. Bucks (1996–2003)
	869	Sea. Sonics (2003–07)
	798	Bos. Celtics (2007–12)
J.J. Redick	549	Orl. Magic (2006–13)
	674	L.A. Clippers (2013–17)
	433	Phi. 76ers (2017–19)
Paul George^	897	Ind. Pacers (2010–17)
	536	Ok.C. Thunder (2017–19)
	419	L.A. Clippers (2019–22)
Ryan Anderson^	533	Orl. Magic (2009–12)
	378	N.O. Hornets Pelicans (2012–16)
	336	Hou. Rockets (2016–18; 2019–20)
Kyle Korver	661	Phi. 76ers (2003–07)
	348	Uta. Jazz (2007–10)
	818	Atl. Hawks (2012–17)
Vince Carter	554	Tor. Raptors (1998–2004)
	638	N.J. Nets (2004–09)
	382	Dal. Mavericks (2011–14)

continued on next page

Jamal Crawford	318	Chi. Bulls (2000–04)
	600	N.Y. Knicks (2004–08)
	662	L.A. Clippers (2012–17)
Kyrie Irving	723	Cle. Cavaliers (2011–17)
	340	Bos. Celtics (2017–19)
	308	Brk. Nets (2019–22)
LeBron James^	1251	Cle. Cavaliers (2003–10; 2014–18)
	365	Mia. Heat (2010–14)
	524	L.A. Lakers (2018–22)
Joe Johnson^	349	Pho. Suns (2002–05)
	900	Atl. Hawks (2005–12)
	516	Brk. Nets (2012–16)
J.R. Smith	768	Den. Nuggets (2006–11)
	443	N.Y. Knicks (2011–15)
	585	Cle. Cavaliers (2015–19)
Eric Gordon^	356	L.A. Clippers (2008–11)
	421	N.O. Hornets-Pelicans (2011–16)
	969	Hou. Rockets (2016–22)
Jason Williams	343	Sac. Kings (1998–2001)
	500	Mem. Grizzlies (2001–05)
	304	Mia. Heat (2005–08)
Bojan Bogdanović^	319	Brk. Nets (2014–17)
	319	Ind. Pacers (2017–19)
	550	Uta. Jazz (2019–22)

^Active.

Multiple Seasons with 200 Three Pointers

9 .... Stephen Curry^	2 .... Mitch Richmond
7 .... Klay Thompson^	2 .... Antoine Walker
7 .... Damian Lillard^	2 .... Peja Stojaković
6 .... James Harden^	2 .... Gilbert Arenas
5 .... Ray Allen	2 .... Kyle Korver
4 .... J.J. Redick	2 .... Rashard Lewis
4 .... Buddy Hield^	2 .... Ryan Anderson^
3 .... Paul George^	2 .... Kyle Lowry^
3 .... Eric Gordon^	2 .... Bradley Beal^
3 .... Kemba Walker^	2 .... Tim Hardaway Jr.^
3 .... Duncan Robinson^	2 .... Terry Rozier^
2 .... Mookie Blaylock	2 .... Trae Young^

^Active.

Fewest Games to 1000 Three Pointers

Games		Career 3P
350	Buddy Hield	1417
369	Stephen Curry	3117
372	Klay Thompson	1912
385	Damian Lillard	2143
435	Robert Covington	1190
457	Dennis Scott	1214
460	Bradley Beal	1434
473	Ray Allen	2973

continued on next page

Games		Career 3P
474	CJ McCollum	1368
476	Gilbert Arenas	1079
481	Paul George	1852
484	Kyrie Irving	1371
484	Eric Gordon	1746
488	Wesley Matthews	1729
488	Peja Stojaković	1760
491	Ryan Anderson	1325
493	Tim Hardaway Jr.	1253
496	James Harden	2593
514	Kemba Walker	1663
516	Bojan Bogdanović	1233

Most 3P in First Three Seasons in League

602	Buddy Hield	2016–17 (148), 2017–18 (176), 2018–19 (278)
599	Damian Lillard	2012–13 (185), 2013–14 (218), 2014–15 (196)
548	Donovan Mitchell	2017–18 (187), 2018–19 (188), 2019–20 (173)
545	Klay Thompson	2011–12 (111), 2012–13 (211), 2013–14 (223)
531	Luka Dončić	2018–19 (168), 2019–20 (171), 2020–21 (192)
530	Duncan Robinson	2018–19 (10), 2019–20 (270), 2020–21 (250)
497	Trae Young	2018–19 (156), 2019–20 (205), 2020–21 (136)
491	Kyle Korver	2003–04 (81), 2004–05 (226*), 2005–06 (184)
455	Ben Gordon	2004–05 (134), 2005–06 (166), 2006–07 (155)
450	Nick Van Exel	1993–94 (123), 1994–95 (183), 1995–96 (144)
432	Jamal Murray	2016–17 (115), 2017–18 (165), 2018–19 (152)
431	Devonte' Graham	2018–19 (34), 2019–20 (218), 2020–21 (179)
427	Bogdan Bogdanović	2017–18 (129), 2018–19 (134), 2019–20 (164)
415	Kirk Hinrich	2003–04 (144), 2004–05 (145), 2005–06 (126)
410	Jayson Tatum	2017–18 (105), 2018–19 (116), 2019–20 (189)
407	Landry Shamet	2018–19 (167), 2019–20 (111), 2020–21 (129)
404	Wesley Person	1994–95 (116), 1995–96 (117), 1996–97 (171)
403	Kevin Huerter	2018–19 (136), 2019–20 (127), 2020–21 (140)
400	Damon Stoudamire	1995–96 (133), 1996–97 (176), 1997–98 (91)

* Led league.

Most 3P, Rookie Season

187 .... Donovan Mitchell, Uta. Jazz, 2017–18
185 .... Damian Lillard*, Por. Blazers, 2012–13
175 .... Saddiq Bey, Det. Pistons, 2020–21
171 .... Anthony Edwards, Min. T'Wolves, 2020–21
168 .... Luka Dončić*, Dal. Mavericks, 2018–19
167 .... Landry Shamet, Phi. 76ers/L.A. Clippers, 2018–19
166 .... Stephen Curry, G.S. Warriors, 2009–10
159 .... Rudy Fernández, Por. Blazers, 2008–09
159 .... Kyle Kuzma, L.A. Lakers, 2017–18
158 .... Kerry Kittles, N.J. Nets, 1996–97
157 .... Jalen Green, Hou. Rockets, 2021–22
156 .... Juan Carlos Navarro, Mem. Grizzlies, 2007–08
156 .... Trae Young, Atl. Hawks, 2018–19
155 .... Allen Iverson*, Phi. 76ers, 1996–97
154 .... Matt Maloney, Hou. Rockets, 1996–97

* Rookie of the Year.

Forwards Leading League in 3P

Dennis Scott, Orl. Magic, 1995–96........................ 267
Antoine Walker, Bos. Celtics, 2000–01.................. 221
Peja Stojaković, Sac. Kings, 2003–04 240
Rashard Lewis, Orl. Magic, 2008–09..................... 220
Ryan Anderson, Orl. Magic, 2011–12 166

Youngest 3P Champion

Age (Birthdate)		3P
22 (Apr. 7)...............	Bo Lamar, S.D. Conquistadors[a], 1973–74	69
23 (May 6)...............	Ryan Anderson, Orl. Magic, 2011–12.............................	166
23 (Mar. 17)............	Kyle Korver, Phi. 76ers, 2004–05	226
24 (Nov. 20)............	Louie Dampier*, Ken. Colonels[a], 1968–69......................	199
24 (Aug. 12)	Antoine Walker, Bos. Celtics, 2000–01	221
24 (Apr. 13)	Quentin Richardson, Pho. Suns, 2004–05	226
24 (Mar. 14)............	Stephen Curry, G.S. Warriors, 2012–13........................	272
24 (Mar. 7)..............	Lester Selvage, Ana. Amigos[a], 1967–68	147
25 (Dec. 2)..............	Dorell Wright, G.S. Warriors, 2010–11.........................	194
25 (Nov. 20)............	Louie Dampier, Ken. Colonels[a], 1969–70	198
25 (Oct. 30)	Glen Combs, Uta. Stars[a], 1971–72	103
25 (Oct. 17)	Mike Bratz, Cle. Cavaliers, 1980–81	57
25 (Sep. 12)............	Vernon Maxwell, Hou. Rockets, 1990–91	172
25 (Aug. 30)	Bill Keller, Ind. Pacers[a], 1972–73	71
25 (Jun. 16).............	Darrell Griffith, Uta. Jazz, 1983–84..............................	91
25 (Mar. 14)............	Stephen Curry, G.S. Warriors, 2013–14........................	261
25 (Jan. 14)	Aaron Brooks, Hou. Rockets, 2009–10	209
25 (Jan. 6)	Gilbert Arenas, Was. Wizards, 2006–07........................	205

[a] ABA.

Oldest 3P Champion

Age (Birthdate)		3P
33 (Mar. 14)............	Stephen Curry, G.S. Warriors, 2021–22	285
32 (Mar. 14)............	Stephen Curry, G.S. Warriors, 2020–21	337
31 (Jul. 23)	Gary Payton, Sea. Sonics, 1999–00	177
31 (Aug. 10)	Don Buse, Ind. Pacers, 1981–82.................................	73
31 (Aug. 24)	Reggie Miller, Ind. Pacers, 1996–97............................	229
30 (Jul. 20)	Ray Allen, Sea. Sonics, 2005–06.................................	269
30 (Aug. 26)	James Harden, Hou. Rockets, 2019–20	299
30 (Sep. 19)............	Raja Bell, Pho. Suns, 2006–07	205
30 (Nov. 29)............	Dee Brown, Tor. Raptors, 1998–99..............................	135
30 (Dec. 7)..............	Larry Bird, Bos. Celtics, 1986–87	90
29 (Aug. 8)	Rashard Lewis, Orl. Magic, 2008–09............................	220
29 (Aug. 10)	John Starks, N.Y. Knicks, 1994–95	217
29 (Aug. 26)	James Harden, Hou. Rockets, 2018–19	378
29 (Dec. 7)..............	Larry Bird, Bos. Celtics, 1985–86	82

Most 3P in a Season, Not Leading League (Runner-Up)

3P	Runner-Up	Season	Leader	3P
354	Stephen Curry, G.S. Warriors	2018–19	James Harden, Hou. Rockets	378
282	Buddy Hield Sac. Kings	2020–21	Stephen Curry, G.S. Warriors	337
276	Klay Thompson G.S. Warriors	2015–16	Stephen Curry, G.S. Warriors	402
271	Buddy Hield Sac. Kings	2019–20	James Harden, Hou. Rockets	299

continued on next page

3P	Runner-Up	Season	Leader	3P
268	Klay Thompson, G.S. Warriors	2016–17	Stephen Curry, G.S. Warriors	324
257	George McCloud, Dal. Mavericks	1995–96	Dennis Scott, Orl. Magic	267
244	Paul George, Ok.C. Thunder	2017–18	Dennis Scott, Orl. Magic	265
239	Klay Thompson, G.S. Warriors	2014–15	Stephen Curry, G.S. Warriors	286
231	Peja Stojaković, N.O. Hornets	2007–08	Jason Richardson, Cha. Bobcats	243
223	Klay Thompson, G.S. Warriors	2013–14	Stephen Curry, G.S. Warriors	261
222	Antoine Walker, Bos. Celtics	2003–04	Ray Allen, Sea. Sonics	229
221	Mookie Blaylock, Atl. Hawks	1996–97	Reggie Miller, Ind. Pacers	229
213	Ryan Anderson, N.O. Hornets	2012–13	Stephen Curry, G.S. Warriors	272
202	Ray Allen, Mil. Bucks/Sea. Sonics	2002–03	Antoine Walker, Bos. Celtics	221

Most Career 3P, Never Leading League

2290	Vince Carter	1830	Chauncey Billups
2282	Jason Terry	1827	Kobe Bryant
2221	Jamal Crawford	1770	Kevin Durant^
2143	Damian Lillard^	1760	Wesley Matthews
2143	Paul Pierce	1746	Eric Gordon^
2140	LeBron James^	1731	Carmelo Anthony^
1988	Jason Kidd	1719	Dale Ellis
1982	Dirk Nowitzki	1685	Steve Nash
1978	Joe Johnson^	1663	Kemba Walker^
1950	J.J. Redick	1561	Danny Green^
1930	J.R. Smith	1544	Chris Paul^
1914	Kyle Lowry	1542	Tim Hardaway
1912	Klay Thompson^	1528	Nick Van Exel
1852	Paul George^	1517	Mike Bibby

^ Active.

Fewest Career Three Pointers for League Leader*

118	Bo Lamar, S.D. Conquistadors^a	led league in 1973–74 with 69
142	Mike Dunleavy, S.A. Spurs	led league in 1982–83 with 67
150	Mike Bratz, Cle. Cavaliers	led league in 1980–81 with 57
211	Brian Taylor, S.D. Clippers	led league in 1979–80 with 90
320	Don Buse, Ind. Pacers	led league in 1981–82 with 73
409	George Lehmann, Car. Cougars^a	led league in 1970–71 with 154
465	Lester Selvage, Ana. Amigos^a	led league in 1967–68 with 147
503	Glen Combs, Uta. Stars^a	led league in 1971–72 ith 103
506	Bill Keller, Ind. Pacers^a	led league in 1972–72 with 71
530	Darrell Griffith, Uta. Jazz	led league in 1983–84 with 91 and in 1984–85 with 92
605	Dee Brown, Tor. Raptors	led league in 1998–99 with 135
617	Dorell Wright, G.S. Warriors	led league in 2010–11 with 194
649	Larry Bird, Bos. Celtics	led league in 1985–86 with 82 and in 1986–87 with 90
820	Aaron Brooks, Hou. Rockets	led league in 2009–10 with 209
949	Michael Adams, Den. Nuggets	led league in 1988–89 with 166 and in 1989–90 with 158
956	Raja Bell**, Pho. Suns	led league in 2006–07 with 205

* The Three Pointer became an official stat in the ABA for the 1967–68 season, and in the NBA for the 1979–80 season.

^a ABA.

** Tied for league lead with Gilbert Arenas, Was. Wizards.

Largest Differential Between Leader in 3P and Runner-Up

Diff	Season	Leader	3P	Runner-Up	3P
+126	2015–16	Stephen Curry, G.S. Warriors	402	Klay Thompson, G.S. Warriors	276
+70	2005–06	Ray Allen, Sea. Sonics	269	Gilbert Arenas, Was. Wizards	199
+68	1969–70	Louie Dampier, Ken. Colonels[a]	198	Glen Combs, Dal. Chaparrals[a]	130
+59	2012–13	Stephen Curry, G.S. Warriors	272	Ryan Anderson, N.O. Hornets	213
+56	2016–17	Stephen Curry, G.S. Warriors	324	Klay Thompson, G.S. Warriors	268
+55	2020–21	Stephen Curry, G.S. Warriors	337	Buddy Hield, Sac. Kings	282
+54	1968–69	Louie Dampier, Ken. Colonels[a]	199	Chico Vaughn, Min. Pipers[a]	145
+53	1983–84	Darrell Griffith, Uta. Jazz	91	Michael Cooper, L.A. Lakers	38
+53	2003–04	Peja Stojakovic, Sac. Kings	240	Baron Davis, N.O. Hornets	187
+51	1970–71	George Lehmann, Car. Cougars[a]	154	Louie Dampier, Ken. Colonels[a]	103
+51	1975–76	Bill Keller, Ind. Pacers[a]	123	Don Buse, Ind. Pacers[a]	72
+47	2014–15	Stephen Curry, G.S. Warriors	286	Klay Thompson, G.S. Warriors	239
+38	2013–14	Stephen Curry, G.S. Warriors	261	Klay Thompson, G.S. Warriors	223
+37	1993–94	Dan Majerle, Pho. Suns	192	Dennis Scott, Orl. Magic	155
+28	1997–98	Wesley Person, Cle. Cavaliers	192	Reggie Miller, Ind. Pacers	164
+28	2011–12	Ryan Anderson, Orl. Magic	166	Jason Terry, Dal. Mavericks	138
+28	2019–20	James Harden, Hou. Rockets	299	Buddy Hield, Sac. Kings	271
+25	1982–83	Mike Dunleavy, S.A. Spurs	67	Allen Leavell, Hou. Rockets	42
+24	2018–19	James Harden, Hou. Rockets	378	Stephen Curry, G.S. Warriors	354

[a] ABA.

Teammates Finishing One-Two in 3P, Season

Season	Team	Leader	3P	Runner-Up	3P
1973–74	S.D. Conquistadors[a]	Bo Lamar	69	Billy Shepherd	65
1974–75	Ind. Pacers[a]	Bill Keller	80	George McGinnis[*]	62
1975–76	Ind. Pacers[a]	Bill Keller	123	Don Buse	72
1992–93	Pho. Suns	Dan Majerle[**]	167	Danny Ainge	150
2013–14	G.S. Warriors	Stephen Curry	261	Klay Thompson	223
2014–15	G.S. Warriors	Stephen Curry	286	Klay Thompson	239
2015–16	G.S. Warriors	Stephen Curry	402	Klay Thompson	276
2016–17	G.S. Warriors	Stephen Curry	324	Klay Thompson	268

[a] ABA.

[*] Tied for second with Warren Jabali, S.D. Conquistadors.

[**] Tied for first with Reggie Miller, Ind. Pacers.

Most 3P, Players 7-Feet or Taller

		Height
1982	Dirk Nowitzki	7-foot-0
1049	Channing Frye	7-foot-0
652	Brook Lopez^	7-foot-0
629	Lauri Markkanen^	7-foot-0
627	Andrea Bargnani	7-foot-0
600	Kristaps Porzingis^	7-foot-3
415	Frank Kaminsky^	7-foot-0
389	Joel Embiid^	7-foot-0
359	Spencer Hawes	7-foot-1
327	Meyers Leonard^	7-foot-0
203	Mo Bamba^	7-foot-0
183	Dragan Bender^	7-foot-0
179	Pau Gasol	7-foot-0

continued on next page

		Height
175	Dewayne Dedmon^	7-foot-0
144	Luke Kornet^	7-foot-2
136	Arvydas Sabonis	7-foot-3
130	Thon Maker^	7-foot-0
121	Donatas Motiejunas^	7-foot-0
115	Aleksej Pokusevski^	7-foot-0
111	Byron Mullens	7-foot-0
110	Alex Len^	7-foot-0
100	Vlade Divac	7-foot-1

^ Active.

Most 3P by Players 6-Foot-10 or Taller, Season

		Height
240	Peja Stojaković, Sac. Kings, 2003–04	6-foot-10
231	Peja Stojaković, N.O. Hornets, 2007–08	6-foot-10
226	Rashard Lewis, Orl. Magic, 2007–08	6-foot-10
220	Rashard Lewis, Orl. Magic, 2008–09	6-foot-10
200	Dāvis Bertāns, Was. Wizards, 2019–20	6-foot-10
192	Kevin Durant, Ok.C. Thunder, 2013–14	6-foot-10
187	Brook Lopez, Mil. Bucks, 2018–19	7-foot-0
186	Danilo Gallinari, N.Y. Knicks, 2009–10	6-foot-10
186	Kevin Durant, Ok.C. Thunder, 2015–16	6-foot-10
178	Clifford Robinson, Por. Blazers, 1995–96	6-foot-10
178	Danilo Gallinari, Ok.C. Thunder, 2019–20	6-foot-10
176	Nikola Vučević, Orl. Magic/Chi. Bulls, 2020–21	6-foot-10
175	Terry Mills, Det. Pistons, 1996–97	6-foot-10
174	Peja Stojaković, Sac. Kings, 2004–05	6-foot-10
173	Rashard Lewis, Sea. Sonics, 2004–05	6-foot-10
173	Kevin Durant, G.S. Warriors, 2017–18	6-foot-10
172	Channing Frye, Pho. Suns, 2009–10	7-foot-0
171	Channing Frye, Pho. Suns, 2010–11	7-foot-0
170	Michael Porter Jr., Den. Nuggets, 2020–21	6-foot-10
169	Dāvis Bertāns, Was. Wizards, 2020–21	6-foot-10
168	Rashard Lewis, Orl. Magic, 2009–10	6-foot-10
166	Hedo Türkoğlu, Orl. Magic, 2007–08	6-foot-10
162	Peja Stojaković, Sac. Kings/Ind. Pacers, 2005–06	6-foot-10
161	Troy Murphy, Ind. Pacers, 2008–09	6-foot-11
161	Danilo Gallinari, L.A. Clippers, 2018–19	6-foot-10
160	Channing Frye, Pho. Suns, 2013–14	7-foot-0
157	Dario Šarić, Phi. 76ers, 2017–18	6-foot-10
155	Peja Stojaković, Sac. Kings, 2002–03	6-foot-10
155	Rasheed Wallace, Det. Pistons, 2005–06	6-foot-10
151	Dirk Nowitzki, Dal. Mavericks, 2000–01	7-foot-0
151	Rashard Lewis, Sea. Sonics, 2006–07	6-foot-10
150	Karl-Anthony Towns, Min. T'Wolves, 2021–22	6-foot-11

Most 3P by a Center, Game

9	Channing Frye, Pho. Suns	vs. Min. T'Wolves (Apr. 11, 2011)
9	Aron Baynes, Pho. Suns	vs. Por. Blazers (Mar. 6, 2020)
8	Brook Lopez, Mil. Bucks	@ Den. Nuggets (Nov. 11, 2018)
7	Channing Frye, Pho. Suns	@ L.A. Clippers (Mar. 3, 2010)

continued on next page

7	Channing Frye, Pho. Suns	vs. Min. T'Wolves (Dec. 15, 2010)
7	Channing Frye, Pho. Suns	@ Was. Wizards (Jan. 21, 2011)
7	Brook Lopez, Brk. Nets	vs. Mia. Heat (Jan. 25, 2017)
7	Brook Lopez, Mil. Bucks	vs. Brk. Nets (Dec. 29, 2018)
7	Brook Lopez, Mil. Bucks	vs. Det. Pistons (Jan. 1, 2019)
7	Karl-Anthony Towns, Min. T'Wolves	@ Brk. Nets (Oct. 23, 2019)
7	Karl-Anthony Towns, Min. T'Wolves	@ Uta. Jazz (Nov. 18, 2019)
7	Myles Turner, Ind. Pacers	vs. N.Y. Knicks (Nov. 3, 2021)
7	Jonas Valančiūnas, N.O. Pelicans	@ L.A. Clippers (Nov. 29, 2021)
7	Mo Bamba, Orl. Magic	@ Phi. 76ers (Jan. 19, 2022)
7	Karl-Anthony Towns, Min. T'Wolves	@ S.A. Spurs (Mar. 14, 2022)

Most 3P, Game

			3P Shooting
14	Klay Thompson, G.S. Warriors	@ Chi. Bulls (Oct. 29, 2018)	14-for-24 (.583)
13	Stephen Curry, G.S. Warriors	vs. N.O. Pelicans (Nov. 7, 2016)	13-for-17 (.765)
13	Zach LaVine, Chi. Bulls	@ Cha. Hornets (Nov. 23, 2019)	13-for-17 (.765)
12	Kobe Bryant, L.A. Lakers	vs. Sea. Sonics (Jan. 7, 2003)	12-for-18 (.667)
12	Donyell Marshall, Tor. Raptors	vs. Phi. 76ers (Mar. 13, 2005)	12-for-19 (.632)
12	Stephen Curry, G.S. Warriors	@ Ok.C. Thunder (Feb. 27, 2016)	12-for-16 (.750)
11	Dennis Scott, Orl. Magic	vs. Atl. Hawks (Apr. 18, 1996)	11-for-17 (.647)
11	J.R. Smith, Den. Nuggets	vs. Sac. Kings (Apr. 13, 2009)	11-for-18 (.611)
11	Stephen Curry, G.S. Warriors*	@ N.Y. Knicks (Feb. 27, 2013)	11-for-13 (.846)
11	Deron Williams, Brk. Nets	vs. Was. Wizards (Mar. 8, 2013)	11-for-16 (.688)
11	Klay Thompson, G.S. Warriors	vs. Sac. Kings (Jan. 23, 2015)	11-for-15 (.733)
11	Kyrie Irving, Cle. Cavaliers	vs. Por. Blazers (Jan. 28, 2015)	11-for-19 (.579)
11	Stephen Curry, G.S. Warriors	@ Was. Wizards (Feb. 3, 2016)	11-for-15 (.733)
11	Stephen Curry, G.S. Warriors	vs. Cha. Hornets (Feb. 1, 2017)	11-for-15 (.733)
11	Stephen Curry, G.S. Warriors	vs. Was. Wizards (Oct. 24, 2018)	11-for-16 (.688)
11	Stephen Curry, G.S. Warriors	@ Dal. Mavericks (Jan. 13, 2019)	11-for-19 (.579)
11	Stephen Curry, G.S. Warriors*	@ Min. T'Wolves (Mar. 29, 2019)	11-for-19 (.579)
11	Buddy Hield, Sac. Kings*	@ Bos. Celtics (Nov. 25, 2019)	11-for-21 (.524)
11	Marcus Smart, Bos. Celtics*	vs. Pho. Suns (Jan. 18, 2020)	11-for-22 (.500)
11	Damian Lillard, Por. Blazers	vs. G.S. Warriors (Jan. 20, 2020)	11-for-20 (.550)
11	Damian Lillard, Por. Blazers	@ Den. Nuggets (Aug. 6, 2020)	11-for-18 (.611)
11	Fred VanVleet, Tor. Raptors	@ Orl. Magic (Feb. 2, 2021)	11-for-14 (.786)
11	Stephen Curry, G.S. Warriors*	@ Dal. Mavericks (Feb. 6, 2021)	11-for-19 (.579)
11	Stephen Curry, G.S. Warriors	@ Ok.C. Thunder (Apr. 14, 2021)	11-for-16 (.688)
11	Stephen Curry, G.S. Warriors*	@ Bos. Celtics (Apr. 17, 2021)	11-for-19 (.579)
11	Stephen Curry, G.S. Warriors	vs. Ok.C. Thunder (May 8, 2021)	11-for-21 (.524)
11	Bojan Bogdanović, Uta. Jazz	@ Ok.C. Thunder (Mar. 6, 2022)	11-for-18 (.611)
11	Malik Beasley, Min. T'Wolves	vs. Ok.C. Thunder (Mar. 9, 2022)	11-for-17 (.647)
11	Robert Covington, L.A. Clippers	@ Mil. Bucks (Apr. 1, 2022)	11-for-18 (.611)

* Team lost game.

Most 3P in a 50-Point Game

			3P Shooting	Pts
14	Klay Thompson, G.S. Warriors	@ Chi. Bulls (Oct. 29, 2018)	14-for-24 (.583)	52
11	Stephen Curry, G.S. Warriors*	@ N.Y. Knicks (Feb. 27, 2013)	11-for-13 (.846)	54
11	Klay Thompson, G.S. Warriors	vs. Sac. Kings (Jan. 23, 2015)	11-for-15 (.733)	52
11	Kyrie Irving, Cle. Cavaliers	vs. Por. Blazers (Jan. 28, 2015)	11-for-19 (.579)	55
11	Stephen Curry, G.S. Warriors	@ Was. Wizards (Feb. 3, 2016)	11-for-15 (.733)	51

continued on next page

			3P Shooting	Pts
11	Stephen Curry, G.S. Warriors	vs. Was. Wizards (Oct. 24, 2018)	11-for-16 (.688)	51
11	Damian Lillard, Por. Blazers	vs. G.S. Warriors (Jan. 20, 2020)	11-for-20 (.550)	61
11	Fred VanVleet, Tor. Raptors	@ Orl. Magic (Feb. 2, 2021)	11-for-14 (.786)	54
11	Stephen Curry, G.S. Warriors*	@ Dal. Mavericks (Feb. 6, 2021)	11-for-19 (.579)	57
10	Terrence Ross, Tor. Raptors*	vs. L.A. Clippers (Jan. 25, 2014)	10-for-17 (.588)	51
10	Stephen Curry, G.S. Warriors	vs. Dal. Mavericks (Feb. 4, 2015)	10-for-16 (.625)	51
10	Stephen Curry, G.S. Warriors	@ Orl. Magic (Feb. 25, 2016)	10-for-15 (.667)	51
10	James Harden, Hou. Rockets	@ Cle. Cavaliers (Dec. 11, 2019)	10-for-18 (.556)	55
10	James Harden, Hou. Rockets	@ Orl. Magic (Dec. 13, 2019)	10-for-15 (.667)	54
10	Stephen Curry, G.S. Warriors	vs. Den. Nuggets (Apr. 12, 2021)	10-for-18 (.556)	53
10	Saddiq Bey, Det. Pistons	@ Orl. Magic (Mar. 17, 2022)	10-for-14 (.714)	51

* Team lost game.

Most Games Hitting Multiple 3P, Career (Regular Season)

847	Ray Allen	569	Dirk Nowitzki
731	Reggie Miller	557	Joe Johnson^
695	Kyle Korver	550	Damian Lillard^
677	Stephen Curry^	546	J.J. Redick
667	Jason Terry	542	Kyle Lowry^
658	James Harden^	520	Kevin Durant^
640	Vince Carter	516	Chauncey Billips
632	Jamal Crawford	514	Rashard Lewis
621	Paul Pierce	511	Dale Ellis
598	LeBron James^	506	J.R. Smith

^ Active.

Longest Consecutive Streak of Games with at Least One 3P*

189	Stephen Curry	79	Joe Harris
157	Stephen Curry	79	Michael Adams
127	Kyle Korver	78	Dennis Scott
99	Jordan Clarkson	77	J.J. Redick
95	Klay Thompson	76	Fred VanVleet
89	Dana Barros	75	Stephen Curry
87	Buddy Hield	72	Fred VanVleet^
83	Karl-Anthony Towns	70	Stephen Curry
79	James Harden		

* Streak is over multiple seasons, where applicable.

^ Active streak, as of conclusion to 2021–22 season.

Most 3P by Players Shooting Lefty

2593	James Harden^	1071	Joe Ingles^
1528	Nick Van Exel	1045	Michael Redd
1495	Manu Ginóbili	1043	D'Angelo Russell^
1489	Mike Conley^	1042	Isaiah Thomas^
1250	C.J. Miles^	1009	Morris Peterson
1248	Derek Fisher	940	Anthony Peeler
1236	Damon Stoudamire	914	Brandon Jennings
1098	Goran Dragić^	849	Sam Perkins
1085	Cuttino Mobley	815	Chris Mullin

^ Active.

Most 3P, Shooting 100% from Three

			Pts
9	Latrell Sprewell, N.Y. Knicks	vs. L.A. Clippers (Feb. 4, 2003)	38
9	Ben Gordon, Chi. Bulls	vs. Was. Wizards (Apr. 14, 2006)	32
9	Ben Gordon, Det. Pistons*	@ Den. Nuggets (Mar. 21, 2012)	45
8	Jeff Hornacek, Uta. Jazz	vs. Sea. Sonics (Nov. 23, 1994)	40
8	Sam Perkins, Sea. Sonics	vs. Tor. Raptors (Jan. 15, 1997)	26
8	Steve Smith, S.A. Spurs	@ Por. Blazers (Nov. 3, 2001)	36
8	Michael Finley, Dal. Mavericks	vs. Cle. Cavaliers (Mar. 26, 2005)	26
7	Darel Carrier, Ken. Colonels[a]	vs. Min. Pipers[a] (Nov. 6, 1968)	48
7	Terry Porter, Por. Blazers	@ G.S. Warriors (Nov. 14, 1992)	40
7	Sam Perkins, Sea. Sonics	vs. Den. Nuggets (Nov. 9, 1993)	28
7	Sasha Danilović, Mia. Heat	@ N.Y. Knicks (Dec. 3, 1996)	21
7	Mitch Richmond, Sac. Kings	@ Bos. Celtics (Feb. 26, 1997)	38
7	Kobe Bryant, L.A. Lakers	vs. Phi. 76ers (Jan. 6, 2006)	48
7	Bobby Jackson, N.O. Hornets	vs. Mia. Heat (Jan. 11, 2008)	25
7	Mo Williams, Cle. Cavaliers	vs. Dal. Mavericks (Nov. 28, 2009)	25
7	Quentin Richardson, Mia. Heat*	vs. Por. Blazers (Dec. 20, 2009)	22
7	Aaron Brooks, Hou. Rockets	vs. Mem. Grizzlies (Mar. 17, 2010)	31
7	Matt Bonner, S.A. Spurs	@ Ok.C. Thunder (Nov. 14, 2010)	21
7	Nate Robinson, Chi. Bulls*	@ Dal. Mavericks (Mar. 30, 2013)	25
7	Kyrie Irving, Cle. Cavaliers	@ S.A. Spurs (Mar. 12, 2015)	57
7	Zach LaVine, Chi. Bulls	vs. Atl. Hawks (Dec. 11, 2019)	35
7	Saddiq Bey, Det. Pistons	@ Bos. Celtics (Feb. 12, 2021)	30
7	Georges Niang, Uta. Jazz	vs. Cha. Hornets (Feb. 22, 2021)	21
7	Bryn Forbes, Mil. Bucks	vs. N.Y. Knicks (Mar. 11, 2021)	21
7	Lauri Markkanen, Chi. Bulls*	vs. Phi. 76ers (Mar. 11, 2021)	23
7	Patty Mills, Brk. Nets*	@ Mil. Bucks (Oct. 19, 2021)	21
7	Mike Conley, Uta. Jazz	vs. Bos. Celtics (Dec. 3, 2021)	29

* Team lost game.
[a] ABA.

Most 3P, Shooting 100%, Game

			FGA	Pts
8	Sam Perkins, Sea. Sonics	vs. Tor. Raptors (Jan. 15, 1997)	8	26
7	Bobby Jackson, N.O. Hornets	vs. Mia. Heat (Jan. 11, 2008)	9	25
7	Quentin Richardson, Mia. Heat*	vs. Por. Blazers (Dec. 20, 2009)	7	22
7	Georges Niang, Uta. Jazz	vs. Cha. Hornets (Feb. 22, 2021)	7	21
6	Trent Tucker, Chi. Bulls	vs. Atl. Hawks (Feb. 27, 1993)	9	24
6	Nick Van Exel, L.A. Lakers	vs. Van. Grizzlies (Nov. 16, 1997)	9	24
6	Mike Miller, Mia. Heat	vs. S.A. Spurs (Jan. 17, 2012)	6	18
6	Chandler Parsons, Hou. Rockets	vs. Brk. Nets (Nov. 29, 2013)	7	21
6	Vince Carter, Mem. Grizzlies	vs. Mil. Bucks (Mar. 13, 2017)	8	24
6	Tony Snell, Det. Pistons	vs. N.Y. Knicks (Nov. 6, 2019)	9	24
6	Wesley Matthews, L.A. Lakers	@ S.A. Spurs (Dec. 30, 2020)	6	18
6	D.J. Augustin, L.A. Lakers	@ Cle. Cavaliers (Mar. 21, 2022)	7	20

* Team lost game.

Most 3P in a Game When Only Shooting from Three (Zero 2P Attempts)

3P			Pts
11	Malik Beasley, Min. T'Wolves	vs. Ok.C. Thunder (Mar. 9, 2022)	33
9	Robert Horry, Hou. Rockets	@ Cle. Cavaliers (Feb. 22, 1996)	27
9	Duncan Robinson, Mia. Heat	vs. Cle. Cavaliers (Nov. 20, 2019)	29
9	Duncan Robinson, Mia. Heat	vs. Orl. Magic (Mar. 4, 2020)	27
9	Dāvis Bertāns, Was. Wizards	vs. Den. Nuggets (Feb. 17, 2021)	35
8	Sam Perkins, Sea. Sonics	vs. Tor. Raptors (Jan. 15, 1997)	26
8	Chris Duhon, Chi. Bulls	@ Atl. Hawks (Apr. 16, 2005)	24
8	Mickaël Piétrus, Orl. Magic*	vs. Tor. Raptors (Nov. 12, 2010)	24
8	Steve Novak, N.Y. Knicks	vs. Bos. Celtics (Apr. 17, 2012)	25
8	J.R. Smith, Cle. Cavaliers	vs. Chi. Bulls (Apr. 5, 2015)	24
8	Danny Green, Tor. Raptors	vs. Mem. Grizzlies (Jan. 19, 2019)	24
8	Duncan Robinson, Mia. Heat*	@ N.O. Pelicans (Mar. 6, 2020)	24
8	Dāvis Bertāns, Was. Wizards*	vs. Mia. Heat (Mar. 8, 2020)	25
8	Wayne Ellington, Det. Pistons	@ Tor. Raptors (Mar. 3, 2021)	25
8	Jae Crowder, Pho. Suns	vs. Hou. Rockets (Apr. 12, 2021)	26
8	Devonte' Graham, N.O. Pelicans	vs. Mil. Bucks (Dec. 17, 2021)	26

* Team lost game.

Youngest Player to Hit a 3P

	Age	
Kobe Bryant, L.A. Lakers	18 years, 75 days	@ Cha. Hornets (Nov. 6, 1996)
Tracy McGrady, Tor. Raptors	18 years, 221 days	@ Was. Wizards (Dec. 31, 1997)
Yaroslav Korolev, L.A. Clippers	18 years, 230 days	@ Cha. Bobcats (Dec. 23, 2005)
C.J. Miles, Uta. Jazz	18 years, 245 days	@ Pho. Suns (Nov. 18, 2005)
Joshua Primo, S.A. Spurs	18 years, 300 days	vs. Orl. Magic (Oct. 20, 2021)
LeBron James, Cle. Cavaliers	18 years, 304 days	@ Pho. Suns (Oct. 30, 2003)
Jonathan Bender, Ind. Pacers	18 years, 314 days	vs. Cle. Cavaliers (Dec. 10, 1999)
Martell Webster, Por. Blazers	18 years, 340 days	vs. N.Y. Knicks (Nov. 9, 2005)
Giannis Antetokounmpo, Mil. Bucks	18 years, 341 days	@ Mia. Heat (Nov. 12, 2013)
Dragan Bender, Pho. Suns	18 years, 344 days	vs. Sac. Kings (Oct. 26, 2016)
Amir Johnson, Det. Pistons	18 years, 351 days	@ Mil. Bucks (Apr. 17, 2006)
Devin Booker, Pho. Suns	18 years, 363 days	vs. Dal. Mavericks (Oct. 28, 2015)
Aleksej Pokusevski, Ok.C. Thunder	19 years, 5 days	vs. N.O. Pelicans (Dec. 31, 2020)
Josh Giddey, Ok.C. Thunder	19 years, 12 days	@ Hou. Rockets (Oct. 22, 2021)
Sekou Doumbouya, Det. Pistons	19 years, 12 days	@ G.S. Warriors (Jan. 4, 2020)
Jonathan Kuminga, G.S. Warriors	19 years, 24 days	vs. Ok.C. Thunder (Oct. 30, 2021)
Darius Miles, L.A. Clippers	19 years, 26 days	vs. Hou. Rockets (Nov. 4, 2000)
Kevin Durant, Sea. Sonics	19 years, 32 days	@ Den. Nuggets (Oct. 31, 2007)
Jaren Jackson Jr., Mem. Grizzlies	19 years, 34 days	vs. Atl. Hawks (Oct. 19, 2018)
Aaron Gordon, Orl. Magic	19 years, 42 days	@ N.O. Pelicans (Oct. 28, 2014)
Michael Kidd-Gilchrist, Cha. Bobcats	19 years, 44 days	@ N.O. Hornets (Nov. 9, 2012)
Brandon Ingram, L.A. Lakers	19 years, 54 days	vs. Hou. Rockets (Oct. 26, 2016)
J.R. Smith, N.O. Hornets	19 years, 58 days	@ Min. T'Wolves (Nov. 6, 2004)
Bruno Caboclo, Tor. Raptors	19 years, 61 days	vs. Mil. Bucks (Nov. 21, 2014)
Kevin Knox, N.Y. Knicks	19 years, 67 days	vs. Atl. Hawks (Oct. 17, 2018)
Lou Williams, Phi. 76ers	19 years, 69 days	@ Pho. Suns (Jan. 4, 2006)
Rashad Vaughn, Mil. Bucks	19 years, 73 days	vs. N.Y. Knicks (Oct. 28, 2015)
Archie Goodwin, Pho. Suns	19 years, 80 days	@ N.O. Pelicans (Nov. 5, 2013)
Noah Vonleh, Cha. Hornets	19 years, 85 days	vs. Dal. Mavericks (Nov. 17, 2014)
Andre Drummond, Det. Pistons	19 years, 88 days	@ Den. Nuggets (Nov. 6, 2012)

Teenagers Hitting Six or More 3P, Game

3P		Age		3P Shooting	Pts
8 ... Anthony Edwards, Min. T'Wolves	19 years, 273 days	vs. Mem. Grizzlies (May 5, 2021)	8-for-9 (.889)	42
8 ... Jalen Green, Hou. Rockets	19 years, 257 days	vs. Bos. Celtics (Oct. 24, 2021)	8-for-10 (.800)	30
7 ... Luka Dončić, Dal. Mavericks	19 years, 303 days	@ N.O. Pelicans (Dec. 28, 2018)	7-for-10 (.700)	34
7 ... Anfernee Simons, Por. Blazers	19 years, 306 days	vs. Sac. Kings (Apr. 10, 2019)	7-for-11 (.636)	37
7 ... Coby White, Chi. Bulls	19 years, 269 days	vs. N.Y. Knicks (Nov. 12, 2019)	7-for-11 (.636)	27
7 ... LaMelo Ball, Cha. Hornets	19 years, 170 days	vs. Hou. Rockets (Feb. 8, 2021)	7-for-12 (.583)	24
7 ... Aleksej Pokusevski, Ok.C. Thunder	19 years, 102 days	vs. Cha. Hornets (Apr. 7, 2021)	7-for-11 (.636)	25
6 ... J.R. Smith, N.O. Hornets	19 years, 198 days	@ Mem. Grizzlies (Mar. 26, 2005)	6-for-9 (.667)	33
6 ... Bradley Beal, Was. Wizards	19 years, 202 days	@ Sac. Kings (Jan. 16, 2013)	6-for-7 (.857)	28
6 ... Bradley Beal, Was. Wizards	19 years, 276 days	vs. Tor. Raptors (Mar. 31, 2013)	6-for-9 (.667)	24
6 ... Devin Booker, Pho. Suns	19 years, 81 days	vs. Ind. Pacers (Jan. 19, 2016)	6-for-11 (.545)	32
6 ... Devin Booker, Pho. Suns	19 years, 95 days	vs. Tor. Raptors (Feb. 2, 2016)	6-for-14 (.429)	27
6 ... Terrance Ferguson, Ok.C. Thunder	19 years, 231 days	@ L.A. Lakers (Jan. 3, 2018)	6-for-9 (.667)	24
6 ... Coby White, Chi. Bulls	19 years, 271 days	@ Mil. Bucks (Nov. 14, 2019)	6-for-13 (.462)	26
6 ... Kevin Porter Jr., Cle. Cavaliers	19 years, 221 days	vs. Hou. Rockets (Dec. 11, 2019)	6-for-9 (.667)	24
6 ... Théo Maledon, Ok.C. Thunder	19 years, 231 days	vs. Brk. Nets (Jan. 29, 2021)	6-for-6 (1.000)	24
6 ... LaMelo Ball, Cha. Hornets	19 years, 203 days	vs. Tor. Raptors (Mar. 13, 2021)	6-for-9 (.667)	23
6 ... Anthony Edwards, Min. T'Wolves	19 years, 221 days	vs. Por. Blazers (Mar. 14, 2021)	6-for-14 (.429)	34
6 ... Aleksej Pokusevski, Ok.C. Thunder	19 years, 141 days	vs. L.A. Clippers (May 16, 2021)	6-for-9 (.667)	29
6 ... Jalen Green, Hou. Rockets	19 years, 317 days	@ Ind. Pacers (Dec. 23, 2021)	6-for-9 (.667)	20
6 ... Moses Moody, G.S. Warriors	19 years, 246 days	@ S.A. Spurs (Feb. 1, 2022)	6-for-10 (.600)	20

Most 3P Before 25th Birthday

862	Bradley Beal	699	Brandon Jennings
827	Jayson Tatum*	696	Klay Thompson
806	D'Angelo Russell	695	LeBron James
803	Devin Booker	676	James Harden
779	Gilbert Arenas	673	Jamal Murray
777	J.R. Smith	660	Ryan Anderson
732	Luka Dončić*	646	Zach LaVine
730	Trae Young	629	Lauri Markkanen*
726	Donovan Mitchell	602	Brandon Knight
701	Kyrie Irving	595	Lonzo Ball*
701	Kevin Durant	563	Kevin Huerter*

* Under 25 years old at the conclusion of the 2021–22 season.

Oldest Player to Hit a 3P

Vince Carter, Atl. Hawks	43 years, 45 days	vs. N.Y. Knicks (Mar. 11, 2020)
Udonis Haslem^, Mia. Heat	41 years, 195 days	vs. Ind. Pacers (Dec. 21, 2021)
John Stockton, Uta. Jazz	41 years, 16 days	vs. Dal. Mavericks (Apr. 11, 2003)
Dirk Nowitzki, Dal. Mavericks	40 years, 295 days	@ S.A. Spurs (Apr. 10, 2019)
Manu Ginóbili, Dal. Mavericks	40 years, 257 days	@ N.O. Pelicans (Apr. 11, 2018)
Jason Terry, Mil. Bucks	40 years, 204 days	@ N.Y. Knicks (Apr. 7, 2018)
Grant Hill, L.A. Clippers	40 years, 190 days	@ Mem. Grizzlies (Apr. 13, 2013)
John Long, Tor. Raptors	40 years, 154 days	@ Phi. 76ers (Jan. 29, 1997)
Jamal Crawford, Brk. Nets	40 years, 137 days	@ Mil. Bucks (Aug. 4, 2020)
Clifford Robinson, N.J. Nets	40 years, 121 days	@ N.Y. Knicks (Apr. 16, 2007)
Kurt Thomas, N.Y. Knicks	40 years, 121 days	vs. Sac. Kings (Feb. 2, 2013)
Steve Nash, L.A. Lakers	40 years, 60 days	vs. Hou. Rockets (Apr. 8, 2014)
Michael Jordan, Was. Wizards	40 years, 51 days	vs. Bos. Celtics (Apr. 9, 2003)
Jason Kidd, N.Y. Knicks	40 years, 23 days	@ Cha. Bobcats (Apr. 15, 2013)

^ Active.

Most 3P from Age 39 On

		Career 3P
399	Vince Carter	2290
202	Dirk Nowitzki	1982
153	Manu Ginóbili	1495
138	Jason Kidd	1988
113	Jason Terry	2282
96	Reggie Miller	2560
88	Derek Fisher	1248
75	Clifford Robinson	1253
62	John Stockton	845
38	Sam Perkins	849
37	Dale Ellis	1719
23	Darrell Armstrong	923

Most 3P Misses, Game

			3P Shooting (Pts)
16	Lester Selvage, Ana. Amigos[a]	@ Den. Rockets[a] (Feb. 15, 1968)	10-for-26 (38)
16	Damon Stoudamire, Por. Blazers	@ G.S. Warriors (Apr. 15, 2005)	5-for-21 (18)
16	James Harden, Hou. Rockets	@ Orl. Magic (Jan. 13, 2019)	1-for-17 (38)
16	James Harden, Hou. Rockets	vs. Sac. Kings (Mar. 30, 2019)	7-for-23 (50)
16	James Harden, Hou. Rockets	vs. N.O. Pelicans (Oct. 26, 2019)	2-for-18 (29)
16	James Harden, Hou. Rockets	@ S.A. Spurs (Dec. 3, 2019)	4-for-20 (50)
16	James Harden, Hou. Rockets	@ Atl. Hawks (Jan. 8, 2020)	4-for-20 (41)
16	James Harden, Hou. Rockets	vs. Ok.C. Thunder (Jan. 20, 2020)	1-for-17 (29)
15	Dennis Scott, Orl. Magic	vs. N.J. Nets (Jan. 9, 1996)	2-for-17 (23)
15	Kobe Bryant, L.A. Lakers	vs. Uta. Jazz (Apr. 13, 2016)	6-for-21 (60)
15	James Harden, Hou. Rockets	@ N.Y. Knicks (Jan. 23, 2019)	5-for-20 (61)
15	Stephen Curry, G.S. Warriors	vs. Mia. Heat (Feb. 17, 2021)	5-for-20 (25)

[a]ABA.

Most 3P in a Loss

11	Stephen Curry, G.S. Warriors	@ N.Y. Knicks (Feb. 27, 2013)
11	Stephen Curry, G.S. Warriors	@ Min. T'Wolves (Mar. 29, 2019)
11	Buddy Hield, Sac. Kings	@ Bos. Celtics (Nov. 25, 2019)
11	Marcus Smart, Bos. Celtics	vs. Pho. Suns (Jan. 18, 2020)
11	Stephen Curry, G.S. Warriors	@ Dal. Mavericks (Feb. 6, 2021)
11	Stephen Curry, G.S. Warriors	@ Bos. Celtics (Apr. 17, 2021)
10	Lester Selvage, Ana. Amigos[a]	@ Den. Rockets[a] (Feb. 15, 1968)
10	George McCloud, Dal. Mavericks	vs. Pho. Suns (Dec. 16, 1995)
10	Chandler Parsons, Hou. Rockets	vs. Mem. Grizzlies (Jan. 24, 2014)
10	Terrence Ross, Tor. Raptors	vs. L.A. Clippers (Jan. 25, 2014)
10	Trevor Ariza, Was. Wizards	@ Hou. Rockets (Feb. 12, 2014)
10	J.R. Smith, N.Y. Knicks	@ Mia. Heat (Apr. 6, 2014)
10	Stephen Curry, G.S. Warriors	vs. Phi. 76ers (Jan. 31, 2019)
10	Terry Rozier, Cha. Hornets	@ Cle. Cavaliers (Dec. 23, 2020)
10	Zach LaVine, Chi. Bulls	@ L.A. Clippers (Jan. 10, 2021)

[a]ABA.

Most 3P Misses, Season

3P		3P Shooting
650	James Harden, Hou. Rockets, 2018–19	378-for-1028 (.368)
544	James Harden, Hou. Rockets, 2019–20	299-for-843 (.355)
494	James Harden, Hou. Rockets, 2016–17	262-for-756 (.347)
484	Stephen Curry, G.S. Warriors, 2015–16	402-for-886 (.454)
471	Kemba Walker, Cha. Hornets, 2018–19	260-for-731 (.356)
465	Stephen Curry, G.S. Warriors, 2016–17	324-for-789 (.411)
465	Paul George, Ok.C. Thunder, 2018–19	292-for-757 (.386)
465	Stephen Curry, G.S. Warriors, 2021–22	285-for-750 (.380)
464	Stephen Curry, G.S. Warriors, 2020–21	337-for-801 (.421)
457	James Harden, Hou. Rockets, 2017–18	265-for-722 (.367)
456	Stephen Curry, G.S. Warriors, 2018–19	354-for-810 (.437)
454	Buddy Hield, Ind. Pacers 2021–22	262-for-716 (.366)
439	Buddy Hield, Sac. Kings, 2020–21	282-for-721 (.391)
429	Damian Lillard, Por. Blazers, 2020–21	275-for-704 (.391)
423	Antoine Walker, Bos. Celtics, 2001–02	222-for-645 (.344)
422	Donovan Mitchell, Uta. Jazz, 2021–22	232-for-654 (.355)
421	George McCloud, Dal. Mavericks, 1995–96	257-for-678 (.379)
421	James Harden, Hou. Rockets, 2015–16	236-for-657 (.359)
421	Jayson Tatum, Bos. Celtics, 2021–22	230-for-651 (.353)
417	Buddy Hield, Sac. Kings, 2019–20	271-for-688 (.394)
415	Eric Gordon, Hou. Rockets, 2016–17	246-for-661 (.372)
407	Jordan Clarkson, Uta. Jazz, 2021–22	190-for-597 (.318)
406	Damian Lillard, Por. Blazers, 2018–19	237-for-643 (.369)
405	Quentin Richardson, Pho. Suns, 2004–05	226-for-631 (.358)
404	Damian Lillard, Por. Blazers, 2019–20	270-for-674 (.401)
402	Damian Lillard, Por. Blazers, 2017–18	227-for-629 (.361)
401	Isaiah Thomas, Bos. Celtics, 2016–17	245-for-646 (.379)
400	Fred VanVleet, Tor. Raptors, 2021–22	242-for-642 (.377)

Most 3P Misses, Career

		3P%			3P%
4583	James Harden^	.361	3265	Kyle Korver	.429
4456	Ray Allen	.400	3248	J.R. Smith	.373
4173	Stephen Curry^	.428	3228	Dirk Nowitzki	.380
4158	Jamal Crawford	.348	3142	Carmelo Anthony^	.355
4046	LeBron James^	.346	2993	Paul George^	.382
3926	Reggie Miller	.395	2974	Trevor Ariza^	.351
3878	Vince Carter	.371	2951	Kemba Walker^	.360
3728	Jason Terry	.380	2939	Wesley Matthews^	.377
3719	Kobe Bryant	.329	2895	Chauncey Billups	.387
3713	Jason Kidd	.349	2878	Antoine Walker	.325
3673	Paul Pierce	.368	2838	Rashard Lewis	.386
3609	Damian Lillard^	.373	2827	Baron Davis	.320
3378	Kyle Lowry^	.368	2803	Tim Hardaway	.355
3353	Joe Johnson^	.371			

^ Active.

Most 3P for One Franchise

3P for Franchise

76ers	885	Allen Iverson
Bucks	1202	Khris Middleton^
Bulls	1049	Kirk Hinrich
Cavaliers	1251	LeBron James
Celtics	1823	Paul Pierce
Clippers	738	Eric Piatkowski
Grizzlies	1086	Mike Conley
Hawks	1050	Mookie Blaylock
Heat	806	Tim Hardaway
Hornets-Bobcats	1283	Kemba Walker
Jazz	1071	Joe Ingles^
Kings	1248	Buddy Hield
Knicks	982	John Starks
Lakers	1827	Kobe Bryant
Magic	981	Dennis Scott
Mavericks	1982	Dirk Nowitzki
Nets	842	Joe Harris^
Nuggets	804	Will Barton^
Pacers	2560	Reggie Miller
Pelicans-Hornets	628	Jrue Holiday
Pistons	990	Joe Dumars
Raptors	1518	Kyle Lowry
Rockets	2029	James Harden
Spurs	1495	Manu Ginóbili
Suns	1051	Steve Nash
Thunder-SuperSonics	1143	Kevin Durant
Timberwolves	779	Karl-Anthony Towns^
Trail Blazers	2143	Damian Lillard^
Warriors	3117	Stephen Curry^
Wizards	1434	Bradley Beal

^ Active with franchise.

Most 3P Against One Franchise

	Career 3P		Total Games Played
76ers	135	Ray Allen	59
Bucks	162	Reggie Miller	79
Bulls	126	Reggie Miller	74
Cavaliers	141	Ray Allen	57
Celtics	129	Reggie Miller	67
Clippers	179	Stephen Curry^	45
Grizzlies	148	Stephen Curry^	35
Hawks	159	Reggie Miller	77
Heat	117	Ray Allen	44
Hornets-Bobcats	130	Ray Allen	47
Jazz	121	Stephen Curry^	35
Kings	144	Stephen Curry^	38
Knicks	126	Kyle Korver	54
Lakers	114	James Harden^	45
Magic	107	Kyle Korver	54

continued on next page

Career 3P			Total Games Played	
Mavericks	137	Stephen Curry^	37
Nets	155	Reggie Miller	70
Nuggets	148	Stephen Curry^	37
Pacers	113	Ray Allen	54
Pelicans-Hornets	139	Stephen Curry^	33
Pistons	111	Reggie Miller	74
Raptors	143	Ray Allen	58
Rockets	127	Stephen Curry^	36
Spurs	103	James Harden^	41
Suns	149	Stephen Curry^	42
Thunder-SuperSonics	160	Stephen Curry^	40
Timberwolves	140	Stephen Curry^	36
Trail Blazers	157	Stephen Curry^	36
Warriors	122	Damian Lillard^	31
Wizards	112	Reggie Miller	69

^ Active.

Players with Highest Differential of Three Pointers to Turnovers, Season (Min. 150 3P)

Diff		3P	TO
+200	Duncan Robinson, Mia. Heat, 2019–20	270	70
+197	Malik Beasley, Min. T'Wolves, 2021–22	240	43
+175	Wayne Ellington, Mia. Heat, 2017–18	227	52
+172	Duncan Robinson, Mia. Heat, 2021–22	232	60
+170	Peja Stojaković, N.O. Hornets, 2007–08	231	61
+169	Duncan Robinson, Mia. Heat, 2020–21	250	81
+162	Stephen Curry, G.S. Warriors, 2018–19	354	192
+154	Patty Mills, Brk. Nets, 2021–22	227	73
+152	Buddy Hield, Sac. Kings, 2020–21	282	130
+149	Ryan Anderson, Hou. Rockets, 2016–17	204	55
+149	Joe Harris, Brk. Nets, 2020–21	211	62
+145	Dennis Scott, Orl. Magic, 1995–96	267	122
+145	J.R. Smith, Cle. Cavaliers, 2015–16	204	59
+143	Tim Hardaway Jr., Dal. Mavericks, 2020–21	207	64
+141	Dāvis Bertāns, Was. Wizards, 2019–20	200	59
+140	Stephen Curry, G.S. Warriors, 2015–16	402	262
+140	Klay Thompson, G.S. Warriors, 2016–17	268	128
+139	J.J. Redick, Phi. 76ers, 2018–19	240	101
+138	Klay Thompson, G.S. Warriors, 2015–16	276	138
+136	Dāvis Bertāns, Was. Wizards, 2020–21	169	33
+136	Evan Fournier, N.Y. Knicks, 2021–22	241	105
+136	Gary Trent Jr., Tor. Raptors, 2021–22	209	73
+135	Tim Hardaway Jr., Dal. Mavericks, 2019–20	204	69
+134	Nick Young, L.A. Lakers, 2016–17	170	36
+132	Buddy Hield, Sac. Kings, 2018–19	278	146
+131	Ben McLemore, Hou. Rockets, 2019–20	181	50
+130	Luke Kennard, L.A. Clippers, 2021–22	190	60

Most Career 3P, Never Turning the Ball Over 250 Times in a Season

3P		Most TO, Season
2560	Reggie Miller	222 (Ind. Pacers, 1989–90)
2450	Kyle Korver	117 (Phi. 76ers, 2006–07)

continued on next page

3P

3P		Most TO, Season
2290	Vince Carter	223 (Tor. Raptors, 2003–04)
2282	Jason Terry	249 (Atl. Hawks, 2002–03)
2221	Jamal Crawford	193 (Chi. Bulls, 2003–04)
2143	Damian Lillard	243 (Por. Blazers, 2012–13)
1982	Dirk Nowitzki	176 (Dal. Mavericks, 2004–05)
1971	Kyle Lowry	225 (Tor. Raptors, 2015–16)
1950	J.J. Redick	138 (Orl. Magic/Mil. Bucks, 2012–13)
1930	J.R. Smith	150 (Den. Nuggets, 2008–09)
1912	Klay Thompson	157 (G.S. Warriors, 2012–13)
1830	Chauncey Billups	189 (Det. Pistons, 2003–04)
1787	Rashard Lewis	158 (Orl. Magic, 2008–09)
1782	Wesley Matthews	138 (Por. Blazers, 2010–11)
1760	Peja Stojaković	153(Sac. Kings, 2003–04)
1746	Eric Gordon	164 (L.A. Clippers, 2008–09)
1719	Dale Ellis	238 (Sea. Sonics, 1986–87)
1663	Kemba Walker	211 (Cha. Hornets, 2018–19)
1608	Jason Richardson	196 (G.S. Warriors, 2003–04)
1605	Trevor Ariza	161 (Hou. Rockets, 2009–10)
1590	Mike Miller	182 (Mem. Grizzlies, 2007–08)
1561	Danny Green	94 (S.A. Spurs, 2012–13)
1559	Glen Rice	182 (Cha. Hornets, 1997–98)
1546	Eddie Jones	169 (L.A. Lakers, 1996–97)
1544	Chris Paul	231 (N.O. Hornets, 2008–09)
1528	Nick Van Exel	221 (Den. Nuggets, 1999–00)
1517	Mike Bibby	248 (Van. Grizzlies, 2000–01)

League 3P, Year by Year·

ABA

Season	3PM	3PA	3P%
1967–68	111	390	.285
1968–69	138	460	.299
1969–70	155	531	.291
1970–71	154	516	.299
1971–72	131	442	.297
1972–73	91	316	.289
1973–74	100	351	.283
1974–75	91	311	.293
1975–76	78	266	.295

NBA

Season	3PM	3PA	3P%	Season	3PM	3PA	3P%
1979–80	64	227	.280	1989–90	179	541	.331
1980–81	41	166	.245	1990–91	187	586	.320
1981–82	49	187	.262	1991–92	207	626	.331
1982–83	44	185	.238	1992–93	247	734	.336
1983–84	49	195	.250	1993–94	270	811	.333
1984–85	73	257	.282	1994–95	450	1255	.359
1985–86	77	274	.282	1995–96	483	1316	.367
1986–87	117	388	.301	1996–97	496	1377	.360
1987–88	130	410	.316	1997–98	360	1042	.346
1988–89	173	537	.323	1998–99	223	658	.339

continued on next page

Season	3PM	3PA	3P%
1999–00	397	1125	353
2000–01	397	1124	.354
2001–02	428	1209	.354
2002–03	421	1204	.349
2003–04	425	1224	.347
2004–05	459	1292	.356
2005–06	470	1310	.358
2006–07	498	1389	.358
2007–08	537	1485	.362
2008–09	545	1486	.367
2009–10	527	1487	.355
2010–11	530	1477	.358

Season	3PM	3PA	3P%
2011–12	423	1213	.349
2012–13	587	1636	.359
2013–14	635	1766	.360
2014–15	643	1838	.350
2015–16	698	1975	.354
2016–17	792	2214	.358
2017–18	860	2378	.362
2018–19	932	2625	.355
2019–20	862	2408	.358
2020–21	914	2494	.367
2021–22	1020	2885	.354

* ABA used the three-point shot throughout it's entirety as a professional league, with the NBA adding the shot for the 1979–80 season.

1998–99: 50-game season.

2011–12: 66-game season.

2019–20: 65-to-75-game season.

2020–21: 72-game season.

Players with Highest Differential of 3P Made to 2P Made, Season

Diff		3P Shooting	2P Shooting	FG%
+217	Duncan Robinson, Mia. Heat, 2019–20	270-for-606 (.446)	53-for-81 (.654)	.470
+185	Duncan Robinson, Mia. Heat, 2020–21	250-for-613 (.408)	65-for-104 (.625)	.439
+174	Duncan Robinson, Mia. Heat, 2021–22	232-for-624 (.372)	58-for-102 (.569)	.399
+169	Wayne Ellington, Mia. Heat, 2017–18	227-for-579 (.392)	58-for-121 (.479)	.407
+161	Buddy Hield, Sac. Kings, 2020–21	282-for-721 (.391)	121-for-271 (.446)	.406
+150	Kyle Korver, Atl. Hawks, 2014–15	221-for-449 (.492)	71-for-151 (.470)	.487
+148	Malik Beasley, Min. T'Wolves, 2021–22	240-for-637 (.377)	92-for-213 (.432)	.391
+145	Dāvis Bertāns, Was. Wizards, 2020–21	169-for-428 (.395)	24-for-50 (.480)	.404
+135	Kyle Korver, Phi. 76ers, 2004–05	226-for-558 (.405)	91-for-201 (.453)	.418
+135	Dāvis Bertāns, Was. Wizards, 2019–20	200-for-472 (.424)	65-for-138 (.471)	.434
+134	Troy Daniels, Pho. Suns, 2017–18	183-for-458 (.400)	49-for-117 (.419)	.403
+130	Patty Mills, Brk. Nets, 2021–22	227-for-568 (.400)	97-for-226 (.429)	.408
+126	Danny Green, Phi. 76ers, 2020–21	175-for-432 (.405)	49-for-112 (.438)	.412
+120	Steve Novak, N.Y. Knicks, 2012–13	149-for-351 (.425)	29-for-79 (.367)	.414
+120	Ben McLemore, Hou. Rockets, 2019–20	181-for-452 (.400)	61-for-93 (.656)	.444
+119	Damon Jones, Mia. Heat, 2004–05	225-for-521 (.432)	106-for-205 (.517)	.456
+113	Max Strus, Mia. Heat, 2021–22	181-for-442 (.410)	68-for-122 (.557)	.441
+106	Kyle Korver, Cle. Cavaliers, 2017–18	164-for-376 (.436)	58-for-108 (.537)	.459
+106	Devonte' Graham, Cha. Hornets, 2020–21	179-for-477 (.375)	73-for-192 (.380)	.377
+103	Danny Green, Tor. Raptors, 2018–19	198-for-435 (.455)	95-for-195 (.487)	.465
+101	Kyle Korver, Atl. Hawks, 2012–13	189-for-414 (.457)	88-for-187 (.471)	.461
+101	C.J. Miles, Tor. Raptors, 2017–18	164-for-454 (.361)	63-for-145 (.434)	.379

Most 3P Last Season in League

158	Carlos Delfino, Hou. Rockets, 2012–13
156	Gerald Green, Hou. Rockets, 2018–19
156	Juan Carlos Navarro, Mem. Grizzlies, 2007–08
133	Kobe Bryant, L.A. Lakers, 2015–16
123	Bill Keller, Ind. Pacers°, 1975–76

continued on next page

116	Ray Allen, Mia. Heat, 2013–14
114	Jason Kidd, N.Y. Knicks, 2012–13
106	Clyde Drexler, Hou. Rockets, 1997–98
104	Trevor Ruffin, Phi. 76ers, 1995–96
99	Kyle Korver, Mil. Bucks, 2019–20
96	Reggie Miller, Ind. Pacers, 2004–05
94	Boštjan Nachbar, N.J. Nets, 2007–08
92	Sergio Rodríguez, Phi. 76ers, 2016–17
89	Joe Dumars, Det. Pistons, 1998–99
88	Derek Fisher, Ok.C. Thunder, 2013–14
87	Matt Barnes, Sac. Kings/G.S. Warriors, 2016–17
86	Marreese Speights, Orl. Magic, 2017–18
86	Dwyane Wade, Mia. Heat, 2018–19
85	Sasha Danilović, Mia. Heat/Dal. Mavericks, 1996–97

Three-Point Average

Highest 3P% by Decade (Min. 100 3P)

NBA

1979-80–1989-90		1990-91–1999-00		2000-01–2009-10	
.423	Mark Price	.459	Steve Kerr	.460	Anthony Morrow
.423	Hersey Hawkins	.441	Hubert Davis	.440	Jason Kapono
.408	Trent Tucker	.434	Dražen Petrović	.440	Hubert Davis
.404	Dale Ellis	.432	Tim Legler	.437	Steve Nash
.404	Craig Hodges	.432	Steve Henson	.437	Stephen Curry
.397	Reggie Miller	.425	B.J. Armstrong	.432	Wesley Person
.394	Byron Scott	.418	Michael Dickerson	.425	Danny Ferry
.389	Jon Sundvold	.415	Eldridge Recasner	.424	Daniel Gibson
.384	Danny Ainge	.414	Dana Barros	.422	Anthony Parker
.382	Craig Ehlo	.412	Dell Curry	.421	Terry Porter

2010-11–2019-20		2020-21–2021-22		ABA 1967-68–1975-76	
.445	Steve Novak	.474	Joe Harris	.377	Darel Carrier
.443	Seth Curry	.451	Tony Snell	.367	Glen Combs
.440	Kyle Korver	.448	Luke Kennard	.365	George Lehmann
.437	Duncan Robinson	.435	Desmond Bane	.358	Louie Dampier
.435	Stephen Curry	.434	Seth Curry	.357	Billy Shepherd
.427	Matt Bonner	.434	Bryn Forbes	.343	Ron Perry
.426	Joe Harris	.422	Marcus Morris	.338	Bill Keller
.422	Ray Allen	.419	Michael Porter Jr.	.338	Steve Jones
.420	J.J. Redick	.418	Bobby Portis	.332	John Roche
.419	Klay Thompson	.414	Norman Powell	.327	Don Buse
		.414	Joe Ingles		

Evolution of Three-Point Average Record

NBA

1979–80......... Fred Brown, Sea. Sonics .... .443
1985–86......... Craig Hodges, Mil. Bucks .... .451
1986–87......... Kiki Vandeweghe, Por. Blazers............ .482
1987–88......... Craig Hodges, Mil. Bucks/Pho. Suns... .491
1988–89......... Jon Sundvold, Mia. Heat................... .521
1994–95......... Steve Kerr, Chi. Bulls .... .524
2009–10......... Kyle Korver, Uta. Jazz .... .536

ABA

1967–68......... Steve Jones, Oak. Oaks..................... .426

Lifetime Three-Point Average of 20-Year Players

Seasons

.380............. Dirk Nowitzki .... 21 (1998–99 — 2018–19)
.371............. Vince Carter.................. 22 (1998–99 — 2019–20)
.348............. Jamal Crawford............ 20 (2000–01 — 2019–20)
.329............. Kobe Bryant.................. 20 (1996–97 — 2015–16)
.275............. Kevin Garnett............... 21 (1995–96 — 2015–16)
.211............. Kevin Willis.................. 21 (1984–85 — 1987–88, 1989–90 — 2004–05, 2006–07)
.096............. Moses Malone............... 21 (1974–75 — 1994–95)
.056............. Kareem Abdul-Jabbar...... 20 (1969–70 — 1988–89)
.000............. Robert Parish................. 21 (1976–77 — 1996–97)

Highest Career 3P% (Min. 500 3P)

.454	Steve Kerr	726-for-1599
.441	Hubert Davis	728-for-1651
.439	Joe Harris^	874-for-1991
.439	Seth Curry^	730-for-1661
.430	Steve Novak	575-for-1337
.429	Kyle Korver	2450-for-5715
.428	Stephen Curry^	3117-for-7290
.428	Steve Nash	1685-for-3939
.425	Luke Kennard^	550-for-1294
.418	Wesley Person	1150-for-2754
.417	Klay Thompson^	1912-for-4587
.417	Anthony Morrow	807-for-1937
.415	J.J. Redick	1950-for-4704
.414	Matt Bonner	797-for-1923
.413	Bryn Forbes^	706-for-1711
.411	Dana Barros	1090-for-2652
.409	Doug McDermott^	723-for-1766
.408	Joe Ingles^	1071-for-2622
.408	Trent Tucker	575-for-1410
.407	Mike Miller	1590-for-3910
.407	José Calderón	920-for-2260
.407	Daniel Gibson	578-for-1419
.406	Raja Bell	956-for-2357
.406	Duncan Robinson^	762-for-1878
.406	Wally Szczerbiak	590-for-1453
.405	Brent Barry	1395-for-3442
.404	Anthony Parker	596-for-1474
.403	Dale Ellis	1719-for-4266
.403	Jeff Hornacek	828-for-2055
.402	Allan Houston	1305-for-3247
.402	Dell Curry	1245-for-3098
.402	Mark Price	976-for-2428
.402	Brandon Rush	522-for-1300
.401	Peja Stojaković	1760-for-4392
.401	Ben Gordon	1171-for-2921
.401	James Jones	776-for-1937
.400	Ray Allen	2973-for-7429
.400	Glen Rice	1559-for-3896
.400	Craig Hodges	563-for-1408

^ Active.

Highest 3P%, Leading League in 3P

3P%		3P
.454	Stephen Curry, G.S. Warriors, 2015–16	402
.453	Stephen Curry, G.S. Warriors, 2012–13	272
.449	Louie Dampier, Ken. Colonels[a], 1968–69	199
.443	Stephen Curry, G.S. Warriors, 2014–15	286
.434	Ray Allen, Mil. Bucks, 2001–02	229
.433	Peja Stojaković, Sac. Kings, 2003–04	240
.430	Wesley Person, Cle. Cavaliers, 1997–98	192
.427	Reggie Miller, Ind. Pacers, 1996–97	229
.427	Larry Bird, Bos. Celtics, 1986–87	90
.425	Dennis Scott, Orl. Magic, 1995–96	267
.424	Stephen Curry, G.S. Warriors, 2013–14	261
.423	Larry Bird, Bos. Celtics, 1985–86	82
.421	Stephen Curry, G.S. Warriors, 2020–21	337
.415	Danny Ainge, Bos. Celtics, 1987–88	148
.414	Louie Dampier, Ken. Colonels[a], 1969–70	198
.413	Raja Bell, Pho. Suns, 2006–07	205
.412	Ray Allen, Sea. Sonics, 2005–06	269
.411	Stephen Curry, G.S. Warriors, 2016–17	324
.406	Jason Richardson, Cha. Bobcats, 2007–08	243
.406	Glen Combs, Uta. Stars[a], 1971–72	103
.405	Kyle Korver, Phi. 76ers, 2004–05	226
.403	George Lehmann*, Car. Cougars[a], 1970–71	154

[a] ABA.

* Also led league in 3P%.

Lowest 3P%, Leading League in 3P

3P%		3P
.279	Bo Lamar, S.D. Conquistadors[a], 1973–74	69
.319	Lester Selvage, Ana. Amigos[a], 1967–68	147
.320	Bill Keller, Ind. Pacers[a], 1972–73	71
.333	Bill Keller, Ind. Pacers[a], 1974–75	80
.337	Vernon Maxwell, Hou. Rockets, 1990–91	172
.337	Mike Bratz, Cle. Cavaliers, 1980–81	57
.340	Gary Payton*, Sea. Sonics, 1999–00	177
.342	Vernon Maxwell, Hou. Rockets, 1991–92	162
.345	Mike Dunleavy*, S.A. Spurs, 1982–83	67
.351	Gilbert Arenas, Was. Wizards, 2006–07	205
.352	Bill Keller, Ind. Pacers[a], 1975–76	123
.355	James Harden, Hou. Rockets, 2019–20	299
.355	John Starks, N.Y. Knicks, 1994–95	217
.356	Michael Adams, Den. Nuggets, 1988–89	166
.358	Quentin Richardson, Pho. Suns, 2004–05	226
.358	Darrell Griffith, Uta. Jazz, 1984–85	92
.361	Darrell Griffith*, Uta. Jazz, 1983–84	91
.366	Michael Adams, Den. Nuggets, 1989–90	158
.367	James Harden, Hou. Rockets, 2017–18	265
.367	Antoine Walker, Bos. Celtics, 2000–01	221
.368	James Harden, Hou. Rockets, 2018–19	378

[a] ABA.

* Also led league in 3P%.

Most 3P Attempts, Season

3P Shooting

1028	James Harden, Hou. Rockets, 2018–19	378-for-1028 (.368)
886	Stephen Curry, G.S. Warriors, 2015–16	402-for-886 (.454)
843	James Harden, Hou. Rockets, 2019–20	299-for-843 (.355)
810	Stephen Curry, G.S. Warriors, 2018–19	354-for-810 (.437)
801	Stephen Curry, G.S. Warriors, 2020–21	337-for-801 (.421)
789	Stephen Curry, G.S. Warriors, 2016–17	324-for-789 (.411)
757	Paul George, Ok.C. Thunder, 2018–19	292-for-757 (.386)
756	James Harden, Hou. Rockets, 2016–17	262-for-756 (.347)
750	Stephen Curry, G.S. Warriors, 2021–22	285-for-750 (.380)
731	Kemba Walker, Cha. Hornets, 2018–19	260-for-731 (.356)
722	James Harden, Hou. Rockets, 2017–18	265-for-722 (.367)
721	Buddy Hield, Sac. Kings, 2020–21	282-for-721 (.391)
716	Buddy Hield, Sac. Kings/Ind. Pacers, 2021–22	262-for-716 (.366)
704	Damian Lillard, Por. Blazers, 2020–21	275-for-704 (.391)
688	Buddy Hield, Sac. Kings, 2019–20	271-for-688 (.394)
678	George McCloud, Dal. Mavericks, 1995–96	257-for-678 (.379)
674	Damian Lillard, Por. Blazers, 2019–20	270-for-674 (.401)
661	Eric Gordon, Hou. Rockets, 2016–17	246-for-661 (.372)
657	James Harden, Hou. Rockets, 2015–16	236-for-657 (.359)
654	Donovan Mitchell, Uta. Jazz, 2021–22	232-for-654 (.355)
653	Ray Allen, Sea. Sonics, 2005–06	269-for-653 (.412)
651	Buddy Hield, Sac. Kings, 2018–19	278-for-651 (.427)
651	Jayson Tatum, Bos. Celtics, 2021–22	230-for-651 (.353)
650	Klay Thompson, G.S. Warriors, 2015–16	276-for-650 (.425)
647	Klay Thompson, G.S. Warriors, 2016–17	268-for-647 (.414)
646	Stephen Curry, G.S. Warriors, 2014–15	286-for-646 (.443)
646	Isaiah Thomas, Bos. Celtics, 2016–17	245-for-646 (.379)
645	Antoine Walker, Bos. Celtics, 2001–02	222-for-645 (.344)
643	Damian Lillard, Por. Blazers, 2018–19	237-for-643 (.369)
642	Fred VanVleet, Tor. Raptors, 2021–22	242-for-642 (.377)
637	Malik Beasley, Min. T'Wolves, 2021–22	240-for-637 (.377)
635	D'Angelo Russell, Brk. Nets, 2018–19	234-for-635 (.369)
631	Quentin Richardson, Pho. Suns, 2004–05	226-for-631 (.358)
629	Damian Lillard, Por. Blazers, 2017–18	227-for-629 (.361)
628	Dennis Scott, Orl. Magic, 1995–96	267-for-628 (.425)
624	Duncan Robinson, Mia. Heat, 2021–22	232-for-624 (.372)
623	Mookie Blaylock, Atl. Hawks, 1995–96	231-for-623 (.371)
619	Evan Fournier, N.Y. Knicks, 2021–22	241-for-619 (.389)
615	Stephen Curry, G.S. Warriors, 2013–14	261-for-615 (.424)
613	Duncan Robinson, Mia. Heat, 2020–21	250-for-613 (.408)
611	John Starks, N.Y. Knicks, 1994–95	217-for-611 (.355)
610	Damian Lillard, Por. Blazers, 2015–16	229-for-610 (.375)
610	Saddiq Bey, Det. Pistons, 2021–22	211-for-610 (.346)
610	Trae Young, Atl. Hawks, 2021–22	233-for-610 (.382)
609	Paul George, Ok.C. Thunder, 2017–18	244-for-609 (.401)
608	Eric Gordon, Hou. Rockets, 2017–18	218-for-608 (.359)
606	Duncan Robinson, Mia. Heat, 2019–20	270-for-606 (.446)
605	J.J. Redick, Phi. 76ers, 2018–19	240-for-605 (.397)
604	Mookie Blaylock, Atl. Hawks, 1996–97	221-for-604 (.366)
603	Antoine Walker, Bos. Celtics, 2000–01	221-for-603 (.367)

continued on next page

3P Shooting

602 .... Kemba Walker, Cha. Hornets, 2016–17 .... 240-for-602 (.399)
602 .... Anthony Edwards, Min. T'Wolves, 2021–22 .... 215-for-602 (.357)
601 .... Kemba Walker, Cha. Hornets, 2017–18 .... 231-for-601 (.384)
600 .... Stephen Curry, G.S. Warriors, 2012–13 .... 272-for-600 (.453)
600 .... Eric Gordon, Hou. Rockets, 2018–19 .... 216-for-600 (.360)

Most 3P Attempts, Career

3P Shooting

7429	Ray Allen	2973-for-7429 (.400)
7290	Stephen Curry^	3197-for-7290 (.428)
7176	James Harden^	2593-for-7176 (.361)
6486	Reggie Miller	2560-for-6486 (.395)
6379	Jamal Crawford	2221-for-6379 (.348)
6186	LeBron James^	2140-for-6186 (.346)
6168	Vince Carter	2290-for-6168 (.371)
6010	Jason Terry	2282-for-6010 (.380)
5816	Paul Pierce	2143-for-5816 (.368)
5752	Damian Lillard^	2143-for-5752 (.373)
5715	Kyle Korver	2450-for-5715 (.429)
5701	Jason Kidd	1988-for-5701 (.349)
5546	Kobe Bryant	1827-for-5546 (.329)
5349	Kyle Lowry^	1971-for-5349 (.368)
5331	Joe Johnson^	1978-for-5331 (.371)
5210	Dirk Nowitzki	1982-for-5210 (.380)
5178	J.R. Smith	1930-for-5178 (.373)
4873	Carmelo Anthony^	1731-for-4873 (.355)
4845	Paul George^	1852-for-4845 (.382)
4721	Wesley Matthews"	1782-for-4721 (.377)
4712	Eric Gordon^	1782-for-4712 (.377)
4704	J.J. Redick	1950-for-4704 (.415)
4625	Rashard Lewis	1787-for-4625 (.386)
4614	Kemba Walker^	1648-for-4614 (.361)
4611	Kevin Durant^	1770-for-4611 (.384)
4587	Klay Thompson^	1912-for-4587 (.417)
4579	Trevor Ariza^	1605-for-4579 (.351)

^ Active.

Most Games with 15 Three-Point Attempts, Career

74	Stephen Curry^	9	J.R. Smith	6	Donovan Mitchell^
54	James Harden^	8	Eric Gordon^	6	Terry Rozier^
22	Damian Lillard^	8	Fred VanVleet^	6	D'Angelo Russell
15	Klay Thompson^	7	Duncan Robinson^	6	Kemba Walker^
12	Buddy Hield^	6	Kobe Bryant	5	Dennis Scott
11	Paul George^	6	George McCloud	5	Russell Westbrook^

^ Active.

Most 3P Attempts, Rookie Season

3PA   **3P Shooting**

550 .... Donovan Mitchell, Uta. Jazz, 2017–18 .... 187-for-550 (.340)
520 .... Anthony Edwards, Min. T'Wolves, 2020–21 .... 171-for-520 (.329)
514 .... Luka Dončić*, Dal. Mavericks, 2018–19 .... 168-for-514 (.327)

continued on next page

3PA | **3P Shooting**

503 .... Damian Lillard*, Por. Blazers, 2012–13 .... 185-for-503 (.368)
482 .... Trae Young, Atl. Hawks, 2018–19 .... 156-for-482 (.324)
461 .... Lester Selvage, Ana. Amigos°, 1967–68 .... 147-for-461 (.319)
460 .... Saddiq Bey, Det. Pistons, 2020–21 .... 175-for-460 (.380)
455 .... Allen Iverson*, Phi. 76ers, 1996–97 .... 155-for-455 (.341)
434 .... Kyle Kuzma, L.A. Lakers, 2017–18 .... 159-for-434 (.366)
458 .... Jalen Green, Hou. Rockets, 2021–22 .... 157-for-458 (.343)
432 .... Juan Carlos Navarro, Mem. Grizzlies, 2007–08 ..... 156-for-432 (.361)
419 .... Kerry Kittles, N.J. Nets, 1996–97 .... 158-for-419 (.377)
401 .... Lauri Markkanen, Chi. Bulls, 2017–18 .... 143-for-401 (.062)
398 .... Rudy Fernández, Por. Blazers, 2008–09 .... 159-for-398 (.399)
396 .... Landry Shamet, Phi. 76ers/L.A. Clippers, 2018–19... 167-for-396 (.422)
391 .... Kendrick Nunn, Mia. Heat, 2019–20 .... 137-for-391 (.350)
388 .... Brandon Jennings, Mil. Bucks, 2009–10 .... 145-for-388 (.374)
381 .... Matt Maloney, Hou. Rockets, 1996–97 .... 154-for-381 (.404)
380 .... Stephen Curry, G.S. Warriors, 2009–10 .... 166-for-380 (.437)
379 .... Buddy Hield, N.O. Pelicans/Sac. Kings, 2016–17.. 148-for-379 (.391)
378 .... O.J. Mayo, Mem. Grizzlies, 2008–09 .... 145-for-378 (.384)
376 .... Coby White, Chi. Bulls, 2019–20 .... 133-for-376 (.354)
370 .... D'Angelo Russell, L.A. Lakers, 2015–16 .... 130-for-370 (.351)
369 .... Kirk Hinrich, Chi. Bulls, 2003–04 .... 144-for-369 (.390)
364 .... Nick Van Exel, L.A. Lakers, 1993–94 .... 123-for-364 (.338)
364 .... Mike Miller*, Orl. Magic, 2000–01 .... 148-for-364 (.407)
364 .... Kevin Knox, N.Y. Knicks, 2018–19 .... 125-for-364 (.343)
363 .... Cade Cunningham, Det. Pistons, 2021–22 .... 114-for-363 (.314)
358 .... Tim Hardaway Jr., N.Y. Knicks, 2013–14 .... 130-for-358 (.363)
358 .... Bones Hyland, Det. Pistons, 2021–22 .... 131-for-358 (.366)
353 .... Kevin Huerter, Atl. Hawks, 2018–19 .... 136-for-353 (.385)
* Rookie of the Year.

Most 3P Attempts, Less Than 100 2P Attempts, Season

3PA | **2PA**

606 .... Duncan Robinson, Mia. Heat, 2019–20 81
452 .... Ben McLemore, Hou. Rockets, 2019–20 93
428 .... Dāvis Bertāns, Was. Wizards, 2020–21 50
386 .... Garrison Mathews, Hou. Rockets, 2021–22 75
372 .... Wayne Ellington, Mia. Heat/Det. Pistons, 2018–19 85
351 .... Steve Novak, N.Y. Knicks, 2012–13 79
325 .... Jason Kidd, N.Y. Knicks, 2012–13 84
316 .... Shane Battier, Mia. Heat, 2012–13 46
296 .... Landry Shamet, L.A. Clippers, 2019–20 95
292 .... Quincy Acy, Brk. Nets, 2017–18 73
287 .... James Jones, Mia. Heat, 2010–11 59
282 .... Steve Novak, N.Y. Knicks, 2011–12 55
280 .... Ben McLemore, Hou. Rockets/L.A. Lakers, 2020–21 85
276 .... Damon Jones, Cle. Cavaliers, 2007–08 87
275 .... Wayne Ellington, Det. Pistons, 2020–21 63
272 .... Anthony Tolliver, Det. Pistons, 2015–16 60
271 .... J.R. Smith, Cle. Cavaliers, 2016–17 85
271 .... Danny Green, Phi. 76ers, 2021–22 49

Most 3P Made, Shooting Under 30%, Career

Career 3P		Career 3P%
549	Dwyane Wade	298
538	Charles Barkley	266
523	Ron Harper	289
503	Corey Brewer	284
450	Josh Smith	285
447	Giannis Antetokounmpo^	288
410	DeMar DeRozan^	288
398	Isiah Thomas	290
398	Jamaal Tinsley	299
373	Reggie Williams	298
326	Derrick Coleman	295
275	Freddie Lewis	280
270	Evan Turner	294
264	Chris Webber	299
263	Josh Jackson^	292
252	Bimbo Coles	267
238	Reggie Theus	252
236	Alvin Robertson	295
219	Jay Humphries	297
210	Charlie Williams	264
208	Tom Gugliotta	284
204	Calbert Cheaney	298

^ Active.

Highest Three-Point Field-Goal Percentage
in Games Shooting 10 or More Three Pointers, Career (Min. 75 Games)

3P%		Games	3P%		Games
.446	J.R. Smith	109	.396	Buddy Hield^	134
.440	CJ McCollum^	76	.394	Bradley Beal^	80
.437	Stephen Curry^	342	.391	Kyle Lowry^	89
.435	Klay Thompson^	127	.390	D'Angelo Russell^	87
.411	Duncan Robinson^	78	.385	Luka Dončić^	83
.410	Ray Allen	114	.373	Eric Gordon^	111
.408	Damian Lillard^	206	.368	James Harden^	266
.400	Kemba Walker^	117	.360	Donovan Mitchell^	93
.398	Paul George^	128	.332	Baron Davis	76

^ Active.

Highest 3PAr·, Season

3PAr		3PA/2PA (FGA)
.895	Dāvis Bertāns, Was. Wizards, 2020–21	428/50 (478)
.890	Wayne Ellington, L.A. Lakers, 2021–22	211/26 (237)
.882	Duncan Robinson, Mia. Heat, 2019–20	606/81 (687)
.880	James Posey, Ind. Pacers, 2010–11	212/29 (241)
.873	Shane Battier, Mia. Heat, 2012–13	316/46 (362)
.863	Keith Bogans, Brk. Nets, 2012–13	245/39 (284)
.860	Duncan Robinson, Mia. Heat, 2021–22	624/102 (726)
.855	Duncan Robinson, Mia. Heat, 2020–21	613/104 (717)

continued on next page

3PAr		3PA/2PA (FGA)
.851	Daequan Cook, Ok.C. Thunder, 2010–11	154/27 (181)
.847	Danny Green, Phi. 76ers, 2021–22	271/49 (320)
.837	Steve Novak, N.Y. Knicks, 2011–12	282/55 (337)
.837	Garrison Mathews, Hou. Rockets, 2021–22	386/75 (461)
.835	Garrison Mathews, Was. Wizards, 2020–21	198/39 (237)
.829	James Jones, Mia. Heat, 2010–11	287/59 (346)
.829	Ben McLemore, Hou. Rockets, 2019–20	452/93 (545)
.827	Wayne Ellington, Mia. Heat, 2017–18	579/121 (700)
.819	Anthony Tolliver, Det. Pistons, 2015–16	272/60 (332)
.817	Jason Kidd, Dal. Mavericks, 2011–12	223/50 (273)
.816	Steve Novak, N.Y. Knicks, 2012–13	351/79 (430)
.814	Wayne Ellington, Mia. Heat/Det. Pistons, 2018–19	372/85 (457)
.814	Wayne Ellington, Det. Pistons, 2020–21	275/63 (338)
.813	Dan Majerle, Pho. Suns, 2001–02	235/54 (289)
.809	Kyle Korver, Mil. Bucks, 2019–20	237/56 (293)
.808	Mychal Mulder, G.S. Warriors, 2020–21	214/51 (265)
.805	Anthony Tolliver, Cha. Bobcats, 2013–14	247/60 (307)
.800	Quincy Acy, Brk. Nets, 2017–18	292/73 (365)

* 3PAr is the "Percentage of FG Attempts from 3-Point Range." (basketball-reference.com)

Highest 3PAr, Career (Min. 5000 FGA)

3PAr		3PA (3P%)	2PA (2P%)	FGA (FG%)
.652	Danny Green^	3908 (.399)	2088 (.461)	5996 (.421)
.642	Robert Covington^	3301 (.360)	1841 (.489)	5142 (.406)
.616	Kyle Korver	5715 (.429)	3562 (.464)	9277 (.442)
.589	Patty Mills^	3716 (.389)	2590 (.479)	6306 (.426)
.584	Wayne Ellington^	3175 (.382)	2266 (.450)	5441 (.410)
.570	Jae Crowder^	3310 (.346)	2498 (.512)	5808 (.417)
.564	Buddy Hield^	3563 (.398)	2749 (.471)	6312 (.430)
.546	Brent Barry	3442 (.405)	2859 (.525)	6301 (.460)
.534	Ryan Anderson	3491 (.380)	3042 (.470)	6533 (.422)
.532	Wesley Matthews^	4721 (.377)	4145 (.470)	8866 (.421)
.527	Steve Blake	2709 (.383)	2436 (.420)	5145 (.401)
.524	J.J. Redick	4704 (.415)	4272 (.482)	8976 (.447)
.520	Terrence Ross^	3415 (.361)	3152 (.478)	6567 (.417)
.519	Tim Hardaway Jr.^	3504 (.358)	3251 (.492)	6755 (.422)
.502	Stephen Curry^	7290 (.428)	7230 (.520)	14,520 (.473)

^ Active.

Most Seasons with a 3PAr of .500 (Min. 1000 Minutes Played)

			Career High	
12	Kyle Korver		.777 (Cle. Cavaliers, 2017–18)	
10	Danny Green		.847 (Phi. 76ers, 2021–22)	
10	Wesley Matthews		.782 (L.A. Lakers, 2020–21)	
8	Dan Majerle		.813 (Pho. Suns, 2001–02)	
8	Shane Battier		.873 (Mia. Heat, 2012–13)	
8	Jae Crowder		.772 (Pho. Suns, 2020–21)	
8	Joe Ingles		.789 (Uta. Jazz, 2021–22)	
8	Robert Covington		.699 (Por. Blazers, 2020–21)	

continued on next page

		Career High
7	Jason Williams	.524 (Sac. Kings, 1998–99)
7	Brent Barry	.675 (S.A. Spurs, 2006–07)
7	Damon Jones	.760 (Cle. Cavaliers, 2007–08)
7	J.R. Smith	.761 (Cle. Cavaliers, 2016–17)
7	Steve Blake	.670 (Por. Blazers, 2014–15)
7	Patrick Beverley	.607 (Hou. Rockets, 2014–15)
7	Trevor Ariza	.710 (Hou. Rockets, 2017–18)
7	Patty Mills	.715 (Brk. Nets, 2021–22)
6	James Posey	.734 (Mia. Heat, 2005–06)
6	J.J. Redick	.629 (N.O. Pelicans, 2019–20)
6	Channing Frye	.710 (Orl. Magic, 2014–15)
6	Randy Foye	.654 (Den. Nuggets, 2014–15)
6	Anthony Tolliver	.830 (Min. T'Wolves, 2018–19)
6	Tony Snell	.665 (Det. Pistons, 2019–20)
6	Terrence Ross	.596 (Orl. Magic, 2019–20)
6	Marvin Williams	.586 (Cha. Hornets, 2018–19)
6	Garrett Temple	.658 (Brk. Nets, 2019–20)
6	Stephen Curry	.613 (G.S. Warriors, 2021–22)
6	Eric Gordon	.654 (Hou. Rockets, 2019–20)
6	Kyle Lowry	.631 (Tor. Raptors, 2017–18)
6	Justin Holiday	.728 (Ind. Pacers/Sac. Kings, 2021–22)

Free Throws

Most Free Throws Made, by Decade

1946–47–1949–50

1530	Joe Fulks
1133	Max Zaslofsky
1099	George Mikan
1028	Ed Sadowski
879	John Logan
845	Kenny Sailors
781	Bob Feerick
682	Stan Miasek
680	Chick Halbert
661	Fred Scolari

1950–51–1959–60

5142	Dolph Schayes
3992	Paul Arizin
3800	Bob Cousy
3415	Neil Johnston
3373	Ed Macauley
3281	Bob Pettit
3259	Larry Foust
2936	Bill Sharman
2822	Harry Gallatin
2760	Vern Mikkelsen

1960–61–1969–70*

6583	Oscar Robertson
5616	Jerry West
4667	Wilt Chamberlain
4643	Elgin Baylor
4201	Bailey Howell
3923	Walt Bellamy
3753	Hal Greer
3618	Lenny Wilkens
3038	Rudy LaRusso
2932	Richie Guerin

1970–71–1979–80*

4505	Dan Issel
3911	Julius Erving
3886	George McGinnis
3802	Tiny Archibald
3732	Kareem Abdul-Jabbar
3630	Elvin Hayes
3588	Rick Barry
3585	Mack Calvin
3566	Pete Maravich
3556	Artis Gilmore

1980–81–1989–90

5903	Moses Malone
5064	Adrian Dantley
3895	Magic Johnson
3853	Tom Chambers
3724	Dominique Wilkins
3625	Alex English
3607	Reggie Theus
3558	Michael Jordan
3370	Jack Sikma
3346	Larry Bird

1990–91–1999–00

5631	Karl Malone
4650	David Robinson
4035	Reggie Miller
3867	Shawn Kemp
3560	Mitch Richmond
3400	Patrick Ewing
3358	Charles Barkley
3284	Detlef Schrempf
3268	Alonzo Mourning
3240	Michael Jordan

continued on next page

2000-01-2009-10		2010-11-2019-20	
5468	Kobe Bryant	6102	James Harden
4924	Paul Pierce	4297	Russell Westbrook
4896	Dirk Nowitzki	4143	Kevin Durant
4805	Allen Iverson	4138	DeMar DeRozan
3924	Corey Maggette	3754	LeBron James
3716	Tim Duncan	3309	Damian Lillard
3650	LeBron James	3098	DeMarcus Cousins
3552	Chauncey Billups	3030	Lou Williams
3353	Dwyane Wade	3016	Anthony Davis
3345	Vince Carter	2974	Blake Griffin

* Includes ABA.

Most Free Throws Made, Season

FT		FT%	FT		FT%
840	Jerry West, L.A. Lakers, 1965–66	.860	736	Oscar Robertson, Cin. Royals, 1966–67	.873
835	Wilt Chamberlain, Phi. Warriors, 1961–62	.613	723	Michael Jordan, Chi. Bulls, 1987–88	.841
833	Michael Jordan, Chi. Bulls, 1986–87	.857	720	James Harden, Hou. Rockets, 2015–16	.860
813	Adrian Dantley, Uta. Jazz, 1983–84	.859	715	James Harden, Hou. Rockets, 2014–15	.868
800	Oscar Robertson, Cin. Royals, 1963–64	.853	714	Charles Barkley, Phi. 76ers, 1987–88	.751
756	Kevin Durant, Ok.C. Thunder, 2009–10	.900	712	Jerry West, L.A. Lakers, 1961–62	.769
754	James Harden, Hou. Rockets, 2018–19	.879	710	Russell Westbrook, Ok.C. Thunder, 2016–17	.845
753	Rick Barry, S.F. Warriors, 1966–67	.884	703	Kevin Durant, Ok.C. Thunder, 2013–14	.873
746	James Harden, Hou. Rockets, 2016–17	.847	703	Karl Malone, Uta. Jazz, 1988–89	.766
742	Oscar Robertson, Cin. Royals, 1965–66	.842	700	Oscar Robertson, Cin. Royals, 1961–62	.803
737	Moses Malone, Phi. 76ers, 1984–85	.815			

Most Free Thows Made, Career

FT		FT%	FT		FT%	FT		FT%
9787	Karl Malone	.742	6349	Charles Barkley	.735	5708	Dwyane Wade	.765
9018	Moses Malone*	.760	6320	Carmelo Anthony^	.814	5512	Russell Westbrook^	.783
8378	Kobe Bryant	.837	6256	Julius Erving*	.777	5423	Hakeem Olajuwon	.712
7836	LeBron James^	.734	6237	Reggie Miller	.888	5394	Lenny Wilkens	.774
7694	Oscar Robertson	.838	6182	Bob Pettit	.761	5392	Patrick Ewing	.740
7327	Michael Jordan	.835	6324	Kevin Durant^	.884	5369	John Havlicek	.815
7240	Dirk Nowitzki	.879	6132	Artis Gilmore*	.698	5356	Elvin Hayes	.670
7160	Jerry West	.814	6057	Wilt Chamberlain	.511	5361	Dwight Howard^	.567
6918	Paul Pierce	.806	6035	David Robinson	.736	5113	Walt Bellamy	.632
7044	James Harden^	.860	6031	Dominique Wilkins	.811	5079	Chet Walker	.796
6832	Adrian Dantley	.818	5935	Shaquille O'Neal	.527	5066	Tom Chambers	.807
6712	Kareem Abdul-Jabbar	.721	5896	Tim Duncan	.696	5193	DeMar DeRozan^	.837
6712	Dolph Schayes	.849	5763	Elgin Baylor	.780	5010	Paul Arizin	.810
6591	Dan Issel*	.793	5737	George Gervin*	.841			
6375	Allen Iverson	.780	5713	Rick Barry*	.893			

^ Active.

* Includes ABA.

Most Free Thows Made, Game

28	Wilt Chamberlain, Phi. Warriors	vs. N.Y. Knicks (Mar. 2, 1962)
28	Adrian Dantley, Uta. Jazz	vs. Hou. Rockets (Jan. 4, 1984)
27	Adrian Dantley, Uta. Jazz	vs. Den. Nuggets (Nov. 25, 1983)
26	Adrian Dantley, Uta. Jazz	vs. Dal. Mavericks (Oct. 31, 1980)
26	Michael Jordan, Chi. Bulls	vs. N.J. Nets (Feb. 26, 1987)
26	Anthony Davis, L.A. Lakers	vs. Mem. Grizzlies (Oct. 29, 2019)
25	Dwight Howard, L.A. Lakers	@ Orl. Magic (Mar. 12, 2013)
24	Frank Selvy, Mil. Hawks	vs. Min. Lakers (Dec. 2, 1954)
24	Tony Jackson, N.J. Americans[a]	@ Ken. Colonels[a] (Nov. 27, 1967)
24	George Thompson, Mem. Tams[a]	@ S.D. Conquistadors[a] (Oct. 14, 1972)
24	Willie Burton, Phi. 76ers	vs. Mia. Heat (Dec. 13, 1994)
24	Allen Iverson, Phi. 76ers	vs. Orl. Magic (Feb. 12, 2005)
24	LeBron James, Cle. Cavaliers	@ Mia. Heat (Mar. 12, 2006)
24	Kevin Durant, Ok.C. Thunder	@ L.A. Clippers (Jan. 23, 2009)
24	DeMar DeRozan, Tor. Raptors	vs. Por. Blazers (Mar. 4, 2016)
24	Devin Booker, Pho. Suns	@ Bos. Celtics (Mar. 24, 2017)
24	James Harden, Hou. Rockets	@ S.A. Spurs (Dec. 3, 2019)

[a] ABA.

Most Free Throws Made without a Miss, Game

24	James Harden, Hou. Rockets	@ S.A. Spurs (Dec. 3, 2019)
23	Rick Barry, Oak. Oaks[a]	@ Ken. Colonels[a] (Feb. 7, 1969)
23	Dominique Wilkins, Atl. Hawks	vs. Chi. Bulls (Dec. 8, 1992)
22	Julius Erving, Vir. Squires[a]	vs. N.Y. Nets[a] (Feb. 8, 1973)
21	Deron Williams, N.J. Nets	@ Cha. Bobcats (Mar. 4, 2012)
21	Kevin Durant, Ok.C. Thunder	@ Dal. Mavericks (Jan. 18, 2013)
20	Rick Barry, Oak. Oaks[a]	@ N.O. Buccaneers[a] (Dec. 9, 1968)
20	Richard Hamilton, Det. Pistons	vs. Cha. Bobcats (Nov. 21, 2004)
20	Amar'e Stoudemire, Pho. Suns	vs. Hou. Rockets (Mar. 22, 2008)
20	Kobe Bryant, L.A. Lakers	@ N.Y. Knicks (Feb. 2, 2009)
19	Bob Pettit, St.L. Hawks	@ Bos. Celtics (Nov. 22, 1961)
19	Willie Somerset, Hou. Mavericks[a]	@ N.O. Buccaneers[a] (Nov. 18, 1968)
19	Jim Eakins, Vir. Squires[a]	vs. Ken. Colonels[a] (Feb. 17, 1974)
19	Bill Cartwright, N.Y. Knicks	vs. K.C. Kings (Nov. 17, 1981)
19	Adrian Dantley, Det. Pistons	vs. Chi. Bulls (Dec. 15, 1987)
19	James Harden, Hou. Rockets	vs. Tor. Raptors (Nov. 14, 2017)
19	James Harden, Hou. Rockets	vs. Det. Pistons (Nov. 21, 2018)
19	Kawhi Leonard, L.A. Clippers	@ Min. T'Wolves (Dec. 13, 2019)

[a] ABA.

Most Consecutive Free Throws Made

		First Game of Streak	Last Game of Streak
97	Micheal Williams, Min. T'Wolves	Mar. 26, 1993	Nov. 9, 1993
87	José Calderón, Tor. Raptors	Apr. 11, 2008	Jan. 30, 2009
82	Dirk Nowitzki, Dal. Mavericks	Mar. 3, 2011	Mar. 27, 2011
81	Mahmoud Abdul Rauf, Den. Nuggets	Mar. 15, 1993	Nov. 16, 1993
80	Stephen Curry, G.S. Warriors	Jun. 7, 2019	Jan. 3, 2021

Most Free Throws Made, Rookie Season

FT%

653	Oscar Robertson*, Cin. Royals, 1960–61	.822
630	Michael Jordan*, Chi. Bulls, 1984–85	.845
613	David Robinson*, S.A. Spurs, 1989–90	.732
604	Dan Issel*, Ken. Colonelsᵃ, 1970–71	.807
603	Connie Hawkins, Pit. Pipersᵃ, 1967–68	.764
577	Wilt Chamberlain*, Phi. Warriors, 1959–60	.582
569	Rick Barry*, S.F. Warriors, 1965–66	.862
551	Doug Moe, N.O. Buccaneersᵃ, 1967–68	.795
549	Walt Bellamy*, Chi. Packers, 1961–62	.644
547	Spencer Haywood*, Den. Rocketsᵃ, 1969–70	.776
541	David Thompson*, Den. Nuggetsᵃ, 1975–76	.794
532	George Mikan, Min. Lakers, 1948–49	.772
532	Elgin Baylor*, Min. Lakers, 1958–59	.777
529	Mack Calvin, L.A. Starsᵃ, 1969–70	.824
518	Stephen Chubin, Ana. Amigosᵃ, 1967–68	.811
507	Earl Monroe*, Bal. Bullets, 1967–68	.781
495	Kelly Tripucka, Det. Pistons, 1981–82	.797
495	Alonzo Mourning, Cha. Hornets, 1992–93	.781
485	Kareem Abdul-Jabbar*, Mil. Bucks, 1969–70	.653
476	Adrian Dantley*, Buf. Braves, 1976–77	.818

ᵃ ABA.

* Rookie of the Year.

Most Free Throws from Age 39 On

642	Karl Malone	642-for-846 (.759)	235	Vince Carter	235-for-303 (.776)
572	Kareem Abdul-Jabbar	572-for-777 (.736)	196	Manu Ginóbili	196-for-238 (.824)
548	John Stockton	548-for-651 (.842)	167	Dikembe Mutombo	167-for-232 (.720)
458	Robert Parish	458-for-646 (.709)	159	Kevin Willis	159-for-234 (.679)
300	Michael Jordan	300-for-367 (.817)	136	Dirk Nowitzki	136-for-158 (.861)
250	Reggie Miller	250-for-268 (.933)			

Most Games without Missing a Free Throw, Minimum 5 FT Attempts, Career*

317	Dirk Nowitzki	191	Chris Paul^	158	Paul Pierce
297	Reggie Miller	179	James Harden^	157	Dan Issel
261	Kevin Durant^	177	George Gervin	157	Mitch Richmond
223	Rick Barry	175	Larry Bird	155	Calvin Murphy
219	Kobe Bryant	174	Stephen Curry^	152	Mack Calvin
210	Chauncey Billups	167	Michael Jordan	151	Magic Johnson
201	Dolph Schayes	164	Oscar Robertson	151	Ricky Pierce
200	Damian Lillard^	161	Jack Sikma	151	Lou Williams^
196	Ray Allen	159	Bill Sharman	151	DeMar DeRozan^

* Includes ABA.

^ Active.

Most Games without Missing a Free Throw, Minimum 10 FT Attempts, Career*

72	Dirk Nowitzki	58	Kobe Bryant	43	Jerry West
64	Kevin Durant^	56	James Harden^	39	Michael Jordan
63	Dolph Schayes	53	Rick Barry	39	Damian Lillard^
61	Oscar Robertson	46	Reggie Miller	37	Chauncey Billups

continued on next page

36	Adrian Dantley	31	Mack Calvin	26	Allen Iverson
34	Magic Johnson	30	Kevin Martin	25	Elgin Baylor
33	Dominique Wilkins	28	Moses Malone	25	Kiki Vandeweghe
32	DeMar DeRozan^	28	Larry Bird	25	Jimmy Butler^
31	Paul Arizin	26	Dan Issel		

* Includes ABA.
^ Active.

In Multiple Seasons, Averaging 10 Free Throw Attempts Per Game

			FTA/G	FT Shooting
11	Wilt Chamberlain	1959–60, Phi. Warriors	13.8	577-for-991 (.582)
		1960–61, Phi. Warriors	13.3	531-for-1054 (.504)
		1961–62, Phi. Warriors	17.0	835-for-1363 (.613)
		1962–63, S.F. Warriors	13.9	660-for-1113 (.593)
		1963–64, S.F. Warriors	12.7	540-for-1016 (.531)
		1964–65, S.F. Warriors/Phi. 76ers	12.1	408-for-880 (.464)
		1965–66, Phi. 76ers	12.4	501-for-976 (.513)
		1966–67, Phi. 76ers	10.8	386-for-875 (.441)
		1967–68, Phi. 76ers	11.4	354-for-932 (.380)
		1968–69, L.A. Lakers	10.6	382-for-857 (.446)
		1969–70, L.A. Lakers	13.1	70-for-157 (.446)
10	Shaquille O'Neal	1993–94, Orl. Magic	10.5	471-for-850 (.554)
		1994–95, Orl. Magic	10.8	455-for-854 (.533)
		1997–98, L.A. Lakers	11.4	359-for-681 (.527)
		1998–99, L.A. Lakers	10.2	269-for-498 (.540)
		1999–00, L.A. Lakers	10.4	432-for-824 (.524)
		2000–01, L.A. Lakers	13.1	499-for-972 (.513)
		2001–02, L.A. Lakers	10.7	398-for-717 (.555)
		2002–03, L.A. Lakers	10.8	451-for-725 (.622)
		2003–04, L.A. Lakers	10.1	331-for-676 (.490)
		2004–05, Mia. Heat	10.5	353-for-765 (.461)
7	Bob Pettit	1955–56, St.L. Hawks	10.5	557-for-757 (.736)
		1957–58, St.L. Hawks	10.6	557-for-744 (.749)
		1958–59, St.L. Hawks	12.2	667-for-879 (.759)
		1959–60, St.L. Hawks	10.0	544-for-722 (.753)
		1960–61, St.L. Hawks	10.6	582-for-804 (.724)
		1961–62, St.L. Hawks	11.6	695-for-901 (.771)
		1962–63, St.L. Hawks	11.2	685-for-885 (.774)
7	Oscar Robertson	1960–61, Cin. Royals	11.2	653-for-794 (.822)
		1961–62, Cin. Royals	11.0	700-for-872 (.803)
		1963–64, Cin. Royals	11.9	800-for-938 (.853)
		1964–65, Cin. Royals	10.6	665-for-793 (.839)
		1965–66, Cin. Royals	11.6	742-for-881 (.842)
		1966–67, Cin. Royals	10.7	736-for-843 (.873)
		1967–68, Cin. Royals	10.2	576-for-660 (.873)
7	James Harden	2012–13, Hou. Rockets	10.2	674-for-792 (.851)
		2014–15, Hou. Rockets	10.2	715-for-824 (.868)
		2015–16, Hou. Rockets	10.2	720-for-837 (.860)
		2016–17, Hou. Rockets	10.9	746-for-881 (.847)
		2017–18, Hou. Rockets	10.1	624-for-727 (.858)
		2018–19, Hou. Rockets	11.0	754-for-858 (.879)
		2019–20, Hou. Rockets	11.8	692-for-800 (.865)

continued on next page

			FTA/G	FT Shooting
6	Moses Malone	1980–81, Hou. Rockets	10.1	609-for-804 (.757)
		1981–82, Hou. Rockets	10.2	630-for-827 (.762)
		1982–83, Phi. 76ers	10.1	600-for-788 (.761)
		1983–84, Phi. 76ers	10.2	545-for-727 (.750)
		1984–85, Phi. 76ers	11.4	737-for-904 (.815)
		1985–86, Phi. 76ers	10.6	617-for-784 (.787)
6	Karl Malone	1988–89, Uta. Jazz	11.5	703-for-918 (.766)
		1989–90, Uta. Jazz	11.1	696-for-913 (.762)
		1990–91, Uta. Jazz	10.8	684-for-888 (.770)
		1991–92, Uta. Jazz	10.7	673-for-865 (.778)
		1992–93, Uta. Jazz	10.2	619-for-836 (.740)
		1997–98, Uta. Jazz	10.2	628-for-825 (.761)
5	Jerry West	1961–62, L.A. Lakers	12.3	712-for-926 (.769)
		1964–65, L.A. Lakers	10.7	648-for-789 (.821)
		1965–66, L.A. Lakers	12.4	840-for-977 (.860)
		1966–67, L.A. Lakers	10.4	602-for-686 (.878)
		1969–70, L.A. Lakers	10.6	647-for-785 (.824)
5	Dwight Howard	2007–08, Orl. Magic	10.9	529-for-897 (.590)
		2008–09, Orl. Magic	10.7	504-for-849 (.594)
		2009–10, Orl. Magic	10.0	483-for-816 (.592)
		2010–11, Orl. Magic	11.7	546-for-916 (.596)
		2011–12, Orl. Magic	10.6	281-for-572 (.491)
4	Adrian Dantley	1981–82, Uta. Jazz	10.1	648-for-818 (.792)
		1982–83, Uta. Jazz	11.3	210-for-248 (.847)
		1983–84, Uta. Jazz	12.0	813-for-946 (.859)
		1985–86, Uta. Jazz	10.5	630-for-796 (.791)
4	David Robinson	1989–90, S.A. Spurs	10.2	613-for-837 (.732)
		1993–94, S.A. Spurs	11.6	693-for-925 (.749)
		1994–95, S.A. Spurs	10.5	656-for-847 (.774)
		1995–96, S.A. Spurs	10.0	626-for-823 (.761)
3	George Mikan	1948–49, Min. Lakers	11.5	532-for-689 (.772)
		1949–50, Min. Lakers	10.7	567-for-728 (.779)
		1950–51, Min. Lakers	10.5	576-for-717 (.803)
3	Paul Arizin	1951–52, Phi. Warriors	10.7	578-for-707 (.818)
		1956–57, Phi. Warriors	10.0	591-for-713 (.829)
		1958–59, Phi. Warriors	10.3	587-for-722 (.813)
3	Neil Johnston	1952–53, Phi. Warriors	11.3	556-for-794 (.700)
		1953–54, Phi. Warriors	10.7	577-for-772 (.747)
		1954–55, Phi. Warriors	10.7	589-for-769 (.766)
3	Elgin Baylor	1959–60, Min. Lakers	11.0	564-for-770 (.732)
		1960–61, L.A. Lakers	11.8	676-for-863 (.783)
		1961–62, L.A. Lakers	13.1	476-for-631 (.754)
3	Walt Bellamy	1961–62, Chi. Packers	10.8	549-for-853 (.644)
		1962–63, Chi. Zephyrs	10.3	553-for-821 (.674)
		1963–64, Bal. Bullets	10.3	537-for-825 (.651)
3	World B. Free	1978–79, S.D. Clippers	11.1	654-for-865 (.756)
		1979–80, S.D. Clippers	11.2	572-for-760 (.753)
		1980–81, G.S. Warriors	10.0	528-for-649 (.814)
3	Allen Iverson	2000–01, Phi. 76ers	10.1	585-for-719 (.814)
		2004–05, Phi. 76ers	10.5	656-for-786 (.835)
		2005–06, Phi. 76ers	11.5	675-for-829 (.814)
3	Kobe Bryant	2004–05, L.A. Lakers	10.1	542-for-664 (.816)

continued on next page

			FTA/G	FT Shooting
		2005–06, L.A. Lakers	10.2	696-for-819 (.850)
		2006–07, L.A. Lakers	10.0	667-for-768 (.868)
3	LeBron James	2005–06, Cle. Cavaliers	10.3	601-for-814 (.738)
		2007–08, Cle. Cavaliers	10.3	549-for-771 (.712)
		2009–10, Cle. Cavaliers	10.2	593-for-773 (.767)
3	Joel Embiid	2018–19, Phi. 76ers	10.1	522-for-649 (.804)
		2020–21, Phi. 76ers	10.7	471-for-548 (.859)
		2021–22, Phi. 76ers	11.8	626-for-766 (.817)
2	Joe Fulks	1946–47, Phi. Warriors	10.0	439-for-601 (.730)
		1948–49, Phi. Warriors	10.6	502-for-638 (.787)
2	Rick Barry	1966–67, S.F. Warriors	10.9	753-for-852 (.884)
		1968–69, Oak. Oaks	13.0	403-for-454 (.888)
2	Connie Hawkins	1967–68, Pit. Pipers[a]	11.3	603-for-789 (.764)
		1968–69, Min. Pipers[a]	11.8	425-for-554 (.767)
2	Michael Jordan	1986–87, Chi. Bulls	11.9	833-for-972 (.857)
		1987–88, Chi. Bulls	10.5	723-for-860 (.841)
2	Charles Barkley	1987–88, Phi. 76ers	11.9	714-for-951 (.751)
		1988–89, Phi. 76ers	10.1	602-for-799 (.753)
2	Dwyane Wade	2005–06, Mia. Heat	10.7	629-for-803 (.783)
		2006–07, Mia. Heat	10.5	432-for-535 (.807)
2	Giannis Antetokounmpo	2019–20, Mil. Bucks	10.0	398-for-629 (.633)
		2021–22, Mil. Bucks	11.5	532-for-738 (.721)

Most Free Throw Attempts, Game

				FT Shooting
39	Dwight Howard, Orl. Magic	@ G.S. Warriors (Jan. 12, 2012)		21-for-39 (.538)
39	Dwight Howard, L.A. Lakers	@ Orl. Magic (Mar. 12, 2013)		25-for-39 (.641)
36	Andre Drummond, Det. Pistons	@ Hou. Rockets (Jan. 20, 2016)		13-for-36 (.361)
34	Wilt Chamberlain, Phi. Warriors	vs. St.L. Hawks (Feb. 22, 1962)		19-for-34 (.559)
34	DeAndre Jordan, L.A. Clippers	vs. Por. Blazers (Nov. 30, 2015)		12-for-34 (.353)
32	Wilt Chamberlain, Phi. Warriors	vs. N.Y. Knicks (Mar. 2, 1962)		28-for-32 (.875)
31	Wilt Chamberlain, Phi. Warriors*	vs. L.A. Lakers (Dec. 8, 1961)		16-for-31 (.516)
31	Adrian Dantley, Uta. Jazz	vs. Den. Nuggets (Nov. 25, 1983)		27-for-31 (.871)
31	Shaquille O'Neal, L.A. Lakers	vs. Chi. Bulls (Nov. 19, 1999)		19-for-31 (.613)
30	Wilt Chamberlain, Phi. Warriors*	@ Cin. Royals (Feb. 13, 1962)		17-for-30 (.567)
30	Jerry West, L.A. Lakers	@ N.Y. Knicks (Oct. 17, 1964)		15-for-30 (.500)
30	Wilt Chamberlain, Phi. 76ers	vs. Sea. Sonics (Dec. 1, 1967)		8-for-30 (.267)
30	Wilt Chamberlain, L.A. Lakers*	@ Phi. 76ers (Oct. 17, 1969)		15-for-30 (.500)
29	Wilt Chamberlain, S.F. Warriors*	vs. L.A. Lakers (Dec. 6, 1963)		15-for-29 (.517)
29	Tony Jackson, N.Y. Nets[a]*	@ Ken. Colonels[a] (Nov. 27, 1967)		24-for-29 (.828)
29	George Thompson, Mem. Tams[a]*	@ S.D. Conquistadors[a] (Oct. 14, 1972)		24-for-29 (.828)
29	World B. Free, S.D. Clippers*	@ Atl. Hawks (Jan. 13, 1979)		22-for-29 (.759)
29	Adrian Dantley, Uta. Jazz	vs. Dal. Mavericks (Oct. 31, 1980)		26-for-29 (.897)
29	Adrian Dantley, Uta. Jazz	vs. Hou. Rockets (Jan. 4, 1984)		28-for-29 (.966)
29	Ben Simmons, Phi. 76ers	vs. Was. Wizards (Nov. 29, 2017)		15-for-29 (.517)

[a] ABA.

* Team lost game.

Most Free Throw Attempts, Missing Them All, Game

11	Shaquille O'Neal, L.A. Lakers*	vs. Sea. Sonics (Dec. 8, 2000)
10	Cliff Barker, Ind. Olympians	vs. Syr. Nationals (Mar. 13, 1951)
10	Wilt Chamberlain, Phi. Warriors	vs. Det. Pistons (Nov. 4, 1960)

continued on next page

9 .... Jim Browne, Den. Nuggets* .... vs. Syr. Nationals (Feb. 23, 1950)
9 .... Wilt Chamberlain, Phi. 76ers .... @ St.L. Hawks (Feb. 19, 1967)
9 .... Truck Robinson, Pho. Suns .... vs. Chi. Bulls (Nov. 28, 1980)
9 .... Dwight Howard, Cha. Hornets* .... @ Mil. Bucks (Oct. 23, 2017)
8 .... Jack Cotton, Den. Nuggets* .... vs. Syr. Nationals (Nov. 21, 1949)
8 .... Elvin Hayes, Hou. Rockets .... vs. Por. Blazers (Mar. 26, 1972)
8 .... Jerome Lane, Cle. Cavaliers .... @ Atl. Hawks (Dec. 29, 1992)
8 .... Chris Gatling, G.S. Warriors* .... vs. Min. T'Wolves (Nov. 15, 1994)
8 .... Eric Montross, Bos. Celtics* .... @ Chi. Bulls (Mar. 30, 1995)
8 .... Dale Davis, Ind. Pacers .... vs. Mil. Bucks (Mar. 13, 1998)
8 .... Tyson Chandler, Chi. Bulls* .... vs. L.A. Lakers (Mar. 13, 2004)
8 .... Nenê, Den. Nuggets .... vs. Min. T'Wolves (Apr. 9, 2011)
8 .... Andre Drummond, Det. Pistons .... vs. Atl. Hawks (Feb. 21, 2014)
8 .... Josh Smith, Det. Pistons* .... @ Pho. Suns (Mar. 21, 2014)
8 .... Hassan Whiteside, Mia. Heat* .... @ Det. Pistons (Jan. 18, 2019)

* Team lost game.

Most Free Throws Missed, Game

			FT Shooting
23	Andre Drummond, Det. Pistons	@ Hou. Rockets (Jan. 20, 2016)	13-for-36 (.361)
22	Wilt Chamberlain, Phi. 76ers	vs. Sea. Sonics (Dec. 1, 1967)	8-for-30 (.267)
22	DeAndre Jordan, L.A. Clippers	vs. Por. Blazers (Nov. 30, 2015)	12-for-34 (.353)
19	Wilt Chamberlain, Phi. 76ers	vs. Chi. Bulls (Jan. 4, 1967)	5-for-24 (.208)
19	Wilt Chamberlain, Phi. 76ers	vs. Sea. Sonics (Dec. 12, 1967)	6-for-25 (.240)
18	Wilt Chamberlain, Phi. Warriors	vs. Syr. Nationals (Nov. 17, 1960)	9-for-27 (.333)
18	Dwight Howard, Orl. Magic	@ G.S. Warriors (Jan. 12, 2012)	21-for-39 (.538)
18	DeAndre Jordan, L.A. Clippers	vs. S.A. Spurs (Feb. 19, 2015)	10-for-28 (.357)
17	Chris Dudley, N.J. Nets	vs. Ind. Pacers (Apr. 14, 1990)	1-for-18 (.056)
17	DeAndre Jordan, L.A. Clippers	vs. Dal. Mavericks (Apr. 10, 2016)	6-for-23 (.261)
16	Wilt Chamberlain, Phi. 76ers	@ Bos. Celtics (Feb. 12, 1967)	8-for-24 (.333)
16	Wilt Chamberlain, L.A. Lakers	@ Chi. Bulls (Dec. 7, 1968)	6-for-22 (.273)
15	Wilt Chamberlain, Phi. Warriors	vs. L.A. Lakers (Dec. 8, 1961)	16-for-31 (.516)
15	Wilt Chamberlain, Phi. Warriors	vs. St.L. Hawks (Feb. 22, 1962)	19-for-34 (.559)
15	Jerry West, L.A. Lakers	@ N.Y. Knicks (Oct. 17, 1964)	15-for-30 (.500)
15	Wilt Chamberlain, S.F. Warriors	vs. L.A. Lakers (Nov. 28, 1964)	6-for-21 (.286)
15	Wilt Chamberlain, Phi. 76ers	vs. Chi. Bulls (Nov. 25, 1967)	4-for-19 (.211)
15	Wilt Chamberlain, Phi. 76ers	@ S.F. Warriors (Jan. 19, 1968)	4-for-19 (.211)
15	Wilt Chamberlain, L.A. Lakers	@ Phi. 76ers (Oct. 17, 1969)	15-for-30 (.500)
15	Shaquille O'Neal, L.A. Lakers	@ Hou. Rockets (Dec. 21, 2000)	7-for-22 (.318)
15	Ben Wallace, Det. Pistons	@ L.A. Clippers (Dec. 11, 2005)	7-for-22 (.318)
15	Dwight Howard, Hou. Rockets	@ Cle. Cavaliers (Mar. 29, 2016)	7-for-22 (.318)

Highest FT% by Decade (Min. 500 FT Attempts)

1946-47 – 1949-50		1950-51 – 1959-60		1960-61 – 1969-70*	
.813	Bobby Wanzer	.881	Bill Sharman	.875	Rick Barry
.807	Max Zaslofsky	.850	Dolph Schayes	.874	Dolph Schayes
.805	Bob Feerick	.844	Al Cervi	.867	Charles Beasley
.795	Fred Scolari	.835	Vince Boryla	.855	Larry Siegfried
.781	Buddy Jeannette	.833	Fred Scolari	.853	Larry Costello
.779	Belus Smawley	.830	Kenny Sears	.851	Tony Jackson
.776	Sonny Hertzberg	.827	Larry Costello	.848	Flynn Robinson

continued on next page

1946–47–1949–50
.776.............................. George Mikan
.774.................................. Walt Budko
.772................................ Chick Reiser

1970–71–1979–80*
.904.................................... Rick Barry
.902......................... Ernie DiGregorio
.886............................. Calvin Murphy
.876..................................... Bill Keller
.871.......................... Jon McGlocklin
.871................................. Mack Calvin
.867................................. Mike Newlin
.866................................ Dick Garrett
.863.................................... Jack Marin
.862................................. Terry Furlow

2000–01–2009–10
.915............................. Reggie Miller
.908................................. Steve Nash
.903.................................... Ray Allen
.900............................. Allan Houston
.897......................... Peja Stojaković
.894......................... Chauncey Billups
.882............................... Kevin Durant
.881............................... Dirk Nowitzki
.881................................ Steve Smith
.880............................... Earl Boykins

* Includes ABA.

** Minimum 150 FT Attempts.

1950–51–1959–60
.827.............................. Fred Schaus
.826................................ Carl Braun
.825........................... Dick Schnittker

1980–81–1989–90
.888................................. Larry Bird
.883................................ Mark Price
.881............................... Mike Newlin
.879............................... Chris Mullin
.874............................... Sam Vincent
.873.................................. Kyle Macy
.871.......................... Kiki Vandeweghe
.869............................... Jeff Malone
.869................................. John Long
.865........................ Hersey Hawkins

2010–11–2019–20
.913........................ Chauncey Billups
.910................................. Steve Nash
.907............................. Stephen Curry
.897..................................... J.J. Redick
.894...................... Malcolm Brogdon
.893................................... Ray Allen
.889............................ Damian Lillard
.889................................ Kevin Martin
.887................................ Dirk Nowitzki
.885................................. Chris Paul

1960–61–1969–70*
.845.......................... Darel Carrier
.837...................... Oscar Robertson
.835........................... Adrian Smith

1990–91–1999–00
.919............................... Mark Price
.909.............. Mahmoud Abdul-Rauf
.896............................. Ricky Pierce
.893........................ Magic Johnson
.892.................... Darrell Armstrong
.892................................ Scott Skiles
.890.............................. Jeff Hornacek
.889............................. Reggie Miller
879.................... Micheal Williams
875............................... Jeff Malone

2020–21–2021–22**
.919................................ Kyrie Irving
.919.......................... Stephen Curry
.915..................... Danielo Gallinari
.914........................... Damian Lillard
.912................................ Jordan Poole
.903............................. Josh Richardson
.900............................... Kevin Durant
.895.................................. Trae Young
.894...................... Khris Middleton
.886........................... Derrick Rose

In Multiple Seasons, Leading League in FT%

7	Bill Sharman	.850	1952–53, Bos. Celtics
		.844	1953–54, Bos. Celtics
		.897	1954–55, Bos. Celtics
		.867	1955–56, Bos. Celtics
		.905	1956–57, Bos. Celtics
		.932	1958–59, Bos. Celtics
		.921	1960–61, Bos. Celtics
7	Rick Barry	.888	1968–69, Oak. Oaksª
		.902	1972–73, G.S. Warriors
		.904	1974–75, G.S. Warriors
		.923	1975–76, G.S. Warriors
		.924	1977–78, G.S. Warriors
		.947	1978–79, Hou. Rockets
		.935	1979–80, Hou. Rockets
5	Reggie Miller	.918	1990–91, Ind. Pacers
		.915	1998–99, Ind. Pacers
		.928	2000–01, Ind. Pacers
		.911	2001–02, Ind. Pacers
		.938	2004–05, Ind. Pacers
4	Larry Bird	.888	1983–84, Bos. Celtics
		.896	1985–86, Bos. Celtics
		.910	1986–87, Bos. Celtics

continued on next page

		.930	....	1989–90, Bos. Celtics
4	Stephen Curry	.934	....	2010–11, G.S. Warriors
		.914	....	2014–15, G.S. Warriors
		.908	....	2015–16, G.S. Warriors
		.921	....	2017–18, G.S. Warriors
3	Dolph Schayes	.904	....	1957–58, Syr. Nationals
		.893	....	1959–60, Syr. Nationals
		.897	....	1961–62, Syr. Nationals
3	Mark Price	.947	....	1991–92, Cle. Cavaliers
		.948	....	1992–93, Cle. Cavaliers
		.906	....	1996–97, G.S. Warriors
2	Bob Feerick	.788	....	1947–48, Was. Capitols
		.859	....	1948–49, Was. Capitols
2	Larry Costello	.881	....	1962–63, Syr. Nationals
		.877	....	1964–65, Phi. 76ers
2	Oscar Robertson	.853	....	1963–64, Cin. Royals
		.873	....	1967–68, Cin. Royals
2	Larry Siegfried	.881	....	1965–66, Bos. Celtics
		.864	....	1968–69, Bos. Celtics
2	Ernie DiGregorio	.902	....	1973–74, Buf. Braves
		.945	....	1976–77, Buf. Braves
2	Mack Calvin	.896	....	1974–75, Den. Rockets[a]
		.888	....	1975–76, Vir. Squires[a]
2	Calvin Murphy	.958	....	1980–81, Hou. Rockets
		.920	....	1982–83, Hou. Rockets
2	Kyle Macy	.899	....	1981–82, Pho. Suns
		.907	....	1984–85, Pho. Suns
2	Mahmoud Abdul-Rauf	.956	....	1993–94, Den. Rockets
		.930	....	1995–96, Den. Rockets
2	Peja Stojaković	.927	....	2003–04, Sac. Kings
		.929	....	2007–08, N.O. Hornets
2	Steve Nash	.921	....	2005–06, Pho. Suns
		.938	....	2009–10, Pho. Suns

[a] ABA.

Highest FT%, Season (Min. 250 FT Attempts)

FT%		FT	FTA
.948	Mark Price, Cle. Cavaliers, 1992–93	289	305
.947	Mark Price, Cle. Cavaliers, 1991–92	270	285
.933	Reggie Miller, Ind. Pacers, 2004–05	250	268
.932	Bill Sharman, Bos. Celtics, 1958–59	342	367
.930	Larry Bird, Bos. Celtics, 1989–90	319	343
.928	Calvin Murphy, Hou. Rockets, 1978–79	246	265
.928	Reggie Miller, Ind. Pacers, 2000–01	323	348
.928	Damian Lillard, Por. Blazers, 2020–21	449	484
.927	Peja Stojaković, Sac. Kings, 2003–04	394	425
.925	Jordan Poole, G.S. Warriors, 2021–22	246	266
.924	Rick Barry, G.S. Warriors, 1977–78	378	409
.923	Rick Barry, G.S. Warriors, 1975–76	287	311
.923	Stephen Curry, G.S. Warriors, 2021–22	275	298
.922	Jack Sikma, Mil. Bucks, 1987–88	321	348
.921	Steve Nash, Pho. Suns, 2005–06	257	279

continued on next page

FT%		FT	FTA
.921	Earl Boykins, Den. Nuggets, 2004–05	279	303
.921	Stephen Curry, G.S. Warriors, 2017–18	278	302
.920	Peja Stojaković, Sac. Kings, 2004–05	253	275

Lowest FT%, Season (Min. 250 FT Attempts)

FT%		FT	FTA
.355	Andre Drummond, Det. Pistons, 2015–16	208	586
.380	Wilt Chamberlain, Phi. 76ers, 1967–68	354	932
.386	Andre Drummond, Det. Pistons, 2016–17	137	355
.389	Andre Drummond, Det. Pistons, 2014–15	142	365
.397	DeAndre Jordan, L.A. Clippers, 2014–15	187	471
.408	Ben Wallace, Chi. Bulls, 2006–07	109	267
.416	Ben Wallace, Det. Pistons, 2005–06	123	296
.418	Andre Drummond, Det. Pistons, 2013–14	137	328
.422	Wilt Chamberlain, L.A. Lakers, 1971–72	221	524
.422	Shaquille O'Neal, Mia. Heat, 2006–07	124	294
.425	Joe Caldwell, Car. Cougars°, 1972–73	172	405
.428	Ben Wallace, Det. Pistons, 2004–05	124	304
.428	DeAndre Jordan, L.A. Clippers, 2013–14	130	374
.430	DeAndre Jordan, L.A. Clippers, 2015–16	160	619
.441	Wilt Chamberlain, Phi. 76ers, 1966–67	266	875
.446	Wilt Chamberlain, L.A. Lakers, 1968–69	386	857

° ABA.

Highest FT%, Career˙ (Min. 1000 FT Attempts)

FT%		FT	FTA
.908	Stephen Curry^	3197	3520
.905	Mahmoud Abdul-Rauf	1051	1161
.904	Steve Nash	3060	3384
.904	Mark Price	2135	2362
.895	Peja Stojaković	2237	2500
.894	Chauncey Billups	4496	5029
.894	Ray Allen	4398	4920
.893	Rick Barry	5713	6397
.893	Damian Lillard^	3917	4388
.892	J.J. Redick	2060	2310
.892	Calvin Murphy	3445	3864
.889	Scott Skiles	1548	1741
.888	Reggie Miller	6237	7026
.886	Larry Bird	3960	4471
.884	Kevin Durant^	6324	7153
.883	Bill Sharman	3143	3559
.882	Kyrie Irving^	2350	2663
.881	Khris Middleton^	1852	2103
.879	Jodie Meeks	883	1004
.879	Dirk Nowitzki	7240	8239
.877	Jeff Hornacek	2973	3390
.877	Kyle Korver	1297	1479
.877	Danilo Gallinari^	2993	3413
.876	Earl Boykins	1255	1433
.875	Ricky Pierce	3389	3871

continued on next page

FT%	FT	FTA
.873 .... Terrell Brandon 1784 2043
.873 .... José Calderón 925 1060
.873 .... Trae Young^ 1808 2072
.872 .... Bill Keller 1202 1378
.872 .... Isaiah Thomas 2339 2682
.872 .... Kiki Vandeweghe 3484 3997
.871 .... Darrell Armstrong 1463 1679
.871 .... Chris Paul^ 4596 5275
.871 .... Jeff Malone 2947 3383
.871 .... Mo Williams 1563 1795
.870 .... Kevin Martin 3561 4091
.870 .... Devin Booker^ 2387 2744
.870 .... Hersey Hawkins 3466 3985
.870 .... Mike Newlin 3005 3456

* Includes ABA.

^ Active.

Lowest FT% Career (Min. 1000 FT Attempts)

FT%	FT	FTA
.414 .... Ben Wallace 1109 2679
.458 .... Chris Dudley 691 1508
.473 .... Andre Drummond^ 1543 3263
.475 .... DeAndre Jordan^ 1694 3563
.511 .... Wilt Chamberlain 6057 11,862
.521 .... Bo Outlaw 957 1837
.527 .... Clint Capela^ 753 1429
.527 .... Shaquille O'Neal 5935 11,252
.528 .... Reggie Evans 1074 2036
.529 .... Michael Smith 626 1183
.531 .... Larry Smith 866 1630
.535 .... Olden Polynice 1146 2141
.547 .... Steven Adams^ 1044 1907
.551 .... Ömer Aşık 585 1062
.553 .... Johnny Green 2335 4226
.557 .... Mason Plumlee^ 1124 2019
.557 .... Greg Anderson 929 1668
.557 .... Andrew Bogut 833 1495
.561 .... Bill Russell 3148 5614
.562 .... Dale Davis 1522 2708
.564 .... Jason Maxiell 685 1214
.564 .... Bismack Biyombo^ 894 1584
.567 .... Ken Norman 1012 1786
.567 .... Dwight Howard^ 5361 9455
.568 .... Mark West 1203 2117
.569 .... Greg Ostertag 833 1465
.570 .... Kwame Brown 998 1750
.570 .... Tom Hawkins 1150 2016
.572 .... Joe Caldwell 2011 3518
.573 .... Toby Kimball 704 1229
.575 .... Bruce Bowen 582 1013
.577 .... Will Perdue 705 1222
.579 .... Elmore Smith 1203 2079

continued on next page

FT%		FT	FTA
.583	Jared Jeffries	604	1036
.583	Ed Davis^	745	1277
.584	Dennis Rodman	1069	1832
.585	Rick Roberson	860	1470
.586	Emeka Okafor	1362	2325
.587	Brendan Haywood	1318	2246
.588	Clifford Ray	1155	1963
.590	Darius Miles	737	1250
.594	Darrall Imhoff	1161	1954
.594	Kendrick Perkins	804	1353
.597	Slick Watts	697	1168
.597	Jon Koncak	613	1027
.597	Alton Lister	1269	2126
.597	Ben Simmons^	809	1354

^ Active.

Highest FT%, Rookie Season (Min. 250 FT Attempts)

FT%		FT	FTA
.879	O.J. Mayo, Mem. Grizzlies, 2008–09	247	281
.873	Derek Anderson, Cle. Cavaliers, 1997–98	275	315
.873	Kevin Durant*, Sea. Sonics, 2007–08	391	448
.872	Charles Beasley, Dal. Chaparrals^a, 1967–68	285	327
.863	Ben Gordon, Chi. Bulls, 2004–05	233	270
.862	Rick Barry*, S.F. Warriors, 1965–66	569	660
.854	Eric Gordon, L.A. Clippers, 2008–09	299	350
.850	Chauncey Billups, Bos. Celtics/Tor. Raptors, 1997–98	226	266
.847	Chris Paul*, N.O.-Ok.C. Hornets, 2005–06	394	465
.846	Keith Van Horn, N.J. Nets, 1997–98	258	305
.845	Michael Jordan*, Chi. Bulls, 1984–85	630	746
.844	Damian Lillard*, Por. Blazers, 2012–13	271	321
.842	John Beasley, Dal. Chaparrals^a, 1967–68	271	322
.840	Devin Booker, Pho. Suns, 2015–16	215	256
.839	Collin Sexton, Cle. Cavaliers, 2018–19	214	255
.836	Larry Bird*, Bos. Celtics, 1979–80	301	360
.835	Howard Komives, N.Y. Knicks, 1964–65	212	254
.835	Joe Hamilton, Tex. Chaparrals^a, 1970–71	233	279
.835	Christian Laettner, Min. T'Wolves, 1992–93	462	553
.833	James Silas, Dal. Chaparrals^a, 1972–73	389	467
.831	Hersey Hawkins, Phi. 76ers, 1988–89	241	290
.830	Walter Davis*, Pho. Suns, 1977–78	387	466
.829	Al Cervi, Syr. Nationals, 1949–50	287	346
.829	Tony Jackson, N.Y. Nets^a, 1967–68	450	543
.829	Larry Johnson*, Cha. Hornets, 1991–92	339	409
.829	Trae Young, Atl. Hawks, 2018–19	343	414
.827	John Brisker, Pit. Pipers^a, 1969–70	329	398
.826	Jonny Flynn, Min. T'Wolves, 2009–10	223	270
.826	Jayson Tatum, Bos. Celtics, 2017–18	213	258
.825	Darel Carrier, Ken. Colonels^a, 1967–68	395	479
.825	Mervin Jackson, L.A. Stars^a, 1968–69	249	302
.825	John Mengelt, Cin. Royals, 1971–72	208	252

^a ABA.

* Rookie of the Year.

Highest Average of Free Throws Made Per Game, Season
(Players Qualifying for FT% Leaderboard)

FT/G		FT%
11.5	Rick Barry, Oak. Oaks[a], 1968–69	.888
10.6	Jerry West, L.A. Lakers, 1965–66	.860
10.4	Wilt Chamberlain, Phi. Warriors, 1961–62	.613
10.3	Adrian Dantley, Uta. Jazz, 1983–84	.859
10.2	James Harden, Hou. Rockets, 2019–20	.865
10.2	Michael Jordan, Chi. Bulls, 1986–87	.857
10.1	Oscar Robertson, Cin. Royals, 1963–64	.853
9.9	Elgin Baylor, L.A. Lakers, 1961–62	.754
9.8	Oscar Robertson, Cin. Royals, 1965–66	.842
9.7	Rick Barry, S.F. Warriors, 1966–67	.884
9.7	James Harden, Hou. Rockets, 2018–19	.879
9.7	Joel Embiid, Phi. 76ers, 2021–22	.819
9.5	Jerry West, L.A. Lakers, 1961–62	.769
9.5	Adrian Dantley, Uta. Jazz, 1982–83	.847
9.4	Allen Iverson, Phi. 76ers, 2005–06	.814
9.3	Bob Pettit, St.L. Hawks, 1958–59	.759
9.3	Elgin Baylor, L.A. Lakers, 1960–61	.783
9.3	Oscar Robertson, Cin. Royals, 1966–67	.873
9.3	Moses Malone, Phi. 76ers, 1984–85	.815
9.2	Oscar Robertson, Cin. Royals, 1960–61	.822
9.2	Kevin Durant, Ok.C. Thunder, 2009–10	.900
9.2	James Harden, Hou. Rockets, 2016–17	.847
9.2	Joel Embiid, Phi. 76ers, 2020–21	.859
9.1	George Yardley, Det. Pistons, 1957–58	.811
9.1	Jerry West, L.A. Lakers, 1966–67	.878
9.0	Connie Hawkins, Min. Pipers[a], 1968–69	.767
9.0	Kevin Martin, Sac. Kings, 2008–09	.867

[a] ABA.

Teammates Finishing One-Two in FT%, Season

Season	Team	Leader	FT%	Runner-Up	FT%
1973–74	Uta. Stars[a]	Jimmy Jones	.884	Ron Boone	.875
1978–79	Hou. Rockets	Rick Barry	.947	Calvin Murphy	.928
1979–80	Hou. Rockets	Rick Barry	.935	Calvin Murphy	.897
1986–87	Bos. Celtics	Larry Bird	.910	Danny Ainge	.897
2021–22	G.S. Warriors	Jordan Poole	.925	Stephen Curry	.923

[a] ABA.

Players Finishing One-Two in FT%, Multiple Seasons

Season	Leader (FT%)	Runner-Up (FT%)
1953–54	Bill Sharman, Bos. Celtics (.844)	Dolph Schayes, Syr. Nationals (.827)
1955–56	Bill Sharman, Bos. Celtics (.867)	Dolph Schayes, Syr. Nationals (.858)
1956–57	Bill Sharman, Bos. Celtics (.905)	Dolph Schayes, Syr. Nationals (.904)
1957–58	Dolph Schayes, Syr. Nationals (.904)	Bill Sharman, Bos. Celtics (.893)
1958–59	Bill Sharman, Bos. Celtics (.932)	Dolph Schayes, Syr. Nationals (.864)
1960–61	Bill Sharman, Bos. Celtics (.921)	Dolph Schayes, Syr. Nationals (.868)

continued on next page

Season	Leader (FT%)	Runner-Up (FT%)
1972–73	Rick Barry, G.S. Warriors (.902)	Calvin Murphy, Hou. Rockets (.888)
1974–75	Rick Barry, G.S. Warriors (.904)	Calvin Murphy, Hou. Rockets (.883)
1975–76	Rick Barry, G.S. Warriors (.923)	Calvin Murphy, Hou. Rockets (.907)
1977–78	Rick Barry, G.S. Warriors (.924)	Calvin Murphy, Hou. Rockets (.918)
1978–79	Rick Barry, Hou. Rockets (.947)	Calvin Murphy, Hou. Rockets (.928)
1979–80	Rick Barry, Hou. Rockets (.935)	Calvin Murphy, Hou. Rockets (.897)
1973–74	Ernie DiGregorio, Buf. Braves (.902)	Rick Barry, G.S. Warriors (.899)
1976–77	Ernie DiGregorio, Buf. Braves (.945)	Rick Barry, G.S. Warriors (.916)
1974–75	Mack Calvin, Den. Nuggets[a] (.896)	James Silas, S.A. Spurs[a] (.885)
1975–76	Mack Calvin, Vir. Squires[a] (.888)	James Silas, S.A. Spurs[a] (.872)
2003–04	Peja Stojaković, Sac. Kings (.927)	Steve Nash, Dal. Mavericks (.916)
2005–06	Steve Nash, Pho. Suns (.921)	Peja Stojaković, Sac. Kings/Ind. Pacers (.915)

[a] ABA.

Assists

Most Assists by Decade

1946-47 – 1949-50

770	Andy Phillip
656	John Logan
631	Kenny Sailors
630	Jim Seminoff
615	Bob Davies
583	George Senesky
572	Ernie Calverley
481	Carl Braun
440	Bob Feerick
426	Belus Smawley

1950-51 – 1959-60

5259	Bob Cousy
3819	Dick McGuire
3012	Slater Martin
2989	Andy Phillip
2292	Carl Braun
2174	Dolph Schayes
2146	Paul Seymour
2130	Jack George
1958	George King
1955	Bill Sharman

1960-61 – 1969-70*

7731	Oscar Robertson
6174	Guy Rodgers
4406	Lenny Wilkens
4023	Jerry West
3455	Hal Greer
3429	Wilt Chamberlain
3311	Bill Russell
3100	Elgin Baylor
2880	Richie Guerin
2649	K.C. Jones

1970-71 – 1979-80*

4748	Tiny Archibald
4717	Norm Van Lier
4534	Kevin Porter
3913	Jo Jo White
3859	Calvin Murphy
3669	Randy Smith
3635	John Havlicek
3594	Dave Bing
3563	Pete Maravich
3562	Rick Barry

1980-81 – 1989-90

8369	Magic Johnson
6985	Isiah Thomas
5678	Maurice Cheeks
5131	Reggie Theus
5075	John Stockton
4588	Larry Bird
4534	Dennis Johnson
4528	Rickey Green
4454	Norm Nixon
4364	Fat Lever

1990-91 – 1999-00

8715	John Stockton
6483	Mark Jackson
5936	Rod Strickland
5621	Tim Hardaway
5548	Gary Payton
5186	Mookie Blaylock
4913	Avery Johnson
4830	Muggsy Bogues
4437	Kevin Johnson
4274	Scottie Pippen

2000-01 – 2009-10

7506	Steve Nash
7075	Jason Kidd
5989	Andre Miller
5190	Baron Davis
4552	Chauncey Billups

2010-11 – 2019-20

6211	Russell Westbrook
6207	Chris Paul
5536	LeBron James
5282	John Wall
5118	James Harden

2020-21 – 2021-22

1331	Trae Young
1324	Chris Paul
1313	Russell Westbrook
1183	Nikola Jokić
1142	James Harden

continued on next page

2000-01–2009-10	2010-11–2019-20	2020-21–2021-22
4186 .... Stephon Marbury	5072 .... Rajon Rondo	1135 .... Luka Dončić
4182 .... Mike Bibby	4749 .... Kyle Lowry	990 .... Dejounte Murray
4012 .... Allen Iverson	4387 .... Ricky Rubio	937 .... Tyrese Haliburton
3963 .... Kobe Bryant	4331 .... Jeff Teague	912 .... Darius Garland
3848 .... Jason Terry	4279 .... Jrue Holiday	884 .... LaMelo Ball

* Includes ABA.

Evolution of Assists Record

1946–47	Ernie Calverly, Pro. Steamrollers	202
1948–49	Bob Davies, Roc. Royals	321
1949–50	Dick McGuire, N.Y. Knicks	386
1950–51	Andy Phillip, Phi. Warriors	414
1951–52	Bob Cousy, Bos. Celtics	539
1952–53	Bob Cousy, Bos. Celtics	547
1954–55	Bob Cousy, Bos. Celtics	557
1955–56	Bob Cousy, Bos. Celtics	642
1959–60	Bob Cousy, Bos. Celtics	715
1961–62	Oscar Robertson, Cin. Royals	899
1966–67	Guy Rodgers, Chi. Bulls	908
1972–73	Tiny Archibald, K.C.-Oma. Kings	910
1978–79	Kevin Porter, Det. Pistons	1099
1984–85	Isiah Thomas, Det. Pistons	1123
1987–88	John Stockton, Uta. Jazz	1128
1989–90	John Stockton, Uta. Jazz	1134
1990–91	John Stockton, Uta. Jazz	1164

Most Assists, Season

1164 .... John Stockton, Uta. Jazz, 1990–91		977 ..... Magic Johnson, L.A. Lakers, 1986–87
1134 .... John Stockton, Uta. Jazz, 1989–90		968 ..... Magic Johnson, L.A. Lakers, 1984–85
1128 .... John Stockton, Uta. Jazz, 1987–88		935 ..... Mark Jackson, Den. Nuggets/Ind. Pacers, 1996–97
1126 .... John Stockton, Uta. Jazz, 1991–92		925 ..... Chris Paul, N.O. Hornets, 2007–08
1123 .... Isiah Thomas, Det. Pistons, 1984–85		916 ..... John Stockton, Uta. Jazz, 1995–96
1118 .... John Stockton, Uta. Jazz, 1988–89		914 ..... Norm Nixon, S.D. Clippers, 1983–84
1099 .... Kevin Porter, Det. Pistons, 1978–79		914 ..... Isiah Thomas, Det. Pistons, 1983–84
1031 .... John Stockton, Uta. Jazz, 1993–94		910 ..... Tiny Archibald, K.C.-Oma. Kings, 1972–73
1011 .... John Stockton, Uta. Jazz, 1994–95		908 ..... Guy Rodgers, Chi. Bulls, 1966–67
991 .... Kevin Johnson, Pho. Suns, 1988–89		907 ..... Magic Johnson, L.A. Lakers, 1985–86
989 .... Magic Johnson, L.A. Lakers, 1990–91		907 ..... Magic Johnson, L.A. Lakers, 1989–90
988 .... Magic Johnson, L.A. Lakers, 1988–89		907 ..... James Harden, Hou. Rockets, 2016–17
987 .... John Stockton, Uta. Jazz, 1992–93		

Most Assists, Career

15,806 .... John Stockton		8966 .... Gary Payton
12,091 .... Jason Kidd		8611 .... Russell Westbrook^
10,977 .... Chris Paul^		8524 .... Andre Miller
10,335 .... Steve Nash		7987 .... Rod Strickland
10,334 .... Mark Jackson		7584 .... Rajon Rondo^
10,141 .... Magic Johnson		7392 .... Maurice Cheeks
10,045 .... LeBron James^		7211 .... Lenny Wilkens
9887 .... Oscar Robertson		7160 .... Terry Porter
9061 .... Isiah Thomas		7095 .... Tim Hardaway

continued on next page

7036	Tony Parker	6454	John Lucas
6955	Bob Cousy	6453	Reggie Theus
6917	Guy Rodgers	6397	James Harden^
6819	Deron Williams	6386	Norm Nixon
6726	Muggsy Bogues	6306	Kobe Bryant
6711	Kevin Johnson	6238	Jerry West
6577	Derek Harper	6135	Scottie Pippen
6476	Tiny Archibald	6125	Clyde Drexler
6471	Stephon Marbury	6114	John Havlicek
6469	Kyle Lowry^	6025	Baron Davis

^ Active.

Assists Leaders by State of Birth

Alabama	Charles Barkley (Leeds)	4215	Nevada	Greg Anthony (Las Vegas)	2997
Alaska	Mario Chalmers (Anchorage)	2412	New Hampshire	Matt Bonner (Concord)	552
Arizona	Sean Elliott (Tucson)	1897	New Jersey	Mike Bibby (Cherry Hill)	5517
Arkansas	Scottie Pippen (Hamburg)	6135	New Mexico	Bill Birdges (Hobbs)	2553
California	Jason Kidd (San Francisco)	12,091	New York	Mark Jackson (Brooklyn)	10,334
Colorado	Chauncey Billups (Denver)	5636	North Carolina	Chris Paul^ (Winston-Salem)	10,977
Connecticut	Calvin Murphy (Norwalk)	4402	North Dakota	Tyler Johnson^ (Grand Forks)	813
Delaware	Walt Hazzard (Wilmington)	3555	Ohio	LeBron James^ (Akron)	10,045
Florida	Vince Carter (Daytona Beach)	4714	Oklahoma	Mark Price (Bartlesville)	4863
Georgia	Derek Harper (Elberton)	6577	Oregon	Damon Stoudamire (Portland)	5371
Hawaii	Red Rocha (Hilo)	1153	Pennsylvania	Guy Rodgers (Philadelphia)	6917
Idaho	Luke Ridnour (Coeur d'Alene)	3713	Rhode Island	Ernie DiGregorio (North Providence)	1594
Illinois	Isiah Thomas (Chicago)	9061	South Carolina	Kevin Garnett (Greenville)	5445
Indiana	Larry Bird (West Baden)	5695	South Dakota	Mike Miller (Mitchell)	2666
Iowa	Kirk Hinrich (Sioux City)	4245	Tennessee	Oscar Robertson (Charlotte)	9887
Kansas	Alvan Adams (Lawrence)	4012	Texas	Mookie Blaylock (Garland)	5972
Kentucky	Rajon Rondo^ (Louisville)	7584	Utah	Byron Scott (Ogden)	2729
Louisiana	Clyde Drexler (New Orleans)	6125	Vermont	N/A	N/A
Maine	Jeff Turner (Bangor)	635	Virginia	Allen Iverson (Hampton)	5624
Maryland	Muggsy Bogues (Baltimore)	6726	Washington	John Stockton (Spokane)	15,806
Massachusetts	Dana Barros (Boston)	2837	West Virginia	Deron Williams (Parkersburg)	6819
Michigan	Magic Johnson (Lansing)	10,141	Wisconsin	Terry Porter (Milwaukee)	7160
Minnesota	Mark Olberding (Melrose)	2332	Wyoming	James Johnson^ (Cheyenne)	1583
Mississippi	Mo Williams (Jackson)	3990			
Missouri	Jo Jo White (St. Louis)	4095	District of Columbia	Dave Bing	5397
Montana	Mike Lewis (Missoula)	1000	Puerto Rico	J.J. Barea (Mayaguez)	3270
Nebraska	Bob Boozer (Omaha)	1237	Virgin Islands	Tim Duncan (St. Croix)	4225

^ Active.

All-Time Assists Leaders by First Letter of Last Name·

A	Archibald, Tiny	6476	I	Iverson, Allen	5624
B	Bogues, Muggsy	6726	J	Jackson, Mark	10,334
C	Cheeks, Maurice	7392	K	Kidd, Jason	12,091
D	Drexler, Clyde	6125	L	Lowry, Kyle^	6469
E	Erving, Julius	5176	M	Miller, Andre	8524
F	Floyd, Sleepy	5175	N	Nash, Steve	10,335
G	Garnett, Kevin	5445	O	Odom, Lamar	3554
H	Hardaway, Tim	7095	P	Paul, Chris^	10,977

continued on next page

Q	Quinn, Chris	455	V	Van Exel, Nick	5777
R	Robertson, Oscar	9887	W	Westbrook, Russell^	8608
S	Stockton, John	15,806	X	N/A	N/A
T	Thomas, Isiah	9061	Y	Young, Trae^	2544
U	Unseld, Wes	3822	Z	Zaslofsky, Max	1093

* Includes ABA.
^ Active.

Most Career Assists by Zodiac Sign

Aquarius (Jan. 20–Feb. 18)	Steve Nash	10,335
Pisces (Feb. 19–Mar. 20)	Andre Miller	8524
Aries (Mar. 21–Apr. 19)	John Stockton	15,806
Taurus (Apr. 20–May 20)	Chris Paul^	10,977
Gemini (May 21–Jun. 21)	Jerry West	6238
Cancer (Jun. 22–Jul. 22)	Rod Strickland	7987
Leo (Jul. 23–Aug. 22)	Magic Johnson	10,141
Virgo (Aug. 23–Sep. 22)	Maurice Cheeks	7392
Libra (Sep. 23–Oct. 23)	Derek Harper	6577
Scorpio (Oct. 24–Nov. 21)	Lenny Wilkens	7211
Sagittarius (Nov. 22–Dec. 21)	Oscar Robertson	9887
Capricorn (Dec. 22–Jan. 19)	LeBron James^	10,045

^ Active.

Multiple Seasons Leading League in Assists

9	John Stockton	Uta. Jazz, 1987–88 (1128)
		Uta. Jazz, 1988–89 (1118)
		Uta. Jazz, 1989–90 (1134)
		Uta. Jazz, 1990–91 (1164)
		Uta. Jazz, 1991–92 (1126)
		Uta. Jazz, 1992–93 (987)
		Uta. Jazz, 1993–94 (1031)
		Uta. Jazz, 1994–95 (1011)
		Uta. Jazz, 1995–96 (916)
8	Bob Cousy	Bos. Celtics, 1952–53 (547)
		Bos. Celtics, 1953–54 (518)
		Bos. Celtics, 1954–55 (557)
		Bos. Celtics, 1955–56 (642)
		Bos. Celtics, 1956–57 (478)
		Bos. Celtics, 1957–58 (463)
		Bos. Celtics, 1958–59 (557)
		Bos. Celtics, 1959–60 (715)
6	Oscar Robertson	Cin. Royals, 1960–61 (690)
		Cin. Royals, 1961–62 (899)
		Cin. Royals, 1963–64 (868)
		Cin. Royals, 1964–65 (861)
		Cin. Royals, 1965–66 (847)
		Cin. Royals, 1968–69 (772)
6	Steve Nash	Pho. Suns, 2004–05 (861)
		Pho. Suns, 2005–06 (826)
		Pho. Suns, 2006–07 (884)
		Pho. Suns, 2009–10 (892)

continued on next page

		Pho. Suns, 2010–11 (855)
		Pho. Suns, 2011–12 (664)
4	Kevin Porter	Was. Bullets, 1974–75 (650)
		Den. Pistons/N.J. Nets, 1977–78 (837)
		Det. Pistons, 1978–79 (1099)
		Was. Bullets, 1980–81 (734)
3	Larry Brown	N.O. Buccaneers[a], 1967–68 (506)
		Oak. Oaks[a], 1968–69 (544)
		Was. Capitols[a], 1969–70 (580)
3	Magic Johnson	L.A. Lakers, 1982–83 (829)
		L.A. Lakers, 1985–86 (907)
		L.A. Lakers, 1986–87 (977)
3	Jason Kidd	Pho. Suns, 1998–99 (539)
		Pho. Suns, 2000–01 (753)
		N.J. Nets, 2002–03 (711)
3	Chris Paul	N.O. Hornets, 2007–08 (925)
		N.O. Hornets, 2008–09 (861)
		L.A. Clippers, 2014–15 (838)
3	Russell Westbrook	Ok.C. Thunder, 2017–18 (820)
		Ok.C. Thunder, 2018–19 (784)
		Was. Wizards, 2020–21 (763)
2	Andy Phillip	Phi. Warriors, 1950–51 (414)
		Phi. Warriors, 1951–52 (539)
2	Guy Rodgers	S.F. Warriors, 1962–63 (825)
		Chi. Bulls, 1966–67 (908)
2	Lenny Wilkens	Sea. Sonics, 1969–70 (683)
		Sea. Sonics, 1971–72 (766)
2	Bill Melchionni	N.Y. Nets[a], 1970–71 (672)
		N.Y. Nets[a], 1971–72 (669)
2	Chuck Williams	S.D. Conquistadors[a], 1972–73 (582)
		Mem. Sounds[a], 1974–75 (576)
2	Don Buse	Ind. Pacers[a], 1975–76 (689)
		Ind. Pacers, 1976–77 (685)
2	Isiah Thomas	Det. Pistons, 1983–84 (914)
		Det. Pistons, 1984–85 (1123)

[a] ABA.

Most Consecutive Seasons Leading League in Assists

9	John Stockton	Uta. Jazz, 1987–88	1128
		Uta. Jazz, 1988–89	1118
		Uta. Jazz, 1989–90	1134
		Uta. Jazz, 1990–91	1164
		Uta. Jazz, 1990–91	1126
		Uta. Jazz, 1991–92	987
		Uta. Jazz, 1992–93	1031
		Uta. Jazz, 1993–94	1011
		Uta. Jazz, 1994–95	916
8	Bob Cousy	Bos. Celtics, 1952–53	547
		Bos. Celtics, 1953–54	518
		Bos. Celtics, 1954–55	557
		Bos. Celtics, 1955–56	642

continued on next page

	Bos. Celtics, 1956–57	478
	Bos. Celtics, 1957–58	463
	Bos. Celtics, 1958–59	557
	Bos. Celtics, 1959–60	715
3 ..... Oscar Robertson	Cin. Royals, 1963–64	868
	Cin. Royals, 1964–65	861
	Cin. Royals, 1965–66	847
3 ..... Steve Nash	Pho. Suns, 2004–05	861
	Pho. Suns, 2005–06	826
	Pho. Suns, 2006–07	884
	Pho. Suns, 2009–10	892
	Pho. Suns, 2010–11	855
	Pho. Suns, 2011–12	664

Largest Differential Between League Leader in Assists and Runner-Up

Diff	Season	Leader	Ast	Runner-Up	Ast
+337	1978–79	Kevin Porter, Det. Pistons	1099	John Lucas, G.S. Warriors	762
+331	1994–95	John Stockton, Uta. Jazz	1011	Kenny Anderson, N.J. Nets	680
+312	1963–64	Oscar Robertson, Cin. Royals	868	Guy Rodgers, S.F. Warriors	556
+296	1964–65	Oscar Robertson, Cin. Royals	861	Guy Rodgers, S.F. Warriors	565
+290	1991–92	John Stockton, Uta. Jazz	1126	Kevin Johnson, Pho. Suns	836
+273	1972–73	Tiny Archibald, K.C.-Oma. Kings	910	Dave Bing, Det. Pistons	637
+260	1987–88	John Stockton, Uta. Jazz	1128	Mark Jackson, N.Y. Knicks	868
+256	1961–62	Oscar Robertson, Cin. Royals	899	Guy Rodgers, Phi. Warriors	643
+252	1992–93	John Stockton, Uta. Jazz	987	Scott Skiles, Orl. Magic	735
+242	1993–94	John Stockton, Uta. Jazz	1031	Mookie Blaylock, Atl. Hawks	789
+233	1959–60	Bob Cousy, Bos. Celtics	715	Guy Rodgers, Phi. Warriors	482
+227	1989–90	John Stockton, Uta. Jazz	1134	Magic Johnson, L.A. Lakers	907
+193	2004–05	Steve Nash, Pho. Suns	861	Stephon Marbury, N.Y. Knicks	668
+185	1955–56	Bob Cousy, Bos. Celtics	642	Jack George, Phi. Warriors	457
+175	1990–91	John Stockton, Uta. Jazz	1164	Magic Johnson, L.A. Lakers	989
+164	1970–71	Norm Van Lier, Cin. Royals	832	Oscar Robertson, Mil. Bucks	668
+161	1979–80	Micheal Ray Richardson, N.Y. Knicks	832	Tiny Archibald, Bos. Celtics	671
+155	1984–85	Isiah Thomas, Det. Pistons	1123	Magic Johnson, L.A. Lakers	968
+150	1952–53	Bob Cousy, Bos. Celtics	547	Andy Phillip, Phi. Warriors/Ft.W. Pistons	397
+142	1967–68	Larry Brown, N.O. Buccaneers[a]	506	Stephen Chubin, Ana. Amigos[a]	364
+141	2020–21	Russell Westbrook, Was. Wizards	763	Chris Paul, Pho. Suns	622
+139	2006–07	Steve Nash, Pho. Suns	884	Deron Williams, Uta. Jazz	745
+136	2008–09	Chris Paul, N.O. Hornets	861	Deron Williams, Uta. Jazz	725
+131	2018–19	Russell Westbrook, Ok.C. Thunder	784	Trae Young, Atl. Hawks	653
+129	1986–87	Magic Johnson, L.A. Lakers	977	Sleepy Floyd, G.S. Warriors	848
+127	1988–89	John Stockton, Uta. Jazz	1118	Kevin Johnson, Pho. Suns	991
+127	1995–96	John Stockton, Uta. Jazz	916	Avery Johnson, S.A. Spurs	789
+127	2005–06	Steve Nash, Pho. Suns	826	Chauncey Billups, Det. Pistons	699
+120	1971–72	Bill Melchionni, N.Y. Nets[a]	669	Larry Brown, Den. Rockets[a]	549
+114	1958–59	Bob Cousy, Bos. Celtics	557	Dick McGuire, N.Y. Knicks	443
+114	2019–20	LeBron James, L.A. Lakers	684	Ricky Rubio, Pho. Suns	570
+111	1956–57	Bob Cousy, Bos. Celtics	478	Jack McMahon, St.L. Hawks	367
+102	1969–70	Larry Brown, Was. Capitols[a]	580	Mack Calvin, L.A. Stars[a]	478
+102	1998–99	Jason Kidd, Pho. Suns	539	Stephon Marbury, Min. T'Wolves/N.J. Nets	437

[a] ABA.

Players Leading League in Assists on Teams with Losing Record

	Team Record	Ast
Ernie Calverley, Pro. Steamrollers, 1946–47	28–32 (.467)	202
Oscar Robertson, Cin. Royals, 1960–61	33–46 (.418)	690
Guy Rodgers, Chi. Bulls, 1966–67	33–48 (.407)	908
Lenny Wilkens, Sea. Sonics, 1969–70	36–46 (.439)	683
Norm Van Lier, Cin. Royals, 1970–71	33–49 (.402)	832
Bill Melchionni, N.Y. Nets[a], 1970–71	40–44 (.476)	672
Tiny Archibald, K.C.-Oma. Kings, 1972–73	36–46 (.439)	910
Chuck Williams, S.D. Conquistadors[a], 1972–73	30–54 (.357)	582
Al Smith, Den. Rockets[a], 1973–74	37–47 (.440)	619
Chuck Williams, Mem. Sounds[a], 1974–75	27–57 (.321)	576
Don Buse, Ind. Pacers[a], 1975–76	39–45 (.464)	689
Don Buse, Ind. Pacers, 1976–77	36–46 (.439)	685
Kevin Porter, Det. Pistons/N.J. Nets, 1977–78	38–44 (.463)/24–58 (.293)	837
Kevin Porter, Det. Pistons, 1978–79	30–52 (.366)	1099
Micheal Ray Richardson, N.Y. Knicks, 1979–80	39–43 (.476)	832
Kevin Porter, Was. Bullets, 1980–81	39–43 (.476)	734
Norm Nixon, S.D. Clippers, 1983–84	25–57 (.305)	914
Mark Jackson, Den. Nuggets/Ind. Pacers, 1996–97	21–61 (.256)/39–43 (.476)	935
Andre Miller, Cle. Cavaliers, 2001–02	29–53 (.354)	882
Stephon Marbury, Pho. Suns/N.Y. Knicks, 2003–04	29–53 (.354)/39–43 (.476)	719
Steve Nash, Pho. Suns, 2010–11	40–42 (.488)	855
Greivis Vásquez, N.O. Hornets, 2012–13	27–55 (.329)	704
Rajon Rondo, Sac. Kings, 2015–16	33–49 (.402)	839
Russell Westbrook, Was. Wizards, 2020–21	34–38 (.472)	763

[a] ABA.

Most Assists, Not Leading League, Season (Runner-Up)

Ast	Runner-Up	Season	Leader	Ast
991	Kevin Johnson, Pho. Suns	1988–89	John Stockton, Uta. Jazz	1118
989	Magic Johnson, L.A. Lakers	1990–91	John Stockton, Uta. Jazz	1164
968	Magic Johnson, L.A. Lakers	1984–85	Isiah Thomas, Det. Pistons	1123
907	Magic Johnson, L.A. Lakers	1989–90	John Stockton, Uta. Jazz	1134
898	Steve Nash. Pho. Suns	2007–08	Chris Paul, N.O. Hornets	925
875	Magic Johnson, L.A. Lakers	1983–84	Norm Nixon, S.D. Clippers/Isiah Thomas, Det. Pistons	914
868	Mark Jackson, N.Y. Knicks	1987–88	John Stockton, Uta. Jazz	1128
860	John Stockton, Uta. Jazz	1996–97	Mark Jackson, Den. Nuggets/Ind. Pacers	935
848	Sleepy Floyd, G.S. Warriors	1986–87	Magic Johnson, L.A. Lakers	977
846	Guy Rodgers, S.F. Warriors	1965–66	Oscar Robertson, Cin. Royals	847
845	Oscar Robertson, Cin. Royals	1966–67	Guy Rodgers, Chi. Bulls	908
840	Russell Westbrook, Ok.C. Thunder	2016–17	James Harden, Hou. Rockets	907
836	Kevin Johnson, Pho. Suns	1991–92	John Stockton, Uta. Jazz	1126
834	Russell Westbrook, Ok.C. Thunder	2015–16	Rajon Rondo, Sac. Kings	839
830	Isiah Thomas, Det. Pistons	1985–86	Magic Johnson, L.A. Lakers	907
808	Jason Kidd, N.J. Nets	2001–02	Andre Miller, Cle. Cavaliers	882

Most Career Assists, Never Leading League

Career Assists		Most Assists, Season		League Leader
7392	Maurice Cheeks	753 (Phi. 76ers, 1985–86)		907 (Magic Johnson, L.A. Lakers)
7160	Terry Porter	831 (Por. Blazers, 1987–88)		1128 (John Stockton, Uta. Jazz)

continued on next page

Career Assists		Most Assists, Season	League Leader
7095	Tim Hardaway	807 (G.S. Warriors, 1991–92)	1126 (John Stockton, Uta. Jazz)
7036	Tony Parker	513 (S.A. Spurs, 2010–11)	855 (Steve Nash, Pho. Suns)
6819	Deron Williams	862 (Uta. Jazz, 2007–08)	925 (Chris Paul, N.O. Hornets)
6726	Muggsy Bogues	867 (Cha. Hornets, 1989–90)	1134 (John Stockton, Uta. Jazz)
6711	Kevin Johnson	991 (Pho. Suns, 1988–89)	1118 (John Stockton, Uta. Jazz)
6577	Derek Harper	634 (Dal. Mavericks, 1987–88)	1128 (John Stockton, Uta. Jazz)
6469	Kyle Lowry^	586 (Tor. Raptors, 2013–14)	721 (John Wall, Was. Wizards)
6454	John Lucas	768 (Hou. Rockets, 1977–78)	837 (Kevin Porter, Det. Pistons/N.J. Nets)
6453	Reggie Theus	788 (Sac. Kings, 1985–86)	907 (Magic Johnson, L.A. Lakers)
6306	Kobe Bryant	481 (L.A. Lakers, 2002–03)	711 (Jason Kidd, N.J. Nets)
6238	Jerry West	747 (L.A. Lakers, 1971–72)	766 (Lenny Wilkens, Sea. Sonics)
6135	Scottie Pippen	572 (Chi. Bulls, 1991–92)	1126 (John Stockton, Uta. Jazz)
6125	Clyde Drexler	600 (Por. Blazers, 1985–86)	907 (Magic Johnson, L.A. Lakers)
6114	John Havlicek	614 (Bos. Celtics, 1971–72)	766 (Lenny Wilkens, Sea. Sonics)
6025	Baron Davis	698 (Cha. Hornets, 2001–02)	882 (Andre Miller, Cle. Cavaliers)

^ Active.

Players Finishing One-Two in Assists, Multiple Seasons

Season	Leader (Ast)	Runner-Up (Ast)
1949–50	Dick McGuire, N.Y. Knicks (386)	Andy Phillip, Chi. Stags (377)
1950–51	Andy Phillip, Phi. Warriors (414)	Dick McGuire, N.Y. Knicks (400)
1951–52	Andy Phillip, Phi. Warriors (539)	Bob Cousy, Bos. Celtics (441)
1952–53	Bob Cousy, Bos. Celtics (547)	Andy Phillip, Phi. Warriors/Ft.W. Pistons (397)
1953–54	Bob Cousy, Bos. Celtics (518))	Andy Phillip, Ft.W. Pistons (449)
1954–55	Bob Cousy, Bos. Celtics (557)	Dick McGuire, N.Y. Knicks (542)
1957–58	Bob Cousy, Bos. Celtics (463)	Dick McGuire, N.Y. Knicks (454)
1958–59	Bob Cousy, Bos. Celtics (557)	Dick McGuire, N.Y. Knicks (443)
1960–61	Oscar Robertson, Cin. Royals (690)	Guy Rodgers, Phi. Warriors (677)
1961–62	Oscar Robertson, Cin. Royals (899)	Guy Rodgers, Phi. Warriors (643)
1962–63	Guy Rodgers, S.F. Warriors (825)	Oscar Robertson, Cin. Royals (758)
1963–64	Oscar Robertson, Cin. Royals (868)	Guy Rodgers, S.F. Warriors (556)
1964–65	Oscar Robertson, Cin. Royals (861)	Guy Rodgers, S.F. Warriors (565)
1965–66	Oscar Robertson, Cin. Royals (847)	Guy Rodgers, S.F. Warriors (846)
1966–67	Guy Rodgers, Chi. Bulls (908)	Oscar Robertson, Cin. Royals (845)
1977–78	Kevin Porter, Det. Pistons/N.J. Nets (837)	John Lucas, Hou. Rockets (768)
1978–79	Kevin Porter, Det. Pistons (1099)	John Lucas, G.S. Warriors (762)
1981–82	Johnny Moore, S.A. Spurs (762)	Magic Johnson, L.A. Lakers (743)
1982–83	Magic Johnson, L.A. Lakers (829)	Johnny Moore, S.A. Spurs (753)
1984–85	Isiah Thomas, Det. Pistons (1123)	Magic Johnson, L.A. Lakers (968)
1985–86	Magic Johnson, L.A. Lakers (907)	Isiah Thomas, Det. Pistons (830)
1987–88	John Stockton, Uta. Jazz (1128)	Mark Jackson, N.Y. Knicks (868)
1996–97	Mark Jackson, Den. Nuggets/Ind. Pacers (935)	John Stockton, Uta. Jazz (860)
1988–89	John Stockton, Uta. Jazz (1118)	Kevin Johnson, Pho. Suns (991)
1991–92	John Stockton, Uta. Jazz (1126)	Kevin Johnson, Pho. Suns (836)

continued on next page

Season	Leader (Ast)	Runner-Up (Ast)
1989–90	John Stockton, Uta. Jazz (1134)	Magic Johnson, L.A. Lakers (907)
1990–91	John Stockton, Uta. Jazz (1164)	Magic Johnson, L.A. Lakers (989)
2003–04	Stephon Marbury, Pho. Suns/N.Y. Knicks (719)	Steve Nash, Dal. Mavericks (687)
2004–05	Steve Nash, Pho. Suns (861)	Stephon Marbury, N.Y. Knicks (668)
2006–07	Steve Nash, Pho. Suns (884)	Deron Williams, Uta. Jazz (745)
2009–10	Steve Nash, Pho. Suns (892)	Deron Williams, Uta. Jazz (798)
2007–08	Chris Paul, N.O. Hornets (925)	Steve Nash, Pho. Suns (898)
2010–11	Steve Nash, Pho. Suns (855)	Chris Paul, N.O. Hornets (782)

Most Seasons with 500 Assists, Career

17	John Stockton	8	Guy Rodgers
16	Jason Kidd	8	Norm Van Lier
13	Mark Jackson	8	Maurice Cheeks
13	Chris Paul^	8	Tim Hardaway
12	Oscar Robertson	8	Stephon Marbury
12	Steve Nash	7	Lenny Wilkens
12	LeBron James^	7	Tiny Archibald
11	Magic Johnson	7	Muggsy Bogues
11	Isiah Thomas	7	Kevin Johnson
10	Gary Payton	7	Rod Strickland
10	Andre Miller	7	Baron Davis
10	Russell Westbrook^	7	Rajon Rondo^
9	Bob Cousy	7	James Harden^
9	Norm Nixon		

^ Active.

Players with 1000 Assists, Season

1099	Kevin Porter, Det. Pistons, 1978–79	1164	John Stockton, Uta. Jazz, 1990–91
1123	Isiah Thomas, Det. Pistons, 1984–85	1126	John Stockton, Uta. Jazz, 1991–92
1128	John Stockton, Uta. Jazz, 1987–88	1031	John Stockton, Uta. Jazz, 1993–94
1118	John Stockton, Uta. Jazz, 1988–89	1011	John Stockton, Uta. Jazz, 1994–95
1134	John Stockton, Uta. Jazz, 1989–90		

Fewest Games to 5000 Assists

Games		Career Assists	Games		Career Assists
460	Oscar Robertson	9887	585	Muggsy Bogues	6726
472	Magic Johnson	10,141	594	Rajon Rondo^	7584
483	John Stockton	15,806	598	Norm Nixon	6386
490	Isiah Thomas	9061	599	Guy Rodgers	6917
510	Chris Paul^	10,977	601	Mark Jackson	10,334
519	Kevin Johnson	6711	603	Stephon Marbury	6471
531	Jason Kidd	12,091	619	Kevin Porter	5314
541	John Wall^	5557	641	Russell Westbrook^	8611
543	Tim Hardaway	7095	646	Tiny Archibald	6476
554	Deron Williams	6819	651	John Lucas	6454

^ Active.

500 Assists, Less Than 500 Points, Season

		Ast	Pts
1969–70	Art Williams, S.D. Rockets	503	446
1986–87	Nate McMillan, Sea. Sonics	583	373
1988–89	Muggsy Bogues, Cha. Hornets	620	423
2020–21	Draymond Green, G.S. Warriors	558	444

Fewest Assists for Players Averaging 20 PPG, Season (Min. 1000 Minutes Played)

Ast		PPG	MP
48	Spencer Haywood, Sea. Sonics, 1970–71	20.6	1162
57	Kristaps Porziņgis, N.Y. Knicks, 2017–18	22.7	1553
60	John Collins, Atl. Hawks, 2019–20	21.6	1363
65	Keith Van Horn, N.J. Nets, 1998–99	21.8	1576
66	Wayman Tisdale, Sac. Kings, 1990–91	20.0	1116
68	Clyde Lovellette, St.L. Hawks, 1961–62	20.9	1192
68	Kristaps Porziņgis, Dal. Mavericks, 2020–21	20.1	1327
71	John Block, S.D. Rockets, 1967–68	20.2	1805
71	Kiki Vandeweghe, Por. Blazers, 1987–88	20.2	1038
71	Christian Wood, Hou. Rockets, 2020–21	21.0	1326
74	Bob Verga, Dal. Chaparrals[a], 1967–68	23.7	1285
74	Alonzo Mourning, Mia. Heat, 1998–99	20.1	1753
76	Alonzo Mourning, Cha. Hornets, 1992–93	21.0	2644
78	Amar'e Stoudemire, Pho. Suns, 2003–04	20.6	2025
79	John Drew, Atl. Hawks, 1980–81	21.7	2075
79	Al Jefferson, Min. T'Wolves, 2008–09	23.1	1836
82	Mike Mitchell, Cle. Cavaliers/S.A. Spurs, 1981–82	20.5	3063
82	Antonio McDyess, Den. Nuggets, 1998–99	21.2	1937
82	Jermaine O'Neal, Ind. Pacers, 2004–05	24.3	1530
82	Amar'e Stoudemire, Pho. Suns, 2009–10	23.1	2838
84	Amar'e Stoudemire, Pho. Suns, 2006–07	20.4	2689
85	Yao Ming, Hou. Rockets, 2005–06	22.3	1949
86	Alonzo Mourning, Cha. Hornets, 1993–94	21.5	2018
88	Michael Redd, Mil. Bucks, 2008–09	21.2	1203
90	Moses Malone, Phi. 76ers, 1985–86	23.8	2706
93	Mike Mitchell, Cle. Cavaliers, 1979–80	22.2	2802
93	Mike Mitchell, S.A. Spurs, 1983–84	23.3	2853
94	Rashard Lewis, Sea. Sonics, 2004–05	20.5	2697
94	Yao Ming, Hou. Rockets, 2006–07	25.0	1624
95	Chris Bosh, Mia. Heat, 2014–15	21.1	1556
96	Moses Malone, Phi. 76ers, 1983–84	22.7	2613
97	George Yardley, Det. Pistons, 1957–58	27.8	2843
97	Jim McDaniels, Car. Cougars[a], 1971–72	26.8	2172
97	John Drew, Uta. Jazz, 1982–83	21.2	1206
98	Travis Grant, S.D. Rockets[a], 1974–75	25.2	1998

[a]ABA.

Players with 1500 Assists on Three Different Teams

Jason Kidd	4211	Dal. Mavericks (1994–96; 2008–11)
	3011	Pho. Suns (1996–2001)
	4620	N.J. Nets (2001–08)

continued on next page

LeBron James	6228	Cle. Cavaliers (2003–10; 2014–18)
	1980	Mia. Heat (2010–14)
	1837	L.A. Lakers (2018–22)
Andre Miller	2015	Cle. Cavaliers (1999–2002)
	2978	Den. Nuggets (2004–06; 2011–14)
	1515	Phi. 76ers (2006–09)

Players with 1200 Assists on Three Different Teams (Excluding Kidd, James, and Miller)

Wilt Chamberlain	1303	Phi.-S.F. Warriors (1959–65)
	1879	Phi. 76ers (1965–68)
	1461	L.A. Lakers (1968–73)
Mark Jackson	4005	N.Y. Knicks (1987–92)
	1402	L.A. Clippers (1992–94)
	3294	Ind. Pacers (1994–96, 1997–2000)
Rod Strickland	1203	S.A. Spurs (1990–92)
	2573	Por. Blazers (1992–96; 2001)
	2712	Was. Bullets-Wizards (1996–2001)
Stephon Marbury	1393	Min. T'Wolves (1996–99)
	1398	N.J. Nets (1999–2001)
	1601	Pho. Suns (2001–04)
	2004	N.Y. Knicks (2004–08)
Baron Davis	1605	Cha.-N.O. Hornets (1999–2005)
	1845	G.S. Warriors (2005–08)
	1398	L.A. Clippers (2008–11)
Chris Paul^	4228	N.O-Ok.C. Hornets (2005–11)
	4023	L.A. Clippers (2011–17)
	1324	Pho. Suns (2020–22)

^ Active.

Most Assists, Game

30	Scott Skiles, Orl. Magic	vs. Den. Nuggets (Dec. 30, 1990)
29	Kevin Porter, N.J. Nets	vs. Hou. Rockets (Feb. 24, 1978)
28	Bob Cousy, Bos. Celtics	vs. Min. Lakers (Feb. 27, 1959)
28	Guy Rodgers, S.F. Warriors	vs. St.L. Hawks (Mar. 14, 1963)
28	John Stockton, Uta. Jazz	vs. S.A. Spurs (Jan. 15, 1991)
27	Geoff Huston, Cle. Cavaliers	vs. G.S. Warriors (Jan. 27, 1982)
27	John Stockton, Uta. Jazz	@ N.Y. Knicks (Dec. 19, 1989)
26	John Stockton, Uta. Jazz	vs. Por. Blazers (Apr. 14, 1988)
25	Ernie DiGregorio, Buf. Braves	@ Por. Blazers (Jan. 1, 1974)
25	Kevin Porter, Det. Pistons	vs. Bos. Celtics (Mar. 9, 1979)
25	Kevin Porter, Det. Pistons	@ Pho. Suns (Apr. 1, 1979)
25	Isiah Thomas, Det. Pistons	vs. Dal. Mavericks (Feb. 13, 1985)
25	Nate McMillan, Sea. Sonics	vs. L.A. Clippers (Feb. 23, 1987)
25	Kevin Johnson, Pho. Suns	vs. S.A. Spurs (Apr. 6, 1994)
25	Jason Kidd, Dal. Mavericks	vs. Uta. Jazz (Feb. 8, 1996)
25	Rajon Rondo, N.O. Pelicans	vs. Brk. Nets (Dec. 27, 2017)
24	Guy Rodgers, Chi. Bulls	vs. N.Y. Knicks (Dec. 21, 1966)
24	Kevin Porter, Was. Bullets	vs. Det. Pistons (Mar. 23, 1980)
24	John Lucas, S.A. Spurs	vs. Den. Nuggets (Apr. 15, 1984)
24	Isiah Thomas, Det. Pistons	@ Was. Bullets (Feb. 7, 1985)
24	John Stockton, Uta. Jazz	@ Hou. Rockets (Jan. 3, 1989)

continued on next page

24	Magic Johnson, L.A. Lakers	vs. Den. Nuggets (Nov. 17, 1989)
24	Magic Johnson, L.A. Lakers	@ Pho. Suns (Jan. 9, 1990)
24	Ramon Sessions, Mil. Bucks	vs. Chi. Bulls (Apr. 14, 2008)
24	Rajon Rondo, Bos. Celtics	vs. N.Y. Knicks (Oct. 29, 2010)
24	Russell Westbrook, Ok.C. Thunder	@ S.A. Spurs (Jan. 10, 2019)
24	Russell Westbrook, Was. Wizards	vs. Ind. Pacers (May 3, 2021)

Most Assists in a Loss

28	Guy Rodgers, S.F. Warriors	vs. St.L. Hawks (Mar. 14, 1963)
27	John Stockton, Uta. Jazz	@ N.Y. Knicks (Dec. 19, 1989)
26	John Stockton, Uta. Jazz	vs. Por. Blazers (Apr. 14, 1990)
25	Kevin Porter, Det. Pistons	@ Pho. Suns (Apr. 1, 1979)
24	Isiah Thomas, Det. Pistons	@ Was. Bullets (Feb. 7, 1985)
24	John Stockton, Uta. Jazz	@ Hou. Rockets (Jan. 3, 1989)
24	Magic Johnson, L.A. Lakers	@ Pho. Suns (Jan. 9, 1990)
24	Ramon Sessions, Mil. Bucks	vs. Chi. Bulls (Apr. 14, 2008)
24	Russell Westbrook, Ok.C. Thunder	@ S.A. Spurs (Jan. 10, 2019)
23	Kevin Porter, Det. Pistons	@ L.A. Lakers (Mar. 30, 1979)
22	Stephen Chubin, Ana. Amigos[a]	vs. Dal. Chaparrals[a] (Jan. 14, 1968)
22	Kevin Porter, Det. Pistons	vs. S.A. Spurs (Dec. 23, 1978)
22	Kevin Porter, Det. Pistons	@ Chi. Bulls (Feb. 27, 1979)
22	John Lucas, G.S. Warriors	@ Den. Nuggets (Feb. 27, 1981)
22	Ennis Whatley, Chi. Bulls	vs. N.Y. Knicks (Jan. 14, 1984)
22	John Stockton, Uta. Jazz	vs. Cle. Cavaliers (Dec. 11, 1989)
22	Magic Johnson, L.A. Lakers	vs. Por. Blazers (Nov. 6, 1990)
22	Tim Hardaway, G.S. Warriors	vs. Orl. Magic (Dec. 16, 1994)
22	Andre Miller, Cle. Cavaliers	vs. Phi. 76ers (Dec. 15, 2001)
22	Steve Nash, Pho. Suns	@ N.Y. Knicks (Jan. 2, 2006)

[a] ABA.

Most Games with 10 Assists, Season

77	John Stockton, Uta. Jazz, 1991–92	60	Magic Johnson, L.A. Lakers, 1986–87
75	John Stockton, Uta. Jazz, 1990–91	60	James Harden, Hou. Rockets, 2016–17
73	John Stockton, Uta. Jazz, 1988–89	59	Magic Johnson, L.A. Lakers, 1983–84
71	John Stockton, Uta. Jazz, 1989–90	59	Steve Nash, Pho. Suns, 2004–05
67	Isiah Thomas, Det. Pistons, 1984–85	59	Chris Paul, N.O. Hornets, 2007–08
67	John Stockton, Uta. Jazz, 1992–93	58	John Stockton, Uta. Jazz, 1995–96
66	John Stockton, Uta. Jazz, 1993–94	57	Isiah Thomas, Det. Pistons, 1983–84
65	Magic Johnson, L.A. Lakers, 1984–85	56	Tiny Archibald, K.C.-Oma. Kings, 1972–73
65	John Stockton, Uta. Jazz, 1994–95	56	Magic Johnson, L.A. Lakers, 1985–86
64	Kevin Johnson, Pho. Suns, 1988–89	56	Mark Jackson, Den. Nuggets/Ind. Pacers, 1996–97
63	John Stockton, Uta. Jazz, 1987–88	56	Steve Nash, Pho. Suns, 2006–07
63	Magic Johnson, L.A. Lakers, 1990–91	55	Norm Nixon, S.D. Clippers, 1983–84
62	Kevin Porter, Det. Pistons, 1978–79	55	Steve Nash, Pho. Suns, 2007–08
62	Magic Johnson, L.A. Lakers, 1988–89	55	Steve Nash, Pho. Suns, 2009–10

Most Games with 10 Assists, Career

863	John Stockton	509	Steve Nash
586	Magic Johnson	478	Oscar Robertson
569	Jason Kidd	438	Isiah Thomas
552	Chris Paul^	411	Mark Jackson

continued on next page

380 .... Russell Westbrook^	281 .... Muggsy Bogues
336 .... Rajon Rondo^	278 .... Guy Rodgers
332 .... Kevin Johnson	270 .... John Wall^
303 .... Rod Strickland	266 .... Norm Nixon
297 .... LeBron James^	262 .... Gary Payton
294 .... Tim Hardaway	257 .... Andre Miller
294 .... Deron Williams	

^ Active.

Most Games with 15 Assists, Season

44 .... John Stockton, Uta. Jazz, 1987–88	24 .... Kevin Johnson, Pho. Suns, 1988–89
42 .... John Stockton, Uta. Jazz, 1989–90	24 .... Magic Johnson, L.A. Lakers, 1988–89
42 .... John Stockton, Uta. Jazz, 1990–91	23 .... Magic Johnson, L.A. Lakers, 1990–91
37 .... Isiah Thomas, Det. Pistons, 1984–85	22 .... Magic Johnson, L.A. Lakers, 1983–84
34 .... John Stockton, Uta. Jazz, 1988–89	22 .... Magic Johnson, L.A. Lakers, 1984–85
31 .... Kevin Porter, Det. Pistons, 1978–79	22 .... Magic Johnson, L.A. Lakers, 1985–86
31 .... John Stockton, Uta. Jazz, 1991–92	22 .... John Stockton, Uta. Jazz, 1993–94
25 .... Magic Johnson, L.A. Lakers, 1986–87	22 .... John Stockton, Uta. Jazz, 1994–95

Most Games with 15 Assists, Career

293 .... John Stockton	87 .... Jason Kidd
189 .... Magic Johnson	82 .... Rajon Rondo^
110 .... Steve Nash	76 .... Kevin Porter
106 .... Oscar Robertson	71 .... Mark Jackson
103 .... Chris Paul^	65 .... Russell Westbrook^
98 .... Isiah Thomas	56 .... Guy Rodgers
87 .... Kevin Johnson	

^ Active.

Least Amount of Games Played Before First 20-Assist Game

Game #		Ast	
12 .... Brevin Knight, Cle. Cavaliers		20 .... vs. Was. Wizards (Nov. 22, 1997)	
14 .... Jamaal Tinsley, Ind. Pacers		23 .... vs. Was. Wizards (Nov. 22, 2001)	
16 .... Ramon Sessions, Mil. Bucks		24 .... vs. Chi. Bulls (Apr. 14, 2008)	
33 .... Ennis Whatley, Chi. Bulls		22 .... vs. N.Y. Knicks (Jan. 14, 1984)	
39 .... Ernie DiGregorio, Buf. Braves		25 .... @ Por. Blazers (Jan. 1, 1974)	
44 .... Nate McMillan, Sea. Sonics		25 .... vs. L.A. Clippers (Feb. 23, 1987)	
57 .... Phil Ford, K.C. Kings		22 .... vs. Mil. Bucks (Feb. 21, 1979)	
58 .... Darren Collison, N.O. Hornets		20 .... vs. G.S. Warriors (Mar. 8, 2010)	
61 .... Oscar Robertson, Cin. Royals		20 .... vs. L.A. Lakers (Feb. 19, 1961)	
61 .... Bobby Washington*, Cle. Cavaliers		20 .... vs. Por. Blazers (Nov. 7, 1971)	
62 .... Gary Grant, L.A. Clippers		20 .... vs. Por. Blazers (Apr. 6, 1989)	

* Includes two games in ABA (1969).

Players with Multiple 19-Assist Games, Never Having a 20-Assist Game

Andy Phillip	Ft.W. Pistons vs. Min. Lakers (Nov. 27, 1954)
	Ft.W. Pistons vs. N.Y. Knicks (Nov. 20, 1955)
Gail Goodrich	Pho. Suns @ Phi. 76ers (Oct. 22, 1969)
	N.O. Jazz @ Mil. Bucks (Nov. 4, 1978)
Don Buse	Ind. Pacersª vs. Den. Nuggetsª (Mar. 10, 1976)
	Ind. Pacersª @ Den. Nuggetsª (Apr. 4, 1976)
Muggsy Bogues	Cha. Hornets @ Bos. Celtics (Apr. 23, 1989)
	Cha. Hornets vs. L.A. Lakers (Nov. 24, 1993)

continued on next page

	Cha. Hornets vs. Mil. Bucks (Feb. 18, 1994)
Michael Adams	Den. Nuggets vs. Pho. Suns (Dec. 15, 1990)
	Was. Bullets @ Sac. Kings (Feb. 12, 1992)
José Calderón	Tor. Raptors vs. Chi. Bulls (Mar. 29, 2009)
	Tor. Raptors vs. Min. T'Wolves (Feb. 4, 2011)
LeBron James^	Cle. Cavaliers @ Atl. Hawks (Feb. 9, 2018)
	L.A. Lakers vs. Orl. Magic (Jan. 15, 2020)
Draymond Green^	G.S. Warriors vs. Cha. Hornets (Feb. 26, 2021)
	G.S. Warriors vs. Den. Nuggets (Apr. 23, 2021)

ªABA.

^ Active.

Most Assists, Rookie Season

868	Mark Jackson*, N.Y. Knicks, 1987–88		619	Sherman Douglas, Mia. Heat, 1989–90
690	Oscar Robertson*, Cin. Royals, 1960–61		611	Chris Paul*, N.O.-Ok.C. Hornets, 2005–06
689	Tim Hardaway, G.S. Warriors, 1989–90		607	Jason Kidd**, Dal. Mavericks, 1994–95
681	Phil Ford*, K.C. Kings, 1978–79		583	Nate McMillan, Sea. Sonics, 1986–87
663	Ernie DiGregorio*, Buf. Braves, 1973–74		574	John Wall, Was. Wizards, 2010–11
662	Ennis Whatley, Chi. Bulls, 1983–84		567	Allen Iverson*, Phi. 76ers, 1996–97
661	Ben Simmons*, Phi. 76ers, 2017–18		565	Isiah Thomas, Det. Pistons, 1981–82
656	Brevin Knight, Cle. Cavaliers, 1997–98		563	Magic Johnson, L.A. Lakers, 1979–80
653	Damon Stoudamire*, Tor. Raptors, 1995–96		555	Kelvin Ransey, Por. Blazers, 1980–81
653	Trae Young, Atl. Hawks, 2018–19		554	Pooh Richardson, Min. T'Wolves, 1989–90
647	Jamaal Tinsley, Ind. Pacers, 2001–02		553	Norm Nixon, L.A. Lakers, 1977–78

* Rookie of the Year.

** Tied for Rookie of the Year with Grant Hill, Det. Pistons.

Most Games with 10 Assists, Rookie Season

48	Mark Jackson*, N.Y. Knicks, 1987–88		25	Ennis Whatley, Chi. Bulls, 1983–84
37	Damon Stoudamire*, Tor. Raptors, 1995–96		25	John Wall, Was. Wizards, 2010–11
35	Oscar Robertson*, Cin. Royals, 1960–61		22	Jason Kidd**, Dal. Mavericks, 1994–95
34	Tim Hardaway, G.S. Warriors, 1989–90		21	Ernie DiGregorio*, Buf. Braves, 1973–74
30	Trae Young, Atl. Hawks, 2018–19		21	Jamaal Tinsley, Ind. Pacers, 2001–02
27	Nate McMillan, Sea. Sonics, 1986–87		21	Chris Paul*, N.O.-Ok.C. Hornets, 2005–06
26	Brevin Knight, Cle. Cavaliers, 1997–98		20	Gary Grant, L.A. Clippers, 1988–89
26	Ben Simmons*, Phi. 76ers, 2017–18		19	Sherman Douglas, Mia. Heat, 1989–90
25	Phil Ford*, K.C. Kings, 1978–79		19	Pooh Richardson, Min. T'Wolves, 1989–90
25	Isiah Thomas, Det. Pistons, 1981–82		19	Kirk Hinrich, Chi. Bulls, 2003–04

* Rookie of the Year.

** Tied for Rookie of the Year with Grant Hill, Det. Pistons.

Most Assists in a Game, Scoring 5 Points or Less (Registering at Least One Point)

Ast				Pts
25	Rajon Rondo, N.O. Pelicans	vs. Brk. Nets (Dec. 27, 2017)	2
22	George McCloud, Den. Nuggets	@ Chi. Bulls (Mar. 26, 2001)	5
21	Kevin Porter, Was. Bullets	vs. L.A. Lakers (Mar. 2, 1975)	4
21	Ennis Whatley, Chi. Bulls	vs. G.S. Warriors (Feb. 23, 1985)	1
21	Steve Nash, Pho. Suns	vs. Cle. Cavaliers (Jan. 11, 2007)	4
20	John Lucas, Hou. Rockets	@ Ind. Pacers (Apr. 8, 1978)	2
20	Nick Van Exel, Den. Nuggets	vs. Sea. Sonics (Dec. 2, 2000)	5

continued on next page

Ast			Pts
20	Andre Miller, Den. Nuggets	vs. Mia. Heat (Dec. 8, 2006)	5
20	Will Bynum, Det. Pistons	vs. Was. Wizards (Mar. 12, 2010)	5
19	John Lucas, G.S. Warriors*	@ N.J. Nets (Feb. 15, 1981)	4
19	John Lucas, Mil. Bucks	vs. N.J. Nets (Apr. 2, 1988)	3
19	John Stockton, Uta. Jazz	@ Chi. Bulls (Jan. 6, 1989)	5
19	Nate McMillan, Sea. Sonics	@ Por. Blazers (Feb. 18, 1989)	3
19	Muggsy Bogues, Cha. Hornets*	@ Bos. Celtics (Apr. 23, 1989)	4
19	Muggsy Bogues, Cha. Hornets*	vs. Mil. Bucks (Feb. 18, 1994)	2
19	Mark Jackson, Ind. Pacers	@ Cha. Hornets (Mar. 28, 1997)	4
19	Rajon Rondo, Bos. Celtics*	@ Atl. Hawks (Dec. 2, 2014)	2
19	Draymond Green, G.S. Warriors	vs. Den. Nuggets (Apr. 23, 2021)	2

* Team lost game.

Most Assists in a Game without Scoring

24	John Lucas, S.A. Spurs	vs. Den. Nuggets (Apr. 15, 1984)
19	Art Williams, S.D. Rockets	vs. Atl. Hawks (Dec. 10, 1969)
15	John Lucas, G.S. Warriors	vs. Det. Pistons (Jan. 10, 1981)
15	Rajon Rondo, Bos. Celtics	vs. Mil. Bucks (Apr. 26, 2012)
14	Fat Lever, Den. Nuggets	vs. L.A. Clippers (Dec. 11, 1985)
14	Greg Anthony, N.Y. Knicks	vs. Orl. Magic (Mar. 8, 1993)
14	Anthony Carter, Den. Nuggets*	@ L.A. Lakers (Jan. 21, 2008)
14	Jamaal Tinsley, Uta. Jazz	vs. Pho. Suns (Nov. 10, 2012)
13	Norm Van Lier, Cin. Royals	vs. L.A. Lakers (Jan. 5, 1971)
13	Dennis Johnson, Bos. Celtics	vs. N.J. Nets (Dec. 2, 1987)
13	Jacque Vaughn, N.J. Nets*	@ Phi. 76ers (Apr. 18, 2006)
13	Chris Duhon, N.Y. Knicks	vs. Min. T'Wolves (Jan. 26, 2010)
13	José Calderón, Tor. Raptors*	@ N.O. Hornets (Jan. 17, 2011)
13	Jason Kidd, Dal. Mavericks*	@ Det. Pistons (Jan. 17, 2011)
13	Jason Kidd, Dal. Mavericks	vs. Min. T'Wolves (Mar. 24, 2011)
13	José Calderón, Tor. Raptors	vs. Por. Blazers (Jan. 2, 2013)
13	Tomáš Satoranský, Was. Wizards	vs. Orl. Magic (Mar. 30, 2022)

* Team lost game.

Most Games with 10 Assists and Zero Turnovers, Career

50	Chris Paul^	20	Mookie Blaylock
46	Muggsy Bogues	19	Maurice Cheeks
44	John Stockton	19	Andre Miller
27	Jason Kidd	19	Steve Nash
26	Mark Jackson	19	Gary Payton
21	José Calderón	19	Nick Van Exel

^ Active.

Most Games Played with at Least One Assist, Career

		Career GP			Career GP
1501	John Stockton	1504	1337	Dirk Nowitzki	1522
1456	Kareem Abdul-Jabbar	1560	1319	Gary Payton	1335
1407	Karl Malone	1476	1304	Tim Duncan	1392
1386	Jason Kidd	1391	1301	Jason Terry	1410
1370	Kevin Garnett	1476	1290	Reggie Miller	1389
1364	LeBron James^	1366	1287	Kobe Bryant	1346
1342	Vince Carter	1541	1283	Mark Jackson	1296

continued on next page

	Career GP			Career GP
1280	Andre Miller	1304	1072	Rod Strickland 1094
1239	Paul Pierce	1343	1065	Michael Jordan 1072
1238	Tony Parker	1254	1063	Hakeem Olajuwon 1238
1233	Jamal Crawford	1327	1060	Shaquille O'Neal 1207
1225	Ray Allen	1300	1058	Jeff Hornacek 1077
1221	Terry Porter	1274	1056	Clyde Drexler 1086
1197	Joe Johnson^	1277	1055	Dennis Johnson 1100
1184	Steve Nash	1217	1048	Artis Gilmore 1329
1179	Andre Iguodala^	1223	1044	Dwyane Wade 1054
1170	Derek Harper	1199	1033	Otis Thorpe 1257
1162	Clifford Robinson	1380	1032	Detlef Schrempf 1136
1155	Derek Fisher	1287	1024	Charles Barkley 1073
1155	Chris Paul^	1155	1018	Russell Westbrook^ 1021
1148	Pau Gasol	1226	1016	Chauncey Billups 1043
1146	Scottie Pippen	1178	1016	Jack Sikma 1107
1121	Carmelo Anthony^	1260	1016	Reggie Theus 1026
1120	Julius Erving	1243	1014	Lou Williams^ 1123
1105	Robert Parish	1611	1013	Horace Grant 1165
1104	Charles Oakley	1282	1009	Kyle Lowry^ 1023
1092	John Havlicek	1270	1008	Manu Ginóbili 1057
1087	Maurice Cheeks	1101	1004	Moses Malone 1455
1084	Alex English	1193	1000	Oscar Robertson 1040

^ Active.

Most Assists by Players 6-foot-10 to 6-foot-11, Season

661	Ben Simmons, Phi. 76ers, 2017–18	6-foot-11
610	Ben Simmons, Phi. 76ers, 2018–19	6-foot-11
599	Nikola Jokić, Den. Nuggets, 2020–21	6-foot-11
584	Nikola Jokić, Den. Nuggets, 2021–22	6-foot-11
580	Nikola Jokić, Den. Nuggets, 2018–19	6-foot-11
512	Nikola Jokić, Den. Nuggets, 2019–20	6-foot-11
495	Kevin Garnett, Min. T'Wolves, 2002–03	6-foot-11
493	Detlef Schrempf, Ind. Pacers, 1992–93	6-foot-10
472	Bill Russell, Bos. Celtics, 1966–67	6-foot-10
466	Kevin Garnett, Min. T'Wolves, 2004–05	6-foot-11
460	Sam Lacey, K.C. Kings, 1979–80	6-foot-10
458	Nikola Jokić, Den. Nuggets, 2017–18	6-foot-11
457	Kevin Durant, G.S. Warriors, 2018–19	6-foot-10
455	Ben Simmons, Phi. 76ers, 2019–20	6-foot-11
445	Kevin Durant, Ok.C. Thunder, 2013–14	6-foot-10
443	Lamar Odom, L.A. Lakers, 2005–06	6-foot-10
434	Giannis Antetokounmpo, Mil. Bucks, 2016–17	6-foot-11
432	Vlade Divac, Sac. Kings, 2003–04	6-foot-11
431	Joakim Noah, Chi. Bulls, 2013–14	6-foot-11
430	Sam Lacey, K.C. Kings, 1978–79	6-foot-10
428	Sam Lacey, K.C.-Oma. Kings, 1974–75	6-foot-10
424	Giannis Antetokounmpo^, Mil. Bucks, 2018–19	6-foot-11
422	Kevin Garnett, Min. T'Wolves, 2001–02	6-foot-11
415	Domantas Sabonis, Ind. Pacers, 2020–21	6-foot-11
413	Kareem Abdul-Jabbar, L.A. Lakers, 1975–76	6-foot-11
410	Bill Russell, Bos. Celtics, 1964–65	6-foot-10
409	Kevin Garnett, Min. T'Wolves, 2003–04	6-foot-11

continued on next page

409 .... Hedo Türkoğlu, Orl. Magic, 2007–08 .... 6-foot-10
407 .... Gerald Govan, Mem. Pros[a], 1970–71 .... 6-foot-10
401 .... Kevin Garnett, Min. T'Wolves, 1999–00 .... 6-foot-11
401 .... Kevin Garnett, Min. T'Wolves, 2000–01 .... 6-foot-11
401 .... Ben Simmons, Phi. 76ers, 2020–21 .... 6-foot-11
[a] ABA.

Most Assists by Players 7-Feet or Taller, Season

702 .... Wilt Chamberlain, Phi. 76ers, 1967–68 .... 7-foot-1
630 .... Wilt Chamberlain, Phi. 76ers, 1966–67 .... 7-foot-1
432 .... Vlade Divac, Sac. Kings, 2003–04 .... 7-foot-1
431 .... Kareem Abdul-Jabbar, L.A. Lakers, 1978–79 .... 7-foot-2
414 .... Wilt Chamberlain, Phi. 76ers, 1965–66 .... 7-foot-1
413 .... Kareem Abdul-Jabbar, L.A. Lakers, 1975–76 .... 7-foot-2
403 .... Wilt Chamberlain, S.F. Warriors, 1963–64 .... 7-foot-1
397 .... Tom Boerwinkle, Chi. Bulls, 1970–71 .... 7-foot-0
386 .... Kareem Abdul-Jabbar, Mil. Bucks, 1973–74 .... 7-foot-2
381 .... David Robinson, S.A. Spurs, 1993–94 .... 7-foot-1
379 .... Kareem Abdul-Jabbar, Mil. Bucks, 1972–73 .... 7-foot-2
371 .... Kareem Abdul-Jabbar, L.A. Lakers, 1979–80 .... 7-foot-2
371 .... Pau Gasol, Mem. Grizzlies, 2005–06 .... 7-foot-0
370 .... Kareem Abdul-Jabbar, Mil. Bucks, 1971–72 .... 7-foot-2

Most Assists by Players 7-Feet or Taller, Career

5660 .... Kareem Abdul-Jabbar 7-foot-2
4643 .... Wilt Chamberlain 7-foot-1
3925 .... Pau Gasol 7-foot-0
3651 .... Dirk Nowitzki 7-foot-0
3541 .... Vlade Divac 7-foot-1
3058 .... Hakeem Olajuwon 7-foot-0
3050 .... Artis Gilmore 7-foot-2
3026 .... Shaquille O'Neal 7-foot-1
2441 .... David Robinson 7-foot-1
2215 .... Patrick Ewing 7-foot-0
2180 .... Robert Parish 7-foot-1
2092 .... Rich Kelley 7-foot-0
2028 .... Brad Daugherty 7-foot-0
2007 .... Tom Boerwinkle 7-foot-0

Most Assists from Age 39 On

1303	John Stockton	311	Michael Jordan
542	Karl Malone	249	Jason Kidd
412	Kareem Abdul-Jabbar	238	Robert Parish
393	Vince Carter	163	Tim Duncan
346	Manu Ginóbili	157	Jason Terry

Most Assists, Last Season in League

629 .... John Stockton, Uta. Jazz, 2002–03
549 .... Larry Brown, Den. Rockets[a], 1971–72
485 .... Dennis Johnson, Bos. Celtics, 1989–90

continued on next page

464 .... Rob Williams, Den. Nuggets, 1983–84
446 .... Oscar Robertson, Mil. Bucks, 1973–74
443 .... Jimmy O'Brien, S.D. Conquistadors[a], 1974–75
417 .... Lionel Hollins, Hou. Rockets, 1984–85
403 .... Maurice Stokes, Cin. Royals, 1957–58
399 .... Isiah Thomas, Det. Pistons, 1993–94
395 .... Kenny Higgs, Den. Nuggets, 1981–82
389 .... K.C. Jones, Bos. Celtics, 1966–67
382 .... Clyde Drexler, Hou. Rockets, 1997–98
378 .... Reggie Theus, N.J. Nets, 1990–91
374 .... Bill Russell, Bos. Celtics, 1968–69
373 .... Keith Jennings, G.S. Warriors, 1994–95
365 .... Wilt Chamberlain, L.A. Lakers, 1972–73
360 .... Deron Williams, Dal. Mavericks/Cle. Cavaliers, 2016–17
358 .... Warren Jabali, S.D. Conquistadors[a], 1974–75
358 .... Dick McGuire, Det. Pistons, 1959–60
357 .... Gail Goodrich, N.O. Jazz, 1978–79
355 .... Bob Davies, Roc. Royals, 1954–55
351 .... Darnell Valentine, Cle. Cavaliers, 1990–91
350 .... Jay Williams, Chi. Bulls, 2002–03

[a] ABA.

Assists Average

Highest APG by Decade

1946-47 – 1949-50

5.7 .... Dick McGuire
5.0 .... Bob Davies
4.9 .... Andy Phillip
4.7 .... Al Cervi
4.0 .... Dolph Schayes
3.9 .... Ralph Beard
3.5 .... Bob Brannum
3.5 .... Ernie Calverley
3.3 .... Bruce Hale
3.3 .... Jim Pollard

1950-51 – 1959-60

7.6 .... Bob Cousy
6.6 .... Guy Rodgers
5.7 .... Dick McGuire
5.5 .... Andy Phillip
5.3 .... Tom Gola
5.3 .... Maurice Stokes
4.8 .... George King
4.8 .... Bob Davies
4.8 .... Larry Costello
4.8 .... Richie Guerin
4.8 .... Ralph Beard

1960-61 – 1969-70*

10.3 .... Oscar Robertson
7.9 .... Guy Rodgers
7.2 .... Bob Cousy
6.9 .... Larry Brown
6.8 .... Walt Frazier
6.2 .... Norm Van Lier
6.2 .... Lenny Wilkens
6.0 .... Art Williams
5.9 .... Jerry West
5.9 .... Dave Bing

1970-71 – 1979-80*

9.0 .... Jerry West
8.0 .... Kevin Porter
8.0 .... John Lucas
8.0 .... Phil Ford
7.9 .... Norm Nixon
7.7 .... Tiny Archibald
7.7 .... Lenny Wilkens
7.5 .... Oscar Robertson
7.3 .... Magic Johnson
7.1 .... Norm Van Lier

1980-81 – 1989-90

11.7 .... Magic Johnson
10.4 .... John Stockton
9.8 .... Isiah Thomas
9.7 .... Kevin Johnson
8.9 .... Mark Jackson
8.7 .... Tim Hardaway
8.5 .... Norm Nixon
8.5 .... Kevin Porter
8.3 .... Nate McMillan
8.2 .... Gary Grant

1990-91 – 1999-00

11.3 .... John Stockton
10.9 .... Magic Johnson
9.3 .... Jason Kidd
8.9 .... Tim Hardaway
8.9 .... Kevin Johnson
8.8 .... Rod Strickland
8.4 .... Mark Jackson
8.4 .... Stephon Marbury
7.9 .... Isiah Thomas
7.7 .... Brevin Knight

continued on next page

2000–01 – 2009–10		2010–11 – 2019–20		2020–21 – 2021–22	
10.0	Chris Paul	9.6	Steve Nash	10.5	James Harden
9.6	Steve Nash	9.2	Chris Paul	9.8	Chris Paul
9.2	Jason Kidd	9.2	John Wall	9.6	Trae Young
9.5	Deron Williams	9.1	Rajon Rondo	9.2	Russell Westbrook
8.2	John Stockton	8.7	Russell Westbrook	8.7	Luka Dončić
7.8	Baron Davis	8.6	Trae Young	8.1	Nikola Jokić
7.7	Terrell Brandon	8.0	Ben Simmons	8.1	Draymond Green
7.3	Stephon Marbury	7.8	Ricky Rubio	7.5	Darius Garland
7.3	Andre Miller	7.7	LeBron James	7.5	Damian Lillard
7.0	LeBron James	7.3	Deron Williams	7.4	Kyle Lowry
		7.3	Luka Dončić		
		7.3	Ja Morant		

* Includes ABA.

Evolution of APG Record

1946–47	Ernie Calverley, Pro. Steamrollers	3.4
1948–49	Bob Davies, Roc. Royals	5.4
1949–50	Andy Phillip, Chi. Stags	5.8
1950–51	Andy Phillip, Phi. Warriors	6.3
1951–52	Andy Phillip, Phi. Warriors	8.2
1955–56	Bob Cousy, Bos. Celtics	8.9
1959–60	Bob Cousy, Bos. Celtics	9.5
1960–61	Oscar Robertson, Cin. Royals	9.7
1961–62	Oscar Robertson, Cin. Royals	11.4
1964–65	Oscar Robertson, Cin. Royals	11.5
1978–79	Kevin Porter, Det. Pistons	13.4
1984–85	Isiah Thomas, Det. Pistons	13.7
1989–90	John Stockton, Uta. Jazz	14.5

Highest APG, Career (Min. 500 Games Played)

		Career GP			Career GP
11.2	Magic Johnson	906	7.9	Rajon Rondo^	957
10.5	John Stockton	1504	7.8	Guy Rodgers	892
9.5	Chris Paul^	1155	7.6	Muggsy Bogues	889
9.5	Oscar Robertson	1040	7.6	Stephon Marbury	846
9.3	Isiah Thomas	979	7.6	Ricky Rubio^	665
9.1	Kevin Johnson	735	7.5	Bob Cousy	924
9.1	John Wall^	613	7.4	Tiny Archibald	876
8.7	Jason Kidd	1391	7.4	LeBron James^	1366
8.5	Steve Nash	1217	7.4	Johnny Moore	520
8.4	Russell Westbrook^	1021	7.3	Rod Strickland	1094
8.3	Norm Nixon	768	7.2	Baron Davis	835
8.2	Tim Hardaway	867	7.0	John Lucas	928
8.1	Kevin Porter	659	7.0	Micheal Ray Richardson	556
8.1	Deron Williams	845	7.0	Norm Van Lier	746
8.0	Mark Jackson	1296			

^ Active.

Highest APG, Season

14.5	John Stockton, Uta. Jazz, 1989–90	13.4	Kevin Porter, Det. Pistons, 1978–79
14.2	John Stockton, Uta. Jazz, 1990–91	13.1	Magic Johnson, L.A. Lakers, 1983–84
13.9	Isiah Thomas, Det. Pistons, 1984–85	12.8	Magic Johnson, L.A. Lakers, 1988–89
13.8	John Stockton, Uta. Jazz, 1987–88	12.6	Magic Johnson, L.A. Lakers, 1984–85
13.7	John Stockton, Uta. Jazz, 1991–92	12.6	Magic Johnson, L.A. Lakers, 1985–86
13.6	John Stockton, Uta. Jazz, 1988–89	12.6	John Stockton, Uta. Jazz, 1993–94

continued on next page

12.5	Magic Johnson, L.A. Lakers, 1990–91
12.3	John Stockton, Uta. Jazz, 1994–95
12.2	Magic Johnson, L.A. Lakers, 1986–87

| 12.2 | Kevin Johnson, Pho. Suns, 1988–89 |
| 12.0 | John Stockton, Uta. Jazz, 1992–93 |

Most Seasons Averaging 10 APG

10	John Stockton
9	Magic Johnson
7	Steve Nash
6	Chris Paul^

5	Oscar Robertson
5	Russell Westbrook^
4	Isiah Thomas
4	Kevin Johnson

| 4 | Deron Williams |
| 4 | Rajon Rondo^ |

^ Active.

Oldest Player to Average 10 APG

Age (Birthdate)		APG
38 (Feb. 7)	Steve Nash, Pho. Suns, 2011–12	10.7
37 (Feb. 7)	Steve Nash, Pho. Suns, 2010–11	11.4
37 (May 6)	Chris Paul, Pho. Suns, 2021–22	10.8
36 (Feb. 7)	Steve Nash, Pho. Suns, 2009–10	11.0
35 (Mar. 23)	Jason Kidd, N.J. Nets/Dal. Mavericks, 2007–08	10.1
35 (Mar. 26)	John Stockton, Uta. Jazz, 1996–97	10.5
35 (Dec. 30)	LeBron James, L.A. Lakers, 2019–20	10.2
34 (Feb. 7)	Steve Nash, Pho. Suns, 2007–08	11.1
34 (Mar. 26)	John Stockton, Uta. Jazz, 1995–96	11.2
33 (Feb. 7)	Steve Nash, Pho. Suns, 2006–07	11.6
33 (Mar. 26)	John Stockton, Uta. Jazz, 1994–95	12.3
32 (Feb. 7)	Steve Nash, Pho. Suns, 2005–06	10.5
32 (Mar. 26)	John Stockton, Uta. Jazz, 1993–94	12.6
32 (Apr. 1)	Mark Jackson, Den. Nuggets/Ind. Pacers, 1996–97	11.4
32 (Aug. 26)	James Harden, Brk. Nets/Phi. 76ers, 2021–22	10.3
32 (Nov. 12)	Russell Westbrook, Was. Wizards, 2020–21	11.7
31 (Feb. 7)	Steve Nash, Pho. Suns, 2004–05	11.5
31 (Mar. 26)	John Stockton, Uta. Jazz, 1992–93	12.0
31 (May 6)	Chris Paul, L.A. Clippers, 2015–16	10.0
31 (Jul. 11)	Rod Strickland, Was. Wizards, 1997–98	10.5
31 (Aug. 14)	Magic Johnson, L.A. Lakers, 1990–91	12.5
31 (Aug. 26)	James Harden, Hou. Rockets/Brk. Nets, 2020–21	10.8
31 (Sep. 1)	Guy Rodgers, Chi. Bulls, 1966–67	11.2
30 (Feb. 22)	Rajon Rondo, Sac. Kings, 2015–16	11.7
30 (Mar. 26)	John Stockton, Uta. Jazz, 1991–92	13.7
30 (May 6)	Chris Paul, L.A. Clippers, 2014–15	10.2
30 (Aug. 14)	Magic Johnson, L.A. Lakers, 1989–90	11.5
30 (Sep. 1)	Guy Rodgers, S.F. Warriors, 1965–66	10.7
30 (Oct. 31)	John Lucas, S.A. Spurs, 1983–84	10.7
30 (Nov. 12)	Russell Westbrook, Ok.C. Thunder, 2018–19	10.7

Youngest Player to Average 10 APG

Age (Birthdate)		APG
22 (May 6)	Chris Paul, N.O. Hornets, 2007–08	11.6
22 (Apr. 30)	Isiah Thomas, Det. Pistons, 1983–84	11.1

continued on next page

Age (Birthdate)		APG
23 (Nov. 24)	Oscar Robertson, Cin. Royals, 1961–62	11.4
23 (Aug. 14)	Magic Johnson, L.A. Laketrs, 1982–83	10.5
23 (Jun. 26)	Deron Williams, Uta. Jazz, 2007–08	10.5
23 (May 6)	Chris Paul, N.O. Hornets, 2008–09	11.0
23 (Mar. 4)	Kevin Johnson, Pho. Suns, 1988–89	12.2
23 (Apr. 30)	Isiah Thomas, Det. Pistons, 1984–85	13.9
23 (Apr. 1)	Mark Jackson, N.Y. Knicks, 1987–88	10.6
24 (Sep. 6)	John Wall, Was. Wizards, 2014–15	10.0
24 (Sep. 2)	Tiny Archibald, K.C.-Oma. Kings, 1972–73	11.4
24 (Aug. 14)	Magic Johnson, L.A. Laketrs, 1983–84	13.1
24 (Jun. 26)	Deron Williams, Uta. Jazz, 2008–09	10.7
24 (May 6)	Chris Paul, N.O. Hornets, 2009–10	10.7
24 (Apr. 30)	Isiah Thomas, Det. Pistons, 1985–86	10.8
24 (Apr. 11)	Micheal Ray Richardson, N.Y. Knicks, 1979–80	10.1
24 (Apr. 1)	Norm Van Lier, Cin. Royals, 1970–71	10.1
24 (Mar. 4)	Kevin Johnson, Pho. Suns, 1989–90	11.4
25 (Nov. 24)	Oscar Robertson, Cin. Royals, 1963–64	11.0
25 (Oct. 13)	Doc Rivers, Atl. Hawks, 1986–87	10.0
25 (Apr. 30)	Isiah Thomas, Det. Pistons, 1986–87	10.0
25 (Sep. 6)	John Wall, Was. Wizards, 2015–16	10.2
25 (Sep. 1)	Tim Hardaway, G.S. Warriors, 1991–92	10.0
25 (Aug. 14)	Magic Johnson, L.A. Laketrs, 1984–85	12.6
25 (Jun. 26)	Deron Williams, Uta. Jazz, 2009–10	10.5
25 (Apr. 21)	Gary Grant, L.A. Clippers, 1989–90	10.0
25 (Apr. 8)	Terry Porter, Por. Blazers, 1987–88	10.1
25 (Mar. 4)	Kevin Johnson, Pho. Suns, 1990–91	10.1
25 (Feb. 22)	Rajon Rondo, Bos. Celtics, 2010–11	11.2
25 (Jan. 9)	Muggsy Bogues, Cha. Hornets, 1989–90	10.7

Rookies Averaging 8 APG

10.6 Mark Jackson, N.Y. Knicks, 1987–88	8.2 Ernie DiGregorio, Buf. Braves, 1973–74
9.7 Oscar Robertson, Cin. Royals, 1960–61	8.2 Nate McMillan, Sea. Sonics, 1986–87
9.3 Damon Stoudamire, Tor. Raptors, 1995–96	8.2 Brevin Knight, Cle. Cavaliers, 1997–98
8.7 Tim Hardaway, G.S. Warriors, 1989–90	8.2 Ricky Rubio, Min. T'Wolves, 2011–12
8.6 Phil Ford, K.C. Kings, 1978–79	8.2 Ben Simmons, Phi. 76ers, 2017–18
8.3 Ennis Whatley, Chi. Bulls, 1983–84	8.1 Jamaal Tinsley, Ind. Pacers, 2001–02
8.3 John Wall, Was. Bullets, 2010–11	8.1 Trae Young, Atl. Hawks, 2018–19

Turnovers

Most Turnovers, Career˙

4788 LeBron James^	3682 Isiah Thomas	3376 Charles Barkley
4524 Karl Malone	3667 Hakeem Olajuwon	3326 Dwyane Wade
4264 Moses Malone	3539 James Harden^	3310 Shaquille O'Neal
4244 John Stockton	3537 Patrick Ewing	3302 Dwight Howard^
4188 Russell Westbrook^	3532 Paul Pierce	3262 Allen Iverson
4010 Kobe Bryant	3506 Magic Johnson	3257 Scottie Pippen
4003 Jason Kidd	3493 Reggie Theus	3183 Robert Parish
3940 Julius Erving	3478 Steve Nash	3179 Kevin Garnett
3926 Artis Gilmore	3381 Tim Duncan	3155 Mark Jackson

continued on next page

3121	....	Andre Miller	3052	....	Carmelo Anthony
3085	....	Ron Boone	3030	....	Gary Payton

* Includes ABA.

^ Active.

Most Time Leading League in Turnovers

6	....	James Harden	....	2012–13: Hou. Rockets	295
				2014–15: Hou. Rockets	321
				2015–16: Hou. Rockets	374
				2016–17: Hou. Rockets	464
				2018–19: Hou Rockets	387
				2019–20: Hou Rockets	308
4	....	George McGinnis	....	1972–73: Ind. Pacers[a]	401
				1973–74: Ind. Pacers[a]	393
				1974–75: Ind. Pacers[a]	422
				1978–79: Den. Nuggets	346
4	....	Russell Westbrook	....	2008–09: Ok.C. Thunder	274
				2010–11: Ok.C. Thunder	316
				2017–78: Ok.C. Thunder	381
				2020–21: Was. Wizards	312
2	....	Larry Brown	....	1967–68: N.O. Buccaneers[a]	355
				1969–70: Was. Capitols[a]	356
2	....	Isiah Thomas	....	1981–82: Det. Pistons	299
				1989–90: Det. Pistons	322
2	....	Jason Kidd	....	1995–96: Dal. Mavericks	328
				2001–02: N.J. Nets	286
2	....	Allen Iverson	....	1996–97: Phi. 76ers	337
				2004–05: Phi. 76ers	344
2	....	Jerry Stackhouse	....	1999–00: Det. Pistons	311
				2000–01: Det. Pistons	326
2	....	Steve Nash	....	2007–08: Pho. Suns	295
				2009–10: Pho. Suns	295
2	....	John Wall	....	2011–12: Was. Wizards	255
				2013–14: Was. Wizards	295

[a] ABA.

Most Turnovers, Season

NBA

464	....	James Harden, Hou. Rockets, 2016–17
438	....	Russell Westbrook, Ok.C. Thunder, 2016–17
387	....	James Harden, Hou. Rockets, 2018–19
381	....	Russell Westbrook, Ok.C. Thunder, 2017–18
374	....	James Harden, Hou. Rockets, 2015–16
366	....	Artis Gilmore, Chi. Bulls, 1977–78
360	....	Kevin Porter, Det. Pistons/N.J. Nets, 1977–78
359	....	Micheal Ray Richardson, N.Y. Knicks, 1979–80
352	....	Ricky Sobers, Ind. Pacers, 1977–78
350	....	Charles Barkley, Phi. 76ers, 1985–86
348	....	Reggie Theus, Chi. Bulls, 1979–80
347	....	LeBron James, Cle. Cavaliers, 2017–18
346	....	Bob McAdoo, N.Y. Knicks, 1977–78

ABA

422	....	George McGinnis, Ind. Pacers, 1974–75
401	....	George McGinnis, Ind. Pacers, 1972–73
393	....	George McGinnis, Ind. Pacers, 1973–74
381	....	Billy Cunningham, Car. Cougars, 1972–73
360	....	Ralph Simpson, Den. Nuggets, 1975–76
356	....	Larry Brown, Was. Capitols, 1969–70
356	....	Mack Calvin, The Floridians, 1970–71
355	....	Ron Boone, Dal. Chaparrals, 1968–69
355	....	Larry Brown, N.O. Buccaneers, 1967–68
346	....	Larry Cannon, Den. Rockets, 1970–71
345	....	Johnny Neumann, Mem. Tams, 1972–73
344	....	Artis Gilmore, Ken. Colonels, 1974–75
342	....	Julius Erving, Vir. Squires, 1971–72

continued on next page

NBA

346................ George McGinnis, Den. Nuggets, 1978–79
345................ Ron Harper, Cle. Cavaliers, 1986–87
344................ Allen Iverson, Phi. 76ers, 2004–05
343................ Isiah Thomas, Det. Pistons, 1986–87
342................ Jeff Ruland, Was. Bullets, 1983–84
342................ Russell Westbrook, Ok.C. Thunder, 2015–16
337................ Kevin Porter, Det. Pistons, 1978–79
337................ Allen Iverson, Phi. 76ers, 1996–97
335................ Ray Williams, K.C. Kings, 1982–83

ABA

341................ Julius Erving, N.Y. Nets, 1973–74
340................ Charlie Scott, Vir. Squires, 1971–72
335................ Ron Boone, Uta. Stars, 1974–75
335................ Artis Gilmore, Ken. Colonels, 1971–72
332................ Warren Jabali, The Floridians, 1971–72
331................ Larry Brown, Oak. Oaks, 1968–69

Most Turnovers in a Game without Scoring

9................ John Lucas, G.S. Warriors* .... vs. Det. Pistons (Jan. 10, 1981)
7................ Del Beshore, Chi. Bulls .... @ Pho. Suns (Dec. 1, 1979)
7................ Bimbo Coles, Mia. Heat .... @ Cle. Cavaliers (Dec. 17, 1991)
7................ Tom Gugliotta, Was. Bullets .... @ N.Y. Knicks (Nov. 24, 1992)
7................ Melvin Booker, Den. Nuggets.................. vs. Phi. 76ers (Dec. 26, 1996)
7................ Danny Fortson, Den. Nuggets* .... vs. L.A. Clippers (Mar. 29, 1999)
7................ Eric Snow, Phi. 76ers .... @ S.A. Spurs (Nov. 25, 2000)
7................ Jason Williams, Sac. Kings .... @ Pho. Suns (Apr. 15, 2001)
7................ José Calderón, Tor. Raptors..................... @ N.O. Hornets (Jan. 17, 2011)
6................ Tim Bassett, N.J. Nets............................ @ S.A. Spurs (Nov. 25, 1978)
6................ Elmore Smith, Cle. Cavaliers*.................. vs. K.C. Kings (Feb. 22, 1979)
6................ Phil Ford, K.C. Kings .... @ Sea. Sonics (Feb. 3, 1982)
6................ Ronnie Lester, Chi. Bulls .... @ Phi. 76ers (Nov. 10, 1982)
6................ James Ray, Den. Nuggets .... @ Was. Bullets (Dec. 9, 1982)
6................ James Bailey, N.Y. Knicks .... @ Phi. 76ers (Dec. 9, 1984)
6................ Jay Humphries, Pho. Suns .... vs. S.A. Spurs (Apr. 9, 1986)
6................ Marc Iavaroni, Uta. Jazz* .... @ Den. Nuggets (Dec. 10, 1986)
6................ Gary Grant, L.A. Clippers .... @ Sac. Kings (Jan. 22, 1990)
6................ Vlade Divac, L.A. Lakers*....................... vs. Sac. Kings (Apr. 5, 1990)
6................ Delaney Rudd, Uta. Jazz .... vs. Pho. Suns (Nov. 2, 1990)
6................ Paul Pressey, S.A. Spurs .... @ L.A. Lakers (Mar. 17, 1991)
6................ Dennis Rodman, S.A. Spurs*.................... @ L.A. Lakers (Jan. 9, 1994)
6................ Chris Dudley, Por. Blazers....................... vs. Van. Grizzlies (Nov. 3, 1995)
6................ Dennis Rodman, Chi. Bulls*.................... vs. Pho. Suns (Dec. 15, 1997)
6................ Larry Hughes, Phi. 76ers*....................... @ Cle. Cavaliers (Dec. 3, 1999)
6................ Dickey Simpkins, Chi. Bulls .... vs. Por. Blazers (Jan. 3, 2000)
6................ Steve Francis, Hou. Rockets..................... vs. Den. Nuggets (Feb. 24, 2000)
6................ Jason Williams, Sac. Kings .... @ Hou. Rockets (Mar. 2, 2000)
6................ Aaron McKie, Phi. 76ers .... @ L.A. Lakers (Mar. 31, 2000)
6................ Michael Olowokandi, L.A. Clippers .... @ Uta. Jazz (Oct. 31, 2000)
6................ Erick Dampier, Dal. Mavericks*................ vs. Atl. Hawks (Nov. 17, 2005)
6................ Kenny Thomas, Sac. Kings....................... @ G.S. Warriors (Nov. 16, 2006)
6................ Damon Stoudamire, Mem. Grizzlies .... @ L.A. Clippers (Jan. 20, 2007)
6................ Armon Johnson, Por. Blazers*.................. vs. Tor. Raptors (Nov. 6, 2010)
6................ Vince Carter, Dal. Mavericks.................... vs. Tor. Raptors (Dec. 20, 2013)
6................ Marcelo Huertas, L.A. Lakers.................... @ Hou. Rockets (Dec. 12, 2015)
6................ Mario Hezonja, N.Y. Knicks..................... vs. Det. Pistons (Apr. 10, 2019)
6................ Draymond Green, G.S. Warriors.............. vs. Dal. Mavericks (Apr. 27, 2021)
6................ Rajon Rondo, L.A. Clippers*..................... vs. Tor. Raptors (May 4, 2021)
6................ Elfrid Payton, Pho. Suns*........................ vs. Cha. Hornets (Dec. 19, 2021)

* Team won game.

Most Consecutive Games with at Least 5 Turnovers, Season

		First Game of Streak	Last Game of Streak
10	Magic Johnson, L.A. Lakers	Jan. 31, 1984	Feb. 18, 1984
10	Allen Iverson, Phi. 76ers	Nov. 29, 1996	Dec. 21, 1996
9	James Harden, Hou. Rockets	Dec. 23, 2016	Jan. 8, 2017
8	Magic Johnson, L.A. Lakers	Nov. 1, 1984	Nov. 16, 1984
8	Shawn Kemp, Sea. Sonics	Jan. 12, 1996	Jan. 27, 1996
8	Russell Westbrook, Ok.C. Thunder	Mar. 18, 2017	Apr. 2, 2017
8	James Harden, Hou. Rockets	Dec. 25, 2018	Jan. 9, 2019
7	Adrian Dantley, Uta. Jazz	Feb. 23, 1984	Mar. 3, 1984
7	Charles Barkley, Phi. 76ers	Dec. 16, 1986	Dec. 27, 1986
7	Damon Stoudamire, Tor. Raptors	Jan. 30, 1996	Feb. 15, 1996
7	Robert Pack, N.J. Nets	Jan. 7, 1997	Jan. 18, 1997
7	Allen Iverson, Phi. 76ers	Nov. 14, 2003	Nov. 26, 2003
7	James Harden, Hou. Rockets	Jan. 20, 2017	Jan. 31, 2017
7	DeMarcus Cousins, N.O. Pelicans	Jan. 6, 2018	Jan. 17, 2018
7	James Harden, Hou. Rockets	Nov. 1, 2019	Nov. 13, 2019
7	James Harden, Brk. Nets	Nov. 10, 2021	Nov. 22, 2021

Most Consecutive Games with 3 or More Turnovers

		First Game of Streak	Last Game of Streak
30	Allen Iverson, Phi. 76ers	Feb. 4, 2005	Apr. 12, 2005
27	Isiah Thomas, Det. Pistons	Dec. 30, 1986	Feb. 22, 1987
25	John Stockton, Uta. Jazz	Mar. 13, 1989	Nov. 11, 1989
25	Kobe Bryant, L.A. Lakers	Nov. 13, 2004	Jan. 10, 2005
25	Luka Dončić, Dal. Mavericks	Mar. 1, 2021	Apr. 27, 2021
23	Isiah Thomas, Det. Pistons	Mar. 22, 1990	Nov. 16, 1990
23	Russell Westbrook, Ok.C. Thunder	Nov. 14, 2016	Dec. 29, 2016
23	James Harden, Hou. Rockets	Dec. 20, 2018	Feb. 4, 2019
22	Magic Johnson, L.A. Lakers	Jan. 12, 1984	Feb. 26, 1984
21	Reggie Theus, K.C. Kings	Dec. 5, 1984	Jan. 13, 1985
21	Magic Johnson, L.A. Lakers	Nov. 4, 1988	Dec. 14, 1988
21	Derrick Coleman, N.J. Nets	Mar. 10, 1992	Nov. 12, 1992
21	Russell Westbrook, Ok.C. Thunder	Jan. 2, 2017	Feb. 11, 2017
21	John Wall, Was. Wizards	Dec. 29, 2017	Oct. 24, 2018
21	James Harden, Hou. Rockets	Apr. 3, 2019	Nov. 24, 2019
20	Eddie Johnson, Atl. Hawks	Feb. 4, 1985	Mar. 19, 1985
20	John Stockton, Uta. Jazz	Mar. 29, 1990	Nov. 16, 1990
20	Allen Iverson, Phi. 76ers	Feb. 23, 2002	Nov. 8, 2002
20	James Harden, Hou. Rockets	Feb. 6, 2015	Mar. 23, 2015

Most Consecutive Games with At Least One Turnover

		First Game of Streak	Last Game of Streak
407	Russell Westbrook	Mar. 16, 2016	Jan. 2, 2022
239	James Harden	Nov. 21, 2016	Dec. 5, 2019
208	Karl Malone	Jan. 9, 1988	Apr. 15, 1990
179	Russell Westbrook	Nov. 3, 2013	Mar. 12, 2016
170	Darius Garland	Nov. 14, 2019	Apr. 8, 2022
157	Joe Barry Carroll	Nov. 17, 1982	Nov. 6, 1985
150	Luka Dončić	Jan. 28, 2020	Apr. 10, 2022
147	Truck Robinson	Nov. 7, 1979	Mar. 22, 1981
146	Paul Pierce	Apr. 9, 2005	Nov. 27, 2007

continued on next page

		First Game of Streak	Last Game of Streak
145	Steve Francis	Apr. 12, 2003	Mar. 15, 2005
144	Reggie Theus	Dec. 7, 1985	Nov. 7, 1987
142	Kobe Bryant	Nov. 26, 2006	Apr. 2, 2008
141	Moses Malone	Nov. 30, 1983	Nov. 6, 1985
137	Allen Iverson	Nov. 22, 2000	Nov. 27, 2002
137	Jalen Rose	Nov. 4, 2002	Mar. 31, 2004
134	Jason Kidd	Feb. 2, 2000	Jan. 8, 2002
132	Shaquille O'Neal	Nov. 6, 1992	Feb. 23, 1994
132	Dwight Howard	Apr. 11, 2010	Mar. 28, 2012
129	Trae Young	Jan. 15, 2021	Apr. 10, 2022
128	Isiah Thomas	Feb. 20, 1985	Dec. 26, 1986
126	LeBron James	Jan. 23, 2016	Nov. 17, 2017
125	Isiah Thomas	Nov. 18, 1983	Feb. 16, 1985
121	Tom Gugliotta	Apr. 16, 1995	Jan. 18, 1997
120	Mark Aguirre	Oct. 27, 1984	Feb. 4, 1986

Most Games with 10 Turnovers, Career

12	Russell Westbrook^	6	Jason Kidd	4	Isiah Thomas
11	James Harden^	4	Kobe Bryant	4	Dwyane Wade
6	Magic Johnson	4	Allen Iverson		

^ Active.

Most Turnovers, Fouling Out of Game

12	Scottie Pippen, Chi. Bulls*	@ N.J. Nets (Feb. 25, 1990)
11	Johnny Neumann, Mem. Tams^a	@ Ken. Colonels^a (Nov. 22, 1972)
11	Hakeem Olajuwon, Hou. Rockets	vs. Den. Nuggets (Apr. 19, 1990)
11	Russell Westbrook, Ok.C. Thunder*	vs. Det. Pistons (Nov. 27, 2015)
10	Mark Aguirre, Dal. Mavericks	vs. Mil. Bucks (Mar. 4, 1983)
10	Rob Williams, Den. Nuggets*	vs. Det. Pistons (Mar. 25, 1983)
10	Mark Aguirre, Dal. Mavericks*	vs. Phi. 76ers (Feb. 15, 1984)
10	George Gervin, S.A. Spurs*	vs. Atl. Hawks (Mar. 20, 1984)
10	Buck Williams, N.J. Nets	@ Ind. Pacers (Dec. 13, 1986)
10	Wayman Tisdale, Sac. Kings	@ Den. Nuggets (Nov. 8, 1989)

* Team won game.
^a ABA.

More Turnovers Than Rebounds, Career (Min. 1750 Rebounds)

Diff		TO	Reb
-377	Norm Nixon	2368	1991
-204	Isiah Thomas	3682	3478
-193	John Stockton	4244	4051
-144	Reggie Theus	3493	3349
-31	Stephon Marbury	2547	2516

Fewest Turnovers, Season (Min. 1500 Minutes Played)

TO		MP
12	Steve Novak, N.Y. Knicks, 2012–13	1641
21	James Jones, Mia. Heat, 2010–11	1549
24	Langston Galloway, Det. Pistons, 2018–19	1745
25	Bruce Bowen, S.A. Spurs, 2008–09	1506
26	T.R. Dunn, Den. Nuggets, 1987–88	1534

continued on next page

TO		MP
28	Kentavious Caldwell-Pope, Det. Pistons, 2013–14	1583
28	Dante Cunningham, N.O. Pelicans, 2016–17	1649
29	Quinton Ross, L.A. Clippers, 2007–08	1505
29	Jodie Meeks, Phi. 76ers, 2011–12	1644
29	Justin Jackson, Dal. Mavericks/Sac. Kings, 2018–19	1614
30	Harvey Grant, Was. Bullets, 1996–97	1604
30	Wayne Ellington, Mia. Heat, 2016–17	1500
30	Javonte Green, Chi. Bulls, 2021–22	1519
31	Tony Snell, Det. Pistons, 2019–20	1641
32	Matt Bonner, Tor. Raptors, 2005–06	1710
33	T.R. Dunn, Den. Nuggets, 1986–87	1932
33	Quinton Ross, L.A. Clippers, 2006–07	1700
33	Maurice Evans, Atl. Hawks/Was. Wizards, 2010–11	1549
33	Dante Cunningham, N.O. Pelicans/Brk. Nets, 2017–18	1562
33	Pat Connaughton, Mil. Bucks, 2020–21	1575
34	Dean Garrett, Min. T'Wolves, 1996–97	1665
34	Shane Battier, Mia. Heat, 2012–13	1786
35	James Jones, Pho. Suns, 2005–06	1772
35	Dante Cunningham, N.O. Pelicans, 2014–15	1652
35	André Roberson, Ok.C. Thunder, 2015–16	1553
35	Pat Connaughton, Mil. Bucks, 2021–22	1691
36	DeSagana Diop, Dal. Mavericks, 2005–06	1510
36	Nick Young, L.A. Lakers, 2016–17	1556
36	Tony Snell, Mil. Bucks, 2017–18	2053
37	Matt Bonner, S.A. Spurs, 2008–09	1928
37	Bryn Forbes, S.A. Spurs, 2017–18	1517
38	Anthony Morrow, Ok.C. Thunder, 2014–15	1806
38	Doug McDermott, Chi. Bulls/Ok.C. Thunder, 2016–17	1508
38	Patrick Patterson, Tor. Raptors, 2016–17	1599
38	Danilo Gallinari, Atl. Hawks, 2021–22	1672
39	Marvin Williams, Atl. Hawks, 2011–12	1500
39	Matisse Thybulle, Phi. 76ers, 2021–22	1685
40	Dale Davis, Por. Blazers, 2003–04	1682
40	Matt Bonner, Tor. Raptors, 2004–05	1553
40	Maurice Evans, L.A. Lakers/Orl. Magic, 2007–08	1720
40	C.J. Miles, Ind. Pacers, 2016–17	1776
40	Justin Jackson, Sac. Kings, 2017–18	1506
40	Langston Galloway, Det. Pistons, 2019–20	1702
40	Reggie Bullock, Dal. Mavericks, 2021–22	1902

Highest Turnover Average, Career (Min. 250 Games)

		Career Games	TO			Career Games	TO
4.1	Russell Westbrook^	1021	4188	3.6	Allen Iverson	914	3262
4.1	Trae Young^	280	1161	3.5	LeBron James^	1366	4788
4.1	Luka Dončić^	264	1080	3.5	Steve Francis	576	2030
3.9	Magic Johnson	906	3506	3.4	Reggie Theus	1026	3493
3.8	Isiah Thomas	979	3682	3.4	Joel Embiid^	328	1109
3.8	James Harden^	942	3539	3.4	Ben Simmons^	275	925
3.8	John Wall	613	2332	3.3	George McGinnis	842	2763
3.8	Warren Jabali	447	1715	3.3	DeMarcus Cousins^	654	2149
3.8	Larry Brown	376	1447	3.3	Micheal Ray Richardson	556	1854
3.7	Jeff Ruland	332	1212	3.2	Julius Erving	1243	3940

continued on next page

	Career Games	TO			Career Games	TO
3.2	Dwyane Wade	1054	3326	3.1	Devin Booker^	477	1492
3.2	Kevin Durant^	939	2964	3.1	Levern Tart	274	841
3.2	Bernard King	874	2791	3.0	Kobe Bryant	1346	4010
3.2	Ray Williams	655	2099	3.0	Artis Gilmore	1329	3926
3.2	Gilbert Arenas	552	1744	3.0	Hakeem Olajuwon	1238	3667
3.1	Karl Malone	1476	4524	3.0	Patrick Ewing	1183	3537
3.1	Charles Barkley	1073	3376	3.0	Ron Boone	1041	3085
3.1	Larry Bird	897	2816	3.0	Stephon Marbury	846	2547
3.1	Stephen Curry^	826	2598	3.0	Mel Daniels	639	1911
3.1	Norm Nixon	768	2368	3.0	Andrew Toney	468	1394
3.1	Kevin Johnson	735	2258	3.0	Ralph Sampson	456	1363
3.1	Glenn Robinson	688	2147				

^ Active.

Highest Turnover Average, Season (Min. 1000 Minutes Played)

5.7 .... James Harden, Hou. Rockets, 2016–17	4.6 .... Allen Iverson, Phi. 76ers, 2004–05
5.4 .... Russell Westbrook, Ok.C. Thunder, 2016–17	4.6 .... James Harden, Hou. Rockets, 2015–16
5.3 .... George McGinnis, Ind. Pacers^a, 1974–75	4.5 .... Billy Cunningham, Car. Cougars^a, 1972–73
5.1 .... Warren Jabali, Was. Capitols^a, 1969–70	4.5 .... Artis Gilmore, Chi. Bulls, 1977–78
5.0 .... Pete Maravich, N.O. Jazz, 1977–78	4.5 .... Ricky Sobers, Ind. Pacers, 1977–78
5.0 .... DeMarcus Cousins, N.O. Pelicans, 2017–18	4.5 .... Russell Westbrook, Ok.C. Thunder, 2018–19
5.0 .... James Harden, Hou. Rockets, 2018–19	4.5 .... James Harden, Hou. Rockets, 2019–20
4.9 .... George McGinnis, Ind. Pacers^a, 1972–73	4.5 .... Russell Westbrook, Hou. Rockets, 2019–20
4.9 .... George McGinnis, Ind. Pacers^a, 1973–74	4.5 .... Luka Dončić, Dal. Mavericks, 2021–22
4.8 .... Jeff Ruland, Was. Bullets, 1984–85	4.4 .... Mack Calvin, The Floridians^a, 1970–71
4.8 .... Russell Westbrook, Ok.C. Thunder, 2017–18	4.4 .... Johnny Neumann, Mem. Tams^a, 1972–73
4.8 .... Trae Young, Atl. Hawks, 2019–20	4.4 .... Kevin Porter, Det. Pistons/N.J. Nets, 1977–78
4.8 .... Russell Westbrook, Was. Wizards, 2020–21	4.4 .... Bob McAdoo, N.Y. Knicks, 1977–78
4.7 .... Ray Williams, K.C. Kings, 1982–83	4.4 .... Micheal Ray Richardson, N.Y. Knicks, 1979–80
4.7 .... Charles Barkley, Phi. 76ers, 1986–87	4.4 .... Charles Barkley, Phi. 76ers, 1985–86
4.7 .... Gary Grant, L.A. Clippers, 1989–90	4.4 .... Allen Iverson, Phi. 76ers, 1996–97
4.6 .... Larry Brown, N.O. Buccaneers^a, 1967–68	4.4 .... Allen Iverson, Phi. 76ers, 2003–04
4.6 .... Ron Boone, Dal. Chaparrals^a, 1968–69	4.4 .... Dwyane Wade, Mia. Heat, 2007–08
4.6 .... Julius Erving, Vir. Squires^a, 1972–73	4.4 .... Russell Westbrook, Ok.C. Thunder, 2014–15
4.6 .... George McGinnis, Den. Nuggets, 1978–79	4.4 .... James Harden, Hou. Rockets, 2017–18
4.6 .... Magic Johnson, L.A. Lakers, 1983–84	4.4 .... James Harden, Brk. Nets/Phi. 76ers, 2021–22
4.6 .... Jeff Ruland, Was. Bullets, 1983–84	

^a ABA.

Average Team Total Turnovers/Turnovers Per Game, Year by Year·

NBA

1973–74 .... 1706 (20.8)	1984–85 .... 1465 (17.9)	1995–96 .... 1298 (15.8)
1974–75 .... 1627 (19.8)	1985–86 .... 1463 (17.8)	1996–97 .... 1285 (15.7)
1975–76 .... 1621 (19.8)	1986–87 .... 1393 (17.0)	1997–98 .... 1270 (15.5)
1976–77 .... 1687 (20.6)	1987–88 .... 1372 (16.7)	1998–99 .... 766 (15.3)
1977–78 .... 1646 (20.1)	1988–89 .... 1412 (17.2)	1999–00 .... 1269 (15.5)
1978–79 .... 1623 (19.8)	1989–90 .... 1317 (16.1)	2000–01 .... 1234 (15.0)
1979–80 .... 1553 (18.9)	1990–91 .... 1315 (16.0)	2001–02 .... 1186 (14.5)
1980–81 .... 1537 (18.7)	1991–92 .... 1275 (15.6)	2002–03 .... 1223 (14.9)
1981–82 .... 1454 (17.7)	1992–93 .... 1305 (15.9)	2003–04 .... 1228 (15.0)
1982–83 .... 1567 (19.1)	1993–94 .... 1312 (16.0)	2004–05 .... 1189 (14.5)
1983–84 .... 1468 (17.9)	1994–95 .... 1308 (15.9)	2005–06 .... 1182 (14.4)

continued on next page

2006–07	1241 (15.1)	2012–13	1192 (14.6)	2018–19	1155 (14.1)
2007–08	1157 (14.1)	2013–14	1201 (14.6)	2019–20	1027 (14.5)
2008–09	1151 (14.0)	2014–15	1177 (14.4)	2020–21	996 (13.8)
2009–10	1166 (14.2)	2015–16	1179 (14.4)	2021–22	1129 (13.8)
2010–11	1169 (14.3)	2016–17	1144 (14.0)		
2011–12	962 (14.6)	2017–18	1170 (14.3)		

* Turnovers became an official NBA stat for the 1977–78 season, though records begin for the 1973–74 season.

1998–99: 50-game season.

2011–12: 66-game season.

2019–20: 65-to-75-game season.

2020–21: 72-game season.

ABA*

1967–68	1341 (17.2)	1970–71	1598 (19.0)	1973–74	1506 (17.9)
1968–69	1473 (18.9)	1971–72	1528 (18.2)	1974–75	1543 (18.4)
1969–70	1637 (19.5)	1972–73	1601 (19.1)	1975–76	1632 (19.5)**

* ABA seasons ranged from 78 games (1967–68, 1968–69) to 84 games (1969–70—1975–76).

** Average includes 7 of 9 ABA teams, as Uta. Stars (16 games) and S.D. Sails (11 games) folded before conclusion of 1975–76 season.

Offensive Miscellany

Most Times Leading League in Offensive Categories

Points

11	Michael Jordan
7	Wilt Chamberlain
5	Kevin Durant^
4	George Gervin
4	James Harden^
4	Kobe Bryant
3	George Mikan
3	Neil Johnston
3	Bob McAdoo
3	Kareem Abdul-Jabbar
3	Shaquille O'Neal

^ Active.

PPG

10	Michael Jordan
7	Wilt Chamberlain
4	Kevin Durant^
4	George Gervin
4	Allen Iverson
3	Bob McAdoo
3	James Harden^
3	Neil Johnston
3	George Mikan
2	Joe Fulks
2	Adrian Dantley
2	Shaquille O'Neal
2	Kobe Bryant
2	Stephen Curry^
2	Paul Arizin
2	Tracy McGrady
2	Kareem Abdul-Jabbar
2	Russell Westbrook
2	Bob Pettit

^ Active.

Field Goals

10	Michael Jordan
7	Wilt Chamberlain
5	Kareem Abdul Jabbar
5	Shaquille O'Neal
5	LeBron James^
4	George Gervin
3	Paul Arizin
3	Alex English

FG%

10	Shaquille O'Neal
9	Wilt Chamberlain
5	DeAndre Jordan^
4	Artis Gilmore
3	Neil Johnston
3	Rudy Gobert^
2	Johnny Green
2	Alex Groza

continued on next page

Field Goals

3	George Mikan
3	Bob Pettit
3	Kobe Bryant
3	Kevin Durant^
2	Cedric Maxwell
2	Buck Williams

^ Active.

FG%

2	Ed Macauley
2	Kenny Sears
2	Gheorghe Mureșan
2	Kevin McHale

^ Active.

Three Pointers

7	Stephen Curry^
3	Ray Allen
3	James Harden^
2	Larry Bird
2	Darrell Griffith
2	Michael Adams
2	Vernon Maxwell
2	Reggie Miller
2	Dan Majerle

^ Active.

3P%

4	Kyle Korver
2	Craig Hodges
2	Steve Kerr
2	Jason Kapono
2	Joe Harris^

^ Active.

Free Throws

8	Karl Malone
6	James Harden^
5	Adrian Dantley
5	Kevin Durant^
4	Oscar Robertson
3	George Mikan
3	Neil Johnston
3	Bob Pettit
3	Tiny Archibald
3	David Robinson
2	Larry Costello
2	Bob Feerick
2	Oscar Robertson
2	Ernie DiGregorio
2	Kyle Macy
2	Peja Stojaković
2	Mahmoud Abdul-Rauf

^ Active.

FT%

7	Bill Sharman
6	Rick Barry
5	Reggie Miller
4	Stephen Curry^
4	Larry Bird
3	Dolph Schayes
3	Mark Price
2	Steve Nash
2	Calvin Murphy
2	Larry Siegfried

^ Active.

Assists

9	John Stockton
8	Bob Cousy
6	Oscar Robertson
6	Steve Nash
4	Kevin Porter
3	Magic Johnson
3	Jason Kidd
3	Chris Paul^
3	Russell Westbrook^
2	Andy Phillip
2	Guy Rodgers
2	Lenny Wilkens
2	Isiah Thomas

^ Active.

APG

9	John Stockton
8	Bob Cousy
7	Oscar Robertson
5	Jason Kidd
5	Steve Nash
5	Chris Paul^
4	Magic Johnson
4	Kevin Porter
3	Rajon Rondo^
3	Andy Phillip
3	Russell Westbrook^

^ Active.

Most Points Scored in a Game without Attempting a Free Throw or Three Pointer

Pts			Shooting
48	Hakeem Olajuwon, Hou. Rockets	vs. Den. Nuggets (Jan. 30, 1997)	24-for-40 (.600)
44	Alex English, Den. Nuggets	vs. Uta. Jazz (Mar. 3, 1984)	22-for-32 (.688)
42	George Gervin, S.A. Spurs	@ Hou. Rockets (Jan. 25, 1985)	21-for-26 (.808)
38	Alex English, Den. Nuggets	@ N.Y. Knicks (Dec. 6, 1988)	19-for-31 (.613)
36	Mike Mitchell, S.A. Spurs	vs. Den. Nuggets (Apr. 13, 1982)	18-for-29 (.621)
36	David Robinson, S.A. Spurs	@ G.S. Warriors (Apr. 8, 1995)	18-for-21 (.857)
34	Alex English, Den. Nuggets	@ Hou. Rockets (Mar. 12, 1985)	17-for-24 (.708)
34	Albert King, N.J. Nets	@ Mil. Bucks (Mar. 25, 1986)	17-for-23 (.739)
34	Chris Mullin, G.S. Warriors	@ N.J. Nets (Nov. 22, 1992)	17-for-28 (.607)
34	Al Jefferson, Uta. Jazz	@ Tor. Raptors (Mar. 9, 2011)	17-for-24 (.708)
32	Toby Knight, N.Y. Knicks	@ S.A. Spurs (Feb. 14, 1980)	16-for-21 (.762)
32	Joe Barry Carroll, G.S. Warriors	vs. L.A. Lakers (Nov. 27, 1980)	16-for-24 (.667)
32	Walter Davis, Pho. Suns	vs. Was. Bullets (Feb. 8, 1981)	16-for-25 (.640)
32	Herb Williams, Ind. Pacers	@ Sea. Sonics (Nov. 22, 1986)	16-for-27 (.593)
32	Michael Jordan, Chi. Bulls	@ Sac. Kings (Nov. 22, 1988)	16-for-20 (.800)
32	Kevin Gamble, Bos. Celtics	@ N.Y. Knicks (Feb. 7, 1991)	16-for-20 (.800)
32	Tim Duncan, S.A. Spurs	@ L.A. Clippers (Dec. 16, 2002)	16-for-29 (.552)
32	Al Jefferson, Cha. Bobcats	@ Bos. Celtics (Apr. 11, 2014)	16-for-26 (.615)

Players Scoring 2000 Points, 175 or Less Turnovers, Season

	Pts	TO
Dan Issel, Ken. Colonels[a], 1973–74	2118	171
Mike Mitchell, Cle. Cavaliers, 1980–81	2012	175
Kiki Vandeweghe, Den. Nuggets, 1983–84	2295	156
Kiki Vandeweghe, Por. Blazers, 1986–87	2122	139
Dominique Wilkins, Atl. Hawks, 1989–90	2138	174
Michael Jordan, Chi. Bulls, 1996–97	2431	166
Vince Carter, Tor. Raptors, 2000–01	2070	167
Dirk Nowitzki, Dal. Mavericks, 2002–03	2011	152
Dirk Nowitzki, Dal. Mavericks, 2005–06	2151	156
Michael Redd, Mil. Bucks, 2005–06	2028	170
Dirk Nowitzki, Dal. Mavericks, 2008–09	2094	157
Dirk Nowitzki, Dal. Mavericks, 2009–10	2027	149
Anthony Davis, N.O. Pelicans, 2017–18	2110	162

[a] ABA.

Players Leading League in Points and Turnovers, Career

	Points Leader	Turnovers Leader
Adrian Dantley	2452: Uta. Jazz, 1980–81	299: Uta. Jazz, 1981–82
	2418: Uta. Jazz, 1983–84	
Allen Iverson	2302: Phi. 76ers, 2004–05	337: Phi. 76ers, 1996–97
		344: Phi. 76ers, 2004–05
George McGinnis	2353: Ind. Pacers[a], 1974–75	401: Ind. Pacers[a], 1972–73
		393: Ind. Pacers[a], 1973–74
		422: Ind. Pacers[a], 1974–75
		346: Den. Nuggets, 1978–79
James Harden	2217: Hou. Rockets, 2014–15	295: Hou. Rockets, 2012–13
	2376: Hou. Rockets, 2015–16	321: Hou. Rockets, 2014–15

continued on next page

	Points Leader	**Turnovers Leader**
	2818: Hou. Rockets, 2018–19	374: Hou. Rockets, 2015–16
	2335: Hou. Rockets, 2019–20	464: Hou. Rockets, 2016–17
		387: Hou. Rockets, 2018–19
		308: Hou. Rockets, 2019–20
Jerry Stackhouse	2380: Det. Pistons, 2000–01	311: Det. Pistons, 1999–00
		326: Det. Pistons, 2000–01
Julius Erving	2299: N.Y. Nets[a], 1973–74	342: Vir. Squires[a], 1971–72
	2462: N.Y. Nets[a], 1975–76	
Paul Pierce	2144: Bos. Celtics, 2001–02	303: Bos. Celtics, 2003–04
Russell Westbrook	2558: Ok.C. Thunder, 2016–17	274: Ok.C Thunder, 2008–09
		316: Ok.C Thunder, 2010–11
		381: Ok.C Thunder, 2017–18
		312: Was. Wizards, 2020–21
Shaquille O'Neal	2315: Orl. Magic, 1994–95	307: Orl. Magic, 1992–93
	1289: L.A. Lakers, 1998–99	
	2344: L.A. Lakers, 1999–00	

[a] ABA.

Players Leading Leading League in Points and Turnovers, Same Season

		Pts	**TO**
1974–75	George McGinnis, Ind. Pacers[a]	2353	422
2000–01	Jerry Stackhouse, Det. Pistons	2380	326
2004–05	Allen Iverson, Phi. 76ers	2302	344
2014–15	James Harden, Hou. Rockets	2217	321
2015–16	James Harden, Hou. Rockets	2376	374
2018–19	James Harden, Hou. Rockets	2818	387
2019–20	James Harden, Hou. Rockets	2335	308

[a] ABA.

Most Points in a Game with Perfect FG%, 3P%, and FT%

			FG	**3P**	**FT**
35	Roger Brown, Ind. Pacers[a]	@ Den. Rockets[a] (Oct. 19, 1971)	13	3	6
32	Gary Payton, Sea. Sonics	@ Cle. Cavaliers (Jan. 4, 1995)	14	1	3
31	Charles Barkley, Phi. 76ers	vs. S.A. Spurs (Mar. 24, 1989)	10	2	9
28	Chris Mullin, G.S. Warriors	@ Mia. Heat (Dec. 1, 1990)	11	1	5
26	Julius Randle, N.O. Pelicans	@ Ok.C. Thunder (Nov. 5, 2018)	10	2	4
26	Ish Smith, Was. Wizards	@ Tor. Raptors (Dec. 20, 2019)	9	4	4
24	Mitchell Butler, Was. Bullets	@ S.A. Spurs (Dec. 12, 1994)	8	2	6
24	Muggsy Bogues, Tor. Raptors	vs. Bos. Celtics (Mar. 3, 2000)	6	4	8
24	Matt Barnes, L.A. Lakers	@ Min. T'Wolves (Nov. 19, 2010)	7	5	5
24	Lance Thomas, N.Y. Knicks	vs. Orl. Magic (Dec. 21, 2015)	9	3	3
24	Vince Carter, Mem. Grizzlies	vs. Mil. Bucks (Mar. 13, 2017)	8	6	2
23	Arvydas Sabonis, Por. Blazers	@ G.S. Warriors (Nov. 29, 1995)	8	3	4
23	Mo Williams, Mil. Bucks	@ Atl. Hawks (Nov. 28, 2007)	9	1	4
22	Blue Edwards, Uta. Jazz	@ Pho. Suns (Feb. 19, 1995)	9	2	2
22	José Calderón, Tor. Raptors	vs. N.O. Hornets (Dec. 14, 2008)	8	5	1
22	Danny Green, S.A. Spurs	@ Dal. Mavericks (Dec. 26, 2013)	7	5	3
22	Kyle Korver, Atl. Hawks	@ N.O. Pelicans (Nov. 6, 2015)	8	4	2
22	Ian Clark, G.S. Warriors	@ Por. Blazers (Nov. 1, 2016)	8	3	3
22	Karl-Anthony Towns, Min. T'Wolves	vs. Atl. Hawks (Dec. 26, 2016)	8	3	3

continued on next page

				FG	3P	FT
22	Jaden McDaniels, Min. T'Wolves	vs. Uta. Jazz (Jan. 30, 2022)		9	3	1
21	Micheal Ray Richardson, N.Y. Knicks	@ Uta. Jazz (Nov. 1, 1979)		9	1	2
21	Dana Barros, Phi. 76ers	@ Orl. Magic (Nov. 5, 1994)		6	3	6
21	Sam Perkins, Sea. Sonics	vs. L.A. Clippers (Dec. 14, 1997)		5	4	7
21	T.J. Warren, Pho. Suns	vs. Dal. Mavericks (Apr. 9, 2017)		8	2	3
21	Dwight Powell, Dal. Mavericks	@ G.S. Warriors (Jan. 14, 2020)		9	1	2
20	Chris Mullin, G.S. Warriors	@ Mil. Bucks (Jan. 18, 1996)		8	2	2
20	David Benoit, Uta. Jazz	vs. Mil. Bucks (Mar. 27, 1996)		6	3	5
20	Pat Garrity, Orl. Magic	@ Tor. Raptors (Apr. 1, 2001)		7	3	3
20	Steve Nash, Pho. Suns	vs. Was. Wizards (Dec. 5, 2010)		8	1	3
20	Steve Nash, Pho. Suns	@ Sac. Kings (Jan. 2, 2011)		8	2	2
20	Terance Mann, L.A. Clippers	@ Tor. Raptors (May 11, 2021)		7	1	5

[a] ABA.

Players Shooting 80% FT%, Under 40% FG%, Career (Min. 500 Games Played)

	FT%	FG%	Career GP
Derek Fisher	.817	.399	1287
Dolph Schayes	.849	.380	996
Bob Cousy	.803	.375	924
Carl Braun	.804	.383	788
Jason Williams	.813	.398	788
Howard Komives	.830	.388	742
Gene Shue	.806	.396	699
Ricky Rubio^	.843	.389	665
Sasha Vujačić	.858	.390	581
Chris Whitney	.875	.395	579
Bobby Wanzer	.802	.393	568
Fred Scolari	.818	.321	534
Darrick Martin	.843	.382	514
Erick Strickland	.826	.392	501
Langston Galloway^	.816	.397	452
Matthew Dellavedova	.840	.386	447

^ Active.

Player with 3P% Higher Than FT%, Season
(Min. 40% Shooting from 3P and FT, 50 3P and FT Attempts)

	3P Shooting	FT Shooting
Bruce Bowen, S.A. Spurs, 2002–03	.441 (101–229)	.404 (36–89)
Sasha Pavlović, Cle. Cavaliers, 2008–09	.410 (48–117)	.463 (25–54)

Hit 175 3P, Shoot 40%, Season

	FG%	3P
Isaiah Canaan, Phi. 76ers, 2015–16	.360	176
Rafer Alston, Hou. Rockets, 2006–07	.375	192
Devonte' Graham, Cha. Hornets, 2020–21	.377	179
Devonte' Graham, Cha. Hornets, 2019–20	.382	218
Antoine Walker, Bos. Celtics, 2002–03	.388	188
Wesley Matthews, Dal. Mavericks, 2015–16	.388	189
Quentin Richardson, Pho. Suns, 2004–05	.389	226

continued on next page

	FG%	3P
Tim Hardaway, Mia. Heat, 2000–01	.392	189
Damon Stoudamire, Por. Blazers, 2004–05	.392	181
Antoine Walker, Bos. Celtics, 2001–02	.394	222
John Starks, N.Y. Knicks, 1994–95	.395	217
Baron Davis, N.O. Hornets, 2003–04	.395	187
Randy Foye, Uta. Jazz, 2012–13	.397	178
Jamal Crawford, N.Y. Knicks, 2004–05	.398	185
Louie Dampier, Ken. Colonels[a], 1969–70	.399	198

[a] ABA.

Higher 3P% than 2P%, Season (Min. 100 3P and 40% 3P%)

Diff		3P% (3P)	2P% (2P)
.082	Shane Battier, Mia. Heat, 2012–13	.430 (136)	.348 (16)
.068	Eric Gordon, N.O. Pelicans, 2014–15	.448 (141)	.380 (144)
.058	Steve Novak, N.Y. Knicks, 2012–13	.425 (149)	.367 (29)
.054	Eric Piatkowski, L.A. Clippers, 2001–02	.466 (111)	.412 (96)
.045	Lindsey Hunter, Det. Pistons, 1995–96	.405 (117)	.360 (122)
.039	James Jones, Mia. Heat, 2010–11	.429 (123)	.390 (23)
.034	Tim Legler, Was. Bullets, 1995–96	.522 (128)	.488 (105)
.032	Jason Kapono, Mia. Heat, 2006–07	.514 (108)	.482 (170)
.032	Randy Foye, Uta. Jazz, 2012–13	.410 (178)	.378 (115)
.029	Jerryd Bayless, Mil. Bucks, 2015–16	.437 (101)	.408 (84)
.027	Steve Smith, S.A. Spurs, 2001–02	.472 (116)	.445 (194)
.026	Chauncey Billups, Det. Pistons, 2005–06	.433 (184)	.407 (239)
.024	Joe Johnson, Pho. Suns, 2004–05	.478 (177)	.454 (367)
.023	Mike Bibby, Atl. Hawks/Was. Wizards, 2010–11	.440 (153)	.417 (95)
.023	Anfernee Simons, Por. Blazers, 2020–21	.426 (120)	.403 (48)
.023	Sam Mack, Van. Grizzlies, 1997–98	.409 (110)	.386 (112)
.022	Kyle Korver, Atl. Hawks, 2014–15	.492 (221)	.470 (71)
.020	Hedo Türkoğlu, S.A. Spurs, 2003–04	.419 (101)	.399 (161)
.019	Daniel Gibson, Cle. Cavaliers, 2007–08	.440 (118)	.421 (83)
.019	Ben Gordon, Chi. Bulls, 2005–06	.435 (166)	.416 (320)
.017	Steve Kerr, Chi. Bulls, 1995–96	.515 (122)	.498 (122)
.015	D.J. Augustin, Cha. Bobcats, 2008–09	.439 (108)	.424 (159)
.014	Matt Carroll, Cha. Bobcats, 2007–08	.436 (105)	.422 (147)
.013	Lindsey Hunter, Det. Pistons, 1999–00	.432 (168)	.419 (211)
.010	Luther Head, Hou. Rockets, 2006–07	.441 (177)	.431 (129)
.009	Kyle Korver, Chi. Bulls, 2011–12	.435 (118)	.426 (60)
.009	Richard Jefferson, S.A. Spurs/G.S. Warriors, 2011–12	.420 (113)	.411 (90)
.005	Jason Kidd, Dal. Mavericks, 2009–10	.425 (176)	.420 (108)
.005	Daniel Gibson, Cle. Cavaliers, 2010–11	.403 (118)	.398 (146)
.004	Stephen Curry, G.S. Warriors, 2012–13	.453 (272)	.449 (354)
.003	Peja Stojaković, N.O. Hornets, 2007–08	.441 (231)	.438 (220)
.003	Damon Jones, Cle. Cavaliers, 2007–08	.417 (115)	.414 (36)
.003	Derek Fisher, L.A. Lakers, 2001–02	.413 (144)	.410 (130)
.003	James Posey, Mia. Heat, 2005–06	.403 (117)	.400 (42)
.002	Cuttino Mobley, Orl. Magic/Sac. Kings, 2004–05	.439 (150)	.437 (258)
.002	Mike Scott, L.A. Clippers/Phi. 76ers, 2018–19	.401 (101)	.399 (67)
.001	Marcus Morris, L.A. Clippers, 2020–21	.473 (140)	.472 (136)
.001	Pat Garrity, Orl. Magic, 2001–02	.427 (169)	.426 (158)

Players Averaging 15 Points, 5 Rebounds, and 5 Assists Per Game with a 90% FT%, Season (Min. 40 Games Played)

	PPG	RPG	APG	FT%
Rick Barry, G.S. Warriors, 1974–75	30.6	5.7	6.2	.904
Rick Barry, G.S. Warriors, 1975–76	21.0	6.1	6.1	.923
Rick Barry, G.S. Warriors, 1976–77	21.8	5.3	6.0	.916
Rick Barry, G.S. Warriors, 1977–78	23.1	5.5	5.4	.924
Larry Bird, Bos. Celtics, 1986–87	28.1	9.2	7.6	.910
Larry Bird, Bos. Celtics, 1987–88	29.9	9.3	6.1	.916
Magic Johnson, L.A. Lakers, 1988–89	22.5	7.9	12.8	.911
Larry Bird, Bos. Celtics, 1989–90	24.3	9.5	7.5	.930
Magic Johnson, L.A. Lakers, 1990–91	19.4	7.0	12.5	.906
Larry Bird, Bos. Celtics, 1991–92	20.2	9.6	6.8	.926
Stephen Curry, G.S. Warriors, 2015–16	30.1	5.4	6.7	.908
Stephen Curry, G.S. Warriors, 2017–18	26.4	5.1	6.1	.921
Chris Paul, Hou. Rockets, 2017–18	18.6	5.4	7.9	.919
Stephen Curry, G.S. Warriors, 2018–19	27.3	5.3	5.2	.916
Stephen Curry, G.S. Warriors, 2020–21	32.0	5.5	5.8	.916

Percent of 2P Field Goals to 3P Field Goals, Season (League Average)

Season	FGM/FGA (FG%)	2PM/2PA (2P%)	3PM/3PA (3P%)	Percent of 2PM to 3PM, Season	Percent of 2PA to 3PA, Season
1979–80	3579/7433 (.481)	3515/7205 (.488)	64/227 (.282)	98.2%/1.8%	96.9%/3.1%
1980–81	3523/7251 (.486)	3482/7085 (.491)	41/166 (.245)	98.8%/1.2%	97.7%/2.3%
1981–82	3554/7236 (.491)	3504/7048 (.497)	49/187 (.262)	98.6%/1.4%	97.4%/2.6%
1982–83	3569/7352 (.485)	3525/7167 (.492)	44/185 (.238)	98.8%/1.2%	97.5%/2.5%
1983–84	3566/7245 (.492)	3517/7050 (.499)	49/195 (.250)	98.6%/1.4%	97.3%/2.7%
1984–85	3588/7306 (.491)	3516/7049 (.499)	73/257 (.282)	98%/2.0%	96.5%/3.5%
1985–86	3542/7268 (.487)	3465/6994 (.495)	77/274 (.282)	97.8%/2.2%	96.2%/3.8%
1986–87	3497/7281 (.480)	3380/6893 (.490)	117/388 (.301)	96.7%/3.3%	94.7%/5.3%
1987–88	3455/7193 (.480)	3326/6783 (.490)	130/410 (.316)	96.3%/3.7%	94.3%/5.7%
1988–89	3482/7295 (.477)	3309/6758 (.490)	173/537 (.323)	95%/5.0%	92.6%/7.4%
1989–90	3404/7146 (.476)	3225/6605 (.488)	179/541 (.331)	94.7%/5.3%	92.4%/7.6%
1990–91	3391/7150 (.474)	3204/6565 (.488)	187/586 (.320)	94.5%/5.5%	91.8%/8.2%
1991–92	3384/7163 (.472)	3177/6537 (.486)	207/626 (.331)	93.9%/6.1%	91.3%/8.7%
1992–93	3335/7048 (.473)	3088/6314 (.489)	247/734 (.336)	92.6%/7.4%	89.6%/10.4%
1993–94	3225/6924 (.466)	2954/6113 (.483)	270/811 (.333)	91.6%/8.4%	88.3%/11.7%
1994–95	3115/6682 (.466)	2665/5427 (.491)	450/1255 (.359)	85.6%/14.4%	81.2%/18.8%
1995–96	3038/6575 (.462)	2555/5259 (.486)	483/1316 (.367)	84.1%/15.9%	80%/20%
1996–97	2958/6503 (.455)	2462/5126 (.480)	496/1377 (.360)	83.2%/16.8%	78.8%/21.2%
1997–98	2944/6536 (.450)	2584/5493 (.470)	360/1042 (.346)	87.8%/22.2%	84%/16%
1998–99	1709/3910 (.437)	1486/3252 (.457)	223/658 (.339)	87%/13%	83.2%/16.8%
1999–00	3020/6732 (.449)	2623/5607 (.468)	397/1125 (.353)	86.9%/13.1%	83.3%/16.7%
2000–01	2926/6609 (.443)	2529/5485 (.461)	397/1124 (.354)	86.4%/13.6%	83%/17%
2001–02	2966/6664 (.445)	2538/5455 (.465)	428/1209 (.354)	85.6%/14.4%	81.9%/18.1%
2002–03	2929/6624 (.442)	2508/5421 (.463)	421/1204 (.349)	85.6%/14.4%	81.8%/18.2%
2003–04	2871/6545 (.439)	2446/5321 (.460)	425/1224 (.347)	85.2%/14.8%	81.3%/18.7%
2004–05	2948/6588 (.447)	2489/5296 (.470)	459/1292 (.356)	84.4%/15.6%	80.4%/19.6%
2005–06	2939/6477 (.454)	2469/5167 (.478)	470/1310 (.358)	84%/16%	79.8%/20.2%
2006–07	2995/6536 (.458)	2498/5147 (.485)	498/1389 (.358)	83.4%/16.6%	78.7%/21.3%
2007–08	3056/6683 (.457)	2518/5199 (.484)	537/1485 (.362)	82.4%/17.6%	77.8%/22.2%

continued on next page

Season	FGM/FGA (FG%)	2PM/2PA (2P%)	3PM/3PA (3P%)	Percent of 2PM to 3PM, Season	Percent of 2PA to 3PA, Season
2008–09	3044/6635 (.459)	2499/5149 (.485)	545/1486 (.367)	82.1%/17.9%	77.6%/22.4%
2009–10	3091/6700 (.461)	2564/5212 (.492)	527/1487 (.355)	83%/17%	77.8%/22.2%
2010–11	3054/6660 (.459)	2525/5183 (.487)	530/1477 (.358)	82.7%/17.3%	77.8%/22.2%
2011–12	2407/5374 (.448)	1930/4401 (.439)	423/1213 (.349)	80.2%/19.8%	81.9%/18.1%
2012–13	3043/6720 (.453)	2456/5085 (.483)	587/1636 (.359)	80.7%/19.3%	75.7%/24.3%
2013–14	3093/6806 (.454)	2458/5040 (.488)	635/1766 (.360)	79.5%/20.5%	74.1%/25.9%
2014–15	3076/6852 (.449)	2433/5014 (.485)	643/1838 (.350)	79.1%/20.9%	73.2%/26.8%
2015–16	3136/6935 (.452)	2437/4960 (.491)	698/1975 (.354)	77.7%/22.3%	71.5%/28.5%
2016–17	3202/7004 (.457)	2410/4790 (.503)	792/2214 (.358)	75.3%/24.7%	68.4%/31.6%
2017–18	3248/7057 (.460)	2388/4679 (.510)	738/1967 (.362)	73.5%/26.5%	66.3%/33.7%
2018–19	3369/7315 (.461)	2437/4691 (.520)	932/2625 (.355)	72.3%/27.7%	64.1%/35.9%
2019–20	2885/6271 (.460)	2023/3862 (.524)	862/2408 (.358)	70.1%/29.9%	61.6%/38.4%
2020–21	2967/6366 (.466)	2053/3872 (.530)	914/2494 (.367)	69.2%/30.8%	60.8%/39.2%
2021–22	3331/7224 (.461)	2311/4340 (.533)	1020/2885 (.354)	69.4%/30.6%	60.1%/39.9%

1998–99: 50-game season.

2011–12: 66-game season.

2019–20: 65-to-75-game season.

2020–21: 72-game season.

Players with 30 Points, 5 Steals, Zero Turnovers, and Perfect FT%, Game

	Pts	Stl	FT
Maurice Lucas, Spirits of St.L.[a] ... vs. Ken. Colonels[a] (Mar. 9, 1975)	30	6	4
Dennis Johnson, Bos. Celtics ... vs. Ind. Pacers (Nov. 13, 1985)	30	6	4
Michael Jordan, Chi. Bulls ... vs. Sac. Kings (Feb. 22, 1991)	34	6	11
Gary Payton, Sea. Sonics ... @ Dal. Mavericks (Nov. 27, 1992)	31	5	8
Doug Christie, Sac. Kings[*] ... vs. L.A. Lakers (Nov. 16, 2000)	32	5	6
Paul George, Ind. Pacers ... @ Dal. Mavericks (Feb. 3, 2012)	30	5	1
OG Anunoby, Tor. Raptors[*] ... @ Den. Nuggets (Mar. 1, 2020)	32	7	5
Gary Trent Jr., Tor. Raptors ... @ Mia. Heat (Jan. 29, 2022)	33	5	2

[a] ABA.

[*] Team lost game.

Most Double-Doubles (Points and Assists), Season

69 ... John Stockton, Uta. Jazz ... 1991–92	57 ... Magic Johnson, L.A. Lakers ... 1990–91
68 ... John Stockton, Uta. Jazz ... 1990–91	56 ... Tiny Archibald, K.C.-Oma. Kings ... 1972–73
67 ... John Stockton, Uta. Jazz ... 1988–89	56 ... Chris Paul, N.O. Hornets ... 2007–08
65 ... Isiah Thomas, Det. Pistons ... 1984–85	53 ... Steve Nash, Pho. Suns ... 2006–07
64 ... John Stockton, Uta. Jazz ... 1989–90	52 ... Oscar Robertson, Cin. Royals ... 1963–64
61 ... Kevin Johnson, Pho. Suns ... 1988–89	52 ... Oscar Robertson, Cin. Royals ... 1964–65
61 ... Magic Johnson, L.A. Lakers ... 1988–89	52 ... Magic Johnson, L.A. Lakers ... 1983–84
60 ... Magic Johnson, L.A. Lakers ... 1984–85	52 ... Magic Johnson, L.A. Lakers ... 1985–86
60 ... James Harden, Hou. Rockets ... 2016–17	52 ... Deron Williams, Uta. Jazz ... 2007–08
59 ... Magic Johnson, L.A. Lakers ... 1986–87	51 ... Oscar Robertson, Cin. Royals ... 1965–66
59 ... John Stockton, Uta. Jazz ... 1994–95	50 ... Oscar Robertson, Cin. Royals ... 1961–62
58 ... John Stockton, Uta. Jazz ... 1987–88	50 ... Kevin Porter, Det. Pistons ... 1978–79
58 ... John Stockton, Uta. Jazz ... 1992–93	50 ... Chris Paul, N.O. Hornets ... 2008–09
58 ... John Stockton, Uta. Jazz ... 1993–94	50 ... Russell Westbrook, Ok.C. Thunder ... 2016–17
57 ... Isiah Thomas, Det. Pistons ... 1983–84	50 ... Russell Westbrook, Was. Wizards ... 2020–21

Most Double-Doubles (Points and Assists), Career

714 .... John Stockton	319 .... Kevin Johnson	242 .... James Harden^
543 .... Magic Johnson	297 .... LeBron James^	226 .... Norm Nixon
491 .... Chris Paul^	279 .... Tim Hardaway	222 .... Tiny Archibald
473 .... Oscar Robertson	275 .... Deron Williams	221 .... Guy Rodgers
436 .... Steve Nash	271 .... Rod Strickland	217 .... Lenny Wilkens
421 .... Isiah Thomas	252 .... John Wall^	210 .... Stephon Marbury
402 .... Jason Kidd	242 .... Mark Jackson	210 .... Rajon Rondo^
370 .... Russell Westbrook^	242 .... Gary Payton	

^ Active.

Players with 10 Assists, 5 Steals, Zero Turnovers, and 5 or Less Points, Game

	Ast	Stl	Pts
Maurice Cheeks, Phi. 76ers .... vs. Chi. Bulls (Nov. 11, 1981) 10		5	4
Doc Rivers, Atl. Hawks .... vs. Por. Blazers (Feb. 28, 1987) 17		7	5
Sidney Lowe, Min. T'Wolves* .... @ G.S. Warriors (Mar. 20, 1990) 17		6	3
Morlon Wiley, Atl. Hawks .... vs. Hou. Rockets (Jan. 6, 1992) 14		5	3
Greg Grant, Phi. 76ers .... vs. Dal. Mavericks (Dec. 6, 1995) 11		6	4
Bobby Hurley, Sac. Kings* .... vs. Pho. Suns (Apr. 10, 1997) 14		5	2
David Wesley, Cha. Hornets* .... @ Mil. Bucks (Dec. 4, 1997) 10		5	2
Eric Snow, Phi. 76ers .... vs. Was. Wizards (Apr. 12, 2000) 10		5	4

* Team lost game.

Player Averaging 50% FG%, 40% 3P%, and 90% FT%, Season
(Min. 1000 Minutes Played)

	FG%	3P%	FT%
Larry Bird, Bos. Celtics, 1986–87 .... .525 .... .400 .... .910			
Larry Bird, Bos. Celtics, 1987–88 .... .527 .... .414 .... .916			
Mark Price, Cle. Cavaliers, 1988–89 .... .526 .... .441 .... .901			
Reggie Miller, Ind. Pacers, 1993–94 .... .503 .... .421 .... .908			
Steve Kerr, Chi. Bulls, 1995–96 .... .506 .... .515 .... .929			
Steve Nash, Pho. Suns, 2005–06 .... .512 .... .439 .... .921			
Dirk Nowitzki, Dal. Mavericks, 2006–07 .... .502 .... .416 .... .904			
José Calderón, Tor. Raptors, 2007–08 .... .519 .... .429 .... .908			
Steve Nash, Pho. Suns, 2007–08 .... .504 .... .470 .... .906			
Steve Nash, Pho. Suns, 2008–09 .... .503 .... .439 .... .933			
Steve Nash, Pho. Suns, 2009–10 .... .507 .... .426 .... .938			
Kevin Durant, Ok.C. Thunder, 2012–13 .... .510 .... .416 .... .905			
Stephen Curry, G.S. Warriors, 2015–16 .... .504 .... .454 .... .908			
Malcolm Brogdon, Mil. Bucks, 2018–19 .... .505 .... .426 .... .928			
Kyrie Irving, Brk. Nets, 2020–21 .... .506 .... .402 .... .922			

Most Four-Point Plays, Career

54 .... Jamal Crawford	17 .... Kobe Bryant	13 .... Ray Allen
36 .... James Harden	17 .... Stephen Curry	10 .... Allen Iverson
25 .... J.J. Redick	14 .... Dirk Nowitzki	
23 .... Reggie Miller	14 .... Kevin Durant	

Highest Box Plus/Minus' (BPM), Season (Min. 20 Minutes Per Game)

BPM		BPM	
13.7	Nikola Jokić**, Den. Nuggets, 2021–22	11.0	James Harden, Hou. Rockets, 2018–19
13.2	LeBron James**, Cle. Cavaliers, 2008–09	10.9	LeBron James, Cle. Cavaliers, 2007–08
13.0	Michael Jordan**, Chi. Bulls, 1987–88	10.9	LeBron James**, Mia. Heat, 2011–12
12.1	Nikola Jokić**, Den. Nuggets, 2020–21	10.8	Michael Jordan, Chi. Bulls, 1986–87
12.0	Michael Jordan**, Chi. Bulls, 1990–91	10.6	Julius Erving**, N.Y. Nets[a], 1975–76
11.9	Michael Jordan, Chi. Bulls, 1988–89	10.6	Dwyane Wade, Mia. Heat, 2008–09
11.9	David Robinson, S.A. Spurs, 1993–94	10.5	Michael Jordan**, Chi. Bulls, 1995–96
11.9	Stephen Curry**, G.S. Warriors, 2015–16	10.5	Tracy McGrady, Orl. Magic, 2002–03
11.8	LeBron James**, Cle. Cavaliers, 2009–10	10.4	Chris Paul, N.O. Hornets, 2007–08
11.7	LeBron James**, Mia. Heat, 2012–13	10.4	Giannis Antetokounmpo**, Mil. Bucks, 2018–19
11.5	Giannis Antetokounmpo**, Mil. Bucks, 2019–20	10.2	Kevin Garnett**, Min. T'Wolves, 2003–04
11.2	Michael Jordan, Chi. Bulls, 1989–90	10.2	Kevin Durant**, Ok.C. Thunder, 2013–14
11.2	Michael Jordan, Chi. Bulls, 1992–93	10.1	Magic Johnson**, L.A. Lakers, 1989–90
11.2	Giannis Antetokounmpo, Mil. Bucks, 2021–22	10.1	Kawhi Leonard, S.A. Spurs, 2017–18
11.1	Russell Westbrook**, Ok.C. Thunder, 2016–17	10.0	Kevin Durant, Ok.C. Thunder, 2014–15
11.0	Chris Paul, N.O. Hornets, 2008–09		

* Box Plus/Minus is "A box score estimate of the points per 1000 possessions a player contributed above a league-average player, translated to an average team." (basketball-reference.com)

** Won MVP.

[a] ABA.

Highest Offensive Win Share' (OWS), Season

OWS		PPG	FG%/3P%/FT%	APG
15.2	Michael Jordan, Chi. Bulls, 1987–88	35.0	.535/.132/.841	5.9
14.9	Michael Jordan, Chi. Bulls, 1990–91	31.5	.539/.312/.851	5.5
14.8	Kevin Durant, Ok.C. Thunder, 2013–14	32.0	.503/.391/.873	5.5
14.7	Michael Jordan, Chi. Bulls, 1989–90	33.6	.526/.376/.848	6.3
14.6	Michael Jordan, Chi. Bulls, 1988–89	32.5	.538/.276/.850	8.0
14.6	LeBron James, Mia. Heat, 2012–13	26.8	.565/.406/.753	7.3
14.2	Michael Jordan, Chi. Bulls, 1995–96	30.4	.495/.427/.834	4.3
13.8	Stephen Curry, G.S. Warriors, 2015–16	30.1	.504/.454/.908	6.7
13.7	LeBron James, Cle. Cavaliers, 2008–09	28.4	.489/.344/.780	7.2
13.6	Kevin Durant, Ok.C. Thunder, 2012–13	28.1	.510/.416/.905	4.6
13.5	Dirk Nowitzki, Dal. Mavericks, 2005–06	26.6	.480/.406/.901	2.8
13.4	Charles Barkley, Phi. 76ers, 1987–88	28.3	.587/.280/.751	3.2
13.3	David Robinson, S.A. Spurs, 1993–94	29.8	.507/.345/.749	4.8
13.3	Michael Jordan, Chi. Bulls, 1996–97	29.6	.486/.374/.833	4.3
13.3	Chris Paul, N.O. Hornets, 2008–09	22.8	.503/.364/.868	11.0
13.3	LeBron James, Cle. Cavaliers, 2009–10	29.7	.503/.333/.767	8.6
13.2	Charles Barkley, Phi. 76ers, 1988–89	25.8	.579/.216/.753	4.1
13.2	Tracy McGrady, Orl. Magic, 2002–03	32.1	.457/.386/.793	5.5
13.2	Chris Paul, N.O. Hornets, 2007–08	21.1	.488/.369/.851	11.6
13.1	Charles Barkley, Phi. 76ers, 1989–90	25.2	.600/.217/.749	3.9
13.0	Adrian Dantley, Uta. Jazz, 1983–84	30.6	.558/.250/.859	3.9
12.9	Chris Paul, L.A. Clippers, 2014–15	19.1	.485/.398/.900	10.2
12.8	Magic Johnson, L.A. Lakers, 1989–90	22.3	.480/.384/.890	11.5
12.7	Chauncey Billups, Det. Pistons, 2005–06	18.5	.418/.433/.894	8.6
12.3	Adrian Dantley, Uta. Jazz, 1980–81	30.7	.559/.286/.806	4.0

continued on next page

OWS		PPG	FG%/3P%/FT%	APG
12.3	LeBron James, Mia. Heat, 2013–14	27.1	.567/.379/.750	6.3
12.2	James Harden, Hou. Rockets, 2014–15	27.4	.440/.375/.868	7.0
12.2	Nikola Jokić, Den. Nuggets, 2020–21	26.4	.566/.388/.868	8.3
12.1	Magic Johnson, L.A. Lakers, 1986–87	23.9	.522/.205/.848	12.2
12.1	Magic Johnson, L.A. Lakers, 1988–89	22.5	.509/.314/.911	12.8
12.1	Michael Jordan, Chi. Bulls, 1991–92	30.1	.519/.270/.832	6.1
12.1	Shaquille O'Neal, Orl. Magic, 1993–94	29.3	.599/.000/.554	2.4
12.1	Karl Malone, Uta. Jazz, 1997–98	27.0	.530/.333/.761	3.9
12.0	Michael Jordan, Chi. Bulls, 1992–93	32.6	.495/.352/.837	5.5
12.0	LeBron James, Cle. Cavaliers, 2005–06	31.4	.480/.335/.738	6.6
11.9	Adrian Dantley, Uta. Jazz, 1981–82	30.3	.570/.333/.792	4.0
11.9	Michael Jordan, Chi. Bulls, 1986–87	37.1	.482/.182/.857	4.6
11.8	Dirk Nowitzki, Dal. Mavericks, 2006–07	24.6	.502/.416/.904	3.4
11.7	Moses Malone, Hou. Rockets, 1981–82	31.1	.519/.000/.762	1.8
11.7	Reggie Miller, Ind. Pacers, 1990–91	22.6	.512/.348/.918	4.0
11.7	Shaquille O'Neal, L.A. Lakers, 1999–00	29.7	.574/.000/.524	3.8
11.6	Karl Malone, Uta. Jazz, 1996–97	27.4	.550/.000/.755	4.5
11.6	Kobe Bryant, L.A. Lakers, 2005–06	35.4	.450/.347/.850	4.5
11.6	James Harden, Hou. Rockets, 2017–18	30.4	.449/.367/.858	8.8
11.5	Ray Allen, Mil. Bucks, 2000–01	22.0	.480/.433/.888	4.6
11.5	Stephen Curry, G.S. Warriors, 2014–15	23.8	.487/.443/.914	7.7
11.5	James Harden, Hou. Rockets, 2016–17	29.1	.440/.347/.847	11.2
11.4	Peja Stojaković, Sac. Kings, 2003–04	24.2	.480/.433/.927	2.1
11.4	James Harden, Hou. Rockets, 2018–19	36.1	.442/.368/.879	7.5
11.3	Amar'e Stoudemire, Pho. Suns, 2004–05	26.0	.559/.188/.733	1.6
11.2	Larry Bird, Bos. Celtics, 1987–88	29.9	.527/.414/.916	6.1
11.2	Magic Johnson, L.A. Lakers, 1990–91	19.4	.477/.320/.906	12.5
11.1	David Robinson, S.A. Spurs, 1995–96	25.0	.516/.333/.761	3.0
11.1	Shaquille O'Neal, L.A. Lakers, 2000–01	28.7	.572/.000/.513	3.7
11.1	Kevin Durant, Ok.C. Thunder, 2009–10	30.1	.476/.365/.900	2.8
11.0	Penny Hardaway, Orl. Magic, 1995–96	21.7	.513/.314/.767	7.1
11.0	Kobe Bryant, L.A. Lakers, 2002–03	30.0	.451/.383/.843	5.9
11.0	Gilbert Arenas, Was. Wizards, 2005–06	29.3	.447/.369/.820	6.1
11.0	Kevin Durant, Ok.C. Thunder, 2015–16	28.2	.505/.387/.898	5.0
11.0	LeBron James, Cle. Cavaliers, 2017–18	27.5	.542/.367/.731	9.1

* Offensive Win Share is "An estimate of the number of wins contributed by a player due to offense." (basketball-reference.com)

Most Points by Players Born in the Same State of the Team They Played For

Georgia	Hawks (Atlanta)	10,371	Josh Smith (College Park)
Massachusetts	Celtics (Boston)	3109	Dana Barros (Boston)
New York	Nets (Brooklyn/Long Island)	7104	Julius Erving[a] (Roosevelt)
New Jersey	Nets (East Rutherford)	3323	Mike O'Koren (Jersey City)
New York	Knicks (Manhattan)	10,449	Carl Braun (Brooklyn)
North Carolina	Hornets/Bobcats (Charlotte)	3289	Kenny Gattison (Wilmington)
Illinois	Bulls (Chicago)	10,233	Jerry Sloan (McLeansboro)
Ohio	Cavaliers (Cleveland)	23,119	LeBron James (Akron)
Texas	Mavericks (Dallas)	3340	Wesley Matthews (San Antonio)
Colorado	Nuggets (Denver)	4378	Chauncey Billups (Denver)
Michigan	Pistons (Detroit)	9023	John Long (Romulus)
California	Warriors (Oakland)	12,347	Klay Thompson^ (Los Angeles)
Pennsylvania	Warriors (Philadelphia)	16,266	Paul Arizin (Philadelphia)

continued on next page

Texas	Rockets (Houston)	1893	Dwight Jones (Houston)
Indiana	Pacers (Indianapolis)	3924	George Hill (Indianapolis)
California	Clippers (Los Angeles/San Diego)	4467	Freeman Williams (Los Angeles)
Tennessee	Grizzlies (Memphis)	3148	Lorenzen Wright (Memphis)
Canada	Raptors (Toronto)	1417	Cory Joseph (Toronto)
California	Lakers (Los Angeles)	13,044	Gail Goodrich (Los Angeles)
Minnesota	Lakers (Minneapolis)	4156	Dick Garmaker (Hibbing)
Minnesota	T'Wolves (Minneapolis)	1310	Randy Breuer (Lake City)
Louisiana	Pelicans/Hornets (New Orleans)	1416	Marcus Thornton (Baton Rouge)
Oklahoma	Thunder (Oklahoma City)	922	Terrance Ferguson (Tulsa)
Washington	Sonics (Seattle)	518	Rod Derline (Elma)
Florida	Magic (Orlando)	8298	Tracy McGrady (Bartow)
Pennsylvania	76ers (Philadelphia)	7673	Fred Carter (Philadelphia)
Arizona	Suns (Phoenix)	819	Bernard Thompson (Phoenix)
Oregon	Blazers (Portland)	6745	Damon Stoudamire (Portland)
California	Kings (Sacramento)	4677	Reggie Theus (Inglewood)
Texas	Spurs (San Antonio)	7325	LaMarcus Aldridge (Dallas)
Utah	Jazz (Salt Lake City)	1396	Tom Chambers (Ogden)
Louisiana	Jazz (New Orleans)	3829	Aaron James (New Orleans)
Washington, D.C.	Wizards/Bullets	2004	Dave Bing (Washington, D.C.)

^ Active with franchise.

ᵃ ABA.

2

DEFENSE

Rebounds

Most Rebounds by Decade*

1950–51–1959–60

9372	Dolph Schayes
7324	Larry Fouse
6814	Bob Pettit
6684	Harry Gallatin
5940	Vern Mikkelsen
5897	Bill Russell
5856	Neil Johnston
5583	Joe Graboski
5333	Clyde Lovellette
5186	Jack Coleman

1960–61–1969–70**

17,392	Wilt Chamberlain
15,723	Bill Russell
10,423	Walt Bellamy
9782	Jerry Lucas
9195	Elgin Baylor
8164	Nate Thurmond
8152	Bailey Howell
7233	Bill Bridges
7154	Ray Scott
6967	Johnny Green

1970–71–1979–80**

11,156	Kareem Abdul-Jabbar
11,075	Elvin Hayes
10,235	Wes Unseld
10,170	Dave Cowens
8765	Sam Lacey
8257	Paul Silas
8242	Bob Lanier
6888	Bob McAdoo
6736	Clifford Ray
6433	Spencer Haywood

1980–81–1989–90

9891	Moses Malone
8737	Bill Laimbeer
8376	Buck Williams
8208	Robert Parish
7776	Jack Sikma
7179	Larry Bird
6892	Larry Smith
6340	James Donaldson
6119	Mychal Thompson
5954	Kevin McHale

1990–91–1999–00

9343	Dennis Rodman
8439	Dikembe Mutombo
8295	Karl Malone
7668	David Robinson
7490	Shawn Kemp
7444	Patrick Ewing
7395	Kevin Willis
7125	Hakeem Olajuwon
6977	Charles Barkley
6615	Shaquille O'Neal

2000–01–2009–10

8869	Tim Duncan
8838	Kevin Garnett
8432	Ben Wallace
7529	Shawn Marion
7108	Dirk Nowitzki
6723	Marcus Camby
6306	Shaquille O'Neal
6297	Antawn Jamison
6189	Dwight Howard
6171	Elton Brand

2010–11–2019–20

8862	DeAndre Jordan
8288	Andre Drummond
7502	Dwight Howard
6552	Kevin Love
6238	LaMarcus Aldridge
6131	DeMarcus Cousins
6110	Nikola Vučević
5764	Marcin Gortat
5547	Serge Ibaka
5544	LeBron James

2020–21–2021–22

1928	Rudy Gobert
1799	Nikola Jokić
1780	Clint Capela
1621	Nikola Vučević
1619	Jonas Valančiūnas
1494	Domantas Sabonis
1449	Giannis Antetokounmpo
1439	Julius Randle
1335	Joel Embiid
1330	Russell Westbrook

* Rebounds were first recorded as a stat in the NBA beginning with the 1950–51 season.

** Includes ABA.

Evolution of Rebounds Record

NBA

1950–51.......... Dolph Schayes, Syr. Nationals...... 1080
1953–54.......... Harry Gallatin, N.Y. Knicks.......... 1098
1955–56.......... Bob Pettit, St.L. Hawks.................. 1164
1956–57.......... Maurice Stokes, Roc. Royals......... 1256
1957–58.......... Bill Russell, Bos. Celtics................ 1564
1958–59.......... Bill Russell, Bos. Celtics................ 1612
1959–60.......... Wilt Chamberlain, Phi. Warriors .. 1941
1960–61.......... Wilt Chamberlain, Phi. Warriors .. 2149

ABA

1967–68 .... Mel Daniels, Min. Muskies 1213
1968–69 .... Mel Daniels, Ind. Pacers 1256
1969–70 .... Spencer Haywood, Den. Rockets 1637

Most Rebounds, Season

NBA

2149 .... Wilt Chamberlain, Phi. Warriors, 1960–61
2052 .... Wilt Chamberlain, Phi. Warriors, 1961–62
1957 .... Wilt Chamberlain, Phi. 76ers, 1966–67
1952 .... Wilt Chamberlain, Phi. 76ers, 1967–68
1946 .... Wilt Chamberlain, S.F. Warriors, 1962–63
1943 .... Wilt Chamberlain, Phi. 76ers, 1965–66
1941 .... Wilt Chamberlain, Phi. Warriors, 1959–60
1930 .... Bill Russell, Bos. Celtics, 1963–64
1878 .... Bill Russell, Bos. Celtics, 1964–65
1868 .... Bill Russell, Bos. Celtics, 1960–61
1843 .... Bill Russell, Bos. Celtics, 1962–63
1790 .... Bill Russell, Bos. Celtics, 1961–62
1787 .... Wilt Chamberlain, S.F. Warriors, 1963–64
1779 .... Bill Russell, Bos. Celtics, 1965–66
1778 .... Bill Russell, Bos. Celtics, 1959–60
1712 .... Wilt Chamberlain, L.A. Lakers, 1968–69
1700 .... Bill Russell, Bos. Celtics, 1966–67
1673 .... Wilt Chamberlain, S.F. Warriors/Phi. 76ers, 1964–65
1668 .... Jerry Lucas, Cin. Royals, 1965–66
1612 .... Bill Russell, Bos. Celtics, 1958–59

ABA

1637 .... Spencer Haywood, Den. Rockets, 1969–70
1538 .... Artis Gilmore, Ken. Colonels, 1973–74
1491 .... Artis Gilmore, Ken. Colonels, 1971–72
1476 .... Artis Gilmore, Ken. Colonels, 1972–73
1475 .... Mel Daniels, Ind. Pacers, 1970–71
1462 .... Mel Daniels, Ind. Pacers, 1969–70
1454 .... Julius Keye, Den. Rockets, 1970–71
1361 .... Artis Gilmore, Ken. Colonels, 1974–75
1332 .... Red Robbins, N.O. Buccaneers, 1969–70
1319 .... Julius Erving, Vir. Squires, 1971–72
1303 .... Artis Gilmore, Ken. Colonels, 1975–76
1297 .... Mel Daniels, Ind. Pacers, 1971–72
1279 .... Swen Nater, S.A. Spurs, 1974–75
1256 .... Mel Daniels, Ind. Pacers, 1968–69
1247 .... Mel Daniels, Ind. Pacers, 1972–73
1217 .... Gerald Govan, N.O. Buccaneers, 1969–70
1213 .... Mel Daniels, Min. Muskies, 1967–68
1213 .... Mike Lewis, Pit. Condors, 1970–71
1209 .... Moses Malone, Uta. Stars, 1974–75
1202 .... Marvin Barnes, Spirits of St.L., 1974–75

Most Rebounds, Career*

23,924 .... Wilt Chamberlain
21,620 .... Bill Russell
17,834 .... Moses Malone
17,440 .... Kareem Abdul-Jabbar
16,330 .... Artis Gilmore
16,279 .... Elvin Hayes
15,091 .... Tim Duncan
14,968 .... Karl Malone
14,715 .... Robert Parish
14,662 .... Kevin Garnett
14,627 .... Dwight Howard^
14,464 .... Nate Thurmond
14,241 .... Walt Bellamy
13,769 .... Wes Unseld

13,748 .... Hakeem Olajuwon
13,099 .... Shaquille O'Neal
13,017 .... Buck Williams
12,942 .... Jerry Lucas
12,849 .... Bob Pettit
12,546 .... Charles Barkley
12,359 .... Dikembe Mutombo
12,357 .... Paul Silas
12,205 .... Charles Oakley
11,954 .... Dennis Rodman
11,901 .... Kevin Willis
11,607 .... Patrick Ewing
11,489 .... Dirk Nowitzki
11,463 .... Elgin Baylor

continued on next page

11,305	Pau Gasol	10,467	Tyson Chandler
11,256	Dolph Schayes	10,444	Dave Cowens
11,133	Dan Issel	10,400	Bill Laimbeer
11,054	Bill Bridges	10,370	Otis Thorpe
10,816	Jack Sikma	10,210	LeBron James^
10,685	Caldwell Jones	10,208	Zach Randolph
10,525	Julius Erving	10,142	DeAndre Jordan^
10,497	David Robinson	10,101	Shawn Marion
10,482	Ben Wallace	10,092	Red Kerr

* Includes ABA.

^ Active.

Rebound Leaders by State of Birth

Alabama	Charles Barkley (Leeds)	12,546
Alaska	Mario Chalmers (Anchorage)	1585
Arizona	Sean Elliott (Tucson)	3204
Arkansas	Paul Silas (Prescott)	12,357
California	Kevin Willis (Los Angeles)	11,901
Colorado	Joe Kleine (Colorado Springs)	3,991
Connecticut	Marcus Camby (Hartford)	9,513
Delaware	Walt Hazzard (Wilmington)	2146
Florida	Artis Gilmore (Chipley)	16,330
Georgia	Dwight Howard^ (Atlanta)	14,627
Hawaii	Cedric Ceballos (Maui)	3258
Idaho	Luke Ridnour (Coeur d'Alene)	1877
Illinois	Dan Issel (Batavia)	11,133
Indiana	Zach Randolph (Marion)	10,208
Iowa	Nick Collison (Orange City)	4701
Kansas	Alvan Adams (Lawrence)	6937
Kentucky	Wes Unseld (Louisville)	13,769
Louisiana	Bill Russell (Monroe)	21,620
Maine	Jeff Turner (Bangor)	2036
Maryland	Jeff Green^ (Cheverly)	4502
Massachusetts	Bill Laimbeer (Boston)	10,400
Michigan	Dave DeBusschere (Detroit)	9618
Minnesota	Kevin McHale (Hibbing)	7122
Mississippi	Sam Lacey (Indianola)	9687
Missouri	David Lee (St. Louis)	7320
Montana	Mike Lewis (Missoula)	4022
Nebraska	Bob Boozer (Omaha)	7119

Nevada	Ricky Davis (Las Vegas)	2550
New Hampshire	Matt Bonner (Concord)	2371
New Jersey	Shaquille O'Neal (Newark)	13,099
New Mexico	Bill Bridges (Hobbs)	11,054
New York	Kareem Abdul-Jabbar (New York)	17,440
North Carolina	Walt Bellamy (New Bern)	14,241
North Dakota	Mark Landsberger (Minot)	2681
Ohio	Nate Thurmond (Akron)	14,464
Oklahoma	Blake Griffin^ (Oklahoma City)	5954
Oregon	A.C. Green (Portland)	9473
Pennsylvania	Wilt Chamberlain (Philadelphia)	23,924
Rhode Island	Marvin Barnes (Providence)	2873
South Carolina	Kevin Garnett (Greenville)	14,662
South Dakota	Mike Miller (Mitchell)	4376
Tennessee	Bailey Howell (Middleton)	9383
Texas	DeAndre Jordan^ (Houston)	10,142
Utah	Tom Chambers (Ogden)	6703
Vermont	N/A	N/A
Virginia	Moses Malone (Petersburg)	17,834
Washington	James Edwards (Seattle)	6004
West Virginia	Hal Greer (Hungington)	5665
Wisconsin	Jim Chones (Racine)	6427
Wyoming	James Johnson^ (Cheyenne)	2676
District of Columbia	Elgin Baylor	11,463
Puerto Rico	J.J. Barea (Mayaguez)	1748
Virgin Islands	Tim Duncan (St. Croix)	15,091

^ Active.

All-Time Rebound Leaders by First Letter of Last Name

A	Abdul-Jabbar, Kareem	17,440	J	Jones, Caldwell	10,685
B	Bellamy, Walt	14,241	K	Kerr, Red	10,092
C	Chamberlain, Wilt	23,924	L	Lucas, Jerry	12,942
D	Duncan, Tim	15,091	M	Malone, Moses	17,834
E	Ewing, Patrick	11,607	N	Nowitzki, Dirk	11,489
F	Foust, Larry	8041	O	Olajuwon, Hakeem	13,748
G	Gilmore, Artis	16,330	P	Parish, Robert	14,715
H	Hayes, Elvin	16,279	Q	Quick, Bob	395
I	Issel, Dan	11,133	R	Russell, Bill	21,620

continued on next page

S .... Silas, Paul 12,357	W .... Williams, Buck 13,017
T .... Thurmond, Nate 14,464	X .... N/A .... N/A
U .... Unseld, Wes 13,769	Y .... Young, Thaddeus^ 6345
V .... Vučević, Nikola^ 7731	Z .... Zeller, Cody ^ 2949

^ Active.

Most Rebounds by Zodiac Sign*

Aquarius (Jan. 20–Feb. 18)	Bill Russell	21,620
Pisces (Feb. 19–Mar. 20)	Wes Unseld	13,769
Aries (Mar. 21–Apr. 19)	Moses Malone	17,834
Taurus (Apr. 20–May 20)	Tim Duncan	15,091
Gemini (May 21–Jun. 21)	Dirk Nowitzki	11,489
Cancer (Jun. 22–Jul.22)	Dikembe Mutombo	12,359
Leo (Jul. 23–Aug. 22)	Wilt Chamberlain	23,924
Virgo (Aug. 23–Sep. 22)	Artis Gilmore	16,330
Libra (Sep. 23–Oct. 23)	Tyson Chandler	10,467
Scorpio (Oct. 24–Nov. 21)	Elvin Hayes	16,279
Sagittarius (Nov. 22–Dec. 21)	Dwight Howard^	14,627
Capricorn (Dec. 22–Jan. 19)	LeBron James^	10,210

* Includes ABA.

^ Active.

Most Times Leading League in Rebounds

11	Wilt Chamberlain	1941	Phi. Warriors, 1959–60
		2149	Phi. Warriors, 1960–61
		2052	Phi. Warriors, 1961–62
		1946	S.F. Warriors, 1962–63
		1943	Phi. 76ers, 1965–66
		1957	Phi. 76ers, 1966–67
		1952	Phi. 76ers, 1967–68
		1712	L.A. Lakers, 1968–69
		1493	L.A. Lakers, 1970–71
		1572	L.A. Lakers, 1971–72
		1526	L.A. Lakers, 1972–73
6	Dwight Howard	1022	Orl. Magic, 2005–06
		1008	Orl. Magic, 2006–07
		1161	Orl. Magic, 2007–08
		1093	Orl. Magic, 2008–09
		1082	Orl. Magic, 2009–10
		785	Orl. Magic, 2011–12
5	Artis Gilmore	1491	Ken. Colonelsª, 1971–72
		1476	Ken. Colonelsª, 1972–73
		1538	Ken. Colonelsª, 1973–74
		1361	Ken. Colonelsª, 1974–75
		1303	Ken. Colonelsª, 1975–76
5	Moses Malone	1444	Hou. Rockets, 1978–79
		1180	Hou. Rockets, 1980–81
		1188	Hou. Rockets, 1981–82
		1194	Phi. 76ers, 1982–83
		1031	Phi. 76ers, 1984–85

continued on next page

4	Bill Russell	1564	Bos. Celtics, 1957–58
		1612	Bos. Celtics, 1958–59
		1930	Bos. Celtics, 1963–64
		1878	Bos. Celtics, 1964–65
4	Dennis Rodman	1530	Det. Pistons, 1991–92
		1132	Det. Pistons, 1992–93
		1367	S.A. Spurs, 1993–94
		1201	Chi. Bulls, 1997–98
4	Dikembe Mutombo	1029	Den. Nuggets, 1994–95
		929	Atl. Hawks, 1996–97
		610	Atl. Hawks, 1998–99
		1157	Atl. Hawks, 1999–00
4	Andre Drummond	1198	Det. Pistons, 2015–16
		1115	Det. Pistons, 2016–17
		1247	Det. Pistons, 2017–18
		1232	Det. Pistons, 2018–19
3	Mel Daniels	1213	Min. Muskies[a], 1967–68
		1256	Ind. Pacers[a], 1968–69
		1475	Ind. Pacers[a], 1970–71

[a] ABA.

Consecutive Seasons Leading League in Rebounds

5	Artis Gilmore	Ken. Colonels[a], 1971–72	1491
		Ken. Colonels[a], 1972–73	1476
		Ken. Colonels[a], 1973–74	1538
		Ken. Colonels[a], 1974–75	361
		Ken. Colonels[a], 1975–76	1303
5	Dwight Howard	Orl. Magic, 2005–06	1022
		Orl. Magic, 2006–07	1008
		Orl. Magic, 2007–08	1161
		Orl. Magic, 2008–09	1093
		Orl. Magic, 2009–10	1082
4	Wilt Chamberlain	Phi. Warriors, 1959–60	1941
		Phi. Warriors, 1960–61	2149
		Phi. Warriors, 1961–62	2052
		S.F. Warriors, 1962–63	1946
		Phi. 76ers, 1965–66	1943
		Phi. 76ers, 1966–67	1957
		L.A. Lakers, 1967–68	1952
		L.A. Lakers, 1968–69	1712
4	Andre Drummond	Det. Pistons, 2015–16	1198
		Det. Pistons, 2016–17	1115
		Det. Pistons, 2017–18	1247
		Det. Pistons, 2018–19	1232
3	Wilt Chamberlain	L.A. Lakers, 1970–71	1493
		L.A. Lakers, 1971–72	1572
		L.A. Lakers, 1972–73	1526
3	Moses Malone	Hou. Rockets, 1980–81	1180
		Hou. Rockets, 1981–82	1188
		Phi. 76ers, 1982–83	1194

continued on next page

3..	Dennis Rodman	Det. Pistons, 1991–92	1530
		Det. Pistons, 1992–93	1132
		S.A. Spurs, 1993–94...	1367
2..	Bill Russell	Bos. Celtics, 1957–58..	1564
		Bos. Celtics, 1958–59..	1612
		Bos. Celtics, 1963–64..	1930
		Bos. Celtics, 1964–65..	1878
2..	Mel Daniels	Min. Muskies[a], 1967–68...................................	1213
		Ind. Pacers[a], 1968–69.....................................	1256
2..	Kareem Abdul-Jabbar.............................	L.A. Lakers, 1975–76	1383
		L.A. Lakers, 1976–77	1090
2..	Charles Oakley.......................................	Chi. Bulls, 1986–87...	1074
		Chi. Bulls, 1987–88...	1066
2..	Hakeem Olajuwon	Hou. Rockets, 1988–89	1105
		Hou. Rockets, 1989–90	1149
2..	Dikembe Mutombo	Atl. Hawks, 1998–99	610
		Atl. Hawks, 1999–00	1157
2..	Kevin Garnett	Min. T'Wolves, 2003–04	1139
		Min. T'Wolves, 2004–05	1108
2..	DeAndre Jordan	L.A. Clippers, 2013–14	1114
		L.A. Clippers, 2014–15	1226
2..	Rudy Gobert	Uta. Jazz, 2019–20	916
		Uta. Jazz, 2020–21	960

[a] ABA.

Largest Differential Between League Leader in Rebounds and Runner-Up

Diff	Season	Leader	Reb	Runner-Up	Reb
+430	1958–59	Bill Russell, Bos. Celtics	1612	Bob Pettit, St.L. Hawks	1182
+401	1978–79	Moses Malone, Hou. Rockets	1444	Artis Gilmore, Chi. Bulls	1043
+392	1967–68	Wilt Chamberlain, Phi. 76ers	1952	Jerry Lucas, Cin. Royals	1560
+348	1957–58	Bill Russell, Bos. Celtics	1564	Bob Pettit, St.L. Hawks	1216
+341	1973–74[a]	Artis Gilmore, Ken. Colonels	1538	George McGinnis, Ind. Pacers	1197
+333	1975–76[a]	Artis Gilmore, Ken. Colonels	1303	Maurice Lucas, Spirits of St.L./Ken. Colonels	970
+295	1993–94	Dennis Rodman, S.A. Spurs	1367	Shaquille O'Neal, Orl. Magic	1072
+281	1960–61	Wilt Chamberlain, Phi. Warriors	2149	Bill Russell, Bos. Celtics	1868
+272	1991–92	Dennis Rodman, Det. Pistons	1530	Kevin Willis, Atl. Hawks	1258
+262	1961–62	Wilt Chamberlain, Phi. Warriors	2052	Bill Russell, Bos. Celtics	1790
+257	1966–67	Wilt Chamberlain, Phi. 76ers	1957	Bill Russell, Bos. Celtics	1700
+229	1972–73[a]	Artis Gilmore, Ken. Colonels	1476	Mel Daniels, Ind. Pacers	1247
+226	1971–72	Wilt Chamberlain, L.A. Lakers	1572	Kareem Abdul-Jabbar, Mil. Bucks	1346
+224	1997–98	Dennis Rodman, Chi. Bulls	1201	Tim Duncan, S.A. Spurs	977
+221	1968–69	Wilt Chamberlain, L.A. Lakers	1712	Wes Unseld, Bal. Bullets	1491
+219	1956–57	Maurice Stokes, Roc. Royals	1256	Bob Pettit, St.L. Hawks	1037
+210	1968–69[a]	Mel Daniels, Ind. Pacers	1256	Skip Thoren, Mia. Floridians	1046
+210	1977–78	Truck Robinson, N.O. Jazz	1288	Dave Cowens, Bos. Celtics	1078
+206	1973–74	Elvin Hayes, Cap. Bullets	1463	Dave Cowens, Bos. Celtics	1257
+205	1964–65	Bill Russell, Bos. Celtics	1878	Wilt Chamberlain, S.F. Warriors/Phi. 76ers	1673

[a] ABA.

Most Rebounds, Not Leading League, Season (Runner-Up)

Reb	Runner-Up	Season	Leader	Reb
1868	Bill Russell, Bos. Celtics	1960–61	Wilt Chamberlain, Phi. Warriors	2149
1843	Bill Russell, Bos. Celtics	1962–63	Wilt Chamberlain, S.F. Warriors	1946
1790	Bill Russell, Bos. Celtics	1961–62	Wilt Chamberlain, Phi. Warriors	2052
1787	Wilt Chamberlain, S.F. Warriors	1963–64	Bill Russell, Bos. Celtics	1930
1779	Bill Russell, Bos. Celtics	1965–66	Wilt Chamberlain, Phi. 76ers	1943
1778	Bill Russell, Bos. Celtics	1959–60	Wilt Chamberlain, Phi. Warriors	1941
1700	Bill Russell, Bos. Celtics	1966–67	Wilt Chamberlain, Phi. 76ers	1957
1673	Wilt Chamberlain, S.F. Warriors/Phi. 76ers	1964–65	Bill Russell, Bos. Celtics	1878
1560	Jerry Lucas, Cin. Royals	1967–68	Wilt Chamberlain, Phi. 76ers	1952
1491	Wes Unseld, Bal. Bullets	1968–69	Wilt Chamberlain, L.A. Lakers	1712
1462	Mel Daniels, Ind. Pacers	1969–70ᵃ	Spencer Haywood, Den. Rockets	1637
1454	Julius Keye, Den. Rockets	1970-71ᵃ	Mel Daniels, Ind. Pacers	1475
1370	Wes Unseld, Bal. Bullets	1969–70	Elvin Hayes, S.D. Rockets	1386
1362	Elvin Hayes, S.D. Rockets	1970–71	Wilt Chamberlain, L.A. Lakers	1493
1349	Nate Thurmond, G.S. Warriors	1972–73	Wilt Chamberlain, L.A. Lakers	1526
1346	Kareem Abdul-Jabbar, Mil. Bucks	1971–72	Wilt Chamberlain, L.A. Lakers	1572
1319	Julius Erving, Vir. Squires	1971–72ᵃ	Artis Gilmore, Ken. Colonels	1491
1279	Swen Nater, S.A. Spurs	1974–75ᵃ	Artis Gilmore, Ken. Colonels	1361
1257	Dave Cowens, Bos. Celtics	1973–74	Elvin Hayes, Was. Capitols	1463
1247	Mel Daniels, Ind. Pacers	1972–73ᵃ	Artis Gilmore, Ken. Colonels	1476
1246	Dave Cowens, Bos. Celtics	1975–76	Kareem Abdul-Jabbar, L.A. Lakers	1383
1216	Bob Pettit, St.L. Hawks	1957–58	Bill Russell, Bos. Celtics	1564
1197	George McGinnis, Ind. Pacers	1973–74ᵃ	Artis Gilmore, Ken. Colonels	1538
1190	Moses Malone, Hou. Rockets	1979–80	Swen Nater, S.D. Clippers	1216
1182	Bob Pettit, St.L. Hawks	1958–59	Bill Russell, Bos. Celtics	1612
1171	DeAndre, Jordan, L.A. Clippers	2017–18	Andre Drummond, Det. Pistons	1247
1149	Sam Lacey, K.C.-Oma. Kings	1974–75	Bob McAdoo, Buf. Braves	1155
1122	Shaquille O'Neal, Orl. Magic	1992–93	Dennis Rodman, S.A. Spurs	1132
1114	DeAndre, Jordan, L.A. Clippers	2016–17	Andre Drummond, Det. Pistons	1115
1102	Kevin Garnett, Min. T'Wolves	2002–03	Ben Wallace, Det. Pistons	1126
1078	Dave Cowens, Bos. Celtics	1977–78	Truck Robinson, N.O. Jazz	1288
1072	Moses Malone, Hou. Rockets	1976–77	Kareem Abdul-Jabbar, L.A. Lakers	1090
1046	Skip Thoren, Mia. Floridians	1968–69ᵃ	Mel Daniels, Ind. Pacers	1256
1043	Artis Gilmore, Chi. Bulls	1978–79	Moses Malone, Hou. Rockets	1444
1038	Jack Sikma, Sea. Sonics	1981–82	Moses Malone, Hou. Rockets	1188
1037	Bob Pettit, St.L. Hawks	1956–57	Maurice Stokes, Roc. Royals	1256
1013	Bill Laimbeer, Det. Pistons	1984–85	Moses Malone, Phi. 76ers	1031

ᵃ ABA.

Players on Losing Teams, Leading League in Rebounds

	Reb	Record
Dolph Schayes, Syr. Nationals, 1950–51	1080	32–34 (.485)
Larry Foust, Ft.W. Pistons, 1951–52	880	29–37 (.439)
Mel Hutchins, Mil. Hawks, 1951–52	880	17–49 (.258)
Neil Johnston, Phi. Warriors, 1954–55	1085	33–39 (.458)
Bob Pettit, St.L. Hawks, 1955–56	1164	33–39 (.458)
Maurice Stokes, Roc. Royals, 1956–57	1256	31–41 (.431)
Wilt Chamberlain, S.F. Warriors, 1962–63	1946	31–49 (.388)
Elvin Hayes, S.D. Rockets, 1969–70	1386	27–55 (.329)
Kareem Abdul-Jabbar, L.A. Lakers, 1975–76	1383	40–42 (.488)

continued on next page

	Reb	Record
Truck Robinson, N.O. Jazz, 1977–78	1288	39–43 (.476)
Swen Nater, S.D. Clippers, 1979–80	1216	35–47 (.427)
Moses Malone, Hou. Rockets, 1980–81	1180	40–42 (.488)
Charles Oakley, Chi. Bulls, 1986–87	1074	40–42 (.488)
Dennis Rodman, Det. Pistons, 1992–93	1132	40–42 (.488)
Dikembe Mutombo, Atl. Hawks, 1999–00	1157	28–54 (.341)
Ben Wallace, Det. Pistons, 2000–01	1052	32–50 (.366)
Dwight Howard, Orl. Magic, 2005–06	1022	36–46 (.439)
Dwight Howard, Orl. Magic, 2006–07	1008	40–42 (.488)
Kevin Love, Min. T'Wolves, 2010–11	1112	17–65 (.207)
Andre Drummond, Det. Pistons, 2016–17	1115	37–45 (.451)
Andre Drummond, Det. Pistons, 2017–18	1247	39–43 (.476)

Most Career Rebounds, Never Leading League

Career Reb		Most Rebounds, Season	League Leader
14,968	Karl Malone	986 (Uta. Jazz, 1987–88)	1066 (Charles Oakley, Chi. Bulls)
14,715	Robert Parish	996 (Bos. Celtics, 1988–89)	1105 (Hakeem Olajuwon, Hou. Rockets)
14,464	Nate Thurmond	1402 (S.F. Warriors, 1968–69)	1712 (Wilt Chamberlain, L.A. Lakers)
14,241	Walt Bellamy	1500 (Chi. Packers, 1961–62)	2052 (Wilt Chamberlain, Phi. Warriors)
13,769	Wes Unseld	1491 (Bal. Bullets, 1968–69)	1712 (Wilt Chamberlain, L.A. Lakers)
13,099	Shaquille O'Neal	1122 (Orl. Magic, 1992–93)	1132 (Dennis Rodman, Det. Pistons)
13,017	Buck Williams	1027 (N.J. Nets, 1982–83)	1194 (Moses Malone, Phi. 76ers)
12,942	Jerry Lucas	1668 (Cin. Royals, 1965–66)	1943 (Wilt Chamberlain, Phi. 76ers)
12,546	Charles Barkley	1026 (Phi. 76ers, 1985–86)	1075 (Bill Laimbeer, Det. Pistons)
12,357	Paul Silas	1039 (Bos. Celtics, 1972–73)	1526 (Wilt Chamerlain, L.A. Lakers)
11,901	Kevin Willis	1258 (Atl. Hawks, 1991–92)	1530 (Dennis Rodman, Det. Pistons)
11,607	Patrick Ewing	980 (N.Y. Knicks, 1992–93)	1132 (Dennis Rodman, Det. Pistons)
11,489	Dirk Nowitzki	791 (Dal. Mavericks, 2002–03)	1126 (Ben Wallace, Det. Pistons)
11,463	Elgin Baylor	1447 (L.A. Lakers, 1960–61)	2149 (Wilt Chamberlain, Phi. Warriors)
11,305	Pau Gasol	919 (Chi. Bulls, 2014–15)	1226 (DeAndre Jordan, L.A. Clippers)
11,133	Dan Issel	1093 (Ken. Colonels[a], 1970–71)	1475 (Mel Daniels, Ind. Pacers[a])
11,054	Bill Bridges	1233 (Atl. Hawks, 1970–71)	1493 (Wilt Chamberlain, L.A. Lakers)
10,816	Jack Sikma	1038 (Sea. Sonics, 1981–82)	1188 (Moses Malone, Hou. Rockets)
10,685	Caldwell Jones	1095 (S.D. Conquistadors[a], 1973–74)	1538 (Artis Gilmore, Ken. Colonels[a])
10,525	Julius Erving	1319 (Vir. Squires[a], 1971–72)	1491 (Artis Gilmore, Ken. Colonels[a])
10,467	Tyson Chandler	928 (N.O. Hornets, 2007–08)	1161 (Dwight Howard, Orl. Magic)
10,444	Dave Cowens	1329 (Bos. Celtics, 1972–73)	1526 (Wilt Chamerlain, L.A. Lakers)
10,370	Otis Thorpe	870 (Hou. Rockets, 1993–94)	1367 (Dennis Rodman, S.A. Spurs)
10,208	Zach Randolph	950 (Mem. Grizzlies, 2009–10)	1082 (Dwight Howard, Orl. Magic)
10,202	LeBron James^	709 (Cle. Cavaliers, 2017–18)	1247 (Andre Drummond, Det. Pistons)
10,101	Shawn Marion	959 (Pho. Suns, 2005–06)	1022 (Dwight Howard, Orl. Magic)
10,092	Red Kerr	1176 (Syr. Nationals, 1961–62)	2052 (Wilt Chamberlain, Phi. Warriors)

^ Active.

[a] ABA.

Players Finishing One-Two in Rebounds, Multiple Seasons

Season	Leader (Reb)	Runner-Up (Reb)
1955–56	Bob Pettit (1164)	Maurice Stokes (1094)
1956–57	Maurice Stokes (1256)	Bob Pettit (1037)

continued on next page

Season	Leader (Reb)	Runner-Up (Reb)
1957–58	Bill Russell (1564)	Bob Pettit (1216)
1958–59	Bill Russell (1612)	Bob Pettit (1182)
1959–60	Wilt Chamberlain (1941)	Bill Russell (1778)
1960–61	Wilt Chamberlain (2149)	Bill Russell (1868)
1961–62	Wilt Chamberlain (2052)	Bill Russell (1790)
1962–63	Wilt Chamberlain (1946)	Bill Russell (1843)
1963–64	Bill Russell (1930)	Wilt Chamberlain (1787)
1964–65	Bill Russell (1878)	Wilt Chamberlain (1673)
1965–66	Wilt Chamberlain (1943)	Bill Russell (1779)
1966–67	Wilt Chamberlain (1957)	Bill Russell (1700)
1979–80	Swen Nater (1216)	Moses Malone (1190)
1980–81	Moses Malone (1180)	Swen Nater (1017)
1990–91	David Robinson (1063)	Dennis Rodman (1026)
1995–96	David Robinson (1000)	Dennis Rodman (952)
1992–93	Dennis Rodman (1132)	Shaquille O'Neal (1122)
1993–94	Dennis Rodman (1367)	Shaquille O'Neal (1072)
1994–95	Dikembe Mutombo (1029)	Shaquille O'Neal (901)
1999–00	Dikembe Mutombo (1157)	Shaquille O'Neal (1078)
2002–03	Ben Wallace (1126)	Kevin Garnett (1102)
2003–04	Kevin Garnett (1139)	Ben Wallace (1006)
2005–06	Dwight Howard (1022)	Kevin Garnett (966)
2006–07	Dwight Howard (1008)	Kevin Garnett (975)
2010–11	Kevin Love (1112)	Dwight Howard (1098)
2011–12	Dwight Howard (785)	Kevin Love (734)
2013–14	DeAndre Jordan (1114)	Andre Drummond (1071)
2014–15	DeAndre Jordan (1226)	Andre Drummond (1104)
2015–16	Andre Drummond (1198)	DeAndre Jordan (1059)
2016–17	Andre Drummond (1115)	DeAndre Jordan (1114)
2017–18	Andre Drummond (1247)	DeAndre Jordan (1171)

Players with 750 Rebounds in Each of First Five Seasons of Career

Kareem Abdul-Jabbar	1969–70 (Mil. Bucks)	1190
	1970–71 (Mil. Bucks)	1311
	1971–72 (Mil. Bucks)	1346
	1972–73 (Mil. Bucks)	1224
	1973–74 (Mil. Bucks)	1178
Elgin Baylor	1958–59 (Min. Lakers)	1050
	1959–60 (Min. Lakers)	1150
	1960–61 (L.A. Lakers)	1447
	1961–62 (L.A. Lakers)	892
	1962–63 (L.A. Lakers)	1146
Walt Bellamy	1961–62 (Chi. Packers)	1500
	1962–63 (Chi. Zephyrs)	1309
	1963–64 (Bal. Bullets)	1361

continued on next page

	1964–65 (Bal. Bullets)	1166
	1965–66 (Bal. Bullets/N.Y. Knicks)	1254
Larry Bird	1979–80 (Bos. Celtics)	852
	1980–81 (Bos. Celtics)	895
	1981–82 (Bos. Celtics)	837
	1982–83 (Bos. Celtics)	870
	1983–84 (Bos. Celtics)	796
Wilt Chamberlain	1959–60 (Phi. Warriors)	2707*
	1960–61 (Phi. Warriors)	3033*
	1961–62 (Phi. Warriors)	4029*
	1962–63 (S.F. Warriors)	3586*
	1963–64 (S.F. Warriors)	2948*
Dave Cowens	1970–71 (Bos. Celtics)	1216
	1971–72 (Bos. Celtics)	1203
	1972–73 (Bos. Celtics)	1329
	1973–74 (Bos. Celtics)	1257
	1974–75 (Bos. Celtics)	958
Mel Daniels	1967–68 (Min. Muskies^a)	1213*
	1968–69 (Ind. Pacers^a)	1256*
	1969–70 (Ind. Pacers^a)	1462
	1970–71 (Ind. Pacers^a)	1475*
	1971–72 (Ind. Pacers^a)	1297
Julius Erving	1971–72 (Vir. Squires^a)	1319
	1972–73 (Vir. Squires^a)	867
	1973–74 (N.Y. Nets^a)	899
	1974–75 (N.Y. Nets^a)	914
	1975–76 (N.Y. Nets^a)	925
Artis Gilmore	1971–72 (Ken. Colonels^a)	1491*
	1972–73 (Ken. Colonels^a)	1476*
	1973–74 (Ken. Colonels^a)	1538*
	1974–75 (Ken. Colonels^a)	1361*
	1975–76 (Ken. Colonels^a)	1303*
Ira Harge	1967–68 (Pit. Pipers^a/Oak Oaks^a)	1038
	1968–69 (Oak. Oaks^a)	816
	1969–70 (Was. Capitols^a)	1177
	1970–71 (Car. Cougars^a/The Floridians^a)	1085
	1971–72 (The Floridians^a/Uta. Stars^a)	780
Elvin Hayes	1968–69 (S.D. Rockets)	1406
	1969–70 (S.D. Rockets)	1386*
	1970–71 (S.D. Rockets)	1362
	1971–72 (Hou. Rockets)	1197
	1972–73 (Bal. Bullets)	1177
Dwight Howard	2004–05 (Orl. Magic)	823
	2005–06 (Orl. Magic)	1022*
	2006–07 (Orl. Magic)	1008*
	2007–08 (Orl. Magic)	1161*
	2008–09 (Orl. Magic)	1093*
Bailey Howell	1959–60 (Det. Pistons)	790
	1960–61 (Det. Pistons)	1111
	1961–62 (Det. Pistons)	996
	1962–63 (Det. Pistons)	910
	1963–64 (Det. Pistons)	776

continued on next page

Larry Kenon	1973–74 (N.Y. Netsª)	962
	1974–75 (N.Y. Netsª)	900
	1975–76 (S.A. Spursª)	897
	1976–77 (S.A. Spurs)	879
	1977–78 (S.A. Spurs)	773
Sam Lacey	1970–71 (Cin. Royals)	913
	1971–72 (Cin. Royals)	968
	1972–73 (K.C.-Oma. Kings)	933
	1973–74 (K.C.-Oma. Kings)	1055
	1974–75 (K.C.-Oma. Kings)	1149
Jerry Lucas	1963–64 (Cin. Royals)	1375
	1964–65 (Cin. Royals)	1321
	1965–66 (Cin. Royals)	1668
	1966–67 (Cin. Royals)	1547
	1967–68 (Cin. Royals)	1560
Dikembe Mutombo	1991–92 (Den. Nuggets)	870
	1992–93 (Den. Nuggets)	1070
	1993–94 (Den. Nuggets)	971
	1994–95 (Den. Nuggets)	1029*
	1995–96 (Den. Nuggets)	871
Swen Nater	1973–74 (Vir. Squiresª/S.A. Spursª)	998
	1974–75 (S.A. Spursª)	1279
	1975–76 (N.Y. Netsª/Vir. Squiresª)	766
	1976–77 (Mil. Bucks)	865
	1977–78 (Buf. Braves)	1029
Bob Netolicky	1967–68 (Ind. Pacersª)	819
	1968–69 (Ind. Pacersª)	798
	1969–70 (Ind. Pacersª)	876
	1970–71 (Ind. Pacersª)	774
	1971–72 (Ind. Pacersª)	764
Hakeem Olajuwon	1984–85 (Hou. Rockets)	974
	1985–86 (Hou. Rockets)	781
	1986–87 (Hou. Rockets)	858
	1987–88 (Hou. Rockets)	959
	1988–89 (Hou. Rockets)	1105*
Billy Paultz	1970–71 (N.Y. Netsª)	940
	1971–72 (N.Y. Netsª)	1035
	1972–73 (N.Y. Netsª)	1015
	1973–74 (N.Y. Netsª)	782
	1974–75 (N.Y. Netsª)	772
Bob Pettit	1954–55 (Mil. Hawks)	994
	1955–56 (St.L. Hawks)	1164*
	1956–57 (St.L. Hawks)	1037
	1957–58 (St.L. Hawks)	1216
	1958–59 (St.L. Hawks)	1182
Clifford Ray	1971–72 (Chi. Bulls)	869
	1972–73 (Chi. Bulls)	797
	1973–74 (Chi. Bulls)	977
	1974–75 (G.S. Warriors)	870
	1975–76 (G.S. Warriors)	776
Willis Reed	1964–65 (N.Y. Knicks)	1175
	1965–66 (N.Y. Knicks)	883

continued on next page

	1966–67 (N.Y. Knicks)	1136
	1967–68 (N.Y. Knicks)	1073
	1968–69 (N.Y. Knicks)	1191
David Robinson	1989–90 (S.A. Spurs)	983
	1990–91 (S.A. Spurs)	1063*
	1991–92 (S.A. Spurs)	829
	1992–93 (S.A. Spurs)	956
	1993–94 (S.A. Spurs)	855
Bill Russell	1956–57 (Bos. Celtics)	943
	1957–58 (Bos. Celtics)	1564*
	1958–59 (Bos. Celtics)	1612*
	1959–60 (Bos. Celtics)	1778
	1960–61 (Bos. Celtics)	1868
Elmore Smith	1971–72 (Buf. Braves)	1184
	1972–73 (Buf. Braves)	946
	1973–74 (L.A. Lakers)	906
	1974–75 (L.A. Lakers)	810
	1975–76 (Mil. Bucks)	893
Nate Thurmond	1963–64 (S.F. Warriors)	790
	1964–65 (S.F. Warriors)	1395
	1965–66 (S.F. Warriors)	1312
	1966–67 (S.F. Warriors)	1382
	1967–68 (S.F. Warriors)	1121
Wes Unseld	1968–69 (Bal. Bullets)	1491
	1969–70 (Bal. Bullets)	1370
	1970–71 (Bal. Bullets)	1253
	1971–72 (Bal. Bullets)	1336
	1972–73 (Bal. Bullets)	1260
Buck Williams	1981–82 (N.J. Nets)	1005
	1982–83 (N.J. Nets)	1027
	1983–84 (N.J. Nets)	1000
	1984–85 (N.J. Nets)	1005
	1985–86 (N.J. Nets)	986

[a] ABA.

* Led league.

Players with 1000 Rebounds in Each of First Five Seasons of Career

Kareem Abdul-Jabbar.... Mil. Bucks: 1969–70 (1190), 1970–71 (1311), 1971–72 (1346), 1972–73 (1224), 1973–74 (1178)

Walt Bellamy................. Chi. Packers-Zephyrs: 1961–62 (1500), 1962–63 (1309)
Bal. Bullets: 1963–64 (1361), 1964–65 (1166)
Bal. Bullets/N.Y. Knicks: 1965–66 (1254)

Wilt Chamberlain.......... Phi.-S.F. Warriors: 1959–60 (1941*), 1960–61 (2149*), 1961–62 (2052*), 1962–63 (1946*), 1963–64 (1787)

Mil Daniels .... Min. Muskies[a]: 1967–68 (1213*)
Ind. Pacers[a]: 1968–69 (1256*), 1969–70 (1462), 1970–71 (1475*), 1971–72 (1297)

Artis Gilmore .... Ken. Colonels[a]: 1971–72 (1491*), 1972–73 (1476*), 1973–74 (1538*), 1974–75 (1361*), 1975–76 (1303*)

Elvin Hayes................... S.D.-Hou. Rockets: 1968–69 (1406), 1969–70 (1386*), 1970–71 (1362), 1971–72 (1197)
Bal. Bullets: 1972–73 (1177)

Jerry Lucas................... Cin. Royals: 1963–64 (1375), 1964–65 (1321), 1965–66 (1668), 1966–67 (1547), 1967–68 (1560)

Wes Unseld.................. Bal. Bullets: 1968–69 (1491), 1969–70 (1370), 1970–71 (1253), 1971–72 (1336), 1972–73 (1260)

* Led league.

[a] ABA.

Most Rebounds for Each Franchise

Hawks	12,849	Bob Pettit
Celtics	21,620	Bill Russell
Nets-Americans*	7576	Buck Williams
Hornets-Bobcats	3516	Emeka Okafor
Bulls	5836	Michael Jordan
Cavaliers	6190	LeBron James
Mavericks	11,489	Dirk Nowitzki
Nuggets-Rockets*	6630	Dan Issel
Pistons	9430	Bill Laimbeer
Warriors	12,771	Nate Thurmond
Rockets	13,382	Hakeem Olajuwon
Pacers*	7643	Mel Daniels
Clippers-Braves	7988	DeAndre Jordan
Lakers	11,463	Elgin Baylor
Grizzlies	5942	Marc Gasol
Heat	5780	Udonis Haslem^
Bucks	7161	Kareem Abdul-Jabbar
Timberwolves	10,718	Kevin Garnett
Pelicans-Hornets	4906	Anthony Davis
Knicks	10,759	Patrick Ewing
Thunder-SuperSonics	7729	Jack Sikma
Magic	8072	Dwight Howard
76ers-Nationals	11,256**	Dolph Schayes
Suns	6937	Alvan Adams
Trail Blazers	5434	LaMarcus Aldridge
Kings-Royals	9353	Sam Lacey
Spurs-Chaparrals*	15,091	Tim Duncan
Raptors	4776	Chris Bosh
Jazz	14,601	Karl Malone
Wizards-Zephyrs-Packers-Bullets	13,769	Wes Unseld

* Includes ABA.

** Does not include rebounds from 1949–50 season.

^ Active with franchise.

Most Rebounds, Game

NBA

55	Wilt Chamberlain, Phi. Warriors	vs. Bos. Celtics (Nov. 24, 1960)
51	Bill Russell, Bos. Celtics	vs. Syr. Nationals (Feb. 5, 1960)
49	Bill Russell, Bos. Celtics	vs. Phi. Warriors (Nov. 16, 1957)
49	Bill Russell, Bos. Celtics	vs. Det. Pistons (Mar. 11, 1965)
45	Wilt Chamberlain, Phi. Warriors	vs. Syr. Nationals (Feb. 6, 1960)
45	Wilt Chamberlain, Phi. Warriors	vs. L.A. Lakers (Jan. 21, 1961)
43	Wilt Chamberlain, Phi. Warriors	vs. N.Y. Knicks (Nov. 10, 1959)
43	Wilt Chamberlain, Phi. Warriors	vs. L.A. Lakers (Dec. 8, 1961)
43	Bill Russell, Bos. Celtics	vs. L.A. Lakers (Jan. 20, 1963)
43	Wilt Chamberlain, Phi. 76ers	vs. Bos. Celtics (Mar. 6, 1965)
42	Wilt Chamberlain, Phi. Warriors	vs. Bos. Celtics (Jan. 15, 1960)
42	Wilt Chamberlain, Phi. Warriors	vs. Det. Pistons (Jan. 25, 1960)
42	Nate Thurmond, S.F. Warriors	vs. Det. Pistons (Nov. 9, 1965)

continued on next page

42	Wilt Chamberlain, Phi. 76ers	vs. Bos. Celtics (Jan. 14, 1966)
42	Wilt Chamberlain, L.A. Lakers	vs. Bos. Celtics (Mar. 7, 1969)
41	Bill Russell, Bos. Celtics	vs. Syr. Nationals (Feb. 12, 1958)
41	Wilt Chamberlain, S.F. Warriors	vs. Det. Pistons (Oct. 26, 1962)
41	Bill Russell, Bos. Celtics	vs. S.F. Warriors (Mar. 14, 1965)
40	Bill Russell, Bos. Celtics	vs. Cin. Royals (Dec. 12, 1958)
40	Wilt Chamberlain, Phi. Warriors	vs. Syr. Nationals (Nov. 4, 1959)
40	Bill Russell, Bos. Celtics	vs. Phi. Warriors (Feb. 12, 1961)
40	Jerry Lucas, Cin. Royals	@ Phi. 76ers (Feb. 29, 1964)
40	Wilt Chamberlain, S.F. Warriors	vs. Det. Pistons (Nov. 22, 1964)
40	Wilt Chamberlain, Phi. 76ers	vs. Bos. Celtics (Dec. 28, 1965)

ABA

40	Artis Gilmore, Ken. Colonels	@ N.Y. Nets (Feb. 3, 1974)
37	George McGinnis, Ind. Pacers	vs. Car. Cougars (Jan. 12, 1974)
35	Manny Leaks, Tex. Chaparrals	vs. Ken. Colonels (Nov. 27, 1970)
34	Mel Daniels, Ind. Pacers	vs. Pit. Pipers (Dec. 20, 1969)
33	Mel Daniels, Ind. Pacers	vs. Mia. Floridians (Mar. 6, 1970)
33	Billy Paultz, N.Y. Nets	vs. Dal. Chaparrals (Dec. 17, 1971)
33	Artis Gilmore, Ken. Colonels	vs. Ind. Pacers (Jan. 3, 1973)
33	George McGinnis, Ind. Pacers	vs. N.Y. Nets (Dec. 5, 1973)
32	Ira Harge, Oak. Oaks	vs. Pit. Pipers (Feb. 9, 1968)
31	Mel Daniels, Ind. Pacers	vs. N.Y. Nets (Mar. 18, 1969)
31	Spencer Haywood, Den. Rockets	@ Ken. Colonels (Nov. 13, 1969)
31	Mel Daniels, Ind. Pacers	vs. N.O. Buccaneers (Jan. 10, 1970)
31	Marvin Barnes, Spirits of St. L.	vs. Mem. Sounds (Jan. 8, 1975)
30	Mel Daniels, Ind. Pacers	@ Ken. Colonels (Oct. 26, 1968)
30	Artis Gilmore, Ken. Colonels	vs. Vir. Squires (Nov. 17, 1971)
30	Mel Daniels, Ind. Pacers	@ The Floridians (Dec. 29, 1971)
30	Artis Gilmore, Ken. Colonels	vs. The Floridians (Feb. 19, 1972)
30	Artis Gilmore, Ken. Colonels	@ Car. Cougars (Nov. 10, 1972)
30	Marvin Barnes, Spirits of St. L.	vs. S.D. Conquistadors (Oct. 29, 1974)

Most Rebounds in an NBA Game (Not Named Wilt Chamberlain or Bill Russell)

42	Nate Thurmond, S.F. Warriors	vs. Det. Pistons (Nov. 9, 1965)
40	Jerry Lucas, Cin. Royals	@ Phi. 76ers (Feb. 29, 1964)
39	Neil Johnston, Phi. Warriors	vs. Syr. Nationals (Dec. 4, 1954)
38	Maurice Stokes, Roc. Royals	vs. Syr. Nationals (Jan. 14, 1956)
37	Nate Thurmond, S.F. Warriors	vs. Bal. Bullets (Oct. 27, 1964)
37	Walt Bellamy, Bal. Bullets	vs. St.L. Hawks (Dec. 4, 1964)
37	Jerry Lucas, Cin. Royals	@ Det. Pistons (Jan. 20, 1965)
37	Nate Thurmond, S.F. Warriors	vs. L.A. Lakers (Dec. 20, 1966)
37	Tom Boerwinkle, Chi. Bulls	vs. Pho. Suns (Jan. 8, 1970)
37	Moses Malone, Hou. Rockets	@ N.O. Jazz (Feb. 9, 1979)
36	George Mikan, Min. Lakers	vs. Roc. Royals (Jan. 20, 1952)
36	George Mikan, Min. Lakers	@ Phi. Warriors (Mar. 4, 1952)
35	Dolph Schayes, Syr. Nationals	@ Phi. Warriors (Dec. 28, 1950)
35	Bob Pettit, St.L. Hawks	vs. Cin. Royals (Mar. 2, 1958)
35	Bob Pettit, St.L. Hawks	vs. Min. Lakers (Jan. 6, 1959)
35	Jerry Lucas, Cin. Royals	vs. Bal. Bullets (Nov. 13, 1965)
35	Elvin Hayes, S.D. Rockets	@ N.Y. Knicks (Jan. 19, 1971)

continued on next page

35	Charles Oakley, Chi. Bulls	vs. Cle. Cavaliers (Apr. 22, 1988)
34	Maurice Stokes, Roc. Royals	vs. St.L. Hawks (Jan. 21, 1956)
34	Gus Johnson, Bal. Bullets	vs. L.A. Lakers (Feb. 9, 1966)
34	Jerry Lucas, Cin. Royals	vs. Chi. Bulls (Feb. 12, 1968)
34	Nate Thurmond, S.F. Warriors	@ Phi. 76ers (Jan. 19, 1969)
34	Nate Thurmond, S.F. Warriors	@ L.A. Lakers (Feb. 2, 1969)
34	Kareem Abdul-Jabbar, L.A. Lakers	vs. Det. Pistons (Dec. 14, 1975)
34	Dennis Rodman, Det. Pistons	vs. Ind. Pacers (Mar. 4, 1992)
34	Rony Seikaly, Mia. Heat	vs. Was. Bullets (Mar. 3, 1993)
33	Harry Gallatin, N.Y. Knicks	@ Ft.W. Pistons (Mar. 15, 1953)
33	Maurice Stokes, Roc. Royals	vs. St.L. Hawks (Jan. 16, 1957)
33	Jerry Lucas, Cin. Royals	vs. N.Y. Knicks (Nov. 29, 1963)
33	Jerry Lucas, Cin. Royals	vs. Phi. 76ers (Feb. 7, 1964)
33	Jerry Lucas, Cin. Royals	@ Bal. Bullets (Nov. 11, 1966)
33	Nate Thurmond, S.F. Warriors	vs. Bal. Bullets (Oct. 27, 1967)
33	Nate Thurmond, S.F. Warriors	@ Phi. 76ers (Nov. 4, 1967)
33	Nate Thurmond, S.F. Warriors	vs. Bos. Celtics (Mar. 4, 1969)
33	Willis Reed, N.Y. Knicks	vs. Cin. Royals (Feb. 2, 1971)
33	Tom Boerwinkle, Chi. Bulls	vs. Mil. Bucks (Mar. 9, 1971)
33	Bob Lanier, Det. Pistons	vs. Sea. Sonics (Dec. 22, 1972)
33	Swen Nater, Mil. Bucks	vs. Atl. Hawks (Dec. 19, 1976)
33	Kevin Willis, Atl. Hawks	vs. Was. Bullets (Feb. 19, 1992)
33	Charles Barkley, Hou. Rockets	@ Pho. Suns (Nov. 2, 1996)

Most Rebounds in a Loss

55	Wilt Chamberlain, Phi. Warriors	vs. Bos. Celtics (Nov. 24, 1960)
43	Wilt Chamberlain, Phi. Warriors	vs. L.A. Lakers (Dec. 8, 1961)
42	Wilt Chamberlain, Phi. Warriors	vs. Bos. Celtics (Jan. 15, 1960)
40	Wilt Chamberlain, S.F. Warriors	vs. Det. Pistons (Nov. 22, 1964)
38	Wilt Chamberlain, S.F. Warriors	vs. Bos. Celtics (Feb. 21, 1963)
38	Bill Russell, Bos. Celtics	vs. L.A. Lakers (Mar. 3, 1965)
37	Wilt Chamberlain, S.F. Warriors	vs. Chi. Zephyrs (Nov. 27, 1962)
37	Wilt Chamberlain, S.F. Warriors	vs. N.Y. Knicks (Nov. 9, 1963)
36	George Mikan, Min. Lakers	@ Phi. Warriors (Mar. 4, 1952)
36	Wilt Chamberlain, Phi. Warriors	@ Bos. Celtics (Dec. 26, 1960)
36	Wilt Chamberlain, Phi. Warriors	@ St.L. Hawks (Jan. 24, 1961)
36	Wilt Chamberlain, Phi. Warriors	@ N.Y. Knicks (Dec. 25, 1961)
36	Bill Russell, Bos. Celtics	@ Det. Pistons (Feb. 2, 1966)
35	Dolph Schayes, Syr. Nationals	@ Phi. Warriors (Dec. 28, 1950)
35	Wilt Chamberlain, Phi. Warriors	@ Bos. Celtics (Jan. 13, 1961)
35	Wilt Chamberlain, Phi. Warriors	vs. Det. Pistons (Mar. 10, 1961)
35	Wilt Chamberlain, L.A. Lakers	vs. S.F. Warriors (Feb. 2, 1969)
35	Manny Leaks, Tex. Chaparrals[a]	vs. Ken. Colonels[a] (Nov. 27, 1970)
35	Elvin Hayes, S.D. Rockets	@ N.Y. Knicks (Jan. 19, 1971)
35	Charles Oakley, Chi. Bulls	vs. Cle. Cavaliers (Apr. 22, 1988)

[a] ABA.

Most 20-Rebound Games, Season

70 ...... Wilt Chamberlain, Phi. Warriors, 1960–61	57 ...... Bill Russell, Bos. Celtics, 1960–61
69 ...... Wilt Chamberlain, Phi. Warriors, 1961–62	57 ...... Bill Russell, Bos. Celtics, 1961–62
67 ...... Wilt Chamberlain, Phi. 76ers, 1965–66	54 ...... Bill Russell, Bos. Celtics, 1962–63
67 ...... Wilt Chamberlain, Phi. 76ers, 1966–67	54 ...... Bill Russell, Bos. Celtics, 1959–60
65 ...... Wilt Chamberlain, Phi. 76ers, 1967–68	52 ...... Bill Russell, Bos. Celtics, 1957–58
64 ...... Bill Russell, Bos. Celtics, 1964–65	52 ...... Wilt Chamberlain, S.F. Warriors, 1963–64
62 ...... Wilt Chamberlain, S.F. Warriors, 1962–63	52 ...... Wilt Chamberlain, L.A. Lakers, 1968–69
62 ...... Wilt Chamberlain, Phi. Warriors, 1959–60	51 ...... Jerry Lucas, Cin. Royals, 1965–66
62 ...... Bill Russell, Bos. Celtics, 1963–64	50 ...... Wilt Chamberlain, S.F. Warriors/Phi. 76ers, 1964–65
59 ...... Bill Russell, Bos. Celtics, 1965–66	

Most 20-Rebound Games, Career

722 ...... Wilt Chamberlain	147 ...... Elvin Hayes
644 ...... Bill Russell	146 ...... Walt Bellamy
251 ...... Jerry Lucas	139 ...... Moses Malone
245 ...... Nate Thurmond	132 ...... Mel Daniels
189 ...... Bob Pettit	127 ...... Kareem Abdul-Jabbar
159 ...... Artis Gilmore	121 ...... Elgin Baylor
159 ...... Dennis Rodman	105 ...... Dave Cowens
159 ...... Wes Unseld	

Most Games with 20 Rebounds and Under 10 Points, Career

100 ...... Dennis Rodman	15 ...... Clyde Lee
70 ...... Bill Russell	14 ...... Larry Smith
27 ...... Wes Unseld	14 ...... Nate Thurmond
24 ...... Wilt Chamberlain	12 ...... Bill Bridges
23 ...... Ben Wallace	12 ...... Dikembe Mutombo
18 ...... Marcus Camby	10 ...... DeAndre Jordan^

^ Active.

Most Rebounds in a Game without Scoring

28 ...... Dennis Rodman, S.A. Spurs ...... @ Cha. Hornets (Dec. 1, 1993)
25 ...... Dennis Rodman, S.A. Spurs ...... @ Pho. Suns (Nov. 10, 1993)
24 ...... Dennis Rodman, S.A. Spurs ...... @ Sac. Kings (Nov. 12, 1993)
21 ...... Dennis Rodman, Chi. Bulls ...... vs. Pho. Suns (Dec. 15, 1997)
20 ...... Happy Hairston, L.A. Lakers ...... vs. Det. Pistons (Oct. 26, 1973)
20 ...... Clyde Lee, G.S. Warriors ...... vs. Chi. Bulls (Mar. 2, 1974)
20 ...... Dennis Rodman, S.A. Spurs ...... @ Uta. Jazz (Dec. 13, 1993)
20 ...... Dennis Rodman, S.A. Spurs ...... vs. Sac. Kings (Jan. 25, 1994)
20 ...... Dennis Rodman, S.A. Spurs ...... vs. Cha. Hornets (Apr. 2, 1994)
20 ...... Reggie Evans, Den. Nuggets ...... @ Tor. Raptors (Mar. 10, 2006)
20 ...... Marcus Camby, Den. Nuggets ...... vs. L.A. Lakers (Dec. 5, 2007)
20 ...... Marcus Camby, Por. Blazers ...... vs. Pho. Suns (Jan. 27, 2012)
19 ...... James Donaldson, Dal. Mavericks ...... @ Sea. Sonics (Jan. 11, 1990)
19 ...... Ömer Aşık, Hou. Rockets ...... @ Atl. Hawks (Nov. 2, 2012)
18 ...... Dennis Rodman, S.A. Spurs ...... vs. Phi. 76ers (Jan. 4, 1994)

continued on next page

17	Ervin Johnson, Den. Nuggets	@ L.A. Clippers (Apr. 12, 1997)
17	Reggie Evans, Sea. Sonics	@ G.S. Warriors (Jan. 28, 2005)
17	Ben Wallace, Det. Pistons	vs. Min. T'Wolves (Feb. 1, 2006)
16	Darrall Imhoff, L.A. Lakers	@ Cin. Royals (Dec. 29, 1965)
16	Clyde Lee, G.S. Warriors	vs. Sea. Sonics (Dec. 26, 1972)
16	Wes Unseld, Was. Bullets	@ N.O. Jazz (Apr. 1, 1975)
16	Caldwell Jones, Phi. 76ers	@ Bos. Celtics (Apr. 3, 1977)
16	Dennis Rodman, S.A. Spurs	vs. Bos. Celtics (Dec. 26, 1993)
16	Dennis Rodman, S.A. Spurs	@ L.A. Lakers (Jan. 9, 1994)
16	Dennis Rodman, S.A. Spurs	vs. Min. T'Wolves (Apr. 11, 1994)
16	Lorenzo Williams, Dal. Mavericks	vs. Pho. Suns (Feb. 7, 1995)
16	Dennis Rodman, Chi. Bulls	@ S.A. Spurs (Mar. 14, 1998)
16	Dale Davis, Ind. Pacers	@ N.Y. Knicks (Feb. 19, 2000)
16	Reggie Evans, Tor. Raptors	vs. N.Y. Knicks (Oct. 27, 2010)
16	Joel Anthony, Mia. Heat	vs. Atl. Hawks (Jan. 18, 2011)
16	Reggie Evans, Brk. Nets	@ Tor. Raptors (Apr. 14, 2013)
16	Bismack Biyombo, Tor. Raptors	@ Was. Wizards (Nov. 28, 2015)

Most Games with 10 Rebounds and Zero Points, Career

27	Dennis Rodman	8	Kendrick Perkins	6	Jeff Foster
23	Ben Wallace	7	George Johnson	6	Marcus Camby
14	Reggie Evans	7	Charles Jones	5	Tree Rollins
8	Clyde Lee	7	Chris Dudley	5	Ömer Aşık
8	Caldwell Jones	6	Wes Unseld		
8	Ervin Johnson	6	Larry Smith		

Players with Multiple 19-Rebound Games, Never Having a 20-Rebound Game, Career

Alvan Adams	Pho. Suns @ Chi. Bulls (Feb. 17, 1976)
	Pho. Suns @ N.O. Jazz (Mar. 30, 1977)
Chris Boucher^	Tor. Raptors vs. Chi. Bulls (Apr. 8, 2021)
	Tor. Raptors vs. Phi. 76ers (Dec. 28, 2021)
Jim Caldwell	Ken. Colonels^a vs. N.J. Nets^a (Mar. 19, 1968)
	Ken. Colonels^a @ Hou. Mavericks^a (Mar. 3, 1969)
Wayne Cooper	Uta. Jazz vs. S.A. Spurs (Mar. 26, 1981)
	Dal. Mavericks vs. S.D. Clippers (Feb. 3, 1982)
	Den. Nuggets vs. Pho. Suns (Dec. 22, 1988)
Adrian Dantley	Buf. Braves @ Mil. Bucks (Oct. 21, 1976)
	Ind. Pacers @ G.S. Warriors (Nov. 9, 1977)
Ed Fleming	Roc. Royals vs. St.L. Hawks (Jan. 13, 1956)
	Min. Lakers @ Bos. Celtics (Feb. 7, 1958)
Fred Hetzel	S.F. Warriors @ Phi. 76ers (Mar. 3, 1966)
	S.F. Warriors vs. Chi. Bulls (Feb. 16, 1967)
Wayne Hightower	Den. Rockets^a vs. Ken. Colonels^a (Apr. 1, 1969)
	Uta. Stars^a vs. Ken. Colonels^a (Dec. 4, 1970)
Mike Mitchell	Cle. Cavaliers vs. Det. Pistons (Dec. 25, 1979)
	Cle. Cavaliers @ Det. Pistons (Mar. 18, 1980)
Craig Raymond	Pit. Pipers^a @ Car. Cougars^a (Nov. 14, 1969)
	L.A. Stars^a vs. Ken. Colonels^a (Feb. 15, 1970)
Pascal Siakam^	Tor. Raptors @ Was. Wizards (Jan. 13, 2019)
	Tor. Raptors vs. L.A. Clippers (Dec. 31, 2021)

continued on next page

Lionel Simmons .... Sac. Kings vs. Por. Blazers (Feb. 6, 1991)

Sac. Kings vs. Dal. Mavericks (Apr. 5, 1992)

Aaron Williams .... N.J. Nets vs. Mia. Heat (Dec. 23, 2000)

N.J. Nets vs. Atl. Hawks (Dec. 26, 2000)

ª ABA.

^ Active.

Shortest Player to Lead League in Rebounds

6-foot-6 .... Mel Hutchins .... Mil. Hawks, 1951–52 (880)

6-foot-6 .... Harry Gallatin .... N.Y. Knicks, 1953–54 (1098)

6-foot-7 .... Maurice Stokes .... Roc. Royals, 1956–57 (1256)

6-foot-7 .... Truck Robinson .... N.O. Jazz, 1977–78 (1288)

6-foot-7 .... Dennis Rodman .... Det. Pistons, 1991–92 (1530), 1992–93 (1132); S.A. Spurs, 1993–94 (1367); Chi. Bulls, 1997–98 (1201)

6-foot-8 .... Dolph Schayes .... Syr. Nationals, 1950–51 (1080)

6-foot-8 .... Neil Johnston .... Phi. Warriors, 1954–55 (1085)

6-foot-8 .... Spencer Haywood ...... Den. Rocketsª, 1969–70 (1637)

6-foot-8 .... Charles Oakley .... Chi. Bulls, 1986–87 (1074), 1987–88 (1066)

6-foot-8 .... Kevin Love .... Min. T'Wolves, 2010–11 (1112)

6-foot-9 .... Larry Foust .... Ft.W. Pistons, 1951–52 (880)

6-foot-9 .... Bob Pettit .... St.L. Hawks (1955–56)

6-foot-9 .... Mel Daniels .... Min. Muskiesª, 1967–68 (1213); Ind. Pacersª, 1968–69 (1256), 1970–71 (1475)

6-foot-9 .... Elvin Hayes .... S.D. Rockets, 1969–70 (1386); Cap. Bullets, 1973–74 (1463)

6-foot-9 .... Bob McAdoo .... Buf. Braves, 1974–75 (1155)

6-foot-9 .... Ben Wallace .... Det. Pistons, 2000–01 (1052), 2002–03 (1126)

ª ABA.

Most Rebounds in a Season, Under 6-Feet Tall

332 .... Willie Somerset, Hou. Mavericksª/N.Y. Netsª, 1968–69 .... 5-foot-8

330 .... Damon Stoudamire, Tor. Raptors, 1996–97 .... 5-foot-10

313 .... Muggsy Bogues, Cha. Hornets, 1993–94 .... 5-foot-3

310 .... Michael Adams, Was. Bullets, 1991–92 .... 5-foot-10

310 .... Damon Stoudamire, Por. Blazers, 2004–05 .... 5-foot-10

308 .... Damon Stoudamire, Por. Blazers, 2003–04 .... 5-foot-10

305 .... Willie Somerset, Hou. Mavericksª, 1967–68 .... 5-foot-8

303 .... Whitey Skoog, Min. Lakers, 1954–55 .... 5-foot-11

303 .... Damon Stoudamire, Por. Blazers, 2000–01 .... 5-foot-10

301 .... Terrell Brandon, Cle. Cavaliers, 1996–97 .... 5-foot-11

298 .... Muggsy Bogues, Cha. Hornets, 1992–93 .... 5-foot-3

298 .... Terrell Brandon, Min. T'Wolves, 2000–01 .... 5-foot-11

298 .... Damon Stoudamire, Tor. Raptors/Por. Blazers, 1997–98 .... 5-foot-10

292 .... Damon Stoudamire, Por. Blazers, 2001–02 .... 5-foot-10

291 .... Whitey Skoog, Min. Lakers, 1955–56 .... 5-foot-11

290 .... Nate Robinson, N.Y. Knicks, 2008–09 .... 5-foot-9

288 .... Slater Martin, N.Y. Knicks/St.L. Hawks, 1956–57 .... 5-foot-10

285 .... Joe Hamilton, Tex. Chaparralsª, 1970–71 .... 5-foot-10

283 .... Michael Adams, Den. Nuggets, 1988–89 .... 5-foot-10

281 .... Damon Stoudamire, Tor. Raptors, 1995–96 .... 5-foot-10

275 .... Ralph Johnson, Ft.W. Pistons, 1950–51 .... 5-foot-11

ª ABA.

Most Career Rebounds by Players 6-Foot-4 or Shorter

8725 .... Jason Kidd 6-foot-4	4786 .... Bob Cousy 6-foot-1
7541 .... Russell Westbrook^ 6-foot-3	4523 .... Fat Lever 6-foot-3
6129 .... Paul Arizin 6-foot-4	4475 .... Kyle Lowry^ 6-foot-0
5665 .... Hal Greer 6-foot-2	4371 .... T.R. Dunn 6-foot-4
5555 .... Cliff Hagan* 6-foot-4	4349 .... Rajon Rondo^ 6-foot-1
5366 .... Jerry West 6-foot-3	4348 .... Ron Boone* 6-foot-2
5269 .... Gary Payton 6-foot-4	4305 .... Sam Jones 6-foot-4
5206 .... Chris Paul^ 6-foot-0	4278 .... Richie Guerin 6-foot-4
5030 .... Lenny Wilkens 6-foot-1	4249 .... Dennis Johnson 6-foot-4
4963 .... Mark Jackson 6-foot-1	4084 ...... Rod Strickland 6-foot-3
4933 .... Dwyane Wade 6-foot-4	4066 .... Alvin Robertson 6-foot-4
4830 .... Walt Frazier 6-foot-4	4051 .... John Stockton 6-foot-1
4795 .... Andre Miller 6-foot-3		

^ Active.

* Includes NBA and ABA statistics.

Most Career Rebounds by Players Under 6-Feet Tall

3039 .... Damon Stoudamire 5-foot-10	1609 .... Dana Barros 5-foot-11
2318 .... Muggsy Bogues 5-foot-3	1506 .... Ty Lawson 5-foot-11
2302 .... Slater Martin 5-foot-10	1446 .... Nate Robinson 5-foot-8
2174 .... Terrell Brandon 5-foot-11	1349 .... Bill Keller[a] 5-foot-10
2103 .... Calvin Murphy 5-foot-9	1321 .... Isaiah Thomas^ 5-foot-9
1900 .... Michael Adams 5-foot-10	1294 .... Johnny Egan 5-foot-11
1805 .... D.J. Augustin^ 5-foot-11	1249 .... Travis Best 5-foot-11
1785 .... Brevin Knight 5-foot-10	1186 .... Chucky Atkins 5-foot-11
1751 .... Avery Johnson 5-foot-10	1133 .... Whitey Skoog 5-foot-11
1748 .... J.J. Barea 5-foot-10	1005 .... Larry Brown[a] 5-foot-9
1742 .... Spud Webb 5-foot-6		

^ Active.

[a] ABA.

Most Rebounds, Rookie Season

NBA

1941 .... Wilt Chamberlain*, Phi. Warriors, 1959–60
1500 .... Walt Bellamy*, Chi. Packers, 1961–62
1491 .... Wes Unseld*, Bal. Bullets, 1968–69
1406 .... Elvin Hayes, S.D. Rockets, 1968–69
1375 .... Jerry Lucas*, Cin. Royals, 1963–64
1216 .... Dave Cowens**, Bos. Celtics, 1970–71
1190 .... Kareem Abdul-Jabbar*, Mil. Bucks, 1969–70
1184 .... Elmore Smith, Buf. Braves, 1971–72
1175 .... Willis Reed*, N.Y. Knicks, 1964–65
1122 .... Shaquille O'Neal*, Orl. Magic, 1992–93
1094 .... Maurice Stokes*, Roc. Royals, 1955–56
1064 .... Gus Johnson, Bal. Bullets, 1963–64
1050 .... Elgin Baylor*, Min. Lakers, 1958–59
1005 .... Buck Williams*, N.J. Nets, 1981–82
994 .... Bob Pettit*, Mil. Hawks, 1954–55
994 .... Larry Smith, G.S. Warriors, 1980–81
989 .... Blake Griffin*, L.A. Clippers, 2010–11

ABA

1637 .... Spencer Haywood*, Den. Rockets, 1969–70
1491 .... Artis Gilmore*, Ken. Colonels, 1971–72
1319 .... Julius Erving, Vir. Squires, 1971–72
1213 .... Mel Daniels*, Min. Muskies, 1967–68
1209 .... Moses Malone, Uta. Stars, 1974–75
1202 .... Marvin Barnes, Spirits of St.L., 1974–75
1095 .... Caldwell Jones, S.D. Conquistadors, 1973–74
1093 .... Dan Issel**, Ken. Colonels, 1970–71
1038 .... Ira Harge, Pit Pipers/Oak. Oaks, 1967–68
998 .... Swen Nater*, Vir. Squires/S.A. Spurs, 1973–74
982 .... John Beasley, Dal. Chaparrals, 1967–68
962 .... Larry Kenon, N.Y. Nets, 1973–74
952 .... Willie Wise, L.A. Stars, 1969–70
945 .... Connie Hawkins, Pit. Pipers, 1967–68
940 .... Billy Paultz, N.Y. Nets, 1970–71
936 .... Jim Hadnot, Oak. Oaks, 1967–68
929 .... Goose Ligon, Ken. Colonels, 1967–68

continued on next page

NBA

983 .... David Robinson*, S.A. Spurs, 1989–90
980 .... Luke Jackson, Phi. 76ers, 1964–65
977 .... Tim Duncan*, S.A. Spurs, 1997–98
974 .... Hakeem Olajuwon, Hou. Rockets, 1984–85
967 .... Lloyd Neal, Por. Blazers, 1972–73
958 .... Ray Felix*, Bal. Bullets, 1953–54
949 .... Pete Cross, Sea. Sonics, 1970–71
943 .... Bill Russell, Bos. Celtics, 1956–57
943 .... Sidney Wicks*, Por. Blazers, 1971–72
913 .... Sam Lacey, Cin. Royals, 1970–71
913 .... Ralph Sampson*, Hou. Rockets, 1983–84

* Rookie of the Year.

** Tied for Rookie of the Year with Geoff Petrie, Por. Blazers.

ABA

894 .... Red Robbins, N.O. Buccaneers, 1967–68
894 .... David Vaughn, Vir. Squires, 1974–75
875 .... Wendell Ladner, Mem. Pros, 1970–71
856 .... Dan Anderson, N.J. Americans, 1967–68
822 .... Keith Swagerty, Hou. Mavericks, 1968–69
819 .... Bob Netolicky, Ind. Pacers, 1967–68
817 .... Gene Moore, Ken. Colonels, 1968–69
816 .... Maurice Lucas, Spirits of St.L., 1974–75
814 .... Jim McDaniels, Car. Cougars, 1971–72
809 .... John Smith, Dal. Chaparrals, 1968–69
804 .... Dave Robisch, Den. Rockets, 1971–72

* Rookie of the Year.

** Tied for Rookie of the Year with Charlie Scott, Vir. Squires.

Players with 10 Rebounds in Each of First Two Career Games

Total Reb		First Game	Second Game
62	Wilt Chamberlain, Phi. Warriors, 1959–60	28	34
42	Wes Unseld, Bal. Bullets, 1968–69	22	20
40	Maurice Stokes, Roc. Royals, 1955–56	20	20
38	Dave Cowens, Bos. Celtics, 1970–71	17	21
38	Artis Gilmore, Ken. Colonelsª, 1971–72	20	18
37	Jerry Lucas, Cin. Royals, 1963–64	17	20
37	Bill Walton, Por. Blazers, 1974–75	24	13
36	Elvin Hayes, S.D. Rockets, 1968–69	12	24
35	Elgin Baylor, Min. Lakers, 1958–59	13	22
35	David Robinson, S.A. Spurs, 1989–90	17	18
34	Elmore Smith, Buf. Braves, 1971–72	16	18
33	Willis Reed, N.Y. Knicks, 1964–65	11	22
33	Kareem Abdul-Jabbar, Mil. Bucks, 1969–70	12	11
33	Dikembe Mutombo, Den. Nuggets, 1991–92	16	17
33	Shaquille O'Neal, Orl. Magic, 1992–93	18	15
31	Buck Williams, N.J. Nets, 1981–82	17	14
30	Adrian Dantley, Buf. Braves, 1976–77	19	11
30	Ralph Sampson, Hou. Rockets, 1983–84	12	18
29	Walt Bellamy, Chi. Packers, 1961–62	18	13
28	Randolph Mahaffey, Ken. Colonelsª, 1967–68	13	15
28	Tom Boerwinkle, Chi. Bulls, 1968–69	12	16
28	Lloyd Neal, Por. Blazers, 1972–73	15	13
28	Brad Daugherty, Cle. Cavaliers, 1986–87	13	15
26	Jim McDaniels, Car. Cougarsª, 1971–72	14	12
26	Bernard King, N.J. Nets, 1977–78	14	12
26	Karl-Anthony Towns, Min. T'Wolves, 2015–16	12	14
25	Randy Denton, Car. Cougarsª, 1971–72	12	13
25	Darrell Arthur, Mem. Grizzlies, 2008–09	15	10
24	Emeka Okafor, Cha. Bobcats, 2004–05	10	14
24	Blake Griffin, L.A. Clippers, 2010–11	14	10
23	Oscar Robertson, Cin. Royals, 1960–61	12	11
23	Paul Silas, St.L. Hawks, 1964–65	13	10
23	Stew Johnson, Ken. Colonelsª, 1967–68	13	10
23	Marques Johnson, Mil. Bucks, 1977–78	12	11
23	Mychal Thompson, Por. Blazers, 1978–79	10	13
23	James Singleton, L.A. Clippers, 2005–06	10	13

continued on next page

Total Reb		First Game	Second Game
22	Rick Barry, S.F. Warriors, 1965–66	10	12
21	Mel Daniels, Min. Muskies[a], 1967–68	10	11
21	Melvin Turpin, Cle. Cavaliers, 1984–85	10	11
21	Al Horford, Atl. Hawks, 2007–08	10	11
21	Ben Simmons, Phi. 76ers, 2017–18	10	11
20	Dwight Howard, Orl. Magic, 2004–05	10	10
20	Nerlens Noel, Phi. 76ers, 2014–15	10	10

[a] ABA.

Youngest Player with an 800-Rebound Season

Age (Birthdate)

19 (Dec. 8)	Dwight Howard, Orl. Magic, 2004–05	823
19 (Mar. 23)	Moses Malone, Uta. Stars[a], 1974–75	1209
20 (Dec. 8)	Dwight Howard, Orl. Magic, 2005–06	1022
20 (Nov. 15)	Karl-Anthony Towns, Min. T'Wolves, 2015–16	858
20 (Sep. 30)	John Drew, Atl. Hawks, 1974–75	836
20 (Aug. 10)	Andre Drummond, Det. Pistons, 2013–14	1071
20 (Apr. 22)	Spencer Haywood, Den. Rockets[a], 1969–70	1637
20 (Mar. 11)	Elton Brand, Chi. Bulls, 1999–00	810
20 (Mar. 6)	Shaquille O'Neal, Orl. Magic, 1992–93	1122
21 (Dec. 13)	Larry Kenon, N.Y. Nets[a], 1973–74	962
21 (Dec. 8)	Dwight Howard, Orl. Magic, 2006–07	1008
21 (Nov. 29)	Julius Randle, L.A. Lakers, 2015–16	829
21 (Nov. 15)	Karl-Anthony Towns, Min. T'Wolves, 2016–17	1007
21 (Aug. 12)	Antoine Walker, Bos. Celtics, 1997–98	836
21 (Aug. 10)	Andre Drummond, Det. Pistons, 2014–15	1104
21 (Jul. 2)	Clark Kellogg, Ind. Pacers, 1982–83	860
21 (Apr. 25)	Tim Duncan, S.A. Spurs, 1997–98	977
21 (Mar. 28)	Rick Barry, S.F. Warriors, 1965–66	850
21 (Mar. 23)	Moses Malone, Buf. Braves/Hou. Rockets, 1976–77	1072
21 (Mar. 16)	Blake Griffin, L.A. Clippers, 2010–11	989
21 (Mar. 8)	Buck Williams, N.J. Nets, 1981–82	1005
21 (Mar. 6)	Shaquille O'Neal, Orl. Magic, 1993–94	1072
21 (Feb. 22)	Julius Erving, Vir. Squires[a], 1971–72	1319
21 (Feb. 8)	Marques Johnson, Mil. Bucks, 1977–78	847

[a] ABA.

Oldest Player with an 800-Rebound Season

Age (Birthdate)

37 (Aug. 30)	Robert Parish, Bos. Celtics, 1990–91	856
36 (May 13)	Dennis Rodman, Chi. Bulls, 1997–98	1201
36 (Aug. 21)	Wilt Chamberlain, L.A. Lakers, 1972–73	1526
36 (Dec. 8)	Johnny Green, Cin. Royals, 1969–70	841
35 (Mar. 22)	Marcus Camby, L.A. Clippers/Por. Blazers, 2009–10	871
35 (May 13)	Dennis Rodman, Chi. Bulls, 1996–97	883
35 (Jun. 25)	Dikembe Mutombo, Phi. 76ers, 2001–02	863
35 (Aug. 21)	Wilt Chamberlain, L.A. Lakers, 1971–72	1572
35 (Aug. 30)	Robert Parish, Bos. Celtics, 1988–89	996
35 (Sep. 21)	Artis Gilmore, S.A. Spurs, 1984–85	846
34 (Feb. 12)	Bill Russell, Bos. Celtics, 1968–69	1484
34 (Mar. 23)	Moses Malone, Atl. Hawks, 1989–90	812

continued on next page

Age (Birthdate)

34 (May 13)	Dennis Rodman, Chi. Bulls, 1995–96	952
34 (Jun. 25)	Dikembe Mutombo, Atl. Hawks/Phi. 76ers, 2000–01	1015
34 (Jul. 6)	Pau Gasol, Chi. Bulls, 2014–15	919
34 (Jul. 24)	Karl Malone, Uta. Jazz, 1997–98	834
34 (Aug. 5)	Patrick Ewing, N.Y. Knicks, 1996–97	834
34 (Aug. 21)	Wilt Chamberlain, L.A. Lakers, 1970–71	1493
34 (Sep. 16)	Elgin Baylor, L.A. Lakers, 1968–69	805
34 (Nov. 17)	Elvin Hayes, Was. Bullets, 1979–80	896

Youngest Player with a 1000-Rebound Season

Age (Birthdate)

19 (Mar. 23)	Moses Malone, Uta. Stars[a], 1974–75	1209
20 (Dec. 8)	Dwight Howard, Orl. Magic, 2005–06	1022
20 (Aug. 10)	Andre Drummond, Det. Pistons, 2013–14	1071
20 (Apr. 22)	Spencer Haywood, Den. Rockets[a], 1969–70	1637
20 (Mar. 6)	Shaquille O'Neal, Orl. Magic, 1992–93	1122
21 (Dec. 8)	Dwight Howard, Orl. Magic, 2006–07	1008
21 (Nov. 15)	Karl-Anthony Towns, Min. T'Wolves, 2016–17	1007
21 (Aug. 10)	Andre Drummond, Det. Pistons, 2014–15	1104
21 (Mar. 23)	Moses Malone, Buf. Braves/Hou. Rockets, 1976–77	1072
21 (Mar. 8)	Buck Williams, N.J. Nets, 1981–82	1005
21 (Mar. 6)	Shaquille O'Neal, Orl. Magic, 1993–94	1072
21 (Feb. 22)	Julius Erving, Vir. Squires[a], 1971–72	1319
22 (Dec. 8)	Dwight Howard, Orl Magic, 2007–08	1161
22 (Nov. 15)	Karl-Anthony Towns, Min. T'Wolves, 2017–18	1012
22 (Oct. 25)	Dave Cowens, Bos. Celtics, 1970–71	1216
22 (Oct. 25)	Dan Issel, Ken. Colonels[a], 1970–71	1093
22 (Sep. 25)	Bob McAdoo, Buf. Braves, 1973–74	1117
22 (Sep. 21)	Artis Gilmore, Ken. Colonels[a], 1971–72	1491
22 (Sep. 7)	Kevin Love, Min. T'Wolves, 2010–11	1112
22 (Aug. 12)	George McGinnis, Ind. Pacers[a], 1972–73	1022
22 (Aug. 10)	Andre Drummond, Det. Pistons, 2015–16	1198
22 (Jul. 27)	Marvin Barnes, Spirits of St.L.[a], 1974–75	1202
22 (Jul. 24)	Walt Bellamy, Chi. Packers, 1961–62	1500
22 (Jun. 25)	Willis Reed, N.Y. Knicks, 1964–65	1175
22 (Jun. 17)	Maurice Stokes, Roc. Royals, 1955–56	1094
22 (May 19)	Dolph Schayes, Syr. Nationals, 1950–51	1080
22 (May 9)	Elmore Smith, Buf. Braves, 1971–72	1184
22 (Apr. 16)	Kareem Abdul-Jabbar, Mil. Bucks, 1969–70	1190
22 (Mar. 14)	Wes Unseld, Bal. Bullets, 1968–69	1491
22 (Mar. 8)	Buck Williams, N.J. Nets, 1982–93	1027
22 (Feb. 20)	Charles Barkley, Phi. 76ers, 1985–86	1026

[a]ABA.

Oldest Player with a 1000-Rebound Season

Age (Birthdate)

36 (May 13)	Dennis Rodman, Chi. Bulls, 1997–98	1201
36 (Aug. 21)	Wilt Chamberlain, L.A. Lakers, 1972–73	1526
35 (Aug. 21)	Wilt Chamberlain, L.A. Lakers, 1971–72	1572
34 (Feb. 12)	Bill Russell, Bos. Celtics, 1968–69	1484
34 (Jun. 25)	Dikembe Mutombo, Atl. Hawks/Phi. 76ers, 2000–01	1015
34 (Aug. 21)	Wilt Chamberlain, L.A. Lakers, 1970–71	1493

continued on next page

Age (Birthdate)

33 (Feb. 12)	Bill Russell, Bos. Celtics, 1967–68	1451
33 (Mar. 14)	Wes Unseld, Was. Bullets, 1979–80	1094
33 (Mar. 22)	Marcus Camby, Den. Nuggets, 2007–08	1037
33 (Jun. 25)	Dikembe Mutombo, Atl. Hawks, 1999–00	1157
32 (Feb. 12)	Bill Russell, Bos. Celtics, 1966–67	1700
32 (Apr. 4)	Bill Bridges, Atl. Hawks/Phi. 76ers, 1971–72	1051
32 (May 13)	Dennis Rodman, S.A. Spurs, 1993–94	1367
32 (Jul. 12)	Paul Silas, Bos. Celtics, 1975–76	1025
32 (Jul. 24)	Walt Bellamy, Atl. Hawks, 1971–72	1049
32 (Aug. 21)	Wilt Chamberlain, L.A. Lakers, 1968–69	1712
32 (Oct. 25)	Zelmo Beaty, Uta. Stars°, 1971–72	1110
32 (Nov. 17)	Elvin Hayes, Was. Bullets, 1977–78	1075
32 (Dec. 8)	Dwight Howard, Cha. Hornets, 2017–18	1012
32 (Dec. 13)	Gus Johnson, Bal. Bullets, 1970–71	1128
31 (Jan. 14)	Swen Nater, S.D. Clippers, 1980–81	1017
31 (Feb. 12)	Bill Russell, Bos. Celtics, 1965–66	1779
31 (Mar. 30)	Jerry Lucas, N.Y. Knicks, 1971–72	1011
31 (Apr. 4)	Bill Bridges, Atl. Hawks, 1970–71	1233
31 (Apr. 16)	Kareem Abdul-Jabbar, L.A. Lakers, 1978–79	1025
31 (May 13)	Dennis Rodman, Det. Pistons, 1992–93	1132
31 (May 31)	Happy Hairston, L.A. Lakers, 1973–74	1040
31 (Jul. 12)	Paul Silas, Bos. Celtics, 1974–75	1025
31 (Jul. 17)	Red Kerr, Phi. 76ers, 1963–64	1017
31 (Jul. 24)	Walt Bellamy, Atl. Hawks, 1970–71	1060
31 (Jul. 25)	Nate Thurmond, G.S. Warriors, 1972–73	1349
31 (Aug. 21)	Wilt Chamberlain, Phi. 76ers, 1967–68	1952
31 (Oct. 25)	Zelmo Beaty, Uta. Stars°, 1970–71	1190
31 (Nov. 17)	Elvin Hayes, Was. Bullets, 1976–77	1029
31 (Dec. 12)	Bob Pettit, St.L. Hawks, 1963–64	1224
31 (Dec. 13)	Gus Johnson, Bal. Bullets, 1969–70	1086

° ABA.

Most Rebounds from Age 39 On

2024	Robert Parish		707	Kevin Willis
1335	Kareem Abdul-Jabbar		596	Dirk Nowitzki
1026	Dikembe Mutombo		497	Michael Jordan
995	Karl Malone		464	John Stockton
839	Vince Carter		447	Tim Duncan

Most Rebounds, Last Season in League

1526	Wilt Chamberlain, L.A. Lakers, 1972–73
1484	Bill Russell, Bos. Celtics, 1968–69
1142	Maurice Stokes, Cin. Royals, 1957–58
946	Happy Hairston, L.A. Lakers, 1974–75
936	Jim Hadnot, Oak. Oaks°, 1967–68
804	Kendall Rhine, Hou. Mavericks°, 1968–69
757	Dave DeBusschere, N.Y. Knicks, 1973–74
749	Harry Gallatin, Det. Pistons, 1957–58
709	Alex Groza, Ind. Olympians, 1950–51
685	Joe Strawder, Det. Pistons, 1967–68

continued on next page

673 .... Wes Unseld, Was. Bullets, 1980–81
672 .... Wayne Embry, Mil. Bucks, 1968–69
662 .... Steve Stipanovich, Ind. Pacers, 1987–88
636 .... Otto Moore, N.O. Jazz, 1976–77
624 .... Rudy LaRusso, S.F. Warriors, 1968–69
621 .... Bob Pettit, St.L. Hawks, 1964–65
618 .... Randolph Mahaffey, Car. Cougars*, 1970–71
610 .... Charlie Tyra, Chi. Packers, 1961–62
607 .... Mike Jackson, Vir. Squires*, 1975–76
586 .... Red Kerr, Bal. Bullets, 1965–66
579 .... George Yardley, Syr. Nationals, 1959–60
570 .... Vern Mikkelsen, Min. Lakers, 1958–59
562 .... Michael Smith, Was. Wizards, 2000–01
553 .... Trooper Washington, N.Y. Nets*, 1972–73
551 .... Dewitt Menyard, Hou. Mavericks*, 1967–68
545 .... Don Barksdale, Bos. Celtics, 1954–55
541 .... Jesse Branson, N.O. Buccaneers*, 1967–68
539 .... Chick Halbert, Was. Capitols/Bal. Bullets, 1950–51
537 .... Eddie Miller, Bal. Bullets, 1953–54
527 .... Paul Arizin, Phi. Warriors, 1961–62
517 .... Bob Harris, Bos. Celtics, 1953–54
515 .... Warren Davis, Mem. Tams*, 1972–73
508 .... Brad Daugherty, Cle. Cavaliers, 1993–94
508 .... David Robinson, S.A. Spurs, 2002–03
* ABA.

Most Offensive Rebounds in a Game without a Defensive Rebound

12 .... Popeye Jones, Dal. Mavericks .... @ L.A. Lakers (Mar. 10, 1994)
11 .... Bill Laimbeer, Det. Pistons .... vs. G.S. Warriors (Jan. 9, 1993)
11 .... Erick Dampier, Dal. Mavericks .... vs. Pho. Suns (Mar. 14, 2007)
10 .... Marty Byrnes, Pho. Suns .... @ Hou. Rockets (Nov. 4, 1978)
10 .... Marques Johnson, Mil. Bucks .... vs. N.J. Nets (Jan. 6, 1981)
10 .... Tony Battie, Den. Nuggets .... @ L.A. Lakers (Jan. 14, 1998)
9 .... Tom Boswell, Den. Nuggets .... vs. S.D. Clippers (Feb. 16, 1979)
9 .... Phil Hubbard, Cle. Cavaliers .... vs. N.J. Nets (Apr. 4, 1982)
9 .... Kent Benson, Det. Pistons .... @ L.A. Lakers (Mar. 23, 1984)
9 .... Michael Brooks, S.D. Clippers .... vs. Dal. Mavericks (Mar. 24, 1983)
9 .... Wayne Cooper, Den. Nuggets .... @ N.Y. Knicks (Dec. 4, 1984)
9 .... Dale Ellis, Sea. Sonics .... @ Ind. Pacers (Nov. 28, 1987)
9 .... Andrew DeClercq, Bos. Celtics .... @ Den. Nuggets (Feb. 10, 1998)
9 .... Clyde Drexler, Por. Blazers .... vs. L.A. Lakers (Mar. 15, 1988)
9 .... Kevin Duckworth, Por. Blazers .... @ G.S. Warriors (Nov. 12, 1988)
9 .... Alton Lister, Sea. Sonics .... vs. L.A. Clippers (Jan. 17, 1989)
9 .... Nazr Mohammed, S.A. Spurs .... @ Ind. Pacers (Feb. 12, 2006)
9 .... Zach Randolph, Por. Blazers .... @ Ind. Pacers (Feb. 8, 2006)

Most Defensive Rebounds in a Game without an Offensive Rebound

21 .... Dirk Nowitzki, Dal. Mavericks .... vs. Sac. Kings (Feb. 23, 2002)
20 .... DeMarcus Cousins, Sac. Kings .... vs. N.O. Pelicans (Apr. 3, 2015)
19 .... David Robinson, S.A. Spurs .... vs. N.J. Nets (Nov. 7, 1994)
19 .... Patrick Ewing, N.Y. Knicks .... @ L.A. Clippers (Nov. 8, 1996)

continued on next page

19	Dirk Nowitzki, Dal. Mavericks	vs. Bos. Celtics (Mar. 20, 2008)
19	Troy Murphy, Ind. Pacers	vs. Was. Wizards (Mar. 24, 2010)
19	Lauri Markkanen, Chi. Bulls	@ Brk. Nets (Jan. 29, 2019)
19	Giannis Antetokounmpo, Mil. Bucks	@ Tor. Raptors (Feb. 25, 2020)
19	Domantas Sabonis, Ind. Pacers	@ Ok.C. Thunder (May 1, 2021)
19	Giannis Antetokounmpo, Mil. Bucks	vs. Ok.C. Thunder (Nov. 19, 2021)
18	Neal Walk, Pho. Suns	@ Was. Capitals (Nov. 4, 1973)
18	Bill Walton, Por. Blazers	vs. Was. Bullets (Dec. 17, 1977)
18	Danilo Gallinari, Den. Nuggets	vs. L.A. Clippers (Nov. 24, 2015)
18	Kevin Love, Cle. Cavaliers	@ Brk. Nets (Jan. 20, 2016)
18	Julius Randle, L.A. Lakers	vs. Den. Nuggets (Mar. 25, 2016)

Players Averaging 5 Offensive and 5 Defensive Rebounds, Season
(Qualified for RPG Leaderboard)

	OR/G	DR/G
Moses Malone, Hou. Rockets, 1976–77	5.3	7.7
Moses Malone, Hou. Rockets, 1977–78	6.4	8.6
Moses Malone, Hou. Rockets, 1978–79	7.2	10.5
Moses Malone, Hou. Rockets, 1979–80	7.0	7.5
Larry Smith, G.S. Warriors, 1980–81	5.3	6.8
Moses Malone, Hou. Rockets, 1980–81	5.9	8.8
Moses Malone, Hou. Rockets, 1981–82	6.9	7.8
Moses Malone, Phi. 76ers, 1982–83	5.7	9.6
Larry Smith, G.S. Warriors, 1984–85	5.1	5.8
Hakeem Olajuwon, Hou. Rockets, 1984–85	5.4	6.5
Charles Barkley, Phi. 76ers, 1986–87	5.7	8.9
Michael Cage, L.A. Clippers, 1987–88	5.2	7.9
Charles Barkley, Phi. 76ers, 1988–89	5.1	7.4
Kevin Willis, Atl. Hawks, 1991–92	5.2	10.4
Dennis Rodman, Det. Pistons, 1991–92	6.4	12.3
Dennis Rodman, Det. Pistons, 1992–93	5.9	12.3
Dennis Rodman, S.A. Spurs, 1993–94	5.7	11.6
Dennis Rodman, S.A. Spurs, 1994–95	5.6	11.2
Dennis Rodman, Chi. Bulls, 1995–96	5.6	9.3
Dennis Rodman, Chi. Bulls, 1996–97	5.8	10.2
Jayson Williams, N.J. Nets, 1997–98	6.8	6.8
Dennis Rodman, Chi. Bulls, 1997–98	5.3	9.8
Andre Drummond, Det. Pistons, 2013–14	5.4	7.8
Andre Drummond, Det. Pistons, 2014–15	5.3	8.1
Andre Drummond, Det. Pistons, 2017–18	5.1	10.9
Andre Drummond, Det. Pistons, 2018–19	5.4	10.2

Most Games with 10 Offensive and 10 Defensive Rebounds, Career

42	Moses Malone	7	Tyson Chandler
32	Dennis Rodman	6	Dikembe Mutombo
14	Andre Drummond^	5	Shaquille O'Neal
11	Larry Smith	5	Kevin Willis
11	Jayson Williams	5	Clint Capela^
7	Charles Barkley		

^ Active.

Offensive and Defensive Rebounds

Offensive Rebounds by Decade[*]
NBA

1973-74–1979-80		1980-81–1989-90		1990-91–1999-00	
2035	Paul Silas	4015	Moses Malone	3185	Dennis Rodman
1990	Elvin Hayes	2889	Larry Smith	2580	Shawn Kemp
1977	Moses Malone	2838	Buck Williams	2554	Dikembe Mutombo
1878	Wes Unseld	2573	Robert Parish	2470	Kevin Willis
1602	Kareem Abdul-Jabbar	2423	Bill Laimbeer	2376	Horace Grant
1584	Clifford Ray	2159	Charles Barkley	2224	Olden Polynice
1564	John Drew	2027	Hakeem Olajuwon	2218	David Robinson
1501	Dave Cowens	1999	Kevin McHale	2192	Charles Oakley
1494	Bob McAdoo	1997	Terry Cummings	2185	Dale Davis
1460	Sidney Wicks	1957	Mychal Thompson	2162	Shaquille O'Neal

2000-01–2009-10		2010-11–2019-20		2020-21–2021-22	
2749	Ben Wallace	2858	Andre Drummond	576	Clint Capela
2318	Tim Duncan	2607	DeAndre Jordan	562	Steven Adams
2310	Elton Brand	2115	Tristan Thompson	481	Rudy Gobert
2080	Erick Dampier	2086	Dwight Howard	481	Jakob Poeltl
2040	Zydrunas Ilgauskas	1894	LaMarcus Aldridge	479	Jonas Valančiūnas
1999	Shaquille O'Neal	1878	Enes Freedom	411	Nikola Jokić
1972	Shawn Marion	1823	Steven Adams	408	Mitchell Robinson
1927	Antawn Jamison	1769	Greg Monroe	406	Ivica Zubac
1911	Jeff Foster	1756	Robin Lopez	395	Andre Drummond
1886	Kevin Garnett	1737	Derrick Favors	388	Jarrett Allen

ABA

1967-68–1969-70		1970-71–1975-76	
1308	Mel Daniels	2177	Artis Gilmore
1161	Red Robbins	2010	Dan Issel
1097	Goose Ligon	1622	Julius Erving
982	Trooper Washington	1571	Wil Jones
963	Bob Netolicky	1562	Mel Daniels
833	Les Hunter	1542	George McGinnis
829	John Beasley	1419	Jim Eakins
753	Warren Davis	1376	Billy Paultz
749	Manny Leaks	1201	Julius Keye
665	Randolph Mahaffey	1194	Dave Robisch

[*] Offensive Rebounds became an official stat in the ABA in 1967–68, and in the NBA in 1973–74.

Evolution of Offensive Rebound Record
NBA

1973–74	Elvin Hayes, Cap. Bullets	354
1974–75	John Drew, Atl. Hawks	357
1975–76	Paul Silas, Bos. Celtics	365
1976–77	Moses Malone, Buf. Braves/Hou. Rockets	437
1978–79	Moses Malone, Hou. Rockets	587

ABA

1967–68	Mel Daniels, Min. Muskies	502
1969–70	Spencer Haywood, Den. Rockets	533

Most Offensive Rebounds, Season

NBA

587 ...... Moses Malone, Hou. Rockets, 1978–79
573 ...... Moses Malone, Hou. Rockets, 1979–80
558 ...... Moses Malone, Hou. Rockets, 1981–82
523 ...... Dennis Rodman, Det. Pistons, 1991–92
474 ...... Moses Malone, Hou. Rockets, 1980–81
453 ...... Dennis Rodman, S.A. Spurs, 1993–94
445 ...... Moses Malone, Phi. 76ers, 1982–83
443 ...... Jayson Williams, N.J. Nets, 1997–98
440 ...... Hakeem Olajuwon, Hou. Rockets, 1984–85
440 ...... Andre Drummond, Det. Pistons, 2013–14
437 ...... Moses Malone, Buf. Braves/Hou. Rockets, 1976–77
437 ...... Andre Drummond, Det. Pistons, 2014–15
433 ...... Larry Smith, G.S. Warriors, 1980–81
423 ...... Andre Drummond, Det. Pistons, 2018–19
421 ...... Dennis Rodman, Chi. Bulls, 1997–98
418 ...... Kevin Willis, Atl. Hawks, 1991–92
405 ...... Larry Smith, G.S. Warriors, 1984–85
403 ...... Charles Barkley, Phi. 76ers, 1988–89

ABA

533 ...... Spencer Haywood, Den. Rockets, 1969–70
502 ...... Mel Daniels, Min. Muskies, 1967–68
478 ...... Artis Gilmore, Ken. Colonels, 1973–74
476 ...... Julius Erving, Vir. Squires, 1971–72
455 ...... Moses Malone, Uta. Stars, 1974–75
449 ...... Artis Gilmore, Ken. Colonels, 1972–73
435 ...... Mike Lewis, Pit. Condors, 1970–71
434 ...... George McGinnis, Ind. Pacers, 1972–73
432 ...... Donald Sidle, Mia. Floridians, 1969–70
427 ...... Manny Leaks, Dal. Chaparrals, 1969–70
427 ...... Red Robbins, N.O. Buccaneers, 1969–70
427 ...... Artis Gilmore, Ken. Colonels, 1974–75
423 ...... Mel Daniels, Ind. Pacers, 1969–70
422 ...... George McGinnis, Ind. Pacers, 1973–74
421 ...... Dan Issel, Ken. Colonels, 1970–71
421 ...... Artis Gilmore, Ken. Colonels, 1971–72
419 ...... Marvin Barnes, Spirits of St.L., 1974–75
407 ...... Zelmo Beaty, Uta. Stars, 1970–71
402 ...... Artis Gilmore, Ken. Colonels, 1975–76

Most Offensive Rebounds, Career

7382 .... Moses Malone
4816 .... Artis Gilmore
4598 .... Robert Parish
4526 .... Buck Williams
4329 .... Dennis Rodman
4260 .... Charles Barkley
4209 .... Shaquille O'Neal
4132 .... Kevin Willis
4124 .... Dwight Howard^
4034 .... Hakeem Olajuwon
3924 .... Charles Oakley
3859 .... Tim Duncan

3808 .... Dikembe Mutombo
3696 .... Dan Issel
3689 .... Julius Erving
3562 .... Karl Malone
3529 .... Tyson Chandler
3467 .... Horace Grant
3446 .... Otis Thorpe
3444 .... Ben Wallace
3401 .... Larry Smith
3354 .... A.C. Green
3304 .... Elton Brand
3303 .... Dale Davis

3279 .... Zach Randolph
3227 .... Michael Cage
3209 .... Kevin Garnett
3184 .... Andre Drummond^
3183 .... Terry Cummings
3143 .... George McGinnis
3085 .... Pau Gasol
3083 .... David Robinson
3026 .... Shawn Kemp
3002 .... P.J. Brown

^ Active.

Most Games with 10 Offensive Rebounds, Season

15 .... Moses Malone, Hou. Rockets, 1981–82
15 .... Jayson Williams, N.J. Nets, 1997–98
14 .... Moses Malone, Hou. Rockets, 1979–80
13 .... Moses Malone, Hou. Rockets, 1978–79
8 .... Marvin Webster, Sea. Sonics, 1977–78
8 .... Dennis Rodman, Chi. Bulls, 1997–98
7 .... Moses Malone, Hou. Rockets, 1977–78
7 .... Moses Malone, Phi. 76ers, 1982–83
7 .... Dennis Rodman, Det. Pistons, 1992–93

7 .... Dennis Rodman, S.A. Spurs, 1993–94
6 .... Larry Smith, G.S. Warriors, 1980–81
6 .... Charles Barkley, Phi. 76ers, 1986–87
6 .... Dennis Rodman, Det. Pistons, 1991–92
6 .... Kevin Willis, Atl. Hawks, 1991–92
6 .... Jayson Williams, N.J. Nets, 1996–97
6 .... Andre Drummond, Det. Pistons, 2013–14
6 .... Andre Drummond, Det. Pistons, 2018–19

Most Games with 10 Offensive Rebounds, Career

91 .... Moses Malone	15 .... Shaquille O'Neal	13 .... Dikembe Mutombo
45 .... Dennis Rodman	15 .... Tyson Chandler	12 .... Buck Williams
27 .... Jayson Williams	14 .... Hakeem Olajuwon	12 .... Zach Randolph
27 .... Andre Drummond^	13 .... Charles Oakley	11 .... Michael Cage
24 .... Charles Barkley	13 .... Kevin Willis	11 .... Horace Grant
19 .... Larry Smith	13 .... David Robinson	10 .... Erik Dampier

^ Active.

Most Consecutive Games with 10 Offensive Rebounds, Season

		First Game of Streak	Last Game of Streak
15	Dennis Rodman, Det. Pistons	Mar. 26, 1993	Apr. 22, 1993
13	Dennis Rodman, S.A. Spurs	Feb. 16, 1995	Mar. 12, 1995
13	Dennis Rodman, Chi. Bulls	Dec. 21, 1996	Feb. 11, 1997
11	Charles Barkley, Phi. 76ers	Mar. 11, 1987	Apr. 1, 1987
10	Dennis Rodman, S.A. Spurs	Jan. 22, 1995	Feb. 8, 1995
10	Elton Brand, L.A. Clippers	Mar. 8, 2002	Mar. 25, 2002
10	Anderson Varejão, Cle. Cavaliers	Nov. 18, 2012	Dec. 5, 2012
9	Charles Barkley, Phi. 76ers	Jan. 17, 1990	Feb. 2, 1990
9	Dennis Rodman, Det. Pistons	Jan. 3, 1992	Jan. 23, 1992
9	Tyrone Hill, Cle. Cavaliers	Dec. 28, 1994	Jan. 17, 1995
9	Andre Drummond. Det. Pistons	Jan. 28, 2014	Feb. 18, 2014
9	Andre Drummond, Det. Pistons	Mar. 31, 2014	Apr. 16, 2014
8	Moses Malone, Phi. 76ers	Oct. 28, 1983	Nov. 13, 1983
8	Larry Smith, G.S. Warriors	Dec. 21, 1986	Jan. 4, 1987
8	Dennis Rodman, Det. Pistons	Feb. 25, 1992	Mar. 10, 1992
8	Jayson Williams, N.J. Nets	Dec. 3, 1997	Dec. 20, 1997

Most Offensive Rebounds, Game

21	Moses Malone, Hou. Rockets	vs. Sea. Sonics (Feb. 11, 1982)
19	Moses Malone, Hou. Rockets	@ N.O. Jazz (Feb. 9, 1979)
18	Tim Bassett, S.D. Conquistadors[a]	@ Ind. Pacers[a] (Mar. 15, 1974)
18	Charles Oakley, Chi. Bulls	vs. Mil. Bucks (Mar. 15, 1986)
18	Dennis Rodman, Det. Pistons	vs. Ind. Pacers (Mar. 4, 1992)
18	Zaza Pachulia, Mil. Bucks	@ Brk. Nets (Mar. 20, 2015)
17	Willie Wise, Uta. Stars	vs. Den. Rockets[a] (Mar. 23, 1971)
17	Jayson Williams, N.J. Nets	vs. Ind. Pacers (Oct. 31, 1997)
16	Mel Daniels, Min. Muskies[a]	@ N.O. Buccaneers[a] (Dec. 28, 1967)
16	Donnie Freeman, Mia. Floridians[a]	@ Pit. Pipers[a] (Mar. 8, 1970)
16	George McGinnis, Ind. Pacers[a]	vs. Car. Cougars[a] (Jan. 12, 1974)
16	Moses Malone, Hou. Rockets	vs. Buf. Braves (Nov. 16, 1977)
16	Moses Malone, Hou. Rockets	vs. Ind. Pacers (Oct. 17, 1979)
16	Larry Smith, G.S. Warriors	vs. Den. Nuggets (Mar. 23, 1986)
16	Charles Barkley, Phi. 76ers	vs. N.Y. Knicks (Mar. 4, 1987)
16	Charles Barkley, Phi. 76ers	vs. Den. Nuggets (Mar. 20, 1987)
16	Charles Oakley, Chi. Bulls	vs. Cle. Cavaliers (Apr. 22, 1988)
16	Terry Cummings, S.A. Spurs	@ G.S. Warriors (Feb. 28, 1990)
16	Kevin Willis, Atl. Hawks	vs. Was. Bullets (Feb. 19, 1992)
16	Andray Blatche, Was. Wizards	vs. Cle. Cavaliers (Apr. 1, 2011)
15	George Johnson, G.S. Warriors	@ Hou. Rockets (Nov. 24, 1976)
15	Swen Nater, Mil. Bucks	vs. Atl. Hawks (Dec. 19, 1976)

continued on next page

15	Mark Landsberger, Chi. Bulls	@ Det. Pistons (Nov. 10, 1978)
15	Moses Malone, Hou. Rockets	vs. S.A. Spurs (Apr. 7, 1979)
15	Moses Malone, Hou. Rockets	vs. Pho. Suns (Dec. 15, 1981)
15	Moses Malone, Phi. 76ers	vs. Bos. Celtics (Mar. 25, 1984)
15	Hakeem Olajuwon, Hou. Rockets	@ N.Y. Knicks (Feb. 14, 1985)
15	Larry Smith, Hou. Rockets	vs. Pho. Suns (Feb. 16, 1991)
15	Jayson Williams, N.J. Nets	vs. Min. T'Wolves (Jan. 9, 1997)
15	Dennis Rodman, Chi. Bulls	vs. L.A. Clippers (Dec. 23, 1997)
15	J.J. Hickson, Den. Nuggets	vs. Por. Blazers (Feb. 25, 2014)
15	Andre Drummond, Det. Pistons	@ G.S. Warriors (Mar. 11, 2015)

ᵃ ABA.

Most Games with 5 Offensive Rebounds, Season

60 .... Dennis Rodman, Det. Pistons, 1991–92	43 .... Larry Smith, G.S. Warriors, 1985–86
50 .... Dennis Rodman, S.A. Spurs, 1993–94	43 .... Charles Barkley, Phi. 76ers, 1987–88
50 .... Andre Drummond, Det. Pistons, 2013–14	43 .... Dennis Rodman, Chi. Bulls, 1995–96
49 .... Hakeem Olajuwon, Hou. Rockets, 1984–85	43 .... Elton Brand, L.A. Clippers, 2001–02
48 .... Moses Malone, Phi. 76ers, 1982–83	43 .... Steven Adams, Ok.C. Thunder, 2017–18
48 .... Jayson Williams, N.J. Nets, 1997–98	43 .... Andre Drummond, Det. Pistons, 2018–19
47 .... Larry Smith, G.S. Warriors, 1980–81	42 .... Dennis Rodman, Det. Pistons, 1992–93
47 .... Andre Drummond, Det. Pistons, 2017–18	42 .... DeAndre Jordan, L.A. Clippers, 2014–15
46 .... Charles Barkley, Phi. 76ers, 1988–89	42 .... Steven Adams, Ok.C. Thunder, 2018–19
45 .... Kevin Willis, Atl. Hawks, 1991–92	41 .... Moses Malone, Was. Bullets, 1987–88
45 .... Dennis Rodman, Chi. Bulls, 1997–98	41 .... Charles Barkley, Phi. 76ers, 1989–90
45 .... Andre Drummond, Det. Pistons, 2014–15	40 .... Moses Malone, Phi. 76ers, 1983–84
44 .... Moses Malone, Phi. 76ers, 1984–85	40 .... Charles Barkley, Phi. 76ers, 1986–87
44 .... Moses Malone, Atl. Hawks, 1988–89	40 .... Michael Cage, L.A. Clippers, 1987–88
43 .... Larry Smith, G.S. Warriors, 1984–85	40 .... Andre Drummond, Det. Pistons, 2015–16

Players with 10 Offensive Rebounds, Zero Defensive Rebounds, Game

12	Popeye Jones, Dal. Mavericks	@ L.A. Lakers (Mar. 10, 1994)
11	Bill Laimbeer, Det. Pistons	vs. G.S. Warriors (Jan. 9, 1993)
11	Erick Dampier, Dal. Mavericks	vs. Pho. Suns (Mar. 14, 2007)
10	Marty Byrnes, Pho. Suns	@ Hou. Rockets (Nov. 4, 1978)
10	Marques Johnson, Mil. Bucks	vs. N.J. Nets (Jan. 6, 1981)
10	Tony Battie, Den. Nuggets	@ L.A. Lakers (Jan. 14, 1998)

Defensive Rebounds by Decade*
NBA

1973–74 – 1979–80		1980–81 – 1989–90		1990–91 – 1999–00	
5673	Kareem Abdul-Jabbar	6314	Bill Laimbeer	6383	Karl Malone
5349	Elvin Hayes	5968	Jack Sikma	6158	Dennis Rodman
4921	Dave Cowens	5876	Moses Malone	5885	Dikembe Mutombo
4666	Bob McAdoo	5737	Larry Bird	5850	Patrick Ewing
4517	Sam Lacey	5635	Robert Parish	5450	David Robinson
4508	Wes Unseld	5538	Buck Williams	5340	Hakeem Olajuwon
3816	Bob Lanier	4605	James Donaldson	4925	Kevin Willis
3486	Clifford Ray	4162	Mychal Thompson	4910	Shawn Kemp
3355	Truck Robinson	4073	Rick Mahorn	4876	Charles Barkley
3213	Paul Silas	4065	Mark Eaton	4453	Shaquille O'Neal

continued on next page

2000–01–2009–10		2010–11–2019–20		2020–21–2021–22	
6952	Kevin Garnett	6255	DeAndre Jordan	1447	Rudy Gobert
6551	Tim Duncan	5430	Andre Drummond	1388	Nikola Jokić
6102	Dirk Nowitzki	5416	Dwight Howard	1333	Nikola Vučević
5683	Ben Wallace	5081	Kevin Love	1230	Julius Randle
5557	Shawn Marion	4713	LeBron James	1218	Giannis Antetokounmpo
5085	Marcus Camby	4566	DeMarcus Cousins	1204	Clint Capela
4732	Lamar Odom	4511	Nikola Vučević	1143	Domantas Sabonis
4432	Dwight Howard	4344	LaMarcus Aldridge	1140	Jonas Valančiūnas
4370	Antawn Jamison	4261	Russell Westbrook	1111	Russell Westbrook
4348	Jermaine O'Neal	4213	Marcin Gortat	1076	Joel Embiid

ABA

1967–68–1969–70		1970–71–1975–76	
2623	Mel Daniels	4992	Arits Gilmore
2089	Red Robbins	4030	Billy Paultz
1989	John Beasley	4001	Mel Daniels
1745	Goose Ligon	3536	Gerald Govan
1530	Bob Netolicky	3416	Dan Issel
1497	Warren Davis	3302	Julius Erving
1423	Gerald Govan	2871	Julius Keye
1390	Ira Harge	2748	Jim Eakins
1380	Trooper Washington	2523	Zelmo Beaty
1321	Les Hunter	2514	George McGinnis

* Defensive Rebounds became an official stat in the ABA in 1967–68, and in the NBA in 1973–74.

Evolution of Defensive Rebound Record

NBA

1973–74 ..... Elvin Hayes, Cap. Bullets 1109
1975–76 ..... Kareem Abdul-Jabbar, L.A. Lakers 1111

ABA

1967–68 ..... Mel Daniels, Min. Muskies 711
1968–69 ..... Mel Daniels, Ind. Pacers 873
1969–70 ..... Spencer Haywood, Den. Rockets 1104

Most Defensive Rebounds, Season

NBA

1111	Kareem Abdul-Jabbar, L.A. Lakers, 1975–76	848	Andre Drummond, Det. Pistons, 2017–18
1109	Elvin Hayes, Cap. Bullets, 1973–74	842	DeAndre Jordan, L.A. Clippers, 2017–18
1007	Dennis Rodman, Det. Pistons, 1991–92	840	Kevin Willis, Atl. Hawks, 1991–92
993	Dave Cowens, Bos. Celtics, 1973–74	836	Bob McAdoo, Buf. Braves, 1973–74
990	Truck Robinson, N.O. Jazz, 1977–78	833	Ben Wallace, Det. Pistons, 2002–03
921	Sam Lacey, K.C.-Oma. Kings, 1974–75	830	Dave Cowens, Bos. Celtics, 1977–78
914	Dennis Rodman, S.A. Spurs, 1993–94	829	DeAndre Jordan, L.A. Clippers, 2014–15
911	Dave Cowens, Bos. Celtics, 1975–76	824	Kareem Abdul-Jabbar, L.A. Lakers, 1976–77
894	Kevin Garnett, Min. T'Wolves, 2003–04	818	Kareem Abdul-Jabbar, L.A. Lakers, 1978–79
891	Kareem Abdul-Jabbar, Mil. Bucks, 1973–74	816	DeAndre Jordan, L.A. Clippers, 2016–17
882	Dwight Howard, Orl. Magic, 2007–08	815	Jack Sikma, Sea. Sonics, 1981–82
861	Kevin Garnett, Min. T'Wolves, 2004–05	813	Nikola Jokić, Den. Nuggets, 2021–22
858	Kevin Garnett, Min. T'Wolves, 2002–03	809	Andre Drummond, Det. Pistons, 2018–19
857	Moses Malone, Hou. Rockets, 1978–79	807	Marcus Camby, Den. Nuggets, 2007–08
853	Dikembe Mutombo, Atl. Hawks, 1999–00	806	Sam Lacey, K.C. Kings, 1975–76
850	Hakeem Olajuwon, Hou. Rockets, 1989–90	805	Bob Lanier, Det. Pistons, 1973–74
848	Bob McAdoo, Buf. Braves, 1974–75	803	Andre Drummond, Det. Pistons, 2015–16

continued on next page

ABA

1060 .... Artis Gilmore, Ken. Colonels, 1973–74
934 .... Artis Gilmore, Ken. Colonels, 1974–75
910 .... Swen Nater, S.A. Spurs, 1974–75
901 .... Artis Gilmore, Ken. Colonels, 1975–76
783 .... Marvin Barnes, Spirits of St.L., 1974–75
775 .... George McGinnis, Ind. Pacers, 1973–74
773 .... Caldwell Jones, S.D. Conquistadors, 1973–74
763 .... Caldwell Jones, S.D. Conquistadors, 1974–75
754 .... Moses Malone, Uta. Stars, 1974–75
730 .... George McGinnis, Ind. Pacers, 1974–75
712 .... Swen Nater, S.A. Spurs/Vir. Squires, 1973–74
673 .... Maurice Lucas, Ken. Colonels/Spirits of St.L., 1975–76
655 .... Mel Daniels, Ind. Pacers, 1973–74
652 .... Billy Paultz, S.A. Spurs, 1975–76
636 .... Julius Erving, N.Y. Nets, 1973–74
630 .... Julius Erving, N.Y. Nets, 1974–75
621 .... Larry Kenon, N.Y. Nets, 1974–75
620 .... Dan Issel, Den. Nuggets, 1975–76
618 .... David Vaughn, Vir. Squires, 1974–75
610 .... Larry Kenon, S.A. Spurs, 1975–76
609 .... Tom Owens, Mem. Sounds/Spirits of St.L., 1974–75
607 .... Caldwell Jones, Ken. Colonels/S.D. Sails/Spirits of St.L., 1975–76

Most Defensive Rebounds, Career

11,453 .... Kevin Garnett	8890 .... Shaquille O'Neal	7764 .... Caldwell Jones
11,406 .... Karl Malone	8855 .... Patrick Ewing	7625 .... Dennis Rodman
11,232 .... Tim Duncan	8609 .... LeBron James^	7581 .... Bill Laimbeer
10,476 .... Dwight Howard^	8551 .... Dikembe Mutombo	7414 .... David Robinson
10,452 .... Moses Malone	8491 .... Buck Williams	7369 .... Shawn Marion
10,117 .... Robert Parish	8286 .... Charles Barkley	7217 .... Larry Bird
10,021 .... Dirk Nowitzki	8281 .... Charles Oakley	7141 .... DeAndre Jordan^
9714 .... Hakeem Olajuwon	8274 .... Jack Sikma	7038 .... Ben Wallace
9417 .... Artis Gilmore	8220 .... Pau Gasol	
9394 .... Kareem Abdul-Jabbar	7769 .... Kevin Willis	

^ Active.

Most Games with 10 Defensive Rebounds, Season

66 .... Dennis Rodman, Det. Pistons, 1991–92	48 .... Kevin Garnett, Min. T'Wolves, 2004–05
61 .... Kareem Abdul-Jabbar, L.A. Lakers, 1975–76	48 .... Kevin Love, Min. T'Wolves, 2010–11
57 .... Dwight Howard, Orl. Magic, 2007–08	47 .... DeAndre Jordan, L.A. Clippers, 2014–15
56 .... Kevin Garnett, Min. T'Wolves, 2003–04	47 .... Joel Embiid, Phi. 76ers, 2018–19
52 .... Dennis Rodman, S.A. Spurs, 1993–94	46 .... Bill Walton, Por. Blazers, 1976–77
51 .... Andre Drummond, Det. Pistons, 2017–18	46 .... Kareem Abdul-Jabbar, L.A. Lakers, 1978–79
51 .... DeAndre Jordan, L.A. Clippers, 2017–18	46 .... Dennis Rodman, Det. Pistons, 1992–93
51 .... Nikola Jokić, Den. Nuggets, 2021–22	45 .... DeAndre Jordan, L.A. Clippers, 2016–17
50 .... Hakeem Olajuwon, Hou. Rockets, 1989–90	45 .... Hassan Whiteside, Mia. Heat, 2016–17
50 .... Kevin Willis, Atl. Hawks, 1991–92	45 .... Andre Drummond, Det. Pistons, 2018–19
49 .... Kevin Garnett, Min. T'Wolves, 2002–03	45 .... Rudy Gobert, Uta. Jazz, 2021–22
49 .... Ben Wallace, Det. Pistons, 2002–03	44 .... Dikembe Mutombo, Atl. Hawks, 1999–00
49 .... Dwight Howard, Orl. Magic, 2010–11	44 .... Marcus Camby, Den. Nuggets, 2007–08

continued on next page

44	Andre Drummond, Det. Pistons, 2015–16		42	Russell Westbrook, Ok.C. Thunder, 2016–17
43	Charles Oakley, Chi. Bulls, 1986–87		41	Shaquille O'Neal, Orl. Magic, 1992–93
43	Kevin Garnett, Min. T'Wolves, 2006–07		41	Kevin Garnett, Min. T'Wolves, 2005–06
43	Giannis Antetokounmpo, Mil. Bucks, 2019–20		40	Bill Walton, Por. Blazers, 1977–78
42	Jack Sikma, Sea. Sonics, 1981–82		40	Dennis Rodman, Chi. Bulls, 1997–98
42	Patrick Ewing, N.Y. Knicks, 1992–93		40	Rudy Gobert, Uta. Jazz, 2020–21

^ Active.

Most Games with 10 Defensive Rebounds, Career

481	Dwight Howard^	328	Patrick Ewing	284	Charles Barkley
443	Kevin Garnett	312	Dikembe Mutombo	268	Kevin Love^
422	Tim Duncan	301	Shaquille O'Neal	267	Marcus Camby
370	Hakeem Olajuwon	292	DeAndre Jordan^	267	Dirk Nowitzki
365	Dennis Rodman	292	Jack Sikma	266	Robert Parish
360	Karl Malone	289	Andre Drummond^	253	Bill Laimbeer

^ Active.

Most Consecutive Games with 10 Defensive Rebounds, Season

		First Game of Streak	Last Game of Streak
20	Kareem Abdul-Jabbar, L.A. Lakers	Nov. 8, 1975	Dec. 18, 1975
18	Dennis Rodman, Det. Pistons	Dec. 1, 1991	Jan. 8, 1992
16	Dennis Rodman, Det. Pistons	Dec. 15, 1992	Jan. 13, 1993
16	Giannis Antetokounmpo, Mil. Bucks	Jan. 16, 2020	Mar. 2, 2020
15	Kevin Willis, Atl. Hawks	Jan. 28, 1992	Feb. 28, 1992
15	Ben Wallace, Det. Pistons	Mar. 4, 2003	Apr. 4, 2003
14	Kevin Love, Min. T'Wolves	Nov. 22, 2010	Dec. 18, 2010
13	Charles Barkley, Phi. 76ers	Mar. 19, 1986	Apr. 13, 1986
13	Dennis Rodman, Det. Pistons	Jan. 11, 1992	Feb. 6, 1992
13	Dennis Rodman, Det. Pistons	Feb. 13, 1992	Mar. 8, 1992
13	Dwight Howard, Orl. Magic	Feb. 22, 2013	Mar. 17, 2013
12	Bill Walton, Por. Blazers	Jan. 10, 1976	Feb. 1, 1976
12	Charles Oakley, Chi. Bulls	Mar. 4, 1987	Mar. 22, 1987
12	DeAndre Jordan, L.A. Clippers	Dec. 9, 2017	Dec. 31, 2017
12	Andre Drummond, Det. Pistons	Jan. 30, 2018	Feb. 26, 2018
11	Kareem Abdul-Jabbar, L.A. Lakers	Dec. 21, 1975	Jan. 7, 1976
11	Russell Westbrook, Ok.C. Thunder	Jan. 24, 2019	Feb. 22, 2019
10	Dennis Rodman, Det. Pistons	Feb. 23, 1993	Mar. 16, 1993
10	Dwight Howard, Orl. Magic	Jan. 26, 2011	Feb. 11, 2011
10	DeAndre Jordan, L.A. Clippers	Feb. 28, 2018	Mar. 18, 2018
10	Joel Embiid, Phi. 76ers	Jan. 21, 2019	Feb. 13, 2019

Most Defensive Rebounds, Game

34	Artis Gilmore, Ken. Colonels[a]	@ N.Y. Nets[a] (Feb. 3, 1974)
29	Kareem Abdul-Jabbar, L.A. Lakers	vs. Det. Pistons (Dec. 14, 1975)
28	Elvin Hayes, Cap. Bullets	@ Atl. Hawks (Nov. 17, 1973)
26	Mel Daniels, Ind. Pacers[a]	@ The Floridians[a] (Dec. 29, 1971)
26	Rony Seikaly, Mia. Heat	vs. Was. Bullets (Mar. 3, 1993)
25	Elvin Hayes, Cap. Bullets	vs. Sea. Sonics (Feb. 27, 1974)
25	Artis Gilmore, Chi. Bulls	vs. S.A. Spurs (Dec. 22, 1978)
25	Robert Parish, G.S. Warriors	vs. N.Y. Knicks (Mar. 30, 1979)

continued on next page

25	Swen Nater, S.D. Clippers	vs. Den. Nuggets (Dec. 14, 1979)
25	Herb Williams, Ind. Pacers	vs. Den. Nuggets (Jan. 23, 1989)
25	Charles Barkley, Hou. Rockets	@ Pho. Suns (Nov. 2, 1996)
25	Shaquille O'Neal, L.A. Lakers	vs. Mil. Bucks (Mar. 21, 2004)
24	Manny Leaks, Tex. Chaparrals[a]	vs. Ken. Colonels[a] (Nov. 27, 1970)
24	Bob McAdoo, Buf. Braves	vs. Por. Blazers (Mar. 10, 1974)
24	Wes Unseld, Was. Bullets	vs. N.O. Jazz (Apr. 6, 1975)
23	Mel Daniels, Ind. Pacers[a]	vs. Pit. Pipers[a] (Dec. 20, 1969)
23	Elvin Hayes, Cap. Bullets	vs. Sea. Sonics (Dec. 2, 1973)
23	Dave Cowens, Bos. Celtics	@ K.C.-Oma. Kings (Jan. 2, 1974)
23	Kareem Abdul-Jabbar, L.A. Lakers	vs. K.C. Kings (Nov. 7, 1976)
23	Bob McAdoo, Buf. Braves	vs. Ind. Pacers (Dec. 7, 1976)
23	Truck Robinson, N.O. Jazz	vs. Pho. Suns (Oct. 28, 1977)
23	Kareem Abdul-Jabbar, L.A. Lakers	@ N.J. Nets (Feb. 3, 1978)
23	Swen Nater, S.D. Clippers	@ K.C. Kings (Jan. 8, 1980)
23	Dennis Rodman, S.A. Spurs	vs. Dal. Mavericks (Jan. 22, 1994)
23	Dikembe Mutombo, Den. Nuggets	vs. Cha. Hornets (Mar. 26, 1996)
23	Tim Duncan, S.A. Spurs	@ Mia. Heat (Feb. 1, 2003)
23	Kevin Garnett, Min. T'Wolves	@ Sac. Kings (Dec. 5, 2003)
23	Kevin Garnett, Min. T'Wolves	vs. Orl. Magic (Jan. 12, 2005)
23	Al Jefferson, Min. T'Wolves	@ Hou. Rockets (Jan. 13, 2010)
23	Dwight Howard, L.A. Lakers	vs. Den. Nuggets (Jan. 6, 2013)
23	Jonas Valančiūnas, Mem. Grizzlies	@ Orl. Magic (Mar. 22, 2019)

[a] ABA.

Most Games in a Season with 10 Defensive Rebounds

66	Dennis Rodman, Det. Pistons, 1991–92		49	Dwight Howard, Orl. Magic, 2010–11
61	Kareem Abdul-Jabbar, L.A. Lakers, 1975–76		48	Kevin Garnett, Min. T'Wolves, 2004–05
57	Dwight Howard, Orl. Magic, 2007–08		48	Kevin Love, Cle. Cavaliers, 2010–11
56	Kevin Garnett, Min. T'Wolves, 2003–04		47	DeAndre Jordan, L.A. Clippers, 2014–15
52	Dennis Rodman, S.A. Spurs, 1993–94		47	Joel Embiid, Phi. 76ers, 2018–19
51	Andre Drummond, Det. Pistons, 2017–18		46	Bill Walton, Por. Blazers, 1976–77
51	DeAndre Jordan, L.A. Clippers, 2017–18		46	Kareem Abdul-Jabbar, L.A. Lakers, 1978–79
51	Nikola Jokić, Uta. Jazz, 2021–22		46	Dennis Rodman, Det. Pistons, 1992–93
50	Hakeem Olajuwon, Hou. Rockets, 1989–90		45	DeAndre Jordan, L.A. Clippers, 2016–17
50	Kevin Willis, Atl. Hawks, 1991–92		45	Hassan Whiteside, Mia. Heat, 2016–17
49	Kevin Garnett, Min. T'Wolves, 2002–03		45	Andre Drummond, Det. Pistons, 2018–19
49	Ben Wallace, Det. Pistons, 2002–03		45	Rudy Gobert, Uta. Jazz, 2021–22

Most Games with 10 Defensive Rebounds, Zero Offensive Rebounds, Career

86	Dirk Nowitzki	33	Kevin Love^	26	Paul George^
86	Kevin Durant^	33	Russell Westbrook^	26	Draymond Green^
52	LeBron James^	31	Tim Duncan	26	Julius Randle^
49	Kevin Garnett	31	Marc Gasol	24	Jack Sikma*
41	Karl Malone	30	Patrick Ewing	23	Jason Kidd
39	Larry Bird	30	James Harden^	20	Carlos Boozer
35	Paul Pierce	28	Giannis Antetokounmpo^		

^ Active.

Steals

Most Steals by Decade[*]

1973-74—1979-80		1980-81—1989-90		1990-91—1999-00	
1143	Randy Smith	1709	Maurice Cheeks	1806	Mookie Blaylock
1104	Rick Barry	1477	Isiah Thomas	1746	Gary Payton
1010	Chris Ford	1455	Fat Lever	1689	John Stockton
961	Slick Watts	1409	Magic Johnson	1545	Scottie Pippen
952	Calvin Murphy	1335	Alvin Robertson	1339	Hersey Hawkins
884	Fred Brown	1263	Larry Bird	1271	Kendall Gill
853	Sam Lacey	1246	Clyde Drexler	1172	Rod Strickland
846	Larry Steele	1191	Rickey Green	1117	Michael Jordan
829	Paul Westphal	1189	Michael Jordan	1113	Jeff Hornacek
804	Gus Williams	1155	John Stockton	1107	Tim Hardaway

2000-01—2009-10		2010-11—2019-20		2020-21—2021-22	
1483	Jason Kidd	1411	Chris Paul	239	Dejounte Murray
1396	Allen Iverson	1317	Russell Westbrook	220	Chris Paul
1394	Shawn Marion	1234	James Harden	220	Matisse Thybulle
1321	Baron Davis	1153	Thaddeus Young	211	Tyrese Haliburton
1253	Kobe Bryant	1139	Paul George	204	Nikola Jokić
1231	Metta World Peace	1104	Trevor Ariza	204	Robert Covington
1130	Andre Miller	1060	LeBron James	204	Jrue Holiday
1115	Paul Pierce	1053	Stephen Curry	202	Jimmy Butler
1077	Ben Wallace	1053	Ricky Rubio	200	LaMelo Ball
1067	Jason Terry	1003	Kyle Lowry	198	Fred VanVleet

[*] Steals were first recorded as a stat in the NBA/ABA, beginning with the 1973–74 season.

Evolution of Steals Record

NBA

1973–74	Larry Steele, Por. Blazers	217
1974–75	Rick Barry, G.S. Warriors	228
1975–76	Slick Watts, Sea. Sonics	261
1976–77	Don Buse, Ind. Pacers	281
1985–86	Alvin Robertson, S.A. Spurs	301

ABA

1972–73	Billy Cunningham, Car. Cougars	216
1973–74	Ted McClain, Car. Cougars	250
1975–76	Don Buse, Ind. Pacers	346

Most Steals, Season

346	Don Buse, Ind. Pacers[a], 1975–76
301	Alvin Robertson, S.A. Spurs, 1985–86
281	Don Buse, Ind. Pacers, 1976–77
265	Micheal Ray Richardson, N.Y. Knicks, 1979–80
263	John Stockton, Uta. Jazz, 1988–89
261	Slick Watts, Sea. Sonics, 1975–76
260	Alvin Robertson, S.A. Spurs, 1986–87
259	Michael Jordan, Chi. Bulls, 1987–88
250	Ted McClain, Car. Cougars[a], 1973–74
246	Alvin Robertson, Mil. Bucks, 1990–91
244	John Stockton, Uta. Jazz, 1991–92
243	Micheal Ray Richardson, N.J. Nets, 1984–85
243	Alvin Robertson, S.A. Spurs, 1987–88

242	John Stockton, Uta. Jazz, 1987–88
236	Michael Jordan, Chi. Bulls, 1986–87
234	Michael Jordan, Chi. Bulls, 1988–89
234	John Stockton, Uta. Jazz, 1990–91
233	Micheal Williams, Ind. Pacers, 1991–92
232	Micheal Ray Richardson, N.Y. Knicks, 1980–81
232	Scottie Pippen, Chi. Bulls, 1994–95
231	Gary Payton, Sea. Sonics, 1995–96
229	Johnny Moore, S.A. Spurs, 1984–85
228	Rick Barry, G.S. Warriors, 1974–75
227	Michael Jordan, Chi. Bulls, 1989–90
225	Ron Lee, Pho. Suns, 1977–78
225	Allen Iverson, Phi. 76ers, 2002–03

[a] ABA.

Most Steals, Career

3265 .... John Stockton	2075 .... Mookie Blaylock	1699 .... Russell Westbrook^
2684 .... Jason Kidd	1983 .... Allen Iverson	1666 .... Fat Lever
2514 .... Michael Jordan	1957 .... Derek Harper	1648 .... Charles Barkley
2453 .... Chris Paul^	1944 .... Kobe Bryant	1638 .... Gus Williams
2445 .... Gary Payton	1861 .... Isiah Thomas	1628 .... Trevor Ariza^
2310 .... Maurice Cheeks	1859 .... Kevin Garnett	1622 .... Hersey Hawkins
2307 .... Scottie Pippen	1818 .... Don Buse	1620 .... Eddie Jones
2272 .... Julius Erving	1761 .... Andre Iguodala^	1620 .... Dwyane Wade
2207 .... Clyde Drexler	1759 .... Shawn Marion	1616 .... Rod Strickland
2162 .... Hakeem Olajuwon	1752 .... Paul Pierce	1608 .... Mark Jackson
2136 .... LeBron James^	1724 .... Magic Johnson	1603 .... Jason Terry
2112 .... Alvin Robertson	1721 .... Metta World Peace	
2085 .... Karl Malone	1716 .... Ron Harper	

^ Active.

Steals Leaders by State of Birth

Alabama	Charles Barkley (Leeds)	1648	
Alaska	Mario Chalmers (Anchorage)	950	
Arizona	Sean Elliott (Tucson)	576	
Arkansas	Scottie Pippen (Hamburg)	2307	
California	Jason Kidd (San Francisco)	2684	
Colorado	Chauncey Billups (Denver)	1051	
Connecticut	Calvin Murphy (Norwalk)	1165	
Delaware	Donte DiVincenzo^ (Newark)	218	
Florida	Trevor Ariza^ (Miami)	1628	
Georgia	Derek Harper (Elberton)	1957	
Hawaii	Cedric Ceballos (Maui)	450	
Idaho	Luke Ridnour (Coeur d'Alene)	814	
Illinois	Maurice Cheeks (Chicago)	2310	
Indiana	Don Buse (Huntingburg)	1818	
Iowa	Kirk Hinrich (Sioux City)	972	
Kansas	Alvan Adams (Lawrence)	1289	
Kentucky	Rajon Rondo^ (Louisville)	1518	
Louisiana	Clyde Drexler (New Orleans)	2207	
Maine	Jeff Turner (Bangor)	215	
Maryland	Muggsy Bogues (Baltimore)	1369	
Massachusetts	Ron Lee (Boston)	869	
Michigan	Magic Johnson (Lansing)	1724	
Minnesota	Mark Olberding (Melrose)	623	
Mississippi	Monta Ellis (Jackson)	1409	
Missouri	Larry Hughes (St. Louis)	1092	
Montana	Phil Jackson (Deer Lodge)	281	
Nebraska	Fred Hoiberg (Lincoln)	428	

^ Active.

Nevada	Greg Anthony (Las Vegas)	887
New Hampshire	Matt Bonner (Concord)	285
New Jersey	Brevin Knight (Livingston)	1229
New Mexico	André Roberson (Las Cruces)	268
New York	Michael Jordan (Brooklyn)	2514
North Carolina	Chris Paul^ (Winston-Salem)	2453
North Dakota	Tyler Johnson^ (Grand Forks)	288
Ohio	LeBron James^ (Akron)	2136
Oklahoma	John Starks (Tulsa)	951
Oregon	Terrell Brandon (Portland)	1142
Pennsylvania	Kobe Bryant (Philadelphia)	1944
Rhode Island	Marvin Barnes (Providence)	365
South Carolina	Kevin Garnett (Greenville)	1859
South Dakota	Mike Miller (Mitchell)	573
Tennessee	Penny Hardaway (Memphis)	1125
Texas	Mookie Blaylock (Garland)	2075
Utah	Byron Scott (Ogden)	1224
Vermont	N/A	N/A
Virginia	Allen Iverson (Hampton)	1983
Washington	John Stockton (Spokane)	3265
West Virginia	Jason Williams (Belle)	933
Wisconsin	Terry Porter (Milwaukee)	1583
Wyoming	James Johnson (Cheyenne)	569
District of Columbia ...	Kevin Durant^	1021
Puerto Rico	J.J. Barea (Mayaguez)	331
Virgin Islands	Tim Duncan (St. Croix)	1025

All-Time Steals Leaders by First Letter of Last Name

A .... Ariza, Trevor^ 1628	E......... Erving, Julius 2272	I.......... Iverson, Allen 1983
B......... Blaylock, Mookie 2075	F......... Fisher, Derek 1352	J.......... Jordan, Michael 2514
C .... Cheeks, Maurice 2310	G........ Garnett, Kevin 1859	K......... Kidd, Jason 2684
D .... Drexler, Clyde 2207	H .... Harper, Derek 1957	L .... Lever, Fat 1666

continued on next page

M........ Malone, Karl 2085
N........ Nowitzki, Dirk 1210
O........ Olajuwon, Hakeem 2162
P........ Paul, Chris^ 2453
Q........ Quinn, Chis 102

R........ Robertson, Alvin 2112
S........ Stockton, John 3265
T........ Thomas, Isiah 1861
U........ Unseld, Wes.................... 628
V........ Valentine, Darnell............. 910

W........ World Peace, Metta 1721
X........ N/A .... N/A
Y........ Young, Thaddeus^ 535
Z........ Zeller, Cody^ 320

^ Active.

Multiple Seasons Leading League in Steals

5	Chris Paul	N.O.-Ok.C. Hornets, 2005–06	175
		N.O. Hornets, 2007–08	217
		N.O. Hornets, 2008–09	216
		N.O. Hornets, 2010–11	188
		L.A. Clippers, 2011–12	152
4	Micheal Ray Richardson	N.Y. Knicks, 1979–80	265
		N.Y. Knicks, 1980–81	232
		N.Y. Knicks, 1981–82	213
		N.J. Nets, 1984–85	243
3	Alvin Robertson	S.A. Spurs, 1985–86	301
		S.A. Spurs, 1986–87	260
		Mil. Bucks, 1990–91	246
3	Michael Jordan	Chi. Bulls, 1987–88	259
		Chi. Bulls, 1989–90	227
		Chi. Bulls, 1992–93	221
2	Don Buse	Ind. Pacers^a, 1975–76	346
		Ind. Pacers, 1976–77	281
2	Rickey Green	Uta. Jazz, 1982–83	220
		Uta. Jazz, 1983–84	215
2	John Stockton	Uta. Jazz, 1988–89	263
		Uta. Jazz, 1991–92	244
2	Allen Iverson	Phi. 76ers, 2002–03	225
		Phi. 76ers, 2004–05	180
2	Shawn Marion	Pho. Suns, 2003–04	167
		Pho. Suns, 2006–07	156
2	Stephen Curry	G.S. Warriors, 2014–15	163
		G.S. Warriors, 2015–16	169

^a ABA.

Consecutive Seasons Leading League in Steals

3	Micheal Ray Richardson	N.Y. Knicks, 1979–80	265
		N.Y. Knicks, 1980–81	232
		N.Y. Knicks, 1981–82	213
2	Rickey Green	Uta. Jazz, 1982–83	220
		Uta. Jazz, 1983–84	215
2	Alvin Robertson	S.A. Spurs, 1985–86	301
		S.A. Spurs, 1986–87	260
2	Chris Paul	N.O. Hornets, 2007–08	217
		N.O. Hornets, 2008–09	216
		N.O. Hornets, 2010–11	188
		L.A. Clippers, 2011–12	152
2	Stephen Curry	G.S. Warriors, 2014–15	163
		G.S. Warriors, 2015–16	169

Rookies Leading League in Steals

Brevin Knight, Cle. Cavaliers, 1997–98 196
Chris Paul*, N.O.-Ok.C. Hornets, 2005–06 175
* Rookie of the Year.

Most Career Steals, Never Leading League

Career Steals	Most Steals, Single Season	League Leader
2310 .... Maurice Cheeks	209 (1981–82, Phi. 76ers)	213 (Micheal Ray Richardson, N.J. Nets)
2272 .... Julius Erving	207 (1975–76, N.Y. Netsᵃ)	346 (Don Buse, Ind. Pacersᵃ)
2207 .... Clyde Drexler	213 (1988–89, Por. Blazers)	263 (John Stockton, Uta. Jazz)
2162 .... Hakeem Olajuwon	213 (1988–89, Hou. Rockets)	263 (John Stockton, Uta. Jazz)
2136 .... LeBron James^	177 (2004–05, Cle. Cavaliers)	180 (Allen Iverson, Phi. 76ers)
2085 .... Karl Malone	152 (2001–02, Uta. Jazz)	175 (Jason Kidd, N.J. Nets)
1957 .... Derek Harper	187 (1989–90, Dal. Mavericks)	227 (Michael Jordan, Chi. Bulls)
1944 .... Kobe Bryant	181 (2002–03, L.A. Lakers)	225 (Allen Iverson, Phi. 76ers)
1861 .... Isiah Thomas	204 (1983–84, Det. Pistons)	215 (Rickey Green, Uta. Jazz)
1859 .... Kevin Garnett	139 (1997–98, Min. T'Wolves)	196 (Brevin Knight, Cle. Cavaliers)
1761 .... Andre Iguodal	171 (2007–08, Phi. 76ers)	217 (Chris Paul, N.O. Hornets)
1752 .... Paul Pierce	154 (2001–02, Bos. Celtics)	175 (Jason Kidd, N.J. Nets)
1724 .... Magic Johnson	208 (1981–82, L.A. Lakers)	213 (Micheal Ray Richardson, N.J. Nets)
1721 .... Metta World Peace	159 (2002–03, Ind. Pacers)	225 (Allen Iverson, Phi. 76ers)
1716 .... Ron Harper	209 (1986–87, Cle. Cavaliers)	260 (Alvin Robertson, S.A. Spurs)
1699 .... Russell Westbrook^	163 (2015–16, Ok.C. Thunder)	169 (Stephen Curry, G.S. Warriors)

^ Active.

ᵃ ABA.

Most Consecutive Seasons with 150 Steals

10	Maurice Cheeks	Phi. 76ers: 1978–88
10	John Stockton	Uta. Jazz: 1985–95
8	Alvin Robertson	S.A. Spurs: 1985–89; Mil. Bucks: 1989–92
8	Mookie Blaylock	N.J. Nets: 1990–92; Atl. Hawks: 1992–98
7	Michael Jordan	Chi. Bulls: 1986–93
6	Isiah Thomas	Det. Pistons: 1981–87
6	Fat Lever	Den. Nuggets: 1984–90
6	Scottie Pippen	Chi. Bulls: 1989–95
6	Gary Payton	Sea. Sonics: 1992–98
6	Chris Paul	N.O. Hornets: 2010–11; L.A. Clippers: 2011–16
5	Rick Barry	G.S. Warriors: 1973–78
5	Don Buse	Ind. Pacersᵃ: 1974–76; Ind. Pacers: 1976–77; Pho. Suns: 1977–79
5	Clyde Drexler	Por. Blazers: 1984–89
5	Derek Harper	Dal. Mavericks: 1985–90
5	Shawn Marion	Pho. Suns: 2002–07
4	Julius Erving	N.Y. Netsᵃ: 1973–76; Phi. 76ers: 1976–77
4	George McGinnis	Ind. Pacersᵃ: 1973–75; Phi. 76ers: 1975–77
4	Randy Smith	Buf. Braves-S.D. Clippers: 1975–79
4	Micheal Ray Richardson	N.Y. Knicks: 1979–82; G.S. Warriors/N.J. Nets: 1982–83
4	Gus Williams	Sea. Sonics: 1981–85
4	Doug Christie	Sac. Kings: 2000–04
3	Phil Chenier	Cap.-Was. Bullets: 1973–76
3	Larry Steele	Por. Blazers: 1973–76

continued on next page

3	Fatty Taylor	Vir. Squires[a]: 1973–74, 1975–76; Den. Nuggets[a]: 1974–75
3	Bobby Jones	Den. Nuggets[a]: 1974–76; Den. Nuggets: 1976–77
3	Slick Watts	Sea. Sonics: 1974–77
3	Chris Ford	Det. Pistons: 1975–78
3	Quinn Buckner	Mil. Bucks: 1976–79
3	Mike Gale	S.A. Spurs: 1976–79
3	Gus Williams	Sea. Sonics: 1977–80
3	Julius Erving	Phi. 76ers: 1979–82
3	Ray Williams	N.Y. Knicks: 1979–81; N.J. Nets: 1981–82
3	Rickey Green	Uta. Jazz: 1981–84
3	Magic Johnson	L.A. Lakers: 1981–84
3	Hakeem Olajuwon	Hou. Rockets: 1987–90
3	Tim Hardaway	G.S. Warriors: 1989–92
3	Micheal Williams	Ind. Pacers: 1990–92; Min. T'Wolves: 1992–93
3	Nate McMillan	Sea. Sonics: 1992–95
3	Allen Iverson	Phi. 76ers: 2000–03
3	Jason Kidd	Pho. Suns: 2000–01; N.J. Nets: 2001–03

[a] ABA.

Fewest Games Played to 1000 Steals

		Age	Career Stl
352	Alvin Robertson	26 years, 165 days	2112
358	Micheal Ray Richardson	29 years, 328 days	1463
362	Michael Jordan	26 years, 294 days	2514
420	Chris Paul^	25 years, 332 days	2453
420	Maurice Cheeks	29 years, 75 days	2310
421	Mookie Blaylock	28 years, 2 days	2075
426	John Stockton	27 years, 260 days	3265
431	Allen Iverson	27 years, 194 days	1983
433	Isiah Thomas	26 years, 204 days	1861
439	Clyde Drexler	26 years, 220 days	2207
441	Quinn Buckner	27 years, 211 days	1337
449	Fat Lever	27 years, 177 days	1666
453	Eddie Jones	29 years, 90 days	1620
454	Gary Payton	27 years, 195 days	2445
455	Magic Johnson	26 years, 235 days	1724
460	Ron Harper	29 years, 293 days	1716
467	Don Buse*	32 years, 226 days	1818
468	Rick Barry*	35 years, 202 days	1104
470	Gus Williams	30 years, 20 days	1638
473	Metta World Peace	27 years, 146 days	1721
481	Jason Kidd	28 years, 9 days	2684
486	Doc Rivers	28 years, 186 days	1563
492	Johnny Moore	31 years, 357 days	1017
494	Scottie Pippen	28 years, 91 days	2307

* Steals did not become an official stat until the 1973–74 season, which was Don Buse's second professional season/Rick Barry's eighth professional season.

Most Steals for One Franchise

Hawks	1321	Mookie Blaylock
Celtics	1583	Paul Pierce
Nets-Americans*	950	Jason Kidd
Hornets	1067	Muggsy Bogues
Bulls	2306	Michael Jordan
Cavaliers	1376	LeBron James
Mavericks	1551	Derek Harper
Nuggets-Rockets*	1167	Fat Lever
Pistons	1861	Isiah Thomas
Warriors	1367	Stephen Curry
Rockets	2088	Hakeem Olajuwon
Pacers*	1505	Reggie Miller
Clippers-Braves	1072	Randy Smith
Lakers	1944	Kobe Bryant
Grizzlies	1161	Mike Conley
Heat	1492	Dwyane Wade
Bucks	1042	Quinn Buckner
Timberwolves	1315	Kevin Garnett
Pelicans-Hornets	1010	Chris Paul
Knicks	1061	Patrick Ewing
Thunder-SuperSonics	2107	Gary Payton
Magic	1004	Nick Anderson
76ers-Nationals	1942	Maurice Cheeks
Suns	1289	Alvan Adams
Trail Blazers	1795	Clyde Drexler
Kings-Royals	950	Sam Lacey
Spurs-Chaparrals*	1392	Manu Ginóbili
Raptors	873	Kyle Lowry
Jazz	3265	John Stockton
Wizards-Bullets-Zephyrs-Packers	976	John Wall

* Includes both ABA and NBA totals.

Players with 500 Steals on Multiple Teams

			Career Stl
Jason Kidd	954	Dal. Mavericks (1994–96; 2008–11)	2684
	655	Pho. Suns (1996–2001)	
	950	N.J. Nets (2001–08)	
Chris Paul^	1010	N.O-Ok.C. Hornets (2005–11)	2453
	902	L.A. Clippers (2011–17)	
Julius Erving	583	N.Y. Nets[a] (1973–76)	2272
	1508	Phi. 76ers (1976–87)	
Alvin Robertson	1128	S.A. Spurs (1984–89)	2112
	753	Mil. Bucks (1989–93)	
Ron Harper	530	Cle. Cavaliers (1986–89)	1716
	606	L.A. Clippers (1989–94)	
Hersey Hawkins	722	Phi. 76ers (1988–93)	1622
	536	Sea. Sonics (1995–99)	
Eddie Jones	644	L.A. Lakers (1994–99)	1620
	515	Mia. Heat (2000–05)	
Jason Terry	588	Atl. Hawks (1999–2004)	1603
	735	Dal. Mavericks (2004–12)	
Doug Christie	664	Tor. Raptors (1996–2000)	1555
	717	Sac. Kings (2000–05)	
Jeff Hornacek	692	Pho. Suns (1986–92)	1536
	618	Uta. Jazz (1994–2000	
Micheal Ray Richardson	810	N.Y. Knicks (1978–82)	1463
	552	N.J. Nets (1983–86)	
Tim Hardaway	821	G.S. Warriors (1989–96)	1428
	541	Mia. Heat (1996–2001)	
Bobby Jones	660	Den. Rockets-Nuggets* (1974–78)	1387
	727	Phi. 76ers (1978–86)	
Derrick McKey	519	Sea. Sonics (1987–93)	1072
	512	Ind. Pacers (1993–2001)	

^ Active.

[a] ABA.

* Includes both ABA and NBA franchise.

Most Steals, Rookie Season

211 .... Dudley Bradley, Ind. Pacers, 1979–80	165 .... Tim Hardaway, G.S. Warriors, 1989–90
209 .... Ron Harper, Cle. Cavaliers, 1986–87	165 .... Gary Payton, Sea. Soncis, 1990–91
205 .... Mark Jackson*, N.Y. Knicks, 1987–88	160 .... Mario Chalmers, Mia. Heat, 2008–09
196 .... Michael Jordan*, Chi. Bulls, 1984–85	157 .... Allen Iverson*, Phi. 76ers, 1996–97
196 .... Brevin Knight, Cle. Cavaliers, 1997–98	157 .... Kerry Kittles, N.J. Nets, 1996–97
192 .... Quinn Buckner, Mil. Bucks, 1976–77	156 .... Ron Lee, Pho. Suns, 1976–77
190 .... Penny Hardaway, Orl. Magic, 1993–94	154 .... Mark Macon, Den. Nuggets, 1991–92
187 .... Magic Johnson, L.A. Lakers, 1979–80	153 .... Fat Lever, Por. Blazers, 1982–83
175 .... Chris Paul*, N.O.-Ok.C. Hornets, 2005–06	152 .... Stephen Curry, G.S. Warriors, 2009–10
174 .... Maurice Cheeks, Phi. 76ers, 1978–79	151 .... Jason Kidd**, Dal. Mavericks, 1994–95
174 .... Phil Ford*, K.C. Kings, 1978–79	150 .... Isiah Thomas, Det. Pistons, 1981–82
167 .... Bobby Jones, Den. Nuggets, 1974–75	150 .... Willie Anderson, S.A. Spurs, 1988–89

* Rookie of the Year.

** Tied for Rookie of the Year with Grant Hill, Det. Pistons.

ᵃ ABA.

Most Steals from Age 39 On

John Stockton	306	Robert Parish	153	Michael Jordan	135
Vince Carter	207	Jason Kidd	139	Manu Ginóbili	125
Karl Malone	186	Kareem Abdul-Jabbar	135		

Most Steals, Game

12 .... Ted McClain, Car. Cougarsᵃ	.... vs. N.Y. Netsᵃ (Dec. 26, 1973)
11 .... Larry Kenon, S.A. Spurs	.... @ K.C. Kings (Dec. 26, 1976)
11 .... Kendall Gill, N.J. Nets	.... vs. Mia. Heat (Apr. 3, 1999)
10 .... Joe Caldwell, Car. Cougarsᵃ	.... vs. S.D. Conquistadorsᵃ (Dec. 16, 1972)
10 .... Jerry West, L.A. Lakers	.... vs. Sea. Sonics (Dec. 7, 1973)
10 .... Larry Steele, Por. Blazers	.... vs. L.A. Lakers (Nov. 16, 1974)
10 .... Fred Brown, Sea. Sonics	.... @ Phi. 76ers (Dec. 3, 1976)
10 .... Gus Williams, Sea. Sonics	.... @ N.J. Nets (Feb. 22, 1978)
10 .... Eddie Jordan, N.J. Nets	.... @ Phi. 76ers (Mar. 23, 1979)
10 .... Johnny Moore, S.A. Spurs	.... vs. Ind. Pacers (Mar. 6, 1985)
10 .... Fat Lever, Den. Nuggets	.... vs. Ind. Pacers (Mar. 9, 1985)
10 .... Clyde Drexler, Por. Blazers	.... @ Mil. Bucks (Jan. 10, 1986)
10 .... Alvin Robertson, S.A. Spurs	.... vs. Pho. Suns (Feb. 18, 1986)
10 .... Alvin Robertson, S.A. Spurs	.... @ L.A. Clippers (Nov. 22, 1986)
10 .... Ron Harper, Cle. Cavaliers	.... vs. Phi. 76ers (Mar. 10, 1987)
10 .... Michael Jordan, Chi. Bulls	.... vs. N.J. Nets (Jan. 29, 1988)
10 .... Alvin Robertson, S.A. Spurs	.... vs. Hou. Rockets (Jan. 11, 1989)
10 .... Alvin Robertson, Mil. Bucks	.... vs. Uta. Jazz (Nov. 19, 1990)
10 .... Kevin Johnson, Pho. Suns	.... vs. Was. Bullets (Dec. 9, 1993)
10 .... Clyde Drexler, Hou. Rockets	.... vs. Sac. Kings (Nov. 1, 1996)
10 .... Mookie Blaylock, Atl. Hawks	.... vs. Phi. 76ers (Apr. 14, 1998)
10 .... Michael Finley, Dal. Mavericks	.... vs. Phi. 76ers (Jan. 23, 2001)
10 .... Brandon Roy, Por. Blazers	.... vs. Was. Wizards (Jan. 24, 2009)
10 .... Draymond Green, G.S. Warriors	.... @ Mem. Grizzlies (Feb. 10, 2017)
10 .... Lou Williams, L.A. Clippers	.... @ Uta. Jazz (Jan. 20, 2018)
10 .... T.J. McConnell, Ind. Pacers	.... @ Cle. Cavaliers (Mar. 3, 2021)

ᵃ ABA.

Most Steals in a Loss

10 .... Jerry West, L.A. Lakers .... vs. Sea. Sonics (Dec. 7, 1973)
10 .... Eddie Jordan, N.J. Nets .... @ Phi. 76ers (Mar. 23, 1979)
10 .... Clyde Drexler, Por. Blazers .... @ Mil. Bucks (Jan. 10, 1986)
10 .... Ron Harper, Cle. Cavaliers .... vs. Phi. 76ers (Mar. 10, 1987)
10 .... Alvin Robertson, S.A. Spurs .... vs. Hou. Rockets (Jan. 11, 1989)
10 .... Michael Finley, Dal. Mavericks .... vs. Phi. 76ers (Jan. 23, 2001)
10 .... Lou Williams, L.A. Clippers .... @ Uta. Jazz (Jan. 20, 2018)
9 .... Calvin Murphy, Hou. Rockets .... vs. Bos. Celtics (Dec. 14, 1973)
9 .... Slick Watts, Sea. Sonics .... vs. Phi. 76ers (Feb. 23, 1975)
9 .... Quinn Buckner, Mil. Bucks .... vs. Ind. Pacers (Jan. 2, 1977)
9 .... Slick Watts, Sea. Sonics .... vs. Pho. Suns (Mar. 27, 1977)
9 .... Ron Lee, Det. Pistons .... vs. Hou. Rockets (Mar. 16, 1980)
9 .... John Lucas, G.S. Warriors .... vs. L.A. Lakers (Mar. 30, 1980)
9 .... Dudley Bradley, Ind. Pacers .... @ Uta. Jazz (Nov. 10, 1980)
9 .... Micheal Ray Richardson, N.Y. Knicks .... @ Chi. Bulls (Dec. 23, 1980)
9 .... Johnny High, Pho. Suns .... @ Was. Bullets (Jan. 28, 1981)
9 .... Magic Johnson, L.A. Lakers .... vs. Pho. Suns (Nov. 6, 1981)
9 .... Rickey Green, Uta. Jazz .... @ Phi. 76ers (Nov. 27, 1982)
9 .... Darwin Cook, N.J. Nets .... vs. Por. Blazers (Dec. 3, 1983)
9 .... Eric Murdock, Mil. Bucks .... @ Was. Bullets (Apr. 2, 1994)
9 .... Mookie Blaylock, Atl. Hawks .... @ Hou. Rockets (Feb. 17, 1997)
9 .... Andre Miller, Cle. Cavaliers .... vs. Phi. 76ers (Dec. 15, 2001)
9 .... Dirk Nowitzki, Dal. Mavericks .... @ Hou. Rockets (Mar. 7, 2004)

Most Steals in a Game without Scoring

7 .... Ryan Bowen, Den. Nuggets .... @ Sac. Kings (Dec. 6, 2002)
6 .... Ron Lee, Det. Pistons .... vs. Was. Bullets (Nov. 19, 1981)
6 .... Nate McMillan, Sea. Sonics .... @ Bos. Celtics (Feb. 2, 1994)
6 .... Eddie House, L.A. Clippers .... vs. G.S. Warriors (Mar. 21, 2004)
5 .... Dave Wohl, Hou. Rockets .... vs. Por. Blazers (Feb. 24, 1974)
5 .... Lenny Wilkens, Por. Blazers .... vs. Sea. Sonics (Oct. 27, 1974)
5 .... Slick Watts, Sea. Sonics .... vs. Chi. Bulls (Nov. 22, 1974)
5 .... Sam Worthen, Chi. Bulls .... @ Was. Bullets (Dec. 16, 1980)
5 .... Bob Hansen, Uta. Jazz .... @ Pho. Suns (Apr. 3, 1987)
5 .... Muggsy Bogues, Cha. Hornets .... vs. L.A. Lakers (Mar. 16, 1989)
5 .... Elston Turner, Den. Nuggets .... @ Uta. Jazz (Apr. 12, 1989)
5 .... Terrell Brandon, Cle. Cavaliers .... @ Phi. 76ers (Nov. 26, 1991)
5 .... Ben Wallace, Was. Bullets .... vs. Cle. Cavaliers (Feb. 4, 1998)
5 .... Hersey Hawkins, Sea. Sonics .... @ L.A. Lakers (Mar. 20, 1998)
5 .... Bob Sura, Hou. Rockets .... vs. L.A. Clippers (Dec. 26, 2004)
5 .... Luke Ridnour, Sea. Sonics .... vs. L.A. Lakers (Mar. 31, 2006)
5 .... Ben Wallace, Det. Pistons .... vs. Orl. Magic (Jan. 2, 2012)
5 .... Patrick Beverley, Hou. Rockets .... vs. Cle. Cavaliers (Feb. 1, 2014)
5 .... Chris Babb, Bos. Celtics .... @ Det. Pistons (Apr. 5, 2014)
5 .... Joey Dorsey, Hou. Rockets .... @ Sac. Kings (Dec. 11, 2014)
5 .... P.J. Tucker, Hou. Rockets .... vs. Pho. Suns (Mar. 15, 2019)
5 .... Garrison Mathews, Was. Wizards .... vs. Mia. Heat (Mar. 8, 2020)
5 .... Garrett Temple, N.O. Pelicans .... vs. Den. Nuggets (Jan. 28, 2022)
5 .... Gary Payton II, G.S. Warriors .... @ S.A. Spurs (Feb. 1, 2022)

Most Steals by Players Under 6-Feet Tall, Season

196	Brevin Knight, Cle. Cavaliers, 1997–98	5-foot-10
170	Muggsy Bogues, Cha. Hornets, 1991–92	5-foot-3
168	Michael Adams, Den. Nuggets, 1987–88	5-foot-10
166	Michael Adams, Den. Nuggets, 1988–89	5-foot-10
166	Muggsy Bogues, Cha. Hornets, 1989–90	5-foot-3
161	Muggsy Bogues, Cha. Hornets, 1992–93	5-foot-3
161	Terrell Brandon, Min. T'Wolves, 2000–01	5-foot-11
157	Calvin Murphy, Hou. Rockets, 1973–74	5-foot-9
157	Brevin Knight, Cha. Bobcats, 2005–06	5-foot-10
151	Calvin Murphy, Hou. Rockets, 1975–76	5-foot-9
149	Dana Barros, Phi. 76ers, 1994–95	5-foot-11
147	Michael Adams, Den. Nuggets, 1990–91	5-foot-10
145	Michael Adams, Was. Bullets, 1991–92	5-foot-10
144	Calvin Murphy, Hou. Rockets, 1976–77	5-foot-9
143	Calvin Murphy, Hou. Rockets, 1979–80	5-foot-9
138	Terrell Brandon, Cle. Cavaliers, 1996–97	5-foot-11
137	Muggsy Bogues, Cha. Hornets, 1990–91	5-foot-3
134	Terrell Brandon, Min. T'Wolves, 1999–00	5-foot-11
133	Muggsy Bogues, Cha. Hornets, 1993–94	5-foot-3
132	Terrell Brandon, Cle. Cavaliers, 1995–96	5-foot-11
131	Brevin Knight, Cha. Bobcats, 2004–05	5-foot-10
128	Calvin Murphy, Hou. Rockets, 1974–75	5-foot-9
127	Muggsy Bogues, Was. Bullets, 1987–88	5-foot-3
125	Spud Webb, Sac. Kings, 1991–92	5-foot-6

Most Steals by Players Under 6-Feet Tall, Career

1369	Muggsy Bogues	5-foot-3	922	Spud Webb	5-foot-6
1229	Brevin Knight	5-foot-10	740	Dana Barros	5-foot-11
1165	Calvin Murphy	5-foot-9	661	Travis Best	5-foot-11
1142	Terrell Brandon	5-foot-11	636	Ty Lawson	5-foot-11
1081	Michael Adams	5-foot-10	567	D.J. Augustin^	5-foot-11
1007	Avery Johnson	5-foot-10	543	Nate Robinson	5-foot-9
953	Damon Stoudamire	5-foot-10	503	Speedy Claxton	5-foot-11

^ Active.

Most Steals by Players 7-Feet or Taller, Season

213	Hakeem Olajuwon, Hou. Rockets, 1988–89	7-foot-0
174	Hakeem Olajuwon, Hou. Rockets, 1989–90	7-foot-0
162	Hakeem Olajuwon, Hou. Rockets, 1987–88	7-foot-0
158	David Robinson, S.A. Spurs, 1991–92	7-foot-1
150	Hakeem Olajuwon, Hou. Rockets, 1992–93	7-foot-0
140	Hakeem Olajuwon, Hou. Rockets, 1986–87	7-foot-0
139	David Robinson, S.A. Spurs, 1993–94	7-foot-1
138	David Robinson, S.A. Spurs, 1989–90	7-foot-1
134	Hakeem Olajuwon, Hou. Rockets, 1985–86	7-foot-0
134	David Robinson, S.A. Spurs, 1994–95	7-foot-1
133	Hakeem Olajuwon, Hou. Rockets, 1994–95	7-foot-0
128	Vlade Divac, L.A. Lakers, 1992–93	7-foot-1
128	Hakeem Olajuwon, Hou. Rockets, 1993–94	7-foot-0
127	David Robinson, S.A. Spurs, 1990–91	7-foot-1
127	Hakeem Olajuwon, Hou. Rockets, 1991–92	7-foot-0
127	David Robinson, S.A. Spurs, 1992–93	7-foot-1

continued on next page

126	Rich Kelley, N.O. Jazz, 1978–79	7-foot-0
121	Hakeem Olajuwon, Hou. Rockets, 1990–91	7-foot-0
119	Kareem Abdul-Jabbar, L.A. Lakers, 1975–76	7-foot-2
117	Patrick Ewing, N.Y. Knicks, 1988–89	7-foot-0
117	Hakeem Olajuwon, Hou. Rockets, 1996–97	7-foot-0
113	Hakeem Olajuwon, Hou. Rockets, 1995–96	7-foot-0
112	Kareem Abdul-Jabbar, Mil. Bucks, 1973–74	7-foot-2
111	David Robinson, S.A. Spurs, 1995–96	7-foot-1
111	Dirk Nowitzki, Dal. Mavericks, 2002–03	7-foot-0
109	Vlade Divac, L.A. Lakers, 1994–95	7-foot-1
108	Joe Barry Carroll, G.S. Warriors, 1982–83	7-foot-0
106	Vlade Divac, L.A. Lakers, 1990–91	7-foot-1
104	Patrick Ewing, N.Y. Knicks, 1987–88	7-foot-0
103	Kareem Abdul-Jabbar, L.A. Lakers, 1977–78	7-foot-2
103	Joe Barry Carroll, G.S. Warriors, 1983–84	7-foot-0
103	Vlade Divac, Cha. Hornets, 1996–97	7-foot-1
103	Vlade Divac, Sac. Kings, 1999–00	7-foot-1
101	Kareem Abdul-Jabbar, L.A. Lakers, 1976–77	7-foot-2
101	Joe Barry Carroll, G.S. Warriors, 1985–86	7-foot-0
100	Robert Parish, G.S. Warriors, 1978–79	7-foot-1

Most Steals by Players 7-Feet or Taller, Career

2162	Hakeem Olajuwon	7-foot-0	532	Shawn Bradley	7-foot-6
1388	David Robinson	7-foot-1	522	Benoit Benjamin	7-foot-0
1288	Vlade Divac	7-foot-1	512	Tree Rollins	7-foot-1
1219	Robert Parish	7-foot-1	503	Brook Lopez^	7-foot-0
1210	Dirk Nowitzki	7-foot-0	494	Dikembe Mutombo	7-foot-2
1160	Kareem Abdul-Jabbar	7-foot-2	460	Bill Cartwright	7-foot-1
1136	Patrick Ewing	7-foot-0	457	Channing Frye	7-foot-0
958	Kevin Willis	7-foot-0	442	Andrew Bogut	7-foot-0
739	Shaquille O'Neal	7-foot-1	422	Brad Daugherty	7-foot-0
694	Rich Kelley	7-foot-0	421	Zydrunas Ilgauskas	7-foot-3
687	Joe Barry Carroll	7-foot-0	420	James Edwards	7-foot-0
648	Artis Gilmore	7-foot-2	412	Rudy Gobert^	7-foot-1
630	Tyson Chandler^	7-foot-0	390	Ralph Sampson	7-foot-4
606	Pau Gasol	7-foot-0	372	Rik Smits	7-foot-4
542	Jon Koncak	7-foot-0	370	Arvydas Sabonis	7-foot-3

^ Active.

Steals Average

Highest Steals Average by Decade (Min. 100 Games)·

1973-74–1979-80		1980-81–1989-90		1990-91–1999-00	
2.5	Don Buse	2.8	Alvin Robertson	2.5	Mookie Blaylock
2.4	Micheal Ray Richardson	2.8	Michael Jordan	2.5	Alvin Robertson
2.3	Brian Taylor	2.7	Micheal Ray Richardson	2.2	Gary Payton
2.3	Fatty Taylor	2.4	John Stockton	2.2	John Stockton
2.3	Eddie Jordan	2.3	Fat Lever	2.2	Michael Jordan
2.2	Slick Watts	2.3	Clyde Drexler	2.2	Eddie Jones
2.2	Quinn Buckner	2.3	Ron Harper	2.1	Scottie Pippen
2.2	Jerry Sloan	2.2	Maurice Cheeks	2.1	Jason Kidd

continued on next page

2.2 .... Maurice Cheeks	2.2 .... Gary Grant	2.1 .... Allen Iverson
2.1 .... Julius Erving	2.1 .... Isiah Thomas	2.0 .... Nate McMillan
2.1 .... Ron Lee	2.1 .... Doc Rivers	2.0 .... Micheal Williams
2.1 .... Joe Caldwell		2.0 .... Brevin Knight

2000–01–2009–10	**2010–11–2019–20**	**2020–21–2021–22****
2.4 .... Chris Paul	2.1 .... Chris Paul	1.9 .... Jimmy Butler
2.2 .... Allen Iverson	1.9 .... Ricky Rubio	1.8 .... Dejounte Murray
2.0 .... Baron Davis	1.8 .... Russell Westbrook	1.7 .... Matisse Thybulle
2.0 .... Metta World Peace	1.8 .... Kawhi Leonard	1.7 .... Fred VanVleet
2.0 .... Doug Christie	1.7 .... Paul George	1.7 .... Herbert Jones
1.9 .... Jason Kidd	1.7 .... Stephen Curry	1.6 .... Tyrese Haliburton
1.9 .... Rajon Rondo	1.7 .... John Wall	1.6 .... Chris Paul
1.9 .... Terrell Brandon	1.7 .... Monta Ellis	1.6 .... LaMelo Ball
1.8 .... Shawn Marion	1.7 .... Tony Allen	1.6 .... Jrue Holiday
1.8 .... Andre Iguodala	1.7 .... Victor Oladipo	1.6 .... Marcus Smart
1.8 .... Dwyane Wade	1.7 .... Robert Covington	1.6 .... T.J. McConnell
1.8 .... Mookie Blaylock	1.7 .... Ben Simmons	1.6 .... Lonzo Ball
	1.7 .... Jason Kidd	1.6 .... Ben Simmons
		1.6 .... Kawhi Leonard

* Steals were first recorded as a stat in the NBA/ABA, beginning with the 1973–74 season.

** Minimum 50 games.

Evolution of Steals Average Record

NBA

1973–74........ Larry Steele, Por. Blazers 2.7
1974–75........ Rick Barry, G.S. Warriors 2.9
1975–76........ Slick Watts, Sea. Sonics.............3.2
1976–77........ Don Buse, Ind. Pacers................3.5
1985–86........ Alvin Robertson, S.A. Spurs........3.7

ABA

1973–74........... Ted McClain, Car. Cougars........3.0
1975–76........... Don Buse, Ind. Pacers................4.1

Highest Steals Average, Season

4.1.......Don Buse, Ind. Pacers[a], 1975–76
3.7.......Alvin Robertson, S.A. Spurs, 1985–86
3.5.......Don Buse, Ind. Pacers, 1976–77
3.4.......Magic Johnson, L.A. Lakers, 1980–81
3.2.......Micheal Ray Richardson, N.Y. Knicks, 1979–80
3.2.......Alvin Robertson, S.A. Spurs, 1986–87
3.2.......John Stockton, Uta. Jazz, 1988–89
3.2.......Slick Watts, Sea. Sonics, 1975–76
3.2.......Michael Jordan, Chi. Bulls, 1987–88
3.0.......Alvin Robertson, Mil. Bucks, 1990–91
3.0.......Alvin Robertson, S.A. Spurs, 1988–89
3.0.......Ted McClain, Car. Cougars[a], 1973–74
3.0.......John Stockton, Uta. Jazz, 1991–92
3.0.......Micheal Ray Richardson, N.J. Nets, 1984–85
3.0.......Alvin Robertson, S.A. Spurs, 1987–88
3.0.......Nate McMillan, Sea. Sonics, 1993–94
[a] ABA.

3.0.......John Stockton, Uta. Jazz, 1987–88
3.0.......Micheal Williams, Ind. Pacers, 1991–92
2.9.......Micheal Ray Richardson, N.Y. Knicks, 1980–81
2.9.......Scottie Pippen, Chi. Bulls, 1994–95
2.9.......Scottie Pippen, Chi. Bulls, 1993–94
2.9.......Michael Jordan, Chi. Bulls, 1988–89
2.9.......Larry Hughes, Was. Wizards, 2004–05
2.9.......Michael Jordan, Chi. Bulls, 1986–87
2.9.......Rick Barry, G.S. Warriors, 1974–75
2.9.......John Stockton, Uta. Jazz, 1990–91
2.9.......Gary Payton, Sea. Sonics, 1995–96
2.8.......Micheal Ray Richardson, G.S. Warriors/N.J. Nets, 1982–83
2.8.......Michael Jordan, Chi. Bulls, 1992–93
2.8.......Rickey Green, Uta. Jazz, 1982–83
2.8.......Brian Taylor, N.Y. Nets[a], 1974–75
2.8.......Allen Iverson, Phi. 76ers, 2001–02

Multiple Seasons Leading League in Steals Average

6............Chris Paul ............................N.O. Hornets: 2007–08 (2.7), 2008–09 (2.8), 2010–11 (2.4); L.A. Clippers: 2011–12
2.5), 2012–13 (2.4), 2013–14 (2.5)

3............Micheal Ray Richardson ........N.Y. Knicks: 1979–80 (3.2); G.S. Warriors/N.J. Nets: 1982–83 (2.8); N.J. Nets:
1984–85 (3.0)

3............Alvin Robertson ...................S.A. Spurs: 1985–86 (3.7), 1986–87 (3.2); Mil. Bucks: 1990–91 (3.0)

3............Allen Iverson ....Phi. 76ers: 2000–01 (2.5), 2001–02 (2.8), 2002–03 (2.7)

2............Don Buse ....Ind. Pacers°: 1975–76 (4.1); Ind. Pacers: 1976–77 (3.5)

2............Magic Johnson ....................L.A. Lakers: 1980–81 (3.4), 1981–82 (2.7)

2............John Stockton ....Uta. Jazz: 1988–89 (3.2), 1991–92 (3.0)

2............Mookie Blaylock ....Atl. Hawks: 1996–97 (2.7), 1997–98 (2.6)

2............Baron Davis ....N.O Hornets: 2003–04 (2.4); G.S. Warriors: 2006–07 (2.1)

Highest Steals Average, Career

		Career GP				Career GP
2.7	Alvin Robertson	779		2.0	Clyde Drexler	1086
2.6	Micheal Ray Richardson	556		2.0	Gus Williams	825
2.3	Michael Jordan	1072		2.0	Johnny Moore	520
2.3	Mookie Blaylock	889		1.9	Jason Kidd	1391
2.2	John Stockton	1504		1.9	Isiah Thomas	979
2.2	Allen Iverson	914		1.9	Don Buse	966
2.2	Fat Lever	752		1.9	Magic Johnson	906
2.2	Slick Watts	437		1.9	Doug Christie	827
2.1	Chris Paul^	1155		1.9	Nate McMillan	796
2.1	Maurice Cheeks	1101		1.9	Quinn Buckner	719
2.0	Scottie Pippen	1178		1.9	Ron Lee	448

^ Active.

Most Seasons Averaging 2.0 SPG, Career

11	Mookie Blaylock	9	Alvin Robertson	7	Micheal Ray Richardson
10	Maurice Cheeks	9	Allen Iverson	7	Gus Williams
10	Michael Jordan	9	Chris Paul^	7	Jason Kidd
10	John Stockton	8	Gary Payton	7	Metta World Peace

^ Active.

Blocks

Most Blocked Shots by Decade·

1973-74—1979-80		1980-81—1989-90		1990-91—1999-00	
1875	Kareem Abdul-Jabbar	2592	Mark Eaton	2443	Dikembe Mutombo
1396	George Johnson	1658	Tree Rollins	2187	David Robinson
1387	Elvin Hayes	1577	Hakeem Olajuwon	2075	Hakeem Olajuwon
1183	Elmore Smith	1490	Manute Bol	1666	Alonzo Mourning
977	Sam Lacey	1426	Kevin McHale	1655	Patrick Ewing
937	Bob McAdoo	1331	Larry Nance	1520	Shawn Bradley
888	Bob Lanier	1324	Wayne Cooper	1436	Shaquille O'Neal
716	Tree Rollins	1314	Kareem Abdul-Jabbar	1229	Elden Campbell
708	Gar Heard	1300	Robert Parish	1147	Vlade Divac
646	Caldwell Jones	1254	Herb Williams	1120	Shawn Kemp

continued on next page

2000-01 – 2009-10		2010-11 – 2019-20		2020-21 – 2021-22	
1738	Tim Duncan	1575	Serge Ibaka	327	Rudy Gobert
1729	Ben Wallace	1281	DeAndre Jordan	277	Myler Turner
1590	Marcus Camby	1264	Anthony Davis	241	Jakob Poeltl
1476	Jermaine O'Neal	1122	Brook Lopez	225	Robert Williams
1306	Andrei Kirilenko	1088	Dwight Howard	222	Clint Capela
1282	Elton Brand	1030	Rudy Gobert	195	Jaren Jackson Jr.
1254	Shaquille O'Neal	997	Marc Gasol	186	Chris Boucher
1158	Theo Ratliff	994	Hassan Whiteside	178	Mitchell Robinson
1137	Kevin Garnett	939	Roy Hibbert	176	Mo Bamba
1131	Samuel Dalembert	938	Andre Drummond	175	Robert Covington

* Blocks were first recorded as a stat in the NBA/ABA, beginning with the 1973–74 season.

Evolution of Blocks Record

NBA

1973–74 .... Elmore Smith, L.A. Lakers 393
1984–85 .... Mark Eaton, Uta. Jazz 456

ABA

1971–72 .... Artis Gilmore, Ken. Colonels 422

Most Blocks, Season

456 .... Mark Eaton, Uta. Jazz, 1984–85
422 .... Artis Gilmore, Ken. Colonels[a], 1971–72
397 .... Manute Bol, Was. Bullets, 1985–86
393 .... Elmore Smith, L.A. Lakers, 1973–74
376 .... Hakeem Olajuwon, Hou. Rockets, 1989–90
369 .... Mark Eaton, Uta. Jazz, 1985–86
351 .... Mark Eaton, Uta. Jazz, 1983–84
345 .... Manute Bol, G.S. Warriors, 1988–89
343 .... Tree Rollins, Atl. Hawks, 1982–83
342 .... Hakeem Olajuwon, Hou. Rockets, 1992–93
338 .... Kareem Abdul-Jabbar, L.A. Lakers, 1975–76
336 .... Dikembe Mutombo, Den. Nuggets, 1993–94
332 .... Dikembe Mutombo, Den. Nuggets, 1995–96
[a] ABA.

327 .... Patrick Ewing, N.Y. Knicks, 1989–90
321 .... Mark Eaton, Uta. Jazz, 1986–87
321 .... Dikembe Mutombo, Den. Nuggets, 1994–95
320 .... David Robinson, S.A. Spurs, 1990–91
319 .... David Robinson, S.A. Spurs, 1989–90
316 .... Caldwell Jones, S.D. Conquistadors[a], 1973–74
316 .... Kareem Abdul-Jabbar, L.A. Lakers, 1978–79
315 .... Mark Eaton, Uta. Jazz, 1988–89
307 .... Theo Ratliff, Atl. Hawks/Por. Blazers, 2003–04
305 .... David Robinson, S.A. Spurs, 1991–92
304 .... Mark Eaton, Uta. Jazz, 1987–88
304 .... Hakeem Olajuwon, Hou. Rockets, 1991–92
302 .... Manute Bol, Was. Bullets, 1986–87

Most Blocks, Career

3830 .... Hakeem Olajuwon
3289 .... Dikembe Mutombo
3189 .... Kareem Abdul-Jabbar
3178 .... Artis Gilmore
3064 .... Mark Eaton
3020 .... Tim Duncan
2954 .... David Robinson
^ Active.

2894 .... Patrick Ewing
2732 .... Shaquille O'Neal
2542 .... Tree Rollins
2361 .... Robert Parish
2356 .... Alonzo Mourning
2331 .... Marcus Camby
2297 .... Caldwell Jones

2217 .... Dwight Howard^
2137 .... Ben Wallace
2119 .... Shawn Bradley
2086 .... Manute Bol
2082 .... George Johnson
2037 .... Kevin Garnett
2027 .... Larry Nance

Block Leaders by State of Birth

Alabama	Ben Wallace (White Hall)	2137	Nevada	Ricky Davis (Las Vegas)	187
Alaska	Mario Chalmers (Anchorage)	5743	New Hampshire	Matt Bonner (Concord)	213
Arizona	Sean Elliott (Tucson)	284	New Jersey	Shaquille O'Neal (Newark)	2732
Arkansas	Caldwell Jones (McGehee)	2297	New Mexico	Andre Roberson^ (Las Cruces)	199
California	Mark Eaton (Westminster)	3064	New York	Kareem Abdul-Jabbar (New York)	3189
Colorado	Jason Smith (Greeley)	408	North Carolina	Bobby Jones (Charlotte)	1319
Connecticut	Marcus Camby (Hartford)	2331	North Dakota	Tyler Johnson^ (Grand Forks)	140
Delaware	Donte DiVincenzo^ (Newark)	49	Ohio	Herb Williams (Columbus)	1605
Florida	Artis Gilmore (Chipley)	3178	Oklahoma	Antoine Carr (Oklahoma City)	925
Georgia	Dwight Howard^ (Atlanta)	2228	Oregon	Jerami Grant^ (Portland)	615
Hawaii	Cedric Ceballos (Maui)	183	Pennsylvania	Rasheed Wallace (Philadelphia)	1460
Idaho	Luke Ridnour (Coeur d'Alene)	161	Rhode Island	Marvin Barnes (Providence)	438
Illinois	Anthony Davis^ (Chicago)	1413	South Carolina	Kevin Garnett (Greenville)	2037
Indiana	Shawn Kemp (Elkhart)	1279	South Dakota	Mike Miller (Mitchell)	229
Iowa	Raef LaFrentz (Hampton)	919	Tennessee	Lorenzen Wright (Memphis)	572
Kansas	Alvan Adams (Lawrence)	808	Texas	DeAndre Jordan^ (Houston)	1502
Kentucky	Felton Spencer (Louisville)	534	Utah	Tom Chambers (Ogden)	627
Louisiana	Robert Parish (Shreveport)	2361	Vermont	N/A	N/A
Maine	Jeff Turner (Bangor)	85	Virginia	Alonzo Mourning (Chesapeake)	2356
Maryland	Marvin Webster (Baltimore)	881	Washington	James Edwards (Seattle)	867
Massachusetts	Bill Laimbeer (Boston)	965	West Virginia	Deron Williams (Parkersburg)	206
Michigan	Terry Tyler (Detroit)	1342	Wisconsin	Jim Chones (Racine)	774
Minnesota	Kevin McHale (Hibbing)	1690	Wyoming	James Johnson (Cheyenne)	646
Mississippi	George Johnson (Tylertown)	2082			
Missouri	Steve Stipanovich (St. Louis)	380	District of Columbia	Thurl Bailey	1086
Montana	Phil Jackson (Deer Lodge)	199	Puerto Rico	Carlos Arroyo (Fajardo)	26
Nebraska	Fred Hoiberg (Lincoln)	59	Virgin Islands	Tim Duncan (St. Croix)	3020

^ Active.

All-Time Block Leaders by First Letter of Last Name

A	Abdul-Jabbar, Kareem	3189	J	Jones, Caldwell	2297	S	Smith, Josh	1713
B	Bradley, Shawn	2119	K	Kirilenko, Andrei	1461	T	Tyler, Terry	1342
C	Camby, Marcus	2331	L	Lopez, Brook^	1530	U	Udoh, Ekpe	429
D	Duncan, Tim	3020	M	Mutombo, Dikembe	3289	V	Jonas Valančiūnas^	702
E	Eaton, Mark	3064	N	Nance, Larry	2027	W	Wallace, Ben	2137
F	Foyle, Adonal	1193	O	Olajuwon, Hakeem	3830	X	N/A	N/A
G	Gilmore, Artis	3178	P	Parish, Robert	2361	Y	Young, Thaddeus^	448
H	Howard, Dwight^	2228	Q	Quinnett, Brian	25	Z	Zeller, Cody^	321
I	Ibaka, Serge^	1752	R	Robinson, David	2954			

^ Active.

Most Times Leading League in Blocks

5	Dikembe Mutombo	Den. Nuggets, 1993–94	336
		Den. Nuggets, 1994–95	321
		Den. Nuggets, 1995–96	332
		Atl. Hawks, 1996–97	264
		Atl. Hawks, 1997–98	277
4	Kareem Abdul-Jabbar	L.A. Lakers, 1975–76	338
		L.A. Lakers, 1976–77	261
		L.A. Lakers, 1978–79	316

continued on next page

		L.A. Lakers, 1979–80	280
4	Mark Eaton	Uta. Jazz, 1983–84	351
		Uta. Jazz, 1984–85	456
		Uta. Jazz, 1986–87	321
		Uta. Jazz, 1987–88	304
4	Serge Ibaka	Ok.C. Thunder, 2010–11	198
		Ok.C. Thunder, 2011–12	241
		Ok.C. Thunder, 2012–13	242
		Ok.C. Thunder, 2013–14	219
3	Artis Gilmore	Ken. Colonels[a], 1971–72	422
		Ken. Colonels[a], 1972–73	259
		Ken. Colonels[a], 1974–75	258
3	George Johnson	N.J. Nets, 1977–78	274
		S.A. Spurs, 1980–81	278
		S.A. Spurs, 1981–82	234
3	Marcus Camby	Den. Nuggets, 2004–05	199
		Den. Nuggets, 2006–07	231
		Den. Nuggets, 2007–08	285

[a] ABA.

Consecutive Seasons Leading League in Blocks

5	Dikembe Mutombo	Den. Nuggets, 1993–94	336
		Den. Nuggets, 1994–95	321
		Den. Nuggets, 1995–96	332
		Atl. Hawks, 1996–97	264
		Atl. Hawks, 1997–98	277
4	Serge Ibaka	Ok.C. Thunder, 2010–11	198
		Ok.C. Thunder, 2011–12	241
		Ok.C. Thunder, 2012–13	242
		Ok.C. Thunder, 2013–14	219
2	Artis Gilmore	Ken. Colonels[a], 1971–72	422
		Ken. Colonels[a], 1972–73	259
2	Elmore Smith	L.A. Lakers, 1973–74	393
		L.A. Lakers, 1974–75	216
2	Kareem Abdul-Jabbar	L.A. Lakers, 1975–76	338
		L.A. Lakers, 1976–77	261
		L.A. Lakers, 1978–79	316
		L.A. Lakers, 1979–80	280
2	George Johnson	S.A. Spurs, 1980–81	278
		S.A. Spurs, 1981–82	234
2	Mark Eaton	Uta. Jazz, 1983–84	351
		Uta. Jazz, 1984–85	456
		Uta. Jazz, 1986–87	321
		Uta. Jazz, 1987–88	304
2	David Robinson	S.A. Spurs, 1990–91	320
		S.A. Spurs, 1991–92	305
2	Alonzo Mourning	Mia. Heat, 1998–99	180
		Mia. Heat, 1999–00	294
2	Theo Ratliff	Atl. Hawks, 2002–03	262
		Atl. Hawks/Por. Blazers, 2003–04	307
2	Marcus Camby	Den. Nuggets, 2006–07	231

continued on next page

		Den. Nuggets, 2007–08 285
2	Dwight Howard	Orl. Magic, 2008–09 231
		Orl. Magic, 2009–10 228

ᵃ ABA.

Most Career Blocks, Never Leading League

Career Blocks		Most Blocks, Season	League Leader
3020..........	Tim Duncan 237	(2002–03, S.A. Spurs)	262 (Theo Ratliff, Atl. Hawks)
2894..........	Patrick Ewing 327	(1989–90, N.Y. Knicks)........................	376 (Hakeem Olajuwon, Hou. Rockets)
2732..........	Shaquille O'Neal..............286	(1992–93, Orl. Magic)	342 (Hakeem Olajuwon, Hou. Rockets)
2361..........	Robert Parish...................217	(1978–79, G.S. Warriors)	316 (Kareem Abdul-Jabbar, L.A. Lakers)
2037..........	Kevin Garnett...................178	(2003–04, Min. T'Wolves).....................	307 (Theo Ratliff, Atl.Hawks/Por. Blazers)
2027..........	Larry Nance....................243	(1991–92, Cle. Cavaliers)	305 (David Robinson, S.A. Spurs)
1941..........	Julius Erving 204	(1973–74, N.Y. Netsᵃ)	316 (Caldwell Jones, S.D. Conquistadorsᵃ)
1941..........	Pau Gasol.......................169	(2001–02, Mem. Grizzlies)	278 (Ben Wallace, Det. Pistons)
1889..........	Moses Malone..................181	(1976–77, Buf. Braves/Hou. Rockets)......	261 (Kareem Abdul-Jabbar, L.A. Lakers)
1828..........	Elton Brand 201	(2005–06, L.A. Clippers).....................	220 (Andrei Kirilenko, Uta. Jazz)
1771..........	Elvin Hayes 240	(1973–74, Cap. Bullets)	393 (Elmore Smith, L.A. Lakers)
1713..........	Josh Smith 227	(2007–08, Atl. Hawks)........................	285 (Marcus Camby, Den. Nuggets)
1690..........	Kevin McHale.................192	(1982–83, Bos. Celtics)	343 (Tree Rollins, Atl. Hawks)
1631..........	Vlade Divac 180	(1996–97, Cha. Hornets)	264 (Dikembe Mutombo, Atl. Hawks)
1605..........	Herb Williams 184	(1985–86, Ind. Pacers)	397 (Manute Bol, Was. Wizards)
1602..........	Elden Campbell..............212	(1995–96, L.A. Lakers)........................	332 (Dikembe Mutombo, Den. Nuggets)
1581..........	Benoit Benjamin................225	(1987–88, L.A. Clipper).....................	304 (Mark Eaton, Uta. Jazz)
1546..........	Samuel Dalembert............192	(2007–08, Phi. 76ers)........................	285 (Marcus Camby, Den. Nuggets)
1535..........	Wayne Cooper................227	(1985–86, Den. Nuggets)	397 (Manute Bol, Was. Wizards)
1530..........	Brook Lopezˆ 179	(2018–19, Mil. Bucks)	199 (Myles Turner, Ind. Pacers)
1502..........	DeAndre Jordanˆ 203	(2013–14, L.A. Clippers).....................	219 (Serge Ibaka, Ok.C. Thunder)

ˆ Active.

ᵃ ABA.

Players with 500 Blocks on Multiple Teams

			Career Blocks
Dikembe Mutombo	1486	.... Den. Nuggets (1991–96)	 3289
	1094	.... Atl. Hawks (1996–2001)	
Artis Gilmore	1431	.... Ken. Colonelsᵃ (1971–76)	 3178
	1029	.... Chi. Bulls (1976–82)	
	700	.... S.A. Spurs (1982–87)	
Shaquille O'Neal	824	.... Orl. Magic (1992–96)	 2732
	1278	.... L.A. Lakers (1996–2004)	
Robert Parish	549	.... G.S. Warriors (1976–80)	 2361
	1703	.... Bos. Celtics (1980–94)	
Alonzo Mourning	684	.... Cha. Hornets (1992–95)	 2356
	1625	.... Mia. Heat (1995–2002; 2005–08)	
Caldwell Jones	599	.... S.D. Conquistadors-Sailsᵃ (1973–75)	 2297
	926	.... Phi. 76ers (1976–82)	
Manute Bol	908	.... Was. Bullets (1985–88; 1994)	 2086
	592	.... G.S. Warriors (1988–90; 1994–95)	
	580	.... Phi. 76ers (1990–93; 1994)	

Career Blocks

continued on next page

George Johnson	507	G.S. Warriors (1972–77)	2082
	863	N.J. Nets (1977–80; 1984–85)	
	512	S.A. Spurs (1980–82)	
Julius Erving	521	N.Y. Nets[a] (1973–76)	1941
	1293	Phi. 76ers (1976–87)	
Pau Gasol	877	Mem. Grizzlies (2001–08)	1941
	607	L.A. Lakers (2008–14)	
Vlade Divac	834	L.A. Lakers (1989–96; 2004–05)	1631
	523	Sac. Kings (1998–2004)	
Alton Lister	804	Mil. Bucks (1981–86; 1994–95)	1473
	500	Sea. Sonics (1986–89)	
Rasheed Wallace	693	Por. Blazers (1996–2004)	1460
	623	Det. Pistons (2004–09)	
Erick Dampier	728	G.S. Warriors (1997–2004)	1398
	546	Dal. Mavericks (2004–10)	
Bobby Jones	625	Den. Nuggets* (1974–78)	1319
	727	Phi. 76ers (1978–86)	

[a] ABA.

* Includes both ABA and NBA franchises.

Most Blocks, Rookie Season

422	Artis Gilmore*, Ken. Colonels[a], 1971–72		
397	Manute Bol, Was. Bullets, 1985–86	195	Michael Stewart, Sac. Kings, 1997–98
319	David Robinson*, S.A. Spurs, 1989–90	178	Herb Williams, Ind. Pacers, 1981–82
316	Caldwell Jones, S.D. Conquistadors[a], 1973–74	169	Pau Gasol*, Mem. Grizzlies, 2001–02
286	Shaquille O'Neal*, Orl. Magic, 1992–93	167	Hot Rod Williams, Cle. Cavaliers, 1986–87
275	Mark Eaton, Uta. Jazz, 1982–83	164	Chris Webber*, G.S. Warriors, 1993–94
271	Alonzo Mourning, Cha. Hornets, 1992–93	163	Roy Rogers, Van. Grizzlies, 1996–97
220	Hakeem Olajuwon, Hou. Rockets, 1984–85	161	Mitchell Robinson, N.Y. Knicks, 2018–19
218	Tree Rollins, Atl. Hawks, 1977–78	159	Andrei Kirilenko, Uta. Jazz, 2001–02
210	Dikembe Mutombo, Den. Nuggets, 1991–92	153	Tom Burleson, Sea. Sonics, 1974–75
206	Benoit Benjamin, L.A. Clippers, 1985–86	153	Bobby Jones, Den. Nuggets[a], 1974–75
206	Tim Duncan*, S.A. Spurs, 1997–98	151	Kevin McHale, Bos. Celtics, 1980–81
203	Sam Bowie, Por. Blazers, 1984–85	151	Rik Smits, Ind. Pacers, 1988–89
201	Terry Tyler, Det. Pistons, 1978–79	151	Brook Lopez, N.J. Nets, 2008–09
197	Ralph Sampson*, Hou. Rockets, 1983–84		

* Rookie of the Year.

[a] ABA.

Most Blocks from Age 39 On

312	Robert Parish	90	Hakeem Olajuwon	60	Kevin Willis
274	Kareem Abdul-Jabbar	78	Tim Duncan	51	Karl Malone
192	Dikembe Mutombo	63	Dirk Nowitzki		
130	Vince Carter	63	Clifford Robinson		

Most Blocks, Game

17	Elmore Smith, L.A. Lakers	vs. Por. Blazers (Oct. 28, 1973)
15	Manute Bol, Was. Bullets	vs. Atl. Hawks (Jan. 25, 1986)
15	Manute Bol, Was. Bullets	vs. Ind. Pacers (Feb. 26, 1987)
15	Shaquille O'Neal, Orl. Magic	@ N.J. Nets (Nov. 20, 1993)
14	Elmore Smith, L.A. Lakers	vs. Det. Pistons (Oct. 26, 1973)
14	Elmore Smith, L.A. Lakers	vs. Hou. Rockets (Nov. 4, 1973)

continued on next page

14................. Mark Eaton, Uta. Jazz ....vs. Por. Blazers (Jan. 18, 1985)
14................. Mark Eaton, Uta. Jazz ....vs. S.A. Spurs (Feb. 18, 1989)
13................. George Johnson, S.A. Spurs.......................vs. G.S. Warriors (Feb. 24, 1981)
13................. Mark Eaton, Uta. Jazz ....vs. Por. Blazers (Feb. 18, 1983)
13................. Darryl Dawkins, N.J. Nets........................vs. Phi. 76ers (Nov. 5, 1983)
13................. Ralph Sampson, Hou. Rockets ....@ Chi. Bulls (Dec. 9, 1983)
13................. Manute Bol, G.S. Warriors..........................vs. N.J. Nets (Feb. 2, 1990)
13................. Shawn Bradley, Dal. Mavericks ....vs. Por. Blazers (Apr. 7, 1998)
12.................Julius Keye, Den. Rockets[a] ....vs. Vir. Squires[a] (Dec. 14, 1972)
12................. Caldwell Jones, S.D. Conquistadors[a] ....vs. Car. Cougars[a] (Jan. 6, 1974)
12................. Nate Thurmond, Chi. Bulls ....vs. Atl. Hawks (Oct. 18, 1974)
12................. George Johnson, N.J. Nets ,,,,,,,,,...........@ N.O. Jazz (Mar. 21, 1978)
12.................Tree Rollins, Atl. Hawks..............................vs. Por. Blazers (Feb. 21, 1979)
12................. Mark Eaton, Uta. Jazz ....@ Den. Nuggets (Feb. 5, 1983)
12................. Mark Eaton, Uta. Jazz ....vs. Dal. Mavericks (Mar. 17, 1984)
12................. Mark Eaton, Uta. Jazz ....@ Dal. Mavericks (Feb. 26, 1985)
12................. Manute Bol, Was. Bullets ....vs. Mil. Bucks (Dec. 12, 1985)
12................. Mark Eaton, Uta. Jazz ....vs. Por. Blazers (Nov. 1, 1986)
12................. Manute Bol, Was. Bullets ....vs. Cle. Cavaliers (Feb. 5, 1987)
12................. Hakeem Olajuwon, Hou. Rockets................vs. Sea. Sonics (Mar. 10, 1987)
12................. Manute Bol, Was. Bullets ....vs. Bos. Celtics (Mar. 26, 1987)
12................. Manute Bol, G.S. Warriors...........................@ S.A. Spurs (Feb. 22, 1989)
12................. Hakeem Olajuwon, Hou. Rockets................vs. Uta. Jazz (Nov. 11, 1989)
12................. David Robinson, S.A. Spurs.......................vs. Min. T'Wolves (Feb. 23, 1990)
12................. Dikembe Mutombo, Den. Nuggets ....vs. L.A. Clippers (Apr. 18, 1993)
12................. Shawn Bradley, N.J. Nets ....vs. Tor. Raptors (Apr. 17, 1996)
12................. Vlade Divac, Cha. Hornets..........................vs. N.J. Nets (Feb. 12, 1997)
12................. Keon Clark, Tor. Raptors ....vs. Atl. Hawks (Mar. 23, 2001)
12.................JaVale McGee, Was. Wizards....................@ Chi. Bulls (Mar. 15, 2011)
12................. Hassan Whiteside, Mia. Heat.....................@ Chi. Bulls (Jan. 25, 2015)
[a] ABA.

Most Blocks in a Loss

13................. Mark Eaton, Uta. Jazz...............................vs. Por. Blazers (Feb. 18, 1983)
13................. Darryl Dawkins, N.J. Nets.........................vs. Phi. 76ers (Nov. 5, 1983)
13................. Shawn Bradley, Dal. Mavericks ....vs. Por. Blazers (Apr. 7, 1998)
12................. Caldwell Jones, S.D. Conquistadors[a] ....vs. Car. Cougars[a] (Jan. 6, 1974)
12................. George Johnson, N.J. Nets ....@ N.O. Jazz (Mar. 21, 1978)
12................. Mark Eaton, Uta. Jazz...............................@ Den. Nuggets (Feb. 5, 1983)
12................. Hakeem Olajuwon, Hou. Rockets................vs. Sea. Sonics (Mar. 10, 1987)
12................. JaVale McGee, Was. Wizards ....@ Chi. Bulls (Mar. 15, 2011)
11................. Elmore Smith, L.A. Lakers ....vs. G.S. Warriors (Mar. 15, 1974)
11................. Kareem Abdul-Jabbar, L.A. Lakers...............vs. Det. Pistons (Nov. 28, 1978)
11................. Mark Eaton, Uta. Jazz ....vs. Ind. Pacers (Jan. 1, 1985)
11................. Manute Bol, G.S. Warriors.........................@ Phi. 76ers (Jan. 27, 1989)
11................. Dikembe Mutombo, Den. Nuggets ....vs. L.A. Clippers (Apr. 5, 1994)
11................. Shawn Bradley, N.J. Nets ....vs. Was. Bullets (Mar. 14, 1996)
11................. Shawn Bradley, N.J. Nets ....vs. Ind. Pacers (Feb. 6, 1997)
[a] ABA.

Least Amount of Games Before First 10-Block Game

Game #		Blk	
21	Ralph Sampson, Hou. Rockets	13	@ Chi. Bulls (Dec. 9, 1983)
21	Manute Bol, Was. Bullets	12	vs. Mil. Bucks (Dec. 12, 1985)
21	Josh Smith, Phi. 76ers	10	@ Dal. Mavericks (Dec. 18, 2004)
31	Harvey Catchings, Phi. 76ers	10	vs. Atl. Hawks (Mar. 21, 1975)
37	Hassan Whiteside, Mia. Heat	12	@ Chi. Bulls (Jan. 25, 2015)
43	David Robinson, S.A. Spurs	11	@ Cha. Hornets (Feb. 2, 1990)
49	Mark Eaton, Uta. Jazz	12	@ Den. Nuggets (Feb. 5, 1983)
62	Dikembe Mutombo, Den. Nuggets	10	@ Orl. Magic (Mar. 10, 1992)
84	Edgar Jones, Det. Pistons	10	vs. Ind. Pacers (Dec. 17, 1981)
90	Shaquille O'Neal, Orl. Magic	15	@ N.J. Nets (Nov. 20, 1993)

Most Consecutive Games Played Registering a Block

		First Game of Streak	Last Game of Streak
145	Patrick Ewing	Nov. 5, 1988	Mar. 23, 1990
116	Dikembe Mutombo	Jan. 20, 1995	Apr. 2, 1996
94	Mark Eaton	Apr. 7, 1984	Nov. 9, 1985
88	Patrick Ewing	Dec. 19, 1990	Jan. 5, 1992
83	Hakeem Olajuwon	Jan. 7, 1993	Jan. 4, 1994
81	Dikembe Mutombo	Jan. 18, 1994	Jan. 16, 1995
76	Josh Smith	Dec. 12, 2006	Dec. 17, 2007
75	Mark Eaton	Mar. 30, 1983	Mar. 11, 1984
75	Mark Eaton	Mar. 12, 1986	Mar. 4, 1987
73	Hakeem Olajuwon	Mar. 20, 1990	Apr. 21, 1991
71	Mark Eaton	Mar. 5, 1988	Feb. 4, 1989
68	Theo Ratliff	Dec. 27, 1997	Feb. 28, 1999
67	Manute Bol	Dec. 27, 1986	Dec. 3, 1987
66	Hakeem Olajuwon	Feb. 10, 1994	Jan. 13, 1995
65	Theo Ratliff	Oct. 31, 2000	Nov. 22, 2002
64	Hakeem Olajuwon	Jan. 19, 1987	Dec. 12, 1987
64	Myles Turner	Feb. 12, 2020	Apr. 6, 2021
61	David Robinson	Mar. 19, 1991	Jan. 28, 1992
60	Manute Bol	Nov. 23, 1988	Mar. 31, 1989
60	Alonzo Mourning	Nov. 17, 1994	Mar. 25, 1995
60	Alonzo Mourning	Mar. 10, 1999	Jan. 8, 2000
59	Dikembe Mutombo	Feb. 16, 1998	Mar. 27, 1999
57	Alonzo Mourning	Nov. 13, 1992	Mar. 14, 1993
55	David Robinson	Apr. 7, 1978	Feb. 6, 1979
55	Kareem Abdul-Jabbar	Jan. 22, 1990	Nov. 23, 1990
54	Jermaine O'Neal	Apr. 17, 2006	Mar. 3, 2007
53	Hakeem Olajuwon	Mar. 21, 1989	Jan. 12, 1990
52	Kevin McHale	Jan. 19, 1987	Dec. 30, 1987
51	Kevin McHale	Mar. 7, 1974	Feb. 18, 1975
51	Kareem Abdul-Jabbar	Feb. 25, 1986	Dec. 17, 1986
51	Marcus Camby	Nov. 10, 2007	Mar. 5, 2008
50	Billy Paultz	Nov. 23, 1977	Mar. 17, 1978

Most Blocks by Players Under 6-Feet Tall, Season

33.......... Terrell Brandon, Cle. Cavaliers, 1995–96 .... 5-foot-11
30.......... Terrell Brandon, Min. T'Wolves, 1999–00 .... 5-foot-11
30.......... Terrell Brandon, Cle. Cavaliers, 1996–97 .... 5-foot-11
27.......... Terrell Brandon, Cle. Cavaliers, 1992–93 .... 5-foot-11
24.......... Spud Webb, Sac. Kings, 1991–92 .... 5-foot-6
23.......... Facundo Campazzo, Den. Nuggets, 2021–22 .... 5-foot-10
23.......... Spud Webb, Sac. Kings, 1993–94 .... 5-foot-6
22.......... Terrell Brandon, Cle. Cavaliers, 1991–92 .... 5-foot-11
21.......... Terrell Brandon, Min. T'Wolves, 2000–01 .... 5-foot-11
21.......... Avery Johnson, S.A. Spurs, 1995–96 .... 5-foot-10
21.......... Brevin Knight, Cle. Cavaliers, 1999–00 .... 5-foot-10

Most Blocks by Players Under 6-Feet Tall, Career

226.............. Terrell Brandon.....................5-foot-11
154.............. Avery Johnson 5-foot-10
111.............. Spud Webb 5-foot-6
87.............. Brevin Knight 5-foot-10
81 .... Damon Stoudamire...............5-foot-10
67.............. Michael Adams.....................5-foot-10
61 .... Isaiah Thomas^ 5-foot-9
60.............. Travis Best 5-foot-11
52.............. Ty Lawson 5-foot-11
51 .... Calvin Murphy.....................5-foot-9

^ Active.

Most Blocks Per Game, Season

5.6........... Mark Eaton, Uta. Jazz, 1984–85
5.0........... Artis Gilmore, Ken. Colonels^a, 1971–72
5.0........... Manute Bol, Was. Bullets, 1985–86
4.9........... Elmore Smith, L.A. Lakers, 1973–74
4.6........... Mark Eaton, Uta. Jazz, 1985–86
4.6........... Hakeem Olajuwon, Hou. Rockets, 1989–90
4.5........... David Robinson, S.A. Spurs, 1991–92
4.5........... Dikembe Mutombo, Den. Nuggets, 1995–96
4.3........... Tree Rollins, Atl. Hawks, 1982–83
4.3........... Mark Eaton, Uta. Jazz, 1983–84
4.3........... Manute Bol, G.S. Warriors, 1988–89
4.3........... Hakeem Olajuwon, Hou. Rockets, 1991–92
4.2........... Hakeem Olajuwon, Hou. Rockets, 1992–93

4.1........... Kareem Abdul-Jabbar, L.A. Lakers, 1975–76
4.1........... Mark Eaton, Uta. Jazz, 1986–87
4.1........... Dikembe Mutombo, Den. Nuggets, 1993–94
4.0........... Caldwell Jones, S.D. Conquistadors^a, 1973–74
4.0........... Kareem Abdul-Jabbar, L.A. Lakers, 1978–79
4.0........... Patrick Ewing, N.Y. Knicks, 1989–90
3.9........... David Robinson, S.A. Spurs, 1989–90
3.9........... Hakeem Olajuwon, Hou. Rockets, 1990–91
3.9........... David Robinson, S.A. Spurs, 1990–91
3.9........... Dikembe Mutombo, Den. Nuggets, 1994–95
3.9........... Alonzo Mourning, Mia. Heat, 1998–99
3.8........... Mark Eaton, Uta. Jazz, 1988–89

^a ABA.

Defensive Miscellany

Most Times Leading League in Defensive Categories

Rebounds		RPG	
11	Wilt Chamberlain	11	Wilt Chamberlain
6	Dwight Howard	7	Dennis Rodman
5	Moses Malone	6	Moses Malone
4	Bill Russell	5	Bill Russell
4	Dennis Rodman	5	Dwight Howard^

continued on next page

Rebounds

4	Dikembe Mutombo
4	Andre Drummond
2	Elvin Hayes
2	Kareem Abdul-Jabbar
2	Bill Laimbeer
2	Hakeem Olajuwon
2	Charles Oakley
2	David Robinson
2	Kevin Garnett
2	Ben Wallace
2	DeAndre Jordan
2	Rudy Gobert

^ Active.

RPG

4	Andre Drummond^
4	Kevin Garnett
2	DeAndre Jordan^
2	Ben Wallace
2	Dikembe Mutombo
2	George Mikan
2	Hakeem Olajuwon
2	Elvin Hayes

^ Active.

Steals

5	Chris Paul^
4	Micheal Ray Richardson
3	Michael Jordan
3	Alvin Robertson
2	Rickey Green
2	John Stockton
2	Allen Iverson
2	Shawn Marion
2	Stephen Curry^

^ Active.

SPG

6	Chris Paul^
3	Michael Jordan
3	Micheal Ray Richardson
3	Alvin Robertson
3	Allen Iverson
2	Baron Davis
2	Mookie Blaylock
2	John Stockton
2	Magic Johnson

^ Active.

Blocks

5	Dikembe Mutombo
4	Kareem Abdul-Jabbar
4	Mark Eaton
4	Serge Ibaka^
3	George Johnson
3	Marcus Camby
2	Elmore Smith
2	Hakeem Olajuwon
2	Manute Bol
2	David Robinson
2	Alonzo Mourning
2	Theo Ratliff
2	Dwight Howard^
2	Hassan Whiteside^
2	Anthony Davis^
2	Rudy Gobert^

^ Active.

BPG

4	Kareem Abdul-Jabbar
4	Mark Eaton
4	Marcus Camby
3	Theo Ratliff
3	George Johnson
3	Anthony Davis^
3	Dikembe Mutombo
3	Hakeem Olajuwon
2	Dwight Howard^
2	Manute Bol
2	Myler Turner^
2	Alonzo Mourning
2	Serge Ibaka^
2	Hassan Whiteside^

^ Active.

Most Games with 10 Rebounds and 5 Blocks, Season

36	Mark Eaton, Uta. Jazz, 1984–85	26	Dikembe Mutombo, Den. Nuggets, 1995–96
33	Kareem Abdul-Jabbar, L.A. Lakers, 1975–76	26	Marcus Camby, Den. Nuggets, 2007–08
32	Hakeem Olajuwon, Hou. Rockets, 1989–90	24	Elmore Smith, L.A. Lakers, 1973–74
26	Hakeem Olajuwon, Hou. Rockets, 1991–92	24	Tree Rollins, Atl. Hawks, 1982–83
26	Hakeem Olajuwon, Hou. Rockets, 1992–93	24	David Robinson, S.A. Spurs, 1990–91
26	Dikembe Mutombo, Den. Nuggets, 1994–95	22	David Robinson, S.A. Spurs, 1989–90

continued on next page

22.................... David Robinson, S.A. Spurs, 1991–92
21.................... Dikembe Mutombo, Den. Nuggets, 1992–93
21.................... Dikembe Mutombo, Den. Nuggets, 1993–94
21.................... Hakeem Olajuwon, Hou. Rockets, 1993–94
21.................... Ben Wallace, Det. Pistons, 2001–02

20.................... Kareem Abdul-Jabbar, Mil. Bucks, 1973–74
20.................... Kareem Abdul-Jabbar, L.A. Lakers, 1978–79
20.................... Hakeem Olajuwon, Hou. Rockets, 1988–89
20.................... Patrick Ewing, N.Y. Knicks, 1989–90
20.................... Shaquille O'Neal, Orl. Magic, 1992–93

Most Games with 10 Rebounds and 5 Blocks, Career

227.................... Hakeem Olajuwon
190.................... Dikembe Mutombo
148.................... David Robinson
144.................... Kareem Abdul-Jabbar
132.................... Mark Eaton
119.................... Patrick Ewing
110.................... Shaquille O'Neal
105.................... Tim Duncan
104.................... Marcus Camby
89.................... Alonzo Mourning
81.................... Ben Wallace

78.................... Tree Rollins
77.................... Shawn Bradley
67.................... Dwight Howard
57*.................... Artis Gilmore
57.................... Elvin Hayes
57.................... George Johnson
54.................... Elmore Smith
54.................... Jermaine O'Neal
51.................... Benoit Benjamin
51.................... Hassan Whiteside^

^ Active.

* 7 times in ABA and 50 times in NBA.

20 Rebounds and 10 Blocks, Game

		Reb	Blk
Elmore Smith, L.A. Lakers	vs. G.S. Warriors (Mar. 16, 1975)	22	10
Kareem Abdul-Jabbar, L.A. Lakers	vs. Atl. Hawks (Nov. 2, 1975)	23	10
Kareem Abdul-Jabbar, L.A. Lakers	@ Det. Pistons (Dec. 3, 1975)	21	11
Elvin Hayes, Was. Bullets	@ Det. Pistons (Mar. 3, 1978)	27	11
Tree Rollins, Atl. Hawks	vs. Bos. Celtics (Mar. 14, 1980)	23	10
Mark Eaton, Uta. Jazz	vs. Por. Blazers (Jan. 18, 1985)	20	14
Mark Eaton, Uta. Jazz	@ Dal. Mavericks (Feb. 1, 1985)	20	10
Mark Eaton, Uta. Jazz	vs. Por. Blazers (Nov. 1, 1986)	20	12
Hakeem Olajuwon, Hou. Rockets	vs. Uta. Jazz (Nov. 11, 1989)	21	12
Hakeem Olajuwon, Hou. Rockets	vs. Orl. Magic (Dec. 17, 1989)	25	10
Dikembe Mutombo, Den. Nuggets	vs. L.A. Clippers (Apr. 18, 1993)	21	12
Shaquille O'Neal, Orl. Magic	@ N.J. Nets (Nov. 20, 1993)	28	15
Shawn Bradley, Dal. Mavericks	vs. Por. Blazers (Apr. 7, 1998)	22	13
Marcus Camby, Den. Nuggets	vs. Uta. Jazz (Jan. 17, 2008)	24	11
Joakim Noah, Chi. Bulls	vs. Phi. 76ers (Feb. 28, 2013)	21	11

20 Points, 20 Rebounds, and 10 Blocks, Game

		Pts	Reb	Blk
Kareem Abdul-Jabbar, L.A. Lakers	vs. Atl. Hawks (Nov. 2, 1975)	39	23	10
Kareem Abdul-Jabbar, L.A. Lakers	@ Det. Pistons (Dec. 3, 1975)	29	21	11
Elvin Hayes, Was. Bullets	@ Det. Pistons (Mar. 3, 1978)	22	27	11
Hakeem Olajuwon, Hou. Rockets	vs. Uta. Jazz (Nov. 11, 1989)	24	21	12
Hakeem Olajuwon, Hou. Rockets	vs. Orl. Magic (Dec. 17, 1989)	32	25	10
Shaquille O'Neal, Orl. Magic	@ N.J. Nets (Nov. 20, 1993)	24	28	15
Shawn Bradley, Dal. Mavericks	vs. Por. Blazers (Apr. 7, 1998)	22	22	13
Joakim Noah, Chi. Bulls	vs. Phi. 76ers (Feb. 28, 2013)	23	21	11

Multiple Games with 5 Rebounds, 5 Steals, and 5 Blocks

22........... Hakeem Olajuwon	3............. Andrei Kirilenko	2............. Julius Erving
5........... David Robinson	3............. Anthony Davis^	2............. Dwight Howard^
4........... Ben Wallace	2............. Bob McAdoo	2............. Draymond Green^

^ Active.

Players with 10 Steals and 5 Blocks, Game

	Stl	Blk	Reb
Draymond Green, G.S. Warriors................. @ Mem. Grizzlies (Feb. 10, 2017)...............	10	5	11

Players with 150 Blocks, 150 Steals, and 600 Rebounds, Season

	Blk	Stl	Reb
Elvin Hayes, Was. Bullets, 1974–75	187	158	1004
Bobby Jones, Den. Nuggets, 1976–77	162	186	678
Hakeem Olajuwon, Hou. Rockets, 1987–88	214	162	959
Hakeem Olajuwon, Hou. Rockets, 1988–89	282	213	1105
Hakeem Olajuwon, Hou. Rockets, 1989–90	376	174	1149
David Robinson, S.A. Spurs, 1991–92	305	158	829
Hakeem Olajuwon, Hou. Rockets, 1992–93	342	150	1068
Andrei Kirilenko, Uta. Jazz, 2003–04	215	150	629

Players with 250 Blocks and 1000 Rebounds, Season

	Blk	Reb
Artis Gilmore, Ken. Colonels[a], 1971–72	422*	1491*
Artis Gilmore, Ken. Colonels[a], 1972–73	259*	1476*
Kareem Abdul-Jabbar, Mil. Bucks, 1973–74	283	1178
Artis Gilmore, Ken. Colonels[a], 1973–74	287	1538*
Caldwell Jones, S.D. Conquistadors[a], 1973–74	316*	1095
Artis Gilmore, Ken. Colonels[a], 1974–75	258*	1361*
Kareem Abdul-Jabbar, L.A. Lakers, 1975–76	338	1383*
Kareem Abdul-Jabbar, L.A. Lakers, 1976–77	261*	1090*
Kareem Abdul-Jabbar, L.A. Lakers, 1978–79	316*	1025
Hakeem Olajuwon, Hou. Rockets, 1988–89	282	1105*
Hakeem Olajuwon, Hou. Rockets, 1989–90	376*	1149*
David Robinson, S.A. Spurs, 1990–91	320*	1063*
Dikembe Mutombo, Den. Nuggets, 1992–93	287	1070
Hakeem Olajuwon, Hou. Rockets, 1992–93	342*	1068
Shaquille O'Neal, Orl. Magic, 1992–93	286	1122
Dikembe Mutombo, Den. Nuggets, 1994–95	321*	1029*
David Robinson, S.A. Spurs, 1995–96	271	1000*
Dikembe Mutombo, Atl. Hawks, 1999–00	269	1157*
Ben Wallace, Det. Pistons, 2001–02	278*	1039
Marcus Camby, Den. Nuggets, 2007–08	285*	1037

* Led league.

[a] ABA.

3

FOULS

Most Fouls by Decade

* Includes ABA.

Most Personal Fouls, Season

continued on next page

361................. Kevin Kunnert, Hou. Rockets, 1976–77
360................. Goose Ligon, Ken. Colonels[a], 1969–70
358................. Dan Roundfield, Atl. Hawks, 1978–79
358................. Rick Mahorn, Was. Bullets, 1983–84
356................. Charlie Scott, Bos. Celtics, 1975–76
[a] ABA.

353................. Wil Jones, Ken. Colonels[a], 1974–75
353................. Darnell Hillman, Ind. Pacers, 1976–77
350................. Dave Cowens, Bos. Celtics, 1970–71
350................. Lonnie Shelton, N.Y. Knicks, 1977–78

Most Personal Fouls, Career

Career PF		Career GP	F/G
4657	Kareem Abdul-Jabbar	1560	3.0
4578	Karl Malone	1476	3.1
4529*	Artis Gilmore	1329	3.4
4443	Robert Parish	1611	2.8
4436**	Caldwell Jones	1299	3.4
4421	Charles Oakley	1282	3.4
4383	Hakeem Olajuwon	1238	3.5
4267	Buck Williams	1307	3.3
4193	Elvin Hayes	1303	3.2
4175	Clifford Robinson	1380	3.0
4172	Kevin Willis	1424	2.9
4146	Shaquille O'Neal	1207	3.4
4146	Otis Thorpe	1257	3.3
4042	James Edwards	1168	3.5
4034	Patrick Ewing	1183	3.4

* 2986 in NBA and 1543 in ABA.

** 3527 in NBA and 909 in ABA.

Most Foul Outs, Season

Foul Outs		F/G
25	Monk Meineke, Ft.W. Pistons, 1952–53	4.9
25	Steve Johnson, K.C. Kings, 1981–82	4.8
23	Darryl Dawkins, N.J. Nets, 1982–83	4.7
22	Ed Sadowski, Phi. Warriors, 1948–49	4.6
22	Walter Dukes, Det. Pistons, 1958–59	4.6
22	Gene Moore, Ken. Colonels[a], 1969–70	4.6
22	Darryl Dawkins, N.J. Nets, 1983–84	4.8
21	Joe Fulks, Phi. Warriors, 1952–53	4.6
21	Joe Meriweather, Atl. Hawks, 1976–77	4.4
20	Vern Mikkelsen, Min. Lakers, 1957–58	4.2
20	Walter Dukes, Det. Pistons, 1959–60	4.7
20	Walter Dukes, Det. Pistons, 1961–62	4.2
20	George Johnson, N.J. Nets, 1977–78	3.4
19	Cal Christensen, T.C. Blackhawks, 1950–51	4.0
19	Tom Sanders, Bos. Celtics, 1965–66	4.4
19	Joe Strawder, Det. Pistons, 1966–67	4.4
19	Bill Robinzine, K.C. Kings, 1975–76	3.9
19	John Drew, Atl. Hawks, 1978–79	4.2
18	Don Boven, Mil. Hawks, 1951–52	4.1
18	Alex Hannum, Roc. Royals, 1952–53	3.8
18	Bob Lavoy, Ind. Olympians, 1952–53	3.9

continued on next page

Foul Outs   **F/G**

		F/G
18	Joe Graboski, Ind. Olympians, 1952–53	3.8
18	Chuck Share, Mil. Hawks, 1954–55	4.0
18	Paul Arizin, Phi. Warriors, 1961–62	3.9
18	Joe Strawder, Det. Pistons, 1967–68	4.3
18	Norm Van Lier, Cin. Royals, 1969–70	4.1
18	John Brown, Atl. Hawks, 1977–78	3.7
18	Tree Rollins, Atl. Hawks, 1978–79	4.0
18	Ben Poquette, Uta. Jazz, 1980–81	4.2
18	Shawn Bradley, Phi. 76ers, 1994–95	4.1

ᵃ ABA.

Most Foul Outs, Career

118	Vern Mikkelsen	101	Darryl Dawkins	92	Tom Sanders
115	Shawn Kemp	95	James Edwards	91	Tree Rollins
112	Walter Dukes	94	Steve Johnson		
107	Chuck Share	93	Paul Arizin		

Quickest Foul Out, Game

MP

MP		
3	Bubba Wells, Dal. Mavericks	@ Chi. Bulls (Dec. 29, 1997)
4	Med Park, St.L. Hawks	vs. Phi. Warriors (Feb. 24, 1957)
4	Daniel Sparks, Mia. Floridiansᵃ	vs. Oak. Oaksᵃ (Nov. 27, 1968)
5	Dick Farley, Syr. Nationals	vs. St.L. Hawks (Mar. 12, 1956)
5	Mark Bryant, Dal. Mavericks	vs. L.A. Lakers (Dec. 22, 2000)
5	Josh McRoberts, Ind. Pacers	vs. Tor. Raptors (Jan. 16, 2009)
6	Bob Brannum, Bos. Celtics	vs. Roc. Royals (Feb. 10, 1952)
6	Johnny Green, Bal. Bullets	vs. S.F. Warriors (Oct. 28, 1966)
6	Jim Barnes, L.A. Lakers	@ Phi. 76ers (Dec. 2, 1966)
6	Hank Finkel, Bos. Celtics	vs. Mil. Bucks (Nov. 17, 1972)
6	Leonard Gray, Was. Bullets	@ Phi. 76ers (Apr. 9, 1977)
6	Chris Engler, G.S. Warriors	vs. Uta. Jazz (Mar. 5, 1983)
6	Len Elmore, N.Y. Knicks	@ K.C. Kings (Feb. 14, 1984)
6	Sam Mitchell, Min. T'Wolves	vs. L.A. Lakers (Mar. 17, 1990)
6	Rik Smits, Ind. Pacers	vs. Det. Pistons (Nov. 6, 1993)
6	David Vaughn, Orl. Magic	@ Uta. Jazz (Jan. 19, 1996)
6	Loren Meyer, Dal. Mavericks	vs. Mia. Heat (Mar. 12, 1996)
6	Duane Causwell, Sac. Kings	vs. Hou. Rockets (Nov. 5, 1996)
6	Steve Nash, Pho. Suns	@ Por. Blazers (Feb. 11, 1997)
6	Malik Rose, S.A. Spurs	vs. Min. T'Wolves (Nov. 15, 1997)
6	Stromile Swift, Mem. Grizzlies	vs. L.A. Lakers (Mar. 22, 2007)
6	Salah Mejri, Dal. Mavericks	vs. N.O. Pelicans (Feb. 25, 2017)

ᵃ ABA.

Fouls Per Game, Season (Min. 50 Games Played)

F/G   **GP**

F/G		GP
4.9	Monk Meineke, Ft.W. Pistons, 1952–53	68
4.8	Ron Livingstone, Bal. Bullets/Phi. Warriors, 1949–50	54
4.8	Ed Johnson, L.A. Starsᵃ, 1968–69	58
4.8	Steve Johnson, K.C. Kings, 1981–82	78
4.8	Darryl Dawkins, N.J. Nets, 1983–84	81

continued on next page

F/G		GP
4.7	Bob Brannum, She. Red Skins, 1949–50	59
4.7	Walter Dukes, Det. Pistons, 1959–60	66
4.7	Darryl Dawkins, N.J. Nets, 1982–83	81
4.6	Ed Sadowski, Phi. Warriors, 1948–49	60
4.6	Joe Fulks, Phi. Warriors, 1952–53	70
4.6	Walter Dukes, Det. Pistons, 1958–59	72
4.6	Gene Moore, Ken. Colonels[a], 1969–70	83
4.6	Doug Smith, Dal. Mavericks, 1992–93	61
4.5	George Mikan, Min. Lakers, 1950–51	68
4.5	George Mikan, Min. Lakers, 1951–52	64
4.5	Vern Mikkelsen, Min. Lakers, 1954–55	71
4.5	Tom Gola, Phi. Warriors, 1961–62	60
4.5	Bill Bridges, St.L. Hawks, 1967–68	82
4.5	Kevin Kunnert, Hou. Rockets, 1976–77	81
4.5	Bill Robinzine, K.C. Kings, 1978–79	82
4.5	Dan Roundfield, Atl. Hawks, 1978–79	80
4.5	James Edwards, Cle. Cavaliers, 1981–82	77
4.5	Darryl Dawkins, N.J. Nets, 1985–86	51
4.5	Shawn Kemp, Cle. Cavaliers, 1999–00	82

[a] ABA.

Fouls Per Game, Career (Min. 500 Games Played)

F/G		GP	F/G		GP
4.1	Walter Dukes	553	3.8	Steve Johnson	626
4.0	Vern Mikkelsen	699	3.7	Earl Lloyd	560
3.9	Paul Arizin	713	3.7	Bailey Howell	950
3.9	Tom Gola	698	3.7	Tom Meschery	778
3.8	Arnie Risen	637	3.7	Willis Reed	650
3.8	Alex Hannum	516	3.7	Billy Cunningham	770
3.8	Ray Felix	637	3.7	Charlie Scott	717
3.8	Tom Heinsohn	654	3.7	Darnell Hillman	682
3.8	Dave Cowens	766	3.7	Bill Robinzine	529
3.8	George McGinnis	842	3.7	Roy Hinson	507
3.8	Darryl Dawkins	726	3.7	DeMarcus Cousins^	633
3.8	Lonnie Shelton	673			

^ Active.

Fouls Per Game, Career (Min. 1000 Games Played)

F/G		GP	F/G		GP
3.6	Shawn Kemp	1051	3.4	Patrick Ewing	1183
3.5	Sam Lacey	1002	3.4	Charles Oakley	1282
3.5	James Edwards	1168	3.4	Shaquille O'Neal	1207
3.5	Jack Sikma	1107	3.3	Buck Williams	1307
3.5	Hakeem Olajuwon	1238	3.3	Otis Thorpe	1257
3.4	Hal Greer	1122	3.2	Elvin Hayes	1303
3.4	Walt Bellamy	1043	3.2	Calvin Murphy	1002
3.4	Artis Gilmore	1329	3.2	Terry Cummings	1183
3.4	Caldwell Jones	1299	3.2	Vlade Divac	1134
3.4	Maurice Lucas	1021	3.2	Kurt Thomas	1110
3.4	Bill Laimbeer	1068	3.2	Dwight Howard^	1227
3.4	Tom Chambers	1107			

^ Active.

Most Technical Fouls, Career

332...................... Karl Malone	212...................... Dennis Rodman	150...................... Shaquille O'Neal
329...................... Charles Barkley	172...................... Russell Westbrook	146...................... Jermaine O'Neal
317...................... Rasheed Wallace	172...................... Kevin Garnett	
250...................... Gary Payton	166...................... Kobe Bryant	

Players Averaging Minimum 3.5 Fouls and 4.5 Turnovers, Season (Min. 45 Games Played)

Season		F/G	TO/G
1978–79	George McGinnis, Den. Nuggets.............................. 4.2	....	4.6
1983–84	Jeff Ruland, Was. Bullets 3.8	....	4.6
1986–87	Charles Barkley, Phi. 76ers.................................... 3.7	....	4.7
2017–18	DeMarcus Cousins, N.O. Pelicans........................... 3.8	....	5.0

4

GAMES PLAYED

Most Games Played by Decade

1946–47 – 1949–50

235	Chick Halbert
235	Max Zaslofsky
234	Stan Miasek
233	George Senesky
231	Joe Fulks
231	Jim Seminoff
229	Jerry Fleishman
229	Ed Sadowski
228	Sonny Hertzberg
228	John Logan

1950–51 – 1959–60

707	Dolph Schayes
692	Larry Foust
690	Bob Cousy
678	Slater Martin
670	Dick McGuire
650	Bill Sharman
637	Joe Graboski
631	Vern Mikkelsen
596	Chuck Share
574	Ed Macauley

1960–61 – 1969–70*

794	Bob Boozer
793	Bailey Howell
784	Hal Greer
779	Guy Rodgers
765	Johnny Green
758	Tom Sanders
752	Oscar Robertson
727	Walt Bellamy
727	Wilt Chamberlain
727	Don Ohl

1970–71 – 1979–80*

827	Ron Boone
824	Dan Issel
814	Elvin Hayes
813	Paul Silas
812	Billy Paultz
804	Sam Lacey
798	Calvin Murphy
790	Bingo Smith
775	Rick Barry
775	John Johnson

1980–81 – 1989–90

815	Bill Laimbeer
813	Alex English
804	Vinnie Johnson
793	Robert Parish
790	Mychal Thompson
788	Michael Cooper
784	Jack Sikma
781	Reggie Theus
777	Dennis Johnson
777	Moses Malone

1990–91 – 1999–00

789	A.C. Green
786	Gary Payton
785	Karl Malone
775	Reggie Miller
772	Clifford Robinson
771	Mark Jackson
770	Jeff Hornacek
770	John Stockton
763	Hersey Hawkins
758	Sam Mitchell

2000–01 – 009–10

815	Andre Miller
796	Jason Terry
791	Dirk Nowitzki
778	Steve Nash
774	Antawn Jamison
773	Jason Kidd
772	Chauncey Billups
771	Tim Duncan
769	Shawn Marion
763	Paul Pierce

2010–11 – 2019–20

757	James Harden
752	DeAndre Jordan
749	Thaddeus Young
743	DeMar DeRozan
735	Sege Ibaka
721	Robin Lopez
719	Marco Belinelli
717	Taj Gibson
717	LeBron James
715	Kyle Korver

2020–21 – 2021–22

154	Mikal Bridges
152	Saddiq Bey
152	Buddy Hield
151	Duncan Robinson
149	Patty Mills
148	Terance Mann
148	Georges Niang
148	Royce O'Neale
148	Jae'Sean Tate
148	Ivica Zubac

* Includes ABA.

Most Games Played, Career

1611	Robert Parish	1976–97
1560	Kareem Abdul-Jabbar	1969–89
1541	Vince Carter	1998–2020
1522	Dirk Nowitzki	1998–2019
1504	John Stockton	1984–2003
1476	Karl Malone	1985–2004
1476	Kevin Garnett	1995–2016
1455	Moses Malone	1974–95
1424	Kevin Willis	1984–88, 1989–2005, 2006–07
1410	Jason Terry	1999–2018

Most Games Played for Each Active Franchise

Hawks	882	Dominique Wilkins
Celtics	1270	John Havlicek
Nets-Americans*	635	Buck Williams
Hornets-Bobcats	701	Dell Curry
Bulls	930	Michael Jordan
Cavaliers	849	LeBron James
Mavericks	1522	Dirk Nowitzki
Nuggets-Rockets*	837	Alex English
Pistons	1018	Joe Dumars
Warriors	819	Stephen Curry^
Rockets	1177	Hakeem Olajuwon
Pacers*	1389	Reggie Miller
Clippers-Braves	750	DeAndre Jordan
Lakers	1346	Kobe Bryant
Grizzlies	788	Mike Conley
Heat	948	Dwyane Wade
Bucks	711	Junior Bridgeman
Timberwolves	970	Kevin Garnett
Pelicans-Hornets	530	David West
Knicks	1039	Patrick Ewing
Thunder-SuperSonics	999	Gary Payton
Magic	692	Nick Anderson
76ers-Nationals	1122	Hal Greer
Suns	988	Alvan Adams
Trail Blazers	867	Clyde Drexler
Kings-Royals	888	Sam Lacey
Spurs-Chaparrals*	1392	Tim Duncan
Raptors	675	DeMar DeRozan
Jazz	1504	John Stockton
Wizards-Bullets-Zephyrs-Packers	984	Wes Unseld

* Includes both NBA and ABA franchises.

^ Active with franchise.

Winning Percentage for Players Appearing in 1000 Regular-Season Games

W/L%		GP	Wins	Losses
.721	Manu Ginóbili	1057	762	295
.719	Tim Duncan	1392	1001	391
.711	Tony Parker	1254	892	362
.690	Danny Ainge	1042	719	323
.688	Kareem Abdul-Jabbar	1560	1074	486
.688	Scottie Pippen	1178	810	368
.679	Shaquille O'Neal	1207	819	388
.671	Robert Horry	1107	743	364
.663	Derek Fisher	1287	853	434
.659	Michael Jordan	1072	706	366
.657	Dennis Johnson	1100	723	377
.656	Julius Erving	1243	815	428
.654	LeBron James^	1366	894	472
.651	Horace Grant	1165	758	407
.650	Chris Paul^	1155	751	404

continued on next page

W/L%		GP	Wins	Losses
.649	John Havlicek	1270	824	446
.646	Byron Scott	1073	693	380
.645	Karl Malone	1476	952	524
.643	Wilt Chamberlain	1045	672	373
.641	Sam Perkins	1286	824	462
.634	John Stockton	1504	953	551
.630	Rasheed Wallace	1109	699	410
.629	Robert Parish	1611	1014	597
.628	Chet Walker	1032	648	384
.628	Steve Nash	1217	764	453
.627	Vlade Divac	1134	711	423
.621	Paul Silas	1254	779	476
.621	Kobe Bryant	1346	836	510
.620	Don Nelson	1053	653	400
.617	Detlef Schrempf	1136	701	435
.616	Gary Payton*	1335	823	512
.616	Jerome Kersey	1153	710	443
.613	Charles Barkley	1073	658	415
.612	Clyde Drexler	1086	665	421
.612	A.C. Green	1278	782	496
.611	Maurice Cheeks	1101	673	428
.611	Chauncey Billups	1043	637	406
.608	Jeff Hornacek	1077	655	422
.606	Clifford Robinson	1380	836	544
.604	Ron Harper	1009	609	400
.603	Oscar Robertson	1040	627	413
.602	Shawn Kemp	1051	633	418
.602	Paul Millsap^	1085	653	432
.602	Dirk Nowitzki	1522	916	606
.599	Andre Iguodala^	1223	733	490
.598	Terry Porter	1274	762	512
.598	David West	1034	618	416
.595	Shawn Marion	1163	692	471
.593	Avery Johnson	1054	625	429
.591	Hakeem Olajuwon	1238	732	506
.591	Dan Issel	1218	720	498
.588	Elden Campbell^	1044	614	430
.587	LaMarcus Aldridge^	1076	632	444
.586	Kyle Korver	1232	722	510
.586	Dale Davis	1094	641	453
.586	Russell Westbrook^	1021	598	423
.585	Boris Diaw	1064	622	442
.584	Jason Kidd	1391	812	579
.581	Michael Finley	1103	641	462
.581	Ray Allen	1300	755	545
.580	Dwyane Wade	1054	611	443
.578	Joe Dumars	1018	588	430
.573	Dwight Howard^	1242	712	530
.573	Patrick Ewing	1183	678	505
.569	Rashard Lewis	1049	597	452
.568	Tree Rollins	1156	657	499
.567	Mark West	1090	618	472

continued on next page

W/L%		GP	Wins	Losses
.564	Paul Pierce	1343	758	585
.564	Kevin Garnett	1462	825	637
.563	Stacey Augmon	1001	564	437
.563	Bill Laimbeer	1068	601	467
.559	Charles Oakley	1282	717	565
.559	Terry Cummings	1183	661	522
.558	Richard Jefferson	1181	659	522
.556	Hal Greer	1122	624	498
.556	Jack Sikma	1107	615	492
.555	Antonio McDyess	1015	563	452
.554	Rick Barry	1020	565	455
.552	Reggie Miller	1389	767	622
.552	Jermaine O'Neal	1011	558	453
.551	Jason Terry	1410	777	633
.551	Tayshaun Prince	1017	560	457
.550	Kyle Lowry^	1023	563	460
.549	Pau Gasol	1226	673	553
.549	Ben Wallace	1088	597	491
.545	Artis Gilmore	1329	724	605
.544	Buck Williams	1307	711	596
.544	Trevor Ariza^	1118	608	510
.543	Tom Chambers	1107	601	506
.543	Caldwell Jones	1299	705	594
.542	George Gervin	1060	575	485
.542	Mark Jackson	1296	703	593
.537	Carmelo Anthony^	1260	677	583
.536	Moses Malone	1455	780	675
.535	Kurt Thomas	1110	594	516
.535	Rod Strickland	1094	585	509
.534	Kevin Willis	1424	760	664
.533	Nazr Mohammed	1005	536	469
.533	P.J. Brown	1089	580	509
.532	Rick Mahorn	1117	594	523
.529	Grant Hill	1026	543	483
.529	Dominique Wilkins	1074	568	506
.527	Walter Davis	1033	544	489
.526	Tyrone Corbin	1065	560	505
.525	Mike Bibby	1001	526	475
.523	Maurice Lucas	1021	534	487
.522	Billy Paultz	1124	587	537
.520	Joe Johnson^	1277	664	613
.519	Dale Ellis	1209	627	582
.513	Dikembe Mutombo	1196	614	582
.513	Gail Goodrich	1031	529	502
.512	Lenny Wilkens	1077	551	526
.511	Andre Miller	1304	666	638
.509	Vince Carter	1541	785	756
.506	Alex English	1193	604	589
.506	Ron Boone	1041	527	513
.505	Lou Williams^	1123	567	556
.504	Danny Schayes	1138	574	564
.504	James Edwards	1168	589	579

continued on next page

W/L%		GP	Wins	Losses
.504	Glen Rice	1000	504	496
.503	Otis Thorpe	1257	632	625
.503	Zach Randolph	1116	561	555
.502	Eddie Johnson	1199	602	597
.502	Elvin Hayes	1303	654	649
.501	Olden Polynice	1058	530	528
.500	Mike Miller	1032	516	516
.497	Tyson Chandler^	1160	577	583
.496	Zaza Pachulia	1098	545	553
.493	Derek Harper	1199	591	608
.492	Leroy Ellis	1048	516	532
.482	Jeff Green^	1051	507	544
.480	Dell Curry	1083	520	563
.479	Joe Smith	1030	493	537
.475	Juwan Howard	1208	574	634
.475	Michael Cage	1140	541	599
.465	Marvin Williams	1072	499	573
.461	Calvin Murphy	1002	462	540
.459	Jamal Crawford	1327	609	718
.453	Rudy Gay^	1064	482	582
.452	Sam Lacey	1002	453	550
.447	Thaddeus Young^	1085	485	600
.433	Herb Williams	1102	477	625
.427	Johnny Newman	1159	495	664
.422	Walt Bellamy	1043	440	603
.421	Elton Brand	1058	445	613
.418	Antawn Jamison	1083	453	630
.413	Grant Long	1003	414	589
.397	Reggie Theus	1026	407	619
.395	Johnny Green	1057	418	640

^ Active.

Most Seasons Appearing in All Regular Season Games, Career

17...... John Stockton............. 1984–85, 1985–86, 1986–87, 1987–88, 1988–89, 1990–91, 1991–92, 1992–93, 1993–94, 1994–95, 1995–96, 1996–97, 1998–99, 1999–00, 2000–01, 2001–02, 2002–03

15...... A.C. Green 1985–86, 1987–88, 1988–89, 1989–90, 1990–91, 1991–92, 1992–93, 1993–94, 1994–95, 1995–96, 1996–97, 1997–98, 1998–99, 1999–00, 2000–01

12...... Artis Gilmore 1971–72ª, 1972–73ª, 1973–74ª, 1974–75ª, 1975–76ª, 1976–77, 1977–78, 1978–79, 1980–81, 1981–82, 1982–83, 1986–87

11...... Red Kerr 1954–55, 1955–56, 1956–57, 1957–58, 1958–59, 1959–60, 1960–61, 1961–62, 1962–63, 1963–64

10...... Dolph Schayes............ 1950–51, 1952–53, 1953–54, 1954–55, 1955–56, 1956–57, 1957–58, 1958–59, 1959–60, 1960–61

10...... Ron Boone 1968–69ª, 1969–70ª, 1970–71ª, 1971–72ª, 1972–73ª, 1973–74ª, 1974–75ª, 1976–77, 1977–78, 1978–79

10...... Randy Smith 1972–73, 1973–74, 1974–75, 1975–76, 1976–77, 1977–78, 1978–79, 1979–80, 1980–81, 1981–82

10...... Karl Malone 1986–87, 1987–88, 1989–90, 1990–91, 1992–93, 1993–94, 1994–95, 1995–96, 1996–97, 1999–00

10...... Gary Payton.............. 1990–91, 1992–93, 1993–94, 1994–95, 1996–97, 1997–98, 1998–99, 1999–00, 2001–02, 2003–04

continued on next page

10...... Derek Fisher 1997–98, 1998–99, 2002–03, 2003–04, 2005–06, 2006–07, 2007–08, 2008–09, 2009–10, 2010–11

10...... Andre Miller..............1999–00, 2000–01, 2003–04, 2004–05, 2005–06, 2007–08, 2008–09, 2009–10, 2011–12, 2012–13

9........ Harry Gallatin 1949–50, 1950–51, 1951–52, 1952–53, 1953–54, 1954–55, 1955–56, 1956–57, 1957–58

9........ Jack Twyman 1955–56, 1956–57, 1957–58, 1958–59, 1959–60, 1960–61, 1961–62, 1962–63, 1964–65

9........ Wilt Chamberlain........1960–61, 1961–62, 1962–63, 1963–64, 1966–67, 1967–68, 1970–71, 1971–72, 1972–73

9........ Michael Jordan..........1984–85, 1986–87, 1987–88, 1989–90, 1990–91, 1995–96, 1996–97, 1997–98, 2002–03

9........ Otis Thorpe 1984–85, 1986–87, 1987–88, 1988–89, 1989–90, 1990–91, 1991–92, 1993–94, 1995–96

9........ Mark Jackson 1987–88, 1989–90, 1992–93, 1994–95, 1996–97, 1997–98, 2000–01, 2001–02, 2002–03

8........ Jack Coleman 1949–50, 1950–51, 1951–52, 1952–53, 1954–55, 1955–56, 1956–57, 1957–58

8........ Vern Mikkelsen 1949–50, 1951–52, 1952–53, 1953–54, 1955–56, 1956–57, 1957–58, 1958–59

8........ John Havlicek 1962–63, 1963–64, 1966–67, 1967–68, 1968–69, 1971–72, 1974–75, 1977–78

8........ Walt Bellamy 1962–63, 1963–64, 1964–65, 1965–66, 1967–68, 1968–69, 1970–71, 1971–72

8........ Elvin Hayes 1968–69, 1969–70, 1970–71, 1971–72, 1974–75, 1976–77, 1978–79, 1981–82

8........ Jack Sikma 1977–78, 1978–79, 1979–80, 1980–81, 1981–82, 1983–84, 1986–87, 1987–88

8........ Reggie Theus..............1978–79, 1979–80, 1980–81, 1981–82, 1982–83, 1984–85, 1985–86, 1988–89

8........ Terry Tyler 1978–79, 1979–80, 1980–81, 1981–82, 1982–83, 1983–84, 1984–85, 1986–87

8........ Buck Williams.............1981–82, 1982–83, 1984–85, 1985–86, 1986–87, 1989–90, 1992–93, 1994–95

8........ Clifford Robinson 1989–90, 1990–91, 1991–92, 1992–93, 1993–94, 1998–99, 2000–01, 2003–04

8........ Michael Cage.............1989–90, 1990–91, 1991–92, 1992–93, 1993–94, 1994–95, 1995–96, 1996–97

8........ Michael Finley 1995–96, 1996–97, 1997–98, 1998–99, 1999–00, 2000–01, 2006–07, 2007–08

7........ Bobby Wanzer 1948–49, 1950–51, 1951–52, 1952–53, 1953–54, 1954–55, 1955–56

7........ Ray Felix 1953–54, 1954–55, 1955–56, 1956–57, 1957–58, 1958–59, 1961–62

7........ Tom Sanders...............1961–62, 1962–63, 1963–64, 1964–65, 1966–67, 1968–69, 1971–72

7........ Don Nelson 1963–64, 1967–68, 1968–69, 1969–70, 1970–71, 1971–72, 1973–74

7........ James Donaldson 1981–82, 1982–83, 1983–84, 1984–85, 1985–86, 1986–87, 1990–91

7........ Bill Laimbeer...............1982–83, 1983–84, 1984–85, 1985–86, 1986–87, 1987–88, 1990–91

7........ Vinnie Johnson...........1982–83, 1983–84, 1984–85, 1987–88, 1988–89, 1989–90, 1990–91

7........ Sleepy Floyd...............1984–85, 1985–86, 1986–87, 1988–89, 1989–90, 1990–91, 1991–92

7........ Charles Oakley...........1986–87, 1987–88, 1988–89, 1991–92, 1992–93, 1993–94, 1998–99

7........ Mark West 1987–88, 1988–89, 1989–90, 1990–91, 1991–92, 1992–93, 1993–94

7........ Hersey Hawkins..........1989–90, 1993–94, 1994–95, 1995–96, 1996–97, 1997–98, 1998–99

7........ Tayshaun Prince 2003–04, 2004–05, 2005–06, 2006–07, 2007–08, 2008–09, 2012–13

6........ Bob Cousy 1950–51, 1951–52, 1952–53, 1953–54, 1955–56, 1959–60

6........ Larry Foust..................1950–51, 1951–52, 1953–54, 1955–56, 1957–58, 1958–59

6........ Bailey Howell 1959–60, 1964–65, 1966–67, 1967–68, 1969–70, 1970–71

6........ Hal Greer 1960–61, 1962–63, 1963–64, 1965–66, 1967–68, 1968–69

6........ Paul Silas 1967–68, 1973–74, 1974–75, 1977–78, 1978–79, 1979–80

6........ Jim Eakins ....1968–69[a], 1970–71[a], 1971–72[a], 1973–74[a], 1974–75[a], 1976–77

6........ Dick Snyder................1969–70, 1970–71, 1972–73, 1974–75, 1975–76, 1976–77

6........ Dave Robisch..............1971–72[a], 1973–74[a], 1974–75[a], 1975–76[a], 1979–80, 1980–81

6........ Julius Erving................1971–72[a], 1973–74[a], 1974–75[a], 1975–76[a], 1976–77, 1980–81

6........ Jim Chones.................1975–76, 1976–77, 1977–78, 1978–79, 1979–80, 1980–81

6........ Alex English 1977–78, 1981–82, 1982–83, 1983–84, 1986–87, 1988–89

6........ Greg Ballard 1978–79, 1979–80, 1980–81, 1983–84, 1984–85, 1986–87

6........ Michael Cooper..........1979–80, 1982–83, 1983–84, 1984–85, 1985–86, 1986–87

6........ T.R. Dunn 1979–80, 1980–81, 1981–82, 1982–83, 1985–86, 1987–88

6........ Dave Corzine 1980–81, 1981–82, 1982–83, 1983–84, 1984–85, 1986–87

6........ Derek Harper..............1983–84, 1984–85, 1987–88, 1989–90, 1993–94, 1995–96

6........ Thurl Bailey 1985–86, 1987–88, 1988–89, 1989–90, 1990–91, 1991–92

continued on next page

6........ Xavier McDaniel 1985–86, 1986–87, 1988–89, 1991–92, 1992–93, 1993–94
6........ Reggie Miller.............. 1987–88, 1989–90, 1990–91, 1991–92, 1992–93, 1998–99
6........ Terry Porter................. 1987–88, 1991–92, 1995–96, 1996–97, 1997–98, 1998–99
6........ Scottie Pippen............. 1989–90, 1990–91, 1991–92, 1996–97, 1998–99, 1999–00
6........ B.J. Armstrong 1990–91, 1991–92, 1992–93, 1993–94, 1994–95, 1995–96
6........ Dikembe Mutombo...... 1992–93, 1993–94, 1994–95, 1997–98, 1998–99, 1999–00
6........ Johnny Newman 1994–95, 1995–96, 1996–97, 1998–99, 1999–00, 2000–01
6........ Howard Eisley 1996–97, 1997–98, 1998–99, 1999–00, 2000–01, 2002–03
6........ Shandon Anderson...... 1997–98, 1998–99, 1999–00, 2000–01, 2001–02, 2002–03
6........ Mike Bibby................. 1998–99, 1999–00, 2000–01, 2003–04, 2005–06, 2006–07
6........ Bruce Bowen 2000–01, 2002–03, 2003–04, 2004–05, 2005–06, 2006–07
6........ Luis Scola................... 2007–08, 2008–09, 2009–10, 2011–12, 2012–13, 2013–14
5........ Max Zaslofsky 1946–47, 1947–48, 1949–50, 1950–51, 1951–52
5........ Red Rocha................... 1947–48, 1951–52, 1954–55, 1955–56, 1956–57
5........ Arnie Johnson............. 1948–49, 1949–50, 1950–51, 1951–52, 1952–53
5........ George Mikan............. 1948–49, 1949–50, 1950–51, 1952–53, 1953–54
5........ Bob Harrison 1950–51, 1952–53, 1954–55, 1955–56, 1957–58
5........ Slater Martin 1950–51, 1951–52, 1952–53, 1954–55, 1955–56
5........ Joe Graboski 1951–52, 1955–56, 1956–57, 1957–58, 1958–59
5........ Mel Hutchins 1951–52, 1952–53, 1953–54, 1954–55, 1956–57
5........ Carl Braun 1952–53, 1953–54, 1955–56, 1956–57, 1958–59
5........ Jack McMahon 1952–53, 1954–55, 1956–57, 1957–58, 1958–59
5........ Earl Lloyd 1953–54, 1954–55, 1955–56, 1956–57, 1958–59
5........ Gene Shue 1955–56, 1956–57, 1958–59, 1959–60, 1961–62
5........ Adrian Smith 1961–62, 1964–65, 1965–66, 1966–67, 1967–68
5........ Tom Meschery 1961–62, 1963–64, 1965–66, 1967–68, 1968–69
5........ Leroy Ellis................. 1962–63, 1964–65, 1965–66, 1966–67, 1974–75
5........ Zelmo Beaty 1962–63, 1964–65, 1965–66, 1967–68, 1971-72a
5........ Bill Bridges 1963–64, 1967–68, 1969–70, 1970–71, 1972–73
5........ Howard Komives......... 1964–65, 1965–66, 1968–69, 1969–70, 1970–71
5........ Chet Walker 1965–66, 1966–67, 1967–68, 1968–69, 1973–74
5........ Bob Weiss.................. 1967–68, 1969–70, 1970–71, 1971–72, 1972–73
5........ Gerald Govan .... 1967–68[a], 1969–70[a], 1970–71[a], 1972–73[a], 1974–75[a]
5........ Kareem Abdul-Jabbar .. 1969–70, 1970–71, 1975–76, 1976–77, 1979–80
5........ Calvin Murphy............ 1970–71, 1971–72, 1975–76, 1976–77, 1978–79
5........ Jo Jo White 1972–73, 1973–74, 1974–75, 1975–76, 1976–77
5........ George Gervin 1974-75a, 1976–77, 1977–78, 1980–81, 1985–86
5........ Jamaal Wilkes 1974–75, 1975–76, 1978–79, 1979–80, 1981–82
5........ Allan Bristow 1976–77, 1977–78, 1979–80, 1980–81, 1981–82
5........ Moses Malone............. 1976–77, 1978–79, 1979–80, 1990–91, 1991–92
5........ Robert Reid 1978–79, 1980–81, 1984–85, 1985–86, 1988–89
5........ Mike Mitchell.............. 1979–80, 1980–81, 1981–82, 1984–85, 1985–86
5........ Kevin McHale............. 1980–81, 1981–82, 1982–83, 1983–84, 1989–90
5........ Kyle Macy................. 1980–81, 1981–82, 1982–83, 1983–84, 1985–86
5........ Eddie Johnson............. 1982–83, 1983–84, 1984–85, 1985–86, 1992–93
5........ Mark Eaton 1983–84, 1984–85, 1987–88, 1988–89, 1989–90
5........ Hakeem Olajuwon 1984–85, 1988–89, 1989–90, 1992–93, 1998–99
5........ Terry Teagle................ 1985–86, 1986–87, 1989–90, 1990–91, 1991–92
5........ Chris Mullin................ 1986–87, 1988–89, 1990–91, 1997–98, 1998–99
5........ Dennis Rodman........... 1987–88, 1988–89, 1989–90, 1990–91, 1991–92
5........ Detlef Schrempf........... 1987–88, 1990–91, 1992–93, 1994–95, 1998–99
5........ Tyrone Corbin............. 1987–88, 1989–90, 1990–91, 1992–93, 1993–94

continued on next page

5........ Mike Brown............... 1989–90, 1990–91, 1991–92, 1992–93, 1993–94
5........ Vlade Divac 1989–90, 1990–91, 1992–93, 1998–99, 1999–00
5........ Sam Mitchell 1990–91, 1991–92, 1996–97, 1998–99, 2000–01
5........ Avery Johnson 1993–94, 1994–95, 1995–96, 1998–99, 1999–00
5........ Lindsey Hunter 1993–94, 1996–97, 1999–00, 2000–01, 2001–02
5....... Rick Fox...................... 1993–94, 1997–98, 1999–00, 2000–01, 2001–02
5........ Allan Houston 1995–96, 1997–98, 1998–99, 1999–00, 2002–03
5........ Antoine Walker........... 1996–97, 1997–98, 1999–00, 2003–04, 2005–06
5........ Bo Outlaw.................. 1996–97, 1997–98, 1999–00, 2001–02, 2003–04
5........ Ray Allen 1996–97, 1997–98, 1998–99, 1999–00, 2000–01
5........ Kobe Bryant 1998–99, 2002–03, 2007–08, 2008–09, 2010–11
5........ Eric Snow.................. 1999–00, 2002–03, 2003–04, 2005–06, 2006–07
5........ Antawn Jamison.......... 2000–01, 2001–02, 2002–03, 2003–04, 2005–06
5........ Joe Johnson 2002–03, 2003–04, 2004–05, 2005–06, 2007–08
5........ Samuel Dalembert....... 2003–04, 2006–07, 2007–08, 2008–09, 2009–10
5........ Andre Iguodala 2004–05, 2005–06, 2007–08, 2008–09, 2009–10
5........ Dwight Howard 2004–05, 2005–06, 2006–07, 2007–08, 2009–10
5........ Russell Westbrook 2008–09, 2009–10, 2010–11, 2011–12, 2012–13
ᵃ ABA.

Most Games Played, Season

NBA

88...... Walt Bellamy, N.Y. Knicks/Det. Pistons, 1968–69
87...... Tom Henderson, Atl. Hawks/Was. Bullets, 1976–77
86...... McCoy McLemore, Cle. Cavaliers/Mil. Bucks, 1970–71
86...... Gar Heard, Buf. Braves/Pho. Suns, 1975–76
85...... John Tresvant, Det. Pistons/Cin. Royals, 1967–68
85...... Howard Komives, N.Y. Knicks/Det. Pistons, 1968–69
85...... Nate Williams, K.C.-Oma. Kings/N.O. Jazz, 1974–75
85...... Chris Gatling, Orl. Magic/Den. Nuggets, 1999–00
85...... Shareef Abdur-Rahim, Atl. Hawks/Por. Blazers, 2003–04
85...... Theo Ratliff, Atl. Hawks/Por. Blazers, 2003–04
84...... Fred Hetzel, Mil. Bucks/Cin. Royals, 1968–69
84...... Al Tucker, Sea. Sonics/Cin. Royals, 1968–69
84...... Jim Washington, Phi. 76ers/Atl. Hawks, 1971–72
84...... Billy Paultz, S.A. Spurs/Hou. Rockets, 1979–80
84...... Dave Robisch, Cle. Cavaliers/Den. Nuggets, 1980–81
84...... Billy McKinney, Uta. Jazz/Den. Nuggets, 1980–81
84...... Mike Mitchell, Cle. Cavaliers/S.A. Spurs, 1981–82
84...... Tyrone Corbin, Cle. Cavaliers/Pho. Suns, 1987–88
84...... Thurl Bailey, Uta. Jazz/Min. T'Wolves, 1991–92
84...... Casey Jacobsen, Pho. Suns/N.O. Hornets, 2004–05
83...... Flynn Robinson, Chi. Bulls/Mil. Bucks, 1968–69
83...... Leonard Gray, Sea. Sonics/Was. Bullets, 1976–77
83...... Jim Price, Den. Nuggets/Det. Pistons, 1977–78
83...... James Edwards, L.A. Lakers/Ind. Pacers, 1977–78
83...... Phil Hubbard, Det. Pistons/Cle. Cavaliers, 1981–82

83...... Mike Woodson, N.J. Nets/K.C. Kings, 1981–82
83...... Clemon Johnson, Ind. Pacers/Phi. 76ers, 1982–83
83...... James Donaldson, L.A. Clippers/Dal. Mavericks, 1985–86
83...... Mark West, Cle. Cavaliers/Pho. Suns, 1987–88
83...... J.R. Reid, Cha. Hornets/S.A. Spurs, 1992–93
83...... Benoit Benjamin, Van. Grizzlies/Mil. Bucks, 1995–96
83...... Michael Finley, Pho. Suns/Dal. Mavericks, 1996–97
83...... A.C. Green, Pho. Suns/Dal. Mavericks, 1996–97
83...... Aaron McKie, Por. Blazers/Det. Pistons, 1996–97
83...... Mark Jackson, Tor. Raptors/N.Y. Knicks, 2000–01
83...... Jalen Rose, Ind. Pacers/Chi. Bulls, 2001–02
83...... Bo Outlaw, Orl. Magic/Pho. Suns, 2001–02
83...... James Posey, Den. Nuggets/Hou. Rockets, 2002–03
83...... Jarrett Jack, Tor. Raptors/N.O. Hornets, 2010–11
83...... Ramon Sessions, Cha. Bobcats/Mil. Bucks, 2013–14
83...... Josh Smith, Det. Pistons/Hou. Rockets, 2014–15

ABA

90.... Chuck Williams, S.D. Conquistadors/Ken. Colonels, 1973–74
88.... Charlie Williams, Pit. Condors/Mem. Pros, 1970–71
87.... Johnny Neumann, Mem. Tams/Uta. Stars, 1973–74
87.... Dave Robisch, S.D. Sails/Ind. Pacers, 1975–76
86.... Ron Boone, Tex. Chaparrals/Uta. Stars, 1970–71
86.... Glen Combs, Tex. Chaparrals/Uta. Stars, 1970–71
86.... Warren Davis, Car. Cougars/Mem. Pros, 1971–72
86.... Steve Jones, Car. Cougars/Den. Rockets, 1973–74
86.... Maurice Lucas, Spirits of St.L./Ken. Colonels, 1975–76

Youngest Player to Appear in a Game*

18 years, 6 days	Andrew Bynum, L.A. Lakers	@ Den. Nuggets (Nov. 2, 2005)
18 years, 53 days	Jermaine O'Neal, Por. Blazers	@ Den. Nuggets (Dec. 5, 1996)
18 years, 72 days	Kobe Bryant, L.A. Lakers	vs. Min. T'Wolves (Nov. 3, 1996)
18 years, 133 days	Darko Miličić, Det. Pistons	@ Mia. Heat (Oct. 31, 2003)
18 years, 139 days	Stan Brown, Phi. Warriors	vs. Pro. Steamrollers (Nov. 13, 1947)
18 years, 160 days	Tracy McGrady, Tor. Raptors	@ Mia. Heat (Oct. 31, 1997)
18 years, 181 days	Yaroslav Korolev, L.A. Clippers	vs. Atl. Hawks (Nov. 3, 2005)
18 years, 156 days	Bill Willoughby, Atl. Hawks	vs. N.O. Jazz (Oct. 23, 1975)
18 years, 217 days	Andris Biedriņš, G.S. Warriors	vs. Uta. Jazz (Nov. 5, 2004)
18 years, 241 days	C.J. Miles, Uta. Jazz	vs. N.Y. Knicks (Nov. 14, 2005)
18 years, 268 days	Amir Johnson, Det. Pistons	@ Min. T'Wolves (Jan. 24, 2006)
18 years, 289 days	Darryl Dawkins, Phi. 76ers	vs. L.A. Lakers (Oct. 27, 1975)
18 years, 296 days	Joe Graboski, Chi. Stags	vs. Bal. Bullets (Nov. 6, 1948)
18 years, 300 days	Joshua Primo, S.A. Spurs	vs. Orl. Magic (Oct. 20, 2021)
18 years, 303 days	LeBron James, Cle. Cavaliers	@ Sac. Kings (Oct. 29, 2003)
18 years, 314 days	Jonathan Bender, Ind. Pacers	vs. Cle. Cavaliers (Dec. 10, 1999)
18 years, 325 days	Jim Browne, Chi. Stags	@ Ft.W. Pistons (Nov. 21, 1948)
18 years, 328 days	Giannis Antetokounmpo, Mil. Bucks	@ N.Y. Knicks (Oct. 30, 2013)
18 years, 330 days	Eddy Curry, Chi. Bulls	vs. Ind. Pacers (Oct. 31, 2001)
18 years, 331 days	Dwight Howard, Orl. Magic	vs. Mil. Bucks (Nov. 3, 2004)
18 years, 334 days	Josh Smith, Atl. Hawks	@ Pho. Suns (Nov. 3, 2004)
18 years, 335 days	Martell Webster, Por. Blazers	@ Den. Nuggets (Nov. 4, 2005)
18 years, 335 days	Sekou Doumbouya, Det. Pistons	@ Mil. Bucks (Nov. 23, 2019)
18 years, 336 days	Robert Swift, Sea. Sonics	@ L.A. Clippers (Nov. 3, 2004)
18 years, 344 days	Dragan Bender, Pho. Suns	vs. Sac. Kings (Oct. 26, 2016)
18 years, 352 days	Maciej Lampe, Pho. Suns	vs. S.A. Spurs (Jan. 23, 2004)
18 years, 363 days	Devin Booker, Pho. Suns	vs. Dal. Mavericks (Oct. 28, 2015)

* Only includes game in which player was the youngest.

Oldest Player to Appear in a Game*

45 years, 363 days	Nat Hickey, Pro. Steamrollers	@ N.Y. Knicks (Jan. 28, 1948)
44 years, 224 days	Kevin Willis, Dal. Mavericks	@ Sea. Sonics (Apr. 18, 2007)
43 years, 232 days	Robert Parish, Chi. Bulls	vs. N.Y. Knicks (Apr. 19, 1997)
43 years, 45 days	Vince Carter, Atl. Hawks	vs. N.Y. Knicks (Mar. 11, 2020)
42 years, 289 days	Dikembe Mutombo, Hou. Rockets	@ G.S. Warriors (Apr. 10, 2009)
42 years, 7 days	Kareem Abdul-Jabbar, L.A. Lakers	vs. Sea. Sonics (Apr. 23, 1989)
41 years, 200 days	Udonis Haslem, Mia. Heat	vs. Orl. Magic (Dec. 26, 2021)
41 years, 150 days	Bob Cousy, Cin. Royals	vs. Pho. Suns (Jan. 6, 1970)
41 years, 75 days	Herb Williams, N.Y. Knicks	@ Ind. Pacers (May 2, 1999)
41 years, 21 days	John Stockton, Uta. Jazz	@ Sac. Kings (Apr. 16, 2003)
41 years, 16 days	Charles Jones, Hou. Rockets	vs. Pho Suns (Apr. 19, 1998)

* Only includes game in which player was the oldest.

Most Games Played from Age 39 On

351 .... Robert Parish	187 .... Dikembe Mutombo	125 .... Jason Terry
299 .... Vince Carter	178 .... John Stockton	123 .... Karl Malone
232 .... Kareem Abdul-Jabbar	134 .... Manu Ginóbili	111 .... Clifford Robinson
205 .... Kevin Willis	128 .... Dirk Nowitzki	

5

MINUTES PLAYED

Most Minutes Played by Decade

1950-51—1959-60*

23,574	Bob Cousy
23,525	Dolph Schayes
21,889	Slater Martin
21,186	Joe Graboski
20,255	Bill Sharman
19,529	Larry Foust
19,177	Paul Arizin
18,443	Vern Mikkelsen
18,298	Neil Johnston
18,071	Ed Macauley

1960-61—1969-70**

33,880	Wilt Chamberlain
33,088	Oscar Robertson
30,266	Bill Russell
29,866	Hal Greer
27,839	Elgin Baylor
27,589	Walt Bellamy
27,326	Jerry West
26,692	Bailey Howell
25,817	Lenny Wilkens
24,615	Guy Rodgers

1970-71—1979-80**

33,381	Elvin Hayes
31,380	Kareem Abdul-Jabbar
30,480	Dan Issel
28,778	Rick Barry
28,551	Dave Cowens
28,377	Jo Jo White
28,226	Artis Gilmore
27,743	Sam Lacey
27,596	Wes Unseld
27,533	Julius Erving

1980-81—1989-90

29,018	Alex English
28,634	Moses Malone
27,549	Larry Bird
27,014	Jack Sikma
26,873	Bill Laimbeer
26,559	Magic Johnson
26,424	Dennis Johnson
26,269	Isiah Thomas
26,118	Robert Parish
26,070	Maurice Cheeks

1990-91—1999-00

29,830	Karl Malone
28,190	Gary Payton
28,062	Glen Rice
27,505	Reggie Miller
27,406	Scottie Pippen
26,868	Mitch Richmond
26,808	Mookie Blaylock
26,315	John Stockton
25,920	Hersey Hawkins
25,441	Horace Grant

2000-01—2009-10

29,835	Dirk Nowitzki
29,787	Kobe Bryant
29,147	Antawn Jamison
29,145	Shawn Marion
28,869	Andre Miller
28,721	Paul Pierce
28,576	Jason Kidd
28,162	Kevin Garnett
27,810	Jason Terry
27,537	Tim Duncan

2010-11—2019-20

26,851	James Harden
26,443	LeBron James
26,326	DeMar DeRozan
24,898	Russell Westbrook
24,551	LaMarcus Aldridge
23,285	Kyle Lowry
23,189	Wesley Matthews
23,002	Thaddeus Young
22,817	Trevor Ariza
22,736	Marc Gasol

2020-21—2021-22

5211	Julius Randle
5202	Mikal Bridges
5047	Russell Westbrook
5021	Jayson Tatum
4964	Nikola Jokić
4932	Buddy Hield
4928	RJ Barrett
4841	Terry Rozier
4799	DeMar DeRozan
4780	Anthony Edwards

* Data may be incomplete.

** Includes ABA.

Most Minutes Played, Season

MP		GP	MPG
3882	Wilt Chamberlain, Phi. Warriors, 1961–62	80	48.5
3836	Wilt Chamberlain, Phi. Warriors, 1967–68	82	46.8
3808	Spencer Haywood, Den. Rockets[a], 1969–70	84	45.3
3806	Wilt Chamberlain, S.F. Warriors, 1962–63	80	47.6
3773	Wilt Chamberlain, Phi. Warriors, 1960–61	79	47.8
3737	Wilt Chamberlain, Phi. 76ers, 1965–66	79	47.3
3701	Gerald Govan, N.O. Buccaneers[a], 1969–70	84	44.1
3698	Gerald Govan, Mem. Pros[a], 1970–71	84	44.0
3698	John Havlicek, Bos. Celtics, 1971–72	82	45.1
3695	Elvin Hayes, S.D. Rockets, 1968–69	82	45.1
3689	Wilt Chamberlain, S.F. Warriors, 1963–64	80	46.1
3682	Wilt Chamberlain, Phi. 76ers, 1966–67	81	45.5
3681	Tiny Archibald, K.C.-Oma. Kings, 1972–73	80	46.0
3678	John Havlicek, Bos. Celtics, 1970–71	81	45.4
3669	Wilt Chamberlain, L.A. Lakers, 1968–69	81	45.3
3666	Artis Gilmore, Ken. Colonels[a], 1971–72	84	43.6
3665	Elvin Hayes, S.D. Rockets, 1969–70	82	44.7
3638	Truck Robinson, N.O. Jazz, 1977–78	82	44.4
3634	Julius Keye, Den. Rockets[a], 1970–71	83	43.8
3633	Elvin Hayes, S.D. Rockets, 1970–71	82	44.3
3630	Wilt Chamberlain, L.A. Lakers, 1970–71	82	44.3
3619	Jerry Lucas, Cin. Royals, 1967–68	82	44.1
3616	Rick Barry, N.Y. Nets[a], 1971–72	80	45.2
3611	Larry Jones, The Floridians[a], 1970–71	84	43.0
3602	Elvin Hayes, Cap. Bullets, 1973–74	81	44.5
3583	Kareem Abdul-Jabbar, Mil. Bucks, 1971–72	81	44.2
3570	Dan Issel, Ken. Colonels[a], 1971–72	83	43.0
3559	Oscar Robertson, Cin. Royals, 1963–64	79	45.1
3558	Jerry Lucas, Cin. Royals, 1966–67	81	43.9
3548	Kareem Abdul-Jabbar, Mil. Bucks, 1973–74	81	43.8
3542	Wilt Chamberlain, L.A. Lakers, 1972–73	82	43.2
3539	Bob McAdoo, Buf. Braves, 1974–75	82	43.2
3534	Kareem Abdul-Jabbar, Mil. Bucks, 1969–70	82	43.1
3533	Latrell Sprewell, G.S. Warriors, 1993–94	82	43.1
3531	Dan Issel, Ken. Colonels[a], 1972–73	84	42.0
3521	Oscar Robertson, Cin. Royals, 1962–63	80	44.0
3517	Jerry Lucas, Cin. Royals, 1965–66	79	44.5
3513	Julius Erving, Vir. Squires[a], 1971–72	84	41.8
3503	Oscar Robertson, Cin. Royals, 1961–62	79	44.3
3502	Artis Gilmore, Ken. Colonels[a], 1972–73	84	41.7
3502	Artis Gilmore, Ken. Colonels[a], 1973–74	84	41.7
3500	Bill Russell, Bos. Celtics, 1962–63	78	44.9

[a] ABA.

Most Minutes Played, Career*

MP		MP		MP	
57,446	Kareem Abdul-Jabbar	50,418	Kevin Garnett	48,637	Kobe Bryant
54,852	Karl Malone	50,111	Jason Kidd	47,859	Wilt Chamberlain
52,139	LeBron James^	50,000	Elvin Hayes	47,764	John Stockton
51,368	Dirk Nowitzki	49,444	Moses Malone	47,619	Reggie Miller

continued on next page

MP		MP		MP	
47,368	Tim Duncan	44,236	Joe Johnson^	41,069	Scottie Pippen
47,134	Artis Gilmore	44,222	Hakeem Olajuwon	41,011	Michael Jordan
47,117	Gary Payton	43,886	Oscar Robertson	41,001	Pau Gasol
46,471	John Havlicek	43,514	Carmelo Anthony^	40,726	Bill Russell
46,367	Vince Carter	42,561	Clifford Robinson	40,594	Patrick Ewing
46,344	Ray Allen	42,464	Buck Williams	40,280	Charles Oakley
45,880	Paul Pierce	42,034	Jason Terry	40,268	Andre Miller
45,704	Robert Parish	41,918	Shaquille O'Neal	40,097	Shawn Marion
45,227	Julius Erving	41,784	Dan Issel		

* Includes ABA.
^ Active.

Most Games Playing Full 48 Minutes, Career* (Not Including Overtime Games)

539	Wilt Chamberlain	104	John Havlicek	54	Roger Brown
234	Bill Russell	89	Jerry Lucas	52	Michael Finley
226	Oscar Robertson	87	Kareem Abdul-Jabbar	40	Artis Gilmore
192	Nate Thurmond	75	Tiny Archibald	36	Guy Rodgers
156	Elvin Hayes	63	Walt Bellamy	35	Dave Cowens

* Includes ABA.

Most Minutes Played in a Single Game

MP			Total OT Periods
69	Dale Ellis, Sea. Sonics*	@ Mil. Bucks (Nov. 9, 1989)	5
68	Xavier McDaniel, Sea. Sonics*	@ Mil. Bucks (Nov. 9, 1989)	5
66	Julius Erving, N.Y. Nets^a*	@ S.D. Conquistadors^a (Feb. 14, 1975)	4
64	Norm Nixon, L.A. Lakers*	@ Cle. Cavaliers (Jan. 29, 1980)	3
64	Sleepy Floyd, G.S. Warriors	vs. N.J. Nets (Feb. 1, 1987)	4
63	Paul Arizin, Phi. Warriors	vs. Min. Lakers (Dec. 21, 1951)	3
63	Andy Phillip, Phi. Warriors	vs. Min. Lakers (Dec. 21, 1951)	3
63	Paul Arizin, Phi. Warriors*	@ Bal. Bullets (Dec. 26, 1951)	3
63	Andy Phillip, Phi. Warriors*	@ Bal. Bullets (Dec. 26, 1951)	3
63	Leo Barnhorst, Ind. Olympians	vs. Min. Lakers (Feb. 3, 1953)	3
63	Joe Graboski, Ind. Olympians	vs. Min. Lakers (Feb. 3, 1953)	3
63	George Mikan, Min. Lakers*	@ Ind. Olympians (Feb. 3, 1953)	3
63	Don Henriksen, Bal. Bullets*	vs. N.Y. Knicks (Mar. 11, 1953)	3
63	Ray Felix, Bal. Bullets*	vs. Bos. Celtics (Feb. 22, 1954)	3
63	Bob Houbregs, Bal. Bullets*	vs. Bos. Celtics (Feb. 22, 1954)	3
63	Larry Costello, Syr. Nationals	@ Cin. Royals (Jan. 8, 1959)	3
63	Wilt Chamberlain, Phi. Warriors*	vs. L.A. Lakers (Dec. 8, 1961)	3
63	Wilt Chamberlain, L.A. Lakers*	vs. S.F. Warriors (Feb. 2, 1969)	3
63	Nate Thurmond, S.F. Warriors	@ L.A. Lakers (Feb. 2, 1969)	3
63	Vince Carter, Tor. Raptors*	vs. Sac. Kings (Feb. 23, 2001)	3
62	Jim Baechtold, N.Y. Knicks*	@ Phi. Warriors (Feb. 25, 1955)	3
62	Jay Humphries, Mil. Bucks	vs. Sea. Sonics (Nov. 9, 1989)	5
61	Geoff Petrie, Por. Blazers	vs. Cle. Cavaliers (Oct. 18, 1974)	4
61	Eddie Johnson, Atl. Hawks	@ Sea. Sonics (Feb. 19, 1982)	4
61	Brian Grant, Por. Blazers*	vs. Pho. Suns (Nov. 14, 1997)	4
61	Jalen Rose, Ind. Pacers*	@ Hou. Rockets (Mar. 13, 2001)	3
60	Slater Martin, Min. Lakers	@ Syr. Nationals (Dec. 15, 1955)	3
60	Lenny Wilkens, Por. Blazers	vs. Cle. Cavaliers (Oct. 18, 1974)	4

continued on next page

MP   **Total OT Periods**

60 .... Kareem Abdul-Jabbar, L.A. Lakers* .... @ Cle. Cavaliers (Jan. 29, 1980) 4

60 .... Buck Williams, N.J. Nets* .... @ G.S. Warriors (Feb. 1, 1987) 4

60 .... Cuttino Mobley, Hou. Rockets .... vs. Atl. Hawks (Feb. 22, 2004) 3

60 .... Shawn Marion, Pho. Suns* .... @ N.Y. Knicks (Jan. 2, 2006) 3

60 .... Jamal Crawford, G.S. Warriors* .... vs. Sac. Kings (Jan. 14, 2009) 3

60 .... DeMar DeRozan, Tor. Raptors* .... vs. Uta. Jazz (Nov. 12, 2012) 3

60 .... Jimmy Butler, Chi. Bulls .... @ Orl. Magic (Jan. 15, 2014) 3

60 .... Paul Millsap, Atl. Hawks .... vs. N.Y. Knicks (Jan. 29, 2017) 4

* Team lost game.

ᵃ ABA.

Highest Average MPG, Career (Regular Season)

45.8 .... Wilt Chamberlain	39.2 .... Jerry West	38.4 .... Paul Arizin
42.3 .... Bill Russell	38.8 .... Jerry Lucas	38.4 .... Larry Bird
42.2 .... Oscar Robertson	38.8 .... Bob Pettit	38.4 .... Elvin Hayes
41.1 .... Allen Iverson	38.6 .... Dave Cowens	38.3 .... Michael Jordan
40.0 .... Elgin Baylor	38.6 .... Latrell Sprewell	38.2 .... LeBron James^

^ Active.

Most Minutes Played from Age 39 On (Regular Season)

6977 .... Robert Parish	4309 .... Karl Malone	2695 .... Dirk Nowitzki
6444 .... Kareem Abdul-Jabbar	3031 .... Michael Jordan	2590 .... Manu Ginóbili
6036 .... Vince Carter	2959 .... Dikembe Mutombo	
4841 .... John Stockton	2818 .... Clifford Robinson	

6

AWARDS

Most Valuable Player (MVP)

Unanimous Choice for MVP

2015–16........Stephen Curry, G.S. Warriors

Closest MVP Race*

Diff (Total Points—First-Place Votes)	Season	MVP	Runner-Up
2 (23–21)	1956–57	Bob Cousy, Bos. Celtics	Bob Pettit, St.L. Hawks
12 (33–21)	1955–56	Bob Pettit, St.L. Hawks	Paul Arizin, Phi. Warriors
15.5** (96–80.5)	1977–78	Bill Walton, Por. Blazers	George Gervin, S.A. Spurs
16 (409–393; 52–47)	1975–76	Kareem Abdul-Jabbar, L.A. Lakers	Bob McAdoo, Buf. Braves
22 (636–614; 27–38)	1989–90	Magic Johnson, L.A. Lakers	Charles Barkley, Phi. 76ers
29 (986–957; 63–52)	1996–97	Karl Malone, Uta. Jazz	Michael Jordan, Chi. Bulls
30 (228–198; 33–25)	1957–58	Bill Russell, Bos. Celtics	Dolph Schayes, Syr. Nationals
31 (454–423; 28–20)	1980–81	Julius Erving, Phi. 76ers	Larry Bird, Bos. Celtics
32** (53–21)	1964–65	Bill Russell, Bos. Celtics	Oscar Robertson, Cin. Royals
34 (1066–1032; 65–58)	2004–05	Steve Nash, Pho. Suns	Shaquille O'Neal, Mia. Heat
41 (498–457; 61–51)	1969–70	Willis Reed, N.Y. Knicks	Jerry West, L.A. Lakers
54 (827–773; 44–36)	1998–99	Karl Malone, Uta. Jazz	Alonzo Mourning, Mia. Heat
57 (954–897; 57–45)	2001–02	Tim Duncan, S.A. Spurs	Jason Kidd, N.J. Nets
65.7 (664.5–598.8; 42.5–27.5)	1988–89	Magic Johnson, L.A. Lakers	Michael Jordan, Chi. Bulls
77 (528–451; 74–60)	1973–74	Kareem Abdul-Jabbar, Mil. Bucks	Bob McAdoo, Buf. Braves
80** (181–101; 48–16)	1965–66	Wilt Chamberlain, Phi. 76ers	Jerry West, L.A. Lakers
84 (270–186; 49–15)	1959–60	Wilt Chamberlain, Phi. Warriors	Bill Russell, Bos. Celtics
91 (962–871; 60–43)	2002–03	Tim Duncan, S.A. Spurs	Kevin Garnett, Min. T'Wolves

* From 1955–56 through 1979–80, MVP voting were done by the players (and could not vote for themselves). Voting from 1980–81 to present day is conducted by the media.

** Data incomplete.

Teammates Finishing One-Two in MVP Balloting

	MVP	Runner-Up
Ken. Colonels[a], 1971–72	Artis Gilmore	Dan Issel

[a] ABA.

MVPs Receiving Fewer First-Place Votes Than Runner-Up

	MVP (Votes)	Runner-Up (Votes)
1989–90	Magic Johnson, L.A. Lakers (27)	Charles Barkley, Phi. 76ers (38)

Players Winning MVP Award in Consecutive Seasons

3 .... Bill Russell .... Bos. Celtics (1960–61, 1961–62, 1962–63)
3 .... Wilt Chamberlain .... Phi. 76ers (1965–66, 1966–67, 1967–68)
3 .... Julius Erving .... N.Y. Nets[a] (1973–74, 1974–75*, 1975–76)

continued on next page

3 ....Larry Bird .... Bos. Celtics (1983–84, 1984–85, 1985–86)
2 ....Kareem Abdul-Jabbar .... Mil. Bucks (1970–71, 1971–72); L.A. Lakers (1975–76, 1976–77)
2 ....Moses Malone .... Hou. Rockets (1981–82), Phi. 76ers (1982–83)
2 ....Magic Johnson .... L.A. Lakers (1988–89, 1989–90)
2 ....Michael Jordan .... Chi. Bulls (1990–91, 1991–92)
2 ....Tim Duncan........................ S.A. Spurs (2001–02, 2002–03)
2 ....Steve Nash .... Pho. Suns (2004–05, 2005–06)
2 ....LeBron James .... Cle. Cavaliers (2008–09, 2009–10); Mia. Heat (2011–12, 2012–13)
2 ....Stephen Curry.................... G.S. Warriors (2014–15, 2015–16)
2 ....Giannis Antetokounmpo .... Mil. Bucks (2018–19, 2019–20)
2 ....Nikola Jokić........................ Den. Nuggets (2020–21, 2021–22)

ª ABA.

* Tied for MVP with George McGinnis, Ind. Pacers.

Players with Multiple MVP Awards

6.................... Kareem Abdul-Jabbar .... Mil. Bucks, 1970–71
                                                         Mil. Bucks, 1971–72
                                                         Mil. Bucks, 1973–74
                                                         L.A. Lakers, 1975–76
                                                         L.A. Lakers, 1976–77
                                                         L.A. Lakers, 1979–80

5.................... Bill Russell .... Bos. Celtics, 1957–58
                                                         Bos. Celtics, 1960–61
                                                         Bos. Celtics, 1961–62
                                                         Bos. Celtics, 1962–63
                                                         Bos. Celtics, 1964–65

5.................... Michael Jordan .... Chi. Bulls, 1987–88
                                                         Chi. Bulls, 1990–91
                                                         Chi. Bulls, 1991–92
                                                         Chi. Bulls, 1995–96
                                                         Chi. Bulls, 1997–98

4.................... Wilt Chamberlain........................... Phi. Warriors, 1959–60
                                                         Phi. 76ers, 1965–66
                                                         Phi. 76ers, 1966–67
                                                         Phi. 76ers, 1967–68

4.................... Julius Erving.................................... N.Y. Netsª, 1973–74
                                                         N.Y. Netsª, 1974–75*
                                                         N.Y. Netsª, 1975–76
                                                         Phi. 76ers, 1980–81

4.................... LeBron James .... Cle. Cavaliers, 2008–09
                                                         Cle. Cavaliers, 2009–10
                                                         Mia. Heat, 2011–12
                                                         Mia. Heat, 2012–13

3.................... Moses Malone .... Hou. Rockets, 1978–79
                                                         Hou. Rockets, 1981–82
                                                         Phi. 76ers, 1982–83

3.................... Larry Bird .... Bos. Celtics, 1983–84
                                                         Bos. Celtics, 1984–85
                                                         Bos. Celtics, 1985–86

3.................... Magic Johnson............................... L.A. Lakers, 1986–87
                                                         L.A. Lakers, 1988–89
                                                         L.A. Lakers, 1989–90

continued on next page

2.....................Bob Pettit.. St.L. Hawks, 1955–56
St.L. Hawks, 1958–59

2.....................Mel Daniels .... Ind. Pacers[a], 1968–69
Ind. Pacers[a], 1970–71

2.....................Karl Malone .... Uta. Jazz, 1996–97
Uta. Jazz, 1998–99

2.....................Tim Duncan .... S.A. Spurs, 2001–02
S.A. Spurs, 2002–03

2.....................Steve Nash..................................... Pho. Suns, 2004–05
Pho. Suns, 2005–06

2.....................Stephen Curry................................. G.S. Warriors, 2014–15
G.S. Warriors, 2015–16

2.....................Giannis Antetokounmpo................... Mil. Bucks, 2018–19
Mil. Bucks, 2019–20

2.....................Nikola Jokić.................................... Den. Nuggets, 2020–21
Den. Nuggets, 2021–22

[a] ABA.

* Tied for MVP with George McGinnis, Ind. Pacers.

MVP on Team with Losing Record

Record

Bob Pettit, St.L. Hawks, 1955–56 .... 33–39 (.458)
Kareem Abdul-Jabbar, L.A. Lakers, 1975–76 .... 40–42 (.488)

Player Winning MVP Award in Both ABA and NBA

ABA   **NBA**

Julius Erving .... N.Y Nets (1973–74, 1974–75, 1975–76) ....Phi. 76ers (1980–81)

Oldest MVP

Age (Birthdate)
35 (Jul. 24) .... Karl Malone, Uta. Jazz, 1998–99
34 (Feb. 17) .... Michael Jordan, Chi. Bulls, 1997–98
33 (Jul. 24) .... Karl Malone, Uta. Jazz, 1996–97
32 (Feb. 17) .... Michael Jordan, Chi. Bulls, 1995–96
32 (Apr. 16) .... Kareem Abdul-Jabbar, L.A. Lakers, 1979–80
31 (Jan. 21)............. Hakeem Olajuwon, Hou. Rockets, 1993–94
31 (Feb. 7) .... Steve Nash, Pho. Suns, 2005–06
31 (Aug. 21)........... Wilt Chamberlain, Phi. 76ers, 1967–68
30 (Feb. 7) .... Steve Nash, Pho. Suns, 2004–05
30 (Feb. 12) .... Bill Russell, Bos. Celtics, 1964–65
30 (Feb. 22) .... Julius Erving, Phi. 76ers, 1980–81
30 (Aug. 14)........... Magic Johnson, L.A. Lakers, 1989–90
30 (Aug. 21)........... Wilt Chamberlain, Phi. 76ers, 1966–67

Youngest MVP

Age (Birthdate)
22 (Oct. 4) ...... Derrick Rose, Chi. Bulls, 2010–11
22 (Mar. 14).... Wes Unseld, Bal. Bullets, 1968–69
23 (Dec. 12) ... Bob Pettit, St.L. Hawks, 1955–56
23 (Sept. 25) ... Bob McAdoo, Buff. Braves, 1974–75
23 (Aug. 21).... Wilt Chamberlain, Phi. Warriors, 1959–60
23 (Apr. 16) .... Kareem Abdul-Jabbar, Mil. Bucks, 1970–71
23 (Mar. 23).... Moses Malone, Hou. Rockets, 1978–79
23 (Feb. 12) .... Bill Russell, Bos. Celtics, 1957–58
24 (Dec. 30) .... LeBron James, Cle. Cavaliers, 2008–19
24 (Dec. 6) ...... Giannis Antetokounmpo, Mil. Bucks, 2018–19
24 (Oct. 25) .... Dave Cowens, Bos. Celtics, 1972–73
24 (Apr. 16) .... Kareem Abdul-Jabbar, Mil. Bucks, 1971–72
24 (Feb. 17) .... Michael Jordan, Chi. Bulls, 1987–88

Rookies Winning MVP Award

1959–60 .... Wilt Chamberlain, Phi. Warriors
1967–68 .... Connie Hawkins, Pit. Pipers[a]
1968–69 .... Wes Unseld, Bal. Bullets
1969–70 .... Spencer Haywood, Den. Rockets[a]
1971–72 .... Artis Gilmore, Ken. Colonels[a]

[a] ABA.

MVPs Born Outside the Continental United States

		Country
1993–94	Hakeem Olajuwon, Hou. Rockets.....	Nigeria
2001–02	Tim Duncan, S.A. Spurs	U.S. Virgin Islands
2002–03	Tim Duncan, S.A. Spurs	U.S. Virgin Islands
2004–05	Steve Nash, Pho. Suns....................	South Africa
2005–06	Steve Nash, Pho. Suns....................	South Africa
2006–07	Dirk Nowitzki, Dal. Mavericks	Germany
2018–19	Giannis Antetokounmpo, Mil. Bucks..	Greece
2019–20	Giannis Antetokounmpo, Mil. Bucks..	Greece
2020–21	Nikola Jokić, Den. Nuggets.............	Serbia
2021–22	Nikola Jokić, Den. Nuggets.............	Serbia

Players Winning MVP Award with Two Different Teams

Wilt Chamberlain.................	Phi. Warriors, 1959–60
	Phi. 76ers, 1965–66, 1966–67, 1967–68
Kareem Abdul-Jabbar	Mil. Bucks, 1970–71, 1971–72, 1973–74
	L.A. Lakers, 1975–76, 1976–77, 1979–80
Julius Erving..........................	N.Y. Nets[a], 1973–74, 1974–75[*], 1975–76
	Phi. 76ers, 1980–81
Moses Malone	Hou. Rockets, 1978–79, 1981–82
	Phi. 76ers, 1982–83
LeBron James	Cle. Cavaliers, 2008–09, 2009–10
	Mia. Heat, 2011–12, 2012–13

[a] ABA.

[*] Tied for MVP with George McGinnis, Ind. Pacers.

Players Winning MVP, Changing Teams Following Season

MVP Season		MVP Team	New Team	Reason
1967–68	Wilt Chamberlain	Phi. 76ers	L.A. Lakers	Traded.
1975–76	Julius Erving	N.Y. Nets[a]	Phi. 76ers	Player rights sold.
1977–78	Bill Walton	Por. Blazers	S.D. Clippers	Missed 1978–79 season with injury; signed as a free agent with Clippers for 1979–80 season (Blazers received compensation).
1981–82	Moses Malone	Hou. Rockets	Phi. 76ers	Traded.
1997–98	Michael Jordan	Chi. Bulls	Was. Wizards	Retired for three seasons (1998–2001), joined Wizards as a free agent.
2009–10	LeBron James	Cle. Cavaliers	Mia. Heat	Free agent.

[a] ABA.

Players Winning MVP in First Season with New Team

1975–76	Kareem Abdul-Jabbar, L.A. Lakers
1982–83	Moses Malone, Phi. 76ers
1992–93	Charles Barkley, Pho. Suns
2004–05	Steve Nash, Pho. Suns

Most Times Runner Up for MVP

Runner-Up			MVP
4................	Jerry West	1965–66 (L.A. Lakers)	Wilt Chamberlain, Phi. 76ers
		1969–70 (L.A. Lakers)	Willis Reed, N.Y. Knicks

continued on next page

Runner-Up		MVP
	1970–71 (L.A. Lakers)	Kareem Abdul-Jabbar, Mil. Bucks
	1971–72 (L.A. Lakers)	Kareem Abdul-Jabbar, Mil. Bucks
4 .... Larry Bird	1980–81 (Bos. Celtics)	Julius Erving, Phi. 76ers
	1981–82 (Bos. Celtics)	Moses Malone, Hou. Rockets
	1982–83 (Bos. Celtics)	Moses Malone, Hou. Rockets
	1987–88 (Bos. Celtics)	Michael Jordan, Chi. Bulls
4 .... LeBron James	2005–06 (Cle. Cavaliers)	Steve Nash, Pho. Suns
	2013–14 (Mia. Heat)	Kevin Durant, Ok.C. Thunder
	2017–18 (Cle. Cavaliers)	James Harden, Hou. Rockets
	2019–20 (L.A. Lakers)	Giannis Antetokounmpo, Mil. Bucks
3 .... Michael Jordan	1986–87 (Chi. Bulls)	Magic Johnson, L.A. Lakers
	1988–89 (Chi. Bulls)	Magic Johnson, L.A. Lakers
	1996–97 (Chi. Bulls)	Karl Malone, Uta. Jazz
3 .... Kevin Durant	2009–10 (Ok.C. Thunder)	LeBron James, Cle. Cavaliers
	2011–12 (Ok.C. Thunder)	LeBron James, Mia. Heat
	2012–13 (Ok.C. Thunder)	LeBron James, Mia. Heat
3 .... James Harden	2014–15 (Hou. Rockets)	Stephen Curry, G.S. Warriors
	2016–17 (Hou. Rockets)	Russell Westbrook, Ok.C. Thunder
	2018–19 (Hou. Rockets)	Giannis Antetokounmpo, Mil. Bucks
2 .... Bob Pettit	1956–57 (St.L. Hawks)	Bob Cousy, Bos. Celtics
	1960–61 (St.L. Hawks)	Bill Russell, Bos. Celtics
2 .... Bill Russell	1958–59 (Bos. Celtics)	Bob Pettit, St.L. Hawks
	1959–60 (Bos. Celtics)	Wilt Chamberlain, Phi. Warriors
2 .... Wilt Chamberlain	1961–62 (Phi. Warriors)	Bill Russell, Bos. Celtics
	1963–64 (Phi. Warriors)	Oscar Robertson, Cin. Royals
2 .... Julius Erving	1972–73 (Vir. Squires[a])	Billy Cunningham, Car. Cougars[a]
	1979–80 (Phi. 76ers)	Kareem Abdul-Jabbar, L.A. Lakers
2 .... Bob McAdoo	1973–74 (Buf. Braves)	Kareem Abdul-Jabbar, Mil. Bucks
	1975–76 (Buf. Braves)	Kareem Abdul-Jabbar, L.A. Lakers
2 .... George Gervin	1977–78 (S.A. Spurs)	Bill Walton, Por. Blazers
	1978–79 (S.A. Spurs)	Moses Malone, Hou. Rockets
2 .... Magic Johnson	1984–85 (L.A. Lakers)	Larry Bird, Bos. Celtics
	1990–91 (L.A. Laketrs)	Michael Jordan, Chi. Bulls
2 .... David Robinson	1993–94 (S.A. Spurs)	Hakeem Olajuwon, Hou. Rockets
	1995–96 (S.A. Spurs)	Michael Jordan, Chi. Bulls
2 .... Shaquille O'Neal	1994–95 (Orl. Magic)	David Robinson, S.A. Spurs
	2004–05 (Mia. Heat)	Steve Nash, Pho. Suns
2 .... Kevin Garnett	1999–00 (Min. T'Wolves)	Shaquille O'Neal, L.A. Lakers
	2002–03 (Min. T'Wolves)	Tim Duncan, S.A. Spurs
2 .... Tim Duncan	2000–01 (S.A. Spurs)	Allen Iverson, Phi. 76ers
	2003–04 (S.A. Spurs)	Kevin Garnett, Min. T'Wolves
2 .... Joel Embiid	2020–21 (Phi. 76ers)	Nikola Jokić, Den. Nuggets
	2021–22 (Phi. 76ers)	Nikola Jokić, Den. Nuggets

[a] ABA.

Left-Handed MVPs

1957–58	Bill Russell, Bos. Celtics		1971–72	Artis Gilmore, Ken. Colonels[a]
1960–61	Bill Russell, Bos. Celtics		1972–73	Dave Cowens, Bos. Celtics
1961–62	Bill Russell, Bos. Celtics		1972–73	Billy Cunningham, Car. Cougars[a]
1962–63	Bill Russell, Bos. Celtics		1994–95	David Robinson, S.A. Spurs
1964–65	Bill Russell, Bos. Celtics		2017–18	James Harden, Hou. Rockets
1969–70	Willis Reed, N.Y. Knicks			

a ABA.

Lowest Points Average in Season Winning MVP Award

13.8.................... West Unseld, Bal. Bullets, 1968–69
14.1.................... Bill Russell, Bos. Celtics, 1964–65
15.5.................... Steve Nash, Pho. Suns, 2004–05
16.6.................... Bill Russell, Bos. Celtics, 1957–58
16.8.................... Bill Russell, Bos. Celtics, 1962–63
16.9.................... Bill Russell, Bos. Celtics, 1960–61
18.8.................... Steve Nash, Pho. Suns, 2005–06
18.9.................... Bill Walton, Por. Blazers, 1977–78
18.9.................... Bill Russell, Bos. Celtics, 1961–62
20.5.................... Dave Cowens, Bos. Celtics, 1972–73
20.6.................... Bob Cousy, Bos. Celtics, 1956–57
21.0.................... Mel Daniels, Ind. Pacers[a], 1970–71
21.7.................... Willis Reed, N.Y. Knicks, 1969–70
[a] ABA.

Highest Points Average in Season Winning MVP Award

37.6 .... Wilt Chamberlain, Phi. Warriors, 1959–60
35.0 .... Michael Jordan, Chi. Bulls, 1987–88
34.8 .... Kareem Abdul-Jabbar, Mil. Bucks, 1971–72
34.5 .... Bob McAdoo, Buf. Braves, 1974–75
33.5 .... Wilt Chamberlain, Phi. 76ers, 1965–66
32.0 .... Kevin Durant, Ok.C. Thunder, 2013–14
31.7 .... Kareem Abdul-Jabbar, Mil. Bucks, 1970–71
31.6 .... Russell Westbrook, Ok.C. Thunder, 2016–17
31.5 .... Michael Jordan, Chi. Bulls, 1990–91
31.4 .... Oscar Robertson, Cin. Royals, 1963–64
31.1 .... Moses Malone, Hou. Rockets, 1981–82
31.1 .... Allen Iverson, Phi. 76ers, 2000–01
30.4 .... Michael Jordan, Chi. Bulls, 1995–96
30.4 .... James Harden, Hou. Rockets, 2017–18
30.1 .... Michael Jordan, Chi. Bulls, 1991–92
30.1 .... Stephen Curry, G.S. Warriors, 2015–16
30.0 .... Spencer Haywood, Den. Rockets[a], 1969–70
[a] ABA.

Lowest Rebound Average in Season Winning MVP Award

3.3...................... Steve Nash, Pho. Suns, 2004–05
3.8...................... Allen Iverson, Phi. 76ers, 2000–01
4.1...................... Derrick Rose, Chi. Bulls, 2010–11
4.2...................... Steve Nash, Pho. Suns, 2005–06
4.3...................... Stephen Curry, G.S. Warriors, 2014–15
4.8...................... Bob Cousy, Bos. Celtics, 1956–57
5.4...................... James Harden, Hou. Rockets, 2017–18
5.4...................... Stephen Curry, G.S. Warriors, 2015–16
5.5...................... Michael Jordan, Chi. Bulls, 1987–88
5.8...................... Michael Jordan, Chi. Bulls, 1997–98
6.0...................... Michael Jordan, Chi. Bulls, 1990–91
6.3...................... Kobe Bryant, L.A. Lakers, 2007–08
6.3...................... Magic Johnson, L.A. Lakers, 1986–87
6.4...................... Michael Jordan, Chi. Bulls, 1991–92
6.6...................... Magic Johnson, L.A. Lakers, 1989–90
6.6...................... Michael Jordan, Chi. Bulls, 1995–96

Highest Rebound Average in Season Winning MVP Award

27.0 .... Wilt Chamberlain, Phi. Warriors, 1959–60
24.6 .... Wilt Chamberlain, Phi. 76ers, 1965–66
24.2 .... Wilt Chamberlain, Phi. 76ers, 1966–67
24.1 .... Bill Russell, Bos. Celtics, 1964–65
23.9 .... Bill Russell, Bos. Celtics, 1960–61
23.8 .... Wilt Chamberlain, Phi. 76ers, 1967–68
23.6 .... Bill Russell, Bos. Celtics, 1962–63
23.6 .... Bill Russell, Bos. Celtics, 1961–62
22.7 .... Bill Russell, Bos. Celtics, 1957–58
19.5 .... Spencer Haywood, Den. Rockets[a], 1969–70
18.2 .... Wes Unseld, Bal. Bullets, 1968–69
18.0 .... Mel Daniels, Ind. Pacers[a], 1970–71
[a] ABA.

Lowest Assist Average in Season Winning MVP Award

1.3............... Moses Malone, Phi. 76ers, 1982–83
1.5............... Mel Daniels, Ind. Pacers[a], 1968–69
1.8............... Moses Malone, Hou. Rockets, 1978–79
1.8............... Moses Malone, Hou. Rockets, 1981–82
2.0............... Willis Reed, N.Y. Knicks, 1969–70
2.2............... Bob McAdoo, Buf. Braves, 1974–75
2.3............... Wilt Chamberlain, Phi. Warriors, 1959–60
2.3............... Spencer Haywood, Den. Rockets[a], 1969–70
2.6............... Wes Unseld, Bal. Bullets, 1968–69
2.6............... Bob Pettit, St.L. Hawks, 1955–56

Highest Assist Average in Season Winning MVP Award

12.8 .... Magic Johnson, L.A. Lakers, 1988–89
12.2 .... Magic Johnson, L.A. Lakers, 1986–87
11.5 .... Magic Johnson, L.A. Lakers, 1989–90
11.5 .... Steve Nash, Pho. Suns, 2004–05
11.0 .... Oscar Robertson, Cin. Royals, 1963–64
10.5 .... Steve Nash, Pho. Suns, 2005–06
10.4 .... Russell Westbrook, Ok.C. Thunder, 2016–17
8.8............ James Harden, Hou. Rockets, 2017–18
8.6............ Wilt Chamberlain, Phi. 76ers, 1967–68
8.6............ LeBron James, Cle. Cavaliers, 2009–10

continued on next page

Lowest Assist Average in Season Winning MVP Award

2.7 .... Artis Gilmore, Ken. Colonels[a], 1971–72
2.9 .... Bill Russell, Bos. Celtics, 1957–56
2.9 .... David Robinson, S.A. Spurs, 1994–95
[a] ABA.

Highest Assist Average in Season Winning MVP Award

8.3 .... Nikola Jokić, Den. Nuggets, 2020–21
7.9 .... Nikola Jokić, Den. Nuggets, 2021–22
7.8 .... Wilt Chamberlain, Phi. 76ers, 1966–67
7.7 .... Derrick Rose, Chi. Bulls, 2010–11
7.7 .... Stephen Curry, G.S. Warriors, 2014–15
7.5 .... Bob Cousy, Bos. Celtics, 1956–57

Lowest Blocks Average in Season Winning MVP Award

0.1 .... Steve Nash, Pho. Suns, 2004–05
0.2 .... Steve Nash, Pho. Suns, 2005–06
0.2 .... Stephen Curry, G.S. Warriors, 2014–15
0.2 .... Stephen Curry, G.S. Warriors, 2015–16
0.3 .... Magic Johnson, L.A. Lakers, 1988–89
0.3 .... Allen Iverson, Phi. 76ers, 2000–01
0.4 .... Magic Johnson, L.A. Lakers, 1989–90
0.4 .... Russell Westbrook, Ok.C. Thunder, 2016–17
0.5 .... Magic Johnson, L.A. Lakers, 1986–87
0.5 .... Michael Jordan, Chi. Bulls, 1995–96
0.5 .... Michael Jordan, Chi. Bulls, 1997–98
0.5 .... Kobe Bryant, L.A. Lakers, 2007–08
0.6 .... Larry Bird, Bos. Celtics, 1985–86
0.6 .... Karl Malone, Uta. Jazz, 1996–97
0.6 .... Karl Malone, Uta. Jazz, 1998–99
0.6 .... Derrick Rose, Chi. Bulls, 2010–11
0.7 .... George McGinnis, Ind. Pacers[a], 1974–75
0.7 .... Kevin Durant, Ok.C. Thunder, 2013–14
0.7 .... James Harden, Hou. Rockets, 2017–18
0.7 .... Nikola Jokić, Den. Nuggets, 2020–21
0.8 .... Dirk Nowitzki, Dal. Mavericks, 2006–07
0.8 .... LeBron James, Mia. Heat, 2011–12
0.9 .... Larry Bird, Bos. Celtics, 1983–84
0.9 .... Michael Jordan, Chi. Bulls, 1991–92
0.9 .... LeBron James, Mia. Heat, 2012–13
0.9 .... Nikola Jokić, Den. Nuggets, 2021–22
[a] ABA.

Highest Blocks Average in Season Winning MVP Award

5.0 .... Artis Gilmore, Ken. Colonels[a], 1971–72
4.1 .... Kareem Abdul-Jabbar, L.A. Lakers, 1975–76
3.7 .... Hakeem Olajuwon, Hou. Rockets, 1993–94
3.5 .... Kareem Abdul-Jabbar, Mil. Bucks, 1973–74
3.4 .... Kareem Abdul-Jabbar, L.A. Lakers, 1979–80
3.2 .... Kareem Abdul-Jabbar, L.A. Lakers, 1976–77
3.2 .... David Robinson, S.A. Spurs, 1994–95
3.0 .... Shaquille O'Neal, L.A. Lakers, 1999–00
2.9 .... Tim Duncan, S.A. Spurs, 2002–03
2.5 .... Bill Walton, Por. Blazers, 1977–78
2.5 .... Tim Duncan, S.A. Spurs, 2001–02
2.4 .... Julius Erving, N.Y. Nets[a], 1973–74
2.2 .... Kevin Garnett, Min. T'Wolves, 2003–04
2.1 .... Bob McAdoo, Buf. Braves, 1974–75
[a] ABA.

Lowest Steals Average in Season Winning MVP Award

0.5 .... Shaquille O'Neal, L.A. Lakers, 1999–00
0.7 .... Tim Duncan, S.A. Spurs, 2001–02
0.7 .... Tim Duncan, S.A. Spurs, 2002–03
0.7 .... Dirk Nowitzki, Dal. Mavericks, 2006–07
0.8 .... Steve Nash, Pho. Suns, 2005–06
0.9 .... Moses Malone, Hou. Rockets, 1981–82
1.0 .... Bill Walton, Por. Blazers, 1977–78
1.0 .... Moses Malone, Hou. Rockets, 1978–79
1.0 .... Kareem Abdul-Jabbar, L.A. Lakers, 1979–80
1.0 .... Steve Nash, Pho. Suns, 2004–05
1.0 .... Derrick Rose, Chi. Bulls, 2010–11
1.0 .... Giannis Antetokounmpo, Mil. Bucks, 2019–20

Highest Steals Average in Season Winning MVP Award

3.2 .... Michael Jordan, Chi. Bulls, 1987–88
2.7 .... Michael Jordan, Chi. Bulls, 1990–91
2.6 .... Billy Cunningham, Car. Cougars[a], 1972–73
2.6 .... George McGinnis, Ind. Pacers[a], 1974–75
2.5 .... Julius Erving, N.Y. Nets[a], 1975–76
2.5 .... Allen Iverson, Phi. 76ers, 2000–01
2.3 .... Julius Erving, N.Y. Nets[a], 1973–74
2.3 .... Michael Jordan, Chi. Bulls, 1991–92
2.2 .... Julius Erving, N.Y. Nets[a], 1974–75
2.2 .... Michael Jordan, Chi. Bulls, 1995–96
2.1 .... Julius Erving, Phi. 76ers, 1980–81
2.1 .... Stephen Curry, G.S. Warriors, 2015–16
2.0 .... Larry Bird, Bos. Celtics, 1985–86
2.0 .... Stephen Curry, G.S. Warriors, 2014–15
[a] ABA.

Lowest FT% in Season
Winning MVP Award

.380............. Wilt Chamberlain, Phi. 76ers, 1967–68
.441............. Wilt Chamberlain, Phi. 76ers, 1966–67
.513............. Wilt Chamberlain, Phi. 76ers, 1965–66
.519............. Bill Russell, Bos. Celtics, 1957–58
.524............. Shaquille O'Neal, L.A. Lakers, 1999–00
.550............. Bill Russell, Bos. Celtics, 1960–61
.555............. Bill Russell, Bos. Celtics, 1962–63
.573............. Bill Russell, Bos. Celtics, 1964–65
.582............. Wilt Chamberlain, Phi. Warriors, 1959–60
.595............. Bill Russell, Bos. Celtics, 1961–62
.604............. Mel Daniels, Ind. Pacers[a], 1968–69
.605............. Wes Unseld, Bal. Bullets, 1968–69
.633............. Giannis Antetokounmpo, Mil. Bucks, 2019–20
.646............. Artis Gilmore, Ken. Colonels[a], 1971–72
.679............. Mel Daniels, Ind. Pacers[a], 1970–71
.689............. Kareem Abdul-Jabbar, Mil. Bucks, 1971–72
.690............. Kareem Abdul-Jabbar, Mil. Bucks, 1970–71
.701............. Kareem Abdul-Jabbar, L.A. Lakers, 1976–77
.702............. Kareem Abdul-Jabbar, Mil. Bucks, 1973–74
.703............. Kareem Abdul-Jabbar, L.A. Lakers, 1975–76
.710............. Tim Duncan, S.A. Spurs, 2002–03
.716............. Hakeem Olajuwon, Hou. Rockets, 1993–94
.720............. Bill Walton, Por. Blazers, 1977–78
.724............. George McGinnis, Ind. Pacers[a], 1974–75
.729............. Giannis Antetokounmpo, Mil. Bucks, 2018–19
.736............. Bob Pettit, St.L. Hawks, 1955–56
.739............. Moses Malone, Hou. Rockets, 1978–79

[a] ABA.

Highest FT% in Season
Winning MVP Award

.921 .... Steve Nash, Pho. Suns, 2005–06
.914 .... Stephen Curry, G.S. Warriors, 2014–15
.911 .... Magic Johnson, L.A. Lakers, 1988–89
.908 .... Stephen Curry, G.S. Warriors, 2015–16
.904 .... Dirk Nowitzki, Dal. Mavericks, 2006–07
.896 .... Larry Bird, Bos. Celtics, 1985–86
.890 .... Magic Johnson, L.A. Lakers, 1989–90
.888 .... Larry Bird, Bos. Celtics, 1983–84
.887 .... Steve Nash, Pho. Suns, 2004–05
.882 .... Larry Bird, Bos. Celtics, 1984–85
.873 .... Kevin Durant, Ok.C. Thunder, 2013–14
.868 .... Nikola Jokić, Den. Nuggets, 2020–21
.858 .... Derrick Rose, Chi. Bulls, 2010–11
.858 .... James Harden, Hou. Rockets, 2017–18
.853 .... Oscar Robertson, Cin. Royals, 1963–64
.851 .... Michael Jordan, Chi. Bulls, 1990–91
.848 .... Magic Johnson, L.A. Lakers, 1986–87
.845 .... Russell Westbrook, Ok.C. Thunder, 2016–17
.841 .... Michael Jordan, Chi. Bulls, 1987–88
.840 .... Kobe Bryant, L.A. Lakers, 2007–08
.834 .... Michael Jordan, Chi. Bulls, 1995–96
.832 .... Michael Jordan, Chi. Bulls, 1991–92
.821 .... Bob Cousy, Bos. Celtics, 1956–57
.814 .... Allen Iverson, Phi. 76ers, 2000–01
.810 .... Nikola Jokić, Den. Nuggets, 2021–22
.805 .... Bob McAdoo, Buf. Braves, 1974–75
.801 .... Julius Erving, N.Y. Nets[a], 1975–76

[a] ABA.

Winning MVP, Leading League in Points

	Pts
Bob Pettit, St.L. Hawks, 1955–56	1849
Bob Pettit, St.L. Hawks, 1958–59	2105
Wilt Chamberlain, Phi. Warriors, 1959–60	2707
Wilt Chamberlain, Phi. 76ers, 1965–66	2649
Spencer Haywood, Den. Rockets[a], 1969–70	2519
Kareem Abdul-Jabbar, Mil. Bucks, 1970–71	2596
Kareem Abdul-Jabbar, Mil. Bucks, 1971–72	2822
Julius Erving, N.Y. Nets[a], 1973–74	2299
Bob McAdoo, Buf. Braves, 1974–75	2831
George McGinnis*, Ind. Pacers[a], 1974–75	2353
Julius Erving, N.Y. Nets[a], 1975–76	2462
Michael Jordan, Chi. Bulls, 1987–88	2868
Michael Jordan, Chi. Bulls, 1990–91	2580
Michael Jordan, Chi. Bulls, 1991–92	2404
Michael Jordan, Chi. Bulls, 1995–96	2491
Michael Jordan, Chi. Bulls, 1997–98	2357
Shaquille O'Neal, L.A. Lakers, 1999–00	2344
Kevin Garnett, Min. T'Wolves, 2003–04	1987
Kobe Bryant, L.A. Lakers, 2007–08	2323

continued on next page

	Pts
Kevin Durant, Ok.C. Thunder, 2013–14	2593
Russell Westbrook, Ok.C. Thunder, 2016–17	2558

^a ABA.

* Tied with Julius Erving, N.Y. Nets.

Fewest Minutes Played, Winning MVP

MP		GP	MPG
1832	Karl Malone, Uta. Jazz, 1998–99*	49	37.4
1917	Giannis Antetokounmpo, Mil. Bucks, 2019–20**	63	30.4
1929	Bill Walton, Por. Blazers, 1977–78	58	33.3
2326	LeBron James, Mia. Heat, 2011–12	62	37.5
2358	Giannis Antetokounmpo, Mil. Bucks, 2018–19	72	32.8
2364	Bob Cousy, Bos. Celtics, 1956–57	64	36.9
2476	Nikola Jokić, Den. Nuggets, 2021–22	41	33.5
2488	Nikola Jokić, Den. Nuggets, 2020–21	72	34.6
2551	James Harden, Hou. Rockets, 2017–18	72	35.4
2573	Steve Nash, Pho. Suns, 2004–05	75	34.3
2613	Stephen Curry, G.S. Warriors, 2014–15	80	32.7
2640	Bill Russell, Bos. Celtics, 1957–58	69	38.3
2700	Stephen Curry, G.S. Warriors, 2015–16	79	34.2
2794	Bob Pettit, St.L. Hawks, 1955–56	72	38.8
2796	Steve Nash, Pho. Suns, 2005–06	79	35.4
2802	Russell Westbrook, Ok.C. Thunder, 2016–17	81	34.6
2820	Dirk Nowitzki, Dal. Mavericks, 2006–07	78	36.2
2859	Charles Barkley, Pho. Suns, 1992–93	76	37.6
2873	Bob Pettit, St.L. Hawks, 1958–59	72	39.9
2874	Julius Erving, Phi. 76ers, 1980–81	82	35.0
2877	LeBron James, Mia. Heat, 2012–13	76	37.9
2886	Magic Johnson, L.A. Lakers, 1988–89	77	37.5
2904	Magic Johnson, L.A. Lakers, 1986–87	80	36.3
2922	Moses Malone, Phi. 76ers, 1982–83	78	37.5
2934	Mel Daniels, Ind. Pacers^a, 1968–69	76	38.6
2937	Magic Johnson, L.A. Lakers, 1989–90	79	37.2
2966	LeBron James, Cle. Cavaliers, 2009–10	76	39.0
2970	Wes Unseld, Bal. Bullets, 1968–69	82	36.2
2979	Allen Iverson, Phi. 76ers, 2000–01	71	42.0
2998	Karl Malone, Uta. Jazz, 1996–97	82	36.6

* Lockout-shortened season.

** Covid-shortened season.

^a ABA.

Most Turnovers in MVP-Winning Season

438 Russell Westbrook, Ok.C. Thunder, 2016–17	307 Julius Erving, N.Y. Nets^a, 1975–76
422* George McGinnis, Ind. Pacers^a, 1974–75	301 Julius Erving, N.Y. Nets^a, 1974–75
381 Billy Cunningham, Car. Cougars^a, 1972–73	300 Magic Johnson, L.A. Lakers, 1986–87
341 Julius Erving, N.Y. Nets^a, 1973–74	297 Kareem Abdul-Jabbar, L.A. Lakers, 1979–80
335 Artis Gilmore, Ken. Colonels^a, 1971–72	297 Moses Malone, Hou. Rockets, 1981–82
326 Moses Malone, Hou. Rockets, 1978–79	289 Magic Johnson, L.A. Lakers, 1989–90
315 James Harden, Hou. Rockets, 2017–18	285 Kevin Durant, Ok.C. Thunder, 2013–14
312 Magic Johnson, L.A. Lakers, 1988–89	281 Nikola Jokić, Den. Nuggets, 2021–22

continued on next page

278............ Derrick Rose, Chi. Bulls, 2010–11

276............ Steve Nash, Pho. Suns, 2005–06

272............ Mel Daniels, Ind. Pacers^a, 1968–69

271............ Hakeem Olajuwon, Hou. Rockets, 1993–94

268............ Giannis Antetokounmpo, Mil. Bucks, 2018–19

266............ Larry Bird, Bos. Celtics, 1985–86

266............ Julius Erving, Phi. 76ers, 1980–81

264............ Moses Malone, Phi. 76ers, 1982–83

263............ Tim Duncan, S.A. Spurs, 2001–02

262............ Stephen Curry, G.S. Warriors, 2015–16

261............ LeBron James, Cle. Cavaliers, 2009–10

257............ Kobe Bryant, L.A. Lakers, 2007–08

253............ Spencer Haywood, Den. Rockets^a, 1969–70

252............ Michael Jordan, Chi. Bulls, 1987–88

* Led league.

^a ABA.

Teams with Most Different MVPs

4.............76ers ....Wilt Chamberlain (1965–66, 1966–67, 1967–68)

Julius Erving (1980–81)

Moses Malone (1982–83)

Allen Iverson (2000–01)

4.............Celtics ....Bill Russell (1957–58, 1960–61, 1961–62, 1962–63, 1964–65)

Bob Cousy (1956–57)

Dave Cowens (1972–73)

Larry Bird (1983–84, 1984–85, 1985–86)

4.............Lakers................Kareem Abdul-Jabbar (1975–76, 1976–77, 1979–80)

Magic Johnson (1986–87, 1988–89, 1989–90)

Kobe Bryant (2007–08)

Shaquille O'Neal (1999–00)

3.............Rockets..............Moses Malone (1978–79, 1981–82)

Hakeem Olajuwon (1993–94)

James Harden (2017–18)

2.............Bulls..................Michael Jordan (1987–88, 1990–91, 1991–92, 1995–96, 1997–98)

Derrick Rose (2010–11)

2.............Bucks.................Kareem Abdul-Jabbar (1970–71, 1971–72, 1973–74)

Giannis Antetokounmpo (2018–19, 2019–20)

2.............Pacers*...............Mel Daniels (1968–69, 1970–71)

George McGinnis (1974–75**)

2.............Spurs..................David Robinson (1994–95)

Tim Duncan (2001–02, 2002–03)

2.............Suns...................Charles Barkley (1992–93)

Steve Nash (2004–05, 2005–06)

2.............Thunder..............Kevin Durant (2013–14)

Russell Westbrook (2016–17)

2.............Warriors.............Wilt Chamberlain (1959–60)

Stephen Curry (2014–15, 2015–16)

* ABA Pacers. Franchise has not had an NBA MVP.

** Tied with Julius Erving, N.Y. Nets.

Teams with Consecutive MVPs

Bos. Celtics.............. Bob Cousy (1956–57), Bill Russell (1957–58)

Bill Russell (1960–61, 1961–62, 1962–63)

Larry Bird (1983–84, 1984–85, 1985–86)

Phi. 76ers................ Wilt Chamberlain (1965–66, 1966–67, 1967–68)

Mil. Bucks................ Kareem Abdul-Jabbar (1970–71, 1971–72)

Giannis Antetokounmpo (2018–19, 2019–20)

N.Y. Nets^a .... Julius Erving (1973–74, 1974–75*, 1975–76)

continued on next page

L.A. Lakers .... Kareem Abdul-Jabbar (1975–76, 1976–77)

Magic Johnson (1988–89, 1989–90)

Chi. Bulls .... Michael Jordan (1990–91, 1991–92)

S.A. Spurs .... Tim Duncan (2001–02, 2002–03)

Pho. Suns .... Steve Nash (2004–05, 2005–06)

Cle. Cavaliers .... LeBron James (2008–09, 2009–10)

Mia. Heat .... LeBron James (2011–12, 2012–13)

G.S. Warriors .... Stephen Curry (2014–15, 2015–16)

Den. Nuggets .... Nikola Jokić (2020–21, 2021–22)

ᵃ ABA.

ᵇ Tied with George McGinnis, Ind. Pacers

Players Winning League and Finals MVP, Same Season

Connie Hawksins, Pit. Pipersᵃ, 1967–68

Willis Reed, N.Y. Knicks, 1969–70

Kareem Abdul-Jabbar, Mil. Bucks, 1970–71

Julius Erving, N.Y. Netsᵃ, 1973–74

Julius Erving, N.Y. Netsᵃ, 1975–76

Moses Malone, Phi. 76ers, 1982–83

Larry Bird, Bos. Celtics, 1983–84

Larry Bird, Bos. Celtics, 1985–86

Magic Johnson, L.A. Lakers, 1986–87

ᵃ ABA.

Michael Jordan, Chi. Bulls, 1990–91

Michael Jordan, Chi. Bulls, 1991–92

Hakeem Olajuwon, Hou. Rockets, 1993–94

Michael Jordan, Chi. Bulls, 1995–96

Michael Jordan, Chi. Bulls, 1997–98

Shaquille O'Neal, L.A. Lakers, 1999–00

Tim Duncan, S.A. Spurs, 2002–03

LeBron James, Mia. Heat, 2011–12

LeBron James, Mia. Heat, 2012–13

Rookie of the Year (ROY)

ROY on Team Other Than the One Drafted By

Drafted By

1947–48 .... Paul Hoffman, Bal. Bullets .... Tor. Huskies (5th Round) .... Tor. Huskies folded before season; signed with Bal. Bullets.

1993–94 .... Chris Webber, G.S. Warriors .... Orl. Magic (1st Round, 1st Pick) .... Traded by Orl. Magic, on draft day, to G.S. Warriors.

1998–99 .... Vince Carter, Tor. Raptors .... G.S. Warriors (1st Round, 5th Pick) ...... Traded by G.S. Warriors, on draft day, to Tor. Raptors.

1999–00 .... Steve Francis, Hou. Rockets .... Van. Grizzlies (1st Round, 2nd Pick) ..... Traded by Van. Grizzlies to Hou. Rockets (in three-team trade with Orl. Magic).

2001–02 .... Pau Gasol, Mem. Grizzlies .... Atl. Hawks (1st Round, 3rd Pick) .... Traded by Atl. Hawks, on draft day, to (then) Van. Grizzlies.

2006–07 .... Brandon Roy, Por. Blazers .... Min. T'Wolves (1st Round, 6th Pick) ..... Traded by Min. T'Wolves, on draft day, to Por. Blazers.

2014–15 .... Andrew Wiggins, Min. T'Wolves .... Cle. Cavaliers (1st Round, 1st Pick) ...... Traded by Cle. Cavaliers to Min. T'Wolves (in three-team trade with Phi. 76ers).

2018–19 .... Luka Dončić, Dal. Mavericks .... Atl. Hawks (1st Round, 3rd Pick) .... Traded by Atl. Hawks, on draft day, to Dal. Mavericks.

Teams with Consecutive ROY Award Winners

Chi. Packers-Zephyrs .... Walt Bellamy (1961–62), Terry Dischinger (1962–63)

Bal. Bullets .... Earl Monroe (1967–68), Wes Unseld (1968–69)

continued on next page

Por. Blazers .... Geoff Petrie* (1970–71), Sidney Wicks (1971–72)
Ken. Colonels° .... Dan Issel** (1970–71), Artis Gilmore (1971–72)
Buf. Braves .... Bob McAdoo (1972–73), Ernie DiGregorio (1973–74)
Mil. Bucks .... Andrew Wiggins (2014–15), Karl-Anthony Towns (2015–16)
* Tied with Dave Cowens, Bos. Celtics.
** Tied with Charlie Scott, Vir. Squires.
° ABA.

ROY Born Outside the Continental United States

		Country
1985–86	Patrick Ewing, N.Y. Knicks	Jamaica
1997–98	Tim Duncan, S.A. Spurs	U.S. Virgin Islands
2001–02	Pau Gasol, Mem. Grizzles	Spain
2011–12	Kyrie Irving, Cle. Cavaliers	Australia
2014–15	Andrew Wiggins, Min. T'Wolves	Canada
2017–18	Ben Simmons, Phi. 76ers	Australia
2018–19	Luka Dončić, Dal. Mavericks	Slovenia

Players Winning ROY and Team Winning Championship, Same Season

1947–48 .... Paul Hoffman, Bal. Bullets
1956–57 .... Tom Heinsohn, Bos. Celtics
° ABA.

1968–69 .... Warren Jabali, Oak. Oaks°
1974–75 .... Jamaal Wilkes, G.S. Warriors

Winning ROY, Leading League in . . .

Points .... 1959–60: Wilt Chamberlain, Phi. Warriors (2707)
 1969–70: Kareem Abdul-Jabbar, Mil. Bucks (2361)
 1969–70: Spencer Haywood, Den. Rockets° (2519)
 1970–71: Dan Issel, Ken. Colonels° (2480)
 1984–85: Michael Jordan, Chi. Bulls (2313)

Field Goals Made .... 1959–60: Wilt Chamberlain, Phi. Warriors (1065)
 1967–68: Mel Daniels, Min. Muskies° (669)
 1969–70: Kareem Abdul-Jabbar, Mil. Bucks (938)
 1969–70: Spencer Haywood, Den. Rockets° (986)
 1970–71: Dan Issel, Ken. Colonels° (938)

Field Goals Attempted .... 1959–60: Wilt Chamberlain, Phi. Warriors (2311)
 1967–68: Mel Daniels, Min. Muskies° (1640)
 1969–70: Spencer Haywood, Den. Rockets° (1998)

Free Throws Attempted .... 1959–60: Wilt Chamberlain, Phi. Warriors (991)

Assists ....1960–61: Oscar Robertson, Cin. Royals (690)
 1973–74: Ernie DiGregorio, Buf. Braves (663)

Total Rebounds .... 1951–52: Mel Hutchins*, Mil. Hawks (880)
 1959–60: Wilt Chamberlain, Phi. Warriors (1941)
 1967–68: Mel Daniels, Min. Muskies° (1213)
 1969–70: Spencer Haywood, Den. Rockets° (1637)
 1971–72: Artis Gilmore, Ken. Colonels° (1491)

Offensive Rebounds .... 1967–68: Mel Daniels, Min. Muskies° (502)
 1969–70: Spencer Haywood, Den. Rockets° (533)
 1999–00: Elton Brand, Chi. Bulls (348)

Defensive Rebounds .... 1967–68: Mel Daniels, Min. Muskies° (711)
 1969–70: Spencer Haywood, Den. Rockets° (1104)

continued on next page

1971–72: Artis Gilmore, Ken. Colonels[a] (1070)

Steals ....2005–06: Chris Paul, N.O.-Ok.C. Hornets (175)

Blocks...................................1971–72: Artis Gilmore, Ken. Colonels[a] (422)

Fouls ....1952–53: Monk Meineke, Ft.W. Pistons (334)

1970–71: Dave Cowens, Bos. Celtics (350)

Turnovers ....1992–93: Shaquille O'Neal, Orl. Magic (307)

1996–97: Allen Iverson, Phi. 76ers (337)

Minutes Played ....1959–60: Wilt Chamberlain, Phi. Warriors (3338)

1969–70: Spencer Haywood, Den. Rockets[a] (3808)

1971–72: Artis Gilmore, Ken. Colonels[a] (3666)

2012–13: Damian Lillard, Por. Blazers (3167)

Field Goal Percentage.............1949–50: Alex Groza, Ind. Olympians (.478)

1961–62: Walt Bellamy, Chi. Packers (.519)

1963–64: Jerry Lucas, Cin. Royals (.527)

1971–72: Artis Gilmore, Ken. Colonels[a] (.598)

1973–74: Swen Nater, Vir. Squires[a]/S.A. Spurs[a] (.552)

Points Average ....1959–60: Wilt Chamberlain, Phi. Warriors (37.6)

1969–70: Spencer Haywood, Den. Rockets[a] (30.0)

1970–71: Dan Issel, Ken. Colonels[a] (29.9)

Free Throw Percentage ....1973–74: Ernie DiGregorio, Buf. Braves (.902)

Assists Average ....1960–61: Oscar Robertson, Cin. Royals (9.7)

1973–74: Ernie DiGregorio, Buf. Braves (8.2)

Rebounds Average..................1955–56: Maurice Stokes, Roc. Royals (16.3)

1959–60: Wilt Chamberlain, Phi. Warriors (27.0)

1967–68: Mel Daniels, Min. Muskies[a] (15.6)

1969–70: Spencer Haywood, Den. Rockets[a] (19.5)

1971–72: Artis Gilmore, Ken. Colonels[a] (17.8)

Minutes Average.....................1959–60: Wilt Chamberlain, Phi. Warriors (46.4)

1969–70: Spencer Haywood, Den. Rockets[a] (45.3)

* Tied for Rookie of the Year with Bill Tosheff, Ind. Olympians.

[a] ABA.

Winning ROY, Making All-Star Team

1950–51	Paul Arizin, Phi. Warriors	1970-71[a]	Dan Issel*, Ken. Colonels
1953–54	Ray Felix, Bal. Bullets	1971–72	Sidney Wicks, Por. Blazers
1954–55	Bob Pettit, Mil. Hawks	1971-72[a]	Artis Gilmore, Ken. Colonels
1955–56	Maurice Stokes, Roc. Royals	1973-74[a]	Swen Nater, Vir. Squires/S.A. Spurs
1956–57	Tom Heinsohn, Bos. Celtics	1974-75[a]	Marvin Barnes, Spirits of St.L.
1958–59	Elgin Baylor, Min. Lakers	1975–76	Alvan Adams, Pho. Suns
1959–60	Wilt Chamberlain, Phi. Warriors	1975-76[a]	David Thompson, Den. Nuggets
1960–61	Oscar Robertson, Cin. Royals	1977–78	Walter Davis, Pho. Suns
1961–62	Walt Bellamy, Chi. Packers	1979–80	Larry Bird, Bos. Celtics
1962–63	Terry Dischinger, Chi. Zephyrs	1981–82	Buck Williams, N.J. Nets
1963–64	Jerry Lucas, Cin. Royals	1983–84	Ralph Sampson, Hou. Rockets
1964–65	Willis Reed, N.Y. Knicks	1984–85	Michael Jordan, Chi. Bulls
1965–66	Rick Barry, S.F. Warriors	1985–86	Patrick Ewing, N.Y. Knicks
1968–69	Wes Unseld, Bal. Bullets	1989–90	David Robinson, S.A. Spurs
1969–70	Kareem Abdul-Jabbar, Mil. Bucks	1992–93	Shaquille O'Neal, Orl. Magic
1969-70[a]	Spencer Haywood, Den. Rockets	1994–95	Grant Hill, Det. Pistons
1970–71	Geoff Petrie, Por. Blazers	1997–98	Tim Duncan, S.A. Spurs
1970-71[a]	Charlie Scott*, Vir. Squires	2010–11	Blake Griffin, L.A. Clippers

* Tied for Rookie of the Year.

[a] ABA.

Least Amount of Points Scored, Winning ROY

767.......... Malcolm Brogdon, Mil. Bucks, 2016–17
803........... LaMelo Ball, Cha. Hornets, 2020–21
912.......... Woody Sauldsberry, Phi. Warriors, 1957–58
913.......... Vince Carter, Tor. Raptors, 1998–99
922.......... Jason Kidd, Dal. Mavericks, 1994–95
944.......... Kyrie Irving, Cle. Cavaliers, 2011–12
955.......... Brandon Roy, Por. Blazers, 2006–07
962.......... Brian Taylor, N.Y. Nets[a], 1972–73
975.......... Mike Miller, Orl. Magic, 2000–01
998.......... Patrick Ewing, N.Y. Knicks, 1985–86
1105.......... Emeka Okafor, Cha. Bobcats, 2004–05

[a] ABA.
1998–99: 50-game season.
2011–12: 66-game season.
2019–20: 65-to-75-game season.
2020–21: 72-game season.

1106.......... Amar'e Stoudemire, Pho. Suns, 2002–03
1114.......... Mark Jackson, N.Y. Knicks, 1987–88
1114.......... Swen Nater, Vir. Squires[a]/S.A. Spurs[a], 1973–74
1125.......... Maurice Stokes, Roc. Royals, 1955–56
1131.......... Wes Unseld, Bal. Bullets, 1968–69
1134.......... Scottie Barnes, Tor. Raptors, 2021–22
1163.......... Tom Heinsohn, Bos. Celtics, 1956–57
1164.......... Jamaal Wilkes, G.S. Warriors, 1974–75
1167.......... Michael Carter-Williams, Phi. 76ers, 2013–14
1193.......... Ja Morant, Mem. Grizzlies, 2019–20

Lowest FT%, Winning ROY

.532 .... Chris Webber, G.S. Warriors, 1993–94
.560 .... Ben Simmons, Phi. 76ers, 2017–18
.575 .... Mel Daniels, Min. Muskies[a], 1967–68
.582 .... Wilt Chamberlain, Phi. Warriors, 1959–60
.592 .... Shaquille O'Neal, Orl. Magic, 1992–93
.605 .... Wes Unseld, Bal. Bullets, 1968–69
.609 .... Emeka Okafor, Cha. Bobcats, 2004–05
.615 .... Woody Sauldsberry, Phi. Warriors, 1957–58
.624 .... Buck Williams, N.J. Nets, 1981–82
.638 .... Ray Felix, Bal. Bullets, 1953–54
.642 .... Blake Griffin, L.A. Clippers, 2010–11
.644 .... Walt Bellamy, Chi. Packers, 1961–62
.644 .... Mel Hutchins, Mil. Hawks, 1951–52
.646 .... Artis Gilmore, Ken. Colonels[a], 1971–72
.653 .... Kareem Abdul-Jabbar, Mil. Bucks, 1969–70
.661 .... Amar'e Stoudemire, Pho. Suns, 2002–03
.661 .... Ralph Sampson, Hou. Rockets, 1983–84
.662 .... Tim Duncan, S.A. Spurs, 1997–98
.662 .... Paul Hoffman, Bal. Bullets, 1947–48
.670 .... Marvin Barnes, Spirits of St.L.[a], 1974–75
.684 .... Warren Jabali, Oak. Oaks[a], 1968–69
.685 .... Elton Brand, Chi. Bulls, 1999–00
.698 .... Jason Kidd, Dal. Mavericks, 1994–95

[a] ABA.

Highest FT%, Winning ROY

.902 .... Ernie DiGregorio, Buf. Braves, 1973–74
.873 .... Kevin Durant, Sea. Sonics, 2007–08
.872 .... Kyrie Irving, Cle. Cavaliers, 2011–12
.865 .... Malcolm Brogdon, Mil. Bucks, 2016–17
.862 .... Rick Barry, S.F. Warriors, 1965–66
.847 .... Chris Paul, N.O.-Ok.C. Hornets, 2005–06
.845 .... Michael Jordan, Chi. Bulls, 1984–85
.844 .... Damian Lillard, Por. Blazers, 2012–13
.838 .... Brandon Roy, Por. Blazers, 2006–07
.836........... Larry Bird, Bos. Celtics, 1979–80
.830 .... Walter Davis, Pho. Suns, 1977–78
.829 .... Larry Johnson, Cha. Hornets, 1991–92
.824 .... Bill Tosheff, Ind. Olympians, 1951–52
.822 .... Oscar Robertson, Cin. Royals, 1960–61
.818 .... Adrian Dantley, Buf. Braves, 1976–77
.813 .... Phil Ford, K.C. Kings, 1978–79
.811 .... Karl-Anthony Towns, Min. T'Wolves, 2015–16
.810 .... Mitch Richmond, G.S. Warriors, 1988–89
.807 .... Dan Issel, Ken. Colonels[a], 1970–71
.804 .... Howie Shannon, Pro. Steamrollers, 1948–49

[a] ABA.

Defensive Player of the Year (DPOY)

Players Winning Multiple DPOY Awards

Dikembe Mutombo .... Den. Nuggets, 1994–95
Atl. Hawks, 1996–97, 1997–98
Atl. Hawks/Phi. 76ers, 2000–01

continued on next page

Ben Wallace..................... Det. Pistons, 2001–02
                              Det. Pistons, 2002–03
                              Det. Pistons, 2004–05
                              Det. Pistons, 2005–06
Dwight Howard............... Orl. Magic, 2008–09
                              Orl. Magic, 2009–10
                              Orl. Magic, 2010–11
Mark Eaton .... Uta. Jazz, 1984–85
                              Uta. Jazz, 1988–89
Sidney Moncrief .... Mil. Bucks, 1982–83
                              Mil. Bucks, 1983–84
Dennis Rodman .... Det. Pistons, 1989–90
                              Det. Pistons, 1990–91
Hakeem Olajuwon............ Hou. Rockets, 1992–93
                              Hou. Rockets, 1993–94
Alonzo Mourning .... Mia. Heat, 1998–99
                              Mia Heat, 1999–00
Kawhi Leonard .... S.A. Spurs, 2014–15
                              S.A. Spurs, 2015–16
Rudy Gobert.................... Uta. Jazz, 2017–18
                              Uta. Jazz, 2018–19

Players Winning Consecutive DOPY Awards

3 .... Dwight Howard............ Orl. Magic: 2008–09, 2009–10, 2010–11
2 .... Sidney Moncrief........... Mil. Bucks: 1982–83, 1983–84
2 .... Dennis Rodman............ Det. Pistons: 1989–90, 1990–91
2 .... Hakeem Olajuwon........ Hou. Rockets: 1992–93, 1993–94
2 .... Dikembe Mutombo .... Atl. Hawks: 1996–97, 1997–98
2 .... Alonzo Mourning .... Mia. Heat: 1998–99, 1999–00
2 .... Ben Wallace................. Det. Pistons: 2004–05, 2005–06
2 .... Kawhi Leonard............. S.A. Spurs: 2014–15, 2015–16
2 .... Rudy Gobert .... Uta. Jazz: 2017–18, 2018–19

Sixth Man of the Year

Players Winning Multiple Sixth Man of the Year Awards

Kevin McHale..................... Bos. Celtics, 1983–84
                              Bos. Celtics, 1984–85
Ricky Pierce......................... Mil. Bucks, 1986–87
                              Mil. Bucks, 1989–90
Detlef Schrempf .... Ind. Pacers, 1990–91
                              Ind. Pacers, 1991–92
Jamal Crawford .... Atl. Hawks, 2009–10
                              L.A. Clippers, 2013–14
                              L.A. Clippers, 2015–16
Lou Williams .... Tor. Raptors, 2014–15
                              L.A. Clippers, 2017–18
                              L.A. Clippers, 2018–19

Players Winning Consecutve Sixth Man Awards

Kevin McHale.............. Bos. Celtics: 1983–84, 1984–85
Detlef Schrempf .... Ind. Pacers: 1990–91, 1991–92
Lou Williams .... L.A. Clippers: 2017–18, 2018–19

Players Winning Sixth Man, Winning Additional Award in Other Seasons

Sixth Man	Additional Award
Bill Walton, Bos. Celtics, 1985–86 ....MVP: Por. Blazers, 1977–78	
Mike Miller, Mem. Grizzlies, 2005–06 ....ROY: Orl. Magic, 2000–01	
James Harden, Ok.C. Thunder, 2011–12 ....MVP: Hou. Rockets, 2017–18	

Highest PPG, Winning Sixth Man Award

PPG		MPG
23.0 .... Ricky Pierce, Mil. Bucks, 1989–90...............	29.0
22.6 .... Lou Williams, L.A. Clippers, 2017–18	32.8
21.5 .... Eddie Johnson, Pho. Suns, 1988–89............	29.2
20.7 .... Tyler Herro, Mia. Heat, 2021–22................	32.6
20.0 .... Lou Williams, L.A. Clippers, 2018–19	26.6
19.8 .... Kevin McHale, Bos. Celtics, 1984–85..........	33.6
19.6 .... Jason Terry, Dal. Mavericks, 2008–09	33.7
19.5 .... Ricky Pierce, Mil. Bucks, 1986–87..............	31.7
19.5 .... Manu Ginóbili, S.A. Spurs, 2007–08	31.1
19.1 .... Clifford Robinson, Por. Blazers, 1992–93.....	31.4
18.6 .... Jamal Crawford, L.A. Clippers, 2013–14.....	30.3
18.6 .... Montrezl Harrell, L.A. Clippers, 2019–20.....	27.8
18.4 .... Kevin McHale, Bos. Celtics, 1983–84..........	31.4
18.4 .... Jordan Clarkson, Uta. Jazz, 2020–21..........	26.7
18.1 .... Leandro Barbosa, Pho. Suns, 2006–07	32.7
18.1 .... J.R. Smith, N.Y. Knicks, 2012–13	33.5
18.0 .... Jamal Crawford, Atl. Hawks, 2009–10	31.1

All-League First Team

Most First-Team All-League Appearances, Career

13	LeBron James^	10	Elgin Baylor	9	Larry Bird
11	Kobe Bryant	10	Michael Jordan	9	Rick Barry*
11	Karl Malone	10	Bob Pettit	9	Julius Erving*
10	Kareem Abdul-Jabbar	10	Bob Cousy	8	Shaquille O'Neal
10	Jerry West	9	Oscar Robertson	7	Wilt Chamberlain

^Active.

* Four in ABA and five in NBA.

Most Consecutive First-Team All-League Appearances
NBA

11..... Karl Malone..................... 1988–89, 1989–90, 1990–91, 1991–92, 1992–93, 1993–94, 1994–95, 1995–96, 1996–97, 1997–98, 1998–99

11..... LeBron James 2007–08, 2008–09, 2009–10, 2010–11, 2011–12, 2012–13, 2013–14, 2014–15, 2015–16, 2016–17, 2017–18

10..... Bob Cousy...................... 1951–52, 1952–53, 1953–54, 1954–55, 1955–56, 1956–57, 1957–58, 1958–59, 1959–60, 1960–61

9..... Bob Pettit 1955–56, 1956–57, 1957–58, 1958–59, 1959–60, 1960–61, 1961–62, 1962–63, 1963–64

9..... Oscar Robertson.............. 1960–61, 1961–62, 1962–63, 1963–64, 1964–65, 1965–66, 1966–67, 1967–68, 1968–69

9..... Larry Bird 1979–80, 1980–81, 1981–82, 1982–83, 1983–84, 1984–85, 1985–86, 1986–87, 1987–88

9..... Magic Johnson................ 1982–83, 1983–84, 1984–85, 1985–86, 1986–87, 1987–88, 1988–89, 1989–90, 1990–91

8..... Tim Duncan..................... 1997–98, 1998–99, 1999–00, 2000–01, 2001–02, 2002–03, 2003–04, 2004–05

continued on next page

8....... Kobe Bryant..................... 2005–06, 2006–07, 2007–08, 2008–09, 2009–10, 2010–11, 2011–12, 2012–13
7....... Elgin Baylor 1958–59, 1959–60, 1960–61, 1961–62, 1962–63, 1963–64, 1964–65
7....... Michael Jordan 1986–87, 1987–88, 1988–89, 1989–90, 1990–91, 1991–92, 1992–93
7....... Shaquille O'Neal 1999–00, 2000–01, 2001–02, 2002–03, 2003–04, 2004–05, 2005–06
6....... George Mikan 1948–49, 1949–50, 1950–51, 1951–52, 1952–53, 1953–54
6....... Jerry West...................... 1961–62, 1962–63, 1963–64, 1964–65, 1965–66, 1966–67
5....... George Gervin............... 1977–78, 1978–79, 1979–80, 1980–81, 1981–82
5....... Dwight Howard.............. 2007–08, 2008–09, 2009–10, 2010–11, 2011–12
5....... Kevin Durant 2009–10, 2010–11, 2011–12, 2012–13, 2013–14
4....... Max Zaslofsky................ 1946–47, 1947–48, 1948–49, 1949–50
4....... Bob Davies 1948–49, 1949–50, 1950–51, 1951–52
4....... Dolph Schayes 1951–52, 1952–53, 1953–54, 1954–55
4....... Neil Johnston 1952–53, 1953–54, 1954–55, 1955–56
4....... Bill Sharman 1955–56, 1956–57, 1957–58, 1958–59
4....... Kareem Abdul-Jabbar........ 1970–71, 1971–72, 1972–73, 1973–74
4....... John Havlicek.................. 1970–71, 1971–72, 1972–73, 1973–74
4....... Charles Barkley 1987–88, 1988–89, 1989–90, 1990–91
4....... Jason Kidd..................... 1998–99, 1999–00, 2000–01, 2001–02
4....... James Harden 2016–17, 2017–18, 2018–19, 2019–20
4....... Giannis Antetokounmpo 2018–19, 2019–20, 2020–21, 2021–22

ABA

5................ Artis Gilmore...............1971–72, 1972–73, 1973–74, 1974–75, 1975–76
4................ Mel Daniels.................1967–68, 1968–69, 1969–70, 1970–71
4................ Rick Barry 1968–69, 1969–70, 1970–71, 1971–72
4................ Julius Erving 1972–73, 1973–74, 1974–75, 1975–76

Rookies Named to All-League First Team

NBA

1946–47	Bob Feerick, Was. Capitols
1946–47	Joe Fulks, Phi. Warrriors
1946–47	Bones McKinney, Was. Capitols
1946–47	Stan Miasek, Det. Falcons
1946–47	Max Zaslofsky, Chi. Stags
1948–49	Bob Davies, Roc. Royals
1948–49	George Mikan, Min. Lakers
1948–49	Jim Pollard, Min. Lakers
1949–50	Alex Groza*, Ind. Olympians
1954–55	Bob Pettit*, Mil. Hawks
1958–59	Elgin Baylor*, Min. Lakers
1959–60	Wilt Chamberlain*, Phi. Warriors
1960–61	Oscar Robertson*, Cin. Royals
1965–66	Rick Barry*, S.F. Warriors
1968–69	Wes Unseld*, Bal. Bullets
1979–80	Larry Bird*, Bos. Celtics
1997–98	Tim Duncan*, S.A. Spurs

* Rookie of the Year.

ABA

1967–68	Mel Daniels*, Min. Muskies
1967–68	Connie Hawkins, Pip. Pipers
1967–68	Doug Moe, N.O. Buccaneers
1967–68	Charlie Williams, Pit. Pipers
1969–70	Spencer Haywood*, Den. Rockets
1970–71	Charlie Scott**, Vir. Squires
1971–72	Artis Gilmore*, Ken. Colonels

* Rookie of the Year.

** Tied with Dan Issel, Ken. Colonels.

Most Seasons Before First All-League First Team Appearance
NBA

		First Season	All-NBA First Team
10	John Stockton	1984–85	1993–94
9	John Havlicek	1962–63	1970–71
9	Gail Goodrich	1965–66	1973–74
9	Clyde Drexler	1983–84	1991–92
9	Steve Nash	1996–97	2004–05
9	Paul George	2010–11	2018–19
8	Gary Payton	1990–91	1997–98
8	Chris Webber	1993–94	2000–01
8	DeAndre Jordan	2008–09	2015–16
8	Russell Westbrook	2008–09	2015–16
7	Elvin Hayes	1968–69	1974–75
7	Bernard King	1977–78	1983–84
7	Kevin McHale	1980–81	1986–87
7	Chris Mullin	1985–86	1991–92
7	Mark Price	1986–87	1992–93
7	Scottie Pippen	1987–88	1993–94
7	Tim Hardaway*	1989–90	1996–97
7	Alonzo Mourning	1992–93	1998–99
7	Dirk Nowitzki	1998–99	2004–05
7	Joakim Noah	2007–08	2013–14
7	Marc Gasol	2008–09	2014–15
7	Devin Booker	2015–16	2021–22
6	Harry Gallatin	1948–49	1953–54
6	Bill Sharman	1950–51	1955–56
6	Gene Shue	1954–55	1959–60
6	Willis Reed	1964–65	1969–70
6	Pete Maravich	1970–71	1975–76
6	George Gervin**	1972–73	1977–78
6	Gus Williams***	1975–76	1981–82
6	Shaquille O'Neal	1992–93	1997–98
6	Dwyane Wade	2003–04	2008–09
6	Stephen Curry	2009–10	2014–15
6	Damian Lillard	2012–13	2017–18
6	Giannis Antetokounmpo	2013–14	2018–19
5	Larry Foust	1950–51	1954–55
5	George Yardley	1953–54	1957–58
5	Bill Melchionni****	1966–67	1971–72
5	Paul Westphal	1972–73	1976–77
5	Dennis Johnson	1976–77	1980–81
5	Patrick Ewing	1985–86	1989–90
5	Jason Kidd	1994–95	1998–99
5	Kevin Garnett	1995–96	1999–00
5	Tracy McGrady	1997–98	2001–02
5	Amar'e Stoudamire	2002–03	2006–07
5	James Harden	2009–10	2013–14
5	Kawhi Leonard	2011–12	2015–16

continued on next page

		First Season	All-NBA First Team
5	Jayson Tatum	2017–18	2021–22

* Missed 1993–94 season with an injury.

** Began career in ABA, before joining NBA in 1975–76, via league merger.

*** Held out for 1980–81 season.

**** Missed 1968–69 season.

ABA

		First Season	All-ABA First Team
8	Billy Cunningham*	1965–66	1972–73
7	Ron Boone	1968–69	1974–75
6	Donnie Freeman	1967–68	1971–72
6	Ralph Simpson	1970–71	1975–76
5	Warren Jabali	1968–69	1972–73

* Began career in NBA before joining ABA in 1972–73.

Largest Gap Between All-NBA First Team Appearances

Seasons

6	Tim Duncan	2006–07	2012–13
4	Paul Arizin	1951–52	1955–56
4	Bill Russell	1958–59	1962–63
4	Allen Iverson	2000–01	2004–05
4	Kevin Garnett	2003–04	2007–08
4	Chris Paul	2007–08	2011–12
4	Kevin Durant	2013–14	2017–18
4	Kawhi Leonard	2016–17	2020–21

Elected to All-NBA First Team, Different Positions

Dolph Schayes.......... Forward: 1951–52; 1952–53; 1954–55; 1956–57
Center: 1953–54

Bob Pettit .... Forward: 1954–55; 1955–56; 1958–59; 1959–60; 1960–61; 1961–62; 1962–63; 1963–64
Center: 1956–57; 1957–58

Tim Duncan .... Forward: 1997–98; 1998–99; 1999–00; 2000–01; 2001–02; 2002–03; 2003–04; 2004–05; 2006–07
Center: 2012–13

Tracy McGrady .... Forward: 2001–02
Guard: 2002–03

Players Chosen to Both All-NBA and All-ABA First Team

	NBA	ABA
Connie Hawkins	1969–70	1967–68; 1968–69
Julius Erving	1977–78; 1979–80; 1980–81; 1981–82; 1982–83	1972–73; 1973–74; 1974–75; 1975–76
Rick Barry	1965–66; 1966–67; 1973–74; 1974–75; 1975–76	1968–69; 1969–70; 1970–71; 1971–72
Billy Cunningham	1968–69; 1969–70; 1970–71	1972–73
Spencer Haywood	1971–72; 1972–73	1969–70
George McGinnis	1975–76	1973–74; 1974–75

All-Defensive First Team

Most All-Defensive First-Team Appearances

10................ Bobby Jones**	6................ Don Buse**	4................ Jerry Sloan
9................ Michael Jordan	6................ Dennis Johnson	4................ Artis Gilmore*
9................ Gary Payton	6................ Rudy Gobert^	4................ Sidney Moncrief
9................ Kevin Garnett	5................ John Havlicek	4................ Maurice Cheeks
9................ Kobe Bryant	5................ Kareem Abdul-Jabbar	4................ Joe Dumars
8................ Scottie Pippen	5................ Michael Cooper	4................ David Robinson
8................ Tim Duncan	5................ Hakeem Olajuwon	4................ Jason Kidd
7................ Walt Frazier	5................ Bruce Bowen	4................ Dwight Howard^
7................ Dennis Rodman	5................ Ben Wallace	4................ Draymond Green^
7................ Chris Paul^	5................ LeBron James^	4................ Giannis Antetokounmpo^
6................ Dave DeBusschere	4................ Jerry West	

* Only includes ABA.

** Includes both NBA and ABA.

^ Active.

Most Consecutive All-Defensive First-Team Appearances

10.............. Bobby Jones.............Den. Nuggets^a: 1974–76; Den. Nuggets: 1976–78; Phi. 76ers: 1978–84
9.............. Gary Payton.............Sea. Sonics: 1993–2002
8.............. Scottie Pippen.............Chi. Bulls: 1991–99
7.............. Walt Frazier.............N.Y. Knicks: 1968–75
6.............. Dave DeBusschere.............Det. Pistons/N.Y. Knicks: 1968–69; N.Y. Knicks: 1969–74
6.............. Don Buse.............Ind. Pacers^a: 1974–76; Ind. Pacers: 1976–77; Pho. Suns: 1977–80
6.............. Michael Jordan.............Chi. Bulls: 1987–93
6.............. Kobe Bryant.............L.A. Lakers: 2005–11
6.............. Chris Paul.............L.A. Clippers: 2011–17
6.............. Rudy Gobert.............Uta. Jazz: 2016–22
5.............. John Havlicek.............Bos. Celtics: 1971–76
5.............. Dennis Johnson.............Sea. Sonics: 1978–80; Pho. Suns: 1980–83
5.............. Dennis Rodman.............Det. Pistons: 1988–93
5.............. Tim Duncan.............S.A. Spurs: 1998–2003
5.............. Kevin Garnett.............Min. T'Wolves: 1999–2005
5.............. Ben Wallace.............Det. Pistons: 2001–06
5.............. Bruce Bowen.............S.A. Spurs: 2003–08
5.............. LeBron James.............Cle. Cavaliers: 2008–10; Mia. Heat: 2010–13
4.............. Jerry West.............L.A. Lakers: 1969–73
4.............. Artis Gilmore.............Ken. Colonels^a: 1972–76
4.............. Maurice Cheeks.............Phi. 76ers: 1982–86
4.............. Sidney Moncrief.............Mil. Bucks: 1982–86
4.............. Dwight Howard.............Orl. Magic: 2008–12
4.............. Giannis Antetokounmpo.....Mil. Bucks: 2018–22

^a ABA.

Teams with Three All-Defensive First Teamers, Same Season

		Record
N.Y. Knicks*, 1969–70 .... Dave DeBusschere, Walt Frazier, Willis Reed		60–22 (.732)
Bos. Celtics*, 1975–76 .... Dave Cowens, John Havlicek, Paul Silas		54–28 (.659)
Por. Blazers, 1977–78 .... Lionel Hollins, Maurice Lucas, Bill Walton		58–24 (.707)

continued on next page

			Record
Phi. 76ers*, 1982–83	Bobby Jones, Moses Malone, Maurice Cheeks		65–17 (.793)
Chi. Bulls*, 1995–96	Michael Jordan, Scottie Pippen, Dennis Rodman		72–10 (.878)

* Won championship.

Teams Winning Championship without a First-Team All-Defensive Player

	Record	PPG, Lg. Avg.	Points for/Points Against, Season
Mil. Bucks, 1970–71	66–16 (.805)	112.4	118.4/106.2
G.S. Warriors, 1974–75	48–34 (.585)	102.6	108.5/105.2
Was. Bullets, 1977–78	44–38 (.537)	108.5	110.3/109.4
Bos. Celtics, 1980–81	62–20 (.756)	108.1	109.9/104.0
Bos. Celtics, 1983–84	62–20 (.756)	110.1	112.1/105.6
Hou. Rockets, 1994–95	47–35 (.573)	101.4	103.5/101.4
L.A. Lakers, 2000–01	56–26 (.683)	94.8	100.6/97.2
L.A. Lakers, 2001–02	58–24 (.707)	95.5	101.3/94.1
Mia. Heat, 2005–06	52–30 (.634)	97.0	99.9/96.0
Dal. Mavericks, 2010–11	57–25 (.695)	99.6	100.2/96.0
S.A. Spurs, 2013–14	62–20 (.756)	101.0	105.4/97.6
Cle. Cavaliers, 2015–16	57–25 (.695)	102.7	104.3/98.3
G.S. Warriors, 2017–18	58–24 (.707)	106.3	113.5/107.5
Tor. Raptors, 2018–19	58–24 (.707)	111.2	114.4/108.4

All-Rookie First Team

Teams with Multiple First-Team All-Rookies

		Record
Bal. Bullets, 1963–64	Gus Johnson, Rod Thorn	31–49 (.388)
N.Y. Knicks, 1964–65	Jim Barnes, Howard Komives, Willis Reed*	31–49 (.388)
S.F. Warriors, 1965–66	Rick Barry*, Fred Hetzel	35–45 (.438)
N.Y. Knicks, 1967–68	Walt Frazier, Phil Jackson	43–39 (.524)
Sea. Sonics, 1967–68	Bob Rule, Al Tucker	23–59 (.280)
Mil. Bucks, 1969–70	Kareem Abdul-Jabbar*, Bob Dandridge	56–26 (.683)
L.A. Stars^a, 1969–70	Mack Calvin, Willie Wise	43–41 (.512)
N.Y. Nets^a, 1972–73	Jim Chones, Brian Taylor*	30–54 (.357)
Spirits of St.L.^a, 1974–75	Marvin Barnes*, Gus Gerard	32–52 (.381)
Pho. Suns, 1975–76	Alvan Adams*, John Shumate**	42–40 (.512)
G.S. Warriors, 1980–81	Joe Barry Carroll, Larry Smith	39–43 (.476)
Det. Pistons, 1981–82	Isiah Thomas, Kelly Tripuck^a	39–43 (.476)
Cle. Cavaliers, 1986–87	Brad Daugherty, Ron Harper, Hot Rod Williams	31–51 (.378)
Cle. Cavaliers, 1997–98	Zydrunas Ilgauskas, Brevin Knght	47–35 (.573)
Mem. Grizzlies, 2001–02	Shane Battier, Pau Gasol*	23–59 (.280)
Chi. Bulls, 2004–05	Luol Deng, Ben Gordon	47–35 (.573)
Por. Blazers, 2006–07	Brandon Roy*, LaMarcus Aldridge	32–50 (.390)
Tor. Raptors, 2006–07	Andrea Bargnani, Jorge Garbajosa	27–55 (.329)
Sea. Sonics, 2007–08	Kevin Durant*, Jeff Green	20–62 (.244)
Phi. 76ers, 2016–17	Joel Embiid, Dario Šarić	28–54 (.341)
Mem. Grizzlies, 2019–20	Brandon Clarke, Ja Morant*	34–39 (.466)

* Rookie of the Year.

** Played 43 games with Pho. Suns and 32 games with Buf. Braves.

^a ABA.

Consecutive Seasons Having a First-Team All-Rookie
NBA

Chi. Zephyrs-Bal. Bullets .... 1962–63: Terry Dischinger; 1963–64: Gus Johnson, Rod Thorn; 1964–65: Wali Jones
1966–67: Jack Martin; 1967–68: Earl Monroe; 1968–69: Wes Unseld; 1969–70: Mike Davis

N.Y. Knicks .... 1963–64: Art Heyman; 1964–65: Jim Barnes, Howard Komives, Willis Reed; 1965–66: Dick
Van Arsdale; 1966–67: Cazzie Russell; 1967–68: Walt Frazier, Phil Jackson
2015–16: Kristaps Porziņģis; 2016–17: Willy Hernangómez

Phi. 76ers .... 1964–65: Luke Jackson; 1965–66: Billy Cunningham
2013–14: Michael Carter-Williams; 2014–15: Nerlens Noel; 2015–16: Jahlil Okafor;
2016–17: Joel Embiid, Dario Šarić; 2017–18: Ben Simmons

Det. Pistons .... 1964–65: Joe Caldwell; 1965–66: Tom Van Arsdale; 1966–67: Dave Bing
1994–95: Grant Hill; 1995–96: Jerry Stackhouse

Sea. Sonics .... 1967–68: Bob Rule, Al Tucker; 1968–69: Art Harris

L.A. Lakers .... 1968–69: Bill Hewitt; 1969–70: Dick Garrett
1982–83: James Worthy; 1983–84: Byron Scott

Bos. Celtics .... 1969–70: Jo Jo White; 1970–71: Dave Cowens
1979–80: Larry Bird; 1980–81: Kevin McHale
1996–97: Antoine Walker; 1997–98: Ron Mercer; 1998–99: Paul Pierce

Por. Blazers .... 1970–71: Geoff Petrie; 1971–72: Sidney Wicks; 1972–73: Lloyd Neal
1978–79: Ron Brewer, Mychal Thompson; 1979–80: Calvin Natt*; 1980–81: Kelvin Ransey

Cle. Cavaliers .... 1971–72: Austin Carr; 1972–73: Dwight Davis
2011–12: Kyrie Irving; 2012–13: Dion Waiters

Buf. Braves .... 1971–72: Elmore Smith; 1972–73: Bob McAdoo; 1973–74: Ernie DiGregorio
1975–76: John Shumate**; 1976–77: Adrian Dantley

K.C.-Oma. Kings .... 1973–74: Ron Behagen; 1974–75: Scott Wedman

Atl. Hawks .... 1973–74: John Brown; 1974–75: John Drew

G.S. Warriors .... 1974–75: Jamaal Wilkes; 1975–76: Gus Williams
1988–89: Mitch Richmond; 1989–90: Tim Hardaway
2000–01: Marc Jackson; 2001–02: Jason Richardson
2011–12: Klay Thompson; 2012–13: Harrison Barnes

Pho. Suns .... 1975–76: Alvan Adams, John Shumate**; 1976–77: Ron Lee; 1977–78: Walter Davis

Hou. Rockets .... 1975–76: Joe Meriweather; 1976–77: John Lucas
1983–84: Ralph Sampson; 1984–85: Hakeem Olajuwon

Chi. Bulls .... 1978–79: Reggie Theus; 1979–80: David Greenwood
1984–85: Michael Jordan; 1985–86: Charles Oakley
2003–04: Kirk Hinrich; 2004–05: Luol Deng, Ben Gordon
2008–09: Derrick Rose; 2009–10: Taj Gibson

Ind. Pacers .... 1982–83: Clark Kellogg; 1983–84: Steve Stipanovich

S.A. Spurs .... 1987–88: Greg Anderson; 1988–89: Willie Anderson; 1989–90: David Robinson
2010–11: Gary Neal; 2011–12: Kawhi Leonard

Cha. Hornets .... 1990–91: Kendall Gill; 1991–92: Larry Johnson; 1992–93: Alonzo Mourning

Den. Nuggets .... 1991–92: Dikembe Mutombo; 1992–93: LaPhonso Ellis
2002–03: Nenê; 2003–04: Carmelo Anthony

Min. T'Wolves .... 1992–93: Christian Laettner; 1993–94: Isaiah Rider
2014–15: Andrew Wiggins; 2015–16: Karl-Anthony Towns

Orl. Magic .... 1992–93: Shaquille O'Neal; 1993–94: Penny Hardaway
2013–14: Victor Oladipo; 2014–15: Elfrid Payton

Mil. Bucks .... 1993–94: Vin Baker; 1994–95: Glenn Robinson

Dal. Mavericks .... 1993–94: Jamal Mashburn; 1994–95: Jason Kidd

Tor. Raptors .... 1995–96: Damon Stoudamire; 1996–97: Marcus Camby
2005–06: Charlie Villanueva; 2006–07: Andrea Bargnani, Jorge Garbajosa

continued on next page

L.A. Clippers .... 1999–00: Lamar Odom; 2000–01: Darius Miles

Mem. Grizzlies............................. 2001–02: Shane Battier, Pau Gasol; 2002–03: Drew Gooden***

2018–19: Jaren Jackson Jr.; 2019–20: Brandon Clarke, Ja Morant

Mia. Heat .... 2002–03: Caron Butler; 2003–04: Dwyane Wade

Sea. Sonics-Ok.C. Thunder .... 2007–08: Kevin Durant, 'Jeff Green; 2008–09: Russell Westbrook

Sac. Kings .... 2009–10: Tyreke Evans; 2010–11: DeMarcus Cousins

* Played 53 games with N.J. Nets and 25 games with Por. Blazers.

** Played 43 games with Pho. Suns and 32 games with Buf. Braves.

*** Played 51 games with Mem. Grizzlies and 19 games with Orl. Magic.

ABA

Ken. Colonels.. 1967–68: Louie Dampier; 1968–69: Gene Moore

1970–71: Dan Issel; 1971–72: Artis Gilmore

Oak. Oaks-Was. Capitols-Vir. Squires .... 1968–69: Warren Jabali; 1969–70: Mike Barrett; 1970–71: Charlie Scott; 1971–72:

Julius Erving; 1972–73: George Gervin; 1973–74: Swen Nater*

L.A. Stars .... 1968–69: Larry Miller; 1970–71: Mack Calvin, Willie Wise

Den. Rockets .... 1968–69: Walter Piatkowski; 1969–70: Spencer Haywood

Mem. Pros.. 1970–71: Wendell Ladner; 1971–72: Johnny Neumann

N.Y. Nets.. 1971–72: John Roche; 1972–73: Jim Chones, Brian Taylor; 1973–74: Larry Kenon,

John Williamson

Dal. Chaparrals-S.A. Spurs .... 1972–73: James Silas; 1973–74: Swen Nater*

Den. Rockets-Nuggets................................. 1973–74: Mike Green; 1974–75: Bobby Jones; 1975–76: David Thompson

Spirits of St.L. .... 1974–75: Marvin Barnes, Gus Gerard; 1975–76: M.L. Carr

* Played 62 games with S.A. Spurs and 17 games with Vir. Squires.

Awards Miscellany

Players Winning Multiple Awards, Same Season

Wilt Chamberlain, Phi. Warriors (1959–60) .... Rookie of the Year, Most Valuable Player

Wes Unseld, Bal. Bullets (1968–69)............................ Rookie of the Year, Most Valuable Player

Alvin Robertson, S.A. Spurs (1985–86) .... Most Improved, Defensive Player of the Year

Michael Jordan, Chi. Bulls (1987–88)........................ Most Valuable Player, Defensive Player of the Year

Hakeem Olajuwon, Hou. Rockets (1993–94) .... Most Valuable Player, Defensive Player of the Year

Darrell Armstrong, Orl. Magic (1998–99) .... Sixth Man, Most Improved

Giannis Antetokounmpo, Mil. Bucks (2019–20) .... Most Valuable Player, Defensive Player of the Year

Players Winning Most Different Awards, Career

Bob Pettit .... ROY: 1954–55 (Mil. Hawks); MVP: 1955–56, 1958–59 (St.L. Hawks)

Wilt Chamberlain .... ROY: 1959–60 (Phi. Warriors); MVP: 1959–60 (Phi. Warriors), 1965–66, 1966–67, 1967–68 (Phi. 76ers)

Oscar Robertson .... ROY: 1960–61 (Cin. Royals); MVP: 1963–64 (Cin. Royals)

Willis Reed...................... ROY: 1964–65 (N.Y. Knicks); MVP: 1969–70 (N.Y. Knicks)

Wes Unseld...................... ROY: 1968–69 (Bal. Bullets); MVP: 1968–69 (Bal. Bullets)

Bob McAdoo.................... ROY: 1972–73 (Buf. Braves); MVP: 1974–75 (Buf. Braves)

Bill Walton .... MVP: 1977–78 (Por. Blazers); Sixth Man: 1985–86 (Bos. Celtics)

Larry Bird........................ ROY: 1979–80 (Bos. Celtics); MVP: 1983–84, 1984–85, 1985–86 (Bos. Celtics)

Michael Jordan................. ROY: 1984–85 (Chi. Bulls); DPOY: 1987–88 (Chi. Bulls); MVP: 1987–88, 1990–91, 1991–92,

1995–96, 1997–98 (Chi. Bulls)

Alvin Robertson .... DPOY: 1985–86 (S.A. Spurs); Most Improved: 1985–86 (S.A. Spurs)

David Robinson .... ROY: 1989–90 (S.A. Spurs); DPOY: 1991–92 (S.A. Spurs); MVP: 1994–95 (S.A. Spurs)

Shaquille O'Neal.............. ROY: 1992–93 (Orl. Magic); MVP: 1999–00 (L.A. Lakers)

Hakeem Olajuwon .... DPOY: 1992–93, 1993–94 (Hou. Rockets); MVP: 1993–94 (Hou. Rockets)

continued on next page

Allen Iverson .... ROY: 1996–97 (Phi. 76ers); MVP: 2000–01 (Phi. 76ers)
Tim Duncan .... ROY: 1997–98 (S.A. Spurs); 2001–02, 2002–03 (S.A. Spurs)
Darrell Armstrong .... Sixth Man: 1998–99 (Orl. Magic); Most Improved: 1998–99 (Orl. Magic)
Mike Miller .... ROY: 2000–01 (Orl. Magic); Sixth Man: 2005–06 (Mem. Grizzlies)
Kevin Garnett .... MVP: 2003–04 (Min. T'Wolves); DPOY: 2007–08 (Bos. Celtics)
LeBron James .... ROY: 2003–04 (Cle. Cavaliers); MVP: 2008–09, 2009–10 (Cle. Cavaliers); 2011–12, 2012–13 (Mia. Heat)
Kevin Durant .... ROY: 2007–08 (Sea. Sonics); MVP: 2013–14 (Ok.C. Thunder)
Derrick Rose .... ROY: 2008–09 (Chi. Bulls); MVP: 2010–11 (Chi. Bulls)
James Harden .... Sixth Man: 2011–12 (Ok.C. Thunder); MVP: 2017–18 (Hou. Rockets)
Giannis Antetokounmkpo ... Most Improved: 2016–17 (Mil. Bucks); MVP: 2018–19, 2019–20 (Mil. Bucks); DPOY: 2019–20 (Mil. Bucks)
Ja Morant .... ROY: 2019–20 (Mem. Grizzlies); Most Improved: 2021–22 (Mem. Grizzlies)

Teammates Winning Multiple Awards, Same Season

Bos. Celtics, 1956–57 .... MVP: Bob Cousy; ROY: Tom Heinsohn
Cin. Royals, 1963–64 .... MVP: Oscar Robertson; ROY: Jerry Lucas
Phi. 76ers, 1982–83 .... MVP: Moses Malone; Sixth Man: Bobby Jones
Bos. Celtics, 1983–84 .... MVP: Larry Bird; Sixth Man: Kevin McHale
Bos. Celtics, 1984–85 .... MVP: Larry Bird; Sixth Man: Kevin McHale
Bos. Celtics, 1985–86 .... MVP: Larry Bird; Sixth Man: Bill Walton
L.A. Lakers, 1986–87 .... MVP: Magic Johnson; DPOY: Michael Cooper
Pho. Suns, 1988–89 .... Sixth Man: Eddie Johnson; Most Improved: Kevin Johnson
Chi. Bulls, 1995–96 .... MVP: Michael Jordan; Sixth Man: Toni Kukoč
Atl. Hawks, 1997–98 .... DPOY: Dikembe Mutombo; Most Improved: Alan Henderson
Phi. 76ers, 2000–01 .... MVP: Allen Iverson; DPOY: Dikembe Mutombo*; Sixth Man: Aaron McKie
Orl. Magic, 2000–01 .... ROY: Mike Miller; Most Improved: Tracy McGrady
Det. Pistons, 2001–02 .... DPOY: Ben Wallace; Sixth Man: Corliss Williamson
Pho. Suns, 2005–06 .... MVP: Steve Nash; Most Improved: Boris Diaw
Uta. Jazz, 2020–21 .... DPOY: Rudy Gobert; Sixth Man: Jordan Clarkson
* Split season between the Atl. Hawks (49 games) and Phi. 76ers (26 games).

Players Winning ROY and MVP, Same Season

Wilt Chamberlain, Phi. Warriors, 1959–60
Wes Unseld, Bal. Bullets, 1968–69

Winning ROY, MVP the Following Season

	ROY	MVP
Bob Pettit	1954–55, Mil. Hawks	1955–56, St.L. Hawks
Kareem Abdul-Jabbar	1969–70, Mil. Bucks	1970–71, Mil. Bucks

7

COACHES

Regular Season

Most Games Coached, Career*

2487	Lenny Wilkens	1332–1155 (.536)	1369	Nate McMillan^	731–638 (.534)
2398	Don Nelson	1335–1063 (.557)	1364	John MacLeod	707–657 (.518)
2338	Larry Brown	1327–1011 (.568)	1329	Mike Dunleavy	613–716 (.461)
2050	Bill Fitch	944–1106 (.460)	1299	Red Holzman	696–603 (.536)
2045	Gregg Popovich^	1344–701 (.657)	1246	Flip Saunders	654–592 (.525)
2024	Jerry Sloan	1221–803 (.603)	1215	Mike Fratello	667–548 (.549)
1999	George Karl	1175–824 (.588)	1213	Alex Hannum	649–564 (.535)
1952	Dick Motta	935–1017 (.479)	1199	Mike D'Antoni	672–527 (.560)
1904	Pat Riley	1210–694 (.636)	1170	Alvin Gentry^	534–636 (.456)
1791	Rick Adelman	1042–749 (.582)	1157	Doug Moe	628–529 (.543)
1778	Doc Rivers^	1043–735 (.587)	1113	Erik Spoelstra^	660–453 (.593)
1647	Jack Ramsay	864–783 (.525)	1107	Slick Leonard	573–534 (.512)
1645	Gene Shue	784–861 (.477)	1101	Byron Scott	454–647 (.412)
1640	Phil Jackson	1155–485 (.704)	1087	Hubie Brown	528–559 (.486)
1607	Cotton Fitzsimmons	832–775 (.518)	1075	Al Attles	557–518 (.518)
1607	Rick Carlisle^	861–746 (.536)	1075	Chuck Daly	638–437 (.593)
1417	Red Auerbach	938–479 (.662)	1013	Del Harris	556–457 (.549)
1388	Kevin Loughery	642–746 (.463)	1003	Terry Stotts	517–486 (.515)

* Includes ABA.

^ Active.

Winningest Coach by State of Birth*

Alabama	Pete Myers (Mobile)	0	Massachusetts	Vinny Del Negro (Springfield)	210
Alaska	Mike Dunlap (Fairbanks)	21	Michigan	Don Nelson (Muskegon)	1335
Arizona	Mike Budenholzer^ (Holbrook)	426	Minnesota	Dave Joerger (Staples)	245
Arkansas	Paul Silas (Prescott)	387	Mississippi	Babe McCarthy (Baldwyn)	284
California	Rick Adelman (Lynwood)	1042	Missouri	Cotton Fitzsimmons (Hannibal)	832
Colorado	J.B. Bickerstaff^ (Denver)	156	Montana	Phil Jackson (Deer Lodge)	1155
Connecticut	Tom Thibodeau^ (New Britain)	430	Nebraska	Fred Hoiberg (Lincoln)	115
Delaware	N/A	N/A	Nevada	Bill Berry (Winnemucca)	0
Florida	Frank Johnson (Weirsdale)	63	New Hampshire	Robert Rolfe (Penacook)	17
Georgia	Sam Mitchell (Columbus)	185	New Jersey	Mike Fratello (Hackensack)	667
Hawaii	Red Rocha (Hilo)	65	New Mexico	James Borrego^ (Albuquerque)	148
Idaho	Phil Johnson (Grace)	236	New York	Lenny Wilkens (Brooklyn)	1332
Illinois	Jerry Sloan (McLeansboro)	1221	North Carolina	Nate McMillan^ (Raleigh)	731
Indiana	Gregg Popovich (East Chicago)	1344	North Dakota	N/A	N/A
Iowa	Bill Fitch (Davenport)	944	Ohio	Flip Saunders (Cleveland)	654
Kansas	Lionel Hollins (Ark City)	262	Oklahoma	Bob Bass (Tulsa)	311
Kentucky	Bernie Bickerstaff (Benham)	419	Oregon	Danny Ainge (Eugene)	136
Louisiana	Bill Russell (Monroe)	341	Pennsylvania	George Karl (Penn Hills)	1175
Maine	Steve Clifford (Island Falls)	292	Rhode Island	Albert Soar (Alton)	2
Maryland	Gene Shue (Baltimore)	784	South Carolina	Tyrone Corbin (Columbia)	119

continued on next page

South Dakota	N/A	N/A	
Tennessee	Tom Marshall (Coldwater)	35	
Texas	K.C. Jones (Taylor)	552	
Utah	Dick Motta (Midvale)	935	
Vermont	N/A	N/A	
Virginia	Monty Williams^ (Fredericksburg)	322	
Washington	Quin Snyder^ (Mercer Island)	372	
West Virginia	Mike D'Antoni (Mullens)	672	

Wisconsin	Tom Nissalke (Madison)	371
Wyoming	Jimmy Darden (Cheyenne)	11
District of Columbia	Eddie Jordan	257
Puerto Rico	N/A	N/A
Virgin Islands	N/A	N/A

* Includes ABA.
^ Active.

Winningest Coach by First Letter of Last Name*

A .... Adelman, Rick 1042	J .... Jackson, Phil 1155	S .... Sloan, Jerry 1221
B .... Brown, Larry 1327	K .... Karl, George 1175	T .... Tomjanovich, Rudy 527
C .... Carlisle, Rick 835	L .... Loughery, Kevin 642	U .... Unseld, Wes 202
D .... D'Antoni, Mike 672	M .... Motta, Dick 935	V .... Van Gundy, Stan 554
E .... Egan, Johnny 129	N .... Nelson, Don 1335	W .... Wilkens, Lenny 1332
F .... Fitch, Bill 944	O .... O'Brien, Jim 303	X .... N/A .... N/A
G .... Gentry, Alvin 534	P .... Popovich, Gregg 1344	Y .... Young, Verl 23
H .... Holzman, Red 696	Q .... N/A .... N/A	Z .... Zaslofsky, Max 103
I .... Issel, Dan 180	R .... Riley, Pat 1210	

* Includes ABA.

Winningest Coach by Zodiac Sign*

Aquarius (Jan. 20–Feb. 18) .... Gregg Popovich^ ..1344	Leo (Jul. 23–Aug. 22) .... Larry Brown 1327
Pisces (Feb. 19–Mar. 20) .... Pat Riley 1210	Virgo (Aug. 23–Sep. 22) .... Red Auerbach 938
Aries (Mar. 21–Apr. 19) .... Jerry Sloan 1221	Libra (Sep. 23–Oct. 23) .... Doc Rivers^ 1043
Taurus (Apr. 20–May 20) .... Don Nelson 1335	Scorpio (Oct. 24–Nov. 21) .... Lenny Wilkens 1332
Gemini (May 21–Jun. 21) .... Rick Adelman 1042	Sagittarius (Nov. 22–Dec. 21) ...... Phil Jackson 1155
Cancer (Jun. 22–Jul.22) .... Alex Hannum 649	Capricorn (Dec. 22–Jan. 19) .... Jeff Van Gundy 430

* Includes ABA.
^ Active.

Most Career Wins* (Regular Season and Playoffs)

1628 .... Gregg Popovich^	1037 .... Red Auerbach	754 .... John MacLeod
1427 .... Larry Brown	999 .... Bill Fitch	726 .... Mike D'Antoni
1412 .... Lenny Wilkens	991 .... Dick Motta	713 .... Chuck Daly
1410 .... Don Nelson	924 .... Rick Carlisle^	701 .... Flip Saunders
1384 .... Phil Jackson	908 .... Jack Ramsay	694 .... Alex Hannum
1381 .... Pat Riley	867 .... Cotton Fitzsimmons	687 .... Mike Fratello
1319 .... Jerry Sloan	814 .... Gene Shue	661 .... Doug Moe
1255 .... George Karl	759 .... Nate McMillan^	651 .... Mike Dunleavy
1147 .... Doc Rivers^	756 .... Erik Spoelstra^	
1121 .... Rick Adelman	754 .... Red Holzman	

* Includes ABA.
^ Active.

Most Career Regular-Season Wins*

1344 .... Gregg Popovich^	1221 .... Jerry Sloan	1043 .... Doc Rivers^
1335 .... Don Nelson	1210 .... Pat Riley	1042 .... Rick Adelman
1332 .... Lenny Wilkens	1175 .... George Karl	944 .... Bill Fitch
1327 .... Larry Brown	1155 .... Phil Jackson	938 .... Red Auerbach

continued on next page

935.............................. Dick Motta	667.............................. Mike Fratello	557.............................. Al Attles
864.............................. Jack Ramsay	660.............................. Erik Spoelstra^	556.............................. Del Harris
861.............................. Rick Carlisle^	654.............................. Flip Saunders	554.............................. Stan Van Gundy
832.............................. Cotton Fitzsimmons	649.............................. Alex Hannum	552.............................. K.C. Jones
784.............................. Gene Shue	642.............................. Kevin Loughery	534.............................. Alvin Gentry^
731.............................. Nate McMillan^	638.............................. Chuck Daly	528.............................. Hubie Brown
707.............................. John MacLeod	628.............................. Doug Moe	527.............................. Rudy Tomjanovich
696.............................. Red Holzman	613.............................. Mike Dunleavy	521.............................. Scott Brooks
672.............................. Mike D'Antoni	573.............................. Slick Leonard	517.............................. Terry Stotts

* Includes ABA.

^ Active.

Most Games Coached, Losing Record*

2050............. Bill Fitch........................ 944–1106 (.460)	1170............. Alvin Gentry^ .... 534–636 (.456)
1952............. Dick Motta .... 935–1017 (.479)	1087............. Hubie Brown .... 528–559 (.486)
1645............. Gene Shue........................ 784–861 (.477)	982............. Dwane Casey^ .... 477–505 (.486)
1388............. Kevin Loughery............... 642–746 (.463)	958............. Scott Skiles .... 478–480 (.499)
1329............. Mike Dunleavy .... 613–716 (.461)	937............. Bernie Bickerstaff............. 419–518 (.447)

* Includes ABA.

^ Active.

Most Career Regular-Season Wins, Under .500 Winning Percentage*

944............... Bill Fitch........................ 944–1106 (.460)	419............... Bernie Bickerstaff............. 419–518 (.447)
935............... Dick Motta .... 935–1017 (.479)	387............... Paul Silas .... 387–488 (.442)
784............... Gene Shue........................ 784–861 (.477)	371............... Tom Nissalke.................. 371–508 (.422)
642............... Kevin Loughery............... 642–746 (.463)	337............... Don Chaney .... 337–494 (.406)
613............... Mike Dunleavy .... 613–716 (.461)	328............... Jim Lynam .... 328–392 (.456)
534............... Alvin Gentry^ .... 534–636 (.456)	323............... Chris Ford..................... 323–376 (.462)
528............... Hubie Brown .... 528–559 (.486)	315............... Mike Woodson................ 315–365 (.463)
478............... Scott Skiles...................... 478–480 (.499)	305............... Maurice Cheeks .... 305–315 (.492)
477............... Dwane Casey^ .... 477–505 (.486)	303............... Jim O'Brien .... 303–327 (.481)
454............... Byron Scott .... 454–647 (.412)	300............... Jack McMahon................ 300–343 (.467)

* Includes ABA.

^ Active.

Most Wins in First Season as Head Coach

	Record
67 .... Steve Kerr, G.S. Warriors*, 2014–15 .... 67–15 (.817)	
62 .... Tom Thibodeau, Chi. Bulls, 2010–11 .... 62–20 (.756)	
60 .... Bill Russell, Bos. Celtics, 1966–67 .... 60–21 (.741)	
60 .... LaDell Andersen, Uta. Stars^a, 1971–72 .... 60–24 (.714)	
58 .... Mike Dunleavy, L.A. Lakers, 1990–91 .... 58–24 (.707)	
58 .... Larry Bird, Ind. Pacers, 1997–98 .... 58–24 (.707)	
58 .... Nick Nurse, Tor. Raptors*, 2018–19 .... 58–24 (.707)	
58 .... Hubie Brown, Ken. Colonels^a*, 1974–75 .... 58–26 (.690)	
57 .... Larry Brown, Car. Cougars^a, 1972–73............................ 57–27 (.679)	
56 .... Chris Ford, Bos. Celtics, 1990–91 .... 56–26 (.683)	
55 .... Jack Ramsay, Phi. 76ers, 1968–69 .... 55–27 (.671)	
55 .... Phil Jackson, Chi. Bulls, 1989–90 .... 55–27 (.671)	
55 .... Billy Donovan, Ok.C. Thunder, 2015–16........................ 55–27 (.671)	
54 .... Vince Cazzetta, Pit. Pipers^a*, 1967–68........................... 54–24 (.692)	
54 .... Matt Guokas, Phi. 76ers, 1985–86 .... 54–28 (.659)	

continued on next page

		Record
53	Billy Cunningham (53–23**), Phi. 76ers, 1977–78	55–27 (.671)
53	Jerry West, L.A. Lakers, 1976–77	53–29 (.646)
53	David Blatt, Cle. Cavaliers, 2014–15	53–29 (.646)
52	Butch van Breda Kolff, L.A. Lakers, 1967–68	52–30 (.634)
51	Al Cervi, Syr. Nationals, 1949–50	51–13 (.797)
51	Ime Udoka, Bos. Celtics, 2021–22	51–31 (.622)
50	Paul Westhead (50–18**), L.A. Lakers*, 1979–80	60–22 (.732)
50	Pat Riley (50–21**), L.A. Lakers*, 1981–82	57–25 (.695)
50	Brian Hill, Orl. Magic, 1993–94	50–32 (.610)
50	Rick Carlisle, Det. Pistons, 2001–02	50–32 (.610)
50	Mike Brown, Cle. Cavaliers, 2005–06	50–32 (.610)
50	Dave Joerger, Mem. Grizzlies, 2013–14	50–32 (.610)
49	Red Holzman, Was. Capitols, 1946–47	49–11 (.817)
49	Neil Johnston, Phi. Warriors, 1959–60	49–26 (.653)
49	Frank McGuire, Phi. Warriors, 1961–62	49–31 (.613)
49	Mike Schyler, Por. Blazers, 1986–87	49–33 (.598)
49	Maurice Cheeks, Por. Blazers, 2001–02	49–33 (.598)
48	Babe McCarthy, N.O. Buccaneersª, 1967–68	48–30 (.615)
48	Harry Gallatin, St.L. Hawks, 1962–63	48–32 (.600)
48	Cotton Fitzsimmons, Pho. Suns, 1970–71	48–34 (.585)
48	Jeff Hornacek, Pho. Suns, 2013–14	48–34 (.585)
48	Steve Nash, Brk. Nets, 2020–21	48–24 (.667)
46	Cliff Hagan, Dal. Chaparralsª, 1967–68	46–32 (.590)
46	Joe Mullaney, L.A. Lakers, 1969–70	46–36 (.561)
46	Monty Williams, N.O. Hornets, 2010–11	46–36 (.561)

* Team won championship.

** Record after taking over for previously fired coach.

ª ABA.

Most Wins for Coach in First Season with New Team

		Record
69	Bill Sharman, L.A. Lakers, 1971–72	69–13 (.841)
68	Alex Hannum, Phi. 76ers, 1966–67	68–13 (.840)
68	Joe Mullaney, Ken. Colonelsª, 1971–72	68–16 (.810)
67	Phil Jackson, L.A. Lakers*, 1999–00	67–15 (.817)
65	Larry Brown, Den. Nuggetsª, 1974–75	65–19 (.774)
64	Flip Saunders, Det. Pistons, 2005–06	64–18 (.780)
62	K.C. Jones, Bos. Celtics*, 1983–84	62–20 (.756)
62	Bob Hill, S.A. Spurs, 1994–95	62–20 (.756)
61	Bill Fitch, Bos. Celtics, 1979–80	61–21 (.744)
61	Rick Carlisle, Ind. Pacers, 2003–04	61–21 (.744)
60	Alex Hannum, Oak. Oaksª, 1968–69	60–18 (.769)
60	Mike Budenholzer, Mil. Bucks, 2018–19	60–22 (.732)
57	Lenny Wilkens, Atl. Hawks, 1993–94	57–25 (.695)
57	Doc Rivers, L.A. Clippers, 2013–14	57–25 (.695)
55	Jack McMahon, Cin. Royals, 1963–64	55–25 (.688)
55	Kevin Loughery, N.Y. Netsª, 1973–74	55–29 (.655)
55	Cotton Fitzsimmons, Pho. Suns, 1988–89	55–27 (.671)
55	Rick Adelman, Hou. Rockets, 2007–08	55–27 (.671)
55	Mike D'Antoni, Hou. Rockets, 2016–17	55–27 (.671)
54	Dave Cowens, Cha. Hornets, 1996–97	54–28 (.659)
54	Larry Brown, Det. Pistons, 2003–04	54–28 (.659)
53	Babe McCarthy, Ken. Colonelsª, 1973–74	53–31 (.631)

continued on next page

		Record
53	John MacLeod, Dal. Mavericks, 1987–88	53–29 (.646)
52	Stan Albeck, S.A. Spurs, 1980–81	52–30 (.634)
52	Stan Van Gundy, Orl. Magic, 2007–08	52–30 (.634)
52	Frank Vogel, L.A. Lakers*, 2019–20	52–19 (.732)
52	Jason Kidd, Dal. Mavericks, 2021–22	52–30 (.634)
51	Paul Seymour, St.L. Hawks, 1960–61	51–28 (.646)
51	Joe Mullaney, Uta. Starsª, 1973–74	51–33 (.607)
51	Pat Riley, N.Y. Knicks, 1991–92	51–31 (.622)
50	Jim Pollard, Min. Muskiesª, 1967–68	50–28 (.641)
50	Rick Carlisle, Dal. Mavericks, 2008–09	50–32 (.610)
49	Tom Nissalke, Hou. Rockets, 1976–77	49–33 (.598)
49	Jack Ramsay, Por. Blazers*, 1976–77	49–33 (.598)
49	Chuck Daly, Det. Pistons, 1983–84	49–33 (.598)
49	Scott Brooks, Was. Wizards, 2016–17	49–33 (.598)
49	Doc Rivers, Phi. 76ers, 2020–21	49–23 (.681)
48	Alex Hannum, S.F. Warriors, 1963–64	48–32 (.600)
48	Dick Motta, Was. Bullets, 1976–77	48–34 (.585)
48	Cotton Fitzsimmons, K.C. Kings, 1978–79	48–34 (.585)
48	Del Harris, L.A. Lakers, 1994–95	48–34 (.585)
47	K.C. Jones, Cap. Bullets, 1973–74	47–35 (.573)
47	Mike Fratello, Cle. Cavaliers, 1993–94	47–35 (.573)
47	Larry Brown, Ind. Pacers, 1993–94	47–35 (.573)
47	Lenny Wilkens, Tor. Raptors, 2000–01	47–35 (.573)
47	Tyronn Lue, L.A. Clippers, 2020–21	47–35 (.573)
46	Cotton Fitzsimmons, Atl. Hawks, 1972–73	46–36 (.561)
46	Doug Collins, Det. Pistons, 1995–96	46–36 (.561)
46	Mike Dunleavy, Por. Blazers, 1997–98	46–36 (.561)

* Team won championship.

ª ABA.

Coaches Winning 500 Games with One Franchise

			Years with Franchise
Don Nelson	540	Mil. Bucks	1976–87
Jerry Sloan	1127	Uta. Jazz	1988–2011
Gregg Popovich^	1344	S.A. Spurs	1996–2022
Gene Shue	522	Bal.-Was. Bullets	1966–73; 1980–86
Phil Jackson	545	Chi. Bulls	1989–98
	610	L.A. Lakers	1999–2011
Rick Carlisle	555	Dal. Mavericks	2008–21
Red Auerbach	1192	Bos. Celtics	1950–66
John MacLeod	579	Pho. Suns	1973–87
Red Holzman	613	N.Y. Knicks	1967–82
Erik Spoelstra^	660	Mia. Heat	2008–22
Al Attles	557	S.F.-G.S. Warriors	1969–83
Rudy Tomjanovich	503	Hou. Rockets	1991–2003
Pat Riley	533	L.A. Lakers	1981–90

^ Active with franchise.

Coaches Winning 200 Games with Three Different Franchises

			Years with Franchise
Lenny Wilkens	478	Sea. Sonics	1969–85
	316	Cle. Cavaliers	1986–93
	310	Atl. Hawks	1993–2000

continued on next page

<table>
<tr><td></td><td></td><td></td><td>**Years with Franchise**</td></tr>
<tr><td>Don Nelson</td><td>540</td><td>Mil. Bucks</td><td>1976–87</td></tr>
<tr><td></td><td>422</td><td>G.S. Warriors</td><td>1988–95</td></tr>
<tr><td></td><td>339</td><td>Dal. Mavericks</td><td>1997–2005</td></tr>
<tr><td>Pat Riley</td><td>533</td><td>L.A. Lakers</td><td>1981–90</td></tr>
<tr><td></td><td>223</td><td>N.Y. Knicks</td><td>1991–95</td></tr>
<tr><td></td><td>454</td><td>Mia. Heat</td><td>1995–2008</td></tr>
<tr><td>George Karl</td><td>384</td><td>Sea. Sonics</td><td>1991–98</td></tr>
<tr><td></td><td>205</td><td>Mil. Bucks</td><td>1998–2003</td></tr>
<tr><td></td><td>423</td><td>Den. Nuggets</td><td>2004–13</td></tr>
<tr><td>Bill Fitch</td><td>304</td><td>Cle. Cavaliers</td><td>1970–79</td></tr>
<tr><td></td><td>242</td><td>Bos. Celtics</td><td>1979–83</td></tr>
<tr><td></td><td>216</td><td>Hou. Rockets</td><td>1983–88</td></tr>
</table>

Most Wins for Each Franchise

Hawks	327	Richie Guerin	Heat	660	Erik Spoelstra^
Celtics	795	Red Auerbach	Bucks	540	Don Nelson
Nets-Americans*	297	Levin Loughery	Timberwolves	427	Flip Saunders
Hornets-Bobcats	207	Allan Bristow	Pelicans-Hornets	203	Byron Scott
Bulls	545	Phil Jackson	Knicks	613	Red Holzman
Cavaliers	316	Lenny Wilkens	Thunder-SuperSonics	478	Lenny Wilkens
Mavericks	555	Rick Carlisle	Magic	267	Brian Hill
Nuggets*	432	Doug Moe	76ers-Nationals	454	Billy Cunningham
Pistons	467	Chuck Daly	Suns	579	John MacLeod
Warriors	557	Al Attles	Trail Blazers	453	Jack Ramsay
Rockets	503	Rudy Tomjanovich	Kings-Royals	395	Rick Adelman
Pacers*	529	Slick Leonard	Spurs*	1344	Gregg Popovich^
Clippers-Braves	356	Doc Rivers	Raptors	320	Dwane Casey
Lakers	610	Phil Jackson	Jazz	1127	Jerry Sloan
Grizzlies	214	Lionel Hollins	Wizards-Zephyrs-Packers-Bullets	522	Gene Shue

^ Active with franchise.

* Includes ABA.

1000 Wins as Coach, 3500 Points as Player

	Wins	Points			Wins	Points
Rick Adelman	1042	3579		Pat Riley	1210	3906
Larry Brown*	1098	4229		Doc Rivers^	1043	9377
Phil Jackson	1155	5428		Jerry Sloan	1221	10,571
Don Nelson	1335	10,898		Lenny Wilkens	1332	17,772

* Playing career in ABA; coached in ABA and NBA.

^ Active.

Coaches Never Experiencing a Losing Season (Min. Three Winning Seasons)

	Winning Seasons	Record
Phil Jackson	20	1155–485 (.704)
Billy Cunningham	8	454–196 (.698)
Joe Lapchick	7	326–247 (.569)
Danny Ainge	4	136–90 (.602)
Larry Bird	3	147–67 (.687)
Harold Olsen	3	95–63 (.601)
Jerry West	3	145–101 (.589)
George Senesky	3	119–97 (.551)

Coaches Winning 60 Games for Multiple Franchises

Rick Adelman	Por. Blazers, 1990–91	63–19 (.768)
	Sac. Kings, 2001–02	61–21 (.744)
Mike Budenholzer	Atl. Hawks, 2014–15	60–22 (.732)
	Mil. Bucks, 2018–19	60–22 (.732)
Mike D'Antoni	Hou. Rockets, 2017–18	65–17 (.793)
	Pho. Suns, 2004–05	62–20 (.756)
	Pho. Suns, 2006–07	61–21 (.744)
Alex Hannum	Phi. 76ers*, 1966–67	68–13 (.840)
	Phi. 76ers, 1967–68	62–20 (.756)
	Oak. Oaksª*, 1968–69	60–18 (.769)
Brian Hill	S.A. Spurs, 1994–95	62–20 (.756)
	Orl. Magic, 1995–96	60–22 (.732)
Phil Jackson	Chi. Bulls*, 1990–91	61–21 (.744)
	Chi. Bulls*, 1991–92	67–15 (.817)
	Chi. Bulls*, 1995–96	72–10 (.878)
	Chi. Bulls*, 1996–97	69–13 (.841)
	Chi. Bulls*, 1997–98	62–20 (.756)
	L.A. Lakers*, 1999–00	67–15 (.817)
	L.A. Lakers*, 2008–09	65–17 (.793)
K.C. Jones	Was. Bullets, 1974–75	60–22 (.732)
	Bos. Celtics*, 1983–84	62–20 (.756)
	Bos. Celtics, 1984–85	63–19 (.768)
	Bos. Celtics*, 1985–86	67–15 (.817)
Don Nelson	Mil. Bucks, 1980–81	60–22 (.732)
	Dal. Mavericks, 2002–03	60–22 (.732)
Pat Riley	L.A. Lakers*, 1984–85	62–20 (.756)
	L.A. Lakers, 1985–86	62–20 (.756)
	L.A. Lakers*, 1986–87	65–17 (.793)
	L.A. Lakers*, 1987–88	62–20 (.756)
	L.A. Lakers, 1989–90	63–19 (.768)
	N.Y. Knicks, 1992–93	60–22 (.732)
	Mia. Heat, 1996–97	61–21 (.744)

* Won championship.
ª ABA.

Coaches Winning 60 Games and Losing 60 Games in a Season

	60-Win Season	Record	60-Loss Season	Record
Larry Brown	Den. Nuggetsª, 1974–75	65–19 (.774)	S.A. Spurs, 1988–89	21–61 (.256)
	Den. Nuggetsª, 1975–76	60–24 (.714)		
Bill Fitch	Bos. Celtics, 1979–80	61–21 (.744)	Cle. Cavaliers, 1970–71	15–67 (.183)
	Bos. Celtics, 1980–81	62–20 (.756)	N.J. Nets, 1989–90	17–65 (.207)
	Bos. Celtics, 1981–82	63–19 (.768)	L.A. Clippers, 1994–95	17–65 (.207)
			L.A. Clippers, 1997–98	17–65 (.207)
Alex Hannum	Phi. 76ers, 1966–67	68–13 (.840)	S.F. Warriors, 1964–65	17–63 (.213)
	Phi. 76ers, 1967–68	62–20 (.756)		
	Oak. Oaksª, 1968–69	60–18 (.769)		
Del Harris	L.A. Lakers, 1997–98	61–21 (.744)	Hou. Rockets, 1982–83	14–68 (.171)
Brian Hill	S.A. Spurs, 1994–95	62–20 (.756)	Van. Grizzlies, 1997–98	19–63 (.232)
	Orl. Magic, 1995–96	60–22 (.732)		

continued on next page

	60-Win Season	Record	60-Loss Season	Record
Pat Riley	L.A. Lakers, 1984–85	62–20 (.756)	Mia. Heat, 2007–08	15–67 (.183)
	L.A. Lakers, 1985–86	62–20 (.756)		
	L.A. Lakers, 1986–87	65–17 (.793)		
	L.A. Lakers, 1987–88	62–20 (.756)		
	L.A. Lakers, 1989–90	63–19 (.768)		
	N.Y. Knicks, 1992–93	60–22 (.732)		
	Mia. Heat, 1996–97	61–21 (.744)		
Flip Saunders	Det. Pistons, 2005–06	64–18 (.780)	Min. T'Wolves, 2014–15	16–66 (.195)

ª ABA.

Most Career Regular-Season Losses·

		Record				Record
1155	Lenny Wilkens	1332–1155 (.536)		746	Kevin Loughery	642–746 (.463)
1106	Bill Fitch	944–1106 (.460)		746	Rick Carlisle^	861–746 (.536)
1063	Don Nelson	1335–1063 (.557)		735	Doc Rivers^	1043–735 (.587)
1017	Dick Motta	935–1017 (.479)		716	Mike Dunleavy	613–716 (.461)
1011	Larry Brown	1327–1011 (.568)		701	Gregg Popovich^	1344–701 (.657)
861	Gene Shue	784–861 (.477)		694	Pat Riley	1210–694 (.636)
824	George Karl	1175–824 (.588)		657	John MacLeod	707–657 (.518)
803	Jerry Sloan	1221–803 (.603)		647	Byron Scott	454–647 (.412)
783	Jack Ramsay	864–783 (.525)		638	Nate McMillan^	731–638 (.534)
775	Cotton Fitzsimmons	832–775 (.518)		636	Alvin Gentry^	534–636 (.456)
749	Rick Adelman	1042–749 (.582)		603	Red Holzman	696–603 (.536)

· Includes ABA.

^ Active.

Coaches Fired After 50-Win Seasons

	50-Win Season	Record	Outcome
David Blatt	Cle. Cavaliers, 2014–15	53–29 (.646)	Fired 12 games into 1998–99 season (6–6).
Hubie Brown	Atl. Hawks, 1979–80	50–32 (.610)	Fired after season.
Larry Brown	S.A. Spurs, 1990–91	55–27 (.671)	Fired 14 games into 1961–62 season (5–9).
Mike Brown	Cle. Cavaliers, 2009–10	61–21 (.744)	Fired 41 games into 2015–16 season (30–11)
Rick Carlisle	Det. Pistons, 2002–03	50–32 (.610)	Fired after season.
Dwane Casey	Tor. Raptors, 2017–18	59–23 (.720)	Fired 6 games into 2018–19 season (0–6).
Don Chaney	Hou. Rockets, 1990–91	52–30 (.634)	Fired after season.
Doug Collins	Det. Pistons, 1996–97	54–28 (.659)	Fired 45 games into 1997–98 season (21–24).
Dave Cowens	Cha. Hornets, 1997–98	51–31 (.622)	Fired 49 games into 1996–97 season (24–25).
Mike Dunleavy	Por. Blazers, 2000–01	50–32 (.610)	Fired 47 games into 1988–89 season (25–22).
Del Harris	L.A. Lakers, 1997–98	61–21 (.744)	Fired after season.
Bob Hill	S.A. Spurs, 1995–96	59–23 (.720)	Fired 33 games into 1995–96 season (14–19).
Brian Hill	Orl. Magic, 1995–96	60–22 (.732)	Fired 11 games into 2015–16 season (4–7).
Mark Jackson	G.S. Warriors, 2013–14	51–31 (.622)	Fired after season.
Avery Johnson	Dal. Mavericks, 2007–08	51–31 (.622)	Fired 52 games into 1991–92 season (26–26).
George Karl	Sea. Sonics, 1997–98	61–21 (.744)	Fired after season.
George Karl	Den. Nuggets, 2012–13	57–25 (.695)	Fired 45 games into 1994–95 season (14–31).
John Lucas	S.A. Spurs, 1993–94	55–27 (.671)	Fired 11 games into 1981–82 season (7–4)
Tyronn Lue	Cle. Cavaliers, 2017–18	50–32 (.610)	Fired after season.
Babe McCarthy	Ken. Colonelsª, 1973–74	53–31 (.631)	Fired after season.
Kevin McHale	Hou. Rockets, 2014–15	56–26 (.683)	Fired 79 games into 1980–81 season (31–48).
Don Nelson	G.S. Warriors, 1993–94	50–32 (.610)	Fired 51 games into 2004–05 season (25–26).

continued on next page

50-Win Season	Record	Outcome
Jimmy Rodgers............. Bos. Celtics, 1989–90 .... 52–30 (.634) ....Fired 18 games into 1996–97 season (3–15).		
Flip Saunders .... Min. T'Wolves, 2003–04 .... 58–24 (.707) ....Fired after season.		
Flip Saunders .... Det. Pistons, 2007–08 .... 59–23 (.720) ....Fired after season.		
Dolph Schayes............. Phi. 76ers, 1965–66 .... 55–25 (.688) ....Fired 38 games into 1991–92 season (21–17).		
Mike Schuler .... Por. Blazers, 1987–88 .... 53–29 (.646) ....Fired after season.		
Paul Seymour .... St.L. Hawks, 1960–61 .... 51–28 (.646) ....Fired after season.		
Gene Shue.................. Phi. 76ers, 1976–77 .... 50–32 (.610) ....Fired after season.		
Tom Thibodeau .... Chi. Bulls, 2014–15 .... 50–32 (.610) ....Fired 15 games into 1998–99 season (4–11).		
Jeff Van Gundy........... Hou. Rockets, 2006–07 .... 52–30 (.634) ....Fired after season.		
Paul Westhead .... L.A. Lakers, 1980–81 .... 54–28 (.659) ....Fired after season.		
Paul Westphal .... Pho. Suns, 1994–95 .... 59–23 (.720) ....Fired after season.		

[a] ABA.

Coaching Most Teams

11........ Larry Brown .... Car. Cougars[a] (1972–74), Den. Nuggets[a] (1974–76), Den. Nuggets (1976–79), N.J. Nets (1981–83), S.A. Spurs (1988–92), L.A. Clippers (1991–93), Ind. Pacers (1993–97), Phi. 76ers (1997–2003), Det. Pistons (2003–05), N.Y. Knicks (2005–06), Cha. Bobcats (2008–11)

7.......... Kevin Loughery............... Phi. 76ers (1972–73), N.Y. Nets[a] (1973–76), N.Y.-N.J. Nets (1976–81), Atl. Hawks (1981–83), Chi. Bulls (1983–85), Was. Bullets (1985–88), Mia. Heat (1991–95)

6.......... Alex Hannum................. St.L. Hawks (1956–58), Syr. Nationals (1960–63), S.F. Warriors (1963–66), Phi. 76ers (1966–68), Oak. Oaks[a] (1968–69), S.D. Rockets (1969–71), Den. Nuggets (1971–74)

6.......... Lenny Wilkens................ Sea. Sonics (1969–72; 1977–85), Por. Blazers (1974–76), Cle. Cavaliers (1986–93), Atl. Hawks (1993–2000), Tor. Raptors (2000–03), N.Y. Knicks (2003–05)

6.......... Tom Nissalke .... Dal. Chaparrals-S.A. Spurs[a] (1971–72; 1973–75), Sea. Sonics (1972–73), Uta. Stars[a] (1974–76), Hou. Rockets (1976–79), Uta. Jazz (1979–82), Cle. Cavaliers (1982–84)

6.......... George Karl .... Cle. Cavaliers (1984–86), G.S. Warriors (1986–88), Sea. Sonics (1991–98), Mil. Bucks (1998–2003), Den. Nuggets (2004–13), Sac. Kings (2014–16)

6.......... Alvin Gentry[^]................. Mia. Heat (1994–95), Det. Pistons (1997–2000), L.A. Clippers (2000–03), Pho. Suns (2008–13), N.O. Pelicans (2015–20), Sac. Kings (2021–22)

5.......... Butch van Breda Kolff ...... L.A. Lakers (1967–69), Det. Pistons (1969–72), Pho. Suns (1972–73), Mem. Tams[a] (1973–74), N.O. Jazz (1974–77)

5.......... Dick Motta..................... Chi. Bulls (1968–76), Was. Bullets (1976–80), Dal. Mavericks (1980–87; 1994–96), Sac. Kings (1989–92), Den. Nuggets (1996–97)

5.......... Stan Albeck .... Den. Rockets[a] (1970–71), Cle. Cavaliers (1979–80), S.A. Spurs (1980–83), N.J. Nets (1983–85), Chi. Bulls (1985–86)

5.......... Bill Fitch .... Cle. Cavaliers (1970–79), Bos. Celtics (1979–83), Hou. Rockets (1983–88), N.J. Nets (1989–92), L.A. Clippers (1994–98)

5.......... Cotton Fitzsimmons.......... Pho. Suns (1970–72; 1988–97), Atl. Hawks (1972–76), Buf. Braves (1977–78), K.C. Kings (1978–84), S.A. Spurs (1984–86)

5.......... Bernie Bickerstaff............. Sea. Sonics (1985–90), Den. Nuggets (1994–97), Was. Bullets-Wizards (1996–99), Cha. Bobcats (2004–07)

5.......... Rick Adelman.................. Por. Blazers (1988–94), G.S. Warriors (1995–97), Sac. Kings (1998–2006), Hou. Rockets (2007–11), Min. T'Wolves (2011–14)

5.......... Mike D'Antoni................. Den. Nuggets (1998–99), Pho. Suns (2003–08), N.Y. Knicks (2008–12), L.A. Lakers (2012–14), Hou. Rockets (2016–20)

[a] ABA.

[^] Active.

Career One-Game Coaches

Lew Hayman .... Tor. Huskies @ Por. Steamrollers (Nov. 30, 1946) ...... Lost

Bob Staak .... Was. Bullets @ Den. Nuggets (Feb. 5, 1997) .... Lost

Coaches with Same Initials as Team They Coached

Dick Motta, Dal. Mavericks (1980–87; 1994–96)
Mike Budenholzer^, Mil. Bucks (2018–22)
^ Active with franchise.

Playoffs

Most Career Playoff Victories

	W/L%			W/L%			W/L%
229....... Phil Jackson	.688	81......... K.C. Jones	.587	58......... Red Holzman..............	.552
171....... Pat Riley	.606	80......... Lenny Wilkens.............	.449	56......... Dick Motta	.444
170....... Gregg Popovich^	.599	80......... George Karl	.432	55......... Mike Budenholzer^.......	.556
120....... Larry Brown*	.518	79......... Rick Adelman	.503	55......... Bill Fitch	.505
104....... Doc Rivers^	.510	75......... Chuck Daly.................	.595	54......... Mike D'Antoni	.491
99....... Red Auerbach.............	.589	75......... Don Nelson	.452	51......... Tyronn Lue^	.638
98....... Jerry Sloan	.485	66......... Billy Cunningham	.629	51......... Rudy Tomjanovich	.567
96....... Erik Spoelstra^	.596	63......... Rick Carlisle^	.474		
93....... Steve Kerr^	.732	60......... John Kundla................	.632		

^ Active.

* Includes ABA.

Winning Percentage for Coaches Winning Championships

			Record	Championships
.704	....	Phil Jackson........................	1155–485...........	11
.698	....	Billy Cunningham.................	454–196	1
.692	....	Vince Cazzetta°.....................	54–24.............	1
.682	....	Steve Kerr^..........................	429–200	3
.674	....	K.C. Jones...........................	522–252	2
.662	....	Red Auerbach......................	938–479	9
.657	....	Gregg Popovich^	1344–701	5
.636	....	Pat Riley.............................	1210–694.............	5
.620	....	Les Harrison	295–181	1
.619	....	Tom Heinsohn	427–263	2
.604	....	Nick Nurse^	186–122	1
.595	....	Tyronn Lue^	217–148	1
.593	....	Erik Spoelstra^	660–453	2
.593	....	Chuck Daly	638–437	2
.592	....	Mike Budenholzer^................	426–293	1
.589	....	Larry Costello	430–300	1
.587	....	Doc Rivers^	1043–735	1
.583	....	John Kundla	423–302	5
.575	....	Al Cervi.............................	326–241	1
.569	....	Bill Sharman**	466–353	2
.568	....	Larry Brown**	1327–1011.............	1
.559	....	Rudy Tomjanovich	527–416	2
.551	....	George Senesky	119–97	1
.540	....	Bill Russell	341–290	2
.536	....	Lenny Wilkens	1332–1155.............	1
.536	....	Rick Carlisle^......................	861–746	1
.536	....	Red Holzman........................	696–603	2

continued on next page

		Record	Championships
.535	Alex Hannum**	649–564	3
.526	Frank Vogel	431–389	1
.525	Jack Ramsay	864–783	1
.518	Slick Leonard*	573–534	3
.518	Al Attles	557–518	1
.486	Hubie Brown*	528–559	1
.479	Dick Motta	935–1017	1
.463	Kevin Loughery*	642–746	2
.460	Bill Fitch	944–1106	1
.453	Eddie Gottlieb	263–318	1
.450	Paul Westhead	183–224	1
.440	Buddy Jeannette	136–173	1

^ Active.

* Coached in both NBA and ABA; won championship in ABA only.

** Won championship in both NBA and ABA.

ª Only coached in ABA (one season).

Winning Championship as Both Coach and Player

	As Coach	As Player
Larry Brown	Det. Pistons: 2004	Oak. Oaksª: 1969
Rick Carlisle	Dal. Mavericks: 2011	Bos. Celtics: 1986
Billy Cunningham	Phi. 76ers: 1983	Phi. 76ers: 1967
Tom Heinsohn	Bos. Celtics: 1974, 1976	Bos. Celtics: 1957, 1959, 1960, 1961, 1962, 1963, 1964, 1965
Red Holzman	N.Y. Knicks: 1970, 1973	Roc. Royals: 1951
Phil Jackson	Chi. Bulls: 1991, 1992, 1993, 1996, 1997, 1998	N.Y. Knicks: 1973
Buddy Jeannette*	Bal. Bullets: 1948	Bal. Bullets: 1948
K.C. Jones	Bos. Celtics: 1984, 1986	Bos. Celtics: 1959, 1960, 1961, 1962, 1963, 1964, 1965, 1966
Steve Kerr	G.S. Warriors: 2015, 2017, 2018	Chi. Bulls: 1996, 1997, 1998
Tyronn Lue	Cle. Cavaliers: 2016	L.A. Lakers: 2001
Pat Riley	L.A. Lakers: 1982, 1985, 1987, 1988	L.A. Lakers: 1972
Bill Russell	Bos. Celtics: 1968, 1969	Bos. Celtics: 1957, 1959, 1960, 1961, 1962, 1963, 1964, 1965, 1966, 1968, 1969
George Senesky	Phi. Warriors: 1956	Phi. Warriors: 1947
Bill Sharman	Uta. Starsª: 1971	Bos. Celtics: 1957, 1959, 1960, 1961

ª ABA.

* Player-Coach.

Championship-Winning Coaches Who Never Played in the BAA/NBA/ABA

Coach	Championships	Team (Championship Year)
Red Auerbach	9	Bos. Celtics (1957, 1959, 1960, 1961, 1962, 1963, 1964, 1965, 1966)
Mike Budenholzer^	1	Mil. Bucks (2021)
Chuck Daly	2	Det. Pistons (1989, 1990)
Bill Fitch	1	Bos. Celtics (1981)
Eddie Gottlieb	1	Phi. Warriors (1947)
Les Harrison	1	Roc. Royals (1951)
John Kundl	5	Min. Lakers (1949, 1950, 1952, 1953, 1954)
Dick Motta	1	Was. Bullets (1978)

continued on next page

Coach	Championships	Team (Championship Year)
Nick Nurse^	1	Tor. Raptors (2019)
Gregg Popovich^	5	S.A. Spurs (1999, 2003, 2005, 2007, 2014)
Jack Ramsay	1	Por. Blazers (1977)
Erik Spoelstra^	2	Mia. Heat (2012; 2013)
Frank Vogel^	1	L.A. Lakers (2020)
Paul Westhead	1	L.A. Lakers (1980)

^ Active.

Coaches Undefeated in Finals Play

		Finals Record
Al Attles	G.S. Warriors, 1974–75	4–0*

* Only finals appearance.

Coaches Winning Championship in First Season as a Head Coach

	Championship-Winning Team	Total Games as Head Coach	Record in First Season
Buddy Jeannette	Bal. Bullets, 1947–48	48	28–20 (.583)
John Kundla	Min. Lakers, 1948–49	60	44–16 (.733)
George Senesky	Phi. Warriors, 1955–56	72	45–27 (.625)
Vince Cazzetta	Pit. Pipers^a, 1967–68	78	54–24 (.692)
Hubie Brown	Ken. Colonels^a, 1974–75	84	58–26 (.690)
Paul Westhead*	L.A. Lakers, 1979–80	68	50–18 (.735)
Pat Riley	L.A. Lakers, 1981–82	71	50–21 (.704)
Steve Kerr	G.S. Warriors, 2014–15	82	67–15 (.817)
Tyronn Lue*	Cle. Cavaliers, 2015–16	41	27–14 (.659)
Nick Nurse	Tor. Raptors, 2018–19	82	58–24 (.707)

^a ABA.

* Hired midseason.

Fewest Regular-Season Games Coached Before First Championship

	Total Games Coached	Championship Team	Record (Up to Championship)
Tyronn Lue	41	Cle. Cavaliers, 2015–16	27–14 (.659)
Buddy Jeannette	48	Bal. Bullets, 1947–48	28–20 (.583)
Eddie Gottlieb	60	Phi. Warriors, 1946–47	35–25 (.583)
John Kundla	60	Min. Lakers, 1948–49	44–16 (.733)
Paul Westhead	68	L.A. Lakers, 1979–80	50–18 (.735)
Pat Riley	71	L.A. Lakers, 1981–82	50–21 (.704)
George Senesky	72	Phi. Warriors, 1955–56	45–27 (.625)
Vince Cazzetta	78	Pit. Pipers^a, 1967–68	54–24 (.692)
Nick Nurse	82	Tor. Raptors, 2018–19	58–24 (.707)
Steve Kerr	82	G.S. Warriors, 2014–15	67–15 (.817)
Hubie Brown	84	Ken. Colonels^a, 1974–75	58–26 (.690)
Alex Hannum	103	St.L. Hawks, 1957–58	56–47 (.544)
Kevin Lougherty	115	N.Y. Nets^a, 1973–74	60–55 (.522)
Bill Russell	163	Bos. Celtics, 1967–68	114–49 (.699)
Phil Jackson	164	Chi. Bulls, 1990–91	116–48 (.707)
Rudy Tomjanovich	194	Hou. Rockets, 1993–94	129–51 (.665)
Gregg Popovich	196	S.A. Spurs, 1998–99	110–86 (.561)
Les Harrison	196	Roc. Royals, 1950–51	137–59 (.699)
Larry Costello	246	Mil. Bucks, 1970–71	149–97 (.606)
Slick Leonard	275	Ind. Pacers^a, 1969–70	145–130 (.527)

* Replaced fired coach midseason.

^a ABA.

Most Regular-Season Games Coached Before First Championship

	Total Games Coached	Championship Team	Record (Up to Championship)
Larry Brown	1982	Det. Pistons, 2003–04	1162–820 (.586)
Bill Fitch	902	Bos. Celtics, 1980–81	427–475 (.473)
Dick Motta	820	Was. Bullets, 1977–78	448–372 (.546)
Jack Ramsay	738	Por. Blazers, 1976–77	381–357 (.516)
Rick Carlisle	738	Dal. Mavericks, 2010–11	443–295 (.600)
Red Auerbach	719	Bos. Celtics, 1956–57	428–291 (.595)
Doc Rivers	667	Bos. Celtics, 2007–08	339–328 (.508)
Frank Vogel	666	L.A. Lakers, 2019–20	356–310 (.535)
Mike Budenholzer	637	Mil. Bucks, 2020–21	375–262 (.589)
Lenny Wilkens	552	Sea. Sonics, 1978–79	290–262 (.525)
Chuck Daly	533	Det. Pistons, 1988–89	319–214 (.598)

Most Games Coached, Never Winning Championship*

2398	Don Nelson	1364	John MacLeod	1170	Alvin Gentry^
2024	Jerry Sloan	1369	Nate McMillan^	1107	Slick Leonard
1999	George Karl	1329	Mike Dunleavy	1101	Byron Scott
1791	Rick Adelman	1246	Flip Saunders	1087	Hubie Brown
1645	Gene Shue	1215	Mike Fratello	1013	Del Harris
1607	Cotton Fitzsimmons	1199	Mike D'Antoni	1003	Terry Stotts
1388	Kevin Loughery	1157	Doug Moe		

* Includes ABA.

^ Active.

Most Career Victories, No Playoff Appearances

Career Wins		Record	Career Wins		Record
573	Slick Leonard	573–534 (.512)	109	Scotty Robertson	109–178 (.308)
283	Al Bianchi	283–392 (.419)	108	Jay Triano	108–200 (.351)
166	Luke Walton	166–241 (.408)	108	Eric Musselman	108–138 (.439)
161	Jeff Hornacek	161–216 (.427)	97	Ron Rothstein	97–231 (.296)
141	Bob Cousy	141–207 (.405)	95	Johnny Bach	95–172 (.356)
137	James Borrego^	148–183 (.447)	93	Keith Smart	93–170 (.354)

^ Active.

Most Coaching Victories, Never Winning Championship

1335	Don Nelson	784	Gene Shue	654	Flip Saunders
1221	Jerry Sloan	707	John MacLeod	628	Mike Dunleavy
1175	George Karl	702	Nate McMillan^	613	Del Harris
1042	Rick Adelman	672	Mike D'Antoni		
832	Cotton Fitzsimmons	667	Mike Fratello		

^ Active.

Most Playoff Victories, Never Winning Champioship

98	Jerry Sloan	54	Mike D'Antoni^	47	Flip Saunders
80	George Karl	49	Scott Brooks^	47	Mike Brown^
79	Rick Adelman	48	Stan Van Gundy	44	Jeff Van Gundy
75	Don Nelson	47	John MacLeod		

^ Active.

Most Career Playoff Losses

		Win%			Win%			Win%
115	Larry Brown	.511	104	Phil Jackson	.688	91	Don Nelson	.452
114	Gregg Popovich^	.599	104	Jerry Sloan	.485	78	Rick Adelman	.503
111	Pat Riley	.606	100	Doc Rivers^	.510	70	Rick Carlisle^	.474
105	George Karl	.432	98	Lenny Wilkens	.449	70	Dick Motta	.444

* Includes ABA.

^ Active.

Most Finals Appearances, Never Winning Championship

4	Fred Schaus	1961–62	L.A. Lakers vs. Bos. Celtics (3–4)
		1962–63	L.A. Lakers vs. Bos. Celtics (2–4)
		1964–65	L.A. Lakers vs. Bos. Celtics (1–4)
		1965–66	L.A. Lakers vs. Bos. Celtics (3–4)
3	Joe Lapchick	1950–51	N.Y. Knicks vs. Roc. Royals (3–4)
		1951–52	N.Y. Knicks vs. Min. Lakers (3–4)
		1952–53	N.Y. Knicks vs. Min. Lakers (1–4)
3	Joe Mullaney	1969–70	L.A. Lakers vs. N.Y. Knicks (3–4)
		1972–73	Ken. Colonels* vs. Ind. Pacers* (3–4)
		1973–74	Uta. Stars* vs. N.Y. Nets* (1–4)
2	Charles Eckman	1954–55	Ft.W. Pistons vs. Syr. Nationals (3–4)
		1955–56	Ft.W. Pistons vs. Phi. Warriors (1–4)
2	Butch van Breda Kolff	1967–68	L.A. Lakers vs. Bos. Celtics (2–4)
		1968–69	L.A. Lakers vs. Bos. Celtics (3–4)
2	Gene Shue	1970–71	Bal. Bullets vs. Mil. Bucks (0–4)
		1976–77	Phi. 76ers vs. Por. Blazers (2–4)
2	Rick Adelman	1989–90	Por. Blazers vs. Det. Pistons (1–4)
		1991–92	Por. Blazers vs. Chi. Bulls (2–4)
2	Jerry Sloan	1996–97	Uta. Jazz vs. Chi. Bulls (2–4)
		1997–98	Uta. Jazz vs. Chi. Bulls (2–4)
2	Byron Scott	2001–02	N.J. Nets vs. L.A. Lakers (0–4)
		2002–03	N.J. Nets vs. S.A. Spurs (2–4)

* ABA.

Awards

Highest Career Winning Percentage for COY

Win% (W–L)

.704 (1155–485)	Phil Jackson	1995–96: Chi. Bulls
.692 (54–24)	Vince Cazzetta	1967–68: Pit. Pipers*
.687 (147–67)	Larry Bird	1997–98: Ind. Pacers
.682 (429–200)	Steve Kerr^	2015–16: G.S. Warriors
.662 (938–479)	Red Auerbach	1964–65: Bos. Celtics
.657 (1344–701)	Gregg Popovich^	2002–03, 2011–12, 2013–14: S.A. Spurs
.652 (45–24)	Joe Belmont	1969–70*: Den. Rockets*
.636 (1210–694)	Pat Riley	1989–90: L.A. Lakers; 1992–93: N.Y. Knicks; 1996–97: Mia. Heat
.619 (427–263)	Tom Heinsohn	1972–73: Bos. Celtics
.616 (347–216)	Mike Brown	2008–09: Cle. Cavaliers
.604 (186–122)	Nick Nurse^	2019–20: Tor. Raptors
.592 (426–293)	Mike Budenholzer^	2014–15: Atl. Hawks; 2018–19: Mil. Bucks

continued on next page

Win% (W—L)

.588 (1175–824)..... George Karl.............2012–13: Den. Nuggets

.587 (1043–735)..... Doc Rivers^ ....1999–00: Orl. Magic

.577 (254–186)....... Avery Johnson ....2005–06: Dal. Mavericks

.572 (430–322)....... Tom Thibodeau^ ....2010–11: Chi. Bulls; 2020–21: N.Y. Knicks

.569 (466–353)....... Bill Sharman.............1969–70*: L.A. Stars^a; 1971–72: L.A. Lakers

.569 (322–244)....... Joe Mullaney............1973–74*: Uta. Stars^a

.568 (1327–1011)... Larry Brown ....1972–73: Car. Cougars^a; 1974–75, 1975–76: Den. Nuggets^a; 2000–01: Phi. 76ers

.560 (672–527)....... Mike D'Antoni ....2004–05: Pho. Suns; 2016–17: Hou. Rockets

.557 (1335–1063)... Don Nelson..............1982–83, 1984–85: Mil. Bucks; 1991–92: G.S. Warriors

.557 (521–414)....... Scott Brooks^.........2009–10: Ok.C. Thunder

.549 (667–548)....... Mike Fratello ....1985–86: Atl. Hawks

.549 (556–457)....... Del Harris ....1994–95: L.A. Lakers

.543 (628–529)....... Doug Moe ....1987–88: Den. Nuggets

.536 (1332–1155)... Lenny Wilkens ....1993–94: Atl. Hawks

.536 (861–746)....... Rick Carlisle^..........2001–02: Det. Pistons

.536 (696–603)....... Red Holzman ....1969–70: N.Y. Knicks

.535 (649–564)....... Alex Hannum ....1963–64: S.F. Warriors; 1968–69: Oak. Oaks^a

.531 (136–120)....... Harry Gallatin ....1962–63: St.L. Hawks

.530 (179–159)....... Mike Schuler ....1986–87: Por. Blazers

.529 (327–291)....... Richie Guerin ....1967–68: St.L. Hawks

.523 (147–134)....... Ray Scott ....1973–74: Det. Pistons

.519 (322–299)....... Monty Williams^.......2021–22: Pho. Suns

.518 (832–775)....... Cotton Fitzsimmons ...1978–79: K.C. Kings; 1988–89: Pho. Suns

.496 (280–284)....... Babe McCarthy ....1973–74*: Ken. Colonels^a

.486 (477–505)....... Dwane Casey^ ....2017–18: Tor. Raptors

.485 (277–294)....... Frank Layden ....1983–84: Uta. Jazz

.479 (935–1017)..... Dick Motta ....1970–71: Chi. Bulls

.477 (784–861)....... Gene Shue...............1968–69, 1981–82: Bal.-Was.Bullets

.467 (151–172)....... Dolph Schayes..........1965–66: Phi. 76ers

.461 (613–716)....... Mike Dunleavy ....1998–99: Por. Blazers

.461 (424–495)....... Hubie Brown ....1977–78: Atl. Hawks; 2003–04: Mem. Grizzlies

.460 (944–1106)..... Bill Fitch..................1975–76: Cle. Cavaliers; 1979–80: Bos. Celtics

.435 (236–307)....... Phil Johnson ....1974–75: K.C.-Oma. Kings

.433 (185–242)....... Sam Mitchell ....2006–07: Tor. Raptors

.422 (371–508)....... Tom Nissalke............1971–72: Dal. Chaparrals^a; 1976–77: Hou. Rockets

.419 (283–392)....... Al Bianchi ....1970–71: Vir. Squires^a

.412 (454–647)....... Byron Scott...............2007–08: N.O. Hornets

.406 (337–494)....... Don Chaney.............1990–91: Hou. Rockets

.387 (136–215)....... Jack McKinney ....1980–81: Ind. Pacers

.329 (93–190).........Red Kerr ....1966–67: Chi. Bulls

^ Active.

^a ABA.

* Tied for Coach of the Year.

Winning COY in Both ABA and NBA

	ABA Team	NBA Team
Larry Brown..................	Car. Cougars, 1972–73 (57–27) ....Phi. 76ers, 2000–01 (56–26)	
	Den. Nuggets, 1974–75 (65–19)	
	Den. Nuggets, 1975–76 (60–24)	
Tom Nissalke	Dal. Chaparrals, 1971–72 (42–42, .500)...........Hou. Rockets, 1976–77 (49–33)	
Bill Sharman.................	L.A. Stars, 1969–70** (43–41)...........................L.A. Lakers*, 1971–72 (69–13)	
Alex Hannum	Oak. Oaks*, 1968–69 (60–18)...........................S.F. Warriors, 1963–64 (48–32)	

* Won championship.

** Tied for COY with Joe Belmont, Den. Rockets.

Winning COY with Two Different Teams

		Record
Bill Fitch	Cle. Cavaliers, 1975–76	49–33
	Bos. Celtics, 1979–80	61–21
Cotton Fitzsimmons	K.C. Kings, 1978–79	48–34
	Pho. Suns, 1988–89	55–27
Don Nelson	Mil. Bucks, 1982–83	51–31
	Mil. Bucks, 1984–85	59–23
	G.S. Warriors, 1991–92	55–27
Hubie Brown	Atl. Hawks, 1977–78	41–41
	Mem. Grizzlies, 2003–04	50–32
Mike Budenholzer	Atl. Hawks, 2014–15	60–22
	Mil. Bucks, 2018–19	60–22
Mike D'Antoni	Pho. Suns, 2004–05	62–20
	Hou. Rockets, 2016–17	55–27
Pat Riley	L.A. Lakers, 1989–90	63–19
	N.Y. Knicks, 1992–93	60–22
	Mia. Heat, 1996–97	61–21
Tom Thibodeau	Chi. Bulls, 2010–11	62–20
	N.Y. Knicks, 2020–21	41–31

Winning Multiple COY Awards

Hubie Brown	Atl. Hawks: 1977–78
	Mem. Grizzlies: 2003–04
Larry Brown	Car. Cougars[a]: 1972–73
	Den. Nuggets[a]: 1974–75, 1975–76
	Phi. 76ers: 2000–01
Mike Budenholzer^	Atl. Hawks: 2014–15
	Mil. Bucks: 2018–19
Mike D'Antoni	Pho. Suns: 2004–05
	Hou. Rockets: 2016–17
Bill Fitch	Cle. Cavaliers: 1975–76
	Bos. Celtics: 1979–80
Cotton Fitzsimmons	K.C. Kings: 1978–79
	Pho. Suns: 1988–89
Alex Hannum	S.F. Warriors: 1963–64
	Oak. Oaks[a]: 1968–69
Don Nelson	Mil. Bucks: 1982–83, 1984–85
	G.S. Warriors: 1991–92
Tom Nissalke	Dal. Chaparrals[a]: 1971–72
	Hou. Rockets: 1976–77
Gregg Popovich^	S.A. Spurs: 2002–03, 2011–12, 2013–14
Pat Riley	L.A. Lakers: 1989–89
	N.Y. Knicks: 1992–93
	Mia. Heat: 1996–97
Bill Sharman	L.A. Stars[a]: 1969–70
	L.A. Lakers: 1971–72
Gene Shue	Bal.-Was. Bullets: 1968–69, 1981–82
Tom Thibodeau^	Chi. Bulls: 2010–11
	N.Y. Knicks: 2020–21

[a] ABA.

COY, .500 Record or Lower, Season

1966–67 ....Red Kerr, Chi. Bulls............................33–48 (.407)
1971–72 ....Tom Nissalke, Dal. Chaparrals^a..........42–42 (.500)
1977–78 ....Hubie Brown, Atl. Hawks ....41–41 (.500)
1999–00 ....Doc Rivers, Orl. Magic ....41–41 (.500)
^a ABA.

Won COY, Losing Record Next Season

	COY Season	Following Season
Alex Hannum, G.S. Warriors	1963–64: 48–32	1964–65: 17–63
Red Kerr, Chi. Bulls	1966–67*: 33–48	1967–68: 29–53
Ray Scott, Det. Pistons	1973–74: 52–30	1974–75: 40–42
Phil Johnson, K.C.-Oma.-K.C. Kings	1974–75: 44–38	1975–76: 31–51
Tom Nissalke, Hou. Rockets	1976–77: 49–33	1977–78: 28–54
Jack McKinney, Ind. Pacers	1980–81: 44–38	1981–82: 35–47
Nick Nurse, Tor. Raptors	2019–20: 53–19	2020–21: 27–45
Tom Thibodeau, N.Y. Knicks	2020–21: 41–35	2021–22: 37–45

* Inaugural season.

Winning COY and Championship, Same Season

1964–65	Red Auerbach, Bos. Celtics	1995–96	Phil Jackson, Chi. Bulls
1969–70	Red Holzman, Bos. Celtics	2002–03	Gregg Popovich, S.A. Spurs
1971–72	Bill Sharman, L.A. Lakers	2013–14	Gregg Popovich, S.A. Spurs

Winning Both COY and MVP

	COY	MVP
Larry Bird	Ind. Pacers, 1997–98	Bos. Celtics, 1983–84
		Bos. Celtics, 1984–85
		Bos. Celtics, 1985–86

8

RELATIVES

Hall of Famers Whose Sons Played in the NBA

Father	Son(s)
Rick Barry (1965–67, 1968–80)	Jon Barry (1992–2006)
	Brent Barry (1995–2009)
	Drew Barry (1997–2000)
Patrick Ewing (1985–2002)	Patrick Ewing Jr. (2010–11)
Tim Hardaway (1989–2003)	Tim Hardaway Jr. (2013–22)
George Karl* (1973–78)	Coby Karl (2007–08, 2009–10)
Al McGuire* (1951–55)	Allie McGuire (1973)
George Mikan (1948–54, 1955–56)	Larry Mikan (1970–71)
Gary Payton (1990–2007)	Gary Payton II (2016–22)
Arvydas Sabonis (1995–2001, 2002–03)	Domantas Sabonis (2016–22)
Dolph Schayes (1949–64)	Danny Schayes (1981–99)
John Stockton (1984–2003)	David Stockton (2015, 2018)
Bill Walton (1974–78, 1979–80, 1982–87)	Luke Walton (2003–13)

* Inducted to HOF as a Coach.

Players with Two Sons Who Played in the NBA

Father	Sons
Rick Barry (1965–67, 1968–80)	Jon Barry (1992–2006)
	Brent Barry (1995–2009)
	Drew Barry (1997–2000)
Harvey Grant (1988–99)	Jerami Grant (2014–22)
	Jerian Grant (2015–20)
Dell Curry (1986–2002)	Stephen Curry (2009–22)
	Seth Curry (2013–22)
Jim Paxson (1956–58)	Jim Paxson (1979–90)
	John Paxson (1983–94)
Mychal Thompson (1978–91)	Klay Thompson (2011–19, 2021–22)
	Mychel Thompson (2011–12)

Father and Son Drafted in the First Round

Father	Son(s)	Draft Year	Pick	Team
Greg Anthony		1991	12th Overall	N.Y. Knicks
	Cole Anthony	2020	15th Overall	Orl. Magic
Rick Barry		1965	4th Overall	S.F. Warriors
	Jon Barry	1992	21st Overall	Bos. Celtics
	Brent Barry	1995	15th Overall	Den. Nuggets
Ron Brewer		1978	7th Overall	Por. Blazers
	Ronnie Brewer	2006	14th Overall	Uta. Jazz
Joe Bryant		1975	14th Overall	G.S. Warriors
	Kobe Bryant	1996	13th Overall	Cha. Hornets
Norm Cook		1976	16th Overall	Bos. Celtics
	Brian Cook	2003	24th Overall	L.A. Lakers

continued on next page

Father	Son(s)	Draft Year	Pick	Team
Dell Curry		1986	15th Overall	Uta. Jazz
	Stephen Curry	2009	7th Overall	G.S. Warriors
LeRoy Ellis		1962	8th Overall	L.A. Lakers
	LeRon Ellis	1991	22nd Overall	L.A. Clippers
Bob Ferry		1959	7th Overall	St.L. Hawks
	Danny Ferry	1989	2nd Overall	L.A. Clippers
Harvey Grant		1988	12th Overall	Was. Bullets
	Jerian Grant	2015	19th Overall	Was. Wizards
Tim Hardaway		1986	14th Overall	G.S. Warriors
	Tim Hardaway Jr.	2013	24th Overall	N.Y. Knicks
Stan Love		1971	9th Overall	Bal. Bullets
	Kevin Love	2008	5th Overall	Mem. Grizzlies
Scott May		1976	2nd Overall	Chi. Bulls
	Sean May	2005	13th Overall	Cha. Bobcats
Larry Nance		1981	20th Overall	Pho. Suns
	Larry Nance Jr.	2015	27th Overall	L.A. Lakers
Sonny Parker		1976	17th Overall	G.S. Warriors
	Jabari Parker	2014	2nd Overall	Mil. Bucks
Arvydas Sabonis*		1986	24th Overall	Por. Blazers
	Domatas Sabonis	2016	11th Overall	Orl. Magic
Dolph Schayes		1948	4th Overall	N.Y. Knicks
	Danny Schayes	1981	13th Overall	Uta. Jazz
Mychal Thompson		1978	1st Overall	Por. Blazers
	Klay Thompson	2011	11th Overall	G.S. Warriors
Jimmy Walker		1967	1st Overall	Det. Pistons
	Jalen Rose	1994	13th Overall	Den. Nuggets
Mitchell Wiggins		1983	23rd Overall	Ind. Pacers
	Andrew Wiggins	2014	1st Overall	Cle. Cavaliers

* Also drafted in 1985 by Por. Blazers (4th Round, 77th Overall).

Father and Son Both Playing for the Same Team

Team	Father	Son(s)
Hou. Rockets	Rick Barry (1978–80)	Brent Barry (2008–09), Jon Barry (2004–06)
G.S. Warriors	Rick Barry (1972–78)	Jon Barry (1995–96)
N.Y. Knicks	Henry Bibby (1972–75)	Mike Bibby (2011–12)
Chi. Bulls	Ron Brewer (1985)	Ronnie Brewer (2010–12, 2014)
Uta. Jazz	Corey Crowder (1991–92)	Jae Crowder (2018–19)
Mil. Bucks	Mike Dunleavy (1983–85, 1988–90)	Mike Dunleavy Jr. (2011–13)
Dal. Mavericks	Tim Hardaway (2001–02)	Tim Hardaway Jr. (2019–22)
Hou. Rockets	John Lucas (1976–78, 1984–86, 1989–90)	John Lucas III (2005–07)
L.A. Lakers	Wes Matthews (1986–88)	Wesley Matthews (2020–21)
N.Y. Knicks	Al McGuire (1951–54)	Allie McGuire (1973–74)
Cle. Cavaliers	Larry Nance (1988–94)	Larry Nance Jr. (2017–21)
Mil. Bucks	Gary Payton (2003)	Gary Payton II (2016–17
L.A. Lakers	Gary Payton (2003–04)	Gary Payton II (2018)
Det. Pistons	Walker Russell (1982–84, 1985, 1988)	Walker Russell Jr. (2011–12)
Uta. Jazz	John Stockton (1984–2003)	David Stockton (2018)
S.A. Spurs	Collis Temple* (1974–75)	Garrett Temple (2010)
N.Y. Knicks	Ernie Vandeweghe (1949–54, 1956)	Kiki Vandeweghe (1989–92)

* Played for ABA Spurs.

Father and Son Both Winning Championships

Father		Son	
Rick Barry	G.S. Warriors, 1974–75	Brent Barry	S.A. Spurs, 2004–05, 2006–07
Matt Guokas	Phi. Warriors, 1946–47	Matt Guokas Jr.	Phi. 76ers, 1966–67
Gary Payton	Mia. Heat, 2005–06	Gary Payton II	G.S. Warriors, 2021–22
Mychal Thompson	L.A. Lakers, 1986–87, 1987–88	Klay Thompson	G.S. Warriors, 2014–15, 2016–17, 2017–18, 2021–22
Bill Walton	Por. Blazers, 1976–77; Bos. Celtics, 1985–86	Luke Walton	L.A. Lakers, 2008–09, 2009–10

Most Career Games Played by Father-Son Combination˙ (Min. 500 Games Each)

Total	Father	GP	Son	GP
2134	Dolph Schayes (1949–64)	996	Danny Schayes (1981–99)	1138
1952	Joe Bryant (1975–83)	606	Kobe Bryant (1996–2016)	1346
1932	Rick Barry (1965–80)	1020	Brent Barry (1995–2009)	912
1903	Dell Curry (1986–2002)	1083	Stephen Curry^ (2009–22)	820
1841	Rick Barry (1965–80)	1020	Jon Barry (1992–2006)	821
1676	Henry Bibby (1972–81)	675	Mike Bibby (1998–2012)	1001
1621	Jimmy Walker (1967–76)	698	Jalen Rose (1994–2007)	923
1582	Mychal Thompson (1979–91)	935	Klay Thompson^ (2011–22)	647
1551	Bob Ferry (1959–69)	634	Danny Ferry (1990–2003)	917
1519	Doc Rivers (1983–96)	864	Austin Rivers^ (2012–22)	655

* Includes ABA.

^ Active.

Most Career Minutes Played by Father-Son Combination (Min. 9000 Minutes Each)

Total	Father	MP	Son	MP
61,796	Rick Barry (1965–80)	38,153	Brent Barry (1995–2009)	23,643
61,482	Joe Bryant (1975–83)	12,845	Kobe Bryant (1996–2016)	48,637
52,033	Rick Barry (1965–80)	38,153	Jon Barry (1992–2006)	13,880
51,910	Dell Curry (1986–2002)	23,549	Stephen Curry^ (2009–22)	28,361
51,775	Dolph Schayes (1949–64)	29,800**	Danny Schayes (1981–99)	21,975
51,515	Jimmy Walker (1967–76)	23,590	Jalen Rose (1994–2007)	27,925
49,437	Henry Bibby (1972–81)	15,475	Mike Bibby (1998–2012)	33,962
49,045	Mychal Thompson (1979–91)	27,764	Klay Thompson^ (2011–22)	21,281
46,463	Tim Hardaway (1989–2003)	30,626	Tim Hardaway Jr.^ (2013–22)	15,837
40,224	Larry Nance (1981–94)	30,697	Larry Nance Jr.^ (2015–22)	9527
39,409	Doc Rivers (1983–96)	23,567	Austin Rivers^ (2012–22)	15,842
37,075	Gerald Wilkins (1985–99)	26,084	Damien Wilkins (2004–18)	10,991
36,651	Wes Matthews (1980–91)	9305	Wesley Matthews^ (2009–22)	27,346
35,768	Mike Dunleavy (1976–90)	8428	Mike Dunleavy Jr. (2002–17)	27,340
34,964	Harvey Grant (1988–99)	20,510	Jerami Grant^ (2014–22)	14,454
34,436	Ed Manning (1967–76)	10,234	Danny Manning (1988–2003)	24,202
33,039	Dell Curry (1986–2002)	23,549	Seth Curry^ (2013–22)	9490
32,710	Gerald Henderson (1979–92)	18,856	Gerald Henderson Jr. (2009–17)	13,854
30,961	Bob Ferry (1959–69)	12,828	Danny Ferry (1990–2003)	18,133

* Includes ABA.

** Stats incomplete.

^ Active.

Most Career Points by Father-Son Combination· (Min. 500 Points Each)

Total	Father	Pts	Son	Pts
38,895	Joe Bryant (1975–83)	5252	Kobe Bryant (1996–2016)	33,643
33,767	Rick Barry (1965–80)	25,279	Brent Barry (1995–2009)	8488
32,734	Dell Curry (1986–2002)	12,670	Stephen Curry^ (2009–22)	20,064
29,994	Rick Barry (1965–80)	25,279	Jon Barry (1992–2006)	4715
27,218	Dolph Schayes (1949–64)	18,438	Danny Schayes (1981–99)	8780
25,457	Mychal Thompson (1979–91)	12,810	Klay Thompson^ (2011–22)	12,647
24,875	Jimmy Walker (1967–76)	11,655	Jalen Rose (1994–2007)	13,220
23,522	Tim Hardaway (1989–2003)	15,373	Tim Hardaway Jr.^ (2013–22)	8149
22,553	Gary Payton (1990–2007)	21,813	Gary Payton II^ (2016–22)	740
20,473	Henry Bibby (1972–81)	5775	Mike Bibby (1998–2012)	14,698
18,897	Larry Nance (1981–94)	15,687	Larry Nance Jr.^ (2015–22)	3210
18,115	Ernie Vandeweghe (1949–56)	2135	Kiki Vandeweghe (1980–93)	15,980
16,915	Dell Curry (1986–2002)	12,670	Seth Curry^ (2013–22)	4245
16,038	Glenn Robinson (1994–2005)	14,234	Glenn Robinson III^ (2015–22)	1804
15,908	Ed Manning (1967–76)	3541	Danny Manning (1988–2003)	12,367
15,884	Stan Love (1972–75)	1579	Kevin Love^ (2008–22)	14,305
15,396	Mitchell Wiggins (1983–92)	3877	Andrew Wiggins^ (2014–22)	11,519
15,340	Gerald Wilkins (1985–99)	11,736	Damien Wilkins (2004–18)	3604
15,118	Doc Rivers (1983–96)	9377	Austin Rivers^ (2012–22)	5741
14,575	Wes Matthews (1980–91)	3654	Wesley Matthews^ (2009–22)	10,921
14,544	Mike Dunleavy (1976–90)	3496	Mike Dunleavy Jr. (2002–17)	11,048
14,110	Harvey Grant (1988–99)	7781	Jerami Grant^ (2014–22)	6329
13,760	Gerald Henderson (1979–92)	7773	Gerald Henderson Jr. (2009–17)	5987
12,219	Bob Ferry (1959–69)	5780	Danny Ferry (1990–2003)	6439
11,851	Sonny Parker (1976–82)	4471	Jabari Parker^ (2014–22)	4380
11,590	Arvydas Sabonis (1995–2003)	5629	Domatis Sabonis^ (2016–22)	5961
11,163	Wayne Champan (1968–72)	1432	Rex Chapman (1988–2000)	9731
11,098	John Lucas (1976–90)	9951	John Lucas III (2005–17)	1147
10,440	Kenyon Martin (2000–15)	9325	Kenyon Martin Jr.^ (2020–22)	1115
9911	Ron Brewer (1978–86)	5971	Ronnie Brewer (2006–14)	3940
9473	Harvey Grant (1988–99)	7781	Jerian Grant^ (2015–22)	1692
8864	Bill Walton (1974–87)	6215	Luke Walton (2003–13)	2649
7941	Winston Garland (1987–95)	4799	Darius Garland^ (2019–22)	3142
7352	Terry Davis (1989–2001)	3061	Ed Davis^ (2010–22)	4291
7164	Greg Anthony (1991–2002)	5497	Cole Anthony^ (2020–22)	1667
7118	Gary Trent (1995–2004)	4366	Gary Trent Jr.^ (2018–22)	2752
5588	Jaren Jackson (1989–2002)	2370	Jaren Jackson Jr.^ (2018–22)	3218
4376	Rick Brunson (1997–2006)	1090	Jalen Brunson^ (2018–22)	3286
3747	Darren Daye (1983–88)	2225	Austin Daye (2009–15)	1522

· Includes ABA.

^ Active.

Most Career Field Goals by Father-Son Combination· (Min. 1000 Field Goals Each)

Total	Father	FG	Son	FG
13,812	Joe Bryant (1975–83)	2093	Kobe Bryant (1996–2016)	11,719
12,591	Rick Barry (1965–80)	9695	Brent Barry (1995–2009)	2896
11,965	Dell Curry (1986–2002)	5090	Stephen Curry^ (2009–22)	6875
11,290	Rick Barry (1965–80)	9695	Jon Barry (1992–2006)	1595
8857	Dolph Schayes (1949–64)	5863	Danny Schayes (1981–99)	2994
9949	Mychal Thompson (1979–91)	5191	Klay Thompson^ (2011–22)	4758

continued on next page

Total	Father	FG	Son	FG
9476	Jimmy Walker (1967–76)	4624	Jalen Rose (1994–2007)	4852
8492	Tim Hardaway (1989–2003)	5640	Tim Hardaway Jr.^ (2013–22)	2852
7559	Henry Bibby (1972–81)	2149	Mike Bibby (1998–2012)	5410
7693	Larry Nance (1981–94)	6370	Larry Nance Jr.^ (2015–22)	1323
6645	Dell Curry (1986–2002)	5090	Seth Curry^ (2013–22)	1555
6544	Ed Manning (1967–76)	1518	Danny Manning (1988–2003)	5026
6098	Gerald Wilkins (1985–99)	4754	Damien Wilkins (2004–18)	1344

* Includes ABA.
^ Active.

Most Career Three Pointers by Father-Son Combination· (Min. 150 Three Pointers Each)

Total	Father	3P	Son	3P
4362	Dell Curry (1986–2002)	1245	Stephen Curry^ (2009–22)	3117
2795	Tim Hardaway (1989–2003)	1542	Tim Hardaway Jr.^ (2013–22)	1253
2795	Tim Hardaway (1989–2003)	1542	Tim Hardaway Jr.^ (2013–22)	1253
1975	Dell Curry (1986–2002)	1245	Seth Curry^ (2013–22)	730
1571	Rick Barry (1965–80)	176	Brent Barry (1995–2009)	1395
1107	Doc Rivers (1983–96)	361	Austin Rivers^ (2012–22)	746
800	Greg Anthony (1991–2002)	610	Cole Anthony^ (2020–22)	190
687	Jaren Jackson (1989–2002)	346	Jaren Jackson Jr.^ (2018–22)	341
623	Gerald Wilkins (1985–99)	418	Damien Wilkins (2004–18)	205
452	Gerald Henderson (1979–92)	203	Gerald Henderson Jr. (2009–17)	249
407	John Lucas (1976–90)	244	John Lucas III (2005–17)	163

* Includes ABA.
^ Active.

Most Career Assists by Father-Son Combination· (Min. 1000 Assists Each)

Total	Father	Ast	Son	Ast
8190	Tim Hardaway (1989–2003)	7095	Tim Hardaway Jr.^ (2013–22)	1095
7844	Rick Barry (1965–80)	4952	Brent Barry (1995–2009)	2892
7776	Henry Bibby (1972–81)	2259	Mike Bibby (1998–2012)	5517
7355	Joe Bryant (1975–83)	1049	Kobe Bryant (1996–2016)	6306
7297	Dell Curry (1986–2002)	1909	Stephen Curry^ (2009–22)	5388
6736	Rick Barry (1965–80)	4952	Jon Barry (1992–2006)	1784
5956	Jimmy Walker (1967–76)	2429	Jalen Rose (1994–2007)	3527
4371	Dolph Schayes (1949–64)	3072	Danny Schayes (1981–99)	1299
4150	Gerald Henderson (1979–92)	3141	Gerald Henderson Jr. (2009–17)	1009
4063	Doc Rivers (1983–96)	2625	Austin Rivers^ (2012–22)	1438

^ Active.

Most Career Rebounds by Father-Son Combination· (Min. 1500 Rebounds Each)

Total	Father	Reb	Son	Reb
16,927	Dolph Schayes (1949–64)	11,256**	Danny Schayes (1981–99)	5671
9929	Larry Nance (1981–94)	7352	Larry Nance Jr.^ (2015–22)	2577
9643	Rick Barry (1965–80)	6863	Brent Barry (1995–2009)	2780
9488	Joe Bryant (1975–83)	2441	Kobe Bryant (1996–2016)	7047
9206	Mychal Thompson (1979–91)	6951	Klay Thompson^ (2011–22)	2255
8376	Rick Barry (1965–80)	6863	Jon Barry (1992–2006)	1513
7503	Terry Davis (1989–2001)	2887	Ed Davis^ (2010–22)	4616
7332	Ed Manning (1967–76)	2717	Danny Manning (1988–2003)	4615
7251	Arvydas Sabonis (1995–2003)	3436	Domatis Sabonis^ (2016–22)	3815

continued on next page

Total	Father	Reb	Son	Reb
6511	Bill Walton (1974–87)	4923	Luke Walton (2003–13)	1588
6455	Dell Curry (1986–2002)	2617	Stephen Curry^ (2009–22)	3838
5893	Bob Ferry (1959–69)	3343	Danny Ferry (1990–2003)	2550
5625	Harvey Grant (1988–99)	3436	Jerami Grant^ (2014–22)	2189
5053	Jimmy Walker (1967–76)	1860	Jalen Rose (1994–2007)	3193

* Includes ABA.

** Stats incomplete.

^ Active.

Most Career Steals by Father-Son Combination (Min. 400 Steals Each)

Total	Father	Stl	Son	Stl
2463	Joe Bryant (1975–83)	519	Kobe Bryant (1996–2016)	1944
2352	Dell Curry (1986–2002)	985	Stephen Curry^ (2009–22)	1367
2059	Rick Barry (1965–80)	1104	Brent Barry (1995–2009)	955
2029	Doc Rivers (1983–96)	1563	Austin Rivers^ (2012–22)	466
1826	Rick Barry (1965–80)	1104	Jon Barry (1992–2006)	722
1733	Henry Bibby (1972–81)	561	Mike Bibby (1998–2012)	1172
1356	Larry Nance (1981–94)	872	Larry Nance Jr.^ (2015–22)	484
1338	Gerald Wilkins (1985–99)	907	Damien Wilkins (2004–18)	431
1333	Wes Matthews (1980–91)	444	Wesley Matthews^ (2009–22)	889
1278	Mychal Thompson (1979–91)	701	Klay Thompson^ (2011–22)	577
1102	Ron Brewer (1978–86)	480	Ronnie Brewer (2006–14)	622

^ Active.

Most Career Blocks by Father-Son Combination (Min. 100 Blocks Each)

Total	Father	Blk	Son	Blk
2226	Larry Nance (1981–94)	2027	Larry Nance Jr.^ (2015–22)	199
1422	Mychal Thompson (1979–91)	1073	Klay Thompson^ (2011–22)	349
1136	Bill Walton (1974–87)	1034	Luke Walton (2003–13)	102
1043	Harvey Grant (1988–99)	428	Jerami Grant^ (2014–22)	615
841	Joe Bryant (1975–83)	201	Kobe Bryant (1996–2016)	640
715	Terry Davis (1989–2001)	149	Ed Davis^ (2010–22)	566
678	Arvydas Sabonis (1995–2003)	494	Domatis Sabonis^ (2016–22)	184
522	Rick Barry (1965–80)	269	Brent Barry (1995–2009)	253
459	Doc Rivers (1983–96)	351	Austin Rivers^ (2012–22)	108
425	Dell Curry (1986–2002)	238	Stephen Curry^ (2009–22)	187

^ Active.

Fathers Coaching Against Sons

Father (Team)	Son	Games	Son's Record	Scoring High
Mike Dunleavy (L.A. Clippers)	Mike Dunleavy Jr.	18	6–12 (.333)	22: G.S. Warriors* @ L.A. Clippers (Jan. 29, 2005)
George Karl (Den. Nuggets)	Coby Karl	1	1–0 (1.000)	1: L.A. Lakers vs. Den. Nuggets (Jan. 21, 2008)
Doc Rivers (L.A. Clippers/Phi. 76ers)	Austin Rivers	14	6–8 (.429)	19: N.O. Pelicans @ L.A. Clippers* (Mar. 1, 2014)
Butch van Breda Kolff (N.Y. Knicks)	Jan van Breda Kolff	28	8–20 (.286)	25: N.J. Nets* @ N.Y. Knicks (Feb. 24, 1979)

* Team lost game.

Fathers Coaching Sons

Father	Son	Team
Doc Rivers	Austin Rivers	L.A. Clippers, 2015–18 (243 games)

Brothers Drafted in First Round

	Draft	Round, Pick		Draft	Round, Pick
Sam Stith	1960	1st Round, 56th Overall	Kareem Rush	2002	1st Round, 20th Overall
Tom Stith	1961	1st Round, 2nd Overall	Brandon Rush	2008	1st Round, 13th Overall
Russ Lee	1972	1st Round, 6th Overall	Brook Lopez	2008	1st Round, 10th Overall
Ron Lee	1976	1st Round, 10th Overall	Robin Lopez	2008	1st Round, 15th Overall
Gene Short	1975	1st Round, 9th Overall	Jrue Holiday	2009	1st Round, 17th Overall
Purvis Short	1978	1st Round, 5th Overall	Aaron Holiday	2018	1st Round, 23rd Overall
Bernard King	1977	1st Round, 7th Overall	Jeff Teague	2009	1st Round, 19th Overall
Albert King	1981	1st Round, 10th Overal	Marquis Teague	2012	1st Round, 29th Overall
Jim Paxson	1979	1st Round, 12th Overall	Markieff Morris	2011	1st Round, 13th Overall
John Paxson	1983	1st Round, 19th Overall	Marcus Morris	2011	1st Round, 14th Overall
Dudley Bradley	1979	1st Round, 13th Overall	Tyler Zeller	2012	1st Round, 17th Overall
Charles Bradley	1981	1st Round, 23rd Overall	Cody Zeller	2013	1st Round, 4th Overall
Chuck Person	1986	1st Round, 4th Overall	Miles Plumlee	2012	1st Round, 26th Overall
Wesley Person	1994	1st Round, 23rd Overall	Mason Plumlee	2013	1st Round, 22nd Overall
Horace Grant	1987	1st Round, 10th Overall	Lonzo Ball	2017	1st Round, 2nd Overall
Harvey Grant	1988	1st Round, 12th Overall	LaMelo Ball	2020	1st Round, 3rd Overall
Jon Barry	1992	1st Round, 21st Overall			
Brent Barry	1995	1st Round, 15th Overall			

Twins Who Played in the NBA

Collins	Jason, center/forward (2001–14)		Martin	Cody, forward (2019–22)
	Jarron, center (2001–11)			Caleb, forward (2019–22)
Graham	Joey, forward (2005–11)		Morris	Marcus, forward (2011–22)
	Stephen, guard (2005–11)			Markieff, forward (2011–22)
Grant	Horace, forward/center (1987–2004)		Thomas	Charles, guard (1991–92)
	Harvey, forward (1988–99)			Carl, guard (1991–92, 1996–98)
Harrison	Aaron, guard (2015–18)		Van Arsdale	Tom, guard/forward (1965–77)
	Andrew, guard (2016–19)			Dick, guard (1965–77)
Lopez	Brook, center (2008–22)		Wear	Travis, forward (2014–15, 2017–18)
	Robin, center (2008–22)			David, forward (2014)

Most Career Games Played by Brothers*

2117	Pau Gasol	1226	1850	Tom Van Arsdale	929	1556	Jim Paxson	784
	Marc Gasol	891		Dick Van Arsdale	921		John Paxson	774
2025	Caldwell Jones	1299	1807	Brook Lopez^	868	1480	Gus Williams	825
	Charles Jones	726		Robin Lopez^	939		Ray Williams	655
1974	Dominique Wilkins	1074	1793	Jon Barry	821	1433	Marcus Morris^	718
	Gerald Wilkins	900		Brent Barry	912		Markieff Morris^	715
1948	Horace Grant	1165	1676	Chuck Person	943	1415	Justin Holiday^	576
	Harvey Grant	783		Wesley Person	733		Jrue Holiday^	839

* Includes ABA.

^ Active.

Most Career Minutes Played by Brothers*

69,720....Paul Gasol............. 41,001	49,668....Chuck Person 28,941	38,614....Jim Paxson............. 21,357
Marc Gasol 28,719	Wesley Person........ 20,727	John Paxson........... 17,257
64,197....Dominique Wilkins... 38,113	46,765....Brook Lopez^ 26,192	37,851....Stephen Curry^....... 28,361
Gerald Wilkins....... 26,084	Robin Lopez^ 20,573	Seth Curry^ 9490
60,453....Tom Van Arsdale.... 28,682	44,107....Gus Williams 25,645	37,175....Marcus Morris^ 19,451
Dick Van Arsdale.... 31,771	Ray Williams.......... 18,462	Markieff Morris^ 17,724
59,131....Horace Grant......... 38,621	42,253....Bernard King.......... 29,417	
Harvey Grant......... 20,510	Albert King 12,836	
57,012....Caldwell Jones 35,081	41,966....Justin Holiday^ 14,149	
Wil Jones............... 21,931	Jrue Holiday^ 27,817	

* Includes ABA.

^ Active.

Most Career Points by Brothers*

38,404....Dominique Wilkins ...26,668	24,251....Gus Williams 14,093	18,723....Caldwell Jones 10,241
Gerald Wilkins....... 11,736	Ray Williams.......... 10,158	Wil Jones.................. 8482
33,408....Paul Gasol 20,894	24,309....Stephen Curry^....... 20,064	18,591....Justin Holiday^ 5005
Marc Gasol 12,514	Seth Curry^ 4245	Jrue Holiday^ 13,586
29,311....Tom Van Arsdale..... 14,232	22,443....Brook Lopez^ 14,247	16,743....Marcus Morris^ 8921
Dick Van Arsdale.... 15,079	Robin Lopez^ 8196	Markieff Morris^ 7822
27,271....George Gervin....... 26,595	22,050....Chuck Person 13,858	
Derrick Gervin............. 676	Wesley Person........... 8192	
26,125....Bernard King.......... 19,655	20,777....Horace Grant......... 12,996	
Albert King 6470	Harvey Grant............ 7781	

* Includes ABA.

^ Active.

Most Career Field Goals by Brothers*

147,17....Dominique Wilkins..... 9963	10,539....Bernard King............. 7830	8704.......Chuck Person 5576
Gerald Wilkins.......... 4754	Albert King 2709	Wesley Person........... 3128
12,615....Paul Gasol 7980	9755....Gus Williams 5793	8430.......Stephen Curry^.......... 6875
Marc Gasol 4635	Ray Williams............. 3962	Seth Curry^ 1555
10,918....Tom Van Arsdale....... 5505	8872....Brook Lopez^ 5443	7631.......Caldwell Jones 4090
Dick Van Arsdale....... 5413	Robin Lopez^ 3429	Wil Jones.................. 3541
10,625....George Gervin....... 10,368	8784....Horace Grant............. 5439	7104.......Justin Holiday^ 1745
Derrick Gervin............. 257	Harvey Grant............ 3345	Jrue Holiday^ 5359

* Includes ABA.

^ Active.

Most Career Three Pointers by Brothers

3847.......Stephen Curry^.......... 3117	2076.......Jon Barry 657	1250.......Derek Fisher.............. 1248
Seth Curry^ 730	Brent Barry............... 1395	Duane Washington 2
2370.......Chuck Person 1220	1747.......Marcus Morris^ 1140	1129.......Dominique Wilkins....... 711
Wesley Person........... 1150	Markieff Morris^.......... 607	Gerald Wilkins............ 418
2149.......Justin Holiday^ 979	1339.......Mark Price 976	1101.......Goran Dragic^ 1098
Jrue Holiday^ 1170	Brent Price 363	Zoran Dragic 3

^ Active.

Most Career Assists by Brothers

8376	Gus Williams	4597	6099	Mark Price	4863	5013	Brad Davis	4709
	Ray Williams	3779		Brent Price	1236		Mickey Davis	304
6921	Paul Gasol	3925	5374	Dominique Wilkins	2677	4259	Goran Dragic^	4254
	Marc Gasol	2996		Gerald Wilkins	2697		Zoran Dragic	5
6233	Justin Holiday^	860	5142	Tom Van Arsdale	2085			
	Jrue Holiday^	5373		Dick Van Arsdale	3057			
6220	Stephen Curry^	5388	5058	Jim Paxson	2300			
	Seth Curry^	832		John Paxson	2758			

^ Active.

Most Career Rebounds by Brothers*

17,909	Paul Gasol	11,305	7322	Bernard King	5060	5473	Mason Plumlee^	3911
	Marc Gasol	6604		Albert King	2262		Miles Plumlee	1562
16,245	Caldwell Jones	10,685	7165	Chuck Person	4763	5061	Jrue Holiday^	3361
	Wil Jones	5560		Wesley Person	2402		Justin Holiday^	1700
12,879	Horace Grant	9443	7012	Markieff Morris^	3714	4769	Cody Zeller^	2949
	Harvey Grant	3436		Marcus Morris^	3298		Tyler Zeller	1820
10,011	Brook Lopez	5407	6399	Giannis Antetokounmpo^	6149	4681	Stephen Curry^	3838
	Robin Lopez	4604		Thanasis Antetokounmpo^	250		Seth Curry^	843
9815	Dominique Wilkins	7169	5956	Blake Griffin^	5954			
	Gerald Wilkins	2646		Taylor Griffin	2			
7749	Tom Van Arsdale	3942	5777	George Gervin*	5602			
	Dick Van Arsdale	3807		Derrick Gervin	175			

* Includes ABA.
^ Active.

Most Career Steals by Brothers*

2836	Gus Williams	1638	1696	Brent Barry	722	1365	Derek Fisher	1352
	Ray Williams	1198		Jon Barry	955		Duane Washington	13
2285	Dominique Wilkins	1378	1641	Stephen Curry^	1367	1322	George Gervin	1283
	Gerald Wilkins	907		Seth Curry^	274		Derrick Gervin	39
1826	Jrue Holiday^	1267	1468	Jim Paxson	951	1318	Bernard King	866
	Justin Holiday^	559		John Paxson	517		Albert King	452
1742	Horace Grant	1143	1398	Marc Gasol	792	1154	Caldwell Jones	685
	Harvey Grant	599		Paul Gasol	606		Wil Jones	469

* Includes ABA.
^ Active.

Most Career Blocks by Brothers*

3431	Caldwell Jones	2297	1073	George Gervin	1047	685	Jrue Holiday	430
	Charles Jones	1134		Derrick Gervin	26		Justin Holiday^	255
3195	Paul Gasol	1941	880	Giannis Antetokounmpo^	856	573	Markieff Morris^	369
	Marc Gasol	1254		Thanasis Antetokounmpo^	24		Marcus Morris^	204
2564	Brook Lopez^	1530	850	Dominique Wilkins	642	562	Cody Zeller^	321
	Robin Lopez^	1034		Gerald Wilkins	208		Tyler Zeller	241
1564	Horace Grant	1136	848	Mason Plumlee^	592	522	Willie Anderson	342
	Harvey Grant	428		Miles Plumlee	256		Shandon Anderson	180

* Includes ABA.
^ Active.

9

ALL-STAR GAME

Most Career ASG Appearancs[*]

19...................... Kareem Abdul-Jabbar	13...................... Dwyane Wade	11...................... Magic Johnson
18...................... Kobe Bryant	12...................... Dolph Schayes	11...................... Patrick Ewing
18...................... LeBron James[^]	12...................... Bill Russell	11...................... Charles Barkley
16...................... Julius Erving	12...................... Oscar Robertson	11...................... Allen Iverson
15...................... Shaquille O'Neal	12...................... Rick Barry	11...................... Chris Bosh
15...................... Kevin Garnett	12...................... Elvin Hayes	10...................... Paul Arizin
15...................... Tim Duncan	12...................... George Gervin	10...................... Hal Greer
14...................... Jerry West	12...................... Larry Bird	10...................... Clyde Drexler
14...................... Michael Jordan	12...................... Isiah Thomas	10...................... John Stockton
14...................... Karl Malone	12...................... Hakeem Olajuwon	10...................... David Robinson
14...................... Dirk Nowitzki	12...................... Chris Paul[^]	10...................... Jason Kidd
13...................... Bob Cousy	12...................... Kevin Durant[^]	10...................... Ray Allen
13...................... Wilt Chamberlain	11...................... Bob Pettit	10...................... Paul Pierce
13...................... John Havlicek	11...................... Elgin Baylor	10...................... Carmelo Anthony[^]
13...................... Moses Malone	11...................... Artis Gilmore	10...................... James Harden[^]

[*] Includes both NBA and ABA.

[^] Active.

Least Amount of Games Played, Voted to ASG

4...... Grant Hill, Orl. Magic 2000–01	18...... Michael Jordan, Chi. Bulls......................... 1985–86
5...... Yao Ming[*], Hou. Rockets 2010–11	19...... Penny Hardaway, Orl. Magic 1997–98
6...... Kobe Bryant, L.A. Lakers 2013–14	27...... Kevin Durant, Ok.C. Thunder.................... 2014–15
13...... Alonzo Mourning, Mia. Heat.................... 2000–01	28...... Allen Iverson[*], Mem. Grizzlies/Phi. 76ers.... 2009–10

[*] Last season in NBA.

ASG Record

NBA

Team LeBron	5–0 (1.000)
East	37–29 (.561)
West	29–37 (.439)
Team Giannis..............	0–2 (.000)
Team Durant	0–2 (.000)
Team Stephen	0–1 (.000)

ABA

East	5–3 (.625)
West	3–5 (.375)
Denver	1–0 (1.000)
All Stars	0–1 (.000)

Oldest Player Selected to ASG

Age (Birthdate)

41 (Apr. 16) ...... Kareem Abdul-Jabbar, L.A. Lakers, 1988–89

40 (Apr. 16) ...... Kareem Abdul-Jabbar, L.A. Lakers, 1987–88

40 (Jun. 19) .... Dirk Nowitzki, Dal. Mavericks, 2018–19

39 (Feb. 17) ...... Michael Jordan, Was. Wizards, 2002–03

39 (Jun. 19) .... Kareem Abdul-Jabbar, L.A. Lakers, 1986–87

38 (Feb. 17) ...... Michael Jordan, Was. Wizards, 2001–02

38 (Apr. 16) ...... Kareem Abdul-Jabbar, L.A. Lakers, 1985–86

Youngest Player Selected to ASG

Age (Birthdate)

19 (Mar. 23)......... Moses Malone, Uta. Stars[a], 1974–75

19 (Aug. 23) .... Kobe Bryant, L.A. Lakers, 1997–98

20 (Apr. 22)......... Spencer Haywood, Den. Rockets[a], 1969–70

20 (Aug. 14) .... Magic Johnson, L.A. Lakers, 1979–80

20 (Apr. 30)......... Isiah Thomas, Det. Pistons, 1981–82

20 (Mar. 6)........... Shaquille O'Neal, Orl. Magic, 1992–93

20 (May 19)......... Kevin Garnett, Min. T'Wolves, 1996–97

continued on next page

Age (Birthdate)

38 (Apr. 25) ...... Tim Duncan, S.A. Spurs, 2014–15
38 (Jul. 24) .... Karl Malone, Uta. Jazz, 2001–02
37 (Jan. 17) .... Dwyane Wade, Mia. Heat, 2018–19
37 (Feb. 7) .... Steve Nash, Pho. Suns, 2011–12
36 (Jul. 24) .... Karl Malone, Uta. Jazz, 1999–00
37 (Dec. 8) .... Johnny Green, Cin. Royals, 1970–71
37 (Apr. 8) .... John Havlicek, Bos. Celtics, 1977–78
37 (Apr. 16) ...... Kareem Abdul-Jabbar, L.A. Lakers, 1984–85
37 (May 6) .... Chris Paul, Pho. Suns, 2021–22
37 (Jul. 24) .... Karl Malone, Uta. Jazz, 2000–01
37 (Aug. 23)...... Kobe Bryant, L.A. Lakers, 2015–16
37 (Aug. 30)...... Robert Parish, Bos. Celtics, 1990–91
36 (Feb. 22) ...... Julius Erving, Phi. 76ers, 1986–87
36 (Mar. 6)........ Shaquille O'Neal, Pho. Suns, 2008–09
36 (Mar. 23)...... Jason Kidd, Dal. Mavericks, 2009–10
36 (Apr. 8) .... John Havlicek, Bos. Celtics, 1976–77
36 (Apr. 16) ...... Kareem Abdul-Jabbar, L.A. Lakers, 1983–84
36 (Apr. 25) ...... Tim Duncan, S.A. Spurs, 2012–13
36 (May 19) ...... Kevin Garnett, Bos. Celtics, 2012–13
36 (Aug. 23)..... Kobe Bryant, L.A. Lakers, 2014–15
37 (Mar. 26)...... John Stockton, Uta. Jazz, 1999–00
36 (Aug. 21)...... Wilt Chamberlain, L.A. Lakers, 1972–73
36 (Jun. 19) ...... Dirk Nowitzki, Dal. Mavericks, 2014–15
36 (Aug. 30)...... Robert Parish, Bos. Celtics, 1989–90
36 (Sep. 21) ...... Artis Gilmore, S.A. Spurs, 1985–86
36 (Dec. 9) .... Cliff Hagan, Dal. Chaparrals[a], 1967–68
36 (Dec. 30) ..... LeBron James, L.A. Lakers, 2020–21
35 (Jan. 5)......... Alex English, Den. Nuggets, 1988–89
35 (Feb. 7) .... Steve Nash, Pho. Suns, 2009–10
35 (Feb. 22) ...... Julius Erving, Phi. 76ers, 1985–86
35 (Apr. 8) .... John Havlicek, Bos. Celtics, 1975–76
35 (Apr. 16) ...... Kareem Abdul-Jabbar, L.A. Lakers, 1982–83
35 (May 6) .... Chris Paul, Pho. Suns, 2020–21
35 (May 28) ...... Jerry West, L.A. Lakers, 1973–74
35 (Jun. 19) .... Dirk Nowitzki, Dal. Mavericks, 2013–14
35 (Jun. 25) .... Dikembe Mutombo, Phi. 76ers, 2001–02
35 (Jul. 6) .... Pau Gasol, Chi. Bulls, 2015–16
35 (Jul. 20) .... Ray Allen, Bos. Celtics, 2010–11
35 (Aug. 6)........ David Robinson, S.A. Spurs, 2000–01
35 (Aug. 21)...... Wilt Chamberlain, L.A. Lakers, 1971–72
35 (Aug. 23)...... Kobe Bryant, L.A. Lakers, 2013–14
35 (Sep. 16) ...... Elgin Baylor, L.A. Lakers, 1969–70
35 (Oct. 28) ...... Lenny Wilkens, Cle. Cavaliers, 1972–73
35 (Dec. 7) .... Larry Bird, Bos. Celtics, 1991–92
35 (Dec. 30) ...... LeBron James, L.A. Lakers, 2019–20
[a] ABA.

Age (Birthdate)

20 (Dec. 30).........LeBron James, Cle. Cavaliers, 2004–05
20 (Mar. 23).........Kyrie Irving, Cle. Cavaliers, 2012–13
20 (Mar. 11).........Anthony Davis, N.O. Pelicans, 2013–14
20 (Feb. 28) ....Luka Dončić, Dal. Mavericks, 2019–20
20 (Jul. 6).............Zion Williamson, N.O. Pelicans, 2020–21
20 (Aug. 22) ....LaMelo Ball, Cha. Hornets, 2021–22
21 (Mar. 28).........Rick Barry, S.F. Warriors, 1965–66
21 (Feb. 22).........Julius Erving, Vir. Squires[a], 1971–72
21 (Dec. 13).........Larry Kenon, N.Y. Netsa, 1973–74
21 (Apr. 27).........George Gervin, Vir. Squires[a]/S.A. Spursa, 1973–74
21 (Sep. 30).........John Drew, Atl. Hawks, 1975–76
21 (Jul. 13)...........David Thompson, Den. Nuggets[a], 1975–76
21 (Jul. 19)...........Alvan Adams, Pho. Suns, 1975–76
21 (Mar. 8)...........Buck Williams, N.J. Nets, 1981–82
21 (Apr. 30)..........Isiah Thomas, Det. Pistons, 1982–83
21 (Feb. 17).........Michael Jordan, Chi. Bulls, 1984–85
21 (Mar. 6)...........Shaquille O'Neal, Orl. Magic, 1993–94
21 (Aug. 12).........Antoine Walker, Bos. Celtics, 1997–98
21 (May 19).........Kevin Garnett, Min. T'Wolves, 1997–98
21 (Apr. 25).........Tim Duncan, S.A. Spurs, 1997–98
21 (Aug. 23).........Kobe Bryant, L.A. Lakers, 1999–00
21 (Mar. 24).........Tracy McGrady, Orl. Magic, 2000–01
21 (Dec. 30).........LeBron James, Cle. Cavaliers, 2005–06
21 (Mar. 24).........Chris Bosh, Tor. Raptors, 2005–06
21 (Dec. 8)...........Dwight Howard, Orl. Magic, 2006–07
21 (Oct. 4)...........Derrick Rose, Chi. Bulls, 2009–10
21 (Sep. 29).........Kevin Durant, Ok.C. Thunder, 2009–10
21 (Mar. 16).........Blake Griffin, L.A. Clippers, 2010–11
21 (Mar. 23).........Kyrie Irving, Cle. Cavaliers, 2013–14
21 (Mar. 11).........Anthony Davis, N.O. Pelicans, 2014–15
21 (Sep. 19).........Trae Young, Atl. Hawks, 2019–20
21 (Mar. 3)...........Jayson Tatum, Bos. Celtics, 2019–20
21 (Feb. 28) .... Luka Dončić, Dal. Mavericks, 2020–21
[a] ABA.

Winning MVP, Not Making All-Star Team

	PPG	RPG	APG	FG%
Karl Malone, Uta. Jazz, 1998–99	23.8	9.4	4.1	.493

Most ASG Appearances, Not in HOF

ASG		ASG		ASG	
14	Dirk Nowitzki*	6	Lou Hudson	5	Tim Hardaway
13	Dwyane Wade*	6	Shawn Kemp	5	Marques Johnson
8	Vince Carter**	6	Jermaine O'Neal	5	Rudy LaRusso
8	Larry Foust	6	Tony Parker*	5	Don Ohl
6	Larry Costello	6	Amar'e Stoudemire	5	Gene Shue
6	Walter Davis	5	Chauncey Billups		
6	Pau Gasol*	5	Brad Daugherty		

* Hall of Fame Eligible in 2023.

** Hall of Fame Eligible in 2024.

Winners of the ASG 3P Contest

1986	Larry Bird, Bos. Celtics
1987	Larry Bird, Bos. Celtics
1988	Larry Bird, Bos. Celtics
1989	Dale Ellis, Sea. Sonics
1990	Craig Hodges, Chi. Bulls
1991	Craig Hodges, Chi. Bulls
1992	Craig Hodges, Chi. Bulls
1993	Mark Price, Cle. Cavaliers
1994	Mark Price, Cle. Cavaliers
1995	Glen Rice, Mia. Heat
1996	Tim Legler, Was. Bullets
1997	Steve Kerr, Chi. Bulls
1998	Jeff Hornacek, Uta. Jazz
2000	Jeff Hornacek, Uta. Jazz
2001	Ray Allen, Mil. Bucks
2002	Peja Stojaković, Sac. Kings
2003	Peja Stojaković, Sac. Kings
2004	Voshon Lenard, Den. Nuggets
2005	Quentin Richardson, Pho. Suns
2006	Dirk Nowitzki, Dal. Mavericks
2007	Jason Kapono, Mia. Heat
2008	Jason Kapono, Tor. Raptors
2009	Daequan Cook, Mia. Heat
2010	Paul Pierce, Bos. Celtics
2011	James Jones, Mia. Heat
2012	Kevin Love, Min. T'Wolves
2013	Kyrie Irving, Cle. Cavaliers
2014	Marco Belinelli, S.A. Spurs
2015	Stephen Curry, G.S. Warriors
2016	Klay Thompson, G.S. Warriors
2017	Eric Gordon, Hou. Rockers
2018	Devin Booker, Pho. Suns
2019	Joe Harris, Brk. Nets
2020	Buddy Hield, Sac. Kings
2021	Stephen Curry, G.S. Warriors
2022	Karl-Anthony Towns, Min. T'Wolves

Lockout-shortened season in 1999 (no ASG).

Winners of the ASG Slam Dunk Contest

1984	Larry Nance, Pho. Suns
1985	Dominique Wilkins, Atl. Hawks
1986	Spud Webb, Atl. Hawks
1987	Michael Jordan, Chi. Bulls
1988	Michael Jordan, Chi. Bulls
1989	Kenny Walker, N.Y. Knicks
1990	Dominique Wilkins, Atl. Hawks
1991	Dee Brown, Bos. Celtics
1992	Cedric Ceballos, Pho. Suns
1993	Harold Miner, Mia. Heat
1994	Isaiah Rider, Min. T'Wolves
1995	Harold Miner, Mia. Heat
1996	Brent Barry, L.A. Clippers
1997	Kobe Bryant, L.A. Lakers
2000	Vince Carter, Tor. Raptors
2001	Desmond Mason, Sea. Sonics
2002	Jason Richardson, G.S. Warriors
2003	Jason Richardson, G.S. Warriors
2004	Fred Jones, Ind. Pacers
2005	Josh Smith, Atl. Hawks
2006	Nate Robinson, N.Y. Knicks
2007	Gerald Green, Bos. Celtics
2008	Dwight Howard, Orl. Magic
2009	Nate Robinson, N.Y. Knicks
2010	Nate Robinson, N.Y. Knicks
2011	Blake Griffin, L.A. Clippers
2012	Jeremy Evans, Uta. Jazz
2013	Terrence Ross, Tor. Raptors
2014	John Wall, Was. Wizards
2015	Zach LaVine, Min. T'Wolves
2016	Zach LaVine, Min. T'Wolves
2017	Glenn Robinson III, Ind. Pacers
2018	Donovan Mitchell, Uta. Jazz
2019	Hamidou Diallo, Ok.C. Thunder
2020	Derrick Jones Jr., Mia. Heat
2021	Anfernee Simons, Por. Blazers
2022	Obi Toppin, N.Y. Knicks

WNBA-NBA 2Ball Competition replaced the 1998 Slam Dunk Contest

Lockout-shortened season in 1999 (no ASG).

Most Points, Game

52..... Anthony Davis, N.O. Pelicans (West), 2017
50..... Stephen Curry, G.S. Warriors (Team LeBron), 2022
42..... Wilt Chamberlain, Phi. Warriors (East), 1962
41..... Russell Westbrook, Ok.C. Thunder (West), 2015
41..... Paul George, Ind. Pacers (East), 2016
41..... Russell Westbrook, Ok.C. Thunder (West), 2017
40..... Michael Jordan, Chi. Bulls (East), 1988
38..... Rick Barry, S.F. Warriors (West), 1967
38..... Kevin Durant, Ok.C. Thunder (West), 2014
38..... Blake Griffin, L.A. Clippers (West), 2014

38..... Giannis Antetokounmpo, Mil. Bucks (Team Giannis), 2019
37..... Kevin Garnett, Min. T'Wolves (West), 2003
37..... Kobe Bryant, L.A. Lakers (West), 2011
36..... Tracy McGrady, Hou. Rockets (West), 2006
36..... Kevin Durant, Ok.C. Thunder (West), 2012
36..... LeBron James, Mia. Heat (East), 2012
36..... Joel Embiid, Phi. 76ers (Team Durant), 2022
35..... Allen Iverson, Phi. 76ers (East), 2003
35..... Giannis Antetokounmpo, Mil. Bucks (Team LeBron), 2021

Most Points, Career

413	LeBron James^	218	Elgin Baylor	179	John Havlicek
321	Julius Erving	202	Shaquille O'Neal	176	Magic Johnson
290	Kobe Bryant	194	Russell Westbrook^	177	George Gervin
262	Michael Jordan	191	Wilt Chamberlain	174	Giannis Antetokounmpo^
251	Kareem Abdul-Jabbar	188	Dwyane Wade	160	Jerry West
250	Kevin Durant^	185	Isiah Thomas	158	Kevin Garnett
246	Oscar Robertson	185	Carmelo Anthony^		
224	Bob Pettit	180	Stephen Curry^		

^ Active.

Most Three Pointers, Game

27............... Stephen Curry, G.S. Warriors (Team LeBron), 2022
19............... Paul George, Ind. Pacers (East), 2016
17............... Kevin Durant, Ok.C. Thunder (West), 2014
17............... Russell Westbrook, Ok.C. Thunder (West), 2016
17............... Damian Lillard, Por. Blazers (Team LeBron), 2019
17............... Stephen Curry, G.S. Warriors (Team Giannis), 2019
16............... Stephen Curry, G.S. Warriors (Team LeBron), 2021
16............... Damian Lillard, Por. Blazers (Team LeBron), 2021
14............... Kawhi Leonard, L.A. Clippers (Team LeBron), 2020
13............... Carmelo Anthony, N.Y. Knicks (East), 2014
13............... Carmelo Anthony, N.Y. Knicks (East), 2015
13............... Stephen Curry, G.S. Warriors (West), 2016
13............... Russell Westbrook, Ok.C. Thunder (West), 2017
13............... James Harden, Hou. Rockets (Team Stephen), 2018
13............... James Harden, Hou. Rockets (Team LeBron), 2019
13............... James Harden, Brk. Nets (Team Durant), 2021

Most Three Pointers, Career

47..................................... Stephen Curry^
40..................................... LeBron James^
39..................................... James Harden^
30..................................... Kevin Durant^
28..................................... Paul George^
23..................................... Damian Lillard^
22..................................... Kobe Bryant
22..................................... Ray Allen
22..................................... Chris Paul^
22..................................... Russell Westbrook^
18..................................... Kyrie Irving^
17..................................... Carmelo Anthony^
17..................................... Klay Thompson^
16..................................... Kawhi Leonard^

^ Active.

Most Rebounds, Game

27............... Bob Pettit, St.L. Hawks (West), 1962
26............... Bob Pettit, St.L. Hawks (West), 1958
25............... Wilt Chamberlain, Phi. Warriors (East), 1960
24............... Bob Pettit, St.L. Hawks (West), 1956
24............... Wilt Chamberlain, Phi. Warriors (East), 1962
24............... Bill Russell, Bos. Celtics (East), 1963
22............... Wilt Chamberlain, Phi. 76ers (East), 1967
22............... Charles Barkley, Phi. 76ers (East), 1991
22............... Dikembe Mutombo, Atl. Hawks (East), 2001

Most Rebounds, Career

197..................................... Wilt Chamberlain
178..................................... Bob Pettit
149..................................... Kareem Abdul-Jabbar
139..................................... Bill Russell
136..................................... Tim Duncan
109..................................... LeBron James^
108..................................... Moses Malone
105..................................... Dolph Schayes
99..................................... Elgin Baylor

continued on next page

Most Rebounds, Game

21............... Bill Russell, Bos. Celtics (East), 1964
20............... Wilt Chamberlain, S.F. Warriors (West), 1964
20............... Dave Cowens, Bos. Celtics (East), 1972
19............... Wilt Chamberlain, S.F. Warriors (West), 1963
19............... Jerry Lucas, Cin. Royals (East), 1966
18............... Harry Gallatin, N.Y. Knicks (East), 1954
18............... Wilt Chamberlain, Phi. Warriors (East), 1961
18............... Zelmo Beaty, St.L. Hawks (West), 1966
18............... Nate Thurmond, S.F. Warriors (West), 1967
18............... Moses Malone, Was. Bullets (East), 1987
17............... Walt Bellamy, Chi. Packers (West), 1962
17............... Bob Pettit, St.L. Hawks (West), 1964

Most Assists, Game

22............... Magic Johnson, L.A. Lakers (West), 1984
19............... Magic Johnson, L.A. Lakers (West), 1988
17............... John Stockton, Uta. Jazz (West), 1989
16............... Magic Johnson, L.A. Lakers (West), 1983
16............... Chris Paul, L.A. Clippers (West), 2016
16............... Chris Paul, Pho. Suns (Team LeBron), 2021
15............... Isiah Thomas, Det. Pistons (East), 1984
15............... Magic Johnson, L.A. Lakers (West), 1985
15............... Magic Johnson, L.A. Lakers (West), 1986
15............... Isiah Thomas, Det. Pistons (East), 1988
15............... John Stockton, Uta. Jazz (West), 1993
15............... Gary Payton, Sea. Sonics (West), 1995
15............... Chris Paul, L.A. Clippers (West), 2013
15............... Chris Paul, L.A. Clippers (West), 2015

Most Steals, Game

8................. Rick Barry, G.S. Warriors (West), 1975
7................. Larry Bird, Bos. Celtics (East), 1986
6................. Eddie Johnson, Atl. Hawks (East), 1980
6................. Sidney Moncrief, Mil. Bucks, 1983
6................. Dwyane Wade, Mia. Heat (East), 2007
6................. Kobe Bryant, L.A. Lakers (West), 2007

Most Blocks, Game

6................. Kareem Abdul-Jabbar, L.A. Lakers (West), 1980
5................. Patrick Ewing, N.Y. Knicks (East), 1990
5................. Hakeem Olajuwon, Hou. Rockets (West), 1994

Most Rebounds, Career

97.................................... Shaquille O'Neal
94.................................... Hakeem Olajuwon
92.................................... Elvin Hayes
88.................................... Kevin Garnett
81.................................... Dave Cowens
79.................................... Larry Bird
78.................................... Bob Cousy
75.................................... Kobe Bryant
75.................................... Carmelo Anthony^
^ Active.

Most Assists, Career

128................................... Chris Paul^
127................................... Magic Johnson
106................................... LeBron James^
97.................................... Isiah Thomas
86.................................... Bob Cousy
81.................................... Oscar Robertson
73.................................... Gary Payton
71.................................... John Stockton
70.................................... Kobe Bryant
69.................................... Jason Kidd
64.................................... Kyrie Irving^
58.................................... Dwyane Wade
56.................................... Allen Iverson
55.................................... Jerry West
54.................................... Michael Jordan
52.................................... James Harden^
51.................................... Kareem Abdul-Jabbar
^ Active.

Most Steals, Career

38.................................... Kobe Bryant
37.................................... Michael Jordan
31.................................... Isiah Thomas
27.................................... Dwyane Wade
26.................................... Chris Paul^
24.................................... Jason Kidd
23.................................... Larry Bird
22.................................... LeBron James^
21.................................... Magic Johnson
21.................................... Allen Iverson
^ Active.

Most Blocks, Career

31.................................... Kareem Abdul-Jabbar
23.................................... Hakeem Olajuwon
19.................................... Shaquille O'Neal

continued on next page

Most Blocks, Game

4................ Elvin Hayes, Was. Bullets (East), 1980
4................ Kareem Abdul-Jabbar, L.A. Lakers (West), 1981
4................ Kareem Abdul-Jabbar, L.A. Lakers (West), 1983
4................ Kevin McHale, Bos. Celtics (East), 1986
4................ Kevin McHale, Bos. Celtics (East), 1987
4................ Michael Jordan, Chi. Bulls (East), 1988
4................ Patrick Ewing, N.Y. Knicks (East), 1991
4................ Shaquille O'Neal, Orl. Magic (East), 1994
4................ Dikembe Mutombo, Den. Nuggetrs (West), 1995
4................ Alonzo Mourning, Mia. Heat (East), 2000
4................ Jermaine O'Neal, Ind. Pacers (East), 2003
4................ Dirk Nowitzki, Dal. Mavericks (West), 2005

Most Blocks, Career

16................... Patrick Ewing
13................... David Robinson
12................... Kevin McHale
11................... Julius Erving
11................... Kevin Garnett
10................... Dikembe Mutombo

Players with Multiple ASG MVP Awards

4.................. Bob Pettit 1956, 1958, 1959*, 1962
4.................. Kobe Bryant 2002, 2007, 2009**, 2011
3.................. Oscar Robertson 1961, 1964, 1969
3.................. Michael Jordan 1988, 1996, 1998
3.................. Shaquille O'Neal 2000***, 2004, 2009****
3.................. LeBron James 2006, 2008, 2018
2.................. Bob Cousy 1954, 1957
2.................. Julius Erving 1977, 1983
2.................. Isiah Thomas 1984, 1986
2.................. Karl Malone 1989, 1993*****
2.................. Magic Johnson 1990, 1992
2.................. Allen Iverson 2001, 2005
2.................. Kevin Durant 2012, 2019
2.................. Russell Westbrook 2015, 2016
2.................. David Thompson 1976a, 1979

* Tied with Elgin Baylor.
** Tied with Shaquille O'Neal.
*** Tied with Tim Duncan.
**** Tied with Kobe Bryant.
***** Tied with John Stockton.
a ABA.

10

PLAYOFFS/FINALS

Players

Scoring

Most Playoff Points, Career*

		Career Playoff Games			Career Playoff Games
7631	LeBron James^	266	3180	Paul Pierce	170
5987	Michael Jordan	179	3116	Dennis Johnson	180
5762	Kareem Abdul-Jabbar	237	3054	Manu Ginóbili	218
5640	Kobe Bryant	220	3022	James Worthy	143
5250	Shaquille O'Neal	216	2972	Reggie Miller	144
5172	Tim Duncan	251	2968	Stephen Curry^	112
4761	Karl Malone	193	2963	Clyde Drexler	145
4580	Julius Erving	189	2934	Dan Issel	133
4457	Jerry West	153	2909	Sam Jones	154
4454	Kevin Durant^	151	2870	Rick Barry	105
4045	Tony Parker	226	2865	Kawhi Leonard^	135
3954	Dwyane Wade	177	2833	Charles Barkley	123
3897	Larry Bird	164	2820	Robert Parish	184
3776	John Havlicek	172	2813	Patrick Ewing	139
3755	Hakeem Olajuwon	145	2749	Ray Allen	171
3701	Magic Johnson	190	2727	Russell Westbrook^	111
3663	Dirk Nowitzki	145	2673	Bill Russell	165
3642	Scottie Pippen	208	2666	Chris Paul^	129
3623	Elgin Baylor	134	2601	Kevin Garnett	143
3607	Wilt Chamberlain	160	2571	Richard Hamilton	130
3191	James Harden^	137	2526	Chauncey Billups	146
3182	Kevin McHale	169			

* Includes ABA.

^ Active.

Most Points in Finals, Career

1679	Jerry West	1037	Tom Heinsohn	741	George Mikan
1562	LeBron James^	1020	John Havlicek	716	Larry Bird
1317	Kareem Abdul-Jabbar	971	Magic Johnson	713	Bob Cousy
1176	Michael Jordan	937	Kobe Bryant	709	Bob Pettit
1161	Elgin Baylor	928	Stephen Curry^	708	Tim Duncan
1151	Bill Russell	865	Shaquille O'Neal		
1143	Sam Jones	754	James Worthy		

^ Active.

Most Playoff Points, Season

759	Michael Jordan, Chi. Bulls*, 1991–92		638	Charles Barkley, Pho. Suns, 1992–93
748	LeBron James, Cle. Cavaliers, 2017–18		634	Giannis Antetokounmpo, Mil. Bucks*, 2020–21
732	Kawhi Leonard, Tor. Raptors*, 2018–19		633	Kobe Bryant, L.A. Lakers, 2007–08
725	Hakeem Olajuwon, Hou. Rockets*, 1994–95		632	Larry Bird, Bos. Celtics*, 1983–84
723	Allen Iverson, Phi. 76ers, 2000–01		622	Larry Bird, Bos. Celtics, 1986–87
707	Shaquille O'Neal, L.A. Lakers*, 1999–00		620	Stephen Curry, G.S. Warriors, 2018–19
697	LeBron James, Mia. Heat*, 2011–12		620	Dirk Nowitzki, Dal. Mavericks, 2005–06
695	Kobe Bryant, L.A. Lakers*, 2008–09		615	Jayson Tatum, Bos. Celtics, 2021–22
680	Michael Jordan, Chi. Bulls*, 1997–98		608	Kevin Durant, G.S. Warriors*, 2017–18
671	Kobe Bryant, L.A. Lakers*, 2009–10		602	Stephen Curry, G.S. Warriors*, 2021–22
666	Michael Jordan, Chi. Bulls*, 1992–93		601	LeBron James, Cle. Cavaliers, 2014–15
664	Hakeem Olajuwon, Hou. Rockets*, 1993–94		601	Devin Booker, Pho. Suns, 2020–21
654	Dwyane Wade, Mia. Heat*, 2005–06			

* Won championship.

Fewest Games to 1000 Playoff Points

28	Michael Jordan	35	Allen Iverson	37	LeBron James
29	Wilt Chamberlain	35	Donovan Mitchell	37	Kevin Durant
30	Rick Barry	36	Tracy McGrady	38	Bob McAdoo
32	Elgin Baylor	36	Anthony Davis	38	Dominique Wilkins
34	Oscar Robertson	37	Jerry West	38	Karl Malone
34	Kareem Abdul-Jabbar	37	Rick Barry	38	Vince Carter
34	Julius Erving	37	Roger Brown	39	Shaquille O'Neal
35	George Mikan	37	Dan Issel	39	Stephen Curry
35	George Gervin	37	Hakeem Olajuwon	39	Nikola Jokić

Fewest Games to 2500 Playoff Points

72	Michael Jordan	92	Hakeem Olajuwon	108	Julius Erving
80	Elgin Baylor	97	Stephen Curry	110	John Havlicek
82	Jerry West	98	Dwyane Wade	111	Kobe Bryant
83	Kareem Abdul-Jabbar	98	Dirk Nowitzki	112	James Harden
88	LeBron James	100	Russell Westbrook	115	Patrick Ewing
88	Kevin Durant	104	Charles Barkley	117	James Worthy
91	Wilt Chamberlain	105	Larry Bird	119	Clyde Drexler
91	Shaquille O'Neal	105	Tim Duncan	119	Paul Pierce
92	Karl Malone	107	Reggie Miller		

Most Field Goals Made in Finals, Career

612	Jerry West	438	Michael Jordan	339	Magic Johnson
588	LeBron James^	415	Bill Russell	333	Kobe Bryant
544	Kareem Abdul-Jabbar	408	Tom Heinsohn	314	James Worthy
458	Sam Jones	390	John Havlicek	300	Stephen Curry^
442	Elgin Baylor	340	Shaquille O'Neal		

^ Active.

Most Playoff Games with 30 Points, Career*

118	LeBron James^	75	Kareem Abdul-Jabbar	60	Elgin Baylor
109	Michael Jordan	74	Jerry West	55	Shaquille O'Neal
88	Kobe Bryant	71	Kevin Durant^	54	Karl Malone

continued on next page

53......................	Hakeem Olajuwon	43......................	Larry Bird	33.................	George Gervin
51......................	Stephen Curry^	42......................	Wilt Chamberlain	33.................	Kawhi Leonard^
49......................	Julius Erving	36......................	Allen Iverson	32.................	Giannis Antetokounmpo^
48......................	Rick Barry	36......................	Tim Duncan	30.................	John Havlicek
46......................	Dirk Nowitzki	34......................	Dwyane Wade		
45......................	James Harden^	33......................	Bob Pettit		

* Includes ABA.

^ Active.

Youngest Player to Score 30 Points in a Playoff Game

	Age		Pts	Round, Game
Moses Malone, Uta. Stars^a...............20 years, 17 days ....vs. Den. Nuggets^a (Apr. 9, 1975)			30 ....ABA WD Semifinals, Gm. 3	
Derrick Rose, Chi. Bulls...................20 years, 196 days ....@ Bos. Celtics (Apr. 18, 2009)			36 ....EC First Round, Gm. 1	
Brandon Jennings, Mil. Bucks ....20 years, 206 days ....@ Atl. Hawks (Apr. 17, 2010)			34 ....EC First Round, Gm. 1	
Tyler Herro, Mia. Heat.....................20 years, 247 days ....vs. Bos. Celtics (Sep. 23, 2020)............			37 ....EC Finals, Gm. 4	
Anthony Edwards, Min. T'Wolves .....20 years, 254 days ....@ Mem. Grizzlies (Apr. 16, 2022)........			36 ....WC First Round, Gm. 1	
Magic Johnson, L.A. Lakers...............20 years, 276 days ....@ Phi. 76ers (May 16, 1980)...............			42 ....NBA Finals, Gm. 6	
Spencer Haywood, Den. Rockets^a.....20 years, 360 days ....vs. Was. Capitols^a (Apr. 17, 1970).......			32 ....ABA WD Semifinals, Gm. 1	
Daniel Gibson, Cle. Cavaliers ....21 years, 95 days ....vs. Det. Pistons (Jun. 2, 2007)...........			31 ....EC Finals, Gm. 6	
LeBron James, Cle. Cavaliers...........21 years, 113 days ....vs. Was. Wizards (Apr. 22, 2006)........			32 ....EC First Round, Gm. 1	
Luguentz Dort, Ok.C. Thunder ....21 years, 136 days ....@ Hou. Rockets (Sep. 2, 2020)...........			30 ....WC First Round, Gm. 7	
Tyrese Maxey, Phi. 76ers.................21 years, 163 days ....vs. Tor. Raptors (Apr. 16, 2022)........			38 ....EC First Round, Gm. 1	
Luka Dončić, Dal. Mavericks............21 years, 171 days ....@ L.A. Clippers (Aug. 17, 2020)........			42 ....WC First Round, Gm. 1	
Jaylen Brown, Bos. Celtics ....21 years, 175 days ....vs. Mil. Bucks (Apr. 17, 2018)...........			30 ....EC First Round, Gm. 2	
Carl Braun, N.Y. Knicks...................21 years, 187 days ....vs. Was. Capitols (Mar. 31, 1949)			30 ....ED Finals, Gm. 2	
Kevin Durant, Ok.C. Thunder ....21 years, 203 days ....@ L.A. Lakers (Apr. 20, 2010)			32 ....WC First Round, Gm. 2	
Donovan Mitchell, Uta. Jazz............21 years, 228 days ....vs. Ok.C. Thunder (Apr. 23, 2018)			33 ....WC First Round, Gm. 4	
George McGinnis, Ind. Pacers^a ....@ Uta. Stars^a (Apr. 15, 1972) ....21 years, 247 days			31 ....WD Finals, Gm. 1	
Kobe Bryant, L.A. Lakers.................21 years, 248 days ....vs. Sac. Kings (Apr. 27, 2000)			32 ....WC First Round, Gm. 2	
David Thompson, Den. Nuggets^a .....21 years, 284 days ....vs. Ken. Colonels^a (Apr. 22, 1976)			34 ....ABA SF, Gm. 5	
Ja Morant, Mem. Grizzlies...............21 years, 289 days ....@ Uta. Jazz (May 26, 2021)...............			47 ....WC First Round, Gm. 2	
Alvan Adams, Pho. Suns..................21 years, 316 days ....vs. Bos. Celtics (May 30, 1976)............			33 ....NBA Finals, Gm. 3	
Bradley Beal, Was. Wizards............21 years, 317 days ....vs. Atl. Hawks (May 11, 2015).............			34 ....EC Semifinals, Gm. 4	
Tracy McGrady, Orl. Magic.............21 years, 333 days ....@ Mil. Bucks (Apr. 22, 2001)...............			33 ....EC First Round, Gm. 1	
Tony Parker, S.A. Spurs ....21 years, 354 days ....vs. L.A. Lakers (May 5, 2004)...............			30 ....WC Semifinals, Gm. 2	
Tim Duncan, S.A. Spurs..................21 years, 363 days ....@ Pho. Suns (Apr. 23, 1998)...............			32 ....WC First Round, Gm. 1	

^a ABA.

Oldest Player to Score 30 Points in a Playoff Game

	Age		Pts	Round, Game
Karl Malone, L.A. Lakers.................40 years, 276 days ....@ Hou. Rockets (Apr. 25, 2004)			30 ....WC First Round, Gm. 4	
Kareem Abdul-Jabbar, L.A. Lakers....40 years, 59 days ....vs. Bos. Celtics (Jun. 14, 1987).............			32 ....NBA Finals, Gm. 6	
Reggie Miller, Ind. Pacers ....39 years, 247 days ....vs. Bos. Celtics (Apr. 28, 2005)........			33 ....EC First Round, Gm. 3	
Eddie Johnson, Hou. Rockets...........38 years, 22 days ....vs. Uta. Jazz (May 23, 1997)...............			31 ....WC Finals, Gm. 3	
Richie Guerin, Atl. Hawks................37 years, 325 days ....@ L.A. Lakers (Apr. 19, 1970).............			31 ....WD Finals, Gm. 4	
Tim Duncan, S.A. Spurs...................37 years, 54 days ....@ Mia. Heat (Jun. 18, 2013)...............			30 ....NBA Finals, Gm. 6	
John Havlicek, Bos. Celtics...............37 years, 12 days ....@ Phi. 76ers (Apr. 20, 1977)			31 ....EC Semifinals, Gm. 2	
Chris Paul, Pho. Suns ....36 years, 357 days ....@ N.O. Pelicans (Apr. 28, 2022)..........			33 ....WC First Round, Gm. 6	
Dirk Nowitzki, Dal. Mavericks.........36 years, 309 days ....vs. Hou. Rockets (Apr. 24, 2015)...........			34 ....WC First Round, Gm. 3	
Sam Cassell, L.A. Clippers...............36 years, 179 days ....@ Pho. Suns (May 16, 2006)			32 ....WC Semifinals, Gm. 5	

continued on next page

	Age		Pts	Round, Game
Steve Nash, Pho. Suns	36 years, 85 days	vs. S.A. Spurs (May 3, 2010)	33	WC Semifinals, Gm. 1
Charles Barkley, Hou. Rockets	36 years, 82 days	vs. L.A. Lakers (May 13, 1999)	30	WC First Round, Gm. 3
Jamal Crawford, L.A. Clippers	36 years, 40 days	@ Por. Blazers (Apr. 29, 2016)	32	WC First Round, Gm. 6
Al Horford, Bos. Celtics	35 years, 340 days	@ Mil. Bucks (May 9, 2022)	30	EC Semifinals, Gm. 4
LeBron James, L.A. Lakers	35 years, 284 days	vs. Mia. Heat (Oct. 9, 2020)	40	NBA Finals, Gm. 5
Ray Allen, Bos. Celtics	35 years, 276 days	@ N.Y. Knicks (Apr. 22, 2011)	32	EC First Round, Gm. 3
Elgin Baylor, L.A. Lakers	35 years, 227 days	vs. N.Y. Knicks (May 1, 1970)	30	NBA Finals, Gm. 4
Dan Issel, Den. Nuggets	35 years, 182 days	vs. Uta. Jazz (Apr. 24, 1984)	32	WC First Round, Gm. 4
Clifford Robinson, Det. Pistons	35 years, 140 days	vs. Bos. Celtics (May 5, 2002)	30	EC Semifinals, Gm. 1
Kevin McHale, Bos. Celtics	35 years, 133 days	vs. Cha. Hornets (May 1, 1993)	30	EC First Round, Gm. 2
Michael Jordan, Chi. Bulls	35 years, 117 days	@ Uta. Jazz (Jun. 14, 1998)	45	NBA Finals, Gm. 6
Alex English, Den. Nuggets	35 years, 115 days	@ Pho. Suns (Apr. 30, 1989)	36	WC First Round, Gm. 2

Most Playoff Games with 40 Points, Career

38	Michael Jordan	14	Kevin Durant^	11	Hakeem Olajuwon
28	LeBron James^	13	Kobe Bryant	10	Allen Iverson
20	Jerry West	13	Wilt Chamberlain		
14	Elgin Baylor	12	Shaquille O'Neal		

^ Active.

Youngest Player to Score 40 Points in a Playoff Game

	Age		Pts	Round, Game
Magic Johnson, L.A. Lakers	20 years, 276 days	@ Phi. 76ers (May 16, 1980)	42	NBA Finals, Gm. 6
Spencer Haywood, Den. Rockets°	20 years, 362 days	@ Was. Capitols° (Apr. 19, 1970)	45	ABA WD Semifinals, Gm. 3
LeBron James, Cle. Cavaliers	21 years, 119 days	@ Was. Wizards (Apr. 28, 2006)	41	EC First Round, Gm. 3
Luka Dončić, Dal. Mavericks	21 years, 171 days	@ L.A. Clippers (Aug. 17, 2020)	42	WC First Round, Gm. 1
Ja Morant, Mem. Grizzlies	21 years, 289 days	@ Uta. Jazz (May 26, 2021)	47	WC First Round, Gm. 2
David Thompson, Den. Nuggets°	21 years, 290 days	vs. Ken. Colonels° (Apr. 28, 1976)	40	ABA Semifinals, Gm. 7
Tracy McGrady, Orl. Magic	21 years, 339 days	vs. Mil. Bucks (Apr. 28, 2001)	42	EC First Round, Gm. 3
Julius Erving, Vir. Squires°	22 years, 42 days	@ The Floridians° (Apr. 4, 1972)	53	ABA ED Semifinals, Gm. 3
Glen Combs, Dal. Chaparrals°	22 years, 167 days	vs. N.O. Buccaneers° (Apr. 15, 1969)	40	ABA WD Semifinals, Gm. 6
Dan Issel, Ken. Colonels°	22 years, 172 days	@ Vir. Squires (Apr. 15, 1971)	46	ABA ED Finals, Gm. 1
Amar'e Stoudemire, Pho. Suns	22 years, 174 days	vs. Dal. Mavericks (May 9, 2005)	40	WC Semifinals, Gm. 1
Russell Westbrook, Ok.C. Thunder	22 years, 178 days	@ Mem. Grizzlies (May 9, 2011)	40	WC Semifinals, Gm. 4
Bob McAdoo, Buf. Braves	22 years, 193 days	vs. Bos. Celtics (Apr. 6, 1974)	44	EC Semifinals, Gm. 4
Kevin Durant, Ok.C. Thunder	22 years, 200 days	vs. Den. Nuggets (Apr. 17, 2011)	41	WC First Round, Gm. 1
Derrick Rose, Chi. Bulls	22 years, 214 days	@ Atl. Hawks (May 6, 2011)	44	EC Semifinals, Gm. 3
Warren Jabali, Oak. Oaks°	22 years, 222 days	@ Den. Rockets° (Apr. 8, 1969)	42	ABA WD Semifinals, Gm. 3
Marvin Barnes, Spirits of St.L.°	22 years, 253 days	@ N.Y. Nets° (Apr. 6, 1975)	41	ABA ED Semifinals, Gm. 1
Kobe Bryant, L.A. Lakers	22 years, 263 days	@ Sac. Kings (May 13, 2001)	48	WC Semifinals, Gm. 4
Mack Calvin, L.A. Stars°	22 years, 269 days	vs. Dal. Chaparrals° (Apr. 22, 1970)	44	ABA WD Semifinals, Gm. 4
Trae Young, Atl. Hawks	22 years, 277 days	@ Mil. Bucks (Jun. 23, 2021)	48	EC Finals, Gm. 1
Chuck Person, Ind. Pacers	22 years, 308 days	vs. Atl. Hawks (May 1, 1987)	40	EC First Round, Gm. 4
Billy Knight, Ind. Pacers°	22 years, 317 days	@ Den. Nuggets° (Apr. 22, 1975)	44	ABA WD Finals, Gm. 2
Dirk Nowitzki, Dal. Mavericks	22 years, 329 days	@ S.A. Spurs (May 14, 2001)	42	WC Semifinals, Gm. 5
Kareem Abdul-Jabbar, Mil. Bucks	22 years, 352 days	vs. Phi. 76ers (Apr. 3, 1970)	46	ED Semifinals, Gm. 5
George Gervin, S.A. Spurs°	22 years, 352 days	vs. Ind. Pacers° (Apr. 14, 1975)	42	ABA WD Semifinals, Gm. 5

° ABA.

Oldest Player to Score 40 Points in a Playoff Game

	Age		Pts	Round, Game
Karl Malone, Uta. Jazz	36 years, 273 days	vs. Sea. Sonics (Apr. 22, 2000)	50	WC First Round, Gm. 1
Chris Paul, Pho. Suns	36 years, 55 days	@ L.A. Clippers (Jun. 30, 2021)	41	WC Finals, Gm. 6
LeBron James, L.A. Lakers	35 years, 284 days	vs. Mia. Heat (Oct. 9, 2020)	40	NBA Finals, Gm. 5
Reggie Miller, Ind. Pacers	35 years, 243 days	@ Phi. 76ers (Apr. 24, 2001)	41	EC First Round, Gm. 2
Michael Jordan, Chi. Bulls	35 years, 117 days	@ Uta. Jazz (Jun. 14, 1998)	45	NBA Finals, Gm. 6
Sam Cassell, Min. T'Wolves	34 years, 168 days	vs. Sac. Kings (May 4, 2004)	40	WC Semifinals, Gm. 1
Stephen Curry, G.S. Warriors	34 years, 88 days	@ Bos. Celtics (Jun. 10, 2022)	43	NBA Finals, Gm. 4
John Havlicek, Bos. Celtics	33 years, 360 days	vs. Buf. Braves (Apr. 3, 1974)	43	EC Semifinals, Gm. 3
Paul Arizin, Phi. Warriors	33 years, 341 days	vs. Syr. Nationals (Mar. 16, 1962)	43	ED Semifinals, Gm. 1
Ray Allen, Bos. Celtics	33 years, 284 days	@ Chi. Bulls (Apr. 30, 2009)	51	EC First Round, Gm. 6
Sam Jones, Bos. Celtics	33 years, 277 days	@ N.Y. Knicks (Mar. 28, 1967)	51	ED Semifinals, Gm. 4
Kobe Bryant, L.A. Lakers	33 years, 272 days	@ Ok.C. Thunder (May 21, 2012)	42	WC Semifinals, Gm. 5
Wilt Chamberlain, L.A. Lakers	33 years, 258 days	vs. N.Y. Knicks (May 6, 1970)	45	NBA Finals, Gm. 6
Kareem Abdul-Jabbar, L.A. Lakers	33 years, 28 days	vs. Phi. 76ers (May 14, 1980)	40	NBA Finals, Gm. 5
Rick Barry, G.S. Warriors	33 years, 27 days	vs. L.A. Lakers (Apr. 24, 1977)	40	WC Semifinals, Gm. 3

Youngest Player to Score 40 Points in a Finals Game

	Age		Pts	Game (Result)
Magic Johnson, L.A. Lakers	20 years, 276 days	@ Phi. 76ers, May 16, 1980	42	6 (Win)
Rick Barry, S.F. Warriors	23 years, 21 days	vs. Phi. 76ers, Apr. 18, 1967	55	3 (Win)
Rick Barry, S.F. Warriors	23 years, 23 days	vs. Phi. 76ers, Apr. 20, 1967	43	4 (Loss)
Rick Barry, S.F. Warriors	23 years, 27 days	vs. Phi. 76ers, Apr. 24, 1967	44	6 (Loss)
Russell Westbrook, Ok.C. Thunder	23 years, 220 days	@ Mia. Heat, Jun. 19, 2012	43	4 (Loss)
Jerry West, L.A. Lakers	23 years, 315 days	@ Bos. Celtics, Apr. 8, 1962	40	2 (Win)
Kyrie Irving, Cle. Cavaliers	24 years, 82 days	@ G.S. Warriors, Jun. 13, 2016	41	5 (Win)
Dwyane Wade, Mia. Heat	24 years, 147 days	vs. Dal. Mavericks, Jun. 13, 2006	42	3 (Win)
Dwyane Wade, Mia. Heat	24 years, 152 days	vs. Dal. Mavericks, Jun. 18, 2006	43	5 (Win)
Devin Booker, Pho. Suns	24 years, 257 days	@ Mil. Bucks, Jul. 14, 2021	42	4 (Loss)
Devin Booker, Pho. Suns	24 years, 260 days	vs. Mil. Bucks, Jul. 17, 2021	40	5 (Loss)
George Mikan, Min. Lakers	24 years, 290 days	vs. Was. Capitols, Apr. 4, 1949	42	1 (Win)
Jerry West, L.A. Lakers	24 years, 324 days	vs. Bos. Celtics, Apr. 17, 1963	42	3 (Win)
Kyrie Irving, Cle. Cavaliers	25 years, 78 days	vs. G.S. Warriors, Jun. 9, 2017	40	4 (Win)
Bob Pettit, St.L. Hawks	25 years, 121 days	vs. Bos. Celtics, Apr. 12, 1958	50	6 (Win)
George Mikan, Min. Lakers	25 years, 309 days	vs. Syr. Nationals, Apr. 23, 1950	40	6 (Win)
Allen Iverson, Phi. 76ers	25 years, 364 days	@ L.A. Lakers, Jun. 6, 2001	48	1 (Win)

Oldest Player to Score 40 Points in a Finals Game

	Age		Pts	Game (Result)
LeBron James, L.A. Lakers	35 years, 284 days	vs. Mia. Heat (Oct. 9, 2020)	40	5 (Loss)
Michael Jordan, Chi. Bulls	35 years, 117 days	@ Uta. Jazz (Jun. 14, 1998)	45	6 (Win)
Stephen Curry, G.S. Warriors	34 years, 88 days	@ Bos. Celtics (Jun. 10, 2022)	43	4 (Win)
Wilt Chamberlain, L.A. Lakers	33 years, 258 days	vs. N.Y. Knicks (May 6, 1970)	45	6 (Win)
Kareem Abdul-Jabbar, L.A. Lakers	33 years, 28 days	vs. Phi. 76er (May 14, 1980)	40	5 (Win)
Elgin Baylor, L.A. Lakers	31 years, 220 days	@ Bos. Celtics (Apr. 24, 1966)	41	5 (Win)
Jimmy Butler, Mia. Heat	31 years, 20 days	vs. L.A. Lakers (Oct. 4, 2020)	40	3 (Loss)
Jerry West, L.A. Lakers	30 years, 342 days	vs. Bos. Celtics (May 5, 1969)	42	7 (Loss)
Kobe Bryant, L.A. Lakers	30 years, 285 days	vs. Orl. Magic (Jun. 4, 2009)	40	1 (Win)
Charles Barkley, Pho. Suns	30 years, 111 days	vs. Chi. Bulls (Jun. 11, 1993)	42	2 (Loss)
Shaquille O'Neal, L.A. Lakers	30 years, 93 days	vs. N.J. Nets (Jun. 7, 2002)	40	2 (Win)

Youngest Player to Score 50 Points in a Playoff Game

	Age		Pts	Round, Game
Julius Erving, Vir. Squires[a]	22 years, 42 days	@ The Floridians[a] (Apr. 4, 1972)	53	ABA ED Semifinals, Gm. 3
Rick Barry, S.F. Warriors	23 years, 21 days	vs. Phi. 76ers (Apr. 18, 1967)	55	NBA Finals, Gm. 3
Michael Jordan, Chi. Bulls	23 years, 62 days	@ Bos. Celtics (Apr. 20, 1986)	63	EC First Round, Gm. 2
Jayson Tatum, Bos. Celtics	23 years, 86 days	vs. Brk. Nets (May 28, 2021)	50	EC First Round, Gm. 3
Jamal Murray, Den. Nuggets	23 years, 182 days	@ Uta. Jazz (Aug. 23, 2020)	50	WC First Round, Gm. 4
Bob McAdoo, Buf. Braves	23 years, 205 days	vs. Was. Bullets (Apr. 18, 1975)	50	EC Semifinals, Gm. 4
Wilt Chamberlain, Phi. Warriors	23 years, 206 days	vs. Syr. Nationals (Mar. 14, 1960)	53	ED Semifinals, Gm. 3
Donovan Mitchell, Uta. Jazz	23 years, 345 days	@ Den. Nuggets (Aug. 17, 2020)	57	WC First Round, Gm. 1
Vince Carter, Tor. Raptors	24 years, 105 days	vs. Phi. 76ers (May 11, 2001)	50	EC Semifinals, Gm. 3
Bob Cousy, Bos. Celtics	24 years, 224 days	vs. Syr. Nationals (Mar. 21, 1953)	50	EC Semifinals, Gm. 2
George McGinnis, Ind. Pacers[a]	24 years, 243 days	vs. S.A. Spurs[a] (Apr. 12, 1975)	51	ABA WD Semifinals, Gm. 4
Bob Pettit, St.L. Hawks	25 years, 121 days	vs. Bos. Celtics (Apr. 12, 1958)	50	NBA Finals, Gm. 6
Allen Iverson, Phi. 76ers	25 years, 336 days	vs. Tor. Raptors (May 9, 2001)	54	EC Semifinals, Gm. 2
Dominique Wilkins, Atl. Hawks	26 years, 97 days	vs. Det. Pistons (Apr. 19, 1986)	50	EC First Round, Gm. 2
Giannis Antetokounmpo, Mil. Bucks	26 years, 226 days	vs. Pho. Suns (Jul. 20, 2021)	50	NBA Finals, Gm. 6
Billy Cunningham, Phi. 76ers	26 years, 302 days	vs. Mil. Bucks (Apr. 1, 1970)	50	EC Semifinals, Gm. 4
Jerry West, L.A. Lakers	26 years, 312 days	vs. Bal. Bullets (Apr. 5, 1965)	52	WD Finals, Gm. 2

[a] ABA.

Oldest Player to Score 50 Points in a Playoff Game

	Age		Pts	Round, Game
Karl Malone, Uta. Jazz	36 years, 273 days	vs. Sea. Sonics (Apr. 22, 2000)	50	WC First Round, Gm. 1
Michael Jordan, Chi. Bulls	34 years, 69 days	vs. Was. Bullets (Apr. 27, 1997)	55	EC First Round, Gm. 2
Ray Allen, Bos. Celtics	33 years, 284 days	@ Chi. Bulls (Apr. 30, 2009)	51	EC First Round, Gm. 6
Sam Jones, Bos. Celtics	33 years, 277 days	@ N.Y. Knicks (Mar. 28, 1967)	51	ED Semifinals, Gm. 4
LeBron James, Cle. Cavaliers	33 years, 152 days	@ G.S. Warriors (May 31, 2018)	51	NBA Finals, Gm. 1
John Havlicek, Bos. Celtics	32 years, 358 days	vs. Atl. Hawks (Apr. 1, 1973)	54	EC Semifinals, Gm. 1
Charles Barkley, Pho. Suns	31 years, 73 days	@ G.S. Warriors (May 4, 1994)	56	WC First Round, Gm. 3
Jerry West, L.A. Lakers	30 years, 330 days	vs. Bos. Celtics (Apr. 23, 1969)	53	NBA Finals, Gm. 1
Damian Lillard, Por. Blazers	30 years, 321 days	@ Den. Nuggets (Jun. 1, 2021)	55	WC First Round, Gm. 5
Kevin Durant, G.S. Warriors	30 years, 209 days	@ L.A. Clippers (Apr. 26, 2019)	50	WC First Round, Gm. 6
Russell Westbrook, Ok.C. Thunder	28 years, 158 days	@ Hou. Rockets (Apr. 19, 2017)	51	WC First Round, Gm. 2
Isaiah Thomas, Bos. Celtics	28 years, 84 days	vs. Was. Wizards (May 2, 2017)	53	EC Semifinals, Gm. 2
Rick Barry, N.Y. Nets[a]	28 years, 4 days	@ Ken. Colonels[a] (Apr. 1, 1972)	50	ABA ED Semifinals, Gm. 1

[a] ABA.

Most Points Scored by Player in a Finals Game

NBA

Game 1

53... Jerry West, L.A. Lakers ... vs. Bos. Celtics (Apr. 23, 1969)
51... LeBron James, Cle. Cavaliers* ... @ G.S. Warriors (May 31, 2018)
48... Allen Iverson, Phi. 76ers ... @ L.A. Lakers (Jun. 6, 2001)
44... Shaquille O'Neal, L.A. Lakers* ... vs. Phi. 76ers (Jun. 6, 2001)
44... LeBron James, Cle. Cavaliers* ... @ G.S. Warriors (Jun. 4, 2015)
43... Shaquille O'Neal, L.A. Lakers ... vs. Ind. Pacers (Jun. 7, 2000)
42... George Mikan, Min. Lakers ... vs. Was. Capitols (Apr. 4, 1949)
41... Jerry West, L.A. Lakers ... @ Bos. Celtics (Apr. 17, 1966)
40... Kobe Bryant, L.A. Lakers ... vs. Orl. Magic (Jun. 4, 2009)
39... Michael Jordan, Chi. Bulls ... vs. Por. Blazers (Jun. 3, 1992)

* Team lost game.

Game 2

45... Jerry West, L.A. Lakers* ... @ Bos. Celtics (Apr. 19, 1965)
43... John Havlicek, Bos. Celtics* ... @ L.A. Lakers (Apr. 25, 1969)
42... Charles Barkley, Pho. Suns* ... vs. Chi. Bulls (Jun. 11, 1993)
42... Michael Jordan, Chi. Bulls ... @ Pho. Suns (Jun. 11, 1993)
42... Giannis Antetokounmpo, Mil. Bucks* ... @ Pho. Suns (Jul. 8, 2021)
41... Jerry West, L.A. Lakers ... vs. Bos. Celtics (Apr. 25, 1969)
40... Cliff Hagan, St.L. Hawks* ... @ Bos. Celtics (Apr. 5, 1961)
40... Jerry West, L.A. Lakers ... @ Bos. Celtics (Apr. 8, 1962)
40... Shaquille O'Neal, L.A. Lakers ... vs. Ind. Pacers (Jun. 9, 2000)
40... Shaquille O'Neal, L.A. Lakers ... vs. N.J. Nets (Jun. 7, 2002)

* Team lost game.

continued on next page

Game 3

55... Rick Barry, S.F. Warriors .... vs. Phi. 76ers (Apr. 18, 1967)
47... Stephen Curry, G.S. Warriors* ... vs. Tor. Raptors (Jun. 5, 2019)
44... Michael Jordan, Chi. Bulls* .... vs. Pho. Suns (Jun. 13, 1993)
43... Kevin Durant, G.S. Warriors ...... @ Cle. Cavaliers (Jun. 6, 2018)
43... Jerry West, L.A. Lakers .... vs. Bos. Celtics (Apr. 21, 1965)
42... Jerry West, L.A. Lakers .... vs. Bos. Celtics (Apr. 17, 1963)
42... Dwyane Wade, Mia. Heat .... vs. Dal. Mavericks (Jun. 13, 2006)
41... Giannis Antetokounmpo, Mil. Bucks ... vs. Pho. Suns (Jul. 11, 2021)
40... LeBron James, Cle. Cavaliers ..... vs. G.S. Warriors (Jun. 9, 2015)
40... Jimmy Butler, Mia. Heat .... vs. L.A. Lakers (Oct. 4, 2020)

* Team lost game.

Game 4

55... Michael Jordan, Chi. Bulls .... vs. Pho. Suns (Jun. 16, 1993)
53... Stephen Curry, G.S. Warriors .... @ Bos. Celtics (Jun. 10, 2022)
45... Jerry West, L.A. Lakers* .... vs. Bos. Celtics (Apr. 22, 1966)
43... Rick Barry, S.F. Warriors* .... vs. Phi. 76ers (Apr. 20, 1967)
43... Russell Westbrook, Ok.C. Thunder* ... @ Mia. Heat (Jun. 19, 2012)
42... Devin Booker, Pho. Suns* .... @ Mil. Bucks (Jul. 14, 2021)
40... Bob Pettit, St.L. Hawks* .... vs. Bos. Celtics (Apr. 9, 1961)
40... Jerry West, L.A. Lakers* .... @ Bos. Celtics (Apr. 29, 1969)
40... James Worthy, L.A. Lakers* .... vs. Det. Pistons (Jun. 13, 1989)
40... Kyrie Irving, Cle. Cavaliers .... vs. G.S. Warriors (Jun. 9, 2017)
40... Khris Middleton, Mil. Bucks .... vs. Pho. Suns (Jul. 14, 2021)

* Team lost game.

Game 5

61... Elgin Baylor, L.A. Lakers .... @ Bos. Celtics (Apr. 14, 1962)
46... Michael Jordan, Chi. Bulls .... @ Por. Blazers (Jun. 12, 1992)
43... Elgin Baylor, L.A. Lakers .... @ Bos. Celtics (Apr. 21, 1963)
43... Dwyane Wade, Mia. Heat .... vs. Dal. Mavericks (Jun. 18, 2006)
41... Elgin Baylor, L.A. Lakers .... @ Bos. Celtics (Apr. 24, 1966)
41... Michael Jordan, Chi. Bulls* ...... vs. Pho. Suns (Jun. 18, 1993)
41... Kyrie Irving, Cle. Cavaliers .... @ G.S. Warriors (Jun. 13, 2016)
41... LeBron James, Cle. Cavaliers ..... @ G.S. Warriors (Jun. 13, 2016)
41... LeBron James, Cle. Cavaliers* ... @ G.S. Warriors (Jun. 12, 2017)
40... Kareem Abdul-Jabbar, L.A. Lakers .... vs. Phi. 76ers (May 14, 1980)
40... LeBron James, Cle. Cavaliers* ... @ G.S. Warriors (Jun. 14, 2015)
40... LeBron James, L.A. Lakers* .... vs. Mia. Heat (Oct. 9, 2020)
40... Devin Booker, Pho. Suns* .... vs. Mil. Bucks (Jul. 17, 2021)

* Team lost game.

Game 6

50... Bob Pettit, St.L. Hawks .... vs. Bos. Celtics (Apr. 12, 1958)
50... Giannis Antetokounmpo, Mil. Bucks ... vs. Pho. Suns (Jul. 20, 2021)
45... Wilt Chamberlain, L.A. Lakers ... vs. N.Y. Knicks (May 6, 1970)
45... Michael Jordan, Chi. Bulls .... @ Uta. Jazz (Jun. 14, 1998)
44... Rick Barry, S.F. Warriors* .... vs. Phi. 76ers (Apr. 24, 1967)
43... Isiah Thomas, Det. Pistons* .... @ L.A. Lakers (Jun. 19, 1988)
42... Magic Johnson, L.A. Lakers .... @ Phi. 76ers (May 16, 1980)
41... Shaquille O'Neal, L.A. Lakers ... vs. Ind. Pacers (Jun. 19, 2000)
41... LeBron James, Cle. Cavaliers ..... vs. G.S. Warriors (Jun. 16, 2016)
40... George Mikan, Min. Lakers .... vs. Syr. Nationals (Apr. 23, 1950)
40... John Havlicek, Bos. Celtics .... @ L.A. Lakers (May 2, 1968)
40... Julius Erving, Phi. 76ers* .... @ Por. Blazers (Jun. 5, 1977)

* Team lost game.

Most Points in a Finals Game 7

				Outcome
42	Jerry West*, L.A. Lakers	vs. Bos. Celtics (May 5, 1969)	Lost
41	Elgin Baylor, L.A. Lakers	@ Bos. Celtics (Apr. 18, 1962)	Lost
39	Bob Pettit, St.L. Hawks	@ Bos. Celtics (Apr. 13, 1957)	Lost
37	Tom Heinsohn, Bos. Celtics	vs. St.L. Hawks (Apr. 13, 1957)	Won
37	LeBron James*, Mia. Heat	vs. S.A. Spurs (Jun. 20, 2013)	Won
36	Jerry West, L.A. Lakers	@ Bos. Celtics (Apr. 28, 1966)	Lost
36	Walt Frazier, N.Y. Knicks	vs. L.A. Lakers (May 8, 1970)	Won
36	James Worthy*, L.A. Lakers	vs. Det. Pistons (Jun. 21, 1988)	Won
35	Jerry West, L.A. Lakers	@ Bos. Celtics (Apr. 18, 1962)	Lost
32	Draymond Green, G.S. Warriors	vs. Cle. Cavaliers (Jun. 19, 2016)	Lost
30	Bill Russell, Bos. Celtics	vs. L.A. Lakers (Apr. 18, 1962)	Won
29	Kareem Abdul-Jabbar, L.A. Lakers	@ Bos. Celtics (Jun. 12, 1984)	Lost
28	Jerry West, L.A. Lakers	@ N.Y. Knicks (May 8, 1970)	Lost
28	Dave Cowens, Bos. Celtics	@ Mil. Bucks (May 12, 1974)	Won
27	Sam Jones, Bos. Celtics	vs. L.A. Lakers (Apr. 18, 1962)	Won
27	Marvin Webster, Sea. Sonics	vs. Was. Bullets (Jun. 7, 1978)	Lost
27	LeBron James*, Cle. Cavaliers	@ G.S. Warriors (Jun. 19, 2016)	Won
26	John Havlicek, Bos. Celtics	@ L.A. Lakers (May 5, 1969)	Won
26	Kareem Abdul-Jabbar, Mil. Bucks	vs. Bos. Celtics (May 12, 1974)	Lost
26	Kyrie Irving, Cle. Cavaliers	@ G.S. Warriors (Jun. 19, 2016)	Won

continued on next page

			Outcome
25	Bill Russell, Bos. Celtics	vs. L.A. Lakers (Apr. 28, 1966)	Won
25	Joe Dumars, Det. Pistons	@ L.A. Lakers (Jun. 21, 1988)	Lost
25	Hakeem Olajuwon*, Hou. Rockets	vs. N.Y. Knicks (Jun. 22, 1994)	Won
25	Tim Duncan*, S.A. Spurs	vs. Det. Pistons (Jun. 23, 2005)	Won

* Finals MVP.

ABA

Game 1

47... Julius Erving, N.Y. Nets .... vs. Uta. Stars (Apr. 30, 1974)
45... Julius Erving, N.Y. Nets .... @ Den. Nuggets (May 1, 1976)
41... Red Robbins, N.O. Buccaneers*... @ Pit. Pipers (Apr. 18, 1968)
40... Gary Bradds, Oak. Oaks .... vs. Ind. Pacers (Apr. 30, 1969)
39... Connie Hawkins, Pit. Pipers .... vs. N.O. Buccaneers (Apr. 18, 1968)
36... Darel Carrier, Ken. Colonels* ..... @ Uta. Stars (May 3, 1971)
35... George McGinnis, Ind. Pacers*... @ Ken. Colonels (May 13, 1975)
34... Rick Barry, N.Y. Nets* .... @ Ind. Pacers (May 6, 1972)
33... Bob Netolicky, Ind. Pacers*........ @ Oak. Oaks (Apr. 30, 1969)
33... Freddie Lewis, Ind. Pacers .... vs. N.Y. Nets (May 6, 1972)
33... Dan Issel, Ken. Colonels*........... vs. Ind. Pacers (Apr. 28, 1973)

Game 2

48... Julius Erving, N.Y. Nets*........... @ Den. Nuggets (May 4, 1976)
40... Zelmo Beaty, Uta. Stars .... vs. Ken. Colonels (May 5, 1971)
40... Dan Issel, Ken. Colonels*.......... @ Uta. Stars (May 5, 1971)
39... Roger Brown, Ind. Pacers .... @ Oak. Oaks (May 2, 1969)
36... Bob Netolicky, Ind. Pacers .... @ Oak. Oaks (May 2, 1969)
35... Freddie Lewis, Ind. Pacers .... @ Oak. Oaks (May 2, 1969)
32... Bob Netolicky, Ind. Pacers .... vs. L.A. Stars (May 17, 1970)
32... Julius Erving, N.Y. Nets .... vs. Uta. Stars (May 4, 1974)
31... Warren Jabali, Oak. Oaks*........ vs. Ind. Pacers (May 2, 1969)
31... Mel Daniels, Ind. Pacers .... vs. L.A. Stars (May 17, 1970)

Game 3

44... Rick Barry, N.Y. Nets* .... vs. Ind. Pacers (May 12, 1972)
41... Artis Gilmore, Ken. Colonels ..... @ Ind. Pacers (May 17, 1975)
37... Warren Jabali, Oak. Oaks .... @ Ind. Pacers (May 3, 1969)
34... George Stone, L.A. Stars .... vs. Ind. Pacers (May 18, 1970)
32... David Thompson, Den. Nuggets* ... @ N.Y. Nets (May 6, 1976)
31... Julius Erving, N.Y. Nets .... vs. Den. Nuggets (May 6, 1976)
30... Red Robbins, N.O. Buccaneers... vs. Pit. Pipers (Apr. 24, 1968)
30... George McGinnis, Ind. Pacers... @ N.Y. Nets (May 12, 1972)
29... Roger Brown, Ind. Pacers* .... vs. Oak. Oaks (May 3, 1969)
29... Mel Daniels, Ind. Pacers* .... vs. Oak. Oaks (May 3, 1969)
29... Willie Wise, Uta. Stars* .... @ Ken. Colonels (May 7, 1971)

Game 4

53... Roger Brown, Ind. Pacers .... @ L.A. Stars (May 19, 1970)
47... Connie Hawkins, Pit. Pipers....... @ N.O. Buccaneers (Apr. 25, 1968)
34... Willie Wise, Uta. Stars* .... @ Ken. Colonels (May 8, 1971)
34... Julius Erving, N.Y. Nets .... vs. Den. Nuggets (May 8, 1976)
33... Louie Dampier, Ken. Colonels .... vs. Uta. Stars (May 8, 1971)
30... Warren Jabali, Oak. Oaks .... @ Ind. Pacers (May 5, 1969)
30... Billy Paultz, N.Y. Nets .... vs. Ind. Pacers (May 15, 1972)
27... Doug Moe, Oak. Oaks .... @ Ind. Pacers (May 5, 1969)
27... Darel Carrier, Ken. Colonels ...... vs. Uta. Stars (May 8, 1971)
26... Rick Barry, N.Y. Nets .... vs. Ind. Pacers (May 15, 1972)

Game 5

40... Billy Knight, Ind. Pacers* .... @ Ken. Colonels (May 22, 1975)
39... Warren Jabali, Oak. Oaks .... vs. Ind. Pacers (May 7, 1969)
39... Roger Brown, Ind. Pacers* .... vs. L.A. Stars (May 23, 1970)
37... Julius Erving, N.Y. Nets* .... @ Den. Nuggets (May 11, 1976)
34... Willie Wise, Uta. Stars* .... @ N.Y. Nets (May 10, 1974)
33... Freddie Lewis, Ind. Pacers* .... @ Oak. Oaks (May 7, 1969)
33... Mack Calvin, L.A. Stars .... @ Ind. Pacers (May 23, 1970)
32... Zelmo Beaty, Uta. Stars............. vs. Ken. Colonels (May 12, 1971)
33... Dan Issel, Ken. Colonels*........... @ Uta. Stars (May 12, 1971)
33... Rick Barry, N.Y. Nets* .... @ Ind. Pacers (May 18, 1972)

Game 6

45... Roger Brown, Ind. Pacers .... @ L.A. Stars (May 25, 1970)
42... David Thompson, Den. Nuggets* ... @ N.Y. Nets (May 13, 1976)
41... Connie Hawkins, Pit. Pipers....... @ N.O. Buccaneers (May 1, 1968)
34... Willie Wise, Uta. Stars* .... @ Ken. Colonels (May 15, 1971)
32... Roger Brown, Ind. Pacers .... @ N.Y. Nets (May 20, 1972)
31... Cincy Powell, Ken. Colonels ...... vs. Uta. Stars (May 15, 1971)
31... Julius Erving, N.Y. Nets .... vs. Den. Nuggets (May 13, 1976)
30... Dan Issel, Den. Nuggets*........... @ N.Y. Nets (May 13, 1976)
29... Artis Gilmore, Ken. Colonele ..... @ Ind. Pacers (May 10, 1973)
28... George Stone, L.A. Stars*.......... vs. Ind. Pacers (May 25, 1970)
28... John Williamson, N.Y. Nets....... vs. Den. Nuggets (May 13, 1976)

Game 7

41... Dan Issel, Ken. Colonels*........... @ Uta. Stars (May 18, 1971)
36... Zelmo Beaty, Uta. Stars............. vs. Ken. Colonels (May 18, 1971)
35... Charlie Williams, Pit. Pipers ...... vs. N.O. Buccaneers (May 4, 1968)
31... Darel Carrier, Ken. Colonels*..... @ Uta. Stars (May 18, 1971)
28... Doug Moe, N.O. Buccaneers* ... @ Pit. Pipers (May 4, 1968)

27... George McGinnis, Ind. Pacers... @ Ken. Colonels (May 12, 1973)
22... Red Robbins, N.O. Buccaneers*... @ Pit. Pipers (May 4, 1968)
22... Willie Wise, Uta. Stars .... vs. Ken. Colonels (May 18, 1971)
20... Connie Hawkins, Pit. Pipers....... vs. N.O. Buccaneers (May 4, 1968)
20... Glen Combs, Uta. Stars .... vs. Ken. Colonels (May 18, 1971)

* Team lost game.

Players Shooting 100% from the Field in a Playoff Game (Min. 10 Shots)

	FG	Round, Game	Pts
Don Nelson, Bos. Celtics*	10-for-10	Eastern Conference Semifinals, Game 4 ......@ Buf. Braves (Apr. 6, 1974)	24
Larry McNeill, K.C.-Oma. Kings	12-for-12	Western Conference Semifinals, Game 2 ....vs. Chi. Bulls (Apr. 13, 1975)	28
Scott Wedman, Bos. Celtics	11-for-11	NBA Finals, Game 1 ....vs. L.A. Lakers (May 27, 1985)	26
Serge Ibaka, Ok.C. Thunder	11-for-11	Western Conference Finals, Game 4 ....vs. S.A. Spurs (Jun. 2, 2012)	26
Nenê, Hou. Rockets	12-for-12	Western Conference First Round, Game 4....@ Ok.C. Thunder (Apr. 23, 2017)	28
Chris Paul, Pho. Suns	14-for-14	Western Conference First Round, Game 6....@ N.O. Pelicans (Apr. 28, 2022)	33

* Team lost game.

Most Points in a Playoff Game, Playing Less Than 30 Minutes

	MP	Round, Game
38.... LaMarcus Aldridge, S.A. Spurs	29:32	Western Conference Semifinals, Gm. 1....... vs. Ok.C. Thunder (Apr. 30, 2016)
38.... Kevin Durant, G.S. Warriors	29:31	Western Conference First Round, Gm. 3 ..... @ L.A. Clippers (Apr. 18, 2019)
37.... Stephen Curry, G.S. Warriors	29:43	Western Conference First Round, Gm. 4 ..... @ Por. Blazers (Apr. 24, 2017)
36.... Nick Van Exel, Dal. Mavericks	29:59	Western Conference Semifinals, Gm. 2....... vs. Sac. Kings (May 8, 2003)
36.... Joel Embiid, Phi. 76ers	27:54	Eastern Conference First Round, Gm. 3....... @ Was. Wizards (May 29, 2021)
35.... Michael Jordan, Chi. Bulls	29:00	Eastern Conference First Round, Gm. 1....... vs. Atl. Hawks (Apr. 30, 1993)
35.... Blake Griffin, L.A. Clippers	29:32	Western Conference First Round, Gm. 2 ..... vs. G.S. Warriors (Apr. 21, 2014)
35.... Paul George, L.A. Clippers	24:55	Western Conference First Round, Gm. 5 ..... vs. Dal. Mavericks (Aug. 25, 2020)
34.... Cliff Hagan, St.L. Hawks*	26:00	Western Divison Finals, Gm. 2.................. @ L.A. Lakers (Apr. 2, 1963)
34.... Tom Heinsohn, Bos. Celtics	28:00	Eastern Division Finals, Gm. 5 .... vs. Cin. Royals (Apr. 6, 1963)
34.... Mark Aguirre, Det. Pistons	29:00	Eastern Conference Semifinals, Gm. 4........ vs. Bos. Celtics (May 13, 1991)
34.... Eddie Johnson, Sea. Sonics*	26:00	Western Conference Finals, Gm. 7............ @ Pho. Suns (Jun. 5, 1993)
34.... Kirk Hinrich, Chi. Bulls	25:00	Eastern Conference First Round, Gm. 2....... vs. Was. Wizards (Apr. 27, 2005)
34.... Nate Robinson, Chi. Bulls	28:32	Eastern Conference First Round, Gm. 4 ..... vs. Brk. Nets (Apr. 27, 2013)
34.... Stephen Curry, G.S. Warriors	22:57	Western Conference First Round, Gm. 2 ..... vs. Den. Nuggets (Apr. 18, 2022)
33.... Cazzie Russell, G.S. Warriors	28:00	Western Conference Finals, Gm. 4............. vs. L.A. Lakers (Apr. 23, 1973)
33.... Joel Embiid, Phi. 76ers	28:09	Eastern Conference Semifinals, Gm. 3........ vs. Tor. Raptors (May 2, 2019)
32.... John Havlicek, Bos. Celtics	26:00	Eastern Division Semifinals, Gm. 1 .... vs. N.Y. Knicks (Mar. 21, 1967)
32.... Kareem Abdul-Jabbar, L.A. Lakers	29:00	NBA Finals, Gm. 6.............................. vs. Bos. Celtics (Jun. 14, 1987)
32.... Jason Terry, Dal. Mavericks	25:14	Western Conference Semifinals, Gm. 4....... vs. L.A. Lakers (May 8, 2011)
32.... Chris Paul, L.A. Clippers	27:44	Western Conference Semifinals, Gm. 1....... @ Ok.C. Thunder (May 5, 2014)
32.... Kawhi Leonard, S.A. Spurs	28:30	Western Conference First Round, Gm. 3 ..... vs. L.A. Clippers (Apr. 24, 2015)
32.... Kawhi Leonard, L.A. Clippers	29:50	Western Conference First Round, Gm. 5 ..... vs. Dal. Mavericks (Aug. 25, 2020)
31.... Tom Heinsohn, Bos. Celtics	25:00	Eastern Division Finals, Gm. 3 .... vs. Phi. Warriors (Mar. 28, 1962)
31.... Cliff Hagan, St.L. Hawks	27:00	Western Divison Finals, Gm. 1.................. vs. Det. Pistons (Mar. 20, 1963)
31.... George Gervin, S.A. Spurs	29:00	Eastern Conference Semifinals, Gm. 1........ vs. Phi. 76ers (Apr. 15, 1979)
31.... Byron Scott, L.A. Lakers	29:00	Western Conference Semifinals, Gm. 2....... vs. Por. Blazers (Apr. 30, 1985)
31.... Kevin McHale, Bos. Celtics	28:00	Eastern Conference First Round, Gm. 2....... vs. N.Y. Knicks (Apr. 28, 1990)
31.... Eddie Johnson, Hou. Rockets	27:34	Western Conference Finals, Gm. 3............. vs. Uta. Jazz (May 23, 1997)
31.... Chris Webber, Sac. Kings*	29:19	Western Conference Semifinals, Gm. 2....... @ Dal. Mavericks (May 8, 2003)
31.... Daniel Gibson, Cle. Cavaliers	29:02	Eastern Conference Finals, Gm. 6.............. vs. Det. Pistons (Jun. 2, 2007)
31.... Eddie House, Bos. Celtics	27:35	Eastern Conference Semifinals, Gm. 2........ vs. Orl. Magic (May 6, 2009)
31.... Anthony Davis, L.A. Lakers	29:21	Western Conference First Round, Gm. 2 ..... vs. Por. Blazers (Aug. 20, 2020)
31.... James Harden, Hou. Rockets	28:24	Western Conference First Round, Gm. 5 ..... vs. Ok.C. Thunder (Aug. 29, 2020)
31.... Devin Booker, Pho. Suns*	24:47	Western Conference First Round, Gm. 2 ..... vs. N.O. Pelicans (Apr. 19, 2022)
30.... Henry Logan, Oak. Oaks^a	28:00	Western Division Finals, Gm. 1 .... vs. N.O. Buccaneers^a (Apr. 19, 1969)
30.... Walter Davis, Pho. Suns	28:00	Western Conference First Round, Gm. 3 ..... @ Den. Nuggets (Apr. 24, 1982)
30.... Andrew Toney, Phi. 76ers	28:00	Eastern Conference Finals, Gm. 2.............. @ Bos. Celtics (May 12, 1982)

continued on next page

	MP	Round, Game
30.... Terry Teagle, G.S. Warriors	29:00	Western Conference First Round, Gm. 3 ..... vs. Uta. Jazz (Apr. 29, 1987)
30.... LeBron James, L.A. Lakers	28:18	Western Conference First Round, Gm. 4 ..... @ Por. Blazers (Aug. 24, 2020)
30.... Joel Embiid, Phi. 76ers	29:46	Eastern Conference First Round, Gm. 1....... vs. Was. Wizards (May 23, 2021)
30.... Donovan Mitchell, Uta. Jazz	29:25	Western Conference First Round, Gm. 5 ..... vs. Mem. Grizzlies (Jun. 2, 2021)
30.... Sperncer Dinwiddie, Dal. Mavericks	25:24	Western Conference Semifinals, Gm. 7....... @ Pho. Suns (May 15, 2022)

* Team lost game.

ᵃ ABA.

Most Field Goal Attempts without Hitting a Shot, Game

		Round, Game	Pts
14...... Chick Reiser, Bal. Bullets	@ Phi. Warriors (Apr. 10, 1948)	BAA Finals, Gm. 1	3
14...... Dennis Johnson, Sea. Sonics	vs. Was. Bullets (Jun. 7, 1978)	NBA Finals, Gm. 7	4
13...... Giff Roux, St.L. Bombers	@ Phi. Warriors (Mar. 27, 1948)	BAA Semifinals, Gm. 3	0
13...... Ray Allen, Bos. Celtics	vs. L.A. Lakers (Jun. 8, 2010)	NBA Finals, Gm. 3	2
12...... Tom Gola, Phi. Warriors	@ Bos. Celtics (Mar. 23, 1958)	ED Finals, Gm. 3	3
12...... Guy Rodgers, S.F. Warriors	@ Bos. Celtics (Apr. 18, 1964)	NBA Finals, Gm. 1	2
12...... Paul Pressey, Mil. Bucks	@ Bos. Celtics (May 5, 1987)	EC Semifinals, Gm. 1	2
12...... Nate Robinson, Chi. Bulls	vs. Mia. Heat (May 13, 2013)	EC Semifinals, Gm. 4	0
12...... Trevor Ariza, Hou. Rockets	vs. G.S. Warriors (May 28, 2018)	WC Finals, Gm. 7	0
11...... Bob Doll, St.L. Bombers	vs. Phi. Warriors (Apr. 6, 1948)	BAA Semifinals, Gm. 7	0
11...... Harry Gallatin, N.Y. Knicks	vs. Roc. Royals (Apr. 11, 1951)	NBA Finals, Gm. 3	1
11...... Walt Hazzard, L.A. Lakers	@ S.F. Warriors (Mar. 26, 1967)	WD Semifinals, Gm. 3	3
11...... George McGinnis, Ind. Pacersᵃ	@ Den. Rocketsᵃ (Apr. 6, 1972)	ABA WD Semifinals, Gm. 4	5
11...... Fred Brown, Sea. Sonics	vs. L.A. Lakers (Apr. 27, 1980)	WC Finals, Gm. 4	1
11...... Henry Walker, N.Y. Knicks	@ Bos. Celtics (Apr. 19, 2011)	EC First Round, Gm. 2	2
10...... Art Hillhouse, Phi. Warriors	@ St.L. Bombers (Apr. 5, 1947)	BAA Quarterfinals, Gm. 2	5
10...... Dick Schulz, Bal. Bullets*	@ Phi. Warriors (Apr. 13, 1948)	BAA Finals, Gm. 2	2
10...... Cliff Barker, Ind. Olympians	@ Min. Lakers (Mar. 25, 1951)	WD Semifinals, Gm. 3	0
10...... Freddie Lewis, Ind. Pacersᵃ*	vs. L.A. Starsᵃ (May 17, 1970)	ABA Finals, Gm. 2	0
10...... Rick Mount, Ind. Pacersᵃ*	vs. Den. Rocketsᵃ (Mar. 31, 1972)	ABA WD Semifinals, Gm. 1	0
10...... Bob Wilkerson, Den. Nuggets	vs. Mil. Bucks (Apr. 28, 1978)	WC Semifinals, Gm. 5	0
10...... Vinnie Johnson, Det. Pistons	@ Chi. Bulls (Jun. 1, 1990)	EC Finals, Gm. 6	2
10...... Patrick Ewing, N.Y. Knicks	@ Ind. Pacers (May 28, 1994)	EC Finals, Gm. 3	1
10...... Charles Barkley, Pho. Suns	@ Hou. Rockets (May 13, 1995)	WC Semifinals, Gm. 3	5
10...... Marvin Williams, Cha. Hornets	@ Mia. Heat (Apr. 20, 2016)	EC First Round, Gm. 2	0
10...... Reggie Bullock, Dal. Mavericks	vs. G.S. Warriors (May 22, 2022)	WC Finals, Gm. 3	0

ᵃ ABA.

* Team won game.

Most Points Scored in First Career Playoff Game

NBA

42......... Luka Dončić, Dal. Mavericks*	@ L.A. Clippers (Aug. 17, 2020)	WC First Round, Gm. 3
37......... George Mikan, Min. Lakers	vs. Chi. Stags (Mar. 23, 1949)	BAA WD Semifinals, Gm. 1
36......... Kareem Abdul-Jabbar, Mil. Bucks	vs. Phi. 76ers (Mar. 25, 1970)	ED Semifinals, Gm. 1
36......... Gary Brokaw, Mil. Bucks	vs. Det. Pistons (Apr. 13, 1976)	WC First Round, Gm. 1
36......... Derrick Rose, Chi. Bulls	@ Bos. Celtics (Apr. 18, 2009)	EC First Round, Gm. 1
36......... Anthony Edwards, Min. T'Wolves	@ Mem. Grizzlies (Apr. 16, 2022)	WC First Round, Gm. 1
35......... Wilt Chamberlain, Phi. Warriors	vs. Syr. Nationals (Mar. 11, 1960)	ED Semifinals, Gm. 1
35......... Chris Paul, N.O. Hornets	vs. Dal. Mavericks (Apr. 19, 2008)	WC First Round, Gm. 1
35......... Anthony Davis, N.O. Pelicans*	@ G.S. Warriors (Apr. 18, 2015)	WC First Round, Gm. 1
34......... Connie Simmons, Bal. Bullets	vs. N.Y. Knicks (Mar. 27, 1948)	BAA Quarterfinals, Gm. 1

continued on next page

34......... Ray Scott, Det. Pistons ....vs. Cin. Royals (Mar. 16, 1962)..........WD Semifinals, Gm. 1
34......... Brandon Jennings, Mil. Bucks* ....@ Atl. Hawks (Apr. 17, 2010) ....EC First Round, Gm. 1
34......... Devin Booker, Pho. Suns ....vs. L.A. Lakers (May 23, 2021)...........WC First Round, Gm. 1
33......... Joe Caldwell, St.L. Hawks ....@ Bal. Bullets (Mar. 24, 1966)..........WD Semifinals, Gm. 1
32......... Earl Monroe, Bal. Bullets* ....vs. N.Y. Knicks (Mar. 27, 1969)..........ED Semifinals, Gm. 1
32......... Tim Duncan, S.A. Spurs ....@ Pho. Suns (Apr. 23, 1998)...............EC First Round, Gm. 1
32......... LeBron James, Cle. Cavaliers ....vs. Was. Wizards (Apr. 22, 2006).......EC First Round, Gm. 1
32......... Trae Young, Atl. Hawks ....@ N.Y. Knicks (May 23, 2021)...........EC First Round, Gm. 1
31......... Elvin Hayes, S.D. Rockets* ....@ Atl. Hawks (Mar. 27, 1969)...........WD Semifinals, Gm. 1
31......... Walter Davis, Pho. Suns* ....vs. Mil. Bucks (Apr. 11, 1978)............WC First Round, Gm. 1
31......... Paul Pierce, Bos. Celtics ....vs. Phi. 76ers (Apr. 21, 2002)............EC First Round, Gm. 1
31......... Damian Lillard, Por. Blazers ....@ Hou. Rockets (Apr. 20, 2014) ....WC First Round, Gm. 1
31......... Dillon Brooks, Mem. Grizzlies ....@ Uta. Jazz (May 23, 2021) ....WC First Round, Gm. 1
* Team lost game.

ABA

46......... Levern Tart, N.Y. Nets..............................@ Ken. Colonels (Apr. 17, 1970)............ ED Semifinals, Gm. 1
44......... Mel Daniels, Min. Muskies......................vs. Ken. Colonels (Mar. 24, 1968).......... ED Semifinals, Gm. 1
42......... Willie Somerset, Hou. Mavericks* ....@ Dal. Chaparrals (Mar. 23, 1968) .... WD Semifinals, Gm. 1
41......... Marvin Barnes, Spirits of St.L.* ....@ N.Y. Nets (Apr. 6, 1975)................... ED Semifinals, Gm. 1
38......... Connie Hawkins, Pit. Pipers ....vs. Ind. Pacers (Mar. 25, 1968).............. ED Semifinals, Gm. 1
34......... Mike Barrett, Was. Capitols* ....@ Den. Rockets (Apr. 17, 1970) .... WD Semifinals, Gm. 1
32......... Roger Brown, Ind. Pacers* ....@ Pit. Pipers (Mar. 25, 1968)................ ED Semifinals, Gm. 1
32......... Spencer Haywood, Den. Rockets..............vs. Was. Capitols (Apr. 17, 1970) .... WD Semifinals, Gm. 1
32......... Julius Erving, Vir. Squires ....vs. The Floridians (Mar. 31, 1972)........... ED Semifinals, Gm. 1
31......... Larry Brown, N.O. Buccaneers.................vs. Den. Rockets (Mar. 26, 1968) .... WD Semifinals, Gm. 1
31......... John Roche, N.Y. Nets..............................@ Ken. Colonels (Apr. 1, 1972)............. ED Semifinals, Gm. 1
30......... Artis Gilmore, Ken. Colonels*..................vs. N.Y. Nets (Apr. 1, 1972) .... ED Semifinals, Gm. 1
30......... Len Elmore, Ind. Pacers...........................@ S.A. Spurs (Apr. 5, 1975).................. WD Semifinals, Gm. 1
29......... Darel Carrier, Ken. Colonels* ....@ Min. Muskies (Mar. 24, 1968) .... ED Semifinals, Gm. 1
29......... Charlie Williams, Pit. Pipers.....................vs. Ind. Pacers (Mar. 25, 1968) .... ED Semifinals, Gm. 1
28......... John Beasley, Dal. Chaparrals..................vs. Hou. Mavericks (Mar. 23, 1968) .... WD Semifinals, Gm. 1
28......... Warren Jabali, Oak. Oaks........................vs. Den. Rockets (Apr. 5, 1969) .... WD Semifinals, Gm. 1
27......... Bob Netolicky, Ind. Pacers* ....@ Pit. Pipers (Mar. 25, 1968) .... ED Semifinals, Gm. 1
26......... Jimmy Jones, N.O. Buccaneers.................vs. Den. Rockets (Mar. 26, 1968) .... WD Semifinals, Gm. 1
26......... Dan Issel, Ken. Colonels ....vs. The Floridians (Apr. 2, 1971)............. ED Semifinals, Gm. 1
26......... Ralph Simpson, Den. Rockets* ....@ Ind. Pacers (Mar. 31, 1972) .... WD Semifinals, Gm. 1
26......... Randy Denton, Uta. Stars*.......................@ Den. Nuggets (Apr. 6, 1975) .... WD Semifinals, Gm. 1
* Team lost game.

Most Points Scored in First Career Finals Game

NBA

48 ....Allen Iverson, Phi. 76ers ....@ L.A. Lakers (Jun. 6, 2001)
42 ....George Mikan, Min. Lakers ....vs. Was. Capitols (Apr. 4, 1949)
37 ....Joe Fulks, Phi. Warriors ....vs. Chi. Stags (Apr. 16, 1947)
37 ....Bob Pettit, St.L. Hawks ....@ Bos. Celtics (Mar. 30, 1957)
37 ....Rick Barry, S.F. Warriors* ....@ Phi. 76ers (Apr. 14, 1967)
37 ....Willis Reed, N.Y. Knicks ....vs. L.A. Lakers (Apr. 24, 1970)
36 ....Bill Sharman, Bos. Celtics* ....vs. St.L. Hawks (Mar. 30, 1957)
36 ....Michael Jordan, Chi. Bulls* ....vs. L.A. Lakers (Jun. 2, 1991)
36 ....Kevin Durant, Ok.C. Thunder ....vs. Mia. Heat (Jun. 12, 2012)
34 ....Jim Pollard, Min. Lakers ....vs. N.Y. Knicks (Apr. 12, 1952)

continued on next page

34 .... Elgin Baylor, Min. Lakers* .... @ Bos. Celtics (Apr. 4, 1959)
34 .... Adrian Dantley, Det. Pistons .... @ L.A. Lakers (Jun. 7, 1988)
34 .... Anthony Davis, L.A. Lakers .... vs. Mia. Heat (Sep. 30, 2020)
33 .... Cliff Hagan, St.L. Hawks .... @ Bos. Celtics (Mar. 29, 1958)
33 .... Hakeem Olajuwon, Hou. Rockets* .... @ Bos. Celtics (May 26, 1986)
33 .... James Worthy, L.A. Lakers .... vs. Bos. Celtics (Jun. 2, 1987)
33 .... Tim Duncan, S.A. Spurs .... vs. N.Y. Knicks (Jun. 16, 1999)
32 .... Hal Greer, Phi. 76ers .... vs. S.F. Warriors (Apr. 14, 1967)
32 .... Gus Williams, Sea. Sonics* .... @ Was. Bulelts (May 20, 1979)
32 .... Shawn Kemp, Sea. Sonics* .... @ Chi. Bulls (Jun. 5, 1996)
32 .... Jason Terry, Dal. Mavericks .... vs. Mia. Heat (Jun. 8, 2006)
32 .... Pascal Siakam, Tor. Raptors .... vs. G.S. Warriors (May 30, 2019)
32 .... Chris Paul, Pho. Suns .... vs. Mil. Bucks (Jul. 6, 2021)
31 .... Kareem Abdul-Jabbar, Mil. Bucks .... vs. Bal. Bullets (Apr. 21, 1971)
30 .... Wali Jones, Phi. 76ers .... vs. S.F. Warriors (Apr. 14, 1967)
30 .... Gail Goodrich, L.A. Lakers .... vs. N.Y. Knicks (May 1, 1973)
30 .... Doug Collins, Phi. 76ers .... vs. Por. Blazers (May 22, 1977)
30 .... Fred Brown, Sea. Sonics .... vs. Was. Bullets (May 21, 1978)

* Team lost game.

ABA

47 .... Julius Erving, N.Y. Nets .... vs. Uta. Stars (Apr. 30, 1974)
45 .... Red Robbins, N.O. Buccaneers* .... @ Pit. Pipers (Apr. 18, 1968)
41 .... Gary Bradds, Oak. Oaks .... vs. Ind. Pacers (Apr. 30, 1969)
40 .... Connie Hawkins, Pit. Pipers .... vs. N.O. Buccaneers (Apr. 18, 1968)
39 .... Darel Carrier, Ken. Colonels* .... @ Uta. Stars (May 3, 1971)
36 .... Bob Netolicky, Ind. Pacers* .... @ Oak. Oaks (Apr. 30, 1969)
33 .... Doug Moe, N.O. Buccaneers* .... @ Pit. Pipers (Apr. 18, 1968)
30 .... David Thompson, Den. Nuggets* .... vs. N.Y. Nets (May 1, 1976)
30 .... Warren Jabali, Oak. Oaks .... vs. Ind. Pacers (Apr. 30, 1969)
29 .... John Roche, N.Y. Nets* .... @ Ind. Pacers (May 6, 1972)
28 .... Dan Issel, Ken. Colonels* .... @ Uta. Stars (May 3, 1971)
27 .... Art Heyman, Pit. Pipers .... vs. N.O. Buccaneers (Apr. 18, 1968)
26 .... Charlie Williams, Pit. Pipers .... vs. N.O. Buccaneers (Apr. 18, 1968)
26 .... Zelmo Beaty, Uta. Stars .... vs. Ken. Colonels (May 3, 1971)

* Team lost game.

Highest PPG in Each Finals Game

Game 1 (Min. 4 GP)

PPG		Points (GP)
33.3	Shaquille O'Neal	200 (6)
33.0	Michael Jordan	198 (6)
32.0	Julius Erving	192 (6)
29.6	Elgin Baylor	207 (7)
28.9	Jerry West	260 (9)
28.2	LeBron James	282 (10)
26.8	George Mikan	134 (5)
26.3	Cliff Hagan	105 (4)
26.0	Bob Pettit	104 (4)
25.7	Tim Duncan	154 (6)
25.6	Stephen Curry	128 (5)
25.0	Freddie Lewis	100 (4)
24.3	Kobe Bryant	170 (7)

Game 2 (Min. 4 GP)

PPG		Points (GP)
36.3	Michael Jordan	218 (6)
32.0	Jerry West	288 (9)
29.2	Shaquille O'Neal	175 (6)
28.5	Dan Issel	114 (4)
27.8	LeBron James	278 (10)
26.8	Julius Erving	161 (6)
26.0	Larry Bird	130 (5)
25.3	Cliff Hagan	101 (4)
25.0	Stephen Curry	125 (5)
24.6	Kareem Abdul-Jabbar	246 (10)
24.3	Kobe Bryant	170 (7)
23.8	Bob Pettit	95 (4)
23.8	Bob Dandridge	95 (4)

continued on next page

Game 1 (Min. 4 GP)

23.2	Scottie Pippen	139 (6)
22.8	Bill Sharman	114 (5)
22.8	Larry Bird	114 (5)
22.3	Dan Issel	89 (4)
21.9	John Havlicek	175 (8)
21.8	James Worthy	131 (6)
21.6	Kareem Abdul-Jabbar	216 (10)

Game 2 (Min. 4 GP)

23.3	John Havlicek	163 (7)
23.0	George McGinnis	92 (4)
22.9	Elgin Baylor	160 (7)
22.8	James Worthy	137 (6)
22.2	Roger Brown	111 (5)
21.5	Klay Thompson	129 (6)
21.4	Dwyane Wade	107 (5)

Game 3 (Min. 4 GP)

PPG		Points (GP)
31.4	Jerry West	283 (9)
30.8	Michael Jordan	185 (6)
29.2	Kobe Bryant	175 (6)
28.0	Bob Pettit	112 (4)
27.8	George Mikan	139 (5)
27.7	LeBron James	277 (10)
26.8	Stephen Curry	161 (6)
26.8	Dwyane Wade	134 (5)
26.0	Shaquille O'Neal	156 (6)
24.8	Julius Erving	149 (6)
23.5	Bob Dandridge	94 (4)
23.4	Kareem Abdul-Jabbar	234 (10)
23.3	Dan Issel	93 (4)
23.0	Elgin Baylor	161 (7)
22.6	Larry Bird	113 (5)
22.3	John Havlicek	156 (7)
21.5	Wilt Chamberlain	129 (6)
20.8	George McGinnis	83 (4)
20.7	James Worthy	124 (6)
20.0	Freddie Lewis	80 (4)

Game 4 (Min. 4 GP)

PPG		Points (GP)
32.3	Michael Jordan	194 (6)
30.8	Jerry West	277 (9)
30.3	Shaquille O'Neal	182 (6)
30.2	Stephen Curry	181 (6)
29.3	Bob Pettit	117 (4)
27.0	Dwyane Wade	135 (5)
26.9	Elgin Baylor	188 (7)
25.2	Dennis Johnson	151 (6)
24.9	Kobe Bryant	174 (7)
24.8	Cliff Hagan	99 (4)
24.6	LeBron James	246 (10)
24.2	Julius Erving	145 (6)
24.1	Magic Johnson	193 (8)
23.5	Roger Brown	94 (4)
23.0	Dan Issel	92 (4)
22.4	Bill Sharman	112 (5)
22.3	Kareem Abdul-Jabbar	223 (10)
21.3	Tom Heinsohn	192 (9)
21.0	James Worthy	126 (6)
21.0	George Mikan	105 (5)
21.0	Larry Bird	105 (5)

Game 5 (Min. 4 GP)

PPG		Points (GP)
34.8	Michael Jordan	209 (6)
33.0	Elgin Baylor	198 (6)
32.6	LeBron James	261 (8)
30.6	Julius Erving	153 (5)
28.6	Stephen Curry	143 (5)
28.3	Bob Pettit	113 (4)
27.9	Jerry West	251 (9)
26.3	Freddie Lewis	105 (4)
26.0	Kareem Abdul-Jabbar	182 (7)
25.5	Shaquille O'Neal	102 (4)
25.3	Dan Issel	101 (4)
25.2	Kobe Bryant	151 (6)
24.4	Dwyane Wade	122 (5)
23.4	Tim Duncan	117 (5)
23.0	Cliff Hagan	92 (4)
22.0	Wilt Chamberlain	132 (6)
22.0	George Mikan	110 (5)
21.5	Tom Heinsohn	172 (8)
21.4	Klay Thompson	107 (5)
21.2	Dennis Johnson	127 (6)
21.2	Larry Bird	106 (5)

Game 6 (Min. 3 GP)

PPG		Points (GP)
35.7	Bob Pettit	107 (3)
34.4	Michael Jordan	172 (5)
32.0	Julius Erving	128 (4)
31.8	George Mikan	127 (4)
30.8	LeBron James	154 (5)
29.8	Jerry West	179 (6)
27.5	Stephen Curry	110 (4)
27.0	Roger Brown	81 (3)
26.2	Kareem Abdul-Jabbar	157 (6)
25.7	Wilt Chamberlain	77 (3)
25.6	Larry Bird	128 (5)
25.0	John Havlicek	150 (6)
24.8	Elgin Baylor	149 (6)
24.7	Kobe Bryant	74 (3)
24.5	James Worthy	98 (4)
24.3	Dan Issel	73 (3)
24.0	Tim Duncan	72 (3)
22.3	Cliff Hagan	67 (3)
22.3	Dwyane Wade	67 (3)
22.0	Dolph Schayes	66 (3)
22.0	Jamaal Wilkes	66 (3)

continued on next page

Game 7 (Min. 2 GP)

PPG		Points (GP)		PPG		Points (GP)
35.3	Jerry West	141 (4)		20.5	Manu Ginóbili	41 (2)
32.0	LeBron James	64 (2)		20.4	Bill Russell	102 (5)
30.5	Bob Pettit	61 (2)		20.0	Arnie Risen	40 (2)
28.5	James Worthy	57 (2)		19.7	Kareem Abdul-Jabbar	59 (3)
26.5	Dan Issel	53 (2)		19.5	Wilt Chamberlain	39 (2)
24.5	Elgin Baylor	98 (4)		19.3	John Havlicek	58 (3)
24.5	Tim Duncan	49 (2)		17.5	Red Robbins	35 (2)
22.8	Sam Jones	91 (4)		17.5	Magic Johnson	35 (2)
22.3	Tom Heinsohn	67 (3)		16.5	George Mikan	33 (2)
21.5	Cliff Hagan	43 (2)		16.5	Bob Dandridge	33 (2)
21.0	Frank Ramsey	63 (3)				

Three Pointers

Most Career 3P, Playoffs

561	Stephen Curry^		314	Danny Green^		254	Kyle Korver
451	Klay Thompson^		294	J.R. Smith		236	Jason Kidd
432	LeBron James^		292	Kobe Bryant		235	Chris Paul^
385	Ray Allen		285	Derek Fisher		228	Kawhi Leonard
369	James Harden^		276	Paul Pierce		221	Jason Terry
344	Kevin Durant^		267	Chauncey Billups		206	Jae Crowder^
324	Manu Ginóbili		261	Robert Horry		200	Scottie Pippen
320	Reggie Miller		258	Paul George^		200	Michael Finley

^ Active.

Most Career 3P, Finals

152	Stephen Curry^		43	Kevin Durant^		30	Kyrie Irving^
106	Klay Thompson^		42	Michael Jordan		29	Jae Crowder^
101	LeBron James^		42	Manu Ginóbili		28	Jason Kidd
59	Danny Green^		41	Andre Iguodala^		27	Danny Ainge
59	J.R. Smith		36	Mario Chalmers		27	Toni Kukoč
56	Robert Horry		35	Michael Cooper		27	Shane Battier
55	Ray Allen		35	Draymond Green^		26	Rashard Lewis
48	Kobe Bryant		34	Kawhi Leonard^		26	Mike Miller
48	Derek Fisher		30	Scottie Pippen		26	Kevin Love^

^ Active.

Most 3P, Playoff Game

			Round, Game	Pts
12	Damian Lillard, Por. Blazers*	@ Den. Nuggets (Jun. 1, 2021)	WC First Round, Game 5	55
11	Klay Thompson, G.S. Warriors	@ Ok.C. Thunder (May 28, 2016)	WC Finals, Game 6	41
10	Damian Lillard, Por. Blazers	vs. Ok.C. Thunder (Apr. 23, 2019)	WC First Round, Game 5	50
9	Bill Keller, Ind. Pacers^a	vs. S.A. Spurs^a (Apr. 1, 1974)	WD Series, Games 2	39
9	Rex Chapman, Pho. Suns	@ Sea. Sonics (Apr. 25, 1997)	WC First Round, Game 1	42
9	Vince Carter, Tor. Raptors	vs. Phi. 76ers (May 11, 2001)	EC Semifinals, Game 3	50
9	Ray Allen, Mil. Bucks	vs. Phi. 76ers (Jun. 1, 2001)	EC Finals, Game 6	41
9	Ray Allen, Bos. Celtics*	@ Chi. Bulls (Apr. 30, 2009)	EC First Round, Game 6	51
9	Jason Terry, Dal. Mavericks	vs. L.A. Lakers (May 8, 2011)	WC Semifinals, Game 4	32
9	Klay Thompson, G.S. Warriors	vs. Hou. Rockets (May 26, 2018)	WC Finals, Game 6	35
9	Stephen Curry, G.S. Warriors	vs. Cle. Cavaliers (Jun. 3, 2018)	NBA Finals, Game 2	33

continued on next page

			Round, Game	Pts
9.......	Stephen Curry, G.S. Warriors............	vs. Por. Blazers (May 14, 2019)	WC Finals, Game 1	36
9.......	Jamal Murray, Den. Nuggets*	@ Uta. Jazz (Aug. 23, 2020).....................	EC First Round, Game 4	50
9.......	Donovan Mitchell, Uta. Jazz*	vs. Den. Nuggets (Aug. 30, 2020)	EC First Round, Game 6	44
9.......	Jamal Murray, Den. Nuggets*	@ Uta. Jazz (Aug. 30, 2020)...................	EC First Round, Game 6	50
9.......	Damian Lillard, Por. Blazers*	@ Den. Nuggets (May 24, 2021)...............	EC First Round, Game 2	42
9.......	Bojan Bogdanović, Uta. Jazz*	vs. L.A. Clippers (Jun. 16, 2021)...............	WC Semifinals, Game 5...................	32
9.......	Donovan Mitchell, Uta. Jazz*	@ L.A. Clippers (Jun. 18, 2021)	WC Semifinals, Game 6...................	39

* Lost game.

ᵃ ABA.

Most 3P, Finals Game

			Game	Pts
9...........	Stephen Curry, G.S. Warriors*	vs. Cle. Cavaliers (Jun. 3, 2018)	Game 2, Win	33
8...........	Ray Allen, Bos. Celtics...........................	@ L.A. Lakers (Jun. 6, 2010)	Game 2, Win	32
7...........	Roger Brown, Ind. Pacersᵃ*	@ L.A. Starsᵃ (Mar 25, 1970)	Game 6, Win	45
7...........	Kenny Smith, Hou. Rockets*	@ Orl. Magic (Jun. 7, 1995)	Game 1, Win	23
7...........	Scottie Pippen, Chi. Bulls*	@ Uta. Jazz (Jun. 6, 1997)	Game 3, Loss	27
7...........	Ray Allen, Bos. Celtics*	vs. L.A. Lakers (Jun. 17, 2008).........................	Game 6, Win	26
7...........	Mike Miller, Mia. Heat*	vs. Ok.C. Thunder (Jun. 21, 2012)...................	Game 5, Win	23
7...........	Danny Green, S.A. Spurs	vs. Mia. Heat (Jun. 11, 2013)...........................	Game 3, Win	27
7...........	Stephen Curry, G.S. Warriors*	@ Cle. Cavaliers (Jun. 9, 2015)	Game 3, Loss	27
7...........	Stephen Curry, G.S. Warriors*	vs. Cle. Cavaliers (Jun. 14, 2015)	Game 5, Win	37
7...........	Stephen Curry, G.S. Warriors	@ Cle. Cavaliers (Jun. 10, 2016)	Game 4, Win	38
7...........	Kyrie Irving, Cle. Cavaliers	vs. G.S. Warriors (Jun. 9, 2017)	Game 4, Win	40
7...........	J.R. Smith, Cle. Cavaliers.....................	@ G.S. Warriors (Jun. 12, 2017)	Game 5, Loss	25
7...........	Stephen Curry, G.S. Warriors*	@ Cle. Cavaliers (Jun. 8, 2018)	Game 4, Win	37
7...........	Klay Thompson, G.S. Warriors...............	@ Tor. Raptors (Jun. 10, 2019).......................	Game 5, Win	26
7...........	Duncan Robinson, Mia. Heat	@ L.A. Lakers (Oct. 9, 2020)	Game 5, Win	26
7...........	Devin Booker, Pho. Suns	vs. Mil. Bucks (Jul. 8, 2021)...........................	Game 2, Win	31
7...........	Stephen Curry, G.S. Warriors*	vs. Bos. Celtics (Jun. 2, 2022)........................	Game 1, Loss	34
7...........	Stephen Curry, G.S. Warriors*	@ Bos. Celtics (Jun. 10, 2022)	Game 4, Win	43

* Won championship.

ᵃ ABA.

Most 3P Attempts without Hitting a Three, Game

			Round, Game	Shooting	Pts
11.....	John Starks, N.Y. Knicks	@ Hou. Rockets (Jun. 22, 1994)	NBA Finals, Gm. 7	2-for-18 (.111)...........	8
11.....	James Harden, Hou. Rockets*	vs. G.S. Warriors (May 24, 2018).........	WCF, Gm. 5	5-for-21 (.238).........	19
10.....	Terry Rozier, Bos. Celtics	vs. Cle. Cavaliers (May 27, 2018)	ECF, Gm. 7	2-for-14 (.143)...........	4
10.....	Eric Gordon, Hou. Rockets*	vs. Ok.C. Thunder (Aug. 20, 2020)	WCF, Gm. 2	6-for-20 (.300).........	15
9.......	Rashard Lewis, Orl. Magic*	vs. Tor. Raptors (Apr. 22, 2008)	ECFR, Gm. 2	7-for-21 (.333).........	18
9.......	Derrick Rose, Chi. Bulls*	vs. Ind. Pacers (Apr. 16, 2011)	ECFR, Gm. 1	10-for-23 (.435).......	39
9.......	Joe Johnson, Atl. Hawks*	vs. Bos. Celtics (Apr. 29, 2012)............	ECFR, Gm. 1	3-for-15 (.200)...........	11
9.......	Trevor Ariza, Hou. Rockets	vs. G.S. Warriors (May 28, 2018).........	WCF, Gm. 7	0-for-12 (.000)...........	0
9.......	Donovan Mitchell, Uta. Jazz	@ Hou. Rockets (Apr. 24, 2019)...........	WCFR, Gm. 5	4-for-22 (.182)...........	12
9.......	Luguentz Dort, Ok.C. Thunder......	@ Hou. Rockets (Aug. 29, 2020)	WCFR, Gm. 5	3-for-16 (.188)...........	6
9.......	Khris Middleton, Mil. Bucks	vs. Atl. Hawks (Jun. 23, 2021)	ECF, Gm. 1	6-for-23 (.261).........	15
9.......	Stephen Curry, G.S. Warriors*	vs. Bos. Celtics (Jun. 13, 2022)	NBA Finals, Gm. 5	7-for-22 (.318).........	16
8.......	Michael Jordan, Chi. Bulls	@ Mia. Heat (May 26, 1997)	ECF, Gm. 4	9-for-35 (.257).........	29
8.......	Allen Iverson, Phi. 76ers..............	vs. Mil. Bucks (May 24, 2001)	ECF, Gm. 2	5-for-26 (.192).........	16

continued on next page

		Round, Game	Shooting	Pts
8.......	Greg Buckner, Den. Nuggets* ......vs. L.A. Clippers (Apr. 27, 2006)...........WCFR, Gm. 3		3-for-12 (.250)........	13
8.......	Ray Allen, Bos. Celtics ....vs. L.A. Lakers (Jun. 8, 2010) ....NBA Finals, Gm. 3		0-for-13 (.000)...........	2
8.......	Kevin Durant, Ok.C. Thunder.......vs. Dal. Mavericks (May 21, 2011) ....WCF, Gm. 3		7-for-22 (.318)........	24
8.......	Kevin Durant, Ok.C. Thunder......@ Mem. Grizzlies (Apr. 24, 2014) ....WCFR, Gm. 3		10-for-27 (.370).......	30
8.......	J.R. Smith, Cle. Cavaliers.............vs. G.S. Warriors (Jun. 11, 2015)..........NBA Finals, Gm. 4		2-for-12 (.167)...........	4
8.......	Chris Paul, Hou. Rockets*............vs. Min. T'Wolves (Apr. 25, 2018).........WCFR, Gm. 5		6-for-16 (.375).............	12
8.......	Danilo Gallinari, L.A. Clippers .....vs. G.S. Warriors (Apr. 18, 2019).........WCFR, Gm. 3		2-for-13 (.154)...........	9
8.......	Jordan Clarkson, Uta. Jazz ....vs. Mem. Grizzlies (May 23, 2021)......WCFR, Gm. 1		5-for-16 (.313)........	14
8.......	James Harden, Brk. Nets* ....vs. Mil. Bucks (Jun. 15, 2021) ....ECSF, Gm. 5		1-for-10 (.100)...........	5

* Team won game.
ECFR: Eastern Conference First Round
WCFR: Western Conference First Round

ECSF: Eastern Conference Semifinals
ECF: Eastern Conference Finals
WCF: Western Conference Finals

Free Throws

Highest Playoff FT%, Career (Min. 100 Free Throw Attempts)

		FT Shooting	GP
.950	Gordon Hayward.............................	113-for-119	29
.944	Mark Price.....................................	202-for-214	47
.932	Calvin Murphy	165-for-177	51
.911	Bill Sharman	370-for-406	78
.907	Hersey Hawkins	292-for-322	74
.907	Kiki Vandeweghe	235-for-259	68
.901	Danilo Gallinari	154-for-171	48
.900	Steve Nash.....................................	396-for-440	120
.900	Peja Stojaković...............................	261-for-290	95
.900	Devin Booker	180-for-200	32
.900	Jamal Murray..................................	126-for-140	33
.895	Kyle Korver....................................	128-for-143	145
.893	Reggie Miller	770-for-862	144
.892	Dirk Nowitzki..................................	1074-for-1204	145
.892	Stephen Curry.................................	647-for-725	134
.891	Kyrie Irving....................................	294-for-330	74
.890	Larry Bird	901-for-1012	164
.890	Brandon Bass.................................	146-for-164	59
.890	Marco Belinelli	97-for-109	65
.889	Vince Boryla	120-for-135	33
.888	Reggie Jackson	111-for-125	69
.887	Damian Lillard................................	368-for-415	61
.886	Jeff Hornacek.................................	488-for-551	140
.886	Howard Eisley.................................	93-for-105	88
.885	Glenn Robinson..............................	92-for-104	39
.884	Allan Houston	268-for-303	63
.883	Ray Allen.......................................	508-for-575	171
.882	Wally Szczerbiak	135-for-153	54
.880	Chauncey Billups............................	785-for-892	146
.880	Ron Boone.....................................	256-for-291	84
.880	Bobby Wanzer................................	212-for-241	38
.879	J.J. Redick.....................................	197-for-224	110
.875	Travis Best	105-for-120	63

Most Playoff Games Hitting 10 Free Throws without a Miss, Career

13.................. Dirk Nowitzki	7..................... Paul George^	5..................... Dominique Wilkins
11.................. Larry Bird	7..................... Stephen Curry^	5..................... Kevin Johnson
11.................. Chauncey Billups	6..................... Rick Barry	5..................... Kobe Bryant
9.................. Michael Jordan	6..................... Magic Johnson	5..................... LeBron James^
9.................. James Harden^	6..................... Paul Pierce	5..................... Kawhi Leonard^
9.................. Kevin Durant^	5..................... Oscar Robertson	
7.................. Dolph Schayes	5..................... Julius Erving	

^ Active.

Assists

Most Career Playoff Assists·

		GP			GP
2346.................. Magic Johnson		190	922.................. Maurice Cheeks		133
1919.................. LeBron James^		266	905.................. Mark Jackson		131
1839.................. John Stockton		182	891.................. Clyde Drexler		145
1263.................. Jason Kidd		158	874.................. Russell Westbrook^		111
1143.................. Tony Parker		226	870.................. Dwyane Wade		177
1136.................. Rajon Rondo		134	841.................. Julius Erving		189
1073.................. Chris Paul^		129	831.................. Chauncey Billups		146
1062.................. Larry Bird		164	827.................. Manu Ginóbili		218
1061.................. Steve Nash		120	825.................. John Havlicek		172
1048.................. Scottie Pippen		208	819.................. James Harden^		137
1040.................. Kobe Bryant		220	811.................. Gary Payton		154
1022.................. Michael Jordan		179	770.................. Bill Russell		165
1006.................. Dennis Johnson		180	769.................. Oscar Robertson		86
987.................. Isiah Thomas		111	767.................. Kareem Abdul-Jabbar		237
970.................. Jerry West		153	764.................. Tim Duncan		251
937.................. Bob Cousy		109	754.................. Draymond Green^		123
935.................. Kevin Johnson		105			

· Includes ABA.

^ Active.

Most Playoff Games with 10 Assists, Career

143.................. Magic Johnson	48.................. Isiah Thomas	24.................. Dennis Johnson
100.................. John Stockton	38.................. Bob Cousy	24.................. Deron Williams
54.................. Steve Nash	36.................. Russell Westbrook^	24.................. James Harden^
54.................. Chris Paul^	35.................. Oscar Robertson	22.................. Clyde Drexler
50.................. Jason Kidd	31.................. Mark Jackson	21.................. Norm Nixon
49.................. LeBron James^	25.................. Maurice Cheeks	20.................. Michael Jordan
49.................. Rajon Rondo^	25.................. Jerry West	
48.................. Kevin Johnson	24.................. Larry Bird	

^ Active.

Most Playoff Games with 15 Assists, Career

49.................. Magic Johnson	10.................. Kevin Johnson	6.................. Chris Paul^
27.................. John Stockton	7.................. Johnny Moore	6.................. Doc Rivers
13.................. Rajon Rondo^	6.................. Bob Cousy	5.................. Oscar Robertson
11.................. Steve Nash	6.................. Jason Kidd	

^ Active.

Most Assists in Finals, Career

584................. Magic Johnson	228................. Dennis Johnson	195................. John Havlicek
430................. LeBron James^	219................. Draymond Green^	187................. Kobe Bryant
306................. Jerry West	209................. Michael Jordan	187................. Larry Bird
265................. Bill Russell	207................. Scottie Pippen	126................. Rajon Rondo^
239................. Bob Cousy	204................. Stephen Curry^	

^ Active.

Most Assists in a Finals Game

21....... Magic Johnson, L.A. Lakers..........1984 NBA Finals, Game 3 ....vs. Bos. Celtics ....Won Game/Lost Finals
20....... Magic Johnson, L.A. Lakers..........1987 NBA Finals, Game 2 ....vs. Bos. Celtics ....Won Game/Won Finals
20....... Magic Johnson, L.A. Lakers..........1991 NBA Finals, Game 5 ....vs. Chi. Bulls ....Lost Game/Lost Finals
19....... Bob Cousy, Bos. Celtics ....1957 NBA Finals, Game 5 ....vs. St.L. Hawks ....Won Game/Won Finals
19....... Bob Cousy, Bos. Celtics ....1959 NBA Finals, Game 3 ....@ Min. Lakers ....Won Game/Won Finals
19....... Walt Frazier, N.Y. Knicks.............1970 NBA Finals, Game 7 ....vs. L.A. Lakers ....Won Game/Won Finals
19....... Magic Johnson, L.A. Lakers..........1987 NBA Finals, Game 6 ....vs. Bos. Celtics ....Won Game/Won Finals
19....... Magic Johnson, L.A. Lakers..........1988 NBA Finals, Game 6 ....vs. Det. Pistons ....Won Game/Won Finals
18....... Jerry West, L.A. Lakers ....1970 NBA Finals, Game 4 ....vs. N.Y. Knicks ....Won Game/Lost Finals
17....... Magic Johnson, L.A. Lakers..........1984 NBA Finals, Game 4 ....vs. Bos. Celtics ....Lost Game/Lost Finals
17....... Magic Johnson, L.A. Lakers..........1985 NBA Finals, Game 5 ....vs. Bos. Celtics ....Won Game/Won Finals
17....... Dennis Johnson, Bos. Celtics ....1985 NBA Finals, Game 5 ....@ L.A. Lakers ....Lost Game/Lost Finals
17....... Robert Reid, Hou. Rockets...........1986 NBA Finals, Game 5 ....vs. Bos. Celtics ....Won Game/Lost Finals
17....... Magic Johnson, L.A. Lakers..........1988 NBA Finals, Game 5 ....@ Det. Pistons ....Lost Game/Won Finals
16....... Magic Johnson, L.A. Lakers..........1985 NBA Finals, Game 3 ....vs. Bos. Celtics ....Won Game/Won Finals
16....... Rajon Rondo, Bos. Celtics ....2008 NBA Finals, Game 2 ....vs. L.A. Lakers ....Won Game/Won Finals
15....... Bob Cousy, Bos. Celtics ....1959 NBA Finals, Game 2 ....vs. Min. Lakers ....Won Game/Won Finals
15....... Magic Johnson, L.A. Lakers..........1984 NBA Finals, Game 7 ....@ Bos. Celtics ....Lost Game/Lost Finals

Rebounds

Most Career Playoff Rebounds

		GP			GP
4104................. Bill Russell		165	1527................. Paul Silas		163
3913................. Wilt Chamberlain		160	1473................. Dwight Howard^		125
2859................. Tim Duncan		251	1465................. Magic Johnson		190
2508................. Shaquille O'Neal		216	1457................. Horace Grant		170
2481................. Kareem Abdul-Jabbar		237	1454................. Ben Wallace		130
2391................. LeBron James^		266	1446................. Dirk Nowitzki		145
2062................. Karl Malone		193	1445................. Charles Oakley		144
1777................. Wes Unseld		119	1435................. Patrick Ewing		139
1765................. Robert Parish		184	1400................. Moses Malone*		100
1724................. Elgin Baylor		134	1370................. Zelmo Beaty*		115
1683................. Larry Bird		164	1361................. Robert Horry		244
1676................. Dennis Rodman		169	1305................. Bill Bridges		113
1621................. Hakeem Olajuwon		145	1304................. Bob Pettit		88
1611................. Julius Erving*		189	1301................. David Robinson		123
1608................. Mel Daniels*		109	1285................. Dave Cowens		89
1583................. Scottie Pippen		208	1267................. Artis Gilmore*		100
1582................. Charles Barkley		123	1255................. Dan Issel*		133
1534................. Kevin Garnett		143	1253................. Kevin McHale		169
1182................. Kevin Durant^		155			

* Includes ABA statistics.

^ Active.

Most Playoff Games with 15 Rebounds, Career*

161	Bill Russell	44	Mel Daniels	31	George McGinnis
149	Wilt Chamberlain	44	Moses Malone	29	Dolph Schayes
60	Wes Unseld	43	Artis Gilmore	28	Hakeem Olajuwon
58	Kareem Abdul-Jabbar	41	Dwight Howard^	27	Zelmo Beaty
56	Tim Duncan	37	Charles Barkley	27	Dave DeBusschere
55	Shaquille O'Neal	35	Bill Bridges	27	Elvin Hayes
47	Elgin Baylor	35	Ben Wallace	25	Walt Bellamy
45	Dave Cowens	33	Nate Thurmond		
44	Bob Pettit	33	Dennis Rodman		

* Includes ABA.

^ Active.

Most Rebounds in Finals, Career

1718	Bill Russell	507	Kareem Abdul-Jabbar	397	Magic Johnson
862	Wilt Chamberlain	473	Tom Heinsohn	393	Shaquille O'Neal
593	Elgin Baylor	452	Tim Duncan		
561	LeBron James^	416	Bob Pettit		

^ Active.

Steals

Most Career Playoff Steals

		GP			GP
454	LeBron James^	266	258	Karl Malone	193
395	Scottie Pippen	208	275	Chris Paul^	177
376	Michael Jordan	179	247	Dennis Johnson	180
358	Magic Johnson	190	245	Hakeem Olajuwon	145
338	John Stockton	182	240	Kawhi Leonard^	135
310	Kobe Bryant	220	247	James Harden^	149
302	Jason Kidd	158	234	Isiah Thomas	111
296	Larry Bird	164	228	Rajon Rondo^	134
295	Maurice Cheeks	133	226	Byron Scott	183
292	Manu Ginóbili	218	222	Draymond Green	145
287	Julius Erving*	189	217	Andre Iguodala^	170
278	Clyde Drexler	145	216	Gary Payton	154
276	Robert Horry	244	210	Stephen Curry	128
273	Dwyane Wade	177	204	Paul Pierce	170
272	Derek Fisher	259	203	Michael Cooper	168

* Includes ABA.

^ Active.

Most Steals in Finals, Career

102	Magic Johnson	62	Michael Jordan	49	Robert Horry
93	LeBron James^	59	Michael Cooper	48	Dennis Johnson
67	Scottie Pippen	59	Draymond Green^	46	Danny Ainge
65	Kobe Bryant	55	Stephen Curry^		
63	Larry Bird	53	Dwyane Wade		

^ Active.

Blocks

Most Career Playoff Blocks

		GP			GP
568	Tim Duncan	251	251	Dikembe Mutombo	101
476	Kareem Abdul-Jabbar	237	250	Ben Wallace	130
472	Hakeem Olajuwon	145	248	Dwight Howard^	125
459	Shaquille O'Neal	216	237	Caldwell Jones*	125
312	David Robinson	123	233	Pau Gasol	136
309	Robert Parish	184	225	Robert Horry	244
303	Patrick Ewing	139	225	Rasheed Wallace	177
293	Julius Erving*	189	222	Elvin Hayes	96
292	Serge Ibaka^	146	215	Alonzo Mourning	95
281	Kevin McHale	169	210	Mark Eaton	74
252	LeBron James^	266	202	Draymond Green	145

* Includes ABA.

^ Active.

Most Blocks in Finals, Career

116	Kareem Abdul-Jabbar	54	Hakeem Olajuwon	42	Caldwell Jones
81	Tim Duncan	46	LeBron James^	40	Julius Erving
62	Shaquille O'Neal	44	Kevin McHale		
54	Robert Parish	43	Robert Horry		

^ Active.

Games/Minutes

Most Career Playoff Games Played*

266	LeBron James^	183	Byron Scott	165	Bill Russell
259	Derek Fisher	182	John Stockton	165	Danny Green^
251	Tim Duncan	180	Dennis Johnson	164	Larry Bird
244	Robert Horry	179	Michael Jordan	163	Paul Silas
237	Kareem Abdul-Jabbar	177	Rasheed Wallace	160	Wilt Chamberlain
226	Tony Parker	177	Dwyane Wade	158	Jason Kidd
220	Kobe Bryant	177	Andre Iguodala^	155	Kevin Durant^
218	Manu Ginóbili	172	John Havlicek	154	Sam Jones
216	Shaquille O'Neal	171	Ray Allen	154	Gary Payton
208	Scottie Pippen	170	Horace Grant	153	Jerry West
193	Danny Ainge	170	Paul Pierce	153	A.C. Green
193	Karl Malone	169	Kevin McHale	152	Serge Ibaka^
190	Magic Johnson	169	Dennis Rodman	151	Bobby Jones
189	Julius Erving	168	Michael Cooper	150	Don Nelson
184	Robert Parish	167	Sam Perkins		

* Includes ABA.

^ Active.

Most Games Played in Finals, Career

70	Bill Russell	55	LeBron James^	47	John Havlicek
64	Sam Jones	52	Tom Heinsohn	46	Michael Cooper
56	Kareem Abdul-Jabbar	50	Magic Johnson		
55	Jerry West	47	Frank Ramsey		

^ Active.

Most Playoff Games Playing Full 48 Minutes, Career* (Not Including Overtime Games)

104 .... Wilt Chamberlain	13 .... Nate Thurmond
92 .... Bill Russell	13 .... Freddie Lewis
45 .... John Havlicek	13 .... Bob Love
21 .... Oscar Robertson	13 .... Allen Iverson
17 .... Kareem Abdul-Jabbar	11 .... Moses Malone
17 .... Dave Cowens	10 .... Roger Brown
14 .... Elvin Hayes	10 .... Artis Gilmore

* Includes ABA.

Youngest Player to Appear in a Playoff Game*

18 years, 191 days	Andrew Bynum, L.A. Lakers	@ Pho. Suns (May 6, 2006)
18 years, 194 days	Jermaine O'Neal, Por. Blazers	@ L.A. Lakers (Apr. 25, 1997)
18 years, 245 days	Kobe Bryant, L.A. Lakers	vs. Por. Blazers (Apr. 25, 1997)
18 years, 303 days	Darko Miličić, Det. Pistons	vs. Mil. Bucks (Apr. 18, 2004)
19 years, 68 days	Joe Graboski, Chi. Stags	vs. Min. Lakers (Mar. 24, 1949)
19 years, 88 days	Jonathan Bender, Ind. Pacers	vs. Mil. Bucks (Apr. 27, 2000)
19 years, 285 days	Gerald Wallace, Sac. Kings	vs. Dal. Mavericks (May 4, 2002)
19 years, 290 days	Talen Horton-Tucker, L.A. Lakers	@ Hou. Rockets (Sep. 10, 2020)
19 years, 304 days	Thaddeus Young, Phi. 76ers	@ Det. Pistons (Apr. 20, 2008)
19 years, 312 days	Anfernee Simons, Por. Blazers	vs. Ok.C. Thunder (Apr. 16, 2019)
19 years, 313 days	Zhaire Smith, Phi. 76ers	vs. Brk. Nets (Apr. 13, 2019)
19 years, 320 days	Markelle Fultz, Phi. 76ers	vs. Mia. Heat (Apr. 14, 2018)
19 years, 324 days	Stanley Johnson, Det. Pistons	@ Cle. Cavaliers (Apr. 17, 2016)
19 years, 325 days	Carmelo Anthony, Den. Nuggets	@ Min. T'Wolves (Apr. 18, 2004)
19 years, 333 days	Terrance Ferguson, Ok.C. Thunder	vs. Uta. Jazz (Apr. 15, 2018)
19 years, 338 days	Tony Parker, S.A. Spurs	vs. Sea. Sonics (Apr. 20, 2002)
19 years, 342 days	Džanan Musa, Brk. Nets	@ Phi. 76ers (Apr. 15, 2019)
19 years, 345 days	Enes Freedom, Uta. Jazz	@ S.A. Spurs (Apr. 29, 2012)
19 years, 354 days	Mark Olberding, S.A. Spursº	@ N.Y. Netsº (Apr. 9, 1976)

* Only includes game in which player was the youngest.

º ABA.

Oldest Player to Appear in a Playoff Game*

43 years, 254 days	Robert Parish, Chi. Bulls	@ Atl. Hawks (May 11, 1997)
42 years, 300 days	Dikembe Mutombo, Hou. Rockets	@ Por. Blazers (Apr. 21, 2009)
42 years, 58 days	Kareem Abdul-Jabbar, L.A. Lakers	vs. Det. Pistons (Jun. 13, 1989)
41 years, 252 days	Kevin Willis, S.A. Spurs	@ L.A. Lakers (May 15, 2004)
41 years, 129 days	Herb Williams, N.Y. Knicks	vs. S.A. Spurs (Jun. 25, 1999)
41 years, 35 days	John Stockton, Uta. Jazz	@ Sac. Kings (Apr. 30, 2003)
41 years, 30 days	Charles Jones, Hou. Rockets	@ Uta. Jazz (May 3, 1998)
40 years, 325 days	Karl Malone, L.A. Lakers	@ Det. Pistons (Jun. 13, 2004)
40 years, 270 days	Manu Ginóbili, S.A. Spurs	@ G.S. Warriors (Apr. 24, 2018)
40 years, 244 days	Rick Mahorn, Phi. 76ers	vs. Ind. Pacers (May 23, 1999)
40 years, 225 days	Jason Terry, Mil. Bucks	@ Bos. Celtics (Apr. 28, 2018)
40 years, 210 days	Grant Hill, L.A. Clippers	@ Mem. Grizzlies (May 3, 2013)
40 years, 187 days	James Edwards, Chi. Bulls	@ Orl. Magic (May 27, 1996)
40 years, 147 days	Clifford Robinson, N.J. Nets	vs. Cle. Cavaliers (May 12, 2007)
40 years, 91 days	Vince Carter, Mem. Grizzlies	vs. S.A. Spurs (Apr. 27, 2017)
40 years, 56 days	Jason Kidd, N.Y. Knicks	@ Ind. Pacers (May 18, 2013)

continued on next page

40 years, 54 days .... Andre Miller, S.A. Spurs .... @ Ok.C. Thunder (May 12, 2016)

40 years, 21 days .... Charles Jones, Hou. Rockets .... vs. Min. T'Wolves (Apr. 24, 1997)

40 years, 17 days .... Tim Duncan, S.A. Spurs .... @ Ok.C. Thunder (May 12, 2016)

40 years, 3 days .... Danny Schayes, Orl. Magic .... @ Phi. 76ers (May 13, 1999)

* Only includes game in which player was the oldest.

Youngest Player to Appear in a Finals Game*

18 years, 356 days .... Darko Miličić, Det. Pistons** .... vs. L.A. Lakers (Jun. 10, 2004)

19 years, 129 days .... Jonathan Bender, Ind. Pacers .... @ L.A. Lakers (Jun. 7, 2000)

20 years, 131 days .... Darryl Dawkins, Phi. 76ers .... vs. Por. Blazers (May 22, 1977)

20 years, 254 days .... Tyler Herro, Mia. Heat .... @ L.A. Lakers (Sep. 30, 2020)

20 years, 264 days .... Magic Johnson, L.A. Lakers** .... vs. Phi. 76ers (May 4, 1980)

20 years, 316 days .... Bruce Seals, Uta. Stars^a .... @ N.Y. Nets^a (Apr. 30, 1974)

21 years, 18 days .... Tony Parker, S.A. Spurs** .... vs. N.J. Nets (Jun. 4, 2003)

21 years, 75 days .... Bob O'Brien, Phi. Warriors .... vs. Bal. Bullets (Apr. 10, 1948)

21 years, 100 days .... Daniel Gibson, Cle. Cavaliers .... @ S.A. Spurs (Jun. 7, 2007)

21 years, 130 days .... Max Zaslofsky, Chi. Stags .... @ Phi. Warriors (Apr. 16, 1947)

21 years, 138 days .... Larry Kenon, N.Y. Nets^a** .... vs. Uta. Stars^a (Apr. 30, 1974)

21 years, 147 days .... Ante Žižić, Cle. Cavaliers .... @ G.S. Warriors (May 31, 2018)

21 years, 169 days .... Vern Mikkelsen, Min. Lakers** .... @ Syr. Nationals (Apr. 8, 1950)

21 years, 188 days .... Jordan Farmar, L.A. Lakers .... @ Bos. Celtics (Jun. 5, 2008)

21 years, 197 days .... Shannon Brown, Cle. Cavaliers .... vs. S.A. Spurs (Jun. 14, 2007)

21 years, 213 days .... Johnny Davis, Por. Blazers** .... @ Phi. 76ers (May 22, 1977)

21 years, 219 days .... Patrick McCaw, G.S. Warriors** .... vs. Cle. Cavaliers (Jun. 1, 2017)

21 years, 220 days .... Andrew Bynum, L.A. Lakers** .... vs. Orl. Magic (Jun. 4, 2009)

21 years, 268 days .... George McGinnis, Ind. Pacers^a** .... vs. N.Y. Nets^a (May, 6, 1972)

21 years, 289 days .... Kobe Bryant, L.A. Lakers** .... vs. Ind. Pacers (Jun. 7, 2000)

21 years, 290 days .... Cory Joseph, S.A. Spurs .... @ Mia. Heat (Jun. 6, 2013)

21 years, 293 days .... David Thompson, Den. Nuggets^a .... vs. N.Y. Nets^a (May 1, 1976)

21 years, 309 days .... Alvan Adams, Pho. Suns .... @ Bos. Celtics (May 23, 1976)

21 years, 324 days .... Dolph Schayes, Syr. Nationals .... vs. Min. Lakers (Apr. 8, 1950)

21 years, 342 days .... Kawhi Leonard, S.A. Spurs .... @ Mia. Heat (Jun. 6, 2013)

21 years, 346 days .... Jacob Evans, G.S. Warriors .... @ Tor. Raptors (May 30, 2019)

21 years, 349 days .... Richard Jefferson, N.J. Nets .... @ L.A. Lakers (Jun. 5, 2002)

* Only includes game in which player was the youngest.

** Team won championship.

^a ABA.

Oldest Player to Appear in a Finals Game*

42 years, 58 days .... Kareem Abdul-Jabbar, L.A. Lakers .... vs. Det. Pistons (Jun. 13, 1989)

41 years, 129 days .... Herb Williams, N.Y. Knicks .... vs. S.A. Spurs (Jun. 25, 1999)

40 years, 325 days .... Karl Malone, L.A. Lakers .... @ Det. Pistons (Jun. 13, 2004)

40 years, 282 days .... Kevin Willis, S.A. Spurs** .... vs. N.J. Nets (Jun. 15, 2003)

39 years, 135 days .... Juwan Howard, Mia. Heat** .... vs. Ok.C. Thunder (Jun. 21, 2012)

39 years, 5 days .... Sam Perkins, Ind. Pacers .... @ L.A. Lakers (Jun. 19, 2000)

38 years, 330 days .... Ray Allen, Mia. Heat .... @ S.A. Spurs (Jun. 15, 2014)

38 years, 247 days .... P.J. Brown, Bos. Celtics** .... vs. L.A. Lakers (Jun. 17, 2008)

38 years, 210 days .... Sam Cassell, Bos. Celtics** .... @ L.A. Lakers (Jun. 15, 2008)

38 years, 81 days .... Jason Kidd, Dal. Mavericks** .... @ Mia. Heat (Jun. 12, 2011)

38 years, 72 days .... Charles Jones, Hou. Rockets** .... vs. Orl. Magic (Jun. 14, 1995)

38 years, 51 days .... Tim Duncan, S.A. Spurs** .... vs. Mia. Heat (Jun. 15, 2014)

continued on next page

37 years, 358 days	Darrell Armstrong, Dal. Mavericks	@ Mia. Heat (Jun. 15, 2006)
37 years, 322 days	Gary Payton, Mia. Heat**	@ Dal. Mavericks (Jun. 20, 2006)
37 years, 320 days	Tony Massenburg, S.A. Spurs**	@ Det. Pistons (Jun. 16, 2005)
37 years, 317 days	Derek Fisher, Ok.C. Thunder	@ Mia. Heat (Jun. 21, 2012)
37 years, 313 days	David Robinson, S.A. Spurs**	vs. N.J. Nets (Jun. 15, 2003)
37 years, 283 days	David West, G.S. Warriors**	@ Cle. Cavaliers (Jun. 8, 2018)
37 years, 261 days	Steve Kerr, S.A. Spurs**	vs. N.J. Nets (Jun. 15, 2003)
37 years, 146 days	Ron Harper, L.A. Lakers**	@ Phi. 76ers (Jun. 15, 2001)
37 years, 101 days	Michael Finley, Bos. Celtics	@ L.A. Lakers (Jun. 15, 2010)
37 years, 95 days	Matt Barnes, G.S. Warriors**	vs. Cle. Cavaliers (Jun. 12, 2017)
37 years, 83 days	Kyle Korver, Cle. Cavaliers	vs. G.S. Warriors (Jun. 8, 2018)
37 years, 32 days	Dennis Rodman, Chi. Bulls**	@ Uta. Jazz (Jun. 14, 1998)

* Only includes game in which player was the oldest.

** Team won championship.

Most Minutes Played in Playoffs, Career*

11,035	LeBron James^	6823	Robert Horry	5481	Gary Payton
9370	Tim Duncan	6697	Dwyane Wade	5365	Byron Scott
8851	Kareem Abdul-Jabbar	6398	John Stockton	5362	Klay Thompson^
8641	Kobe Bryant	6321	Jerry West	5323	James Harden^
8105	Scottie Pippen	6259	Kevin Durant^	5321	Chauncey Billups
8098	Shaquille O'Neal	6229	Paul Pierce	5308	Reggie Miller
7907	Karl Malone	6177	Robert Parish	5297	James Worthy
7758	Tony Parker	6172	Horace Grant	5283	Kevin Garnett
7559	Wilt Chamberlain	6088	Jason Kidd	5266	Andre Iguodala^
7538	Magic Johnson	6075	Manu Ginóbili	5207	Patrick Ewing
7497	Bill Russell	6064	Ray Allen	5192	Chris Paul^
7474	Michael Jordan	5895	Dirk Nowitzki	5108	Charles Oakley
7352	Julius Erving	5838	Rasheed Wallace	5103	Al Horford^
6994	Dennis Johnson	5749	Hakeem Olajuwon	5080	Draymond Green^
6886	Larry Bird	5716	Kevin McHale	5039	Richard Hamilton
6860	John Havlicek	5572	Clyde Drexler	5038	Danny Ainge
6856	Derek Fisher	5510	Elgin Baylor		

* Includes ABA.

^ Active.

Most Minutes Played in Finals, Career

3185	Bill Russell	1580	Kobe Bryant	1223	Klay Thompson^
2374	Jerry West	1506	Michael Jordan	1211	Robert Horry
2335	LeBron James^	1483	Dennis Johnson	1209	Derek Fisher
2082	Kareem Abdul-Jabbar	1469	Scottie Pippen	1163	Frank Ramsey
2044	Magic Johnson	1406	Michael Cooper	1125	Tom Sanders
1872	John Havlicek	1346	James Worthy	1125	Dwyane Wade
1871	Sam Jones	1345	Tim Duncan	1050	Tony Parker
1850	Elgin Baylor	1327	Stephen Curry^	1048	Danny Ainge
1656	Wilt Chamberlain	1326	Larry Bird	1037	Bob Pettit
1639	Bob Cousy	1269	Draymond Green^	1020	Robert Parish
1602	Tom Heinsohn	1269	Shaquille O'Neal	1009	Kevin McHale

^ Active.

Player Miscellany

Highest Playoff Plus-Minus, Career

+1310............. LeBron James^	+668............... Kawhi Leonard^	+578............... Chauncey Billups
+1090............. Tim Duncan	+638............... Shaquille O'Neal	+555............... Kobe Bryant
+1005............. Draymond Green^	+615............... Danny Green^	+451............... Tayshaun Prince
+951............... Manu Ginóbili	+595............... Klay Thompson^	+432............... Dwyane Wade
+898............... Stephen Curry^	+590............... Robert Horry	+415............... Richard Hamilton
+725............... Derek Fisher	+586............... Ray Allen	+404............... Kyrie Irving^
+719............... Kevin Durant^	+581............... Tony Parker	

^ Active.

Lowest Playoff Plus-Minus, Career

-373................. DeMar DeRozan^	-235................ Damian Lillard^	-197................ Monte Morris^
-288................. Carmelo Anthony^	-234................ Evan Turner^	-194................ Robin Lopez^
-284................. Marvin Williams	-219................ Jeff Teague^	-188................ Marcus Camby
-270................. Joe Johnson^	-213................ Caron Butler	-188................ Kirk Hinrich
-262................. Josh Smith	-210................ LaMarcus Aldridge^	-184................ Amir Johnson
-250................. Wesley Matthews^	-205................ Thaddeus Young^	-181................ Jason Williams
-243................. Andre Miller	-202................ Evan Fournier^	-181................ Thabo Sefolosha

^ Active.

Most Playoff Double-Doubles, Season

	GP	PPG	RPG/APG
22.................. Charles Barkley, Pho. Suns, 1992–93	24	26.6	13.6
22.................. Tim Duncan, S.A. Spurs, 2002–03	24	24.7	15.4
22.................. Dwight Howard, Orl. Magic, 2008–09	23	20.7	15.6
21.................. Shaquille O'Neal, L.A. Lakers, 1999–00	23	30.7	15.4
20.................. Moses Malone, Hou. Rockets, 1980–81	21	26.8	14.5
19.................. Magic Johnson, L.A. Lakers, 1984–85	19	17.5	15.2*
19.................. Magic Johnson, L.A. Lakers, 1987–88	24	19.9	12.6*
19.................. Patrick Ewing, N.Y. Knicks, 1993–94	25	21.9	11.7
18.................. Wilt Chamberlain, L.A. Lakers, 1969–70	18	22.1	22.2
18.................. Dave Cowens, Bos. Celtics, 1975–76	18	21.0	16.4
18.................. Bill Walton, Por. Blazers, 1976–77	19	18.2	15.2
18.................. Larry Bird, Bos. Celtics, 1983–84	23	27.5	11.0
18.................. Magic Johnson, L.A. Lakers, 1983–84	21	18.2	13.5*
18.................. Shaquille O'Neal, Orl. Magic, 1994–95	21	25.7	11.9
18.................. Tim Duncan, S.A. Spurs, 2004–05	23	23.6	12.4
18.................. Giannis Antetokounmpo, Mil. Bucks, 2020–21	21	30.2	12.8
17.................. Bill Russell, Bos. Celtics, 1967–68	19	14.4	22.8
17.................. Marvin Webster, Sea. Sonics, 1977–78	22	16.1	13.1
17.................. Elvin Hayes, Was. Bullets, 1977–78	21	21.8	13.3
17.................. Dikembe Mutombo, Phi. 76ers, 2000–01	23	13.9	13.7
17.................. Shaquille O'Neal, L.A. Lakers, 2003–04	22	21.5	13.2
17.................. Kevin Garnett, Min. T'Wolves, 2003–04	18	24.3	14.6
17.................. Kevin Garnett, Bos. Celtics, 2007–08	26	20.4	10.5

* Assists per game.

Most Playoff Double-Doubles, Career

164 .... Tim Duncan	100 .... Hakeem Olajuwon	79 .... Patrick Ewing
157 .... Magic Johnson	98 .... Elgin Baylor	75 .... Dirk Nowitzki
143 .... Wilt Chamberlain	97 .... Larry Bird	73 .... Elvin Hayes
142 .... Shaquille O'Neal	95 .... Robert Parish	72 .... Zelmo Beaty
137 .... Bill Russell	92 .... Charles Barkley	72 .... Mel Daniels
130 .... LeBron James^	87 .... John Stockton	72 .... Dwight Howard^
124 .... Karl Malone	86 .... Kevin Garnett	
119 .... Kareem Abdul-Jabbar	80 .... Moses Malone	

^ Active.

Players with Most Finals Double-Doubles·

56 .... Bill Russell	20 .... Mel Daniels	12 .... Draymond Green^
43 .... Magic Johnson	20 .... George McGinnis	11 .... Willie Wise
36 .... Elgin Baylor	19 .... Tom Heinsohn	11 .... Artis Gilmore
35 .... LeBron James^	19 .... Dan Issel	11 .... Kevin McHale
30 .... Wilt Chamberlain	15 .... Cliff Hagan	11 .... Pau Gasol
27 .... Tim Duncan	15 .... Julius Erving	10 .... Tom Sanders
24 .... Kareem Abdul-Jabbar	14 .... George Mikan	10 .... Jerry West
24 .... Shaquille O'Neal	13 .... Robert Parish	10 .... Dave DeBusschere
23 .... Bob Pettit	13 .... Scottie Pippen	10 .... Wes Unseld
22 .... Larry Bird	12 .... John Havlicek	10 .... Moses Malone
21 .... Bob Cousy	12 .... Hakeem Olajuwon	

* Includes ABA.

^ Active.

Most Playoff Triple-Doubles, Career

30 .... Magic Johnson	11 .... Jason Kidd	10 .... Draymond Green^
28 .... LeBron James^	10 .... Larry Bird	9 .... Wilt Chamberlain
12 .... Russell Westbrook^	10 .... Rajon Rondo^	8 .... Oscar Robertson

^ Active.

Players with Triple-Doubles in Finals

			Pts	Reb	Ast
Charles Barkley	Pho. Suns @ Chi. Bulls	Game 4 (Jun. 16, 1993)	32	12	10
Elgin Baylor	L.A. Lakers vs. N.Y. Knicks	Game 3 (Apr. 29, 1970)	13	12	11
Larry Bird	Bos. Celtics @ Hou. Rockets	Game 3 (Jun. 1, 1986)	25	15	11
	Bos. Celtics vs. Hou. Rockets	Game 6* (Jun. 8, 1986)	29	11	12
Jimmy Butler	Mia. Heat vs. L.A. Lakers	Game 3* (Oct. 4, 2020)	40	11	13
	Mia. Heat @ L.A. Lakers	Game 5* (Oct. 9, 2020)	35	12	11
Wilt Chamberlain	Phi. 76ers vs. S.F. Warriors	Game 1* (Apr. 14, 1967)	16	33	10
	Phi. 76ers vs. S.F. Warriors	Game 2* (Apr. 16, 1967)	10	38	10
Bob Cousy	Bos. Celtics @ St.L. Hawks	Game 4* (Apr. 5, 1958)	24	13	10
	Bos. Celtics vs. Min. Lakers	Game 2* (Apr. 5, 1959)	21	11	15
Dave Cowens	Bos. Celtics vs. Pho. Suns	Game 1* (May 23, 1976)	25	21	10
Stephen Curry	G.S. Warriors vs. Cle. Cavaliers	Game 2* (Jun. 4, 2017)	32	10	11
Tim Duncan	S.A. Spurs vs. N.J. Nets	Game 6* (Jun. 15, 2003)	21	20	10
Kevin Durant	G.S. Warriors @ Cle. Cavaliers	Game 4* (Jun. 8, 2018)	20	12	10
Walt Frazier	N.Y. Knicks vs. L.A. Lakers	Game 2 (Apr. 27, 1970)	11	12	11
	N.Y. Knicks @ L.A. Lakers	Game 1* (Apr. 26, 1972)	14	12	11

continued on next page

			Pts	Reb	Ast
Artis Gilmore	Ken. Colonels[a] vs. Ind. Pacers[a]	Game 5 (May 8, 1973)	17	17	11
Draymond Green	G.S. Warriors @ Cle. Cavaliers	Game 6* (Jun. 16, 2015)	16	11	10
	G.S. Warriors @ Tor. Raptors	Game 1 (May 30, 2019)	10	10	10
	G.S. Warriors vs. Tor. Raptors	Game 6 (Jun. 13, 2019)	11	19	13
LeBron James	Mia. Heat @ Dal. Mavericks	Game 5 (Jun. 9, 2011)	17	10	10
	Mia. Heat vs. Ok.C. Thunder	Game 5* (Jun. 21, 2012)	26	11	13
	Mia. Heat vs. S.A. Spurs	Game 1 (Jun. 6, 2013)	18	18	10
	Mia. Heat vs. S.A. Spurs	Game 6* (Jun. 18, 2013)	32	10	11
	Cle. Cavaliers @ G.S. Warriors	Game 2* (Jun. 7, 2015)	39	16	11
	Cle. Cavaliers @ G.S. Warriors	Game 5 (Jun. 14, 2015)	40	14	11
	Cle. Cavaliers @ G.S. Warriors	Game 7* (Jun. 19, 2016)	27	11	11
	Cle. Cavaliers @ G.S. Warriors	Game 2 (Jun. 4, 2017)	29	11	14
	Cle. Cavaliers vs. G.S. Warriors	Game 4* (Jun. 9, 2017)	31	10	11
	Cle. Cavaliers vs. G.S. Warriors	Game 3 (Jun. 6, 2018)	33	10	11
	L.A. Lakers @ Mia. Heat	Game 6* (Oct. 11, 2020)	28	14	10
Magic Johnson	L.A. Lakers vs. Phi. 76ers	Game 5* (May 14, 1980)	14	15	10
	L.A. Lakers vs. Phi. 76ers	Game 6* (Jun. 8, 1982)	13	13	13
	L.A. Lakers vs. Bos. Celtics	Game 3* (Jun. 3, 1984)	14	11	21
	L.A. Lakers vs. Bos. Celtics	Game 4 (Jun. 6, 1984)	20	11	17
	L.A. Lakers vs. Bos. Celtics	Game 4 (Jun. 5, 1985)	20	11	12
	L.A. Lakers @ Bos. Celtics	Game 6* (Jun. 9, 1985)	14	10	14
	L.A. Lakers @ Chi. Bulls	Game 1* (Jun. 2, 1991)	19	10	11
	L.A. Lakers vs. Chi. Bulls	Game 5 (Jun. 12, 1991)	16	11	20
Jason Kidd	N.J. Nets @ L.A. Lakers	Game 1 (Jun. 5, 2002)	23	10	10
Scottie Pippen	Chi. Bulls @ Pho. Suns	Game 2* (Jun. 11, 1993)	15	12	12
Rajon Rondo	Bos. Celtics @ L.A. Lakers	Game 2* (Jun. 6, 2010)	19	12	10
Bill Russell	Bos. Celtics @ L.A. Lakers	Game 6* (Apr. 16, 1962)	19	24	10
	Bos. Celtics vs. L.A. Lakers	Game 2* (Apr. 19, 1965)	23	25	10
Jerry West	L.A. Lakers vs. Bos. Celtics	Game 7 (May 5, 1969)	42	13	12
James Worthy	L.A. Lakers vs. Det. Pistons	Game 7* (Jun. 21, 1988)	36	16	10
Wes Unseld	Bal. Bullets vs. Mil. Bucks	Game 4 (Apr. 30, 1971)	11	23	10

* Team won game.

[a] ABA.

Multiple Playoff Games with 30 Points, 10 Rebounds, and 10 Assists

15	LeBron James^	3	George McGinnis	2	Stephen Curry^
8	Oscar Robertson	2	Charles Barkley	2	Luka Dončić^
6	Russell Westbrook^	2	Jimmy Butler^	2	Nikola Jokic^
3	James Harden^	2	Wilt Chamberlain		

^ Active.

Multiple Playoff Games with 40 Points and 20 Rebounds

12	Wilt Chamberlain	4	Shaquille O'Neal	2	George McGinnis
5	Elgin Baylor	3	Kareem Abdul-Jabbar	2	Hakeem Olajuwon

40 Points and 10 Rebounds in a Finals Game, Team Losing the Game

		Pts	Reb
Cliff Hagan, St.L. Hawks	@ Bos. Celtics, Apr. 5, 1961 (Gm. 2)	40	17
Bob Pettit, St.L. Hawks	vs. Bos. Celtics, Apr. 9, 1961 (Gm. 4)	40	18
Elgin Baylor, L.A. Lakers	@ Bos. Celtics, Apr. 18, 1962 (Gm. 7)	41	22

continued on next page

		Pts	Reb
John Havlicek, Bos. Celtics*	@ L.A. Lakers, Apr. 25, 1969 (Gm. 2)	43	12
Jerry West, L.A. Lakers	vs. Bos. Celtics, May 5, 1969 (Gm. 7)	42	13
Charles Barkley, Pho. Suns	vs. Chi. Bulls, Jun. 11, 1993 (Gm. 2)	42	13
Shaquille O'Neal, L.A. Lakers*	vs. Phi. 76ers, Jun. 6, 2001 (Gm. 1)	44	20
LeBron James, Cle. Cavaliers	@ G.S. Warriors, Jun. 14, 2015 (Gm. 5)	40	14
LeBron James, Cle. Cavaliers	@ G.S. Warriors, Jun. 12, 2017 (Gm. 5)	41	13
LeBron James, L.A. Lakers*	vs. Mia. Heat, Oct. 9, 2020 (Gm. 5)	40	13
Giannis Antetokounmpo, Mil. Bucks*	@ Pho. Suns, Jul. 8, 2021 (Gm. 2)	42	12

* Won championship.

Most Turnovers in a Single Postseason

TO		GP	TO/G
100	Jayson Tatum, Bos. Celtics**, 2021–22	24	4.2
94	LeBron James, Cle. Cavaliers**, 2017–18	22	4.3
90	Dwyane Wade, Mia. Heat*, 2005–06	23	3.9
87	Larry Bird, Bos. Celtics*, 1983–84	23	3.8
85	Isiah Thomas, Det. Pistons**, 1987–88	23	3.7
85	Shaquille O'Neal, Mia. Heat*, 2005–06	23	3.7
84	Kevin Johnson, Pho. Suns**, 1992–93	23	3.7
84	LeBron James, L.A. Lakers*, 2019–20	21	4.0
83	Magic Johnson, L.A. Lakers*, 1987–88	24	3.5
83	Patrick Ewing, N.Y. Knicks**, 1993–94	25	3.3
83	Hakeem Olajuwon, Hou. Rockets*, 1993–94	23	3.6
83	Russell Westbrook, Ok.C. Thunder, 2013–14	19	4.4
83	Draymond Green, G.S. Warriors**, 2018–19	22	3.8
82	Paul Pierce, Bos. Celtics*, 2007–08	26	3.2
82	Stephen Curry, G.S. Warriors*, 2014–15	21	3.9
82	LeBron James, Cle. Cavaliers**, 2014–15	20	4.1
81	Michael Jordan, Chi. Bulls*, 1991–92	22	3.7
81	LeBron James, Mia. Heat*, 2011–12	23	3.5
81	Devin Booker, Pho. Suns**, 2020–21	22	3.7
80	Shawn Kemp, Sea. Sonics**, 1995–96	20	4.0
79	Magic Johnson, L.A. Lakers**, 1983–84	21	3.8
79	Jason Kidd, N.J. Nets**, 2002–03	20	4.0
79	Kobe Bryant, L.A. Lakers*, 2009–10	23	3.4
78	Richard Hamilton, Det. Pistons**, 2004–05	25	3.1
78	Russell Westbrook, Ok.C. Thunder, 2010–11	17	4.6
78	Russell Westbrook, Ok.C. Thunder, 2015–16	18	4.3
77	Magic Johnson, L.A. Lakers, 1990–91	19	4.1
77	James Harden, Hou. Rockets, 2014–15	17	4.5
76	Magic Johnson, L.A. Lakers*, 1984–85	19	4.0
76	Tim Duncan, S.A. Spurs*, 2002–03	24	3.2
75	Kevin Garnett, Min. T'Wolves, 2003–04	18	4.2
75	Paul George, Ind. Pacers, 2012–13	19	3.9
75	Stephen Curry, G.S. Warriors**, 2015–16	18	4.2
75	LeBron James, Cle. Cavaliers*, 2015–16	21	3.6

* Won championship.

** Lost championship.

Youngest Player to Win an NBA Championship

Age (Birthdate)

18 (Jun. 20) .... Darko Miličić, Det. Pistons, 2003–04
19 (Nov. 25)....... Talen Horton-Tucker, L.A. Lakers, 2019–20
20 (Feb. 6) .... Kevon Looney, G.S. Warriors, 2016–17
20 (May 17) .... Tony Parker, S.A. Spurs, 2002–03
20 (Aug. 14)....... Magic Johnson, L.A. Lakers, 1979–80
20 (Dec. 2) .... Dorell Wright, Mia. Heat, 2005–06
21 (Feb. 6) .... Kevon Looney, G.S. Warriors, 2017–18
21 (Feb. 22) .... Rajon Rondo, Bos. Celtics, 2007–08
21 (Mar. 10)....... Jackie Butler, S.A. Spurs, 2006–07
21 (Mar. 20)...... Phil Walker, Was. Bullets, 1977–78
21 (Mar. 29)...... Carl Meinhold, Bal. Bullets, 1947–48
21 (Apr. 4) .... Stanislav Medvedenko, L.A. Lakers, 2000–01
21 (Apr. 19) .... Gabe Pruitt, Bos. Celtics, 2007–08

Age (Birthdate)

21 (Apr. 30) .... Rick Weitzman, Bos. Celtics, 1967–68
21 (May 2) .... Jamaal Wilkes, G.S. Warriors, 1974–75
21 (Jun. 30)........ Damian Jones, G.S. Warriors, 2016–17
21 (Jul. 17) .... OG Anunoby, Tor. Raptors, 2018–19
21 (Aug. 23)....... Kobe Bryant, L.A. Lakers, 1999–00
21 (Oct. 21) .... Johnny Davis, Por. Blazers, 1976–77
21 (Oct. 21) .... Vern Mikkelsen, Min. Lakers, 1949–50
21 (Oct. 25) .... Patrick McCaw, G.S. Warriors, 2016–17
21 (Oct. 27) .... Andrew Bynum, L.A. Lakers, 2008–09
22 (Jun. 30) .... Damian Jones, G.S. Warriors, 2017–18
22 (Sep. 9) .... Jordan Nwora, Mil. Bucks, 2020–21
22 (Nov. 20)....... Kostas Antetokounmpo, L.A. Lakers, 2019–20

Oldest Player to Win an NBA Championship

Age (Birthdate)

43 (Aug. 30)....... Robert Parish, Chi. Bulls, 1996–97
40 (Sep. 6) .... Kevin Willis, S.A. Spurs, 2002–03
40 (Nov. 22)....... James Edwards, Chi. Bulls, 1995–96
40 (Apr. 16) .... Kareem Abdul-Jabbar, L.A. Lakers, 1987–88
39 (Feb. 7) .... Juwan Howard, Mia. Heat, 2012–13
39 (Apr. 16) ...... Kareem Abdul-Jabbar, L.A. Lakers, 1986–87
38 (Feb. 7) .... Juwan Howard, Mia. Heat, 2011–12
38 (Oct. 14) .... P.J. Brown, Bos. Celtics, 2007–08
38 (Nov. 18)...... Sam Cassell, Bos. Celtics, 2007–08
37 (Jan. 20)........ Ron Harper, L.A. Lakers, 2000–01
37 (Mar. 23)...... Jason Kidd, Dal. Mavericks, 2010–11
37 (Apr. 3) .... Charles Jones, Hou. Rockets, 1994–95

Age (Birthdate)

37 (Apr. 16) .... Kareem Abdul-Jabbar, L.A. Lakers, 1984–85
37 (Apr. 25) .... Tim Duncan, S.A. Spurs, 2013–14
37 (Jul. 20) .... Ray Allen, Mia. Heat, 2012–13
37 (Jul. 23) .... Gary Payton, Mia. Heat, 2005–06
37 (Jul. 31) .... Tony Massenburg, 2004–05
37 (Aug. 6)......... David Robinson, S.A. Spurs, 2002–03
37 (Sep. 27) .... Steve Kerr, S.A. Spurs, 2002–03
37 (Oct. 29) .... David West, G.S. Warriors, 2017–18
36 (Mar. 9)........ Matt Barnes, G.S. Warriors, 2016–17
36 (Jul. 28) .... Man Ginóbili, S.A. Spurs, , 2013–14
36 (Aug. 25)....... Robert Horry, S.A. Spurs, 2006–07
36 (Oct. 29) .... David West, G.S. Warriors, 2016–17

Players with Most Rings

11.................. Bill Russell .... Bos. Celtics (1957, 1959–1966, 1968–1969)
10................. Sam Jones................................ Bos. Celtics (1959–1966, 1968–1969)
8.................. Tom Heinsohn .... Bos. Celtics (1957, 1959–1965)
8.................. K.C. Jones................................ Bos. Celtics (1959–1966)
8.................. Satch Sanders.......................... Bos. Celtics (1961–1966, 1968–1969)
8.................. John Havlicek .... Bos. Celtics (1963–1966, 1968–1969, 1974, 1976)
7.................. Jim Loscutoff .... Bos. Celtics (1957, 1959–1964)
7.................. Frank Ramsey .... Bos. Celtics (1957, 1959–1964)
7.................. Robert Horry............................ Hou. Rockets (1994–1995), L.A. Lakers (2000–2002), S.A. Spurs (2005, 2007)
6.................. Bob Cousy .... Bos. Celtics (1957, 1959–1963)
6.................. Kareem Abdul-Jabbar .... Mil. Bucks (1971), L.A. Lakers (1980, 1982, 1985, 1987–1988)
6.................. Michael Jordan .... Chi. Bulls (1991–1993, 1996–1998)
6.................. Scottie Pippen .... Chi. Bulls (1991–1993, 1996–1998)
5.................. George Mikan .... Min. Lakers (1949–1950, 1952–1954)
5.................. Jim Pollard.............................. Min. Lakers (1949–1950, 1952–1954)
5.................. Slater Martin .... Min. Lakers (1950, 1952–1954), St.L. Hawks (1958)
5.................. Larry Siegfried .... Bos. Celtics (1964–1966, 1968–1969)
5.................. Don Nelson .... Bos. Celtics (1966, 1968–1969, 1974, 1976)

continued on next page

5................. Michael Cooper........................ L.A. Lakers (1980, 1982, 1985, 1987—1988)
5................. Magic Johnson.......................... L.A. Lakers (1980, 1982, 1985, 1987—1988)
5................. Dennis Rodman........................ Det. Pistons (1989—1990), Chi. Bulls (1996—1998)
5................. Ron Harper............................... Chi. Bulls (1996—1998), L.A. Lakers (2000—2001)
5................. Steve Kerr .... Chi. Bulls (1996—1998), S.A. Spurs (1999, 2003)
5................. Kobe Bryant .... L.A. Lakers (2000—2002, 2009—2010)
5................. Derek Fisher .... L.A. Lakers (2000—2002, 2009—2010)
5................. Tim Duncan .... S.A. Spurs (1999, 2003, 2005, 2007, 2014)

Players Winning Championships with Three Different Teams

Robert Horry .... Hou. Rockets (1994—1995), L.A. Lakers (2000, 2002), S.A. Spurs (2005, 2007)
John Salley .... Det. Pistons (1989, 1990), Chi. Bulls (1996), L.A. Lakers (2000)
LeBron James .... Mia. Heat (2012, 2013), Cle. Cavaliers (2016), L.A. Lakers (2020)
Danny Green .... S.A. Spurs (2014), Tor. Raptors (2019), L.A. Lakers (2020)

Playing for Two Different Finals Champions in Successive Years

Pep Saul.................... Roc. Royals, 1950–51 .... Min. Lakers, 1951–52
Steve Kerr.................... Chi. Bulls, 1997–98................. S.A. Spurs, 1998–99
Patrick McCaw............ G.S. Warriors, 2017–18.......... Tor. Raptors, 2018–19
Danny Green .... Tor. Raptors, 2018–19 .... L.A. Lakers, 2019–20

Players Winning NCAA and NBA Championships

	NCAA Championship	**NBA Championship**
Kareem Abdul-Jabbar	UCLA (1967, 1968, 1969)	Mil. Bucks (1971); L.A. Lakers (1980, 1982, 1985, 1987, 1988)
Lucius Allen	UCLA (1967, 1968)	Mil. Bucks (1971)
Derek Anderson	Kentucky (1996)	Mia. Heat (2006)
Shane Battier	Duke (2001)	Mia. Heat (2012, 2013)
Henry Bibby	UCLA (1970, 1971, 1972)	N.Y. Knicks (1973)
Ron Bonham	Cincinatti (1962)	Bos. Celtics (1965, 1966)
Corey Brewer	Florida (2006, 2007)	Dal. Mavericks (2011)
Quinn Buckner	Indiana (1976)	Bos. Celtics (1984)
Mario Chalmers	Kansas (2008)	Mia. Heat (2012, 2013)
Arnie Ferrin	Utah (1944)	Min. Lakers (1949, 1950)
Bob Cousy	Holy Cross (1947)	Bos. Celtics (1957, 1959, 1960, 1961, 1962, 1963)
Danny Green	UNC (2009)	S.A. Spurs (2014); Tor. Raptors (2019); L.A. Lakers (2020)
Frank Ramsey	Kentucky (1951)	Bos. Celtics (1957, 1959, 1960, 1961, 1962, 1963, 1964)
Marreese Speights	Florida (2007)	G.S. Warriors (2015)
Bill Russell	San Francisco (1955, 1956)	Bos. Celtics (1957, 1959, 1960, 1961, 1962, 1963, 1964, 1965, 1966, 1968, 1969)
Magic Johnson	Michigan State (1979)	L.A. Lakers (1980, 1982, 1985, 1987, 1988)
Glen Rice	Michigan (1989)	L.A. Lakers (2000)
K.C. Jones	San Francisco (1955, 1956)	Bos. Celtics (1959, 1960, 1961, 1962, 1963, 1964, 1965, 1966)
Richard Hamilton	UConn (1999)	Det. Pistons (2004)
John Havlicek	Ohio State (1960)	Bos. Celtics (1963, 1964, 1965, 1966, 1968, 1969)
Jason Terry	Kentucky (1997)	Dal. Mavericks (2011)
Michael Jordan	UNC (1982)	Chi. Bulls (1991, 1992, 1993, 1996, 1997, 1998)
Gail Goodrich	UCLA (1965)	L.A. Lakers (1972)
Antoine Walker	Kentucky (1996, 1998)	Mia. Heat (2006)
Bill Walton	UCLA (1972, 1973	Por. Blazers (1977); Bos. Celtics (1986)
Isiah Thomas	Indiana (1981)	Det. Pistons (1989, 1990)

continued on next page

	NCAA Championship	NBA Championship
James Worthy	UNC (1982)	L.A. Lakers (1985, 1987, 1988)
Jerry Lucas	Ohio State (1960)	N.Y. Knicks (1973)
Lucius Allen	UCLA (1967, 1968)	Mil. Bucks (1971)
Keith Erickson	UCLA (1969, 1970, 1971)	L.A. Lakers (1972)
Jamaal Wilkes	UCLA (1972, 1973)	G.S. Warriors (1975); L.A. Lakers (1980, 1982, 1985)
Tom Thacker	Cincinnati (1961, 1962)	Bos. Celtics (1968); Ind. Pacers[a] (1970)
Billy Thompson	Louisville (1986)	L.A. Lakers (1987)
Tom Gola	La Salle (1954)	Phi. Warriors (1956)
Cliff Hagan	Kentucky (1951)	St.L. Hawks (1958)
Dahntay Jones	Duke (2001)	Cle. Cavaliers (2016)
Sasha Kaun	Kansas (2008)	Cle. Cavaliers (2016)
Butch Lee	Marquette (1977)	L.A. Lakers (1980)
Clyde Lovellette	Kansas (1952)	Min. Lakers (1954); Bos Celtics (1963, 1964)
Nazr Mohammed	Kentucky (1996, 1998)	S.A. Spurs (2005)
Rodney McCray	Louisville (1980)	Chi. Bulls (1993)
Rick Robey	Kentucky (1978)	Bos. Celtics (1981)
Brandon Rush	Kansas (2008)	G.S. Warriors (2015)
Larry Siegfried	Ohio State (1960)	Bos. Celtics (1964. 1965. 1966. 1968. 1969)
Lou Tsioropoulos	Kentucky (1954)	Bos. Celtics (1957, 1959)
Milt Wagner	Louisville (1986)	L.A. Lakers (1988)
Corliss Williamson	Arkansas (1994)	Det. Pistons (2004)

^ Active.

[a] ABA.

Awards

Most Times Named Finals MVP·

6	Michael Jordan	1990–91: Chi. Bulls
		1991–92: Chi. Bulls
		1992–93: Chi. Bulls
		1995–96: Chi. Bulls
		1996–97: Chi. Bulls
		1997–98: Chi. Bulls
4	LeBron James	2011–12: Mia. Heat
		2012–13: Mia. Heat
		2015–16: Cle. Cavaliers
		2019–20: L.A. Lakers
3	Magic Johnson	1979–80: L.A. Lakers
		1981–82: L.A. Lakers
		1986–87: L.A. Lakers
3	Tim Duncan	1998–99: S.A. Spurs
		2002–03: S.A. Spurs
		2004–05: S.A. Spurs
3	Shaquille O'Neal	1999–00: L.A. Lakers
		2000–01: L.A. Lakers
		2001–02: L.A. Lakers
2	Willis Reed	1969–70: N.Y. Knicks
		1972–73: N.Y. Knicks
2	Kareem Abdul-Jabbar	1970–71: Mil. Bucks
		1984–85: L.A. Lakers

continued on next page

2	Julius Erving**	1973–74: N.Y. Nets
		1975–76: N.Y. Nets
2	Larry Bird	1983–84: Bos. Celtics
		1985–86: Bos. Celtics
2	Hakeem Olajuwon	1993–94: Hou. Rockets
		1994–95: Hou. Rockets
2	Kawhi Leonard	2013–14: S.A. Spurs
		2018–19: Tor. Raptors
2	Kobe Bryant	2008–09: L.A. Lakers
		2009–10: L.A. Lakers
2	Kevin Durant	2016–17: G.S. Warriors
		2017–18: G.S. Warriors

* First awarded in NBA for 1968–69 Finals.

** ABA Playoff MVP Award was first awarded in 1968. In each occasion, the MVP was from the team that won the ABA championship.

Career Points by Finals MVP

Finals MVP

38,387	Kareem Abdul-Jabbar	Mil. Bucks, 1970–71; L.A. Lakers, 1984–85
37,062	LeBron James	Mia. Heat, 2011–12, 2012–13; Cle. Cavaliers, 2015–16; L.A. Lakers, 2019–20
33,646	Kobe Bryant	L.A. Lakers, 2008–09, 2009–10
32,292	Michael Jordan	Chi. Bulls, 1990–91, 1991–92, 1992–93, 1995–96, 1996–97, 1997–98
31,560	Dirk Nowitzki	Dal. Mavericks, 2010–11
31,419	Wilt Chamberlain	L.A. Lakers, 1971–72
29,580	Moses Malone	Phi. 76ers, 1982–83
28,596	Shaquille O'Neal	L.A. Lakers, 1999–00, 2000–01, 2001–02
26,946	Hakeem Olajuwon	Hou. Rockets, 1993–94, 1994–95
26,496	Tim Duncan	S.A. Spurs, 1998–99, 2002–03, 2004–05
26,397	Paul Pierce	Bos. Celtics, 2007–08
26,395	John Havlicek	Bos. Celtics, 1973–74
25,526	Kevin Durant	G.S. Warriors, 2016–17, 2017–18
25,279	Rick Barry	G.S. Warriors, 1974–75
25,192	Jerry West	L.A. Lakers, 1968–69
23,165	Dwyane Wade	Mia. Heat, 2005–06
21,791	Larry Bird	Bos. Celtics, 1983–84, 1985–86
20,064	Stephen Curry	G.S. Warriors, 2021–22
19,473	Tony Parker	S.A. Spurs, 2006–07
18,822	Isiah Thomas	Det. Pistons, 1989–90
17,707	Magic Johnson	L.A. Lakers, 1979–80, 1981–82, 1986–87
16,401	Joe Dumars	Det. Pistons, 1988–89
16,320	James Worthy	L.A. Lakers, 1987–88
15,802	Chauncey Billups	Det. Pistons, 2003–04
15,535	Dennis Johnson	Sea. Sonics, 1978–79
14,399	Jo Jo White	Bos. Celtics, 1975–76
14,321	Giannis Antetokounmpo	Mil. Bucks, 2020–21
13,951	Andre Iguodala	G.S. Warriors, 2014–15
12,183	Willis Reed	N.Y. Knicks, 1969–70, 1972–73
11,085	Kawhi Leonard	S.A. Spurs, 2013–14; Tor. Raptors, 2018–19
10,624	Wes Unseld	Was. Bullets, 1977–78
10,465	Cedric Maxwell	Bos. Celtics, 1980–81
6215	Bill Walton	Por. Blazers, 1976–77

Players Winning League and Finals MVP, Same Season

Willis Reed, N.Y. Knicks, 1969–70

Kareem Abdul-Jabbar, Mil. Bucks, 1970–71

Moses Malone, Phi. 76ers, 1982–83

Larry Bird, Bos. Celtics, 1983–84

Larry Bird, Bos. Celtics, 1985–86

Magic Johnson, L.A. Lakers, 1986–87

Michael Jordan, Chi. Bulls, 1990–91

Michael Jordan, Chi. Bulls, 1991–92

Hakeem Olajuwon, Hou. Rockets, 1993–94

Michael Jordan, Chi. Bulls, 1995–96

Michael Jordan, Chi. Bulls, 1997–98

Shaquille O'Neal, L.A. Lakers, 1999–00

Tim Duncan, S.A. Spurs, 2002–03

LeBron James, Mia. Heat, 2011–12

LeBron James, Mia. Heat, 2012–13

Players Winning League MVP, All-Star Game MVP, and Finals MVP, Same Season

Willis Reed, N.Y. Knicks, 1969–70

Michael Jordan, Chi. Bulls, 1995–96

Michael Jordan, Chi. Bulls, 1997–98

Shaquille O'Neal*, L.A. Lakers, 1999–00

* Tied for ASG MVP with Tim Duncan.

Coaches

Championship-Winning Coaches Who Never Played in the BAA/NBA/ABA

Eddie Gottlieb ....Phi. Warriors: 1947

John Kundla ....Min. Lakers: 1949, 1950, 1952, 1953, 1954

Les Harrison ....Roc. Royals: 1951

Red Auerbach ....Bos. Celtics: 1957, 1959, 1960, 1961, 1962, 1963, 1964, 1965, 1966

Vince Cazzetta ....Pit. Pipers^a: 1968

Hubie Brown ....Ken. Colonels^a: 1975

Jack Ramsay..................Por. Blazers: 1977

Dick Motta ....Was. Bullets: 1978

Paul Westhead ..............L.A. Lakers: 1980

Bill Fitch........................Bos. Celtics: 1981

Chuck Daly ....Det. Pistons: 1989, 1990

Gregg Popovich^ ...........S.A. Spurs: 1999, 2003, 2005, 2007, 2014

Erik Spoelstra^...............Mia. Heat: 2012, 2013

Nick Nurse^ ....Tor. Raptors: 2019

Frank Vogel^ .................L.A. Lakers: 2020

Mike Budenholzer^ ....Mil. Bucks: 2021

a ABA.

^ Active.

Most Championship Rings, Player and Coach

	Player		Coach
12...........	Phil Jackson ..............N.Y. Knicks (1973)...		Chi. Bulls (1991–93, 1996–98); L.A. Lakers (2000–02, 2008–09)
11...........	Bill Russell.................Bos. Celtics (1957, 1959–66, 1968–69)		Bos. Celtics* (1968–69)
10...........	Tom Heinsohn ....Bos. Celtics (1957, 1959–65)...............................		Bos. Celtics (1974, 1976)
10...........	K.C. Jones ....Bos. Celtics (1959–66)..		Bos. Celtics (1984, 1986)
9.............	Steve Kerr................Chi. Bulls (1996–98); S.A. Spurs (1999, 2003)......		G.S. Warriors (2015, 2017–18, 2022)
6.............	Bill Sharman ....Bos. Celtics (1957, 1959–61)...............................		Uta. Stars^a (1971); L.A. Lakers (1972)
6.............	Pat Riley ..................L.A. Lakers (1972)...		L.A. Lakers (1982, 1985, 1987–88); Mia. Heat (2006)
3.............	Red Holzman ....Roc. Royals (1951)		N.Y. Knicks (1970, 1973)
3.............	Tyronn Lue ...............L.A. Lakers (2000–01)...		Cle. Cavaliers (2016)

continued on next page

Player	Coach
2............. George Senseky........ Phi. Warriors (1947)	Phi. Warriors (1956)
2............. Larry Costello............ Phi. 76ers (1967)	Mil. Bucks (1971)
2............. Billy Cunningham ...... Phi. 76ers (1967)	Phi. 76ers (1983)
2............. Larry Brown .... Oak. Oaksᵃ (1969)...	Det. Pistons (2004)
2............. Rick Carlisle.............. Bos. Celtics (1986)...	Dal. Mavericks (2011)
1............. Buddy Jeannette .... Bal. Bullets (1948)...	Bal. Bullets* (1948)

* Was a Player-Coach.

ABA.

Teams

Most Playoff Games Played, Season

26......... Bos. Celtics*, 2007–08 .... ECFR vs. Atl. Hawks (4–3); ECSF vs. Cle. Cavaliers (4–3); ECF vs. Det. Pistons (4–2); NBA Finals vs. L.A. Lakers (4–2)

25......... Det. Pistons, 2004–05 .... ECFR vs. Phi. 76ers (4–1); ECSF vs. Ind. Pacers (4–2); ECF vs. Mia. Heat (4–3); NBA Finals vs. S.A. Spurs (3–4)

25......... N.Y. Knicks, 1993–94 .... ECFR vs. N.J. Nets (3–1); ECSM vs. Chi. Bulls (4–3); ECF vs. Ind. Pacers (4–3); NBA Finals vs. Hou. Rockets (3–4)

24......... Bos. Celtics, 2009–10 .... ECFR vs. Mia. Heat (4–1); ECSM vs. Cle. Cavaliers (4–2); ECF vs. Orl. Magic (4–2); NBA Finals vs. L.A. Lakers (3–4)

24......... G.S. Warriors, 2015–16 .... WCFR vs. Hou. Rockets (4–1); WCSF vs. Por. Blazers (4–1); WCF vs. OK.C. Thunder (4–3); NBA Finals vs. Cle. Cavaliers (3–4)

24......... L.A. Lakers*, 1987–88 .... WCFR vs. S.A. Spurs (3–0); WCSF vs. Uta. Jazz (4–3); WCF vs. Dal. Mavericks; NBA Finals vs. Det. Pistons (4–3)

24......... Orl. Magic, 2008–09............ ESFR vs. Phi. 76ers (4–2); ECSF vs. Bos. Celtics; ECF vs. Cle. Cavaliers (4–2); NBA Finals vs. L.A. Lakers (1–4)

24......... Pho. Suns, 1992–93.............. WCFR vs. L.A. Lakers (3–2); WCSF vs. S.A. Spurs (4–2); WCF vs. Sea. Sonics (4–3); NBA Finals vs. Chi. Bulls (2–4)

24......... S.A. Spurs*, 2002–03 .... WCFR vs. Pho. Suns (4–2); WCSF vs. L.A. Lakers (4–2); WCF vs. Dal. Mavericks (4–2); NBA Finals vs. N.J. Nets (4–2)

24......... Tor Raptors*, 2018–19........... ECFR vs. Orl. Magic (4–1); EXSF vs. Phi. 76ers (4–3); ECF vs. Mil. Bucks (4–2); NBA Finals vs. G.S. Warriors (4–2)

ECFR: Eastern Conference First Round WCFR: Western Conference First Round

ECSM: Eastern Conference Semifinals WCSM: Western Conference Semifinals

ECF: Eastern Conference Finals WCF: Western Conference Finals

* Won championship.

Teams with .500 Record, Making Playoffs and Winning at Least One Series*

Team (Seed)	Record	Opponent (Seed), Record	Round	Series
Bos. Celtics (#3), 1954–55	36–36	N.Y. Knicks (#2), 38–34	ED Semifinals	Won (2–1)
Phi. 76ers (#3), 1964–65	40–40	Cin. Royals (#2), 48–32	ED Semifinals	Won (3–1)
Hou. Rockets (#4), 1974–75	41–41	N.Y. Knicks (#5), 40–42	EC First Round	Won (2–1)
Hou. Rockets (#4), 1979–80	41–41	S.A. Spurs (#5), 41–41	EC First Round	Won (2–1)
Pho. Suns (#6), 1983–84	41–41	Por. Blazers (#3), 48–34	WC First Round	Won (3–2)
		Uta. Jazz (#2), 45–37	WC Semifinals	Won (4–2)
Uta. Jazz (#6), 1984–85	41–41	Hou. Rockets (#3), 48–34	WC First Round	Won (3–2)
N.J. Nets (#6), 2006–07	41–41	Tor. Raptors (#3), 47–35	EC First Round	Won (4–2)

* Does not include tiebreakers.

Teams with Losing Record, Making Playoffs and Winning at Least One Series[*]

Team (Seed)	Record	Opponent (Seed), Record	Round	Series
Syr. Nationals (#4), 1950–51	32–34	Phi. Warriors (#1), 40–26	ED Semifinals	Won (2–0)
Syr. Nationals (#3), 1955–56	35–37	Bos. Celtics (#2), 39–33	ED Semifinals	Won (2–1)
St.L. Hawks (#3), 1955–56	33–39	Min. Lakers (#2), 33–39	WD Semifinals	Won (2–1)
Min. Lakers (#2), 34–38, 1956–67	34–38	Ft.W. Pistons (#3), 34–38	WD Semifinals	Won (2–0)
St.L. Hawks (#1), 1956–57	34–38	Min. Lakers (#2), 34–38	WD Finals	Won (3–0)
Det. Pistons (#2), 1957–58	33–39	Cin. Royals (#3), 33–39	WD Semifinals	Won (2–0)
Syr. Nationals (#3), 1958–59	35–37	N.Y. Knicks (#2), 40–32	ED Semifinals	Won (2–0)
Min. Lakers (#2), 1958–59	33–39	Det. Pistons (#3), 28–44	WD Semifinals	Won (2–1)
		St.L. Hawks (#1), 49–23	WD Finals	Won (4–2)
Min. Lakers (#3), 1959–60	25–50	Det. Pistons (#2), 30–45	WD Semifinals	Won (2–0)
L.A. Lakers (#2), 1960–61	36–43	Det. Pistons (#3), 34–45	WD Semifinals	Won (3–2)
Syr. Nationals, 1960–61	38–41	Phi. Warriors (#2), 46–33	ED Semifinals	Won (3–0)
Det. Pistons (#3), 1961–62	37–43	Cin. Royals (#2), 43–37	WD Semifinals	Won (3–1)
Bal. Bullets (#3), 1964–65	37–43	St.L. Hawks (#2), 45–35	WD Semifinals	Won (3–1)
St.L. Hawks (#3), 1965–66	36–44	Bal. Bullets (#2), 38–42	WD Semifinals	Won (3–0)
St.L. Hawks (#2), 1966–67	39–42	Chi. Bulls (#4), 33–48	WD Semifinals	Won (3–0)
Hou. Rockets (#6), 1980–81	40–42	L.A. Lakers (#3), 54–28	WC First Round	Won (2–1)
		S.A. Spurs (#2), 52–30	WC Semifinals	Won (4–3)
		K.C. Kings (#5), 40–42	WC Finals	Won (4–1)
K.C. Kings (#5), 1980–81	40–42	Por. Blazers (#4), 45–37	WC First Round	Won (2–1)
		Pho. Suns (#1), 57–25	WC Semifinals	Won (4–3)
Sea. Sonics (#7), 1986–87	39–43	Dal. Mavericks (#2), 55–27	WC First Round	Won (3–1)
		Hou. Rockets (#6), 42–40	WC Semifinals	Won (4–2)

[*] Does not include tiebreakers.

Biggest Playoff Blowouts

Diff		Score	
58	Min. Lakers vs. St.L. Hawks	133–75	WDSF, Gm. 2 (Mar. 19, 1956)
58	Den. Nuggets @ N.O. Hornets	121–63	WCFR, Gm. 4 (Apr. 27, 2009)
56	L.A. Lakers @ G.S. Warriors	126–70	WCF, Gm. 3 (Apr. 21, 1973)
54	Chi. Bulls @ Mil. Bucks	120–66	ECFR, Gm. 6 (Apr. 30, 2015)
50	Mil. Bucks vs. S.F. Warriors	136–86	WCSF, Gm. 5 (Apr. 4, 1971)
47	Vir. Squires[a] vs. N.Y. Nets[a]	138–91	ABA EDF, Gm. 1 (Apr. 13, 1972)
47	L.A. Lakers vs. S.A. Spurs	135–88	WCFR, Gm. 1 (Apr. 17, 1986)
47	Orl. Magic vs. Bos. Celtics	124–77	ECFR, Gm. 1 (Apr. 28, 1995)
44	St.L. Hawks @ Det. Pistons	145–101	WDF, Gm. 4 (Mar. 25, 1958)
44	L.A. Lakers vs. Den. Nuggets	153–109	WCF, Gm. 5 (May 22, 1985)
44	Sea. Sonics vs. Pho. Suns	122–78	WCFR, Gm. 2 (Apr. 27, 1997)
44	Cle. Cavaliers @ Bos. Celtics	130–86	ECF, Gm. 2 (May 19, 2017)
43	L.A. Lakers vs. Dal. Mavericks	134–91	WCSF, Gm. 1 (Apr. 28, 1984)
43	Det. Pistons vs. Was. Bullets	128–85	ECFR, Gm. 2 (Apr. 26, 1987)
43	Orl. Magic vs. Atl. Hawks	114–71	ECSF, Gm. 1 (May 4, 2010)
43	L.A. Clippers vs. Dal. Mavericks	154–111	WCFR, Gm. 5 (Aug. 25, 2020)
42	Chi. Bulls vs. Uta. Jazz	96–54	NBA Finals, Gm. 3 (Jun. 7, 1998)
41	Chi. Bulls vs. N.Y. Knicks	126–85	ECFR, Gm. 1 (Apr. 25, 1991)
41	G.S. Warriors vs. Hou. Rockets	126–85	WCF, Gm. 3 (May 20, 2018)
40	L.A. Lakers @ S.F. Warriors	118–78	WDSF, Gm. 6 (Apr. 5, 1969)
40	Phi. 76ers vs. N.Y. Knicks	130–90	ECSF, Gm. 1 (Apr. 16, 1978)
40	Bos. Celtics vs. Phi. 76ers	121–81	ECF, Gm. 1 (May 9, 1982)
40	S.A. Spurs vs. Den. Nuggets	145–105	WCSF, Gm. 5 (May 4, 1983)

continued on next page

Diff		Score	
40	Dal. Mavericks vs. Hou. Rockets	116–76	WCFR, Gm. 7 (May 7, 2005)
40	L.A. Lakers vs. Hou. Rockets	118–78	WCSF, Gm. 5 (May 12, 2009)
40	L.A. Clippers vs. G.S. Warriors	138–98	WCFR, Gm. 2 (Apr. 21, 2014)

ᵃ ABA.

ECFR: NBA Eastern Conference First Round

ECSF: NBA Eastern Conference Semifinals

ECF: NBA Eastern Conference Finals

WCFR: NBA Western Conference First Round

WCSF: NBA Western Conference Semifinals

WCF: NBA Western Conference Finals

WDSF: NBA Western Division Semifinals

WDF: NBA Western Division Finals

ABA EDF: ABA Eastern Division Finals

Biggest Finals Blowouts

Diff			Final Score
42	Chi. Bulls* vs. Uta. Jazz	Game 3 (Jun. 7, 1998)	96–54
39	Bos. Celtics* vs. L.A. Lakers	Game 6 (Jun. 17, 2008)	131–92
36	S.A. Spurs vs. Mia. Heat*	Game 3 (Jun. 11, 2013)	113–77
35	Was. Bullets* vs. Sea. Sonics	Game 6 (Jun. 4, 1978)	117–82
34	Bos. Celtics* vs. St.L. Hawks	Game 1 (Apr. 2, 1961)	129–95
34	Bos. Celtics vs. L.A. Lakers*	Game 1 (May 27, 1985)	148–114
33	Bos. Celtics vs. L.A. Lakers*	Game 5 (Apr. 25, 1965)	129–96
33	Phi. 76ers vs. L.A. Lakers*	Game 5 (Jun. 6, 1982)	135–102
33	L.A. Lakers vs. Bos. Celtics*	Game 3 (Jun. 3, 1984)	137–104
33	Chi. Bulls* vs. Por. Blazers	Game 1 (Jun. 3, 1992)	122–89
33	Ind. Pacers vs. L.A. Lakers*	Game 5 (Jun. 16, 2000)	120–87
33	G.S. Warriors vs. Cle. Cavaliers*	Game 2 (Jun. 5, 2016)	110–77
32	Bos. Celtics* vs. L.A. Lakers	Game 1 (Apr. 18, 1965)	142–110
32	Por. Blazers* vs. Phi. 76ers	Game 4 (May 31, 1977)	130–98
31	Phi. 76ers* vs. S.F. Warriors	Game 2 (Apr. 16, 1967)	126–95
31	Det. Pistons vs. S.A. Spurs*	Game 4 (Jun. 16, 2005)	102–71
30	Cle. Cavaliers* vs. G.S. Warriors	Game 3 (Jun. 8, 2016)	120–90

* Won championship.

Biggest Game 7 Blowouts

Diff		Score	
40	Dal. Mavericks vs. Hou. Rockets	116–76	Western Conference First Round (May 7, 2005)
39	Phi. Warriors @ St.L. Bombers	85–46	BAA Semifinals (Apr. 6, 1948)
35	L.A. Lakers vs. Pho. Suns	129–94	Western Division Semifinals (Apr. 9, 1970)
34	Bos. Celtics vs. Atl. Hawks	99–65	Eastern Conference First Round (May 4, 2008)
33	Mia. Heat vs. Cha. Hornets	106–73	Eastern Conference First Round (May 1, 2016)
33	Dal. Mavericks @ Pho. Suns	123–90	Western Conference Semifinals (May 15, 2022)
31	Pho. Suns vs. L.A. Lakers	121–90	Western Conference First Round (May 6, 2006)
29	Chi. Bulls vs. N.Y. Knicks	110–81	Eastern Conference Semifinals (May 17, 1992)
28	Bos. Celtics vs. Mil. Bucks	109–81	Eastern Conference Semifinals (May 15, 2022)
27	Ind. Pacers @ Bos. Celtics	97–70	Western Conference First Round (May 7, 2005)
27	Tor. Raptors vs. Mia. Heat	116–89	Eastern Conference Semifinals (May 15, 2016)
24	Den. Rocketsᵃ vs. Was. Capitolsᵃ	143–119	ABA Western Division Semifinals (Apr. 28, 1970)
24	Orl. Magic vs. Ind. Pacers	105–81	Eastern Conference Finals (Jun. 4, 1995)
23	Den. Nuggetsᵃ vs. Ken. Colonelsᵃ	133–110	ABA Semifinals (Apr. 28, 1976)
23	Mia. Heat vs. Ind. Pacers	99–76	Eastern Conference Finals (Jun. 3, 2013)
23	S.A. Spurs vs. Dal. Mavericks	119–96	Western Conference First Round (May 4, 2014)
22	Uta. Starsᵃ vs. Ind. Pacersᵃ	109–87	ABA Western Division Finals (Apr. 27, 1974)
21	Det. Pistons vs. N.J. Nets	90–69	Eastern Conference Semifinals (May 20, 2004)
21	Atl. Hawks vs. Mil. Bucks	95–74	Eastern Conference First Round (May 2, 2010)
20	Pho. Suns vs. L.A. Clippers	127–107	Western Conference Semifinals (May 22, 2006)

Franchise Record in Game 7

NBA

	Playoffs	Finals		Playoffs	Finals
Timberwolves	1–0 (1.000)	N/A	Trail Blazers	2–2 (.500)	N/A
Celtics	26–9 (.743)	7–1 (.875)	Knicks	7–8 (.467)	1–3 (.250)
Cavaliers	5–2 (.714)	1–0 (1.000)	Bulls	4–6 (.400)	N/A
Lakers	16–8 (.667)	4–5 (.444)	Suns	4–6 (.400)	N/A
Magic	2–1 (.667)	N/A	Spurs	4–7 (.364)	1–1 (.500)
Mavericks	5–3 (.625)	N/A	Hawks	5–9 (.357)	0–2 (.000)
Wizards-Bullets	6–4 (.600)	1–0 (.1000)	76ers-Nationals	6–11 (.353)	1–1 (.500)
Rockets	7–5 (.583)	1–0 (1.000)	Pacers	3–6 (.333)	N/A
Nuggets	4–3 (.571)	N/A	Kings-Royals	2–4 (.333)	1–0 (1.000)
Heat	6–5 (.545)	1–0 (1.000)	Bucks	3–9 (.250)	1–0 (1.000)
Thunder-SuperSonics	6–5 (.545)	0–1 (.000)	Nets	1–3 (.250)	N/A
Pistons	5–5 (.500)	0–3 (.000)	Grizzlies	0–3 (.000)	N/A
Warriors	5–5 (.500)	0–1 (.000)	Hornets	0–2 (.000)	N/A
Clippers	4–4 (.500)	N/A	Pelicans-Hornets	0–2 (.000)	N/A
Jazz	3–3 (.500)	N/A	Bombers	0–1 (.000)	N/A
Raptors	3–3 (.500)	N/A			

ABA

	Playoffs	Finals		Playoffs	Finals
Floridians	1–0 (1.000)	N/A	Nuggets-Rockets	2–3 (.400)	N/A
Pacers	6–2 (.750)	1–0 (1.000)	Colonels	2–4 (.333)	0–2 (.000)
Stars	3–1 (.750)	1–0 (1.000)	Oaks-Capitols-Squires	1–2 (.333)	N/A
Nets	2–1 (.667)	N/A	Spurs-Chaparrals	0–3 (.000)	N/A
Pipers	1–1 (.500)	1–0 (1.000)	Cougars	0–1 (.000)	N/A
Buccaneers	1–1 (.500)	0–1 (.000)			

Lowest Playoff Seed, Winning Championship

		Record
#6 Seed	Hou. Rockets, 1994–95	47–35 (.573)
#4 Seed	Bos. Celtics, 1968–69	48–34 (.585)

Most Regular-Season Losses, Winning Championship

		Record			Record
38	Was. Bullets, 1977–78	44–38 (.537)	33	Ind. Pacers[a], 1972–73	51–33 (.607)
37	Ind. Pacers[a], 1971–72	47–37 (.560)	33	Por. Blazers, 1976–77	49–33 (.598)
35	Hou. Rockets, 1994–95	47–35 (.573)	31	St.L. Hawks, 1957–58	41–31 (.569)
34	Bos. Celtics, 1968–69	48–34 (.585)	30	Sea. Sonics, 1978–79	52–30 (.634)
34	G.S. Warriors, 1974–75	48–34 (.585)	30	Mia. Heat, 2005–06	52–30 (.634)

[a] ABA.

Most Regular-Season Wins, Not Winning Championship

	Record	Champ
G.S. Warriors*, 2015–16	73–9 (.890)	Cle. Cavaliers
Bos. Celtics, 1972–73	68–14 (.830)	N.Y. Knicks
Ken. Colonels[a], 1971–72	68–16 (.810)	Ind. Pacers[a]
Dal. Mavericks, 2006–07	67–15 (.817)	S.A. Spurs
S.A. Spurs, 2015–16	67–15 (.817)	Cle. Cavaliers

continued on next page

	Record	Champ
Cle. Cavaliers, 2008–09	66–16 (.805)	L.A. Lakers
Hou. Rockets, 2017–18	65–17 (.793)	G.S. Warriors
Den. Nuggets[a], 1974–75	65–19 (.774)	Ken. Colonels[a]
Sea. Sonics*, 1995–96	64–18 (.780)	Chi. Bulls
Uta. Jazz*, 1996–97	64–18 (.780)	Chi. Bulls
Det. Pistons, 2005–06	64–18 (.780)	Mia. Heat
Mil. Bucks, 1971–72	63–19 (.768)	L.A. Lakers
Bos. Celtics, 1981–82	63–19 (.768)	L.A. Lakers
Bos. Celtics*, 1984–85	63–19 (.768)	L.A. Lakers
L.A. Lakers, 1989–90	63–19 (.768)	Det. Pistons
Por. Blazers, 1990–91	63–19 (.768)	Chi. Bulls
Sea. Sonics, 1993–94	63–19 (.768)	Hou. Rockets
S.A. Spurs, 2005–06	63–19 (.768)	Mia. Heat
Phi. 76ers, 1967–68	62–20 (.756)	Bos. Celtics
Phi. 76ers, 1980–81	62–20 (.756)	Bos. Celtics
L.A. Lakers, 1985–86	62–20 (.756)	Bos. Celtics
Pho. Suns*, 1992–93	62–20 (.756)	Chi. Bulls
S.A. Spurs, 1994–95	62–20 (.756)	Hou. Rockets
Uta. Jazz*, 1997–98	62–20 (.756)	Chi. Bulls
Pho. Suns, 2004–05	62–20 (.756)	S.A. Spurs
Bos. Celtics, 2008–09	62–20 (.756)	L.A. Lakers
Chi. Bulls, 2010–11	62–20 (.756)	Dal. Mavericks
Bos. Celtics, 1979–80	61–20 (.753)	L.A. Lakers
Mia. Heat, 1996–97	61–21 (.744)	Chi. Bulls
L.A. Lakers, 1997–98	61–21 (.744)	Chi. Bulls
Sea. Sonics, 1997–98	61–21 (.744)	Chi. Bulls
Sac. Kings, 2001–02	61–21 (.744)	L.A. Lakers
Ind. Pacers, 2003–04	61–21 (.744)	Det. Pistons
Pho. Suns, 2006–07	61–21 (.744)	S.A. Spurs
Cle. Cavaliers, 2009–10	61–21 (.744)	L.A. Lakers
S.A. Spurs, 2010–11	61–21 (.744)	Dal. Mavericks
S.A. Spurs, 2016–17	61–21 (.744)	G.S. Warriors
Bos. Celtics, 1966–67	61–21 (.744)	Phi. 76ers
L.A. Lakers*, 1972–73	60–22 (.732)	N.Y. Knicks
Mil. Bucks, 1972–73	60–22 (.732)	N.Y. Knicks
Bos. Celtics, 1974–75	60–22 (.732)	G.S. Warriors
Was. Bullets, 1974–75	60–22 (.732)	G.S. Warriors
Mil. Bucks, 1980–81	60–22 (.732)	Bos. Celtics
N.Y. Knicks, 1992–93	60–22 (.732)	Chi. Bulls
Uta. Jazz, 1994–95	60–22 (.732)	Hou. Rockets
Orl. Magic, 1995–96	60–22 (.732)	Chi. Bulls
Dal. Mavericks, 2002–03	60–22 (.732)	S.A. Spurs
Dal. Mavericks*, 2005–06	60–22 (.732)	Mia. Heat
Ok.C. Thunder, 2012–13	60–22 (.732)	Mia. Heat
Atl. Hawks, 2014–15	60–22 (.732)	G.S. Warriors
Mil. Bucks, 2018–19	60–22 (.732)	Tor. Raptors
Uta. Stars[a], 1971–72**	60–24 (.714)	Ind. Pacers[a]
Den. Nuggets[a]*, 1975–76**	60–24 (.714)	N.Y. Nets[a]

* Lost in Finals.

[a] ABA.

Fewest Playoff Losses, Winning Championship

Four-Round Playoff (1949–50, 1976–78, 1983–2022)

1.........L.A. Lakers, 2000–01 ....WCFR vs. Por. Blazers (3–0); WCSF vs. Sac. Kings (4–0); WCF vs. S.A. Spurs (4–0); NBA Finals vs. Phi. 76ers (4–1)

1.........G.S. Warriors, 2016–17.........WCFR vs. Por. Blazers (4–0); WCSF vs. Uta. Jazz; WCF vs. S.A. Spurs (4–0); NBA Finals vs. Cle. Cavaliers (4–1)

2.........Min. Lakers, 1949–50 ....CDSF vs. Chi. Stags (2–0); CDF vs. Ft.W. Pistons (2–0); SF vs. And. Packers (2–0); NBA Finals vs. Syr. Nationals (4–2)

2.........Det. Pistons, 1988–89 ....ECFR vs. Bos. Celtics (3–0); ECSF vs. Mil. Bucks (4–0); ESF vs. Chi. Bulls (4–2); NBA Finals vs. L.A. Lakers (4–0)

2.........Chi. Bulls, 1990–91 ....ECFR vs. N.Y. Knicks (3–0); ECSF vs. Phi. 76ers (4–1); ESF vs. Det. Pistons (4–0); NBA Finals vs. L.A. Lakers (4–1)

2.........S.A. Spurs, 1998–99..............WCFR vs. Min. T'Wolves (3–1); WCSF vs. L.A. Lakers (4–0); WCF vs. Por. Blazers (4–0); NBA Finals vs. N.Y. Knicks (4–1)

3.........Bos. Celtics, 1985–86 ....ECFR vs. Chi. Bulls (3–0); ECSF vs. Atl. Hawks (4–1); ECF vs. Mil. Bucks (4–0); NBA Finals vs. Hou. Rockets (4–2)

3.........L.A. Lakers, 1986–87 ....WCFR vs. Den. Nuggets (3–0); WCSF vs. G.S. Warriors (4–1); WCF vs. Sea. Sonics (4–0); NBA Finals vs. Bos. Celtics (4–2)

3.........Chi. Bulls, 1995–96 ....ECFR vs. Mia. Heat (3–0); ECSF vs. N.Y. Knicks (4–1); ESF vs. Orl. Magic (4–0); NBA Finals vs. Sea. Sonics (4–2)

3.........L.A. Lakers, 2001–02 ....WCFR vs. Por. Blazers (3–0); WCSF vs. S.A. Spurs (4–1); WCF vs. Sac. Kings (4–3); NBA Finals vs. N.J. Nets (4–0)

4.........L.A. Lakers, 1984–85 ....WCFR vs. Pho. Suns (3–0); WCSF vs. Por. Blazers (4–1); WCF vs. Den. Nuggets (4–1); NBA Finals vs. Bos. Celtics (4–2)

4.........Chi. Bulls, 1992–93 ....ECFR vs. Atl. Hawks (3–0); ECSF vs. Cle. Cavaliers (4–0); ECF vs. N.Y. Knicks (4–2); NBA Finals vs. Pho. Suns (4–2)

4.........Chi. Bulls, 1996–97 ....ECFR vs. Was. Bullets (3–0); ECSF vs. Atl. Hawks (4–1); ECF vs. Mia. Heat (4–1); NBA Finals vs. Uta. Jazz (4–2)

4.........S.A. Spurs, 2006–07..............WCFR vs. Den. Nuggets, (4–1); WCSF vs. Pho. Suns (4–2); WCF vs. Uta. Jazz (4–1); NBA Finals vs. Cle. Cavaliers (4–0)

ECFR: Eastern Conference First Round	WCFR Western Conference First Round	SF: NBA Semifinals
ECSF: Eastern Conference Semifinals	WCSF: Western Conference Semifinals	CDSF: Central Division Semifinals
ECF: Eastern Conference Finals	WCF: Western Conference Finals	CDF: Central Division Finals

Three-Round Playoff (1946–51, 1952–53, 1965–76, 1978–83)

1.........Phi. 76ers, 1982–83 ....ECSF vs. N.Y. Knicks (4–0); ECF vs. Mil. Bucks (4–1); NBA Finals vs. L.A. Lakers (4–0)

2.........Phi. Warriors, 1946–47.........BAA QF vs. St.L. Bombers (2–1); BAA SF vs. N.Y. Knicks (2–0); BAA Finals vs. Chi. Stags (4–1)

2.........Min. Lakers, 1948–49 ....BAA WDSF vs. Chi. Stags (2–0); BAA WDF vs. Roc. Royals (2–0); BAA Finals vs. Was. Capitols (4–2)

2.........Mil. Bucks, 1970–71 ....WCSF vs. S.F. Warriors (4–1); WCF vs. L.A. Lakers (4–1); NBA Finals vs. Bal. Bullets (4–0)

2.........N.Y. Nets[a], 1973–74 ....ABA EDSF vs. Vir. Squires (4–1); ABA EDF vs. Ken. Colonels (4–0); ABA Finals vs. Uta. Stars (4–1)

2.........L.A. Lakers, 1981–82 ....WCSF vs. Pho. Suns (4–0); WCF vs. S.A. Spurs (4–0); NBA Finals vs. Phi. 76ers (4–2)

3.........Bal. Bullets, 1947–48 ....BAA QF vs. N.Y. Knicks (2–1); BAA SF vs. Chi. Stags (2–0); BAA Finals vs. Phi. Warriors (4–2)

3.........Min. Lakers, 1952–53 ....WDSF vs. Ind. Olympians (2–0); WDF vs. Ft.W. Pistons (3–2); NBA Finals vs. N.Y. Knicks (4–1)

3.........Ind. Pacers[a], 1969–70............ABA EDSF vs. Car. Cougars (4–0); ABA EDF vs. Ken. Colonels (4–1); ABA Finals vs. L.A. Stars (4–2)

3.........L.A. Lakers, 1971–72 ....WCSF vs. Chi. Bulls (4–0); WCF vs. Mil. Bucks (4–2); NBA Finals vs. N.Y. Knicks (4–1)

3.........Ken. Colonels[a], 1974–75........ABA EDSF vs. Mem. Sounds (4–1); ABA EDF vs. Spirits of St.L. (4–1); ABA Finals vs. Ind. Pacers (4–1)

continued on next page

4.........Pit. Pipers*a*, 1967–68 ....ABA EDSF vs. Ind. Pacers (3–0); ABA EDF vs. Min. Muskies (4–1); ABA Finals vs.
     N.O. Buccaneers (4–3)
4.........Oak. Oaks*a*, 1968–69 ....ABA WDSF vs. Den. Rockets (4–3); ABA WDF vs. N.O. Buccaneers (4–0); ABA Finals vs.
     Ind. Pacers (4–1)
4.........L.A. Lakers, 1979–80 ....WCSF vs. Pho. Suns (4–1); WCF vs. Sea. Sonics (4–1); NBA Finals vs. Phi. 76ers (4–2)
a ABA.

BAA QF—BAA Quarterfinals	EDSF—NBA Eastern Division Semfinals	WCSF—NBA Western Conference Semifinals
BAA SF—BAA Semifinals	EDF—NBA Eastern Division Finals	WCF—NBA Western Conference Finals
BAA WDSF—BAA Western Division Semifinals	WDSF—NBA Western Division Semifinals	ABA EDSF—ABA Eastern Division Semifinals
BAA WDF—BAA Western Division Finals	WDF—NBA Western Division Finals	ABA EDF—ABA Eastern Division Finals

Two-Round Playoff (1951–52; 1953–65; 1975–76 (ABA)

2 .... Bos. Celtics, 1960–61 ....EDF vs. Syr. Nationals (4–1); NBA Finals vs. St.L. Hawks (4–1)
2 .... Bos. Celtics, 1963–64 ....EDF vs. Cin. Royals (4–1); NBA Finals vs. S.F. Warriors (4–1)
3 .... Phi. Warriors, 1955–56 ....EDF vs. Syr. Nationals (3–2); NBA Finals vs. Ft.W. Pistons (4–1)
3 .... Bos. Celtics, 1956–57 ....EDF vs. Syr. Nationals (3–0); NBA Finals vs. St.L. Hawks (4–3)
3 .... St.L. Hawks, 1957–58 ....WDF vs. Det. Pistons (4–1); NBA Finals vs. Bos. Celtics (4–2)
3 .... Bos. Celtics, 1958–59 ....EDF vs. Syr. Nationals (4–3); NBA Finals vs. Min. Lakers (4–0)

EDF: Eastern Division Finals
WDF: Western Division Finals

Teams Winning Championship, Winning All Playoff Road Games

L.A. Lakers, 2000–01....... WC First Round.............. WC Semifinals.................WC Finals..................... NBA Finals
    Por. Blazers (Gm. 3) .... Sac. Kings (Gm. 4–5).........S.A. Spurs (Gm. 1–2)...... Phi. 76ers (Gm. 3–5)

Teams Sweeping Finals

	Winning Team	Losing Team		Winning Team	Losing Team
1958–59	Bos. Celtics	Min. Lakers	1994–95	Hou. Rockets	Orl. Magic
1970–71	Mil. Bucks	Bal. Bullets	2001–02	L.A. Lakers	N.J. Nets
1974–75	G.S. Warriors	Was. Bullets	2006–07	S.A. Spurs	Cle. Cavaliers
1982–83	Phi. 76ers	L.A. Lakers	2017–18	G.S. Warriors	Cle. Cavaliers
1988–89	Det. Pistons	L.A. Lakers			

Teams' Overall Won–Lost Percentage in NBA Finals Games Played

	Record		Record
Bulls (6 appearances, 6–0)	24–11 (.686)	Hawks (4 appearances, 1–3)	11–14 (.440)
Spurs (6 appearances, 5–1)	23–11 (.676)	Sonics/Thunder (4 appearances, 1–3)	10–13 (.435)
Raptors (1 appearances, 1–0)	4–2 (.666)	Knicks (8 appearances, 2–6)	20–28 (.417)
Bucks (3 appearances, 2–1)	11–6 (.647)	Trail Blazers (3 appearances, 1–2)	7–10 (.412)
Bullets (1 appearances, 1–0)	4–2 (.600)	Bullets/Wizards (4 appearances, 1–3)	8–13 (.381)
Celtics (22 appearances, 17–5)	79–56 (.585)	Suns (3 appearances, 0–3)	6–12 (.333)
Warriors (12 appearances, 7–5)	38–27 (.585)	Jazz (2 appearances, 0–2)	4–8 (.333)
Royals/Kings (1 appearances, 1–0)	4–3 (.571)	Pacers (1 appearances, 0–1)	2–4 (.333)
Pistons (7 appearances, 3–4)	22–18 (.550)	Capitols (1 appearances, 0–1)	2–4 (.333)
Rockets (4 appearances, 2–2)	12–11 (.522)	Cavaliers (5 appearances, 1–4)	7–19 (.269)
Lakers (32 appearances, 17–15)	93–92 (.503)	Nets (2 appearances, 0–2)	2–8 (.200)
Mavericks (2 appearances, 1–1)	6–6 (.500)	Stags (1 appearances, 0–1)	1–4 (.200)
Heat (6 appearances, 3–3)	17–18 (.486)	Magic (2 appearances, 0–2)	1–8 (.111)
Nationals/76ers (9 appearances, 3–6)	24–29 (.453)		

Teams Leading League in Scoring, Winning Championship

		Pts			Pts
1948–49	Min. Lakers*	5042	1971–72	L.A. Lakers	9920
1949–50	Min. Lakers	5717	1974–75	G.S. Warriors	8898
1956–57	Bos. Celtics	7599	1995–96	Chi. Bulls	8625
1958–59	Bos. Celtics	8379	1996–97	Chi. Bulls	8458
1959–60	Bos. Celtics	9337	2014–15	G.S. Warriors	9016
1966–67	Phi. 76ers	10,143	2016–17	G.S. Warriors	9503
1967–68	Pit. Pipersª	8731	2017–18	G.S. Warriors	9304
1968–69	Oak. Oaksª	9866	2020–21	Mil. Bucks	8649
1970–71	Mil. Bucks	9710			

* Tied in scoring with Roc. Royals.

ª ABA.

Highest PPG for Team Winning Championship

126.5 Oak. Oaksª, 1968–69	119.7 Bos. Celtics, 1960–61	116.4 Bos. Celtics, 1958–59
125.2 Phi. 76ers, 1966–67	119.0 Uta. Starsª, 1970–71	116.1 Bos. Celtics, 1967–68
124.5 Bos. Celtics, 1959–60	118.8 Bos. Celtics, 1962–63	115.9 G.S. Warriors, 2016–17
121.1 Bos. Celtics, 1961–62	118.4 Mil. Bucks, 1970–71	115.1 L.A. Lakers, 1979–80
121.0 L.A. Lakers, 1971–72	118.2 L.A. Lakers, 1984–85	115.0 N.Y. Knicks, 1969–70
120.1 Mil. Bucks, 2019–20	117.8 L.A. Lakers, 1986–87	

ª ABA.

Lowest PPG for Team Winning Championship (Shot-Clock Era*)

90.1 Det. Pistons, 2003–04	98.5 S.A. Spurs, 2006–07	100.8 L.A. Lakers, 1999–00
91.1 Syr. Nationals, 1954–55	98.5 Mia. Heat, 2011–12	101.1 Hou. Rockets, 1993–94
92.8 S.A. Spurs, 1998–99	99.9 Mia. Heat, 2005–06	101.3 L.A. Lakers, 2001–02
95.8 S.A. Spurs, 2002–03	100.2 Dal. Mavericks, 2010–11	101.7 L.A. Lakers, 2009–10
96.2 S.A. Spurs, 2004–05	100.5 Bos. Celtics, 2007–08	102.9 Mia. Heat, 2012–13
96.7 Chi. Bulls, 1997–98	100.6 L.A. Lakers, 2000–01	

* Shot clock was introduced for the 1954–55 season.

Lowest FG% for Team Winning Finals (Shot-Clock Era)

1954–55 Syr. Nationals .372	1955–56 Phi. Warriors .410	1962–63 Bos. Celtics .427
1956–57 Bos. Celtics .383	1963–64 Bos. Celtics .413	1968–69 Bos. Celtics .431
1957–58 St.L. Hawks .388	1964–65 Bos. Celtics .414	2003–04 Det. Pistons .435
1952–53 Min. Lakers .390	1965–66 Bos. Celtics .417	1967–68 Bos. Celtics .440
1958–59 Bos. Celtics .395	1959–60 Bos. Celtics .417	1967–68 Pit. Pipersª .429
1960–61 Bos. Celtics .398	1961–62 Bos. Celtics .423	1975–76 Bos. Celtics .446

ª ABA.

Team Leading League in FT%, Winning Championship

		FT%	Lg. Avg.
1953–54	Min. Lakers	.731	.709
1968–69	Oak. Oaksª	.759	.760
1970–71	Uta. Starsª	.784	.751
2017–18	G.S. Warriors	.815	.767

ª ABA.

Highest FT% for Teams Winning Championship

FT%		Lg. Avg.	FT%		Lg. Avg.
.815	G.S. Warriors, 2017–18	.767	.780	Bos. Celtics, 1975–76	.751
.804	Tor. Raptors, 2018–19	.766	.777	Dal. Mavericks, 2010–11	.763
.800	Bos. Celtics, 1973–74	.771	.775	L.A. Lakers, 1979–80	.764
.794	Bos. Celtics, 1985–86	.756	.775	Mia. Heat, 2011–12	.752
.792	Bos. Celtics, 1983–84	.760	.771	Bos. Celtics, 2007–08	.755
.789	L.A. Lakers, 1986–87	.763	.770	L.A. Lakers, 2008–09	.771
.789	L.A. Lakers, 1987–88	.766	.769	Det. Pistons, 1988–89	.768
.788	G.S. Warriors, 2016–17	.772	.768	G.S. Warriors, 1974–75	.765
.785	S.A. Spurs, 2013–14	.756	.768	G.S. Warriors, 2014–15	.750
.784	Uta. Stars[a], 1970–71	.751	.766	Bos. Celtics, 1958–59	.756
.780	N.Y. Knicks, 1972–73	.758	.765	L.A. Lakers, 2009–10	.759

[a] ABA.

Teams Winning Championship, FT% Lower Than League Average

		FT%	Lg. Avg.
1956–57	Bos. Celtics	.750	.751
1957–58	St.L. Hawks	.715	.746
1959–60	Bos. Celtics	.734	.735
1962–63	Bos. Celtics	.725	.727
1966–67	Phi. 76ers	.680	.732
1967–68	Pit. Pipers[a]	.714	.717
1969–70	N.Y. Knicks	.733	.751
1969–70	Ind. Pacers[a]	.741	.744
1970–71	Mil. Bucks	.742	.745
1971–72	L.A. Lakers	.734	.748
1971–72	Ind. Pacers[a]	.749	.759
1972–73	Ind. Pacers[a]	.739	.746
1973–74	N.Y. Nets[a]	.754	.760
1974–75	Ken. Colonels[a]*	.730	.767
1975–76	N.Y. Nets[a]	.761	.771
1977–78	Was. Bullets*	.711	.752
1981–82	L.A. Lakers	.717	.746
1984–85	L.A. Lakers	.763	.764
1989–90	Det. Pistons	.761	.764
1990–91	Chi. Bulls	.760	.765
1991–92	Chi. Bulls	.744	.759
1992–93	Chi. Bulls	.733	.754
1998–99	S.A. Spurs	.698	.728
1999–00	L.A. Lakers	.696	.750
2000–01	L.A. Lakers*	.683	.748
2001–02	L.A. Lakers*	.699	.752
2002–03	S.A. Spurs	.725	.758
2004–05	S.A. Spurs	.724	.756
2005–06	Mia. Heat	.700	.745
2006–07	S.A. Spurs	.751	.752
2008–09	L.A. Lakers	.770	.771
2015–16	Cle. Cavaliers	.748	.757
2019–20	L.A. Lakers	.729	.773
2020–21	Mil. Bucks	.760	.778

* Lowest in league.

Most Turnovers in a Season, Making Finals

TO		Lg. Avg.	TO		Lg. Avg.
1915	Phi. 76ers, 1976–77	1687	1655	N.Y. Nets[a], 1971–72	1528
1852	Pho. Suns, 1975–76	1621	1639	Ken. Colonels[a], 1974–75	1543
1837	Oak. Oaks[a], 1968–69	1473	1613	N.Y. Nets[a], 1975–76	1632**
1796	Ind. Pacers[a], 1971–72	1528	1612	Bos. Celtics, 1973–74	1706
1757	Ind. Pacers[a], 1972–73	1601	1609	G.S. Warriors, 1974–75	1627
1757	Por. Blazers, 1976–77*	1687	1609	Bos. Celtics, 1975–76	1621
1755	Den. Nuggets, 1975–76	1621	1580	Por. Blazers, 1976–77	1687
1716	N.Y. Nets[a], 1973–74	1506	1577	Was. Bullets, 1977–78	1646
1716	G.S. Warriors, 1974–75*	1627	1537	L.A. Lakers, 1979–80	1553
1708	Phi. 76ers, 1979–80	1553	1529	Bos. Celtics, 1980–81	1537
1694	Mil. Bucks, 1973–74	1706	1524	L.A. Lakers, 1984–85	1465

[a] ABA

* Team won championship.

** Average includes 7 of 9 ABA teams, as Uta. Stars (16) and S.D. Sails (11) played less than 20 games for 1975–76 season.

Teams Winning NBA Finals in First Year in New Arena

Team	Arena	Opponent	Series
Uta. Stars[a]*	Salt Palace, 1970–71	Ken. Colonels[a]	4 games to 3
Sea. Sonics	Kingdome, 1978–79	Was. Bullets	4 games to 1
Det. Pistons	The Palace of Auburn Hills, 1988–89	L.A. Lakers	4 games to 0
L.A. Lakers	STAPLES Center, 1999–00	Ind. Pacers	4 games to 2
S.A. Spurs	SBC Center, 2002–03	N.J. Nets	4 games to 2

[a] ABA.

* Previous season spent as the L.A. Stars.

First Players Elected to Hall of Fame from Each Position*

Point Guard .... Andy Phillip, 1961

Shooting Guard .... Bill Sharman/Tom Gola, 1976

Small Forward .... Elgin Baylor/Jim Pollard/
Cliff Hagan/Paul Arizin, 1977

Power Forward .... Bob Pettit, 1971

Center .... George Mikan, 1959

* Played professionally in BAA/NBA.

Elected to HOF in Multiple Capacities

Charles Barkley .... Player (2006)
Team** (2010)

Walt Bellamy .... Player (1993)
Team* (2010)

Larry Bird .... Player (1998)
Team** (2010)

Chuck Daly .... Coach (1994)
Team** (2010)

Clyde Drexler .... Player (2004)
Team** (2010)

Patrick Ewing .... Player (2008)
Team** (2010)

Don Haskins .... Coach (1997)
Team*** (2007)

Tom Heinsohn .... Player (1986)
Coach (2015)

Magic Johnson .... Player (2002)
Team** (2010)

Michael Jordan .... Player (2009)
Team** (2010)

Mike Krzyzewski .... Coach (2001)
Team** (2010)

Arthur Lonborg .... Coach (1973)
Team* (2010)

Jerry Lucas .... Player (1980)
Team* (2010)

Karl Malone .... Player (2010)
Team** (2010)

John McLendon .... Contributor (1979)
Coach (2016)

Chris Mullin .... Player (2011)
Team** (2010)

Pete Newell .... Coach (1979)
Team* (2010)

Scottie Pippen .... Player (2010)
Team** (2010)

Oscar Robertson .... Player (1980)
Team* (2010)

David Robinson .... Player (2009)
Team** (2010)

Bill Sharman .... Player (1976)
Coach (2004)

John Stockton .... Player (2009)
Team** (2010)

Jerry West .... Player (1980)
Team* (2010)

Lenny Wilkens .... Player (1989)
Coach (1998)
Team** (2010)

John Wooden .... Player (1960)
Coach (1973)

* Member of the 1960 USA Men's Olympic team, elected to the HOF in 2010.
** Member of the 1992 USA Men's Olympic team, elected to the HOF in 2010.
*** Member of the 1966 Texas Western team, elected to the HOF in 2007.

Hall of Famers Who Played in the ABA

Rick Barry .... Oak. Oaks (1968–69); Was. Capitols (1969–70); N.Y. Nets (1970–72)

Zelmo Beaty .... Uta.-L.A. Stars (1970–74)

Larry Brown* .... N.O. Buccaneers (1967–68); Oak. Oaks-Was. Capitols (1968–70); Vir. Squires (1970–71); Den. Rockets (1971–72)

Roger Brown .... Ind. Pacers (1967–74; 1975); Mem. Sounds/Uta. Stars (1974–75)

Billy Cunningham .... Car. Cougars (1972–74)

Louie Dampier .... Ken. Colonels (1967–76)

Mel Daniels .... Min. Muskies (1967–68); Ind. Pacers (1968–74); Mem. Sounds (1974–75)

Julius Erving .... Vir. Squires (1971–73); N.Y. Nets (1973–76)

George Gervin .... Vir. Squires (1972–74); S.A. Spurs (1974–76)

Artis Gilmore .... Ken. Colonels (1971–76)

Cliff Hagan .... Dal. Chaparrals (1967–70)

Connie Hawkins .... Pit.-Min. Pipers (1967–69)

Spencer Haywood ..... Den. Rockets (1969–70)

continued on next page

Dan Issel..................Ken. Colonels (1970–75); Den. Nuggets (1975–76)
Gus Johnson..............Ind. Pacers (1972–73)
Bobby Jones..............Den. Nuggets (1974–76)
Moses Malone..........Uta. Stars (1974–75); Spirits of St.L. (1975–76)
George McGuinnis ....Ind. Pacers (1971–75)
Charlie Scott ....Vir. Squires (1970–72)
David Thompson........Den. Nuggets (1975–76)
* Inducted to HOF as Coach (2002).

Hall of Famers Who Did Not Play College Basketball

	Draft Year	High School/Country
Kevin Garnett	1995	Mauldin HS (SC), Farragut Career Academy (IL)
Kobe Bryant	1996	Lower Merion (PA)
Tracy McGrady	1997	Auburndale (FL), Mount Zion Christian Academy (NC)
Vlade Divac	1989	Serbia
Yao Ming	2002	China
Arvydas Sabonis	1985, 1986	Lithuania
Dražen Petrović	1986	Croatia
Šarūnas Marčiulionis	1987	Lithuania
Dino Radja	1989	Croatia

Hall of Famers Who Were Drafted #1 Overall

Draft Year		Drafting Team	College/Country
1958	Elgin Baylor	Min. Lakers	Seattle University
1960	Oscar Robertson	Cin. Royals	Cincinnati
1961	Walt Bellamy	Chi. Packers	Indiana
1968	Elvin Hayes	S.D. Rockets	Houston
1969	Kareem Abdul-Jabbar	Mil. Bucks	UCLA
1970	Bob Lanier	Det. Pistons	St. Bonaventure
1974	Bill Walton	Por. Blazers	UCLA
1975	David Thompson*	Atl. Hawks	NC State
1979	Magic Johnson	L.A. Lakers	Michigan State
1982	James Worthy	L.A. Lakers	UNC
1983	Ralph Sampson	Hou. Rockets	Virginia
1984	Hakeem Olajuwon	Hou. Rockets	Houston
1985	Patrick Ewing	N.Y. Knicks	Georgetown
1987	David Robinson	S.A. Spurs	United States Naval Academy
1992	Shaquille O'Neal	Orl. Magic	LSU
1996	Allen Iverson	Phi. 76ers	Georgetown
1997	Tim Duncan	S.A. Spurs	Wake Forest
2002	Yao Ming	Hou. Rockets	China

* Played first professional season in ABA.

Hall of Famers Drafted in the Second Round or Later*

Draft Year		Drafting Team	Round/Pick
1947	Harry Gallatin	Bal. Bullets	4/40
1947	Andy Phillip	Chi. Stags	5/47
1947	Jim Pollard	Chi. Stags	7/62
1948	Harry Gallatin	N.Y. Knicks	2/NA**
1949	Harry Gallatin	N.Y. Knicks	2/20

continued on next page

Draft Year		Drafting Team	Round/Pick
1949	Slater Martin	Min. Lakers	3/NA**
1950	Chuck Cooper	Bos. Celtics	2/13
1950	Bill Sharman	Was. Capitols	2/17
1953	Cliff Hagan	Bos. Celtics	3/21
1954	Richie Guerin	N.Y. Knicks	2/17
1955	Jack Twyman	Roc. Royals	2/10
1955	K.C. Jones	Min. Lakers	11/85
1956	K.C. Jones	Bos. Celtics	2/14
1956	Sam Jones	Min. Lakers	8/59
1956	Elgin Baylor	Min. Lakers	14/91
1958	Hal Greer	Syr. Nationals	2/14
1962	Chet Walker	Syr. Nationals	2/14
1963	Gus Johnson	Bal. Bullets	2/11
1964	Willis Reed	N.Y. Knicks	2/10
1967	Louie Dampier	Cin. Royals	4/38
1969	Bob Dandridge	Mil. Bucks	4/45
1970	Calvin Murphy	S.D. Rockets	2/18
1970	Tiny Archibald	Cin. Royals	2/19
1970	Charlie Scott	Bos. Celtics	7/106
1970	Dan Issel	Det. Pistons	8/122
1971	Spencer Haywood	Buf. Braves	2/30
1971	Artis Gilmore	Chi. Bulls	7/117
1973	George McGinnis	Phi. 76ers	2/22
1974	George Gervin	Pho. Suns	3/40
1976	Alex English	Mil. Bucks	2/23
1976	Dennis Johnson	Sea. Sonics	2/29
1977	Lusia Harris***	N.O. Jazz	7/137
1978	Maurice Cheeks	Phi. 76ers	2/36
1985	Arvydas Sabonis	Atl. Hawks	4/77
1986	Dennis Rodman	Det. Pistons	2/27
1986	Dražen Petrović	Por. Blazers	3/60
1987	Šarūnas Marčiulionis	G.S. Warriors	6/127
1989	Dino Radja	Bos. Celtics	2/40
1990	Toni Kukoč	Chi. Bulls	2/29
1999	Manu Ginóbili	S.A. Spurs	2/57

* Elected to Hall of Fame as a Player.

** Exact pick unavailable.

*** Only woman drafted in NBA history.

Teams with Most HOFers

37	Celtics	20	Wizards-Packers-Zephyrs-Bullets	11	Bulls
28	Lakers	20	Warriors	11	Nuggets-Rockets
23	Hawks	19	Kings-Royals	11	Spurs-Chaparrals
23	Knicks	16	Bucks	11	Suns
22	Pistons	13	Nets-Americans	10	Thunder-SuperSonics
21	76ers-Nationals	12	Rockets		

Winning Rookie of the Year, Elected to Hall of Fame

ROY		Inducted to HOF
1950–51	Paul Arizin, Phi. Warriors	1978
1954–55	Bob Pettit, Mil. Hawks	1971

continued on next page

ROY		Inducted to HOF
1955–56	Maurice Stokes, Roc. Royals	2004
1956–57	Tom Heinsohn, Bos. Celtics	1986*
1958–59	Elgin Baylor, Min. Lakers	1977
1959–60	Wilt Chamberlain, Phi. Warriors	1979
1960–61	Oscar Robertson, Cin. Royals	1980
1961–62	Walt Bellamy, Chi. Packers	1993
1963–64	Jerry Lucas, Cin. Royals	1980
1964–65	Willis Reed, N.Y. Knicks	1982
1965–66	Rick Barry, S.F. Warriors	1987
1966–67	Dave Bing, Det. Pistons	1990
1967–68	Earl Monroe, Bal. Bullets	1990
1967–68	Mel Daniels, Min. Muskies[a]	2012
1968–69	Wes Unseld, Bal. Bullets	1988
1969–70	Kareem Abdul-Jabbar, Mil. Bucks	1995
1969–70	Spencer Haywood, Den. Rockets[a]	2015
1970–71	Dave Cowens, Bos. Celtics	1991
1970–71	Dan Issel, Ken. Colonels[a]	1993
1970–71	Charlie Scott, Vir. Squires[a]	2018
1971–72	Artis Gilmore, Ken. Colonels[a]	2011
1972–73	Bob McAdoo, Buf. Braves	2000
1974–75	Jamaal Wilkes, G.S. Warriors	2012
1975–76	David Thompson, Den. Nuggets[a]	1996
1976–77	Adrian Dantley, Buf. Braves	2008
1979–80	Larry Bird, Bos. Celtics	1998
1983–84	Ralph Sampson, Hou. Rockets	2012
1984–85	Michael Jordan, Chi. Bulls	2009
1985–86	Patrick Ewing, N.Y. Knicks	2008
1988–89	Mitch Richmond, G.S. Warriors	2014
1989–90	David Robinson, S.A. Spurs	2009
1992–93	Shaquille O'Neal, Orl. Magic	2016
1993–94	Chris Webber, G.S. Warriors	2021
1994–95	Grant Hill, Det. Pistons	2018
1994–95	Jason Kidd, Dal. Mavericks	2018
1996–97	Allen Iverson, Phi. 76ers	2016
1997–98	Tim Duncan, S.A. Spurs	2020

* Inducted to HOF as a Coach in 2015.

[a] ABA.

Offensive Marks for Hall of Famers (Includes ABA)

Most Points		Fewest Points	
38,387......Kareem Abdul-Jabbar	25,279 .....Rick Barry	997 .... Buddy Jeannette	6594 .....Bob Davies
36,928......Karl Malone	25,279 .....Reggie Miller	1591.... Al Cervi	6683 .....Dennis Rodman
33,643......Kobe Bryant	25,192 .....Jerry West	2611.... Bob Houbregs	6924 .....Bobby Wanzer
32,292......Michael Jordan	24,941 .....Artis Gilmore	2725.... Chuck Cooper	7039 .....Ralph Sampson
31,419......Wilt Chamberlain	24,815 .....Patrick Ewing	3315.... Maurice Stokes	7337 .....Slater Martin
30,026......Julius Erving	24,505 .....Ray Allen	3733.... Dino Radja	7633 .....Arnie Risen
29,580......Moses Malone	24,368 .....Allen Iverson	4461.... Dražen Petrović	7871 .....Tom Gola
28,596......Shaquille O'Neal	23,757 ....Charles Barkley	4631.... Šarūnas Marčiulionis	8003 .....Joe Fulks
27,482......Dan Issel	23,334 .....Robert Parish	5011.... K.C. Jones	8378 .....Frank Ramsey
27,313......Elvin Hayes	23,177 .....Adrian Dantley	5629.... Arvydas Sabonis	8843 .....Harry Gallatin
26,946......Hakeem Olajuwon	23,149 .....Elgin Baylor	5762.... Jim Pollard	9063 .....George Yardley

continued on next page

Most Points

26,710 .... Oscar Robertson	22,195 .... Clyde Drexler
26,668 .... Dominique Wilkins	21,813 .... Gary Payton
26,595 .... George Gervin	21,791 .... Larry Bird
26,496 .... Tim Duncan	21,586 .... Hal Greer
26,397 .... Paul Pierce	20,941 .... Walt Bellamy
26,395 .... John Havlicek	20,880 .... Bob Pettit
26,071 .... Kevin Garnet	20,790 .... David Robinson
25,613 .... Alex English	20,497 .... Mitch Richmond

Fewest Points

5921 .... Dick McGuire
6215 .... Bill Walton
6254 .... Ben Wallace
6384 .... Andy Phillip
9217 .... Bill Bradley
9247 .... Yao Ming
9810 .... Toni Kukoč

Highest PPG

30.1 ...... Wilt Chamberlain	24.6 ...... Kareem Abdul-Jabbar
30.1 ...... Michael Jordan	24.3 ...... Larry Bird
27.4 ...... Elgin Baylor	24.3 ...... Adrian Dantley
27.0 ...... Jerry West	24.2 ...... Julius Erving
26.7 ...... Allen Iverson	24.2 ...... Pete Maravich
26.4 ...... Bob Pettit	23.7 ...... Shaquille O'Neal
25.7 ...... Oscar Robertson	23.1 ...... George Mikan
25.1 ...... George Gervin	22.8 ...... Paul Arizin
25.0 ...... Kobe Bryant	22.7 ...... David Thompson
25.0 ...... Karl Malone	22.6 ...... Dan Issel
24.8 ...... Rick Barry	22.5 ...... Bernard King
24.8 ...... Dominique Wilkins	

Lowest PPG

5.7 .... Ben Wallace
6.7 .... Chuck Cooper
7.2 .... Buddy Jeannette
7.3 .... Dennis Rodman
7.4 .... K.C. Jones
7.9 .... Al Cervi
8.0 .... Dick McGuire
9.1 .... Andy Phillip
9.3 .... Bob Houbregs
9.8 .... Slater Martin
9.8 .... Dikembe Mutombo
10.8 .... Wes Unseld

Highest FG%

.582 ...... Shaquille O'Neal	.516 .... Karl Malone
.582 ...... Artis Gilmore	.516 .... Walt Bellamy
.560 ...... Bobby Jones	.515 .... John Stockton
.559 ...... Kareem Abdul-Jabbar	.514 .... Bob Lanier
.554 ...... Kevin McHale	.512 .... Hakeem Olajuwon
.541 ...... Charles Barkley	.509 .... Chris Mullin
.540 ...... Adrian Dantley	.509 .... Wes Unseld
.540 ...... Wilt Chamberlain	.507 .... Alex English
.537 ...... Robert Parish	.506 .... Dražen Petrović
.527 ...... Alonzo Mourning	.506 .... Tim Duncan
.524 ...... Yao Ming	.506 .... Julius Erving
.523 ...... Maurice Cheeks	.505 .... David Thompson
.521 ...... Dennis Rodman	.505 .... Šarūnas Marčiulionis
.521 ...... James Worthy	.504 .... Patrick Ewing
.521 ...... Bill Walton	.504 .... George Gervin
.520 ...... Magic Johnson	.504 .... Paul Westphal
.518 ...... Bernard King	.503 .... Bob McAdoo
.518 ...... Dikembe Mutombo	.502 .... Sidney Moncrief
.518 ...... David Robinson	.500 .... Arvydas Sabonis

Lowest FG%

.302 ..... Joe Fulks	.389 .... Dick McGuire
.339 ..... Chuck Cooper	.393 .... Bobby Wanzer
.341 ..... Buddy Jeannette	.398 .... Harry Gallatin
.351 ..... Maurice Stokes	.399 .... Frank Ramsey
.359 ..... Al Cervi	.400 .... Jason Kidd
.360 ..... Jim Pollard	.403 .... Vern Mikkelsen
.364 ..... Slater Martin	.404 .... Bob Houbregs
.368 ..... Andy Phillip	.404 .... George Mikan
.375 ..... Bob Cousy	.405 .... Tom Heinsohn
.378 ..... Bob Davies	.416 .... Richie Guerin
.378 ..... Guy Rodgers	.421 .... Nate Thurmond
.380 ..... Dolph Schayes	.421 .... Paul Arizin
.381 ..... Arnie Risen	.422 .... George Yardley
.383 ..... Carl Braun	.425 .... Allen Iverson
.387 ..... K.C. Jones	

continued on next page

Highest FT%

.904	Steve Nash	.832	Alex English
.900	Rick Barry	.831	Sidney Moncrief
.894	Ray Allen	.826	John Stockton
.892	Calvin Murphy	.820	Pete Maravich
.888	Reggie Miller	.820	Paul Westphal
.886	Larry Bird	.818	Adrian Dantley
.883	Bill Sharman	.815	John Havlicek
.865	Chris Mullin	.814	Jerry West
.850	Mitch Richmond	.811	Dominique Wilkins
.849	Dolph Schayes	.810	Tiny Archibald
.849	Jack Sikma	.810	Paul Arizin
.848	Magic Johnson	.807	Gail Goodrich
.844	George Gervin	.807	Earl Monroe
.843	Joe Dumars	.806	Paul Pierce
.841	Dražen Petrović	.804	Carl Braun
.840	Bill Bradley	.804	Frank Ramsey
.839	Al Cervi	.803	Bob Cousy
.838	Oscar Robertson	.803	Sam Jones
.837	Kobe Bryant	.802	Bobby Wanzer
.835	Michael Jordan	.801	Hal Greer
.834	Jo Jo White	.800	Spencer Haywood
.833	Yao Ming		

Lowest FT%

.414	Ben Wallace	.660	Don Barksdale
.511	Wilt Chamberlain	.661	Ralph Sampson
.527	Shaquille O'Neal	.667	Nate Thurmond
.561	Bill Russell	.670	Elvin Hayes
.565	Mel Daniels	.684	Dikembe Mutombo
.584	Dennis Rodman	.692	Alonzo Mourning
.595	John Thompson	.692	Vlade Divac
.632	Walt Bellamy	.695	Andy Phillip
.633	Wes Unseld	.696	Tim Duncan
.644	Dick McGuire	.698	Maurice Stokes
.647	K.C. Jones	.699	Gus Johnson
.649	Chris Webber	.699	Arnie Risen
.651	George McGinnis	.699	Dave DeBusschere
.660	Bill Walton		

Most 3P

2973	Ray Allen	990	Joe Dumars
2560	Reggie Miller	978	Scottie Pippen
2143	Paul Pierce	845	John Stockton
1988	Jason Kidd	827	Clyde Drexler
1827	Kobe Bryant	815	Chris Mullin
1685	Steve Nash	794	Louie Dampier
1542	Tim Hardaway	731	Toni Kukoč
1495	Manu Ginóbili	711	Dominique Wilkins
1326	Mitch Richmond	649	Larry Bird
1132	Gary Payton	581	Michael Jordan
1081	Tracy McGrady	538	Charles Barkley
1059	Allen Iverson		

Fewest 3P

0	Bobby Jones	7	Ben Wallace
0	Dikembe Mutombo	7	Jamaal Wilkes
0	Robert Parish	8	Moses Malone
0	Dino Radja	10	Ralph Sampson
0	Bill Walton	18	Alex English
1	Dave Cowens	19	Patrick Ewing
1	Spencer Haywood	22	Alonzo Mourning
1	Shaquille O'Neal	23	Bernard King
1	Jo Jo White	25	Hakeem Olajuwon
2	Bob Dandridge	25	David Robinson
2	Bob Lanier	29	Dan Issel
2	Yao Ming	30	Tim Duncan
3	Mel Daniels	41	Kevin McHale
3	Artis Gilmore	47	Charlie Scott
3	Wes Unseld		

Highest 3P% (Min. 100 3P Attempts)

.437	Dražen Petrović	.338	Tracy McGrady
.428	Steve Nash	.335	Chris Bosh
.400	Ray Allen	.335	Toni Kukoč
.395	Reggie Miller	.329	Kobe Bryant
.388	Mitch Richmond	.328	Jack Sikma
.384	Chris Mullin	.328	Arvydas Sabonis
.384	John Stockton	.327	Michael Jordan
.382	Joe Dumars	.326	Scottie Pippen

Lowest 3P% (Min. 100 3P Attempts)

.152	Patrick Ewing	.261	Kevin McHale
.172	Bernard King	.266	Charles Barkley
.172	Dennis Johnson	.271	George Gervin
.179	Tim Duncan	.273	George McGinnis
.202	Hakeem Olajuwon	.274	Karl Malone
.204	Dan Issel	.275	Paul Westphal
.231	Dennis Rodman	.275	Kevin Garnett
.235	Vlade Divac	.284	Sidney Moncrief

continued on next page

.376 Larry Bird	.321 Roger Brown	.241 James Worthy	.290 Isiah Thomas
.369 Šarūnas Marčiulionis	.319 Dominique Wilkins	.250 David Robinson	.297 Rick Barry
.369 Manu Ginóbili	.318 Clyde Drexler	.253 Charlie Scott	.298 Julius Erving
.368 Paul Pierce	.317 Gary Payton	.255 Maurice Cheeks	.299 Chris Webber
.358 Louie Dampier	.314 Grant Hill	.255 David Thompson	
.355 Tim Hardaway	.313 Allen Iverson		
.349 Jason Kidd	.303 Magic Johnson		

Most Assists

15,806	John Stockton	6238	Jerry West
12,091	Jason Kidd	6135	Scottie Pippen
10,335	Steve Nash	6125	Clyde Drexler
10,141	Magic Johnson	6114	John Havlicek
9887	Oscar Robertson	5695	Larry Bird
9061	Isiah Thomas	5660	Kareem Abdul-Jabbar
8966	Gary Payton	5633	Michael Jordan
7392	Maurice Cheeks	5624	Allen Iverson
7211	Lenny Wilkens	5499	Dennis Johnson
7095	Tim Hardaway	5445	Kevin Garnett
6955	Bob Cousy	5397	Dave Bing
6917	Guy Rodgers	5248	Karl Malone
6476	Tiny Archibald	5176	Julius Erving
6306	Kobe Bryant	5040	Walt Frazier

Fewest Assists

287	Buddy Jeannette	807	Šarūnas Marčiulionis
356	Dino Radja	815	George Yardley
500	Bob Houbregs	946	Alonzo Mourning
587	Joe Fulks	964	Arvydas Sabonis
648	Al Cervi	1026	Tom Sanders
701	Dražen Petrović	1038	Ralph Sampson
734	Chuck Cooper	1058	Arnie Risen
769	Yao Ming	1062	Maurice Stokes
795	George Karl	1097	Clyde Lovellette

Highest APG

11.0	Magic Johnson	6.3	Larry Bird
11.0	John Stockton	6.2	Allen Iverson
10.0	Oscar Robertson	6.1	Walt Frazier
9.0	Isiah Thomas	6.0	Dave Bing
8.7	Jason Kidd	5.7	Dick McGuire
8.5	Steve Nash	5.6	Clyde Drexler
8.2	Tim Hardaway	5.4	Pete Maravich
7.8	Guy Rodgers	5.4	Andy Phillip
7.5	Bob Cousy	5.3	Maurice Stokes
7.4	Tiny Archibald	5.3	Michael Jordan
6.7	Gary Payton	5.2	Scottie Pippen
6.7	Maurice Cheeks	5.0	Richie Guerin
6.7	Lenny Wilkens	5.0	Dennis Johnson
6.7	Jerry West		

Lowest APG

1.0	Dikembe Mutombo	1.7	Arnie Risen
1.1	Phil Jackson	1.7	Kevin McHale
1.1	Tom Sanders	1.7	George Yardley
1.1	Alonzo Mourning	1.8	Dennis Rodman
1.2	Joe Fulks	1.8	Harry Gallatin
1.3	Ben Wallace	1.8	Bob Houbregs
1.3	Moses Malone	1.8	Mel Daniels
1.4	Robert Parish	1.8	Chuck Cooper
1.4	Wayne Embry	1.8	Frank Ramsey
1.5	Zelmo Beaty	1.8	Willis Reed
1.6	Clyde Lovellette	1.8	Spencer Haywood
1.6	Yao Ming	1.8	Elvin Hayes
1.6	Dino Radja	1.9	Patrick Ewing

Defensive Marks for Hall of Famers[*]

Most Rebounds

23,924	Wilt Chamberlain	12,942	Jerry Lucas
21,620	Bill Russell	12,849	Bob Pettit
17,834	Moses Malone	12,546	Charles Barkley
17,440	Kareem Abdul-Jabbar	12,359	Dikembe Mutombo
16,330	Artis Gilmore	11,954	Dennis Rodman
16,279	Elvin Hayes	11,607	Patrick Ewing
15,091	Tim Duncan	11,463	Elgin Baylor
14,968	Karl Malone	11,256	Dolph Schayes
14,715	Robert Parish	11,133	Dan Issel

Fewest Rebounds

669	Dražen Petrović	2354	Bill Bradley
819	Šarūnas Marčiulionis	2395	Andy Phillip
980	Bob Davies	2399	K.C. Jones
1552	Bob Houbregs	2431	Chuck Cooper
1580	Paul Westphal	2446	David Thompson
1883	Dino Radja	2543	Louie Dampier
1979	Bobby Wanzer	2747	Pete Maravich
2046	Tiny Archibald	2784	Dick McGuire
2103	Calvin Murphy	2793	Bill Sharman

continued on next page

14,662.... Kevin Garnett	10,816 ..... Jack Sikma	2122 .... Carl Braun	2796 .... Earl Monroe
14,464.... Nate Thurmond	10,525 ..... Julius Erving	2203 .... Joe Dumars	2846 .... Charlie Scott
14,241.... Walt Bellamy	10,497 ..... David Robinson	2302 .... Slater Martin	2855 .... Tim Hardaway
13,769.... Wes Unseld	10,482 ..... Ben Wallace		
13,748.... Hakeem Olajuwon	10,444 ..... Dave Cowens		
13,099.... Shaquille O'Neal			

Highest RPG

23.0........ Wilt Chamberlain	11.3.........Neil Johnston
23.0........ Bill Russell	11.3.........Dolph Schayes
17.0........ Maurice Stokes	11.2.........Kareem Abdul-Jabbar
16.0........ Bob Pettit	11.1.........Hakeem Olajuwon
15.6........ Jerry Lucas	11.0.........Dave DeBusschere
15.0........ Nate Thurmond	11.0.........George McGinnis
14.9........ Mel Daniels	10.9.........Zelmo Beaty
14.0........ Wes Unseld	10.9.........Shaquille O'Neal
13.7........ Walt Bellamy	10.8.........Tim Duncan
13.6........ Dave Cowens	10.6.........David Robinson
13.5........ Elgin Baylor	10.5.........Bill Walton
13.1........ Dennis Rodman	10.4.........Billy Cunningham
12.9........ Willis Reed	10.3.........Spencer Haywood
12.5........ Elvin Hayes	10.3.........Dikembe Mutombo
12.3........ Artis Gilmore	10.1.........Bob Lanier
12.3........ Moses Malone	10.1.........Karl Malone
12.1........ Gus Johnson	10.0.........Larry Bird
11.7........ Charles Barkley	10.0.........Kevin Garnett

Lowest RPG

1.3............... Al Cervi
1.9............... Paul Westphal
2.1............... Calvin Murphy
2.1............... Bob Davies
2.2............... Joe Dumars
2.3............... Šarūnas Marčiulionis
2.3............... Dražen Petrović
2.3............... Tiny Archibald
2.6............... Louie Dampier
2.7............... Carl Braun
2.7............... John Stockton
2.8............... Maurice Cheeks
2.8............... Joe Fulks
3.0............... Earl Monroe
3.0............... Reggie Miller
3.0............... Steve Nash

Most Steals

3265....... John Stockton	1983........ Allen Iverson
2684....... Jason Kidd	1944........ Kobe Bryant
2514....... Michael Jordan	1861........ Isiah Thomas
2445....... Gary Payton	1859........ Kevin Garnett
2310....... Maurice Cheeks	1752........ Paul Pierce
2307....... Scottie Pippen	1724........ Magic Johnson
2272....... Julius Erving	1648........ Charles Barkley
2207....... Clyde Drexler	1556........ Larry Bird
2162....... Hakeem Olajuwon	1530........ Chris Mullin
2085....... Karl Malone	1505........ Reggie Miller

Fewest Steals

52 ...... Walt Bellamy*	407 ...... Louie Dampier*
67 ...... Dave DeBusschere*	414 ...... Alonzo Mourning
125 ..... Nate Thurmond*	459 ...... Šarūnas Marčiulionis
189 ..... Yao Ming	483 ...... Dave Bing*
201 ..... Dino Radja	494 ...... Dikembe Mutombo
265 ..... Dražen Petrović	516 ...... Lou Hudson*
344 ..... Kevin McHale	545 ...... Gail Goodrich*
355 ..... Spencer Haywood*	587 ...... Pete Maravich*
370 ..... Arvydas Sabonis	595 ...... David Thompson
380 ..... Bill Walton	599 ...... Dave Cowens
390 ..... Ralph Sampson	

* Career began before steals were an official statistic.

Most Blocks

3830....... Hakeem Olajuwon	1889 .... Moses Malone
3289....... Dikembe Mutombo	1771 .... Elvin Hayes
3189....... Kareem Abdul-Jabbar	1690 .... Kevin McHale
3178....... Artis Gilmore	1631 .... Vlade Divac
3020....... Tim Duncan	1319 .... Bobby Jones
2954....... David Robinson	1200 .... Chris Webber
2894....... Patrick Ewing	1147 .... Bob McAdoo
2732....... Shaquille O'Neal	1145 .... Karl Malone
2361....... Robert Parish	1100 .... Bob Lanier
2356....... Alonzo Mourning	1048 ...... Jack Sikma
2137....... Ben Wallace	1047 .... George Gervin
2037....... Kevin Garnett	1034 .... Bill Walton
1941....... Julius Erving	

Fewest Blocks

27 .... Dražen Petrović	83 ...... Joe Dumars
31 .... Šarūnas Marčiulionis	89 ...... Dave Bing*
39 .... Dave DeBusschere*	98 ...... Lou Hudson*
48 .... Walt Bellamy*	102 ...... Steve Nash
51 .... Calvin Murphy*	108 ...... Pete Maravich*
63 .... Walt Frazier*	112 ...... Jo Jo White*
72 .... Gail Goodrich*	129 ..... Tim Hardaway
81 .... Tiny Archibald*	150 ...... Adrian Dantley

* Career began before blocks were an official statistic.

Additional Marks for Hall of Famers*

Most Games Played

1611	Robert Parish	1178	Scottie Pippen
1560	Kareem Abdul-Jabbar	1134	Vlade Divac
1504	John Stockton	1122	Hal Greer
1476	Karl Malone	1107	Jack Sikma
1462	Kevin Garnett	1101	Maurice Cheeks
1455	Moses Malone	1100	Dennis Johnson
1392	Tim Duncan	1088	Ben Wallace
1391	Jason Kidd	1086	Clyde Drexler
1389	Reggie Miller	1077	Lenny Wilkens
1346	Kobe Bryant	1074	Dominique Wilkins
1343	Paul Pierce	1073	Charles Barkley
1335	Gary Payton	1072	Michael Jordan
1329	Artis Gilmore	1060	George Gervin
1303	Elvin Hayes	1057	Manu Ginóbili
1300	Ray Allen	1045	Wilt Chamberlain
1270	John Havlicek	1043	Walt Bellamy
1243	Julius Erving	1040	Oscar Robertson
1238	Hakeem Olajuwon	1032	Chet Walker
1218	Dan Issel	1031	Gail Goodrich
1217	Steve Nash	1026	Grant Hill
1207	Shaquille O'Neal	1020	Rick Barry
1196	Dikembe Mutombo	1018	Joe Dumars
1193	Alex English	1002	Calvin Murphy
1183	Patrick Ewing		

Fewest Games Played

139	Buddy Jeannette
202	Al Cervi
202	Maurice Stokes
224	Dino Radja
281	Bob Houbregs
290	Dražen Petrović
363	Šarūnas Marčiulionis
409	Chuck Cooper
438	Jim Pollard
439	George Mikan
456	Ralph Sampson
462	Bob Davies
468	Bill Walton
470	Arvydas Sabonis
472	George Yardley
486	Yao Ming
489	Joe Fulks

Most Minutes Played

57,446	Kareem Abdul-Jabbar	46,471	John Havlicek
54,852	Karl Malone	46,344	Ray Allen
50,418	Kevin Garnett	45,880	Paul Pierce
50,111	Jason Kidd	45,704	Robert Parish
50,000	Elvin Hayes	45,227	Julius Erving
49,444	Moses Malone	44,222	Hakeem Olajuwon
48,637	Kobe Bryant	43,886	Oscar Robertson
47,859	Wilt Chamberlain	41,918	Shaquille O'Neal
47,764	John Stockton	41,784	Dan Issel
47,619	Reggie Miller	41,069	Scottie Pippen
47,368	Tim Duncan	41,011	Michael Jordan
47,134	Artis Gilmore	40,726	Bill Russell
47,117	Gary Payton	40,594	Patrick Ewing

Fewest Minutes Played

6725	Bob Houbregs	15,767	George Yardley
7308	Dino Radja	15,813	Harry Gallatin
7544	Maurice Stokes	15,818	Yao Ming
7669	Dražen Petrović	17,170	Dick McGuire
7964	Chuck Cooper	17,501	K.C. Jones
8123	Šarūnas Marčiulionis	18,071	Ed Macauley
11,375	Arvydas Sabonis	18,298	Neil Johnston
12,128	Bobby Wanzer	18,409	Carl Braun
12,690	Arnie Risen	18,443	Vern Mikkelsen
13,250	Bill Walton	19,075	Clyde Lovellette
13,591	Ralph Sampson	19,254	Tom Heinsohn
15,330	Frank Ramsey	19,406	David Thompson
15,378	Andy Phillip		

Highest Marks for Players Not in Hall of Fame (Includes ABA)

Points

31,560	Dirk Nowitzki**	19,591	Clifford Robinson	19,015	Reggie Theus
25,728	Vince Carter****	19,521	Walter Davis	19,004	Dale Ellis
23,165	Dwyane Wade**	19,473	Tony Parker**	18,881	Jason Terry*
20,894	Pau Gasol**	19,460	Terry Cummings	18,578	Zach Randolph*
20,049	Tom Chambers	19,419	Jamal Crawford***	18,458	Mark Aguirre
20,042	Antawn Jamison	19,202	Eddie Johnson	18,336	Glen Rice

* Hall of Fame Eligible in 2022.

** Hall of Eligible in 2023.

*** Hall of Fame Eligible in 2024.

continued on next page

Three Pointers

2450............... Kyle Korver***	1830............... Chauncey Billups	1590............... Mike Miller
2290............... Vince Carter***	1787............... Rashard Lewis	1559............... Glen Rice
2282............... Jason Terry*	1760............... Peja Stojaković	1546............... Eddie Jones
2221............... Jamal Crawford***	1719............... Dale Ellis	1528............... Nick Van Exel
1982............... Dirk Nowitzki**	1608............... Jason Richardson	1517............... Mike Bibby

* Hall of Fame Eligible in 2022.
** Hall of Fame Eligible in 2023.
*** Hall of Fame Eligible in 2024.

Free Throw Percentage (Min. 500 FT Attempts)

.905............. Mahmoud Abdul-Rauf........ 1051-for-1161	.875............. Ricky Pierce 3389-for-3871
.904............. Mark Price 2135-for-2362	.875............. Chris Whitney 732-for-837
.902............. Ernie DiGregorio 461-for-511	.873............. Terrell Brandon 1784-for-2043
.895............. Peja Stojaković................. 2237-for-2500	.873............. José Calderón 925-for-1060
.894............. Chauncey Billups 4496-for-5029	.873............. Kyle Macy 717-for-821
.892............. J.J. Redick 2060-for-2310	.872............. Kiki Vandeweghe............. 3484-for-3997
.889............. Scott Skiles...................... 1548-for-1741	.871............. Jeff Malone 2947-for-3383
.880............. Anthony Morrow 608-for-691	.871............. Mo Williams 1563-for-1795
.879............. Dirk Nowitzki 7240-for-8239	.871............. Darrell Armstrong 1463-for-1679
.877............. Jeff Hornacek 2973-for-3390	.870............. Kevin Martin 3561-for-4091
.877............. Kyle Korver 1297-for-1479	.870............. Hersey Hawkins................ 3466-for-3985
.876............. Earl Boykins 1255-for-1433	.870............. Mike Newlin 3005-for-3456

Assists

10,334............ Mark Jackson	6819............... Deron Williams	6454............... John Lucas
8524............. Andre Miller	6726............... Muggsy Bogues	6453............... Reggie Theus
7987............ Rod Strickland	6711............... Kevin Johnson	6386............... Norm Nixon
7160............ Terry Porter	6577............... Derek Harper	6025............... Baron Davis
7036............ Tony Parker*	6471............... Stephon Marbury	

* Hall of Fame Eligible in 2023.

Rebounds

13,017............ Buck Williams	10,482............. Ben Wallace	9687............... Sam Lacey
12,357............ Paul Silas	10,467............. Tyson Chandler***	9513............... Marcus Camby
12,205............ Charles Oakley	10,400............. Bill Laimbeer	9473............... A.C. Green
11,901............ Kevin Willis	10,370............. Otis Thorpe	9443............... Horace Grant
11,489............ Dirk Nowitzki**	10,208............. Zach Randolph*	9083............... Johnny Green
11,305............ Pau Gasol**	10,101............. Shawn Marion	9040............... Elton Brand
11,054............ Bill Bridges	10,092............. Red Kerr	8834............... Shawn Kemp

* Hall of Fame Eligible in 2022.
** Hall of Fame Eligible in 2023.
*** Hall of Fame Eligible in 2024.

Steals

2112............... Alvin Robertson	1716............... Ron Harper	1620............... Dwyane Wade**
2075............... Mookie Blaylock	1666............... Fat Lever	1616............... Rod Strickland
1957............... Derek Harper	1638............... Gus Williams	1608............... Mark Jackson
1759............... Shawn Marion	1622............... Hersey Hawkins	1603............... Jason Terry*
1721............... Metta World Peace	1620............... Eddie Jones	

* Hall of Fame Eligible in 2022.
** Hall of Fame Eligible in 2023.

continued on next page

Blocks

3064 .... Mark Eaton	2086 .... Manute Bol	1941 .... Pau Gasol*
2542 .... Tree Rollins	2082 .... George Johnson	1828 .... Elton Brand
2331 .... Marcus Camby	2027 .... Larry Nance	1820 .... Jermaine O'Neal
2119 .... Shawn Bradley	1968 .... Theo Ratliff	

* Hall of Fame Eligible in 2023.

Minutes Played

51,368 .... Dirk Nowitzki**	40,097 .... Shawn Marion	37,638 .... Antawn Jamison
46,367 .... Vince Carter	39,822 .... Otis Thorpe	36,654 .... Juwan Howard
45,880 .... Paul Pierce	39,121 .... Mark Jackson	36,598 .... Sam Perkins
42,561 .... Clifford Robinson	38,994 .... Jamal Crawford	36,552 .... A.C. Green
42,464 .... Buck Williams	38,621 .... Horace Grant	36,243 .... Rasheed Wallace
42,034 .... Jason Terry	38,362 .... Kevin Willis	35,773 .... Dwyane Wade
41,001 .... Pau Gasol	38,279 .... Tony Parker	35,354 .... Terry Porter
40,280 .... Charles Oakley	37,996 .... Michael Finley	35,270 .... Latrell Sprewell
40,268 .... Andre Miller	37,786 .... Derek Harper	

Games Played

1541 .... Vince Carter	1257 .... Otis Thorpe	1159 .... Johnny Newman
1522 .... Dirk Nowitzki	1254 .... Tony Parker	1156 .... Tree Rollins
1424 .... Kevin Willis	1254 .... Paul Silas	1153 .... Jerome Kersey
1410 .... Jason Terry	1232 .... Kyle Korver	1140 .... Michael Cage
1380 .... Clifford Robinson	1226 .... Pau Gasol	1138 .... Danny Schayes
1327 .... Jamal Crawford	1209 .... Dale Ellis	1136 .... Detlef Schrempf
1307 .... Buck Williams	1208 .... Juwan Howard	1124 .... Billy Paultz
1304 .... Andre Miller	1199 .... Derek Harper	1117 .... Rick Mahorn
1299 .... Caldwell Jones	1199 .... Eddie Johnson	1116 .... Zach Randolph
1296 .... Mark Jackson	1183 .... Terry Cummings	1110 .... Kurt Thomas
1287 .... Derek Fisher	1181 .... Richard Jefferson	1109 .... Rasheed Wallace
1286 .... Sam Perkins	1168 .... James Edwards	1107 .... Tom Chambers
1282 .... Charles Oakley	1165 .... Horace Grant	1107 .... Robert Horry
1278 .... A.C. Green	1163 .... Shawn Marion	1103 .... Michael Finley
1274 .... Terry Porter	1160 .... Tyson Chandler	1102 .... Herb Williams

Most Coaching Victories, Not in Hall of Fame*

1175 .... George Karl	667 .... Mike Fratello	557 .... Al Attles
935 .... Dick Motta	654 .... Flip Saunders	554 .... Stan Van Gundy
832 .... Cotton Fitzsimmons	642 .... Kevin Loughery	552 .... K.C. Jones
784 .... Gene Shue	628 .... Doug Moe	516 .... Terry Stotts
707 .... John MacLeod	613 .... Mike Dunleavy	

* Includes ABA.

Won-Lost Percentage of Hall of Famers Elected as Players Who Coached Professionally

		Teams Managed	Career W-L
.698	Billy Cunningham	Phi. 76ers, 1977–85	454–196
.687	Larry Bird	Ind. Pacers, 1997–2000	147–67
.667	Bob Pettit	St.L. Hawks, 1961–62	4–2
.650	Ed Macauley	St.L. Hawks, 1958–60	89–48

continued on next page

		Teams Managed	Career W-L
.643	K.C. Jones	S.D. Conquistadors[a], 1972–73	552–306
		Cap.-Was. Bullets, 1973–76	
		Bos. Celtics, 1983–88	
		Sea. Sonics, 1990–92	
.619	Tom Heinsohn*	Bos. Celtics, 1969–78	427–263
.617	Neil Johnston	Phi. Warriors, 1959–61	95–59
.600	Andy Phillip	St.L. Hawks, 1958–59	6–4
.597	Steve Nash^	Brk. Nets, 2020–22	92–62
.589	Jerry West	L.A. Lakers, 1976–79	145–101
.575	Al Cervi	Syr. Nationals, 1949–57	326–241
		Phi. Warriors, 1958–59	
.569	Bill Sharman*	S.F. Warriors, 1966–68	466–353
		L.A.-Uta. Stars[a], 1968–71	
		L.A. Lakers, 1971–76	
.569	Joe Lapchick	N.Y. Knicks, 1947–56	326–247
.556	Kevin McHale	Min. T'Wolves, 2004–05; 2008–09	232–185
		Hou. Rockets, 2011–16	
.548	Cliff Hagan	Dal. Chaparrals[a], 1967–70	109–90
.540	Bill Russell*	Bos. Celtics, 1966–69	341–290
		Sea. Sonics, 1973–77	
		Sac. Kings, 1987–88	
.536	Lenny Wilkens*	Sea. Sonics, 1969–72; 1977–85	1332–1155
		Por. Blazers, 1974–76	
		Cle. Cavaliers, 1986–93	
		Atl. Hawks, 1993–2000	
		Tor. Raptors, 2000–03	
		N.Y. Knicks, 2003–05	
.533	Paul Westphal	Pho. Suns, 1992–96	318–279
		Sea. Sonics, 1998–2001	
		Sac. Kings, 2009–12	
.531	Harry Gallatin	St.L. Hawks, 1962–65	136–120
		N.Y. Knicks, 1964–66	
.529	Richie Guerin	St.L.-Atl. Hawks, 1964–72	327–291
.516	Jason Kidd^	Brk. Nets, 2013–14	235–220
		Mil. Bucks, 2014–18	
		Dal. Mavericks, 2021–22	
.500	Vern Mikkelsen	Min. Pipers[a], 1968–69	6–6
.492	Maurice Cheeks	Por. Blazers, 2001–05	305–315
		Phi. 76ers, 2005–09	
.478	Frank Ramsey	Ken. Colonels[a], 1970–71	32–35
.467	Dolph Schayes	Phi. 76ers, 1963–66	151–172
		Buf. Braves, 1970–72	
.464	Dan Issel	Den. Nuggets, 1992–95; 1999–2002	180–208
.459	Dutch Dehnert	Cle. Rebels, 1946–47	17–20
.457	Dave Cowens	Bos. Celtics, 1978–79	161–191
		Cha. Hornets, 1996–99	
		G.S. Warriors, 2000–02	
.456	Isiah Thomas	Ind. Pacers, 2000–03	187–223
		N.Y. Knicks, 2006–08	
.441	Jim Pollard	Min. Lakers, 1959–60	130–165
		Chi. Packers, 1961–62	
		Min. Muskies-Mia. Floridians[a], 1967–70	

continued on next page

		Teams Managed	Career W-L
.440	Wilt Chamberlain	S.D. Conquistadors°, 1973–74	37–47
.430	Dick McGuire	Det. Pistons, 1959–63	197–261
		N.Y. Knicks, 1965–68	
.427	Buddy Jeannette	Bal. Bullets, 1947–51	151–203
		Bal. Bullets, 1964–65; 1966–67	
		Pit. Pipers°, 1969–70	
.419	Bobby Wanzer	Roc.-Cin. Royals, 1955–59	98–136
.405	Bob Cousy	Cin. Royals, 1969–72	141–207
		K.C.-Oma. Kings, 1972–74	
.398	Willis Reed	N.Y. Knicks, 1977–79	82–124
		N.J. Nets, 1987–89	
.389	Elgin Baylor	N.O. Jazz, 1974–75; 1976–79	86–135
.389	Honey Russell	Bos. Celtics, 1946–48	42–66
.378	Slater Martin	St.L. Hawks, 1956–57	37–61
		Hou. Mavericks°, 1967–69	
.369	Wes Unseld	Was. Bullets, 1987–94	202–345
.356	Dave DeBusschere	Det. Pistons, 1964–67	79–143
.324	Bob Lanier	G.S. Warriors, 1994–95	12–25
.333	Dennis Johnson	L.A. Clippers, 2002–03	8–16
.315	Carl Braun	N.Y. Knicks, 1959–61	40–87
.313	Magic Johnson	L.A. Lakers, 1993–94	5–11
.231	George Mikan	Min. Lakers, 1957–58	9–30
.000	Mel Daniels	Ind. Pacers, 1988–89	0–2

° Elected to Hall of Fame as both Player and Coach.

^ Active.

12

Team Won-Loss Percentage by Decade

1946–47–1949–50 (BAA/NBA)

Syr. Nationals	51–13 (.797)
Roc. Royals	96–32 (.750)
Min. Lakers	95–33 (.742)
Was. Capitols	147–89 (.623)
Chi. Stags	145–92 (.612)
Ind. Olympians	39–25 (.609)
And. Packers	37–27 (.578)
N.Y. Knicks	131–105 (.555)
St.L. Bombers	122–115 (.515)
Cle. Rebels	30–30 (.500)
Phi. Warriors	116–120 (.492)
Ft.W. Pistons	62–66 (.484)
Bal. Bullets	82–94 (.466)
T.C. Blackhawks	29–35 (.453)
Bos. Celtics	89–147 (.377)
Tor. Huskies	22–38 (.367)
She. Red Skins	22–40 (.355)
Det. Falcons	20–40 (.333)
Wat. Hawks	19–43 (.306)
Ind. Jets	18–42 (.300)
Pro. Steamrollers	46–122 (.274)
Pit. Ironmen	15–45 (.250)
Den. Nuggets	11–51 (.177)

1950–51–1959–60

Bos. Celtics	445–268 (.624)
Syr. Nationals	398–312 (.561)
N.Y. Knicks	375–334 (.529)
Min. Lakers	362–349 (.509)
Phi. Warriors	347–361 (.490)
Ft.W.-Det. Pistons	342–368 (.482)
Roc.-Cin. Royals	332–379 (.467)
Ind. Olympians	93–112 (.454)
T.C. Blackhawks-Mil.-St.L. Hawks	319–393 (.448)
Was. Capitols	10–25 (.286)
Bal. Bullets	76–198 (.277)

1960–61–1969–70

Bos. Celtics	546–260 (.677)
Syr. Nationals-Phi. 76ers	483–323 (.599)
L.A. Lakers	468–338 (.581)
St.L.-Atl. Hawks	446–360 (.553)
Cin. Royals	421–385 (.522)
Mil. Bucks	83–81 (.506)
Phi.-S.F. Warriors	384–422 (.476)
N.Y. Knicks	347–459 (.431)
Chi. Packers-Zephyrs-Bal. Bullets	312–415 (.429)
Chi. Bulls	134–193 (.410)
Det. Pistons	314–492 (.390)
Sea. Sonics	89–157 (.362)
Pho. Suns	55–109 (.335)
S.D. Rockets	79–167 (.321)

1970–71–1979–80

Eastern Conference

Bos. Celtics	504–316 (.615)
Mil. Bucks	485–335 (.591)
Bal.-Cap.-Was. Bullets	472–348 (.576)
N.Y. Knicks	437–383 (.533)
Chi. Bulls	429–391 (.523)
Phi. 76ers	402–418 (.490)
Atl. Hawks	381–439 (.465)
Det. Pistons	367–453 (.448)
Ind. Pacers*	142–186 (.433)
Cle. Cavaliers	341–479 (.416)
N.Y.-N.J. Nets*	117–211 (.357)

Western Conference

L.A. Lakers	499–321 (.609)
S.A. Spurs*	185–143 (.564)
S.F.-G.S. Warriors	441–379 (.538)
Denver Nuggets*	175–153 (.534)
Sea. Sonics	428–392 (.522)
Pho. Suns	427–393 (.521)
S.D.-Hou. Rockets	385–435 (.470)
Cin. Royals-K.C.-Oma-K.C. Kings	373–447 (.455)
Por. Blazers	360–460 (.439)
Buf. Braves**-S.D. Clippers	337–483 (.411)
N.O.-Uta. Jazz	185–307 (.376)

1967–68–1975–76

American Basketball Association (ABA)

Ken. Colonels	448–296 (.602)
Ind. Pacers	427–317 (.574)
Den. Rockets-Nuggets	413–331 (.555)
Ana. Amigos-L.A.-Uta. Stars	366–310 (.541)
Dal.-Tex Chaparrals-S.A. Spurs	378–366 (.508)
N.J. Americans-N.Y. Nets	374–370 (.503)
Mln. Muskies-Mia.-The Floridians	189–219 (.463)
Hou. Mavericks-Car. Cougars-Spirits of St.L.	334–410 (.449)
Pit.-Min. Pipers-Pit. Condors	180–228 (.441)
Oak. Oaks-Was. Capitols-Vir. Squires	326–417 (.439)
N.O. Buccaneers-Mem.Pros-Tams-Sounds	275–385 (.417)
S.D. Conquistadors-Sails	101–162 (.384)

* Joined the NBA, from the ABA, in 1976–77.

** Buf. Braves were in the Eastern Conference until moving to S.D. for the 1978–79 season.

continued on next page

1980-81—1989-90

Eastern Conference

Bos. Celtics .... 583–237 (.711)

Phi. 76ers .... 529–291 (.645)

Mil. Bucks .... 517–303 (.630)

Det. Pistons .... 466–354 (.568)

Atl. Hawks .... 440–380 (.537)

Chi. Bulls .... 394–426 (.480)

Was. Bullets .... 389–431 (.474)

N.Y. Knicks .... 380–440 (.463)

Cle. Cavaliers .... 331–489 (.404)

N.J. Nets .... 329–491 (.401)

Ind. Pacers .... 322–498 (.393)

Cha. Hornets .... 39–125 (.238)

Orl. Magic .... 18–64 (.220)

Mia. Heat .... 33–131 (.201)

Western Conference

L.A. Lakers .... 594–226 (.724)

Por. Blazers .... 463–357 (.565)

Den. Nuggets .... 443–377 (.540)

Pho. Suns .... 438–382 (.534)

Sea. Sonics .... 409–411 (.499)

Uta. Jazz .... 408–412 (.498)

Dal. Mavericks .... 405–415 (.494)

Hou. Rockets .... 402–418 (.490)

S.A. Spurs .... 402–418 (.490)

G.S. Warriors .... 345–475 (.421)

K.C.-Sac. Kings .... 324–496 (.395)

S.D.-L.A. Clippers .... 251–569 (.306)

Min. T'Wolves .... 22–60 (.268)

1990-91—1999-00

Eastern Conference

Chi. Bulls .... 520–268 (.660)

N.Y. Knicks .... 486–302 (.617)

Ind. Pacers .... 459–329 (.582)

Atl. Hawks .... 434–354 (.551)

Cle. Cavaliers .... 424–364 (.538)

Orl. Magic .... 420–368 (.533)

Mia. Heat .... 415–373 (.527)

Cha. Hornets .... 413–375 (.524)

Det. Pistons .... 394–394 (.500)

Bos. Celtics .... 360–428 (.457)

N.J. Nets .... 330–458 (.419)

Mil. Bucks .... 325–463 (.412)

Phi. 76ers .... 302–486 (.383)

Was. Bullets-Wizards .... 294–494 (.373)

Tor. Raptors .... 135–243 (.357)

Western Conference

Uta. Jazz .... 542–246 (.688)

Sea. Sonics .... 515–273 (.654)

Pho. Suns .... 502–286 (.637)

Por. Blazers .... 495–293 (.628)

S.A. Spurs .... 493–295 (.626)

L.A. Lakers .... 489–299 (.621)

Hou. Rockets .... 465–323 (.590)

G.S. Warriors .... 334–454 (.424)

Sac. Kings .... 317–471 (.402)

Min. T'Wolves .... 290–498 (.368)

Den. Nuggets .... 279–509 (.354)

L.A. Clippers .... 267–521 (.339)

Dal. Mavericks .... 239–549 (.303)

Van. Grizzlies .... 78–300 (.206)

2000-01—2009-10

Eastern Conference

Det. Pistons .... 482–338 (.588)

Bos. Celtics .... 445–375 (.543)

Orl. Magic .... 432–388 (.527)

Cle. Cavaliers .... 425–395 (.518)

Ind. Pacers .... 416–404 (.507)

Mia. Heat .... 413–407 (.504)

Phi. 76ers .... 404–416 (.493)

N.J. Nets .... 386–434 (.471)

Mil. Bucks .... 380–440 (.463)

Tor. Raptors .... 367–453 (.448)

Cha. Hornets/Cha. Bobcats* ...... 90–74 (.549)/188–304 (.382)

Chi. Bulls .... 341–479 (.416)

Was. Wizards .... 334–486 (.407)

Atl. Hawks .... 327–493 (.399)

N.Y. Knicks .... 327–493 (.399)

Western Conference

S.A. Spurs .... 573–247 (.699)

Dal. Mavericks .... 563–257 (.687)

L.A. Lakers .... 520–300 (.634)

Pho. Suns .... 492–328 (.600)

Uta. Jazz .... 459–361 (.560)

Hou. Rockets .... 448–372 (.546)

Sac. Kings .... 437–383 (.533)

Den. Nuggets .... 422–398 (.515)

Por. Blazers .... 415–405 (.506)

N.O.-N.O-Ok.C. Hornets .... 325–331 (.495)

Sea. Sonics-Ok.C. Thunder .... 377–443 (.460)

Min. T'Wolves .... 376–444 (.459)

G.S. Warriors .... 326–494 (.398)

Van.-Mem. Grizzlies .... 326–494 (.398)

L.A. Clippers .... 320–500 (.390)

* The Cha. Hornets moved to N.O. for the 2002–03 season. The expansion Cha. Bobcats began play for the 2004–05 season.

continued on next page

2010–11—2019–20

Eastern Conference		Western Conference	
Mia. Heat	477–318 (.600)	S.A. Spurs	541–252 (.682)
Bos. Celtics	454–339 (.573)	Ok.C. Thunder	509–285 (.641)
Tor. Raptors	453–341 (.571)	G.S. Warriors	494–293 (.628)
Ind. Pacers	450–344 (.567)	Hou. Rockets	490–304 (.617)
Chi. Bulls	409–378 (.520)	L.A. Clippers	484–310 (.610)
Mil. Bucks	395–400 (.497)	Por. Blazers	436–360 (.548)
Atl. Hawks	390–399 (.494)	Den. Nuggets	430–365 (.541)
Was. Wizards	352–442 (.443)	Van.-Mem. Grizzlies	422–373 (.531)
Cle. Cavaliers	346–441 (.440)	Uta. Jazz	414–380 (.521)
Phi. 76ers	331–464 (.416)	Dal. Mavericks	408–389 (.512)
Det. Pistons	326–462 (.414)	L.A. Lakers	358–435 (.451)
N.J.-Brk. Nets	323–471 (.407)	N.O. Hornets-Pelicans	348–446 (.438)
Cha. Hornets	320–467 (.407)	Pho. Suns	306–489 (.385)
Orl. Magic	321–474 (.404)	Min. T'Wolves	292–494 (.372)
N.Y. Knicks	316–472 (.401)	Sac. Kings	293–501 (.369)

2020–21—2021–22

Eastern Conference		Western Conference	
Phi. 76ers	100–54 (.649)	Pho. Suns	115–39 (.747)
Mil. Bucks	97–57 (.630)	Uta. Jazz	101–53 (.656)
Mia. Heat	93–61 (.604)	Den. Nuggets	95–59 (.617)
Brk. Nets	92–62 (.597)	Dal. Mavericks	94–60 (.610)
Bos. Celtics	87–67 (.565)	Mem. Grizzlies	94–60 (.610)
Atl. Hawks	84–70 (.545)	G.S. Warriors	92–62 (.597)
N.Y. Knicks	78–76 (.506)	L.A. Clippers	89–65 (.578)
Chi. Bulls	77–77 (.500)	L.A. Lakers	75–79 (.487)
Cha. Bobcats-Hornets	76–78 (.494)	Min. T'Wolves	69–85 (.448)
Tor. Raptors	75–79 (.487)	Por. Blazers	69–85 (.448)
Was. Wizards	69–85 (.448)	N.O. Pelicans	67–87 (.435)
Cle. Cavaliers	66–88 (.429)	S.A. Spurs	67–87 (.435)
Ind. Pacers	59–95 (.383)	Sac. Kings	61–93 (.396)
Det. Pistons	43–111 (.279)	Ok.C. Thunder	46–108 (.299)
Orl. Magic	43–111 (.279)	Hou. Rockets	37–117 (.240)

All-Time Regular-Season Record for Each Franchise

BAA/NBA

	Wins	Losses	W/L%
Spurs	2261	1442	.611
Lakers	3460	2380	.592
Celtics	3513	2437	.590
Jazz	2109	1759	.545
Suns	2335	2026	.535
Thunder-SuperSonics	2373	2069	.534
Trail Blazers	2238	1960	.533
Heat	1431	1290	.526
Bucks	2282	2079	.523
76ers-Nationals	3000	2777	.519

continued on next page

	Wins	Losses	W/L%
Rockets	2306	2136	.519
Bulls	2304	2212	.510
Mavericks	1709	1670	.506
Pacers	1848	1856	.499
Nuggets	1844	1861	.498
Hawks-Blackhawks	2850	2923	.494
Warriors	2879	3060	.485
Knicks	2877	3064	.484
Raptors	1030	1116	.480
Pistons	2796	3038	.479
Magic	1234	1405	.468
Cavaliers	1933	2256	.461
Pelicans-Hornets	740	864	.461
Kings-Royals	2654	3187	.454
Wizards-Bullets-Packers-Zephyrs	2222	2701	.451
Hornets-Bobcats	1126	1423	.442
Grizzlies	920	1227	.429
Nets	1577	2127	.426
Clippers-Braves	1748	2448	.417
Timberwolves	1049	1581	.399

ABA

	Wins	Losses	W/L%
Colonels	448	296	.602
Pacers	427	317	.574
Nuggets	413	331	.555
Stars-Amigos	366	310	.541
Spurs-Chaparrals	378	366	.508
Nets-Americans	374	370	.503
The Floridians-Muskies	189	219	.463
Spirits of St.L.-Mavericks-Cougars	334	410	.449
Condors-Pipers	180	228	.441
Squires-Oaks-Capitols	326	417	.439
Sounds-Buccaneers-Pros-Tams	275	385	.417
Sails-Conquistadors	101	162	.384

Team with Highest Winning Percentage, Season

.890 ... G.S. Warriors**, 2015–16 ... 73–9
.878 ... Chi. Bulls*, 1995–96 ... 72–10
.841 ... L.A. Lakers*, 1971–72 ... 69–13
.841 ... Chi. Bulls*, 1996–97 ... 69–13
.840 ... Phi. 76ers*, 1966–67 ... 68–13
.829 ... Bos. Celtics, 1972–73 ... 68–14
.817 ... Bos. Celtics*, 1985–86 ... 67–15
.817 ... Chi. Bulls*, 1991–92 ... 67–15
.817 ... L.A. Lakers*, 1999–00 ... 67–15
.817 ... Dal. Mavericks, 2006–07 ... 67–15
.817 ... G.S. Warriors*, 2014–15 ... 67–15
.817 ... S.A. Spurs, 2015–16 ... 67–15
.817 ... G.S. Warriors*, 2016–17 ... 67–15
.817 ... Was. Capitols, 1946–47 ... 49–11

Team with Lowest Winning Percentage, Season

.106 ... Cha. Bobcats, 2011–12 ... 7–59
.110 ... Phi. 76ers, 1972–73 ... 9–73
.122 ... Phi. 76ers, 2015–16 ... 10–72
.125 ... Pro. Steamrollers, 1947–48 ... 6–42
.134 ... Dal. Mavericks, 1992–93 ... 11–71
.134 ... Den. Nuggets, 1997–98 ... 11–71
.146 ... L.A. Clippers, 1986–87 ... 12–70
.146 ... N.J. Nets, 2009–10 ... 12–70
.159 ... Atl. Hawks, 2004–05 ... 13–69
.159 ... Dal. Mavericks, 1993–94 ... 13–69
.160 ... Van. Grizzlies, 1998–99 ... 8–42
.171 ... Hou. Rockets, 1982–83 ... 14–68
.171 ... Van. Grizzlies, 1996–97 ... 14–68
.174 ... Phi. Warriors, 1952–53 ... 12–57

continued on next page

.810........... Ken. Colonels[a], 1971–72 68–16
.805........... Mil. Bucks*, 1970–71 66–16
.805........... Bos. Celtics*, 2007–08.................66–16
.805........... Cle. Cavaliers, 2008–09...............66–16
.805........... Mia. Heat*, 2012–13 66–16
.797........... Syr. Nationals**, 1949–50...........51–13
.793........... Phi. 76ers*, 1982–83 65–17
.793........... L.A. Lakers*, 1986–87.................65–17
.793........... L.A. Lakers*, 2008–09.................65–17
.793........... Hou. Rockets, 2017–18................65–17
.787........... Bos. Celtics*, 1959–60.................59–16
.780........... Sea. Sonics**, 1995–96 64–18
.780........... Uta. Jazz**, 1996–97...................64–18
.780........... Det. Pistons, 2005–06..................64–18
.780........... Pho. Suns, 2021–22 64–18
.775........... Bos. Celtics*, 1964–65.................62–18

* Won NBA Finals.
** Lost NBA Finals.
[a] ABA.

.177 .... Den. Nuggets**, 1949–50...........11–51
.179 .... Vir. Squires[a], 1974–75 15–69
.180 .... L.A. Clippers, 1998–99 9–41
.181 .... Vir. Squires[a], 1975–76 15–68
.183 .... Bos. Celtics, 1996–97 15–67
.183 .... Chi. Bulls, 2000–01 15–67
.183 .... Cle. Cavaliers*, 1970–71 15–67
.183 .... Cle. Cavaliers, 1981–82 15–67
.183 .... Dal. Mavericks*, 1980–81 15–67
.183 .... L.A. Clippers, 1999–00 15–67
.183 .... Mia. Heat*, 1988–89 15–67
.183 .... Mia. Heat, 2007–08 15–67
.183 .... Mil. Bucks, 2013–14..................15–67
.183 .... Min. T'Wolves, 1991–92 15–67
.183 .... Min. T'Wolves, 2009–10 15–67
.183 .... S.D. Rockets*, 1967–68...............15–67
.183 .... Van. Grizzlies*, 1995–96 15–67
.195 .... Det. Pistons, 1979–80 16–66
.195 .... Min. T'Wolves, 2014–15 16–66
.195 .... Pho. Suns*, 1968–69..................16–66
.195 .... Tor. Raptors, 1997–98................16–66

* Inaugural season.
** Only season of existence.
[a] ABA.

Largest Increase in Games Won by Team, Following Season

Diff		Record (Season)	Record (Season)
+42	Bos. Celtics	66–16 (2007–08)	24–58 (2006–07)
+38	Oak. Oaks[a]	60–18 (1968–69)	22–56 (1967–68**)
+36	L.A. Lakers	67–15 (1999–00)	31–19 (1998–99*)
+36	S.A. Spurs	56–26 (1997–98)	20–62 (1996–97)
+35	S.A. Spurs	56–26 (1989–90)	21–61 (1988–89)
+33	Pho. Suns	62–20 (2004–05)	29–53 (2003–04)
+32	Bos. Celtics	61–21 (1979–80)	29–53 (1978–79)
+29	Mil. Bucks	56–26 (1969–70)	27–55 (1968–69**)
+28	Den. Nuggets-Rockets[a]	65–19 (1974–75)	37–47 (1973–74)
+28	Mia. Heat	43–39 (2008–09)	15–67 (2007–08)
+27	Brk.-N.J. Nets	49–33 (2012–13)	22–44 (2011–12)
+27	Ok.C. Thunder	50–32 (2009–10)	23–59 (2008–09)
+27	Pho. Suns	55–27 (1988–89)	28–54 (1987–88)
+26	N.J. Nets	52–30 (2001–02)	26–56 (2000–01)
+26	Den. Nuggets	43–39 (2003–04)	17–65 (2002–03)
+26	Mil. Bucks	41–41 (2014–15)	15–67 (2013–14)
+26	Pho. Suns	53–29 (1999–00)	27–23 (1998–99*)
+25	N.Y. Nets[a]	55–29 (1973–74)	30–54 (1972–73)
+25	Min. T'Wolves	50–32 (1999–00)	25–25 (1998–99*)

* Strike-shortened 50-game season.
** Inaugural season.
[a] ABA.

Largest Decrease in Games Won by Team, Following Season

Diff		Record (Season)	Record (Season)
−49	Chi. Bulls	13–37 (1998–99*)	62–20 (1997–98)
−42	G.S. Warriors	15–50 (2019–20)	57–25 (2018–19)
−42	Cle. Cavaliers	19–63 (2010–11)	61–21 (2009–10)
−39	S.A. Spurs	20–62 (1996–97)	59–23 (1995–96)
−36	Sea. Sonics	25–25 (1998–99*)	61–21 (1997–98)
−33	N.Y. Nets**	22–60 (1976–77)	55–29 (1975–76)
−32	Hou. Rockets	14–68 (1982–83)	46–36 (1981–82)
−31	S.F. Warriors	17–63 (1964–65)	48–32 (1963–64)
−31	Cle. Cavaliers	19–63 (2018–19)	50–32 (2017–18)
−30	L.A. Lakers	31–19 (1998–99*)	61–21 (1997–98)
−29	Mia. Heat	15–67 (2007–08)	44–38 (2006–07)
−29	Pho. Suns	27–23 (1998–99*)	56–26 (1997–98)
−27	N.J. Nets	16–34 (1998–99*)	43–39 (1997–98)
−27	Cha. Bobcats	7–59 (2011–12)	34–48 (2010–11)
−27	Mem. Grizzlies	22–60 (2006–07)	49–33 (2005–06)
−26	Tor. Raptors	27–45 (2020–21)	53–19 (2019–20)
−25	Cha. Hornets	26–24 (1998–99*)	51–31 (1997–98)
−25	Cle. Cavaliers	22–28 (1998–99*)	47–35 (1997–98)
−25	Ind. Pacers	33–17 (1998–99*)	58–24 (1997–98)
−25	N.O. Hornets	21–45 (2011–12)	46–36 (2010–11)
−25	Uta. Jazz	37–13 (1998–99*)	62–20 (1997–98)

* Strike-shortened 50-game season.

** Nets last season in ABA was 1975–76, and first year in NBA was 1976–77.

First Place One Season, Last Place the Following Season

	First Place	Last Place		First Place	Last Place
S.F. Warriors	1963–64 (48–32)	1964–65 (17–63)	Mia. Heat	2006–07 (44–38)	2007–08 (15–67)
Den. Rockets[a]	1969–70 (51–33)	1970–71 (30–54)	Cle. Cavaliers	2009–10 (61–21)	2010–11 (19–63)
Mil. Bucks	1973–74 (59–23)	1974–75 (38–44)	Cle. Cavaliers	2017–18 (50–32)	2018–19 (19–63)
L.A. Lakers	1973–74 (47–35)	1974–75 (30–52)	G.S. Warriors	2018–19 (57–25)	2019–20 (15–50)
Hou. Rockets	1976–77 (49–33)	1977–78 (28–54)	Tor. Raptors	2019–20 (53–19)	2020–21 (27–45)
Chi. Bulls	1997–98* (62–20)	1998–99** (13–37)	Hou. Rockets	2019–20 (44–28)	2020–21 (17–55)

[a] ABA.

* Won championship.

** Strike-shortened 50-game season.

Last Place One Season, First Place the Following Season

	Last Place	First Place		Last Place	First Place
Bal. Bullets	1967–68 (36–46)	1968–69 (57–25)	Bos. Celtics	1978–79 (29–53)	1979–80 (61–21)
Oak. Oaks[a]	1967–68 (22–56)	1968–69* (60–18)	Bos. Celtics	2006–07 (24–58)	2007–08* (66–16)
Den. Rockets-Nuggets[a]	1973–74 (37–47)	1974–75 (65–19)	Tor. Raptors	2012–13 (34–48)	2013–14 (48–34)
Mil. Bucks	1974–75 (38–44)	1975–76 (38–44)	Den. Nuggets	2017–18 (46–36)	2018–19 (54–28)
			Atl. Hawks	2019–20 (20–47)	2020–21 (41–31)

[a] ABA.

* Won championship.

Regular-Season Record for Active Teams in Inaugural Season[*]

	Record
Phi. Warriors, 1946–47	35–25 (.583)
N.Y. Knickerbockers, 1946–47	33–27 (.550)
Bos. Celtics, 1946–47	22–38 (.367)
Roc. Royals (Kings), 1948–49	45–15 (.750)
Ft.W. Pistons, 1948–49	22–38 (.367)
Min. Lakers, 1948–49[**]	44–16 (.733)
T.C. Blackhawks (Hawks), 1949–50	29–35 (.453)
Syr. Nationals (76ers), 1949–50[***]	51–13 (.797)
Chi. Packers (Wizards), 1961–62	18–62 (.225)
Chi. Bulls, 1966–67	33–48 (.407)
Dal. Chaparrals[a] (Spurs), 1967–68	46–32 (.590)
Den. Rockets[a] (Nuggets), 1967–68	45–33 (.577)
Ind. Pacers[a], 1967–68	38–40 (.487)
N.J. Americans[a] (Nets), 1967–68	36–42 (.462)
Sea. Sonics (Thunder), 1967–68	23–59 (.280)
S.D. Rockets, 1967–68	15–67 (.183)

	Record
Mil. Bucks, 1968–69	27–55 (.329)
Pho. Suns, 1968–69	16–66 (.195)
Por. Blazers, 1970–71	29–53 (.354)
Buf. Braves (Clippers), 1970–71	22–60 (.268)
Cle. Cavaliers, 1970–71	15–67 (.183)
N.O. Jazz, 1974–75	23–59 (.280)
Dal. Mavericks, 1980–81	15–67 (.183)
Cha. Hornets, 1988–89	20–62 (.244)
Mia. Heat, 1988–89	15–67 (.183)
Min. T'Wolves, 1989–90	22–60 (.268)
Orl. Magic, 1989–90	18–64 (.220)
Tor. Raptors, 1995–96	21–62 (.253)
Van. Grizzlies, 1995–96	15–67 (.183)
N.O. Hornets (Pelicans)[****], 2002–03	47–35 (.573)
Cha. Bobcats (Hornets), 2004–05	18–64 (.220)

[*] Franchise's first year of existence. This includes former ABA franchises.

[**] Won championship.

[***] Lost championship.

[****] The Cha. Hornets moved to N.O. beginning in the 2002–03 season. Now the Pelicans, they are considered a separate franchise from the original Hornets.

[a] ABA.

Largest Point Differential, Season

Diff		Record	Points For	Points Against
+739	Bos. Celtics[*], 1961–62	60–20 (.750)	9687	8948
+772	Bos. Celtics[*], 1985–86	67–15 (.817)	9359	8587
+841	Bos. Celtics[*], 2007–08	66–16 (.805)	8245	7404
+746	Chi. Bulls[*], 1990–91	61–21 (.744)	9024	8278
+856	Chi. Bulls[*], 1991–92	67–15 (.817)	9011	8155
+1004	Chi. Bulls[*], 1995–96	72–10 (.878)	8625	7621
+886	Chi. Bulls[*], 1996–97	69–13 (.841)	8458	7572
+732	Cle. Cavaliers, 2008–09	66–16 (.805)	8223	7491
+882	G.S. Warriors[**], 2015–16	73–9 (.890)	9421	8539
+828	G.S. Warriors[*], 2014–15	67–15 (.817)	9016	8188
+954	G.S. Warriors[*], 2016–17	67–15 (.817)	9503	8549
+754	Ken. Colonels[a], 1971–72	68–16 (.810)	9743	8989
+1007	L.A. Lakers[*], 1971–72	69–13 (.841)	9920	8913
+763	L.A. Lakers[*], 1986–87	65–17 (.793)	9656	8893
+701	L.A. Lakers[*], 1999–00	67–15 (.817)	8267	7566
+700	L.A. Lakers, 1972–73[**]	60–22 (.732)	9159	8459
+1005	Mil. Bucks[*], 1970–71	66–16 (.805)	9710	8705
+915	Mil. Bucks, 1971–72	63–19 (.768)	9400	8485
+741	Mil. Bucks, 1985–86	57–25 (.695)	9390	8649
+727	Mil. Bucks, 2018–19	60–22 (.732)	9686	8959
+736	Mil. Bucks, 2019–20	56–17 (.767)	8663	7927
+745	N.Y. Knicks[*], 1969–70	60–22 (.732)	9427	8682
+755	Ok.C. Thunder, 2012–13	60–22 (.732)	8669	7914
+765	Phi. 76ers[*], 1966–67	68–13 (.840)	10,143	9378

continued on next page

Diff		Record	Points For	Points Against
+705	Phi. 76ers, 1967–68	62–20 (.756)	10,051	9346
+712	Por. Blazers, 1990–91	63–19 (.768)	9407	8695
+872	S.A. Spurs, 2015–16	67–15 (.817)	8490	7618
+745	Sea. Sonics, 1993–94	63–19 (.768)	8687	7942
+721	Uta. Jazz**, 1996–97	64–18 (.780)	8454	7733

* Won championship.

** Lost championship.

ᵃ ABA.

Worst Point Differential, Season

Diff		Record	Points For	Points Against
-1246	Dal. Mavericks, 1992–93	11–71 (.134)	8141	9387
-991	Phi. 76ers, 1972–73	9–73 (.110)	8540	9531
-966	Den. Nuggets, 1997–98	11–71 (.134)	7300	8266
-951	Hou. Rockets, 1982–83	14–68 (.171)	8145	9096
-945	L.A. Clippers, 1999–00	15–67 (.183)	7546	8491
-937	L.A. Clippers, 1986–87	12–70 (.146)	8566	9503
-921	Mia. Heat*, 1988–89	15–67 (.183)	8016	8937
-918	Cha. Bobcats, 2011–12	7–59 (.106)	5739	6657
-916	Cle. Cavaliers, 1970–71	15–67 (.183)	8373	9289
-895	Den. Nuggets, 1990–91	20–62 (.244)	9829	10,723
-857	Phi. 76ers, 2013–14	19–63 (.232)	8155	9012
-846	L.A. Clippers, 1987–88	17–65 (.207)	8103	8949
-839	Phi. 76ers, 2015–16	10–72 (.122)	7988	8827
-839	Van. Grizzlies, 1996–97	14–68 (.171)	7313	8152
-820	Phi. 76ers, 1995–96	18–64 (.220)	7746	8566
-818	Van. Grizzlies*, 1995–96	15–67 (.183)	7362	8180
-813	L.A. Clippers, 1988–89	21–61 (.256)	8712	9525
-798	Por. Blazers, 1971–72	18–64 (.220)	8759	9557
-797	Mia. Heat, 1989–90	18–64 (.220)	8247	9044
-796	Atl. Hawks, 2004–05	13–69 (.159)	7605	8401
-789	Cle. Cavaliers, 2002–03	17–65 (.207)	7495	8284
-788	Cle. Cavaliers, 2018–19	19–63 (.232)	8567	9355
-787	Min. T'Wolves, 2009–10	15–67 (.183)	8051	8838
-784	L.A. Lakers, 2015–16	17–65 (.207)	7982	8766
-775	Por. Blazers, 2005–06	21–61 (.256)	7285	8060
-771	Chi. Bulls, 1999–00	17–65 (.207)	6952	7723
-768	Pho. Suns, 2017–18	21–61 (.256)	8522	9290
-766	Ok.C. Thunder, 2020–21	22–50 (.306)	7560	8326
-766	Pho. Suns, 2018–19	19–63 (.232)	8815	9581
-764	N.Y. Knicks, 2014–15	17–65 (.207)	7535	8299

* Inaugural season.

Teams Finishing .500 or Higher, Lowest Point Differential

W/L%	Diff		Points For	Points Against	Record
.549	-61	Det. Pistons, 1970–71	9029	9090	45–37
.537	-162	Bos. Celtics, 1976–77	8572	8734	44–38
.537	-85	Det. Pistons, 1976–77	8970	9055	44–38
.537	-82	Brk. Nets, 2013–14	8079	8161	44–38
.537	-64	Mil. Bucks, 1989–90	8691	8755	44–38
.526	-53	Dal. Chaparralsᵃ, 1968–69	8657	8710	41–37

continued on next page

W/L%	Diff		Points For	Points Against	Record
.524	-146	S.D. Clippers, 1978–79	9278	9424	43–39
.524	-90	L.A. Lakers, 1991–92	8229	8319	43–39
.524	-89	Sea. Sonics, 1974–75	8451	8540	43–39
.524	-78	Atl. Hawks, 1982–83	8335	8413	43–39
.524	-71	Atl. Hawks, 1992–93	8814	8885	43–39
.524	-70	Atl. Hawks, 2016–17	8459	8529	43–39
.524	-61	Phi. 76ers, 2004–05	8128	8189	43–39
.524	-54	Was. Capitols[a], 1969–70	9929	9983	44–40
.512	-192	G.S. Warriors, 1986–87	9188	9380	42–40
.512	-184	Mem. Grizzlies, 2015–16	8126	8310	42–40
.512	-141	Hou. Rockets, 1991–92	8366	8507	42–40
.512	-121	Chi. Bulls, 2015–16	8335	8456	42–40
.512	-112	Was. Bullets, 1986–87	8690	8802	42–40
.500	-134	S.F. Warriors, 1968–69	8947	9081	41–41
.500	-134	Chi. Bulls, 2009–10	7993	8127	41–41
.500	-118	S.F. Warriors, 1970–71	8783	8901	41–41
.500	-84	Cin. Royals, 1968–69	9392	9476	41–41
.500	-63	N.J. Nets, 2006–07	8001	8064	41–41
.500	-62	Hou. Rockets, 1997–98	8099	8161	41–41
.500	-53	Ind. Pacers, 1986–87	8698	8751	41–41

[a] ABA.

Teams Winning 50 Games in a Season, Three Years in a Row

Atl. Hawks 1985–86 (50–32), 1986–87 (57–25), 1987–88 (50–32), 1988–89 (52–30)

Bos. Celtics 1958–59* (52–20), 1959–60* (59–16), 1960–61* (57–22), 1961–62* (60–20), 1962–63* (58–22), 1963–64* (59–21), 1964–65* (62–18), 1965–66* (54–26), 1966–67 (60–21), 1967–68* (54–28); 1971–72 (56–26), 1972–73 (68–14), 1973–74* (56–26), 1974–75 (60–22), 1975–76* (54–28); 1979–80 (61–21), 1980–81* (62–20), 1981–82 (63–19), 1982–83 (56–26), 1983–84* (62–20), 1984–85 (63–19), 1985–86* (67–15), 1986–87 (59–23), 1987–88 (57–25); 1989–90 (52–30), 1990–91 (56–26), 1991–92 (51–31); 2007–08* (66–16), 2008–09 (62–20), 2009–10 (50–32), 2010–11 (56–26)

N.Y. Nets[a] 1973–74 (55–29), 1974–75 (58–26), 1975–76 (55–29)

Chi. Bulls 1970–71 (51–31), 1971–72 (57–25), 1972–73 (51–31), 1973–74 (54–28); 1989–90 (55–27), 1990–91* (61–21), 1991–92* (67–15), 1992–93* (57–25), 1993–94 (55–27); 1995–96* (72–10), 1996–97* (69–13), 1997–98* (62–20)

Cle. Cavaliers 2014–15 (53–29), 2015–16* (57–25), 2016–17 (51–31), 2017–18 (50–32)

Dal. Mavericks 2000–01 (53–29), 2001–02 (57–25), 2002–03 (60–22), 2003–04 (52–30), 2004–05 (58–24), 2005–06 (60–22), 2006–07 (67–15), 2007–08 (51–31), 2008–09 (50–32), 2009–10 (57–25), 2010–11* (57–25)

Den. Nuggets 1974-75a (65–19), 1975-76a (60–24), 1976–77 (50–32); 2007–08 (50–32), 2008–09 (54–28), 2009–10 (53–29), 2010–11 (50–32)

Det. Pistons 1986–87 (52–30), 1987–88 (54–28), 1988–89* (63–19), 1989–90* (59–23), 1990–91 (50–32); 2001–02 (50–32), 2002–03 (50–32), 2003–04* (54–28), 2004–05 (54–28), 2005–06 (64–18), 2006–07 (53–29), 2007–08 (59–23)

G.S. Warriors 2013–14 (51–31), 2014–15* (67–15), 2015–16 (73–9), 2016–17* (67–15), 2017–18* (58–24), 2018–19 (57–25)

Hou. Rockets 2006–07 (52–30), 2007–08 (55–27), 2008–09 (53–29); 2016–17 (55–27), 2017–18 (65–17), 2018–19 (53–29)

L.A. Clippers 2012–13 (56–26), 2013–14 (57–25), 2014–15 (56–26), 2015–16 (53–29), 2016–17 (51–31)

L.A. Lakers 1979–80* (60–22), 1980–81 (54–28), 1981–82* (57–25), 1982–83 (58–24), 1983–84 (54–28), 1984–85* (62–20), 1985–86 (62–20), 1986–87* (65–17), 1987–88* (62–20), 1989–90 (63–19), 1990–91 (58–24); 1995–96 (53–29), 1996–97 (56–26), 1997–98 (61–21); 1999–00* (67–15), 2000–01* (56–26), 2001–02* (61–21), 2002–03 (50–32), 2003–04 (56–26)

continued on next page

Mem. Grizzlies....... 2012–13 (56–26), 2013–14 (50–32), 2014–15 (55–27)

Mil. Bucks.............. 1969–70 (56–26), 1970–71* (66–16), 1971–72 (63–19), 1972–73 (60–22), 1973–74 (59–23); 1980–81 (60–22), 1981–82 (55–27), 1982–83 (51–31), 1983–84 (50–32), 1984–85 (59–23), 1985–86 (57–25), 1986–87 (50–32)

Min. T'Wolves........ 2001–02 (50–32), 2002–03 (51–31), 2003–04 (58–24)

N.Y. Knicks 1968–69 (54–28), 1969–70* (60–22), 1970–71 (52–30); 1991–92 (51–31), 1992–93 (60–22), 1993–94 (57–25), 1994–95 (55–27)

Sea. Sonics............ 1992–93 (55–27), 1993–94 (63–19), 1994–95 (57–25), 1995–96 (64–18), 1996–97 (57–25), 1997–98 (61–21)

Orl. Magic............. 1993–94 (50–32), 1994–95 (57–25), 1995–96 (60–22); 2007–08 (52–30), 2008–09 (59–23), 2009–10 (59–23), 2010–11 (52–30)

Phi. 76ers 1965–66 (55–25), 1966–67* (68–13), 1967–68 (62–20), 1968–69 (55–27); 1979–80 (59–23), 1980–81 (62–20), 1981–82 (58–24), 1982–83* (65–17), 1983–84 (52–30), 1984–85 (58–24), 1985–86 (54–28)

Pho. Suns............... 1989–90 (54–28), 1990–91 (55–27), 1991–92 (53–29), 1992–93 (62–20), 1993–94 (56–26), 1994–95 (59–23); 2004–05 (62–20), 2005–06 (54–28), 2006–07 (61–21), 2007–08 (55–27)

Por. Blazers........... 1989–90 (59–23), 1990–91 (63–19), 1991–92 (57–25), 1992–93 (51–31)

Sac. Kings 2000–01 (55–27), 2001–02 (61–21), 2002–03 (59–23), 2003–04 (55–27), 2004–05 (50–32)

S.A. Spurs.............. 1993–94 (55–27), 1994–95 (62–20), 1995–96 (59–23); 1999–00 (53–29), 2000–01 (58–24), 2001–02 (58–24), 2002–03* (60–22), 2003–04 (57–25), 2004–05* (59–23), 2005–06 (63–19), 2006–07* (58–24), 2007–08 (56–26), 2008–09 (54–28), 2009–10 (50–32), 2010–11 (61–21), 2011–12 (50–16), 2012–13 (58–24), 2013–14 (62–20), 2014–15 (55–27), 2015–16 (67–15), 2016–17 (61–21)

Tor. Raptors 2015–16 (56–26), 2016–17 (51–31), 2017–18 (59–23), 2018–19* (58–24), 2019–20 (53–19)

Uta. Jazz 1988–89 (51–31), 1989–90 (55–27), 1990–91 (54–28), 1991–92 (55–27); 1993–94 (53–29), 1994–95 (60–22), 1995–96 (55–27), 1996–97 (64–18), 1997–98 (62––20)

Ken. Colonels^a....... 1971–72 (68–16), 1972–73 (56–28), 1973–74 (53–31), 1974–75* (58–26)

Uta. Stars^a............. 1970–71* (57–27), 1971–72 (60–24), 1972–73 (55–29), 1973–74 (51–33)

* Won championship.

^a ABA.

Most Home Wins, Season

		Record
40	Bos. Celtics*, 1985–86	67–15 (.817)
40	S.A. Spurs, 2015–16	67–15 (.817)
39	Bos. Celtics**, 1986–87	59–23 (.720)
39	Orl. Magic**, 1994–95	57–25 (.695)
39	Chi. Bulls*, 1995–96	72–10 (.878)
39	Chi. Bulls*, 1996–97	69–13 (.841)
39	Cle. Cavaliers, 2008–09	66–16 (.805)
39	G.S. Warriors*, 2014–15	67–15 .817)
39	G.S. Warriors**, 2015–16	73–9 (.890)
38	Sea. Sonics**, 1995–96	64–18 (.780)
38	Uta. Jazz**, 1996–97	64–18 (.780)
38	S.A. Spurs*, 2004–05	59–23 (.720)
38	Den. Nuggets, 2012–13	57–25 (.695)
37	L.A. Lakers, 1976–77	53–29 (.646)
37	Phi. 76ers, 1977–78	55–27 (.671)
37	L.A. Lakers*, 1979–80	60–22 (.732)
37	Pho. Suns, 1979–80	55–27 (.671)
37	Phi. 76ers, 1980–81	62–20 (.756)
37	L.A. Lakers*, 1986–87	65–17 (.793)
37	Det. Pistons*, 1988–89	63–19 (.768)

Most Road Wins, Season

		Record
34	G.S. Warriors**, 2015–16	73–9 (.890)
33	Chi. Bulls*, 1995–96	72–10 (.878)
32	Bos. Celtics, 1972–73	68–14 (.829)
32	Bos. Celtics, 1974–75	60–22 (.732)
32	Mia. Heat, 1996–97	61–21 (.744)
31	L.A. Lakers*, 1971–72	69–13 (.841)
31	Chi. Bulls*, 1991–92	67–15 (.817)
31	L.A. Lakers*, 1999–00	67–15 (.817)
31	Pho. Suns, 2004–05	62–20 (.756)
31	Dal. Mavericks, 2006–07	67–15 (.817)
31	Bos. Celtics*, 2007–08	66–16 (.805)
31	G.S. Warriors, 2016–17	57–25 (.695)
31	Hou. Rockets, 2017–18	65–17 (.793)
30	Phi. 76ers*, 1982–83	65–17 (.793)
30	Chi. Bulls*, 1996–97	69–13 (.841)
30	S.A. Spurs*, 2013–14	62–20 (.756)
30	S.A. Spurs, 2016–17	61–21 (.744)
29	Bos. Celtics*, 1983–84	62–20 (.756)
29	S.A. Spurs, 1994–95	60–22 (.732)
29	Por. Blazers, 1999–00	59–23 (.720)

continued on next page

	Record
37............Cle. Cavaliers, 1988–89	57–25 (.695)
37............L.A. Lakers, 1989–90	63–19 (.768)
37............Uta. Jazz, 1991–92	55–27 (.671)
37............N.Y. Knicks, 1992–93	60–22 (.732)
37............Sea. Sonics, 1993–94	63–19 (.768)
37............Orl. Magic, 1995–96	60–22 (.732)
37............Chi. Bulls*, 1997–98	62–20 (.756)
37............Det. Pistons, 2005–06	64–18 (.780)
37............Uta. Jazz, 2007–08	54–28 (.659)
37............Mia. Heat*, 2012–13	66–16 (.805)

* Won NBA Finals.
** Lost NBA Finals.

	Record
29 .... Dal. Mavericks, 2004–05	58–24 (.707)
29 .... S.A. Spurs, 2005–06	63–19 (.768)
29 .... L.A. Lakers*, 2008–09	65–17 (.793)
29 .... Mia. Heat*, 2012–13	66–16 (.805)
29 .... G.S. Warriors*, 2017–18	58–24 (.707)
28 .... Pho. Suns, 2006–07	61–21 (.744)
28 .... Mia. Heat**, 2010–11	58–24 (.707)
28 .... Dal. Mavericks*, 2010–11	57–25 (.695)
28 .... G.S. Warriors*, 2014–15	67–15 .817)
28 .... Bos. Celtics, 2017–18	55–27 (.671)

* Won NBA Finals.
** Lost NBA Finals.

Most Home Losses, Season

	Record
35............ Dal. Mavericks, 1993–94	13–69 (.159)
34............ Dal. Mavericks, 1992–93	11–71 (.134)
34............ Phi. 76ers, 2015–16	10–72 (.122)
33............ S.D. Rockets*, 1967–68	15–67 (.183)
33............ Van. Grizzlies, 1996–97	14–68 (.171)
32............ Den. Nuggets, 1997–98	11–71 (.134)
33............ N.J. Nets, 2009–10	12–70 (.146)
32............ Cle. Cavaliers, 1981–82	15–67 (.183)
32............ Hou. Rockets, 1982–83	14–68 (.171)
32............ L.A. Clippers, 1986–87	12–70 (.146)
32............ Min. T'Wolves, 1991–92	15–67 (.183)
32............ Tor. Raptors, 1997–98	16–66 (.195)
32............ Atl. Hawks, 2004–05	13–69 (.159)
32............ Mia. Heat, 2007–08	15–67 (.183)
32............ Min. T'Wolves, 2014–15	16–66 (.195)
32............ Chi. Bulls, 2018–19	22–60 (.268)
32............ N.Y. Knicks, 2018–19	17–65 (.207)

* First season as expansion franchise.

Most Road Losses, Season

	Record
40 .... Sac. Kings, 1990–91	25–57 (.305)
39 .... Den. Nuggets, 1997–98	11–71 (.134)
38 .... N.O. Jazz*, 1974–75	23–59 (.280)
38 .... Det. Pistons, 1979–80	16–66 (.195)
38 .... L.A. Clippers, 1986–87	12–70 (.146)
38 .... L.A. Clippers, 1987–88	17–65 (.207)
38 .... N.J. Nets, 1987–88	19–63 (.232)
38 .... Mia. Heat*, 1988–89	15–67 (.183)
38 .... S.A. Spurs, 1988–89	21–61 (.256)
38 .... Den. Nuggets, 1990–91	20–62 (.244)
38 .... Cle. Cavaliers, 2002–03	17–65 (.207)
38 .... Chi. Bulls, 2002–03	30–52 (.366)
38 .... Was. Wizards, 2010–11	23–59 (.280)
38 .... Phi. 76ers, 2015–16	10–72 (.122)
37 .... Cle. Cavaliers*, 1970–71	15–67 (.183)
37 .... N.O. Jazz, 1978–79	26–56 (.317)
37 .... Dal. Mavericks*, 1980–81	15–67 (.183)
37 .... G.S. Warriors, 1987–88	20–62 (.244)
37 .... L.A. Clippers, 1988–89	21–61 (.256)
37 .... N.J. Nets, 1989–90	17–65 (.207)
37 .... Dal. Mavericks, 1992–93	11–71 (.134)
37 .... L.A. Clippers, 1994–95	17–65 (.207)
37 .... Bos. Celtics, 1996–97	15–67 (.183)
37 .... Den. Nuggets, 2002–03	17–65 (.207)
37 .... Atl. Hawks, 2004–05	13–69 (.159)
37 .... Cha. Bobcats*, 2004–05	18–64 (.220)
37 .... N.J. Nets, 2009–10	12–70 (.146)
37 .... Orl. Magic, 2013–14	23–59 (.280)
36 .... Van. Grizzlies*, 1995–96	15–67 (.183)
36 .... Mil. Bucks, 2013–14	15–67 (.183)
36 .... L.A. Lakers, 2015–16	17–65 (.207)

* First season as expansion franchise.

Most Consecutive Regular-Season Wins, Single Season

	Record			Record
33.............. L.A. Lakers*, 1971–72	.............69–13 (.841)		18.............. Chi. Bulls*, 1995–96	.................72–10 (.878)
28.............. G.S. Warriors*, 2014–15	...........67–15 (.817)		18.............. Mil. Bucks, 2019–20	.................56–17 (.767)
27.............. Mia. Heat*, 2012–13	.................66–16 (.805)		18.............. Pho. Suns, 2021–22	...................64–18 (.780)
22.............. Hou. Rockets, 2007–08	.............55–27 (.671)		17.............. Was. Capitols, 1946–47	............49–11 (.817)
20.............. Mil. Bucks*, 1970–71	.................66–16 (.805)		17.............. Bos. Celtics*, 1959–60	..............59–16 (.787)
19.............. L.A. Lakers*, 1999–00	...............67–15 (.817)		17.............. S.A. Spurs, 1995–96	.................59–23 (.720)
19.............. Bos. Celtics, 2008–09	...............62–20 (.756)		17.............. Dal. Mavericks, 2006–07	.........67–15 (.817)
19.............. S.A. Spurs*, 2013–14	.................62–20 (.756)		17.............. Pho. Suns, 2006–07	...................61–21 (.744)
19.............. Atl. Hawks, 2014–15	.................60–22 (.732)		17.............. L.A. Clippers, 2012–13	..............56–26 (.683)
18.............. N.Y. Knicks*, 1969–70	...............60–22 (.732)		17.............. Hou. Rockets, 2017–18	..............65–17 (.793)
18.............. Bos. Celtics, 1981–82	...............63–19 (.768)			

* Won championship.

Most Consecutive Regular-Season Losses, Single Season

	Record			Record
26.............. Cle. Cavaliers, 2010–11	.............19–63 (.232)		19.............. L.A. Clippers, 1988–89	.............21–61 (.256)
26.............. Phi. 76ers, 2013–14	.................19–63 (.232)		19.............. Dal. Mavericks, 1992–93	...........11–71 (.134)
23.............. Van. Grizzlies*, 1995–96	...........15–67 (.183)		19.............. Van. Grizzlies*, 1995–96	...........15–67 (.183)
23.............. Den. Nuggets, 1997–98	.............11–71 (.134)		19.............. Orl. Magic, 2003–04	.................21–61 (.256)
23.............. Cha. Bobcats, 2011–12	.................7–59 (.106)		19.............. Mem. Grizzlies, 2017–18	...........22–60 (.268)
20.............. Phi. 76ers, 1972–73	...................9–73 (.110)		18.............. Uta. Jazz, 1981–82	...................25–57 (.305)
20.............. Dal. Mavericks, 1993–94	...........13–69 (.159)		18.............. Bos. Celtics, 2006–07	...............24–58 (.293)
20.............. Hou. Rockets, 2020–21	.............17–55 (.236)		18.............. Cha. Bobcats, 2012–13	.............21–61 (.256)
19.............. S.D. Clippers, 1981–82	.............17–65 (.207)		18.............. N.Y. Knicks, 2018–19	...............17–65 (.207)

* Inaugural season.

Most Points in a Single Game (Including Overtime)

Points	Score		OT Periods
370	186–184	Det. Pistons @ Den. Nuggets (Dec. 13, 1983)	3OT
342	176–166	S.D. Conquistadorsᵃ vs. N.Y. Netsᵃ (Feb. 14, 1975)	4OT
337	171–166	S.A. Spurs vs. Mil. Bucks (Mar. 6, 1982	3OT
329	168–161	Chi. Bulls @ Atl. Hawks (Mar. 1, 2019	4OT
320	162–158	Was. Capitolsᵃ @ Dal. Chaparralsᵃ (Mar. 13, 1970	2OT
320	162–158	G.S. Warriors @ Den. Nuggets (Nov. 2, 1990	N/A
318	163–155	Den. Nuggets vs. S.A. Spurs (Jan. 11, 1984	N/A
318	161–157	Pho. Suns @ N.J. Nets (Dec. 7, 2006	2OT
317	159–158	Hou. Rockets @ Was. Wizards (Oct. 30, 2019	N/A
316	169–147	Phi. Warriors vs. N.Y. Knicks (Mar. 2, 1962	N/A
316	165–151	Cin. Royals vs. S.D. Rockets (Mar. 12, 1970	N/A
316	173–143	Pho. Suns vs. Den. Nuggets (Nov. 10, 1990	N/A
315	160–155	Mia. Floridiansᵃ vs. Dal. Chaparralsᵃ (Mar. 22, 1970	N/A
314	161–153	S.A. Spurs vs. Den. Nuggets (Nov. 7, 1990	N/A
313	172–141	Ind. Pacersᵃ vs. L.A. Starsᵃ (Feb. 1, 1969	N/A
312	173–139	Bos. Celtics vs. Min. Lakers (Feb. 27, 1959	N/A
312	157–155	Was. Capitolsᵃ @ Dal. Chaparralsᵃ (Mar. 20, 1970	N/A
312	177–135	Ind. Pacersᵃ vs. Pit. Pipersᵃ (Apr. 12, 1970	N/A
311	163–148	Syr. Nationals vs. S.F. Warriors (Mar. 10, 1963	N/A
311	158–153	Tex Chaparralsᵃ vs. Den. Nuggetsᵃ (Mar. 5, 1971	3OT

continued on next page

Points	Score		OT Periods
311	156–155	Chi. Bulls @ Por. Blazers (Mar. 16, 1984	4OT
311	157–154	S.A. Spurs vs. Den. Nuggets (Apr. 15, 1984	N/A
310	157–153	S.A. Spurs @ Was. Wizards (Feb. 25, 2022)	2OT
309	155–154	Mil. Bucks vs. Sea. Sonics (Nov. 9, 1989	5OT
307	154–153	Cle. Cavaliers vs. L.A. Lakers (Jan. 29, 1980	4OT
306	156–150	Pit. Condors[a] @ Tex. Chaparrals[a] (Nov. 13, 1970	1OT
305	162–143	Den. Nuggets vs. Por. Blazers (Feb. 13, 1981	N/A
305	155–150	Den. Nuggets vs. Ind. Pacers (Dec. 28, 1982	1OT
303	155–148	Ind. Pacers[a] @ Car. Cougars[a] (Dec. 11, 1970	2OT
303	156–147	Dal. Mavericks @ Hou. Rockets (Apr. 11, 1995	2OT
301	154–147	S.A. Spurs vs. Ok.C. Thunder (Jan. 10, 2019	2OT
300	156–144	Den. Nuggets[a] vs. S.A. Spurs[a] (Mar. 8, 1975	1OT

[a] ABA.

Fewest Points Scored in a Game (Shot-Clock Era)

Pts		Score
56	Mia. Heat @ Cha. Hornets (Dec. 20, 2000)	65–56
57	Mil. Hawks n. Bos. Celtics (Feb. 27, 1955)	62–57
57	Phi. 76ers vs. Mia. Heat (Feb. 21, 1996)	66–57
59	Cle. Cavaliers @ S.A. Spurs (Mar. 25, 1997)	64–59
60	Por. Blazers @ N.J. Nets (Nov. 9, 2004)	64–60
62	Uta. Jazz @ Det. Pistons (Mar. 13, 2005)	64–62
65	Mia. Heat @ Van. Grizzlies (Jan. 13, 1996)	69–65
65	Mia. Heat vs. S.A. Spurs (Feb. 1, 2003)	67–65
65	Ok.C. Thunder vs. Hou. Rockets (Nov. 16, 2014)	69–65
66	Syr. Nationals n. Ft.W. Pistons (Jan. 25, 1955)	69–66
66	Dal. Mavericks @ Uta. Jazz (Dec. 12, 1997)	68–66

n.: Neutral site.

Most Points Scored in a Regulation Loss

Pts		Score
158	Den. Nuggets vs. G.S. Warriors (Nov. 2, 1990)	162–158
158	Was. Wizards vs. Hou. Rockets (Oct. 30, 2019)	159–158
155	Dal. Chaparrals[a] vs. Was. Capitols[a] (Mar. 20, 1970)	157–155
155	Dal. Chaparrals[a] @ Mia. Floridians[a] (Mar. 22, 1970)	160–155
155	S.A. Spurs @ Den. Nuggets (Jan. 11, 1984)	163–155
154	Den. Nuggets @ S.A. Spurs (Apr. 15, 1984)	157–154
153	Den. Nuggets @ S.A. Spurs (Nov. 7, 1990)	161–153
151	S.D. Rockets @ Cin. Royals (Mar. 12, 1970)	165–151
148	S.F. Warriors @ Syr. Nationals (Mar. 10, 1963)	163–148
148	Den. Nuggets vs. Uta. Jazz (Feb. 10, 1982)	151–148

[a] ABA.

Most Points Scored in an Overtime Loss

Pts		Score	OT Periods
184	Den. Nuggets vs. Det. Pistons (Dec. 13, 1983)	186–184	3
166	N.Y. Nets[a] @ S.D. Conquistadors[a] (Feb. 14, 1975)	176–166	4
166	Mil. Bucks @ S.A. Spurs (Mar. 6, 1982)	171–166	3
161	Atl. Hawks vs. Chi. Bulls (Mar. 1, 2019)	168–161	4

continued on next page

Pts		Score	OT Periods
158 .... Dal. Chaparrals^a vs. Was. Capitols^a (Mar. 13, 1970)		162–158	2
157 .... N.J. Nets vs. Pho. Suns (Dec. 7, 2006)		161–157	2
155 .... Por. Blazers vs. Chi. Bulls (Mar. 16, 1984)		156–155	4
154 .... Sea. Sonics @ Mil. Bucks (Nov. 9, 1989)		155–154	5
153 .... Den. Rockets^a @ Tex. Chaparrals^a (Mar. 5, 1971)		158–153	3
153 .... L.A. Lakers @ Cle. Cavaliers (Jan. 29, 1980)		154–153	4

^a ABA.

Most Points Scored in the First Quarter

Pts	Score
51 .... G.S. Warriors @ Den. Nuggets (Jan. 15, 2019)	142–111
50 .... Syr. Nationals @ S.F. Warriors (Dec. 16, 1962)	144–137
50 .... Bos. Celtics vs. Den. Nuggets (Feb. 5, 1982)	145–144
50 .... Uta. Jazz vs. Den. Nuggets (Apr. 10, 1982)	151–136
50 .... Mil. Bucks vs. Orl. Magic (Nov. 16, 1989)	132–113
50 .... Pho. Suns vs. Den. Nuggets (Nov. 10, 1990)	173–143
50 .... Mil. Bucks vs. Was. Wizards (Feb. 6, 2019)	148–129
50 .... Por. Blazers vs. Hou. Rockets (May 10, 2019)	140–129
49 .... Atl. Hawks vs. N.J. Nets (Jan. 5, 1985)	124–114
49 .... Por. Blazers vs. S.A. Spurs (Nov. 25, 1990)	117–103
49 .... Cha. Hornets vs. Ind. Pacers (Feb. 2, 2018)	133–126
49 .... Sac. Kings vs. N.O. Pelicans (Aug. 6, 2020)	140–125

Most Points Scored in the Second Quarter

Pts	Score
57 .... Pho. Suns vs. Den. Nuggets (Nov. 10, 1990)	173–143
52 .... Bal. Bullets vs. Det. Pistons (Dec. 18, 1965)	143–114
50 .... S.D. Clippers vs. Uta. Jazz (Apr. 14, 1984)	146–128
50 .... S.A. Spurs @ Hou. Rockets (Nov. 17, 1984)	133–141
49 .... Dal. Mavericks* @ N.J. Nets (Dec. 2, 2009)	117–101
49 .... N.Y. Knicks vs. Atl. Hawks (Oct. 17, 2018)	126–107
49 .... Mil. Bucks vs. Phi. 76ers (Oct. 24, 2018)	123–108
49 .... Phi. 76ers @ Was. Wizards (Jan. 6, 2021)	141–136
48 .... Syr. Nationals vs. Det. Pistons (Feb. 12, 1961)	148–122
48 .... S.L. Hawks @ Det. Pistons (Jan. 1, 1962)	145–139
48 .... L.A. Lakers vs. Den. Nuggets (Apr. 9, 1982)	153–128
48 .... G.S. Warriors @ Chi. Bulls (Oct. 29, 2018)	149–124
48 .... Den. Nuggets vs. Hou. Rockets (Feb. 1, 2019)	136–122
48 .... Sac. Kings* @ Por. Blazers (Apr. 10, 2019)	131–136
48 .... Hou. Rockets* @ N.O. Pelicans (Jan. 30, 2021)	126–112

* Lost game.

Most Points Scored in the Third Quarter

Pts	Score
57 .... G.S. Warriors vs. Sac. Kings (Mar. 4, 1989)	155–143
55 .... Mem. Grizzlies vs. N.O. Pelicans (Apr. 9, 2022)	141–114
54 .... Atl. Hawks @ S.D. Rockets (Feb. 11, 1970)	155–131
54 .... Ind. Pacers vs. Den. Nuggets (Nov. 9, 2010)	144–113
51 .... Syr. Nationals vs. Det. Pistons (Mar. 2, 1963)	152–128
51 .... Cin. Royals n. Phi. 76ers (Feb. 28, 1964)	134–132

continued on next page

Pts		Score
51	Sea. Sonics vs. Bal. Bullets (Feb. 13, 1970)	141–138
51	Den. Nuggets vs. S.D. Clippers (Jan. 6, 1982)	136–114
51	L.A. Lakers vs. N.Y. Knicks (Mar. 25, 2014)	127–96
50	St.L. Hawks vs. S.F. Warriors (Dec. 8, 1962)	145–129
50	Syr. Nationals @ Det. Pistons (Feb. 8, 1963)	162–135
50	G.S. Warriors vs. L.A. Clippers (Feb. 23, 2017)	123–113
50	G.S. Warriors @ Ok.C. Thunder (Apr. 14, 2021)	147–109

n.: Neutral site.

Most Points Scored in the Fourth Quarter

Pts		Score
58	Buf. Braves* @ Bos. Celtics (Oct. 20, 1972)	126–118
54	Bos. Celtics vs. S.D. Rockets (Feb. 25, 1970)	147–124
53	Phi. 76ers @ Sea. Sonics (Dec. 20, 1967)	160–122
53	N.Y. Knicks* n. Sea. Sonics (Dec. 26, 1967)	137–135
53	Det. Pistons vs. Cin. Royals (Jan. 7, 1972)	151–132
53	S.D. Clippers* vs. Hou. Rockets (Feb. 9, 1982)	129–121
53	S.A. Spurs* @ Den. Nuggets (Jan. 11, 1984)	163–155
53	Mil. Bucks* @ Cle. Cavaliers (Nov. 12, 1991)	119–113
52	Bos. Celtics vs. Min. Lakers (Feb. 27, 1959)	173–139
51	Syr. Nationals vs. Det. Pistons (Jan. 13, 1963)	148–114
51	Dal. Mavericks @ G.S. Warriors (Jan. 15, 1985)	149–104
51	Brk. Nets @ Bos. Celtics (Mar. 3, 2020)	129–120 (OT)
50	Cin. Royals* @ N.Y. Knicks (Dec. 19, 1964)	133–105
50	Cin. Royals* @ Bal. Bullets (Jan. 29, 1971)	145–118
50	Det. Pistons @ Chi. Bulls (Jan. 22, 1980)	145–131
50	G.S. Warriors vs. L.A. Clippers (Mar. 7, 1989)	138–112
50	G.S. Warriors vs. Por. Blazers (Mar. 21, 1989)	151–127
50	Sea. Sonics vs. Mia. Heat (Jan. 5, 1990)	140–110
50	Hou. Rockets @ Den. Nuggets (Jan. 10, 1991)	156–133

* Lost game.

n.: Neutral site.

Most Points Scored in an Overtime Period

Pts		Score
25	N.J. Nets @ L.A. Clippers (Nov. 30, 1996)	106–95
24	Sac. Kings vs. Uta. Jazz (Mar. 17, 1990)	122–109
23	L.A. Clippers vs. Pho. Suns (Nov. 12, 1988)	138–127
23	Dal. Mavericks @ L.A. Lakers (Dec. 12, 1990)	112–97
23	Ind. Pacers vs. G.S. Warriors (Mar. 31, 1991)	127–120
23	Dal. Mavericks @ Hou. Rockets (Apr. 11, 1995)	156–147
23	Hou. Rockets* vs. Dal. Mavericks (Apr. 11, 1995)	156–147
23	Den. Nuggets @ Pho. Suns (Dec. 23, 1996)	112–109
23	N.Y. Knicks @ Was. Wizards (Feb. 19, 2008)	113–100

* Lost game in 2OT.

Most Lopsided Regular-Season Victories

Diff		Score
73	Mem. Grizzlies vs. Ok.C. Thunder (Dec. 2, 2021)	152–79
68	Cle. Cavaliers vs. Mia. Heat (Dec. 17, 1991)	148–80

continued on next page

Diff		Score
65	Ind. Pacers vs. Por. Blazers (Feb. 27, 1998)	124–59
63	L.A. Lakers vs. G.S. Warriors (Mar. 19, 1972)	162–99
62	Syr. Nationals vs. N.Y. Knicks (Dec. 25, 1960)	162–100
62	G.S. Warriors vs. Sac. Kings (Nov. 2, 1991)	153–91
61	Cha. Hornets vs. Mem. Grizzlies (Mar. 22, 2018)	140–79
59	G.S. Warriors vs. Ind. Pacers (Mar. 19, 1977)	150–91
59	Mil. Bucks vs. Det. Pistons (Dec. 26, 1978)	143–84
58	Mil. Bucks vs. Sac. Kings (Dec. 15, 1985)	140–82
58	Sac. Kings vs. Dal. Mavericks (Dec. 29, 1992)	139–81
57	Ind. Pacers @ Ok.C. Thunder (May 1, 2021)	152–95
56	L.A. Lakers vs. Det. Pistons (Nov. 12, 1966)	144–88
56	Chi. Bulls vs. Por. Blazers (Feb. 20, 1976)	130–74
56	Mil. Bucks vs. N.O. Jazz (Mar. 14, 1979)	158–102
56	Sea. Sonics @ Hou. Rockets (Dec. 6, 1986)	136–80
56	Sac. Kings vs. Phi. 76ers (Jan. 2, 1993)	154–98
56	Sea. Sonics vs. Phi. 76ers (Mar. 6, 1993)	149–93
56	Bos. Celtics @ Chi. Bulls (Dec. 8, 2018)	133–77
55	Pho. Suns vs. Sac. Kings (Apr. 17, 1989)	140–85
55	L.A. Lakers vs. Cle. Cavaliers (Jan. 11, 2011)	112–57

Most Games Scoring 100 Points, Season

NBA

		Record
82	Den. Nuggets, 1981–82	46–36 (.561)
81	L.A. Lakers*, 1971–72	69–13 (.841)
81	Den. Nuggets, 1986–87	37–45 (.451)
80	Phi. 76ers*, 1966–67	68–13 (.840)
80	S.F. Warriors, 1966–67	44–37 (.543)
80	N.Y. Knicks, 1966–67	36–45 (.444)
80	Phi. 76ers, 1969–70	42–40 (.512)
80	S.A. Spurs, 1978–79	48–34 (.585)
80	S.A. Spurs, 1979–80	41–41 (.500)
80	Den. Nuggets, 1983–84	38–44 (.463)
80	S.A. Spurs, 1983–84	37–45 (.451)
80	Den. Nuggets, 1984–85	52–30 (.634)

* Won championship.

ABA

		Record
84	Vir. Squires, 1970–71	55–29 (.655)
82	Car. Cougars, 1972–73	57–27 (.679)
81	Den. Rockets, 1970–71	30–54 (.357)
80	Ken. Colonels, 1970–71	44–40 (.524)
80	Tex. Chaparrals, 1970–71	30–54 (.357)
80	Vir. Squires, 1971–72	45–39 (.536)
80	Pit. Condors, 1971–72	25–59 (.298)
79	Ind. Pacers, 1970–71	58–26 (.690)
79	Uta. Stars*, 1970–71	57–27 (.679)
79	Pit. Condors, 1970–71	36–48 (.429)
79	Den. Nuggets, 1975–76	60–24 (.714)

* Won championship.

Most Consecutive Games Scoring 100 Points

Games		First Game of Streak	Last Game of Streak	Record During Streak	PPG–Opp. PPG
136	Den. Nuggets	Jan. 21, 1981	Dec. 8, 1982	74–62 (.544)	126–126
129	S.A. Spurs	Dec. 12, 1978	Mar. 14, 1980	71–58 (.550)	119–117
87	Ken. Colonels[a]	Dec. 12, 1970	Dec. 17, 1971	47–40 (.540)	120–118
85	Vir. Squires[a]	Oct. 17, 1970	Oct. 15, 1971	56–29 (.659)	123–120
83	Mil. Bucks	Feb. 23, 2019	Feb. 28, 2020	67–16 (.807)	121–109
81	Cin. Royals	Nov. 18, 1960	Nov. 21, 1961	35–46 (.432)	120–122
81	Oak. Oaks[a]	Mar. 20, 1968	Apr. 4, 1969	60–21 (.741)	126–119
80	S.A. Spurs	Feb. 4, 1983	Feb. 3, 1984	43–37 (.538)	118–116
79	Cin. Royals	Dec. 6, 1961	Dec. 2, 1962	44–35 (.557)	123–121
78	N.Y. Knicks	Oct. 23, 1966	Oct. 17, 1967	35–43 (.449)	117–119
78	Phi. 76ers	Nov. 8, 1966	Oct. 27, 1967	66–12 (.846)	125–116
76	Syr. Nationals	Nov. 4, 1961	Oct. 26, 1962	41–35 (.539)	121–119
75	Den. Nuggets	Dec. 2, 1986	Oct. 26, 1962	34–41 (.453)	117–117

[a] ABA.

Most Consecutive Games Scoring Under 100 Points (Shot-Clock Era)

Games		First Game of Streak	Last Game of Streak	Record During Streak	PPG–Opp. PPG
35	Mia. Heat	Oct. 31, 2001	Jan. 14, 2002	9–26 (.257)	84–89
31	Chi. Bulls	May 3, 1999	Jan. 5, 2000	3–28 (.097)	83–96
29	Orl. Magic	Dec. 13, 1997	Feb. 16, 1998	9–20 (.310)	86–92
27	G.S. Warriors	Dec. 18, 1997	Feb. 13, 1998	3–24 (.111)	85–96
26	Cle. Cavaliers	Mar. 28, 1999	Nov. 3, 1999	9–17 (.346)	84–88
26	Mia. Heat	Mar. 16, 1999	May 1, 1999	15–11 (.577)	88–84
26	Por. Blazers	Nov. 2, 2005	Dec. 23, 2005	8–18 (.308)	87–95
26	Uta. Jazz	Mar. 24, 2005	Nov. 19, 2005	9–17 (.346)	88–94
25	Atl. Hawks	Dec. 16, 2003	Feb. 4, 2004	9–16 (.360)	86–91
25	Chi. Bulls	Apr. 14, 2000	Dec. 11, 2000	2–23 (.080)	84–97
25	Mil. Hawks	Dec. 18, 1954	Jan. 30, 1955	10–15 (.400)	87–88
25	Phi. 76ers	Nov. 15, 2003	Jan. 5, 2004	10–15 (.400)	85–87
25	Uta. Jazz	Jan. 9, 2004	Feb. 25, 2004	11–14 (.440)	86–89

Lowest FG%, Winning Game (Shot-Clock Era)

FG%		Team Shooting	Opp Shooting	Score
.277	Min. Lakers vs. St.L. Hawks (Dec. 29, 1955*)	23-for-83	25-for-86 (.291)	74–71
.277	Dal. Mavericks @ Van. Grizzlies (Nov. 13, 1995)	26-for-94	38-for-91 (.418)	94–89
.280	Phi. Warriors vs. N.Y. Knicks (Nov. 10, 1956)	30-for-107	28-for-78 (.359)	83–81
.281	N.Y. Knicks vs. Phi. Warriors (Dec. 27, 1955)	25-for-89	23-for-81 (.284)	80–79
.281	Phi. Warriors vs. Roc. Royals (Jan. 2, 1956*)	45-for-160	35-for-138 (.254)	130–100
.286	Orl. Magic vs. Phi. 76ers (Mar. 15, 1999)	26-for-91	27-for-77 (.351)	74–73
.286	Chi. Bulls vs. L.A. Clippers (Feb. 19, 2000)	22-for-77	30-for-78 (.385)	74–72
.288	Hou. Rockets @ Ok.C. Thunder (Nov. 16, 2014)	23-for-80	20-for-68 (.294)	69–65
.292	Den. Nuggets vs. S.A. Spurs (Oct. 29, 2003)	28-for-96	26-for-97 (.268)	80–72
.293	Syr. Nationals vs. Phi. Warriors (Nov. 16, 1954*)	29-for-99	27-for-78 (.346)	86–85
.293	Syr. Nationals vs. St.L. Hawks (Nov. 15, 1957)	27-for-92	25-for-80 (.313)	91–86
.295	St.L. Hawks @ Syr. Nationals (Nov. 4, 1956)	28-for-95	25-for-76 (.329)	78–76
.299	Phi. Warriors vs. Bos. Celtics (Dec. 25, 1956*)	29-for-97	30-for-93 (.323)	89–82

continued on next page

FG%		Team Shooting	Opp Shooting	Score
.299	Phi. Warriors vs. St.L. Hawks (Jan. 2, 1958)	32-for-107	35-for-92 (.380)	95–93
.299	Bos. Celtics n. Min. Lakers (Jan. 11, 1959)	35-for-117	39-for-99 (.394)	109–106*
.300	Syr. Nationals vs. St.L. Hawks (Nov. 20, 1955)	27-for-90	30-for-85 (.353)	84–80
.300	Min. Lakers vs. Roc. Royals (Feb. 19, 1956)	30-for-100	30-for-101 (.297)	100–93
.301	Sac. Kings vs. Ind. Pacers (Jan. 18, 2012)	28-for-93	34-for-78 (.436)	92–88
.302	Dal. Mavericks vs. Van. Grizzlies (Dec. 28, 1995)	32-for-106	37-for-87 (.425)	103–101**
.303	Phi. Warriors vs. Syr. Nationals (Dec. 4, 1954)	33-for-109	28-for-94 (.298)	79–73
.303	Atl. Hawks @ Min. T'Wolves (Apr. 12, 1997)	23-for-76	22-for-73 (.301)	80–66
.304	Roc. Royals vs. Phi. Warriors (Nov. 7, 1956)	31-for-102	22-for-67 (.328)	81–80
.304	Tor. Raptors vs. N.Y. Knicks (Mar. 21, 1999)	31-for-102	30-for-76 (.395)	85–81*
.304	Chi. Bulls vs. Den. Nuggets (Mar. 24, 2000)	24-for-79	25-for-75 (.333)	70–68
.305	Syr. Nationals vs. Ft.W. Pistons (Feb. 5, 1956)	29-for-95	25-for-79 (.316)	90–85
.305	Atl. Hawks @ N.J. Nets (Apr. 5, 1996)	25-for-82	28-for-95 (.295)	82–70
.306	Chi. Bulls vs. S.A. Spurs (Nov. 3, 1997)	33-for-108	34-for-85 (.400)	87–83*
.306	N.O. Hornets @ Hou. Rockets (Apr. 1, 2005)	22-for-72	24-for-78 (.308)	76–73
.307	Cha. Hornets vs. Ind. Pacers (Jan. 17, 2015)	31-for-101	30-for-84 (.357)	80–71*
.309	Ken. Colonelsᵃ @ Mia. Floridiansᵃ (Oct. 26, 1969)	34-for-110	34-for-113 (.301)	92–85
.309	Phi. 76ers vs. N.Y. Knicks (Jan. 4, 1974)	30-for-97	34-for-84 (.405)	78–75

n: Neutral site.

* Overtime victory.

** Double-overtime victory.

ᵃ ABA.

Highest FG%, Season

		Record			Record
.545	L.A. Lakers*, 1984–85	62–20 (.756)	.516	L.A. Lakers*, 1986–87	65–17 (.793)
.532	L.A. Lakers, 1983–84	54–28 (.659)	.514	Phi. 76ers, 1980–81	62–20 (.756)
.529	L.A. Lakers*, 1979–80	60–22 (.732)	.513	S.A. Spurs, 1984–85	41–41 (.500)
.528	L.A. Lakers, 1982–83	58–24 (.707)	.512	Pho. Suns, 1978–79	50–32 (.610)
.522	L.A. Lakers, 1985–86	62–20 (.756)	.512	L.A. Lakers, 1980–81	54–28 (.659)
.521	Bos. Celtics, 1987–88	57–25 (.695)	.512	Bos. Celtics, 1990–91	56–26 (.683)
.520	Den. Nuggets, 1981–82	46–36 (.561)	.512	Uta. Jazz, 1994–95	60–22 (.732)
.518	Phi. 76ers, 1981–82	58–24 (.707)	.510	Chi. Bulls*, 1990–91	61–21 (.744)
.517	L.A. Lakers, 1978–79	47–35 (.573)	.509	Mil. Bucks*, 1970–71	66–16 (.805)
.517	L.A. Lakers*, 1981–82	57–25 (.695)	.509	Den. Nuggetsᵃ, 1974–75	65–19 (.774)
.517	Bos. Celtics, 1986–87	59–23 (.720)	.509	Pho. Suns, 1983–84	41–41 (.500)

* Won championship.

ᵃ ABA.

Highest FG%, Losing Record

		Record			Record
.506	S.A. Spurs, 1983–84	37–45 (.451)	.501	Chi. Bulls, 1981–82	34–48 (.415)
.506	S.A. Spurs, 1985–86	35–47 (.427)	.500	K.C. Kings, 1980–81	40–42 (.488)
.504	K.C. Kings, 1984–85	31–51 (.378)	.500	S.D. Clippers, 1981–82	17–65 (.207)
.503	Mil. Bucks, 1978–79	38–44 (.463)	.500	Chi. Bulls, 1984–85	38–44 (.463)
.503	Pho. Suns, 1985–86	32–50 (.390)			

Teams Scoring 10,000 Points, Season

NBA

1961–62...... Phi. Warriors...............................10,035	1981–82...... Den. Nuggets............................10,371
1966–67...... Phi. 76ers*................................10,143	1982–83...... Den. Nuggets............................10,105
1967–68...... Phi. 76ers.................................10,051	1983–84...... Den. Nuggets............................10,147

* Won championship.

ABA*

1969–70...... Dal. Chaparrals.........................10,077	1970–71...... Ind. Pacers...............................10,002
1970–71...... Vir. Squires 10,355	1970–71...... Pit. Condors 10,001
1970–71...... Ken. Colonels...........................10,264	1971–72...... Pit. Condors 10,016
1970–71...... Tex. Chaparrals 10,207	1975–76...... Den. Nuggets............................10,237

* ABA had 78-game seasons from 1967–69, and 84-game seasons thereafter.

Teams Scoring 9500 or More Points in a Season, Having a Losing Record

Pts		Record	Pts		Record
10,147.............	Den. Nuggets, 1983–84	38–44 (.463)	9627................	Bal. Bullets, 1967–68...............	36–46 (.439)
9986.............	Den. Nuggets, 1980–81	37–45 (.451)	9616................	Cin. Royals, 1969–70..............	36–46 (.439)
9862.............	S.A. Spurs, 1983–84	37–45 (.451)	9589................	Sea. Sonics, 1969–70	36–46 (.439)
9828.............	Den. Nuggets, 1990–91	20–62 (.244)	9586................	Syr. Nationals, 1960–61..........	38–41 (.481)
9786.............	Pho. Suns, 1969–70	39–43 (.476)	9569................	Den. Nuggets, 1986–87	37–45 (.451)
9764.............	L.A. Lakers, 1966–67...............	36–45 (.444)	9562................	Cin. Royals, 1967–68..............	39–43 (.476)
9732.............	S.D. Rockets, 1969–70	27–55 (.329)	9534................	G.S. Warriors, 1989–90..........	37–45 (.451)
9732.............	Sea. Sonics, 1967–68	23–59 (.280)	9511................	Cin. Royals, 1970–71..............	33–49 (.402)
9725.............	Det. Pistons, 1967–68..............	40–42 (.488)	9508................	St.L. Hawks, 1961–62..............	29–51 (.363)

Highest 3P%, Season

NBA

3P%		Record	3P%		Record
.428................	Cha. Hornets, 1996–97	54–28 (.659)	.396................	Sea. Sonics, 1997–98	61–21 (.744)
.416................	G.S. Warriors, 2015–16..........	73–9 (.890)	.396................	Mia. Heat*, 2012–13	66–16 (.805)
.412................	Pho. Suns, 2009–10	54–28 (.659)	.393................	Pho. Suns, 2004–05	62–20 (.756)
.411................	L.A. Clippers, 2020–21............	47–25 (.653)	.393................	Pho. Suns, 2007–08	55–27 (.671)
.407................	Cle. Cavaliers, 1989–90..........	42–40 (.512)	.393................	Cle. Cavaliers, 2008–09..........	66–16 (.805)
.407................	Was. Bulelts, 1995–96............	39–43 (.476)	.393................	S.A. Spurs, 2011–12	50–16 (.758)
.407................	S.A. Spurs, 2000–01	58–24 (.707)	.392................	S.A. Spurs, 1995–96	59–23 (.720)
.404................	Det. Pistons, 1995–96.............	46–36 (.561)	.392................	Ind. Pacers, 1999–00	56–26 (.683)
.403................	Chi. Bulls*, 1995–96..............	72–10 (.878)	.392................	Tor. Raptors, 2007–08	41–41 (.500)
.403................	G.S. Warriors, 2012–13	47–35 (.573)	.392................	G.S. Warriors, 2010–11	36–46 (.439)
.401................	Sac. Kings, 2003–04	55–27 (.671)	.392................	S.A. Spurs, 2018–19	48–34 (.585)
.399................	Sea. Sonics, 2000–01	44–38 (.537)	.392................	Brk. Nets, 2020–21	48–24 (.667)
.399................	Pho. Suns, 2005–06	54–28 (.659)	.392................	N.Y. Knicks, 2020–21..............	41–31 (.569)
.399................	Pho. Suns, 2006–07	61–21 (.744)	.391................	Sac. Kings, 1996–97...............	34–48 (.415)
.398................	G.S. Warriors*, 2014–15	67–15 (.817)	.391................	Dal. Mavericks, 1999–00........	40–42 (.488)
.397................	Cha. Hornets, 1994–95	50–32 (.610)	.391................	S.A. Spurs, 2016–17...............	61–21 (.744)
.397................	Bos. Celtics, 2008–09.............	62–20 (.756)	.391................	G.S. Warriors*, 2017–18..........	58–24 (.707)
.397................	S.A. Spurs, 2010–11	61–21 (.744)	.390................	Ind. Pacers, 1997–98	58–24 (.707)
.397................	S.A. Spurs*, 2013–14	62–20 (.756)			

continued on next page

ABA

3P%		Record
.358	Ken. Colonels, 1969–70	45–39 (.536)
.356	Uta. Stars, 1971–72	60–24 (.714)
.356	Mem. Sounds, 1974–75	27–57 (.321)
.353	Ken. Colonels, 1968–69	42–36 (.538)
.344	Car. Cougars, 1970–71	34–50 (.405)
.343	Ken. Colonels, 1971–72	68–16 (.810)
.336	Dal. Chaparrals, 1971–72	42–42 (.500)
.335	Ken. Colonels, 1975–76	46–38 (.548)
.330	Dal. Chaparrals, 1972–73	28–56 (.333)
.329	Den. Rockets, 1973–74	37–47 (.440)

3P%		Record
.324	Ind. Pacers, 1975–76	39–45 (.464)
.323	Ken. Colonels, 1970–71	44–40 (.524)
.322	L.A. Stars, 1968–69	33–45 (.423)
.320	Dal. Chaparrals, 1969–70	45–39 (.536)
.317	The Floridians, 1971–72	36–48 (.429)
.316	Dal. Chaparrals, 1968–69	41–37 (.526)
.316	N.Y. Nets*, 1973–74	55–29 (.655)
.315	N.O. Buccaneers, 1968–69	46–32 (.590)
.315	Ind. Pacers, 1973–74	46–38 (.548)

* Won championship.

Most 3P Made, Game*

3P		3P Shooting
29	Mil. Bucks @ Mia. Heat (Dec. 29, 2020)	29-for-51 (.569)
28	Hou. Rockets @ Ok.C. Thunder (Feb. 1, 2021)	28-for-52 (.538)
28	Uta. Jazz vs. Cha. Hornets (Feb. 22, 2021)	28-for-55 (.509)
27	Hou. Rockets vs. Pho. Suns (Apr. 7, 2019)	27-for-57 (.474)
27	Brk. Nets @ Sac. Kings (Feb. 15, 2021)	27-for-47 (.574)
27	G.S. Warriors vs. Ok.C. Thunder (May 8, 2021)	27-for-54 (.500)
27	Uta. Jazz vs. Bos. Celtics (Dec. 3, 2021)	27-for-51 (.529)
26	Hou. Rockets vs. Was. Wizards (Dec. 19, 2018)	26-for-55 (.473)
26	Hou. Rockets @ Sac. Kings (Apr. 2, 2019)	26-for-61 (.426)
26	Min. T'Wolves vs. L.A. Clippers (Feb. 8, 2020)	26-for-44 (.591)
26	Uta. Jazz @ Cha. Hornets (Feb. 5, 2021)	26-for-50 (.520)
26	Uta. Jazz vs. Orl. Magic (Apr. 3, 2021)	26-for-55 (.473)
26	Mil. Bucks vs. N.Y. Knicks (Nov. 10, 2021)	26-for-50 (.520)
25	Cle. Cavaliers @ Atl. Hawks (Mar. 3, 2017)	25-for-46 (.543)
25	Hou. Rockets vs. L.A. Lakers (Jan. 19, 2019)	25-for-68 (.368)
25	Hou. Rockets vs. Atl. Hawks (Nov. 30, 2019)	25-for-51 (.490)
25	Hou. Rockets @ G.S. Warriors (Feb. 20, 2020)	25-for-49 (.510)
25	L.A. Clippers vs. N.O. Pelicans (Aug. 1, 2020)	25-for-47 (.532)
25	Uta. Jazz @ Mil. Bucks (Jan. 8, 2021)	25-for-53 (.472)
25	Chi. Bulls vs. N.O. Pelicans (Feb. 10, 2021)	25-for-47 (.532)
25	Dal. Mavericks vs. N.O. Pelicans (Feb. 12, 2021)	25-for-45 (.556)
25	Pho. Suns vs. Hou. Rockets (Apr. 12, 2021)	25-for-45 (.556)
25	Hou. Rockets vs. Mil. Bucks (Apr. 29, 2021)	25-for-46 (.543)
25	Hou. Rockets** @ Mil. Bucks (May 7, 2021)	25-for-53 (.472)
25	Atl. Hawks @ Min. T'Wolves (Dec. 6, 2021)	25-for-49 (.510)
25	Uta. Jazz @ Min. T'Wolves (Dec. 8, 2021)	25-for-54 (.463)
25	Bos. Celtics @ Phi. 76ers (Feb. 15, 2022)	25-for-45 (.556)

* Includes overtime, where applicable.

** Team lost game.

Teammates Scoring 40 Points in a Game, Regular Season

Pts	Player	Player	
98*	51–Kiki Vandeweghe	47–Alex English	Den. Nuggets** vs. Det. Pistons (Dec. 13, 1983)
95*	50–George Gervin	45–Mike Michell	S.A. Spurs vs. Mil. Bucks (Mar. 6, 1982)
91	51–Kevin Durant	40–Russell Westbrook	Ok.C. Thunder vs. Den. Nuggets (Feb. 19, 2012)

continued on next page

Pts	Player	Player	
88*	47–Isiah Thomas	41–John Long	Det. Pistons @ Den. Nuggets (Dec. 13, 1983)
88	45–Paul George	43–Russell Westbrook	Ok.C. Thunder vs. Uta. Jazz (Feb. 22, 2019)
86	43–Elgin Baylor	43–Jerry West	L.A. Lakers @ S.F. Warriors (Feb. 11, 1970)
86	45–Pete Maravich	41–Nate Williams	N.O. Jazz vs. Den. Nuggets (Apr. 10, 1977)
85	43–Adrian Dantley	42–John Drew	Uta. Jazz vs. Det. Pistons (Mar. 19, 1984)
85	45–Russell Westbrook	40–Kevin Durant	Ok.C. Thunder vs. Min. T'Wolves (Mar. 23, 2012)
84	44–Michael Jordan	40–Scottie Pippen	Chi. Bulls @ Ind. Pacers (Feb. 18, 1996)
83	43–Paul Westphal	40–Walter Davis	Pho. Suns @ Bos. Celtics (Jan. 5, 1978)
81	41–Gus Johnson	40–Walt Bellamy	Bal. Bullets vs. L.A. Lakers (Nov. 14, 1964)
81	41–Andrew Wiggins	40–Karl-Anthony Towns	Min. T'Wolves** @ L.A. Lakers (Apr. 9, 2017)

* Game went into triple overtime.

** Team lost game.

Team with Three Players Averaging 20 PPG in Same Season (Min. 1000 Minutes Played)

	Season	Players	PPG	Record
St. L. Hawks	1959–60	Bob Pettit	26.1	46–29 (.613)
		Cliff Hagan	24.8	
		Clyde Lovelette	20.8	
	1960–61	Bob Pettit	27.9	51–28 (.646)
		Cliff Hagan	22.1	
		Clyde Lovellette	22.0	
	1961–62	Bob Pettit	31.1	29–51 (.363)
		Cliff Hagan	22.9	
		Clyde Lovellette	20.9	
Bos. Celtics	1966–67	Sam Jones	22.1	60–21 (.741)
		John Havlicek	21.4	
		Bailey Howell	20.0	
	2019–20	Jayson Tatum	23.4	48–24 (.667)
		Kemba Walker	20.4	
		Jaylen Brown	20.3	
Brk. Nets	2020–21	Kevin Durant	26.9	48–24 (.667)
		Kyrie Irving	26.9	
		James Harden	24.6	
Chi. Bulls	1969–70	Chet Walker	21.5	39–43 (.476)
		Bob Love	21.0	
		Clem Haskins	20.3	
Den. Nuggets	1980–81	David Thompson	25.5	37–45 (.451)
		Alex English	23.8	
		Dan Issel	21.9	
	1981–82	Alex English	25.4	46–36 (.561)
		Dan Issel	22.9	
		Kiki Vandeweghe	21.5	
	1982–83	Alex English	28.4	45–37 (.549)
		Kiki Vandeweghe	26.7	
		Dan Issel	21.6	
Det. Pistons	1971–72	Bob Lanier	25.7	26–56 (.317)
		Dave Bing	22.6	
		Jimmy Walker	21.3	
S.F. Warriors	1968–69	Jeff Mullins	22.8	41–41 (.500)
		Nate Thurmond	21.5	
		Rudy LaRusso	20.7	

continued on next page

	Season	Players	PPG	Record
G.S. Warriors	1971–72	Jeff Mullins	21.5	51–31 (.622)
		Cazzie Russell	21.4	
		Nate Thurmond	21.4	
	1990–91	Chris Mullin	25.7	44–38 (.567)
		Mitch Richmond	23.9	
		Tim Hardaway	22.9	
	2007–08	Baron Davis	21.8	48–34 (.585)
		Monta Ellis	20.2	
		Stephen Jackson	20.1	
	2016–17	Stephen Curry	25.3	67–15* (.817)
		Kevin Durant	25.1	
		Klay Thompson	22.3	
Ind. Pacers	1968–69ª	Mel Daniels	24.0	44–34 (.564)
		Roger Brown	21.0	
		Freddie Lewis	20.3	
	2020–21	Malcolm Brogdon	21.2	34–38 (.472)
		Caris LeVert	20.7	
		Domantas Sabonis	20.3	
L.A. Lakers	1968–69	Jerry West	25.9	55–27 (.671)
		Elgin Baylor	24.8	
		Wilt Chamberlain	20.5	
	1969–70	Jerry West	31.2	46–36 (.561)
		Elgin Baylor	24.0	
		Happy Hairston	20.6	
	1980–81	Kareem Abdul-Jabbar	26.2	54–28 (.659)
		Jamaal Wilkes	22.6	
		Magic Johnson	21.6	
N.O. Pelicans	2018–19	Anthony Davis	25.9	33–49 (.402)
		Julius Randle	21.4	
		Jrue Holiday	21.2	
Sea. Sonics	1986–87	Dale Ellis	24.9	39–43 (.476)
		Tom Chambers	23.3	
		Xavier McDaniel	23.0	
	1987–88	Dale Ellis	25.8	44–38 (.537)
		Xavier McDaniel	21.4	
		Tom Chambers	20.4	
Pho. Suns	1969–70	Connie Hawkins	24.6	39–43 (.476)
		Dick Van Arsdale	21.3	
		Gail Goodrich	20.0	
	1988–89	Tom Chambers	25.7	55–27 (.671)
		Eddie Johnson	21.5	
		Kevin Johnson	20.4	
Sac. Kings	2013–14	DeMarcus Cousins	22.7	28–54 (.341)
		Isaiah Thomas	20.3	
		Rudy Gay	20.1	
Tex. Chaparralsª	1970–71	Donnie Freeman	23.6	30–54 (.357)
		Glen Combs	20.5	
		Ron Boone	20.3	
N.O. Jazz	1978–79	Truck Robinson	24.2	26–56 (.317)
		Spencer Haywood	24.0	
		Pete Maravich	22.6	

continued on next page

	Season	Players	PPG	Record
Pit. Pipers[a]	1967–68	Connie Hawkins	26.8	54–24* (.692)
		Charles Williams	20.8	
		Art Heyman	20.1	
Pit. Condors[a]	1971–72	John Brisker	28.9	25–59 (.300)
		George Thompson	27.0	
		George Carter	21.4	
Hou. Mavericks[a]	1968–69	Bob Verga	24.7	23–55 (.295)
		Willie Somerset	23.5	
		Stew Johnson	20.6	
Spirits of St. L.[a]	1975–76	Marvin Barnes	24.1	35–49 (.417)
		Ron Boone	21.0	
		Maurice Lucas	20.4	

* Won championship.
[a] ABA.

Most Games with 40 Three-Point Attempts, Season

		Record				Record
63	Hou. Rockets, 2018–19	53–29 (.646)		34	Mil. Bucks, 2018–19	60–22 (.732)
59	Hou. Rockets, 2019–20	44–28 (.611)		34	Cha. Hornets, 2021–22	43–39 (.524)
52	Hou. Rockets, 2017–18	65–17 (.793)		32	Min. T'Wolves, 2019–20	19–45 (.297)
52	Min. T'Wolves, 2021–22	46–36 (.561)		32	Uta. Jazz, 2021–22	49–33 (.598)
51	Uta. Jazz, 2020–21	52–20 (.634)		32	Hou. Rockets, 2021–22	20–62 (.244)
49	Dal. Mavericks, 2019–20	43–32 (.573)		31	Dal. Mavericks, 2020–21	42–30 (.583)
45	G.S. Warriors*, 2021–22	53–29 (.646)		31	Bos. Celtics, 2021–22	51–31 (.622)
45	Por. Blazers, 2020–21	42–30 (.583)		31	Mil. Bucks, 2021–22	51–31 (.622)
41	Hou. Rockets, 2016–17	55–27 (.671)		30	Mil. Bucks, 2019–20	56–17 (.767)
41	Hou. Rockets, 2020–21	17–55 (.236)		30	G.S. Warriors, 2020–21	42–30 (.583)
41	Uta. Jazz, 2021–22	49–33 (.598)		30	Tor. Raptors, 2020–21	27–45 (.375)
40	Hou. Rockets, 2021–22	20–62 (.244)				

* Won championship.

Most Games with 25 Assists, Season

		Record				Record
74	L.A. Lakers*, 1984–85	62–20 (.756)		68	G.S. Warriors**, 2018–19	57–25 (.695)
73	Pho. Suns, 1978–79	50–32 (.610)		67	Den. Nuggets, 1983–84	38–44 (.463)
71	L.A. Lakers**, 1982–83	58–24 (.707)		66	Phi. 76ers, 1980–81	62–20 (.756)
71	G.S. Warriors*, 2016–17	67–15 (.817)		66	Det. Pistons, 1985–86	46–36 (.561)
70	Pho. Suns, 1984–85	36–46 (.439)		66	G.S. Warriors*, 2017–18	58–24 (.707)
70	Bos. Celtics, 1985–86	67–15 (.817)		65	Mil. Bucks, 1978–79	38–44 (.463)
69	L.A. Lakers**, 1983–84	54–28 (.659)		65	L.A. Lakers*, 1979–80	60–22 (.732)
69	Bos. Celtics**, 1986–87	59–23 (.720)		65	L.A. Lakers, 1985–86	62–20 (.756)
69	Bos. Celtics, 1989–90	52–30 (.634)		65	Por. Blazers, 1986–87	49–33 (.598)
68	Bos. Celtics, 1987–88	57–25 (.695)		65	Cha. Hornets, 1991–92	31–51 (.378)
68	Uta. Jazz, 1987–88	47–35 (.573)		65	G.S. Warriors**, 2015–16	73–9 (.890)

* Won championship.

** Lost championship.

Most Games with 10 Blocks, Season

	Record			Record
35............... Was. Bullets, 1985–86 ....39–43 (.476)			23............... Was. Bullets, 1986–87 ....42–40 (.512)	
29............... Uta. Jazz, 1984–85 ....41–41 (.500)			23............... Uta. Jazz, 1987–88 ....47–35 (.573)	
28............... Den. Nuggets, 1993–94 ....42–40 (.512)			23............... Cle. Cavaliers, 1991–92.............57–25 (.695)	
28............... Den. Nuggets, 1999–00 ....35–47 (.427)			23............... Ok.C. Thunder*, 2011–12............47–19 (.712)	
25............... Phi. 76ers, 1983–84 ....52–30 (.634)			20............... G.S. Warriors, 1988–89.............43–39 (.524)	
25............... Sac. Kings, 1991–92..................29–53 (.354)			22............... N.J. Nets, 1990–91 ....26–56 (.317)	
24............... Uta. Jazz, 1985–86 ....42–40 (.512)			22............... N.J. Nets, 1991–92 ....40–42 (.488)	
24............... Den. Nuggets, 1994–95 ....41–41 (.500)			22............... Ok.C. Thunder, 2012–13............60–22 (.732)	
24............... Tor. Raptors, 1997–98 ....16–66 (.195)				

* Lost championship.

Most Games with 50 Total Rebounds, Season (Beginning with 1973–74 Season[W])

NBA

	Record
59............. Bos. Celtics*, 1973–74.............. 56–26 (.683)	
56............. L.A. Lakers, 1973–74................ 47–35 (.573)	
50............. N.O. Jazz, 1977–78 .... 39–43 (.476)	
49............. G.S. Warriors, 1973–74 .... 44–38 (.537)	
49............. Bos. Celtics*, 1975–76 .... 54–28 (.659)	
48............. Bos. Celtics, 1974–75 .... 60–22 (.732)	
48............. G.S. Warriors*, 1974–75 .... 48–34 (.585)	
47............. G.S. Warriors, 1975–76 .... 59–23 (.720)	
45............. Bos. Celtics, 1976–77 .... 44–38 (.537)	
45............. Mil. Bucks, 2018–19 .... 60–22 (.732)	
44............. Was. Bullets*, 1977–78 .... 44–38 (.537)	
44............. Was. Bullets**, 1978–79 ....54–28 (.659)	
44............. Chi. Bulls, 1975–76.................. 24–58 (.293)	
43............. Mil. Bucks, 2019–20 .... 56–17 (.767)	
42............. Cap. Bullets, 1973–74 .... 48–34 (.585)	
42............. Sea. Sonics, 1973–74 .... 36–46 (.439)	
42............. Bos. Celtics, 1977–78.............. 30–52 (.366)	
41............. L.A. Lakers, 1974–75................ 30–52 (.366)	
41............. Den. Nuggets, 1990–91 .... 20–62 (.244)	
40............. Mil. Bucks**, 1973–74 .... 59–23 (.720)	
40............. Pho. Suns, 1974–75 .... 30–52 (.366)	
40............. Ok.C. Thunder, 2015–16 .... 55–27 (.671)	

W Season after Wilt Chamberlain's last year.

* Team won championship.

** Team lost championship.

ABA

	Record
52 .... Ind. Pacers, 1975–76 ....39–45 (.464)	
51 .... Ken. Colonels, 1975–76 ....46–38 (.548)	
49 .... Ind. Pacers**, 1974–75 ....45–39 (.536)	
48 .... Ind. Pacers, 1973–74 ....46–38 (.548)	
47 .... Ken. Colonels, 1973–74 ....53–31 (.631)	
47 .... Ken. Colonels*, 1974–75 ....58–26 (.690)	
46 .... Spirits of St.L., 1975–76 ....35–49 (.417)	
38 .... S.A. Spurs, 1974–75 ....51–33 (.607)	
37 .... Spirits of St.L., 1974–75 ....32–52 (.381)	
33 .... N.Y. Nets*, 1975–76 ....55–29 (.655)	
33 .... S.A. Spurs, 1975–76 ....50–34 (.595)	
31 .... Vir. Squires, 1973–74................28–56 (.333)	

* Team won championship.

** Team lost championship.

Most Turnovers, Season[T]

TO		Record	TO		Record
2011............Den. Nuggets, 1976–77 .... 50–32 (.610)			1873............N.J. Nets, 1982–83..................... 49–33 (.598)		
1991............Was. Capitols[a], 1969–70 .... 44–40 (.524)			1867............Por. Blazers, 1975–76 .... 37–45 (.451)		
1915............Phi. 76ers*, 1976–77 .... 50–32 (.610)			1861............N.J. Nets, 1978–79..................... 37–45 (.451)		
1913............L.A. Lakers, 1973–74................... 47–35 (.573)			1858............Det. Pistons, 1977–78.................. 38–44 (.463)		

continued on next page

TO		Record	TO		Record
1852............	Pho. Suns**, 1975–76	42–40 (.512)	1823............	Por. Blazers, 1973–74	27–55 (.329)
1837............	Oak. Oaksᵃ*, 1968–69	60–18 (.769)	1821............	Den. Nuggetsᵃ, 1974–75	65–19 (.774)
1833............	Por. Blazers, 1974–75	38–44 (.463)	1819............	Vir. Squiresᵃ, 1972–73	42–42 (.500)
1830............	Pho. Suns, 1976–77	34–48 (.415)	1813............	Chi. Bulls, 1978–79	31–51 (.378)
1828............	Buf. Braves, 1973–74	42–40 (.512)	1802............	N.O. Jazz, 1974–75	23–59 (.280)
1823............	Atl. Hawks, 1973–74	35–47 (.427)			

ᵀ Turnovers became an official stat beginning with the 1977–78 season, though data for the ABA is available from the 1968–69 season, and in the NBA from the 1973–74 season..

ᵃ ABA.

* Won championship.

** Lost championship.

In Multiple Seasons, Leading League in Turnovers

5	Phi. 76ers	1983–84 (1628), 2013–14 (1384), 2014–15 (1453), 2016–17 (1366), 2017–18 (1353)
3	Den. Nuggets	1976–77 (2011), 1991–92 (1447), 2002–03 (1514)
3	Det. Pistons	1977–78 (1858), 1979–80 (1742), 1980–81 (1759)
3	N.J. Nets	1978–79 (1861), 1981–82 (1650), 1982–83 (1873)
3	Mia. Heat	1988–89 (1728), 1989–90 (1557), 1990–91 (1551)
3	Min. T'Wolves	1993–94 (1478), 2009–10 (1333), 2010–11 (1398)
3	N.Y. Knicks	1996–97 (1462), 2005–06 (1449), 2006–07 (1405)
3	Ok.C. Thunder	2008–09 (1330), 2011–12 (1079), 2020–21 (1162)
2	Por. Blazers	1974–75 (1833), 1975–76 (1867)
2	Pho. Suns	1985–86 (1763), 2015–16 (1410)
2	Cle. Cavaliers	1986–87 (1619), 1997–98 (1418)
2	G.S. Warriors	1994–95 (1497), 2001–02 (1378)
2	Chi. Bulls	1999–00 (1557), 2004–05 (1371)
2	Was. Wizards	2000–01 (1391), 2003–04 (1439)
2	Hou. Rockets	2012–13 (1348), 2021–22 (1351)

Most Fouls in a Regulation NBA Game (Shot-Clock Era)

Fouls	Teams (PF)	Date	Foul Outs
81	Ind. Pacers* (41) vs. K.C. Kings (40)	Oct. 22, 1977	6 (3: Ind. Pacers; 3: K.C. Kings)
81	S.A. Spurs* (45) vs. Uta. Jazz (36)	Nov. 8, 1997	3 (S.A. Spurs)
80	Syr. Nationals* (42) vs. N.Y. Knicks (38)	Nov. 24, 1962	5 (2: Syr. Nationals; 3: N.Y. Knicks)
80	Den. Nuggets (42) @ N.O. Jazz* (38)	Apr. 10, 1977	6 (3: Den. Nuggets; 3: N.O. Jazz)
80	Pho. Suns (41) vs. Den. Nuggets* (39)	Oct. 29, 1985	2 (1: Pho. Suns; 1: Den. Nuggets)
79	Por. Blazers (42) @ Atl. Hawks* (37)	Jan. 16, 1977	7 (4: Por. Blazers; 3: Atl. Hawks)
79	K.C. Kings* (41) @ Dal. Mavericks (38)	Nov. 20, 1982	4 (2: K.C. Kings; 2: Dal. Mavericks)
79	Det. Pistons (42) @ N.Y. Knicks* (37)	Oct. 27, 1984	2 (1: Det. Pistons; 1: N.Y. Knicks)
78	K.C. Kings (43) @ S.A. Spurs* (35)	Nov. 17, 1983	2 (1: K.C. Kings; 1: S.A. Spurs)
77	Den. Nuggets* (40) @ G.S. Warriors (37)	Oct. 25, 1985	4 (G.S. Warriors)
77	N.Y. Knicks (46) @ Pho. Suns* (31)	Dec. 3, 1987	4 (2: N.Y. Knicks; 2: Pho. Suns)
76	Sea. Sonics (43) vs. S.D. Rockets* (33)	Dec. 28, 1967	2 (Sea. Sonics)
76	Sea. Sonics (42) @ Pho. Suns* (34)	Oct. 21, 1972	6 (4: Sea. Sonics; 2: Pho. Suns)
76	L.A. Lakers (40) @ Det. Pistons* (36)	Feb. 20, 1974	5 (3: L.A. Lakers; 2: Det. Pistons)
76	K.C. Kings* (41) @ Den. Nuggets (35)	Nov. 11, 1978	8 (5: K.C. Kings; 3: Den. Nuggets)
76	Mil. Bucks* (40) @ N.J. Nets (36)	Nov. 11, 1981	2 (N.J. Nets)
76	G.S. Warriors (41) vs. Phi. 76ers* (35)	Dec. 29, 1981	4 (G.S. Warriors)
76	Pho. Suns (40) vs. Atl. Hawks* (36)	Nov. 6, 1985	1 (Pho. Suns)

* Won game.

Players Who Played for Three or More California Teams

Matt Barnes................. L.A. Clippers, 2003–04, 2012–15; Sac. Kings, 2004–05, 2016–17; G.S. Warriors, 2006–08, 2017; L.A. Lakers, 2010–12

Jon Barry .... G.S. Warriors, 1995–96; L.A. Lakers, 1997–98; Sac. Kings, 1998–2001

Kent Bazemore^ .... G.S. Warriors, 2012–14, 2020–21; L.A. Lakers, 2014, 2021–22; Sac. Kings, 2020

Steve Blake .... L.A. Clippers, 2009–10; L.A. Lakers, 2010–14; G.S. Warriors, 2014

Chucky Brown .... L.A. Lakers, 1991–92; G.S. Warriors, 2001; Sac. Kings, 2001–02

Caron Butler................ L.A. Lakers, 2004–05; L.A. Clippers, 2011–13; Sac. Kings, 2015–16

Doug Christie .... L.A. Lakers, 1992–94; Sac. Kings, 2000–05; L.A. Clippers, 2006–07

Darren Collison^ .... L.A. Clippers, 2013–14; Sac. Kings, 2014–17; L.A. Lakers, 2021–22

Lester Conner .... G.S. Warriors, 1982–86; L.A. Clippers, 1992–93; L.A. Lakers, 1994–95

DeMarcus Cousins^ .... Sac. Kings, 2010–17; G.S. Warriors, 2018–19; L.A. Clippers, 2021

Ike Diogu .... G.S. Warriors, 2005–07; Sac. Kings, 2009; L.A. Clippers, 2010–11

Larry Drew .... Sac. Kings, 1985–86; L.A. Clippers, 1986–88; L.A. Lakers, 1989–91

Jordan Farmar .... L.A. Lakers, 2006–10, 2013–14; L.A. Clippers, 2014–15; Sac. Kings, 2016–17

Wenyen Gabriel^ .... Sac. Kings, 2019–20; L.A. Clippers, 2021–22; L.A. Lakers, 2022

Jim Jackson .... G.S. Warriors, 1998; Sac. Kings, 2002–03; L.A. Lakers, 2006

Antawn Jamison........... G.S. Warriors, 1998–2003; L.A. Lakers, 2012–13; L.A. Clippers, 2013–14

Damian Jones^ .... G.S. Warriors, 2016–19; L.A. Lakers, 2021; Sac. Kings, 2021–22

Tony Massenburg.......... G.S. Warriors, 1992; L.A. Clippers, 1994–95; Sac. Kings, 2003–04

Mikki Moore .... L.A. Clippers, 2004–05; Sac. Kings, 2007–09; G.S. Warriors, 2009–10, 2011–12

Josh Powell.................. G.S. Warriors, 2007; L.A. Clippers, 2007–08; L.A. Lakers, 2008–10

Vladimir Radmanović .... L.A. Clippers, 2006; L.A. Lakers, 2006–09; G.S. Warriors, 2009–11

Mitch Richmond........... G.S. Warriors, 1988–91; Sac. Kings, 1991–98; L.A. Lakers, 2001–02

Rajon Rondo^ .... Sac. Kings, 2015–16; L.A. Lakers, 2018–20, 2021–22; L.A. Clippers, 2021

Derek Smith................. G.S. Warriors, 1982–83; S.D.-L.A. Clippers, 1983–86; Sac. Kings, 1987–89

Mike Smrek................. L.A. Lakers, 1986–88; G.S. Warriors, 1989–90, 1991–92; L.A. Clippers, 1990–91

Ronny Turiaf .... L.A. Lakers, 2005–08; G.S. Warriors, 2008–10; L.A. Clippers, 2012–13

^ Active.

13

DRAFT

College with the Most #1 Overall Picks in Draft

School		Draft Year	Team
4 .... Duke	Art Heyman .... 1963 .... N.Y. Knicks
	Elton Brand .... 1999 .... Chi. Bulls
	Kyrie Irving .... 2011 .... Cle. Cavaliers
	Zion Williamson .... 2019 .... N.O. Pelicans
	Paolo Banchero .... 2022 .... Orl. Magic
3 .... Kentucky	John Wall .... 2010 .... Was. Wizards
	Anthony Davis .... 2012 .... N.O. Hornets
	Karl-Anthony Towns ...... 2015 .... Min. Timberwolves
2 .... Cincinnati	Oscar Robertson .... 1960 .... Cin. Royals
	Kenyon Martin .... 2000 .... N.J. Nets
2 .... Duquesne	Dick Ricketts .... 1955 .... St.L. Hawks
	Si Green .... 1956 .... Roc. Royals
2 .... Georgetown	Patrick Ewing .... 1985 .... N.Y. Knicks
	Allen Iverson .... 1996 .... Phi. 76ers
2 .... Houston	Elvin Hayes .... 1968 .... S.D. Rockets
	Hakeem Olajuwon .... 1984 .... Hou. Rockets
2 .... Indiana	Walt Bellamy .... 1961 .... Chi. Packers
	Kent Benson .... 1977 .... Mil. Bucks
2 .... Kansas	Danny Manning .... 1988 .... L.A. Clippers
	Andrew Wiggins .... 2014 .... Cle. Cavaliers
2 .... Kansas State	Howie Shannon .... 1949 .... Pro. Steamrollers
	Bob Boozer .... 1959 .... Cin. Royals
2 .... LSU	Shaquille O'Neal .... 1992 .... Orl. Magic
	Ben Simmons .... 2016 .... Phi. 76ers
2 .... Maryland	John Lucas .... 1976 .... Hou. Rockets
	Joe Smith .... 1995 .... G.S. Warriors
2 .... Michigan	Cazzie Russell .... 1966 .... N.Y. Knicks
	Chris Webber .... 1993 .... Orl. Magic
2 .... Purdue	Joe Barry Carroll .... 1980 .... G.S. Warriors
	Glenn Robinson .... 1994 .... Mil. Bucks
2 .... Texas-El Paso	Clifton McNeeley .... 1947 .... Pit. Ironmen
	Jim Barnes .... 1964 .... N.Y. Knicks
2 .... UCLA	Kareem Abdul-Jabbar .... 1969 .... Mil. Bucks
	Bill Walton .... 1974 .... Por. Trail Blazers
2 .... UNC	James Worthy .... 1982 .... L.A. Lakers
	Brad Daugherty .... 1986 .... Cle. Cavaliers
2 .... UNLV	Larry Johnson .... 1991 .... Cha. Hornets
	Anthony Bennett .... 2013 .... Cle. Cavaliers
2 .... Utah	Bill McGill .... 1962 .... Chi. Zephyrs
	Andrew Bogut .... 2005 .... Mil. Bucks
2 .... West Virginia	Mark Workman .... 1952 .... Mil. Hawks
	Hot Rod Hundley .... 1957 .... Cin. Royals

Least Amount of Points Scored for #1 Overall Draft Pick*

Career Pts**	Draft Year	Drafting Team		Career GP**
44	1948	Providence Steamrollers	Andy Tonkovich	17
386	1952	Milwaukee Hawks	Mark Workman	79
658	2013	Cleveland Cavaliers	Anthony Bennett	151
840	2007	Portland Trail Blazers	Greg Oden	105
1114	2021	Detroit Pistons	Cade Cunningham^	64
1323	1949	Providence Steamrollers	Howie Shannon	122
1423	2017	Philadelphia 76ers	Markelle Fultz^	131
1430	1972	Portland Trail Blazers	LaRue Martin	271
1974	1955	St. Louis Hawks	Dick Ricketts	212
2187	2019	New Orleans Pelicans	Zion Williamson^	85
2325	1953	Philadelphia Warriors	Ernie Beck	371
2925	2020	Minnesota Timberwolves	Anthony Edwards^	144
3094	1962	Chicago Zephyrs	Bill McGill	295
3625	1957	Cincinnati Royals	Hot Rod Hundley	431
3843	2018	Phoenix Suns	Deandre Ayton^	236
3997	1964	New York Knicks	Jim Barnes	454
4030	1963	New York Knicks	Art Heyman	310
4035	2001	Washington Wizards	Kwame Brown	607
4135	1998	Los Angeles Clippers	Michael Olowokandi	500
4382	2016	Philadelphia 76ers	Ben Simmons^	275
4494	1989	Sacramento Kings	Pervis Ellison	474
4636	1956	Rochester Royals	Si Green	504
4658	1965	San Francisco Warriors	Fred Hetzel	416
4928	1950	Boston Celtics	Chuck Share	596
6120	1954	Baltimore Bullets	Frank Selvy	565
6168	1977	Milwaukee Bucks	Kent Benson	680
6215	1974	Portland Trail Blazers	Bill Walton	468
6808	2005	Milwaukee Bucks	Andrew Bogut	706
7039	1983	Houston Rockets	Ralph Sampson	456
7427	1973	Philadelphia 76ers	Doug Collins	415
7873	2006	Toronto Raptors	Andrea Bargnani	550
9247	2002	Houston Rockets	Yao Ming	486
9325	2000	New Jersey Nets	Kenyon Martin	757
9951	1976	Houston Rockets	John Lucas	928

* Clifton McNeeley was drafted by the Pit. Ironmen in 1947, but chose to forego a playing career to become a head coach. Gene Melchiorre was drafted by the Bal. Bullets in 1951, but due to being involved in a point shaving scandal while in college, was banned for life from playing professional basketball by then-NBA President Maurice Podoloff. They are the only two players to be drafted first overall, though never play in the NBA.

** Players taken #1 overall in NBA Draft, but stats include ABA points/games, where applicable.

^ Active.

Highest Amount of Points Scored for #1 Overall Draft Pick·

Career Pts		Draft Year	Drafting Team	Career GP
38,387	Kareem Abdul-Jabbar	1969	Mil. Bucks	1560
37,062	LeBron James^	2003	Cle. Cavaliers	1366
28,596	Shaquille O'Neal	1992	Orl. Magic	1207
27,313	Elvin Hayes	1968	S.D. Rockets	1303
26,946	Hakeem Olajuwon	1984	Hou. Rockets	1238
26,710	Oscar Robertson	1960	Cin. Royals	1040
26,496	Tim Duncan	1997	S.A. Spurs	1392

continued on next page

Career Pts		Draft Year	Drafting Team	Career GP
24,815	Patrick Ewing	1985	N.Y. Knicks	1183
24,368	Allen Iverson	1996	Phi. 76ers	914
23,149	Elgin Baylor	1958	Min. Lakers	846
20,941	Walt Bellamy	1961	Chi. Packers	1043
20,790	David Robinson	1987	S.A. Spurs	987
19,485	Dwight Howard^	2004	Orl. Magic	1242
19,248	Bob Lanier	1970	Det. Pistons	959
18,458	Mark Aguirre	1981	Dal. Mavericks	923
17,707	Magic Johnson	1979	L.A. Lakers	906
17,182	Chris Webber	1993	Orl. Magic	831
16,827	Elton Brand	1999	Chi. Bulls	1058
16,320	James Worthy	1982	L.A. Lakers	926
14,343	Blake Griffin^	2009	L.A. Clippers	724
14,089	Kyrie Irving^	2011	Cle. Cavaliers	611
14,390	Anthony Davis^	2012	N.O. Hornets	604

* Includes ABA.

^ Active.

First Player Drafted by Expansion Franchise

Draft		Team	Round, Pick	College
1961	Walt Bellamy	Chi. Packers	1,1	Indiana
1966	Dave Schellhase	Chi. Bulls	1,10	Purdue
1967	Al Tucker	Sea. Sonics	1,6	Oklahoma Baptist University
1967	Pat Riley	S.D. Rockets	1,7	Kentucky
1968	Charlie Paulk	Mil. Bucks	1,7	Northeastern State University
1968	Gary Gregor	Pho. Suns	1,8	South Carolina
1970	John Johnson	Cle. Cavaliers	1,7	Iowa
1970	Geoff Petrie	Por. Blazers	1,8	Princeton
1970	John Hummer	Buf. Braves	1,15	Princeton
1974	Aaron James	N.O. Jazz	1,28	Grambling State University
1980	Kiki Vandeweghe	Dal. Mavericks	1,11	UCLA
1988	Rex Chapman	Cha. Hornets	1,8	Kentucky
1988	Rony Seikaly	Mia. Heat	1,9	Syracuse
1989	Pooh Richardson	Min. T'Wolves	1,10	UCLA
1989	Nick Anderson	Orl. Magic	1,11	Illinois
1995	Bryant Reeves	Van. Grizzlies	1,6	Oklahoma State
1995	Damon Stoudamire	Tor. Raptors	1,7	Arizona
2004	Emeka Okafor	Cha. Bobcats	1,2	UConn

Players Taken in Multiple Expansion Drafts

	Expansion Team (Draft)	Previous Team
John Barnhill	Chi. Bulls (1966)	Det. Pistons
	S.D. Rockets (1967)	Bal. Bullets
	Pho. Suns (1968)	S.D. Rockets
Nate Bowman	Chi. Bulls (1966)	Cin. Royals
	Sea. Sonics (1967)	Phi. 76ers
Len Chappell	Chi. Bulls (1966)	N.Y. Knicks
	Mil. Bucks (1968)	Det. Pistons
	Cle. Cavaliers (1970)	Mil. Bucks

continued on next page

	Expansion Team (Draft)	Previous Team
Barry Clemens	Chi. Bulls (1966)	N.Y. Knicks
	N.O. Jazz (1974)	Cle. Cavaliers
Don Kojis	Chi. Bulls (1966)	Det. Pistons
	S.D. Rockets (1967)	Chi. Bulls
McCoy McLemore	Chi. Bulls (1966)	S.F. Warriors
	Pho. Suns (1968)	Chi. Bulls
	Cle. Cavaliers (1970)	Det. Pistons
Tom Thacker	Chi. Bulls (1966)	Cin. Royals
	Mil. Bucks (1968)	Bos. Celtics
Gerry Ward	Chi. Bulls (1966)	Phi. 76ers
	S.D. Rockets (1967)	Chi. Bulls
Jim Barnett	S.D. Rockets (1967)	Bos. Celtics
	N.O. Jazz (1974)	G.S. Warriors
John Block	S.D. Rockets (1967)	L.A. Lakers
	N.O. Jazz (1974)	K.C.-Oma. Kings
Dave Gambee	S.D. Rockets (1967)	Phi. 76ers
	Mil. Bucks (1968)	S.D. Rockets
Toby Kimball	S.D. Rockets (1967)	Bos. Celtics
	N.O. Jazz (1974)	Phi. 76ers
Jon McGlocklin	S.D. Rockets (1967)	Cin. Royals
	Mil. Bucks (1968)	S.D. Rockets
Dorie Murrey	Sea. Sonics (1967)	Det. Pistons
	Por. Blazers (1970)	Sea. Sonics
Em Bryant	Pho. Suns (1968)	N.Y. Knicks
	Buf. Braves (1970)	Bos. Celtics
Paul Long	Pho. Suns (1968)	Det. Pistons
	Buf. Braves (1970)	Det. Pistons
George Wilson	Sea. Sonics (1967)	Chi. Bulls
	Pho. Suns (1968)	Sea. Sonics
	Buf. Braves (1970)	Phi. 76ers
Bud Olsen	Sea. Sonics (1967)	S.F. Warriors
	Mil. Bucks (1968)	Sea. Sonics
Bob Weiss	Sea. Sonics (1967)	Phi. 76ers
	Mil. Bucks (1968)	Sea. Sonics
Stan McKenzie	Pho. Suns (1968)	Bal. Bullets
	Por. Blazers (1970)	Pho. Suns
Johnny Egan	Mil. Bucks (1968)	Bal. Bullets
	Cle. Cavaliers (1970)	L.A. Lakers
Fred Hetzel	Mil. Bucks (1968)	S.F. Warriors
	Por. Blazers (1970)	Phi. 76ers
Bingo Smith	Cle. Cavaliers (1970)	S.D. Rockets
	Dal. Mavericks (1980)	S.D. Clippers
Arvid Kramer	Dal. Mavericks (1980)	Den. Nuggets
	Mia. Heat (1988)	Dal. Mavericks

14

MISCELLANY

Players with 5 Points, 5 Rebounds, 5 Assists, 5 Steals, and 5 Blocks in a Single Game

	Pts	Reb	Ast	Stl	Blk
George Johnson*, N.J. Nets .... @ Was. Bullets (Mar. 26, 1978)...............	10	12	6	6	5
George Gervin, S.A. Spurs .... vs. Cle. Cavaliers (Apr. 8, 1979)	21	5	6	5	5
Julius Erving, Phi. 76ers .... vs. S.A. Spurs (Dec. 5, 1979)	28	7	10	5	5
Hakeem Olajuwon*, Hou. Rockets .... vs. Sea. Sonics (Mar. 10, 1987)	38	17	6	7	12
Hakeem Olajuwon, Hou. Rockets .... vs. G.S. Warriors (Mar. 3, 1990).............	29	18	9	5	11
Hakeem Olajuwon*, Hou. Rockets .... vs. Dal. Mavericks (Apr. 11, 1992)	19	13	6	5	5
David Robinson, S.A. Spurs .... vs. Mil. Bucks (Nov. 10, 1992)	29	9	5	5	10
Derrick Coleman, N.J. Nets .... vs. Phi. 76ers (Jan. 15, 1993)	21	10	7	5	5
Hakeem Olajuwon, Hou Rockets .... vs. Min. T'Wolves (Apr. 22, 1993)	33	13	5	5	5
Hakeem Olajuwon, Hou. Rockets .... vs. N.J. Nets (Nov. 5, 1993)	24	19	6	5	5
Hakeem Olajuwon, Hou. Rockets .... @ Min. T'Wolves (Dec. 30, 1993)............	34	10	5	5	8
Vlade Divac, L.A. Lakers .... vs. Phi. 76ers (Feb. 22, 1995)...............	19	12	8	5	5
Jamaal Tinsley*, Ind. Pacers .... vs. Min. T'Wolves (Nov. 16, 2001)	12	9	15	6	5
Andrei Kirilenko*, Uta. Jazz .... @ Hou. Rockets (Dec. 3, 2003)...............	19	5	7	8	5
Andrei Kirilenko, Uta. Jazz .... vs. N.Y. Knicks (Dec. 10, 2003)...............	10	12	6	6	5
Marcus Camby, Den. Nuggets .... vs. Uta. Jazz (Jan. 9, 2004)...................	8	11	5	5	8
Andrei Kirilenko, Uta. Jazz .... vs. L.A. Lakers (Jan. 3, 2006)...............	14	8	9	6	7
Nicolas Batum, Por. Blazers .... vs. N.O. Hornets (Dec. 16, 2012)............	11	5	10	5	5
Draymond Green, G.S. Warriors .... @ Bos. Celtics (Dec. 11, 2015)................	24	11	8	5	5
Anthony Davis*, N.O. Pelicans .... @ Phi. 76ers (Nov. 21, 2018)	12	16	6	5	5
Jusuf Nurkić, Por. Blazers .... @ Sac. Kings (Jan. 1, 2019)...................	24	23	7	5	5

* Team lost game.

Players with 15 Points, 15 Rebounds, and 15 Assists, Game

	Pts	Reb	Ast
Richie Guerin, N.Y. Knicks .... vs. Syr. Nationals (Dec. 20, 1960)............	21	15	17
Oscar Robertson, Cin. Royals...................... vs. Det. Pistons (Dec. 25, 1960)	32	15	16
Oscar Robertson, Cin. Royals*...................... vs. Det. Pistons (Jan. 12, 1961)	31	15	16
Oscar Robertson, Cin. Royals*...................... vs. Phi. Warriors (Feb. 22, 1961)	39	15	18
Oscar Robertson, Cin. Royals...................... vs. Chi. Packers (Nov. 10, 1961)...............	40	15	16
Oscar Robertson, Cin. Royals*...................... vs. Phi. Warriors (Nov. 21, 1961)...............	25	16	18
Oscar Robertson, Cin. Royals...................... vs. Chi. Packers (Dec. 11, 1961)...............	32	15	20
Oscar Robertson, Cin. Royals...................... vs. St.L. Hawks (Feb. 10, 1962)................	32	21	16
Oscar Robertson, Cin. Royals...................... vs. Phi. Warriors (Feb. 13, 1962)	42	15	18
Oscar Robertson, Cin. Royals*...................... vs. Det. Pistons (Feb. 17, 1962)................	30	15	18
Oscar Robertson, Cin. Royals...................... vs. St.L. Hawks (Feb. 20, 1962)................	31	20	16
Guy Rodgers, S.F. Warriors........................... vs. Det. Pistons (Oct. 26, 1962)................	23	20	17
Oscar Robertson, Cin. Royals*...................... @ Bos. Celtics (Feb. 19, 1963)................	35	17	17
Oscar Robertson, Cin. Royals...................... vs. St.L. Hawks (Dec. 25, 1963)	37	15	16
Oscar Robertson, Cin. Royals...................... vs. Bos. Celtics (Mar. 5, 1964)................	27	15	17

continued on next page

	Pts	Reb	Ast
Donnie Butcher, Det. Pistons ....vs. N.Y. Knicks (Mar. 14, 1964) ....19...............15................15			
Oscar Robertson, Cin. Royals.....................vs. N.Y. Knicks (Jan. 6, 1965) ....28...............20................16			
Oscar Robertson, Cin. Royals.....................vs. Phi. 76ers (Jan. 8, 1965) ....26...............15................16			
Wilt Chamberlain, Phi. 76ers.....................vs. Det. Pistons (Nov. 26, 1966) ....26...............24................15			
Wilt Chamberlain, Phi. 76ers.....................vs. Cin. Royals (Feb. 17, 1967)...............15...............22................17			
Wilt Chamberlain, Phi. 76ers.....................vs. Bal. Bullets (Mar. 18, 1967)...............26...............17................15			
Connie Hawkins, Pit. Pipers[a] ....@ Ind. Pacers (Jan. 17, 1968)...................28...............16................18			
Wilt Chamberlain, Phi. 76ers.....................vs. Det. Pistons (Feb. 2, 1968)................22...............25................21			
Wilt Chamberlain, Phi. 76ers.....................vs. S.F. Warriors (Feb. 4, 1968) ....19...............27................16			
Walt Frazier, N.Y. Knicks...........................vs. Phi. 76ers (Feb. 10, 1968)................23...............15................15			
Wilt Chamberlain, Phi. 76ers.....................vs. Sea. Sonics (Feb. 14, 1968) ....35...............24................15			
Wilt Chamberlain, Phi. 76ers.....................vs. S.D. Rockets (Mar. 5, 1968)................31...............21................15			
Wilt Chamberlain, Phi. 76ers*....................vs. Cin. Royals (Mar. 19, 1968)...............22...............27................19			
Micheal Ray Richardson, N.Y. Knicks*..........vs. Ind. Pacers (Mar. 13, 1980)...............15...............16................16			
Micheal Ray Richardson, N.Y. Knicks............vs. Cle. Cavaliers (Mar. 21, 1981) ....27...............15................19			
Magic Johnson, L.A. Lakers*.......................vs. Den. Nuggets (Mar. 29, 1981)...........33...............15................17			
Larry Bird, Bos. Celtics ....vs. Atl. Hawks (Jan. 13, 1982)................28...............19................15			
Larry Bird, Bos. Celtics ....vs. Was. Bullets (Apr. 1, 1987)................30...............17................15			
Magic Johnson, L.A. Lakers*.......................@ Den. Nuggets (Apr. 1, 1989)...............20...............17................15			
Magic Johnson, L.A. Lakers........................vs. Den. Nuggets (Apr. 18, 1989) ....24...............17................17			
Jason Kidd, Dal. Mavericks.........................vs. L.A. Clippers (Jan. 30, 1996) ....21...............16................16			
Jason Kidd, Dal. Mavericks.........................@ Atl. Hawks (Feb. 26, 2010)..................19...............16................17			
Rajon Rondo, Bos. Celtics ....vs. N.Y. Knicks (Mar. 4, 2012) ....18...............17................20			
Russell Westbrook, Ok.C. Thunder ....vs. G.S. Warriors (Jan. 16, 2015) ....17...............15................16			
James Harden, Hou. Rockets ....vs. N.Y. Knicks (Dec. 31, 2016) ....53...............16................17			
Russell Westbrook, Ok.C. Thunder ....vs. L.A. Lakers (Feb. 24, 2017).................17...............18................17			
Russell Westbrook, Ok.C. Thunder ....@ Phi. 76ers (Dec. 15, 2017) ....27...............17................15			
Nikola Jokić, Den. Nuggets.........................@ Mil. Bucks (Feb. 15, 2018)....................30...............15................17			
Russell Westbrook, Ok.C. Thunder ....vs. Cle. Cavaliers (Nov. 28, 2018) ....23...............18................15			
Russell Westbrook, Ok.C. Thunder ....@ Brk. Nets (Dec. 5, 2018)........................21...............15................17			
Russell Westbrook, Ok.C. Thunder ....vs. N.O. Pelicans (Jan. 24, 2019) ....23...............17................16			
Russell Westbrook, Ok.C. Thunder ....vs. Orl. Magic (Feb. 5, 2019) ....16...............15................16			
Russell Westbrook, Ok.C. Thunder ....vs. L.A. Lakers (Apr. 2, 2019)...................20...............20................21			
Giannis Antetokounmpo, Mil. Bucks..............vs. Por. Blazers (Nov. 21, 2019)...............24...............19................15			
Luka Dončić, Dal. Mavericks ....@ Sac. Kings (Jan. 15, 2020).....................25...............15................17			
Luka Dončić, Dal. Mavericks*......................vs. Chi. Bulls (Jan. 17, 2021) ....36...............16................15			
Russell Westbrook, Was. Wizards ....@ Ind. Pacers (May 8, 2021) ....33...............19................15			

* Team lost game.
[a] ABA.

Players with 25 Points, 10 Rebounds, 15 Assists, and 5 Steals, Game

	Pts	Reb	Ast	Stl
Magic Johnson, L.A. Lakers*......................vs. Den. Nuggets (Mar. 29, 1981).............33..........15..........17..........6				
Jason Kidd, N.J. Nets*..............................vs. Orl. Magic (Feb. 23, 2003).................26..........11..........15..........6				
Chris Paul, N.O.-Ok.C. Hornets* ....vs. Chi. Bulls (Dec. 1, 2006)....................25..........11..........18..........5				
Chris Paul, N.O. Hornets........................vs. Phi. 76ers (Jan. 26, 2009) ....27..........10..........15..........7				
James Harden, Hou. Rockets*..................vs. Dal. Mavericks (Nov. 28, 2018) ....25..........11..........17..........6				
James Harden, Phi. 76ers ....@ N.Y. Knicks (Feb. 27, 2022) ....29..........10..........16..........5				

* Team lost game.

Players with 20 Points, 20 Rebounds, and 10 Blocks, Game

		Pts	Reb	Blk
Kareem Abdul-Jabbar, L.A. Lakers	vs. Atl. Hawks (Nov. 2, 1975)	39	23	10
Kareem Abdul-Jabbar, L.A. Lakers	@ Det. Pistons (Dec. 3, 1975)	29	21	11
Elvin Hayes, Was. Bullets	@ Det. Pistons (Mar. 3, 1978)	22	27	11
Hakeem Olajuwon, Hou. Rockets	vs. Uta. Jazz (Nov. 11, 1989)	24	21	12
Hakeem Olajuwon, Hou. Rockets	vs. Orl. Magic (Dec. 17, 1989)	32	25	10
Shaquille O'Neal, Orl. Magic	@ N.J. Nets (Nov. 20, 1993)	24	28	15
Shawn Bradley, Dal. Mavericks*	vs. Por. Blazers (Apr. 7, 1998)	22	22	13
Joakim Noah, Chi. Bulls	vs. Phi. 76ers (Feb. 28, 2013)	23	21	11

* Team lost game.

Players with 55 Points and 15 Rebounds in a Game, Not Named Wilt Chamberlain*

		Pts	Reb
George Mikan, Min. Lakers	vs. Roc. Royals (Jan. 20, 1952)	61	36
Elgin Baylor, Min. Lakers	vs. Bos. Celtics (Nov. 8, 1959)	64	17
Elgin Baylor, L.A. Lakers	@ N.Y. Knicks (Nov. 15, 1960)	71	25
Elgin Baylor, L.A. Lakers	vs. Syr. Nationals (Jan. 24, 1961)	56	20
Elgin Baylor, L.A. Lakers	@ Det. Pistons (Feb. 16, 1961)	57	26
Bob Pettit, St.L. Hawks	@ Det. Pistons (Feb. 18, 1961)	57	28
Elgin Baylor, L.A. Lakers	@ Phi. Warriors (Dec. 8, 1961)	63	31
Rick Barry, S.F. Warriors**	@ N.Y. Knicks (Dec. 14, 1965)	57	15
Rick Barry, S.F. Warriors	@ Cin. Royals (Oct. 29, 1966)	57	15
Mel Daniels, Ind. Pacers[a]	vs. N.Y. Nets[a] (Mar. 18, 1969)	56	31
Kareem Abdul-Jabbar, Mil. Bucks	vs. Bos. Celtics (Dec. 10, 1971)	55	18
Zelmo Beaty, Uta. Stars[a]	vs. Pit. Condors[a] (Feb. 21, 1972)	63	15
George McGinnis, Ind. Pacers[a]	@ Dal. Chaparrals[a] (Nov. 28, 1972)	58	16
Julius Erving, Vir. Squires[a]	vs. N.Y. Nets[a] (Feb. 8, 1973)	58	15
Julius Erving, N.Y. Nets[a]**	@ S.D. Conquistadors[a] (Feb. 14, 1975)	63	23
Purvis Short, G.S. Warriors	vs. S.A. Spurs (Jan. 7, 1984)	57	15
Kevin McHale, Bos. Celtics	vs. Det. Pistons (Mar. 3, 1985)	56	16
Karl Malone, Uta. Jazz	vs. Mil. Bucks (Jan. 27, 1990)	61	18
Michael Jordan, Chi. Bulls	@ Cle. Cavaliers (Mar. 28, 1990)	69	18
Shaquille O'Neal, L.A. Lakers	@ L.A. Clippers (Mar. 6, 2000)	61	23
Anthony Davis, N.O. Pelicans	@ Det. Pistons (Feb. 21, 2016)	59	20
Karl-Anthony Towns, Min. T'Wolves	vs. Atl. Hawks (Mar. 28, 2018)	56	15
James Harden, Hou. Rockets	@ N.Y. Knicks (Jan. 23, 2019)	61	15
Karl-Anthony Towns, Min. T'Wolves	@ S.A. Spurs (Mar. 14, 2022)	60	17

* Chamberlain accomplished this feat 68 times.

** Team lost game.

[a] ABA.

Players with 30 Points, 5 Steals, Zero Turnovers, and Perfect FT%, Game

		Pts	Stl	FT
Dennis Johnson, Bos. Celtics	vs. Ind. Pacers (Nov. 13, 1985)	30	6	4-for-4
Michael Jordan, Chi. Bulls	vs. Sac. Kings (Feb. 22, 1991)	34	6	11-for-11
Gary Payton, Sea. Sonics	@ Dal. Mavericks (Nov. 27, 1992)	31	5	8-for-8
Doug Christie, Sac. Kings*	vs. L.A. Lakers (Nov. 16, 2000)	32	5	6-for-6
Paul George, Ind. Pacers	@ Dal. Mavericks (Feb. 3, 2012)	30	5	1-for-1
OG Anunoby, Tor. Raptors*	@ Den. Nuggets (Mar. 1, 2020)	32	7	5-for-5
Gary Trent Jr., Tor. Raptors	@ Mia. Heat (Jan. 29, 2022)	33	5	2-for-2

* Team lost game.

Players with 10 Assists, 5 Steals, Zero Turnovers, and 5 or Less Points, Game

		Ast	Stl	Pts
Maurice Cheeks, Phi. 76ers	vs. Chi. Bulls (Nov. 11, 1981)	10	5	4
Doc Rivers, Atl. Hawks	vs. Por. Blazers (Feb. 28, 1987)	17	7	5
Sidney Lowe, Min. T'Wolves*	@ G.S. Warriors (Mar. 20, 1990)	17	6	3
Morlon Wiley, Atl. Hawks	vs. Hou. Rockets (Jan. 6, 1992)	14	5	3
Greg Grant, Phi. 76ers	vs. Dal. Mavericks (Dec. 6, 1995)	11	6	4
Bobby Hurley, Sac. Kings*	vs. Pho. Suns (Apr. 10, 1997)	14	5	2
David Wesley, Cha. Hornets*	@ Mil. Bucks (Dec. 4, 1997)	10	5	2
Eric Snow, Phi. 76ers	vs. Was. Wizards (Apr. 12, 2000)	10	5	4

* Team lost game.

Players with 10 Turnovers, Scoring Under 10 Points, Game

		TO	Pts
Kevin Porter, N.J. Nets	@ Phi. 76ers (Nov. 9, 1977)	12	8
Bob Dandridge, Was. Bullets	@ G.S. Warriors (Feb. 7, 1978)	11	6
Bob Gross, Por. Blazers	@ Pho. Suns (Nov. 16, 1979)	10	6
Kenny Carr, Cle. Cavaliers	vs. Mil. Bucks (Feb. 6, 1981)	10	10
Magic Johnson, L.A. Lakers*	@ Pho. Suns (Nov. 14, 1981)	10	8
Rob Williams, Den. Nuggets*	vs. Det. Pistons (Mar. 25, 1983)	10	8
Ralph Sampson, G.S. Warriors*	@ Cle. Cavaliers (Feb. 4, 1988)	10	8
John Lucas, Mil. Bucks*	@ Was. Bullets (Feb. 15, 1988)	10	9
Kevin Edwards, Mia. Heat	@ Por. Blazers (Jan. 3, 1989)	11	8
Magic Johnson, L.A. Lakers*	vs. Dal. Mavericks (Apr. 15, 1991)	11	7
Pooh Richardson, Ind. Pacers	@ G.S. Warriors (Dec. 4, 1993)	11	9
Mark Jackson, Ind. Pacers*	@ Bos. Celtics (Apr. 12, 1998)	10	2

* Team won game.

Players Leading League in Points and Turnovers, Same Season

	Pts	TO
Jerry Stackhouse, Det. Pistons, 2000–01	2380	326
Allen Iverson, Phi. 76ers, 2004–05	2302	344
James Harden, Hou. Rockets, 2014–15	2217	321
James Harden, Hou. Rockets, 2015–16	2376	374

Most Games Registering at Least One Point, Rebound, Assist, Steal, and Block, Career

787	Hakeem Olajuwon	495	Michael Jordan	424	Robert Parish
723	Kevin Garnett	481	Vlade Divac	423	Elton Brand
586	David Robinson	467	Josh Smith	421	Dwight Howard^
577	Tim Duncan	458	Shawn Marion	419	Ben Wallace
559	LeBron James^	456	Clifford Robinson	418	Clyde Drexler
524	Kareem Abdul-Jabbar	437	Chris Webber	408	Charles Barkley
521	Karl Malone	432	Larry Nance	400	Andrei Kirilenko
514	Scottie Pippen	430	Dwyane Wade		
506	Patrick Ewing	429	Shaquille O'Neal		

^ Active.

Most Games Registering at Least One Point, Rebound, Assist, Steal, Block, Free Throws Made, and Three Pointer Made, Career

400................. LeBron James^	178................. Carmelo Anthony^	146................. Rasheed Wallace
314................. Kevin Durant^	176................. Shawn Marion	145................. Charles Barkley
290................. Paul Pierce	176................. Rudy Gay^	144................. Antoine Walker
277................. James Harden^	173................. Clyde Drexler	142................. Josh Smith
257................. Vince Carter	170................. Jason Kidd	141................. Manu Ginóbili
255................. Dirk Nowitzki	167................. Metta World Peace	141................. Kawhi Leonard^
222................. Eddie Jones	156................. Larry Bird	141................. Giannis Antetokounmpo^
214................. Kobe Bryant	151................. Michael Jordan	140................. Baron Davis
192................. Scottie Pippen	150................. Jrue Holiday^	140................. Andre Iguodala^
191................. Clifford Robinson	149................. Paul George^	
186................. Tracy McGrady	148................. Rashard Lewis	

^ Active.

Teammates with the Highest Combined PPG, Season

Total PPG	Team	Player	PPG	Player	PPG
72.3	Phi. Warriors, 1961–62	Wilt Chamberlain	50.4	Paul Arizin	21.9
69.1	L.A. Lakers**, 1961–62	Jerry West	30.8	Elgin Baylor	38.3
61.9	Vir. Squires^a, 1971–72	Charlie Scott	34.6	Julius Erving	27.3
61.6	Phi. Warriors, 1960–61	Wilt Chamberlain	38.4	Paul Arizin	23.2
61.5	Hou. Rockets, 2019–20	James Harden	34.3	Russell Westbrook	27.2
61.1	L.A. Lakers**, 1962–63	Jerry West	27.1	Elgin Baylor	34.0
59.9	Phi. Warriors, 1959–60	Wilt Chamberlain	37.6	Paul Arizin	22.3
58.5	L.A. Lakers**, 1969–70	Jerry West	31.2	Wilt Chamberlain	27.3
58.1	L.A. Lakers**, 1964–65	Jerry West	31.0	Elgin Baylor	27.1
57.5	L.A. Lakers, 2002–03	Shaquille O'Neal	27.5	Kobe Bryant	30.0
57.2	L.A. Lakers*, 2000–01	Shaquille O'Neal	28.7	Kobe Bryant	28.5
56.2	Phi. 76ers, 1965–66	Wilt Chamberlain	33.5	Hal Greer	22.7
55.9	Pit. Condors^a, 1971–72	John Brisker	28.9	George Thompson	27.0
55.8	Cin. Royals, 1960–61	Oscar Robertson	30.5	Jack Twyman	25.3
55.8	Den. Nuggets, 1983–84	Alex English	26.4	Kiki Vandeweghe	29.4
55.5	Oak. Oaks^a*, 1968–69	Rick Barry	34.0	Warren Jabali	21.5
55.3	L.A. Lakers, 1966–67	Jerry West	28.7	Elgin Baylor	26.6
55.2	L.A. Lakers**, 1969–70	Jerry West	31.2	Elgin Baylor	24.0
55.1	Den. Nuggets, 1982–83	Alex English	28.4	Kiki Vandeweghe	26.7
54.9	Den. Rockets^a, 1969–70	Spencer Haywood	30.0	Larry Jones	24.9
54.5	N.Y. Knicks, 1961–62	Willie Naulls	25.0	Richie Guerin	29.5
54.4	Ken. Colonels^a, 1971–72	Dan Issel	30.6	Artis Gilmore	23.8
54.2	Bos. Celtics, 1986–87	Larry Bird	28.1	Kevin McHale	26.1
54.1	L.A. Lakers**, 1963–64	Jerry West	28.7	Elgin Baylor	25.4
54.0	St.L. Hawks, 1961–62	Bob Pettit	31.1	Cliff Hagan	22.9
53.8	Ok.C. Thunder, 2013–14	Kevin Durant	32.0	Russell Westbrook	21.8
53.8	Brk. Nets, 2020–21	Kyrie Irving	26.9	Kevin Durant	26.9
53.7	Cin. Royals, 1961–62	Oscar Robertson	30.8	Jack Twyman	22.9
53.5	Ok.C. Thunder, 2014–15	Kevin Durant	25.4	Russell Westbrook	28.1
53.5	Was. Wizards, 2020–21	Russell Westbrook	22.2	Bradley Beal	31.3
53.4	Chi. Zephyrs, 1962–63	Walt Bellamy	27.9	Terry Dischinger	25.5
53.3	N.O. Pelicans, 2017–18	Anthony Davis	28.1	DeMarcus Cousins	25.2
53.3	G.S. Warriors**, 2018–19	Stephen Curry	27.3	Kevin Durant	26.0

continued on next page

Total PPG	Team	Player	PPG	Player	PPG
53.2	Atl. Hawks, 1972–73	Lou Hudson	27.1	Pete Maravich	26.1
53.2	S.A. Spurs, 1979–80	George Gervin	33.1	Larry Kenon	20.1
53.2	Phi. 76ers, 2005–06	Allen Iverson	33.0	Chris Webber	20.2
53.1	Atl. Hawks, 1973–74	Lou Hudson	25.4	Pete Maravich	27.7
53.0	S.A. Spurs, 1976–77	George Gervin	23.1	Larry Kenon	29.9
52.9	St.L. Hawks*, 1958–59	Bob Pettit	29.2	Cliff Hagan	23.7
52.9	Buf. Braves, 1975–76	Randy Smith	21.8	Bob McAdoo	31.1
52.9	Uta. Jazz, 1982–83	Adrian Dantley	30.7	Darrell Griffith	22.2
52.8	Cin. Royals, 1965–66	Oscar Robertson	31.3	Jerry Lucas	21.5
52.8	G.S. Warriors*, 2017–18	Stephen Curry	26.4	Kevin Durant	26.4
52.5	N.Y. Nets^a**, 1971–72	Rick Barry	31.5	Bill Melchionni	21.0
52.5	Bos. Celtics, 1987–88	Larry Bird	29.9	Kevin McHale	22.6
52.4	L.A. Lakers*, 2001–02	Shaquille O'Neal	27.2	Kobe Bryant	25.2
52.3	L.A. Lakers**, 1967–68	Jerry West	26.3	Elgin Baylor	26.0
52.2	L.A. Lakers*, 1999–00	Shaquille O'Neal	29.7	Kobe Bryant	22.5
52.2	Mia. Heat**, 2010–11	Dwyane Wade	25.5	LeBron James	26.7
52.2	G.S. Warriors**, 2015–16	Stephen Curry	30.1	Klay Thompson	22.1
52.2	Por. Blazers, 2019–20	Damian Lillard	30.0	CJ McCollum	22.2
52.1	Den. Nuggets, 2007–08	Allen Iverson	26.4	Carmelo Anthony	25.7
52.0	St.L. Hawks, 1961–62	Bob Pettit	31.1	Clyde Lovellette	20.9
51.9	Uta. Jazz, 1982–83	Adrian Dantley	30.7	John Drew	21.2
51.9	Dal. Mavericks, 1983–84	Mark Aguirre	29.5	Rolando Blackman	22.4
51.9	Por. Blazers, 2020–21	Damian Lillard	28.8	CJ McCollum	23.1
51.8	Cin. Royals, 1964–65	Oscar Robertson	30.4	Jerry Lucas	21.4
51.7	L.A. Lakers*, 1971–72	Jerry West	25.8	Gail Goodrich	25.9
51.7	S.A. Spurs, 1978–79	George Gervin	29.6	Larry Kenon	22.1
51.7	Cle. Cavaliers**, 2014–15	LeBron James	25.3	Kyrie Irving	26.4
51.7	Ok.C. Thunder, 2015–16	Kevin Durant	28.2	Russell Westbrook	23.5
51.6	Den. Nuggets, 1990–91	Michael Adams	26.5	Orlando Woolridge	25.1
51.6	Ok.C. Thunder**, 2011–12	Kevin Durant	28.0	Russell Westbrook	23.6
51.5	The Floridians^a, 1970–71	Mack Calvin	27.2	Larry Jones	24.3
51.4	L.A. Lakers*, 2019–20	LeBron James	25.3	Anthony Davis	26.1
51.3	L.A. Lakers**, 1969–70	Wilt Chamberlain	27.3	Elgin Baylor	24.0
51.3	Uta. Jazz, 1980–81	Adrian Dantley	30.7	Darrell Griffith	20.6
51.3	Ok.C. Thunder, 2012–13	Kevin Durant	28.1	Russell Westbrook	23.2
51.2	Den. Nuggets, 1984–85	Alex English	27.9	Calvin Natt	23.3
51.1	Chi. Bulls, 1984–85	Michael Jordan	28.2	Orlando Woolridge	22.9
51.1	Chi. Bulls*, 1991–92	Michael Jordan	30.1	Scottie Pippen	21.0
51.1	Bos. Celtics, 2020–21	Jayson Tatum	26.4	Jaylen Brown	24.7
50.9	St.L. Hawks**, 1959–60	Bob Pettit	26.1	Cliff Hagan	24.8
50.9	S.D. Rockets, 1968–69	Elvin Hayes	28.4	Don Kojis	22.5
50.9	Ok.C. Thunder, 2018–19	Paul George	28.0	Russell Westbrook	22.9
50.8	N.O. Pelicans, 2020–21	Zion Williamson	27.0	Brandon Ingram	23.8
50.7	Cin. Royals, 1967–68	Oscar Robertson	29.2	Jerry Lucas	21.5
50.7	L.A. Lakers**, 1968–69	Jerry West	25.9	Elgin Baylor	24.8
50.6	Mil. Bucks, 1969–70	Kareem Abdul-Jabbar	28.8	Flynn Robinson	21.8
50.6	Bos. Celtics, 1971–72	John Havlicek	27.5	Jo Jo White	23.1
50.5	Was. Capitols^a, 1969–70	Rick Barry	27.7	Warren Jabali	22.8
50.4	Sea. Sonics, 1970–71	Bob Rule	29.8	Spencer Haywood	20.6
50.4	G.S. Warriors*, 2016–17	Stephen Curry	25.3	Kevin Durant	25.1
50.4	Mil. Bucks, 2019–20	Giannis Antetokounmpo	29.5	Khris Middleton	20.9

continued on next page

Total PPG	Team	Player	PPG	Player	PPG
50.2	Bos. Celtics, 1970–71	John Havlicek	28.9	Jo Jo White	21.3
50.2	Orl. Magic**, 1994–95	Shaquille O'Neal	29.3	Penny Hardaway	20.9
50.0	St.L. Hawks**, 1960–61	Bob Pettit	27.9	Cliff Hagan	22.1
50.0	Den. Nuggets, 1982–83	Alex English	28.4	Dan Issel	21.6
50.0	Por. Blazers, 2016–17	Damian Lillard	27.0	CJ McCollum	23.0

* Won championship.

** Lost championship.

ª ABA.

Players Averaging 25 Points, 10 Rebounds, 5 Assists, and 50% Field Goal Percentage, Season

	PPG	RPG	APG	FG%
Oscar Robertson, Cin. Royals, 1962–63	28.3	10.4	9.5	.518
Wilt Chamberlain, S.F. Warriors, 1963–64	36.9	22.3	5.0	.524
Wilt Chamberlain, Phi. 76ers, 1965–66	33.5	24.6	5.2	.540
Julius Erving, N.Y. Netsª, 1973–74	27.4	10.7	5.2	.512
Julius Erving, N.Y. Netsª, 1974–75	27.9	10.9	5.5	.506
Kareem Abdul-Jabbar, L.A. Lakers, 1975–76	27.7	16.9	5.0	.529
Julius Erving, N.Y. Netsª, 1975–76	29.3	11.0	5.0	.507
Larry Bird, Bos. Celtics, 1984–85	28.7	10.5	6.6	.522
Charles Barkley, Pho. Suns, 1992–93	25.6	12.2	5.1	.520
Giannis Antetokounmpo, Mil. Bucks, 2018–19	27.7	12.5	5.9	.578
Giannis Antetokounmpo, Mil. Bucks, 2019–20	29.5	13.6	5.6	.553
Giannis Antetokounmpo, Mil. Bucks, 2020–21	28.1	11.0	5.9	.569
Nikola Jokić, Den. Nuggets, 2020–21	26.4	10.8	8.3	.566
Nikola Jokić, Den. Nuggets, 2021–22	27.1	13.8	7.9	.583
Giannis Antetokounmpo, Mil. Bucks, 2021–22	29.9	11.6	5.8	.553

ª ABA.

Players Averaging 25 Points, 10 Rebounds, and 5 Assists in Consecutive Seasons

		PPG	RPG	APG
Oscar Robertson	Cin. Royals, 1960–61	30.5	10.1	9.7
	Cin. Royals, 1961–62	30.8	12.5	11.4
	Cin. Royals, 1962–63	28.3	10.4	9.5
Julius Erving	N.Y. Netsª, 1973–74*	27.4	10.7	5.2
	N.Y. Netsª, 1974–75**	27.9	10.9	5.5
	N.Y. Netsª, 1975–76*	29.3	11.0	5.0
Russell Westbrook	Ok.C. Thunder, 2016–17*	31.6	10.7	10.4
	Ok.C. Thunder, 2017–18	25.4	10.1	10.3
Giannis Antetokounmpo	Mil. Bucks, 2018–19*	27.7	12.5	5.9
	Mil. Bucks, 2019–20*	29.5	13.6	5.6
	Mil. Bucks, 2020–21	28.1	11.0	5.9
	Mil. Bucks, 2021–22	29.9	11.6	5.8
Nikola Jokić	Den. Nuggets, 2020–21*	26.4	10.8	8.3
	Den. Nuggets, 2021–22*	27.1	13.8	7.9

* Most Valuable Player.

** Tied for MVP Award with George McGinnis, Ind. Pacers.

ª ABA.

Players with 750 Rebounds, Shooting 85% from the Free-Throw Line, Season

	Reb	FT%
Dolph Schayes, Syr. Nationals, 1955–56	891	.858
Dolph Schayes, Syr. Nationals, 1956–57	1008	.904
Dolph Schayes, Syr. Nationals, 1957–58	1022	.904
Dolph Schayes, Syr. Nationals, 1958–59	962	.864
Kenny Sears, N.Y. Knicks, 1959–60	876	.868
Dolph Schayes, Syr. Nationals, 1959–60	959	.893
Dolph Schayes, Syr. Nationals, 1960–61	960	.868
Oscar Robertson, Cin. Royals, 1963–64	783	.853
Rick Barry, S.F. Warriors, 1965–66	850	.862
Byron Beck, Den. Rockets[a], 1970–71	884	.868
Dave Robisch, Ind. Pacers[a]/S.D. Sails[a], 1975–76	794	.850
Larry Kenon, S.A. Spurs, 1977–78	773	.854
Larry Bird, Bos. Celtics, 1980–81	895	.863
Jack Sikma, Sea. Sonics, 1981–82	1038	.855
Larry Bird, Bos. Celtics, 1981–82	837	.863
Jack Sikma, Sea. Sonics, 1983–84	911	.856
Bill Laimbeer, Det. Pistons, 1983–84	1003	.866
Larry Bird, Bos. Celtics, 1983–84	796	.888
Larry Bird, Bos. Celtics, 1984–85	842	.882
Larry Bird, Bos. Celtics, 1985–86	805	.896
Bill Laimbeer, Det. Pistons, 1986–87	955	.894
Bill Laimbeer, Det. Pistons, 1987–88	832	.874
Mike Gminski, N.J. Nets/Phi. 76ers, 1987–88	814	.906
Mike Gminski, Phi. 76ers, 1988–89	769	.871
Bill Laimbeer, Det. Pistons, 1989–90	780	.854
Dirk Nowitzki, Dal. Mavericks, 2001–02	755	.853
P.J. Brown, Cha. Hornets, 2001–02	786	.858
Dirk Nowitzki, Dal. Mavericks, 2002–03	791	.881
Shawn Marion, Pho. Suns, 2002–03	773	.851
Dirk Nowitzki, Dal. Mavericks, 2004–05	757	.869
Yao Ming, Hou. Rockets, 2008–09	761	.866
Kevin Love, Min. T'Wolves, 2010–11	1112	.850
Karl-Anthony Towns, Min. T'Wolves, 2017–18	1012	.858
Nikola Jokić, Den. Nuggets, 2017–18	803	.850
Nikola Jokić, Den. Nuggets, 2020–21	780	.868

[a] ABA.

Players Averaging 15 Points, 5 Rebounds, and 5 Assists Per Game, with a 90% Free Throw Percentage, Season (Min. 40 Games Played)

	PPG	RPG	APG	FT%
Rick Barry, G.S. Warriors, 1974–75	30.6	5.7	6.2	.904
Rick Barry, G.S. Warriors, 1975–76	21.0	6.1	6.1	.923
Rick Barry, G.S. Warriors, 1976–77	21.8	5.3	6.0	.916
Rick Barry, G.S. Warriors, 1977–78	23.1	5.5	5.4	.924
Larry Bird, Bos. Celtics, 1986–87	28.1	9.2	7.6	.910
Larry Bird, Bos. Celtics, 1987–88	29.9	9.3	6.1	.916
Magic Johnson, L.A. Lakers, 1988–89	22.5	7.9	12.8	.911
Larry Bird, Bos. Celtics, 1989–90	24.3	9.5	7.5	.930

continued on next page

	PPG	RPG	APG	FT%
Magic Johnson, L.A. Lakers, 1990–91	19.4	7.0	12.5	.906
Larry Bird, Bos. Celtics, 1991–92	20.2	9.6	6.8	.926
Stephen Curry, G.S. Warriors, 2015–16	30.1	5.4	6.7	.908
Stephen Curry, G.S. Warriors, 2017–18	26.4	5.1	6.1	.921
Chris Paul, Hou. Rockets, 2017–18	18.6	5.4	7.9	.919
Stephen Curry, G.S. Warriors, 2018–19	27.3	5.3	5.2	.916
Stephen Curry, G.S. Warriors, 2020–21	32.0	5.5	5.8	.916
Stephen Curry, G.S. Warriors, 2021–22	25.5	5.2	6.3	.923
Kevin Durant, Brk. Nets, 2021–22	29.9	7.4	6.4	.910

Players with 20,000 Points, 10,000 Rebounds, 3000 Assists, 1000 Blocks, and 500 Steals, Career

	Pts	Reb	Ast	Blk	Stl
Kareem Abdul-Jabbar	38,387	17,440	5660	3189	1160
Tim Duncan	26,496	15,091	4225	3020	1025
Julius Erving*	30,026	10,525	5176	1941	2272
Kevin Garnett	26,071	14,662	5445	2037	1859
Pau Gasol	20,894	11,305	3925	1941	606
Artis Gilmore*	24,941	16,330	3050	3178	648
LeBron James^	37,062	10,210	10,045	1041	2136
Karl Malone	36,928	14,968	5248	1145	2085
Dirk Nowitzki	31,560	11,489	3651	1281	1210
Shaquille O'Neal	28,596	13,099	3026	2732	739
Hakeem Olajuwon	26,946	13,748	3058	3830	2162

* Includes ABA.

^ Active.

Most Double-Doubles (Points and Rebounds), Season

81	Wilt Chamberlain, Phi. 76ers, 1966–67
80	Wilt Chamberlain, Phi. Warriors, 1961–62
80	Wilt Chamberlain, S.F. Warriors, 1962–63
80	Wilt Chamberlain, S.F. Warriors, 1963–64
80	Wilt Chamberlain, Phi. 76ers, 1967–68
79	Wilt Chamberlain, Phi. Warriors, 1960–61
79	Wilt Chamberlain, Phi. 76ers, 1965–66
79	Jerry Lucas, Cin. Royals, 1967–68
79	Elvin Hayes, S.D. Rockets, 1969–70
78	Elvin Hayes, S.D. Rockets, 1968–69
78	Kareem Abdul-Jabbar, Mil. Bucks, 1971–72
77	Walt Bellamy, Chi. Packers, 1961–62
77	Kareem Abdul-Jabbar, Mil. Bucks, 1970–71
77	Elvin Hayes, S.D. Rockets, 1970–71
77	Kareem Abdul-Jabbar, L.A. Lakers, 1975–76
77	Moses Malone, Hou. Rockets, 1978–79

^ Active.

Most Double-Doubles (Points and Rebounds), Career

972*	Moses Malone
966	Wilt Chamberlain
885	Elvin Hayes
882	Kareem Abdul-Jabbar
841	Tim Duncan
828**	Artis Gilmore
811	Karl Malone
774	Hakeem Olajuwon
771	Bill Russell
748	Dwight Howard^
741	Kevin Garnett
732	Walt Bellamy
727	Shaquille O'Neal
706	Charles Barkley

* 894 in NBA, 78 in ABA.

** 461 in NBA, 367 in ABA.

Most 20–20 Games
(Points and Rebounds), Season

69........... Wilt Chamberlain, Phi. Warriors, 1960–61
69........... Wilt Chamberlain, Phi. Warriors, 1961–62
65........... Wilt Chamberlain, Phi. 76ers, 1965–66
62........... Wilt Chamberlain, Phi. Warriors, 1959–60
62........... Wilt Chamberlain, S.F. Warriors, 1962–63
52........... Wilt Chamberlain, S.F. Warriors, 1963–64
47........... Wilt Chamberlain, S.F. Warriors/Phi. 76ers, 1964–65
47........... Wilt Chamberlain, Phi. 76ers, 1966–67
41........... Elgin Baylor, L.A. Lakers, 1960–61
41........... Wilt Chamberlain, Phi. 76ers, 1967–68
38........... Bob Pettit, St.L. Hawks, 1960–61
35........... Walt Bellamy, Chi. Packers, 1961–62
31........... Moses Malone, Hou. Rockets, 1978–79
30........... Bill Russell, Bos. Celtics, 1961–62
29........... Bob Pettit, St.L. Hawks, 1961–62
29........... Wilt Chamberlain, L.A. Lakers, 1968–69
28........... Jerry Lucas, Cin. Royals, 1965–66
27........... Kareem Abdul-Jabbar, L.A. Lakers, 1975–76
26........... Artis Gilmore, Ken. Colonelsᵃ, 1971–72

ᵃ ABA.

Most 20–20 Games
(Points and Rebounds), Career

589.......................... Wilt Chamberlain
196.......................... Bill Russell
171.......................... Bob Pettit
144.......................... Nate Thurmond
138.......................... Jerry Lucas
124.......................... Walt Bellamy
120.......................... Elvin Hayes
120.......................... Kareem Abdul-Jabbar
120.......................... Moses Malone
117.......................... Elgin Baylor
116.......................... Artis Gilmore
94........................... Mel Daniels
61........................... Dave Cowens
55........................... Willis Reed
51........................... Dwight Howard^
46........................... Bob Lanier
44........................... Andre Drummond^
43........................... Bob McAdoo
42........................... Dolph Schayes
42........................... Hakeem Olajuwon
42........................... Charles Barkley

^ Active.

Longest Streak of Consecutive Double-Doubles

		First Game of Streak	Last Game of Streak
53	Kevin Love	Nov. 22, 2010	Mar. 11, 2011
37	John Stockton	Feb. 27, 1989	Nov. 29, 1989
37	Kevin Garnett	Feb. 1, 2006	Nov. 6, 2006
36	Russell Westbrook	Mar. 13, 2021	May 16, 2021
33	Dwight Howard	Jan. 21, 2011	Apr. 1, 2011
28	Charles Barkley	Dec. 10, 1986	Feb. 3, 1987
27	Blake Griffin	Nov. 20, 2010	Jan. 17, 2011
26	Hakeem Olajuwon	Mar. 14, 1991	Nov. 9, 1991
25	John Stockton	Jan. 29, 1991	Mar. 23, 1991
24	David Lee	Jan. 14, 2009	Mar. 4, 2009
24	Nikola Jokić	Jan. 25, 2022	Mar. 18, 2022
23	Charles Barkley	Feb. 16, 1987	Apr. 1, 1987
23	Russell Westbrook	Jan. 6, 2019	Feb. 28, 2019
22	Joel Embiid	Jan. 21, 2019	Oct. 28, 2019
21	Kevin Willis	Jan. 24, 1992	Mar. 11, 1992
20	John Stockton	Apr. 2, 1991	Nov. 15, 1991
20	Dwight Howard	Jan. 15, 2010	Feb. 26, 2010
20	Giannis Antetokounmpo	Jan. 16, 2020	Aug. 2, 2020
20	Nikola Jokić	Dec. 23, 2020	Jan. 31, 2021

Most Triple-Doubles, Season

42.............Russell Westbrook, Ok.C. Thunder, 2016–17
41.............Oscar Robertson, Cin. Royals, 1961–62
38.............Russell Westbrook, Was. Wizards, 2020–21

34.............Russell Westbrook, Ok.C. Thunder, 2018–19
31.............Wilt Chamberlain, Phi. 76ers, 1967–68
26.............Oscar Robertson*, Cin. Royals, 1960–61

continued on next page

26.............Oscar Robertson, Cin. Royals, 1963–64	22.............Wilt Chamberlain, Phi. 76ers, 1966–67
25.............Russell Westbrook, Ok.C. Thunder, 2017–18	22.............James Harden, Hou. Rockets, 2016–17
22.............Oscar Robertson, Cin. Royals, 1964–65	20.............Oscar Robertson, Cin. Royals, 1962–63

* Rookie season.

Most Triple-Doubles, Career

194.................Russell Westbrook^	69..................James Harden^	29...................John Havlicek
182.................Oscar Robertson	59..................Larry Bird	29...................Grant Hill
138.................Magic Johnson	46..................Luka Dončić^	29...................Giannis Antetokounmpo^
107.................Jason Kidd	43..................Fat Lever	28...................Michael Jordan
105.................LeBron James^	32..................Rajon Rondo^	25...................Elgin Baylor
78.................Wilt Chamberlain	32..................Ben Simmons^	25...................Clyde Drexler
76.................Nikola Jokić^	31..................Draymond Green^	

^ Active.

Player Averaging a Triple-Double, Season

	PPG	RPG	APG
Oscar Robertson, Cin. Royals, 1961–62	30.8	12.5	11.4
Russell Westbrook, Ok.C. Thunder, 2016–17	31.6	10.7	10.4
Russell Westbrook, Ok.C. Thunder, 2017–18	25.4	10.1	10.3
Russell Westbrook, Ok.C. Thunder, 2018–19	22.9	11.1	10.7
Russell Westbrook, Was. Wizards, 2020–21	22.2	11.5	11.7

Most Games with 30 Points, 10 Rebounds, and 10 Assists, Career

106............Oscar Robertson	21..............Wilt Chamberlain	16..............Michael Jordan
48............Russell Westbrook^	21..............Luka Dončić^	12..............Nikola Jokic^
37............LeBron James^	17..............Larry Bird	10..............Giannis Antetokounmpo^
35............James Harden^	17..............Magic Johnson	

^ Active.

Fewest Games Played Before First Career Triple-Double (Points, Rebounds, Assists)

Game #				Pts	Reb	Ast
1	Oscar Robertson, Cin. Royals	vs. L.A. Lakers (Oct. 19, 1960)		21	12	10
4	Art Williams, S.D. Rockets*	vs. Sea. Sonics (Oct. 21, 1967)		17	15	13
4	Ben Simmons, Phi. 76ers	@ Det. Pistons (Oct. 23, 2017)		21	12	10
5	Magic Johnson, L.A. Lakers	vs. G.S. Warriors (Oct. 28, 1979)		15	10	10
6	Guy Rodgers, Phi. Warriors	vs. N.Y. Knicks (Dec. 26, 1958)		28	11	12
6	John Wall, Was. Wizards	vs. Hou. Rockets (Nov. 10, 2010)		19	10	13
7	Jay Williams, Chi. Bulls	vs. N.J. Nets (Nov. 9, 2002)		26	14	13
9	Jim Tucker, Syr. Nationals	vs. N.Y. Knicks (Feb. 20, 1955)		12	10	12
10	LaMelo Ball, Cha. Hornets	vs. Atl. Hawks (Jan. 9, 2021)		22	12	11
11	Tom Gola, Phi. Warriors	vs. Min. Lakers (Dec. 6, 1955)		13	12	15
11	Norm Van Lier, Cin. Royals	vs. S.D. Rockets (Nov. 5, 1969)		13	10	11
11	Damon Stoudamire, Tor. Raptors	vs. Sea. Sonics (Nov. 21, 1995)		20	12	11
11	Cade Cunningham, Det. Pistons*	vs. L.A. Lakers (Nov. 21, 2021)		13	12	10
13	Elgin Baylor, Min. Lakers	vs. Syr. Nationals (Nov. 20, 1958)		37	14	10
13	Alvan Adams, Pho. Suns	vs. Por. Blazers (Nov. 28, 1975)		17	10	11
14	Larry Bird, Bos. Celtics	vs. Det. Pistons (Nov. 14, 1979)		23	19	10
14	Jamaal Tinsley, Ind. Pacers	vs. Was. Wizards (Nov. 22, 2001)		19	11	23
14	Markelle Fultz, Phi. 76ers	vs. Mil. Bucks (Apr. 11, 2018)		13	10	10
15	Michael Carter-Williams, Phi. 76ers	vs. Orl. Magic (Dec. 3, 2013)		27	12	10

* Team lost game.

Youngest Player to Achieve First Career Triple-Double

Age		Pts	Reb	Ast
19 years, 84 days	Josh Giddey, Ok.C. Thunder ... vs. Dal. Mavericks (Jan. 2, 2022)	17	13	14
19 years, 140 days	LaMelo Ball, Cha. Hornets ... vs. Atl. Hawks (Jan. 9, 2021)	22	12	11
19 years, 317 days	Markelle Fultz, Phi. 76ers ... vs. Mil. Bucks (Apr. 11, 2018)	13	10	10
19 years, 327 days	Luka Dončić, Dal. Mavericks ... @ Mil. Bucks (Jan. 21, 2019)	18	11	10
20 years, 15 days	Lonzo Ball, L.A. Lakers ... @ Mil. Bucks (Nov. 11, 2017)	19	12	13
20 years, 20 days	LeBron James, Cle. Cavaliers ... @ Por. Blazers (Jan. 19, 2005)	27	11	10
20 years, 34 days	Dennis Smith Jr., Dal. Mavericks ... @ N.O. Pelicans (Dec. 29, 2017)	21	10	10
20 years, 54 days	Lamar Odom, L.A. Clippers ... @ Hou. Rockets (Dec. 30, 1999)	10	13	10
20 years, 57 days	Cade Cunningham, Det. Pistons ... vs. L.A. Lakers (Nov. 21, 2021)	13	12	10
20 years, 65 days	John Wall, Was. Wizards ... vs. Hou. Rockets (Nov. 10, 2010)	19	10	13
20 years, 75 days	Magic Johnson, L.A. Lakers ... vs. G.S. Warriors (Oct. 28, 1979)	15	10	10
20 years, 110 days	Russell Westbrook, Ok.C. Thunder ... vs. Dal. Mavericks (Mar. 2, 2009)	17	10	10
20 years, 125 days	Lamar Odom, L.A. Clippers ... vs. Cha. Hornets (Mar. 10, 2000)	10	10	11
20 years, 129 days	Shareef Abdur-Rahim, Van. Grizzlies ... @ Pho. Suns (Apr. 19, 1997)	26	10	10
20 years, 171 days	Trae Young, Atl. Hawks ... vs. Brk. Nets (Mar. 9, 2019)	23	10	11
20 years, 172 days	Tyreke Evans, Sac. Kings ... vs. Tor. Raptors (Mar. 10, 2010)	19	10	10
20 years, 183 days	Ja Morant, Mem. Grizzlies ... @ Was. Wizards (Feb. 9, 2020)	27	10	10
20 years, 214 days	Tony Wroten, Phi. 76ers ... vs. Hou. Rockets (Nov. 13, 2013)	18	10	11
20 years, 235 days	Jrue Holiday, Phi. 76ers ... @ N.J. Nets (Feb. 2, 2011)	11	10	11
20 years, 247 days	Antoine Walker, Bos. Celtics ... vs. Cha. Hornets (Apr. 16, 1997)	23	10	10
20 years, 297 days	Chris Webber, G.S. Warriors ... vs. L.A. Clippers (Dec. 23, 1993)	22	12	12
20 years, 316 days	De'Aaron Fox, Sac. Kings ... @ Atl. Hawks (Nov. 1, 2018)	31	10	15
20 years, 330 days	Spencer Haywood, Den. Rockets[a] ... @ Ind. Pacers (Mar. 18, 1970)	20	17	11
20 years, 331 days	Chris Paul, N.O.-Ok.C. Hornets ... @ Tor. Raptors (Apr. 2, 2006)	24	12	12

[a] ABA.

Players with Quadruple-Double

		Pts	Reb	Ast	Blk
Nate Thurmond, Chi. Bulls	vs. Atl. Hawks (Oct. 18, 1974)	22	14	13	12
Hakeem Olajuwon, Hou. Rockets	vs. G.S. Warriors (Mar. 3, 1990)	29	18	10	11
Hakeem Olajuwon, Hou. Rockets	vs. Mil. Bucks (Mar. 29, 1990)	18	16	10	11
David Robinson, S.A. Spurs	vs. Det. Pistons (Feb. 17, 1994)	34	10	10	10

Unlucky Quadruple Double (10 or More Points, Rebounds, Assists, and Turnovers)

		Pts	Reb	Ast	TO
Magic Johnson, L.A. Lakers	vs. Cle. Cavaliers (Nov. 11, 1979)	24	16	12	10
Clyde Drexler, Por. Blazers	@ Atl. Hawks (Mar. 5, 1985)	13	11	10	10
Charles Barkley, Phi. 76ers	vs. N.J. Nets (Mar. 27, 1987)	28	15	10	10
Jason Kidd, Pho. Suns*	vs. N.Y. Knicks (Nov. 17, 2000)	18	12	10	14
Russell Westbrook, Ok.C. Thunder	vs. N.O. Pelicans (Dec. 4, 2016)	28	17	12	10
James Harden, Hou. Rockets	@ Tor. Raptors (Jan. 8, 2017)	40	10	11	10
Russell Westbrook, Ok.C. Thunder*	@ Min. T'Wolves (Jan. 13, 2017)	21	11	12	10
Russell Westbrook, Ok.C. Thunder*	@ G.S. Warriors (Jan. 18, 2017)	27	15	13	10
James Harden, Hou. Rockets	@ Sac. Kings (Apr. 9, 2017)	35	11	15	10
LeBron James, Cle. Cavaliers	vs. Ind. Pacers (Jan. 26, 2018)	26	11	11	11
Russell Westbrook, Ok.C. Thunder*	@ Chi. Bulls (Dec. 7, 2018)	24	17	13	10
Blake Griffin, Det. Pistons*	vs. Mil. Bucks (Dec. 17, 2018)	19	10	11	10
Russell Westbrook, Ok.C. Thunder	@ Hou. Rockets (Feb. 9, 2019)	21	12	11	10

continued on next page

		Pts	Reb	Ast	TO
James Harden, Hou. Rockets*	@ Cha. Hornets (Mar. 7, 2020)	30	10	14	10
Nikola Jokić, Den. Nuggets*	@ Sac. Kings (Dec. 29, 2020)	26	10	12	10
Russell Westbrook, L.A. Lakers*	@ Ok.C. Thunder (Oct. 27, 2021)	20	14	13	10

* Team lost game.

Highest Plus-Minus, Season

		Record
+1070	Draymond Green, G.S. Warriors, 2015–16	73–9 (.890)
+1022	Stephen Curry, G.S. Warriors, 2015–16	73–9 (.890)
+1015	Stephen Curry, G.S. Warriors*, 2016–17	67–15 (.817)
+920	Stephen Curry, G.S. Warriors*, 2014–15	67–15 (.817)
+870	LeBron James, Cle. Cavaliers, 2008–09	66–16 (.805)
+839	Draymond Green, G.S. Warriors*, 2014–15	67–15 (.817)
+836	Klay Thompson, G.S. Warriors, 2015–16	73–9 (.890)
+820	Draymond Green, G.S. Warriors*, 2016–17	67–15 (.817)
+818	Michael Jordan, Chi. Bulls*, 1996–97	69–13 (.841)
+807	Scottie Pippen, Chi. Bulls*, 1996–97	69–13 (.841)
+801	Klay Thompson, G.S. Warriors*, 2016–17	67–15 (.817)
+785	Paul Pierce, Bos. Celtics*, 2007–08	66–16 (.805)
+778	Dirk Nowitzki, Dal. Mavericks, 2002–03	60–22 (.732)
+776	Klay Thompson, G.S. Warriors*, 2014–15	67–15 (.817)
+775	Jeff Hornacek, Uta. Jazz, 1996–97	64–18 (.780)
+768	Karl Malone, Uta. Jazz, 1996–97	64–18 (.780)
+748	Tim Duncan, S.A. Spurs*, 2006–07	58–24 (.707)
+736	Kevin Garnett, Bos. Celtics*, 2007–08	66–16 (.805)
+734	Chris Paul, L.A. Clippers, 2014–15	56–26 (.683)
+728	Rudy Gobert, Uta. Jazz, 2020–21	52–20 (.722)
+721	Kevin Durant, Ok.C. Thunder, 2012–13	60–22 (.732)
+720	LeBron James, Mia. Heat*, 2012–13	66–16 (.805)
+711	Kevin Durant, G.S. Warriors*, 2016–17	67–15 (.817)
+706	Shaquille O'Neal, L.A. Lakers*, 1999–00	67–15 (.817)

* Team won championship.

Lowest Plus-Minus, Season

		Record
-756	Dean Garrett, Den. Nuggets, 1997–98	11–71 (.134)
-711	Michael Olowokandi, L.A. Clippers, 1999–00	15–67 (.183)
-684	Roy Hibbert, L.A. Lakers, 2015–16	17–65 (.207)
-681	Julius Randle, L.A. Lakers, 2015–16	17–65 (.207)
-672	Collin Sexton, Cle. Cavaliers, 2018–19	19–63 (.232)
-651	Kevin Durant, Sea. Sonics, 2007–08	20–62 (.244)
-650	Thaddeus Young, Phi. 76ers, 2013–14	19–63 (.232)
-647	Elton Brand, Chi. Bulls, 1999–00	17–65 (.207)
-641	Cedi Osman, Cle. Cavaliers, 2018–19	19–63 (.232)
-638	Ricky Davis, Cle. Cavaliers, 2002–03	17–65 (.207)
-637	Kevin Knox II, N.Y. Knicks, 2018–19	17–65 (.207)
-628	Jordan Clarkson, L.A. Lakers, 2015–16	17–65 (.207)
-627	Jonny Flynn, Min. T'Wolves, 2009–10	15–67 (.183)
-621	Theo Maledon, Ok.C. Thunder, 2020–21	22–50 (.306)
-619	Tyrone Nesby, L.A. Clippers, 1999–00	15–67 (.183)
-604	LaPhonso Ellis, Den. Nuggets, 1997–98	11–71 (.134)

continued on next page

		Record
-596	Shareef Abdul-Rahim, Van. Grizzlies, 1996–97	14–68 (.171)
-595	Brook Lopez, N.J. Nets, 2009–10	12–70 (.146)
-593	Ricky Davis, Mia. Heat, 2007–08	15–67 (.183)
-589	Maurice Taylor, L.A. Clippers, 1999–00	15–67 (.183)
-580	Derek Anderson, L.A. Clippers, 1999–00	15–67 (.183)
-571	Kobe Bryant, L.A. Lakers, 2015–16	17–65 (.207)
-566	Al Thornton, L.A. Clippers, 2008–09	19–63 (.232)
-559	Antoine Walker, Bos. Celtics, 1996–97	15–67 (.183)

Highest Box Plus/Minus* (BPM), Season

13.7 ... Nikola Jokić**, Den. Nuggets, 2021–22	11.0 ... James Harden, Hou. Rockets, 2018–19
13.2 ... LeBron James**, Cle. Cavaliers, 2008–09	10.9 ... LeBron James, Cle. Cavaliers, 2007–08
13.0 ... Michael Jordan**, Chi. Bulls, 1987–88	10.9 ... LeBron James**, Mia. Heat, 2011–12
12.0 ... Michael Jordan**, Chi. Bulls, 1990–91	10.8 ... Michael Jordan, Chi. Bulls, 1986–87
11.9 ... Michael Jordan, Chi. Bulls, 1988–89	10.6 ... Julius Erving**, N.Y. Nets[a], 1975–76
11.9 ... David Robinson, S.A. Spurs, 1993–94	10.6 ... Dwyane Wade, Mia. Heat, 2008–09
11.9 ... Stephen Curry**, G.S. Warriors, 2015–16	10.5 ... Michael Jordan**, Chi. Bulls, 1995–96
11.8 ... LeBron James**, Cle. Cavaliers, 2009–10	10.5 ... Tracy McGrady, Orl. Magic, 2002–03
11.7 ... LeBron James**, Mia. Heat, 2012–13	10.4 ... Chris Paul, N.O. Hornets, 2007–08
11.7 ... Nikola Jokić**, Den. Nuggets, 2020–21	10.4 ... Giannis Antetokounmpo**, Mil. Bucks, 2018–19
11.5 ... Giannis Antetokounmpo**, Mil. Bucks, 2019–20	10.2 ... Kevin Garnett, Min**. T'Wolves, 2003–04
11.2 ... Michael Jordan, Chi. Bulls, 1989–90	10.2 ... Kevin Durant**, Ok.C. Thunder, 2013–14
11.2 ... Michael Jordan, Chi. Bulls, 1992–93	10.1 ... Magic Johnson**, L.A. Lakers, 1989–90
11.2 ... Giannis Antetokounmpo, Mil. Bucks, 2021–22	10.1 ... Kawhi Leonard, S.A. Spurs, 2017–18
11.1 ... Russell Westbrook**, Ok.C. Thunder, 2016–17	10.0 ... Kevin Durant, Ok.C. Thunder, 2014–15
11.0 ... Chris Paul, N.O. Hornets, 2008–09	

* Box Plus/Minus is "A box score estimate of the points per 100 possessions a player contributed above a league-average player, translated to an average team." (basketball-reference.com)

** Won MVP.

[a] ABA.

Highest Win Share, Season[WS]

WS

25.4	Kareem Abdul-Jabbar*, Mil. Bucks, 1971–72
25.0	Wilt Chamberlain, S.F. Warriors, 1963–64
23.4	George Mikan, Min. Lakers, 1950–51
23.1	Wilt Chamberlain, Phi. Warriors, 1961–62
22.3	Kareem Abdul-Jabbar*, Mil. Bucks, 1970–71
21.9	Wilt Chamberlain*, Phi. 76ers, 1966–67
21.9	Kareem Abdul-Jabbar, Mil. Bucks, 1972–73
21.4	Wilt Chamberlain*, Phi. 76ers, 1965–66
21.2	Michael Jordan*, Chi. Bulls, 1987–88
21.1	George Mikan, Min. Lakers, 1949–50
20.9	George Mikan, Min. Lakers, 1948–49
20.9	Wilt Chamberlain, S.F. Warriors, 1962–63
20.6	Oscar Robertson*, Cin. Royals, 1963–64
20.4	Wilt Chamberlain*, Phi. 76ers, 1967–68
20.4	Michael Jordan*, Chi. Bulls, 1995–96
20.3	Michael Jordan*, Chi. Bulls, 1990–91
20.3	LeBron James*, Cle. Cavaliers, 2008–09

Highest Win Share, Career

WS

273.4	Kareem Abdul-Jabbar
249.5	LeBron James
247.3	Wilt Chamberlain
234.6	Karl Malone
214.0	Michael Jordan
207.7	John Stockton
206.4	Tim Duncan
206.3	Dirk Nowitzki
198.9	Chris Paul
191.4	Kevin Garnett
189.7	Artis Gilmore
189.2	Oscar Robertson
181.7	Shaquille O'Neal
181.1	Julius Erving
179.1	Moses Malone
178.7	David Robinson
177.2	Charles Barkley

continued on next page

WS

20.0	David Robinson, S.A. Spurs, 1993–94
19.8	Artis Gilmore* **, Ken. Colonels[a], 1971–72
19.8	Michael Jordan, Chi. Bulls, 1988–89
19.3	LeBron James*, Mia. Heat, 2012–13
19.2	Kevin Durant*, Ok.C. Thunder, 2013–14
19.0	Michael Jordan, Chi. Bulls, 1989–90
18.9	Kevin Durant, Ok.C. Thunder, 2012–13
18.8	Wilt Chamberlain, Phi. Warriors, 1960–61
18.6	Bob Feerick, Was. Capitols, 1946–47
18.6	Shaquille O'Neal*, L.A. Lakers, 1999–00
18.5	Artis Gilmore, Ken. Colonels[a], 1972–73
18.5	LeBron James*, Cle. Cavaliers, 2009–10
18.4	Kareem Abdul-Jabbar*, Mil. Bucks, 1973–74
18.3	Neil Johnston, Phi. Warriors, 1953–54
18.3	David Robinson, S.A. Spurs, 1995–96
18.3	Michael Jordan, Chi. Bulls, 1996–97
18.3	Kevin Garnett*, Min. T'Wolves, 2003–04
18.3	Chris Paul, N.O. Hornets, 2008–09
18.2	Wilt Chamberlain, L.A. Lakers, 1972–73
18.0	Alex Groza, Ind. Olympians, 1950–51
17.9	Alex Groza**, Ind. Olympians, 1949–50
17.9	Connie Hawkins*, Pit. Pipers[a], 1967–68
17.9	Stephen Curry*, G.S. Warriors, 2015–16
17.8	Bob McAdoo*, Buf. Braves, 1974–75
17.8	Kareem Abdul-Jabbar, L.A. Lakers, 1976–77
17.8	Tim Duncan*, S.A. Spurs, 2001–02
17.8	Chris Paul, N.O. Hornets, 2007–08
17.7	Julius Erving*, N.Y. Nets[a], 1975–76
17.7	Michael Jordan*, Chi. Bulls, 1991–92
17.7	Dirk Nowitzki, Dal. Mavericks, 2005–06
17.6	Julius Erving*, N.Y. Nets[a], 1974–75
17.5	David Robinson*, S.A. Spurs, 1994–95
17.4	Oscar Robertson, Cin. Royals, 1966–67
17.3	Bill Russell, Bos. Celtics, 1963–64
17.3	Charles Barkley, Phi. 76ers, 1989–90
17.2	Michael Jordan, Chi. Bulls, 1992–93
17.1	Jerry West, L.A. Lakers, 1965–66
17.1	Spencer Haywood* **, Den. Rockets[a], 1969–70
17.0	Wilt Chamberlain* **, Phi. Warriors, 1959–60
17.0	Oscar Robertson, Cin. Royals, 1964–65
17.0	Kareem Abdul-Jabbar*, L.A. Lakers, 1975–76
17.0	David Robinson, S.A. Spurs, 1990–91
16.9	Bill Russell*, Bos. Celtics, 1964–65
16.9	Oscar Robertson, Cin. Royals, 1965–66
16.9	Michael Jordan, Chi. Bulls, 1986–87
16.9	Shaquille O'Neal, Orl. Magic, 1993–94
16.8	Oscar Robertson, Cin. Royals, 1962–63
16.7	Jerry West, L.A. Lakers, 1964–65
16.7	Charles Barkley, Phi. 76ers, 1987–88
16.7	Karl Malone*, Uta. Jazz, 1996–97
16.5	Julius Erving*, N.Y. Nets[a], 1973–74

WS

174.4	Reggie Miller
172.7	Kobe Bryant
163.5	Bill Russell
162.8	Hakeem Olajuwon
162.6	Jerry West
157.8	Dan Issel
155.8	Magic Johnson
155.2	Kevin Durant
150.0	Paul Pierce
149.6	James Harden
147.0	Robert Parish
145.8	Larry Bird
145.5	Gary Payton
145.1	Ray Allen
144.1	Pau Gasol
142.4	Dolph Schayes
141.7	Dwight Howard
138.6	Jason Kidd
136.0	Bob Pettit
135.6	Clyde Drexler
134.2	Adrian Dantley
131.7	John Havlicek
130.0	Walt Bellamy
129.7	Steve Nash
128.9	Rick Barry
126.4	Patrick Ewing
125.3	Vince Carter
125.1	Scottie Pippen
124.9	Shawn Marion
120.8	Chauncey Billups
120.8	Elvin Hayes
120.7	Dwyane Wade
120.2	Stephen Curry
120.1	Buck Williams
118.2	Horace Grant
117.5	Dominique Wilkins
117.4	Chet Walker
117.1	Bob Lanier
117.0	Dikembe Mutombo
116.3	George Gervin
115.7	LaMarcus Aldridge
114.8	Bailey Howell
113.5	Walt Frazier
113.0	Kevin McHale
112.5	Jack Sikma
111.3	Tony Parker
110.4	Terry Porter
110.1	Wes Unseld
109.6	Elton Brand
109.6	Larry Nance
109.5	Detlef Schrempf

continued on next page

WS

16.5............. Magic Johnson*, L.A. Lakers, 1989–90
16.5............. Tim Duncan*, S.A. Spurs, 2002–03
16.4............. Karl Malone, Uta. Jazz, 1997–98
16.4............. James Harden, Hou. Rockets, 2014–15
16.3............. Joe Fulks, Phi. Warriors, 1946–47
16.3............. Walt Bellamy**, Chi. Packers, 1961–62
16.3............. LeBron James, Cle. Cavaliers, 2005–06
16.3............. Dirk Nowitzki*, Dal. Mavericks, 2006–07
16.2............. Artis Gilmore, Ken. Colonelsª, 1974–75
16.1............. Jimmy Jones, N.O. Buccaneersª, 1968–69
16.1............. Magic Johnson*, L.A. Lakers, 1988–89
16.1............. Charles Barkley, Phi. 76ers, 1988–89
16.1............. Dirk Nowitzki, Dal. Mavericks, 2002–03
16.1............. Tracy McGrady, Orl. Magic, 2002–03
16.1............. Kevin Garnett, Min. T'Wolves, 2004–05
16.1............. Kevin Durant, Ok.C. Thunder, 2009–10
16.1............. Chris Paul, L.A. Clippers, 2014–15
16.0............. Paul Arizin, Phi. Warriors, 1951–52
16.0............. Zelmo Beaty, Uta. Jazz, 1970–71
15.9............. Ed Macauley, Bos. Celtics, 1950–51
15.9............. Magic Johnson*, L.A. Lakers, 1986–87
15.9............. Karl Malone, Uta. Jazz, 1989–90
15.9............. LeBron James, Mia. Heat, 2013–14
15.8............. Wilt Chamberlain, L.A. Lakers, 1971–72
15.8............. Dan Issel, Ken. Colonelsª, 1972–73
15.8............. Larry Bird*, Bos. Celtics, 1985–86
15.8............. Hakeem Olajuwon, Hou. Rockets, 1992–93
15.8............. Michael Jordan*, Chi. Bulls, 1997–98
15.7............. Larry Bird*, Bos. Celtics, 1984–85
15.7............. Stephen Curry*, G.S. Warriors, 2014–15
15.6............. Oscar Robertson, Cin. Royals, 1961–62
15.6............. Walt Frazier, N.Y. Knicks, 1970–71
15.6............. John Stockton, Uta. Jazz, 1988–89
15.6............. Kevin Garnett, Min. T'Wolves, 2002–03
15.6............. Dirk Nowitzki, Dal. Mavericks, 2004–05
15.6............. LeBron James, Mia. Heat, 2010–11
15.6............. Nikola Jokić*, Den. Nuggets, 2020–21
15.5............. Bill Russell*, Bos. Celtics, 1961–62
15.5............. Karl Malone, Uta. Jazz, 1990–91
15.5............. Chauncey Billups, Den. Nuggets, 2005–06
15.4............. Neil Johnston, Phi. Warriors, 1954–55
15.4............. Moses Malone*, Hou. Rockets, 1981–82
15.4............. Magic Johnson, L.A. Lakers, 1990–91
15.4............. Karl Malone, Uta. Jazz, 1992–93
15.4............. James Harden*, Hou. Rockets, 2017–18
15.3............. Neil Johnston, Phi. Warriors, 1952–53
15.3............. Bob McAdoo, Buf. Braves, 1973–74
15.3............. Karl Malone, Uta. Jazz, 1999–00
15.3............. Kobe Bryant, L.A. Lakers, 2005–06
15.2............. Jerry West, L.A. Lakers, 1969–70
15.2............. Larry Bird, Bos. Celtics, 1986–87
15.2............. Karl Malone, Uta. Jazz, 1988–89

WS

108.9...................... Jeff Hornacek
108.8...................... Paul Arizin
108.7...................... George Mikan
108.5...................... Carmelo Anthony
106.5...................... Russell Westbrook
106.4...................... Manu Ginóbili
106.4...................... Otis Thorpe
106.0...................... Zelmo Beaty
106.0...................... Chris Bosh
105.6...................... Bill Laimbeer
105.4...................... Sam Perkins
105.1...................... Rasheed Wallace
104.6...................... Kyle Lowry
104.2...................... Elgin Baylor
103.5...................... Maurice Cheeks
102.7...................... Hal Greer
102.1...................... Tyson Chandler
102.0...................... Jason Terry
100.8...................... Andre Miller
100.7...................... Alex English
100.6...................... Eddie Jones
100.4...................... Ed Macauley
100.3...................... Al Horford
100.3...................... Andre Iguodala

continued on next page

WS

15.2............. LeBron James, Cle. Cavaliers, 2007–08
15.2............. James Harden, Hou. Rockets, 2018–19
15.2............. Nikola Jokić, Den. Nuggets, 2021–22
15.1............. Wilt Chamberlain, S.F. Warriors/Phi. 76ers, 1964–65
15.1............. Zelmo Beaty, Uta. Jazz, 1971–72
15.1............. Artis Gilmore, Ken. Colonels[a], 1975–76
15.1............. Moses Malone[*], Phi. 76ers, 1982–83
15.1............. David Robinson[**], S.A. Spurs, 1989–90
15.1............. Karl Malone, Uta. Jazz, 1991–92
15.1............. Karl Malone, Uta. Jazz, 1995–96
15.0............. Walt Frazier, N.Y. Knicks, 1969–70
15.0............. Larry Bird, Bos. Celtics, 1987–88
15.0............. James Harden, Hou. Rockets, 2016–17

[*] WS Win Share is "an estimate of the number of wins contributed by a player." (basketball-reference.com)

[*] MVP.

[**] Rookie of the Year.

[a] ABA.

Teams Having Multiple Players with a Win Share of 10, Season

			Record
Min. Lakers, 1951–52[*]	George Mikan (14.4)	Vern Mikkelsen (13.2)	40–26 (.606)
Min. Lakers, 1952–53[*]	George Mikan (14.6)	Vern Mikkelsen (12.0)	48–22 (.686)
Bos. Celtics, 1953–54	Ed Macauley (14.6)	Bill Sharman (10.4)	42–30 (.583)
Phi. Warriors, 1955–56[*]	Neil Johnston (13.9)	Paul Arizin (12.2)	45–27 (.625)
Phi. Warriors, 1956–57	Neil Johnston (13.7)	Paul Arizin (12.1)	37–35 (.514)
Bos. Celtics, 1957–58	Bill Russell (11.3)	Frank Ramsey (10.0)	49–23 (.681)
St.L. Hawks, 1957–58[*]	Bob Pettit (11.0)	Cliff Hagan (10.0)	41–31 (.569)
St.L. Hawks, 1958–59	Bob Pettit (14.8)	Cliff Hagan (11.7)	49–23 (.681)
St.L. Hawks, 1959–60	Cliff Hagan (11.8)	Bob Pettit (11.5)	46–29 (.613)
St.L. Hawks, 1960–61	Bob Pettit (14.9)	Cliff Hagan (10.8)	51–28 (.646)
Cin. Royals, 1963–64	Oscar Robertson (20.6)	Jerry Lucas (12.7)	55–25 (.688)
Bal. Bullets, 1963–64	Walt Bellamy (14.4)	Terry Dischinger (11.3)	31–49 (.388)
Bos. Celtics, 1964–65[*]	Bill Russell (16.9)	Sam Jones (12.8)	62–18 (.775)
Bal. Bullets, 1964–65	Walt Bellamy (12.1)	Bailey Howell (10.9)	37–43 (.463)
Bos. Celtics, 1965–66[*]	Bill Russell (11.7)	Sam Jones (10.0)	54–26 (.675)
Phi. 76ers, 1966–67[*]	Wilt Chamberlain (21.9)	Chet Walker (10.1)	68–13 (.840)
Bos. Celtics, 1966–67	Bill Russell (12.2)	Bailey Howell (11.8)	60–21 (.741)
Phi. 76ers, 1967–68	Wilt Chamberlain (20.4)	Hal Greer (11.2)	62–20 (.756)
St.L. Hawks, 1967–68	Zelmo Beaty (11.8)	Lenny Wilkens (10.1)	56–26 (.683)
N.Y. Knicks, 1967–68	Walt Bellamy (11.1)	Willis Reed (10.0)	43–39 (.524)
Cin. Royals, 1967–68	Oscar Robertson (12.3)	Jerry Lucas (10.1)	39–43 (.476)
L.A. Lakers, 1968–69	Wilt Chamberlain (14.7)	Jerry West (10.8)	55–27 (.671)
N.Y. Knicks, 1968–69	Willis Reed (14.7)	Walt Frazier (12.7)	54–28 (.659)
Bos. Celtics, 1968–69[*]	Bailey Howell (11.3)	Bill Russell (10.9)	48–34 (.585)
N.Y. Knicks, 1969–70[*]	Walt Frazier (15.0)	Willis Reed (14.6)	60–22 (.732)
N.O. Buccaneers[a], 1969–70	Red Robbins (10.7)	Jimmy Jones (10.3)	42–42 (.500)
Den. Rockets[a], 1969–70	Spencer Haywood (17.1)	Larry Jones (10.6)	51–33 (.607)
Mil. Bucks, 1970–71[*]	Kareem Abdul-Jabbar (22.3)	Oscar Robertson (12.4)	66–16 (.805)
N.Y. Knicks, 1970–71	Walt Frazier (15.6)	Willis Reed (10.6)	52–30 (.634)
L.A. Lakers, 1970–71	Jerry West (12.8)	Wilt Chamberlain (12.6)	48–34 (.585)
Phi. 76ers, 1970–71	Archie Clark (11.4)	Billy Cunningham (10.0)	47–35 (.573)

continued on next page

Record

Ind. Pacers[a], 1970–71	Mel Daniels (11.4)	Roger Brown (10.9)		58–26 (.690)
L.A. Lakers, 1971–72*	Wilt Chamberlain (15.8)	Jerry West (13.3)	Gail Goodrich (12.3)	69–13 (.841)
Ken. Colonels[a], 1971–72	Artis Gilmore (19.8)	Dan Issel (13.5)		68–16 (.810)
Uta. Stars[a], 1971–72	Zelmo Beaty (15.1)	Willie Wise (11.2)		60–24 (.714)
Bos. Celtics, 1971–72	John Havlicek (12.4)	Dave Cowens (10.4)		56–26 (.683)
Pho. Suns, 1971–72	Paul Silas (11.0)	Dick Van Arsdale (10.4)		49–33 (.598)
N.Y. Knicks, 1971–72	Walt Frazier (14.5)	Jerry Lucas (11.2)		48–34 (.585)
Bos. Celtics, 1972–73	John Havlicek (12.1)	Dave Cowens (12.0)	Paul Silas (11.5)	68–14 (.829)
L.A. Lakers, 1972–73	Wilt Chamberlain (18.2)	Jerry West (10.6)		60–22 (.732)
Car. Cougars[a], 1972–73	Billy Cunningham (11.9)	Mack Calvin (10.4)		57–27 (.679)
Ken. Colonels[a], 1972–73	Artis Gilmore (18.5)	Dan Issel (15.8)		56–28 (.667)
Bal. Bullets, 1972–73	Mike Riordan (11.1)	Wes Unseld (10.7)		52–30 (.634)
Den. Rockets[a], 1972–73	Warren Jabali (10.7)	Dave Robisch (10.1)		47–37 (.560)
Ken. Colonels[a], 1973–74	Dan Issel (13.8)	Artis Gilmore (12.7)		53–31 (.631)
Was. Bullets, 1974–75	Elvin Hayes (12.5)	Wes Unseld (10.6)		60–22 (.732)
Ken. Colonels[a], 1974–75*	Artis Gilmore (16.2)	Louie Damipier (10.1)		58–26 (.690)
N.Y. Nets[a], 1974–75	Julius Erving (17.6)	Larry Kenon (10.0)		58–26 (.690)
Den. Nuggets[a], 1975–76	Dan Issel (12.5)	David Thompson (12.4)	Bobby Jones (10.2)	60–24 (.714)
Den. Nuggets, 1976–77	Bobby Jones (11.0)	Dan Issel (10.9)	David Thompson (10.7)	50–32 (.610)
Den. Nuggets, 1977–78	David Thompson (10.7)	Dan Issel (11.1)		48–34 (.585)
Bos. Celtics, 1979–80	Cedric Maxwell (12.2)	Larry Bird (11.2)		61–21 (.744)
L.A. Lakers, 1979–80*	Kareem Abdul-Jabbar (14.8)	Magic Johnson (10.5)	Jamaal Wilkes (10.0)	60–22 (.732)
Bos. Celtics, 1980–81*	Cedric Maxwell (11.0)	Robert Parish (10.9)	Larry Bird (10.8)	62–20 (.756)
Bos. Celtics, 1981–82	Larry Bird (12.5)	Robert Parish (10.0)		63–19 (.768)
L.A. Lakers, 1981–82*	Magic Johnson (12.9)	Kareem Abdul-Jabbar (10.7)		57–25 (.695)
Sea. Sonics, 1981–82	Jack Sikma (12.6)	Gus Williams (10.2)		52–30 (.634)
Phi. 76ers, 1982–83*	Moses Malone (15.1)	Julius Erving (10.9)		65–17 (.793)
L.A. Lakers, 1982–83	Magic Johnson (12.5)	Kareem Abdul-Jabbar (10.9)		58–24 (.707)
Bos. Celtics, 1982–83	Larry Bird (14.0)	Robert Parish (10.8)		56–26 (.683)
Mil. Bucks, 1982–83	Sidney Moncrief (13.2)	Marques Johnson (10.7)		51–31 (.622)
Den. Nuggets, 1982–83	Kiki Vandeweghe (11.0)	Alex English (10.3)		45–37 (.549)
Bos. Celtics, 1983–84*	Larry Bird (13.6)	Kevin McHale (10.5)	Robert Parish (10.5)	62–20 (.756)
Bos. Celtics, 1984–85	Larry Bird (15.7)	Kevin McHale (11.0)		63–19 (.768)
L.A. Lakers, 1984–85*	Magic Johnson (12.7)	Kareem Abdul-Jabbar (11.2)		62–20 (.756)
Mil. Bucks, 1984–85	Sidney Moncrief (11.2)	Terry Cummings (10.7)		59–23 (.720)
Bos. Celtics, 1985–86*	Larry Bird (15.8)	Kevin McHale (11.0)		67–15 (.817)
L.A. Lakers, 1985–86	Magic Johnson (12.1)	Kareem Abdul-Jabbar (10.8)		62–20 (.756)
Bos. Celtics, 1986–87	Larry Bird (15.2)	Kevin McHale (14.8)		59–23 (.720)
Atl. Hawks, 1986–87	Dominique Wilkins (12.2)	Doc Rivers (10.3)		57–25 (.695)
Det. Pistons, 1986–87	Bill Laimbeer (10.5)	Adrian Dantley (10.3)		52–30 (.634)
Por. Blazers, 1986–87	Kiki Vandeweghe (10.8)	Clyde Drexler (10.3)		49–33 (.598)
L.A. Lakers, 1987–88*	Magic Johnson (10.9)	Byron Scott (10.7)		62–20 (.756)
Bos. Celtics, 1987–88	Larry Bird (15.0)	Kevin McHale (10.2)		57–25 (.695)
Uta. Jazz, 1987–88	John Stockton (14.1)	Karl Malone (10.1)		47–35 (.573)
Cle. Cavaliers, 1988–89	Larry Nance (10.3)	Ron Harper (10.2)		57–25 (.695)
Atl. Hawks, 1988–89	Moses Malone (10.7)	Dominique Wilkins (10.4)		52–30 (.634)
Uta. Jazz, 1988–89	John Stockton (15.6)	Karl Malone (15.2)		51–31 (.622)
Bos. Celtics, 1988–89	Robert Parish (10.5)	Kevin McHale (10.1)		42–40 (.512)
L.A. Lakers, 1989–90	Magic Johnson (16.5)	James Worthy (10.6)		63–19 (.768)
Por. Blazers, 1989–90	Terry Porter (11.7)	Clyde Drexler (11.6)		59–23 (.720)
Uta. Jazz, 1989–90	Karl Malone (15.9)	John Stockton (14.4)		55–27 (.671)
Pho. Suns, 1989–90	Kevin Johnson (11.6)	Tom Chambers (11.2)		54–28 (.659)

continued on next page

			Record
Por. Blazers, 1990–91	Terry Porter (13.0)	Clyde Drexler (12.4)	63–19 (.768)
Chi. Bulls, 1990–91*	Michael Jordan (20.3)	Scottie Pippen (11.2) .... Horace Grant (10.3)	61–21 (.744)
Uta. Jazz, 1990–91	Karl Malone (15.5)	John Stockton (14.0)	54–28 (.659)
Chi. Bulls, 1991–92*	Michael Jordan (17.7)	Horace Grant (14.1) .... Scottie Pippen (12.7)*	67–15 (.817)
Cle. Cavaliers, 1991–92	Larry Nance (12.2)	Brad Daugherty (11.7)	57–25 (.695)
Uta. Jazz, 1991–92	Karl Malone (15.1)	John Stockton (13.4)	55–27 (.671)
Por. Blazers, 1991–92	Clyde Drexler (12.8)	Terry Porter (10.6)	57–25 (.671)
Pho. Suns, 1991–92	Jeff Hornacek (11.6)	Kevin Johnson (10.0)	53–29 (.646)
Cle. Cavaliers, 1992–93	Brad Daugherty (12.7)	Larry Nance (10.7)	54–28 (.659)
Uta. Jazz, 1992–93	Karl Malone (15.4)	John Stockton (10.6)	47–35 (.573)
Ind. Pacers, 1992–93	Reggie Miller (11.3)	Detlef Schrempf (10.4)	41–41 (.500)
N.Y. Knicks, 1993–94	Patrick Ewing (13.1)	Charles Oakley (10.5)	57–25 (.695)
Chi. Bulls, 1993–94	Scottie Pippen (11.2)	Horace Grant (10.0)	55–27 (.671)
Atl. Hawks, 1993–94	Mookie Blaylock (10.2)	Kevin Willis (10.2)	57–25 (.671)
Uta. Jazz, 1993–94	Karl Malone (13.4)	John Stockton (13.2)	53–29 (.646)
Uta. Jazz, 1994–95	John Stockton (13.9)	Karl Malone (13.8) .... Jeff Hornacek (10.1)	60–22 (.732)
Orl. Magic, 1994–95	Shaquille O'Neal (14.0)	Penny Hardaway (10.7)	57–25 (.695)
Sea. Sonics, 1994–95	Detlef Schrempf (12.9)	Gary Payton (11.7) .... Shawn Kemp (10.6)	57–25 (.695)
Chi. Bulls, 1994–95	Scottie Pippen (11.8)	Toni Kukoč (10.0)	47–35 (.573)
Chi. Bulls, 1995–96*	Michael Jordan (20.4)	Scottie Pippen (12.3) .... Toni Kukoč (10.1)	72–10 (.878)
Sea. Sonics, 1995–96	Gary Payton (11.5)	Shawn Kemp (11.2)	64–18 (.780)
Uta. Jazz, 1995–96	Karl Malone (15.1)	John Stockton (13.0) .... Jeff Hornacek (10.2)	55–27 (.671)
Chi. Bulls, 1996–97*	Michael Jordan (18.3)	Scottie Pippen (13.1)	69–13 (.841)
Uta. Jazz, 1996–97	Karl Malone (16.7)	John Stockton (13.6) .... Jeff Hornacek (10.2)	64–18 (.780)
Sea. Sonics, 1996–97	Gary Payton (12.9)	Hersey Hawkins (10.9) .... Shawn Kemp (10)	57–25 (.695)
Atl. Hawks, 1996–97	Mookie Blaylock (12.5)	Christian Laettner (11.6) .... Dikembe Mutombo (11.3)	56–26 (.683)
Cha. Hornets*, 1996–97	Anthony Mason (11.4)	Glen Rice (10.8)	54–28 (.659)
L.A. Lakers, 1997–98	Shaquille O'Neal (10.2)	Eddie Jones (10.1)	61–21 (.744)
Sea. Sonics, 1997–98	Gary Payton (12.5)	Detlef Schrempf (10.4) .... Vin Baker (10.4)	61–21 (.744)
S.A. Spurs, 1997–98	David Robinson (13.8)	Tim Duncan (12.8)	56–26 (.683)
Atl. Hawks, 1997–98	Dikembe Mutombo (10.8)	Steve Smith (10.2)	50–32 (.610)
L.A. Lakers, 1999–00*	Shaquille O'Neal (18.6)	Kobe Bryant (10.6)	67–15 (.817)
Uta. Jazz, 1999–00	Karl Malone (15.3)	John Stockton (11.2)	55–27 (.671)
S.A. Spurs, 1999–00	Tim Duncan (13.0)	David Robinson (12.7)	53–29 (.646)
S.A. Spurs, 2000–01	Tim Duncan (13.2)	David Robinson (12.1)	58–24 (.707)
L.A. Lakers, 2000–01*	Shaquille O'Neal (14.9)	Kobe Bryant (11.3)	56–26 (.683)
Sac. Kings, 2000–01	Chris Webber (11.0)	Peja Stojaković (10.1)	55–27 (.671)
Uta. Jazz, 2000–01	Karl Malone (13.1)	John Stockton (10.8)	53–29 (.646)
L.A. Lakers, 2001–02*	Shaquille O'Neal (13.2)	Kobe Bryant (12.7)	58–24 (.770)
S.A. Spurs, 2001–02	Tim Duncan (17.8)	David Robinson (10.1)	58–24 (.707)
Sea. Sonics, 2001–02	Gary Payton (12.6)	Brent Barry (12.1)	45–37 (.549)
Dal. Mavericks, 2002–03	Dirk Nowitzki (16.1)	Steve Nash (11.6)	60–22 (.732)
L.A. Lakers, 2002–03	Kobe Bryant (14.9)	Shaquille O'Neal (13.2)	50–32 (.610)
Min. T'Wolves, 2003–04	Kevin Garnett (18.3)	Sam Cassell (12.1)	58–24 (.707)
Sac. Kings, 2003–04	Peja Stojaković (13.5)	Brad Miller (10.0)	55–27 (.671)
Det. Pistons, 2003–04*	Chauncey Billups (11.3)	Ben Wallace (10.2)	54–28 (.659)
Pho. Suns, 2004–05	Amar'e Stoudamire (14.6)	Shawn Marion (12.5) .... Steve Nash (10.9)	62–20 (.756)
Mia. Heat, 2004–05	Shaquille O'Neal (11.0)	Dwyane Wade (11.0)	59–23 (.720)
S.A. Spurs, 2004–05*	Tim Duncan (11.2)	Manu Ginóbili (11.0)	59–23 (.720)
Hou. Rockets, 2004–05	Tracy McGrady (12.0)	Yao Ming (10.7)	51–31 (.622)
Det. Pistons, 2005–06	Chauncey Billups (15.5)	Ben Wallace (10.1)	64–18 (.780)
Pho. Suns, 2005–06	Shawn Marion (14.6)	Steve Nash (12.4)	54–28 (.659)

continued on next page

Record

N.J. Nets, 2005–06	Richard Jefferson (11.7)	Jason Kidd (10.1)	49–33 (.598)
Dal. Mavericks, 2006–07	Dirk Nowitzki (16.3)	Jason Terry (10.8)	67–15 (.817)
Pho. Suns, 2006–07	Steve Nash (12.6)	Shawn Marion (12.0)	Amar'e Stoudamire (11.2) ...61–21 (.744)
S.A. Spurs, 2006–07*	Tim Duncan (13.0)	Manu Ginóbili (10.6)	58–24 (.707)
Chi. Bulls, 2006–07	Luol Deng (11.3)	Kirk Hinrich (10.1)	49–33 (.598)
Bos. Celtics, 2007–08*	Kevin Garnett (12.9)	Paul Pierce (12.4)	66–16 (.805)
N.O. Hornets, 2007–08	Chris Paul (17.8)	Tyson Chandler (10.0)	56–26 (.683)
S.A. Spurs, 2007–08	Tim Duncan (11.1)	Manu Ginóbili (11.1)	56–26 (.683)
Pho. Suns, 2007–08	Amar'e Stoudamire (14.6)	Steve Nash (10.5)	55–27 (.671)
Uta. Jazz, 2007–08	Deron Williams (11.3)	Carlos Boozer (10.2)	54–28 (.659)
Tor. Raptors, 2007–08	José Calderón (10.2)	Chris Bosh (10.1)	41–41 (.500)
L.A. Lakers, 2008–09*	Pau Gasol (13.9)	Kobe Bryant (12.7)	65–17 (.793)
Bos. Celtics, 2008–09	Ray Allen (11.1)	Paul Pierce (10.3)	62–20 (.756)
Mia. Heat, 2010–11	LeBron James (15.6)	Dwyane Wade (12.8)	Chris Bosh (10.3)............58–24 (.707)
L.A. Lakers, 2010–11	Pau Gasol (14.7)	Lamar Odom (10.1)	57–25 (.695)
Bos. Celtics, 2010–11	Paul Pierce (11.6)	Ray Allen (10.0)	56–26 (.683)
Ok.C. Thunder, 2012–13	Kevin Durant (18.9)	Russell Westbrook (11.6)	60–22 (.732)
L.A. Clippers, 2012–13	Chris Paul (13.9)	Blake Griffin (10.6)	56–26 (.683)
L.A. Clippers, 2013–14	Blake Griffin (12.2)	Chris Paul (12.2)	DeAndre Jordan (11.1)...57–25 (.695)
L.A. Clippers, 2014–15	Chris Paul (16.1)	DeAndre Jordan (12.8)	56–26 (.683)
Cle. Cavaliers, 2014–15	LeBron James (10.4)	Kyrie Irving (10.4)	53–29 (.646)
Chi. Bulls, 2014–15	Jimmy Butler (11.2)	Paul Gasol (10.4)	50–32 (.610)
G.S. Warriors, 2015–16	Stephen Curry (17.9)	Draymond Green (11.1)	73–9 (.890)
S.A. Spurs, 2015–16	Kawhi Leonard (13.7)	LaMarcus Aldridge (10.1)	67–15 (.817)
Ok.C. Thunder, 2015–16	Kevin Durant (14.5)	Russell Westbrook (14)	55–27 (.671)
L.A. Clippers, 2015–16	Chris Paul (12.7)	DeAndre Jordan (11.5)	53–29 (.646)
G.S. Warriors, 2016–17*	Stephen Curry (12.6)	Kevin Durant (12.0)	67–15 (.817)
L.A. Clippers, 2016–17	DeAndre Jordan (11.8)	Chris Paul (10.6)	51–31 (.622)
Uta. Jazz, 2016–17	Rudy Gobert (14.3)	Gordon Hayward (10.4)	51–31 (.622)
Hou. Rockets, 2017–18	James Harden (15.4)	Clint Capela (10.2)	Chris Paul (10.2) ....65–17 (.793)
Hou. Rockets, 2018–19	James Harden (15.2)	Clint Capela (10.8)	53–29 (.646)

* Won championship.

ᵃ ABA.

Highest Player Efficiency Rating˙ (PER), Season (Min. 60 Games)

PER		PER	
31.9	Giannis Antetokounmpo, Mil. Bucks, 2019–20	31.6	LeBron James, Mia. Heat, 2012–13
31.8	Wilt Chamberlain, S.F. Warriors, 1962–63	31.5	Stephen Curry, G.S. Warriors, 2015–16
31.7	Wilt Chamberlain, Phi. Warriors, 1961–62	31.3	Nikola Jokić, Den. Nuggets, 2020–21
31.7	Michael Jordan, Chi. Bulls, 1987–88	31.2	Michael Jordan, Chi. Bulls, 1989–90
31.7	LeBron James, Cle. Cavaliers, 2008–09	31.1	Michael Jordan, Chi. Bulls, 1988–89
31.6	Wilt Chamberlain, S.F. Warriors, 1963–64	31.1	Giannis Antetokounmpo, Mil. Bucks, 2009–10
31.6	Michael Jordan, Chi. Bulls, 1990–91		

˙ Player Efficiency Rating is "A measure of per-minute production standardized such that the league average is 15." (basketball-reference.com)

Highest Player Efficiency Rating (PER), Career (Min. 500 Games)

PER		PER		PER	
27.9	Michael Jordan	26.4	Shaquille O'Neal	25.3	Kevin Durant^
27.3	LeBron James^	26.2	Wilt Chamberlain	24.9	Neil Johnston
27.1	Nikola Jokić^	26.2	David Robinson	24.6	Chris Paul^
26.9	Anthony Davis^	25.4	Bob Pettit	24.6	Kareem Abdul-Jabbar

continued on next page

PER

24.6................. Charles Barkley

24.5................. James Harden^

^ Active.

PER

24.5................. Giannis Antetokounmpo^

24.2................. Tim Duncan

PER

24.1................. Magic Johnson

Highest Value Over Replacement Player* (VORP), Season

VORP

12.5............ Michael Jordan, Chi. Bulls, 1987–88

11.8............ LeBron James, Cle. Cavaliers, 2008–09

11.4............ Michael Jordan, Chi. Bulls, 1988–89

11.4............ David Robinson, S.A. Spurs, 1993–94

10.8............ Michael Jordan, Chi. Bulls, 1990–91

VORP

10.6............ Michael Jordan, Chi. Bulls, 1986–87

10.6............ Michael Jordan, Chi. Bulls, 1989–90

10.3............ LeBron James, Cle. Cavaliers, 2009–10

10.2............ Michael Jordan, Chi. Bulls, 1992–93

10.0............ Kevin Garnett, Min. T'Wolves, 2003–04

* VORP (available since the 1973–74 season in the NBA) is "a box score estimate of the points per 100 TEAM possessions that a player contributed above a replacement-level (-2.0) player, translated to an average team and prorated to an 82-game season. Multiply by 2.70 to convert to wins over replacement." (basketball-reference.com)

Highest Value Over Replacement Player (VORP), Career

VORP

142.6.............. LeBron James^

116.1.............. Michael Jordan

106.5.............. John Stockton

99.0.............. Karl Malone

96.9.............. Kevin Garnett

93.7.............. Chris Paul^

91.1.............. Tim Duncan

^ Active.

VORP

85.7................. Kareem Abdul-Jabbar

84.8................. Dirk Nowitzki

82.0................. David Robinson

80.5................. Charles Barkley

80.1................. Kobe Bryant

80.0................. Magic Johnson

77.2................. Larry Bird

VORP

76.4................. Kevin Durant^

75.5................. Shaquille O'Neal

74.4................. Hakeem Olajuwon

73.4................. Jason Kidd

72.0................. James Harden^

70.2................. Clyde Drexler

Youngest Player to...

Register a Point....................18 years, 24 days............Andrew Bynum, L.A. Lakers ....vs. Chi. Bulls (Nov. 20, 2005)

Register a Free Throw............18 years, 24 days............Andrew Bynum, L.A. Lakers ....vs. Chi. Bulls (Nov. 20, 2005)

Register a Three Pointer........18 years, 75 days............Kobe Bryant, L.A. Lakers ....@ Cha. Hornets (Nov. 6, 1996)

Register a Rebound ....18 years, 6 days............Andrew Bynum, L.A. Lakers ....@ Den. Nuggets (Nov. 2, 2005)

Register an Assist................18 years, 20 days............Andrew Bynum, L.A. Lakers ....vs. N.Y. Knicks (Nov. 16, 2005)

Register a Block..................18 years, 6 days............Andrew Bynum, L.A. Lakers ....@ Den. Nuggets (Nov. 2, 2005)

Register a Steal....................18 years, 82 days............Kobe Bryant, L.A. Lakers ....@ S.A. Spurs (Nov. 13, 1996)

Oldest Player to...

Register a Point....................45 years, 362 days.......... Nat Hickey, Pro. Steamrollers..............vs. St.L. Bombers (Jan. 27, 1948)

Register a Free Throw............45 years, 362 days.......... Nat Hickey, Pro. Steamrollers..............vs. St.L. Bombers (Jan. 27, 1948)

Register a Three Pointer........43 years, 45 days.......... Vince Carter, Atl. Hawks ....vs. N.Y. Knicks (Mar. 11, 2020)

Register a Rebound ....44 years, 224 days.......... Kevin Willis, Dal. Mavericks ....@ Sea. Sonics (Apr. 18, 2007)

Register an Assist................44 years, 219 days.......... Kevin Willis, Dal. Mavericks ....vs. Uta. Jazz (Apr. 13, 2007)

Register a Block..................44 years, 213 days.......... Kevin Willis, Dal. Mavericks ....vs. Por. Blazers (Apr. 7, 2007)

Register a Steal....................44 years, 224 days.......... Kevin Willis, Dal. Mavericks ....@ Sea. Sonics (Apr. 18, 2007)

Shortest Players to Appear in a Game

5-foot-3 .... Muggsy Bogues 1987–2001

Penny Early° 1968–69

5-foot-5 .... Earl Boykins 1998–2012

5-foot-6 .... Mel Hirsch 1946–47

continued on next page

	Spud Webb........................1985–98	
5-foot-7	Jerry Dover[a] 1971–72	
	Greg Grant 1989–96	
	Keith Jennings....................1992–95	
	Red Klotz 1947–48	
	Wat Misak[a]........................1947–48	
	Monte Towe 1975–77	
5-foot-8	Charlie Criss 1977–85	
	Dino Martin........................1946–48	
	Willie Somerset 1965–69	

5-foot-9	Larry Brown[a]............................1967–72
	Howie Carl...............................1961–62
	Chris Clemons...........................2019–20
	Kay Felder...............................2016–18
	Charlie Hoefer 1946–48
	Lionel Malamed[a] 1948–49
	Ed Melvin 1946–47
	Calvin Murphy 1970–83
	Angelo Musi 1946–49
	Ralph O'Brien 1951–53
	Nate Robinson 2005–16
	Gene Rock................................1947–48
	Yuta Tabuse 2004–05
	Isaiah Thomas**.........................2011–22
	Murray Wier.............................1949–50
	Willie Worsley[a].........................1968–69

[a] ABA.

* Early, a female basketball player, appeared in one game for the Kentucky Colonels (Nov. 27, 1968).

^ Active.

Tallest Players to Appear in a Game

7-foot-7	Manute Bol 1985–95
	Gheorghe Mureşan 1993–2000
7-foot-6	Shawn Bradley 1993–2005
	Yao Ming 2002–11
7-foot-5	Sim Bhullar........................2014–15
	Tacko Fall^ 2019–22
	Chuck Nevitt 1982–94
	Pavel Podkolzin 2004–06
	Slavo Vraneš 2003–04
7-foot-4	Mark Eaton 1982–93
	Priest Lauderdale..................1996–98
	Ralph Sampson....................1983–92
	Rik Smits 1988–2000

7-foot-3	Randy Breuer......................1983–94
	Keith Closs 1997–2000
	Swede Halbrook.................1960–62
	Zydrunas Ilgauskas...............1997–2011
	Boban Marjanović^ 2015–22
	Tibor Pleiß...........................2015–16
	Kristaps Porziņģis^...............2015–22
	Aleksandar Radojević...........1999–2005
	Peter John Ramos 2004–05
	Arvydas Sabonis.................1995–2003
	Ha Seung-Jin 2004–06
	Edy Tavares..........................2015–17
	Hasheem Thabeet 2009–14

^ Active.

Most Common Last Name

80...................... Williams	34...................... Jackson	20...................... Wright
72...................... Johnson	27...................... Robinson	19...................... Taylor
61...................... Smith	26...................... Green	19...................... Thompson
59...................... Jones	26...................... Thomas	18...................... King
46...................... Brown	24...................... Anderson	18...................... White
42...................... Davis	22...................... Martin	

Number of Professional Players by First Letter of Last Name

A 175	F 150	K.......... 175	O 96	S........... 434	W 386
B........... 480	G 254	L 199	P.......... 225	T...........198	X......... N/A
C 308	H 358	M......... 475	Q 8	U 11	Y............ 21
D 247	I............... 26	N......... 107	R 256	V 59	Z............ 20
E........... 109	J............. 246				

Players Born on Leap Year Day (February 29)

	Birth Year		Birth Year
John Chaney, forward/center (1949–50)	1920	Vonteego Cummings, guard (1999–2002)	1976
Chucky Brown, forward (1989–2002)	1968	Tyrese Haliburton^, guard (2020–22)	2000

^ Active.

Players Winning Basketball's "Triple Crown"·

Player	NCAA Championship	NBA Finals	Olympic Gold Medal
Clyde Lovellette	Kansas (1952)	Min. Lakers (1954); Bos. Celtics (1963, 1964)	1952
Bill Russell	San Francisco (1955, 1956)	Bos. Celtics (1957, 1959, 1960, 1961, 1962, 1963, 1964, 1965, 1966, 1968, 1969)	1956
K.C. Jones	San Francisco (1955, 1956)	Bos. Celtics (1959, 1960, 1961, 1962, 1963, 1964, 1965, 1966)	1956
Jerry Lucas	Ohio State (1960, 1961, 1962)	N.Y. Knicks (1973)	1960
Magic Johnson	Michigan State (1979)	L.A. Lakers (1980, 1982, 1985, 1987, 1988)	1992
Michael Jordan	North Carolina (1982)	Chi. Bulls (1991, 1992, 1993, 1996, 1997, 1998)	1992
Quinn Buckner	Indiana (1976)	Bos. Celtics (1984)	1976
Anthony Davis	Kentucky (2012)	L.A. Lakers (2020)	2012

* Triple Crown consists of winning an NCAA Championship, NBA Finals, and Olympic gold medal.

Players Who Also Played for the Harlem Globetrotters

Willie Gardner	Nat Clifton	Connie Hawkins	Red Klotz
Wilt Chamberlain	Smokey Gaines	Andy Johnson	Woody Sauldsberry

Playing Most Seasons with One Address (One Club, One City in League)

21	Dirk Nowitzki, Dal. Mavericks, 1998–2019	13	Bill Russell, Bos. Celtics, 1956–69
20	Kobe Bryant, L.A. Lakers, 1996–2016	13	Satch Sanders, Bos. Celtics, 1960–73
19	John Stockton, Uta. Jazz, 1984–2003	13	Fred Brown, Sea. Sonics, 1971–84
19	Tim Duncan, S.A. Spurs, 1997–2016	13	Alvan Adams, Pho. Suns, 1975–88
19	Udonis Haslem^, Mia. Heat, 2003–22	13	Larry Bird, Bos. Celtics, 1979–92
18	Reggie Miller, Ind. Pacers, 1987–2005	13	Magic Johnson, L.A. Lakers, 1979–91, 1996
16	John Havlicek, Bos. Celtics, 1962–78	13	Kevin McHale, Bos. Celtics, 1980–93
16	Manu Ginóbili, S.A. Spurs, 2002–18	13	Isiah Thomas, Det. Pistons, 1981–94
14	Jerry West, L.A. Lakers, 1960–74	13	Jeff Foster, Ind. Pacers, 1999–2012
14	Joe Dumars, Det. Pistons, 1985–99	13	Stephen Curry^, G.S. Warriors, 2009–22
14	David Robinson, S.A. Spurs, 1989–2003		

^ Active with franchise.

Teammates the Longest

Games

1412	John Stockton and Karl Malone, Uta. Jazz (1984–2003)
1002	Tim Duncan and Tony Parker, S.A. Spurs (2001–16)
940	Robert Parish and Kevin McHale, Bos. Celtics (1980–93)
933	Tony Parker and Manu Ginóbili, S.A. Spurs (2002–18)
878	Bill Laimbeer and Isiah Thomas, Det. Pistons (1982–94)
858	Tim Duncan and Manu Ginóbili, S.A. Spurs (2002–16)
849	Reggie Miller and Rik Smits, Ind. Pacers (1988–2000)
848	John Havlicek and Don Nelson, Bos. Celtics (1965–76)
847	Kobe Bryant and Derek Fisher, L.A. Lakers (1996–2004, 2007–12)

continued on next page

Games

796..............	Brad Davis and Rolando Blackman, Dal. Mavericks (1981–92)
789..............	Larry Bird and Robert Parish, Bos. Celtics (1980–92)
770..............	Magic Johnson and Michael Cooper, L.A. Lakers (1979–90)
769..............	Terry Porter and Jerome Kersey, Por. Blazers (1985–95))
761..............	Kareem Abdul-Jabbar and Michael Cooper, L.A. Lakers (1978–89)
757..............	Bill Laimbeer and Vinnie Johnson, Det. Pistons (1982–91)
755..............	Larry Bird and Kevin McHale, Bos. Celtics (1980–92)
754..............	John Havlicek and Tom Sanders, Bos. Celtics (1962–73)
741..............	Calvin Murphy and Rudy Tomjanovich, S.D.-Hou. Rockets (1970–71)
726..............	Jerome Kersey and Clyde Drexler, Por. Blazers (1984–95)
721..............	Derek Harper and Rolando Blackman, Dal. Mavericks (1983–93)
717..............	Byron Scott and James Worthy, L.A. Lakers (1983–93)
710..............	Alex English and T.R. Dunn, Den. Nuggets (1980–90)
707..............	John Stockton and Mark Eaton, Uta. Jazz (1984–93)
703..............	Walter Davis and Alvan Adams, Pho. Suns (1977–88)
691..............	Michael Jordan and Scottie Pippen, Chi. Bulls (1987–93, 1994–98)
689..............	Dwyane Wade and Udonis Haslem, Mia. Heat (2003–16, 2018–19)
688..............	Bill Bradley and Walt Frazier, N.Y. Knicks (1967–77)
685..............	Magic Johnson and Kareem Abdul-Jabbar, L.A. Lakers (1979–89)

Players Who Played for Both Philadelphia Warriors and Philadelphia 76ers

Wilt Chamberlain	Phi. Warriors, 1959–62	Phi. 76ers, 1964–68
Larry Costello	Phi. Warriors, 1954–55; 1956–57	Phi. 76ers, 1963–65; 1966–68

Players Who Played for Both Minneapolis and Los Angeles Lakers

Slick Leonard	Min. Lakers, 1956–60	L.A. Lakers, 1960–61
Frank Selvy	Min. Lakers, 1957–58; 1959–60	L.A. Lakers, 1960–64
Jim Krebs	Min. Lakers, 1957–60	L.A. Lakers, 1960–64
Hot Rod Hundley	Min. Lakers, 1957–60	L.A. Lakers, 1960–63
Elgin Baylor	Min. Lakers, 1958–60	L.A. Lakers, 1960–72
Bobby Smith	Min. Lakers, 1959–60	L.A. Lakers, 1961–62
Rudy LaRusso	Min. Lakers, 1959–60	L.A. Lakers, 1960–67
Tom Hawkins	Min. Lakers, 1959–60	L.A. Lakers, 1960–62; 1966–69
Ray Felix	Min. Lakers, 1959–60	L.A. Lakers, 1960–62; 1966–69

Players Who Played for Both San Diego Clippers and San Diego Rockets

Bingo Smith	S.D. Rockets, 1969–70	S.D. Clippers, 1979–80

Players Who Played for Both New Orleans and Utah Jazz

Pete Maravich	N.O. Jazz, 1974–79	Uta. Jazz, 1979
Rich Kelley	N.O. Jazz, 1975–79	Uta. Jazz, 1982–85
James Hardy	N.O. Jazz, 1978–79	Uta. Jazz, 1979–82

Players Who Played for Both Vancouver and Memphis Grizzlies

Isaac Austin	Van. Grizzlies, 2000–01	Mem. Grizzlies, 2001–02
Michael Dickerson	Van. Grizzlies, 1999–2001	Mem. Grizzlies, 2001–03
Grant Long	Van. Grizzlies, 1999–2001	Mem. Grizzlies, 2001–02
Tony Massenburg	Van. Grizzlies, 1997–99; 2000–01	Mem. Grizzlies, 2001–02
Stromile Swift	Van. Grizzlies, 2000–01	Mem. Grizzlies, 2001–05; 2006–08

Players Who Played for Both Seattle SuperSonics and Oklahoma City Thunder

Nick Collison	Sea. Sonics, 2004–08	Ok.C. Thunder, 2008–18
Kevin Durant	Sea. Sonics, 2007–08	Ok.C. Thunder, 2008–16
Jeff Green	Sea. Sonics, 2007–08	Ok.C. Thunder, 2008–11
Desmond Mason	Sea. Sonics, 2000–03	Ok.C. Thunder, 2008–09
Kevin Ollie	Sea. Sonics, 2002–03	Ok.C. Thunder, 2009–10
Johan Petro	Sea. Sonics, 2005–08	Ok.C. Thunder, 2008–09
Mouhamed Sene	Sea. Sonics, 2006–08	Ok.C. Thunder, 2008–09
Robert Swift	Sea. Sonics, 2004–06; 2007–08	Ok.C. Thunder, 2008–09
Chris Wilcox	Sea. Sonics, 2005–08	Ok.C. Thunder, 2008–09
Damien Wilkins	Sea. Sonics, 2004–08	Ok.C. Thunder, 2008–09
Earl Watson	Sea. Sonics, 2006–08	Ok.C. Thunder, 2008–09
Mike Wilks	Sea. Sonics, 2005–07	Ok.C. Thunder, 2009–10

Number of Players to Wear a Uniform Number, and First Player to Do So

#	Number of Players	First Season Worn	First Worn By
00	49	1976–77	Robert Parish, G.S. Warriors
03	3	1949–50	Pep Saul, Roc. Royals
07	1	1950–51	Paul Noel, Roc. Royals
09	1	1948–49	Bobby Wanzer, Roc. Royals
0	124	1947–48	Johnny Jorgensen, Chi. Stags
1	242	1970–71	Oscar Robertson, Mil. Bucks
2	230	1947–48	Belus Smawley, St.L. Bombers
3	350	1946–47	8 Players
4	323	1946–47	10 Players
5	361	1946–47	15 Players
6	260	1946–47	12 Players
7	331	1946–47	12 Players
8	286	1946–47	11 Players
9	296	1946–47	11 Players
10	332	1946–47	11 Players
11	384	1946–47	13 Players
12	421	1946–47	13 Players
13	209	1946–47	5 Players
14	340	1946–47	16 Players
15	346	1946–47	13 Players
16	124	1946–47	8 Players
17	164	1946–47	8 Players
18	132	1946–47	5 Players
19	104	1946–47	5 Players
20	348	1946–47	Ed Sadowski, Tor. Huskies Ralph Siewert, Tor. Huskies
21	317	1946–47	Roy Hurley, Tor. Huskies Buddy O'Grady, Was. Capitols
22	323	1946–47	5 Players
23	245	1946–47	Fred Scolari, Was. Capitols Red Wallace, Tor. Huskies
24	276	1946–47	Harold Brown, Det. Falcons Jerry Kelly, Bos. Celtics
25	235	1948–49	Ward Williams, Ft.W. Pistons
26	58	1946–47	Tony Jaros, Chi. Stags

continued on next page

#	Number of Players	First Season Worn	First Worn By
27	57	1947–48	Chick Reiser, Bal. Bullets
28	44	1947–48	Mike Bloom, Bal. Bullets
29	26	1947–48	Kleggie Hermsen, Bal. Bullets
30	233	1947–48	Elmer Gainer, Bal. Bullets
31	192	1947–48	John Abramovic, Bal. Bullets
			Carl Meinhold, Bal. Bullets
32	232	1947–48	Paul Hoffman, Bal. Bullets
33	244	1946–47	Harold Johnson, Det. Falcons
34	225	1946–47	George Pearcy, Det. Falcons
35	182	1947–48	Grady Lewis, Bal. Bullets
			Irv Rothenberg, Bal. Bullets
36	19	1948–49	Ralph Hamilton, Ft.W. Pistons
37	9	1948–49	Jack Smiley, Ft.W. Pistons
38	11	1970–71	Ron Knight, Por. Blazers
39	6	1984–85	Caldwell Jones, Chi. Bulls
40	170	1948–49	Ray Lumpp, Ind. Jets
41	108	1960–61	Win Wilfong, Cin. Royals
42	167	1963–64	Nate Thurmond, S.F. Warriors
43	103	1962–63	Terry Dischinger, Chi. Zephyrs
			Howie Montgomery, S.F. Warriors
44	223	1946–47	Henry Pearcy, Det. Falcons
			Art Stolkey, Det. Falcons
45	124	1967–68	5 Players
46	7	1973–74	Dennis Bell, N.Y. Knicks
47	6	1967–68	Dave Lattin, S.F. Warriors
48	2	1970–71	Walt Gilmore, Por. Blazers
49	3	1989–90	Mel McCants, L.A. Lakers
50	124	1948–49	John Mandic, Ind. Jets
51	42	1960–61	Hub Reed, Cin. Royals
			Mike Farmer, Cin. Royals
52	82	1946–47	John Janisch, Det. Falcons
53	29	1971–72[a]/1975–76	Artis Gilmore, Ken. Colonels[a]
			Darryl Dawkins, Phi. 76ers
			Rich Kelley, N.O. Jazz
54	82	1960–61	Howie Jolliff, L.A. Lakers
55	112	1946–47	Howie McCarty, Det. Falcons
56	3	2003–04	Francisco Elson, Den. Nuggets
			Brandon Hunter, Bos. Celtics
57	1	2013–14	Hilton Armstrong, G.S. Warriors
58	N/A		
59	1	2021–22	Rayjon Tucker, Mil. Bucks
60	3	1948–49	Walt Kirk, Ind. Jets
			Dick Wehr, Ind. Jets
61	2	1961–62	Bevo Nordmann, Cin. Royals
62	2	1946–47	Bob Dille, Det. Falcons
63	1	2015–16	Coty Clarke, Bos. Celtics
64	N/A		
65	1	1949–50	George Ratkovicz, Syr. Nationals
66	5	1946–47	Grady Lewis, Det. Falcons
67	2	1946–47	Moe Becker, Det. Falcons
68	1	1946–47	Milt Schoon, Det. Falcons
69	N/A		

continued on next page

#	Number of Players	First Season Worn	First Worn By
70	8	1948–49	Jack Eskridge, Ind. Jets
71	4	1961–62	Bob Wiesenhahn, Cin. Royals
72	1	2009–10	Jason Kapono, Phi. 76ers
73	1	1998–99	Dennis Rodman, L.A. Lakers
74	N/A		
75	N/A		
76	1	1993–94	Shawn Bradley, Phi. 76ers
77	15	1948–49	John Mahnken, Ind. Jets
			Blackie Towery, Ind. Jets
78	N/A		
79	N/A		
80	N/A		
81	2	2017–18	José Calderón, Cle. Cavaliers
82	N/A		
83	1	2011–12	Craig Smith, Por. Blazers
84	2	2006–07	Chris Webber, Det. Pistons
85	1	2010–11	Baron Davis, Cle. Cavaliers
86	2	2010–11	Semih Erden, Bos. Celtics
			Chris Johnson, Bos. Celtics
87	N/A		
88	8	2004–05	Antoine Walker, Bos. Celtics
89	2	1953–54	Clyde Lovellette, Min. Lakers
90	2	2004–05	Drew Gooden, Cle. Cavaliers
91	4	2004–05	Metta World Peace, Ind. Pacers
92	2	2009–10	DeShawn Stevenson, Dal. Mavericks
93	2	2005–06	Metta World Peace, Sac. Kings
94	2	2012–13	Evan Fournier, Den. Nuggets
95	2	2016–17	DeAndre' Bembry, Atl. Hawks
96	2	1949–50	Don Ray, T.C. Blackhawks
97	1	2021–22	Brodric Thomas, Bos. Celtics
98	4	1946–47	Chet Aubuchon, Det. Falcons
99	7	1946–47	Ariel Maughan, Det. Falcons

ᵃ ABA.

PART 2
Team-by-Team Histories

1

EASTERN CONFERENCE

Atlanta Hawks

Dates of Operation: (as the St. Louis Hawks) 1949–68 (19 seasons)
Overall Record: 698 wins, 720 losses (.492)
Arenas: Wharton Field House, 1949–51; Milwaukee Arena, 1951–55; Kiel Auditorium, 1955–58
Other Names: Tri-Cities Blackhawks, 1949–51; Milwaukee Hawks, 1951–55; St. Louis Hawks, 1955–68

Dates of Operation: (as the Atlanta Hawks) 1968–present (54 seasons)
Overall Record: 2152 wins, 2203 losses (.494)
Arenas: Alexander Memorial Coliseum, 1968–72; Omni Coliseum, 1972–97; Georgia Dome, 1997–99; State Farm Arena (formerly Philips Arena, 1999–2018), 1999–present (capacity: 16,600)

Year-by-Year Finishes

Year	Finish	Wins	Losses	Percentage	Games Behind	Head Coach	Attendance
				Tri-Cities Blackhawks **Western Division**			
1949–50	3rd	29	35	.453	10.0	Roger Potter (1–6), Red Auerbach (28–29)	N/A
1950–51	5th	25	43	.368	12.0	Dave McMillan (9–14), John Logan (2–1), Mike Todorovich (14–28)	101,331
				Milwaukee Hawks			
1951–52	5th	17	49	.258	24.0	Doxie Moore	
1952–53	5th	27	44	.380	21.5	Fuzzy Levane	136,673
1953–54	4th	21	51	.292	25.0	Fuzzy Levane (11–35), Red Holzman (10–16)	60,210
1954–55	4th	26	46	.361	17.0	Red Holzman	60,991
				St. Louis Hawks			
1955–56	2nd (Tie)	33	39	.458	4.0	Red Holzman	156,009
1956–57	1st (Tie)	34	38	.472	—	Red Holzman (14–19), Slater Martin (5–3), Alex Hannum (15–16)	217,300
1957–58	1st	41	31	.569	+8.0	Alex Hannum	224,512
1958–59	1st	49	23	.681	+16.0	Andy Phillip (6–4), Ed Macauley (43–19)	265,000
1959–60	1st	46	29	.613	+16.0	Ed Macauley	277,502
1960–61	1st	51	28	.646	+15.0	Paul Seymour	291,084

Year	Finish	Wins	Losses	Percentage	Games Behind	Head Coach	Attendance
1961–62	4th	29	51	.363	25.0	Paul Seymour (5–9), Fuzzy Levane (20–40), Bob Pettit (4–2)	256,747
1962–63	2nd	48	32	.600	5.0	Harry Gallatin	284,849
1963–64	2nd	46	34	.575	2.0	Harry Gallatin	290,840
1964–65	2nd	45	35	.563	4.0	Harry Gallatin (17–16), Richie Guerin (28–19)	265,645
1965–66	3rd	36	44	.450	9.0	Richie Guerin	267,008
1966–67	2nd	39	42	.481	5.0	Richie Guerin	198,039
1967–68	1st	56	26	.683	+4.0	Richie Guerin	201,215

Atlanta Hawks

Year	Finish	Wins	Losses	Percentage	Games Behind	Head Coach	Attendance
1968–69	2nd	48	34	.585	7.0	Richie Guerin	178,979
1969–70	1st	48	34	.585	+2.0	Richie Guerin	197,990

Eastern Conference Central Division

Year	Finish	Wins	Losses	Percentage	Games Behind	Head Coach	Attendance
1970–71	2nd	36	46	.439	6.0	Richie Guerin	245,910
1971–72	2nd	36	46	.439	2.0	Richie Guerin	230,784
1972–73	2nd	46	36	.561	6.0	Cotton Fitzsimmons	304,802
1973–74	2nd	35	47	.427	12.0	Cotton Fitzsimmons	312,128
1974–75	4th	31	51	.378	29.0	Cotton Fitzsimmons	205,341
1975–76	5th	29	53	.354	20.0	Cotton Fitzsimmons (28–46), Gene Tormohlen (1–7)	227,815
1976–77	6th	31	51	.378	18.0	Hubie Brown	214,775
1977–78	4th	41	41	.500	11.0	Hubie Brown	304,050
1978–79	3rd	46	36	.561	2.0	Hubie Brown	329,064
1979–80	1st	50	32	.610	+9.0	Hubie Brown	449,843
1980–81	4th	31	51	.378	29.0	Hubie Brown (31–48), Mike Fratello (0–3)	362,699
1981–82	2nd	42	40	.512	13.0	Kevin Loughery	314,593
1982–83	2nd	43	39	.524	8.0	Kevin Loughery	292,126
1983–84	3rd	40	42	.488	10.0	Mike Fratello	286,049
1984–85	5th	34	48	.415	25.0	Mike Fratello	290,746
1985–86	2nd	50	32	.610	7.0	Mike Fratello	377,351
1986–87	1st	57	25	.695	+5.0	Mike Fratello	549,526
1987–88	2nd (Tie)	50	32	.610	4.0	Mike Fratello	572,460
1988–89	3rd	52	30	.634	11.0	Mike Fratello	644,291
1989–90	6th	41	41	.500	18.0	Mike Fratello	573,711
1990–91	4th	43	39	.524	18.0	Bob Weiss	529,161
1991–92	5th	38	44	.463	29.0	Bob Weiss	511,803
1992–93	4th	43	39	.524	14.0	Bob Weiss	491,229
1993–94	1st	57	25	.695	+2.0	Lenny Wilkens	537,547
1994–95	4th (Tie)	42	40	.512	10.0	Lenny Wilkens	504,807
1995–96	4th (Tie)	46	36	.561	26.0	Lenny Wilkens	496,668
1996–97	2nd	56	26	.683	13.0	Lenny Wilkens	549,414
1997–98	4th	50	32	.610	12.0	Lenny Wilkens	610,615
1998–99	2nd	31	19	.620	2.0	Lenny Wilkens	331,831
1999–00	7th	28	54	.341	28.0	Lenny Wilkens	600,954
2000–01	7th	25	57	.305	27.0	Lon Kruger	560,330
2001–02	6th	33	49	.402	17.0	Lon Kruger	506,110
2002–03	5th	35	47	.427	15.0	Lon Kruger (11–16), Terry Stotts (24–31)	528,655
2003–04	7th	28	54	.341	33.0	Terry Stotts	565,728

Year	Finish	Wins	Losses	Percentage	Games Behind	Head Coach	Attendance
					Southeast Division		
2004–05	5th	13	69	.159	46.0	Mike Woodson	586,390
2005–06	4th (Tie)	26	56	.317	26.0	Mike Woodson	617,817
2006–07	5th	30	52	.366	14.0	Mike Woodson	639,375
2007–08	3rd	37	45	.451	15.0	Mike Woodson	667,518
2008–09	2nd	47	35	.573	12.0	Mike Woodson	686,688
2009–10	2nd	53	29	.646	6.0	Mike Woodson	678,375
2010–11	3rd	44	38	.537	14.0	Larry Drew	641,596
2011–12	2nd	40	26	.606	6.0	Larry Drew	501,593
2012–13	2nd	44	38	.537	22.0	Larry Drew	620,146
2013–14	4th	38	44	.463	16.0	Mike Budenholzer	587,927
2014–15	1st	60	22	.732	+14.0	Mike Budenholzer	713,909
2015–16	1st (Tie)	48	34	.585	—	Mike Budenholzer	690,150
2016–17	2nd	43	39	.524	6.0	Mike Budenholzer	654,306
2017–18	5th	24	58	.293	20.0	Mike Budenholzer	590,769
2018–19	5th	29	53	.354	13.0	Lloyd Pierce	628,440
2019–20	5th	20	47	.299	21.0	Lloyd Pierce	545,453
2020–21	1st	41	31	.569	+1.0	Lloyd Pierce (14–20), Nate McMillan (27–11)	59,288
2021–22	2nd (Tie)	43	39	.524	10.0	Nate McMillan	672,742

1998–99: 50-game season.

2011–12: 66-game season.

2019–20: 65-to-75-game season.

2020–21: 72-game season.

Awards

Most Valuable Player

Bob Pettit, center, 1955–56 (St.L.)

Bob Pettit, forward, 1958–59 (St.L.)

Rookie of the Year

Mel Hutchins*, center, 1951–52 (Mil.)

Bob Pettit, forward, 1954–55 (Mil.)

* Tied with Bill Tosheff, Ind. Olympians.

Defensive Player of the Year

Dikembe Mutombo, center, 1996–97

Dikembe Mutombo, center, 1997–98

Dikembe Mutombo*, center, 2000–01

* 49 games with Atl. Hawks and 26 games with Phi. 76ers.

Sixth Man of the Year

Jamal Crawford, guard, 2009–10

Most Improved Player

Alan Henderson, forward, 1997–98

All-NBA First Team

Bob Pettit, 1954–55 (Mil.)

Bob Pettit, 1955–56 (St.L.)

Bob Pettit, 1956–57 (St.L.)

Bob Pettit, 1957–58 (St.L.)

Bob Pettit, 1958–59 (St.L.)

Bob Pettit, 1959–60 (St.L.)

Bob Pettit, 1960–61 (St.L.)

Bob Pettit, 1961–62 (St.L.)

Bob Pettit, 1962–63 (St.L.)

Bob Pettit, 1963–64 (St.L.)

Dominique Wilkins, 1985–86

All-Defensive First Team

Dan Roundfield, 1979–80

Dan Roundfield, 1981–82

Dan Roundfield, 1982–83

Tree Rollins, 1983–84

Mookie Blaylock, 1993–94

Mookie Blaylock, 1994–95

Dikembe Mutombo, 1996–97

Dikembe Mutombo, 1997–98

Dikembe Mutombo, 2000–01*

*49 games with Atl. Hawks and 26 games with Phi. 76ers.

All-Rookie First Team

Zelmo Beaty, 1962–63 (St.L.)

Lou Hudson, 1966–67 (St.L.)

Pete Maravich, 1970–71

John Brown, 1973–74

John Drew, 1974–75

Dominique Wilkins, 1982–83

Stacey Augmon, 1991–92

Al Horford, 2007–08

Trae Young, 2018–19

Coach of the Year

Harry Gallatin, 1962–63 (St.L.)

Richie Guerin, 1967–68 (St.L.)

Hubie Brown, 1977–78

Mike Fratello, 1985–86

Lenny Wilkens, 1993–94

Mike Budenholzer, 2014–15

Hall of Famers Who Played for the Blackhawks/Hawks

Zelmo Beaty, center, 1962–69 (St.L.-Atl.)

Walt Bellamy, center, 1969–74

Maurice Cheeks, guard, 1991–92

Chuck Cooper, forward, 1954–56 (Mil.-St.L.)

Richie Guerin, guard, 1963–67 (St.L.); 1968–70

Alex Hannum, forward, 1954–57 (Mil.-St.L.)

Cliff Hagan, forward, 1956–66 (St.L.)

Connie Hawkins, forward, 1975–76

Red Holzman, guard, 1953–54 (Mil.)
Bob Houbregs, forward, 1953–54 (Mil.)
Lou Hudson, forward-guard, 1966–77
  (St.L.-Atl.)
Toni Kukoč, forward, 2000–02
Clyde Lovellette, center, 1958–62 (St.L.)
Ed Macauley, center, 1956–59 (St.L)
Moses Malone, center, 1988–91
Pete Maravich, guard, 1970–74
Slater Martin, guard, 1956–60 (St.L.)
Tracy McGrady, guard, 2011–12
Sidney Moncrief, guard, 1990–91
Dikembe Mutombo, center, 1996–2001
Bob Pettit, forward-center, 1954–65
  (Mil.-St.L.)
Lenny Wilkens, guard, 1960–68 (St.L.)
Dominique Wilkins, forward, 1982–94

Retired Numbers

TT .... Ted Turner
9 .... Bob Pettit
21 .... Dominique Wilkins
23 .... Lou Hudson
44 .... Pete Maravich
55 .... Dikembe Mutombo

League Leaders, Offense

Points

Bob Pettit, 1955–56 .... 1849 (St.L.)
Bob Pettit, 1958–59 .... 2105 (St.L.)
Trae Young, 2021–22 2155

Three Pointers

Assists

Trae Young, 2021–22 737

Scoring Average

Dominique Wilkins, 1985–86 .... 30.3

Field Goal Percantage

Bob Pettit, 1955–56 (St.L.) 25.7
Bob Pettit, 1958–59 (St.L.) 29.2

Three Point Percentage

Kyle Korver, 2013–14 .... .472
Kyle Korver, 2014–15 .... .492
Kyle Korver*, 2016–17 .... .451
*.409 with Atl. Hawks and .485 with
  Cle. Cavaliers.

Free Throw Percentage

Assists Average

League Leaders, Defense

Offensive Rebounds

John Drew, 1974–75 357
Moses Malone, 1989–90 364
Dikembe Mutombo*, 2000–01 307
Clint Capela, 2020–21 297
* 188 with Atl. Hawks and 119 with Phi. 76ers.

Defensive Rebounds

Dikembe Mutombo, 1998–99 418
Dikembe Mutombo, 1999–00 853

Total Rebounds

Mel Hutchins, 1951–52 (Mil.) 880
Bob Pettit, 1955–56 (St.L.) 1164
Dikembe Mutombo, 1996–97 929
Dikembe Mutombo, 1998–99 610
Dikembe Mutombo, 1999–00 1157

Steals

Mookie Blaylock, 1996–97 212

Blocks

Tree Rollins, 1982–83 343
Dikembe Mutombo, 1996–97 264
Dikembe Mutombo, 1997–98 277
Theo Ratliff, 2002–03 262
Theo Ratliff*, 2003–04 307
* 166 with Atl. Hawks and 141 with Por. Blazers.

Rebounds Average

Dikembe Mutombo, 1999–00 .... 14.1
Dikembe Mutombo*, 2000–01 .... 13.5
Clint Capela, 2020–21 .... 14.3
* 14.1 with Atl. Hawks and 12.4 with Phi. 76ers.

Steals Average

Mookie Blaylock, 1996–97 .... 2.72
Mookie Blaylock, 1997–98 .... 2.61

Blocks Average

Tree Rollins, 1982–83 .... 4.3
Theo Ratliff, 2002–03 .... 3.2
Theo Ratliff*, 2003–04 .... 3.6
* 3.1 with Atl. Hawks and 4.4 with Por. Blazers.

Feats

50-Point Game

57 .... Bob Pettit (@ Det. Pistons),
  Feb. 18, 1961 (St.L)
57 .... Lou Hudson (vs. Chi. Bulls),
  Nov. 10, 1969
57 ... Dominique Wilkins (vs. N.J. Nets),
  Apr. 10, 1986
57 ... Dominique Wilkins (vs. Chi. Bulls),
  Dec. 10, 1986

56 .... Trae Young (@ Por. Blazers),
  Jan. 3, 2022
55 .... Cliff Hagan (vs. Cin. Royals),
  Feb. 11, 1962
54 ...Dominique Wilkins (vs. Bos. Celtics),
  Feb. 3, 1987
53 ...Dominique Wilkins (vs. L.A. Clippers),
  Jan. 12, 1987
52 .... Bob Pettit (vs. Bos. Celtics),
  Jan. 20, 1959 (St.L)
52 .... Bob Pettit (vs. Bal. Bullets),
  Nov. 16, 1963 (St.L)
52 ...Dominique Wilkins (vs. N.Y. Knicks),
  Dec. 7, 1991
51 .... Bob Pettit (vs. Syr. Nationals),
  Dec. 21, 1957 (St.L)
51 .... Bob Pettit (@ Phi. Warriors),
  Dec. 6, 1961 (St.L.)
51 ... Dominique Wilkins (vs. Sac. Kings),
  Feb. 16, 1988
50 .... Bob Pettit (vs. Det. Pistons),
  Jan. 11, 1959 (St.L)
50 .... Pete Maravich (vs. Phi. 76ers),
  Jan. 16, 1972
50 ...Pete Maravich (vs. Cle. Cavaliers),
  Feb. 5, 1972
50 .... John Drew (vs. Den. Nuggets),
  Dec. 30, 1978
50 ...Dominique Wilkins (vs. Det. Pistons),
  Mar. 1, 1988
50 ... Shareef Abdur-Rahim (vs. Det. Pistons),
  Nov. 23, 2001
50 .... Trae Young (vs. Mia. Heat),
  Feb. 20, 2020

20-Assist Game

23 .... Mookie Blaylock (vs. Uta. Jazz),
  Mar. 6, 1993
21 .... Doc Rivers (vs. Phil. 76ers),
  Mar. 4, 1986

30-Rebound Game

35 ....Bob Pettit (vs. Cin. Royals),
  Mar. 2, 1958 (St.L)
35 .... Bob Pettit (vs. Min. Lakers),
  Jan. 6, 1959 (St.L)
33 .... Kevin Willis (vs. Was. Bullets),
  Feb. 19, 1992
31 .... Mel Hutchins (vs. Min. Lakers),
  Mar. 2, 1952 (Mil.)
31 .... Bob Pettit (vs. N.Y. Knicks),
  Nov. 15, 1955 (St.L)

31 .... Bob Pettit (vs. Det. Pistons),
Nov. 17, 1960 (St.L)

31 .... Bob Pettit (vs. Chi. Packers),
Dec. 30, 1961 (St.L)

31 ...Kevin Willis (@ Dal. Mavericks),
Dec. 3, 1991

30 ....Chuck Share (vs. Bos. Celtics),
Feb. 15, 1955 (Mil.)

30 .... Bob Pettit (vs. Ft.W. Pistons),
Jan. 19, 1956 (St.L.)

30 .... Bob Pettit (vs. Phi. Warriors),
Nov. 14, 1958 (St.L.)

30 ....Bob Pettit (vs. Cin. Royals),
Feb. 28, 1960 (St.L.)

30 .... Bob Pettit (@ Phi. Warriors),
Dec. 6, 1991 (St.L.)

8-Steal Game

10 ...Mookie Blaylock (vs. Phi. 76ers),
Apr. 14, 1998

9 ...Mookie Blaylock (@ Hou. Rockets),
Feb. 17, 1997

8 .... Lou Hudson (vs. Phi. 76ers),
Dec. 26, 1973

8 .... John Drew (@ Phi. 76ers),
Dec. 5, 1980

8 ...Eddie Johnson (vs. Chi. Bulls), Feb. 26,
1982

8 ....Doc Rivers (vs. Por. Blazers),
Dec. 4, 1985

8 ....Doc Rivers (@ Mia. Heat),
Nov. 24, 1989

8 .... Mookie Blaylock (vs. Chi. Bulls),
Apr. 9, 1993

8 ... Mookie Blaylock (vs. Min. T'Wolves),
Mar. 1, 1994

8 .... Mookie Blaylock (@ Phi. 76ers),
Apr. 9, 1997

8 ... Mookie Blaylock (@ Orl. Magic),
Feb. 3, 1998

8 ... Speedy Claxton (vs. Cle. Cavaliers),
Dec. 27, 2006

10-Block Game

12 ....Tree Rollins (vs. Por. Blazers),
Feb. 21, 1979

11 .... Tree Rollins (vs. Ind. Pacers),
Nov. 27, 1982

11 ...Dikembe Mutombo (vs. N.J. Nets),
Feb. 15, 2000

10 ....Tree Rollins (vs. Bos. Celtics),
Mar. 14, 1980

10 ....Tree Rollins (@ Chi. Bulls),
Dec. 21, 1982

10 ....Tree Rollins (@ N.J. Nets),
Jan. 17, 1983

10 ....Tree Rollins (vs. Cle. Cavaliers),
Mar. 29, 1983

10 ....Tree Rollins (vs. Chi. Bulls),
Nov. 4, 1983

10 .... Tree Rollins (@ Was. Bullets),
Dec. 13, 1983

10 .... Josh Smith (@ Dal. Mavericks),
Dec. 18, 2004

10 .... Clint Capela (@ Min. T'Wolves),
Jan. 22, 2021

Multiple Triple-Doubles in a Single Season

4 ....Bill Bridges, 1969–70

3 ....Doc Rivers, 1987–88

2 ....Tree Rollins, 1982–83

2 .... Mookie Blaylock, 1993–94

2 .... Mookie Blaylock, 1994–95

2 .... Mookie Blaylock, 1997–98

2 .... Toni Kukoč, 2000–01

2 .... Bob Sura, 2003–04

2 .... Trae Young, 2019–20

Postseason Play

1950 Western Division Semifinals
vs. And. Packers, lost (2–1)

1956 Western Division Second Place
Tiebreaker vs. Min. Lakers, won
Western Division Semifinals
vs. Min. Lakers, won (2–1)
Western Division Finals
vs. Ft.W. Pistons, lost (3–2)

1957 Western Division Tiebreaker
vs. Ft.W. Pistons, won
Western Division Tiebreaker
vs. Min. Lakers, won
Western Division Finals
vs. Min. Lakers, won (3–0)
NBA Finals vs. Bos. Celtics,
lost (4–3)

1958 Western Division Finals
vs. Det. Pistons, won (4–1)
NBA Finals vs. Bos. Celtics,
won (4–2)

1959 Western Division Finals
vs. Min. Lakers, lost (4–2)

1960 Western Division Finals
vs. Min. Lakers, won (4–3)
NBA Finals vs. Bos. Celtics,
lost (4–3)

1961 Western Division Finals
vs. L.A. Lakers, won (4–3)

NBA Finals vs. Bos. Celtics,
lost (4–1)

1963 Western Division Semifinals
vs. Det. Pistons, won (3–1)
Western Division Finals
vs. L.A. Lakers, lost (4–3)

1964 Western Division Semifinals
vs. L.A. Lakers, won (3–2)
Western Division Finals
vs. S.F. Warriors, lost (4–3)

1965 Western Division Semifinals
vs. Bal. Bullets, lost (3–1)

1966 Western Division Semifinals
vs. Bal. Bullets, won (3–0)
Western Division Finals
vs. L.A. Lakers, lost (4–3)

1967 Western Division Semifinals
vs. Chi. Bulls, won (3–0)
Western Division Finals
vs. S.F. Warriors, lost (4–2)

1968 Western Division Semifinals
vs. S.F. Warriors, lost (4–2)

1969 Western Division Semifinals
vs. S.D. Rockets, won (4–2)
Western Division Finals
vs. L.A. Lakers, lost (4–1)

1970 Western Division Semifinals
vs. Chi. Bulls, won (4–1)
Western Division Finals
vs. L.A. Lakers, lost (4–0)

1971 Eastern Conference Semifinals
vs. N.Y. Knicks, lost (4–1)

1972 Eastern Conference Semifinals
vs. Bos. Celtics, lost (4–2)

1973 Eastern Conference Semifinals
vs. Bos. Celtics, lost (4–2)

1978 Eastern Conference First Round
vs. Was. Bullets, lost (2–0)

1979 Eastern Conference First Round
vs. Hou. Rockets, won (2–0)
Eastern Conference Semifinals
vs. Was. Bullets, lost (4–3)

1980 Eastern Conference Semifinals
vs. Phi. 76ers, lost (4–1)

1982 Eastern Conference First Round
vs. Phi. 76ers, lost (2–0)

1983 Eastern Conference First Round
vs. Bos. Celtics, lost (2–1)

1984 Eastern Conference First Round
vs. Mil. Bucks, lost (3–2)

1986 Eastern Conference First Round
vs. Det. Pistons, won (3–1)

Eastern Conference Semifinals
vs. Bos. Celtics, lost (4–1)

1987 Eastern Conference First Round
vs. Ind. Pacers, won (3–1)
Eastern Conference Semifinals
vs. Det. Pistons, lost (4–1)

1988 Eastern Conference First Round
vs. Mil. Bucks, won (3–2)
Eastern Conference Semifinals
vs. Bos. Celtics, lost (4–3)

1989 Eastern Conference First Round
vs. Mil. Bucks, won (3–2)

1991 Eastern Conference First Round
vs. Det. Pistons, lost (3–2)

1993 Eastern Conference First Round
vs. Chi. Bulls, lost (3–0)

1994 Eastern Conference First Round
vs. Mia. Heat, won (3–2)
Eastern Conference Semifinals
vs. Ind. Pacers, lost (4–2)

1995 Eastern Conference First Round
vs. Ind. Pacers, lost (3–0)

1996 Eastern Conference First Round
vs. Ind. Pacers, won (3–2)
Eastern Conference Semifinals
vs. Orl. Magic, lost (4–1)

1997 Eastern Conference First Round
vs. Det. Pistons, won (3–2)
Eastern Conference Semifinals
vs. Chi. Bulls, lost (4–1)

1998 Eastern Conference First Round
vs. Cha. Hornets, lost (3–1)

1999 Eastern Conference First Round
vs. Det. Pistons, won (3–2)
Eastern Conference Semifinals
vs. N.Y. Knicks, lost (4–0)

2008 Eastern Conference First Round
vs. Bos. Celtics, lost (4–3)

2009 Eastern Conference First Round
vs. Mia. Heat, won (4–3)
Eastern Conference Semifinals
vs. Cle. Cavaliers, lost (4–0)

2010 Eastern Conference First Round
vs. Mil. Bucks, won (4–3)
Eastern Conference Semifinals
vs. Orl. Magic, lost (4–0)

2011 Eastern Conference First Round
vs. Orl. Magic, won (4–2)
Eastern Conference Semifinals
vs. Chi. Bulls, lost (4–2)

2012 Eastern Conference First Round
vs. Bos. Celtics, lost (4–2)

2013 Eastern Conference First Round
vs. Ind. Pacers, lost (4–0)

2014 Eastern Conference First Round
vs. Ind. Pacers, lost (4–3)

2015 Eastern Conference First Round
vs. Brk. Nets, won (4–2)
Eastern Conference Semifinals
vs. Was. Wizards, won (4–2)
Eastern Conference Finals
vs. Cle. Cavaliers, lost (4–0)

2016 Eastern Conference First Round
vs. Bos. Celtics, won (4–2)
Eastern Conference Semifinals
vs. Cle. Cavaliers, lost (4–0)

2017 Eastern Conference First Round
vs. Was. Wizards, lost (4–2)

2021 Eastern Conference First Round
vs. N.Y. Knicks, won (4–1)
Eastern Conference Semifinals
vs. Phi. 76ers, won (4–3)
Eastern Conference Finals
vs. Mil. Bucks, lost (4–2)

2022 Eastern Conference First Round
vs. Mia. Heat, lost (4–1)

Boston Celtics

Dates of Operation: 1946–present (76 seasons)
Overall Record: 3513 wins, 2437 losses (.590)
Arenas: Boston Garden, 1946–95; TD Garden (formerly FleetCenter, 1995–2005; TD Banknorth Garden; 2005–09); 1995–present (capacity: 19,156)

Year-by-Year Finishes

Year	Finish	Wins	Losses	Percentage	Games Behind	Head Coach	Attendance
				BAA Eastern Division			
1946–47	5th (Tie)	22	38	.367	27.0	Honey Russell	108,240
1947–48	3rd	20	28	.417	7.0	Honey Russell	90,264
1948–49	5th	25	35	.417	13.0	Doggie Julian	144,275
				NBA Eastern Division			
1949–50	6th	22	46	.324	31.0	Doggie Julian	110,552
1950–51	2nd	39	30	.565	2.5	Red Auerbach	197,888
1951–52	2nd	39	27	.591	1.0	Red Auerbach	160,167
1952–53	3rd	46	25	.648	1.5	Red Auerbach	161,808
1953–54	2nd (Tie)	42	30	.583	2.0	Red Auerbach	156,912
1954–55	3rd	36	36	.500	7.0	Red Auerbach	175,675
1955–56	2nd	39	33	.542	6.0	Red Auerbach	209,645
1956–57	1st	44	28	.611	+6.0	Red Auerbach	262,918
1957–58	1st	49	23	.681	+8.0	Red Auerbach	240,943
1958–59	1st	52	20	.722	+12.0	Red Auerbach	244,642
1959–60	1st	59	16	.787	+10.0	Red Auerbach	209,374
1960–61	1st	57	22	.722	+11.0	Red Auerbach	201,569
1961–62	1st	60	20	.750	+11.0	Red Auerbach	191,855
1962–63	1st	58	22	.725	+10.0	Red Auerbach	262,581
1963–64	1st	59	21	.738	+4.0	Red Auerbach	223,347
1964–65	1st	62	18	.775	+14.0	Red Auerbach	246,529
1965–66	2nd	54	26	.675	1.0	Red Auerbach	246,189
1966–67	2nd	60	21	.741	8.0	Bill Russell	322,690
1967–68	2nd	54	28	.659	8.0	Bill Russell	320,788
1968–69	4th	48	34	.585	9.0	Bill Russell	322,130
1969–70	6th	34	48	.415	26.0	Tom Heinsohn	277,632
				Eastern Conference Atlantic Division			
1970–71	3rd	44	38	.537	8.0	Tom Heinsohn	313,768
1971–72	1st	56	26	.683	+8.0	Tom Heinsohn	346,701
1972–73	1st	68	14	.829	+11.0	Tom Heinsohn	423,234
1973–74	1st	56	26	.683	+7.0	Tom Heinsohn	355,261
1974–75	1st	60	22	.732	+11.0	Tom Heinsohn	486,270
1975–76	1st	54	28	.659	+8.0	Tom Heinsohn	539,589
1976–77	2nd	44	38	.537	6.0	Tom Heinsohn	517,391
1977–78	3rd	32	50	.390	23.0	Tom Heinsohn (11–23), Tom Sanders (21–27)	437,937
1978–79	5th	29	53	.354	25.0	Tom Sanders (2–12), Dave Cowens (27–41)	417,926
1979–80	1st	61	21	.744	+2.0	Bill Fitch	596,349
1980–81	1st (Tie)	62	20	.756	—	Bill Fitch	595,454

Year	Finish	Wins	Losses	Percentage	Games Behind	Head Coach	Attendance
1981–82	1st	63	19	.768	+5.0	Bill Fitch	612,711
1982–83	2nd	56	26	.683	9.0	Bill Fitch	621,829
1983–84	1st	62	20	.756	+10.0	K.C. Jones	606,857
1984–85	1st	63	19	.768	+5.0	K.C. Jones	610,547
1985–86	1st	67	15	.817	+13.0	K.C. Jones	610,571
1986–87	1st	59	23	.720	+14.0	K.C. Jones	611,222
1987–88	1st	57	25	.695	+19.0	K.C. Jones	611,231
1988–89	3rd	42	40	.512	10.0	Jimmy Rodgers	611,537
1989–90	2nd	52	30	.634	1.0	Jimmy Rodgers	611,537
1990–91	1st	56	26	.683	+12.0	Chris Ford	611,537
1991–92	1st (Tie)	51	31	.622	—	Chris Ford	610,776
1992–93	2nd	48	34	.585	12.0	Chris Ford	608,495
1993–94	5th	32	50	.390	25.0	Chris Ford	604,867
1994–95	3rd	35	47	.427	22.0	Chris Ford	606,070
1995–96	5th	33	49	.402	27.0	M.L. Carr	730,842
1996–97	7th	15	67	.183	46.0	M.L. Carr	664,022
1997–98	6th	36	46	.439	19.0	Rick Pitino	739,422
1998–99	5th	19	31	.380	14.0	Rick Pitino	440,602
1999–00	5th	35	47	.427	17.0	Rick Pitino	683,608
2000–01	5th	36	46	.439	20.0	Rick Pitino (12–22), Jim O'Brien (24–24)	629,201
2001–02	2nd	49	33	.598	3.0	Jim O'Brien	659,751
2002–03	3rd	44	38	.537	5.0	Jim O'Brien	709,049
2003–04	4th	36	46	.439	11.0	Jim O'Brien (22–24), John Carroll (14–22)	664,248
2004–05	1st	45	37	.549	+2.0	Doc Rivers	656,081
2005–06	3rd	33	49	.402	16.0	Doc Rivers	692,873
2006–07	5th	24	58	.293	23.0	Doc Rivers	690,576
2007–08	1st	66	16	.805	+25.0	Doc Rivers	763,584
2008–09	1st	62	20	.756	+21.0	Doc Rivers	763,584
2009–10	1st	50	32	.610	+10.0	Doc Rivers	763,584
2010–11	1st	56	26	.683	+14.0	Doc Rivers	763,584
2011–12	1st	39	27	.591	+3.0	Doc Rivers	614,592
2012–13	3rd	41	40	.506	12.5	Doc Rivers	744,960
2013–14	4th	25	57	.305	23.0	Brad Stevens	742,400
2014–15	2nd	40	42	.488	9.0	Brad Stevens	721,350
2015–16	2nd	48	34	.585	8.0	Brad Stevens	749,076
2016–17	1st	53	29	.646	+2.0	Brad Stevens	760,690
2017–18	2nd	55	27	.671	4.0	Brad Stevens	763,584
2018–19	3rd	49	33	.598	9.0	Brad Stevens	763,584
2019–20	2nd	48	24	.667	5.0	Brad Stevens	610,864
2020–21	4th	36	36	.500	13.0	Brad Stevens	30,067
2021–22	1st (Tie)	51	31	622	—	Ime Udoka	727,928

1998–99: 50-game season.

2011–12: 66-game season.

2019–20: 65-to-75-game season.

2020–21: 72-game season.

Awards

Most Valuable Player
Bob Cousy, guard, 1956–57
Bill Russell, center, 1957–58
Bill Russell, center, 1960–61
Bill Russell, center, 1961–62
Bill Russell, center, 1962–63
Bill Russell, center, 1964–65
Dave Cowens, center, 1972–73
Larry Bird, forward, 1983–84
Larry Bird, forward, 1984–85
Larry Bird, forward, 1985–86

Rookie of the Year
Tom Heinsohn, forward, 1956–57
Dave Cowens, center, 1970–71*
Larry Bird, forward, 1979–80
* Tied with Geoff Petrie, Por. Blazers.

Defensive Player of the Year
Kevin Garnett, forward, 2007–08
Marcus Smart, guard, 2021–22

Sixth Man of the Year
Kevin McHale, forward, 1983–84
Kevin McHale, forward, 1984–85
Bill Walton, center, 1985–86

Most Improved Player
none

All-NBA First Team
Ed Sadowski, 1947–48
Ed Macauley, 1950–51
Bob Cousy, 1951–52
Ed Macauley, 1951–52
Bob Cousy, 1952–53
Ed Macauley, 1952–53
Bob Cousy, 1953–54
Bob Cousy, 1954–55
Bob Cousy, 1955–56
Bill Sharman, 1955–56
Bob Cousy, 1956–57
Bill Sharman, 1956–57
Bob Cousy, 1957–58
Bill Sharman, 1957–58
Bob Cousy, 1958–59
Bill Russell, 1958–59
Bill Sharman, 1958–59
Bob Cousy, 1959–60
Bob Cousy, 1960–61
Bill Russell, 1962–63
Bill Russell, 1964–65
John Havlicek, 1970–71
John Havlicek, 1971–72
John Havlicek, 1972–73

John Havlicek, 1973–74
Larry Bird, 1979–80
Larry Bird, 1980–81
Larry Bird, 1981–82
Larry Bird, 1982–83
Larry Bird, 1983–84
Larry Bird, 1984–85
Larry Bird, 1985–86
Larry Bird, 1986–87
Kevin McHale, 1986–87
Larry Bird, 1987–88
Kevin Garnett, 2007–08
Jayson Tatum, 2021–22

All-Defensive First Team
Bill Russell, 1968–69
John Havlicek, 1971–72
John Havlicek, 1972–73
John Havlicek, 1973–74
John Havlicek, 1974–75
Paul Silas, 1974–75
Dave Cowens, 1975–76
John Havlicek, 1975–76
Paul Silas, 1975–76
Kevin McHale, 1985–86
Dennis Johnson, 1986–87
Kevin McHale, 1986–87
Kevin McHale, 1987–88
Kevin Garnett, 2007–08
Kevin Garnett, 2008–09
Rajon Rondo, 2009–10
Kevin Garnett, 2010–11
Rajon Rondo, 2010–11
Avery Bradley, 2015–16
Marcus Smart, 2018–19
Marcus Smart, 2019–20

All-Rookie First Team
John Havlicek, 1962–63
Jo Jo White, 1969–70
Dave Cowens, 1970–71
Larry Bird, 1979–80
Kevin McHale, 1980–81
Dee Brown, 1990–91
Antoine Walker, 1996–97
Ron Mercer, 1997–98
Paul Pierce, 1998–99
Jayson Tatum, 2017–18

Coach of the Year
Red Auerbach, 1964–65
Tom Heinsohn, 1972–73
Bill Fitch, 1979–80

Hall of Famers Who Played for the Celtics
Ray Allen, guard, 2009–12
Tiny Archibald, guard, 1978–83
Dave Bing, guard, 1977–78
Larry Bird, forward, 1979–92
Carl Braun, guard, 1961–62
Chuck Cooper, forward, 1950–54
Bob Cousy, guard, 1950–63
Dave Cowens, center, 1970–80
Wayne Embry, center, 1966–68
Kevin Garnett, forward-center, 2007–13
Artis Gilmore, center, 1987–88
John Havlicek, forward-guard, 1962–78
Tommy Heinsohn, forward, 1956–65
Bob Houbregs, center, 1954–55
Bailey Howell, forward, 1966–70
Dennis Johnson, guard, 1983–90
K.C. Jones, guard, 1958–67
Sam Jones, guard-forward, 1957–69
Clyde Lovellette, center, 1962–64
Ed Macauley, center 1950–56
Pete Maravich, guard, 1979–80
Bob McAdoo, center, 1978–79
Kevin McHale, forward, 1980–93
Shaquille O'Neal, center, 2010–11
Robert Parish, center, 1980–94
Andy Philip, guard 1956–58
Paul Pierce, forward-guard, 1998–2013
Dino Radja, forward-center, 1993–97
Frank Ramsey, forward-guard, 1954–55; 1956–64
Arnie Risen, center, 1955–58
Bill Russell, center, 1956–69
Charlie Scott, guard, 1975–78
Bill Sharman, guard, 1951–61
Bill Walton, center, 1985–87
Paul Westphal, guard, 1972–75
Jo Jo White, guard, 1969–79
Dominique Wilkins, forward, 1994–95

Retired Numbers
JL.................................... Jim Loscutoff
JM .... Johnny Most
00.................................. Robert Parish
1................................. Walter Brown
2.............................. Red Auerbach
3............................... Dennis Johnson
5.................................Kevin Garnett
6...................................... Bill Russell
10...................................... Jo Jo White
14...................................... Bob Cousy
15..............................Tom Heinsohn

16	Tom Sanders
17	John Havlicek
18	Dave Cowens
19	Don Nelson
21	Bill Sharman
22	Ed Macauley
23	Frant Ramsey
24	Sam Jones
25	K.C. Jones
31	Cedric Maxwell
32	Kevin McHale
33	Larry Bird
34	Paul Pierce
35	Reggie Lewis

League Leaders, Offense

Points

Paul Pierce, 2001–02 2144

Three Pointers

Larry Bird, 1985–86 82
Larry Bird, 1986–87 90
Danny Ainge, 1987–88 148
Antoine Walker, 2000–01 221

Assists

Bob Cousy, 1952–53 547
Bob Cousy, 1953–54 518
Bob Cousy, 1954–55 557
Bob Cousy, 1955–56 642
Bob Cousy, 1956–57 478
Bob Cousy, 1957–58 463
Bob Cousy, 1958–59 557
Bob Cousy, 1959–60 715

Scoring Average

Field Goal Percantage

Ed Macauley, 1952–53 .... .452
Ed Macauley, 1953–54 .... .486
Don Nelson, 1974–75 .... .539
Cedric Maxwell, 1978–79 .... .584
Cedric Maxwell, 1979–80 .... .609
Kevin McHale, 1986–87 .... .604
Kevin McHale, 1987–88 .... .604

Three Point Percentage

Free Throw Percentage

Bill Sharman, 1952–53 .... .850
Bill Sharman, 1953–54 .... .844
Bill Sharman, 1954–55 .... .897
Bill Sharman, 1955–56 .... .867

Bill Sharman, 1956–57 .... .905
Bill Sharman, 1958–59 .... .932
Bill Sharman, 1960–61 .... .921
Larry Siegfried, 1965–66 .... .881
Larry Siegfried, 1968–69 .... .864
Larry Bird, 1983–84 .... .888
Larry Bird, 1985–86 .... .896
Larry Bird, 1986–87 .... .910
Larry Bird, 1989–90 .... .930
Brad Wanamaker, 2019–20 .... .927

Assists Average

Bob Cousy, 1952–53 .... 7.7
Bob Cousy, 1953–54 .... 7.2
Bob Cousy, 1954–55 .... 7.9
Bob Cousy, 1955–56 .... 8.9
Bob Cousy, 1956–57 .... 7.5
Bob Cousy, 1957–58 .... 7.1
Bob Cousy, 1958–59 .... 8.6
Bob Cousy, 1959–60 .... 9.5
Rajon Rondo, 2011–12 .... 11.7
Rajon Rondo, 2012–13 .... 11.1

League Leaders, Defense

Offensive Rebounds

Paul Silas, 1975–76 365

Defensive Rebounds

Total Rebounds

Bill Russell, 1957–58 1564
Bill Russell, 1958–59 1612
Bill Russell, 1963–64 1930
Bill Russell, 1964–65 1878

Steals

Rajon Rondo, 2009–10 189

Blocks

Rebounds Average

Bill Russell, 1956–57 .... 19.7
Bill Russell, 1957–58 .... 22.7
Bill Russell, 1958–59 .... 23.0
Bill Russell, 1963–64 .... 24.7
Bill Russell, 1964–65 .... 24.1

Steals Average

Rajon Rondo, 2009–10 .... 2.3

Blocks Average

Feats

50-Point Game

60 .... Larry Bird (@ Atl. Hawks),
Mar. 12, 1985

60 .... Jayson Tatum (vs. S.A. Spurs),
Apr. 30, 2021
56 .... Kevin McHale (vs. Det. Pistons),
Mar. 3, 1985
53 .... Larry Bird (vs. Ind. Pacers),
Mar. 30, 1983
53 ... Jayson Tatum (vs. Min. T'Wolves),
Apr. 9, 2021
52 .... Isaiah Thomas (vs. Mia. Heat),
Dec. 30, 2016
51 .... Sam Jones (@ Det. Pistons),
Oct. 29, 1965
51 ... Jayson Tatum (@ Was. Wizards),
Jan. 23, 2022
50 .... Larry Bird (@ Dal. Mavericks),
Mar. 10, 1986
50 .... Larry Bird (vs. Atl. Hawks),
Nov. 10, 1989
50 .... Paul Pierce (vs. Cle. Cavaliers),
Feb. 15, 2006
50 .... Jaylen Brown (vs. Orl. Magic),
Jan. 2, 2022

20-Assist Game

28 .... Bob Cousy (vs. Min. Lakers),
Feb. 27, 1959
24 .... Rajon Rondo (vs. N.Y. Knicks),
Oct. 29, 2010
23 .... Tiny Archibald (vs. Den. Nuggets),
Feb. 5, 1982
23 .... Rajon Rondo (vs. S.A. Spurs),
Jan. 5, 2011
22 ... Sherman Douglas (@ Phi. 76ers),
Apr. 3, 1994
21 .... Bob Cousy (vs. St.L. Hawks),
Dec. 21, 1960
21 ... Sherman Douglas (vs. Sac. Kings),
Dec. 8, 1993
20 .... Rajon Rondo (vs. N.Y. Knicks),
Mar. 4, 2012
20 .... Rajon Rondo (vs. Atl. Hawks),
Apr. 11, 2012
20 .... Rajon Rondo (vs. Phi. 76ers),
Nov. 9, 2012
20 .... Rajon Rondo (vs. Tor. Raptors),
Nov. 17, 2012

30-Rebound Game

51 .... Bill Russell (vs. Syr. Nationals),
Feb. 5, 1960
49 .... Bill Russell (vs. Phi. Warriors),
Nov. 16, 1957
49 .... Bill Russell (vs. Det. Pistons),
Mar. 11, 1965

43.............. Bill Russell (vs. L.A. Lakers),
Jan. 20, 1963

41.......... Bill Russell (vs. Syr. Nationals),
Feb. 12, 1958

41........... Bill Russell (vs. S.F. Warriors),
Mar. 14, 1965

40................Bill Russell (vs. Cin. Royals),
Dec. 12, 1958

40.......... Bill Russell (vs. Phi. Warriors),
Feb. 12, 1961

39.............. Bill Russell (vs. Det. Pistons),
Jan. 25, 1959

39................Bill Russell (vs. N.Y. Knicks),
Dec. 19, 1959

39................Bill Russell (vs. N.Y. Knicks),
Dec. 21, 1961

38.......... Bill Russell (vs. Phi. Warriors),
Feb. 23, 1958

38.............. Bill Russell (vs. N.Y. Knicks),
Dec. 4, 1959

38................Bill Russell (@ N.Y. Knicks),
Jan. 30, 1965

38................Bill Russell (vs. L.A. Lakers),
Mar. 3, 1965

37.......... Bill Russell (vs. Syr. Nationals),
Jan. 4, 1960

37.............. Bill Russell (vs. L.A. Lakers),
Nov. 12, 1960

37.......... Bill Russell (vs. Syr. Nationals),
Dec. 15, 1960

37.............. Bill Russell (vs. N.Y. Knicks),
Feb. 1, 1961

37...........Bill Russell (vs. Syr. Nationals),
Mar. 13, 1962

37................Bill Russell (vs. St.L. Hawks),
Dec. 23, 1966

36.......... Bill Russell (vs. Syr. Nationals),
Feb. 14, 1959

36.......... Bill Russell (vs. Syr. Nationals),
Feb. 22, 1962

36............. Bill Russell (@ S.F. Warriors),
Jan. 8, 1963

36............. Bill Russell (vs. Syr. Nationals),
Mar. 17, 1963

36.............. Bill Russell (vs. Phi. 76ers),
Mar. 3, 1964

36.............. Bill Russell (vs. Cin. Royals),
Mar. 21, 1965

36................Bill Russell (vs. Cin. Royals),
Oct. 16, 1965

36..............Bill Russell (@ Det. Pistons),
Feb. 2, 1966

36................Bill Russell (@ Det. Pistons),
Oct. 18, 1968

35.......... Bill Russell (@ Phi. Warriors),
Feb. 15, 1958

35..............Bill Russell (vs. Min. Lakers),
Mar. 3, 1959

35.......... Bill Russell (vs. Phi. Warriors),
Nov. 7, 1959

35................Bill Russell (vs. St.L. Hawks),
Jan. 27, 1960

35............. Bill Russell (vs. N.Y. Knicks),
Feb. 3, 1961

35.......... Bill Russell (vs. Syr. Nationals),
Oct. 27, 1962

35................ Bill Russell (vs. L.A. Lakers),
Nov. 27, 1965

34...........Bill Russell (vs. Phi. Warriors),
Dec. 26, 1956

34.......... Bill Russell (vs. Syr. Nationals),
Feb. 5, 1957

34...............Bill Russell (vs. N.Y. Knicks),
Dec. 26, 1957

34.......... Bill Russell (vs. Syr. Nationals),
Feb. 1, 1959

34............. Bill Russell (vs. Min. Lakers),
Feb. 3, 1960

34.............. Bill Russell (vs. St.L. Hawks),
Nov. 16, 1960

34.......... Bill Russell (vs. Phi. Warriors),
Jan. 13, 1961

34................ Bill Russell (vs. L.A. Lakers),
Nov. 18, 1961

34.............. Bill Russell (vs. Cin. Royals),
Jan. 12, 1962

34.............. Bill Russell (@ St.L. Hawks),
Nov. 9, 1963

34............. Bill Russell (vs. Bal. Bullets),
Feb. 6, 1964

34................Bill Russell (vs. L.A. Lakers),
Feb. 11, 1964

34.............. Bill Russell (@ Det. Pistons),
Jan. 2, 1965

34.............. Bill Russell (@ Bal. Bullets),
Dec. 25, 1965

33.......... Bill Russell (vs. Phi. Warriors),
Jan. 31, 1958

33................Bill Russell (@ N.Y. Knicks),
Dec. 25, 1958

33.......... Bill Russell (vs. Syr. Nationals),
Dec. 29, 1958

33......... Bill Russell (vs. Syr. Nationals),
Mar. 4, 1959

33............. Bill Russell (@ Min. Lakers),
Dec. 6, 1959

33...........Bill Russell (vs. Phi. Warriors),
Feb. 13, 1960

33............. Bill Russell (vs. Phi. Warriors),
Mar. 2, 1960

33................Bill Russell (@ N.Y. Knicks),
Dec. 30, 1960

33.............. Bill Russell (vs. N.Y. Knicks),
Feb. 11, 1961

33................Bill Russell (vs. Det. Pistons),
Oct. 21, 1961

33................ Bill Russell (vs. L.A. Lakers),
Mar. 11, 1962

33............. Bill Russell (@ S.F. Warriors),
Jan. 2, 1963

33.............. Bill Russell (@ S.F. Warriors),
Feb. 21, 1963

33................Bill Russell (@ Phi. 76ers),
Nov. 1, 1963

33............. Bill Russell (vs. Cin. Royals),
Feb. 2, 1964

33............. Bill Russell (@ N.Y. Knicks),
Feb. 8, 1964

33......... Bill Russell (@ S.F. Warriors),
Feb. 15, 1964

33.............. Bill Russell (@ St.L. Hawks),
Nov. 24, 1966

33................Bill Russell (@ Chi. Bulls),
Dec. 30, 1966

33............. Bill Russell (vs. L.A. Lakers),
Nov. 3, 1967

32.......... Bill Russell (vs. Syr. Nationals),
Dec. 30, 1956

32.............. Bill Russell (@ Cin. Royals),
Nov. 8, 1957

32................Bill Russell (@ Det. Pistons),
Feb. 20, 1959

32................Bill Russell (@ Det. Pistons),
Feb. 19, 1960

32......... Bill Russell (vs. Phi. Warriors),
Feb. 23, 1960

32.............. Bill Russell (vs. Det. Pistons),
Jan. 27, 1961

32.............. Bill Russell (vs. L.A. Lakers),
Dec. 26, 1961

32.............. Bill Russell (vs. Cin. Royals),
Nov. 12, 1962

32......... Bill Russell (vs. Syr. Nationals),
Feb. 1, 1963

32........... Bill Russell (vs. S.F. Warriors),
Nov. 30, 1963

32............... Bill Russell (vs. Cin. Royals),
Jan. 10, 1964

32............. Bill Russell (vs. Det. Pistons),
Mar. 8, 1964

32.......... Bill Russell (vs. S.F. Warriors),
Feb. 10, 1967

32.......... Dave Cowens (vs. Hou. Rockets),
Mar. 20, 1973

31............ Bill Russell (vs. Ft.W. Pistons),
Jan. 6, 1957

31................ Bill Russell (vs. Min. Lakers),
Nov. 29, 1959

31.......... Bill Russell (vs. Syr. Nationals),
Jan. 5, 1960

31.......... Bill Russell (vs. Syr. Nationals),
Dec. 1, 1962

31.............. Bill Russell (vs. L.A. Lakers),
Dec. 7, 1962

31................ Bill Russell (vs. St.L. Hawks),
Nov. 11, 1963

31.............. Bill Russell (vs. L.A. Lakers),
Nov. 13, 1963

31................Bill Russell (@ Phi. 76ers),
Dec. 13, 1963

31................ Bill Russell (@ Phi. 76ers),
Jan. 11, 1964

31.............. Bill Russell (vs. L.A. Lakers),
Jan. 17, 1964

31.............. Bill Russell (@ Cin. Royals),
Jan. 22, 1964

31..........Bill Russell (vs. S.F. Warriors),
Feb. 28, 1964

31................Bill Russell (vs. Det. Pistons),
Dec. 25, 1964

31.............. Bill Russell (vs. L.A. Lakers),
Jan. 24, 1965

31.............. Bill Russell (vs. L.A. Lakers),
Jan. 12, 1966

31................ Bill Russell (@ Cin. Royals),
Mar. 10, 1966

30............Bill Russell (@ Det. Pistons),
Nov. 21, 1957

30..........Bill Russell (vs. Syr. Nationals),
Nov. 30, 1957

30..............Bill Russell (vs. Det. Pistons),
Nov. 1, 1958

30..............Bill Russell (@ N.Y. Knicks),
Dec. 2, 1958

30.............. Bill Russell (vs. N.Y. Knicks),
Jan. 14, 1959

30................Bill Russell (vs. Min. Lakers),
Feb. 26, 1960

30.............. Bill Russell (vs. L.A. Lakers),
Dec. 17, 1960

30.............. Bill Russell (vs. Cin. Royals),
Dec. 20, 1960

30.......... Bill Russell (vs. Phi. Warriors),
Jan. 29, 1961

30............ Bill Russell (vs. Chi. Zephyrs),
Nov. 20, 1962

30................Bill Russell (vs. Cin. Royals),
Dec. 15, 1962

30.......... Bill Russell (vs. S.F. Warriors),
Dec. 26, 1962

30................Bill Russell (vs. St.L. Hawks),
Jan. 24, 1963

30.............. Bill Russell (@ N.Y. Knicks),
Mar. 3, 1963

30................ Bill Russell (@ Cin. Royals),
Oct. 17, 1963

30............ Bill Russell (vs. St.L. Hawks),
Dec. 11, 1963

30.............. Bill Russell (vs. Phi. 76ers),
Jan. 12, 1964

30............. Bill Russell (vs. St.L. Hawks),
Jan. 23, 1964

30.............. Bill Russell (vs. L.A. Lakers),
Nov. 13, 1964

30.............. Bill Russell (@ St.L. Hawks),
Dec. 19, 1964

30............ Bill Russell (vs. Det. Pistons),
Dec. 27, 1964

30............ Bill Russell (vs. Cin. Royals),
Jan. 17, 1965

30.......... Bill Russell (vs. S.F. Warriors),
Jan. 22, 1965

30................Bill Russell (@ Cin. Royals),
Oct. 28, 1965

30............ Bill Russell (@ S.F. Warriors),
Jan. 3, 1967

30.............. Bill Russell (vs. Cin. Royals),
Oct. 23, 1968

30................ Bill Russell (vs. Phi. 76ers),
Nov. 1, 1968

30.............. Bill Russell (@ Det. Pistons),
Feb. 12, 1969

8-Steal Game

9................ Larry Bird (@ Uta. Jazz),
Feb. 18, 1985

9.............. Paul Pierce (vs. Mia. Heat),
Dec. 3, 1999

8................ Larry Bird (@ N.J. Nets),
Oct. 25, 1985

8................... Larry Bird (vs. N.J. Nets),
Jan. 3, 1986

8........ Rajon Rondo (vs. Mem. Grizzlies),
Mar. 23, 2011

8.............. Marcus Smart (vs. Phi. 76ers),
Feb. 15, 2017

8...............Kyrie Irving (vs. Mia. Heat),
Jan. 21, 2019

10-Block Game
none

Multiple Triple-Doubles in a Single Season

10........................Larry Bird, 1985–86
10........................Larry Bird, 1989–90
8.................. John Havlicek, 1970–71
8.................. John Havlicek, 1971–72
8.................. Larry Bird, 1984–85
7.................. John Havlicek, 1969–70
7....................Larry Bird, 1983–84
6....................Rajon Rondo, 2011–12
5.................. Bill Russell, 1966–67
5....................Larry Bird, 1980–81
5....................Larry Bird, 1986–87
5.............. Antoine Walker, 2000–01
5....................Rajon Rondo, 2012–13
4....................Bob Cousy, 1955–56
4....................Bob Cousy, 1959–60
4....................Larry Bird, 1982–83
3....................Bob Cousy, 1954–55
3....................Bob Cousy, 1958–59
3.................. Bill Russell, 1963–64
3.................. Bill Russell, 1968–69
3.................. John Havlicek, 1973–74
3....................Larry Bird, 1981–82
3....................Larry Bird, 1990–91
3....................Rajon Rondo, 2010–11
3.................. Paul Pierce, 2012–13
3....................Rajon Rondo, 2014–15
3....................Evan Turner, 2014–15
2....................Bob Cousy, 1951–52
2.................. Bill Russell, 1964–65
2.................. Bill Russell, 1965–66
2.................. John Havlicek, 1972–73
2.................. Dave Cowens, 1973–74
2.................. Dave Cowens, 1977–78
2....................Larry Bird, 1987–88
2.............. Antoine Walker, 1996–97
2.............. Antoine Walker, 2001–02
2.............. Antoine Walker, 2002–03
2.................. Paul Pierce, 2004–05
2....................Rajon Rondo, 2008–09
2....................Rajon Rondo, 2009–10
2....................Jaylen Brown, 2021–22

Postseason Play

1948 BAA Quarterfinals
vs. Chi. Stags, lost (2–1)
1951 NBA Eastern Division Semifinals
vs. N.Y. Knicks, lost (2–0)
1952 Eastern Division Semifinals
vs. N.Y. Knicks, lost (2–1)
1953 Eastern Division Semifinals
vs. Syr. Nationals, won (2–0)
Eastern Division Finals
vs. N.Y. Knicks, lost (3–1)
1954 (Advanced from Eastern Division
Round Robin)
Eastern Division Finals
vs. Syr. Nationals, lost (2–0)
1955 Eastern Division Semifinals
vs. N.Y. Knicks, won (2–1)
Eastern Division Finals
vs. Syr. Nationals, lost (3–1)
1956 Eastern Division Semifinals
vs. Syr. Nationals, won (2–1)
1957 Eastern Division Finals
vs. Syr. Nationals, lost (3–0)
NBA Finals vs. St.L. Hawks,
won (4–3)
1958 Eastern Division Finals
vs. Phi. Warriors, won (4–1)
NBA Finals vs. St.L. Hawks,
lost (4–2)
1959 Eastern Division Finals
vs. Syr. Nationals, won (4–3)
NBA Finals vs. Min. Lakers,
won (4–0)
1960 Eastern Division Finals
vs. Phi. Warriors, won (4–2)
NBA Finals vs. St.L. Hawks,
won (4–3)
1961 Eastern Division Finals
vs. Syr. Nationals, won (4–1)
NBA Finals vs. St.L. Hawks,
won (4–1)
1962 Eastern Division Finals
vs. Phi. Warriors, won (4–3)
NBA Finals vs. L.A. Lakers,
won (4–3)
1963 Eastern Division Finals
vs. Cin. Royals, won (4–3)
NBA Finals vs. L.A. Lakers,
won (4–2)
1964 Eastern Division Finals
vs. Cin. Royals, won (4–1)
NBA Finals vs. S.F. Warriors,
won (4–1)

1965 Eastern Division Finals
vs. Phi. 76ers, won (4–3)
NBA Finals vs. L.A. Lakers,
won (4–1)
1966 Eastern Division Semifinals
vs. Cin. Royals, won (3–2)
Eastern Division Finals
vs. Phi. 76ers, won (4–1)
NBA Finals vs. L.A. Lakers,
won (4–3)
1967 Eastern Division Semifinals
vs. N.Y. Knicks, won (3–1)
Eastern Division Finals
vs. Phi. 76ers, lost (4–1)
1968 Eastern Division Semifinals
vs. Det. Pistons, won (4–2)
Eastern Division Finals
vs. Phi. 76ers, won (4–3)
NBA Finals vs. L.A. Lakers,
won (4–2)
1969 Eastern Division Semifinals
vs. Phi. 76ers, won (4–1)
Eastern Division Finals
vs. N.Y. Knicks, won (4–2)
NBA Finals vs. L.A. Lakers,
won (4–3)
1972 Eastern Conference Semifinals
vs. Atl. Hawks, won (4–2)
Eastern Conference Finals
vs. N.Y. Knicks, lost (4–1)
1973 Eastern Conference Semifinals
vs. Atl. Hawks, won (4–2)
Eastern Conference Finals
vs. N.Y. Knicks, lost (4–3)
1974 Eastern Conference Semifinals
vs. Buf. Braves, won (4–2)
Eastern Conference Finals
vs. N.Y. Knicks, won (4–1)
NBA Finals vs. Mil. Bucks,
won (4–3)
1975 Eastern Conference Semifinals
vs. Hou. Rockets, won (4–1)
Eastern Conference Finals
vs. Was. Bullets, lost (4–2)
1976 Eastern Conference Semifinals
vs. Buf. Braves, won (4–2)
Eastern Conference Finals
vs. Cle. Cavaliers, won (4–2)
NBA Finals vs. Pho. Suns,
won (4–2)
1977 Eastern Conference First Round
vs. S.A. Spurs, won (2–0)

Eastern Conference Semifinals
vs. Phi. 76ers, lost (4–3)
1980 Eastern Conference Semifinals
vs. Hou. Rockets, won (4–0)
Eastern Conference Finals
vs. Phi. 76ers, lost (4–1)
1981 Eastern Conference Semifinals
vs. Chi. Bulls, won (4–0)
Eastern Conference Finals
vs. Phi. 76ers, won (4–3)
NBA Finals vs. Hou. Rockets,
won (4–2)
1982 Eastern Conference Semifinals
vs. Was. Bullets, won (4–1)
Eastern Conference Finals
vs. Phi. 76ers, lost (4–3)
1983 Eastern Conference First Round
vs. Atl. Hawks, won (2–1)
Eastern Conference Semifinals
vs. Mil. Bucks, lost (4–0)
1984 Eastern Conference First Round
vs. Was. Bullets, won (3–1)
Eastern Conference Semifinals
vs. N.Y. Knicks, won (4–3)
Eastern Conference Finals
vs. Mil. Bucks, won (4–1)
NBA Finals vs. L.A. Lakers,
won (4–3)
1985 Eastern Conference First Round
vs. Cle. Cavaliers, won (3–1)
Eastern Conference Semifinals
vs. Det. Pistons, won (4–2)
Eastern Conference Finals
vs. Phi. 76ers, won (4–1)
NBA Finals vs. L.A. Lakers,
lost (4–2)
1986 Eastern Conference First Round
vs. Chi. Bulls, won (3–0)
Eastern Conference Semifinals
vs. Atl. Hawks, won (4–1)
Eastern Conference Finals
vs. Mil. Bucks, won (4–0)
NBA Finals vs. Hou. Rockets,
won (4–2)
1987 Eastern Conference First Round
vs. Chi. Bulls, won (3–0)
Eastern Conference Semifinals
vs. Mil. Bucks, won (4–3)
Eastern Conference Finals
vs. Det. Pistons, won (4–3)
NBA Finals vs. L.A. Lakers,
lost (4–2)

1988 Eastern Conference First Round
      vs. N.Y. Knicks, won (3–1)
      Eastern Conference Semifinals vs.
      Atl. Hawks, won (4–3)
      Eastern Conference Finals vs. Det.
      Pistons, lost (4–2)

1989 Eastern Conference First Round
      vs. Det. Pistons, lost (3–0)

1990 Eastern Conference First Round
      vs. N.Y. Knicks, lost (3–2)

1991 Eastern Conference First Round
      vs. Ind. Pacers, won (3–2)
      Eastern Conference Semifinals vs.
      Det. Pistons, lost (4–2)

1992 Eastern Conference First Round
      vs. Ind. Pacers, won (3–0)
      Eastern Conference Semifinals vs.
      Cle. Cavaliers, lost (4–3)

1993 Eastern Conference First Round
      vs. Cha. Hornets, lost (3–1)

1995 Eastern Conference First Round
      vs. Orl. Magic, lost (3–1)

2002 Eastern Conference First Round
      vs. Phi. 76ers, won (3–2)
      Eastern Conference Semifinals vs.
      Det. Pistons, won (4–1)
      Eastern Conference Finals vs. N.J.
      Nets, lost (4–2)

2003 Eastern Conference First Round
      vs. Ind. Pacers, won (4–2)
      Eastern Conference Semifinals vs.
      N.J. Nets, lost (4–0)

2004 Eastern Conference First Round
      vs. Ind. Pacers, lost (4–0)

2005 Eastern Conference First Round
      vs. Ind. Pacers, lost (4–3)

2008 Eastern Conference First Round
      vs. Atl. Hawks, won (4–3)
      Eastern Conference Semifinals vs.
      Cle. Cavaliers, won (4–3)
      Eastern Conference Finals vs. Det.
      Pistons, won (4–2)
      NBA Finals vs. L.A. Lakers, won
      (4–2)

2009 Eastern Conference First Round
      vs. Chi. Bulls, won (4–3)
      Eastern Conference Semifinals vs.
      Orl. Magic, lost (4–3)

2010 Eastern Conference First Round
      vs. Mia. Heat, won (4–1)
      Eastern Conference Semifinals vs.
      Cle. Cavaliers, won (4–2)
      Eastern Conference Finals vs. Orl.
      Magic, won (4–2)
      NBA Finals vs. L.A. Lakers, lost
      (4–3)

2011 Eastern Conference First Round
      vs. N.Y. Knicks, won (4–0)
      Eastern Conference Semifinals vs.
      Mia. Heat, lost (4–1)

2012 Eastern Conference First Round
      vs. Atl. Hawks, won (4–2)
      Eastern Conference Semifinals vs.
      Phi. 76ers, won (4–3)
      Eastern Conference Finals vs. Mia.
      Heat, lost (4–3)

2013 Eastern Conference First Round
      vs. N.Y. Knicks, lost (4–2)

2015 Eastern Conference First Round
      vs. Cle. Cavaliers, lost (4–0)

2016 Eastern Conference Semifinals
      vs. Phi. 76ers, lost (4–2)

2017 Eastern Conference First Round
      vs. Chi. Bulls, won (4–2)
      Eastern Conference Semifinals vs.
      Was. Wizards, won (4–3)
      Eastern Conference Finals vs. Cle.
      Cavaliers, lost (4–1)

2018 Eastern Conference First Round
      vs. Mil. Bucks, won (4–3)
      Eastern Conference Semifinals vs.
      Phi. 76ers, won (4–1)
      Eastern Conference Finals vs. Cle.
      Cavaliers, lost (4–3)

2019 Eastern Conference First Round
      vs. Ind. Pacers, won (4–0)
      Eastern Conference Semifinals vs.
      Mil. Bucks, lost (4–1)

2020 Eastern Conference First Round
      vs. Phi. 76ers, won (4–0)
      Eastern Conference Semifinals vs.
      Tor. Raptors, won (4–3)
      Eastern Conference Finals vs. Mia.
      Heat, lost (4–2)

2021 Eastern Conference First Round
      vs. Brk. Nets, lost (4–1)

2022 Eastern Conference First Round vs.
      Brk. Nets, won (4–0)
      Eastern Conference Semifinals vs.
      Mil. Bucks, won (4–3)
      Eastern Conference Finals vs. Mia.
      Heat, (won (4–3)
      NBA Finals vs. G.S. Warriors,
      lost (4–2)

Brooklyn Nets

ABA Dates of Operation: (as the New York Nets) 1967–76 (9 seasons)
Overall Record: 374 wins, 370 losses (.503)
Arenas: Teaneck Armory, 1967–68; Long Island Arena, 1968–69; Island Garden, 1969–71; Nassau
  Veterans Memorial Coliseum, 1971–76
Other Name: New Jersey Americans, 1967–68

NBA Dates of Operation: (as the Brooklyn Nets) 1977–present (46 seasons)
Overall Record: 1577 wins, 2127 losses (.426)
Arenas: Nassau Veterans Memorial Coliseum, 1976–77; Rutgers Athletic Center, 1977–81; Izod
  Center (formerly Brendan Byrne Arena, 1981–96; Continental Airlines Arena, 1996–2007), 1981–
  2010; Prudential Center, 2010–12; Barclays Center, 2012–present (capacity: 17,732)
Other Names: New York Nets, 1976–77; New Jersey Nets, 1977–2012

Year-by-Year Finishes

Year	Finish	Wins	Losses	Percentage	Games Behind	Head Coach	Attendance*
				New Jersey Americans **ABA Eastern Division**			
1967–68	4th (Tie)	36	42	.462	18.0	Max Zaslofsky	80,091
				New York Nets			
1968–69	5th	17	61	.218	27.0	Max Zaslofsky	42,668
1969–70	4th	39	45	.464	20.0	York Larese	151,244
1970–71	3rd	40	44	.476	15.0	Lou Carnesecca	199,231
1971–72	3rd	44	40	.524	24.0	Lou Carnesecca	275,529
1972–73	4th	30	54	.357	27.0	Lou Carnesecca	289,596
1973–74	1st	55	29	.655	+2.0	Kevin Loughery	374,752
1974–75	1st (Tie)	58	26	.690	—	Kevin Loughery	383,673
				American Basketball Association			
1975–76	2nd	55	29	.655	5.0	Kevin Loughery	324,958
				NBA Eastern Conference Atlantic Division			
1976–77	5th	22	60	.268	28.0	Kevin Loughery	317,952
				New Jersey Nets			
1977–78	5th	24	58	.293	31.0	Kevin Loughery	199,090
1978–79	3rd	37	45	.451	17.0	Kevin Loughery	198,990
1979–80	5th	34	48	.415	27.0	Kevin Loughery	257,418
1980–81	5th	24	58	.293	38.0	Kevin Loughery (12–23), Bob MacKinnon (12–35)	301,900
1981–82	3rd	44	38	.537	19.0	Larry Brown	560,734
1982–83	3rd	49	33	.598	16.0	Larry Brown (47–29), Bill Blair (2–4)	530,801
1983–84	4th	45	37	.549	17.0	Stan Albeck	499,496
1984–85	3rd	42	40	.512	21.0	Stan Albeck	502,177
1985–86	3rd (Tie)	39	43	.476	28.0	Dave Wohl	482,854
1986–87	4th (Tie)	24	58	.293	35.0	Dave Wohl	452,704
1987–88	5th	19	63	.232	38.0	Dave Wohl (2–13), Bob MacKinnon (10–29), Willis Reed (7–21)	476,054

Year	Finish	Wins	Losses	Percentage	Games Behind	Head Coach	Attendance
1988–89	5th	26	56	.317	26.0	Willis Reed	378,397
1989–90	6th	17	65	.207	36.0	Bill Fitch	473,760
1990–91	5th	26	56	.317	30.0	Bill Fitch	480,786
1991–92	3rd	40	42	.488	11.0	Bill Fitch	517,356
1992–93	3rd	43	39	.524	17.0	Chuck Daly	620,416
1993–94	3rd	45	37	.549	12.0	Chuck Daly	658,304
1994–95	5th	30	52	.366	27.0	Butch Beard	684,102
1995–96	6th	30	52	.366	30.0	Butch Beard	638,144
1996–97	5th	26	56	.317	35.0	John Calipari	670,628
1997–98	2nd (Tie)	43	39	.524	12.0	John Calipari	718,514
1998–99	7th	16	34	.320	17.0	John Calipari (3–17), Don Casey (13–17)	400,387
1999–00	6th	31	51	.378	21.0	Don Casey	643,631
2000–01	6th	26	56	.317	30.0	Byron Scott	556,573
2001–02	1st	52	30	.634	3.0	Byron Scott	564,194
2002–03	1st	49	33	.598	1.0	Byron Scott	622,574
2003–04	1st	47	35	.573	5.0	Byron Scott (22–20), Lawrence Frank (25–15)	613,051
2004–05	3rd	42	40	.512	3.0	Lawrence Frank	618,681
2005–06	1st	49	33	.598	11.0	Lawrence Frank	691,543
2006–07	2nd	41	41	.500	6.0	Lawrence Frank	693,955
2007–08	4th	34	48	.415	32.0	Lawrence Frank	641,921
2008–09	3rd	34	48	.415	28.0	Lawrence Frank	621,062
2009–10	5th	12	70	.146	38.0	Lawrence Frank (0–16), Tom Barrise (0–2), Kiki Vandeweghe (12–52)	537,230
2010–11	4th	24	58	.293	32.0	Avery Johnson (24–58)	581,378
2011–12	5th	22	44	.333	17.0	Avery Johnson (24–58)	460,719
Brooklyn Nets							
2012–13	2nd	49	33	.598	5.0	Avery Johnson (14–14), P.J. Carlesimo (35–19)	704,702
2013–14	2nd	44	38	.537	4.0	Jason Kidd	707,331
2014–15	3rd	38	44	.463	11.0	Lionel Hollins	698,529
2015–16	4th	21	61	.256	35.0	Lionel Hollins (10–27), Tony Brown (11–34)	620,142
2016–17	5th	20	62	.244	33.0	Kenny Atkinson	632,608
2017–18	5th	28	54	.341	31.0	Kenny Atkinson	640,010
2018–19	4th	42	40	.512	16.0	Kenny Atkinson	612,597
2019–20	4th	35	37	.486	18.0	Kenny Atkinson (28–34), Jacque Vaughn (7–3)	524,907
2020–21	2nd	48	24	.667	1.0	Steve Nash	30,491
2021–22	4th	44	38	.537	7.0	Steve Nash	711,539

1998–99: 50-game season.
2011–12: 66-game season.
2019–20: 65-to-75-game season.
2020–21: 72-game season.
(ABA Attendance totals are unofficial, and numbers include when listed as home team.)

Awards

ABA Most Valuable Player

Julius Erving, forward, 1973–74

Julius Erving, forward, 1974–75*

Julius Erving, forward, 1975–76

* Tied with George McGinnis, Ind. Pacers.

NBA Most Valuable Player

ABA Rookie of the Year

Brian Taylor, guard, 1972–73

NBA Rookie of the Year

Buck Williams, forward, 1981–82 (N.J.)

Derrick Coleman, forward, 1990–91 (N.J.)

All-ABA First Team

Rick Barry, 1970–71

Rick Barry, 1971–72

Bill Melchionni, 1971–72

Julius Erving, 1973–74

Julius Erving, 1974–75

Julius Erving, 1975–76

All-NBA First Team

Jason Kidd, 2001–02 (N.J.)

Jason Kidd, 2003–04 (N.J.)

All-ABA Defensive First Team

Mike Gale, 1973–74*

Brian Taylor, 1974–75

Julius Erving, 1975–76

Brian Taylor, 1975–76

* 32 games with N.Y. Nets and 48 games with Ken. Colonels.

All-NBA Defensive First Team

Jason Kidd, 2001–02

Jason Kidd, 2005–06

All-ABA Rookie First Team

John Roche, 1971–72

Jim Chones, 1972–73

Brian Taylor, 1972–73

Larry Kenon, 1973–74

John Williamson, 1973–74

Kim Hughes, 1975–76

All-NBA Rookie First Team

Bernard King, 1977–78 (N.J.)

Calvin Natt, 1979–80* (N.J.)

Buck Williams, 1981–82 (N.J.)

Derrick Coleman, 1990–91 (N.J.)

Keith Van Horn, 1997–98 (N.J.)

Kenyon Martin, 2000–01 (N.J.)

Brook Lopez, 2008–09 (N.J.)

Mason Plumlee, 2013–14

* 53 games with N.J. Nets and 25 games with Por. Blazers.

ABA Coach of the Year

NBA Coach of the Year

Hall of Famers Who Played for the Americans/Nets

Tiny Archibald, guard, 1976–77 (N.Y.)

Rick Barry, foward, 1970–72 (ABA)

Maurice Cheeks, guard, 1992–93 (N.J.)

Mel Daniels, center, 1976–77 (N.Y.)

Julius Erving, foward, 1973–76 (ABA)

Kevin Garnett, center-forward, 2013–15

Jason Kidd, guard, 2001–08 (N.J.)

Bernard King, forward, 1977–79; 1992–93 (N.J.)

Bob McAdoo, forward, 1980–81 (N.J.)

Alonzo Mourning, center, 2003–05

Dikembe Mutombo, center, 2002–03 (N.J.)

Dražen Petrović, guard, 1990–93 (N.J.)

Paul Pierce, forward, 2013–14

Retired Numbers

3 .... Dražen Petrović

5 .... Jason Kidd

23 .... John Williamson

25 .... Bill Melchionni

32 .... Julius Erving

52 .... Buck Williams

League Leaders, Offense

Points

Julius Erving, 1973–74 (ABA)....... 2299

Julius Erving, 1975–76 (ABA)....... 2462

Three Pointers

Assists

Bill Melchionni, 1970–71 (ABA)...... 672

Kevin Porter*, 1977–78 (N.J.) 837

Jason Kidd, 2002–03 (N.J.)............ 711

*801 with N.J. Nets and 36 with Det. Pistons.

Scoring Average

Julius Erving, 1973–74 (ABA)........ 27.4

Julius Erving, 1975–76 (ABA)........ 29.3

Field Goal Percantage

Mikki Moore, 2006–07 (N.J.) .... .609

Three Point Percentage

Brian Taylor, 1975–76 (ABA) .... .421

Joe Harris, 2018–19..................... .474

Joe Harris, 2020–21..................... .475

Free Throw Percentage

Assists Average

Bill Melchionni, 1970–71 (ABA)....... 8.3

Bill Melchionni, 1971–72 (ABA)....... 8.4

Kevin Porter*, 1977–78 .... 10.2

Jason Kidd, 2002–03 (N.J.)............. 8.9

Jason Kidd, 2003–04 (N.J.)............. 9.2

*10.8 with N.J. Nets and 4.5 with Det. Pistons.

League Leaders, Defense

Offensive Rebounds

Buck Williams, 1983–84 (N.J.) 355

Jayson Williams, 1997–98 (N.J.) 443

Defensive Rebounds

Total Rebounds

Steals

Brian Taylor, 1974–75 (ABA) 221

Eddie Jordan, 1978–79 (N.J.) 201

Micheal Ray Richardson, 1984–85 (N.J.)..................................... 243

Kendall Gill, 1998–99 (N.J.) 134

Jason Kidd, 2001–02 (N.J.)............. 175

Blocks

George Johnson, 1977–78 (N.J.)..... 274

Rebounds Average

Steals Average

Brian Taylor, 1974–75 (ABA) 2.8

Micheal Ray Richardson*, 1982–83 (N.J.)...................................... 2.8

Micheal Ray Richardson, 1984–85 (N.J.)...................................... 3.0

Kendall Gill, 1998–99 (N.J.) 2.7

*2.6 with N.J. Nets and 3.1 with G.S. Warriors.

Blocks Average

George Johnson, 1977–78 (N.J.)..... 3.4

Shawn Bradley*, 1996–97 .... 3.4

*4.0 with N.J. Nets and 2.7 with Dal. Mavericks.

Feats

50-Point Game

63... Julius Erving (@ S.D. Conquistadors), Feb. 14, 1975 (ABA)

60............... Kyrie Irving (@ Orl. Magic), Mar. 15, 2022

57... Deron Williams (@ Cha. Bobcats), Mar. 4, 2012 (N.J.)

55............ Kevin Durant (@ Atl. Hawks), Apr. 2, 2022

54.............. Kyrie Irving (vs. Chi. Bulls), Jan. 31, 2020

53.............. Rick Barry (vs. Pit. Condors), Jan. 15, 1971 (ABA)

52......... Mike Newlin (vs. Bos. Celtics), Dec. 16, 1979 (N.J.)

52......... Ray Williams (@ Det. Pistons), Apr. 17, 1982 (N.J.)

51............... Rick Barry (vs. Uta. Stars), Mar. 28, 1971 (ABA)

51.......... Rick Barry (@ Car. Cougars), Nov. 19, 1971 (ABA)

51.. Julius Erving (vs. S.D. Conquistadors), Feb. 22, 1975 (ABA)

51............. Julius Erving (vs. S.A. Spurs), Jan. 18, 1976 (ABA)

51...............Vince Carter (@ Mia. Heat), Dec. 23, 2005 (N.J.)

51............. Caris LeVert (@ Bos. Celtics), Mar. 3, 2020

51........ Kevin Durant (@ Det. Pistons), Dec. 12, 2021

50............... Rick Barry (vs. Uta. Stars), Feb. 16, 1972 (ABA)

50........ John Williamson (@ Ind. Pacers), Apr. 4, 1978 (N.J.)

50... Stephon Marbury (vs. L.A. Lakers), Feb. 13, 2001 (N.J.)

50.......... Kyrie Irving (@ Cha. Hornets), Mar. 8, 2022

50..........Kyrie Irving (vs. Min. T'Wolves), Oct. 23, 2019

20-Assist Game

29.......... Kevin Porter (vs. Hou. Rockets), Feb. 24, 1978 (N.J.)

22........ Robert Pack (vs. Dal. Mavericks), Nov. 23, 1996 (N.J.)

21... Deron Williams (vs. Min. T'Wolves), Apr. 5, 2011 (N.J.)

20............ Kevin Porter (vs. S.A. Spurs), Dec. 7, 1977 (N.J.)

20.............. Kevin Porter (vs. K.C. Kings), Jan. 22, 1978 (N.J.)

20......... Kevin Porter (@ Den. Nuggets), Apr. 5, 1978 (N.J.)

20........ Stephon Marbury (vs. Ind. Pacers), Apr. 25, 1999 (N.J.)

20...Deron Williams (@ G.S. Warriors), Mar. 30, 2012 (N.J.)

30-Rebound Game

33...Billy Paultz (vs. Dal. Chaparrals), Dec. 17, 1971 (ABA)

8-Steal Game

11.............. Kendall Gill (vs. Mia. Heat), Apr. 3, 1999 (N.J.)

10.......... Eddie Jordan (@ Phi. 76ers), Mar. 23, 1979 (N.J.)

9............ Darwin Cook (vs. Por. Blazers), Dec. 3, 1983 (N.J.)

9... Micheal Ray Richardson (vs. Ind. Pacers), Oct. 30, 1985 (N.J.)

8............. Eddie Jordan (vs. Pho. Suns), Jan. 4, 1978 (N.J.)

8......... Eddie Jordan (@ Por. Blazers), Mar. 17, 1979 (N.J.)

8............... Eddie Jordan (@ Chi. Bulls), Oct. 23, 1979 (N.J.)

8............ Eddie Jordan (vs. L.A. Lakers), Feb. 8, 1980 (N.J.)

8.............. Eddie Jordan (@ Ind. Pacers), Feb. 13, 1980 (N.J.)

8.............. Eddie Jordan (vs. Uta. Jazz), Feb. 14, 1980 (N.J.)

8...............Ray Williams (vs. Ind. Pacers), Nov. 8, 1981 (N.J.)

8............... Darwin Cook (@ Pho. Suns), Nov. 26, 1982 (N.J.)

8... Micheal Ray Richardson (vs. Por. Blazers), Mar. 13, 1983 (N.J.)

8.. Micheal Ray Richardson (vs. Phi. 6ers), Apr. 10, 1984 (N.J.)

8............ Micheal Ray Richardson (@ L.A. Clippers), Nov. 13, 1984 (N.J.)

8.. Micheal Ray Richardson (vs. Phi. 76ers), Nov. 1, 1985 (N.J.)

8...............Lester Conner (@ S.A. Spurs), Mar. 9, 1989 (N.J.)

10-Block Game

13.......... Darryl Dawkins (vs. Phi. 76ers), Nov. 5, 1983 (N.J.)

12.......... George Johnson (@ N.O. Jazz), Mar. 21, 1978 (N.J.)

12...Shawn Bradley (vs. Tor. Raptors), Apr. 17, 1996 (N.J.)

11... Shawn Bradley (vs. Was. Bullets), Mar. 14, 1996 (N.J.)

11...Shawn Bradley (vs. Bos. Celtics), Dec. 21, 1996 (N.J.)

11...Shawn Bradley (vs. Ind. Pacers), Feb. 6, 1997 (N.J.)

10........ George Johnson (vs. Atl. Hawks), Oct. 26, 1977 (N.J.)

10... George Johnson (vs. Ind. Pacers), Mar. 4, 1980 (N.J.)

10...........Shawn Bradley (vs. Pho. Suns), Mar. 12, 1996 (N.J.)

10.......... Shawn Bradley (vs. Bos. Celtics), Apr. 19, 1996 (N.J.)

10........ Shawn Bradley (@ Orl. Magic), Nov. 8, 1996 (N.J.)

10... Shawn Bradley (vs. Dal. Mavericks), Nov. 23, 1996 (N.J.)

Multiple Triple-Doubles in a Single Season

12.............. Jason Kidd, 2006–07 (N.J.)

12.............. Jason Kidd, 2007–08 (N.J.)

12..................James Harden, 2020–21

9.............. Jason Kidd, 2003–04 (N.J.)

9................James Harden, 2021–22*

8............. Jason Kidd, 2001–02 (N.J.)

8............. Jason Kidd, 2004–05 (N.J.)

8............. Jason Kidd, 2005–06 (N.J.)

4............. Jason Kidd, 2002–03 (N.J.)

4..................James Harden, 2021–22

4.................. Kevin Durant, 2021–22

3.......... Lester Conner, 1988–89 (N.J.)

3...... Kenny Anderson, 1993–94 (N.J.)

3........ Shawn Bradley, 1995–96 (N.J.)

2...........Julius Erving, 1973–74 (ABA)

2...........Julius Erving, 1974–75 (ABA)

2.... Micheal Ray Richardson, 1984–85 (N.J.)

2...... Kenny Anderson, 1992–93 (N.J.)

2...... Rumeal Robinson, 1992–93 (N.J.)

2.....Derrick Coleman, 1993–94 (N.J.)

2....... Shawn Bradley, 1996–97 (N.J.)

2............ Jim Jackson, 1996–97 (N.J.)

2...........Vince Carter, 2006–07 (N.J.)

* Had 11 Triple-Doubles for 2021–22 season: 9 with Brk. Nets and 2 with Phi. 76ers.

Postseason Play

1970　ABA Eastern Division Semifinals vs. Ken. Colonels, lost (4–3)

1971　ABA Eastern Division Semifinals vs. Vir. Squires, lost (4–2)

1972　ABA Eastern Division Semifinals vs. Ken. Colonels, won (4–2)

　　　ABA Eastern Division Finals vs. Vir. Squires, won (4–3)

　　　ABA Finals vs. Ind. Pacers, lost (4–2)

1973 ABA Eastern Division Semifinals
vs. Car. Cougars, lost (4–1)

1974 ABA Eastern Division Semifinals
vs. Vir. Squires, won (4–1)
ABA Eastern Division Finals
vs. Ken. Colonels, won (4–0)
ABA Finals vs. Uta. Stars,
won (4–1)

1975 ABA Eastern Division Tiebreaker
vs. Ken. Colonels, won
ABA Eastern Division Semifinals
vs. Spirits of St.L., lost (4–1)

1976 ABA Semifinals vs. S.A. Spurs,
won (4–3)
ABA Finals vs. Den. Nuggets,
lost (4–2)

1979 NBA Eastern Conference First Round
vs. Phi. 76ers, lost (2–0)

1982 Eastern Conference First Round
vs. Was. Bullets, lost (2–0)

1983 Eastern Conference First Round
vs. N.Y. Knicks, lost (2–0)

1984 Eastern Conference First Round
vs. Phi. 76ers, won (3–2)
Eastern Conference Semifinals
vs. Mil. Bucks, lost (4–2)

1985 Eastern Conference First Round
vs. Det. Pistons, lost (3–0)

1986 Eastern Conference First Round
vs. Mil. Bucks, lost (3–0)

1992 Eastern Conference First Round
vs. Cle. Cavaliers, lost (3–1)

1993 Eastern Conference First Round
vs. Cle. Cavaliers, lost (3–2)

1994 Eastern Conference First Round
vs. N.Y. Knicks, lost (3–1)

1998 Eastern Conference First Round
vs. Chi. Bulls, lost (3–0)

2002 Eastern Conference First Round
vs. Ind. Pacers, won (3–2)
Eastern Conference Semifinals
vs. Cha. Hornets, won (4–1)
Eastern Conference Finals
vs. Bos. Celtics, won (4–2)
NBA Finals vs. L.A. Lakers,
lost (4–0)

2003 Eastern Conference First Round
vs. Mil. Bucks, won (4–2)
Eastern Conference Semifinals
vs. Bos. Celtics, won (4–0)
Eastern Conference Finals
vs. Det. Pistons, won (4–0)
NBA Finals vs. S.A. Spurs,
lost (4–2)

2004 Eastern Conference First Round
vs. N.Y. Knicks, won (4–0)
Eastern Conference Semifinals
vs. Det. Pistons, lost (4–3)

2005 Eastern Conference First Round
vs. Mia. Heat, lost (4–0)

2006 Eastern Conference First Round
vs. Ind. Pacers, won (4–2)
Eastern Conference Semifinals
vs. Mia. Heat, lost (4–1)

2007 Eastern Conference First Round
vs. Tor. Raptors, won (4–2)
Eastern Conference Semifinals
vs. Cle. Cavaliers, lost (4–2)

2013 Eastern Conference First Round
vs. Chi. Bulls, lost (4–3)

2014 Eastern Conference First Round
vs. Tor. Raptors, won (4–3)
Eastern Conference Semifinals
vs. Mia. Heat, lost (4–1)

2015 Eastern Conference First Round
vs. Atl. Hawks, lost (4–2)

2019 Eastern Conference First Round
vs. Phi. 76ers, lost (4–1)

2020 Eastern Conference First Round
vs. Tor. Raptors, lost (4–0)

2021 Eastern Conference First Round
vs. Bos. Celtics, won (4–1)
Eastern Conference Semifinals
vs. Mil. Bucks, lost (4–3)

2022 Eastern Conference First Round
vs. Bos. Celtics, lost (4–0)

Charlotte Hornets

Dates of Operation: 1988–2002; 2004–present (32 seasons)
Overall Record: 1126 wins, 1423 losses (.442)
Arenas: Charlotte Coliseum, 1988–2002; 2004–05; Spectrum Center (formerly Charlotte Bobcats
    Arena, 2005–08; Time Warner Cable Arena, 2008–16), 2005–present (capacity: 19,077)
Other Name: Charlotte Bobcats, 2004–14

Year-by-Year Finishes

Year	Finish	Wins	Losses	Percentage	Games Behind	Head Coach	Attendance
Eastern Conference Atlantic Division							
1988–89	6th	20	62	.244	32.0	Dick Harter	949,858
Western Conference Midwest Division							
1989–90	7th	19	63	.232	37.0	Dick Harter (8–32), Gene Littles (11–31)	979,941
Eastern Conference Central Division							
1990–91	7th	26	56	.317	35.0	Gene Littles	978,141
1991–92	6th (Tie)	31	51	.378	36.0	Allan Bristow	971,618
1992–93	3rd	44	38	.537	13.0	Allan Bristow	971,880
1993–94	5th	41	41	.500	16.0	Allan Bristow	971,609
1994–95	2nd	50	32	.610	2.0	Allan Bristow	971,618
1995–96	6th	41	41	.500	31.0	Allan Bristow	985,722
1996–97	3rd (Tie)	54	28	.659	15.0	Dave Cowens	985,722
1997–98	3rd	51	31	.622	11.0	Dave Cowens	959,634
1998–99	5th	26	24	.520	7.0	Dave Cowens (4–11), Paul Silas (22–13)	480,807
1999–00	2nd	49	33	.598	7.0	Paul Silas	732,827
2000–01	4rd	46	36	.561	6.0	Paul Silas	615,424
2001–02	2nd	44	38	.537	6.0	Paul Silas	462,738
Charlotte Bobcats							
Eastern Conference Southeast Division							
2004–05	4th	18	64	.220	41.0	Bernie Bickerstaff	591,701
2005–06	4th (Tie)	26	56	.317	26.0	Bernie Bickerstaff	671,011
2006–07	4th	33	49	.402	11.0	Bernie Bickerstaff	637,520
2007–08	4th	32	50	.390	20.0	Sam Vincent	603,403
2008–09	4th	35	47	.427	24.0	Larry Brown	597,548
2009–10	4th	44	38	.537	15.0	Larry Brown	648,520
2010–11	4th	34	48	.415	24.0	Larry Brown (9–19), Paul Silas (25–29)	649,694
2011–12	5th	7	59	.106	39.0	Paul Silas	486,984
2012–13	4th	21	61	.256	45.0	Mike Dunlap	628,293
2013–14	3rd	43	39	.524	11.0	Steve Clifford	636,268
Charlotte Hornets							
2014–15	4th	33	49	.402	27.0	Steve Clifford	704,886
2015–16	1st (Tie)	48	34	.585	—	Steve Clifford	716,894
2016–17	4th	36	46	.439	13.0	Steve Clifford	710,643
2017–18	3rd	36	46	.439	8.0	Steve Clifford	671,404
2018–19	2nd (Tie)	39	43	.476	3.0	James Borrego	676,570
2019–20	3rd	23	42	.354	17.0	James Borrego	478,591
2020–21	4th	33	39	.458	8.0	James Borrego	68,255
2021–22	2nd (Tie)	43	39	.524	10.0	James Borrego	700,755

1998–99: 50-game season.
2011–12: 66-game season.
2019–20: 65-to-75-game season.
2020–21: 72-game season.

Awards

Most Valuable Player
none

Rookie of the Year
Larry Johnson, forward, 1991–92
Emeka Okafor, center, 2004–05
   (Bobcats)
LaMelo Ball, guard, 2020–21

Defensive Player of the Year
none

Sixth Man of the Year
Dell Curry, guard, 1993–94

Most Improved Player
none

All-NBA First Team
none

All-Defensive First Team
Gerald Wallace, 2009–10 (Bobcats)

All-Rookie First Team
Kendall Gill, 1990–91
Larry Johnson, 1991–92
Alonzo Mourning, 1992–93
Emeka Okafor, 2004–05 (Bobcats)
LaMelo Ball, 2020–21

Coach of the Year
none

Hall of Famers Who Played for the Hornets/Bobcats
Vlade Divac, center, 1996–98
Alonzo Mourning, center, 1992–95
Robert Parish, center, 1994–96

Retired Numbers
13.....................................Bobby Phills

League Leaders, Offense

Points
none

Three Pointers
Jason Richardson, 2007–08
   (Bobcats)................................. 243

Assists
none

Scoring Average
none

Field Goal Percantage
none

Three Point Percentage
Glen Rice, 1996–97 .... .471

Free Throw Percentage
none

Assists Average
none

League Leaders, Defense

Offensive Rebounds
none

Defensive Rebounds
none

Total Rebounds
none

Steals
Eddie Jones, 1999–00 192

Blocks
none

Rebounds Average
none

Steals Average
Eddie Jones, 1999–00 .... 2.7
Gerald Wallace, 2005–06 (Bobcats)... 2.5

Blocks Average
none

Feats

50-Point Game
60.......... Kemba Walker (vs. Phi. 76ers),
   Nov. 17, 2018
52......... Kemba Walker (vs. Uta. Jazz),
   Jan. 18, 2016

20-Assist Game
20......... Brevin Knight (@ Cle. Cavaliers),
   Jan. 11, 2005 (Bobcats)

30-Rebound Game
30...........Dwight Howard (@ Brk. Nets),
   Mar. 21, 2018

8-Steal Game
9............... Eddie Jones (vs. Ind. Pacers),
   Nov. 4, 1999
8................Brevin Knight (@ Orl. Magic),
   Mar. 24, 2005 (Bobcats)
8..........Gerald Wallace (vs. Mil. Bucks),
   Jan. 13, 2006 (Bobcats)

8..........Jason Richardson (@ N.J. Nets),
   Apr. 15, 2008 (Bobcats)
8...Kemba Walker (vs. Dal. Mavericks),
   Nov. 10, 2012 (Bobcats)

10-Block Game
12.............. Vlade Divac (vs. N.J. Nets),
   Feb. 12, 1997
10......... Emeka Okafor (@ N.Y. Knicks),
   Jan. 12, 2007 (Bobcats)

Multiple Triple-Doubles in a Single Season
5........................LaMelo Ball, 2021–22
4.................. Anthony Mason, 1996–97
3.................. Anthony Mason, 1999–00
2..................... Larry Johnson, 1992–93
2........................Kendall Gill, 1995–96
2........................Baron Davis, 2000–01
2.................. Nicholas Batum, 2015–16
2.................. Nicholas Batum, 2017–18
2........................LaMelo Ball, 2021–22

Postseason Play

1993	Eastern Conference First Round
	vs. Bos. Celtics, won (3–1)
	Eastern Conference Semifinals
	vs. N.Y. Knicks, lost (4–1)
1995	Eastern Conference First Round
	vs. Chi. Bulls, lost (3–1)
1997	Eastern Conference First Round
	vs. N.Y. Knicks, lost (3–0)
1998	Eastern Conference First Round
	vs. Atl. Hawks, won (3–1)
	Eastern Conference Semifinals
	vs. Chi. Bulls, lost (4–1)
2000	Eastern Conference First Round
	vs. Phi. 76ers, lost (3–1)
2001	Eastern Conference First Round
	vs. Mia. Heat, won (3–0)
	Eastern Conference Semifinals
	vs. Mil. Bucks, lost (4–3)
2002	Eastern Conference First Round
	vs. Orl. Magic, won (3–1)
	Eastern Conference Semifinals
	vs. N.J. Nets, lost (4–1)
2010	Eastern Conference First Round
	vs. Orl. Magic, lost (4–0)
2014	Eastern Conference First Round
	vs. Mia. Heat, lost (4–0)
2016	Eastern Conference First Round
	vs. Mia. Heat, lost (4–3)

Chicago Bulls

Dates of Operation: 1966–present (56 seasons)
Overall Record: 2304 wins, 2212 losses (.510)
Arenas: International Amphitheatre, 1966–67; Chicago Stadium, 1967–94; United Center, 1994–present (capacity: 20,917)

Year-by-Year Finishes

Year	Finish	Wins	Losses	Percentage	Games Behind	Head Coach	Attendance
				Western Division			
1966–67	4th	33	48	.407	11.0	Red Kerr	171,793
1967–68	4th	29	53	.354	27.0	Red Kerr	131,165
1968–69	5th	33	49	.402	22.0	Dick Motta	151,608
1969–70	3rd (Tie)	39	43	.476	9.0	Dick Motta	331,668
				Western Conference Midwest Division			
1970–71	2nd	51	31	.622	15.0	Dick Motta	414,857
1971–72	2nd	57	25	.695	6.0	Dick Motta	435,282
1972–73	2nd	51	31	.622	9.0	Dick Motta	424,944
1973–74	2nd	54	28	.659	5.0	Dick Motta	334,183
1974–75	1st	47	35	.573	+3.0	Dick Motta	438,860
1975–76	4th	24	58	.293	14.0	Dick Motta	258,406
1976–77	2nd (Tie)	44	38	.537	6.0	Ed Badger	476,636
1977–78	3rd	40	42	.488	8.0	Ed Badger	548,844
1978–79	5th	31	51	.378	17.0	Larry Costello (20–36), Scotty Robertson (11–15)	368,968
1979–80	3rd (Tie)	30	52	.366	19.0	Jerry Sloan	363,605
				Eastern Conference Central Division			
1980–81	2nd	45	37	.549	15.0	Jerry Sloan	391,118
1981–82	5th	34	48	.415	21.0	Jerry Sloan (19–32), Phil Johnson (0–1), Rod Thorn (15–15)	372,613
1982–83	4th	28	54	.341	23.0	Paul Westhead	296,411
1983–84	5th	27	55	.329	23.0	Kevin Loughery	256,430
1984–85	3rd	38	44	.463	21.0	Kevin Loughery	487,297
1985–86	4th	30	52	.366	27.0	Stan Albeck	469,226
1986–87	5th	40	42	.488	17.0	Doug Collins	650,818
1987–88	2nd (Tie)	50	32	.610	4.0	Doug Collins	740,411
1988–89	5th	47	35	.573	16.0	Doug Collins	736,962
1989–90	2nd	55	27	.671	4.0	Phil Jackson	752,564
1990–91	1st	61	21	.744	+11.0	Phil Jackson	757,745
1991–92	1st	67	15	.817	+10.0	Phil Jackson	759,980
1992–93	1st	57	25	.695	+3.0	Phil Jackson	759,656
1993–94	2nd	55	27	.671	2.0	Phil Jackson	760,816
1994–95	3rd	47	35	.573	5.0	Phil Jackson	926,218
1995–96	1st	72	10	.878	+20.0	Phil Jackson	969,149
1996–97	1st	69	13	.841	+13.0	Phil Jackson	978,457
1997–98	1st	62	20	.756	+4.0	Phil Jackson	983,444
1998–99	8th	13	37	.260	20.0	Tim Floyd	560,012
1999–00	8th	17	65	.207	39.0	Tim Floyd	907,064

Year	Finish	Wins	Losses	Percentage	Games Behind	Head Coach	Attendance
2000–01	8th	15	67	.183	37.0	Tim Floyd	888,654
2001–02	8th	21	61	.256	29.0	Tim Floyd (4–21), Bill Berry (0–2), Bill Cartwright (17–38)	776,311
2002–03	6th	30	52	.366	20.0	Bill Cartwright	804,309
2003–04	8th	23	59	.280	38.0	Bill Cartwright (4–10), Pete Myers (0–2), Scott Skiles (19–47)	809,177
2004–05	2nd	47	35	.573	7.0	Scott Skiles	828,384
2005–06	3rd (Tie)	41	41	.500	23.0	Scott Skiles	868,720
2006–07	3rd	49	33	.598	4.0	Scott Skiles	912,364
2007–08	4th	33	49	.402	26.0	Scott Skiles (9–16), Pete Myers (0–1), Jim Boylan (24–32)	901,502
2008–09	2nd	41	41	.500	25.0	Vinny Del Negro	868,667
2009–10	3rd	41	41	.500	20.0	Vinny Del Negro	849,760
2010–11	1st	62	20	.756	+25.0	Tom Thibodeau	893,462
2011–12	1st	50	16	.758	+8.0	Tom Thibodeau	731,326
2012–13	2nd	45	37	.549	4.5	Tom Thibodeau	896,944
2013–14	2nd	48	34	.585	8.0	Tom Thibodeau	890,370
2014–15	2nd	50	32	.610	3.0	Tom Thibodeau	886,612
2015–16	4th	42	40	.512	15.0	Fred Hoiberg	894,659
2016–17	4th	41	41	.500	10.0	Fred Hoiberg	888,882
2017–18	5th	27	55	.329	23.0	Fred Hoiberg	851,824
2018–19	4th	22	60	.268	38.0	Fred Hoiberg (5–19), Jim Boylen (17–41)	823,475
2019–20	3rd	22	43	.338	30.0	Jim Boylen	639,352
2020–21	3rd	31	41	.431	15.0	Billy Donovan	13,655
2021–22	2nd	46	36	.561	5.0	Billy Donovan	856,148

1998–99: 50-game season.

2011–12: 66-game season.

2019–20: 65-to-75-game season.

2020–21: 72-game season.

Awards

Most Valuable Player

Michael Jordan, guard, 1987–88

Michael Jordan, guard, 1990–91

Michael Jordan, guard, 1991–92

Michael Jordan, guard, 1995–96

Michael Jordan, guard, 1997–98

Derrick Rose, guard, 2010–11

Rookie of the Year

Michael Jordan, guard, 1984–85

Elton Brand, forward, 1999–00

Derrick Rose, guard 2008–09

Defensive Player of the Year

Michael Jordan, 1987–88

Joakim Noah, 2013–14

Sixth Man of the Year

Toni Kukoč, forward, 1995–96

Ben Gordon, guard, 2004–05

Most Improved Player

Jimmy Butler, guard, 2014–15

All-NBA First Team

Michael Jordan, 1986–87

Michael Jordan, 1987–88

Michael Jordan, 1988–89

Michael Jordan, 1989–90

Michael Jordan, 1990–91

Michael Jordan, 1991–92

Michael Jordan, 1992–93

Scottie Pippen, 1993–94

Scottie Pippen, 1994–95

Michael Jordan, 1995–96

Scottie Pippen, 1995–96

Michael Jordan, 1996–97

Michael Jordan, 1997–98

Derrick Rose, 2010–11

Joakim Noah, 2013–14

All-Defensive First Team

Jerry Sloan, 1968–69

Jerry Sloan, 1971–72

Jerry Sloan, 1973–74

Norm Van Lier, 1973–74

Jerry Sloan, 1974–75

Norm Van Lier, 1975–76

Norm Van Lier, 1976–77

Michael Jordan, 1987–88

Michael Jordan, 1988–89

Michael Jordan, 1989–90

Michael Jordan, 1990–91
Michael Jordan, 1991–92
Scottie Pippen, 1991–92
Michael Jordan, 1992–93
Scottie Pippen, 1992–93
Scottie Pippen, 1993–94
Scottie Pippen, 1994–95
Michael Jordan, 1995–96
Scottie Pippen, 1995–96
Dennis Rodman, 1995–96
Michael Jordan, 1996–97
Scottie Pippen, 1996–97
Michael Jordan, 1997–98
Scottie Pippen, 1997–98
Scottie Pippen, 1998–99
Joakim Noah, 2012–13
Joakim Noah, 2013–14

All-Rookie First Team
Erwin Mueller, 1966–67
Clifford Ray, 1971–72
Scott May, 1976–77
Reggie Theus, 1978–79
David Greenwood, 1979–80
Quintin Dailey, 1982–83
Michael Jordan, 1984–85
Charles Oakley, 1985–86
Elton Brand, 1999–00
Kirk Hinrich, 2003–04
Luol Deng, 2004–05
Ben Gordon, 2004–05
Derrick Rose, 2008–09
Taj Gibson, 2009–10
Nikola Mirotić, 2014–15
Lauri Markkanen, 2017–18

Coach of the Year
Red Kerr, 1966–67
Dick Motta, 1970–71
Phil Jackson, 1995–96
Tom Thibodeau, 2010–11

Hall of Famers Who Played for the Bulls
George Gervin, guard, 1985–86
Artis Gilmore, center, 1976–82; 1987–88
Michael Jordan, guard, 1984–93; 1994–98
Toni Kukoč, forward, 1993–2000
Robert Parish, center, 1996–97
Scottie Pippen, forward, 1987–98; 2003–04
Guy Rodgers, guard, 1966–68

Dennis Rodman, forward, 1995–98
Nate Thurmond, center, 1974–76
Chet Walker, forward, 1969–75
Ben Wallace, center, 2006–08

Retired Numbers
JK .... Jerry Krause
PJ.. Phil Jackson
4.. Jerry Sloan
10.. Bob Love
23................................ Michael Jordan
33................................ Scottie Pippen

League Leaders, Offense
Points
Michael Jordan, 1984–85 2313
Michael Jordan, 1986–87 3041
Michael Jordan, 1987–88 2868
Michael Jordan, 1988–89 2633
Michael Jordan, 1989–90 2753
Michael Jordan, 1990–91 2580
Michael Jordan, 1991–92 2404
Michael Jordan, 1992–93 2541
Michael Jordan, 1995–96 2491
Michael Jordan, 1996–97 2431
Michael Jordan, 1997–98 2357

Three Pointers
none

Assists
Guy Rodgers, 1966–67 908

Scoring Average
Michael Jordan, 1986–87 .... 37.1
Michael Jordan, 1987–88 .... 35.0
Michael Jordan, 1988–89 .... 32.5
Michael Jordan, 1989–90 .... 33.6
Michael Jordan, 1990–91 .... 31.5
Michael Jordan, 1991–92 .... 30.1
Michael Jordan, 1992–93 .... 32.6
Michael Jordan, 1995–96 .... 30.4
Michael Jordan, 1996–97 .... 29.7
Michael Jordan, 1997–98 .... 28.7

Field Goal Percantage
Artis Gilmore, 1980–81 .... .670
Artis Gilmore, 1981–82 .... .652
Eddie Curry, 2002–03 .... .585

Three Point Percentage
B.J. Armstrong, 1992–93 .... .453
Steve Kerr, 1994–95 .... .524

Free Throw Percentage
Chet Walker, 1970–71 .... .859

Assists Average
Guy Rodgers, 1966–67 .... 11.2

League Leaders, Defense
Offensive Rebounds
Dennis Rodman, 1995–96 356
Dennis Rodman, 1996–97 320
Elton Brand, 1999–00 348

Defensive Rebounds
Charles Oakley, 1986–87 775
Charles Oakley, 1987–88 740
Dennis Rodman, 1997–98 780

Total Rebounds
Charles Oakley, 1986–87 1074
Charles Oakley, 1987–88 1066
Dennis Rodman, 1997–98 1201

Steals
Michael Jordan, 1987–88 259
Michael Jordan, 1989–90 227
Michael Jordan, 1992–93 221
Scottie Pippen, 1994–95 232

Blocks
none

Rebounds Average
Dennis Rodman, 1995–96 .... 14.9
Dennis Rodman, 1996–97 .... 16.1
Dennis Rodman, 1997–98 .... 15.0

Steals Average
Michael Jordan, 1987–88 .... 3.2
Michael Jordan, 1989–90 .... 2.8
Michael Jordan, 1992–93 .... 2.8
Scottie Pippen, 1994–95 .... 2.9

Blocks Average
none

Feats
50-Point Game
69... Michael Jordan (@ Cle. Cavaliers), Jan. 16, 1986
64 .... Michael Jordan (vs. Orl. Magic), Jan. 16, 1993
61 .... Michael Jordan (@ Det Pistons), Mar. 4, 1987)
61 .... Michael Jordan (vs. Atl. Hawks), Apr. 16, 1987
59 .... Michael Jordan (@ Det. Pistons), Apr. 3, 1988
58 .... Michael Jordan (vs. N.J. Nets), Feb. 26, 1987

57...Michael Jordan (vs. Was. Bullets),
Dec. 23, 1992

56............. Chet Walker (vs. Cin. Royals),
Feb. 6, 1972

56.......... Michael Jordan (vs. Phi. 76ers),
Mar. 24, 1987

55......... Michael Jordan (@ N.Y. Knicks),
Mar. 28, 1995

54... Michael Jordan (vs. Cle. Cavaliers),
Nov. 3, 1989

54.......... Michael Jordan (@ L.A. Lakers),
Nov. 20, 1992

53... Michael Jordan (vs. Por. Blazers),
Jan. 8, 1987

53......... Michael Jordan (vs. Ind. Pacers),
Apr. 12, 1987

53......... Michael Jordan (vs. Pho. Suns),
Jan. 21, 1989

53......... Michael Jordan (vs. Det. Pistons),
Mar. 7, 1996

53............... Jimmy Butler (@ Phi. 76ers),
Jan. 14, 2016

52... Michael Jordan (vs. Cle. Cavaliers),
Dec. 17, 1987

52...Michael Jordan (vs. Por. Blazers),
Feb. 26, 1988

52......... Michael Jordan (@ Bos. Celtics),
Nov. 9, 1988

52.......... Michael Jordan (@ Phi. 76ers),
Nov. 16, 1988

52... Michael Jordan (@ Den. Nuggets),
Nov. 26, 1988

52.......... Michael Jordan (@ Orl. Magic),
Dec. 20, 1989

52... Michael Jordan (vs. Cha. Hornets),
Mar. 12, 1993

52........ Jimmy Butler (vs. Cha. Hornets),
Jan. 2, 2017

51... Michael Jordan (@ Was. Bullets),
Mar. 19, 1992

51......... Michael Jordan (vs. N.Y. Knicks),
Jan. 21, 1997

50......... Michael Jordan (@ N.Y. Knicks),
Nov. 1, 1986

50...Michael Jordan (@ Mil. Bucks),
Apr. 13, 1987

50... Michael Jordan (vs. Bos. Celtics),
Mar. 18, 1988

50......... Michael Jordan (vs. Mil. Bucks),
Feb. 16, 1989

50... Michael Jordan (vs. Den. Nuggets),
Mar. 24, 1992

50.......... Michael Jordan (@ Mia. Heat),
Nov. 6, 1996

50........ Jamal Crawford (@ Tor. Raptors),
Apr. 11, 2004

50.............. Zach LaVine (@ Atl. Hawks),
Apr. 9, 2021

50...DeMar DeRozan (vs. L.A. Clippers),
Mar. 31, 2022

20-Assist Game

24.......... Guy Rodgers (vs. N.Y. Knicks),
Dec. 21, 1966

22..........Ennis Whatley (vs. N.Y. Knicks),
Jan. 14, 1984

22...............Ennis Whatley (Atl. Hawks),
Mar. 3, 1984

21.......... Clem Haskins (vs. Bos. Celtics),
Dec. 6, 1969

21...Ennis Whatley (vs. G.S. Warriors),
Feb. 23, 1985

20..........Guy Rodgers (vs. S.F. Warriors),
Oct. 18, 1966

30-Rebound Game

37..........Tom Boerwinkle (vs. Pho. Suns),
Jan. 8, 1970

35...Charles Oakley (vs. Cle. Cavaliers),
Apr. 22, 1988

33.......... Tom Boerwinkle (vs. Mil. Bucks),
Mar. 9, 1971

8-Steal Game

10........ Michael Jordan (vs. N.J. Nets),
Jan. 29, 1988

9.......... Michael Jordan (@ Bos. Celtics),
Nov. 9, 1988

9............. Michael Jordan (vs. N.J. Nets),
Apr. 2, 1993

9.............. Scottie Pippen (vs. Atl. Hawks),
Mar. 8, 1994

8...Norm Van Lier (@ G.S. Warriors),
Nov. 8, 1973

8... Michael Jordan (vs. Cle. Cavaliers),
Feb. 22, 1987

8......... Michael Jordan (vs. N.Y. Knicks),
Mar. 6, 1987

8.......... Michael Jordan (vs. Phi. 76ers),
Mar. 24, 1987

8......... Michael Jordan (vs. N.Y. Knicks),
Apr. 8, 1988

8........ Michael Jordan (vs. Bos. Celtics),
Jan. 15, 1989

8..........Scottie Pippen (vs. Orl. Magic),
Dec. 14, 1989

8......... Michael Jordan (vs. Mil. Bucks),
Apr. 13, 1990

8............ Michael Jordan (vs. N.Y. Knicks),
Dec. 7, 1990

8.......... Michael Jordan (vs. Phi. 76ers),
Apr. 20, 1993

8............. Scottie Pippen (@ Ind. Pacers),
Apr. 8, 1994

8.......... Scottie Pippen (vs. Mil. Bucks),
Mar. 17, 1995

8............... Randy Brown (@ Bos. Celtics),
Apr. 11, 1999

8...Metta World Peace (vs. Van. Grizzlies),
Feb. 24, 2001

8... Metta World Peace (@ Sea. Sonics),
Feb. 2, 2002

10-Block Game

12......... Nate Thurmond (vs. Atl. Hawks),
Oct. 18, 1974

11.......... Arits Gilmore (vs. Atl. Hawks),
Dec. 20, 1977

11.......... Joakim Noah (vs. Phi. 76ers),
Feb. 28, 2013

Multiple Triple-Doubles in a Single Season

15.................Michael Jordan, 1988–89

4................ Mickey Johnson, 1978–79

4.................Michael Jordan, 1992–93

4....................Joakim Noah, 2013–14

3.................Michael Jordan, 1984–85

3..................Scottie Pippen, 1990–91

2....................Jimmy Butler, 2015–16

2....................Jimmy Butler, 2016–17

2.................... Guy Rodgers, 1966–67

2.............. Tom Boerwinkle, 1970–71

2.................Nate Thurmond, 1974–75

2...............Charles Oakley, 1986–87

2.................Michael Jordan, 1987–88

2.................Michael Jordan, 1991–92

2..................Scottie Pippen, 1991–92

2..................Scottie Pippen, 1993–94

2..................Scottie Pippen, 1995–96

2...................Joakim Noah, 2012–13

2........................ Pau Gasol, 2015–16

Postseason Play

1967 Western Division Semifinals
     vs. St.L. Hawks, lost (3–0)

1968 Western Division Semifinals
     vs. L.A. Lakers, lost (4–1)

1970 Western Division Semifinals
     vs. Atl. Hawks, lost (4–1)

1971	Western Division Semifinals
	vs. L.A. Lakers, lost (4–3)
1972	Western Division Semifinals
	vs. L.A. Lakers, lost (4–0)
1973	Western Division Semifinals
	vs. L.A. Lakers, lost (4–3)
1974	Western Division Semifinals
	vs. Det. Pistons, won (4–3)
	Western Division Finals
	vs. Mil. Bucks, lost (4–0)
1975	Western Division Semifinals
	vs. K.C.-Oma. Kings, won (4–2)
	Western Division Finals
	vs. G.S. Warriors, lost (4–3)
1977	Western Conference First Round
	vs. Por. Blazers, lost (2–1)
1981	Eastern Conference First Round
	vs. N.Y. Knicks, won (2–0)
	Eastern Conference Semifinals
	vs. Bos. Celtics, lost (4–0)
1985	Eastern Conference First Round
	vs. Mil. Bucks, lost (3–1)
1986	Eastern Conference First Round
	vs. Bos. Celtics, lost (3–0)
1987	Eastern Conference First Round
	vs. Bos. Celtics, lost (3–0)
1988	Eastern Conference First Round
	vs. Cle. Cavaliers, won (3–2)
	Eastern Conference Semifinals
	vs. Det. Pistons, lost (4–1)
1989	Eastern Conference First Round
	vs. Cle. Cavaliers, won (3–2)
	Eastern Conference Semifinals
	vs. N.Y. Knicks, won (4–2)
	Eastern Conference Finals
	vs. Det. Pistons, lost (4–2)
1990	Eastern Conference First Round
	vs. Mil. Bucks, won (3–1)
	Eastern Conference Semifinals
	vs. Phi. 76ers, won (4–1)
	Eastern Conference Finals
	vs. Det. Pistons, lost (4–3)
1991	Eastern Conference First Round
	vs. N.Y. Knicks, won (3–0)

Eastern Conference Semifinals
vs. Phi. 76ers, won (4–1)
Eastern Conference Finals
vs. Det. Pistons, won (4–0)
NBA Finals vs. L.A. Lakers,
won (4–1)

1992	Eastern Conference First Round
	vs. Mia. Heat, won (3–0)
	Eastern Conference Semifinals
	vs. N.Y. Knicks, won (4–3)
	Eastern Conference Finals
	vs. Cle. Cavaliers, won (4–2)
	NBA Finals vs. Por. Blazers,
	won (4–2)
1993	Eastern Conference First Round
	vs. Atl. Hawks, won (3–0)
	Eastern Conference Semifinals
	vs. Cle. Cavaliers, won (4–0)
	Eastern Conference Finals
	vs. N.Y. Knicks, won (4–2)
	NBA Finals vs. Pho. Suns,
	won (4–2)
1994	Eastern Conference First Round
	vs. Cle. Cavaliers, won (3–0)
	Eastern Conference Semifinals
	vs. N.Y. Knicks, lost (4–3)
1995	Eastern Conference First Round
	vs. Cha. Hornets, won (3–1)
	Eastern Conference Semifinals
	vs. Orl. Magic, won (4–2)
1996	Eastern Conference First Round
	vs. Mia. Heat, won (3–0)
	Eastern Conference Semifinals
	vs. N.Y. Knicks, won (4–1)
	Eastern Conference Finals
	vs. Orl. Magic, won (4–0)
	NBA Finals vs. Sea. Sonics,
	won (4–2)
1997	Eastern Conference First Round
	vs. Was. Bullets, won (3–0)
	Eastern Conference Semifinals
	vs. Atl. Hawks, won (4–1)
	Eastern Conference Finals
	vs. Mia. Heat, won (4–1)

NBA Finals vs. Uta. Jazz,
won (4–2)

1998	Eastern Conference First Round
	vs. N.J. Nets, won (3–0)
	Eastern Conference Semifinals
	vs. Cha. Hornets, won (4–1)
	Eastern Conference Finals
	vs. Ind. Pacers, won (4–3)
	NBA Finals vs. Uta. Jazz,
	won (4–2)
2005	Eastern Conference First Round
	vs. Was. Wizards, lost (4–2)
2006	Eastern Conference First Round
	vs. Mia. Heat, lost (4–2)
2007	Eastern Conference First Round
	vs. Mia. Heat, won (4–0)
	Eastern Conference Semifinals
	vs. Det. Pistons, lost (4–2)
2009	Eastern Conference First Round
	vs. Bos. Celtics, lost (4–3)
2010	Eastern Conference First Round
	vs. Cle. Cavaliers, lost (4–1)
2011	Eastern Conference First Round
	vs. Ind. Pacers, won (4–1)
	Eastern Conference Semifinals
	vs. Atl. Hawks, won (4–2)
	Eastern Conference Finals
	vs. Mia. Heat, lost (4–1)
2012	Eastern Conference First Round
	vs. Phi. 76ers, lost (4–2)
2013	Eastern Conference First Round
	vs. Brk. Nets, won (4–3)
	Eastern Conference Semifinals
	vs. Mia. Heat, lost (4–1)
2014	Eastern Conference First Round
	vs. Was. Wizards, lost (4–1)
2015	Eastern Conference First Round
	vs. Mil. Bucks, won (4–2)
	Eastern Conference Semifinals
	vs. Cle. Cavaliers, lost (4–2)
2017	Eastern Conference First Round
	vs. Bos. Celtics, lost (4–2)
2022	Eastern Conference First Round
	vs. Mil. Bucks, lost (4–1)

Cleveland Cavaliers

Dates of Operation: 1970–present (52 seasons)
Overall Record: 1933 wins, 2256 losses (.461)
Arenas: Cleveland Arena, 1970–74; Richfield Coliseum, 1974–94; Rocket Mortgage FieldHouse
(formerly Gund Arena, 1994–2006; Quicken Loans Arena, 2006–19), 1994–present (capacity:
19,432)
Other Name: Cavs

Year-by-Year Finishes

Year	Finish	Wins	Losses	Percentage	Games Behind	Head Coach	Attendance
				Eastern Conference Central Division			
1970–71	4th	15	67	.183	27.0	Bill Fitch	144,252
1971–72	4th	23	59	.280	15.0	Bill Fitch	214,119
1972–73	4th	32	50	.390	20.0	Bill Fitch	186,477
1973–74	4th	29	53	.354	18.0	Bill Fitch	164,520
1974–75	3rd	40	42	.488	20.0	Bill Fitch	334,582
1975–76	1st	49	33	.598	+1.0	Bill Fitch	519,010
1976–77	4th	43	39	.524	6.0	Bill Fitch	570,445
1977–78	3rd	43	39	.524	9.0	Bill Fitch	454,961
1978–79	4th (Tie)	30	52	.366	18.0	Bill Fitch	325,616
1979–80	4th (Tie)	37	45	.451	13.0	Stan Albeck	322,788
1980–81	5th	28	54	.341	32.0	Bill Musselman (25–46), Don Delaney (3–8)	224,499
1981–82	6th	15	67	.183	40.0	Don Delaney (4–11), Bob Kloppenburg (0–3), Chuck Daly (9–32), Bill Musselman (2–21)	232,421
1982–83	5th	23	59	.280	28.0	Tom Nissalke	160,537
1983–84	4th	28	54	.341	22.0	Tom Nissalke	208,094
1984–85	4th	36	46	.439	23.0	George Karl	324,004
1985–86	5th	29	53	.354	28.0	George Karl (25–42), Gene Littles (4–11)	391,842
1986–87	6th	31	51	.378	26.0	Lenny Wilkens	447,125
1987–88	4th (Tie)	42	40	.512	12.0	Lenny Wilkens	504,847
1988–89	2nd	57	25	.695	6.0	Lenny Wilkens	721,426
1989–90	4th (Tie)	42	40	.512	17.0	Lenny Wilkens	695,710
1990–91	6th	33	49	.402	28.0	Lenny Wilkens	623,735
1991–92	2nd	57	25	.695	10.0	Lenny Wilkens	677,408
1992–93	2nd	54	28	.659	3.0	Lenny Wilkens	751,465
1993–94	3rd (Tie)	47	35	.573	10.0	Mike Fratello	753,686
1994–95	4th	43	39	.524	9.0	Mike Fratello	833,580
1995–96	3rd	47	35	.573	25.0	Mike Fratello	730,095
1996–97	5th	42	40	.512	27.0	Mike Fratello	692,684
1997–98	5th	47	35	.573	15.0	Mike Fratello	694,629
1998–99	7th	22	28	.440	11.0	Mike Fratello	352,992
1999–00	6th	32	50	.390	24.0	Randy Wittman	603,702
2000–01	6th	30	52	.366	22.0	Randy Wittman	650,775
2001–02	7th	29	53	.354	21.0	John Lucas	596,115
2002–03	8th	17	65	.207	33.0	John Lucas (8–34), Keith Smart (9–31)	471,374

Year	Finish	Wins	Losses	Percentage	Games Behind	Head Coach	Attendance
2003–04	5th	35	47	.427	26.0	Paul Silas	749,790
2004–05	4th	42	40	.512	12.0	Paul Silas (34–30), Brendan Malone (8–10)	784,249
2005–06	2nd	50	32	.610	14.0	Mike Brown	792,391
2006–07	2nd	50	32	.610	3.0	Mike Brown	837,883
2007–08	2nd	45	37	.549	14.0	Mike Brown	839,074
2008–09	1st	66	16	.805	+25.0	Mike Brown	841,000
2009–10	1st	61	21	.744	+15.0	Mike Brown	843,042
2010–11	5th	19	63	.232	43.0	Byron Scott	824,595
2011–12	5th	21	45	.318	29.0	Byron Scott	525,577
2012–13	5th	24	58	.293	25.5	Byron Scott	663,882
2013–14	3rd	33	49	.402	23.0	Mike Brown	710,522
2014–15	1st	53	29	.646	+3.0	David Blatt	843,042
2015–16	1st	57	25	.695	+12.0	D. Blatt (30–11), Tyronn Lue (27–14)	843,042
2016–17	1st	51	31	.622	+9.0	Tyronn Lue	843,042
2017–18	1st	50	32	.610	+2.0	Tyronn Lue	843,042
2018–19	5th	19	63	.232	41.0	Tyronn Lue (0–6), Larry Drew (19–57)	793,337
2019–20	5th	19	46	.292	33.0	John Beilein (14–40), J.B. Bickerstaff (5–6)	643,008
2020–21	4th	22	50	.306	24.0	J.B. Bickerstaff	91,476
2021–22	3rd	44	38	.537	7.0	J.B. Bickerstaff	758,228

1998–99: 50-game season.

2011–12: 66-game season.

2019–20: 65-to-75-game season.

2020–21: 72-game season.

Awards

Most Valuable Player
LeBron James, forward, 2008–09
LeBron James, forward, 2009–10

Rookie of the Year
LeBron James, forward, 2003–04
Kyrie Irving, guard, 2011–12

Defensive Player of the Year
none

Sixth Man of the Year
none

Most Improved Player
none

All-NBA First Team
Mark Price, 1992–93
LeBron James, 2005–06
LeBron James, 2007–08
LeBron James, 2008–09
LeBron James, 2009–10
LeBron James, 2014–15
LeBron James, 2015–16

LeBron James, 2016–17
LeBron James, 2017–18

All-Defensive First Team
Larry Nance, 1988–89
LeBron James, 2008–09
LeBron James, 2009–10

All-Rookie First Team
Austin Carr, 1971–72
Dwight Davis, 1972–73
Brad Daugherty, 1986–87
Ron Harper, 1986–87
Hot Rod Williams, 1986–87
Zydrunas Ilgauskas, 1997–98
Brevin Knight, 1997–98
Andre Miller, 1999–00
LeBron James, 2003–04
Kyrie Irving, 2011–12
Dion Waiters, 2012–13
Evan Mobley, 2021–22

Coach of the Year
Bill Fitch, 1975–76

Mike Brown, 2008–09

Hall of Famers Who Played for the Cavaliers
Walt Frazier, guard, 1977–80
Shaquille O'Neal, center, 2009–10
Nate Thurmond, center, 1975–77
Ben Wallace, forward, 2007–09
Lenny Wilkens, guard, 1972–74

Retired Numbers
7 .... Bing Smith
11 .... Zydrunas Ilgauskas
22 .... Larry Nance
25 .... Mark Price
34 .... Austin Carr
42 .... Nate Thurmond
43 .... Brad Daugherty

League Leaders, Offense
Points
LeBron James, 2017–18 2251

Three Pointers
Mike Bratz, 1980–81 57
Wesley Person, 1997–98 192

Assists
Andre Miller, 2001–02 882

Scoring Average
LeBron James, 2007–08 .... 30.0

Field Goal Percentage
none

Three Point Percentage
Steve Kerr, 1989–90 .... .507
Kyle Korver*, 2016–17 .... .451
*.485 with Cle. Cavaliers and .409 with Atl. Hawks.

Free Throw Percentage
Mark Price, 1991–92 .... .947
Mark Price, 1992–93 .... .948

Assists Average
Andre Miller, 2001–02 .... 10.9

League Leaders, Defense
Offensive Rebounds
Zydrunas Ilgauskas, 2004–05 299

Defensive Rebounds
none

Total Rebounds
none

Steals
Brevin Knight, 1997–98 196

Blocks
none

Rebounds Average
Andre Drummond*, 2019–20 .... 15.2
*11.1 with Cle. Cavaliers and 15.8 with Det. Pistons.

Steals Average
none

Blocks Average
none

Feats
50-Point Game
57 .... Kyrie Irving (@ S.A. Spurs), Mar. 12, 2015
57 .... LeBron James (@ Was. Wizards), Nov. 3, 2017
56 .... LeBron James (@ Tor. Raptors), Mar. 20, 2005

55 .... LeBron James (@ Mil. Bucks), Feb. 20, 2009
55 .... Kyrie Irving (vs. Por. Blazers), Jan. 28, 2015
52 .... LeBron James (@ Mil. Bucks), Dec. 10, 2005
52 .... LeBron James (@ N.Y. Knicks), Feb. 4, 2009
51 .... LeBron James (@ Uta. Jazz), Jan. 21, 2006
51 .... LeBron James (@ Mem. Grizzlies), Jan. 15, 2008
51 .... LeBron James (@ Sac. Kings), Mar. 13, 2009
50 .... Walt Wesley (vs. Cin. Royals), Feb. 19, 1971
50 .... LeBron James (@ N.Y. Knicks), Mar. 5, 2008

20-Assist Game
27 .... Geoff Huston (vs. G.S. Warriors), Jan. 27, 1982
22 .... Andre Miller (vs. Phil. 76ers), Dec. 15, 2001
20 ...Bobby Washington (vs. Por. Blazers), Nov. 7, 1971
20 .... Lenny Wilkens (vs. Sea. Sonics), Nov. 27, 1973
20 .... Geoff Huston (vs. Ind. Pacers), Feb. 3, 1982
20 .... Mark Price (vs. Atl. Hawks), Apr. 4, 1990
20 .... Brevin Knight (vs. Was. Bullets), Nov. 22, 1997

30-Rebound Game
none

8-Steal Game
10 .... Ron Harper (vs. Phi. 76ers), Mar. 10, 1987
9 .... Andre Miller (vs. Phi. 76ers), Dec. 15, 2001
8 .... Foots Walker (@ N.Y. Knicks), Oct. 25, 1977
8 .... Randy Smith (@ Hou. Rockets), Nov. 28, 1979
8 .... Randy Smith (vs. Det. Pistons), Oct. 14, 1980
8 .... Ron Harper (@ Phi. 76ers), Dec. 17, 1986
8 .... Ron Harper (vs. Atl. Hawks), Jan. 29, 1987

8 .... Brevin Knight (vs. Phi. 76ers), Jan. 24, 1998
8 .... Delonte West (vs. Mil. Bucks), Mar. 4, 2009

10-Block Game
11 .... Larry Nance (vs. N.Y. Knicks), Jan. 7, 1989

Multiple Triple-Doubles in a Single Season
18 .... LeBron James, 2017–18
13 .... LeBron James, 2016–17
7 .... LeBron James, 2007–08
7 .... LeBron James, 2008–09
5 .... LeBron James, 2005–06
4 .... LeBron James, 2004–05
4 .... LeBron James, 2009–10
3 .... Andre Miller, 2001–02
3 .... LeBron James, 2015–16
2 .... LeBron James, 2014–15

Postseason Play
1976 Eastern Conference Semifinals
vs. Was. Bullets, won (4–3)
Eastern Conference Finals
vs. Bos. Celtics, lost (4–2)
1977 Eastern Conference First Round
vs. Was. Bullets, lost (2–1)
1978 Eastern Conference First Round
vs. N.Y. Knicks, lost (2–0)
1985 Eastern Conference First Round
vs. Bos. Celtics, lost (3–1)
1988 Eastern Conference First Round
vs. Chi. Bulls, lost (3–2)
1989 Eastern Conference First Round
vs. Chi. Bulls, lost (3–2)
1990 Eastern Conference First Round
vs. Phi. 76ers, lost (3–2)
1992 Eastern Conference First Round
vs. N.J. Nets, won (3–1)
Eastern Conference Semifinals
vs. Bos. Celtics, won (4–3)
Eastern Conference Finals
vs. Chi. Bulls, lost (4–2)
1993 Eastern Conference First Round
vs. N.J. Nets, won (3–2)
Eastern Conference Semifinals
vs. Chi. Bulls, lost (4–0)
1994 Eastern Conference First Round
vs. Chi. Bulls, lost (3–0)
1995 Eastern Conference First Round
vs. N.Y. Knicks, lost (3–1)

1996   Eastern Conference First Round
        vs. N.Y. Knicks, lost (3–0)
1998   Eastern Conference First Round
        vs. Ind. Pacers, lost (3–1)
2006   Eastern Conference First Round
        vs. Was. Wizards, won (4–2)
        Eastern Conference Semifinals
        vs. Det. Pistons, lost (4–3)
2007   Eastern Conference First Round
        vs. Was. Wizards, won (4–2)
        Eastern Conference Semifinals
        vs. N.J. Nets, won (4–2)
        Eastern Conference Finals
        vs. Det. Pistons, won (4–2)
        NBA Finals vs. S.A. Spurs,
        lost (4–0)
2008   Eastern Conference First Round
        vs. Was. Wizards, won (4–2)
        Eastern Conference Semifinals
        vs. Bos. Celtics, lost (4–3)
2009   Eastern Conference First Round
        vs. Det. Pistons, won (4–0)

Eastern Conference Semifinals
vs. Atl. Hawks, won (4–0)
Eastern Conference Finals
vs. Orl. Magic, lost (4–2)
2010   Eastern Conference First Round
        vs. Chi. Bulls, won (4–1)
        Eastern Conference Semifinals
        vs. Bos. Celtics, lost (4–2)
2015   Eastern Conference First Round
        vs. Bos. Celtics, won (4–0)
        Eastern Conference Semifinals
        vs. Chi. Bulls, won (4–2)
        Eastern Conference Finals
        vs. Atl. Hawks, won (4–0)
        NBA Finals vs. G.S. Warriors,
        lost (4–2)
2016   Eastern Conference First Round
        vs. Det. Pistons, won (4–0)
        Eastern Conference Semifinals
        vs. Atl. Hawks, won (4–0)
        Eastern Conference Finals
        vs. Tor. Raptors, won (4–2)

NBA Finals vs. G.S. Warriors,
won (4–3)
2017   Eastern Conference First Round
        vs. Ind. Pacers, won (4–0)
        Eastern Conference Semifinals
        vs. Tor. Raptors, won (4–0)
        Eastern Conference Finals
        vs. Bos. Celtics, won (4–1)
        NBA Finals vs. G.S. Warriors,
        lost (4–1)
2018   Eastern Conference First Round
        vs. Ind. Pacers, won (4–3)
        Eastern Conference Semifinals
        vs. Tor. Raptors, won (4–0)
        Eastern Conference Finals
        vs. Bos. Celtics, won (4–3)
        NBA Finals vs. G.S. Warriors,
        lost (4–0)

Detroit Pistons

Dates of Operation: (as the Fort Wayne Pistons) 1948–57 (9 seasons)
Overall Record: 313 wins, 306 losses (.506)
Arenas: North Side High School Gym, 1948–52; Allen County War Memorial Coliseum, 1952–57

Dates of Operation: (as the Detroit Pistons) 1957–present (65 seasons)
Overall Record: 2483 wins, 2732 losses (.476)
Arenas: Detroit Olympia, 1957–61; Cobo Arena, 1961–78; Pontiac Silverdome, 1978–88; The Palace of Auburn Hills, 1988–2017; Little Caesars Arena, 2017–present (capacity: 20,332)

Year-by-Year Finishes

Year	Finish	Wins	Losses	Percentage	Games Behind	Head Coach	Attendance
				Fort Wayne Pistons			
				BAA Western Division			
1948–49	5th	22	38	.367	23.0	Cal Bennett (0–6),	N/A
						Curly Armstrong (22–32)	
				NBA Central Division			
1949–50	3rd (Tie)	40	28	.588	11.0	Murray Mendenhall	N/A
				Western Division			
1950–51	3rd	32	36	.471	12.0	Murray Mendenhall	107,019
1951–52	4th	29	37	.439	12.0	Paul Birch	N/A
1952–53	3rd	36	33	.522	11.5	Paul Birch	N/A
1953–54	3rd	40	32	.556	6.0	Paul Birch	113,889
1954–55	1st	43	29	.597	+3.0	Charles Eckman	96,641
1955–56	1st	37	35	.514	+4.0	Charles Eckman	128,102
1956–57	1st (Tie)	34	38	.472	—	Charles Eckman	108,054
				Detroit Pistons			
1957–58	2nd (Tie)	33	39	.458	8.0	Charles Eckman (9–16),	134,411
						Red Rocha (24–23)	
1958–59	3rd	28	44	.389	21.0	Red Rocha	119,351
1959–60	2nd	30	45	.400	16.0	Red Rocha (13–21),	178,007
						Dick McGuire (17–24)	
1960–61	3rd	34	45	.430	17.0	Dick McGuire	164,230
1961–62	3rd	37	43	.463	17.0	Dick McGuire	143,081
1962–63	3rd	34	46	.425	19.0	Dick McGuire	144,150
1963–64	5th	23	57	.288	25.0	Charles Wolf	100,386
1964–65	4th	31	49	.388	18.0	Charles Wolf (2–9),	121,239
						Dave DeBusschere (29–40)	
1965–66	5th	22	58	.275	23.0	Dave DeBusschere	120,013
1966–67	5th	30	51	.370	14.0	Dave DeBusschere (28–45),	193,782
						Donnie Butcher (2–6)	
				Eastern Division			
1967–68	4th	40	42	.488	22.0	Donnie Butcher	224,164
1968–69	6th	32	50	.390	25.0	Donnie Butcher (10–12),	201,433
						Paul Seymour (22–38)	
1969–70	7th	31	51	.378	29.0	Butch van Breda Kolff	167,648

Year	Finish	Wins	Losses	Percentage	Games Behind	Head Coach	Attendance
				Eastern Conference Midwest Division			
1970–71	4th	45	37	.549	21.0	Butch van Breda Kolff	283,913
1971–72	4th	26	56	.317	37.0	Butch van Breda Kolff (6–4), Terry Dischinger (0–2), Earl Lloyd (20–50)	188,763
1972–73	3rd	40	42	.488	20.0	Earl Lloyd (2–5), Ray Scott (38–37)	212,094
1973–74	3rd	52	30	.634	7.0	Ray Scott	300,565
1974–75	3rd	40	42	.488	7.0	Ray Scott	307,180
1975–76	2nd	36	46	.439	2.0	Ray Scott (17–25), Herb Brown (19–21)	251,352
1976–77	2nd (Tie)	44	38	.537	6.0	Herb Brown	303,792
1977–78	4th	38	44	.463	10.0	Herb Brown (9–15), Bob Kauffman (29–29)	223,382
				Central Division			
1978–79	4th (Tie)	30	52	.366	18.0	Dick Vitale	389,936
1979–80	6th	16	66	.195	34.0	Dick Vitale (4–8), Richie Adubato (12–58)	333,233
1980–81	6th	21	61	.256	39.0	Scotty Robertson	228,348
1981–82	3rd	39	43	.476	16.0	Scotty Robertson	391,205
1982–83	3rd	37	45	.451	14.0	Scotty Robertson	482,571
1983–84	2nd	49	33	.598	1.0	Chuck Daly	652,865
1984–85	2nd	46	36	.561	13.0	Chuck Daly	691,550
1985–86	3rd	46	36	.561	11.0	Chuck Daly	695,233
1986–87	2nd	52	30	.634	5.0	Chuck Daly	907,520
1987–88	1st	54	28	.659	+4.0	Chuck Daly	1,066,505
1988–89	1st	63	19	.768	+6.0	Chuck Daly	879,405
1989–90	1st	59	23	.720	+4.0	Chuck Daly	879,705
1990–91	2nd	50	32	.610	11.0	Chuck Daly	879,614
1991–92	3rd	48	34	.585	19.0	Chuck Daly	879,614
1992–93	6th	40	42	.488	17.0	Ron Rothstein	889,614
1993–94	7th	20	62	.244	37.0	Don Chaney	806,641
1994–95	7th	28	54	.341	24.0	Don Chaney	719,090
1995–96	4th (Tie)	46	36	.561	26.0	Doug Collins	730,573
1996–97	3rd (Tie)	54	28	.659	15.0	Doug Collins	784,234
1997–98	6th	37	45	.451	25.0	Doug Collins (21–24), Alvin Gentry (16–21)	794,567
1998–99	3rd	29	21	.580	4.0	Alvin Gentry	444,585
1999–00	4th (Tie)	42	40	.512	14.0	Alvin Gentry (28–30), George Irvine (14–10)	678,470
2000–01	5th	32	50	.390	20.0	George Irvine	607,323
2001–02	1st	50	32	.610	+6.0	Rick Carlisle	760,807
2002–03	1st	50	32	.610	+2.0	Rick Carlisle	839,278
2003–04	2nd	54	28	.659	7.0	Larry Brown	872,902
2004–05	1st	54	28	.659	+7.0	Larry Brown	905,116
2005–06	1st	64	18	.780	+14.0	Flip Saunders	905,116
2006–07	1st	53	29	.646	+3.0	Flip Saunders	905,116
2007–08	1st	59	23	.720	+14.0	Flip Saunders	905,116
2008–09	3rd	39	43	.476	27.0	Michael Curry	896,971
2009–10	5th	27	55	.329	34.0	John Kuester	768,826
2010–11	4th	30	52	.366	32.0	John Kuester	683,080

Year	Finish	Wins	Losses	Percentage	Games Behind	Head Coach	Attendance
2011–12	4th	25	41	.379	25.0	Lawrence Frank	475,638
2012–13	4th	29	53	.354	20.5	Lawrence Frank	606,094
2013–14	4th	29	53	.354	27.0	Maurice Cheeks (21–29), John Loyer (8–24)	616,005
2014–15	5th	32	50	.390	21.0	Stan Van Gundy	625,917
2015–16	3rd	44	38	.537	13.0	Stan Van Gundy	677,138
2016–17	5th	37	45	.451	14.0	Stan Van Gundy	655,141
2017–18	4th	39	43	.476	11.0	Stan Van Gundy	713,945
2018–19	3rd	41	41	.500	19.0	Dwane Casey	675,963
2019–20	4th	20	46	.303	32.5	Dwane Casey	509,469
2020–21	5th	20	52	.278	26.0	Dwane Casey	14,250
2021–22	5th	23	59	.280	28.0	Dwane Casey	663,556

1998–99: 50-game season.

2011–12: 66-game season.

2019–20: 65-to-75-game season.

2020–21: 72-game season.

Awards

Most Valuable Player

Rookie of the Year

Monk Meineke, forward, 1952–53 (Ft.W.)

Grant Hill, forward, 1994–95

Defensive Player of the Year

Dennis Rodman, forward, 1989–90

Dennis Rodman, forward, 1990–91

Ben Wallace, center, 2001–02

Ben Wallace, center, 2002–03

Ben Wallace, center, 2004–05

Ben Wallace, center, 2005–06

Sixth Man of the Year

Corliss Williamson, forward, 2001–02

Most Improved Player

All-NBA First Team

Larry Foust, 1954–55 (Ft.W.)

George Yardley, 1957–58

Gene Shue, 1960–61

Dave Bing, 1967–68

Dave Bing, 1970–71

Isiah Thomas, 1983–84

Isiah Thomas, 1984–85

Isiah Thomas, 1985–86

Grant Hill, 1996–97

All-Defensive First Team

Dave DeBusschere*, 1968–69

Joe Dumars, 1988–89

Dennis Rodman, 1988–89

Joe Dumars, 1989–90

Dennis Rodman, 1989–90

Dennis Rodman, 1990–91

Joe Dumars, 1991–92

Dennis Rodman, 1991–92

Joe Dumars, 1992–93

Dennis Rodman, 1992–93

Ben Wallace, 2001–02

Ben Wallace, 2002–03

Ben Wallace, 2003–04

Ben Wallace, 2004–05

Ben Wallace, 2005–06

* 29 games with Det. Pistons and 47 games with N.Y. Knicks.

All-Rookie First Team

Dave DeBusschere, 1962–63

Joe Caldwell, 1964–65

Tom Van Arsdale, 1965–66

Dave Bing, 1966–67

Bob Lanier, 1970–71

Terry Tyler, 1978–79

Isiah Thomas, 1981–82

Kelly Tripucka, 1981–82

Grant Hill, 1994–95

Jerry Stackhouse, 1995–96

Brandon Knight, 2011–12

Saddiq Bey, 2020–21

Cade Cunningham, 2021–22

Coach of the Year

Ray Scott, 1973–74

Rick Carlisle, 2001–02

Hall of Famers Who Played for the Pistons

Walt Bellamy, center, 1968–70

Dave Bing, guard, 1966–75

Chuck Cooper, forward, 1955–56 (Ft.W.)

Adrian Dantley, forward, 1986–89

Dave DeBusschere, forward, 1962–69

Joe Dumars, guard, 1985–99

Harry Gallatin, forward, 1957–58

Alex Hannum, forward, 1956–57 (Ft.W.)

Grant Hill, forward, 1994–2000

Bob Houbregs, center, 1954–58 (Ft.W.-Det.)

Bailey Howell, forward, 1959–64

Allen Iverson, guard, 2008–09

Bob Lanier, center, 1970–80

Bob McAdoo, forward, 1979–81

Tracy McGrady, guard, 2010–11

Dick McGuire, guard, 1957–60

Andy Phillip, guard, 1952–56 (Ft.W.)

Dennis Rodman, forward, 1986–93

Isiah Thomas, guard, 1981–94

Ben Wallace, center, 2000–06; 2009–12

Chris Webber, forward, 2006–07

George Yardley, forward, 1953–59 (Ft.W.-Det.)

Retired Numbers

JM ....Jack McCloskey

WD..........................William Davidson

1.............................Chauncey Billups

2....................................Chuck Daly

3.................................. Ben Wallace

4.....................................Joe Dumars

10..............................Dennis Rodman

11...................................Isiah Thomas

15..............................Vinnie Johnson

16.......................................Bob Lanier

21..Dave Bing
32.............................Richard Hamilton
40...................................Bill Laimbeer

League Leaders, Offense
Points
George Yardley, 1957–58 2001
Dave Bing, 1967–68.................... 2142
Jerry Stackhouse, 2000–01 2380

Three Pointers
none

Assists
Kevin Porter*, 1977–78 837
Kevin Porter, 1978–79................. 1099
Isiah Thomas, 1983–84.................. 914
Isiah Thomas, 1984–85............... 1123
*36 with Det. Pistons and 801 with N.J. Nets.

Scoring Average
George Yardley, 1957–58 .... 27.8

Field Goal Percentage
Larry Foust, 1954–55 (Ft.W.)......... .487
Dennis Rodman, 1988–89............. .595

Three Point Percentage
Richard Hamilton, 2005–06 .... .458
José Calderón*, 2012–13 .... .461
*.502 with Det. Pistons and .429 with Tor. Raptors.

Free Throw Percentage
none

Assists Average
Kevin Porter*, 1977–78 .... 10.2
Kevin Porter, 1978–79................. 13.4
Isiah Thomas, 1984–85................. 13.9
*4.5 with Det. Pistons and 10.8 with N.J. Nets.

League Leaders, Defense
Offensive Rebounds
Dennis Rodman, 1990–91.............. 361
Dennis Rodman, 1991–92.............. 523
Dennis Rodman, 1992–93.............. 367
Ben Wallace, 2002–03 293
Ben Wallace, 2005–06 301
Andre Drummond, 2013–14.......... 440
Andre Drummond, 2014–15.......... 437
Andre Drummond, 2015–16.......... 395
Andre Drummond, 2016–17.......... 345
Andre Drummond, 2017–18.......... 399
Andre Drummond, 2018–19.......... 423

Defensive Rebounds
Bill Laimbeer, 1985–86................. 770
Dennis Rodman, 1991–92............ 1007
Ben Wallace, 2000–01 749
Andre Drummond, 2015–16.......... 803
Andre Drummond, 2017–18.......... 848
Andre Drummond, 2018–19.......... 809

Total Rebounds
Larry Foust, 1951–52 (Ft.W.).......... 880
Bill Laimbeer, 1983–84................ 1003
Bill Laimbeer, 1985–86................ 1075
Dennis Rodman, 1991–92............ 1530
Dennis Rodman, 1992–93............ 1132
Ben Wallace, 2000–01 1052
Ben Wallace, 2002–03 1126
Andre Drummond, 2015–16.......... 1198
Andre Drummond, 2016–17......... 1115
Andre Drummond, 2017–18.......... 1247
Andre Drummond, 2018–19......... 1232

Steals
none

Blocks
Ben Wallace, 2001–02 278

Rebounds Average
Bill Laimbeer, 1985–86................. 13.1
Dennis Rodman, 1991–92............. 18.7
Dennis Rodman, 1992–93............. 18.3
Ben Wallace, 2001–02 .... 13.0
Ben Wallace, 2002–03 .... 15.4
Andre Drummond, 2015–16.......... 14.8
Andre Drummond, 2017–18.......... 16.0
Andre Drummond, 2018–19.......... 15.6
Andre Drummond*, 2019–20 .... 15.2
*15.8 with Det. Pistons and 11.1 with Cle. Cavaliers.

Steals Average
M.L. Carr, 1978–79 .... 2.5

Blocks Average
Ben Wallace, 2001–02 .... 3.5

Feats
50-Point Game
57.......... Jerry Stackhouse (@ Chi. Bulls), Apr. 3, 2001
56.......... Kelly Tripucka (vs. Chi. Bulls), Jan. 29, 1983
54................ Dave Bing (vs. Chi. Bulls), Feb. 21, 1971
52...George Yardley (vs. Syr. Nationals), Feb. 4, 1958

51......... George Yardley (@ Bos. Celtics), Jan. 15, 1958
51...Richard Hamilton (@ N.Y. Knicks), Dec. 27, 2006
50................ Blake Griffin (vs. Phi. 76ers), Oct. 23, 2018
51................Saddiq Bey (@ Orl. Magic), Mar. 17, 2022

20-Assist Game
25..............Kevin Porter (vs. Bos. Celtics), Mar. 9, 1979
25............. Kevin Porter (@ Pho. Suns), Apr. 1, 1979
25........ Isiah Thomas (vs. Dal. Mavericks), Feb. 13, 1985
24.......... Isiah Thomas (@ Was. Bullets), Feb. 7, 1985
23.......... Kevin Porter (vs. Hou. Rockets), Dec. 27, 1978
23................Kevin Porter (@ L.A. Lakers), Mar. 30, 1979
22.......... Kevin Porter (vs. S.A. Spurs), Dec. 23, 1978
22................Kevin Porter (@ Chi. Bulls), Feb. 27, 1979
21...........Kevin Porter (@ Hou. Rockets), Feb. 6, 1979
21.......... Isiah Thomas (@ K.C. Kings), Dec. 22, 1984
21.......... Isiah Thomas (vs. Was. Bullets), Apr. 12, 1985
21...Brandon Jennings (vs. Orl. Magic), Jan. 21, 2015
20............Kevin Porter (vs. Bos. Celtics), Nov. 20, 1976
20............Kevin Porter (vs. L.A. Lakers), Nov. 15, 1978
20...........Kevin Porter (vs. Ind. Pacers), Mar. 17, 1979
20.......... Isiah Thomas (@ Atl. Hawks), Feb. 28, 1984
20..........Isiah Thomas (vs. L.A. Lakers), Jan. 13, 1985
20.......... Isiah Thomas (@ Atl. Hawks), Jan. 22, 1985
20.......... Isiah Thomas (vs. L.A. Clippers), Mar. 11, 1985
20............ Isiah Thomas (@ Mil. Bucks), Apr. 4, 1985
20.......... Will Bynum (vs. Was. Wizards), Mar. 12, 2010
20... Reggie Jackson (vs. Mem. Grizzlies), Mar. 17, 2015

30-Rebound Game

34.......... Dennis Rodman (vs. Ind. Pacers),
Mar. 4, 1992

33........... Bob Lanier (vs. Sea. Sonics),
Dec. 22, 1972

32......... Larry Foust (vs. Syr. Nationals),
Jan. 5, 1954 (Ft.W.)

32.......... Walter Dukes (vs. N.Y. Knicks),
Dec. 13, 1959

32........ Bailey Howell (vs. Phi. Warriors),
Nov. 5, 1960

32... Dennis Rodman (@ Cha. Hornets),
Jan. 28, 1992

31...Happy Hairston (vs. S.D. Rockets),
Feb. 8, 1969

31.......... Dennis Rodman (@ Sac. Kings),
Mar. 14, 1992

30......... Walter Dukes (vs. Phi. Warriors),
Jan. 17, 1959

30.......... Bailey Howell (vs. L.A. Lakers),
Nov. 25, 1960

8-Steal Game

9................. Earl Tatum (@ L.A. Lakers),
Nov. 28, 1978

9................. Ron Lee (vs. Hou. Rockets),
Mar. 16, 1980

8........... Chris Ford (vs. G.S. Warriors),
Mar. 25, 1977

8........................ Ron Lee (@ Phi. 76ers),
Mar. 17, 1980

10-Block Game

10........... Edgar Jones (vs. Ind. Pacers),
Dec. 17, 1981

10......... Ben Wallace (@ Mil. Bucks),
Feb. 24, 2002

10........... Ben Wallace (vs. Mia. Heat),
Nov. 20, 2002

Multiple Triple-Doubles in a Single Season

13........................ Grant Hill, 1996–97

10........................ Grant Hill, 1995–96

4........................ Grant Hills, 1997–98

3........................ Bob Lanier, 1973–74

2........................ Dave Bing, 1974–75

2.................... Isiah Thomas, 1984–85

2.................... Isiah Thomas, 1986–87

2..................... Reggie Jackson, 2014–15

2..................... Blake Griffin, 2018–19

2................. Mason Plumlee, 2020–21

2........... Cade Cunningham, 2021–22

Postseason Play

1951 Central Divison Third Place
Tiebreaker vs. Chi. Stags, won
Central Divison Semifinals
vs. Roc. Royals, won (2–0)
Central Division Finals
vs. Min. Lakers, lost (2–0)

1952 Western Division Semifinals
vs. Roc. Royals, lost (2–0)

1953 Western Division Semifinals
vs. Roc. Royals, won (2–1)
Western Division Finals
vs. Min. Lakers, lost (3–2)

1954 Western Division Round Robin,
eliminated

1955 Western Division Finals
vs. Min. Lakers, won (3–1)
NBA Finals vs. Syr. Nationals,
won (4–3)

1956 Western Division Finals
vs. St.L. Hawks, won (3–2)
NBA Finals vs. Phi. Warriors,
lost (4–1)

1957 Western Division Tiebreaker
vs. St.L. Hawks, won
Western Division Semifinals
vs. Min. Lakers, lost (2–0)

1958 Western Division Semifinals
vs. Cin. Royals, won (2–0)
Western Division Finals
vs. St.L. Hawks, lost (4–1)

1959 Western Division Semifinals
vs. Min. Lakers, lost (2–1)

1960 Western Division Semifinals
vs. Min. Lakers, lost (2–0)

1961 Western Division Semifinals
vs. L.A. Lakers, lost (3–2)

1962 Western Division Semifinals
vs. Cin. Royals, won (3–1)
Western Division Finals
vs. L.A. Lakers, lost (4–2)

1963 Western Division Semifinals
vs. St.L. Hawks, lost (3–1)

1968 Eastern Division Semifinals
vs. Bos. Celtics, lost (4–2)

1974 Western Conference Semifinals
vs. Chi. Bulls, lost (4–3)

1975 Western Conference First Round
vs. Sea. Sonics, lost (2–1)

1976 Western Conference First Round
vs. Mil. Bucks, won (2–1)

Western Conference Semifinals
vs. G.S. Warriors, lost (4–2)

1977 West Conference First Round
vs. G.S. Warriors, lost (2–1)

1984 Eastern Conference First Round
vs. N.Y. Knicks, lost (3–2)

1985 Eastern Conference First Rounds
vs. N.J. Nets, won (3–0)
Eastern Conference Semifinals
vs. Bos. Celtics, lost (4–2)

1986 Eastern Conference Semifinals
vs. Atl. Hawks, lost (3–1)

1987 Eastern Conference First Round
vs. Was. Bullets, won (3–0)
Eastern Conference Semifinals
vs. Atl. Hawks, won (4–1)
Eastern Conference Finals
vs. Bos. Celtics, lost (4–3)

1988 Eastern Conference First Round
vs. Was. Bullets, won (3–2)
Eastern Conference Semifinals
vs. Chi. Bulls, won (4–1)
Eastern Conference Finals
vs. Bos. Celtics, won (4–2)
NBA Finals vs. L.A. Lakers,
lost (4–3)

1989 Eastern Conference First Round
vs. Bos. Celtics, won (3–0)
Eastern Conference Semifinals
vs. Mil. Bucks, won (4–0)
Eastern Conference Finals
vs. Chi. Bulls, won (4–2)
NBA Finals vs. L.A. Lakers,
won (4–0)

1990 Eastern Conference First Round
vs. Ind. Pacers, won (3–0)
Eastern Conference Semifinals
vs. N.Y. Knicks, won (4–1)
Eastern Conference Finals
vs. Chi. Bulls, won (4–3)
NBA Finals vs. Por. Blazers,
won (4–1)

1991 Eastern Conference First Round
vs. Atl. Hawks, won (3–2)
Eastern Conference Semifinals
vs. Bos. Celtics, won (4–2)
Eastern Conference Finals
vs. Chi. Bulls, lost (4–0)

1992 Eastern Conference First Round
vs. N.Y. Knicks, lost (3–2)

1996 Eastern Conference First Round
vs. Orl. Magic, lost (3–0)

1997   Eastern Conference First Round
      vs. Atl. Hawks, lost (3–2)

1999   Eastern Conference First Round
      vs. Atl. Hawks, lost (3–2)

2000   Eastern Conference First Round
      vs. Mia. Heat, lost (3–0)

2002   Eastern Conference First Round
      vs. Tor. Raptors, won (3–2)
      Eastern Conference Semifinals
      vs. Bos. Celtics, lost (4–1)

2003   Eastern Conference First Round
      vs. Orl. Magic, won (4–3)
      Eastern Conference Semifinals
      vs. Phi. 76ers, won (4–2)
      Eastern Conference Finals
      vs. N.J. Nets, lost (4–0)

2004   Eastern Conference First Round
      vs. Mil. Bucks, won (4–1)
      Eastern Conference Semifinals
      vs. N.J. Nets, won (4–3)

Eastern Conference Finals
vs. Ind. Pacers, won (4–2)
NBA Finals vs. L.A. Lakers,
won (4–1)

2005   Eastern Conference First Round
      vs. Phi. 76ers, won (4–1)
      Eastern Conference Semifinals
      vs. Ind. Pacers, won (4–2)
      Eastern Conference Finals
      vs. Mia. Heat, won (4–3)
      NBA Finals vs. S.A. Spurs,
      lost (4–3)

2006   Eastern Conference First Round
      vs. Mil. Bucks, won (4–1)
      Eastern Conference Semifinals
      vs. Cle. Cavaliers, won (4–3)
      Eastern Conference Finals
      vs. Mia. Heat, lost (4–2)

2007   Eastern Conference First Round
      vs. Orl. Magic, won (4–0)

Eastern Conference Semifinals
vs. Chi. Bulls, won (4–2)
Eastern Conference Finals
vs. Cle. Cavaliers, lost (4–2)

2008   Eastern Conference First Round
      vs. Phi. 76ers, won (4–2)
      Eastern Conference Semifinals
      vs. Orl. Magic, won (4–1)
      Eastern Conference Finals
      vs. Bos. Celtics, lost (4–2)

2009   Eastern Conference First Round
      vs. Cle. Cavaliers, lost (4–0)

2016   Eastern Conference First Round
      vs. Cle. Cavaliers, lost (4–0)

2019   Eastern Conference First Round
      vs. Mil. Bucks, lost (4–0)

Indiana Pacers

ABA Dates of Operation: 1967–76 (9 seasons)
Overall Record: 427 wins, 317 losses (.574)
Arenas: Indiana State Fair Coliseum, 1967–74; Market Square Arena, 1974–76

NBA Dates of Operation: 1976–present (46 seasons)
Overall Record: 1848 wins, 1856 losses (.499)
Arenas: Market Square Arena, 1976–99; Gainbridge Fieldhouse (formerly Conseco Fieldhouse, 1999–2011; Bankers Life Fieldhouse, 2011–21), 1999–present (capacity: 17,923)

Year-by-Year Finishes

Year	Finish	Wins	Losses	Percentage	Games Behind	Head Coach	Attendance
				ABA Eastern Division			
1967–68	3rd	38	40	.487	16.0	Larry Staverman	201,522
1968–69	1st	44	34	.564	+1.0	Larry Staverman (2–7), Slick Leonard (42–27)	237,789
1969–70	1st	59	25	.702	+14.0	Slick Leonard	321,861
				Western Division			
1970–71	1st	58	26	.690	+1.0	Slick Leonard	339,666
1971–72	2nd	47	37	.560	13.0	Slick Leonard	359,821
1972–73	2nd	51	33	.607	4.0	Slick Leonard	352,638
1973–74	2nd	46	38	.548	5.0	Slick Leonard	309,740
1974–75	3rd	45	39	.536	20.0	Slick Leonard	360,559
				American Basketball Association			
1975–76	5th	39	45	.464	21.0	Slick Leonard	316,892
				NBA Western Conference Midwest Division			
1976–77	5th	36	46	.439	14.0	Slick Leonard	432,726
1977–78	5th (Tie)	31	51	.378	17.0	Slick Leonard	501,759
1978–79	3rd (Tie)	38	44	.463	10.0	Slick Leonard	367,160
				Eastern Conference Central Division			
1979–80	4th (Tie)	37	45	.451	13.0	Slick Leonard	433,402
1980–81	3rd	44	38	.537	16.0	Jack McKinney	415,339
1981–82	4th	35	47	.427	20.0	Jack McKinney	309,633
1982–83	6th	20	62	.244	31.0	Jack McKinney	188,642
1983–84	6th	26	56	.317	24.0	Jack McKinney	410,626
1984–85	6th	22	60	.268	37.0	George Irvine	438,377
1985–86	6th	26	56	.317	31.0	George Irvine	460,969
1986–87	4th	41	41	.500	16.0	Jack Ramsay	521,007
1987–88	6th	38	44	.463	16.0	Jack Ramsay	502,244
1988–89	6th	28	54	.341	35.0	Jack Ramsay (0–7), Mel Daniels (0–2), George Irvine (6–14), Dick Versace (22–31)	335,298
1989–90	4th (Tie)	42	40	.512	17.0	Dick Versace	518,923
1990–91	5th	41	41	.500	20.0	Dick Versace (9–16), Bob Hill (32–25)	465,650
1991–92	4th	40	42	.488	27.0	Bob Hill	517,352
1992–93	5th	41	41	.500	16.0	Bob Hill	530,891

407

Year	Finish	Wins	Losses	Percentage	Games Behind	Head Coach	Attendance
1993–94	3rd (Tie)	47	35	.573	10.0	Larry Brown	531,812
1994–95	1st	52	30	.634	+2.0	Larry Brown	654,428
1995–96	2nd	52	30	.634	20.0	Larry Brown	673,967
1996–97	6th	39	43	.476	30.0	Larry Brown	636,735
1997–98	2nd	58	24	.707	4.0	Larry Bird	645,302
1998–99	1st	33	17	.660	+2.0	Larry Bird	404,536
1999–00	1st	56	26	.683	+7.0	Larry Bird	752,145
2000–01	4th	41	41	.500	11.0	Isiah Thomas	731,800
2001–02	3rd (Tie)	42	40	.512	8.0	Isiah Thomas	686,537
2002–03	2nd	48	34	.585	2.0	Isiah Thomas	670,461
2003–04	1st	61	21	.744	+7.0	Rick Carlisle	678,326
2004–05	3rd	44	38	.537	10.0	Rick Carlisle	696,764
2005–06	3rd (Tie)	41	41	.500	23.0	Rick Carlisle	663,368
2006–07	4th	35	47	.427	18.0	Rick Carlisle	629,750
2007–08	3rd	36	46	.439	23.0	Jim O'Brien	501,092
2008–09	4th	36	46	.439	30.0	Jim O'Brien	581,472
2009–10	4th	32	50	.390	29.0	Jim O'Brien	582,295
2010–11	2nd	37	45	.451	25.0	Jim O'Brien (17–27), Frank Vogel (20–18)	555,077
2011–12	2nd	42	24	.636	8.0	Frank Vogel	467,561
2012–13	1st	49	32	.605	+4.5	Frank Vogel	626,069
2013–14	1st	56	26	.683	+8.0	Frank Vogel	717,542
2014–15	4th	38	44	.463	15.0	Frank Vogel	691,434
2015–16	2nd	45	37	.549	12.0	Frank Vogel	690,733
2016–17	2nd (Tie)	42	40	.512	9.0	Nate McMillan	684,578
2017–18	2nd	48	34	.585	2.0	Nate McMillan	658,119
2018–19	2nd	48	34	.585	12.0	Nate McMillan	689,310
2019–20	2nd	45	28	.616	11.0	Nate McMillan	529,008
2020–21	2nd	34	38	.472	12.0	Nate Bjorkgren	N/A
2021–22	4th	25	57	.305	26.0	Rick Carlisle	588,743

1998–99: 50-game season.

2011–12: 66-game season.

2019–20: 65-to-75-game season.

2020–21: 72-game season.

(ABA Attendance totals are unofficial, and numbers include when listed as home team.)

Awards

ABA Most Valuable Player
Mel Daniels, center, 1968–69
Mel Daniels, center, 1970–71
George McGinnis, forward, 1974–75*

*Tied with Julius Erving, N.Y. Nets.

NBA Most Valuable Player
none

ABA Rookie of the Year
none

NBA Rookie of the Year
Chuck Person, forward, 1986–87

Defensive Player of the Year
Metta World Peace, forward, 2003–04

Sixth Man of the Year
Detlef Schrempf, forward, 1990–91

Detlef Schrempf, forward, 1991–92

Most Improved Player
Jalen Rose, guard, 1999–00
Jermaine O'Neal, forward, 2001–02
Danny Granger, forward, 2008–09
Paul George, forward, 2012–13
Victor Oladipo, guard, 2017–18

All-ABA First Team
Mel Daniels, 1968–69
Mel Daniels, 1969–70
Roger Brown, 1970–71
Mel Daniels, 1970–71
George McGinnis, 1973–74
George McGinnis, 1974–75
Billy Knight, 1975–76

All-NBA First Team
none

All-ABA Defensive First Team
Bob Netolicky, 1967–68
George McGinnis, 1971–72
Billy Knight, 1974–75
Don Buse, 1974–75
Don Buse, 1975–76
Don Buse, 1976–77

All-NBA Defensive First Team
Metta World Peace, 2003–04
Metta World Peace, 2005–06*
Paul George, 2013–14
Victor Oladipo, 2017–18

* 16 games with Ind. Pacers and 40 games with Sac. Kings.

All-ABA Rookie First Team
Bob Netolicky, 1967–68
George McGinnis, 1971–72
Billy Knight, 1974–75

All-NBA Rookie First Team
Clark Kellogg, 1982–83
Steve Stipanovich, 1983–84
Chuck Person, 1986–87
Rik Smits, 1988–89

ABA Coach of the Year
none

NBA Coach of the Year
Jack McKinney, 1980–81
Larry Bird, 1997–98

Hall of Famers Who Played for the Pacers
Roger Brown, forward, 1967–75 (ABA)
Mel Daniels, center, 1968–74 (ABA)
Adrian Dantley, forward, 1977–78
Alex English, forward, 1978–80
Tim Hardaway, guard, 2002–03
Gus Johnson, forward, 1972–73 (ABA)
George McGinnis, forward, 1971–75 (ABA); 1979–82
Reggie Miller, guard, 1987–2005
Chris Mullin, forward-guard, 1997–2000

Retired Numbers
30 .... George McGinnis
31 .... Reggie Miller
34 .... Mel Daniels
35 .... Roger Brown
529 .... Slick Leonard

League Leaders, Offense
Points
George McGinnis, 1974–75 (ABA) ... 2353

Three Pointers
Bill Keller, 1972–73 (ABA) 71
Bill Keller, 1974–75 (ABA) 80
Bill Keller, 1975–76 (ABA) 123
Don Buse, 1981–82 73
Reggie Miller, 1992–93 167
Reggie Miller, 1996–97 229

Assists
Don Buse, 1975–76 (ABA) 689
Don Buse, 1976–77 685
Mark Jackson*, 1996–97 935
*294 with Ind. Pacers and 641 with Den. Nuggets.

Scoring Average
George McGinnis, 1974–75 (ABA) 29.8

Field Goal Percantage
Three Point Percentage
Darren Collison, 2017–18 .... .468

Free Throw Percentage
Bill Keller, 1972–73 (ABA) .... .870
Reggie Miller, 1990–91 .... .918
Chris Mullin, 1997–98 .... .939
Reggie Miller, 1998–99 .... .915
Reggie Miller, 2000–01 .... .928
Reggie Miller, 2001–02 .... .911
Reggie Miller, 2004–05 .... .933

Assists Average
Don Buse, 1975–76 (ABA) 8.2
Don Buse, 1976–77 .... 8.5
Mark Jackson*, 1996–97 .... 11.4
*9.8 with Ind. Pacers and 12.3 with Den. Nuggets.

League Leaders, Defense
Offensive Rebounds
none

Defensive Rebounds
none

Total Rebounds
none

Steals
Don Buse, 1975–76 (ABA) 346
Don Buse, 1976–77 281
Victor Oladipo, 2017–18 177
T.J. McConnell, 2020–21 128

Blocks
Jermaine O'Neal, 2000–01 228
Myles Turner, 2018–19 199

Rebounds Average
Mel Daniels, 1968–69 (ABA) 16.5
Mel Daniels, 1970–71 (ABA) 18.0

Steals Average
Don Buse, 1975–76 (ABA) 4.1
Don Buse, 1976–77 .... 3.5
Victor Oladipo, 2017–18 .... 2.4

Blocks Average
Myles Turner, 2018–19 .... 2.7
Myles Turner, 2020–21 .... 3.4

Feats
50-Point Game
58 ... George McGinnis (@ Dal. Chaparrals), Nov. 28, 1972 (ABA)
57 .... Reggie Miller (@ Cha. Hornets), Nov. 28, 1992
56 .... Mel Daniels (vs. N.Y. Nets), Mar. 18, 1969 (ABA)
55 .... Jermaine O'Neal (vs. Mil. Bucks), Jan. 4, 2005
53 .... T.J. Warren (vs. Phi. 76ers), Aug. 1, 2020

52 ... George McGinnis (vs. Car. Cougars), Jan. 12, 1974 (ABA)
52 .... Billy Knight (@ S.A. Spurs), Nov. 11, 1980

20-Assist Game
23. Jamaal Tinsley (vs. Was. Wizards), Nov. 22, 2001
21 .... Roger Brown (vs. Mem. Tams), Oct. 26, 1973 (ABA)
20 .... Jalen Rose (@ Cle. Cavaliers), Apr. 18, 2001

30-Rebound Game
37 ... George McGinnis (vs. Car. Cougars), Jan. 12, 1974 (ABA)
34 .... Mel Daniels (vs. Pit. Pipers), Dec. 20, 1969 (ABA)
33 .... Mel Daniels (vs. Mia. Floridians), Mar. 6, 1970 (ABA)
33 .... George McGinnis (vs. N.Y. Nets), Dec. 5, 1973 (ABA)
31 .... Mel Daniels (vs. N.Y. Nets), Mar. 18, 1969 (ABA)
31 .. Mel Daniels (vs. N.O. Buccaneers), Jan. 10, 1970 (ABA)
30 .... Mel Daniels (@ Ken. Colonels), Oct. 26, 1968 (ABA)
30 .... Mel Daniels (@ The Floridians), Dec. 29, 1971 (ABA)

8-Steal Game
10 ... T.J. McConnell (@ Cle. Cavaliers), Mar. 3, 2021
9 .... Dudley Bradley (@ Uta. Jazz), Nov. 10, 1980
9 ... Dudley Bradley (vs. Cle. Cavaliers), Nov. 29, 1980
8 ... George McGinnis (@ Dal. Chaparrals), Nov. 28, 1972 (ABA)
8 .... Don Buse (vs. Cle. Cavaliers), Dec. 3, 1976
8 .... Don Buse (vs. N.O. Jazz), Mar. 27, 1977
8 .... Micheal Williams (vs. Mil. Bucks), Jan. 12, 1991
8 .... Micheal Williams (vs. Chi. Bulls), Dec. 30, 1991
8 ... Metta World Peace (vs. Mia. Heat), Mar. 31, 2002
8 ... Metta World Peace (vs. Dal. Mavericks), Mar. 24, 2004
8 .... Jamaal Tinsley (@ Det. Pistons), Nov. 19, 2004

10-Block Game
18 ... Jermaine O'Neal (vs. Tor. Raptors), Jan. 22, 2003

10...Darnell Hillman (vs. The Floridians),
Mar. 12, 1972 (ABA)
10..........Roy Hibbert (vs. N.O. Hornets),
Nov. 21, 2012

Multiple Triple-Doubles in a Single Season

9......George McGinnis, 1974–75 (ABA)
9..............Domantas Sabonis, 2020–21
5...............Lance Stephenson, 2013–14
5..............Domantas Sabonis, 2021–22
4..................Detlef Schrempf, 1992–93
4..............Domantas Sabonis, 2019–20
3......................Vern Fleming, 1987–88
2............Roger Brown, 1968–69 (ABA)
2.................Mickey Johnson, 1979–80
2....................Mark Jackson, 1996–97
2....................Jamaal Tinsley, 2001–02

Postseason Play

1968 ABA Eastern Division Semifinals
vs. Pit. Pipers, lost (3–0)
1969 ABA Eastern Division Semifinals
vs. Ken. Colonels, won (4–3)
ABA Eastern Division Finals
vs. Mia. Floridians, won (4–1)
ABA Finals vs. Oak. Oaks,
lost (4–1)
1970 ABA Eastern Division Semifinals
vs. Car. Cougars, won (4–0)
ABA Eastern Division Finals
vs. Ken. Colonels, won (4–1)
ABA Finals vs. L.A. Stars,
won (4–2)
1971 ABA Western Division Semifinals
vs. Mem. Pros, won (4–0)
ABA Western Division Finals
vs. Uta. Stars, lost (4–3)
1972 ABA Western Division Semifinals
vs. Den. Rockets, won (4–3)
ABA Western Division Finals
vs. Uta. Stars, won (4–3)
ABA Finals vs. N.Y. Nets,
won (4–2)
1973 ABA Western Division Semifinals
vs. Den. Rockets, won (4–1)
ABA Western Division Finals
vs. Uta. Stars, won (4–2)
ABA Finals vs. Ken. Colonels,
won (4–3)
1974 ABA Western Division Semifinals
vs. S.A. Spurs, won (4–3)

ABA Western Division Finals
vs. Uta. Stars, lost (4–3)
1975 ABA Western Division Semifinals
vs. S.A. Spurs, won (4–2)
ABA Western Division Finals
vs. Den. Nuggets, won (4–3)
ABA Finals vs. Ken. Colonels,
lost (4–1)
1976 ABA First Round vs. Ken. Colonels,
lost (2–1)
1981 NBA Eastern Conference First Round
vs. Phi. 76ers, lost (2–0)
1987 Eastern Conference First Round
vs. Atl. Hawks, lost (3–1)
1990 Eastern Conference First Round
vs. Det. Pistons, lost (3–0)
1991 Eastern Conference First Round
vs. Bos. Celtics, lost (3–2)
1992 Eastern Conference First Round
vs. Bos. Celtics, lost (3–0)
1993 Eastern Conference First Round
vs. N.Y. Knicks, lost (3–1)
1994 Eastern Conference First Round
vs. Orl. Magic, won (3–0)
Eastern Conference Semifinals
vs. Atl. Hawks, won (4–2)
Eastern Conference Finals
vs. N.Y. Knicks, lost (4–3)
1995 Eastern Conference First Round
vs. Atl. Hawks, won (3–0)
Eastern Conference Semifinals
vs. N.Y. Knicks, won (4–3)
Eastern Conference Finals
vs. Orl. Magic, lost (4–3)
1996 Eastern Conference First Round
vs. Atl. Hawks, lost (3–2)
1998 Eastern Conference First Round
vs. Cle. Cavaliers, won (3–1)
Eastern Conference Semifinals
vs. N.Y. Knicks, won (4–1)
Eastern Conference Finals
vs. Chi. Bulls, lost (4–3)
1999 Eastern Conference First Round
vs. Mil. Bucks, won (3–0)
Eastern Conference Semifinals
vs. Phi. 76ers, won (4–0)
Eastern Conference Finals
vs. N.Y. Knicks, lost (4–2)
2000 Eastern Conference First Round
vs. Mil. Bucks, won (3–2)
Eastern Conference Semifinals
vs. Phi. 76ers, won (4–2)

Eastern Conference Finals
vs. N.Y. Knicks, lost (4–2)
NBA Finals vs. L.A. Lakers,
lost (4–2)
2001 Eastern Conference First Round
vs. Phi. 76ers, lost (3–1)
2002 Eastern Conference First Round
vs. N.J. Nets, lost (3–2)
2003 Eastern Conference First Round
vs. Bos. Celtics, lost (4–2)
2004 Eastern Conference First Round
vs. Bos. Celtics, won (4–0)
Eastern Conference Semifinals
vs. Mia. Heat, won (4–2)
Eastern Conference Finals
vs. Det. Pistons, lost (4–2)
2005 Eastern Conference First Round
vs. Bos. Celtics, won (4–3)
Eastern Conference Semifinals
vs. Det. Pistons, lost (4–2)
2006 Eastern Conference First Round
vs. N.J. Nets, lost (4–2)
2011 Eastern Conference First Round
vs. Chi. Bulls, lost (4–1)
2012 Eastern Conference First Round
vs. Orl. Magic, won (4–1)
Eastern Conference Semifinals
vs. Mia. Heat, lost (4–2)
2013 Eastern Conference First Round
vs. Atl. Hawks, won (4–2)
Eastern Conference Semifinals
vs. N.Y. Knicks, won (4–2)
Eastern Conference Finals
vs. Mia. Heat, lost (4–3)
2014 Eastern Conference First Round
vs. Atl. Hawks, won (4–3)
Eastern Conference Semifinals
vs. Was. Wizards, won (4–2)
Eastern Conference Finals
vs. Mia. Heat, lost (4–2)
2016 Eastern Conference First Round
vs. Tor. Raptors, lost (4–3)
2017 Eastern Conference First Round
vs. Cle. Cavaliers, lost (4–0)
2018 Eastern Conference First Round
vs. Cle. Cavaliers, lost (4–3)
2019 Eastern Conference First Round
vs. Bos. Celtics, lost (4–0)
2020 Eastern Conference First Round
vs. Mia. Heat, lost (4–0)

Miami Heat

Dates of Operation: 1988–present (34 seasons)
Overall Record: 1431 wins, 1290 losses (.526)
Arenas: Miami Arena, 1988–99; FTX Arena (formerly American Airlines Arena, 1999–2021), 1999–present (capacity: 19,600)

Year-by-Year Finishes

Year	Finish	Wins	Losses	Percentage	Games Behind	Head Coach	Attendance
Western Conference Midwest Division							
1988–89	6th	15	67	.183	36.0	Ron Rothstein	612,754
Eastern Conference Atlantic Division							
1989–90	5th	18	64	.220	35.0	Ron Rothstein	615,328
1990–91	6th	24	58	.293	32.0	Ron Rothstein	615,328
1991–92	4th	38	44	.463	13.0	Kevin Loughery	613,583
1992–93	5th	36	46	.439	24.0	Kevin Loughery	614,915
1993–94	4th	42	40	.512	15.0	Kevin Loughery	617,242
1994–95	4th	32	50	.390	25.0	Kevin Loughery (17–29), Alvin Gentry (15–21)	598,761
1995–96	3rd	42	40	.512	18.0	Pat Riley	606,088
1996–97	1st	61	21	.744	+4.0	Pat Riley	615,160
1997–98	1st	55	27	.671	+12.0	Pat Riley	614,861
1998–99	1st (Tie)	33	17	.660	—	Pat Riley	378,813
1999–00	1st	52	30	.634	+2.0	Pat Riley	706,725
2000–01	2nd	50	32	.610	6.0	Pat Riley	678,186
2001–02	6th	36	46	.439	16.0	Pat Riley	655,549
2002–03	7th	25	57	.305	24.0	Pat Riley	628,242
2003–04	2nd	42	40	.512	5.0	Stan Van Gundy	624,809
Southeast Division							
2004–05	1st	59	23	.720	+14.0	Stan Van Gundy	815,143
2005–06	1st	52	30	.634	+10.0	Stan Van Gundy (11–10), Pat Riley (41–20)	818,149
2006–07	1st	44	38	.537	+3.0	Pat Riley	808,541
2007–08	5th	15	67	.183	37.0	Pat Riley	798,004
2008–09	3rd	43	39	.524	16.0	Eric Spoelstra	748,778
2009–10	3rd	47	35	.573	12.0	Eric Spoelstra	726,935
2010–11	1st	58	24	.707	+6.0	Eric Spoelstra	810,930
2011–12	1st	46	20	.697	+6.0	Eric Spoelstra	657,855
2012–13	1st	66	16	.805	+22.0	Eric Spoelstra	819,290
2013–14	1st	54	28	.659	+10.0	Eric Spoelstra	811,036
2014–15	3rd	37	45	.451	23.0	Eric Spoelstra	808,223
2015–16	1st (Tie)	48	34	.585	—	Eric Spoelstra	809,350
2016–17	3rd	41	41	.500	8.0	Eric Spoelstra	805,400
2017–18	1st	44	38	.537	+1.0	Eric Spoelstra	804,850
2018–19	2nd (Tie)	39	43	.476	3.0	Eric Spoelstra	805,264
2019–20	1st	44	29	.603	+11.0	Eric Spoelstra	629,771
2020–21	2nd	40	32	.556	1.0	Eric Spoelstra	N/A
2021–22	1st	53	29	.646	+10.0	Erik Spoelstra	804,761

1998–99: 50-game season.

2011–12: 66-game season.

2019–20: 65-to-75-game season.

2020–21: 72-game season.

Awards

Most Valuable Player
LeBron James, forward, 2011–12
LeBron James, forward, 2012–13

Rookie of the Year
none

Defensive Player of the Year
Alonzo Mourning, center, 1998–99
Alonzo Mourning, center, 1999–00

Sixth Man of the Year
Tyler Herro, guard, 2021–22

Most Improved Player
Rony Seikaly, center, 1989–90
Isaac Austin, center, 1996–97

All-NBA First Team
Tim Hardaway, 1996–97
Alonzo Mourning, 1998–99
Shaquille O'Neal, 2004–05
Shaquille O'Neal, 2005–06
Dwyane Wade, 2008–09
Dwyane Wade, 2009–10
LeBron James, 2010–11
LeBron James, 2011–12
LeBron James, 2012–13
LeBron James, 2013–14

All-Defensive First Team
Alonzo Mourning, 1998–99
Alonzo Mourning, 1999–00
LeBron James, 2010–11
LeBron James, 2011–12
LeBron James, 2012–13

All-Rookie First Team
Sherman Douglas, 1989–90
Steve Smith, 1991–92
Caron Butler, 2002–03
Dwyane Wade, 2003–04
Michael Beasley, 2008–09
Kendrick Nunn, 2019–20

Coach of the Year
Pat Riley, 1996–97

Hall of Famers Who Played for the Heat
Ray Allen, guard, 2012–14

Chris Bosh, forward-center, 2010–16
Tim Hardaway, guard, 1996–2001
Alonzo Mourning, center, 1995–2002;
  2005–08
Shaquille O'Neal, center, 2004–08
Gary Payton, guard, 2005–07

Retired Numbers
1 .... Chris Bosh
3 .... Dwyane Wade
10 .... Tim Hardaway
13 .... Dan Marino
23 .... Michael Jordan
32 .... Shaquille O'Neal
33 .... Alonzo Mourning

League Leaders, Offense

Points
Dwyane Wade, 2008–09 2386

Three Pointers
none

Assists
none

Scoring Average
Dwyane Wade, 2008–09 .... 30.2

Field Goal Percantage
Shaquille O'Neal, 2004–05 .... .601
Shaquille O'Neal, 2005–06 .... .600

Three Point Percentage
Jon Sundvold, 1988–89 .... .522
Jason Kapono, 2006–07 .... .514

Free Throw Percentage
none

Assists Average
none

League Leaders, Defense

Offensive Rebounds
none

Defensive Rebounds
none

Total Rebounds
none

Steals
none

Blocks
Alonzo Mourning, 1998–99 180
Alonzo Mourning, 1999–00 294
Hassan Whiteside, 2015–16 269

Rebounds Average
Hassan Whiteside, 2016–07 .... 14.1

Steals Average
Jimmy Butler, 2020–21 .... 2.1

Blocks Average
Alonzo Mourning, 1998–99 .... 3.9
Alonzo Mourning, 1999–00 .... 3.7
Hassan Whiteside, 2015–16 .... 3.7

Feats

50-Point Game
61 .... LeBron James (vs. Cha. Bobcats),
  Mar. 3, 2014
56 .... Glen Rice (vs. Orl. Magic),
  Apr. 15, 1995
51 .... LeBron James (@ Orl. Magic),
  Feb. 3, 2011
50 ... Alonzo Mourning (vs. Was. Bullets),
  Mar. 29, 1996
50 .... Dwyane Wade (@ Orl. Magic),
  Feb. 22, 2009
50 .... Dwyane Wade (vs. Uta. Jazz),
  Mar. 14, 2009
55 .... Dwyane Wade (vs. N.Y. Knicks),
  Apr. 12, 2009

20-Assist Game
none

30-Rebound Game
34 .... Rony Seikaly (vs. Was. Bullets),
  Mar. 3, 1993

8-Steal Game
9 .... Mario Chalmers (vs. Phi. 76ers),
  Nov. 5, 2008
8 .... Tim Hardaway (vs. Atl. Hawks),
  Dec. 12, 1997
8 ... Dwyane Wade (vs. Dal. Mavericks),
  Nov. 15, 2013

8..........Mario Chalmers (@ N.Y. Knicks), Feb. 2, 2015

10-Block Game

12......... Hassan Whiteside (@ Chi. Bulls), Jan. 25, 2015

11...Hassan Whiteside (@ Den. Nuggets), Jan. 15, 2016

10...Hassan Whiteside (vs. Min. T'Wolves), Nov. 17, 2015

10...Hassan Whiteside (@ Cha. Hornets), Feb. 5, 2016

Multiple Triple-Doubles in a Single Season

4......................LeBron James, 2010–11

4......................LeBron James, 2012–13

4......................Jimmy Butler, 2020–21

4......................Jimmy Butler, 2021–22

3.............. Hassan Whiteside, 2015–16

3....................Bam Adebayo, 2019–20

3....................Jimmy Butler, 2019–20

2................. Dwyane Wade, 2005–06

2....................Bam Adebayo, 2020–21

2........................ Kyle Lowry, 2021–22

Postseason Play

1992 Eastern Conference First Round
vs. Chi. Bulls, lost (3–0)

1994 Eastern Conference First Round
vs. Atl. Hawks, lost (3–2)

1996 Eastern Conference First Round
vs. Chi. Bulls, lost (3–0)

1997 Eastern Conference First Round
vs. Orl. Magic, won (3–2)
Eastern Conference Semifinals
vs. N.Y. Knicks, won (4–3)
Eastern Conference Finals
vs. Chi. Bulls, lost (4–1)

1998 Eastern Conference First Round
vs. N.Y. Knicks, lost (3–2)

1999 Eastern Conference First Round
vs. N.Y. Knicks, lost (3–2)

2000 Eastern Conference First Round
vs. Det. Pistons, won (3–0)
Eastern Conference Semifinals
vs. N.Y. Knicks, lost (4–3)

2001 Eastern Conference First Round
vs. Cha. Hornets, lost (3–0)

2004 Eastern Conference First Round
vs. N.O. Hornets, won (4–3)
Eastern Conference Semifinals
vs. Ind. Pacers, lost (4–2)

2005 Eastern Conference First Round
vs. N.J. Nets, won (4–0)
Eastern Conference Semifinals
vs. Was. Wizards, won (4–0)
Eastern Conference Finals
vs. Det. Pistons, lost (4–3)

2006 Eastern Conference First Round
vs. Chi. Bulls, won (4–2)
Eastern Conference Semifinals
vs. N.J. Nets, won (4–1)
Eastern Conference Finals
vs. Det. Pistons, won (4–2)
NBA Finals vs. Dal. Mavericks, won (4–2)

2007 Eastern Conference First Round
vs. Chi. Bulls, lost (4–0)

2009 Eastern Conference First Round
vs. Atl. Hawks, lost (4–3)

2010 Eastern Conference First Round
vs. Bos. Celtics, lost (4–1)

2011 Eastern Conference First Round
vs. Phi. 76ers, won (4–1)
Eastern Conference Semifinals
vs. Bos. Celtics, won (4–1)
Eastern Conference Finals
vs. Chi. Bulls, won (4–1)
NBA Finals vs. Dal. Mavericks, lost (4–2)

2012 Eastern Conference First Round
vs. N.Y. Knicks, won (4–1)
Eastern Conference Semifinals
vs. Ind. Pacers, won (4–2)

Eastern Conference Finals
vs. Bos. Celtics, won (4–3)
NBA Finals vs. Ok.C. Thunder, won (4–1)

2013 Eastern Conference First Round
vs. Mil. Bucks, won (4–0)
Eastern Conference Semifinals
vs. Chi. Bulls, won (4–1)
Eastern Conference Finals
vs. Ind. Pacers, won (4–3)
NBA Finals vs. S.A. Spurs, lost (4–3)

2014 Eastern Conference First Round
vs. Cha. Bobcats, won (4–0)
Eastern Conference Semifinals
vs. Brk. Nets, won (4–1)
Eastern Conference Finals
vs. Ind. Pacers, won (4–2)
NBA Finals vs. S.A. Spurs, lost (4–1)

2016 Eastern Conference First Round
vs. Cha. Hornets, won (4–3)
Eastern Conference Semifinals
vs. Tor. Raptors, lost (4–3)

2018 Eastern Conference First Round
vs. Phi. 76ers, lost (4–1)

2020 Eastern Conference First Round
vs. Ind. Pacers, won (4–0)
Eastern Conference Semifinals
vs. Mil. Bucks, won (4–1)
Eastern Conference Finals
vs. Bos. Celtics, won (4–2)
NBA Finals vs. L.A. Lakers, lost (4–2)

2021 Eastern Conference First Round
vs. Mil. Bucks, lost (4–0)

2022 Eastern Conference First Round
vs. Atl. Hawks, won (4–1)
Eastern Conference Semifinals
vs. Phi. 76ers, won (4–2)
Eastern Conference Finals
vs. Bos. Celtics, lost (4–3)

Milwaukee Bucks

Dates of Operation: 1968–present (54 seasons)
Overall Record: 2282 wins, 2079 losses (.523)
Arenas: MECCA Arena (formerly Milwaukee Arena, 1968–75), 1968–88; BMO Harris Bradley Center
(formerly Bradley Center, 1988–2012), 1988–2018; Fiserv Forum, 2018–present (capacity: 17,341)

Year-by-Year Finishes

Year	Finish	Wins	Losses	Percentage	Games Behind	Head Coach	Attendance
				Eastern Division			
1968–69	7th	27	55	.329	30.0	Larry Costello	212,362
1969–70	2nd	56	26	.683	4.0	Larry Costello	360,650
				Western Conference Midwest Division			
1970–71	1st	66	16	.805	+15.0	Larry Costello	378,106
1971–72	1st	63	19	.768	+6.0	Larry Costello	372,439
1972–73	1st	60	22	.732	+9.0	Larry Costello	372,951
1973–74	1st	59	23	.720	+5.0	Larry Costello	373,135
1974–75	4th	38	44	.463	9.0	Larry Costello	425,173
1975–76	1st	38	44	.463	+2.0	Larry Costello	426,784
1976–77	6th	30	52	.366	20.0	Larry Costello (3–15), Don Nelson (27–37)	396,947
1977–78	2nd	44	38	.537	4.0	Don Nelson	435,057
1978–79	3rd (Tie)	38	44	.463	10.0	Don Nelson	443,926
1979–80	1st	49	33	.598	+2.0	Don Nelson	446,972
				Eastern Conference Central Division			
1980–81	1st	60	22	.732	+15.0	Don Nelson	448,366
1981–82	1st	55	27	.671	+13.0	Don Nelson	443,288
1982–83	1st	51	31	.622	+8.0	Don Nelson	425,572
1983–84	1st	50	32	.610	+1.0	Don Nelson	393,301
1984–85	1st	59	23	.720	+13.0	Don Nelson	422,924
1985–86	1st	57	25	.695	+7.0	Don Nelson	443,064
1986–87	3rd	50	32	.610	7.0	Don Nelson	451,797
1987–88	4th (Tie)	42	40	.512	12.0	Del Harris	441,615
1988–89	4th	49	33	.598	14.0	Del Harris	700,984
1989–90	3rd	44	38	.537	15.0	Del Harris	659,602
1990–91	3rd	48	34	.585	13.0	Del Harris	673,687
1991–92	6th (Tie)	31	51	.378	36.0	Del Harris (8–9), Frank Hamblen (23–42)	635,515
1992–93	7th	28	54	.341	29.0	Mike Dunleavy	660,939
1993–94	6th	20	62	.244	37.0	Mike Dunleavy	634,047
1994–95	6th	34	48	.415	18.0	Mike Dunleavy	670,720
1995–96	7th	25	57	.305	47.0	Mike Dunleavy	647,088
1996–97	7th	33	49	.402	36.0	Chris Ford	634,999
1997–98	7th	36	46	.439	26.0	Chris Ford	638,034
1998–99	4th	28	22	.560	5.0	George Karl	381,948
1999–00	4th (Tie)	42	40	.512	14.0	George Karl	628,605
2000–01	1st	52	30	.634	+5.0	George Karl	683,125
2001–02	5th	41	41	.500	9.0	George Karl	745,305
2002–03	4th	42	40	.512	8.0	George Karl	665,966

Year	Finish	Wins	Losses	Percentage	Games Behind	Head Coach	Attendance
2003–04	3rd (Tie)	41	41	.500	20.0	Terry Porter	690,180
2004–05	5th	30	52	.366	24.0	Terry Porter	637,009
2005–06	5th	40	42	.488	24.0	Terry Stotts	681,337
2006–07	5th	28	54	.341	25.0	Terry Stotts (23–41), Larry Krystkowiak (5–13)	663,629
2007–08	5th	26	56	.317	33.0	Larry Krystkowiak	639,421
2008–09	5th	34	48	.415	32.0	Scott Skiles	630,976
2009–10	2nd	46	36	.561	15.0	Scott Skiles	619,453
2010–11	3rd	35	47	.427	27.0	Scott Skiles	631,912
2011–12	3rd	31	35	.470	19.0	Scott Skiles	485,717
2012–13	3rd	38	44	.463	11.5	Scott Skiles (16–16), Jim Boylan (22–28)	616,469
2013–14	5th	15	67	.183	41.0	Larry Drew	552,067
2014–15	3rd	41	41	.500	12.0	Jason Kidd	593,910
2015–16	5th	33	49	.402	24.0	Jason Kidd	621,808
2016–17	2nd (Tie)	42	40	.512	9.0	Jason Kidd	648,952
2017–18	3rd	44	38	.537	6.0	Jason Kidd (23–22), Joe Prunty (21–16)	685,303
2018–19	1st	60	22	.732	+12.0	Mike Budenholzer	721,692
2019–20	1st	56	17	.767	+11.0	Mike Budenholzer	549,036
2020–21	1st	46	26	.639	+12.0	Mike Budenholzer	64,780
2021–22	1st	51	31	.622	+5.0	Mike Budenholzer	715,581

1998–99: 50-game season.

2011–12: 66-game season.

2019–20: 65-to-75-game season.

2020–21: 72-game season.

Awards

Most Valuable Player

Kareem Abdul-Jabbar, center, 1970–71
Kareem Abdul-Jabbar, center, 1971–72
Kareem Abdul-Jabbar, center, 1973–74
Giannis Antetokounmpo, forward, 2018–19
Giannis Antetokounmpo, forward, 2019–20

Rookie of the Year

Kareem Abdul-Jabbar, center, 1969–70
Malcolm Brogdon, guard, 2016–17

Defensive Player of the Year

Sidney Moncrief, guard, 1982–83
Sidney Moncrief, guard, 1983–84
Giannis Antetokounmpo, forward, 2019–20

Sixth Man of the Year

Ricky Pierce, guard, 1986–87
Ricky Pierce, guard, 1989–90

Most Improved Player

Giannis Antetokounmpo, forward, 2016–17

All-NBA First Team

Kareem Abdul-Jabbar, 1971–72
Kareem Abdul-Jabbar, 1970–71
Kareem Abdul-Jabbar, 1972–73
Kareem Abdul-Jabbar, 1973–74
Marques Johnson, 1978–79
Sidney Moncrief, 1982–83
Giannis Antetokounmpo, 2018–19
Giannis Antetokounmpo, 2019–20
Giannis Antetokounmpo, 2020–21
Giannis Antetokounmpo, 2021–22

All-Defensive First Team

Kareem Abdul-Jabbar, 1973–74
Kareem Abdul-Jabbar, 1974–75
Sidney Moncrief, 1982–83
Sidney Moncrief, 1983–84
Sidney Moncrief, 1984–85
Paul Pressey, 1984–85
Sidney Moncrief, 1985–86

Paul Pressey, 1985–86
Alvin Robertson, 1990–91
Giannis Antetokounmpo, 2018–19
Eric Bledsoe, 2018–19
Giannis Antetokounmpo, 2019–20
Giannis Antetokounmpo, 2020–21
Jrue Holiday, 2020–21

All-Rookie First Team

Kareem Abdul-Jabbar, 1969–70
Bob Dandridge, 1969–70
Marques Johnson, 1977–78
Vin Baker, 1993–94
Glenn Robinson, 1994–95
Andrew Bogut, 2005–06
Brandon Jennings, 2009–10
Malcolm Brogdon, 2016–17

Coach of the Year

Don Nelson, 1982–83
Don Nelson, 1984–85
Mike Budenholzer, 2018–19

Hall of Famers Who Played for the Bucks
Kareem Abdul-Jabbar, center, 1969–75
Ray Allen, guard, 1996–2003
Tiny Archibald, guard, 1983–84
Dave Cowens, forward, 1982–83
Bob Dandridge, forward, 1969–77;
    1981–82
Adrian Dantley, forward, 1990–91
Wayne Embry, center, 1968–69
Alex English, forward, 1976–78
Toni Kukoč, forward, 2002–06
Bob Lanier, center, 1979–84
Moses Malone, center, 1991–93
Sidney Moncrief, guard, 1979–89
Gary Payton, guard, 2002–03
Oscar Robertson, guard, 1970–74
Guy Rodgers, guard, 1968–70
Jack Sikma, center, 1986–91

Retired Numbers
1 .... Oscar Robertson
2 .... Junior Bridgeman
4 .... Sidney Moncrief
8 .... Marques Johnson
10 .... Bob Dandridge
14 .... Jon McGlocklin
16 .... Bob Lanier
32 .... Brian Winters
33 .... Kareem Abdul-Jabbar

League Leaders, Offense
Points
Kareem Abdul-Jabbar, 1969–70... 2361
Kareem Abdul-Jabbar, 1970–71... 2596
Kareem Abdul-Jabbar, 1971–72... 2822

Three Pointers
Ray Allen, 2001–02 229
Ray Allen*, 2002–03 201
*123 with Mil. Bucks and 78 with Sea. Sonics.

Assists
none

Scoring Average
Kareem Abdul-Jabbar, 1970–71.... 34.8
Kareem Abdul-Jabbar, 1971–72.... 31.7

Field Goal Percentage
none

Three Point Percentage
Craig Hodges, 1985–86 .... .451
Craig Hodges*, 1987–88 .... .491
Dell Curry, 1998–99 .... .476
George Hill, 2019–20 .... .460
*.466 with Mil. Bucks and .544 with Pho. Suns.

Free Throw Percentage
Flynn Robinson, 1969–70 .... .898
Jack Sikma, 1987–88 .... .922
Malcolm Brogdon, 2018–19 .... .928

Assists Average
none

Offensive Rebounds
none

League Leaders, Defense
Defensive Rebounds
Giannis Antetokounmpo, 2019–20.. 716

Total Rebounds
none

Steals
Alvin Robertson, 1990–91 246

Blocks
none

Rebounds Average
none

Steals Average
Alvin Robertson, 1990–91 .... 3.0

Blocks Average
Kareem Abdul-Jabbar, 1974–75 ...... 3.6
Andrew Bogut, 2010–11 .... 2.6

Feats
50-Point Game
57 .... Michael Redd (vs. Uta. Jazz),
    Nov. 11, 2006
55 ... Kareem Abdul-Jabbar (vs. Bos. Celtics),
    Dec. 10, 1971
55 ... Brandon Jennings (vs. G.S. Warriors),
    Nov. 14, 2009
53 ... Kareem Abdul-Jabbar (@ Cle. Cavaliers),
    Nov. 4, 1970
53 ... Kareem Abdul-Jabbar (@ Bos. Celtics),
    Jan. 27, 1971
53 ... Kareem Abdul-Jabbar (@ Cle. Cavaliers),
    Feb. 9, 1972
53 ... Kareem Abdul-Jabbar (vs. Phi. 76ers),
    Feb. 18, 1972
52 ... Kareem Abdul-Jabbar (vs. Atl. Hawks),
    Jan. 2, 1975
52 .... Michael Redd (vs. Chi. Bulls),
    Mar. 4, 2007
52 ... Giannis Antetokounmpo (vs. Phi. 76ers),
    Mar. 17, 2019
51 ... Kareem Abdul-Jabbar (vs. Sea. Sonics),
    Feb. 21, 1970

51 ... Kareem Abdul-Jabbar (@ Bos. Celtics),
    Feb. 13, 1972
51 ... Khris Middleton (vs. Was. Wizards),
    Jan. 28, 2020
50 ... Kareem Abdul-Jabbar (@ L.A. Lakers),
    Mar. 17, 1972
50 ... Kareem Abdul-Jabbar (vs. Por. Blazers),
    Jan. 19, 1975
50 ... Giannis Antetokounmpo (vs. Uta. Jazz),
    Nov. 25, 2019
50 ... Giannis Antetokounmpo (vs. Ind. Pacers),
    Feb. 15, 2022

20-Assist Game
24 .... Ramon Sessions (vs. Chi. Bulls),
    Apr. 14, 2008
21 .... Guy Rodgers (vs. Det. Pistons),
    Oct. 31, 1968

30-Rebound Game
33 .... Swen Nater (vs. Atl. Hawks),
    Dec. 19, 1976
30 ... Kareem Abdul-Jabbar (@ Bos. Celtics),
    Feb. 28, 1971

8-Steal Game
10 .... Alvin Robertson (vs. Uta. Jazz),
    Nov. 19, 1990
9 .... Quinn Buckner (vs. Ind. Pacers),
    Jan. 2, 1977
9 .... Eric Murdock (@ Was. Bullets),
    Apr. 2, 1994
8 .... Quinn Buckner (vs. N.Y. Nets),
    Nov. 27, 1976
8 .... Alvin Robertson (@ Mia. Heat),
    Nov. 6, 1990

10-Block Game
10 ... Kareem Abdul-Jabbar (vs. Det. Pistons),
    Nov. 3, 1973
10 .... Larry Sanders (@ Min. T'Wolves),
    Nov. 30, 2012

Multiple Triple-Doubles in a Single Season
7 ...... Giannis Antetokounmpo, 2020–21
5 ...... Giannis Antetokounmpo, 2015–16
5 ...... Giannis Antetokounmpo, 2018–19
4 ...... Giannis Antetokounmpo, 2019–20
4 ...... Giannis Antetokounmpo, 2021–22
3 .... Oscar Robertson, 1970–71
3 .... Kareem Abdul-Jabbar, 1973–74
3 .... Alvin Robertson, 1990–91
3 ...... Giannis Antetokounmpo, 2016–17
2 .... Kareem Abdul-Jabbar, 1972–73
2 .... Oscar Robertson, 1973–74

2...................Sidney Moncrief, 1983–84
2...................Sidney Moncrief, 1984–85
2....................... Paul Pressey, 1986–87
2....................... Paul Pressey, 1987–88
2.................. Alvin Robertson, 1989–90
2.........................Sam Cassell, 2002–03

Postseason Play

1970 Eastern Division Semifinals
vs. Phi. 76ers, won (4–1)
Eastern Division Finals
vs. N.Y. Knicks, lost (4–1)
1971 Western Conference Semifinals
vs. S.F. Warriors, won (4–1)
Western Conference Finals
vs. L.A. Lakers, won (4–1)
NBA Finals vs. Bal. Bullets,
won (4–0)
1972 Western Conference Semifinals
vs. G.S. Warriors, won (4–1)
Western Conference Finals
vs. L.A. Lakers, lost (4–2)
1973 Western Conference Semifinals
vs. G.S. Warriors, lost (4–2)
1974 Western Conference Semifinals
vs. L.A. Lakers, won (4–1)
Western Conference Finals
vs. Chi. Bulls, won (4–0)
NBA Finals vs. Bos. Celtics,
lost (4–3)
1976 Western Conference First Round
vs. Det. Pistons, lost (2–1)
1978 Western Conference First Round
vs. Pho. Suns, won (2–0)
Western Conference Semifinals
vs. Den. Nuggets, lost (4–3)
1980 Western Conference Semifinals
vs. Sea. Sonics, lost (4–3)
1981 Eastern Conference Semifinals
vs. Phi. 76ers, lost (4–3)
1982 Eastern Conference Semifinals
vs. Phi. 76ers, lost (4–2)

1983 Eastern Conference Semifinals
vs. Bos. Celtics, won (4–0)
Eastern Conference Finals
vs. Phi. 76ers, lost (4–1)
1984 Eastern Conference First Round
vs. Atl. Hawks, won (3–2)
Eastern Conference Semifinals
vs. N.J. Nets, won (4–2)
Eastern Conference Finals
vs. Bos. Celtics, lost (4–1)
1985 Eastern Conference First Round
vs. Chi. Bulls, won (3–1)
Eastern Conference Semifinals
vs. Phi. 76ers, lost (4–0)
1986 Eastern Conference First Round
vs. N.J. Nets, won (3–0)
Eastern Conference Semifinals
vs. Phi. 76ers, won (4–3)
Eastern Conference Finals
vs. Bos. Celtics, lost (4–0)
1987 Eastern Conference First Round
vs. Phi. 76ers, won (3–2)
Eastern Conference Semifinals
vs. Bos. Celtics, lost (4–3)
1988 Eastern Conference First Round
vs. Atl. Hawks, lost (3–2)
1989 Eastern Conference First Round
vs. Atl. Hawks, won (3–2)
Eastern Conference Semifinals
vs. Det. Pistons, lost (4–0)
1990 Eastern Conference First Round
vs. Chi. Bulls, lost (3–1)
1991 Eastern Conference First Round
vs. Phi. 76ers, lost (3–0)
1999 Eastern Conference First Round
vs. Ind. Pacers, lost (3–0)
2000 Eastern Conference First Round
vs. Ind. Pacers, lost (3–2)
2001 Eastern Conference First Round
vs. Orl. Magic, won (3–1)
Eastern Conference Semifinals
vs. Cha. Hornets, won (4–3)

Eastern Conference Finals
vs. Phi. 76ers, lost (4–3)
2003 Eastern Conference First Round
vs. N.J. Nets, lost (4–2)
2004 Eastern Conference First Round
vs. Det. Pistons, lost (4–1)
2006 Eastern Conference First Round
vs. Det. Pistons, lost (4–1)
2010 Eastern Conference First Round
vs. Atl. Hawks, lost (4–3)
2013 Eastern Conference First Round
vs. Mia. Heat, lost (4–0)
2015 Eastern Conference First Round
vs. Chi. Bulls, lost (4–2)
2017 Eastern Conference First Round
vs. Tor. Raptors, lost (4–2)
2018 Eastern Conference First Round
vs. Bos. Celtics, lost (4–3)
2019 Eastern Conference First Round
vs. Det. Pistons, won (4–0)
Eastern Conference Semifinals
vs. Bos. Celtics, won (4–1)
Eastern Conference Finals
vs. Tor. Raptors, lost (4–2)
2020 Eastern Conference First Round
vs. Orl. Magic, won (4–1)
Eastern Conference Semifinals
vs. Mia. Heat, lost (4–1)
2021 Eastern Conference First Round
vs. Mia. Heat, won (4–0)
Eastern Conference Semifinals vs.
Brk. Nets, won (4–3)
Eastern Conference Finals
vs. Atl. Hawks, won (4–2)
NBA Finals vs. Pho. Suns,
won (4–2)
2022 Eastern Conference First Round
vs. Chi. Bulls, won (4–1)
Eastern Conference Semifinals
vs. Bos. Celtics, lost (4–3)

New York Knicks

Dates of Operation: 1946–present (76 seasons)
Overall Record: 2877 wins, 3064 losses (.484)
Arenas: Madison Square Garden (III), 1946–68; Madison Square Garden (IV), 1968–present
(capacity: 19,812)
Other Name: Knickerbockers

Year-by-Year Finishes

Year	Finish	Wins	Losses	Percentage	Games Behind	Head Coach	Attendance
				BAA Eastern Division			
1946–47	3rd	33	27	.550	16.0	Neil Cohalan	129,329
1947–48	2nd	26	22	.542	1.0	Joe Lapchick	165,155
1948–49	2nd	32	28	.533	6.0	Joe Lapchick	211,284
				NBA Eastern Division			
1949–50	2nd	40	28	.588	13.0	Joe Lapchick	186,682
1950–51	3rd	36	30	.545	4.0	Joe Lapchick	146,347
1951–52	3rd	37	29	.561	3.0	Joe Lapchick	140,746
1952–53	1st	47	23	.671	+0.5	Joe Lapchick	195,240
1953–54	1st	44	28	.611	+2.0	Joe Lapchick	221,079
1954–55	2nd	38	34	.528	5.0	Joe Lapchick	214,125
1955–56	3rd (Tie)	35	37	.486	10.0	Joe Lapchick (26–25), Vince Boryla (9–12)	273,641
1956–57	4th	36	36	.500	8.0	Vince Boryla	288,998
1957–58	4th	35	37	.486	14.0	Vince Boryla	268,304
1958–59	2nd	40	32	.556	12.0	Fuzzy Levane	326,674
1959–60	4th	27	48	.360	32.0	Fuzzy Levane (8–19), Carl Braun (19–29)	335,578
1960–61	4th	21	58	.266	36.0	Carl Braun	326,895
1961–62	4th	29	51	.363	31.0	Eddie Donovan (29–51)	265,153
1962–63	4th	21	59	.263	37.0	Eddie Donovan (29–51)	302,775
1963–64	4th	22	58	.275	37.0	Eddie Donovan (29–51)	293,704
1964–65	4th	31	49	.388	31.0	Eddie Donovan (12–26), Harry Gallatin (19–23)	322,870
1965–66	4th	30	50	.375	25.0	Harry Gallatin (6–15), Dick McGuire (24–35)	369,812
1966–67	4th	36	45	.444	32.0	Dick McGuire	410,057
1967–68	3rd	43	39	.524	19.0	Dick McGuire (15–23), Red Holzman (28–16)	534,568
1968–69	3rd	54	28	.659	3.0	Red Holzman	569,153
1969–70	1st	60	22	.732	+4.0	Red Holzman	761,226
				Eastern Conference Atlantic Division			
1970–71	1st	52	30	.634	+5.0	Red Holzman	763,487
1971–72	2nd	48	34	.585	8.0	Red Holzman	785,298
1972–73	2nd	57	25	.695	11.0	Red Holzman	790,031
1973–74	2nd	49	33	.598	7.0	Red Holzman	784,433
1974–75	3rd	40	42	.488	20.0	Red Holzman	760,786
1975–76	4th	38	44	.463	16.0	Red Holzman	672,745
1976–77	3rd	40	42	.488	28.0	Red Holzman	644,811

Year	Finish	Wins	Losses	Percentage	Games Behind	Head Coach	Attendance
1977–78	2nd	43	39	.524	12.0	Willis Reed	626,815
1978–79	4th	31	51	.378	23.0	Willis Reed (6–8), Red Holzman (25–43)	545,715
1979–80	3rd (Tie)	39	43	.476	22.0	Red Holzman	508,597
1980–81	3rd	50	32	.610	12.0	Red Holzman	544,641
1981–82	5th	33	49	.402	30.0	Red Holzman	451,140
1982–83	4th	44	38	.537	21.0	Hubie Brown	438,823
1983–84	3rd	47	35	.573	15.0	Hubie Brown	487,649
1984–85	5th	24	58	.293	39.0	Hubie Brown	457,137
1985–86	5th	23	59	.280	44.0	Hubie Brown	592,484
1986–87	4th (Tie)	24	58	.293	35.0	Hubie Brown (4–12), Bob Hill (20–46)	538,048
1987–88	2nd (Tie)	38	44	.463	19.0	Rick Pitino	586,752
1988–89	1st	52	30	.634	+6.0	Rick Pitino	746,851
1989–90	3rd	45	37	.549	8.0	Stu Jackson	730,432
1990–91	3rd	39	43	.476	17.0	Stu Jackson (7–8), John MacLeod (32–35)	654,962
1991–92	1st (Tie)	51	31	.622	—	Pat Riley	726,608
1992–93	1st	60	22	.732	+12.0	Pat Riley	804,840
1993–94	1st	57	25	.695	+7.0	Pat Riley	810,193
1994–95	2nd	55	27	.671	2.0	Pat Riley	810,283
1995–96	2nd	47	35	.573	13.0	Don Nelson (34–25), Jeff Van Gundy (13–10)	810,283
1996–97	2nd	57	25	.695	4.0	Jeff Van Gundy	790,520
1997–98	2nd (Tie)	43	39	.524	12.0	Jeff Van Gundy	810,283
1998–99	4th	27	23	.540	6.0	Jeff Van Gundy	494,075
1999–00	2nd	50	32	.610	2.0	Jeff Van Gundy	810,103
2000–01	3rd	48	34	.585	8.0	Jeff Van Gundy	810,283
2001–02	7th	30	52	.366	22.0	Jeff Van Gundy (10–9), Don Chaney (20–43)	810,283
2002–03	5th (Tie)	37	45	.451	12.0	Don Chaney	779,479
2003–04	3rd	39	43	.476	8.0	Don Chaney (15–24), Herb Williams (1–0), Lenny Wilkens (23–19)	785,739
2004–05	4th (Tie)	33	49	.402	12.0	Lenny Wilkens (17–22), Herb Williams (16–27)	800,144
2005–06	5th	23	59	.280	26.0	Larry Brown	776,176
2006–07	4th	33	49	.402	14.0	Isiah Thomas	770,617
2007–08	5th	23	59	.280	43.0	Isiah Thomas	783,739
2008–09	5th	32	50	.390	30.0	Mike D'Antoni	790,801
2009–10	3rd	29	53	.354	21.0	Mike D'Antoni	799,550
2010–11	2nd	42	40	.512	14.0	Mike D'Antoni	808,879
2011–12	2nd	36	30	.545	3.0	Mike D'Antoni (18–24), Mike Woodson (18–6)	652,179
2012–13	1st	54	28	.659	+5.0	Mike Woodson	780,353
2013–14	3rd	37	45	.451	11.0	Mike Woodson	812,292
2014–15	5th	17	65	.207	32.0	Derek Fisher	812,292
2015–16	3rd	32	50	.390	24.0	Derek Fisher (23–31), Kurt Rambis (9–19)	812,292
2016–17	3rd	31	51	.378	22.0	Jeff Hornacek	810,741
2017–18	4th	29	53	.354	30.0	Jeff Hornacek	792,608
2018–19	5th	17	65	.207	41.0	David Fizdale	779,087

Year	Finish	Wins	Losses	Percentage	Games Behind	Head Coach	Attendance
2019–20	5th	21	45	.318	29.0	David Fizdale (4–18), Mike Miller (17–27)	620,789
2020–21	3rd	41	31	.569	8.0	Tom Thibodeau	42,131
2021–22	5th	37	45	.451	14.0	Tom Thibodeau	763,484

1998–99: 50-game season.
2011–12: 66-game season.
2019–20: 65-to-75-game season.
2020–21: 72-game season.

Awards

Most Valuable Player
Willis Reed, center, 1969–70

Rookie of the Year
Willis Reed, center, 1964–65
Patrick Ewing, center, 1985–86
Mark Jackson, guard, 1987–88

Defensive Player of the Year
Tyson Chandler, center, 2011–12

Sixth Man of the Year
Anthony Mason, forward, 1994–95
John Starks, guard, 1996–97
J.R. Smith, guard, 2012–13

Most Improved Player
Julius Randle, forward, 2020–21

All-NBA First Team
Harry Gallatin, 1953 54
Walt Frazier, 1969–70
Willis Reed, 1969–70
Walt Frazier, 1971–72
Walt Frazier, 1973–74
Walt Frazier, 1974–75
Bernard King, 1983–84
Bernard King, 1984–85
Patrick Ewing, 1989–90

All-Defensive First Team
Dave DeBusschere*, 1968–69
Walt Frazier, 1968–69
Dave DeBusschere, 1969–70
Walt Frazier, 1969–70
Willis Reed, 1969–70
Dave DeBusschere, 1970–71
Walt Frazier, 1970–71
Dave DeBusschere, 1971–72
Walt Frazier, 1971–72
Dave DeBusschere, 1972–73
Walt Frazier, 1972–73
Dave DeBusschere, 1973–74
Walt Frazier, 1973–74

Walt Frazier, 1974–75
Micheal Ray Richardson, 1979–80
Micheal Ray Richardson, 1980–81
Charles Oakley, 1993–94
Tyson Chandler, 2012–13
* 47 games with N.Y. Knicks and 29 games with Det. Pistons.

All-Rookie First Team
Art Heyman, 1963–64
Jim Barnes, 1964–65
Howard Komives, 1964–65
Wilils Reed, 1964–65
Dick Van Arsdale, 1965–66
Cazzie Russell, 1966–67
Walt Frazier, 1967–68
Phil Jackson, 1967–68
Bill Cartwright, 1979–80
Darrell Walker, 1983–84
Patrick Ewing, 1985–86
Mark Jackson, 1987–88
Channing Frye, 2005–06
Landry Fields, 2010–11
Tim Hardaway Jr., 2013–14
Kristaps Porziņģis, 2015–16
Willy Hernangómez, 2016–17

Coach of the Year
Red Holzman, 1969–70
Pat Riley, 1992–93

Hall of Famers Who Played for the Knicks
Walt Bellamy, center, 1965–69
Bill Bradley, forward, 1967–77
Carl Braun, guard, 1947–50; 1952–61
Maurice Cheeks, guard, 1989–91
Dave DeBusschere, forward, 1968–74
Patrick Ewing, center, 1985–2000
Walt Frazier, guard, 1967–77
Harry Gallatin, forward, 1948–57
Tom Gola, guard-forward, 1962–66
Richie Guerin, guard, 1956–64

Spencer Haywood, forward, 1975–79
Jason Kidd, guard, 2012–13
Bernard King, forward, 1982–85; 1986–87
Jerry Lucas, center-forward, 1971–74
Slater Martin, guard, 1956–57
Bob McAdoo, center-forward, 1976–79
Tracy McGrady, guard, 2009–10
Alfred McGuire, guard, 1951–54
Dick McGuire, guard, 1949–57
Earl Monroe, guard, 1971–80
Dikembe Mutombo, center, 2003–04
Willis Reed, center-forward, 1964–74
Paul Westphal, guard, 1981–84

Retired Numbers
10	Walt Frazier
12	Dick Barnett
15	Dick McGuire
15	Earl Monroe
19	Willis Reed
22	Dave DeBusschere
24	Bill Bradley
33	Patrick Ewing
613	Red Holzman

League Leaders, Offense

Points
none

Three Pointers
John Starks, 1994–95 217

Assists
Dick McGuire, 1949–50 386
Micheal Ray Richardson, 1979–80 .. 832
Stephon Marbury*, 2003–04 719
* 438 with N.Y. Knicks and 281 with Pho. Suns

Scoring Average
Bernard King, 1984–85 .... 32.9
Carmelo Anthony, 2012–13 .... 28.7

Field Goal Percentage

Kenny Sears, 1958–59 .... .490

Kenny Sears, 1959–60 .... .477

Tyson Chandler, 2011–12 .... .679

Mitchell Robinson, 2019–20 .... .742

Three Point Percentage

Campy Russell, 1981–82 .... .439

José Calderón, 2011–12 .... .472

Free Throw Percentage

Allan Houston, 2002–03 .... .919

Assists Average

Micheal Ray Richardson, 1979–80. 10.2

League Leaders, Defense

Offensive Rebounds

Defensive Rebounds

Patrick Ewing, 1992–93 789

Total Rebounds

Harry Gallatin, 1953–54 1098

Steals

Micheal Ray Richardson, 1979–80.. 265

Micheal Ray Richardson, 1980–81.. 232

Micheal Ray Richardson, 1981–82.. 213

Blocks

Rebounds Average

Harry Gallatin, 1953–54 .... 15.3

Steals Average

Micheal Ray Richardson, 1979–80... 3.2

Blocks Average

Feats

50-Point Game

62...Carmelo Anthony (vs. Cha. Bobcats),
Jan. 24, 2014

60 .... Bernard King (vs. N.J. Nets),
Dec. 25, 1984

57...Richie Guerin (vs. Syr. Nationals),
Dec. 11, 1959

55 .... Bernard King (vs. N.J. Nets),
Feb. 16, 1985

53 .... Willis Reed (@ L.A. Lakers),
Nov. 1, 1967

53 .... Allan Houston (@ L.A. Lakers),
Feb. 16, 2003

52 .... Bernard King (vs. Ind. Pacers),
Nov. 24, 1984

52 .... Jamal Crawford (vs. Bos. Celtics),
Jan. 26, 2007

51 .... Richie Guerin (vs. Bos. Celtics),
Feb. 14, 1962

51 .... Patrick Ewing (vs. Bos. Celtics),
Mar. 24, 1990

50 ....Richie Guerin (@ Phi. Warriors),
Feb. 25, 1962

50 .... Bernard King (@ S.A. Spurs),
Jan. 31, 1984

50 .... Bernard King (@ Dal. Mavericks),
Feb. 1, 1984

50 .... Patrick Ewing (vs. Cha. Hornets),
Dec. 1, 1990

50 .... Allan Houston (vs. Mil. Bucks),
Mar. 16, 2003

50 ....Carmelo Anthony (@ Mia. Heat),
Apr. 2, 2013

20-Assist Game

22 .... Chris Duhon (vs. G.S. Warriors),
Nov. 29, 2008

21 .... Richie Guerin (vs. St.L. Hawks),
Dec. 12, 1958

30-Rebound Game

33 ....Harry Gallatin (@ Ft.W. Pistons),
Mar. 15, 1953

33 .... Willis Reed (vs. Cin. Royals),
Feb. 2, 1971

31 .... Harry Gallatin (vs. Ft.W. Pistons),
Nov. 30, 1954

30...Harry Gallatin (vs. Ft.W. Pistons),
Jan. 16, 1954

30 .... Harry Gallatin (vs. Bal. Bullets),
Feb. 6, 1954

30 .... Ray Felix (vs. Ft.W. Pistons),
Feb. 17, 1955

30 .... Willis Reed (vs. Bal. Bullets),
Nov. 12, 1970

8-Steal Game

9...Micheal Ray Richardson (@ Chi. Bulls),
Dec. 23, 1980

8...Micheal Ray Richardson (vs. S.A. Spurs),
Jan. 6, 1981

8 .... Chris McNealy (vs. Was. Bullets),
Mar. 4, 1986

8 .... Sergio Rodríguez (vs. Mil. Bucks),
Feb. 22, 2010

10-Block Game

10 ....Joe Meriweather (@ Atl. Hawks),
Dec. 12, 1979

10...Dikembe Mutombo (vs. N.J. Nets),
Jan. 4, 2004

Multiple Triple-Doubles in a Single Season

8 .... Walt Frazier, 1968–69

7 ...... Micheal Ray Richardson, 1979–80

7 ...... Micheal Ray Richardson, 1981–82

6 .... Richie Guerin, 1961–62

6 .... Julius Randle, 2020–21

5 .... Richie Guerin, 1960–61

4 .... Walt Frazier, 1970–71

4 .... Jerry Lucas, 1972–73

4 ...... Micheal Ray Richardson, 1980–81

2 .... Richie Guerin, 1957–58

2 .... Richie Guerin, 1959–60

2 ....Walt Bellamy, 1966–67

2 .... Walt Frazier, 1967–68

2 .... Walt Frazier, 1969–70

2 .... Walt Frazier, 1973–74

2 .... Walt Frazier, 1974–75

2 .... Mark Jackson, 1987–88

2 .... Mark Jackson, 1988–89

2 ....Immanuel Quickley, 2021–22

Postseason Play

1947 BAA Quarterfinals vs. Cle. Rebels,
won (2–1)

BAA Semifinals vs. Phi. Warriors,
lost (2–0)

1948 BAA Quarterfinals vs. Bal. Bullets,
lost (2–1)

1949 BAA Eastern Division Semifinals
vs. Bal. Bullets, won (2–1)

BAA Eastern Division Finals
vs. Was. Capitols, lost (2–1)

1950 NBA Eastern Division Semifinals
vs. Was. Capitols, won (2–0)

NBA Eastern Division Finals
vs. Syr. Nationals, lost (2–1)

1951 Eastern Division Semifinals
vs. Bos. Celtics, won (2–0)

Eastern Division Finals
vs. Syr. Nationals, won (3–2)

NBA Finals vs. Roc. Royals,
lost (4–3)

1952 Eastern Division Semifinals
vs. Bos. Celtics, won (2–1)

Eastern Division Finals
vs. Syr. Nationals, won (3–1)

NBA Finals vs. Min. Lakers,
lost (4–3)

1953 Eastern Division Semifinals
vs. Bal. Bullets, won (2–0)
Eastern Division Finals
vs. Bos. Celtics, won (3–1)
NBA Finals vs. Min. Lakers,
lost (4–1)

1954 Eastern Division Round Robin,
eliminated

1955 Eastern Division Semifinals
vs. Bos. Celtics, lost (2–1)

1956 Eastern Division Third Place
Tiebreaker
vs. Syr. Nationals, lost

1959 Eastern Division Semifinals
vs. Syr. Nationals, lost (2–0)

1967 Eastern Division Semifinals
vs. Bos. Celtics, lost (3–1)

1968 Eastern Division Semifinals
vs. Phi. 76ers, lost (4–2)

1969 Eastern Division Semifinals
vs. Bal. Bullets, won (4–0)
Eastern Division Finals
vs. Bos. Celtics, lost (4–2)

1970 Eastern Division Semifinals
vs.Bal. Bullets, won (4–3)
Eastern Division Finals
vs. Mil. Bucks, won (4–1)
NBA Finals vs. L.A. Lakers,
won (4–3)

1971 Eastern Conference Semifinals
vs. Atl. Hawks, won (4–1)
Eastern Conference Finals
vs. Bal. Bullets, lost (4–3)

1972 Eastern Conference Semifinals
vs. Bal. Bullets, won (4–2)
Eastern Conference Finals
vs. Bos. Celtics, won (4–1)
NBA Finals vs. L.A. Lakers,
lost (4–1)

1973 Eastern Conference Semifinals
vs. Bal. Bullets, won (4–1)
Eastern Conference Finals
vs. Bos. Celtics, won (4–3)
NBA Finals vs. L.A. Lakers,
won (4–1)

1974 Eastern Conference Semifinals
vs. Cap. Bullets, won (4–3)

Eastern Conference Finals
vs. Bos. Celtics, lost (4–1)

1975 Eastern Conference First Round
vs. Hou. Rockets, lost (2–1)

1978 Eastern Conference First Round
vs. Cle. Cavaliers, won (2–0)
Eastern Conference Semifinals
vs. Phi. 76ers, lost (4–0)

1981 Eastern Conference First Round
vs. Chi. Bulls, lost (2–0)

1983 Eastern Conference First Round
vs. N.J. Nets, won (2–0)
Eastern Conference Semifinals
vs. Phi. 76ers, lost (4–0)

1984 Eastern Conference First Round
vs. Det. Pistons, won (3–2)
Eastern Conference Semifinals
vs. Bos. Celtics, lost (4–3)

1988 Eastern Conference First Round
vs. Bos. Celtics, lost (3–1)

1989 Eastern Conference First Round
vs. Phi. 76ers, won (3–0)
Eastern Conference Semifinals
vs. Chi. Bulls, lost (4–2)

1990 Eastern Conference First Round
vs. Bos. Celtics, won (3–2)
Eastern Conference Semifinals
vs. Det. Pistons, lost (4–1)

1991 Eastern Conference First Round
vs. Chi. Bulls, lost (3–0)

1992 Eastern Conference First Round
vs. Det. Pistons, won (3–2)
Eastern Conference Semifinals
vs. Chi. Bulls, lost (4–3)

1993 Eastern Conference First Round
vs. Ind. Pacers, won (3–1)
Eastern Conference Semifinals
vs. Cha. Hornets, won (4–1)
Eastern Conference Finals
vs. Chi. Bulls, lost (4–2)

1994 Eastern Conference First Round
vs. N.J. Nets, won (3–1)
Eastern Conference Semifinals
vs. Chi. Bulls, won (4–3)
Eastern Conference Finals
vs. Ind. Pacers, won (4–3)
NBA Finals vs. Hou. Rockets,
lost (4–3)

1995 Eastern Conference First Round
vs. Cle. Cavaliers, won (3–1)
Eastern Conference Semifinals
vs. Ind. Pacers, lost (4–3)

1996 Eastern Conference First Round
vs. Cle. Cavaliers, won (3–0)
Eastern Conference Semifinals
vs. Chi. Bulls, lost (4–1)

1997 Eastern Conference First Round
vs. Cha. Hornets, won (3–0)
Eastern Conference Semifinals
vs. Mia. Heat, lost (4–3)

1998 Eastern Conference First Round
vs. Mia. Heat, won (3–2)
Eastern Conference Semifinals
vs. Ind. Pacers, lost (4–1)

1999 Eastern Conference First Round
vs. Mia. Heat, won (3–2)
Eastern Conference Semifinals
vs. Atl. Hawks, won (4–0)
Eastern Conference Finals
vs. Ind. Pacers, won (4–)
NBA Finals vs. S.A. Spurs,
lost (4–1)

2000 Eastern Conference First Round
vs. Tor. Raptors, won (3–0)
Eastern Conference Semifinals
vs. Mia. Heat, won (4–3)
Eastern Conference Finals
vs. Ind. Pacers, lost (4–2)

2001 Eastern Conference First Round
vs. Tor. Raptors, lost (3–2)

2004 Eastern Conference First Round
vs. N.J. Nets, lost (4–0)

2011 Eastern Conference First Round
vs. Bos. Celtics, lost (4–0)

2012 Eastern Conference First Round
vs. Mia. Heat, lost (4–1)

2013 Eastern Conference First Round
vs. Bos. Celtics, won (4–2)
Eastern Conference Semifinals
vs. Ind. Pacers, lost (4–2)

2021 Eastern Conference First Round
vs. Atl. Hawks, lost (4–1)

Orlando Magic

Dates of Operation: 1989–present (33 seasons)
Overall Record: 1234 wins, 1405 losses (.468)
Arenas: Amway Arena (formerly Orlando Arena, 1989–99; TD Waterhouse Centre, 1999–2006),
1989–2010; Amway Center, 2010–present (capacity: 18,846)

Year-by-Year Finishes

Year	Finish	Wins	Losses	Percentage	Games Behind	Head Coach	Attendance
Eastern Conference Central Division							
1989–90	7th	18	64	.220	41.0	Matt Guokas	617,468
Western Conference Midwest Division							
1990–91	4th	31	51	.378	24.0	Matt Guokas	617,668
Eastern Conference Atlantic Division							
1991–92	7th	21	61	.256	30.0	Matt Guokas	621,191
1992–93	4th	41	41	.500	19.0	Matt Guokas	621,191
1993–94	2nd	50	32	.610	7.0	Brian Hill	626,931
1994–95	1st	57	25	.695	+2.0	Brian Hill	656,410
1995–96	1st	60	22	.732	+13.0	Brian Hill	707,168
1996–97	3rd	45	37	.549	16.0	Brian Hill (24–25), Richie Adubato (21–12)	711,311
1997–98	5th	41	41	.500	14.0	Chuck Daly	667,322
1998–99	1st (Tie)	33	17	.660	—	Chuck Daly	411,091
1999–00	4th	41	41	.500	11.0	Doc Rivers	576,409
2000–01	4th	43	39	.524	13.0	Doc Rivers	605,031
2001–02	3rd	44	38	.537	8.0	Doc Rivers	621,121
2002–03	4th	42	40	.512	7.0	Doc Rivers	605,901
2003–04	7th	21	61	.256	26.0	Doc Rivers (1–10), Johnny Davis (20–51)	589,144
Southeast Division							
2004–05	3rd	36	46	.439	23.0	Johnny Davis (31–33), Chris Jent (5–13)	597,942
2005–06	3rd	36	46	.439	16.0	Brian Hill	638,005
2006–07	3rd	40	42	.488	4.0	Brian Hill	700,887
2007–08	1st	52	30	.634	+9.0	Stan Van Gundy	709,346
2008–09	1st	59	23	.720	+12.0	Stan Van Gundy	698,768
2009–10	1st	59	23	.720	+6.0	Stan Van Gundy	715,901
2010–11	2nd	52	30	.634	6.0	Stan Van Gundy	777,852
2011–12	3rd	37	29	.561	9.0	Stan Van Gundy	623,587
2012–13	5th	20	62	.244	46.0	Jacque Vaughn	722,716
2013–14	5th	23	59	.280	31.0	Jacque Vaughn	666,046
2014–15	5th	25	57	.305	35.0	Jacque Vaughn (15–37), James Borrego (10–20)	688,194
2015–16	5th	35	47	.427	13.0	Scott Skiles	719,275
2016–17	5th	29	53	.354	20.0	Frank Vogel	727,875
2017–18	4th	25	57	.305	19.0	Frank Vogel	734,531
2018–19	1st	42	40	.512	+3.0	Steve Clifford	720,024
2019–20	2nd	33	40	.452	11.0	Steve Clifford	529,870
2020–21	5th	21	51	.292	20.0	Steve Clifford	126,463

Year	Finish	Wins	Losses	Percentage	Games Behind	Head Coach	Attendance
2021–22	5th	22	60	.268	31.0	Jamahl Mosley	622,881

1998–99: 50-game season.
2011–12: 66-game season.
2019–20: 65-to-75-game season.
2020–21: 72-game season.

Awards

Most Valuable Player
none

Rookie of the Year
Shaquille O'Neal, center, 1992–93
Mike Miller, forward, 2000–01

Defensive Player of the Year
Dwight Howard, center, 2008–09
Dwight Howard, center, 2009–10
Dwight Howard, center, 2010–11

Sixth Man of the Year
Darrell Armstrong, guard, 1998–99

Most Improved Player
Scott Skiles, guard, 1990–91
Darrell Armstrong, guard, 1998–99
Tracy McGrady, guard, 2000–01
Hedo Türkoğlu, forward, 2007–08
Ryan Anderson, forward, 2011–12

All-NBA First Team
Penny Hardaway, 1994–95
Penny Hardaway, 1995–96
Tracy McGrady, 2001–02
Tracy McGrady, 2002–03
Dwight Howard, 2007–08
Dwight Howard, 2008–09
Dwight Howard, 2009–10
Dwight Howard, 2010–11
Dwight Howard, 2011–12

All-Defensive First Team
Dwight Howard, 2008–09
Dwight Howard, 2009–10
Dwight Howard, 2010–11
Dwight Howard, 2011–12

All-Rookie First Team
Dennis Scott, 1990–91
Shaquille O'Neal, 1992–93
Penny Hardaway, 1993–94
Matt Harpring, 1998–99
Mike Miller, 2000–01
Drew Gooden, 2002–03*
Dwight Howard, 2004–05

Victor Oladipo, 2013–14
Elfrid Payton, 2014–15
Franz Wagner, 2021–22

* 19 games with Orl. Magic and 51 games with Mem. Grizzlies.

Coach of the Year
Doc Rivers, 1999–00

Hall of Famers Who Played for the Magic
Patrick Ewing, center, 2001–02
Grant Hill, forward, 2000–03; 2004–07
Tracy McGrady, guard, 2000–04
Shaquille O'Neal, center, 1992–96
Ben Wallace, forward, 1999–00
Dominique Wilkins, forward, 1998–99

Retired Numbers
6.........................The Fans (Sixth Man)

League Leaders, Offense

Points
Shaquille O'Neal, 1994–95 2315

Three Pointers
Dennis Scott, 1995–96.................. 267
Rashard Lewis, 2008–09 220
Ryan Anderson, 2011–12 166

Assists
none

Scoring Average
Shaquille O'Neal, 1994–95 .... 29.3
Tracy McGrady, 2002–03............. 32.1
Tracy McGrady, 2003–04............. 28.0

Field Goal Percantage
Shaquille O'Neal, 1993–94 .... .599
Dwight Howard, 2009–10............. .612

Three Point Percentage
none

Free Throw Percentage
none

Assists Average
none

League Leaders, Defense

Offensive Rebounds
Dwight Howard, 2008–09............. 336

Defensive Rebounds
Dwight Howard, 2007–08............. 882
Dwight Howard, 2008–09............. 757
Dwight Howard, 2009–10............. 798
Dwight Howard, 2010–11............. 789
Dwight Howard, 2011–12............. 585

Total Rebounds
Dwight Howard, 2005–06........... 1022
Dwight Howard, 2006–07........... 1008
Dwight Howard, 2007–08........... 1161
Dwight Howard, 2008–09........... 1093
Dwight Howard, 2009–10........... 1082
Dwight Howard, 2011–12............. 785

Steals
none

Blocks
Dwight Howard, 2008–09............. 231
Dwight Howard, 2009–10............. 228

Rebounds Average
Dwight Howard, 2007–08............. 14.2
Dwight Howard, 2008–09............. 13.8
Dwight Howard, 2009–10............. 13.2
Dwight Howard, 2011–12............. 14.5

Steals Average
none

Blocks Average
Dwight Howard, 2008–09............... 2.9
Dwight Howard, 2009–10............... 2.8

Feats

50-Point Game
62... Tracy McGrady (vs. Was. Wizards), Mar. 10, 2004
53...Shaquille O'Neal (vs. Min. T'Wolves), Apr. 20, 1994
52..........Tracy McGrady (vs. Chi. Bulls), Feb. 21, 2003
51...Tracy McGrady (@ Den. Nuggets), Nov. 14, 2003

50..........Nick Anderson (@ N.J. Nets),
Apr. 23, 1993

50...Tracy McGrady (vs. Was. Wizards),
Mar. 8, 2002

20-Assist Game

30.......... Scott Skiles (vs. Den. Nuggets),
Dec. 30, 1990

21...........Scott Skiles (@ Cle. Cavaliers),
Apr. 16, 1993

20...........Scott Skiles (vs. Den. Nuggets),
Mar. 8, 1991

20..............Scott Skiles (vs. Por. Blazers),
Dec. 1, 1993

30-Rebound Game

8-Steal Game

8...Nick Anderson (@ Was. Bullets), Nov.
12, 1991

10-Block Game

15...Shaquille O'Neal (@ N.J. Nets), Nov.
20, 1993

10...Dwight Howard (@ Ok.C. Thunder),
Nov. 12, 2008

**Multiple Triple-Doubles in a Single
Season**

5.......................Elfrid Payton, 2016–17

2................... Hedo Türkoğlu, 2007–08

2.......................Elfrid Payton, 2014–15

Postseason Play

1994   Eastern Conference First Round
vs. Ind. Pacers, lost (3–0)

1995   Eastern Conference First Round
vs. Bos. Celtics, won (3–1)
Eastern Conference Semifinals
vs. Chi. Bulls, won (4–2)
Eastern Conference Finals
vs. Ind. Pacers, won (4–3)
NBA Finals vs. Hou. Rockets,
lost (4–0)

1996   Eastern Conference First Round
vs. Det. Pistons, won (3–0)
Eastern Conference Semifinals
vs. Atl. Hawks, won (4–1)
Eastern Conference Finals
vs. Chi. Bulls, lost (4–0)

1997   Eastern Conference First Round
vs. Mia. Heat, lost (3–2)

1999   Eastern Conference First Round
vs. Phi. 76ers, lost (3–1)

2001   Eastern Conference First Round
vs. Mil. Bucks, lost (3–1)

2002   Eastern Conference First Round
vs. Cha. Hornets, lost (3–1)

2003   Eastern Conference First Round
vs. Det. Pistons, lost (4–3)

2007   Eastern Conference First Round
vs. Det. Pistons, lost (4–0)

2008   Eastern Conference First Round
vs. Tor. Raptors, won (4–1)
Eastern Conference Semifinals
vs. Det. Pistons, lost (4–1)

2009   Eastern Conference First Round
vs. Phi. 76ers, won (4–2)
Eastern Conference Semifinals vs.
Bos. Celtics, won (4–3)
Eastern Conference Finals
vs. Cle. Cavaliers, won (4–2)
NBA Finals vs. L.A. Lakers,
lost (4–1)

2010   Eastern Conference First Round
vs. Cha. Bobcats, won (4–0)
Eastern Conference Semifinals
vs. Atl. Hawks, won (4–0)
Eastern Conference Finals
vs. Bos. Celtics, lost (4–2)

2011   Eastern Conference First Round
vs. Atl. Hawks, lost (4–2)

2012   Eastern Conference First Round
vs. Ind. Pacers, lost (4–1)

2019   Eastern Conference First Round
vs. Tor. Raptors, lost (4–1)

2020   Eastern Conference First Round
vs. Mil. Bucks, lost (4–1)

Philadelphia 76ers

Dates of Operation: (as the Syracuse Nationals) 1949–63 (14 seasons)
Overall Record: 576 wins, 437 losses (.569)
Arenas: State Fair Coliseum, 1949–51; Onondaga County War Memorial, 1951–63

Dates of Operation: (as the Phiadelphia 76ers) 1963–present (59 seasons)
Overall Record: 2424 wins, 2340 losses (.509)
Arenas: Convention Hall, 1963–67; Wachovia Center (formerly The Spectrum, 1967–94; CoreStates Spectrum, 1994–98; First Union Center, 1998–2003) 1967–2010; Wells Fargo Center, 2010–present (capacity: 20,478)
Other Name: Sixers

Year-by-Year Finishes

Year	Finish	Wins	Losses	Percentage	Games Behind	Head Coach	Attendance
				Syracuse Nationals **Eastern Division**			
1949–50	1st	51	13	.797	+13.0	Al Cervi	N/A
1950–51	4th	32	34	.485	8.0	Al Cervi	174,094
1951–52	1st	40	26	.606	+1.0	Al Cervi	N/A
1952–53	2nd	47	24	.662	0.5	Al Cervi	N/A
1953–54	2nd (Tie)	42	30	.583	2.0	Al Cervi	N/A
1954–55	1st	43	29	.597	+5.0	Al Cervi	N/A
1955–56	3rd (Tie)	35	37	.486	10.0	Al Cervi	140,714
1956–57	2nd	38	34	.528	6.0	Al Cervi (4–8), Paul Seymour (34–26)	118,883
1957–58	2nd	41	31	.569	8.0	Paul Seymour	112,386
1958–59	3rd	35	37	.486	17.0	Paul Seymour	107,455
1959–60	3rd	45	30	.600	14.0	Paul Seymour	110,000
1960–61	3rd	38	41	.481	19.0	Alex Hannum	112,394
1961–62	3rd	41	39	.513	19.0	Alex Hannum	112,486
1962–63	2nd	48	32	.600	10.0	Alex Hannum	161,593
				Philadelphia 76ers			
1963–64	3rd	34	46	.425	25.0	Dolph Schayes	108,271
1964–65	3rd	40	40	.500	22.0	Dolph Schayes	108,729
1965–66	1st	55	25	.688	+1.0	Dolph Schayes	145,372
1966–67	1st	68	13	.840	+8.0	Alex Hannum	246,275
1967–68	1st	62	20	.756	+8.0	Alex Hannum	304,631
1968–69	2nd	55	27	.671	2.0	Jack Ramsay	361,161
1969–70	4th	42	40	.512	18.0	Jack Ramsay	311,976
				Eastern Conference Atlantic Division			
1970–71	2nd	47	35	.573	5.0	Jack Ramsay	336,815
1971–72	3rd	30	52	.366	26.0	Jack Ramsay	326,493
1972–73	4th	9	73	.110	59.0	Roy Rubin (4–47), Kevin Loughery (5–26)	182,921
1973–74	4th	25	57	.305	31.0	Gene Shue	171,159
1974–75	4th	34	48	.415	26.0	Gene Shue	296,721
1975–76	2nd (Tie)	46	36	.561	8.0	Gene Shue	509,699
1976–77	1st	50	32	.610	+6.0	Gene Shue	632,949
1977–78	1st	55	27	.671	+12.0	Gene Shue (2–4), Billy Cunningham (53–23)	644,456

Year	Finish	Wins	Losses	Percentage	Games Behind	Head Coach	Attendance
1978–79	2nd	47	35	.573	7.0	Billy Cunningham	506,485
1979–80	2nd	59	23	.720	2.0	Billy Cunningham	479,727
1980–81	1st (Tie)	62	20	.756	–	Billy Cunningham	469,355
1981–82	2nd	58	24	.707	5.0	Billy Cunningham	498,901
1982–83	1st	65	17	.793	+9.0	Billy Cunningham	612,203
1983–84	2nd	52	30	.634	10.0	Billy Cunningham	588,139
1984–85	2nd	58	24	.707	5.0	Billy Cunningham	575,415
1985–86	2nd	54	28	.659	13.0	Matt Guokas	513,459
1986–87	2nd	45	37	.549	14.0	Matt Guokas	587,748
1987–88	4th	36	46	.439	21.0	Matt Guokas (20–23), Jim Lynam (16–23)	505,245
1988–89	2nd	46	36	.561	6.0	Jim Lynam	531,715
1989–90	1st	53	29	.646	+1.0	Jim Lynam	565,926
1990–91	2nd	44	38	.537	12.0	Jim Lynam	624,582
1991–92	5th	35	47	.427	16.0	Jim Lynam	574,137
1992–93	6th	26	56	.317	34.0	Doug Moe (19–37), Fred Carter (7–19)	515,284
1993–94	6th	25	57	.305	32.0	Fred Carter	491,769
1994–95	6th	24	58	.293	33.0	John Lucas	507,806
1995–96	7th	18	64	.220	42.0	John Lucas	476,016
1996–97	6th	22	60	.268	39.0	Johnny Davis	610,974
1997–98	7th	31	51	.378	24.0	Larry Brown	655,417
1998–99	3rd	28	22	.560	5.0	Larry Brown	436,444
1999–00	3rd	49	33	.598	3.0	Larry Brown	756,956
2000–01	1st	56	26	.683	+6.0	Larry Brown	805,692
2001–02	4th	43	39	.524	9.0	Larry Brown	842,976
2002–03	2nd	48	34	.585	1.0	Larry Brown	807,097
2003–04	5th	33	49	.402	14.0	Randy Ayers (21–31), Chris Ford (12–18)	788,128
2004–05	2nd	43	39	.524	2.0	Jim O'Brien	732,686
2005–06	2nd	38	44	.463	11.0	Maurice Cheeks	677,278
2006–07	3rd	35	47	.427	12.0	Maurice Cheeks	608,603
2007–08	3rd	40	42	.488	26.0	Maurice Cheeks	609,675
2008–09	2nd	41	41	.500	21.0	Maurice Cheeks (9–14), Tony DiLeo (32–27)	647,898
2009–10	4th	27	55	.329	23.0	Eddie Jordan	583,219
2010–11	3rd	41	41	.500	15.0	Doug Collins	604,823
2011–12	3rd	35	31	.530	4.0	Doug Collins	577,597
2012–13	4th (Tie)	34	48	.415	20.0	Doug Collins	685,412
2013–14	5th	19	63	.232	29.0	Brett Brown	568,632
2014–15	4th	18	64	.220	31.0	Brett Brown	571,572
2015–16	5th	10	72	.122	46.0	Brett Brown	614,650
2016–17	4th	28	54	.341	25.0	Brett Brown	710,557
2017–18	3rd	52	30	.634	7.0	Brett Brown	833,503
2018–19	2nd	51	31	.622	7.0	Brett Brown	838,342
2019–20	3rd	43	30	.589	10.5	Brett Brown	639,491
2020–21	1st	49	23	.681	+1.0	Doc Rivers	68,583
2021–22	1st (Tie)	51	31	.622	–	Doc Rivers	846,867

1998–99: 50-game season.

2011–12: 66-game season.

2019–20: 65-to-75-game season.

2020–21: 72-game season.

Awards

Most Valuable Player

Wilt Chamberlain, center, 1965–66
Wilt Chamberlain, center, 1966–67
Wilt Chamberlain, center, 1967–68
Julius Erving, forward, 1980–81
Moses Malone, center, 1982–83
Allen Iverson, guard, 2000–01

Rookie of the Year

Allen Iverson, guard, 1996–97
Michael Carter-Williams, guard, 2013–14
Ben Simmons, guard, 2017–18

Defensive Player of the Year

Dikembe Mutombo*, center, 2000–01

*26 games with Phi. 76ers and 49 games with Atl. Hawks.

Sixth Man of the Year

Bobby Jones, forward, 1982–83
Aaron McKie, forward, 2000–01

Most Improved Player

Dana Barros, guard, 1994–95

All-NBA First Team

Dolph Schayes, 1951–52 (Syr.)
Dolph Schayes, 1952–53 (Syr.)
Dolph Schayes, 1953–54 (Syr.)
Dolph Schayes, 1954–55 (Syr.)
Dolph Schayes, 1956–57 (Syr.)
Dolph Schayes, 1957–58 (Syr.)
Wilt Chamberlain, 1965–66
Wilt Chamberlain, 1966–67
Wilt Chamberlain, 1967–68
Billy Cunningham, 1968–69
Billy Cunningham, 1969–70
Billy Cunningham, 1970–71
George McGinnis, 1975–76
Julius Erving, 1977–78
Julius Erving, 1979–80
Julius Erving, 1980–81
Julius Erving, 1981–82
Julius Erving, 1982–83
Moses Malone, 1982–83
Moses Malone, 1984–85
Charles Barkley, 1987–88
Charles Barkley, 1988–89
Charles Barkley, 1989–90
Charles Barkley, 1990–91
Allen Iverson, 1998–99
Allen Iverson, 2000–01
Allen Iverson, 2004–05

All-Defensive First Team

Bobby Jones, 1978–79
Bobby Jones, 1979–80
Bobby Jones, 1980–81
Caldwell Jones, 1980–81
Bobby Jones, 1981–82
Caldwell Jones, 1981–82
Maurice Cheeks, 1982–83
Bobby Jones, 1982–83
Moses Malone, 1982–83
Maurice Cheeks, 1983–84
Bobby Jones, 1983–84
Maurice Cheeks, 1984–85
Maurice Cheeks, 1985–86
Robert Covington, 2017–18
Dikembe Mutombo, 2000–01*
Ben Simmons, 2019–20
Ben Simmons, 2020–21

* 26 games with Phi. 76ers and 49 games with Atl. Hawks.

All-Rookie First Team

Chet Walker, 1962–63 (Syr.)
Luke Jackson, 1964–65
Billy Cunningham, 1965–66
Freddie Boyd, 1972–73
Charles Barkley, 1984–85
Hersey Hawkins, 1988–89
Allen Iverson, 1996–97
Andre Iguodala, 2004–05
Michael Carter-Williams, 2013–14
Nerlens Noel, 2014–15
Jahlil Okafor, 2015–16
Joel Embiid, 2016–17
Dario Šarić, 2016–17
Ben Simmons, 2017–18

Coach of the Year

Dolph Schayes, 1965–66
Larry Brown, 2000–01

Hall of Famers Who Played for the Nationals/76ers

Charles Barkley, forward, 1984–92
Al Cervi, guard, 1949–53 (Syr.)
Wilt Chamberlain, center, 1964–68
Maurice Cheeks, guard, 1978–89
Billy Cunningham, forward, 1965–72; 1974–76
Julius Erving, forward, 1976–87
Hal Greer, guard, 1958–73 (Syr.-Phi.)
Alex Hannum, forward, 1949–51 (Syr.)
Bailey Howell, forward, 1970–71
Allen Iverson, guard, 1996–2007; 2009–10

Bobby Jones, forward, 1978–86
Toni Kukoč, forward, 1999–2001
Earl Lloyd, forward, 1952–58 (Syr.)
Moses Malone, center, 1982–86; 1993–94
Bob McAdoo, center, 1985–86
George McGinnis, forward, 1975–78
Dikembe Mutombo, center, 2000–02
Dolph Schayes, forward-center, 1949–64 (Syr.-Phi.)
Chet Walker, forward, 1962–69 (Syr.-Phi.)
Chris Webber, forward, 2004–07
George Yardley, forward, 1958–60 (Syr.)

Retired Numbers

DZ .... Dave Zinkoff
2 .... Moses Malone
3 .... Allen Iverson
4 .... Dolph Schayes
6 .... Julius Erving
10 .... Maurice Cheeks
13 .... Wilt Chamberlain
15 .... Hal Greer
24 .... Bobby Jones
32 .... Billy Cunningham
34 .... Charles Barkley

League Leaders, Offense

Points

Wilt Chamberlain*, 1964–65 2534
Wilt Chamberlain, 1965–66 2649
Allen Iverson, 2004–05 2302

*1054 with Phi. 76ers and 1480 with S.F. Warriors.

Three Pointers

Kyle Korver, 2004–05 226

Assists

Wilt Chamberlain, 1967–68 702

Scoring Average

Wilt Chamberlain*, 1964–65 .... 34.7
Wilt Chamberlain, 1965–66 .... 33.5
Allen Iverson, 1998–99 .... 26.8
Allen Iverson, 2000–01 .... 31.1
Allen Iverson, 2001–02 .... 31.4
Allen Iverson, 2004–05 .... 30.7
Joel Embiid, 2021–22 .... 30.6

* 30.1 with Phi. 76ers and 38.9 with S.F. Warriors.

Field Goal Percentage

Wilt Chamberlain*, 1964–65 .... .510
Wilt Chamberlain, 1965–66 .... .540
Wilt Chamberlain, 1966–67 .... .683

Wilt Chamberlain, 1967–68.......... .595

* .528 with Phi. 76ers and .499 with S.F. Warriors.

Three Point Percentage
none

Free Throw Percentage
Dolph Schayes, 1957–58 (Syr.) ..... .904
Dolph Schayes, 1959–60 (Syr.) ..... .893
Dolph Schayes, 1961–62 (Syr.) ..... .897
Larry Costello, 1962–63 (Syr.)....... .881
Larry Costello, 1964–65................. .877
Kyle Korver, 2006–07.................... .914

Assists Average
none

League Leaders, Defense
Offensive Rebounds
Moses Malone, 1982–83................ 445
Charles Barkley, 1986–87.............. 390
Charles Barkley, 1987–88.............. 385
Charles Barkley, 1988–89.............. 403
Dikembe Mutombo*, 2000–01........ 307
*119 with Phi. 76ers and 188 with Atl. Hawks.

Defensive Rebounds
Moses Malone, 1982–83................ 749

Total Rebounds
Dolph Schayes, 1950–51 (Syr.) 1080
Wilt Chamberlain, 1965–66......... 1943
Wilt Chamberlain, 1966–67......... 1957
Wilt Chamberlain, 1967–68......... 1952
Moses Malone, 1982–83.............. 1194
Moses Malone, 1984–85.............. 1031

Steals
Allen Iverson, 2002–03................. 225
Allen Iverson, 2004–05................. 180

Blocks
none

Rebounds Average
Dolph Schayes, 1950–51 (Syr.) 16.4
Wilt Chamberlain, 1965–66.......... 24.6
Wilt Chamberlain, 1966–67.......... 24.2
Wilt Chamberlain, 1967–68.......... 23.8
Moses Malone, 1982–83............... 15.3
Moses Malone, 1983–84............... 13.4
Moses Malone, 1984–85............... 13.1
Charles Barkley, 1986–87............. 14.6
Dikembe Mutombo*, 2000–01....... 13.5
*12.4 with Phi. 76ers and 14.1 with Atl. Hawks.

Steals Average
Allen Iverson, 2000–01.................... 2.5
Allen Iverson, 2001–02.................... 2.8

Allen Iverson, 2002–03................... 2.7
Ben Simmons, 2019–20 .... 2.1

Blocks Average
Theo Ratliff, 2000–01 .... 3.7

Feats
50-Point Game
68...Wilt Chamberlain (@ Chi. Bulls), Dec. 16, 1967
65... Wilt Chamberlain (vs. L.A. Lakers), Feb. 7, 1966
62... Wilt Chamberlain (vs. S.F. Warriors), Mar. 3, 1966
60......... Allen Iverson (vs. Orl. Magic), Feb. 12, 2005
58...Wilt Chamberlain (vs. Cin. Royals), Feb. 13, 1967
58......... Allen Iverson (vs. Hou. Rockets), Jan. 15, 2002
54......... Allen Iverson (@ Cle. Cavaliers), Jan. 6, 2001
54......... Allen Iverson (@ Det. Pistons), Dec. 18, 2004
53...Wilt Chamberlain (vs. Det. Pistons), Oct. 23, 1965
53...Wilt Chamberlain (vs. L.A. Lakers), Jan. 25, 1966
53... Wilt Chamberlain (@ Sea. Sonics), Dec. 20, 1967
53... Wilt Chamberlain (vs. L.A. Lakers), Mar. 18, 1968
53......... Willie Burton (vs. Mia. Heat), Dec. 13, 1994
53......... Allen Iverson (@ Atl. Hawks), Dec. 23, 2005
52... Wilt Chamberlain (vs. Sea. Sonics), Dec. 1, 1967
51...Wilt Chamberlain (@ Bal. Bullets), Mar. 14, 1965
51......... Moses Malone (vs. Det. Pistons), Nov. 14, 1984
51.......... Allen Iverson (vs. Tor. Raptors), Jan. 21, 2001
51.............. Allen Iverson (vs. Uta. Jazz), Dec. 20, 2004
50......... Dolph Schayes (@ Bos. Celtics), Feb. 1, 1959 (Syr.)
50.............. Hal Greer (vs. Bos. Celtics), Feb. 21, 1964
50...Wilt Chamberlain (vs. N.Y. Knicks), Jan. 2, 1966
50..........Dana Barros (vs. Hou. Rockets), Mar. 14, 1995
50......... Allen Iverson (@ Cle. Cavaliers), Apr. 12, 1997

50............ Allen Iverson (vs. Sac. Kings), Feb. 6, 2000
50.......... Allen Iverson (vs. Atl. Hawks), Nov. 29, 2003
50................Joel Embiid (vs. Chi. Bulls), Feb. 19, 2021
50.............. Joel Embiid (vs. Orl. Magic), Jan. 19, 2022

20-Assist Game
21...Wilt Chamberlain (vs. Det. Pistons), Feb. 2, 1968
21.......... Maurice Cheeks (vs. N.J. Nets), Oct. 30, 1982

30-Rebound Game
43...Wilt Chamberlain (vs. Bos. Celtics), Mar. 6, 1965
42...Wilt Chamberlain (vs. Bos. Celtics), Jan. 14, 1966
40... Wilt Chamberlain (vs. Bos. Celtics), Dec. 28, 1965
38...Wilt Chamberlain (vs. S.F. Warriors), Mar. 2, 1967
38...Wilt Chamberlain (@ Sea. Sonics), Dec. 20, 1967
37...Wilt Chamberlain (vs. S.F. Warriors), Mar. 3, 1966
37... Wilt Chamberlain (vs. Sea. Sonics), Dec. 1, 1967
36...Wilt Chamberlain (vs. Bos. Celtics), Mar. 5, 1966
36... Wilt Chamberlain (vs. St.L. Hawks), Mar. 9, 1966
36...Wilt Chamberlain (vs. Cin. Royals), Feb. 28, 1967
35...Dolph Schayes (@ Phi. Warriors), Dec. 28, 1950 (Syr.)
35...Wilt Chamberlain (vs. Bal. Bullets), Jan. 12, 1968
34...Wilt Chamberlain (vs. Bos. Celtics), Jan. 29, 1965
34.......... Wilt Chamberlain (@ Chi. Bulls), Dec. 16, 1967
33...Wilt Chamberlain (@ L.A. Lakers), Nov. 21, 1965
33...Wilt Chamberlain (vs. Bal. Bullets), Nov. 30, 1965
33...Wilt Chamberlain (vs. Cin. Royals), Dec. 11, 1965
33...Wilt Chamberliin (vs. Chi. Bulls), Nov. 11, 1966
33...Wilt Chamberlain (@ N.Y. Knicks), Jan. 3, 1967
33...Wilt Chamberlain (vs. Bos. Celtics), Nov. 18, 1967

32...Wilt Chamberlain (vs. Det. Pistons), Jan. 22, 1965

32...Wilt Chamberlain (vs. N.Y. Knicks), Feb. 20, 1965

32...Wilt Chamberlain (vs. Bos. Celtics), Nov. 12, 1965

32...Wilt Chamberlain (vs. Cin. Royals), Dec. 26, 1966

32...Wilt Chamberlain (vs. Bos. Celtics), Dec. 28, 1966

32...Wilt Chamberlain (vs. Det. Pistons), Feb. 23, 1968

32...Wilt Chamberlain (vs. L.A. Lakers), Mar. 18, 1968

32...........Bill Bridges (vs. Sea. Sonics), Mar. 19, 1972

31...Wilt Chamberlain (vs. St.L. Hawks), Feb. 4, 1965

31...Wilt Chamberlain (@ S.F. Warriors), Nov. 27, 1965

31...Wilt Chamberlain (vs. L.A. Lakers), Jan. 25, 1966

31...Wilt Chamberlain (@ Bal. Bullets), Feb. 23, 1966

31...Wilt Chamberlain (vs. Bos. Celtics), Oct. 29, 1966

31...Wilt Chamberlain (vs. S.F. Warriors), Nov. 24, 1966

31...Wilt Chamberlain (vs. L.A. Lakers), Dec. 5, 1967

31...Wilt Chamberlain (vs. S.F. Warriors), Feb. 27, 1968

30...................Red Kerr (@ Min. Lakers), Feb. 1, 1958 (Syr.)

30...............Red Kerr (@ Phi. Warriors), Nov. 8, 1958 (Syr.)

30...Wilt Chamberlain (@ Cin. Royals), Feb. 13, 1965

30...Wilt Chamberlain (vs. L.A. Lakers), Feb. 28, 1965

30...Wilt Chamberlain (@ Bos. Celtics), Dec. 3, 1965

30...Wilt Chamberlain (vs. S.F. Warriors), Dec. 26, 1965

30...Wilt Chamberlain (vs. L.A. Lakers), Jan. 7, 1966

30...Wilt Chamberlain (@ Bos. Celtics), Mar. 6, 1966

30...Wilt Chamberlain (vs. N.Y. Knicks), Nov. 16, 1966

30...Wilt Chamberlain (vs. L.A. Lakers), Dec. 2, 1966

30...Wilt Chamberlain (vs. L.A. Lakers), Jan. 20, 1967

30...Wilt Chamberlain (vs. Bal. Bullets), Feb. 24, 1967

30........Wilt Chamberlain (@ Bal. Bullets), Mar. 19, 1967

30...Wilt Chamberlain (vs. L.A. Lakers), Oct. 18, 1967

30.........Wilt Chamberlain (vs. Chi. Bulls), Mar. 12, 1968

8-Steal Game

9........Maurice Cheeks (vs. L.A. Clippers), Jan. 5, 1987

9.........Hersey Hawkins (vs. Bos. Celtics), Jan. 25, 1991

9..........Allen Iverson (vs. Orl. Magic), Mar. 19, 2000

9...............Allen Iverson (vs. L.A. Lakers), Dec. 20, 2002

9...Michael Carter-Williams (vs. Mia. Heat), Oct. 30, 2013

8..........Julius Erving (vs. Was. Bullets), Nov. 12, 1976

8..............Henry Bibby (@ Por. Blazers), Mar. 1, 1977

8..........Maurice Cheeks (vs. Pho. Suns), Mar. 17, 1984

8..........Maurice Cheeks (vs. S.A. Spurs), Nov. 7, 1986

8.........Hersey Hawkins (vs. Mil. Bucks), Dec. 4, 1990

8...............Allen Iverson (@ Atl. Hawks), Mar. 29, 2003

8..............Allen Iverson (@ Chi. Bulls), Nov. 7, 2003

8...Thaddeus Young (vs. Ok.C. Thunder), Jan. 25, 2014

8...Robert Covington (@ Hou. Rockets), Nov. 27, 2015

10-Block Game

10.....Harvey Catchings (vs. Atl. Hawks), Mar. 21, 1975

10...............Manute Bol (@ Sac. Kings), Feb. 14, 1991

10..........Dikembe Mutombo (@ Chi. Bulls), Dec. 1, 2001

Multiple Triple-Doubles in a Single Season

31............ Wilt Chamberlain, 1967–68

22............ Wilt Chamberlain, 1966–67

12...................Ben Simmons, 2017–18

10...................Ben Simmons, 2018–19

9............ Wilt Chamberlain, 1965–66

6..............Billy Cunningham, 1971–72

6...................Ben Simmons, 2019–20

5...............George McGinnis, 1975–76

5..................Charles Barkley, 1986–87

4...............Billy Cunningham, 1970–71

4....................Ben Simmons, 2020–21

3..............Billy Cunningham, 1974–75

3.................Andre Iguodala, 2006–07

3.................Andre Iguodala, 2010–11

3......Michael Carter-Williams, 2014–15

2..................Charles Barkley, 1988–89

2..................Charles Barkley, 1989–90

2.......................Aaron McKie, 2000–01

2......................Andre Miller, 2008–09

2......Michael Carter-Williams, 2013–14

2........................ Joel Embiid, 2018–19

2........................ Joel Embiid, 2021–22

2..................James Harden, 2021–22*

* Had 11 Triple-Doubles for 2021–22 season: 2 with Phi. 76ers and 9 with Brk. Nets.

Postseason Play

1950 Eastern Division Semifinals vs. Phi. Warriors, won (2–0)
Eastern Division Finals vs. N.Y. Knicks, won (2–1)
NBA Finals vs. Min. Lakers, lost (4–2)

1951 Eastern Division Semifinals vs. Phi. Warriors, won (2–0)
Eastern Division Finals vs. N.Y. Knicks, lost (3–2)

1952 Eastern Division Semifinals vs. Phi. Warriors, won (2–1)
Eastern Division Finals vs. N.Y. Knicks, lost (3–1)

1953 Eastern Division Semifinals vs. Bos. Celtics, lost (2–0)

1954 Eastern Division Finals vs. Bos. Celtics, won (2–0)
(Advanced from Eastern Division Round Robin)
NBA Finals vs. Min. Lakers, lost (4–3)

1955 Eastern Division Finals vs. Bos. Celtics, won (3–1)
NBA Finals vs. Ft.W. Pistons, won (4–3)

1956 Eastern Division Third Place Tiebreaker vs. N.Y. Knicks, won
Eastern Division Semifinals vs. Bos. Celtics, won (2–1)
Eastern Division Finals vs. Phi. Warriors, lost (3–2)

1957 Eastern Division Semifinals vs. Phi. Warriors, won (2–0)

Eastern Division Finals
vs. Bos. Celtics, lost (3–0)

1958 Eastern Division Semifinals
vs. Phi. Warriors, lost (2–1)

1959 Eastern Division Semifinals
vs. N.Y. Knicks, won (2–0)
Eastern Division Finals
vs. Bos. Celtics, lost (4–3)

1960 Eastern Division Semifinals
vs. Phi. Warriors, lost (2–1)

1961 Eastern Division Semifinals
vs. Phi. Warriors, won (3–0)
Eastern Division Finals
vs. Bos. Celtics, lost (4–1)

1962 Eastern Division Semifinals
vs. Phi. Warriors, lost (3–2)

1963 Eastern Division Semifinals
vs. Cin. Royals, lost (3–2)

1964 Eastern Division Semifinals
vs. Cin. Royals, lost (3–2)

1965 Eastern Division Semifinals
vs. Cin. Royals, won (3–1)
Eastern Division Finals
vs. Bos. Celtics, lost (4–3)

1966 Eastern Division Finals
vs. Bos. Celtics, lost (4–1)

1967 Eastern Division Semifinals
vs. Cin. Royals, won (3–1)
Eastern Division Finals
vs. Bos. Celtics, won (4–1)
NBA Finals vs. S.F. Warriors,
won (4–2)

1968 Eastern Division Semifinals
vs. N.Y. Knicks, won (4–2)
Eastern Division Finals
vs. Bos. Celtics, lost (4–3)

1969 Eastern Division Semifinals
vs. Bos. Celtics, lost (4–1)

1970 Eastern Division Semifinals
vs. Mil. Bucks, lost (4–1)

1971 Eastern Division Semifinals
vs. Bal. Bullets, lost (4–3)

1976 Eastern Conference First Round
vs. Buf. Braves, lost (2–1)

1977 Eastern Conference Semifinals
vs. Bos. Celtics, won (4–3)
Eastern Conference Finals
vs. Hou. Rockets, won (4–2)
NBA Finals vs. Por. Blazers,
lost (4–2)

1978 Eastern Conference Semifinals
vs. N.Y. Knicks, won (4–0)
Eastern Conference Finals
vs. Was. Bullets, lost (4–2)

1979 Eastern Conference First Round
vs. N.J. Nets, won (2–0)
Eastern Conference Semifinals
vs. S.A. Spurs, lost (4–3)

1980 Eastern Conference First Round
vs. Was. Bullets, won (2–0)
Eastern Conference Semifinals
vs. Atl. Hawks, won (4–1)
Eastern Conference Finals
vs. Bos. Celtics, won (4–1)
NBA Finals vs. L.A. Lakers,
lost (4–2)

1981 Eastern Conference First Round
vs. Ind. Pacers, won (2–0)
Eastern Conference Semifinals
vs. Mil. Bucks, won (4–3)
Eastern Conference Finals
vs. Bos. Celtics, lost (4–1)

1982 Eastern Conference First Round
vs. Atl. Hawks, won (2–0)
Eastern Conference Semifinals
vs. Mil. Bucks, won (4–2)
Eastern Conference Finals
vs. Bos. Celtics, won (4–3)
NBA Finals vs. L.A. Lakers,
lost (4–2)

1983 Eastern Conference Semifinals
vs. N.Y. Knicks, won (4–0)
Eastern Conference Finals
vs. Mil. Bucks, won (4–1)
NBA Finals vs. L.A. Lakers,
lost (4–0)

1984 Eastern Conference First Round
vs. N.J. Nets, lost (3–2)

1985 Eastern Conference First Round
vs. Was. Bullets, won (3–1)
Eastern Conference Semifinals
vs. Mil. Bucks, won (4–0)
Eastern Conference Finals
vs. Bos. Celtics, lost (4–1)

1986 Eastern Conference First Round
vs. Was. Bullets, won (3–2)
Eastern Conference Semifinals
vs. Mil. Bucks, lost (4–3)

1987 Eastern Conference First Round
vs. Mil. Bucks, lost (3–2)

1989 Eastern Conference First Round
vs. N.Y. Knicks, lost (3–0)

1990 Eastern Conference First Round
vs. Cle. Cavaliers, won (3–2)
Eastern Conference Semifinals
vs. Chi. Bulls, lost (4–1)

1991 Eastern Conference First Round
vs. Mil. Bucks, won (3–0)
Eastern Conference Semifinals

vs. Chi. Bulls, lost (4–1)

1999 Eastern Conference First Round
vs. Orl. Magic, won (3–1)
Eastern Conference Semifinals
vs. Ind. Pacers, lost (4–0)

2000 Eastern Conference First Round
vs. Cha. Hornets, won (3–1)
Eastern Conference Semifinals
vs. Ind. Pacers, lost (4–2)

2001 Eastern Conference First Round
vs. Ind. Pacers, won (3–1)
Eastern Conference Semifinals
vs. Tor. Raptors, won (4–3)
Eastern Conference Finals
vs. Mil. Bucks, won (4–3)
NBA Finals vs. L.A. Lakers,
lost (4–1)

2002 Eastern Conference First Round
vs. Bos. Celtics, lost (3–2)

2003 Eastern Conference First Round
vs. N.O. Hornets, won (4–2)
Eastern Conference Semifinals
vs. Det. Pistons, lost (4–2)

2005 Eastern Conference First Round
vs. Det. Pistons, lost (4–1)

2008 Eastern Conference First Round
vs. Det. Pistons, lost (4–2)

2009 Eastern Conference First Round
vs. Orl. Magic, lost (4–2)

2011 Eastern Conference First Round
vs. Mia. Heat, lost (4–1)

2012 Eastern Conference First Round
vs. Chi. Bulls, won (4–2)
Eastern Conference Semifinals
vs. Bos. Celtics, lost (4–3)

2018 Eastern Conference First Round
vs. Mia. Heat, won (4–1)
Eastern Conference Semifinals
vs. Bos. Celtics, lost (4–1)

2019 Eastern Conference First Round
vs. Brk. Nets, won (4–1)
Eastern Conference Semifinals
vs. Tor. Raptors, lost (4–3)

2020 Eastern Conference First Round
vs. Bos. Celtics, lost (4–0)

2021 Eastern Conference First Round
vs. Was. Wizards, won (4–1)
Eastern Conference Semifinals
vs. Atl. Hawks, lost (4–3)

2022 Eastern Conference First Round
vs. Tor. Raptors, won (4–2)
Eastern Conference Semifinals
vs. Mia. Heat, lost (4–2)

Toronto Raptors

Dates of Operation: 1995–present (27 seasons)
Overall Record: 1030 wins, 1116 losses (.480)
Arenas: Skydome, 1995–99; Amalie Arena (Tampa, FL), 2020–21; Scotiabank Arena (formerly Air Canada Centre, 1998–2018) 1998–present (capacity: 19,800)

Year-by-Year Finishes

Year	Finish	Wins	Losses	Percentage	Games Behind	Head Coach	Attendance
Eastern Conference Central Division							
1995–96	8th	21	61	.256	51.0	Brendan Malone	950,330
1996–97	8th	30	52	.366	39.0	Darrell Walker	744,550
1997–98	8th	16	66	.195	46.0	Darrell Walker (11–38), Butch Carter (5–28)	674,685
1998–99	6th	23	27	.460	10.0	Butch Carter	439,190
1999–00	3rd	45	37	.549	11.0	Butch Carter	756,496
2000–01	2nd	47	35	.573	5.0	Lenny Wilkens	793,256
2001–02	3rd (Tie)	42	40	.512	8.0	Lenny Wilkens	810,160
2002–03	7th	24	58	.293	26.0	Lenny Wilkens	777,507
2003–04	6th	33	49	.402	28.0	Kevin O'Neill	750,608
Atlantic Division							
2004–05	4th (Tie)	33	49	.402	12.0	Sam Mitchell	703,388
2005–06	4th	27	55	.329	22.0	Sam Mitchell	699,332
2006–07	1st	47	35	.573	+6.0	Sam Mitchell	748,603
2007–00	2nd	41	41	.500	25.0	Sam Mitchell	796,835
2008–09	4th	33	49	.402	29.0	Sam Mitchell (8–9), Jay Triano (25–40)	769,707
2009–10	2nd	40	42	.488	10.0	Jay Triano	733,784
2010–11	5th	22	60	.268	34.0	Jay Triano	680,255
2011–12	4th	23	43	.348	16.0	Dwane Casey	555,584
2012–13	4th (Tie)	34	48	.415	20.0	Dwane Casey	743,936
2013–14	1st	48	34	.585	+4.0	Dwane Casey	748,339
2014–15	1st	49	33	.598	+9.0	Dwane Casey	809,824
2015–16	1st	56	26	.683	+8.0	Dwane Casey	812,863
2016–17	2nd	51	31	.622	2.0	Dwane Casey	813,050
2017–18	1st	59	23	.720	+4.0	Dwane Casey	813,431
2018–19	1st	58	24	.707	+7.0	Nick Nurse	812,822
2019–20	1st	53	19	.736	+5.0	Nick Nurse	633,456
2020–21	5th	27	45	.375	22.0	Nick Nurse	26,024
2021–22	3rd	48	34	.585	3.0	Nick Nurse	547,343

1998–99: 50-game season.

2011–12: 66-game season.

2019–20: 65-to-75-game season.

2020–21: 72-game season.

Awards

Most Valuable Player

Rookie of the Year

Damon Stoudamire, guard, 1995–96

Vince Carter, guard, 1998–99

Scottie Barnes, forward, 2021–22

Defensive Player of the Year

Sixth Man of the Year

Lou Williams, guard, 2014–15

Most Improved Player

Pascal Siakam, forward, 2018–19

All-NBA First Team

All-Defensive First Team

All-Rookie First Team

Damon Stoudamire, 1995–96

Marcus Camby, 1996–97

Vince Carter, 1998–99

Morris Peterson, 2000–01

Chris Bosh, 2003–04

Charlie Villanueva, 2005–06

Andrea Bargnani, 2006–07

Jorge Garbajosa, 2006–07

Scottie Barnes, 2021–22

Coach of the Year

Sam Mitchell, 2006–07

Dwane Casey, 2017–18

Nick Nurse, 2019–20

Hall of Famers Who Played for the Raptors

Chris Bosh, center-forward, 2003–10

Tracy McGrady, guard, 1997–2000

Hakeem Olajuwon, center, 2001–02

Retired Numbers

League Leaders, Offense

Points

Three Pointers

Dee Brown, 1998–99 135

Assists

Scoring Average

Field Goal Percentage

Three Point Percentage

Jason Kapono, 2007–08 .... .483

José Calderón*, 2012–13 .... .461

*.429 with Tor. Raptors and .520 with Det. Pistons.

Free Throw Percentage

José Calderón, 2008–09 .... .981

Assists Average

League Leaders, Defense

Offensive Rebounds

Defensive Rebounds

Total Rebounds

Steals

Blocks

Rebounds Average

Steals Average

Blocks Average

Marcus Camby, 1997–98 .... 3.7

Feats

50-Point Game

54 .... Fred VanVleet (@ Orl. Magic), Feb. 2, 2021

52 .... DeMar DeRozan (vs. Mil. Bucks), Jan. 1, 2018

51 .... Vince Carter (vs. Pho. Suns), Feb. 27, 2000

51 .... Terrence Ross (vs. L.A. Clippers), Jan. 25, 2014

20-Assist Game

30-Rebound Game

8-Steal Game

9 .... Doug Christie (@ Den. Nuggets), Feb. 25, 1997

8 .... Doug Christie (@ Phi. 76ers), Jan. 29, 1997

8 .... Doug Christie (@ Phi. 76ers), Apr. 2, 1997

8 .... Doug Christie (@ Atl. Hawks), Mar. 4, 1999

8 .... Jerome Williams (@ Chi. Bulls), Feb. 26, 2003

8 .... Morris Peterson (@ Cha. Bobcats), Feb. 10, 2006

10-Block Game

12 .... Keon Clark (vs. Atl. Hawks), Mar. 23, 2001

11 .... Marcus Camby (@ N.J. Nets), Apr. 14, 1998

10 .... Marcus Camby (vs. Phi. 76ers), Apr. 19, 1998

Multiple Triple-Doubles in a Single Season

3 .... Kyle Lowry, 2017–18

2 .... Damon Stoudamire, 1996–97

2 .... Marcus Camby, 1997–98

2 .... José Calderón, 2012–13

2 .... Kyle Lowry, 2013–14

2 .... Kyle Lowry, 2014–15

2 .... Kyle Lowry, 2018–19

2 .... Kyle Lowry, 2019–20

2 .... Kyle Lowry, 2020–21

2 .... Pascal Siakam, 2021–22

Postseason Play

2000 Eastern Conference First Round vs. N.Y. Knicks, lost (3–0)

2001 Eastern Conference First Round vs. N.Y. Knicks, won (3–2)

Eastern Conference Semifinals vs. Phi. 76ers, lost (4–3)

2002 Eastern Conference First Round vs. Det. Pistons, lost (3–2)

2007 Eastern Conference First Round vs. N.J. Nets, lost (4–2)

2008 Eastern Conference First Round vs. Orl. Magic, lost (4–1)

2014 Eastern Conference First Round vs. Brk. Nets, lost (4–3)

2015 Eastern Conference First Round vs. Was. Wizards, lost (4–0)

2016 Eastern Conference First Round vs. Ind. Pacers, won (4–3)

Eastern Conference Semifinals vs. Mia. Heat, won (4–3)

Eastern Conference Finals vs. Cle. Cavaliers, lost (4–2)

2017   Eastern Conference First Round
      vs. Mil. Bucks, won (4–2)
    Eastern Conference Semifinals
      vs. Cle. Cavaliers, lost (4–0)

2018   Eastern Conference First Round
      vs. Was. Wizards, won (4–2)
    Eastern Conference Semifinals
      vs. Cle. Cavaliers, lost (4–0)

2019   Eastern Conference First Round
      vs. Orl. Magic, won (4–1)
    Eastern Conference Semifinals
      vs. Phi. 76ers, won (4–3)
    Eastern Conference Finals
      vs. Mil. Bucks, won (4–2)
    NBA Finals vs. G.S. Warriors,
      won (4–2)

2020   Eastern Conference First Round
      vs. Brk. Nets, won (4–0)
    Eastern Conference Semifinals
      vs. Bos. Celtics, lost (4–3)

2022   Eastern Conference First Round
      vs. Phi. 76ers, lost (4–2)

Washington Wizards

Dates of Operation: (as the Chicago Packers-Zephyrs) 1961–63 (2 seasons)
Overall Record: 43 wins, 117 losses (.269)
Arenas: International Amphitheatre, 1961–62; Chicago Coliseum, 1962–63

Dates of Operation: (as the Washington Wizards) 1963–present (59 seasons)
Overall Record: 2179 wins, 2584 losses (.457)
Arenas: Baltimore Civic Center, 1963–73; US Airways Arena (formerly Capital Centre, 1973–93),
   1973–97; Capital One Arena (formerly MCI Center, 1997–2006; Verizon Center, 2006–17),
   1997–present (capacity: 20,356)
Other Names: Baltimore Bullets, 1963–73; Capital Bullets, 1973–74; Washington Bullets, 1974–97

Year-by-Year Finishes

Year	Finish	Wins	Losses	Percentage	Games Behind	Head Coach	Attendance
				Chicago Packers **Western Division**			
1961–62	5th	18	62	.225	36.0	Jim Pollard	103,126
				Chicago Zephyrs			
1962–63	5th	25	55	.313	28.0	Jack McMahon (12–26), Slick Leonard (13–29)	155,290
				Baltimore Bullets			
1963–64	4th	31	49	.388	17.0	Slick Leonard	195,783
1964–65	3rd	37	43	.463	12.0	Buddy Jeannette	187,124
1965–66	2nd	38	42	.475	7.0	Paul Seymour	174,880
				Eastern Division			
1966–67	5th	20	61	.247	48.0	Mike Farmer (1–8), Buddy Jeannette (3–13), Gene Shue (16–40)	129,799
1967–68	6th	36	46	.439	26.0	Gene Shue	171,146
1968–69	1st	57	25	.695	+2.0	Gene Shue	290,147
1969–70	3rd	50	32	.610	10.0	Gene Shue	225,569
				Eastern Conference Central Division			
1970–71	1st	42	40	.512	+6.0	Gene Shue	251,130
1971–72	1st	38	44	.463	+2.0	Gene Shue	272,339
1972–73	1st	52	30	.634	+6.0	Gene Shue	263,660
				Capital Bullets			
1973–74	1st	47	35	.573	+12.0	K.C. Jones	414,202
				Washington Bullets			
1974–75	1st	60	22	.732	+19.0	K.C. Jones	383,775
1975–76	2nd	48	34	.585	1.0	K.C. Jones	440,837
1976–77	2nd	48	34	.585	1.0	Dick Motta	467,745
1977–78	2nd	44	38	.537	8.0	Dick Motta	446,539

Year	Finish	Wins	Losses	Percentage	Games Behind	Head Coach	Attendance
				Atlantic Division			
1978–79	1st	54	28	.659	+7.0	Dick Motta	524,356
1979–80	3rd (Tie)	39	43	.476	22.0	Dick Motta	466,823
1980–81	4th	39	43	.476	23.0	Gene Shue	377,238
1981–82	4th	43	39	.524	20.0	Gene Shue	379,891
1982–83	5th	42	40	.512	23.0	Gene Shue	368,281
1983–84	5th	35	47	.427	27.0	Gene Shue	317,447
1984–85	4th	40	42	.488	23.0	Gene Shue	383,098
1985–86	3rd (Tie)	39	43	.476	28.0	Gene Shue (32–37), Kevin Loughery (7–6)	373,802
1986–87	3rd	42	40	.512	17.0	Kevin Loughery	485,316
1987–88	2nd (Tie)	38	44	.463	19.0	Kevin Loughery (8–19), Wes Unseld (30–25)	433,376
1988–89	4th	40	42	.488	12.0	Wes Unseld	253,980
1989–90	4th	31	51	.378	22.0	Wes Unseld	458,332
1990–91	4th	30	52	.366	26.0	Wes Unseld	443,683
1991–92	6th	25	57	.305	26.0	Wes Unseld	505,988
1992–93	7th	22	60	.268	38.0	Wes Unseld	558,966
1993–94	7th	24	58	.293	33.0	Wes Unseld	619,756
1994–95	7th	21	61	.256	36.0	Jim Lynam	689,463
1995–96	4th	39	43	.476	21.0	Jim Lynam	669,598
1996–97	4th	44	38	.537	17.0	Jim Lynam (22–24), Bob Staak (0–1), Bernie Bickerstaff (22–13)	700,646
				Washington Wizards			
1997–98	4th	42	40	.512	13.0	Bernie Bickerstaff	801,240
1998–99	6th	18	32	.360	15.0	Bernie Bickerstaff (13–19), Jim Brovelli (5–13)	402,481
1999–00	7th	29	53	.354	23.0	Gar Heard (14–30), Darrell Walker (15–23)	616,593
2000–01	7th	19	63	.232	37.0	Leonard Hamilton	638,653
2001–02	5th	37	45	.451	15.0	Doug Collins	847,634
2002–03	5th (Tie)	37	45	.451	12.0	Doug Collins	827,093
2003–04	6th	25	57	.305	22.0	Eddie Jordan	645,363
				Southeast Division			
2004–05	2nd	45	37	.549	14.0	Eddie Jordan	705,069
2005–06	2nd	42	40	.512	10.0	Eddie Jordan	705,062
2006–07	2nd	41	41	.500	3.0	Eddie Jordan	753,283
2007–08	2nd	43	39	.524	9.0	Eddie Jordan	736,461
2008–09	5th	19	63	.232	40.0	Eddie Jordan (1–10), Ed Tapscott (18–53)	681,119
2009–10	5th	26	56	.317	33.0	Flip Saunders	664,398
2010–11	5th	23	59	.280	35.0	Flip Saunders	688,466
2011–12	4th	20	46	.303	26.0	Flip Saunders (2–15), Randy Wittman (18–31)	552,038
2012–13	3rd	29	53	.354	37.0	Randy Wittman	670,070
2013–14	2nd	44	38	.537	10.0	Randy Wittman	698,068
2014–15	2nd	46	36	.561	14.0	Randy Wittman	747,796
2015–16	4th	41	41	.500	7.0	Randy Wittman	725,426
2016–17	1st	49	33	.598	+6.0	Scott Brooks	697,107
2017–18	2nd	43	39	.524	1.0	Scott Brooks	739,302

Year	Finish	Wins	Losses	Percentage	Games Behind	Head Coach	Attendance
2018–19	4th	32	50	.390	10.0	Scott Brooks	716,996
2019–20	4th	25	47	.347	18.5	Scott Brooks	532,702
2020–21	3rd	34	38	.472	7.0	Scott Brooks	19,198
2021–22	4th	35	47	.427	18.0	Wes Unseld Jr.	641,499

1998–99: 50-game season.

2011–12: 66-game season.

2019–20: 65-to-75-game season.

2020–21: 72-game season.

Awards

Most Valuable Player

Wes Unseld, center, 1968–69 (Bal.)

Rookie of the Year

Walt Bellamy, center, 1961–62 (Packers)

Terry Dischinger, forward, 1962–63 (Zephyrs)

Earl Monroe, guard, 1967–68 (Bal.)

Wes Unseld, center, 1968–69 (Bal.)

Defensive Player of the Year

Sixth Man of the Year

Most Improved Player

Pervis Ellison, center, 1991–92 (Was.)

Don MacLean, forward, 1993–94 (Was.)

Gheorghe Mureşan, center, 1995–96 (Was.)

All-NBA First Team

Earl Monroe, 1968–69 (Bal.)

Wes Unseld, 1968–69 (Bal.)

Elvin Hayes, 1974–75 (Was.)

Elvin Hayes, 1976–77 (Was.)

All-Defensive First Team

Gus Johnson, 1969–70 (Bal.)

Gus Johnson, 1970–71 (Bal.)

Bob Dandridge, 1978–79 (Was.)

Larry Hughes, 2004–05

All-Rookie First Team

Terry Dischinger, 1962–63 (Zephyrs)

Gus Johnson, 1963–64 (Bal.)

Rod Thorn, 1963–64 (Bal.)

Wali Jones, 1964–65 (Bal.)

Jack Marin, 1966–67 (Bal.)

Earl Monroe, 1967–68 (Bal.)

Wes Unseld, 1968–69 (Bal.)

Mike Davis, 1969–70 (Bal.)

Phil Chenier, 1971–72 (Bal.)

Nick Weatherspoon, 1973–74 (Cap.)

Mitch Kupchak, 1976–77 (Was.)

Jeff Ruland, 1981–82 (Was.)

Jeff Malone, 1983–84 (Was.)

Tom Gugliotta, 1992–93 (Was.)

John Wall, 2010–11

Bradley Beal, 2012–13

Coach of the Year

Gene Shue, 1968–69 (Bal.)

Gene Shue, 1981–82 (Was.)

Hall of Famers Who Played for the Packers/Zephyrs/Bullets/Wizards

Walt Bellamy, center, 1961–66 (Packers-Zephyrs-Bal.)

Dave Bing, guard, 1975–77 (Was.)

Bob Dandridge, forward, 1977–81 (Was.)

Elvin Hayes, forward, 1972–81 (Bal.-Cap.-Was.)

Spencer Haywood, forward, 1981–83 (Was.)

Bailey Howell, forward, 1964–66 (Bal.)

Gus Johnson, forward, 1963–72 (Bal.)

Michael Jordan, forward, 2001–03

Bernard King, forward, 1987–91 (Was.)

Moses Malone, center, 1986–88 (Was.)

Earl Monroe, guard, 1967–72 (Bal.)

Paul Pierce, forward, 2014–15

Mitch Richmond, guard, 1998–2001

Ralph Sampson, center, 1991–92 (Was.)

Ben Wallace, forward-center, 1996–99 (Was.-Wizards)

Chris Webber, forward-center, 1994–98 (Was.-Wizards)

Wes Unseld, center,1968–81 (Bal.-Cap.-Was.)

Retired Numbers

10 .... Earl Monroe

11 .... Elvin Hayes

25 .... Gus Johnson

41 .... Wes Unseld

45 .... Phil Chenier

League Leaders, Offense

Points

Three Pointers

Gilbert Arenas, 2006–07 205

Assists

Kevin Porter, 1974–75 (Was.) 650

Kevin Porter, 1980–81 (Was.) 734

Rod Strickland, 1997–98 801

John Wall, 2013–14 721

Russell Westbrook, 2020–21 763

Scoring Average

Field Goal Percantage

Walt Bellamy, 1961–62 (Packers) .. .519

Wes Unseld, 1975–76 (Was.) .... .561

Gheorghe Mureşan, 1995–96 (Was.) .... .584

Gheorghe Mureşan, 1996–97 (Was.) .... .604

Three Point Percentage

Tim Legler, 1995–96 .... .522

Free Throw Percentage

Jack Marin, 1971–72 (Bal.) .... .895

Assists Average

Kevin Porter, 1974–75 (Bal.) 8.0

Kevin Porter, 1980–81 (Bal.) 9.1

Rod Strickland, 1997–98 .... 10.5

Russell Westbrook, 2020–21 .... 11.7

League Leaders, Defense

Offensive Rebounds

Elvin Hayes, 1973–74 (Cap.).......... 354

Defensive Rebounds

Elvin Hayes, 1973–74 (Cap.)........ 1109

Total Rebounds
Elvin Hayes, 1973–74 (Cap.)........ 1463

Steals
John Wall, 2016–17...................... 157

Blocks
Manute Bol, 1985–86 (Was.) 397

Rebounds Average
Elvin Hayes, 1973–74 (Cap.)......... 18.1
Wes Unseld, 1974–75 (Was.) 14.8

Steals Average
Larry Hughes, 2004–05 .... 2.9

Blocks Average
Manute Bol, 1985–86 (Was.) 5.0

Feats

50-Point Game
60.......... Gilbert Arenas (@ L.A. Lakers),
    Dec. 17, 2006
60............. Bradley Beal (@ Phi. 76ers),
    Jan. 6, 2021
56.......... Earl Monroe (vs. L.A. Lakers),
    Feb. 13, 1968 (Bal.)
55............... Bradley Beal (vs. Mil. Bucks),
    Feb. 24, 2020
54.......... Gilbert Arenas (@ Pho. Suns),
    Dec. 22, 2006
53.......... Phil Chenier (vs. Por. Blazers),
    Dec. 6, 1972 (Bal.)
53............... Bradley Beal (@ Chi. Bulls),
    Feb. 23, 2020
52........ Bernard King (vs. Den. Nuggets),
    Dec. 29, 1990 (Was.)
52............. John Wall (vs. Orl. Magic),
    Dec. 6, 2016
51...Michael Jordan (vs. Cha. Hornets),
    Dec. 29, 2001
51.......... Gilbert Arenas (vs. Uta. Jazz),
    Jan. 15, 2007
51........... Bradley Beal (@ Por. Blazers),
    Dec. 5, 2017
50............. Moses Malone (@ N.J. Nets),
    Apr. 8, 1987 (Was.)
50............. Bernard King (vs. Uta. Jazz),
    Mar. 6, 1991 (Was.)
50......... Tracy Murray (@ G.S. Warriors),
    Feb. 10, 1998
50............. Bradley Beal (@ Ind. Pacers),
    May 8, 2021

20-Assist Game
24.......... Kevin Porter (vs. Det. Pistons),
    Mar. 23, 1980
24... Russell Westbrook (vs. Ind. Pacers),
    May 3, 2021
22.............. Kevin Porter (vs. Atl. Hawks),
    Mar. 5, 1975
21............. Kevin Porter (vs. L.A. Lakers),
    Mar. 2, 1975
21... Russell Westbrook (vs. Ind. Pacers),
    Mar. 29, 2021
21... Russell Westbrook (vs. Atl. Hawks),
    May 10, 2021
20.......... Kevin Porter (vs. Det. Pistons),
    Oct. 20, 1979
20... Rod Strickland (vs. G.S. Warriors),
    Feb. 10, 1998
20................. John Wall (vs. Chi. Bulls),
    Mar. 17, 2017

30-Rebound Game
37.......... Walt Bellamy (vs. St.L. Hawks),
    Dec. 4, 1964 (Bal.)
34............. Gus Johnson (vs. L.A. Lakers),
    Feb. 9, 1966 (Bal.)
32........... Wes Unseld (vs. Bos. Celtics),
    Mar. 15, 1969 (Bal.)
32...........Gus Johnson (@ N.Y. Knicks),
    Dec. 27, 1970 (Bal.)
32................ Elvin Hayes (@ Atl. Hawks),
    Nov. 17, 1973 (Cap.)
31......... Gus Johnson (vs. S.D. Rockets),
    Jan. 23, 1971 (Bal.)
30.......... Walt Bellamy (vs. Bos. Celtics),
    Jan. 10, 1962 (Packers)
30........... Walt Bellamy (vs. L.A. Lakers),
    Feb. 4, 1962 (Packers)
30.......... Walt Bellamy (vs. L.A. Lakers),
    Feb. 6, 1965 (Bal.)
30.............. Wes Unseld (vs. Mil. Bucks),
    Feb. 14, 1969 (Bal.)
30................ Wes Unseld (@ Chi. Bulls),
    Mar. 20, 1970 (Bal.)
30............. Wes Unseld (vs. N.O. Jazz),
    Apr. 6, 1975 (Was.)

8-Steal Game
9.............. Gus Williams (vs. Atl. Hawks),
    Oct. 30, 1984 (Was.)
9.......... Michael Adams (@ Ind. Pacers),
    Nov. 1, 1991 (Was.)
9.............. John Wall (vs. Phi. 76ers),
    Nov. 2, 2010

8........... Phil Chenier (vs. N.Y. Knicks),
    Nov. 25, 1973 (Cap.)
8............... Wes Unseld (@ Pho. Suns),
    Jan. 24, 1976 (Was.)
8............... John Lucas (@ Pho. Suns),
    Dec. 12, 1981 (Was.)
8...............Frank Johnson (@ Chi. Bulls),
    Oct. 30, 1982 (Was.)
8.......... Dudley Bradley (@ Phi. 76ers),
    Nov. 20, 1984 (Was.)
8......... Tom Gugliotta (vs. Den. Nuggets),
    Mar. 11, 1994 (Was.)
8...........Chris Webber (@ S.A. Spurs),
    Nov. 26, 1997
8.............. Juan Dixon (vs. Ind. Pacers),
    Feb. 20, 2004
8...........Gilbert Arenas (vs. Sac. Kings),
    Mar. 17, 2004

10-Block Game
15............... Manute Bol (vs. Atl. Hawks),
    Jan. 25, 1986 (Was.)
15.............. Manute Bol (vs. Ind. Pacers),
    Feb. 26, 1987 (Was.)
12.............. Manute Bol (vs. Mil. Bucks),
    Dec. 12, 1985 (Was.)
12.......... Manute Bol (vs. Cle. Cavaliers),
    Feb. 5, 1987 (Was.)
12.......... Manute Bol (vs. Bos. Celtics),
    Mar. 26, 1987 (Was.)
12.......... JaVale McGee (@ Chi. Bulls),
    Mar. 15, 2011
11.............. Elvin Hayes (@ Det. Pistons),
    Mar. 3, 1978 (Was.)
10.............. Manute Bol (@ Pho. Suns),
    Jan. 8, 1986 (Was.)
10......... Manute Bol (@ L.A. Clippers),
    Feb. 17, 1986 (Was.)
10................Manute Bol (@ Ind. Pacers),
    Feb. 25, 1986 (Was.)
10......... Manute Bol (vs. G.S. Warriors),
    Jan. 22, 1988 (Was.)
10.......... Charles Jones (@ Orl. Magic),
    Mar. 3, 1990 (Was.)

Multiple Triple-Doubles in a Single Season
38............. Russell Westbrook, 2020–21
9.................. Darrell Walker, 1989–90
4.................. Darrell Walker, 1990–91
4....................... John Wall, 2015–16
3.................. Chris Webber, 1994–95
3.................. Rod Strickland, 1997–98
3.................. Gilbert Arenas, 2003–04

3....................Caron Butler, 2007–08
2.....................Gus Johnson, 1969–70
2.......................Jeff Ruland, 1983–84
2...................... Jeff Ruland, 1985–86
2.................Darrell Walker, 1988–89
2..................Chris Webber, 1996–97
2........................ John Wall, 2013–14
2.....................Bradley Beal, 2018–19

Postseason Play

1965 Western Division Semifinals
vs. St.L. Hawks, won (3–1)
Western Division Finals
vs. L.A. Lakers, lost (4–2)

1966 Eastern Division Semifinals
vs. St.L. Hawks, lost (3–0)

1969 Eastern Division Semifinals
vs. N.Y. Knicks, lost (4–0)

1970 Eastern Division Semifinals
vs. N.Y. Knicks, lost (4–3)

1971 Eastern Conference Semifinals
vs. Phi. 76ers, won (4–3)
Eastern Conference Finals
vs. N.Y. Knicks, won (4–3)
NBA Finals vs. Mil. Bucks,
lost (4–0)

1972 Eastern Conference Semifinals
vs. N.Y. Knicks, lost (4–2)

1973 Eastern Conference Semifinals
vs. N.Y. Knicks, lost (4–1)

1974 Eastern Conference Semifinals
vs. N.Y. Knicks, lost (4–3)

1975 Eastern Conference Semifinals
vs. Buf. Braves, won (4–3)

Eastern Conference Finals
vs. Bos. Celtics, won (4–2)
NBA Finals vs. G.S. Warriors,
lost (4–0)

1976 Eastern Conference Semifinals
vs. Cle. Cavaliers, lost (4–3)

1977 Eastern Conference First Round
vs. Cle. Cavaliers, lost (2–1)

1978 Eastern Conference First Round
vs. Atl. Hawks, won (2–0)
Eastern Conference Semifinals
vs. S.A. Spurs, won (4–2)
Eastern Conference Finals
vs. Phi. 76ers, won (4–2)
NBA Finals vs. Sea. Sonics,
won (4–3)

1979 Eastern Conference Semifinals
vs. Atl. Hawks, won (4–3)
Eastern Conference Finals
vs. S.A. Spurs, won (4–3)
NBA Finals vs. Sea. Sonics,
lost (4–1)

1980 Eastern Conference First Round
vs. Phi. 76ers, lost (2–0)

1982 Eastern Conference First Round
vs. N.J. Nets, won (2–0)
Eastern Conference Semifinals
vs. Bos. Celtics, lost (4–1)

1984 Eastern Conference First Round
vs. Bos. Celtics, lost (3–1)

1985 Eastern Conference First Round
vs. Phi. 76ers, lost (3–1)

1986 Eastern Conference First Round
vs. Phi. 76ers, lost (3–2)

1987 Eastern Conference First Round
vs. Det. Pistons, lost (3–0)

1988 Eastern Conference First Round
vs. Det. Pistons, lost (3–2)

1997 Eastern Conference First Round
vs. Chi. Bulls, lost (3–0)

2005 Eastern Conference First Round
vs. Chi. Bulls, won (4–2)
Eastern Conference Semifinals
vs. Mia. Heat, lost (4–0)

2006 Eastern Conference First Round
vs. Cle. Cavaliers, lost (4–2)

2007 Eastern Conference First Round
vs. Cle. Cavaliers, lost (4–0)

2008 Eastern Conference First Round
vs. Cle. Cavaliers, lost (4–2)

2014 Eastern Conference First Round
vs. Chi. Bulls, won (4–1)
Eastern Conference Semifinals
vs. Ind. Pacers, lost (4–2)

2015 Eastern Conference First Round
vs. Tor. Raptors, won (4–0)
Eastern Conference Semifinals
vs. Atl. Hawks, lost (4–2)

2017 Eastern Conference First Round
vs. Atl. Hawks, won (4–2)
Eastern Conference Semifinals
vs. Bos. Celtics, lost (4–3)

2018 Eastern Conference First Round
vs. Tor. Raptors, lost (4–2)

2021 Eastern Conference First Round
vs. Phi. 76ers, lost (4–1)

2

WESTERN CONFERENCE

Dallas Mavericks

Dates of Operation: 1980–present (42 seasons)
Overall Record: 1709 wins, 1670 losses (.506)
Arenas: Reunion Arena, 1980–2001; American Airlines Center, 2001–present (capacity: 19,200)
Other Name: Mavs

Year-by-Year Finishes

Year	Finish	Wins	Losses	Percentage	Games Behind	Head Coach	Attendance
				Western Conference Midwest Division			
1980–81	6th	15	67	.183	37.0	Dick Motta	319,347
1981–82	5th	28	54	.341	20.0	Dick Motta	380,484
1982–83	4th	38	44	.463	15.0	Dick Motta	487,155
1983–84	2nd	43	39	.524	2.0	Dick Motta	538,162
1984–85	3rd	44	38	.537	8.0	Dick Motta	683,916
1985–86	3rd	44	38	.537	7.0	Dick Motta	693,052
1986–87	1st	55	27	.671	+11.0	Dick Motta	696,333
1987–88	2nd	53	29	.646	1.0	John Macleod	695,592
1988–89	4th	38	44	.463	13.0	John Macleod	695,056
1989–90	3rd	47	35	.573	9.0	John Macleod (5–6) Richie Adubato (42–29)	691,490
1990–91	6th	28	54	.341	27.0	Richie Adubato	683,927
1991–92	5th	22	60	.268	33.0	Richie Adubato	634,380
1992–93	6th	11	71	.134	44.0	Richie Adubato (2–27), Gar Heard (9–44)	554,724
1993–94	6th	13	69	.159	45.0	Quinn Buckner	526,414
1994–95	5th	36	46	.439	26.0	Dick Motta	678,433
1995–96	5th (Tie)	26	56	.317	33.0	Dick Motta	684,138
1996–97	4th	24	58	.293	40.0	Jim Cleamons (24–58)	619,178
1997–98	5th	20	62	.244	42.0	Jim Cleamons (4–12), Don Nelson (16–50)	503,936
1998–99	5th	19	31	.380	18.0	Don Nelson	362,837
1999–00	4th	40	42	.488	15.0	Don Nelson	606,177
2000–01	2nd (Tie)	53	29	.646	5.0	Don Nelson	680,238
2001–02	2nd	57	25	.695	1.0	Don Nelson	802,783
2002–03	1st (Tie)	60	22	.732	—	Don Nelson	816,429

Year	Finish	Wins	Losses	Percentage	Games Behind	Head Coach	Attendance
2003–04	3rd	52	30	.634	6.0	Don Nelson	825,594
Southwest Division							
2004–05	2nd	58	24	.707	1.0	Don Nelson (42–22), Avery Johnson (16–2)	822,533
2005–06	2nd	60	22	.732	3.0	Avery Johnson	824,693
2006–07	1st	67	15	.817	+9.0	Avery Johnson	834,411
2007–08	4th	51	31	.622	5.0	Avery Johnson	831,738
2008–09	3rd	50	32	.610	4.0	Rick Carlisle	821,723
2009–10	1st	55	27	.671	+5.0	Rick Carlisle	819,770
2010–11	2nd	57	25	.695	4.0	Rick Carlisle	824,162
2011–12	3rd	36	30	.545	14.0	Rick Carlisle	671,050
2012–13	4th	41	41	.500	17.0	Rick Carlisle	821,490
2013–14	4th	49	33	.598	13.0	Rick Carlisle	817,982
2014–15	4th	50	32	.610	6.0	Rick Carlisle	827,702
2015–16	2nd (Tie)	42	40	.512	25.0	Rick Carlisle	825,901
2016–17	5th	33	49	.402	28.0	Rick Carlisle	811,366
2017–18	4th	24	58	.293	41.0	Rick Carlisle	811,453
2018–19	3rd (Tie)	33	49	.402	20.0	Rick Carlisle	820,569
2019–20	2nd	43	32	.573	2.5	Rick Carlisle	682,096
2020–21	1st	42	30	.583	+4.0	Rick Carlisle	94,849
2021–22	2nd	52	30	.634	4.0	Jason Kidd	808,037

1998–99: 50-game season.

2011–12: 66-game season.

2019–20: 65-to-75-game season.

2020–21: 72-game season.

Awards

Most Valuable Player
Dirk Nowitzki, forward, 2006–07

Rookie of the Year
Jason Kidd, guard, 1994–95*
Luka Dončić, guard, 2018–19
*Tied with Grant Hill, Det. Pistons.

Defensive Player of the Year
none

Sixth Man of the Year
Roy Tarpley, forward, 1987–88
Antawn Jamison, forward, 2003–04
Jason Terry, guard, 2008–09

Most Improved Player
none

All-NBA First Team
Dirk Nowitzki, 2004–05
Dirk Nowitzki, 2005–06
Dirk Nowitzki, 2006–07
Dirk Nowitzki, 2008–09
Luka Dončić, 2019–20
Luka Dončić, 2020–21
Luka Dončić, 2021–22

All-Defensive First Team
none

All-Rookie First Team
Jay Vincent, 1981–82
Sam Perkins, 1984–85
Roy Tarpley, 1986–87
Jamal Mashburn, 1993–94
Jason Kidd, 1994–95
Luka Dončić, 2018–19

Coach of the Year
Avery Johnson, 2005–06

Hall of Famers Who Played for the Mavericks
Adrian Dantley, forward, 1988–90
Alex English, forward, 1990–91
Tim Hardaway, guard, 2001–02
Jason Kidd, guard, 1994–97; 2007–12
Steve Nash, guard, 1998–2004
Dennis Rodman, forward, 1999–00

Retired Numbers
12.................................Derek Harper
15.......................................Brad Davis
22.............................Rolando Blackman
41.................................Dirk Nowitzki

League Leaders, Offense

Points
none

Three Pointers
none

Assists
none

Scoring Average
none

Field Goal Percantage
none

Three Point Percentage
Hubert Davis, 1999–00.................. .491

Free Throw Percentage
none

Assists Average
none

League Leaders, Defense

Offensive Rebounds
Popeye Jones, 1994–95................. 329

Defensive Rebounds
none

Total Rebounds
none

Steals
none

Blocks
Shawn Bradley, 2000–01 228

Rebounds Average
none

Steals Average
none

Blocks Average
Shawn Bradley*, 1996–97 .... 3.4
*2.7 with Dal. Mavericks and 4.0 with N.J.
Nets.

Feats

50-Point Game
53......... Dirk Nowitzki (vs. Hou. Rockets),
Dec. 12, 2004
51... Dirk Nowitzki (vs. G.S. Warriors),
Mar. 23, 2006
51.......... Luka Dončić (vs. L.A. Clippers),
Feb. 11, 2022
50......... Jamal Mashburn (@ Chi. Bulls),
Nov. 12, 1994
50......... Jim Jackson (@ Den. Nuggets),
Nov. 26, 1994

20-Assist Game
25.............. Jason Kidd (vs. Uta. Jazz),
Feb. 8, 1996
20.............. Jason Kidd (vs. Pho. Suns),
Apr. 5, 2009
20........ Luka Dončić (vs. Was. Wizards),
May 1, 2021

30-Rebound Game
none

8-Steal Game
10......... Michael Finley (vs. Phi. 76ers),
Jan. 23, 2001
9.............. Fat Lever (vs. Was. Bullets),
Feb. 10, 1994
9......... Dirk Nowitzki (@ Hou. Rockets),
Mar. 7, 2004
8.......... Jim Spanarkel (vs. Pho. Suns),
Mar. 10, 1981
8..........Derek Harper (vs. Hou. Rockets),
Nov. 9, 1985
8......... Marquis Daniels (@ Chi. Bulls),
Dec. 13, 2004

10-Block Game
13.......... Shawn Bradley (vs. Por. Blazers),
Apr. 7, 1998
10...........Shawn Bradley (vs. L.A. Lakers),
Mar. 4, 1997

Multiple Triple-Doubles in a Single Season
17.....................Luka Dončić, 2019–20
11.....................Luka Dončić, 2020–21
10.....................Luka Dončić, 2021–22
9.......................Jason Kidd, 1995–96
8.....................Luka Dončić, 2018–19
4.......................Jason Kidd, 1994–95
4.................Michael Finley, 1999–00
3.......................Jason Kidd, 2008–09
2...............Antoine Walker, 2003–04
2.......................Jason Kidd, 2009–10
2.......................Jason Kidd, 2010–11

Postseason Play

1984 Western Conference First Round
vs. Sea. Sonics, won (3–2)
Western Conference Semifinals
vs. L.A. Lakers, lost (4–1)
1985 Western Conference First Round
vs. Por. Blazers, lost (3–1)
1986 Western Conference First Round
vs. Uta. Jazz, won (3–1)
Western Conference Semifinals
vs. L.A. Lakers, lost (4–2)
1987 Western Conference First Round
vs. Sea. Sonics, lost (3–1)
1988 Western Conference First Round
vs. Hou. Rockets, won (3–1)
Western Conference Semifinals
vs. Den. Nuggets, won (4–2)
Western Conference Finals
vs. L.A. Lakers, lost (4–3)
1990 Western Conference First Round
vs. Por. Blazers, lost (3–0)
2001 Western Conference First Round
vs. Uta. Jazz, won (3–2)
Western Conference Semifinals
vs. S.A. Spurs, lost (4–1)
2002 Western Conference First Round
vs. Min. T'Wolves, won (3–0)
Western Conference Semifinals
vs. Sac. Kings, lost (4–1)
2003 Western Conference First Round
vs. Por. Blazers, won (4–3)
Western Conference Semifinals
vs. Sac. Kings, won (4–3)
Western Conference Finals
vs. S.A. Spurs, lost (4–2)

2004 Western Conference First Round
vs. Sac. Kings, lost (4–1)
2005 Western Conference First Round
vs. Hou. Rockets, won (4–3)
Western Conference Semifinals
vs. Pho. Suns, lost (4–2)
2006 Western Conference First Round
vs. Mem. Grizzlies, won (4–0)
Western Conference Semifinals
vs. S.A. Spurs, won (4–3)
Western Conference Finals
vs. Pho. Suns, won (4–2)
NBA Finals vs. Mia. Heat,
lost (4–2)
2007 Western Conference First Round
vs. G.S. Warriors, lost (4–2)
2008 Western Conference First Round
vs. N.O. Hornets, lost (4–1)
2009 Western Conference First Round
vs. S.A. Spurs, won (4–1)
Western Conference Semifinals
vs. Den. Nuggets, lost (4–1)
2010 Western Conference First Round
vs. S.A. Spurs, lost (4–2)
2011 Western Conference First Round
vs. Por. Blazers, won (4–2)
Western Conference Semifinals
vs. L.A. Lakers, won (4–0)
Western Conference Finals
vs. Ok.C. Thunder, won (4–1)
NBA Finals vs. Mia. Heat,
won (4–2)
2012 Western Conference First Round
vs. Ok.C. Thunder, lost (4–0)
2014 Western Conference First Round
vs. S.A. Spurs, lost (4–3)
2015 Western Conference First Round
vs. Hou. Rockets, lost (4–1)
2016 Western Conference First Round
vs. Ok.C. Thunder, lost (4–1)
2020 Western Conference First Round
vs. L.A. Clippers, lost (4–2)
2021 Western Conference First Round
vs. L.A. Clippers, lost (4–3)
2022 Western Conference First Round
vs. Uta. Jazz, won (4–2)
Western Conference Semifinals
vs. Pho. Suns, won (4–3)
Western Conference Finals
vs. G.S. Warriors, lost (4–1)

Denver Nuggets

ABA Dates of Operation: 1967–76 (9 seasons)
Overall Record: 413 wins, 331 losses (.555)
Arenas: Denver Auditorium Arena, 1967–75; McNichols Sports Arena, 1975–76
Other Name: Denver Rockets, 1967–74

NBA Dates of Operation: 1976–present (46 seasons)
Overall Record: 1844 wins, 1861 losses (.498)
Arenas: McNichols Sports Arena, 1976–99; Ball Arena (formerly Pepsi Center, 1999–2020) 1999–present (capacity: 19,520)

Year-by-Year Finishes

Year	Finish	Wins	Losses	Percentage	Games Behind	Head Coach	Attendance
				Denver Rockets **ABA Western Division**			
1967–68	3rd	45	33	.577	3.0	Bob Bass	161,007
1968–69	3rd	44	34	.564	16.0	Bob Bass	169,498
1969–70	1st	51	33	.607	+6.0	John McLendon (9–19), Joe Belmont (42–14)	263,855
1970–71	4th (Tie)	30	54	.357	28.0	Joe Belmont (3–10), Stan Albeck (27–44)	179,106
1971–72	4th	34	50	.405	26.0	Alex Hannum	174,493
1972–73	3rd	47	37	.560	8.0	Alex Hannum	200,224
1973–74	4th (Tie)	37	47	.440	14.0	Alex Hannum	172,630
				Denver Nuggets			
1974–75	1st	65	19	.774	+14.0	Larry Brown	281,810
				American Basketball Association			
1975–76	1st	60	24	.714	+5.0	Larry Brown	535,344
				NBA Western Conference Midwest Division			
1976–77	1st	50	32	.610	+6.0	Larry Brown	703,133
1977–78	1st	48	34	.585	+4.0	Larry Brown	657,673
1978–79	2nd	47	35	.573	1.0	Larry Brown (28–25), Donnie Walsh (19–10)	603,356
1979–80	3rd (Tie)	30	52	.366	19.0	Donnie Walsh	527,208
1980–81	4th	37	45	.451	15.0	Donnie Walsh (11–20), Doug Moe (26–25)	423,287
1981–82	2nd (Tie)	46	36	.561	2.0	Doug Moe	456,857
1982–83	2nd (Tie)	45	37	.549	8.0	Doug Moe	491,253
1983–84	3rd (Tie)	38	44	.463	7.0	Doug Moe	462,407
1984–85	1st	52	30	.634	+4.0	Doug Moe	448,546
1985–86	2nd	47	35	.573	4.0	Doug Moe	531,824
1986–87	4th	37	45	.451	18.0	Doug Moe	494,943
1987–88	1st	54	28	.659	+1.0	Doug Moe	520,881
1988–89	3rd	44	38	.537	7.0	Doug Moe	527,337
1989–90	4th	43	39	.524	13.0	Doug Moe	484,288
1990–91	7th	20	62	.244	35.0	Paul Westhead	438,103
1991–92	4th	24	58	.293	31.0	Paul Westhead	534,323
1992–93	4th	36	46	.439	19.0	Dan Issel	586,407
1993–94	4th	42	40	.512	16.0	Dan Issel	673,738

Year	Finish	Wins	Losses	Percentage	Games Behind	Head Coach	Attendance
1994–95	4th	41	41	.500	21.0	Dan Issel (18–16), Gene Littles (3–13), Bernie Bickerstaff (20–12)	704,011
1995–96	4th	35	47	.427	24.0	Bernie Bickerstaff	675,425
1996–97	5th	21	61	.256	43.0	Bernie Bickerstaff (4–9), Dick Motta (17–52)	340,486
1997–98	7th	11	71	.134	51.0	Bill Hanzlik	380,590
1998–99	6th	14	36	.280	23.0	Mike D'Antoni	296,965
1999–00	5th	35	47	.427	20.0	Dan Issel	637,698
2000–01	6th	40	42	.488	18.0	Dan Issel	619,300
2001–02	6th	27	55	.329	31.0	Dan Issel (9–17), Mike Evans (18–38)	633,846
2002–03	7th	17	65	.207	43.0	Jeff Bzdelik	607,813
2003–04	6th	43	39	.524	15.0	Jeff Bzdelik	721,476
Northwest Division							
2004–05	2nd	49	33	.598	3.0	Jeff Bzdelik (13–15), Michael Cooper (4–10), George Karl (32–8)	723,949
2005–06	1st	44	38	.537	+3.0	George Karl	702,555
2006–07	2nd	45	37	.549	6.0	George Karl	706,437
2007–08	2nd	50	32	.610	4.0	George Karl	711,962
2008–09	1st (Tie)	54	28	.659	—	George Karl	706,165
2009–10	1st	53	29	.646	+3.0	George Karl	737,301
2010–11	2nd	50	32	.610	5.0	George Karl	696,568
2011–12	2nd	38	28	.576	9.0	George Karl	561,966
2012–13	2nd	57	25	.695	3.0	George Karl	730,616
2013–14	4th	36	46	.439	23.0	Brian Shaw	692,898
2014–15	4th	30	52	.366	21.0	Brian Shaw (20–39), Melvin Hunt (10–13)	602,707
2015–16	4th	33	49	.402	22.0	Michael Malone	577,898
2016–17	4th	40	42	.488	11.0	Michael Malone	605,585
2017–18	5th	46	36	.561	3.0	Michael Malone	702,796
2018–19	1st	54	28	.659	+1.0	Michael Malone	756,457
2019–20	1st	46	27	.630	+1.5	Michael Malone	633,153
2020–21	2nd	47	25	.653	5.0	Michael Malone	54,563
2021–22	2nd	48	34	.585	1.0	Michael Malone	695,262

1998–99: 50-game season.

2011–12: 66-game season.

2019–20: 65-to-75-game season.

2020–21: 72-game season.

(ABA Attendance totals are unofficial, and numbers include when listed as home team.)

Awards

ABA Most Valuable Player
Spencer Haywood, forward, 1969–70 (Rockets)

NBA Most Valuable Player
Nikola Jokić, center, 2020–21
Nikola Jokić, center, 2021–22

ABA Rookie of the Year
Spencer Haywood, forward, 1969–70 (Rockets)

David Thompson, forward, 1975–76

NBA Rookie of the Year
none

Defensive Player of the Year
Dikembe Mutombo, center, 1994–95
Marcus Camby, center, 2006–07

Sixth Man of the Year
none

Most Improved Player
Mahmoud Abdul-Rauf, guard, 1992–93

All-ABA First Team
Larry Jones, 1967–68 (Rockets)
Larry Jones, 1968–69 (Rockets)
Spencer Haywood, 1969–70 (Rockets)
Larry Jones, 1969–70 (Rockets)
Warren Jabali, 1972–73 (Rockets)
Mack Calvin, 1974–75
Ralph Sampson, 1975–76

All-NBA First Team
David Thompson, 1976–77
David Thompson, 1977–78
Nikola Jokić, 2018–19
Nikola Jokić, 2020–21
Nikola Jokić, 2021–22

All-ABA Defensive First Team
Julius Keye, 1972–73 (Rockets)
Julius Keye, 1973–74 (Rockets)
Bobby Jones, 1974–75
Bobby Jones, 1975–76

All-NBA Defensive First Team
Bobby Jones, 1976–77
Bobby Jones, 1977–76
Marcus Camby, 2006–07
Marcus Camby, 2007–08

All-ABA Rookie First Team
Walter Piatkowski, 1968–69 (Rockets)
Spencer Haywood, 1969–70 (Rockets)
Mike Green, 1973–74 (Rockets)
Bobby Jones, 1974–75
David Thompson, 1975–76

All-NBA Rookie First Team
Dikembe Mutombo, 1991–92
LaPhonso Ellis, 1992–93
Antonio McDyess, 1995–96
Nenê, 2002–03
Carmelo Anthony, 2003–04
Kenneth Faried, 2011–12
Nikola Jokić, 2015–16

ABA Coach of the Year
Joe Belmont, 1969–70* (Rockets)
Larry Brown, 1974–75
Larry Brown, 1975–76
*Tied with Bill Sharman, L.A. Stars.

NBA Coach of the Year
Doug Moe, 1987–88
George Karl, 2012–13

Hall of Famers Who Played for the Rockets/Nuggets
Alex English, forward, 1980–90
Tim Hardaway, guard, 2002
Spencer Haywood, forward, 1969–70 (ABA)
Dan Issel, center, 1975–85 (ABA/NBA)
Allen Iverson, guard, 2006–09
Bobby Jones, forward, 1975–78 (ABA/NBA)
Šarūnas Marčiulionis, guard, 1996–97
George McGinnis, forward, 1978–80

Dikembe Mutombo, center, 1991–96
Charlie Scott, guard, 1978–80
David Thompson, forward-guard, 1975–82 (ABA/NBA)

Retired Numbers
2 ....Alex English
12 ....Fat Lever
33 ....David Thompson
40 ....Byron Beck
44 .... Dan Issel
55 .... Dikembe Mutombo
432 .... Doug Moe

League Leaders, Offense
Points
Larry Jones, 1968–69
(Rockets/ABA) 2133
Spencer Haywood, 1969–70
(Rockets/ABA) 2519
Alex English, 1982–83 2326
Alex English, 1985–86 2414

Three Pointers
Michael Adams, 1988–89 166
Michael Adams, 1989–90 158

Assists
Al Smith, 1973–74 (Rockets/ABA).... 619
Mark Jackson*, 1996–97 935
*641 with Den. Nuggets and 294 with Ind. Pacers.

Scoring Average
Larry Jones, 1968–69
(Rockets/ABA) 28.4
Spencer Haywood, 1969–70
(Rockets/ABA) 30.0
Alex English, 1982–83 .... 28.4

Field Goal Percentage
Bobby Jones, 1974–75 (ABA) .... .604
Bobby Jones, 1975–76 (ABA) .... .581
Bobby Jones, 1977–78 .... .578
Nenê, 2010–11 .... .615

Three Point Percentage
none

Free Throw Percentage
Mack Calvin, 1974–75 (ABA) .... .896
Mahmoud Abdul-Rauf, 1993–94..... .956
Mahmoud Abdul-Rauf, 1995–96..... .930

Assists Average
Al Smith, 1973–74 (Rockets/ABA) 8.1
Mack Calvin, 1974–75 (ABA) 7.7

Mark Jackson*, 1996–97 .... 11.4
*12.3 with Den. Nuggets and 9.8 with Ind. Pacers.

League Leaders, Defense
Offensive Rebounds
Spencer Haywood, 1969–70
(Rockets/ABA) 533
Danny Fortson, 1998–99............... 210

Defensive Rebounds
Spencer Haywood, 1969–70
(Rockets/ABA) 1104
Julius Keye, 1970–71
(Rockets/ABA) 1084
Ervin Johnson, 1996–97................ 682
Nikola Jokić, 2021–22................... 813

Total Rebounds
Spencer Haywood, 1969–70
(Rockets/ABA) 1637
Dikembe Mutombo, 1994–95 1029
Nikola Jokić, 2021–22................ 1019

Steals
none

Blocks
Dikembe Mutombo, 1993–94 336
Dikembe Mutombo, 1994–95 321
Dikembe Mutombo, 1995–96 332
Marcus Camby, 2004–05............... 199
Marcus Camby, 2006–07............... 231
Marcus Camby, 2007–08............... 285

Rebounds Average
Spencer Haywood, 1969–70
(Rockets/ABA) 19.5

Steals Average
none

Blocks Average
Dikembe Mutombo, 1993–94 .... 4.1
Dikembe Mutombo, 1994–95 .... 3.9
Dikembe Mutombo, 1995–96 .... 4.5
Marcus Camby, 2005–06............... 3.3
Marcus Camby, 2006–07............... 3.3
Marcus Camby, 2007–08............... 3.6

Feats
50-Point Game
73........ David Thompson (@ Det. Pistons), Apr. 9, 1978
59...Spencer Haywood, (vs. L.A. Stars), Apr. 15, 1970 (Rockets/ABA)

54.......... Alex English (vs. Hou. Rockets),
Nov. 19, 1985

54.......... Michael Adams (vs. Mil. Bucks),
Mar. 23, 1991

52........... Larry Jones, (vs. Oak. Oaks),
Nov. 28, 1967 (Rockets/ABA)

52.......... Larry Jones, (vs. Hou. Mavericks),
Mar. 21, 1969 (Rockets/ABA)

51...Kiki Vandeweghe (vs. Det. Pistons),
Dec. 13, 1983

51................ Alex English (@ Mia. Heat),
Mar. 10, 1989

51...Mahmoud Abdul-Rauf (@ Uta. Jazz),
Dec. 7, 1995

51............. Allen Iverson (vs. L.A. Lakers),
Dec. 5, 2007

50......... David Thompson (vs. S.A. Spurs),
Feb. 27, 1976 (ABA)

50......... Kiki Vandeweghe (vs. S.A. Spurs),
Jan. 11, 1984

50...Carmelo Anthony (vs. N.Y. Knicks),
Nov. 27, 2009

50...Carmelo Anthony (vs. Hou. Rockets),
Feb. 7, 2011

50..............Nikola Jokić (@ Sac. Kings),
Feb. 6, 2021

50........ Jamal Murray (@ Cle. Cavaliers),
Feb. 19, 2021

20-Assist Game

23......... Larry Brown (vs. Pit. Condors),
Feb. 20, 1972 (Rockets/ABA)

23.............. Fat Lever (@ G.S. Warriors),
Apr. 21, 1989

22......... Mark Jackson (vs. N.J. Nets),
Jan. 20, 1997

22.......... George McCloud (@ Chi. Bulls),
Mar. 26, 2001

21............... Al Smith (vs. Ken. Colonels),
Feb. 20, 1974 (Rockets/ABA)

20...Mahmoud Abdul-Rauf (@ Pho. Suns),
Nov. 15, 1995

20...........Nick Van Exel (vs. Atl. Hawks),
Nov. 8, 1999

20.......... Nick Van Exel (vs. Sea. Sonics),
Dec. 2, 2000

20.............. Andre Miller (vs. Mia. Heat),
Dec. 8, 2006

30-Rebound Game

31... Spencer Haywood (vs. Ken. Colonels),
Nov. 13, 1969 (Rockets/ABA)

31...Dikembe Mutombo (@ Cha. Hornets),
Mar. 26, 1996

8-Steal Game

10.............. Fat Lever (vs. Ind. Pacers),
Mar. 9, 1985

9..................... T.R. Dunn (@ N.J. Nets),
Jan. 6, 1988

8............... Rob Williams (@ N.J. Nets),
Feb. 17, 1983

8................ T.R. Dunn (@ G.S. Warriors),
Nov. 17, 1983

8............... Fat Lever (vs. K.C. Kings),
Jan. 11, 1985

8..................... Fat Lever (vs. N.J. Nets),
Nov. 24, 1987

8................Fat Lever (vs. Mia. Heat),
Mar. 18, 1989

8............... Ty Lawson (@ Por. Blazers),
Dec. 29, 2011

10-Block Game

12.............. Julius Keye (vs. Vir. Squires),
Dec. 14, 1972 (Rockets/ABA)

12...Dikembe Mutombo (vs. L.A. Clippers),
Apr. 18, 1993

11...Dikembe Mutombo (vs. Por. Blazers),
Nov. 26, 1993

11...Dikembe Mutombo (vs. L.A. Clippers),
Apr. 5, 1994

11...Dikembe Mutombo (vs. Sea. Sonics),
Apr. 7, 1994

11...Dikembe Mutombo (@ Dal. Mavericks),
Nov. 8, 1994

11.......... Marcus Camby (vs. Uta. Jazz),
Jan. 17, 2008

10..........Wayne Cooper (vs. Mia. Heat),
Dec. 30, 1988

10...Dikembe Mutombo (@ Orl. Magic),
Mar. 10, 1992

10...Dikembe Mutombo (vs. G.S. Warriors),
Mar. 25, 1993

10...Dikembe Mutombo (vs. Uta. Jazz),
Dec. 10, 1993

10...Dikembe Mutombo (@ Cle. Cavaliers),
Apr. 2, 1995

10...Dikembe Mutombo (vs. Min. T'Wolves),
Dec. 2, 1995

10.......... Marcus Camby (vs. Mil. Bucks),
Dec. 26, 2007

Multiple Triple-Doubles in a Single Season

19..................... Nikola Jokić, 2021–22

16......................... Fat Lever, 1986–87

16..................... Nikola Jokić, 2020–21

13..................... Nikola Jokić, 2019–20

12.................... Nikola Jokić, 2018–19

11.......................... Fat Lever, 1987–88

10.................... Nikola Jokić, 2017–18

9........................... Fat Lever, 1988–89

6.................... Nikola Jokić, 2016–17

5........................... Fat Lever, 1989–90

4.................... Nikola Jokić, 2021–22

3..................... Alex English, 1981–82

3............ Dikembe Mutombo, 1993–94

2........Warren Jabali, 1972–73 (ABA)

2.............George McGinnis, 1979–80

2.............Dikembe Mutombo, 1992–93

2.............Dikembe Mutombo, 1994–95

2.................. Mark Jackson, 1996–97

2................ Marcus Camby, 2007–08

Postseason Play

1968 ABA Western Division Semifinals
vs. N.O. Buccaneers, lost (3–2)

1969 ABA Western Division Semifinals
vs. Oak. Oaks, lost (4–3)

1970 ABA Western Division Semifinals
vs. Was. Capitols, won (4–3)
ABA Western Division Finals
vs. L.A. Stars, lost (4–1)

1971 ABA Western Division Tiebreaker
vs. Tex. Chaparrals, lost

1972 ABA Western Division Semifinals
vs. Ind. Pacers, lost (4–3)

1973 ABA Western Division Semifinals
vs. Ind. Pacers, lost (4–1)

1974 ABA Western Division Tiebreaker
vs. S.D. Conquistadors, lost

1975 ABA Western Division Semifinals
vs. Uta. Stars, won (4–2)
ABA Western Division Finals
vs. Ind. Pacers, lost (4–3)

1976 ABA Western Division Semifinals
vs. Ken. Colonels, won (4–3)
ABA Western Division Finals
vs. N.Y. Nets, lost (4–2)

1977 NBA Western Conferernce
Semifinals vs. Por. Blazers,
lost (4–2)

1978 Western Conferernce Semifinals
vs. Mil. Bucks, won (4–3)
Western Conference Finals
vs. Sea. Sonics, lost (4–2)

1979 Western Conference First Round
vs. L.A. Lakers, lost (2–1)

1982 Western Conference First Round
vs. Pho. Suns, lost (2–1)

1983 Western Conference First Round
vs. Pho. Suns, won (2–1)
Western Conferernce Semifinals
vs. S.A. Spurs, lost (4–1)

1984 Western Conference First Round
vs. Uta. Jazz, lost (3–2)

1985 Western Conference First Round
vs. S.A. Spurs, won (3–2)
Western Conferernce Semifinals
vs. Uta. Jazz, won (4–1)
Western Conference Finals
vs. L.A. Lakers, lost (4–1)

1986 Western Conference First Round
vs. Por. Blazers, won (3–1)
Western Conferernce Semifinals
vs. Hou. Rockets, lost (4–2)

1987 Western Conference First Round
vs. L.A. Lakers, lost (3–0)

1988 Western Conference First Round
vs. Sea. Sonics, won (3–2)
Western Conferernce Semifinals
vs. Dal. Mavericks, lost (4–2)

1989 Western Conference First Round
vs. Pho. Suns, lost (3–0)

1990 Western Conference First Round
vs. S.A. Spurs, lost (3–0)

1994 Western Conference First Round
vs. Sea. Sonics, won (3–2)
Western Conferernce Semifinals
vs. Uta. Jazz, lost (4–3)

1995 Western Conference First Round
vs. S.A. Spurs, lost (3–0)

2004 Western Conference First Round
vs. Min. T'Wolves, lost (4–1)

2005 Western Conference First Round
vs. S.A. Spurs, lost (4–1)

2006 Western Conference First Round
vs. L.A. Clippers, lost (4–1)

2007 Western Conference First Round
vs. S.A. Spurs, lost (4–1)

2008 Western Conference First Round
vs. L.A. Lakers, lost (4–0)

2009 Western Conference First Round
vs. N.O. Hornets, won (4–1)
Western Conferernce Semifinals
vs. Dal. Mavericks, won (4–1)
Western Conference Finals
vs. L.A. Lakers, lost (4–2)

2010 Western Conference First Round
vs. Uta. Jazz, lost (4–2)

2011 Western Conference First Round
vs. Ok.C. Thunder, lost (4–1)

2012 Western Conference First Round
vs. L.A. Lakers, lost (4–3)

2013 Western Conference First Round
vs. G.S. Warriors, lost (4–2)

2019 Western Conference First Round
vs. S.A. Spurs, won (4–3)
Western Conferernce Semifinals
vs. Por. Blazers, lost (4–3)

2020 Western Conference First Round
vs. Uta. Jazz, won (4–3)
Western Conferernce Semifinals
vs. L.A. Clippers, won (4–3)
Western Conference Finals
vs. L.A. Lakers, lost (4–1)

2021 Western Conference First Round
vs. Por. Blazers, won (4–2)
Western Conferernce Semifinals
vs. Pho. Suns, lost (4–0)

2022 Western Conference First Round
vs. G.S. Warriors, lost (4–1)

Golden State Warriors

Dates of Operation: (as the Philadelphia Warriors) 1946–62 (16 seasons)
Overall Record: 558 wins, 545 losses (.506)
Arenas: Philadelphia Arena, 1946–52; Philadelphia Civic Center, 1952–62

Dates of Operation: (as the Golden State Warriors) 1962–present (60 seasons)
Overall Record: 2321 wins, 2515 losses (.480)
Arenas: Cow Palace, 1962–64; 1967–68; San Francisco Civil Auditorium, 1964–67; Oracle
  Arena (formerly Oakland-Alameda County Coliseum Arena, 1968–96; The Arena in Oakland,
  1997–2004; Oakland Arena, 2004–06), 1968–2019; San Jose Arena, 1996–97; Chase Center,
  2019–present (capacity: 18,064)
Other Name: San Francisco Warriors, 1962–71

Year-by-Year Finishes

Year	Finish	Wins	Losses	Percentage	Games Behind	Head Coach	Attendance
				Philadelphia Warriors **BAA Eastern Division**			
1946–47	2nd	35	25	.583	14.0	Eddie Gottlieb	129,142
1947–48	1st	27	21	.563	+1.0	Eddie Gottlieb	109,095
1948–49	4th	28	32	.467	10.0	Eddie Gottlieb	94,847
				NBA Eastern Division			
1949–50	4th	26	42	.382	27.0	Eddie Gottlieb	63,270
1950–51	1st	40	26	.606	+2.5	Eddie Gottlieb	105,108
1951–52	4th	33	33	.500	7.0	Eddie Gottlieb	96,578
1952–53	5th	12	57	.174	34.5	Eddie Gottlieb	56,882
1953–54	4th	29	43	.403	15.0	Eddie Gottlieb	113,088
1954–55	4th	33	39	.458	10.0	Eddie Gottlieb	123,438
1955–56	1st	45	27	.625	+10.0	George Senesky	164,929
1956–57	3rd	37	35	.514	7.0	George Senesky	158,004
1957–58	3rd	37	35	.514	12.0	George Senesky	156,981
1958–59	4th	32	40	.444	20.0	Al Cervi	153,566
1959–60	2nd	49	26	.653	10.0	Neil Johnston	226,412
1960–61	2nd	46	33	.582	11.0	Neil Johnston	196,223
1961–62	2nd	49	31	.613	11.0	Frank McGuire	161,795
				San Francisco Warriors **Western Division**			
1962–63	4th	31	49	.388	22.0	Bob Feerick	101,218
1963–64	1st	48	32	.600	+2.0	Alex Hannum	132,678
1964–65	5th	17	63	.213	32.0	Alex Hannum	76,963
1965–66	4th	35	45	.438	10.0	Alex Hannum	124,160
1966–67	1st	44	37	.543	+5.0	Bill Sharman	216,352
1967–68	3rd	43	39	.524	13.0	Bill Sharman	185,322
1968–69	3rd	41	41	.500	14.0	George Lee	194,683
1969–70	6th	30	52	.366	18.0	George Lee (22–30), Al Attles (8–22)	189,642
				Western Conference Pacific Division			
1970–71	2nd	41	41	.500	7.0	Al Attles	195,935

Year	Finish	Wins	Losses	Percentage	Games Behind	Head Coach	Attendance
				Golden State Warriors			
1971–72	2nd	51	31	.622	18.0	Al Attles	200,917
1972–73	2nd	47	35	.573	13.0	Al Attles	244,504
1973–74	2nd	44	38	.537	3.0	Al Attles	265,095
1974–75	1st	48	34	.585	+5.0	Al Attles	360,740
1975–76	1st	59	23	.720	+16.0	Al Attles	490,846
1976–77	3rd	46	36	.561	7.0	Al Attles	479,328
1977–78	5th	43	39	.524	15.0	Al Attles	474,715
1978–79	6th	38	44	.463	14.0	Al Attles	427,252
1979–80	6th	24	58	.293	36.0	Al Attles (18–43), Johnny Bach (6–15)	344,483
1980–81	4th	39	43	.476	18.0	Al Attles	412,969
1981–82	4th	45	37	.549	12.0	Al Attles	391,726
1982–83	5th	30	52	.366	28.0	Al Attles	341,365
1983–84	5th	37	45	.451	17.0	Johnny Bach	316,844
1984–85	6th	22	60	.268	40.0	Johnny Bach	300,586
1985–86	6th	30	52	.366	32.0	Johnny Bach	401,205
1986–87	3rd	42	40	.512	23.0	George Karl	423,997
1987–88	5th	20	62	.244	42.0	George Karl (16–48), Ed Gregory (4–14)	440,294
1988–89	4th	43	39	.524	14.0	Don Nelson	587,820
1989–90	5th	37	45	.451	26.0	Don Nelson	616,025
1990–91	4th	44	38	.537	19.0	Don Nelson	616,025
1991–92	2nd	55	27	.671	2.0	Don Nelson	616,025
1992–93	6th	34	48	.415	28.0	Don Nelson	616,025
1993–94	3rd	50	32	.610	13.0	Don Nelson	616,025
1994–95	6th	26	56	.317	33.0	Don Nelson (14–31), Bob Lanier (12–25)	616,025
1995–96	6th	36	46	.439	28.0	Rick Adelman	616,025
1996–97	7th	30	52	.366	27.0	Rick Adelman	621,844
1997–98	6th	19	63	.232	42.0	P.J. Carlesimo	444,922
1998–99	6th	21	29	.420	14.0	P.J. Carlesimo	335,837
1999–00	6th	19	63	.232	48.0	P.J. Carlesimo (6–21), Garry St. Jean (13–42)	509,171
2000–01	7th	17	65	.207	39.0	Dave Cowens	591,981
2001–02	7th	21	61	.256	40.0	Dave Cowens (8–15), Brian Winters (13–46)	593,182
2002–03	6th	38	44	.463	21.0	Eric Musselman	634,935
2003–04	4th (Tie)	37	45	.451	19.0	Eric Musselman	665,648
2004–05	4th (Tie)	34	48	.415	28.0	Mike Montgomery	670,368
2005–06	5th	34	48	.415	20.0	Mike Montgomery	749,185
2006–07	2nd (Tie)	42	40	.512	19.0	Don Nelson	742,267
2007–08	3rd	48	34	.585	9.0	Don Nelson	804,864
2008–09	3rd	29	53	.354	36.0	Don Nelson	776,660
2009–10	4th	26	56	.317	31.0	Don Nelson	739,120
2010–11	3rd	36	46	.439	21.0	Keith Smart	766,398
2011–12	4th	23	43	.348	18.0	Mark Jackson	622,311
2012–13	2nd	47	35	.573	9.0	Mark Jackson	794,320
2013–14	2nd	51	31	.622	6.0	Mark Jackson	803,436
2014–15	1st	67	15	.817	+11.0	Steve Kerr	803,436
2015–16	1st	73	9	.890	+20.0	Steve Kerr	803,436
2016–17	1st	67	15	.817	+16.0	Steve Kerr	803,436

Year	Finish	Wins	Losses	Percentage	Games Behind	Head Coach	Attendance
2017–18	1st	58	24	.707	+16.0	Steve Kerr	803,436
2018–19	1st	57	25	.695	+9.0	Steve Kerr	803,436
2019–20	5th	15	50	.231	34.0	Steve Kerr	614,176
2020–21	4th	39	33	.542	12.0	Steve Kerr	33,457
2021–22	2nd	53	29	.646	11.0	Steve Kerr	740,624

1998–99: 50-game season.

2011–12: 66-game season.

2019–20: 65-to-75-game season.

2020–21: 72-game season.

Awards

Most Valuable Player
Wilt Chamberlain, center, 1959–60 (Phi.)
Stephen Curry, guard, 2014–15
Stephen Curry, guard, 2015–16

Rookie of the Year
Wilt Chamberlain, center, 1959–60 (Phi.)
Woody Sauldsberry, forward, 1957–58 (Phi.)
Paul Arizin, forward, 1950–51 (Phi.)
Rick Barry, forward, 1965–66 (S.F.)
Jamaal Wilkes, forward, 1974–75
Mitch Richmond, guard, 1988–89
Chris Webber, forward, 1993–94

Defensive Player of the Year
Draymond Green, forward, 2016–17

Sixth Man of the Year
none

Most Improved Player
Gilbert Arenas, guard, 2002–03
Monta Ellis, guard, 2006–07

All-NBA First Team
Joe Fulks, 1946–47 (Phi.)
Howie Dallmar, 1947–48 (Phi.)
Joe Fulks, 1947–48 (Phi.)
Joe Fulks, 1948–49 (Phi.)
Paul Arizin, 1951–52 (Phi.)
Neil Johnston, 1952–53 (Phi.)
Neil Johnston, 1953–54 (Phi.)
Neil Johnston, 1954–55 (Phi.)
Paul Arizin, 1955–56 (Phi.)
Neil Johnston, 1955–56 (Phi.)
Paul Arizin, 1956–57 (Phi.)
Wilt Chamberlain, 1959–60 (Phi.)
Wilt Chamberlain, 1960–61 (Phi.)
Wilt Chamberlain, 1961–62 (Phi.)
Wilt Chamberlain, 1963–64 (S.F.)
Rick Barry, 1965–66 (S.F.)

Rick Barry, 1966–67 (S.F.)
Rick Barry, 1973–74
Rick Barry, 1974–75
Rick Barry, 1975–76
Chris Mullin, 1991–92
Latrell Sprewell, 1993–94
Stephen Curry, 2014–15
Stephen Curry, 2015–16
Kevin Durant, 2017–18
Stephen Curry, 2018–19
Stephen Curry, 2020–21

All-Defensive First Team
Nate Thurmond, 1968–69 (S.F.)
Nate Thurmond, 1970–71 (S.F.)
Andre Iguodala, 2013–14
Draymond Green, 2014–15
Draymond Green, 2015–16
Draymond Green, 2016–17
Draymond Green, 2020–21

All-Rookie First Team
Nate Thurmond, 1963–64 (S.F.)
Rick Barry, 1965–66 (S.F.)
Fred Hetzel, 1965–66 (S.F.)
Jamaal Wilkes, 1974–75
Gus Williams, 1975–76
Joe Barry Carroll, 1980–81
Larry Smith, 1980–81
Mitch Richmond, 1988–89
Tim Hardaway, 1989–90
Billy Owens, 1991–92
Chris Webber, 1993–94
Joe Smith, 1995–96
Marc Jackson, 2000–01
Jason Richardson, 2001–02
Stephen Curry, 2009–10
Klay Thompson, 2011–12
Harrison Barnes, 2012–13
Eric Paschall, 2019–20

Coach of the Year
Alex Hannum, 1963–64 (S.F.)
Don Nelson, 1991–92
Steve Kerr, 2015–16

Hall of Famers Who Played for the Warriors
Paul Arizin, forward, 1950–52; 1954–62 (Phi.)
Rick Barry, forward, 1965–67; 1972–78 (S.F.-G.S.)
Wilt Chamberlain, center, 1959–65 (Phi.-S.F.)
Joe Fulks, forward, 1946–54
Tom Gola, guard, 1955–56; 1957–63 (Phi.-S.F.)
Tim Hardaway, guard, 1989–93; 1994–96
Neil Johnston, center, 1951–59 (Phi.)
Bernard King, forward, 1980–82
Jerry Lucas, forward, 1969–71
Šarūnas Marčiulionis, guard-forward, 1989–93
Chris Mullin, guard-forward, 1985–97; 2000–01
Robert Parish, center, 1976–80
Andy Phillip, guard, 1950–53 (Phi.)
Mitch Richmond, guard, 1988–91
Guy Rodgers, guard, 1958–66 (Phi.-S.F.)
Ralph Sampson, center, 1987–89
Nate Thurmond, forward-center, 1963–74 (S.F.-G.S.)
Chris Webber, forward-center, 1993–94; 2007–08
Jo Jo White, guard, 1978–80
Jamaal Wilkes, forward, 1974–77

Retired Numbers
13 .... Wilt Chamberlain
14 .... Tom Meschery
16 .... Al Attles

17.....................................Chris Mullin
24...Rick Barry
42...............................Nate Thurmond

League Leaders, Offense
Points

Joe Fulks, 1946–47 (Phi.)............. 1389
Paul Arizin, 1951–52 (Phi.).......... 1674
Neil Johnston, 1952–53 (Phi.) 1564
Neil Johnston, 1953–54 (Phi.) 1759
Neil Johnston, 1954–55 (Phi.) 1631
Paul Arizin, 1956–57 (Phi.).......... 1817
Wilt Chamberlain, 1959–60 (Phi.) ... 2707
Wilt Chamberlain, 1960–61 (Phi.)... 3033
Wilt Chamberlain, 1961–62 (Phi.)... 4029
Wilt Chamberlain, 1962–63 (S.F.)... 3586
Wilt Chamberlain, 1963–64 (S.F.)... 2948
Wilt Chamberlain*, 1964–65 (S.F.)... 2534
Rick Barry, 1966–67 (S.F.) 2775
Stephen Curry, 2020–21 2015

*1480 with S.F. Warriors and 1054 with Phi. 76ers.

Three Pointers

Dorrell Wright, 2010–11 194
Stephen Curry, 2012–13................. 272
Stephen Curry, 2013–14................. 261
Stephen Curry, 2014–15................. 286
Stephen Curry, 2015–16................. 402
Stephen Curry, 2016–17................. 324
Stephen Curry, 2020–21 337
Stephen Curry, 2021–22................. 285

Assists

Howie Dallmar, 1947–48 (Phi.) 120
Andy Phillip, 1950–51 (Phi.) 414
Andy Phillip, 1951–52 (Phi.) 539
Guy Rodgers, 1962–63 (S.F.) 825

Scoring Average

Joe Fulks, 1946–47 (Phi.).............. 23.2
Joe Fulks, 1947–48 (Phi.).............. 22.1
Paul Arizin, 1951–52 (Phi.)........... 25.4
Neil Johnston, 1952–53 (Phi.) 22.3
Neil Johnston, 1953–54 (Phi.) 24.4
Neil Johnston, 1954–55 (Phi.) 22.7
Paul Arizin, 1956–57 (Phi.)........... 25.6
Wilt Chamberlain, 1959–60 (Phi.) ... 37.6
Wilt Chamberlain, 1960–61 (Phi.) ... 38.4
Wilt Chamberlain, 1961–62 (Phi.)... 50.4
Wilt Chamberlain, 1962–63 (S.F.) ... 44.8
Wilt Chamberlain, 1963–64 (S.F.) ... 36.9
Wilt Chamberlain*, 1964–65 (S.F.)... 34.7
Rick Barry, 1966–67 (S.F.) 35.6
Stephen Curry, 2015–16............... 30.1

Stephen Curry, 2020–21 .... 32.0
*38.9 with S.F. Warriors and 30.1 with Phi. 76ers.

Field Goal Percantage

Paul Arizin, 1951–52 (Phi.)........... .448
Neil Johnston, 1952–53 (Phi.) .... .452
Neil Johnston, 1955–56 (Phi.) .... .457
Neil Johnston, 1956–57 (Phi.) .... .447
Wilt Chamberlain, 1960–61 (Phi.)... .509
Wilt Chamberlain, 1962–63 (S.F.) ... .528
Wilt Chamberlain*, 1964–65 (S.F.)... .510
Chris Gatling, 1994–95 .... .633
Andris Biedriņš, 2007–08 .... .626

* .499 with S.F. Warriors and .528 with Phi. 76ers.

Three Point Percentage

Anthony Morrow, 2008–09 .... .467
Jordan Poole, 2021–22................. .925

Free Throw Percentage

Joe Fulks, 1950–51 (Phi.).............. .855
Rick Barry, 1972–73..................... .902
Rick Barry, 1974–75..................... .904
Rick Barry, 1975–76..................... .923
Rick Barry, 1977–78..................... .924
Mark Price, 1996–97.................... .906
Stephen Curry, 2010–11 .... .934
Stephen Curry, 2014–15............... .914
Stephen Curry, 2015–16............... .908
Stephen Curry, 2017–18............... .921

Assists Average

Andy Phillip, 1950–51 (Phi.) 6.3
Andy Phillip, 1951–52 (Phi.) 8.2
Guy Rodgers, 1962–63 (S.F.) 10.4

League Leaders, Defense
Offensive Rebounds

Larry Smith, 1985–86 384
Erick Dampier, 2003–04 344

Defensive Rebounds

Total Rebounds

Neil Johnston, 1954–55 (Phi.) 1085
Wilt Chamberlain, 1959–60 (Phi.)... 1941
Wilt Chamberlain, 1960–61 (Phi.)... 2149
Wilt Chamberlain, 1961–62 (Phi.)... 2052
Wilt Chamberlain, 1962–63 (S.F.)... 1946

Steals

Rick Barry, 1974–75..................... 228
Stephen Curry, 2014–15............... 163
Stephen Curry, 2015–16............... 169

Blocks

Manute Bol, 1988–89 345

Rebounds Average

Neil Johnston, 1954–55 (Phi.) 15.1
Wilt Chamberlain, 1959–60 (Phi.) ... 27.0
Wilt Chamberlain, 1960–61 (Phi.) ... 27.2
Wilt Chamberlain, 1961–62 (Phi.) ... 25.7
Wilt Chamberlain, 1962–63 (S.F.) ... 24.3

Steals Average

Rick Barry, 1974–75..................... 2.9
Micheal Ray Richardson*, 1982–83 . 2.8
Baron Davis, 2006–07 .... 2.1
Stephen Curry, 2015–16................ 2.1
Draymond Green, 2016–17 .... 2.0
*3.1 with G.S. Warriors and 2.6 with N.J. Nets.

Blocks Average

Manute Bol, 1988–89 .... 4.3

Feats
50-Point Game

100...Wilt Chamberlain (vs. N.Y. Knicks),
    Mar. 2, 1962 (Phi.)
70...Wilt Chamberlain (@ Syr. Nationals),
    Mar. 10, 1963 (S.F.)
67...Wilt Chamberlain (@ St.L. Hawks),
    Feb. 17, 1962 (Phi.)
65... Wilt Chamberlain (@ Cin. Royals),
    Feb. 13, 1962 (Phi.)
65...Wilt Chamberlain (@ St.L. Hawks),
    Feb. 27, 1962 (Phi.)
64...............Rick Barry (vs. Por. Blazers),
    Mar. 26, 1974
63...Wilt Chamberlain (@ Phi. 76ers),
    Nov. 26, 1964 (S.F.)
62... Wilt Chamberlain (@ Bos. Celtics),
    Jan. 14, 1962 (Phi.)
62... Wilt Chamberlain (vs. St.L. Hawks),
    Jan. 17, 1962 (Phi.)
62...Wilt Chamberlain (vs. Syr. Nationals),
    Jan. 21, 1962 (Phi.)
62......... Stephen Curry (vs. Por. Blazers),
    Jan. 3, 2021
61... Wilt Chamberlain (@ Chi. Packers),
    Feb. 28, 1962 (Phi.)
61... Wilt Chamberlain (vs. Cin. Royals),
    Nov. 21, 1962 (S.F.)
61...Wilt Chamberlain (vs. St.L. Hawks),
    Dec. 18, 1962 (S.F.)
60...Wilt Chamberlain (@ L.A. Lakers),
    Dec. 1, 1961 (Phi.)
60... Wilt Chamberlain (vs. L.A. Lakers),
    Dec. 29, 1961 (Phi.)
59... Wilt Chamberlain (vs. N.Y. Knicks),
    Oct. 30, 1962 (S.F.)

59... Wilt Chamberlain (vs. St.L. Hawks),
Dec. 2, 1962 (S.F.)

59... Wilt Chamberlain (vs. L.A. Lakers),
Dec. 6, 1963 (S.F.)

59... Wilt Chamberlain (@ Phi. 76ers),
Jan. 28, 1964 (S.F.)

59... Wilt Chamberlain (@ Det. Pistons),
Feb. 11, 1964 (S.F.)

58... Wilt Chamberlain (vs. Det. Pistons),
Jan. 25, 1960 (Phi.)

58... Wilt Chamberlain (@ N.Y. Knicks),
Feb. 21, 1960 (Phi.)

58... Wilt Chamberlain (@ N.Y. Knicks),
Mar. 4, 1962 (Phi.)

58... Wilt Chamberlain (vs. Det. Pistons),
Jan. 24, 1963 (S.F.)

58... Wilt Chamberlain (@ N.Y. Knicks),
Dec. 15, 1964 (S.F.)

57... Wilt Chamberlain (vs. Chi. Zephyrs),
Nov. 10, 1962 (S.F.)

57.............. Rick Barry (@ N.Y. Knicks),
Dec. 14, 1965 (S.F.)

57.............. Rick Barry (@ Cin. Royals),
Oct. 29, 1966 (S.F.)

57... Stephen Curry (@ Dal. Mavericks),
Feb. 6, 2021

56... Wilt Chamberlain (@ Syr. Nationals),
Mar. 1, 1961 (Phi.)

56... Wilt Chamberlain (vs. Det. Pistons),
Oct. 23, 1962 (S F.)

56... Wilt Chamberlain (@ Cin. Royals),
Feb. 7, 1963 (S.F.)

56... Wilt Chamberlain (@ L.A. Lakers),
Feb. 16, 1963 (S.F.)

56... Wilt Chamberlain (vs. Bal. Bullets),
Dec. 1, 1964 (S.F.)

55... Wilt Chamberlain (vs. Cin. Royals),
Nov. 12, 1959 (Phi.)

55... Wilt Chamberlain (vs. Syr. Nationals),
Oct. 27, 1961 (Phi.)

55... Wilt Chamberlain (vs. Chi. Packers),
Dec. 10, 1961 (Phi.)

55... Wilt Chamberlain (@ Det. Pistons),
Dec. 20, 1961 (Phi.)

55... Wilt Chamberlain (@ St.L. Hawks),
Jan. 7, 1962 (Phi.)

55... Wilt Chamberlain (vs. Chi. Packers),
Jan. 24, 1962 (Phi.)

55.... Wilt Chamberlain (@ N.Y. Knicks),
Jan. 30, 1962 (Phi.)

55... Wilt Chamberlain (vs. L.A. Lakers),
Nov. 2, 1963 (S.F.)

55... Wilt Chamberlain (@ L.A. Lakers),
Mar. 14, 1964 (S.F.)

55.............. Rick Barry (vs. Phi. 76ers),
Jan. 23, 1975

55.............. Rick Barry (vs. N.Y. Knicks),
Mar. 25, 1978

54... Wilt Chamberlain (vs. Det. Pistons),
Dec. 12, 1961 (Phi.)

54... Wilt Chamberlain (vs. Cin. Royals),
Jan. 18, 1962 (Phi.)

54... Wilt Chamberlain (vs. Chi. Zephyrs),
Nov. 9, 1962 (S.F.)

54... Wilt Chamberlain (vs. Cin. Royals),
Mar. 1, 1963 (S.F.)

54... Stephen Curry (vs. N.Y. Knicks),
Feb. 27, 2013

53... Wilt Chamberlain (vs. N.Y. Knicks),
Oct. 21, 1961 (Phi.)

53... Wilt Chamberlain (vs. N.Y. Knicks),
Dec. 27, 1961 (Phi.)

53... Wilt Chamberlain (vs. St.L. Hawks),
Jan. 5, 1962 (Phi.)

53... Wilt Chamberlain (vs. Det. Pistons),
Jan. 19, 1962 (Phi.)

53... Wilt Chamberlain (vs. Cin. Royals),
Feb. 1, 1962 (Phi.)

53... Wilt Chamberlain (vs. Cin. Royals),
Oct. 28, 1962 (S.F.)

53... Wilt Chamberlain (vs. L.A. Lakers),
Nov. 23, 1962 (S.F.)

53... Wilt Chamberlain (vs. St.L. Hawks),
Nov. 29, 1962 (S.F.)

53... Wilt Chamberlain (vs. Det. Pistons),
Nov. 12, 1964 (S.F.)

53... Wilt Chamberlain (vs. Bal. Bullets),
Jan. 3, 1965 (S.F.)

53... Stephen Curry (vs. N.O. Pelicans),
Oct. 31, 2015

53... Stephen Curry (vs. Den. Nuggets),
Apr. 12, 2021

52... Wilt Chamberlain (vs. Cin. Royals),
Jan. 11, 1962 (Phi.)

52... Wilt Chamberlain (vs. Cin. Royals),
Feb. 17, 1964 (S.F.)

52... Wilt Chamberlain (vs. Det. Pistons),
Feb. 18, 1964 (S.F.)

52... Wilt Chamberlain (vs. Cin. Royals),
Feb. 25, 1964 (S.F.)

52... Wilt Chamberlain (vs. N.Y. Knicks),
Nov. 6, 1964 (S.F.)

52.............. Rick Barry (vs. Chi. Bulls),
Feb. 16, 1967 (S.F.)

52... Klay Thompson (vs. Sac. Kings),
Jan. 23, 2015

52.. D'Angelo Russell (vs. Min. T'Wolves),
Nov. 8, 2019

51... Wilt Chamberlain (vs. Det. Pistons),
Dec. 7, 1962 (S.F.)

51... Wilt Chamberlain (vs. Det. Pistons),
Feb. 13, 1963 (S.F.)

51... Wilt Chamberlain (vs. Chi. Zephyrs),
Mar. 6, 1963 (S.F.)

51... Wilt Chamberlain (vs. Det. Pistons),
Mar. 8, 1963 (S.F.)

51.............. Rick Barry (vs. Hou. Rockets),
Jan. 17, 1973

51.............. Rick Barry (vs. Phi. 76ers),
Feb. 23, 1974

51.......... Phil Smith (vs. Pho. Suns),
Jan. 8, 1976

51.......... Phil Smith (vs. Hou. Rockets),
Dec. 11, 1976

51.................. Rick Barry (vs. Phi. 76ers),
Oct. 29, 1977

51. Antawn Jamison (vs. L.A. Lakers), Dec.
6, 2000

51......Stephen Curry (vs. Dal. Mavericks),
Feb. 4, 2015

51.......... Stephen Curry (vs. Orl. Magic),
Feb. 25, 2016

51...... Stephen Curry (vs. Was. Wizards),
Oct. 24, 2018

51.......... Kevin Durant (vs. Tor. Raptors),
Nov. 9, 2018

50....... Neil Johnston (vs. Syr. Nationals),
Feb. 16, 1954 (Phi.)

50... Wilt Chamberlain (vs. Chi. Packers),
Dec. 16, 1961 (Phi.)

50... Wilt Chamberlain (vs. Bos. Celtics),
Jan. 28, 1962 (Phi.)

50... Wilt Chamberlain (vs. Syr. Nationals),
Feb. 4, 1962 (Phi.)

50... Wilt Chamberlain (vs. Chi. Zephyrs),
Jan. 5, 1963 (S.F.)

50... Wilt Chamberlain (vs. L.A. Lakers),
Jan. 10, 1964 (S.F.)

50.............. Rick Barry (vs. St.L. Hawks),
Dec. 8, 1966 (S.F.)

50................ Rick Barry (vs. Cin. Royals),
Dec. 25, 1966 (S.F.)

50.............. Rick Barry (vs. Det. Pistons),
Jan. 14, 1967 (S.F.)

50.............. Rick Barry (vs. Bos. Celtics),
Feb. 14, 1967 (S.F.)

50............ Rick Barry (vs. L.A. Lakers),
Dec. 8, 1973

50............ Bernard King (vs. Phi. 76ers),
Jan. 3, 1981

50... Jamal Crawford (vs. Cha. Bobcats),
Dec. 20, 2008

50............Kevin Durant (vs. Por. Blazers),
Feb. 4, 2018

50...........Stephen Curry (vs. Atl. Hawks),
Nov. 8, 2021

20-Assist Game

28...........Guy Rodgers (vs. St.L. Hawks),
Mar. 14, 1963 (S.F.)

22............John Lucas (@ Den. Nuggets),
Feb. 7, 1981

22... Tim Hardaway (vs. Orl. Magic),
Dec. 16, 1994

20......... Guy Rodgers (vs. L.A. Lakers),
Dec. 1, 1960 (Phi.)

20............ Guy Rodgers (vs. N.Y. Knicks),
Mar. 2, 1962 (Phi.)

20......... Guy Rodgers (vs. Cin. Royals),
Mar. 1, 1963 (S.F.)

30-Rebound Game

55... Wilt Chamberlain (vs. Bos. Celtics),
Nov. 24, 1960 (Phi.)

45... Wilt Chamberlain (vs. Syr. Nationals),
Feb. 6, 1960 (Phi.)

45... Wilt Chamberlain (vs. L.A. Lakers),
Jan. 21, 1961 (Phi.)

43... Wilt Chamberlain (vs. N.Y. Knicks),
Nov. 10, 1959 (Phi.)

43... Wilt Chamberlain (vs. L.A. Lakers),
Dec. 8, 1961 (Phi.)

42... Wilt Chamberlain (vs. Bos. Celtics),
Jan. 15, 1960 (Phi.)

42... Wilt Chamberlain (vs. Det. Pistons),
Jan. 25, 1960 (Phi.) (Phi.)

42... Nate Thurmond (vs. Det. Pistons),
Nov. 9, 1965 (S.F.)

41... Wilt Chamberlain (vs. Det. Pistons),
Oct. 26, 1962 (S.F.)

40... Wilt Chamberlain (vs. Syr. Nationals),
Nov. 4, 1959 (Phi.)

40... Wilt Chamberlain (vs. Det. Pistons),
Nov. 22, 1964 (S.F.)

39... Neil Johnston (vs. Syr. Nationals),
Dec. 4, 1954 (Phi.)

39... Wilt Chamberlain (vs. Cin. Royals),
Dec. 28, 1959 (Phi.)

39... Wilt Chamberlain (vs. Syr. Nationals),
Jan. 13, 1960 (Phi.)

39... Wilt Chamberlain (vs. Bos. Celtics),
Jan. 29, 1960 (Phi.)

39... Wilt Chamberlain (vs. Det. Pistons),
Nov. 4, 1960 (Phi.)

38... Wilt Chamberlain (vs. L.A. Lakers),
Nov. 29, 1960 (Phi.)

38... Wilt Chamberlain (@ Cin. Royals),
Dec. 18, 1960 (Phi.)

38... Wilt Chamberlain (vs. Chi. Packers),
Nov. 25, 1961 (Phi.)

38... Wilt Chamberlain (vs. Bos. Celtics),
Feb. 21, 1963 (S.F.)

37... Wilt Chamberlain (vs. Syr. Nationals),
Jan. 9, 1960 (Phi.)

37... Wilt Chamberlain (@ Cin. Royals),
Jan. 24, 1960 (Phi.)

37... Wilt Chamberlain (vs. Chi. Zephyrs),
Nov. 27, 1962 (S.F.)

37... Wilt Chamberlain (vs. N.Y. Knicks),
Nov. 9, 1963 (S.F.)

37... Nate Thurmond (vs. Bal. Bullets),
Oct. 27, 1964 (S.F.)

37... Nate Thurmond (vs. L.A. Lakers),
Dec. 20, 1966 (S.F.)

36... Wilt Chamberlain (vs. Bos. Celtics),
Jan. 2, 1960 (Phi.)

36... Wilt Chamberlain (@ Bos. Celtics),
Dec. 26, 1960 (Phi.)

36... Wilt Chamberlain (@ St.L. Hawks),
Jan. 24, 1961 (Phi.)

36... Wilt Chamberlain (@ N.Y. Knicks),
Feb. 10, 1961 (Phi.)

36... Wilt Chamberlain (vs. Chi. Packers),
Dec. 9, 1961 (Phi.)

36... Wilt Chamberlain (@ N.Y. Knicks),
Dec. 25, 1961 (Phi.)

36... Wilt Chamberlain (vs. Chi. Packers),
Jan. 13, 1962 (Phi.)

36... Wilt Chamberlain (vs. L.A. Lakers),
Feb. 19, 1963 (S.F.)

35... Wilt Chamberlain (vs. Cin. Royals),
Nov. 8, 1959 (Phi.)

35... Wilt Chamberlain (@ Bos. Celtics),
Nov. 25, 1959 (Phi.)

35... Wilt Chamberlain (vs. St.L. Hawks),
Nov. 11, 1960 (Phi.)

35... Wilt Chamberlain (@ Bos. Celtics),
Jan. 13, 1961 (Phi.)

35... Wilt Chamberlain (vs. Bos. Celtics),
Jan. 14, 1961 (Phi.)

35... Wilt Chamberlain (vs. Det. Pistons),
Mar. 10, 1961 (Phi.)

35... Wilt Chamberlain (vs. N.Y. Knicks),
Oct. 21, 1961 (Phi.)

35... Wilt Chamberlain (@ N.Y. Knicks),
Mar. 4, 1962 (Phi.)

35... Wilt Chamberlain (vs. N.Y. Knicks),
Oct. 30, 1962 (S.F.)

34... Wilt Chamberlain (vs. Det. Pistons),
Oct. 31, 1959 (Phi.)

34... Wilt Chamberlain (vs. N.Y. Knicks),
Nov. 29, 1959 (Phi.)

34... Wilt Chamberlain (vs. Syr. Nationals),
Dec. 25, 1959 (Phi.)

34... Wilt Chamberlain (@ Cin. Royals),
Nov. 21, 1961 (Phi.)

34... Wilt Chamberlain (vs. St.L. Hawks),
Nov. 29, 1962 (S.F.)

34... Wilt Chamberlain (vs. Bal. Bullets),
Dec. 15, 1963 (S.F.)

34.........Nate Thurmond (@ Phi. 76ers),
Jan. 19, 1969 (S.F.)

34... Nate Thurmond (@ L.A. Lakers),
Feb. 2, 1969 (S.F.)

33... Wilt Chamberlain (vs. Min. Lakers),
Nov. 14, 1959 (Phi.)

33... Wilt Chamberlain (vs. Bos. Celtics),
Nov. 26, 1959 (Phi.)

33... Wilt Chamberlain (vs. Min. Lakers),
Dec. 3, 1959 (Phi.)

33... Wilt Chamberlain (vs. Min. Lakers),
Jan. 31, 1960 (Phi.)

33... Wilt Chamberlain (vs. Det. Pistons),
Jan. 3, 1961 (Phi.)

33... Wilt Chamberlain (vs. Bos. Celtics),
Nov. 3, 1961 (Phi.)

33... Wilt Chamberlain (vs. Det. Pistons),
Nov. 4, 1961 (Phi.)

33... Wilt Chamberlain (@ Chi. Packers),
Mar. 14, 1962 (Phi.)

33... Wilt Chamberlain (vs. N.Y. Knicks),
Jan. 14, 1963 (S.F.)

33... Wilt Chamberlain (vs. Cin. Royals),
Mar. 3, 1963 (S.F.)

33... Wilt Chamberlain (vs. Bos. Celtics),
Feb. 15, 1964 (S.F.)

33... Wilt Chamberlain (vs. Phi. 76ers),
Mar. 18, 1964 (S.F.)

33... Nate Thurmond (vs. Bal. Bullets),
Oct. 27, 1967 (S.F.)

33...........Nate Thurmond (@ Phi. 76ers),
Nov. 4, 1967 (S.F.)

33... Nate Thurmond (vs. Bos. Celtics),
Mar. 4, 1969 (S.F.)

32... Wilt Chamberlain (vs. Min. Lakers),
Dec. 30, 1959 (Phi.)

32... Wilt Chamberlain (vs. St.L. Hawks),
Jan. 12, 1961 (Phi.)

32... Wilt Chamberlain (vs. L.A. Lakers),
Oct. 20, 1961 (Phi.)

32... Wilt Chamberlain (vs. L.A. Lakers),
Nov. 17, 1961 (Phi.)

32... Wilt Chamberlain (vs. Chi. Packers),
Jan. 24, 1962 (Phi.)

32... Wilt Chamberlain (@ Bos. Celtics),
Dec. 26, 1962 (S.F.)

32... Wilt Chamberlain (@ Det. Pistons),
Feb. 12, 1963 (S.F.)

32...Wilt Chamberlain (vs. Bos. Celtics),
Jan. 7, 1964 (S.F.)

32... Wilt Chamberlain (vs. Det. Pistons),
Feb. 18, 1964 (S.F.)

32... Wilt Chamberlain (@ Bos. Celtics),
Nov. 25, 1964 (S.F.)

32... Wilt Chamberlain (@ Phi. 76ers),
Nov. 26, 1964 (S.F.)

32... Wilt Chamberlain (vs. N.Y. Knicks),
Dec. 30, 1964 (S.F.)

32... Nate Thurmond (@ Bal. Bullets),
Feb. 28, 1965 (S.F.)

32... Nate Thurmond (vs. Phi. 76ers),
Nov. 26, 1965 (S.F.)

32... Robert Parish (vs. N.Y. Knicks),
Mar. 30, 1979

31... Wilt Chamberlain (vs. N.Y. Knicks),
Dec. 26, 1959 (Phi.)

31...Wilt Chamberlain (@ Syr. Nationals),
Jan. 20, 1960 (Phi.)

31...Wilt Chamberlain (@ Syr. Nationals),
Oct. 22, 1960 (Phi.)

31... Wilt Chamberlain (@ N.Y. Knicks),
Jan. 8, 1961 (Phi.)

31... Wilt Chamberlain (vs. L.A. Lakers),
Feb. 28, 1961 (Phi.)

31... Wilt Chamberlain (vs. N.Y. Knicks),
Mar. 9, 1961 (Phi.)

31... Wilt Chamberlain (vs. Cin. Royals),
Jan. 18, 1962 (Phi.)

31... Wilt Chamberlain (vs. Bos. Celtics),
Feb. 10, 1962 (Phi.)

31... Wilt Chamberlain (vs. Bos. Celtics),
Feb. 24, 1962 (Phi.)

31... Wilt Chamberlain (vs. Bos. Celtics),
Jan. 2, 1963 (S.F.)

31... Wilt Chamberlain (vs. Bos. Celtics),
Jan. 8, 1963 (S.F.)

31... Wilt Chamberlain (vs. Syr. Nationals),
Jan. 27, 1963 (S.F.)

31... Wilt Chamberlain (@ St.L. Hawks),
Feb. 27, 1964 (S.F.)

31...Nate Thurmond (vs. Bos. Celtics),
Jan. 7, 1966 (S.F.)

31........... Larry Smith (vs. Den. Nuggets),
Mar. 28, 1981

30... Woody Sauldsberry (vs. Syr. Nationals),
Feb. 21, 1959 (Phi.)

30...Wilt Chamberlain (@ Cin. Royals),
Feb. 16, 1960 (Phi.)

30... Wilt Chamberlain (vs. Bos. Celtics),
Dec. 27, 1960 (Phi.)

30... Wilt Chamberlain (vs. Bos. Celtics),
Dec. 27, 1960 (Phi.)

30... Wilt Chamberlain (vs. Cin. Royals),
Feb. 3, 1961 (Phi.)

30... Wilt Chamberlain (@ N.Y. Knicks),
Feb. 21, 1961 (Phi.)

30... Wilt Chamberlain (vs. Bos. Celtics),
Nov. 23, 1961 (Phi.)

30... Wilt Chamberlain (@ Bos. Celtics),
Dec. 13, 1961 (Phi.)

30... Wilt Chamberlain (vs. N.Y. Knicks),
Dec. 27, 1961 (Phi.)

30... Wilt Chamberlain (vs. L.A. Lakers),
Dec. 14, 1962 (S.F.)

30... Wilt Chamberlain (vs. Bos. Celtics),
Feb. 26, 1963 (S.F.)

30... Wilt Chamberlain (vs. Bos. Celtics),
Feb. 26, 1963 (S.F.)

30... Wilt Chamberlain (vs. St.L. Hawks),
Dec. 17, 1963 (S.F.)

30... Wilt Chamberlain (@ Bos. Celtics),
Jan. 19, 1964 (S.F.)

30... Wilt Chamberlain (vs. L.A. Lakers),
Nov. 28, 1964 (S.F.)

30... Nate Thurmond (vs. N.Y. Knicks),
Jan. 15, 1965 (S.F.)

30... Nate Thurmond (vs. Cin. Royals),
Dec. 9, 1965 (S.F.)

30... Nate Thurmond (vs. Det. Pistons),
Nov. 14, 1966 (S.F.)

30... Nate Thurmond (vs. St.L. Hawks),
Nov. 21, 1966 (S.F.)

30............... Clyde Lee (@ N.Y. Knicks),
Feb. 20, 1968 (S.F.)

30... Nate Thurmond (vs. S.D. Rockets),
Oct. 18, 1969 (S.F.)

30... George Johnson (@ L.A. Lakers),
Mar. 15, 1974

8-Steal Game

10... Draymond Green (@ Mem. Grizzlies),
Feb. 10, 2017

9............... Rick Barry (vs. Buf. Braves),
Oct. 29, 1974

9................John Lucas (vs. L.A. Lakers),
Mar. 30, 1980

9...Micheal Ray Richardson (vs. S.A. Spurs),
Feb. 5, 1983

8................ Rick Barry (vs. L.A. Lakers),
Mar. 25, 1975

8...............Lorenzo Romar (@ N.J. Nets),
Feb. 25, 1983

8... Winston Garland (vs. Por. Blazers),
Apr. 20, 1988

8.......... Tim Hardaway (vs. Mia. Heat),
Apr. 3, 1991

8.......... Latrell Sprewell (@ Orl. Magic),
Mar. 26, 1995

10-Block Game

13............... Manute Bol (vs. N.J. Nets),
Feb. 2, 1990

12............... Manute Bol (@ S.A. Spurs),
Feb. 22, 1989

11...........George Johnson (@ Chi. Bulls),
Mar. 30, 1976

11........ Robert Parish (vs. Cle. Cavaliers),
Oct. 29, 1978

11............... Manute Bol (@ Phi. 76ers),
Jan. 27, 1989

10........George Johnson (vs. Sea. Sonics),
Apr. 3, 1976

10............ Manute Bol (vs. Por. Blazers),
Nov. 2, 1988

10.............. Manute Bol (@ S.A. Spurs),
Dec. 17, 1988

10........... Manute Bol (@ L.A. Clippers),
Feb. 16, 1989

10............... Manute Bol (@ Uta. Jazz),
Mar. 10, 1989

10.......... Manute Bol (@ L.A. Clippers),
Mar. 12, 1990

Multiple Triple-Doubles in a Single Season

13.............Draymond Green, 2015–16

9...............Tom Gola, 1959–60 (Phi.)

6...........Guy Rodgers, 1960–61 (Phi.)

6.............Draymond Green, 2020–21

5.............Andy Phillip, 1950–51 (Phi.)

5.............Tom Gola, 1955–56 (Phi.)

5......Wilt Chamberlain, 1963–64 (S.F)

5.............Draymond Green, 2016–17

4.............Andy Phillip, 1951–52 (Phi.)

4...........Guy Rodgers, 1962–63 (S.F)

4.................Stephen Curry, 2013–14

3...............Tom Gola, 1957–58 (Phi.)

3...........Guy Rodgers, 1958–59 (Phi.)

3......Wilt Chamberlain, 1962–63 (S.F)

3.......................Rick Barry, 1972–73

3.................Tim Hardaway, 1989–90

3.....................Baron Davis, 2007–08

3.............Draymond Green, 2017–18

2...............Tom Gola, 1961–62 (Phi.)

2............Guy Rodgers, 1965–66 (S.F)

2........Nate Thurmond, 1967–68 (S.F)

2...............Jerry Lucas, 1970–71 (S.F)

2......................Chris Mullin, 1996–97
2................. Stephen Curry, 2015–16
2.................... Kevin Durant, 2017–18
2.................... Kevin Durant, 2018–19
2.............. Draymond Green, 2019–20
2................. Stephen Curry, 2021–22

Postseason Play

1947 BAA Quarterfinals vs. St.L.
Bombers, won (2–1)
BAA Semifinals vs. N.Y. Knicks,
won (2–0)
BAA Finals vs. Chi. Stags,
won (4–1)

1948 BAA Semifinals vs. St.L. Bombers,
won (4–3)
BAA Finals vs. Bal. Bullets,
lost (4–2)

1949 BAA Semifinals vs. Was. Capitols,
lost (2–0)

1950 NBA Eastern Division Semifinals
vs. Syr. Nationals, lost (2–0)

1951 Eastern Division Semifinals
vs. Syr. Nationals, lost (2–0)

1952 Eastern Division Semifinals
vs. Syr. Nationals, lost (2–1)

1956 Eastern Division Finals
vs. Syr. Nationals, won (3–2)
NBA Finals vs. Ft.W. Pistons,
won (4–1)

1957 Eastern Division Semifinals
vs. Syr. Nationals, lost (2–0)

1958 Eastern Division Semifinals
vs. Syr. Nationals, won (2–1)
Eastern Division Finals
vs. Bos. Celtics, lost (4–1)

1960 Eastern Division Semifinals
vs. Syr. Nationals, won (2–1)
Eastern Division Finals
vs. Bos. Celtics, lost (4–2)

1961 Eastern Division Semifinals
vs. Syr. Nationals, lost (3–0)

1962 Eastern Division Semifinals
vs. Syr. Nationals, won (3–2)
Eastern Division Finals
vs. Bos. Celtics, lost (4–3)

1964 Western Division Finals
vs. St.L. Hawks, won (4–3)
NBA Finals vs. Bos. Celtics,
lost (4–1)

1967 Western Division Semifinals
vs. L.A. Lakers, won (3–0)
Western Division Finals

vs. St.L. Hawks, won (4–2)
NBA Finals vs. Phi. 76ers,
lost (4–2)

1968 Western Division Semifinals
vs. St.L. Hawks, won (4–2)
Western Division Finals
vs. L.A. Lakers, lost (4–0)

1969 Western Division Semifinals
vs. L.A. Lakers, lost (4–2)

1971 Western Conference Semifinals
vs. Mil. Bucks, lost (4–1)

1972 Western Conference Semifinals
vs. Mil. Bucks, lost (4–1)

1973 Western Conference Semifinals
vs. Mil. Bucks, won (4–2)
Western Conference Finals
vs. L.A. Lakers, lost (4–1)

1975 Western Conference Semifinals
vs. Sea. Sonics, won (4–2)
Western Conference Finals
vs. Chi. Bulls, won (4–3)
NBA Finals vs. Was. Bullets,
lost (4–0)

1976 Western Conference Semifinals
vs. Det. Pistons, won (4–2)
Western Conference Finals
vs. Pho. Suns, lost (4–3)

1977 Western Conference First Round
vs. Det. Pistons, won (2–1)
Western Conference Semifinals
vs. L.A. Lakers, lost (4–3)

1987 Western Conference First Round
vs. Uta. Jazz, won (3–2)
Western Conference Semifinals
vs. L.A. Lakers, lost (4–1)

1989 Western Conference First Round
vs. Uta. Jazz, won (3–0)
Western Conference Semifinals
vs. Pho. Suns, lost (4–1)

1991 Western Conference First Round
vs. S.A. Spurs, won (3–1)
Western Conference Semifinals
vs. L.A. Lakers, lost (4–1)

1992 Western Conference First Round
vs. Sea. Sonics, lost (3–1)

1994 Western Conference First Round
vs. Pho. Suns, lost (3–0)

2007 Western Conference First Round
vs. Dal. Mavericks, won (4–2)
Western Conference Semifinals
vs. Uta. Jazz, lost (4–1)

2013 Western Conference First Round
vs. Den. Nuggets, won (4–2)

Western Conference Semifinals
vs. S.A. Spurs, lost (4–2)

2014 Western Conference First Round
vs. L.A. Clippers, lost (4–3)

2015 Western Conference First Round
vs. N.O. Pelicans, won (4–0)
Western Conference Semifinals
vs. Mem. Grizzlies, won (4–2)
Western Conference Finals
vs. Hou. Rockets, won (4–1)
NBA Finals vs. Cle. Cavaliers,
won (4–2)

2016 Western Conference First Round
vs. Hou. Rockets, won (4–1)
Western Conference Semifinals
vs. Por. Blazers, won (4–1)
Western Conference Finals
vs. Ok.C. Thunder, won (4–3)
NBA Finals vs. Cle. Cavaliers,
lost (4–3)

2017 Western Conference First Round
vs. Por. Blazers, won (4–0)
Western Conference Semifinals
vs. Uta. Jazz, won (4–0)
Western Conference Finals
vs. S.A. Spurs, won (4–0)
NBA Finals vs. Cle. Cavaliers,
won (4–1)

2018 Western Conference First Round
vs. S.A. Spurs, won (4–1)
Western Conference Semifinals
vs. N.O. Pelicans, won (4–1)
Western Conference Finals
vs. Hou. Rockets, won (4–3)
NBA Finals vs. Cle. Cavaliers,
won (4–0)

2019 Western Conference First Round
vs. L.A. Clippers, won (4–2)
Western Conference Semifinals
vs. Hou. Rockets, won (4–2)
Western Conference Finals
vs. Por. Blazers, won (4–0)
NBA Finals vs. Tor. Raptors,
lost (4–2)

2022 Western Conference First Round
vs. Den. Nuggets, won (4–1)
Western Conference Semifinals
vs. Mem. Grizzlies, won (4–2)
Western Conference Finals
vs. Dal. Mavericks, won (4–1)
NBA Finals vs. Bos. Celtics,
won (4–2)

Houston Rockets

Dates of Operation: (as the San Diego Rockets) 1967–71 (4 seasons)
Overall Record: 119 wins, 209 losses (.363)
Arena: San Diego Sports Arena, 1967–71

Dates of Operation: (as the Houston Rockets) 1971–present (51 seasons)
Overall Record: 2187 wins, 1927 losses (.532)
Arenas: Hofheinz Pavilion, 1971–75; Compaq Center (formerly The Summit, 1975–98), 1975–2003;
Toyota Center, 2003–present (capacity: 18,055)

Year-by-Year Finishes

Year	Finish	Wins	Losses	Percentage	Games Behind	Head Coach	Attendance
				San Diego Rockets **Western Division**			
1967–68	6th	15	67	.183	41.0	Jack McMahon	188,865
1968–69	4th	37	45	.451	18.0	Jack McMahon	248,217
1969–70	7th	27	55	.329	21.0	Jack McMahon (9–17), Alex Hannum (18–38)	232,684
				Western Conference Pacific Division			
1970–71	3rd	40	42	.488	8.0	Alex Hannum	264,206
				Houston Rockets			
1971–72	4th	34	48	.415	35.0	Tex Winter	203,599
				Eastern Conference Central Division			
1972–73	3rd	33	49	.402	19.0	Tex Winter (17–30), Johnny Egan (16–19)	189,773
1973–74	3rd	32	50	.390	15.0	Johnny Egan	158,059
1974–75	2nd	41	41	.500	19.0	Johnny Egan	187,457
1975–76	3rd	40	42	.488	9.0	Johnny Egan	261,518
1976–77	1st	49	33	.598	+1.0	Tom Nissalke	347,920
1977–78	6th	28	54	.341	24.0	Tom Nissalke	384,905
1978–79	2nd	47	35	.573	1.0	Tom Nissalke	434,400
1979–80	2nd (Tie)	41	41	.500	9.0	Del Harris	413,572
				Western Conference Midwest Division			
1980–81	2nd (Tie)	40	42	.488	12.0	Del Harris	385,354
1981–82	2nd (Tie)	46	36	.561	2.0	Del Harris	480,190
1982–83	6th	14	68	.171	39.0	Del Harris	291,315
1983–84	6th	29	53	.354	16.0	Bill Fitch	425,755
1984–85	2nd	48	34	.585	4.0	Bill Fitch	553,014
1985–86	1st	51	31	.622	+4.0	Bill Fitch	604,644
1986–87	3rd	42	40	.512	13.0	Bill Fitch	660,175
1987–88	4th	46	36	.561	8.0	Bill Fitch	681,051
1988–89	2nd	45	37	.549	6.0	Don Chaney	680,728
1989–90	5th	41	41	.500	15.0	Don Chaney	649,702
1990–91	3rd	52	30	.634	3.0	Don Chaney	613,230
1991–92	3rd	42	40	.512	13.0	Don Chaney (26–26), Rudy Tomjanovich (16–14)	592,790
1992–93	1st	55	27	.671	+6.0	Rudy Tomjanovich	554,210
1993–94	1st	58	24	.707	+3.0	Rudy Tomjanovich	615,227

Year	Finish	Wins	Losses	Percentage	Games Behind	Head Coach	Attendance
1994–95	3rd	47	35	.573	15.0	Rudy Tomjanovich	653,389
1995–96	3rd	48	34	.585	11.0	Rudy Tomjanovich	667,840
1996–97	2nd	57	25	.695	7.0	Rudy Tomjanovich	667,685
1997–98	4th	41	41	.500	21.0	Rudy Tomjanovich	670,117
1998–99	3rd	31	19	.620	6.0	Rudy Tomjanovich	407,125
1999–00	6th	34	48	.415	21.0	Rudy Tomjanovich	624,594
2000–01	5th	45	37	.549	13.0	Rudy Tomjanovich	518,555
2001–02	5th	28	54	.341	30.0	Rudy Tomjanovich	481,227
2002–03	5th	43	39	.524	17.0	Rudy Tomjanovich	565,155
2003–04	5th	45	37	.549	13.0	Jeff Van Gundy	640,794
Southwest Division							
2004–05	3rd	51	31	.622	8.0	Jeff Van Gundy	663,444
2005–06	5th	34	48	.415	29.0	Jeff Van Gundy	636,110
2006–07	3rd	52	30	.634	15.0	Jeff Van Gundy	678,362
2007–08	3rd	55	27	.671	1.0	Rick Adelman	718,524
2008–09	2nd	53	29	.646	1.0	Rick Adelman	717,669
2009–10	3rd	42	40	.512	13.0	Rick Adelman	677,658
2010–11	5th	43	39	.524	18.0	Rick Adelman	663,839
2011–12	4th	34	32	.515	16.0	Kevin McHale	506,994
2012–13	3rd	45	37	.549	13.0	Kevin McHale	683,564
2013–14	2nd	54	28	.659	8.0	Kevin McHale	743,082
2014–15	1st	56	26	.683	+1.0	Kevin McHale	747,412
2015–16	4th	41	41	.500	26.0	Kevin McHale (4–7), J.B. Bickerstaff (37–34)	737,244
2016–17	2nd	55	27	.671	6.0	Mike D'Antoni	695,903
2017–18	1st	65	17	.793	+17.0	Mike D'Antoni	732,722
2018–19	1st	53	29	.646	+5.0	Mike D'Antoni	740,392
2019–20	1st	44	28	.611	+2.5	Mike D'Antoni	578,458
2020–21	5th	17	55	.236	25.0	Stephen Silas	117,009
2021–22	5th	20	62	.244	36.0	Stephen Silas	638,977

1998–99: 50-game season.

2011–12: 66-game season.

2019–20: 65-to-75-game season.

2020–21: 72-game season.

Awards

Most Valuable Player

Moses Malone, center, 1978–79
Moses Malone, center, 1981–82
Hakeem Olajuwon, center, 1993–94
James Harden, guard, 2017–18

Rookie of the Year

Ralph Sampson, center, 1983–84
Steve Francis, guard, 1999–00*
*Tied with Elton Brand, Chi. Bulls.

Defensive Player of the Year

Hakeem Olajuwon, center, 1992–93
Hakeem Olajuwon, center, 1993–94

Sixth Man of the Year

Eric Gordon, guard, 2016–17

Most Improved Player

Aaron Brooks, guard, 2009–10

All-NBA First Team

Moses Malone, 1978–79
Moses Malone, 1981–82
Hakeem Olajuwon, 1986–87
Hakeem Olajuwon, 1987–88
Hakeem Olajuwon, 1988–89
Hakeem Olajuwon, 1992–93
Hakeem Olajuwon, 1993–94
Hakeem Olajuwon, 1996–97

James Harden, 2013–14
James Harden, 2014–15
James Harden, 2016–17
James Harden, 2017–18
James Harden, 2018–19
James Harden, 2019–20

All-Defensive First Team

Hakeem Olajuwon, 1986–87
Rodney McCray, 1987–88
Hakeem Olajuwon, 1987–88
Hakeem Olajuwon, 1989–90
Hakeem Olajuwon, 1992–93
Hakeem Olajuwon, 1993–94
Patrick Beverley, 2016–17

All-Rookie First Team

Elvin Hayes, 1968–69 (S.D.)
Calvin Murphy, 1970–71 (S.D.)
Joe Meriweather, 1975–76
John Lucas, 1976–77
Ralph Sampson, 1983–84
Hakeem Olajuwon, 1984–85
Steve Francis, 1999–00
Yao Ming, 2002–03
Luis Scola, 2007–08
Jae'Sean Tate, 2020–21
Jalen Green, 2021–22

Coach of the Year

Tom Nissalke, 1976–77
Don Chaney, 1990–91
Mike D'Antoni, 2016–17

Hall of Famers Who Played for the Rockets

Charles Barkley, forward, 1996–2000
Rick Barry, forward, 1978–80
Clyde Drexler, guard, 1994–98
Elvin Hayes, center, 1968–72; 1981–84 (S.D.-Hou.)
Moses Malone, center, 1976–82
Tracy McGrady, guard, 2004–10
Yao Ming, center, 2002–09; 2010–11
Calvin Murphy, guard, 1970–83 (S.D.-Hou.)
Dikembe Mutombo, center, 2004–09
Hakeem Olajuwon, center, 1984–2001
Scottie Pippen, forward, 1998–99
Ralph Sampson, center-forward, 1983–88

Retired Numbers

CD .... Carroll Dawson
11 .... Yao Ming
22 .... Clyde Drexler
23 .... Calvin Murphy
24 .... Moses Malone
34 .... Hakeem Olajuwon
45 .... Rudy Tomjanovich

League Leaders, Offense
Points

Elvin Hayes, 1968–69 (S.D.) 2327
James Harden, 2014–15 2217
James Harden, 2015–16 2376
James Harden, 2018–19 2818
James Harden, 2019–20 2335

Three Pointers

Vernon Maxwell, 1990–91 172
Vernon Maxwell, 1991–92 162

Aaron Brooks, 2009–10 209
James Harden, 2017–18 265
James Harden, 2018–19 378
James Harden, 2019–20 299

Assists

James Harden, 2016–17 907

Scoring Average

Elvin Hayes, 1968–69 (S.D.) 28.4
James Harden, 2017–18 .... 30.4
James Harden, 2018–19 .... 36.1
James Harden, 2019–20 .... 34.3

Field Goal Percentage

Clint Capela, 2017–18 .... .652

Three Point Percentage

Free Throw Percentage

Rick Barry, 1978–79 .... .947
Rick Barry, 1979–80 .... .935
Calvin Murphy, 1980–81 .... .958
Calvin Murphy, 1982–83 .... .920

Assists Average

James Harden, 2016–17 .... 11.2

League Leaders, Defense
Offensive Rebounds

Moses Malone*, 1976–77 437
Moses Malone, 1977–78 380
Moses Malone, 1978–79 587
Moses Malone, 1979–80 573
Moses Malone, 1980–81 474
Moses Malone, 1981–82 558
Hakeem Olajuwon, 1984–85 440
*437 with Hou. Rockets and 0 with Buf. Braves.

Defensive Rebounds

Moses Malone, 1978–79 857
Hakeem Olajuwon, 1988–89 767
Hakeem Olajuwon, 1989–90 850

Total Rebounds

Elvin Hayes, 1969–70 (S.D.) 1386
Moses Malone, 1978–79 1444
Moses Malone, 1980–81 1180
Moses Malone, 1981–82 1188
Hakeem Olajuwon, 1988–89 1105
Hakeem Olajuwon, 1989–90 1149
Ömer Aşık, 2012–13 956

Steals

James Harden, 2019–20 125

Blocks

Hakeem Olajuwon, 1989–90 376

Hakeem Olajuwon, 1992–93 342

Rebounds Average

Elvin Hayes, 1969–70 (S.D.) 16.9
Moses Malone, 1978–79 .... 17.6
Moses Malone, 1980–81 .... 14.8
Moses Malone, 1981–82 .... 14.7
Hakeem Olajuwon, 1988–89 .... 13.5
Hakeem Olajuwon, 1989–90 .... 14.0

Steals Average

Blocks Average

Hakeem Olajuwon, 1989–90 .... 4.6
Hakeem Olajuwon, 1990–91 .... 4.0
Hakeem Olajuwon, 1992–93 .... 4.2

Feats
50-Point Game

61 .... James Harden (@ N.Y. Knicks), Jan. 23, 2019
61 .... James Harden (vs. S.A. Spurs), Mar. 22, 2019
60 .... James Harden (vs. Orl. Magic), Jan. 30, 2018
60 .... James Harden (vs. Atl. Hawks), Nov. 30, 2019
59 ... James Harden (@ Was. Wizards), Oct. 30, 2019
58 .... James Harden (vs. Brk. Nets), Jan. 16, 2019
58 .... James Harden (vs. Mia. Heat), Feb. 28, 2019
57 .... Calvin Murphy (vs. N.J. Nets), Mar. 18, 1978
57 .. James Harden (vs. Mem. Grizzlies), Jan. 14, 2019
57 .... James Harden (@ Mem. Grizzlies), Mar. 20, 2019
56 .... James Harden (vs. Uta. Jazz), Nov. 5, 2017
55 ... James Harden (@ Cle. Cavaliers), Dec. 11, 2019
54 .... Elvin Hayes (vs. Det. Pistons), Nov. 13, 1968 (S.D.)
54 ... James Harden (@ Was. Wizards), Nov. 26, 2018
54 .... James Harden (@ Orl. Magic), Dec. 13, 2019
53 ... Moses Malone (vs. S.D. Clippers), Feb. 2, 1982
53 .... James Harden (vs. N.Y. Knicks), Dec. 31, 2016

52.. Hakeem Olajuwon (vs. Den. uggets),
Apr. 19, 1990

51... Moses Malone (vs. G.S. Warriors),
Mar. 11, 1981

51... Vernon Maxwell (vs. Cle. Cavaliers),
Jan. 26, 1991

51... Hakeem Olajuwon (vs. Bos. Celtics),
Jan. 18, 1996

51......... James Harden (vs. Sac. Kings),
Apr. 1, 2015

51.......... James Harden (@ Phi. 76ers),
Jan. 27, 2017

51.......... James Harden (vs. L.A. Lakers),
Dec. 20, 2017

51.. James Harden (vs. L.A. Clippers),
Dec. 22, 2017

50........... Elvin Hayes (vs. Sea. Sonics),
Nov. 20, 1970 (S.D.)

50... James Harden (vs. Den. Nuggets),
Mar. 19, 2015

50...........James Harden (vs. Phi. 76ers),
Nov. 27, 2015

50.......... James Harden (vs. L.A. Lakers),
Dec. 13, 2018

50.......... James Harden (vs. Sac. Kings),
Mar. 30, 2019

50......... James Harden (@ S.A. Spurs),
Dec. 3, 2019

50................Eric Gordon (@ Uta. Jazz),
Jan. 27, 2020

50...........Kevin Porter (vs. Mil. Bucks),
Apr. 29, 2021

20-Assist Game

22................ Art Williams (@ Pho. Suns),
Dec. 28, 1968 (S.D.)

22......... Art Williams (vs. S.F. Warriors),
Feb. 14, 1970 (S.D.)

22............... Allen Leavell (vs. N.J. Nets),
Jan. 25, 1983

21.......... Larry Siegfried (@ Por. Blazers),
Nov. 16, 1970 (S.D.)

20.............. John Lucas (@ Ind. Pacers),
Apr. 8, 1978

30-Rebound Game

37......... Moses Malone (@ N.O. Jazz),
Feb. 9, 1979

35...............Elvin Hayes (@ N.Y. Knicks),
Jan. 19, 1971 (S.D.)

33...........Charles Barkley (@ Pho. Suns),
Nov. 2, 1996

32...........Moses Malone (vs. Sea. Sonics),
Feb. 11, 1982

30.............. Elvin Hayes (vs. L.A. Lakers),
Dec. 5, 1970 (S.D.)

8-Steal Game

10......... Clyde Drexler (vs. Sac. Kings),
Nov. 1, 1996

9.........Calvin Murphy (vs. Bos. Celtics),
Dec. 14, 1973

9......... Rafer Alston (vs. Cha. Bobcats),
Feb. 10, 2007

8......................... Ed Ratleff (vs. Chi. Bulls),
Oct. 27, 1973

8.............. Rick Barry (@ Cle. Cavaliers),
Apr. 1, 1979

8.............. Allen Leavell (@ L.A. Lakers),
Feb. 24, 1980

8................Robert Reid (@ Pho. Suns),
Jan. 16, 1981

8...Hakeem Olajuwon (@ Cle. Cavaliers),
Nov. 19, 1987

8......... Allen Leavell (vs. G.S. Warriors),
Feb. 16, 1988

8.........Hakeem Olajuwon (@ Mia. Heat),
Apr. 8, 1989

8... Hakeem Olajuwon (vs. L.A. Clippers),
Nov. 27, 1990

8.......... Steve Francis (@ L.A. Clippers),
Nov. 24, 2002

8......... James Harden (vs. Uta. Jazz),
Mar. 23, 2016

10-Block Game

13...........Ralph Sampson (@ Chi. Bulls),
Dec. 9, 1983

12.. Hakeem Olajuwon (vs. Sea. Sonics),
Mar. 10, 1987

12.. Hakeem Olajuwon (vs. Uta. Jazz),
Nov. 11, 1989

11.. Hakeem Olajuwon (vs. G.S. Warriors),
Jan. 7, 1986

11.. Hakeem Olajuwon (vs. G.S. Warriors),
Mar. 3, 1990

11.. Hakeem Olajuwon (vs. Mil. Bucks),
Mar. 29, 1990

11.. Hakeem Olajuwon (vs. Orl. Magic),
Dec. 20, 1990

10.. Hakeem Olajuwon (vs. S.A. Spurs),
Apr. 21, 1988

10.. Hakeem Olajuwon (vs. Orl. Magic),
Dec. 17, 1989

10.. Hakeem Olajuwon (@ Por. Blazers),
Jan. 3, 1993

10.. Hakeem Olajuwon (@ Van. Grizzlies),
Dec. 13, 1995

10...Hakeem Olajuwon (vs. Dal. Mavericks),
Apr. 13, 1996

Multiple Triple-Doubles in a Single Season

22...................James Harden, 2016–17

8.............Russell Westbrook, 2019–20

7...................James Harden, 2018–19

4........... Hakeem Olajuwon, 1989–90

4...................James Harden, 2014–15

4...................James Harden, 2017–18

4...................James Harden, 2019–20

3.............. Clyde Drexler, 1995–96

3........... Hakeem Olajuwon, 1995–96

3............. Clyde Drexler, 1996–97

3...................James Harden, 2015–16

2...........Art Williams, 1967–68 (S.D.)

2.............. Rodney McCray, 1986–87

2.................Scottie Pippen, 1998–99

2................... Steve Francis, 2000–01

2................... Steve Francis, 2001–02

Postseason Play

1969 Western Division Semifinals
vs. Atl. Hawks, lost (4–2)

1975 Eastern Conference First Round
vs. N.Y. Knicks, won (2–1)
Eastern Conference Semifinals
vs. Bos. Celtics, lost (4–1)

1977 Eastern Conference Semifinals
vs. Was. Bullets, won (4–2)
Eastern Conference Finals
vs. Phi. 76ers, lost (4–2)

1979 Eastern Conference First Round
vs. Atl. Hawks, lost (2–0)

1980 Eastern Conference First Round
vs. S.A. Spurs, won (2–1)
Eastern Conference Semifinals
vs. Bos. Celtics, lost (4–0)

1981 Western Conference First Round
vs. L.A. Lakers, won (2–1)
Western Conference Semifinals
vs. S.A. Spurs, won (4–3)
Western Conference Finals
vs. K.C. Kings, won (4–1)
NBA Finals vs. Bos. Celtics,
lost (4–2)

1982 Western Conference First Round
vs. Sea. Sonics, lost (2–1)

1985 Western Conference First Round
vs. Uta. Jazz, lost (3–2)

1986 Western Conference First Round
vs. Sac. Kings, won (3–0)

Western Conference Semifinals
vs. Den. Nuggets, won (4–2)
Western Conference Finals
vs. L.A. Lakers, won (4–1)
NBA Finals vs. Bos. Celtics,
lost (4–2)

1987 Western Conference First Round
vs. Por. Blazers, won (3–1)
Western Conference Semifinals
vs. Sea. Sonics, lost (4–2)

1988 Western Conference First Round
vs. Dal. Mavericks, lost (3–1)

1989 Western Conference First Round
vs. Sea. Sonics, lost (3–1)

1990 Western Conference First Round
vs. L.A. Lakers, lost (3–1)

1991 Western Conference First Round
vs. L.A. Lakers, lost (3–0)

1993 Western Conference First Round
vs. L.A. Clippers, won (3–2)
Western Conference Semifinals
vs. Sea. Sonics, lost (4–3)

1994 Western Conference First Round
vs. Por. Blazers, won (3–1)
Western Conference Semifinals
vs. Pho. Suns, won (4–3)
Western Conference Finals
vs. Uta. Jazz, won (4–1)
NBA Finals vs. N.Y. Knicks,
won (4–3)

1995 Western Conference First Round
vs. Uta. Jazz, won (3–2)

Western Conference Semifinals
vs. Pho. Suns, won (4–3)
Western Conference Finals
vs. S.A. Spurs, won (4–2)
NBA Finals vs. Orl. Magic,
won (4–0)

1996 Western Conference First Round
vs. L.A. Lakers, won (3–1)
Western Conference Semifinals
vs. Sea. Sonics, lost (4–0)

1997 Western Conference First Round
vs. Min. T'Wolves, won (3–0)
Western Conference Semifinals
vs. Sea. Sonics, won (4–3)
Western Conference Finals
vs. Uta. Jazz, lost (4–2)

1998 Western Conference First Round
vs. Uta. Jazz, lost (3–2)

1999 Western Conference First Round
vs. L.A. Lakers, lost (3–1)

2004 Western Conference First Round
vs. L.A. Lakers, lost (4–1)

2005 Western Conference First Round
vs. Dal. Mavericks, lost (4–3)

2007 Western Conference First Round
vs. Uta. Jazz, lost (4–3)

2008 Western Conference First Round
vs. Uta. Jazz, lost (4–2)

2009 Western Conference First Round
vs. Por. Blazers, won (4–2)
Western Conference Semifinals
vs. L.A. Lakers, lost (4–3)

2013 Western Conference First Round
vs. Ok.C. Thunder, lost (4–2)

2014 Western Conference First Round
vs. Por. Blazers, lost (4–2)

2015 Western Conference First Round
vs. Dal. Mavericks, won (4–1)
Western Conference Semifinals
vs. L.A. Clippers, won (4–3)
Western Conference Finals
vs. G.S. Warriors, lost (4–1)

2016 Western Conference First Round
vs. G.S. Warriors, lost (4–1)

2017 Western Conference First Round
vs. Ok.C. Thunder, won (4–1)
Western Conference Semifinals
vs. S.A. Spurs, lost (4–2)

2018 Western Conference First Round
vs. Min. T'Wolves, won (4–1)
Western Conference Semifinals
vs. Uta. Jazz, won (4–1)
Western Conference Finals
vs. G.S. Warriors, lost (4–3)

2019 Western Conference First Round
vs. Uta. Jazz, won (4–1)
Western Conference Semifinals
vs. G.S. Warriors, lost (4–2)

2020 Western Conference First Round
vs. Ok.C. Thunder, won (4–3)
Western Conference Semifinals
vs. L.A. Lakers, lost (4–1)

Los Angeles Clippers

Dates of Operation: (as the Buffalo Braves) 1970–78 (8 seasons)
Overall Record: 259 wins, 397 losses (.390)
Arena: Buffalo Memorial Auditorium, 1970–78

Dates of Operation: (as the Los Angeles Clippers) 1978–present (44 seasons)
Overall Record: 1489 wins, 2051 losses (.421)
Arenas: San Diego Sports Arena, 1978–84; Los Angeles Memorial Sports Arena, 1984–99;
   Crypto.com Arena (formerly STAPLES Center, 1999–2021), 1999–present (capacity: 19,079)
Other Name: San Diego Clippers, 1978–88

Year-by-Year Finishes

Year	Finish	Wins	Losses	Percentage	Games Behind	Head Coach	Attendance
				Buffalo Braves			
				Eastern Conference Atlantic Division			
1970–71	4th	22	60	.268	30.0	Dolph Schayes	204,053
1971–72	4th	22	60	.268	34.0	Dolph Schayes (0–1), Johnny McCarthy (22–59)	350,852
1972–73	3rd	21	61	.256	47.0	Jack Ramsay	321,710
1973–74	3rd	42	40	.512	14.0	Jack Ramsay	427,270
1974–75	2nd	49	33	.598	11.0	Jack Ramsay	467,267
1975–76	2nd (Tie)	46	36	.561	8.0	Jack Ramsay	418,696
1976–77	4th	30	52	.366	20.0	Tates Locke (16–30), Bob MacKinnon (3–4), Joe Mullaney (11–18)	319,398
1977–78	4th	27	55	.329	28.0	Cotton Fitzsimmons	252,457
				San Diego Clippers			
				Western Conference Pacific Division			
1978–79	5th	43	39	0.524	9.0	Gene Shue	311,789
1979–80	5th	35	47	0.427	25.0	Gene Shue	325,012
1980–81	5th	36	46	0.439	21.0	Paul Silas	257,597
1981–82	6th	17	65	0.207	40.0	Paul Silas	225,036
1982–83	6th	25	57	0.305	33.0	Paul Silas	195,883
1983–84	6th	30	52	0.366	24.0	Jim Lynam	218,534
				Los Angeles Clippers			
1984–85	4th (Tie)	31	51	.378	31.0	Jim Lynam (22–39), Don Chaney (9–12)	384,519
1985–86	3rd (Tie)	32	50	.390	30.0	Don Chaney	337,814
1986–87	6th	12	70	.146	53.0	Don Chaney	316,140
1987–88	6th	17	65	.207	45.0	Gene Shue	345,589
1988–89	7th	21	61	.256	36.0	Gene Shue (10–28), Don Casey (11–33)	286,614
1989–90	6th	30	52	.366	33.0	Don Casey	486,621
1990–91	6th	31	51	.378	32.0	Mike Schuler	522,111
1991–92	5th	45	37	.549	12.0	Mike Schuler (21–24), Mack Calvin (1–1), Larry Brown (23–12)	500,200
1992–93	4th	41	41	.500	21.0	Larry Brown	532,625

Year	Finish	Wins	Losses	Percentage	Games Behind	Head Coach	Attendance
1993–94	7th	27	55	.329	36.0	Bob Weiss	471,034
1994–95	7th	17	65	.207	42.0	Bill Fitch	438,244
1995–96	7th	29	53	.354	35.0	Bill Fitch	405,495
1996–97	5th	36	46	.439	21.0	Bill Fitch	232,895
1997–98	7th	17	65	.207	44.0	Bill Fitch	254,840
1998–99	7th	9	41	.180	26.0	Chris Ford	256,568
1999–00	7th	15	67	.183	52.0	Chris Ford (11–34), Jim Todd (4–33)	559,714
2000–01	6th	31	51	.378	25.0	Alvin Gentry	601,587
2001–02	5th	39	43	.476	22.0	Alvin Gentry	740,185
2002–03	7th	27	55	.329	32.0	Alvin Gentry (19–39), Dennis Johnson (8–16)	706,471
2003–04	7th	28	54	.341	28.0	Mike Dunleavy	665,396
2004–05	3rd	37	45	.451	25.0	Mike Dunleavy	696,181
2005–06	2nd	47	35	.573	7.0	Mike Dunleavy	712,409
2006–07	4th	40	42	.488	21.0	Mike Dunleavy	755,261
2007–08	5th	23	59	.280	34.0	Mike Dunleavy	692,408
2008–09	4th	19	63	.232	46.0	Mike Dunleavy	663,587
2009–10	3rd	29	53	.354	28.0	Mike Dunleavy (21–28), Kim Hughes (8–25)	670,063
2010–11	4th	32	50	.390	25.0	Vinny Del Negro	727,462
2011–12	2nd	40	26	.606	1.0	Vinny Del Negro	634,237
2012–13	1st	56	26	.683	+9.0	Vinny Del Negro	788,293
2013–14	1st	57	25	.695	+6.0	Doc Rivers	787,692
2014–15	2nd	56	26	.683	11.0	Doc Rivers	785,892
2015–16	2nd	53	29	.646	20.0	Doc Rivers	786,910
2016–17	2nd	51	31	.622	16.0	Doc Rivers	782,609
2017–18	2nd	42	40	.512	16.0	Doc Rivers	697,812
2018–19	2nd	48	34	.585	9.0	Doc Rivers	710,327
2019–20	2nd	49	23	.681	3.5	Doc Rivers	610,176
2020–21	2nd	47	25	.653	4.0	Tyronn Lue	13,901
2021–22	3rd	42	40	.512	22.0	Tyronn Lue	694,005

1998–99: 50-game season.

2011–12: 66-game season.

2019–20: 65-to-75-game season.

2020–21: 72-game season.

Awards

Most Valuable Player
Bob McAdoo, center, 1974–75 (Buf.)

Rookie of the Year
Bob McAdoo, forward, 1972–73 (Buf.)
Ernie DiGregorio, guard, 1973–74 (Buf.)
Adrian Dantley, forward, 1976–77 (Buf.)
Terry Cummings, forward, 1982–83 (S.D.)
Blake Griffin, forward, 2010–11

Defensive Player of the Year
none

Sixth Man of the Year
Jamal Crawford, guard, 2013–14
Jamal Crawford, guard, 2015–16
Lou Williams, guard, 2017–18
Lou Williams, guard, 2018–19
Montrezl Harrell, center, 2019–20

Most Improved Player
Bobby Simmons, forward, 2004–05

All-NBA First Team
Bob McAdoo, 1974–75 (Buf.)
Chris Paul, 2011–12

Chris Paul, 2012–13
Chris Paul, 2013–14
DeAndre Jordan, 2015–16
Kawhi Leonard, 2020–21

All-Defensive First Team
Chris Paul, 2011–12
Chris Paul, 2012–13
Chris Paul, 2013–14
DeAndre Jordan, 2014–15
Chris Paul, 2014–15
DeAndre Jordan, 2015–16
Chris Paul, 2015–16

Chris Paul, 2016–17

All-Rookie First Team

Elmore Smith, 1971–72 (Buf.)

Bob McAdoo, 1972–73 (Buf.)

Ernie DiGregorio, 1973–74 (Buf.)

John Shumate, 1975–76* (Buf.)

Adrian Dantley, 1976–77 (Buf.)

Terry Cummings, 1982–83 (S.D.)

Charles Smith, 1988–89

Lamar Odom, 1999–00

Darius Miles, 2000–01

Al Thornton, 207–08

Blake Griffin, 2010–11

* 32 games with Buf. Braves and 43 games
with Pho. Suns.

Coach of the Year

Hall of Famers Who Played for the Braves/Clippers

Adrian Dantley, forward, 1976–77
(Buf.)

Grant Hill, forward, 2012–13

Moses Malone, center, 1976–77 (Buf.)

Bob McAdoo, forward-center, 1972–77
(Buf.)

Paul Pierce, forward, 2015–17

Bill Walton, center, 1979–80; 1982–84
(S.D.-L.A.)

Jamaal Wilkes, forward, 1985–86

Dominique Wilkins, forward, 1993–94

Retired Numbers

League Leaders, Offense

Points

Bob McAdoo, 1973–74 (Buf.)....... 2261

Bob McAdoo, 1974–75 (Buf.)....... 2831

Bob McAdoo, 1975–76 (Buf.)....... 2427

Three Pointers

Brian Taylor, 1979–80 (S.D.)............ 90

Assists

Ernie DiGregorio, 1973–74 (Buf.)... 663

Norm Nixon, 1983–84 (S.D.)......... 914

Chris Paul, 2014–15...................... 838

Scoring Average

Bob McAdoo, 1973–74 (Buf.)........ 30.6

Bob McAdoo, 1974–75 (Buf.)........ 34.5

Bob McAdoo, 1975–76 (Buf.)........ 31.1

Field Goal Percantage

Bob McAdoo, 1973–74 (Buf.)........ .547

John Shumate*, 1975–76 (Buf.) ..... .561

James Donaldson, 1984–85 .... .637

DeAndre Jordan, 2012–13............. .643

DeAndre Jordan, 2013–14............. .676

DeAndre Jordan, 2014–15............. .710

DeAndre Jordan, 2015–16............. .703

DeAndre Jordan, 2016–17............. .714

*.575 with Buf. Braves and .550 with Pho. Suns.

Three Point Percentage

Brian Taylor, 1980–81 (S.D.)......... .383

J.J. Redick, 2015–16 .... .475

Luke Kennard, 2021–22................ .449

Free Throw Percentage

Ernie DiGregorio, 1973–74 (Buf.).. .902

Ernie DiGregorio, 1976–77 (Buf.).. .945

Assists Average

Ernie DiGregorio, 1973–74 (Buf.).... 8.2

Chris Paul, 2013–14..................... 10.7

Chris Paul, 2014–15..................... 10.2

League Leaders, Defense

Offensive Rebounds

Moses Malone*, 1976–77 (Buf.) 437

Elton Brand, 2000–01.................... 396

*0 with Buf. Braves and 437 with Hou. Rockets.

Defensive Rebounds

Swen Nater, 1979–80 (S.D.) 864

Swen Nater, 1980–81 (S.D.) 722

DeAndre Jordan, 2013–14............. 783

DeAndre Jordan, 2014–15............. 829

DeAndre Jordan, 2016–17............. 816

Total Rebounds

Bob McAdoo, 1974–75 (Buf.)....... 1155

Swen Nater, 1979–80 (S.D.) 1216

DeAndre Jordan, 2013–14........... 1114

DeAndre Jordan, 2014–15........... 1226

Steals

Chris Paul, 2011–12...................... 152

Blocks

Rebounds Average

Swen Nater, 1979–80 (S.D.) 15.0

Michael Cage, 1987–88 .... 13.0

DeAndre Jordan, 2013–14............. 13.6

DeAndre Jordan, 2014–15............. 15.0

Steals Average

Chris Paul, 2011–12...................... 2.5

Chris Paul, 2012–13...................... 2.4

Chris Paul, 2013–14...................... 2.5

Blocks Average

Feats

50-Point Game

52.......... Bob McAdoo (vs. Bos. Celtics),
Feb. 22, 1974 (Buf.)

52........... Bob McAdoo (@ Sea. Sonics),
Mar. 17, 1976 (Buf.)

52........ Charles Smith (@ Den. Nuggets),
Dec. 1, 1990

51.......... Bob McAdoo (@ Hou. Rockets),
Mar. 18, 1975 (Buf.)

51......... Freeman Williams (@ Pho. Suns),
Jan. 19, 1980 (S.D.)

50.......... Bob McAdoo (@ Cle. Cavaliers),
Nov. 20, 1975 (Buf.)

50........ Lou Williams (@ G.S. Warriors),
Jan. 10, 2018

20-Assist Game

25...Ernie DiGregorio (@ Por. Blazers),
Jan. 1, 1974 (Buf.)

21...........Norm Nixon (vs. Det. Pistons),
Mar. 18, 1985

21................ Gary Grant (vs. Mil. Bucks),
Nov. 29, 1989

21...............Gary Grant (vs. Sea. Sonics),
Jan. 18, 1990

20..........Norm Nixon (vs. Den. Nuggets),
Apr. 10, 1985

20.......... Norm Nixon (vs. Hou. Rockets),
Dec. 8, 1988

20......... Gary Grant (vs. Por. Blazers),
Apr. 6, 1989

20......... Gary Grant (vs. G.S. Warriors),
Dec. 28, 1989

20.......... Baron Davis (vs. N.Y. Knicks),
Feb. 11, 2009

20.......... Baron Davis (vs. Was. Wizards),
Mar. 18, 2009

20......... Chris Paul (vs. N.O. Pelicans),
Dec. 10, 2016

30-Rebound Game

32.......... Swen Nater (vs. Den. Nuggets),
Dec. 14, 1979 (S.D.)

30............... Swen Nater (vs. N.J. Nets),
Mar. 4, 1978 (Buf.)

30.......... Michael Cage (vs. Sea. Sonics),
Apr. 24, 1988

8-Steal Game

10............... Lou Williams (@ Uta. Jazz),
    Jan. 20, 2018
9............... Doc Rivers (vs. Pho. Suns),
    Nov. 6, 1991
8...............Randy Smith (vs. Phi. 76ers),
    Jan. 22, 1974 (Buf.)
8...............Randy Smith (@ Phi. 76ers),
    Dec. 26, 1975 (Buf.)
8.......... Randy Smith (vs. Atl. Hawks),
    Mar. 22, 1977 (Buf.)
8.............. Randy Smith (@ Pho. Suns),
    Mar. 24, 1977 (Buf.)
8.............. Randy Smith (@ Por. Blazers),
    Dec. 13, 1977 (Buf.)
8............. Randy Smith (vs. S.A. Spurs),
    Feb. 7, 1979 (S.D.)
8.......... Mark Jackson (vs. Ind. Pacers),
    Dec. 13, 1992
8...............Gary Grant (vs. Sea. Sonics),
    Apr. 22, 1993
8............... Gary Grant (@ S.A. Spurs),
    Nov. 22, 1993
8......... Pooh Richardson (@ Orl. Magic),
    Dec. 30, 1994
8............... Malik Sealy (@ Ind. Pacers),
    Mar. 30, 1997
8...............Chris Paul (vs. N.O. Hornets),
    Apr. 22, 2012
8..............Pablo Prigioni (vs. Mia. Heat),
    Jan. 13, 2016
8......... Paul George (vs. Por. Blazers),
    Oct. 25, 2021

10-Block Game

10......... Benoit Benjamin (vs. Mil. Bucks),
    Jan. 29, 1988
10......... Benoit Benjamin (vs. S.A. Spurs),
    Mar. 31, 1989

Multiple Triple-Doubles in a Single Season

4............ Bob Kauffman, 1972–73 (Buf.)
4......................Lamar Odom, 2000–01
3.................... Mark Jackson, 1992–93
3......................Lamar Odom, 1999–00
2............ Bob Kauffman, 1970–71 (Buf.)
2........................ Ron Harper, 1993–94
2......................Blake Griffin, 2010–11
2......................Blake Griffin, 2017–18

Postseason Play

1974	Eastern Conference Semifinals	vs. Bos. Celtics, lost (4–2)
1975	Eastern Conference Semifinals	vs. Was. Bullets, lost (4–3)
1976	Eastern Conference First Round	vs. Phi. 76ers, won (2–1)
	Eastern Conference Semifinals	vs. Bos. Celtics, lost (4–2)
1992	Western Conference First Round	vs. Uta. Jazz, lost (3–2)
1993	Western Conference First Round	vs. Hou. Rockets, lost (3–2)
1997	Western Conference First Round	vs. Uta. Jazz, lost (3–0)
2006	Western Conference First Round	vs. Den. Nuggets, won (4–1)
	Western Conference Semifinals	vs. Pho. Suns, lost (4–3)
2012	Western Conference First Round	vs. Mem. Grizzlies, won (4–3)
	Western Conference Semifinals	vs. S.A. Spurs, lost (4–0)
2013	Western Conference First Round	vs. Mem. Grizzlies, lost (4–2)
2014	Western Conference First Round	vs. G.S. Warriors, won (4–3)
	Western Conference Semifinals	vs. Ok.C. Thunder, lost (4–2)
2015	Western Conference First Round	vs. S.A. Spurs, won (4–3)
	Western Conference Semifinals	vs. Hou. Rockets, lost (4–3)
2016	Western Conference First Round	vs. Por. Blazers, lost (4–2)
2017	Western Conference First Round	vs. Uta. Jazz, lost (4–3)
2019	Western Conference First Round	vs. G.S. Warriors, lost (4–2)
2020	Western Conference First Round	vs. Dal. Mavericks, won (4–2)
	Western Conference Semifinals	vs. Den. Nuggets, lost (4–3)
2021	Western Conference First Round	vs. Dal. Mavericks, won (4–3)
	Western Conference Semifinals	vs. Uta. Jazz, won (4–2)
	Western Conference Finals	vs. Pho. Suns, lost (4–2)

Los Angeles Lakers

Dates of Operation: (as the Minneapolis Lakers) 1948–60 (12 seasons)
Overall Record: 457 wins, 382 losses (.545)
Arenas: Minneapolis Auditorium, 1948–59; Minneapolis Armory, 1959–60

Dates of Operation: (as the Los Angeles Lakers) 1960–present (62 seasons)
Overall Record: 3003 wins, 1998 losses (.600)
Arenas: Los Angeles Memorial Sports Arena, 1960–67; Great Western Forum (formerly The Forum, 1967–88), 1967–99; Crypto.com Arena (formerly STAPLES Center, 1999–2021), 1999–present (capacity: 19,079)

Year-by-Year Finishes

Year	Finish	Wins	Losses	Percentage	Games Behind	Head Coach	Attendance
				Minneapolis Lakers			
				BAA Western Division			
1948–49	2nd	44	16	.733	1.0	John Kundla	N/A
				NBA Central Division			
1949–50	1st (Tie)	51	17	.750	—	John Kundla	N/A
				Western Division			
1950–51	1st	44	24	.647	+3.0	John Kundla	172,410
1951–52	2nd	40	26	.606	1.0	John Kundla	N/A
1952–53	1st	48	22	.686	+4.0	John Kundla	N/A
1953–54	1st	46	26	.639	+2.0	John Kundla	N/A
1954–55	2nd	40	32	.556	3.0	John Kundla	N/A
1955–56	2nd (Tie)	33	39	.458	4.0	John Kundla	112,360
1956–57	1st (Tie)	34	38	.472	—	John Kundla	82,211
1957–58	4th	19	53	.264	22.0	George Mikan (9–30), John Kundla (10–23)	107,874
1958–59	2nd	33	39	.458	16.0	John Kundla	164,197
1959–60	3rd	25	50	.333	21.0	John Castellani (11–25), Jim Pollard (14–25)	106,859
				Los Angeles Lakers			
1960–61	2nd	36	43	.456	15.0	Fred Schaus	151,344
1961–62	1st	54	26	.675	+11.0	Fred Schaus	190,321
1962–63	1st	53	27	.663	+5.0	Fred Schaus	285,462
1963–64	3rd	42	38	.525	6.0	Fred Schaus	322,331
1964–65	1st	49	31	.613	+4.0	Fred Schaus	392,004
1965–66	1st	45	35	.563	+7.0	Fred Schaus	426,467
1966–67	3rd	36	45	.444	8.0	Fred Schaus	435,008
1967–68	2nd	52	30	.634	4.0	Butch van Breda Kolff	421,326
1968–69	1st	55	27	.671	+7.0	Butch van Breda Kolff	483,262
1969–70	2nd	46	36	.561	2.0	Joe Mullaney	536,513
				Western Conference Pacific Division			
1970–71	1st	48	34	.585	+7.0	Joe Mullaney	566,108
1971–72	1st	69	13	.841	+18.0	Bill Sharman	668,340
1972–73	1st	60	22	.732	+13.0	Bill Sharman	664,872
1973–74	1st	47	35	.573	+3.0	Bill Sharman	603,145
1974–75	5th	30	52	.366	18.0	Bill Sharman	474,287
1975–76	4th	40	42	.488	19.0	Bill Sharman	524,976

Year	Finish	Wins	Losses	Percentage	Games Behind	Head Coach	Attendance
1976–77	1st	53	29	.646	+4.0	Jerry West	501,434
1977–78	4th	45	37	.549	13.0	Jerry West	534,017
1978–79	3rd	47	35	.573	5.0	Jerry West	482,611
1979–80	1st	60	22	.732	+4.0	Jack McKinney (10–4), Paul Westhead (50–18)	582,882
1980–81	2nd	54	28	.659	3.0	Paul Westhead	538,865
1981–82	1st	57	25	.695	+5.0	Paul Westhead (7–4), Pat Riley (50–21)	605,236
1982–83	1st	58	24	.707	+5.0	Pat Riley	598,739
1983–84	1st	54	28	.659	+6.0	Pat Riley	622,401
1984–85	1st	62	20	.756	+20.0	Pat Riley	610,361
1985–86	1st	62	20	.756	+22.0	Pat Riley	691,071
1986–87	1st	65	17	.793	+16.0	Pat Riley	681,207
1987–88	1st	62	20	.756	+9.0	Pat Riley	708,477
1988–89	1st	57	25	.695	+2.0	Pat Riley	717,349
1989–90	1st	63	19	.768	+4.0	Pat Riley	712,498
1990–91	2nd	58	24	.707	5.0	Mike Dunleavy	682,024
1991–92	6th	43	39	.524	14.0	Mike Dunleavy	699,240
1992–93	5th	39	43	.476	23.0	Randy Pfund	633,655
1993–94	5th	33	49	.402	30.0	Randy Pfund (27–37), Bill Bertka (1–1), Magic Johnson (5–11)	545,915
1994–95	3rd	48	34	.585	11.0	Del Harris	591,125
1995–96	2nd	53	29	.646	11.0	Del Harris	649,634
1996–97	2nd	56	26	.683	1.0	Del Harris	697,159
1997–98	1st (Tie)	61	21	.744	—	Del Harris	676,101
1998–99	2nd	31	19	.620	4.0	Dell Harris (6–6), Bill Bertka (1–0), Kurt Rambis (24–13)	430,007
1999–00	1st	67	15	.817	+8.0	Phil Jackson	771,420
2000–01	1st	56	26	.683	+1.0	Phil Jackson	776,336
2001–02	2nd	58	24	.707	3.0	Phil Jackson	778,777
2002–03	2nd (Tie)	50	32	.610	9.0	Phil Jackson	777,888
2003–04	1st	56	26	.683	+1.0	Phil Jackson	777,757
2004–05	4th (Tie)	34	48	.415	28.0	Rudy Tomjanovich (24–19), Frank Hamblen (10–29)	770,494
2005–06	3rd	45	37	.549	9.0	Phil Jackson	774,189
2006–07	2nd (Tie)	42	40	.512	19.0	Phil Jackson	778,415
2007–08	1st	57	25	.695	+2.0	Phil Jackson	778,877
2008–09	1st	65	17	.793	+19.0	Phil Jackson	778,877
2009–10	1st	57	25	.695	+3.0	Phil Jackson	778,877
2010–11	1st	57	25	.695	+17.0	Phil Jackson	778,877
2011–12	1st	41	25	.621	+1.0	Mike Brown	626,901
2012–13	3rd	45	37	.549	11.0	Mike Brown (1–4), Bernie Bickerstaff (4–1), Mike D'Antoni (40–32)	778,877
2013–14	5th	27	55	.329	30.0	Mike D'Antoni	771,974
2014–15	5th	21	61	.256	46.0	Byron Scott	768,244
2015–16	5th	17	65	.207	56.0	Byron Scott	778,877
2016–17	4th	26	56	.317	41.0	Luke Walton	776,917
2017–18	3rd	35	47	.427	23.0	Luke Walton	776,327
2018–19	4th	37	45	.451	20.0	Luke Walton	778,877

Year	Finish	Wins	Losses	Percentage	Games Behind	Head Coach	Attendance
2019–20	1st	52	19	.732	+3.5	Frank Vogel	588,907
2020–21	3rd	42	30	.583	9.0	Frank Vogel	23,313
2021–22	4th	33	49	.402	31.0	Frank Vogel	764,631

1998–99: 50-game season.
2011–12: 66-game season.
2019–20: 65-to-75-game season.
2020–21: 72-game season.

Awards

Most Valuable Player
Kareem Abdul-Jabbar, center, 1975–76
Kareem Abdul-Jabbar, center, 1976–77
Kareem Abdul-Jabbar, center, 1979–80
Magic Johnson, guard, 1986–87
Magic Johnson, guard 1988–89
Magic Johnson, guard, 1989–90
Shaquille O'Neal, center, 1999–00
Kobe Bryant, guard, 2007–08

Rookie of the Year
Elgin Baylor, forward, 1958–59 (Min.)

Defensive Player of the Year
Michael Cooper, guard, 1986–87

Sixth Man of the Year
Lamar Odom, forward, 2010–11

Most Improved Player
none

All-NBA First Team
George Mikan, 1948–49 (Min.)
Jim Pollard, 1948–49 (Min.)
George Mikan, 1949–50 (Min.)
Jim Pollard, 1949–50 (Min.)
George Mikan, 1950–51 (Min.)
George Mikan, 1951–52 (Min.)
George Mikan, 1952–53 (Min.)
George Mikan, 1953–54 (Min.)
Elgin Baylor, 1958–59 (Min.)
Elgin Baylor, 1959–60 (Min.)
Elgin Baylor, 1960–61
Jerry West, 1961–62
Elgin Baylor, 1961–62
Elgin Baylor, 1962–63
Jerry West, 1962–63
Elgin Baylor, 1963–64
Jerry West, 1963–64
Elgin Baylor, 1964–65
Jerry West, 1964–65
Jerry West, 1965–66
Elgin Baylor, 1966–67

Jerry West, 1966–67
Elgin Baylor, 1967–68
Elgin Baylor, 1968–69
Jerry West, 1969–70
Jerry West, 1970–71
Jerry West, 1971–72
Jerry West, 1972–73
Gail Goodrich, 1973–74
Kareem Abdul-Jabbar, 1975–76
Kareem Abdul-Jabbar, 1976–77
Kareem Abdul-Jabbar, 1979–80
Kareem Abdul-Jabbar, 1980–81
Magic Johnson, 1982–83
Kareem Abdul-Jabbar, 1983–84
Magic Johnson, 1983–84
Magic Johnson, 1984–85
Kareem Abdul-Jabbar, 1985–86
Magic Johnson, 1985–86
Magic Johnson, 1986–87
Magic Johnson, 1987–88
Magic Johnson, 1988–89
Magic Johnson, 1989–90
Magic Johnson, 1990–91
Shaquille O'Neal, 1997–98
Shaquille O'Neal, 1999–00
Shaquille O'Neal, 2000–01
Kobe Bryant, 2001–02
Shaquille O'Neal, 2001–02
Kobe Bryant, 2002–03
Shaquille O'Neal, 2002–03
Kobe Bryant, 2003–04
Shaquille O'Neal, 2003–04
Kobe Bryant, 2005–06
Kobe Bryant, 2006–07
Kobe Bryant, 2007–08
Kobe Bryant, 2008–09
Kobe Bryant, 2009–10
Kobe Bryant, 2010–11
Kobe Bryant, 2011–12
Kobe Bryant, 2012–13
Anthony Davis, 2019–20
LeBron James, 2019–20

All-Defensive First Team
Jerry West, 1969–70
Jerry West, 1970–71
Wilt Chamberlain, 1971–72
Jerry West, 1971–72
Wilt Chamberlain, 1972–73
Jerry West, 1972–73
Kareem Abdul-Jabbar, 1978–79
Kareem Abdul-Jabbar, 1979–80
Kareem Abdul-Jabbar, 1980–81
Michael Cooper, 1981–82
Michael Cooper, 1983–84
Michael Cooper, 1984–85
Michael Cooper, 1986–87
Michael Cooper, 1987–88
Kobe Bryant, 1999–00
Kobe Bryant, 2002–03
Kobe Bryant, 2003–04
Kobe Bryant, 2005–06
Kobe Bryant, 2006–07
Kobe Bryant, 2007–08
Kobe Bryant, 2008–09
Kobe Bryant, 2009–10
Kobe Bryant, 2010–11
Anthony Davis, 2019–20

All-Rookie First Team
Bill Hewitt, 1968–69
Dick Garrett, 1969–70
Jim Price, 1972–73
Brian Winters, 1974–75
Norm Nixon, 1977–78
Magic Johnson, 1979–80
James Worthy, 1982–83
Byron Scott, 1983–84
Vlade Divac, 1989–90
Eddie Jones, 1994–95
Jordan Clarkson, 2014–15
Kyle Kuzma, 2017–18

Coach of the Year
Bill Sharman, 1971–72
Pat Riley, 1989–90
Del Harris, 1994–95

Hall of Famers Who Played for the Lakers

Kareem Abdul-Jabbar, center, 1975–89

Elgin Baylor, forward, 1958–72 (Min.-L.A.)

Zelmo Beaty, center, 1974–75

Kobe Bryant, guard, 1996–2016

Wilt Chamberlain, center, 1968–73

Adrian Dantley, forward, 1977–79

Vlade Divac, center, 1989–96; 2004–05

Gail Goodrich, guard, 1965–68; 1970–76

Connie Hawkins, forward, 1973–75

Spencer Haywood, forward, 1979–80

Lou Hudson, guard, 1977–79

Magic Johnson, guard, 1979–91; 1995–96

Clyde Lovellette, center, 1953–57 (Min.)

Slater Martin, guard, 1949–56 (Min.)

Karl Malone, forward, 2003–04

Bob McAdoo, center, 1981–85

George Mikan, center, 1948–54; 1955–56 (Min.)

Vern Mikkelsen, forward, 1949–59 (Min.)

Steve Nash, guard, 2012–14

Shaquille O'Neal, center, 1996–2004

Gary Payton, guard, 2003–04

Jim Pollard, forward, 1948–55 (Min.)

Mitch Richmond, guard, 2001–02

Dennis Rodman, forward, 1998–99

Charlie Scott, guard, 1977–78

Jerry West, guard, 1960–74

Jamaal Wilkes, forward, 1977–85

James Worthy, forward, 1982–94

Retired Numbers

CH	Chick Hern
JK	John Kundla
8	Kobe Bryant
13	Wilt Chamberlain
17	Jim Pollard
19	Vern Mikkelsen
22	Elgin Baylor
22	Slater Martin
24	Kobe Bryant
25	Gail Goodrich
32	Magic Johnson
33	Kareem Abdul-Jabbar
34	Clyde Lovellette
34	Shaquille O'Neal
42	James Worthy

44	Jerry West
52	Jamaal Wilkes
99	George Mikan

League Leaders, Offense

Points

George Mikan, 1948–49 (Min.)	1698
George Mikan, 1949–50 (Min.)	1865
George Mikan, 1950–51 (Min.)	1932
Shaquille O'Neal, 1998–99	1289
Shaquille O'Neal, 1999–00	2344
Kobe Bryant, 2002–03	2461
Kobe Bryant, 2005–06	2832
Kobe Bryant, 2006–07	2430
Kobe Bryant, 2007–08	2323

Three Pointers

Assists

Magic Johnson, 1982–83	829
Magic Johnson, 1985–86	907
Magic Johnson, 1986–87	977
LeBron James, 2019–20	684

Scoring Average

George Mikan, 1948–49 (Min.)	28.3
George Mikan, 1949–50 (Min.)	27.4
George Mikan, 1950–51 (Min.)	28.4
Jerry West, 1969–70	31.2
Shaquille O'Neal, 1999–00	29.7
Kobe Bryant, 2005–06	35.4
Kobe Bryant, 2006–07	31.6

Field Goal Percentage

Wilt Chamberlain, 1968–69	.583
Wilt Chamberlain, 1971–72	.649
Wilt Chamberlain, 1972–73	.727
Kareem Abdul-Jabbar, 1976–77	.579
Shaquille O'Neal, 1997–98	.584
Shaquille O'Neal, 1998–99	.576
Shaquille O'Neal, 1999–00	.574
Shaquille O'Neal, 2000–01	.572
Shaquille O'Neal, 2001–02	.579
Shaquille O'Neal, 2003–04	.584

Three Point Percentage

Byron Scott, 1984–85	.433

Free Throw Percentage

Magic Johnson, 1988–89	.911

Assists Average

Jerry West, 1971–72	9.7
Magic Johnson, 1982–83	10.5
Magic Johnson, 1983–84	13.1

Magic Johnson, 1985–86	12.6
Magic Johnson, 1986–87	12.2
LeBron James, 2019–20	10.2

League Leaders, Defense

Offensive Rebounds

Defensive Rebounds

Kareem Abdul-Jabbar, 1975–76	1111
Kareem Abdul-Jabbar, 1976–77	824
Dwight Howard, 2012–13	694

Total Rebounds

George Mikan, 1952–53 (Min.)	1007
Wilt Chamberlain, 1968–69	1712
Wilt Chamberlain, 1970–71	1493
Wilt Chamberlain, 1971–72	1572
Wilt Chamberlain, 1972–73	1526
Kareem Abdul-Jabbar, 1975–76	1383
Kareem Abdul-Jabbar, 1976–77	1090

Steals

Norm Nixon, 1978–79	201

Blocks

Elmore Smith, 1973–74	393
Elmore Smith, 1974–75	216
Kareem Abdul-Jabbar, 1975–76	338
Kareem Abdul-Jabbar, 1976–77	261
Kareem Abdul-Jabbar, 1978–79	316
Kareem Abdul-Jabbar, 1979–80	280

Rebounds Average

George Mikan, 1951–52 (Min.)	13.5
George Mikan, 1952–53 (Min.)	14.4
Wilt Chamberlain, 1968–69	21.1
Wilt Chamberlain, 1970–71	18.2
Wilt Chamberlain, 1971–72	19.2
Wilt Chamberlain, 1972–73	18.6
Kareem Abdul-Jabbar, 1975–76	16.9
Dwight Howard, 2012–13	12.4

Steals Average

Magic Johnson, 1980–81	3.4
Magic Johnson, 1981–82	2.7

Blocks Average

Elmore Smith, 1973–74	4.9
Kareem Abdul-Jabbar, 1975–76	4.1
Kareem Abdul-Jabbar, 1978–79	4.0
Kareem Abdul-Jabbar, 1979–80	3.4

Feats

50-Point Game

81 .... Kobe Bryant (vs. Tor. Raptors), Jan. 22, 2006

71........... Elgin Baylor (@ N.Y. Knicks), Nov. 15, 1960 (Min.)

66... Wilt Chamberlain (vs. Pho. Suns), Feb. 9, 1969

65......... Kobe Bryant (vs. Por. Blazers), Mar. 16, 2007

64........... Elgin Baylor (vs. Bos. Celtics), Nov. 8, 1959 (Min.)

63......... Elgin Baylor (@ Phi. Warriors), Dec. 8, 1961

63............. Jerry West (vs. N.Y. Knicks), Jan. 17, 1962

62....... Kobe Bryant (vs. Dal. Mavericks), Dec. 20, 2005

61........ George Mikan (vs. Roc. Royals), Jan. 20, 1952 (Min.)

61... Shaquille O'Neal (@ L.A. Clippers), Mar. 6, 2000

61............ Kobe Bryant (@ N.Y. Knicks), Feb. 2, 2009

60...Wilt Chamberlain (vs. Cin. Royals), Jan. 26, 1969

60.......... Kobe Bryant (@ Mem. Grizzlies), Mar. 22, 2007

60.............. Kobe Bryant (vs. Uta. Jazz), Apr. 13, 2016

58......... Kobe Bryant (@ Cha. Bobcats), Dec. 29, 2006

57............... Elgin Baylor (@ Det. Pistons), Feb. 16, 1961

56......... Elgin Baylor (vs. Syr. Nationals), Jan. 24, 1961

56........ Kobe Bryant (vs. Mem. Grizzlies), Jan. 14, 2002

56.......... LeBron James (vs. G.S. Warriors), Mar. 3, 2022

55.......... Elgin Baylor (vs. Cin. Royals), Feb. 25, 1959 (Min.)

55.......... Kobe Bryant (vs. Was. Wizards), Mar. 28, 2003

53.......... George Mikan (@ Bal. Bullets), Feb. 26, 1949 (Min.)

53............... Jerry West (vs. Cin. Royals), Jan. 29, 1965

53...Gail Goodrich (vs. K.C.-Oma. Kings), Mar. 28, 1975

53.......... Kobe Bryant (vs. Hou. Rockets), Dec. 15, 2006

53...........Kobe Bryant (vs. Hou. Rockets), Mar. 30, 2007

53... Kobe Bryant (vs. Mem. Grizzlies), Mar. 28, 2008

52.......... Elgin Baylor (vs. Det. Pistons), Oct. 18, 1959 (Min.)

52........... Elgin Baylor (vs. Det. Pistons), Nov. 20, 1960 (Min.)

52......... Elgin Baylor (vs. St.L. Hawks), Dec. 11, 1961

52......... Elgin Baylor (vs. St.L. Hawks), Dec. 13, 1961

52......... Elgin Baylor (vs. Phi. Warriors), Dec. 29, 1961

52......... Elgin Baylor (vs. S.F. Warriors), Dec. 15, 1962

52........ Kobe Bryant (vs. Hou. Rockets), Feb. 18, 2003

52................Kobe Bryant (vs. Uta. Jazz), Nov. 30, 2006

52.......... Kobe Bryant (vs. Dal. Mavericks), Mar. 2, 2008

51.......... George Mikan (vs. N.Y. Knicks), Mar. 13, 1949 (Min.)

51......... George Mikan (@ Roc. Royals), Jan. 14, 1950 (Min.)

51.......... Elgin Baylor (@ Det. Pistons), Nov. 25, 1960 (Min.)

51.......... Elgin Baylor (@ S.F. Warriors), Dec. 14, 1962

51.............. Jerry West (vs. Cin. Royals), Dec. 3, 1965

51................ Jerry West (@ Cin. Royals), Dec. 10, 1965

51.......... Kobe Bryant (@ G.S. Warriors), Dec. 6, 2000

51......... Kobe Bryant (@ Den. Nuggets), Feb. 12, 2003

51.............. Kobe Bryant (@ Sac. Kings), Jan. 19, 2006

51............ Kobe Bryant (@ Pho. Suns), Apr. 7, 2006

51............... LeBron James (@ Mia. Heat), Nov. 18, 2018

50......... Elgin Baylor (vs. Syr. Nationals), Dec. 4, 1961

50.............. Jerry West (vs. Cin. Royals), Jan. 24, 1962

50.......... Rudy LaRusso (vs. St.L. Hawks), Mar. 14, 1962

50......... Elgin Baylor (vs. Syr. Nationals), Dec. 12, 1962

50.............. Elgin Baylor (@ Bos. Celtics), Feb. 13, 1963

50...Cedric Ceballos (vs. Min. T'Wolves), Dec. 20, 1994

50......... Shaquille O'Neal (@ N.J. Nets), Apr. 2, 1998

50.......... Kobe Bryant (@ L.A. Clippers), Jan. 7, 2006

50...........Kobe Bryant (vs. Por. Blazers), Apr. 14, 2006

50.......... Kobe Bryant (vs. Min. T'Wolves), Mar. 18, 2007

50...Kobe Bryant (@ N.O.-Ok.C. Hornets), Mar. 23, 2007

50.......... Kobe Bryant (vs. L.A. Clippers), Apr. 12, 2007

50.......... Kobe Bryant (vs. Sea. Sonics), Apr. 15, 2007

50...Anthony Davis (vs. Min. T'Wolves), Dec. 8, 2019

20-Assist Game

24... Magic Johnson (vs. Den. Nuggets), Nov. 17, 1989

24.......... Magic Johnson (@ Pho. Suns), Jan. 9, 1990

23.............. Jerry West (vs. Phi. 76ers), Feb. 1, 1967

23......... Magic Johnson (vs. Sea. Sonics), Feb. 21, 1984

23... Magic Johnson (@ Dal. Mavericks), Apr. 20, 1988

23......... Nick Van Exel (@ Van. Grizzlies), Jan. 5, 1997

22... Magic Johnson (vs. Cle. Cavaliers), Nov. 17, 1983

22.......... Magic Johnson (vs. Por. Blazers), Nov. 6, 1990

21........ Magic Johnson (@ Atl. Hawks), Jan. 15, 1983

21......... Magic Johnson (@ L.A. Clippers), Dec. 6, 1988

21......... Magic Johnson (vs. Sea. Sonics), Apr. 23, 1989

21......... Magic Johnson (@ Bos. Celtics), Dec. 15, 1989

21......... Magic Johnson (vs. Ind. Pacers), Dec. 16, 1990

20.......... Jerry West (vs. Hou. Rockets), Nov. 7, 1972

20......... Magic Johnson (@ Phi. 76ers), Jan. 5, 1983

20......... Magic Johnson (vs. Mil. Bucks), Jan. 26, 1983

20... Magic Johnson (vs. S.D. Clippers), Mar. 9, 1983

20.......... Magic Johnson (vs. N.J. Nets), Nov. 25, 1983

20.......... Magic Johnson (@ Atl. Hawks), Dec. 18, 1984

20... Magic Johnson (@ Hou. Rockets), Dec. 19, 1984

20... Magic Johnson (vs. L.A. Clippers),
Nov. 20, 1985

20.......... Magic Johnson (vs. Pho. Suns),
Dec. 12, 1985

20... Magic Johnson (@ Hou. Rockets),
Apr. 6, 1986

20... Magic Johnson (vs. Den. Nuggets),
Mar. 10, 1987

20........... Magic Johnson (@ Phi. 76ers),
Nov. 28, 1988

30-Rebound Game

42... Wilt Chamberlain (vs. Bos. Celtics),
Mar. 7, 1969

38... Wilt Chamberlain (vs. Bal. Bullets),
Mar. 9, 1969

36......... George Mikan (vs. Roc. Royals),
Jan. 20, 1952 (Min.)

36.......... George Mikan (@ Phi. Warriors),
Mar. 4, 1952 (Min.)

35... Wilt Chamberlain (vs. S.F. Warriors),
Feb. 2, 1969

34.......... Wilt Chamberlain (vs. Phi. 76ers),
Dec. 19, 1971

34... Kareem Abdul-Jabbar (vs. Det. Pistons),
Dec. 14, 1975

33... Wilt Chamberlain (@ Sea. Sonics),
Feb. 12, 1969

32... Wilt Chamberlain (@ Cin. Royals),
Oct. 22, 1968

32... Wilt Chamberlain (vs. Chi. Bulls),
Mar. 7, 1971

32... Wilt Chamberlain (vs. Cin. Royals),
Oct. 29, 1971

31.......... Elgin Baylor (vs. Phi. Warriors),
Nov. 6, 1958 (Min.)

31.......... Elgin Baylor (@ Phi. Warriors),
Dec. 8, 1961

31.......... Wilt Chamberlain (@ Chi. Bulls),
Oct. 16, 1970

31... Wilt Chamberlain (vs. S.D. Rockets),
Nov. 29, 1970

31... Wilt Chamberlain (vs. Bos. Celtics),
Nov. 14, 1971

31... Wilt Chamberlain (vs. Det. Pistons),
Nov. 26, 1971

31... Wilt Chamberlain (vs. Phi. 76ers),
Feb. 11, 1973

31... Wilt Chamberlain (@ Por. Blazers),
Feb. 17, 1973

30............ Elgin Baylor (vs. Cin. Royals),
Jan. 14, 1961

30... Wilt Chamberlain (@ S.F. Warriors),
Feb. 1, 1969

30... Wilt Chamberlain (vs. Bos. Celtics),
Feb. 20, 1972

30... Kareem Abdul-Jabbar (@ N.J. Nets),
Feb. 3, 1978

30........ Andrew Bynum (@ S.A.Spurs),
Apr. 11, 2012

8-Steal Game

10.............. Jerry West (vs. Sea. Sonics),
Dec. 7, 1973

9.......... Magic Johnson (vs. Pho. Suns),
Nov. 6, 1981

8........ Gail Goodrich (vs. Sea. Sonics),
Feb. 15, 1974

8............. Norm Nixon (@ N.J. Nets),
Nov. 2, 1977

8... Magic Johnson (@ Dal. Mavericks),
Nov. 7, 1980

8................ Eddie Jones (@ Phi. 76ers),
Nov. 26, 1996

10-Block Game

17......... Elmore Smith (vs. Por. Blazers),
Oct. 28, 1973

14.......... Elmore Smith (vs. Det. Pistons),
Oct. 26, 1973

14.......... Elmore Smith (vs. Hou. Rockets),
Nov. 4, 1973

11.......... Elmore Smith (vs. G.S. Warriors),
Mar. 15, 1974

11... Kareem Abdul-Jabbar (vs. Det. Pistons),
Dec. 3, 1975

11... Kareem Abdul-Jabbar (vs. Det. Pistons),
Nov. 28, 1978

11... Kareem Abdul-Jabbar (vs. K.C. Kings),
Nov. 25, 1979

10......... Elmore Smith (@ Hou. Rockets),
Oct. 23, 1973

10.. Elmore Smith (vs. K.C.-Oma. Kings),
Nov. 30, 1973

10........ Elmore Smith (@ Cle. Cavaliers),
Dec. 11, 1973

10... Elmore Smith (vs. G.S. Warriors),
Mar. 16, 1975

10... Kareem Abdul-Jabbar (vs. Atl. Hawks),
Nov. 2, 1975

10... Kareem Abdul-Jabbar (vs. Atl. Hawks),
Jan. 18, 1980

10... Kareem Abdul-Jabbar (vs. Det. Pistons),
Jan. 22, 1982

Multiple Triple-Doubles in a Single Season

18................ Magic Johnson, 1981-82

17................ Magic Johnson, 1988-89

16................ Magic Johnson, 1982-83

13................. Magic Johnson, 1990-91

13................... LeBron James, 2019-20

12................ Magic Johnson, 1983-84

12................ Magic Johnson, 1987-88

11................ Magic Johnson, 1984-85

11................ Magic Johnson, 1986-87

11................ Magic Johnson, 1989-90

10............ Russell Westbrook, 2021-22

8................... LeBron James, 2018-19

7................ Magic Johnson, 1979-80

6................. Elmore Smith, 1973-74

6................ Magic Johnson, 1980-81

6.................. LeBron James, 2021-22

5..................... Elgin Baylor, 1968-69

5....... Kareem Abdul-Jabbar, 1975-76

5.................... Kobe Bryant, 2002-03

5.................... Kobe Bryant, 2004-05

5.................... LeBron James, 2020-21

4.................... Elgin Baylor, 1960-61

4...................... Jerry West, 1961-62

4.................... Elgin Baylor, 1962-63

4............. Wilt Chamberlain, 1968-69

3.................... Elgin Baylor, 1963-64

3...................... Jerry West, 1965-66

3.................... Elgin Baylor, 1967-68

3...... Kareem Abdul-Jabbar, 1978-79

3......... Magic Johnson, 1985-86

3............ Julius Randle, 2016-17

3........... Russell Westbrook, 2021-22

2...................... Jerry West, 1960-61

2..................... Elgin Baylor, 1961-62

2..................... Jerry West, 1962-63

2.................... Elgin Baylor, 1965-66

2............ Wilt Chamberlain, 1970-71

2............ Wilt Chamberlain, 1972-73

2...... Kareem Abdul-Jabbar, 1979-80

2.................... Vlade Divac, 1993-94

2.................... Kobe Bryant, 2000-01

2.................. Lamar Odom, 2005-06

2.................... Kobe Bryant, 2008-09

2.................... Kobe Bryant, 2012-13

2...................... Pau Gasol, 2012-13

2.................... Kobe Bryant, 2014-15

2...................... Lonzo Ball, 2017-18

Postseason Play

1949 BAA Western Division Semifinals
vs. Chi. Stags, won (2-0)
BAA Western Division Finals
vs. Roc. Royals, won (2-0)
BAA Finals vs. Was. Capitols,
won (4-2)

1950 NBA Central Division First Place
Tiebreaker vs. Roc. Royals, won

NBA Central Division Semifinals
vs. Chi. Stags, won (2–0)
NBA Central Division Finals
vs. Ft.W. Pistons, won (2–0)
NBA Semifinals vs. And. Packers,
won (2–0)
NBA Finals vs. Syr. Nationals,
won (4–2)

1951 Western Division Semifinals
vs. Ind. Olympians, won (2–1)
Western Division Finals
vs. Roc. Royals, lost (3–1)

1952 Western Division Semifinals
vs. Ind. Olympians, won (2–0)
Western Division Finals
vs. Roc. Royals, won (3–1)
NBA Finals vs. N.Y. Knicks,
won (4–3)

1953 Western Division Semifinals
vs. Ind. Olympians, won (2–0)
Western Division Finals
vs. Ft.W. Pistons, won (3–2)
NBA Finals vs. N.Y. Knicks,
won (4–1)

1954 Western Division Finals
vs. Roc. Royals, won (2–1)
(Advanced from Western Division
Round Robin)
NBA Finals vs. Syr. Nationals,
won (4–3)

1955 Western Division Semifinals
vs. Roc. Royals, won (2–1)
Western Division Finals
vs. Ft.W. Pistons, lost (3–1)

1956 Western Division Second Place
Tiebreaker vs. St.L. Hawks, won
Western Division Semifinals
vs. St.L. Hawks, lost (2–1)

1957 Western Division Tiebreaker
vs. St.L. Hawks, won
Western Division Semifinals
vs. Ft.W. Pistons, won (2–0)
Western Division Finals
vs. St.L. Hawks, lost (3–0)

1959 Western Division Semifinals
vs. Det. Pistons, won (2–1)
Western Division Finals
vs. St.L. Hawks, won (4–2)
NBA Finals vs. Bos. Celtics,
won (4–0)

1960 Western Division Semifinals
vs. Det. Pistons, won (2–0)
Western Division Finals
vs. St.L. Hawks, lost (4–3)

1961 Western Division Semifinals
vs. Det. Pistons, won (3–2)
Western Division Finals
vs. St.L. Hawks, lost (4–3)

1962 Western Division Finals
vs. Det. Pistons, won (4–2)
NBA Finals vs. Bos. Celtics,
won (4–3)

1963 Western Division Finals
vs. St.L. Hawks, won (4–3)
NBA Finals vs. Bos. Celtics,
won (4–2)

1964 Western Division Semifinals
vs. St.L. Hawks, lost (3–2)

1965 Western Division Finals
vs. Bal. Bullets, won (4–2)
NBA Finals vs. Bos. Celtics,
lost (4–1)

1966 Western Division Finals
vs. St.L. Hawks, won (4–3)
NBA Finals vs. Bos. Celtics,
lost (4–3)

1967 Western Division Semifinals
vs. S.F. Warriors, lost (3–0)

1968 Western Division Semifinals
vs. Chi. Bulls, won (4–1)
Western Division Finals
vs. S.F. Warriors, won (4–0)
NBA Finals vs. Bos. Celtics,
lost (4–2)

1969 Western Division Semifinals
vs. S.F. Warriors, won (4–2)
Western Division Finals
vs. Atl. Hawks, won (4–1)
NBA Finals vs. Bos. Celtics,
lost (4–3)

1970 Western Division Semifinals
vs. Pho. Suns, won (4–3)
Western Division Finals
vs. Atl. Hawks, won (4–0)
NBA Finals vs. N.Y. Knicks,
lost (4–3)

1971 Western Conference Semifinals
vs. Chi. Bulls, won (4–3)
Western Conference Finals
vs. Mil. Bucks, lost (4–1)

1972 Western Conference Semifinals
vs. Chi. Bulls, won (4–0)
Western Conference Finals
vs. Mil. Bucks, won (4–2)
NBA Finals vs. N.Y. Knicks,
won (4–1)

1973 Western Conference Semifinals
vs. Chi. Bulls, won (4–3)

Western Conference Finals
vs. G.S. Warriors, won (4–1)
NBA Finals vs. N.Y. Knicks,
lost (4–1)

1974 Western Conference Semifinals
vs. Mil. Bucks, lost (4–1)

1977 Western Conference Semifinals
vs. G.S. Warriors, won (4–3)
Western Conference Finals
vs. Por. Blazers, lost (4–0)

1978 Western Conference First Round
vs. Sea. Sonics, lost (2–1)

1979 Western Conference First Round
vs. Den. Nuggets, won (2–1)
Western Conference Semifinals
vs. Sea. Sonics, lost (4–1)

1980 Western Conference Semifinals
vs. Pho. Suns, won (4–1)
Western Conference Finals
vs. Sea. Sonics, won (4–1)
NBA Finals vs. Phi. 76ers,
won (4–2)

1981 Western Conference First Round
vs. Hou. Rockets, lost (2–1)

1982 Western Conference Semifinals
vs. Pho. Suns, won (4–0)
Western Conference Finals
vs. S.A. Spurs, won (4–0)
NBA Finals vs. Phi. 76ers,
won (4–2)

1983 Western Conference Semifinals
vs. Por. Blazers, won (4–1)
Western Conference Finals
vs. S.A. Spurs, won (4–2)
NBA Finals vs. Phi. 76ers,
lost (4–0)

1984 Western Conference First Round
vs. K.C. Kings, won (3–0)
Western Conference Semifinals
vs. Dal. Mavericks, won (4–1)
Western Conference Finals
vs. Pho. Suns, won (4–2)
NBA Finals vs. Bos. Celtics,
lost (4–3)

1985 Western Conference First Round
vs. Pho. Suns, won (3–0)
Western Conference Semifinals
vs. Por. Blazers, won (4–1)
Western Conference Finals
vs. Den. Nuggets, won (4–1)
NBA Finals vs. Bos. Celtics,
won (4–2)

1986 Western Conference First Round
vs. S.A. Spurs, won (3–0)

Western Conference Semifinals
vs. Dal. Mavericks, won (4–2)
Western Conference Finals
vs. Hou. Rockets, lost (4–1)
1987 Western Conference First Round
vs. Den. Nuggets, won (3–0)
Western Conference Semifinals
vs. G.S. Warriors, won (4–1)
Western Conference Finals
vs. Sea. Sonics, won (4–0)
NBA Finals vs. Bos. Celtics,
won (4–2)
1988 Western Conference First Round
vs. S.A. Spurs, won (3–0)
Western Conference Semifinals
vs. Uta. Jazz, won (4–3)
Western Conference Finals
vs. Dal. Mavericks, won (4–3)
NBA Finals vs. Det. Pistons,
won (4–3)
1989 Western Conference First Round
vs. Por. Blazers, won (3–0)
Western Conference Semifinals
vs. Sea. Sonics, won (4–0)
Western Conference Finals
vs. Pho. Suns, won (4–0)
NBA Finals vs. Det. Pistons,
lost (4–0)
1990 Western Conference First Round
vs. Hou. Rockets, won (3–1)
Western Conference Semifinals
vs. Pho. Suns, lost (4–1)
1991 Western Conference First Round
vs. Hou. Rockets, won (3–0)
Western Conference Semifinals
vs. G.S. Warriors, won (4–1)
Western Conference Finals
vs. Por. Blazers, won (4–2)
NBA Finals vs. Chi. Bulls,
lost (4–1)
1992 Western Conference First Round
vs. Por. Blazers, lost (3–1)
1993 Western Conference First Round
vs. Pho. Suns, lost (3–2)
1995 Western Conference First Round
vs. Sea. Sonics, won (3–1)
Western Conference Semifinals
vs. S.A. Spurs, lost (4–2)
1996 Western Conference First Round
vs. Hou. Rockets, lost (3–1)
1997 Western Conference First Round
vs. Por. Blazers, won (3–1)

Western Conference Semifinals
vs. Uta. Jazz, lost (4–1)
1998 Western Conference First Round
vs. Por. Blazers, won (3–1)
Western Conference Semifinals
vs. Sea. Sonics, won (4–1)
Western Conference Finals
vs. Uta. Jazz, lost (4–0)
1999 Western Conference First Round
vs. Hou. Rockets, won (3–1)
Western Conference Semifinals
vs. S.A. Spurs, lost (4–0)
2000 Western Conference First Round
vs. Sac. Kings, won (3–2)
Western Conference Semifinals
vs. Pho. Suns, won (4–1)
Western Conference Finals
vs. Por. Blazers, won (4–3)
NBA Finals vs. Ind. Pacers,
won (4–2)
2001 Western Conference First Round
vs. Por. Blazers, won (3–0)
Western Conference Semifinals
vs. Sac. Kings, won (4–0)
Western Conference Finals
vs. S.A. Spurs, won (4–0)
NBA Finals vs. Phi. 76ers,
won (4–1)
2002 Western Conference First Round
vs. Por. Blazers, won (3–0)
Western Conference Semifinals
vs. S.A. Spurs, won (4–1)
Western Conference Finals
vs. Sac. Kings, won (4–3)
NBA Finals vs. N.J. Nets,
won (4–0)
2003 Western Conference First Round
vs. Min. T'Wolves, won (4–2)
Western Conference Semifinals
vs. S.A. Spurs, lost (4–2)
2004 Western Conference First Round
vs. Hou. Rockets, won (4–1)
Western Conference Semifinals
vs. S.A. Spurs, won (4–2)
Western Conference Finals
vs. Min. T'Wolves, won (4–2)
NBA Finals vs. Det. Pistons,
lost (4–1)
2006 Western Conference First Round
vs. Pho. Suns, lost (4–3)
2007 Western Conference First Round
vs. Pho. Suns, lost (4–1)

2008 Western Conference First Round
vs. Den. Nuggets, won (4–0)
Western Conference Semifinals
vs. Uta. Jazz, won (4–2)
Western Conference Finals
vs. S.A. Spurs, won (4–1)
NBA Finals vs. Bos. Celtics,
lost (4–2)
2009 Western Conference First Round
vs. Uta. Jazz, won (4–1)
Western Conference Semifinals
vs. Hou. Rockets, won (4–3)
Western Conference Finals
vs. Den. Nuggets, won (4–2)
NBA Finals vs. Orl. Magic,
won (4–1)
2010 Western Conference First Round
vs. Ok.C. Thunder, won (4–2)
Western Conference Semifinals
vs. Uta. Jazz, won (4–0)
Western Conference Finals
vs. Pho. Suns, won (4–2)
NBA Finals vs. Bos. Celtics,
won (4–3)
2011 Western Conference First Round
vs. N.O. Hornets, won (4–2)
Western Conference Semifinals
vs. Dal. Mavericks, lost (4–0)
2012 Western Conference First Round
vs. Den. Nuggets, won (4–3)
Western Conference Semifinals
vs. Ok.C. Thunder, lost (4–1)
2013 Western Conference First Round
vs. S.A. Spurs, lost (4–0)
2020 Western Conference First Round
vs. Por. Blazers, won (4–1)
Western Conference Semifinals
vs. Hou. Rockets, won (4–1)
Western Conference Finals
vs. Den. Nuggets, won (4–1)
NBA Finals vs. Mia. Heat,
won (4–2)
2021 Western Conference First Round
vs. Pho. Suns, lost (4–2)

Memphis Grizzlies

Dates of Operation: (as the Vancouver Grizzlies) 1995–2001 (6 seasons)
Overall Record: 101 wins, 359 losses (.220)
Arena: General Motors Place, 1995–2001

Dates of Operation: (as the Memphis Grizzlies) 2001–present (21 seasons)
Overall Record: 819 wins, 868 losses (.485)
Arenas: Pyramid Arena, 2001–04; FedExForum, 2004–present (capacity: 18,119)

Year-by-Year Finishes

Year	Finish	Wins	Losses	Percentage	Games Behind	Head Coach	Attendance
				Vancouver Grizzlies			
				Western Conference Midwest Division			
1995–96	7th	15	67	.183	44.0	Brian Winters	654,013
1996–97	7th	14	68	.171	50.0	Brian Winters (8–35), Stu Jackson (6–33)	683,442
1997–98	6th	19	63	.232	43.0	Brian Hill	660,457
1998–99	7th	8	42	.160	29.0	Brian Hill	417,966
1999–00	7th	22	60	.268	33.0	Brian Hill (4–18), Lionel Hollins (18–42)	569,864
2000–01	7th	23	59	.280	35.0	Sidney Lowe	563,218
				Memphis Grizzlies			
2001–02	7th	23	59	.280	35.0	Sidney Lowe	591,030
2002–03	6th	28	54	.341	32.0	Sidney Lowe (0–8), Hubie Brown (28–46)	611,322
2003–04	4th	50	32	.610	8.0	Hubie Brown (50–32)	622,723
				Southwest Division			
2004–05	4th	45	37	.549	14.0	Hubie Brown (5–7), Lionel Hollins (0–4), Mike Fratello (40–26)	691,362
2005–06	3rd	49	33	.598	14.0	Mike Fratello	647,533
2006–07	5th	22	60	.268	45.0	Mike Fratello (6–24), Tony Barone (16–36)	600,836
2007–08	5th	22	60	.268	34.0	Marc Iavaroni	523,578
2008–09	5th	24	58	.293	30.0	Marc Iavaroni (11–30), Johnny Davis (0–2), Lionel Hollins (13–26)	519,895
2009–10	4th	40	42	.488	15.0	Lionel Hollins	552,914
2010–11	3rd (Tie)	46	36	.561	15.0	Lionel Hollins	600,687
2011–12	2nd	41	25	.621	9.0	Lionel Hollins	518,446
2012–13	2nd	56	26	.683	2.0	Lionel Hollins	681,613
2013–14	3rd	50	32	.610	12.0	Dave Joerger	685,458
2014–15	2nd (Tie)	55	27	.671	1.0	Dave Joerger	710,502
2015–16	2nd (Tie)	42	40	.512	25.0	Dave Joerger	701,894
2016–17	3rd	43	39	.524	18.0	David Fizdale	677,314
2017–18	5th	22	60	.268	43.0	David Fizdale (7–12), J.B. Bickerstaff (15–48)	653,863
2018–19	3rd (Tie)	33	49	.402	20.0	J.B. Bickerstaff	638,332
2019–20	3rd	34	39	.466	10.5	Taylor Jenkins	523,297

Year	Finish	Wins	Losses	Percentage	Games Behind	Head Coach	Attendance
2020–21	2nd	38	34	.528	4.0	Taylor Jenkins	61,449
2021–22	1st	56	26	.683	+4.0	Taylor Jenkins	646,785

1998–99: 50-game season.
2011–12: 66-game season.
2019–20: 65-to-75-game season.
2020–21: 72-game season.

Awards

Most Valuable Player
none

Rookie of the Year
Pau Gasol, forward, 2001–02
Ja Morant, guard, 2019–20

Defensive Player of the Year
Marc Gasol, center, 2012–13

Sixth Man of the Year
Mike Miller, guard, 2005–06

Most Improved Player
Ja Morant, guard, 2021–22

All-NBA First Team
Marc Gasol, 2014–15

All-Defensive First Team
Tony Allen, 2011–12
Tony Allen, 2012–13
Tony Allen, 2014–15

All-Rookie First Team
Shareef Abdur-Rahim, 1996–97 (Van.)
Mike Bibby, 1998–99 (Van.)
Shane Battier, 2001–02
Pau Gasol, 2001–02
Drew Gooden, 2002–03*
Rudy Gay, 2006–07
O.J. Mayo, 2008–09
Jaren Jackson Jr., 2018–19
Brandon Clarke, 2019–20
Ja Morant, 2019–20

* 51 games with Mem. Grizzlies and 19 games
with Orl. Magic.

Coach of the Year
Hubie Brown, 2003–04

Hall of Famers Who Played for the Grizzlies
Allen Iverson, guard, 2009–10

Retired Numbers
50.................................Zach Randolph

League Leaders, Offense
Points
none

Three Pointers
none

Assists
none

Scoring Average
none

Field Goal Percantage
none

Three Point Percentage
none

Free Throw Percentage
none

Assists Average
none

League Leaders, Defense
Offensive Rebounds
Steven Adams, 2021–22................ 349

Defensive Rebounds
Zach Randolph, 2009–10............... 330
Zach Randolph, 2012–13............... 310

Total Rebounds
none

Steals
Mike Conley, 2012–13 174

Blocks
Jaren Jackson Jr., 2021–22............ 138

Rebounds Average
none

Steals Average
none

Blocks Average
Jaren Jackson Jr., 2021–22............. 2.3

Feats
50-Point Game
52............... Ja Morant (vs. S.A. Spurs),
Feb. 28, 2022

20-Assist Game
none

30-Rebound Game
none

8-Steal Game
8........... Tony Allen (vs. Cle. Cavaliers),
Apr. 23, 2012

10-Block Game
none

Multiple Triple-Doubles in a Single Season
3......................Delon Wright, 2018–19
2........................Marc Gasol, 2016–17
2.......................... Ja Morant, 2019–20

Postseason Play

2004	Western Conference First Round	
	vs. S.A. Spurs, lost (4–0)	
2005	Western Conference First Round	
	vs. Pho. Suns, lost (4–0)	
2006	Western Conference First Round	
	vs. Dal. Mavericks, lost (4–0)	
2011	Western Conference First Round	
	vs. S.A. Spurs, won (4–2)	
	Western Conference Semifinals	
	vs. Ok.C. Thunder, lost (4–3)	
2012	Western Conference First Round	
	vs. L.A. Clippers, lost (4–3)	
2013	Western Conference First Round	
	vs. L.A. Clippers, won (4–2)	
	Western Conference Semifinals	
	vs. Ok.C. Thunder, won (4–1)	
	Western Conference Finals	
	vs. S.A. Spurs, lost (4–0)	
2014	Western Conference First Round	
	vs. Ok.C. Thunder, lost (4–3)	
2015	Western Conference First Round	
	vs. Por. Blazers, won (4–1)	
	Western Conference Semifinals	
	vs. G.S. Warriors, lost (4–2)	
2016	Western Conference First Round	
	vs. S.A. Spurs, lost (4–0)	
2017	Western Conference First Round	
	vs. S.A. Spurs, lost (4–2)	
2021	Western Conference First Round	
	vs. Uta. Jazz, lost (4–1)	
2022	Western Conference First Round	
	vs. Min. T'Wolves, won (4–2)	
	Western Conference Semifinals	
	vs. G.S. Warriors, lost (4–2)	

Minnesota Timberwolves

Dates of Operation: 1989–present (33 seasons)
Overall Record: 1049 wins, 1581 losses (.399)
Arenas: Hubert H. Humphrey Metrodome, 1989–90; Target Center, 1990–present (capacity: 18,798)
Other Names: T'Wolves, Wolves

Year-by-Year Finishes

Year	Finish	Wins	Losses	Percentage	Games Behind	Head Coach	Attendance
				Western Conference Midwest Division			
1989–90	6th	22	60	.268	34.0	Bill Musselman	1,072,572
1990–91	5th	29	53	.354	26.0	Bill Musselman	779,530
1991–92	6th	15	67	.183	40.0	Jimmy Rodgers	769,035
1992–93	5th	19	63	.232	36.0	Jimmy Rodgers (6–23), Sidney Lowe (13–40)	754,593
1993–94	5th	20	62	.244	38.0	Sidney Lowe	733,419
1994–95	6th	21	61	.256	41.0	Bill Blair	603,518
1995–96	5th (Tie)	26	56	.317	33.0	Bill Blair (6–14), Flip Saunders (20–42)	585,669
1996–97	3rd	40	42	.488	24.0	Flip Saunders	697,727
1997–98	3rd	45	37	.549	17.0	Flip Saunders	738,590
1998–99	4th	25	25	.500	12.0	Flip Saunders	427,974
1999–00	3rd	50	32	.610	5.0	Flip Saunders	690,012
2000–01	4th	47	35	.573	11.0	Flip Saunders	717,371
2001–02	3rd	50	32	.610	8.0	Flip Saunders	731,673
2002–03	3rd	51	31	.622	9.0	Flip Saunders	643,684
2003–04	1st	58	24	.707	+1.0	Flip Saunders	723,071
				Northwest Division			
2004–05	3rd	44	38	.537	8.0	Flip Saunders (25–26), Kevin McHale (19–12)	704,438
2005–06	4th	33	49	.402	11.0	Dwane Casey	662,167
2006–07	3rd (Tie)	32	50	.390	19.0	Dwane Casey (20–20), Randy Wittman (12–30)	655,947
2007–08	4th	22	60	.268	32.0	Randy Wittman	593,537
2008–09	4th	24	58	.293	30.0	Randy Wittman (4–15), Kevin McHale (20–43)	595,013
2009–10	5th	15	67	.183	38.0	Kurt Rambis	619,170
2010–11	5th	17	65	.207	38.0	Kurt Rambis	624,960
2011–12	5th	26	40	.394	21.0	Rick Adelman	577,197
2012–13	5th	31	51	.378	29.0	Rick Adelman	669,956
2013–14	3rd	40	42	.488	19.0	Rick Adelman	597,157
2014–15	5th	16	66	.195	35.0	Flip Saunders	595,652
2015–16	5th	29	53	.354	26.0	Sam Mitchell	581,178
2016–17	5th	31	51	.378	20.0	Tom Thibodeau	607,203
2017–18	4th	47	35	.573	2.0	Tom Thibodeau	699,308
2018–19	5th	36	46	.439	18.0	Tom Thibodeau (19–21), Ryan Saunders (17–25)	627,543
2019–20	5th	19	45	.297	22.5	Ryan Saunders	482,112

Year	Finish	Wins	Losses	Percentage	Games Behind	Head Coach	Attendance
2020–21	4th	23	49	.319	29.0	Ryan Saunders (7–24), Chris Finch (16–25)	15,774
2021–22	3rd	46	36	.561	3.0	Chris Finch	657,148

1998–99: 50-game season.
2011–12: 66-game season.
2019–20: 65-to-75-game season.
2020–21: 72-game season.

Awards

Most Valuable Player
Kevin Garnett, forward, 2003–04

Rookie of the Year
Andrew Wiggins, forward, 2014–15
Karl-Anthony Towns, center, 2015–16

Defensive Player of the Year
none

Sixth Man of the Year
none

Most Improved Player
Kevin Love, forward, 2010–11

All-NBA First Team
Kevin Garnett, 1999–00
Kevin Garnett, 2002–03
Kevin Garnett, 2003–04

All-Defensive First Team
Kevin Garnett, 1999–00
Kevin Garnett, 2000–01
Kevin Garnett, 2001–02
Kevin Garnett, 2002–03
Kevin Garnett, 2003–04
Kevin Garnett, 2004–05

All-Rookie First Team
Pooh Richardson, 1989–90
Christian Laettner, 1992–93
Isiah Rider, 1993–94
Stephon Marbury, 1996–97
Wally Szczerbiak, 1999–00
Randy Foye, 2006–07
Ricky Rubio, 2011–12
Andrew Wiggins, 2014–15
Karl-Anthony Towns, 2015–16
Anthony Edwards, 2020–21

Coach of the Year
none

Hall of Famers Who Played for the Timberwolves
Kevin Garnett, forward, 1995–2007; 2014–16

Retired Numbers

FLIP .... Flip Saunders
2 .... Malik Sealy

League Leaders, Offense

Points
Kevin Garnett, 2003–04 1987

Three Pointers
none

Assists
none

Scoring Average
none

Field Goal Percantage
none

Three Point Percentage
Fred Hoiberg, 2004–05 .... .483

Free Throw Percentage
none

Assists Average
none

League Leaders, Defense

Offensive Rebounds
Kevin Love, 2010–11 330

Defensive Rebounds
Kevin Garnett, 2002–03 858
Kevin Garnett, 2003–04 894
Kevin Garnett, 2004–05 861
Kevin Garnett, 2005–06 752
Kevin Garnett, 2006–07 792

Total Rebounds
Kevin Garnett, 2003–04 1139
Kevin Garnett, 2004–05 1108
Kevin Love, 2010–11 1112

Steals
Ricky Rubio, 2013–14 191

Blocks
none

Rebounds Average
Kevin Garnett, 2003–04 .... 13.9
Kevin Garnett, 2004–05 .... 13.5
Kevin Garnett, 2005–06 .... 12.7
Kevin Garnett, 2006–07 .... 12.8
Kevin Love, 2010–11 .... 15.2

Steals Average
none

Blocks Average
none

Feats

50-Point Game
60... Karl-Anthony Towns (@ S.A. Spurs), Mar. 14, 2022
56... Karl-Anthony Towns (vs. Atl. Hawks), Mar. 28, 2018
52 .... Mo Williams (@ Ind. Pacers), Jan. 13, 2015
51 .... Corey Brewer (vs. Hou. Rockets), Apr. 11, 2014
51 .... Kevin Love (@ Ok.C. Thunder), Mar. 23, 2012
50 .... Derrick Rose (vs. Uta. Jazz), Oct. 31, 2018

20-Assist Game
none

30-Rebound Game
31 .... Kevin Love (vs. N.Y. Knicks), Nov. 12, 2010

8-Steal Game
8 ...... Tyrone Corbin (@ Dal. Mavericks), Mar. 30, 1990
8 .... Terrell Brandon (@ N.J. Nets), Mar. 24, 2000
8 .... Ricky Rubio (@ Mil. Bucks), Apr. 3, 2013
8 .... Ricky Rubio (@ N.Y. Knicks), Dec. 16, 2015

10-Block Game
none

Multiple Triple-Doubles in a Single Season

6..................... Kevin Garnett, 2002–03

3..................... Kevin Garnett, 2006–07

3..........................Kevin Love, 2013–14

2...............Micheal Williams, 1992–93

2.................... Kevin Garnett, 2000–01

2.................... Kevin Garnett, 2003–04

2...................... Ricky Rubio, 2013–14

Postseason Play

1997   Western Conference First Round
vs. Hou. Rockets, lost (3–0)

1998   Western Conference First Round
vs. Sea. Sonics, lost (3–2)

1999   Western Conference First Round
vs. S.A. Spurs, lost (3–1)

2000   Western Conference First Round
vs. Por. Blazers, lost (3–1)

2001   Western Conference First Round
vs. S.A. Spurs, lost (3–1)

2002   Western Conference First Round
vs. Dal. Mavericks, lost (3–0)

2003   Western Conference First Round
vs. L.A. Lakers, lost (4–2)

2004   Western Conference First Round
vs. Den. Nuggets, won (4–1)

Western Conference Semifinals
vs. Sac. Kings, won (4–3)

Western Conference Finals
vs. L.A. Lakers, lost (4–2)

2018   Western Conference First Round
vs. Hou. Rockets, lost (4–1)

2022   Western Conference First Round
vs. Mem. Grizzlies, lost (4–2)

New Orleans Pelicans

Dates of Operation: (as the New Orleans Pelicans) 2002–present (20 seasons)
Overall Record: 740 wins, 864 losses (.461)
Arenas: Ford Center, 2005–07; Smoothie King Center (formerly New Orleans Arena, 2002–05, 2007–13), 2002–05, 2007–present (capacity: 16,867)
Other Names: New Orleans Hornets, 2002–05, 2007–13; New Orleans-Oklahoma City Hornets, 2005–07

Year-by-Year Finishes

Year	Finish	Wins	Losses	Percentage	Games Behind	Head Coach	Attendance
New Orleans Hornets							
Eastern Conference Central Division							
2002–03	3rd	47	35	.573	3.0	Paul Silas	641,683
2003–04	3rd (Tie)	41	41	.500	20.0	Tim Floyd	587,613
Western Conference Southwest Division							
2004–05	5th	18	64	.220	41.0	Byron Scott	583,070
New Orleans-Oklahoma City Hornets							
2005–06	4th	38	44	.463	25.0	Byron Scott	744,920
2006–07	4th	39	43	.476	28.0	Byron Scott	731,165
New Orleans Hornets							
2007–08	1st (Tie)	56	26	.683	—	Byron Scott	581,432
2008–09	4th	49	33	.598	5.0	Byron Scott	695,727
2009–10	5th	37	45	.451	18.0	Byron Scott (3–6), Jeff Bower (34–39)	617,366
2010–11	3rd (Tie)	46	36	.561	15.0	Monty Williams	603,088
2011–12	5th	21	45	.318	29.0	Monty Williams	498,618
2012–13	5th	27	55	.329	31.0	Monty Williams	565,930
New Orleans Pelicans							
2013–14	5th	34	48	.415	28.0	Monty Williams	672,029
2014–15	5th	45	37	.549	11.0	Monty Williams	683,757
2015–16	5th	30	52	.366	37.0	Alvin Gentry	688,549
2016–17	4th	34	48	.415	27.0	Alvin Gentry	663,099
2017–18	2nd	48	34	.585	17.0	Alvin Gentry	673,920
2018–19	3rd (Tie)	33	49	.402	20.0	Alvin Gentry	656,183
2019–20	5th	30	42	.417	14.0	Alvin Gentry	528,172
2020–21	4th	31	41	.431	11.0	Stan Van Gundy	93,120
2021–22	3rd	36	46	.439	20.0	Willie Green	635,941

2011–12: 66-game season.

2019–20: 65-to-75-game season.

2020–21: 72-game season.

Awards

Most Valuable Player
none

Rookie of the Year
Chris Paul, guard, 2005–06 (N.O.-Ok.C.)

Defensive Player of the Year
none

Sixth Man of the Year
none

Most Improved Player
Brandon Ingram, forward, 2019–20

All-NBA First Team
Chris Paul, 2007–08 (N.O.)
Anthony Davis, 2014–15
Anthony Davis, 2016–17
Anthony Davis, 2017–18

All-Defensive First Team
Chris Paul, 2008–09 (N.O.)
Anthony Davis, 2017–18
Jrue Holiday, 2017–18

All-Rookie First Team
Chris Paul, 2005–06 (N.O.-Ok.C.)
Darren Collison, 2009–10 (N.O.)
Anthony Davis, 2012–13 (N.O.)
Buddy Hield, 2016–17*
Zion Williamson, 2019–20

* 57 games with N.O. Pelicans and 25 games with Sac. Kings.

Coach of the Year
Byron Scott, 2007–08 (N.O.)

Hall of Famers Who Played for the Hornets/Pelicans
none

Retired Numbers
7.....................................Pete Maravich

League Leaders, Offense
Points
none

Three Pointers
none

Assists
Chris Paul, 2007–08 (N.O.) 925
Chris Paul, 2008–09 (N.O.) 861
Greivis Vásquez, 2012–13 (N.O.)...... 704

Scoring Average
none

Field Goal Percantage
none

Three Point Percentage
none

Free Throw Percentage
Peja Stojaković, 2007–08 (N.O.).... .929
Brian Roberts, 2013–14 .... .940

Assists Average
Chris Paul, 2007–08 (N.O.) 11.6
Chris Paul, 2008–09 (N.O.) 11.0

League Leaders, Defense
Offensive Rebounds
Tyson Chandler, 2006–07
(N.O.-Ok.C.)........................... 320
Tyson Chandler, 2007–08 (N.O.)...... 322

Defensive Rebounds
none

Total Rebounds
none

Steals
Chris Paul, 2005–06 (N.O.-Ok.C.).... 175
Chris Paul, 2007–08 (N.O.) 217
Chris Paul, 2008–09 (N.O.) 216
Chris Paul, 2010–11 (N.O.) 188

Blocks
Anthony Davis, 2014–15 200
Anthony Davis, 2017–18 193

Rebounds Average
none

Steals Average
Baron Davis, 2003–04 (N.O.) 2.4
Chris Paul, 2007–08 (N.O.) 2.7
Chris Paul, 2008–09 (N.O.) 2.8
Chris Paul, 2010–11 (N.O.) 2.4

Blocks Average
Anthony Davis, 2013–14 .... 2.8
Anthony Davis, 2014–15 .... 2.9
Anthony Davis, 2017–18 .... 2.6

Feats
50-Point Game
59......... Anthony Davis (@ Det. Pistons), Feb. 21, 2016
53......... Anthony Davis (vs. Pho. Suns), Feb. 26, 2018
50... Jamal Mashburn (vs. Mem. Grizzlies), Feb. 21, 2003 (N.O.)
50... Anthony Davis (vs. Den. Nuggets), Oct. 26, 2016

20-Assist Game
25............... Rajon Rondo (vs. Brk. Nets), Dec. 27, 2017
21............... Chris Paul (@ L.A. Lakers), Nov. 6, 2007 (N.O.)
20........... Chris Paul (@ Cle. Cavaliers), Mar. 26, 2008 (N.O.)
20............... Chris Paul (vs. Mil. Bucks), Feb. 27, 2009 (N.O.)
20... Darren Collison (vs. G.S. Warriors), Mar. 8, 2010 (N.O.)

30-Rebound Game
none

8-Steal Game
9......... Chris Paul (vs. Dal. Mavericks), Feb. 20, 2008 (N.O.)
8................... Chris Paul (@ Pho. Suns), Feb. 6, 2008 (N.O.)
8................ Chris Paul (vs. Sac. Kings), Dec. 20, 2008 (N.O.)
8................ Bonzi Wells (vs. Bos. Celtics), Mar. 22, 2008 (N.O.)
8.............Chris Paul (vs. Min. T'Wolves), Dec. 4, 2009 (N.O.)

10-Block Game
10...........Anthony Davis (vs. Uta. Jazz), Mar. 11, 2018

Multiple Triple-Doubles in a Single Season
6................Chris Paul, 2008–09 (N.O.)
6......................Elfrid Payton, 2018–19
3............. DeMarcus Cousins, 2017–18
3......................... Lonzo Ball, 2019–20
2...... Chris Paul, 2005–06 (N.O.-Ok.C.)
2.......Jamal Mashburn, 2002–03 (N.O.)
2......................Rajon Rondo, 2017–18

Postseason Play
2003	Eastern Conference First Round	vs. Phi. 76ers, lost (4–2)
2004	Eastern Conference First Round	vs. Mia. Heat, lost (4–3)
2008	Western Conference First Round	vs. Dal. Mavericks, won (4–1)
	Western Conference Semifinals	vs. S.A. Spurs, lost (4–3)
2009	Western Conference First Round	vs. Den. Nuggets, lost (4–1)
2011	Western Conference First Round	vs. L.A. Lakers, lost (4–2)
2015	Western Conference First Round	vs. G.S. Warriors, lost (4–0)
2018	Western Conference First Round	vs. Por. Blazers, won (4–0)
	Western Conference Semifinals	vs. G.S. Warriors, lost (4–1)
2022	Western Conference First Round	vs. Pho. Suns, lost (4–2)

Oklahoma City Thunder

Dates of Operation: (as the Seattle SuperSonics) 1967–2008 (41 seasons)
Overall Record: 1745 wins, 1585 losses (.524)
Arena: Key Arena (formerly Seattle Center Coliseum, 1967–78) 1967–78, 1985–94, 1995–2008;
 Kingdome, 1978–85; Tacoma Dome, 1994–95
Other Name: Sonics

Dates of Operation: (as the Oklahoma City Thunder) 2008–present (14 seasons)
Overall Record: 628 wins, 484 losses (.565)
Arenas: Paycom Center (formerly Ford Center, 2008–09; Oklahoma City Arena, 2009–10;
 Chesapeake Energy Arena, 2011–21), 2008–present (capacity: 18,203)

Year-by-Year Finishes

Year	Finish	Wins	Losses	Percentage	Games Behind	Head Coach	Attendance
				Seattle SuperSonics			
				Western Division			
1967–68	5th	23	59	.280	33.0	Al Bianchi	202,263
1968–69	6th	30	52	.366	25.0	Al Bianchi	210,232
1969–70	5th	36	46	.439	12.0	Lenny Wilkens	278,444
			Western Conference Pacific Division				
1970–71	4th	38	44	.463	10.0	Lenny Wilkens	372,612
1971–72	3rd	47	35	.573	22.0	Lenny Wilkens	444,302
1972–73	4th	26	56	.317	34.0	Tom Nissalke (13–32),	387,382
						Bucky Buckwalter (13–24)	
1973–74	3rd	36	46	.439	11.0	Bill Russell	491,856
1974–75	2nd	43	39	.524	5.0	Bill Russell	524,692
1975–76	2nd	43	39	.524	16.0	Bill Russell	557,304
1976–77	4th	40	42	.488	13.0	Bill Russell	532,196
1977–78	3rd	47	35	.573	11.0	Bob Hopkins (5–17),	504,668
						Lenny Wilkens (42–18)	
1978–79	1st	52	30	.634	+2.0	Lenny Wilkens	747,243
1979–80	2nd	56	26	.683	4.0	Lenny Wilkens	890,713
1980–81	6th	34	48	.415	23.0	Lenny Wilkens	675,097
1981–82	2nd	52	30	.634	5.0	Lenny Wilkens	721,049
1982–83	3rd	48	34	.585	10.0	Lenny Wilkens	539,622
1983–84	3rd	42	40	.512	12.0	Lenny Wilkens	425,307
1984–85	4th (Tie)	31	51	.378	31.0	Lenny Wilkens	303,344
1985–86	5th	31	51	.378	31.0	Bernie Bickerstaff	329,296
1986–87	4th	39	43	.476	26.0	Bernie Bickerstaff	356,352
1987–88	3rd	44	38	.537	18.0	Bernie Bickerstaff	475,983
1988–89	3rd	47	35	.573	10.0	Bernie Bickerstaff	456,765
1989–90	4th	41	41	.500	22.0	Bernie Bickerstaff	473,277
1990–91	5th	41	41	.500	22.0	K.C. Jones	501,250
1991–92	4th	47	35	.573	10.0	K.C. Jones (18–18),	588,928
						Bob Kloppenburg (2–2),	
						George Karl (27–15)	
1992–93	2nd	55	27	.671	7.0	George Karl	646,589
1993–94	1st	63	19	.768	+7.0	George Karl	601,369
1994–95	2nd	57	25	.695	2.0	George Karl	633,604

Year	Finish	Wins	Losses	Percentage	Games Behind	Head Coach	Attendance
1995–96	1st	64	18	.780	+11.0	George Karl	697,301
1996–97	1st	57	25	.695	+1.0	George Karl	699,952
1997–98	1st (Tie)	61	21	.744	—	George Karl	699,952
1998–99	5th	25	25	.500	10.0	Paul Westphal	426,800
1999–00	4th	45	37	.549	22.0	Paul Westphal	615,730
2000–01	5th	44	38	.537	12.0	Paul Westphal (6–9), Nate McMillan (38–29)	640,847
2001–02	4th	45	37	.549	16.0	Nate McMillan	633,516
2002–03	5th	40	42	.488	19.0	Nate McMillan	637,194
2003–04	4th (Tie)	37	45	.451	19.0	Nate McMillan	625,474
Northwest Division							
2004–05	1st	52	30	.634	+3.0	Nate McMillan	675,490
2005–06	3rd	35	47	.427	9.0	Bob Weiss (13–17), Bob Hill (22–30)	664,157
2006–07	5th	31	51	.378	20.0	Bob Hill (31–51)	654,163
2007–08	5th	20	62	.244	34.0	P.J. Carlesimo	547,556
Oklahoma City Thunder							
2008–09	5th	23	59	.280	31.0	P.J. Carlesimo (1–12), Scott Brooks (22–47)	766,868
2009–10	3rd (Tie)	50	32	.610	3.0	Scott Brooks	738,149
2010–11	1st	55	27	.671	+5.0	Scott Brooks	744,068
2011–12	1st	47	19	.712	+9.0	Scott Brooks	600,699
2012–13	1st	60	22	.732	+3.0	Scott Brooks	746,323
2013–14	1st	59	23	.720	+3.0	Scott Brooks	746,323
2014–15	2nd	45	37	.549	6.0	Scott Brooks	746,323
2015–16	1st	55	27	.671	+11.0	Billy Donovan	746,323
2016–17	2nd	47	35	.573	4.0	Billy Donovan	746,323
2017–18	2nd (Tie)	48	34	.585	1.0	Billy Donovan	746,322
2018–19	4th	49	33	.598	5.0	Billy Donovan	746,323
2019–20	2nd (Tie)	44	28	.611	1.5	Billy Donovan	600,699
2020–21	5th	22	50	.306	30.0	Mark Daigneault	N/A
2021–22	5th	24	58	.293	25.0	Mark Daigneault	595,112

1998–99: 50-game season.
2011–12: 66-game season.
2019–20: 65-to-75-game season.
2020–21: 72-game season.

Awards

Most Valuable Player
Kevin Durant, forward, 2013–14
Russell Westbrook, guard, 2016–17

Rookie of the Year
Kevin Durant, forward, 2007–08 (Sea.)

Defensive Player of the Year
Gary Payton, guard, 1995–96 (Sea.)

Sixth Man of the Year
James Harden, guard, 2011–12

Most Improved Player
Dale Ellis, guard, 1986–87 (Sea.)

All-NBA First Team
Spencer Haywood, 1971–72 (Sea.)
Spencer Haywood, 1972–73 (Sea.)
Gus Williams, 1981–82 (Sea.)
Gary Payton, 1997–98 (Sea.)
Gary Payton, 1999–00 (Sea.)
Kevin Durant, 2009–10
Kevin Durant, 2010–11
Kevin Durant, 2011–12

Kevin Durant, 2012–13
Kevin Durant, 2013–14
Russell Westbrook, 2015–16
Russell Westbrook, 2016–17
Paul George, 2018–19

All-Defensive First Team
Slick Watts, 1975–76 (Sea.)
Dennis Johnson, 1978–79 (Sea.)
Dennis Johnson, 1979–80 (Sea.)
Gary Payton, 1993–94 (Sea.)
Gary Payton, 1994–95 (Sea.)

Gary Payton, 1995–96 (Sea.)
Gary Payton, 1996–97 (Sea.)
Gary Payton, 1997–98 (Sea.)
Gary Payton, 1998–99 (Sea.)
Gary Payton, 1999–00 (Sea.)
Gary Payton, 2000–01 (Sea.)
Gary Payton, 2001–02 (Sea.)
Serge Ibaka, 2011–12
Serge Ibaka, 2012–13
Serge Ibaka, 2013–14
Paul George, 2018–19

All-Rookie First Team
Bob Rule, 1967–68 (Sea.)
Al Tucker, 1967–68 (Sea.)
Art Harris, 1968–69 (Sea.)
Tom Burleson, 1974–75 (Sea.)
Jack Sikma, 1977–78 (Sea.)
Xavier McDaniel, 1985–86 (Sea.)
Derrick McKey, 1987–88 (Sea.)
Kevin Durant, 2007–08 (Sea.)
Jeff Green, 2007–08 (Sea.)
Russell Westbrook, 2008–09

Coach of the Year
Scott Brooks, 2009–10

Hall of Famers Who Played for the SuperSonics/Thunder
Ray Allen, 2002–07 (Sea.)
Patrick Ewing, 2000–01 (Sea.)
Spencer Haywood, 1970–75 (Sea.)
Dennis Johnson, 1976–80 (Sea.)
Šarūnas Marčiulionis, 1994–95 (Sea.)
Gary Payton, 1990–2003 (Sea.)
Jack Sikma, 1977–86 (Sea.)
David Thompson, 1982–84 (Sea.)
Paul Westphal, 1980–81 (Sea.)
Lenny Wilkens, 1968–72 (Sea.)

Retired Numbers
BB .... Bob Blackburn
1 .... Gus Williams
4 .... Nick Collison
10 .... Nate McMillan
19 .... Lenny Wilkens
24 .... Spencer Haywood
32 .... Fred Brown
43 .... Jack Sikma

League Leaders, Offense
Points
Kevin Durant, 2009–10 2472
Kevin Durant, 2010–11 2161
Kevin Durant, 2011–12 1850

Kevin Durant, 2012–13 2280
Kevin Durant, 2013–14 2593
Russell Westbrook, 2016–17 2558

Three Pointers
Gary Payton, 1999–00 (Sea.) 177
Ray Allen*, 2002–03 (Sea.) 201
Ray Allen, 2005–06 (Sea.) 269
*78 with Sea. Sonics and 123 with Mil. Bucks.

Assists
Lenny Wilkens, 1969–70 (Sea.) 683
Lenny Wilkens, 1971–72 (Sea.) 766
Slick Watts, 1975–76 (Sea.) 661
Gary Payton, 1999–00 (Sea.) 732
Russell Westbrook, 2017–18 820
Russell Westbrook, 2018–19 784

Scoring Average
Kevin Durant, 2009–10 .... 30.1
Kevin Durant, 2010–11 .... 27.7
Kevin Durant, 2011–12 .... 28.0
Kevin Durant, 2013–14 .... 32.0
Russell Westbrook, 2014–15 .... 28.2
Russell Westbrook, 2016–17 .... 31.6

Field Goal Percentage
none

Three Point Percentage
Fred Brown, 1979–80 (Sea.) .... .443
Dana Barros, 1991–92 (Sea.) .... .446
Dale Ellis, 1997–98 (Sea.) .... .464
Brent Barry, 2000–01 (Sea.) .... .476

Free Throw Percentage
Kevin Durant, 2012–13 .... .905

Assists Average
Lenny Wilkens, 1969–70 (Sea.) 9.1
Slick Watts, 1975–76 (Sea.) 8.1
Russell Westbrook, 2017–18 .... 10.3
Russell Westbrook, 2018–19 .... 10.7

League Leaders, Defense
Offensive Rebounds
none

Defensive Rebounds
Jack Sikma, 1981–82 (Sea.) 815
Jack Sikma, 1983–84 (Sea.) 686

Total Rebounds
none

Steals
Slick Watts, 1975–76 (Sea.) 261
Nate McMillan, 1993–94 (Sea.) 216

Gary Payton, 1995–96 (Sea.) 231
Paul George, 2018–19 170

Blocks
Serge Ibaka, 2010–11 198
Serge Ibaka, 2011–12 241
Serge Ibaka, 2012–13 242
Serge Ibaka, 2013–14 219

Rebounds Average
none

Steals Average
Slick Watts, 1975–76 (Sea.) 3.2
Nate McMillan, 1993–94 (Sea.) 3.0
Gary Payton, 1995–96 (Sea.) 2.9
Paul George, 2018–19 .... 2.2

Blocks Average
Serge Ibaka, 2011–12 .... 3.7
Serge Ibaka, 2012–13 .... 3.0

Feats
50-Point Game
58 .... Fred Brown (@ G.S. Warriors),
     Mar. 23, 1974 (Sea.)
58 ... Russell Westbrook (vs. Por. Blazers),
     Mar. 7, 2017
57 ... Russell Westbrook (@ Orl. Magic),
     Mar. 29, 2017
54 .... Ray Allen (vs. Uta. Jazz),
     Jan. 12, 2007 (Sea.)
54 ... Kevin Durant (vs. G.S. Warriors),
     Jan. 17, 2014
54 ... Russell Westbrook (@ Ind. Pacers),
     Apr. 12, 2015
53 .... Dale Ellis (@ Mil. Bucks),
     Nov. 9, 1989 (Sea.)
52 .... Kevin Durant (@ Dal. Mavericks),
     Jan. 18, 2013
51 ... Spencer Haywood (vs. K.C.-Oma.
     Kings), Jan. 3, 1973 (Sea.)
51 .... Kevin Durant (vs. Den. Nuggets),
     Feb. 19, 2012
51 .... Kevin Durant (@ Tor. Raptors),
     Mar. 21, 2014
51 .... Russell Westbrook (vs. Pho. Suns),
     Oct. 28, 2016
50 .... Rashard Lewis (@ L.A. Clippers),
     Oct. 31, 2003 (Sea.)
50 ... Russell Westbrook (@ Den. Nuggets),
     Apr. 9, 2017

20-Assist Game
25 ... Nate McMillan (vs. L.A. Clippers),
     Feb. 23, 1987 (Sea.)

30-Rebound Game

30................ Jim Fox (vs. L.A. Lakers),
Dec. 26, 1973 (Sea.)

8-Steal Game

10............. Fred Brown (@ Phi. 76ers),
Dec. 3, 1976 (Sea.)

10...............Gus Williams (@ N.J. Nets),
Feb. 22, 1978 (Sea.)

9................ Slick Watts (vs.Phi. 76ers),
Feb. 23, 1975 (Sea.)

9.................Slick Watts (vs. Pho. Suns),
Mar. 27, 1977 (Sea.)

9......... Gus Williams (@ Was. Bullets),
Jan. 23, 1979 (Sea.)

9................ Jack Sikma (@ K.C. Kings),
Jan. 27, 1982 (Sea.)

8............... Slick Watts (vs. Phi. 76ers),
Dec. 14, 1975 (Sea.)

8.............. Gus Williams (@ Det. Pistons),
Dec. 14, 1977 (Sea.)

8.............. Lonnie Shelton (@ L.A. Lakers),
Dec. 15, 1978 (Sea.)

8..........Gus Williams (vs. S.D. Clippers),
Nov. 29, 1983 (Sea.)

8.......... Nate McMillan (@ Sac. Kings),
Nov. 24, 1993 (Sea.)

8......... Gary Payton (vs. G.S. Warriors),
Dec. 18, 1993 (Sea.)

8.......... Gary Payton (vs. L.A. Clippers),
Mar. 26, 1999 (Sea.)

8... Russell Westbrook (@ G.S. Warriors),
Feb. 6, 2010

10-Block Game

11..........Serge Ibaka (vs. Den. Nuggets),
Feb. 19, 2012

10...............Shawn Kemp (@ L.A. Lakers),
Jan. 18, 1991 (Sea.)

10......... Calvin Booth (vs. Cle. Cavaliers),
Jan. 13, 2004 (Sea.)

10.........Serge Ibaka (@ Dal. Mavericks),
Feb. 1, 2012

10............... Serge Ibaka (@ Sac. Kings),
Feb. 9, 2012

10..........Serge Ibaka (vs. Den. Nuggets),
Feb. 19, 2012

Multiple Triple-Doubles in a Single Season

42............Russell Westbrook, 2016–17

34............Russell Westbrook, 2018–19

25............Russell Westbrook, 2017–18

18............Russell Westbrook, 2015–16

11............Russell Westbrook, 2014–15

5.........Lenny Wilkens, 1968–69 (Sea.)

4.........Lenny Wilkens, 1969–70 (Sea.)

4....................Josh Giddey, 2021–22

3....................Russell Westbrook, 2010–11

3....................Kevin Durant, 2012–13

3....................Kevin Durant, 2013–14

2..............Slick Watts, 1976–77 (Sea.)

2........ Nate McMillan, 1988–89 (Sea.)

2.......... Gary Payton, 1991–92 (Sea.)

2.......... Gary Payton, 1996–97 (Sea.)

2.......... Gary Payton, 1999–00 (Sea.)

2.......... Gary Payton, 2000–01 (Sea.)

2.......... Gary Payton, 2001–02 (Sea.)

2............Russell Westbrook, 2013–14

Postseason Play

1975 Western Conference First Round
vs. Det. Pistons, won (2–1)
Western Conference Semifinals
vs. G.S. Warriors, lost (4–2)

1976 Western Conference Semifinals
vs. Pho. Suns, lost (4–2)

1978 Western Conference First Round
vs. L.A. Lakers, won (2–1)
Western Conference Semifinals
vs. Por. Blazers, won (4–2)
Western Conference Finals
vs. Den. Nuggets, won (4–2)
NBA Finals vs. Was. Bullets,
lost (4–3)

1979 Western Conference Semifinals
vs. L.A. Lakers, won (4–1)
Western Conference Finals
vs. Pho. Suns, won (4–3)
NBA Finals vs. Was. Bullets,
won (4–1)

1980 Western Conference First Round
vs. Por. Blazers, won (2–1)
Western Conference Semifinals
vs. Mil. Bucks, won (4–3)
Western Conference Finals
vs. L.A. Lakers, lost (4–1)

1982 Western Conference First Round
vs. Hou. Rockets, won (2–1)
Western Conference Semifinals
vs. S.A. Spurs, lost (4–1)

1983 Western Conference First Round
vs. Por. Blazers, lost (2–0)

1984 Western Conference First Round
vs. Dal. Mavericks, lost (3–2)

1987 Western Conference First Round
vs. Dal. Mavericks, won (3–1)
Western Conference Semifinals
vs. Hou. Rockets, won (4–2)
Western Conference Finals
vs. L.A. Lakers, lost (4–0)

1988 Western Conference First Round
vs. Den. Nuggets, lost (3–2)

1989 Western Conference First Round
vs. Hou. Rockets, won (3–1)
Western Conference Semifinals
vs. L.A. Lakers, lost (4–0)

1991 Western Conference First Round
vs. Por. Blazers, lost (3–2)

1992 Western Conference First Round
vs. G.S. Warriors, won (3–1)
Western Conference Semifinals
vs. Uta. Jazz, lost (4–1)

1993 Western Conference First Round
vs. Uta. Jazz, won (3–2)
Western Conference Semifinals
vs. Hou. Rockets, won (4–3)
Western Conference Finals
vs. Pho. Suns, lost (4–3)

1994 Western Conference First Round
vs. Den. Nuggets, lost (3–2)

1995 Western Conference First Round
vs. L.A. Lakers, lost (3–1)

1996 Western Conference First Round
vs. Sac. Kings, won (3–1)
Western Conference Semifinals
vs. Hou. Rockets, won (4–0)
Western Conference Finals
vs. Uta. Jazz, won (4–3)
NBA Finals vs. Chi. Bulls,
lost (4–2)

1997 Western Conference First Round
vs. Pho. Suns, won (3–2)
Western Conference Semifinals
vs. Hou. Rockets, lost (4–3)

1998 Western Conference First Round
vs. Min. T'Wolves, won (3–2)
Western Conference Semifinals
vs. L.A. Lakers, lost (4–1)

2000 Western Conference First Round
vs. Uta. Jazz, lost (3–2)

2002 Western Conference First Round
vs. S.A. Spurs, lost (3–2)

2005 Western Conference First Round
vs. Sac. Kings, won (4–1)
Western Conference Semifinals
vs. S.A. Spurs, lost (4–2)

2010　Western Conference First Round
　　　vs. L.A. Lakers, lost (4–2)
2011　Western Conference First Round
　　　vs. Den. Nuggets, won (4–1)
　　　Western Conference Semifinals
　　　vs. Mem. Grizzlies, won (4–3)
　　　Western Conference Finals
　　　vs. Dal. Mavericks, lost (4–1)
2012　Western Conference First Round
　　　vs. Dal. Mavericks, won (4–0)
　　　Western Conference Semifinals
　　　vs. L.A. Lakers, won (4–1)
　　　Western Conference Finals
　　　vs. S.A. Spurs, won (4–2)

　　　NBA Finals vs. Mia. Heat,
　　　lost (4–1)
2013　Western Conference First Round
　　　vs. Hou. Rockets, won (4–2)
　　　Western Conference Semifinals
　　　vs. Mem. Grizzlies, lost (4–1)
2014　Western Conference First Round
　　　vs. Mem. Grizzlies, won (4–3)
　　　Western Conference Semifinals
　　　vs. L.A. Clippers, won (4–2)
　　　Western Conference Finals
　　　vs. S.A. Spurs, lost (4–2)
2016　Western Conference First Round
　　　vs. Dal. Mavericks, won (4–1)

　　　Western Conference Semifinals
　　　vs. S.A. Spurs, won (4–2)
　　　Western Conference Finals
　　　vs. G.S. Warriors, lost (4–3)
2017　Western Conference First Round
　　　vs. Hou. Rockets, lost (4–1)
2018　Western Conference First Round
　　　vs. Uta. Jazz, lost (4–2)
2019　Western Conference First Round
　　　vs. Por. Blazers, lost (4–1)
2020　Western Conference First Round
　　　vs. Hou. Rockets, lost (4–1)

Phoenix Suns

Dates of Operation: 1968–present (54 seasons)
Overall Record: 2335 wins, 2026 losses (.535)
Arenas: Arizona Veterans Memorial Coliseum, 1968–92; Footprint Center (formerly America West Arena, 1992–2006; US Airways Center, 2006–15; Talking Stick Resort Arena, 2015–20; Phoenix Suns Arena, 2020–21), 1992–present (capacity: 16,645)

Year-by-Year Finishes

Year	Finish	Wins	Losses	Percentage	Games Behind	Head Coach	Attendance
Western Division							
1968–69	7th	16	66	.195	39.0	Red Kerr	160,565
1969–70	3rd (Tie)	39	43	.476	9.0	Red Kerr (15–23), Jerry Colangelo (24–20)	281,821
Western Conference Midwest Division							
1970–71	3rd	48	34	.585	18.0	Cotton Fitzsimmons	332,945
1971–72	3rd	49	33	.598	14.0	Cotton Fitzsimmons	342,922
Pacific Division							
1972–73	3rd	38	44	.463	22.0	Butch van Breda Kolff (3–4), Jerry Colangelo (35–40)	342,117
1973–74	4th	30	52	.366	17.0	John MacLeod	284,324
1974–75	4th	32	50	.390	16.0	John MacLeod	253,103
1975–76	3rd	42	40	.512	17.0	John MacLeod	295,293
1976–77	5th	34	48	.415	19.0	John MacLeod	411,294
1977–78	2nd	49	33	.598	9.0	John MacLeod	470,009
1978–79	2nd	50	32	.610	2.0	John MacLeod	465,010
1979–80	3rd	55	27	.671	5.0	John MacLeod	480,659
1980–81	1st	57	25	.695	+3.0	John MacLeod	482,693
1981–82	3rd	46	36	.561	11.0	John MacLeod	486,855
1982–83	2nd	53	29	.646	5.0	John MacLeod	465,603
1983–84	4th	41	41	.500	13.0	John MacLeod	445,788
1984–85	3rd	36	46	.439	26.0	John MacLeod	478,788
1985–86	3rd (Tie)	32	50	.390	30.0	John MacLeod	455,763
1986–87	5th	36	46	.439	29.0	John MacLeod (22–34), Dick Van Arsdale (14–12)	458,347
1987–88	4th	28	54	.341	34.0	John Wetzel	452,354
1988–89	2nd	55	27	.671	2.0	Cotton Fitzsimmons	447,061
1989–90	3rd	54	28	.659	9.0	Cotton Fitzsimmons	578,661
1990–91	3rd	55	27	.671	8.0	Cotton Fitzsimmons	589,591
1991–92	3rd	53	29	.646	4.0	Cotton Fitzsimmons	594,327
1992–93	1st	62	20	.756	+7.0	Paul Westphal	779,943
1993–94	2nd	56	26	.683	7.0	Paul Westphal	779,952
1994–95	1st	59	23	.720	+2.0	Paul Westphal	779,943
1995–96	4th	41	41	.500	23.0	Paul Westphal (14–19), Cotton Fitzsimmons (27–22)	779,943
1996–97	4th	40	42	.488	17.0	Cotton Fitzsimmons (0–8), Danny Ainge (40–34)	779,940
1997–98	3rd	56	26	.683	5.0	Danny Ainge	779,943
1998–99	3rd (Tie)	27	23	.540	8.0	D. Ainge (27–23)	472,283
1999–00	3rd	53	29	.646	14.0	Danny Ainge (13–7), Scott Skiles (40–22)	773,115

Year	Finish	Wins	Losses	Percentage	Games Behind	Head Coach	Attendance
2000–01	3rd	51	31	.622	5.0	Scott Skiles	737,586
2001–02	6th	36	46	.439	25.0	Scott Skiles (25–26), Frank Johnson (11–20)	668,939
2002–03	4th	44	38	.537	15.0	Frank Johnson	666,559
2003–04	6th	29	53	.354	27.0	Frank Johnson (8–13), Mike D'Antoni (21–40)	670,385
2004–05	1st	62	20	.756	+12.0	Mike D'Antoni	726,066
2005–06	1st	54	28	.659	+7.0	Mike D'Antoni	730,179
2006–07	1st	61	21	.744	+19.0	Mike D'Antoni	755,302
2007–08	2nd	55	27	.671	2.0	Mike D'Antoni	755,302
2008–09	2nd	46	36	.561	19.0	Terry Porter (28–23), Alvin Gentry (18–13)	755,302
2009–10	2nd	54	28	.659	3.0	Alvin Gentry	723,582
2010–11	2nd	40	42	.488	17.0	Alvin Gentry	720,249
2011–12	3rd	33	33	.500	8.0	Alvin Gentry	514,718
2012–13	5th	25	57	.305	31.0	Alvin Gentry (13–28), Lindsey Hunter (12–29)	632,913
2013–14	3rd	48	34	.585	9.0	Jeff Hornacek	650,739
2014–15	3rd	39	43	.476	28.0	Jeff Hornacek	693,862
2015–16	4th	23	59	.280	50.0	Jeff Hornacek (14–35), Earl Watson (9–24)	701,405
2016–17	5th	24	58	.293	43.0	Earl Watson	708,639
2017–18	5th	21	61	.256	37.0	Earl Watson (0–3), Jay Triano (21–58)	690,576
2018–19	5th	19	63	.232	38.0	Igor Kokoskov	627,023
2019–20	3rd	34	39	.466	19.0	Monty Williams	550,633
2020–21	1st	51	21	.708	+4.0	Monty Williams	104,027
2021–22	1st	64	18	.780	+11.0	Monty Williams	663,171

1998–99: 50-game season.

2011–12: 66-game season.

2019–20: 65-to-75-game season.

2020–21: 72-game season.

Awards

Most Valuable Player
Charles Barkley, forward, 1992–93
Steve Nash, guard, 2004–05
Steve Nash, guard, 2005–06

Rookie of the Year
Alvan Adams, center, 1975–76
Walter Davis, forward, 1977–78
Amar'e Stoudemire, forward, 2002–03

Defensive Player of the Year
none

Sixth Man of the Year
Eddie Johnson, forward, 1988–89
Danny Manning, forward, 1997–98
Rodney Rogers, forward, 1999–00
Leandro Barbosa, guard, 2006–07

Most Improved Player
Kevin Johnson, guard, 1988–89
Boris Diaw, forward, 2005–06
Goran Dragić, guard, 2013–14

All-NBA First Team
Connie Hawkins, 1969–70
Paul Westphal, 1976–77
Paul Westphal, 1978–79
Paul Westphal, 1979–80
Dennis Johnson, 1980–81
Charles Barkley, 1992–93
Jason Kidd, 1998–99
Jason Kidd, 1999–00
Jason Kidd, 2000–01
Steve Nash, 2004–05
Steve Nash, 2005–06
Steve Nash, 2006–07

Amar'e Stoudemire, 2006–07
Devin Booker, 2021–22

All-Defensive First Team
Don Buse, 1977–78
Don Buse, 1978–79
Don Buse, 1979–80
Dennis Johnson, 1980–81
Dennis Johnson, 1981–82
Dennis Johnson, 1982–83
Jason Kidd, 1998–99
Jason Kidd, 2000–01
Raja Bell, 2006–07

All-Rookie First Team
Gary Gregor, 1968–69
Mike Bantom, 1973–74
Alvan Adams, 1975–76

John Shumate, 1975–76*
Ron Lee, 1976–77
Walter Davis, 1977–78
Armen Gilliam, 1987–88
Michael Finley, 1995–96
Amar'e Stoudemire, 2002–03
Devin Booker, 2015–16
Deandre Ayton, 2018–19

* 43 games with Pho. Suns and 32 games with Buf. Braves.

Coach of the Year
Cotton Fitzsimmons, 1988–89
Mike D'Antoni, 2004–05
Monty Williams, 2021–22

Hall of Famers Who Played for the Suns
Charles Barkley, forward, 1992–96
Gail Goodrich, guard, 1968–70
Connie Hawkins, forward, 1969–74
Grant Hill, forward, 2007–12
Dennis Johnson, guard, 1980–83
Gus Johnson, forward, 1972–73
Jason Kidd, guard, 1996–2001
Steve Nash, guard, 1996–98; 2004–12
Shaquille O'Neal, center, 2007–09
Charlie Scott, guard, 1971–75
Paul Westphal, guard, 1975–80; 1983–84

Retired Numbers
AM .... Al McCoy
JC .... Jerry Colangelo
JM .... John MacLeod
JP .... Joe Proski
5 .... Dick Van Arsdale
6 .... Walter Davis
7 .... Kevin Johnson
9 .... Dan Majerle
13 .... Steve Nash
24 .... Tom Chambers
33 .... Alvan Adams
34 .... Charles Barkley
42 .... Connie Hawkins
44 .... Paul Westphal
832 .... Cotton Fitzsimmons

League Leaders, Offense
Points
none

Three Pointers
Dan Majerle, 1992–93 167
Dan Majerle, 1993–94 192

Quentin Richardson, 2004–05 226
Raja Bell, 2006–07 205

Assists
Jason Kidd, 1998–99 539
Jason Kidd, 2000–01 753
Stephon Marbury*, 2003–04 719
Steve Nash, 2004–05 861
Steve Nash, 2005–06 826
Steve Nash, 2006–07 884
Steve Nash, 2009–10 892
Steve Nash, 2010–11 855
Steve Nash, 2011–12 664

*281 with Pho. Suns and 438 with N.Y. Knicks.

Scoring Average
none

Field Goal Percentage
John Shumate*, 1975–76 .... .561
Mark West, 1989–90 .... .625
Cedric Ceballos, 1992–93 .... .576
Shaquille O'Neal, 2008–09 .... .601

*.550 with Pho. Suns and .575 with Buf. Braves.

Three Point Percentage
Craig Hodges*, 1987–88 .... .491

*.544 with Pho. Suns and .466 with Mil. Bucks.

Free Throw Percentage
Kyle Macy, 1981–82 .... .899
Kyle Macy, 1984–85 .... .907
Steve Nash, 2005–06 .... .921
Steve Nash, 2009–10 .... .938
Chris Paul, 2020–21 .... .934

Assists Average
Jason Kidd, 1998–99 .... 10.8
Jason Kidd, 1999–00 .... 10.1
Jason Kidd, 2000–01 .... 9.8
Steve Nash, 2004–05 .... 11.5
Steve Nash, 2005–06 .... 10.5
Steve Nash, 2006–07 .... 11.6
Steve Nash, 2009–10 .... 11.0
Steve Nash, 2010–11 .... 11.4
Chris Paul, 2021–22 .... 10.8

League Leaders, Defense
Offensive Rebounds
none

Defensive Rebounds
none

Total Rebounds
none

Steals
Ron Lee, 1977–78 225

Shawn Marion, 2003–04 167
Shawn Marion, 2006–07 156

Blocks
none

Rebounds Average
none

Steals Average
Ron Lee, 1977–78 .... 2.7

Blocks Average
none

Feats
50-Point Game
70 .... Devin Booker (@ Bos. Celtics), Mar. 24, 2017
60 .... Tom Chambers (vs. Sea. Sonics), Mar. 24, 1990
59 .... Devin Booker (@ Uta. Jazz), Mar. 25, 2019
56 .... Tom Chambers (@ G.S. Warriors), Feb. 18, 1990
53 .... Tony Delk (@ Sac. Kings), Jan. 2, 2001
51 ... Jamal Crawford (@ Dal. Mavericks), Apr. 9, 2019
50 ... Clifford Robinson (vs. Den. Nuggets), Jan. 16, 2000
50 ... Amar'e Stoudemire (vs. Por. Blazers), Jan. 2, 2005
50 .... Devin Booker (vs. Was. Wizards), Mar. 27, 2019

20-Assist Game
25 .... Kevin Johnson (vs. S.A. Spurs), Apr. 6, 1994
22 .... Steve Nash (@ N.Y. Knicks), Jan. 2, 2006
21 .... Kevin Johnson (@ L.A. Lakers), Feb. 26, 1989
21 .... Steve Nash (vs. Cle. Cavaliers), Jan. 11, 2007
21 .... Steve Nash (@ Det. Pistons), Feb. 8, 2009
20 .... Kevin Johnson (vs. S.A. Spurs), Apr. 15, 1989
20 .... Kevin Johnson (vs. Cha. Hornets), Mar. 21, 1990
20 ... Kevin Johnson (vs. Dal. Mavericks), Apr. 3, 1990
20 .... Kevin Johnson (vs. Uta. Jazz), Apr. 2, 1991

20.......... Kevin Johnson (vs. Por. Blazers),
Mar. 31, 1992

20.............. Steve Nash (vs. Sac. Kings),
Dec. 5, 2006

20.............. Steve Nash (@ L.A. Lakers),
Jan. 17, 2008

20..........Steve Nash (vs. G.S. Warriors),
Oct. 30, 2009

20.............. Steve Nash (@ Phi. 76ers),
Nov. 9, 2009

20.............. Steve Nash (@ L.A. Lakers),
Mar. 22, 2011

30-Rebound Game
none

8-Steal Game
10.......... Kevin Johnson (vs. Was. Bullets),
Dec. 9, 1993

9.............. Johnny High (@ Was. Bullets),
Jan. 28, 1981

8.............. Paul Westphal (@ N.O. Jazz),
Dec. 16, 1977

8.......... Mike Bratz (vs. Cle. Cavaliers),
Feb. 11, 1979

8.......... Alvan Adams (@ Dal. Mavericks),
Nov. 3, 1984

8.............. Alvan Adams (vs. Uta. Jazz),
Dec. 6, 1985

8........ Shawn Marion (vs. Min. T'Wolves),
Feb. 6, 2006

10-Block Game
10.............. Larry Nance (@ Phi. 76ers),
Jan. 4, 1988

10... Amar'e Stoudemire (vs. Uta. Jazz),
Feb. 7, 2004

Multiple Triple-Doubles in a Single Season
7........................ Jason Kidd, 1998–99
7........................ Jason Kidd, 2000–01
6.................. Charles Barkley, 1992–93
5..................... Alvan Adams, 1975–76
5........................ Jason Kidd, 1999–00
4........................ Jason Kidd, 1997–98
4........................ Boris Diaw, 2005–06
3..................... Alvan Adams, 1976–77
3................... Kevin Johnson, 1987–88
3................... Kevin Johnson, 1989–90
2................. Connie Hawkins, 1969–70
2........................ Rich Kelley, 1981–82
2..................... Alvan Adams, 1984–85
2................... Kevin Johnson, 1988–89

2.................... Kevin Johnson, 1996–97
2........................ Jason Kidd, 1996–97
2........................ Eric Bledsoe, 2014–15
2..................... Elfrid Payton, 2017–18
2........................ Ricky Rubio, 2019–20
2........................ Chris Paul, 2021–22

Postseason Play

1970 Western Division Semifinals
vs. L.A. Lakers, lost (4–3)

1976 Western Conference Semifinals
vs. Sea. Sonics, won (4–2)
Western Conference Finals
vs. G.S. Warriors, won (4–3)
NBA Finals vs. Bos. Celtics,
lost (4–2)

1978 Western Conference First Round
vs. Mil. Bucks, lost (2–0)

1979 Western Conference First Round
vs. Por. Blazers, won (2–1)
Western Conference Semifinals
vs. K.C. Kings, won (4–1)
Western Conference Finals
vs. Sea. Sonics, lost (4–3)

1980 Western Conference First Round
vs. K.C. Kings, won (2–1)
Western Conference Semifinals
vs. L.A. Lakers, lost (4–1)

1981 Western Conference Semifinals
vs. K.C. Kings, lost (4–3)

1982 Western Conference First Round
vs. Den. Nuggets, won (2–1)
Western Conference Semifinals
vs. L.A. Lakers, lost (4–0)

1983 Western Conference First Round
vs. Den. Nuggets, lost (2–1)

1984 Western Conference First Round
vs. Por. Blazers, won (3–2)
Western Conference Semifinals
vs. Uta. Jazz, won (4–2)
Western Conference Finals
vs. L.A. Lakers, lost (4–2)

1985 Western Conference First Round
vs. L.A. Lakers, lost (3–0)

1989 Western Conference First Round
vs. Den. Nuggets, won (3–0)
Western Conference Semifinals
vs. G.S. Warriors, won (4–1)
Western Conference Finals
vs. L.A. Lakers, lost (4–0)

1990 Western Conference First Round
vs. Uta. Jazz, won (3–2)

Western Conference Semifinals
vs. L.A. Lakers, won (4–1)
Western Conference Finals
vs. Por. Blazers, lost (4–2)

1991 Western Conference First Round
vs. Uta. Jazz, lost (3–1)

1992 Western Conference First Round
vs. S.A. Spurs, won (3–0)
Western Conference Semifinals
vs. Por. Blazers, lost (4–1)

1993 Western Conference First Round
vs. L.A. Lakers, won (3–2)
Western Conference Semifinals
vs. S.A. Spurs, won (4–2)
Western Conference Finals
vs. Sea. Sonics, won (4–3)
NBA Finals vs. Chi. Bulls,
lost (4–2)

1994 Western Conference First Round
vs. G.S. Warriors, won (3–0)
Western Conference Semifinals
vs. Hou. Rockets, lost (4–3)

1995 Western Conference First Round
vs. Por. Blazers, won (3–0)
Western Conference Semifinals
vs. Hou. Rockets, lost (4–3)

1996 Western Conference First Round
vs. S.A. Spurs, lost (3–1)

1997 Western Conference First Round
vs. Sea. Sonics, lost (3–2)

1998 Western Conference First Round
vs. S.A. Spurs, lost (3–1)

1999 Western Conference First Round
vs. Por. Blazers, lost (3–0)

2000 Western Conference First Round
vs. S.A. Spurs, won (3–1)
Western Conference Semifinals
vs. L.A. Lakers, lost (4–1)

2001 Western Conference First Round
vs. Sac. Kings, lost (3–1)

2003 Western Conference First Round
vs. S.A. Spurs, lost (4–2)

2005 Western Conference First Round
vs. Mem. Grizzlies, won (4–0)
Western Conference Semifinals
vs. Dal. Mavericks, won (4–2)
Western Conference Finals v
s. S.A. Spurs, lost (4–1)

2006 Western Conference First Round
vs. L.A. Lakers, won (4–3)
Western Conference Semifinals
vs. L.A. Clippers, won (4–3)

Western Conference Finals
    vs. Dal. Mavericks, lost (4–2)
2007 Western Conference First Round
    vs. L.A. Lakers, won (4–1)
Western Conference Semifinals
    vs. S.A. Spurs, lost (4–2)
2008 Western Conference First Round
    vs. S.A. Spurs, lost (4–1)
2010 Western Conference First Round
    vs. Por. Blazers, won (4–2)

Western Conference Semifinals
    vs. S.A. Spurs, won (4–0)
Western Conference Finals
    vs. L.A. Lakers, lost (4–2)
2021 Western Conference First Round
    vs. L.A. Lakers, won (4–2)
Western Conference Semifinals
    vs. Den. Nuggets, won (4–0)
Western Conference Finals
    vs. L.A. Clippers, won (4–2)

NBA Finals vs. Mil. Bucks,
    lost (4–2)
2022 Western Conference First Round
    vs. N.O. Pelicans, won (4–2)
Western Conference Semifinals
    vs. Dal. Mavericks, lost (4–3)

Portland Trail Blazers

Dates of Operation: 1970–present (52 seasons)
Overall Record: 2238 wins, 1960 losses (.533)
Arenas: Memorial Coliseum, 1970–95; Moda Center (formerly Rose Garden Arena, 1995–2013),
  1995–present (capacity: 19,393)
Other Name: Blazers

Year-by-Year Finishes

Year	Finish	Wins	Losses	Percentage	Games Behind	Head Coach	Attendance
				Western Conference Pacific Division			
1970–71	5th	29	53	.354	19.0	Rolland Todd	245,383
1971–72	5th	18	64	.220	51.0	Rolland Todd (12–44), Stu Inman (6–20)	279,506
1972–73	5th	21	61	.256	39.0	Jack McCloskey	333,480
1973–74	5th	27	55	.329	20.0	Jack McCloskey	327,495
1974–75	3rd	38	44	.463	10.0	Lenny Wilkens	441,506
1975–76	5th	37	45	.451	22.0	Lenny Wilkens	413,992
1976–77	2nd	49	33	.598	4.0	Jack Ramsay	499,302
1977–78	1st	58	24	.707	+9.0	Jack Ramsay	519,306
1978–79	4th	45	37	.549	7.0	Jack Ramsay	519,306
1979–80	4th	38	44	.463	22.0	Jack Ramsay	519,306
1980–81	3rd	45	37	.549	12.0	Jack Ramsay	519,306
1981–82	5th	42	40	.512	15.0	Jack Ramsay	519,306
1982–83	4th	46	36	.561	12.0	Jack Ramsay	483,974
1983–84	2nd	48	34	.585	6.0	Jack Ramsay	518,306
1984–85	2nd	42	40	.512	20.0	Jack Ramsay	519,306
1985–86	2nd	40	42	.488	22.0	Jack Ramsay	519,306
1986–87	2nd	49	33	.598	16.0	Mike Schuler	519,306
1987–88	2nd	53	29	.646	9.0	Mike Schuler	519,306
1988–89	5th	39	43	.476	18.0	Mike Schuler (25–22), Rick Adelman (14–21)	527,008
1989–90	2nd	59	23	.720	4.0	Rick Adelman	528,132
1990–91	1st	63	19	.768	+5.0	Rick Adelman	528,244
1991–92	1st	57	25	.695	+2.0	Rick Adelman	528,408
1992–93	3rd	51	31	.622	11.0	Rick Adelman	528,408
1993–94	4th	47	35	.573	16.0	Rick Adelman	528,408
1994–95	4th	44	38	.537	15.0	P.J. Carlesimo	529,759
1995–96	3rd	44	38	.537	20.0	P.J. Carlesimo	848,055
1996–97	3rd	49	33	.598	8.0	P.J. Carlesimo	852,798
1997–98	4th	46	36	.561	15.0	Mike Dunleavy	846,559
1998–99	1st	35	15	.700	+4.0	Mike Dunleavy	486,556
1999–00	2nd	59	23	.720	8.0	Mike Dunleavy	835,078
2000–01	4th	50	32	.610	6.0	Mike Dunleavy	831,376
2001–02	3rd	49	33	.598	12.0	Maurice Cheeks	797,821
2002–03	2nd (Tie)	50	32	.610	9.0	Maurice Cheeks	796,258
2003–04	3rd	41	41	.500	15.0	Maurice Cheeks	684,038
				Northwest Division			
2004–05	4th	27	55	.329	25.0	Maurice Cheeks (22–33), Kevin Pritchard (5–22)	680,374

Year	Finish	Wins	Losses	Percentage	Games Behind	Head Coach	Attendance
2005–06	5th	21	61	.256	23.0	Nate McMillan	617,019
2006–07	3rd (Tie)	32	50	.390	19.0	Nate McMillan	670,778
2007–08	3rd	41	41	.500	13.0	Nate McMillan	801,566
2008–09	1st (Tie)	54	28	.659	—	Nate McMillan	841,499
2009–10	3rd (Tie)	50	32	.610	3.0	Nate McMillan	841,499
2010–11	3rd	48	34	.585	7.0	Nate McMillan	840,924
2011–12	4th	28	38	.424	19.0	Nate McMillan (20–23), Kaleb Canales (8–15)	676,384
2012–13	4th	33	49	.402	27.0	Terry Stotts	813,012
2013–14	2nd	54	28	.659	5.0	Terry Stotts	809,612
2014–15	1st	51	31	.622	+6.0	Terry Stotts	798,368
2015–16	2nd	44	38	.537	11.0	Terry Stotts	794,085
2016–17	3rd	41	41	.500	10.0	Terry Stotts	792,029
2017–18	1st	49	33	.598	+1.0	Terry Stotts	795,750
2018–19	2nd	53	29	.646	1.0	Terry Stotts	799,345
2019–20	4th	35	39	.473	11.5	Terry Stotts	628,303
2020–21	3rd	42	30	.583	10.0	Terry Stotts	5,817
2021–22	4th	27	55	.329	22.0	Chauncey Billups	705,608

1998–99: 50-game season.

2011–12: 66-game season.

2019–20: 65-to-75-game season.

2020–21: 72-game season.

Awards

Most Valuable Player

Bill Walton, center, 1977–78

Rookie of the Year

Geoff Petrie, guard, 1970–71*

Sidney Wicks, forward, 1971–72

Brandon Roy, guard, 2006–07

Damian Lillard, guard, 2012–13

*Tied with Dave Cowens, Bos. Celtics.

Defensive Player of the Year

Sixth Man of the Year

Clifford Robinson, forward, 1992–93

Most Improved Player

Kevin Duckworth, center, 1987–88

Zach Randolph, forward, 2003–04

C.J. McCollum, guard, 2015–16

All-NBA First Team

Bill Walton, 1977–78

Clyde Drexler, 1991–92

Damian Lillard, 2017–18

All-Defensive First Team

Bill Walton, 1976–77

Lionel Hollins, 1977–78

Maurice Lucas, 1977–78

Bill Walton, 1977–78

Buck Williams, 1989–90

Buck Williams, 1990–91

All-Rookie First Team

Geoff Petrie, 1970–71

Sidney Wicks, 1971–72

Lloyd Neal, 1972–73

Lionel Hollins, 1975–76

Ron Brewer, 1978–79

Mychal Thompson, 1978–79

Calvin Natt, 1979–80*

Kelvin Ransey, 1980–81

Sam Bowie, 1984–85

Arvydas Sabonis, 1995–96

LaMarcus Aldridge, 2006–07

Brandon Roy, 2006–07

Damian Lillard, 2012–13

* 25 games with Por. Blazers and 53 games with N.J. Nets

Coach of the Year

Mike Schuler, 1986–87

Mike Dunleavy, 1998–99

Hall of Famers Who Played for the Trail Blazers

Clyde Drexler, guard, 1983–95

Dražen Petrović, guard, 1989–91

Scottie Pippen, forward, 2000–03

Arvydas Sabonis, center, 1995–2001; 2002–03

Bill Walton, center, 1974–78

Lenny Wilkens, guard, 1974–75

Retired Numbers

LW ....Larry Weinberg

13.................................Dave Twardzik

14.................................... Lionel Hollins

15...Larry Steele

20...................................Maurice Lucas

22....................................Clyde Drexler

30.. Bob Gross

30....................................Terry Porter

32.................................... Bill Walton

36...................................Lloyd Neal

45.................................. Geoff Petrie

77...................................Jack Ramsay

League Leaders, Offense

Points

Three Pointers

Assists

Scoring Average
none

Field Goal Percantage
Buck Williams, 1990–91 .... .602
Buck Williams, 1991–92 .... .604

Three Point Percentage
Kiki Vandeweghe, 1986–87 .... .482
Tracy Murray, 1993–94 .... .459

Free Throw Percentage
Jamal Crawford, 2011–12 .... .927
C.J. McCollum, 2016–17 .... .912

Assists Average
none

League Leaders, Defense
Offensive Rebounds
Hassan Whiteside, 2019–20 258

Defensive Rebounds
none

Total Rebounds
none

Steals
Larry Steele, 1973–74 217

Blocks
Theo Ratliff*, 2003–04 307
Hassan Whiteside, 2019–20 196
*141 with Por. Blazers and 166 with Atl. Hawks.

Rebounds Average
Bill Walton, 1976–77 .... 14.4

Steals Average
Larry Steele, 1973–74 .... 2.7

Blocks Average
Bill Walton, 1976–77 .... 3.3
Theo Ratliff*, 2003–04 .... 3.6
Hassan Whiteside, 2019–20 .... 2.9
*4.4 with Por. Blazers and 3.1 with Atl. Hawks.

Feats
50-Point Game
61... Damian Lillard (vs. G.S. Warriors),
Jan. 20, 2020
61... Damian Lillard (@ Dal. Mavericks),
Aug. 11, 2020
60 .... Damian Lillard (vs. Brk. Nets),
Nov. 8, 2019
59 .... Damian Lillard (vs. Uta. Jazz),
Apr. 8, 2017

54... Damon Stoudamire (@ N.O. Hornets),
Jan. 14, 2005
52 .... Brandon Roy (vs. Pho. Suns),
Dec. 18, 2008
52 ... Andre Miller (@ Dal. Mavericks),
Jan. 30, 2010
51 .... Geoff Petrie (@ Hou. Rockets),
Jan. 20, 1973
51 .... Geoff Petrie (vs. Hou. Rockets),
Mar. 16, 1973
51... Damian Lillard (vs. G.S. Warriors),
Feb. 19, 2016
51... Damian Lillard (vs. Ok.C. Thunder),
Mar. 7, 2019
51 .... Damian Lillard (vs. Uta. Jazz),
Feb. 1, 2020
51 .... Damian Lillard (vs. Phi. 76ers),
Aug. 9, 2020
50 .... Clyde Drexler (vs. Sac. Kings),
Jan. 6, 1989
50 ... Damian Lillard (@ Tor. Raptors), Mar.
4, 2016
50 .... C.J. McCollum (vs. Chi. Bulls),
Jan. 31, 2018
50 .... Damian Lillard (@ Sac. Kings),
Feb. 9, 2018
50 .... Damian Lillard (vs. Ind. Pacers),
Jan. 26, 2020
50... Damian Lillard (vs. N.O. Pelicans),
Mar. 16, 2021

20-Assist Game
20 .... Rod Strickland (vs. Pho. Suns),
Apr. 5, 1994
20 .... Rod Strickland (vs. Hou. Rockets),
Mar. 30, 1996

30-Rebound Game
30 .... Enes Freedom (vs. Det. Pistons),
Apr. 10, 2021

8-Steal Game
10 .... Larry Steele (vs. L.A. Lakers),
Nov. 16, 1974
10 .... Clyde Drexler (@ Mil. Bucks),
Jan. 10, 1986
10 .... Brandon Roy (vs. Was. Wizards),
Jan. 24, 2009
9 .... Larry Steele (vs. L.A. Lakers),
Mar. 5, 1974
9 .... Larry Steele (vs. Pho. Suns),
Mar. 7, 1975
9 .... Larry Steele (vs. Det. Pistons),
Mar. 14, 1976

8 .... Larry Steele (vs. Cle. Cavaliers),
Feb. 16, 1974
8 .... Larry Steele (vs. N.Y. Knicks),
Nov. 9, 1975
8 .... Larry Steele (vs. K.C. Kings),
Mar. 30, 1976
8 .... Lionel Hollins (vs. N.Y. Knicks),
Jan. 10, 1978
8 .... Darnell Valentine (vs. S.A. Spurs),
Nov. 4, 1982
8... Darnell Valentine (vs. G.S. Warriors),
Oct. 27, 1985
8 .... Clyde Drexler (@ Ind. Pacers),
Nov. 30, 1986
8 .... Clyde Drexler (@ Chi. Bulls),
Feb. 26, 1988
8 .... Terry Porter (vs. Uta. Jazz),
Jan. 30, 1990
8 .... Clyde Drexler (vs. Ind. Pacers),
Dec. 11, 1992

10-Block Game
10 .... Hassan Whiteside (vs. Chi. Bulls),
Nov. 29, 2019

Multiple Triple-Doubles in a Single Season
4 .... Sidney Wicks, 1972–73
4 .... Clyde Drexler, 1985–86
4 .... Clyde Drexler, 1988–89
4 .... Clyde Drexler, 1990–91
3 .... Clyde Drexler, 1986–87
3 .... Terry Porter, 1988–89
2 .... Dale Schlueter, 1971–72
2 .... Sidney Wicks, 1973–74
2 .... Bill Walton, 1975–76
2 .... Bill Walton, 1977–78
2 .... Clyde Drexler, 1984–85
2 .... Terry Porter, 1986–87
2 .... Terry Porter, 1987–88
2 .... Damon Stoudamire, 2004–05
2 .... Nicolas Batum, 2012–13
2 .... Nicolas Batum, 2013–14
2 .... Evan Turner, 2018–19

Postseason Play
1977   Western Conference First Round
vs. Chi. Bulls, won (2–1)
Western Conference Semifinals
vs. Den. Nuggets, won (4–2)
Western Conference Finals
vs. L.A. Lakers, won (4–0)
NBA Finals vs. Phi. 76ers,
won (4–2)

1978 Western Conference Semifinals
vs. Sea. Sonics, lost (4–2)

1979 Western Conference First Round
vs. Pho. Suns, lost (2–1)

1980 Western Conference First Round
vs. Sea. Sonics, lost (2–1)

1981 Western Conference First Round
vs. K.C. Kings, lost (2–1)

1983 Western Conference First Round
vs. Sea. Sonics, won (2–0)

Western Conference Semifinals
vs. L.A. Lakers, lost (4–1)

1984 Western Conference First Round
vs. Pho. Suns, lost (3–2)

1985 Western Conference First Round
vs. Dal. Mavericks, won (3–1)

Western Conference Semifinals
vs. L.A. Lakers, lost (4–1)

1986 Western Conference First Round
vs. Den. Nuggets, lost (3–1)

1987 Western Conference First Round
vs. Hou. Rockets, lost (3–1)

1988 Western Conference First Round
vs. Uta. Jazz, lost (3–1)

1989 Western Conference First Round
vs. L.A. Lakers, lost (3–0)

1990 Western Conference First Round
vs. Dal. Mavericks, won (3–1)

Western Conference Semifinals
vs. S.A. Spurs, won (4–3)

Western Conference Finals
vs. Pho. Suns, won (4–2)

NBA Finals vs. Det. Pistons,
lost (4–1)

1991 Western Conference First Round
vs. Sea. Sonics, won (3–2)

Western Conference Semifinals
vs. Uta. Jazz, won (4–1)

Western Conference Finals
vs. L.A. Lakers, lost (4–2)

1992 Western Conference First Round
vs. L.A. Lakers, won (3–1)

Western Conference Semifinals
vs. Pho. Suns, won (4–1)

Western Conference Finals
vs. Uta. Jazz, won (4–2)

NBA Finals vs. Chi. Bulls,
lost (4–2)

1993 Western Conference First Round
vs. S.A. Spurs, lost (3–1)

1994 Western Conference First Round
vs. Hou. Rockets, lost (3–1)

1995 Western Conference First Round
vs. Pho. Suns, lost (3–0)

1996 Western Conference First Round
vs. Uta. Jazz, lost (3–2)

1997 Western Conference First Round
vs. L.A. Lakers, lost (3–1)

1998 Western Conference First Round
vs. L.A. Lakers, lost (3–1)

1999 Western Conference First Round
vs. Pho. Suns, won (3–0)

Western Conference Semifinals
vs. Uta. Jazz, won (4–2)

Western Conference Finals
vs. S.A. Spurs, lost (4–0)

2000 Western Conference First Round
vs. Min. T'Wolves, won (3–1)

Western Conference Semifinals
vs. Uta. Jazz, won (4–1)

Western Conference Finals
vs. L.A. Lakers, lost (4–3)

2001 Western Conference First Round
vs. L.A. Lakers, lost (3–0)

2002 Western Conference First Round
vs. L.A. Lakers, lost (3–0)

2003 Western Conference First Round
vs. Dal. Mavericks, lost (4–3)

2009 Western Conference First Round
vs. Hou. Rockets, lost (4–2)

2010 Western Conference First Round
vs. Pho. Suns, lost (4–2)

2011 Western Conference First Round
vs. Dal. Mavericks, lost (4–2)

2014 Western Conference First Round
vs. Hou. Rockets won (4–2)

Western Conference Semifinals
vs. S.A. Spurs, lost (4–1)

2015 Western Conference First Round
vs. Mem. Grizzlies, lost (4–1)

2016 Western Conference First Round
vs. L.A. Clippers, won (4–2)

Western Conference Semifinals
vs. G.S. Warriors, lost (4–1)

2017 Western Conference First Round
vs. G.S. Warriors, lost (4–0)

2018 Western Conference First Round
vs. N.O. Pelicans, lost (4–0)

2019 Western Conference First Round
vs. Ok.C. Thunder, won (4–1)

Western Conference Semifinals
vs. Den. Nuggets, won (4–3)

Western Conference Finals
vs. G.S. Warriors, lost (4–0)

2020 Western Conference First Round
vs. L.A. Lakers, lost (4–1)

2021 Western Conference First Round
vs. Den. Nuggets, lost (4–2)

Sacramento Kings

Dates of Operation: (as the Cincinnati Royals) 1948–72 (24 seasons)
Overall Record: 912 wins, 897 losses (.504)
Arenas: Edgerton Park Arena, 1948–55; Rochester Community War Memorial, 1955–57; Cincinnati Gardens, 1957–72
Other Name: Rochester Royals, 1948–57

Dates of Operation: (as the Kansas City Kings) 1972–85 (13 seasons)
Overall Record: 494 wins, 572 losses (.463)
Arenas: Municipal Auditorium, 1972–74; Kemper Arena, 1974–85
Other Name: Kansas City-Omaha Kings, 1972–75

Dates of Operation: (as the Sacramento Kings) 1985–present (37 seasons)
Overall Record: 1248 wins, 1718 losses (.421)
Arenas: ARCO Arena (I), 1985–88; Sleep Train Arena (formerly ARCO Arena II, 1988–2009; Power Balance Pavilion, 2009–12), 1988–2016; Golden 1 Center, 2016–present (capacity: 17,608)

Year-by-Year Finishes

Year	Finish	Wins	Losses	Percentage	Games Behind	Head Coach	Attendance
				Rochester Royals **BAA Western Division**			
1948–49	1st	45	15	.750	+1.0	Les Harrison	121,499
				NBA Central Division			
1949–50	1st (Tie)	51	17	.750	—	Les Harrison	81,872
				Western Division			
1950–51	2nd	41	27	.603	3.0	Les Harrison	N/A
1951–52	1st	41	25	.621	+1.0	Les Harrison	N/A
1952–53	2nd	44	26	.629	4.0	Les Harrison	N/A
1953–54	2nd	44	28	.611	2.0	Les Harrison	N/A
1954–55	3rd	29	43	.403	14.0	Les Harrison	79,285
1955–56	4th	31	41	.431	6.0	Bobby Wanzer	102,468
1956–57	4th	31	41	.431	3.0	Bobby Wanzer	122,502
				Cincinnati Royals			
1957–58	2nd (Tie)	33	39	.458	8.0	Bobby Wanzer	105,590
1958–59	4th	19	53	.264	30.0	Bobby Wanzer (3–15), Tom Marshall (16–38)	68,470
1959–60	4th	19	56	.253	27.0	Tom Marshall	58,244
1960–61	4th	33	46	.418	18.0	Charles Wolf	194,017
1961–62	2nd	43	37	.538	11.0	Charles Wolf	146,468
				Eastern Division			
1962–63	3rd	42	38	.525	16.0	Charles Wolf	137,739
1963–64	2nd	55	25	.688	4.0	Jack McMahon	228,012
1964–65	2nd	48	32	.600	14.0	Jack McMahon	169,570
1965–66	3rd	45	35	.563	10.0	Jack McMahon	208,865
1966–67	3rd	39	42	.481	29.0	Jack McMahon	156,931
1967–68	5th	39	43	.476	23.0	Ed Jucker	124,668
1968–69	5th	41	41	.500	16.0	Ed Jucker	113,822
1969–70	5th	36	46	.439	24.0	Bob Cousy	155,818

Year	Finish	Wins	Losses	Percentage	Games Behind	Head Coach	Attendance
				Eastern Conference Central Division			
1970–71	3rd	33	49	.402	9.0	Bob Cousy	131,734
1971–72	3rd	30	52	.366	8.0	Bob Cousy	151,186
				Kansas City-Omaha Kings			
				Western Conference Midwest Division			
1972–73	4th	36	46	.439	24.0	Bob Cousy	261,860
1973–74	4th	33	49	.402	26.0	Bob Cousy (6–14), Draff Young (0–4), Phil Johnson (27–31)	232,692
1974–75	2nd	44	38	.537	3.0	Phil Johnson	308,906
				Kansas City Kings			
1975–76	3rd	31	51	.378	7.0	Phil Johnson	272,675
1976–77	4th	40	42	.488	10.0	Phil Johnson	330,526
1977–78	5th (Tie)	31	51	.378	17.0	Phil Johnson (13–24), Larry Staverman (18–27)	315,722
1978–79	1st	48	34	.585	+1.0	Cotton Fitzsimmons	442,354
1979–80	2nd	47	35	.573	2.0	Cotton Fitzsimmons	375,387
1980–81	2nd (Tie)	40	42	.488	12.0	Cotton Fitzsimmons	336,385
1981–82	4th	30	52	.366	18.0	Cotton Fitzsimmons	305,665
1982–83	2nd (Tie)	45	37	.549	8.0	Cotton Fitzsimmons	309,597
1983–84	3rd (Tie)	38	44	.463	7.0	Cotton Fitzsimmons	370,270
1984–85	6th	31	51	.378	21.0	Jack McKinney (1–8), Phil Johnson (30–43)	262,813
				Sacramento Kings			
1985–86	5th	37	45	.451	14.0	Phil Johnson	423,653
1986–87	5th	29	53	.354	26.0	Phil Johnson (14–32), Jerry Reynolds (15–21)	423,653
1987–88	6th	24	58	.293	30.0	Bill Russell (17–41), Jerry Reynolds (7–17)	423,653
				Pacific Division			
1988–89	6th	27	55	.329	30.0	Jerry Reynolds	677,197
1989–90	7th	23	59	.280	40.0	Jerry Reynolds (7–21), Dick Motta (16–38)	697,667
1990–91	7th	25	57	.305	38.0	Dick Motta	697,604
1991–92	7th	29	53	.354	28.0	Dick Motta (7–18), Rex Hughes (22–35)	697,574
1992–93	7th	25	57	.305	37.0	Garry St. Jean	709,997
1993–94	6th	28	54	.341	35.0	Garry St. Jean	710,497
1994–95	5th	39	43	.476	20.0	Garry St. Jean	709,997
1995–96	5th	39	43	.476	25.0	Garry St. Jean	709,999
1996–97	6th	34	48	.415	23.0	Garry St. Jean (28–39), Eddie Jordan (6–9)	709,993
1997–98	5th	27	55	.329	34.0	Eddie Jordan	605,443
1998–99	3rd (Tie)	27	23	.540	8.0	Rick Adelman	418,751
1999–00	5th	44	38	.537	23.0	Rick Adelman	720,033
2000–01	2nd	55	27	.671	1.0	Rick Adelman	709,997
2001–02	1st	61	21	.744	+3.0	Rick Adelman	709,997
2002–03	1st	59	23	.720	+9.0	Rick Adelman	709,997
2003–04	2nd	55	27	.671	1.0	Rick Adelman	709,997
2004–05	2nd	50	32	.610	12.0	Rick Adelman	709,997
2005–06	4th	44	38	.537	10.0	Rick Adelman	709,997

Year	Finish	Wins	Losses	Percentage	Games Behind	Head Coach	Attendance
2006–07	5th	33	49	.402	28.0	Eric Musselman	709,997
2007–08	4th	38	44	.463	19.0	Reggie Theus	580,181
2008–09	5th	17	65	.207	48.0	Reggie Theus (6–18), Kenny Natt (11–47)	520,169
2009–10	5th	25	57	.305	32.0	Paul Westphal	543,416
2010–11	5th	24	58	.293	33.0	Paul Westphal	569,496
2011–12	5th	22	44	.333	19.0	Paul Westphal (2–5), Keith Smart (20–39)	478,764
2012–13	4th	28	54	.341	28.0	Keith Smart	563,743
2013–14	4th	28	54	.341	29.0	Michael Malone	667,949
2014–15	4th	29	53	.354	38.0	Michael Malone (11–13), Tyrone Corbin (7–21), George Karl (11–19)	680,049
2015–16	3rd	33	49	.402	40.0	George Karl	707,526
2016–17	3rd	32	50	.390	35.0	Dave Joerger	721,928
2017–18	4th	27	55	.329	31.0	Dave Joerger	714,680
2018–19	3rd	39	43	.476	18.0	Dave Joerger	700,975
2019–20	4th	31	41	.431	21.5	Luke Walton	520,663
2020–21	5th	31	41	.431	20.0	Luke Walton	N/A
2021–22	5th	30	52	.366	34.0	Luke Walton (6–11), Alvin Gentry (24–41)	577,583

1998–99: 50-game season.

2011–12: 66-game season.

2019–20: 65-to-75-game season.

2020–21: 72-game season.

Awards

Most Valuable Player
Oscar Robertson, guard, 1963–64 (Cin.)

Rookie of the Year
Maurice Stokes, center, 1955–56 (Roc.)
Oscar Robertson, guard, 1960–61 (Cin.)
Jerry Lucas, forward, 1963–64 (Cin.)
Phil Ford, guard, 1978–79 (K.C.)
Tyreke Evans, guard, 2009–10

Defensive Player of the Year
none

Sixth Man of the Year
Bobby Jackson, guard, 2002–03

Most Improved Player
none

All-NBA First Team
Bob Davies, 1949–50 (Roc.)
Bob Davies, 1950–51 (Roc.)
Bob Davies, 1951–52 (Roc.)
Oscar Robertson, 1960–61 (Cin.)
Oscar Robertson, 1961–62 (Cin.)
Oscar Robertson, 1962–63 (Cin.)
Oscar Robertson, 1963–64 (Cin.)
Oscar Robertson, 1964–65 (Cin.)
Jerry Lucas, 1964–65 (Cin.)
Oscar Robertson, 1965–66 (Cin.)
Jerry Lucas, 1965–66 (Cin.)
Oscar Robertson, 1966–67 (Cin.)
Oscar Robertson, 1967–68 (Cin.)
Jerry Lucas, 1967–68 (Cin.)
Oscar Robertson, 1968–69 (Cin.)
Tiny Archibald, 1972–73 (K.C.-Oma.)
Tiny Archibald, 1974–75 (K.C.-Oma.)
Tiny Archibald, 1975–76 (K.C.)
Chris Webber, 2000–01

All-Defensive First Team
Doug Christie, 2002–03
Metta World Peace, 2005–06*

* 40 games with Sac. Kings and 16 games with Ind. Pacers.

All-Rookie First Team
Jerry Lucas, 1963–64 (Cin.)
Ron Behagen, 1973–74 (K.C.-Oma.)
Scott Wedman, 1974–75 (K.C.-Oma.)
Phil Ford, 1978–79 (K.C.)
Kenny Smith, 1987–88

Lionel Simmons, 1990–91
Brian Grant, 1994–95
Jason Williams, 1998–99
Tyreke Evans, 2009–10
DeMarcus Cousins, 2010–11
Buddy Hield, 2016–17*
Marvin Bagley, 2018–19
Tyrese Haliburton, 2020–21

* 25 games with Sac. Kings and 57 games with N.O. Pelicans.

Coach of the Year
Phil Johnson, 1974–75 (K.C.-Oma.)
Cotton Fitzsimmons, 1978–79 (K.C.)

Hall of Famers Who Played for the Royals/Kings
Tiny Archibald, guard, 1970–76 (Cin.-K.C.-Oma.-K.C.)
Bob Cousy, guard, 1969–70 (Cin.)
Bob Davies, guard, 1948–55 (Roc.)
Vlade Divac, center, 1998–2004
Wayne Embry, center, 1958–66 (Cin.)
Alex Hannum, forward, 1951–54 (Roc.)
Red Holzman, guard, 1948–53 (Roc.)
Clyde Lovellette, center, 1957–58 (Cin.)

Jerry Lucas, forward, 1963–70 (Cin.)
Šarūnas Marčiulionis, guard, 1995–96
Mitch Richmond, guard, 1991–98
Arnie Risen, center, 1948–55 (Roc.)
Oscar Robertson, guard, 1960–70
(Cin.)
Guy Rodgers, guard, 1967–68 (Cin.)
Ralph Sampson, center, 1989–91
Maurice Stokes, center-forward, 1955–
58 (Roc.-Cin.)
Bobby Wanzer, guard, 1948–57 (Roc.)
Chris Webber, forward, 1998–2005
Jo Jo White, guard, 1980–81 (K.C.)

Retired Numbers

1	Tiny Archibald
2	Mitch Richmond
4	Chris Webber
6	Sixth Man (The Fans)
11	Bob Davies
12	Maurice Stokes
14	Oscar Robertson
16	Peja Stojaković
21	Vlade Divac
27	Jack Twyman
44	Sam Lacey

League Leaders, Offense

Points

Tiny Archibald, 1972–73
(K.C.-Oma.) 2719

Three Pointers

Peja Stojaković, 2003–04 240

Assists

Bob Davies, 1948–49 (Roc.) 321
Oscar Robertson, 1960–61 (Cin.) ... 690
Oscar Robertson, 1961–62 (Cin.) ... 899
Oscar Robertson, 1963–64 (Cin.) ... 868
Oscar Robertson, 1964–65 (Cin.) ... 861
Oscar Robertson, 1965–66 (Cin.) ... 847
Oscar Robertson, 1968–69 (Cin.) ... 772
Norm Van Lier, 1970–71 (Cin.) 832
Tiny Archibald, 1972–73
(K.C.-Oma.) 910
Rajon Rondo, 2015–16 839

Scoring Average

Oscar Robertson, 1967–68 (Cin.)... 29.2
Tiny Archibald, 1972–73
(K.C.-Oma.) 34.0

Field Goal Percantage

Arnie Risen, 1948–49 (Roc.).......... .423

Jack Twyman, 1957–58 (Cin.) .... .452
Jerry Lucas, 1963–64 (Cin.)........... .527
Johnny Green, 1969–70 (Cin.) ...... .559
Johnny Green, 1970–71 (Cin.) ...... .587

Three Point Percentage

Jim Les, 1990–91 .... .461
Anthony Peeler, 2003–04.............. .482

Free Throw Percentage

Bobby Wanzer, 1951–52 (Roc.) .... .904
Oscar Robertson, 1963–64 (Cin.) .. .853
Adrian Smith, 1966–67 (Cin.) .... .903
Oscar Robertson, 1967–68 (Cin.) .. .873
Spud Webb, 1994–95 .... .934
Peja Stojaković, 2003–04 .... .927

Assists Average

Bob Davies, 1948–49 (Roc.)........... 5.4
Oscar Robertson, 1960–61 (Cin.) 9.7
Oscar Robertson, 1961–62 (Cin.)... 11.4
Oscar Robertson, 1963–64 (Cin.)... 11.0
Oscar Robertson, 1964–65 (Cin.)... 11.5
Oscar Robertson, 1965–66 (Cin.)... 11.1
Oscar Robertson, 1966–67 (Cin.) 9.7
Oscar Robertson, 1968–69 (Cin.) 9.8
Norm Van Lier, 1970–71 (Cin.)..... 10.2
Tiny Archibald, 1972–73
(K.C.-Oma.) 11.4
Johnny Moore, 1981–82................. 9.7
Rajon Rondo, 2015–16................. 11.7

League Leaders, Defense

Offensive Rebounds

DeMarcus Cousins, 2011–12.......... 265

Defensive Rebounds

Sam Lacey, 1974–75 (K.C.-Oma.)... 921

Total Rebounds

Maurice Stokes, 1956–57 (Roc.) ... 1256

Steals

Doug Christie, 2000–01 183

Blocks

Rebounds Average

Maurice Stokes, 1955–56 (Roc.) 16.3
Chris Webber, 1998–99 .... 13.0

Steals Average

Blocks Average

Feats

50-Point Game

59 .... Jack Twyman (vs. Min. Lakers),
Jan. 15, 1960 (Cin.)
56 ...Oscar Robertson (vs. L.A. Lakers),
Dec. 18, 1964 (Cin.)
56 ... DeMarcus Cousins (vs. Cha. Hornets),
Jan. 25, 2016
55 .... Tiny Archibald (vs. Por. Blazers),
Feb. 23, 1972 (Cin.)
55 ... DeMarcus Cousins (vs. Por. Blazers),
Dec. 20, 2016
52 .... Tiny Archibald (vs. N.Y. Knicks),
Jan. 9, 1973 (K.C.-Oma.)
52 .... Tiny Archibald (@ Atl. Hawks),
Jan. 27, 1973 (K.C.-Oma.)
51 ... Tiny Archibald (vs. Hou. Rockets),
Nov. 18, 1972 (K.C.-Oma.)
51 .... Chris Webber (vs. Ind. Pacers),
Jan. 5, 2001
50 .... Jack Twyman (vs. St.L. Hawks),
Feb. 28, 1959 (Cin.)
50 .... Oscar Robertson (vs. Phi. 76ers),
Feb. 6, 1965 (Cin.)
50 .... Kevin Martin (@ G.S. Warriors),
Apr. 1, 2009

20-Assist Game

22 ...Oscar Robertson (vs. Syr. Nationals),
Oct. 29, 1961 (Cin.)
22 ...Oscar Robertson (vs. N.Y. Knicks),
Mar. 5, 1966 (Cin.)
22 ....Phil Ford (vs. Mil. Bucks),
Feb. 21, 1979 (K.C.)
21 ... Oscar Robertson (vs. N.Y. Knicks),
Feb. 14, 1964 (Cin.)
21 .... Tiny Archibald (vs. Det. Pistons),
Dec. 15, 1972 (K.C.-Oma.)
21 .... Phil Ford (vs. Pho. Suns),
Feb. 23, 1979 (K.C.)
20 .... Bob Davies (vs. Bos. Celtics),
Jan. 22, 1955 (Roc.)
20 .... Oscar Robertson (vs. L.A. Lakers),
Feb. 19, 1961 (Cin.)
20 ... Oscar Robertson (vs. Chi. Packers),
Dec. 11, 1961 (Cin.)
20 .. Oscar Robertson (vs. S.F. Warriors),
Dec. 28, 1964 (Cin.)
20 ... Oscar Robertson (vs. N.Y. Knicks),
Feb. 28, 1965 (Cin.)
20 .... Oscar Robertson (@ Pho. Suns),
Mar. 4, 1969 (Cin.)

20........ Tiny Archibald (@ Hou. Rockets),
Feb. 9, 1973 (K.C.-Oma.)

20...Tiny Archibald (@ G.S. Warriors),
Mar. 2, 1973 (K.C.-Oma.)

20.......... Rajon Rondo (@ Cha. Hornets),
Nov. 23, 2015

20......... Rajon Rondo (vs. Cha. Hornets),
Jan. 25, 2016

30-Rebound Game

40................ Jerry Lucas (@ Phi. 76ers),
Feb. 29, 1964 (Cin.)

38...Maurice Stokes (vs. Syr. Nationals),
Jan. 14, 1956 (Roc.)

37............... Jerry Lucas (@ Det. Pistons),
Jan. 20, 1965 (Cin.)

35............... Jerry Lucas (vs. Bal. Bullets),
Nov. 13, 1965 (Cin.)

34......... Maurice Stokes (vs. St.L. Hawks),
Jan. 21, 1956 (Roc.)

34................ Jerry Lucas (vs. Chi. Bulls),
Feb. 12, 1968 (Cin.)

33......... Maurice Stokes (vs. St.L. Hawks),
Jan. 16, 1957 (Roc.)

33.......... Jerry Lucas (vs. N.Y. Knicks),
Nov. 29, 1963 (Cin.)

33.............. Jerry Lucas (vs. Phi. 76ers),
Feb. 7, 1964 (Cin.)

33................ Jerry Lucas (@ Bal. Bullets),
Nov. 11, 1966 (Cin.)

32............... Jerry Lucas (vs. Bos. Celtics),
Jan. 25, 1966 (Cin.)

32.............. Jerry Lucas (vs. Bos. Celtics),
Feb. 15, 1966 (Cin.)

32........ Jerry Lucas (vs. Chi. Bulls),
Oct. 21, 1967 (Cin.)

31............... Jerry Lucas (@ Phi. 76ers),
Nov. 28, 1963 (Cin.)

31............. Jerry Lucas (@ Phi. 76ers),
Nov. 7, 1964

31.......... Jerry Lucas (@ S.F. Warriors),
Mar. 6, 1965 (Cin.)

31............... Jerry Lucas (vs. Bos. Celtics),
Oct. 28, 1965 (Cin.)

31................ Jerry Lucas (vs. Phi. 76ers),
Nov. 23, 1966 (Cin.)

31.......... Jerry Lucas (vs. S.F. Warriors),
Jan. 28, 1969 (Cin.)

31.......... Jerry Lucas (vs. S.D. Rockets),
Feb. 12, 1969 (Cin.)

30...Maurice Stokes (vs. Syr. Nationals),
Feb. 1, 1956 (Roc.)

30....... Maurice Stokes (vs. Ft.W. Pistons),
Feb. 1, 1957 (Roc.)

30........ Maurice Stokes (vs. Bos. Celtics),
Nov. 8, 1957 (Cin.)

30................ Jerry Lucas (@ Bos. Celtics),
Mar. 21, 1965 (Cin.)

30............... Jerry Lucas (vs. Det. Pistons),
Nov. 23, 1965 (Cin.)

30.......... Jerry Lucas (vs. S.F. Warriors),
Jan. 29, 1967 (Cin.)

8-Steal Game

8............. Sam Lacey (vs. Por. Blazers),
Feb. 5, 1975 (K.C.-Oma.)

8.......... Danny Ainge (vs. L.A. Clippers),
Apr. 22, 1989

8............... Chris Webber (vs. Uta. Jazz),
Mar. 11, 2001

8.............. Doug Christie (@ S.A. Spurs),
Dec. 8, 2002

10-Block Game
none

Multiple Triple-Doubles in a Single Season

41...... Oscar Robertson, 1961–62 (Cin.)
26...... Oscar Robertson, 1960–61 (Cin.)
26...... Oscar Robertson, 1963–64 (Cin.)
22...... Oscar Robertson, 1964–65 (Cin.)
20...... Oscar Robertson, 1962–63 (Cin.)
13...... Oscar Robertson, 1965–66 (Cin.)
12..........Norm Van Lier, 1970–71 (Cin.)
8........ Maurice Stokes, 1957–58 (Cin.)
8...... Oscar Robertson, 1967–68 (Cin.)
8...... Oscar Robertson, 1968–69 (Cin.)
7...... Oscar Robertson, 1966–67 (Cin.)
6...... Oscar Robertson, 1969–70 (Cin.)
6....................Rajon Rondo, 2015–16
5..................Chris Webber, 1999–00
4..................Chris Webber, 2004–05
3..................Chris Webber, 2002–03
2........Maurice Stokes, 1956–57 (Roc.)
2.....Sam Lacey, 1974–75 (K.C.-Oma.)
2............. Sam Lacey, 1980–81 (K.C.)
2...........Ray Williams, 1982–83 (K.C.)
2..................Rodney McCray, 1988–89
2......................Brad Miller, 2003–04
2............ DeMarcus Cousins, 2014–15
2............ DeMarcus Cousins, 2016–17

Postseason Play

| 1949 | BAA Western Division Semifinals |
| | vs. St.L. Bombers, won (2–0) |

BAA Western Division Finals
vs. Min. Lakers, lost (2–0)

1950 NBA Central Division First-Place
Tiebreaker vs. Min. Lakers, won
NBA Central Division Semifinals
vs. Ft.W. Pistons, lost (2–0)

1951 Western Division Semifinals
vs. Ft.W. Pistons, won (2–1)
Western Division Finals
vs. Min. Lakers, won (3–1)
NBA Finals vs. N.Y. Knicks,
won (4–3)

1952 Western Division Semifinals
vs. Ft.W. Pistons, won (2–0)
Western Division Finals
vs. Min. Lakers, lost (3–1)

1953 Western Division Semifinals
vs. Ft.W. Pistons, lost (2–1)

1954 (Advanced from Western Division
Round Robin)
Western Division Finals
vs. Min. Lakers, lost (2–1)

1955 Western Division Semifinals
vs. Min. Lakers, lost (2–1)

1958 Western Division Semifinals
vs. Det. Pistons, lost (2–0)

1962 Western Division Semifinals
vs. Det. Pistons, lost (3–1)

1963 Eastern Division Semifinals
vs. Syr. Nationals, won (3–2)
Eastern Division Finals
vs. Bos. Celtics, lost (4–3)

1964 Eastern Division Semifinals
vs. Phi. 76ers, won (3–2)
Eastern Division Finals
vs. Bos. Celtics, lost (4–1)

1965 Eastern Division Semifinals
vs. Phi. 76ers, lost (3–1)

1966 Eastern Division Semifinals
vs. Bos. Celtics, lost (3–2)

1967 Eastern Division Semifinals
vs. Phi. 76ers, lost (3–1)

1975 Western Conference Semifinals
vs. Chi. Bulls, lost (4–2)

1979 Western Conference Semifinals
vs. Pho. Suns, lost (4–1)

1980 Western Conference First Round
vs. Pho. Suns, lost (2–1)

1981 Western Conference First Round
vs. Por. Blazers, won (2–1)
Western Conference Semifinals
vs. Pho. Suns, won (4–3)

Western Conference Finals
vs. Hou. Rockets, lost (4–1)

1984 Western Conference First Round
vs. L.A. Lakers, lost (3–0)

1986 Western Conference First Round
vs. Hou. Rockets, lost (3–0)

1996 Western Conference First Round
vs. Sea. Sonics, lost (3–1)

1999 Western Conference First Round
vs. Uta. Jazz, lost (3–2)

2000 Western Conference First Round
vs. L.A. Lakers, lost (3–2)

2001 Western Conference First Round
vs. Pho. Suns, won (3–1)

Western Conference Semifinals
vs. L.A. Lakers, lost (4–0)

2002 Western Conference First Round
vs. Uta. Jazz, won (3–1)

Western Conference Semifinals
vs. Dal. Mavericks, won (4–1)

Western Conference Finals
vs. L.A. Lakers, lost (4–3)

2003 Western Conference First Round
vs. Uta. Jazz, won (4–1)

Western Conference Semifinals
vs. Dal. Mavericks, lost (4–3)

2004 Western Conference First Round
vs. Dal. Mavericks, won (4–1)

Western Conference Semifinals
vs. Min. T'Wolves, lost (4–3)

2005 Western Conference First Round
vs. Sea. Sonics, lost (4–1)

2006 Western Conference First Round
vs. S.A. Spurs, lost (4–2)

San Antonio Spurs

ABA Dates of Operation: 1967–76 (9 seasons)
Overall Record: 378 wins, 366 losses (.508)
Arenas: Moody Coliseum, 1967–73; HemisFair Arena, 1973–76
Other Names: Dallas Chaparrals, 1967–70; 1971–73; Texas Chaparrals, 1970–71

NBA Dates of Operation: 1976–present (46 seasons)
Overall Record: 2261 wins, 1442 losses (.611)
Arenas: HemisFair Arena, 1976–93; Alamodome, 1993–2002; AT&T Center (formerly SBC Center, 2002–06), 2002–present (capacity: 18,418)

Year-by-Year Finishes

Year	Finish	Wins	Losses	Percentage	Games Behind	Head Coach	Attendance*
				Dallas Chaparrals **ABA Western Division**			
1967–68	2nd	46	32	.590	2.0	Cliff Hagan	N/A
1968–69	4th	41	37	.526	19.0	Cliff Hagan	113,371
1969–70	2nd	45	39	.536	6.0	Cliff Hagan (22–21), Max Williams (23–18)	175,035
				Texas Chaparrals			
1970–71	4th (Tie)	30	54	.357	28.0	Max Williams (5–14), Bill Blakeley (25–40)	140,806
				Dallas Chaparrals			
1971–72	3rd	42	42	.500	18.0	Tom Nissalke	150,391
1972–73	5th	28	56	.333	27.0	Babe McCarthy (24–48), Dave Brown (4–8)	102,865
				San Antonio Spurs			
1973–74	3rd	45	39	.536	6.0	Tom Nissalke	261,842
1974–75	2nd	51	33	.607	14.0	Tom Nissalke (18–10), Bob Bass (33–23)	322,543
				American Basketball Association			
1975–76	3rd	50	34	.595	10.0	Bob Bass	339,521
				NBA Eastern Conference Central Division			
1976–77	3rd	44	38	.537	5.0	Doug Moe	336,189
1977–78	1st	52	30	.634	+8.0	Doug Moe	373,707
1978–79	1st	48	34	.585	+1.0	Doug Moe	489,207
1979–80	2nd (Tie)	41	41	.500	9.0	Doug Moe (33–33), Bob Bass (8–8)	468,657
				Western Conference Midwest Division			
1980–81	1st	52	30	.634	+12.0	Stan Albeck	440,553
1981–82	1st	48	34	.585	+2.0	Stan Albeck	434,278
1982–83	1st	53	29	.646	+8.0	Stan Albeck	379,876
1983–84	5th	37	45	.451	8.0	Morris McHone (11–20), Bob Bass (26–25)	375,900
1984–85	4th (Tie)	41	41	.500	11.0	Cotton Fitzsimmons	351,950
1985–86	6th	35	47	.427	16.0	Cotton Fitzsimmons	336,369
1986–87	6th	28	54	.341	27.0	Bob Weiss	341,132

Year	Finish	Wins	Losses	Percentage	Games Behind	Head Coach	Attendance
1987–88	5th	31	51	.378	23.0	Bob Weiss	334,354
1988–89	5th	21	61	.256	30.0	Larry Brown	323,573
1989–90	1st	56	26	.683	+1.0	Larry Brown	586,787
1990–91	1st	55	27	.671	+1.0	Larry Brown	651,965
1991–92	2nd	47	35	.573	8.0	Larry Brown (21–17), Bob Bass (26–18)	658,337
1992–93	2nd	49	33	.598	6.0	Jerry Tarkanian (9–11), Rex Hughes (1–0), John Lucas (39–22)	658,337
1993–94	2nd	55	27	.671	3.0	John Lucas	904,190
1994–95	1st	62	20	.756	+2.0	Bob Hill	920,413
1995–96	1st	59	23	.720	+4.0	Bob Hill	782,701
1996–97	6th	20	62	.244	44.0	Bob Hill (3–15), Gregg Popovich (17–47)	706,641
1997–98	2nd	56	26	.683	6.0	Gregg Popovich	783,455
1998–99	1st (Tie)	37	13	.740	—	Gregg Popovich	527,357
1999–00	2nd	53	29	.646	2.0	Gregg Popovich	884,450
2000–01	1st	58	24	.707	+5.0	Gregg Popovich	913,176
2001–02	1st	58	24	.707	+1.0	Gregg Popovich	906,390
2002–03	1st (Tie)	60	22	.732	—	Gregg Popovich	735,970
2003–04	2nd	57	25	.695	1.0	Gregg Popovich	739,706
Southwest Division							
2004–05	1st	59	23	.720	+1.0	Gregg Popovich	750,970
2005–06	1st	63	19	.768	+1.0	Gregg Popovich	770,677
2006–07	2nd	58	24	.707	9.0	Gregg Popovich	764,823
2007–08	1st (Tie)	56	26	.683	—	Gregg Popovich	761,149
2008–09	1st	54	28	.659	+1.0	Gregg Popovich	749,048
2009–10	2nd	50	32	.610	5.0	Gregg Popovich	741,676
2010–11	1st	61	21	.744	+4.0	Gregg Popovich	750,879
2011–12	1st	50	16	.758	+9.0	Gregg Popovich	607,095
2012–13	1st	58	24	.707	+2.0	Gregg Popovich	755,700
2013–14	1st	62	20	.756	+8.0	Gregg Popovich	755,031
2014–15	2nd (Tie)	55	27	.671	1.0	Gregg Popovich	762,855
2015–16	1st	67	15	.817	+25.0	Gregg Popovich	756,445
2016–17	1st	61	21	.744	+6.0	Gregg Popovich	755,347
2017–18	3rd	47	35	.573	18.0	Gregg Popovich	754,562
2018–19	2nd	48	34	.585	5.0	Gregg Popovich	750,616
2019–20	4th	32	39	.451	11.5	Gregg Popovich	550,515
2020–21	3rd	33	39	.458	9.0	Gregg Popovich	61,053
2021–22	4th	34	48	.415	22.0	Gregg Popovich	615,588

1998–99: 50-game season.

2011–12: 66-game season.

2019–20: 65-to-75-game season.

2020–21: 72-game season.

(ABA Attendance totals are unofficial, and numbers include when listed as home team.)

Awards

ABA Most Valuable Player

NBA Most Valuable Player

David Robinson, center, 1994–95
Tim Duncan, forward, 2001–02
Tim Duncan, forward, 2002–03

ABA Rookie of the Year

Swen Nater*, center, 1973–74

*62 games with S.A. Spurs and 17 games with Vir. Squires.

NBA Rookie of the Year

David Robinson, center, 1989–90
Tim Duncan, forward, 1997–98

Defensive Player of the Year

Alvin Robertson, guard, 1985–86
David Robinson, center, 1991–92
Kawhi Leonard, forward, 2014–15
Kawhi Leonard, forward, 2015–16

Sixth Man of the Year

Manu Ginóbili, guard, 2007–08

Most Improved Player

Alvin Robertson, guard, 1985–86

All-ABA First Team

Donnie Freeman, 1971–72 (Dal.)
James Silas, 1975–76

All-NBA First Team

George Gervin, 1977–78
George Gervin, 1978–79
George Gervin, 1979–80
George Gervin, 1980–81
George Gervin, 1981–82
David Robinson, 1990–91
David Robinson, 1991–92
David Robinson, 1994–95
David Robinson, 1995–96
Tim Duncan, 1997–98
Tim Duncan, 1998–99
Tim Duncan, 1999–00
Tim Duncan, 2000–01
Tim Duncan, 2001–02
Tim Duncan, 2002–03
Tim Duncan, 2003–04
Tim Duncan, 2004–05
Tim Duncan, 2006–07
Tim Duncan, 2012–13
Kawhi Leonard, 2015–16
Kawhi Leonard, 2016–17

All-ABA Defensive First Team

All-NBA Defensive First Team

Alvin Robertson, 1986–87
David Robinson, 1990–91
David Robinson, 1991–92
David Robinson, 1994–95
Dennis Rodman, 1994–95
David Robinson, 1995–96
Tim Duncan, 1998–99
Tim Duncan, 1999–00
Tim Duncan, 2000–01
Tim Duncan, 2001–02
Tim Duncan, 2002–03
Tim Duncan, 2004–05
Tim Duncan, 2006–07
Tim Duncan, 2007–08
Bruce Bowen, 2003–04
Bruce Bowen, 2004–05
Bruce Bowen, 2005–06
Bruce Bowen, 2006–07
Bruce Bowen, 2007–08
Kawhi Leonard, 2014–15
Kawhi Leonard, 2015–16
Kawhi Leonard, 2016–17

All-ABA Rookie First Team

Ron Boone, 1968–69 (Dal.)
Joe Hamilton, 1970–71 (Tex.)
James Silas, 1972–73 (Dal.)
George Gervin, 1972–73
Swen Nater, 1973–74*
Mark Olberding, 1975–76**

* 62 games with S.A. Spurs and 17 games with Vir. Squires.

** 70 games with S.A. Spurs and 11 games with S.D. Sails.

All-NBA Rookie First Team

Greg Anderson, 1987–88
Willie Anderson, 1988–89
David Robinson, 1989–90
Tim Duncan, 1997–98
Tony Parker, 2001–02
Gary Neal, 2010–11
Kawhi Leonard, 2011–12

ABA Coach of the Year

Tom Nissalke, 1971–72 (Dal.)

NBA Coach of the Year

Gregg Popovich, 2002–03
Gregg Popovich, 2011–12
Gregg Popovich, 2013–14

Hall of Famers Who Played for the Chaparrals/Spurs

Maurice Cheeks, guard, 1989–90
Louie Dampier, guard, 1976–79
Tim Duncan, forward-center, 1997–2016
George Gervin, forward-guard, 1973–85 (ABA/NBA)
Artis Gilmore, center, 1982–87
Manu Ginóbili, guard, 2002–18
Cliff Hagan, 1967–70 (ABA)
Moses Malone, center, 1994–95
David Robinson, center, 1989–2003
Dennis Rodman, forward, 1993–95
Dominique Wilkins, forward, 1996–97

Retired Numbers

00 .... Johnny Moore
6 .... Avery Johnson
9 .... Tony Parker
12 .... Bruce Bowen
13 ....James Silas
20 ....Manu Ginóbili
21 .... Tim Duncan
32 .... Sean Elliott
44 ....George Gervin
50 ....David Robinson

League Leaders, Offense

Points

George Gervin, 1977–78 2232
George Gervin, 1978–79 2365
George Gervin, 1979–80 2585
George Gervin, 1981–82 2551
David Robinson, 1993–94 2383

Three Pointers

Mike Dunleavy, 1982–83 67

Assists

Johnny Moore, 1981–82 762

Scoring Average

George Gervin, 1977–78 .... 27.2
George Gervin, 1978–79 .... 29.6
George Gervin, 1979–80 .... 33.1
George Gervin, 1981–82 .... 32.3
David Robinson, 1993–94 .... 29.8

Field Goal Percentage

Swen Nater*, 1973–74 (ABA) .... .552
Artis Gilmore, 1982–83 .... .626
Artis Gilmore, 1983–84 .... .631
Steve Johnson, 1985–86 .... .632

*.551 with S.A. Spurs and .556 with Vir. Squires.

Three Point Percentage

Mike Dunleavy, 1982–83 .... .345

Steve Smith, 2001–02 .... .472

Bruce Bowen, 2002–03 .... .441

Matt Bonner, 2010–11 .... .457

Free Throw Percentage

Charles Beasley, 1967–68 (Dal./ABA).. .872

Assists Average

Johnny Moore, 1981–82 .... 9.7

League Leaders, Defense

Offensive Rebounds

Dennis Rodman, 1993–94 453

Defensive Rebounds

Dennis Rodman, 1993–94 914

David Robinson, 1995–96 681

Tim Duncan, 2001–02 774

Total Rebounds

David Robinson, 1990–91 1063

Dennis Rodman, 1993–94 1367

David Robinson, 1995–96 1000

Tim Duncan, 2001–02 1042

Steals

Alvin Robertson, 1985–86 301

Alvin Robertson, 1986–87 260

Dejounte Murray, 2021–22 138

Blocks

Billy Paultz, 1975–76 (ABA) 253

George Johnson, 1980–81 278

George Johnson, 1981–82 234

David Robinson, 1990–91 320

David Robinson, 1991–92 305

Rebounds Average

Swen Nater, 1974–75 .... 16.4

David Robinson, 1990–91 .... 13.0

Dennis Rodman, 1993–94 .... 17.3

Dennis Rodman, 1994–95 .... 16.8

Steals Average

Alvin Robertson, 1985–86 .... 3.7

Alvin Robertson, 1986–87 .... 3.2

Kawhi Leonard, 2014–15 .... 2.3

Dejounte Murray, 2021–22 .... 2.0

Blocks Average

Billy Paultz, 1975–76 (ABA) 3.1

George Johnson, 1980–81 .... 3.4

George Johnson, 1981–82 .... 3.1

David Robinson, 1991–92 .... 4.5

Feats

50-Point Game

71... David Robinson (@ L.A. Clippers),
Apr. 24, 1994

63......... George Gervin (@ N.O. Jazz),
Apr. 9, 1978

56... LaMarcus Aldridge (vs. Ok.C. Thunder),
Jan. 10, 2019

55......... George Gervin (@ Ind. Pacers),
Jan. 23, 1980

55......... Tony Parker (@ Min. T'Wolves),
Nov. 5, 2008

53...George Gervin (vs. Den. Nuggets),
Jan. 8, 1980

53......... Tim Duncan (vs. Dal. Mavericks),
Dec. 26, 2001

52...George Gervin (vs. S.D. Clippers),
Jan. 11, 1979

52...Terry Cummings (vs. Cha. Hornets),
Jan. 31, 1990

52... David Robinson (vs. Cha. Hornets),
Jan. 16, 1993

51... George Gervin (vs. Mem. Sounds),
Feb. 5, 1975 (ABA)

51.......... Larry Kenon (vs. Det. Pistons),
Mar. 30, 1980

50.......... George Gervin (vs. Mil. Bucks),
Mar. 6, 1982

50... David Robinson (@ Min. T'Wolves),
Feb. 21, 1994

20-Assist Game

24.......... John Lucas (vs. Den. Nuggets),
Apr. 15, 1984

20... Johnny Moore (vs. Den. Nuggets),
Jan. 2, 1982

20......... Johnny Moore (vs. Was. Bullets),
Dec. 10, 1983

20............... John Lucas (@ K.C. Kings),
Dec. 23, 1983

20......... Avery Johnson (vs. L.A. Clippers),
Dec. 10, 1997

20... Avery Johnson (vs. Van. Grizzlies),
Dec. 17, 1997

30-Rebound Game

35... Manny Leaks, (vs. Ken. Colonels),
Nov. 27, 1970 (Tex./ABA)

32...Dennis Rodman (vs. Dal. Mavericks),
Jan. 22, 1994

30... Dennis Rodman (@ Hou. Rockets),
Feb. 21, 1995

8-Steal Game

11............... Larry Kenon (@ K.C. Kings),
Dec. 26, 1976

10..........Johnny Moore (vs. Ind. Pacers),
Mar. 6, 1985

10......... Alvin Robertson (vs. Pho. Suns),
Feb. 18, 1986

10... Alvin Robertson (@ L.A. Clippers),
Nov. 22, 1986

10... Alvin Robertson (vs. Hou. Rockets),
Jan. 11, 1989

9......... Johnny Moore (vs. G.S. Warriors),
Jan. 8, 1985

8............... Mike Gale (@ Phi. 76ers),
Mar. 25, 1977

8.............. Mike Gale (@ Ind. Pacers),
Jan. 18, 1978

8............... Mike Gale (vs. N.J. Nets),
Mar. 7, 1978

8................ Mike Gale (@ Pho. Suns),
Oct. 17, 1978

8...Johnny Moore (vs. Sea. Sonics), Mar.
24, 1985

8..........Johnny Moore (vs. L.A. Lakers),
Apr. 3, 1985

8.........Alvin Robertson (vs. Sac. Kings),
Feb. 16, 1986

8......... Alvin Robertson (@ N.Y. Knicks),
Dec. 22, 1986

8......... Alvin Robertson (vs. Chi. Bulls),
Dec. 5, 1987

8... Alvin Robertson (vs. L.A. Clippers),
Mar. 16, 1988

8......... Alvin Robertson (vs. Det. Pistons),
Mar. 25, 1988

8..........Tim Duncan (@ Den. Nuggets),
Feb. 9, 2000

8......... Manu Ginóbili (vs. L.A. Lakers),
Jan. 23, 2008

8...Dejounte Murray (vs. G.S. Warriors),
Feb. 8, 2021

10-Block Game

13...George Johnson (vs. G.S. Warriors),
Feb. 24, 1981

12... David Robinson (vs. Min. T'Wolves),
Feb. 23, 1990

11... David Robinson (@ Cha. Hornets),
Feb. 2, 1990

11.......... David Robinson (vs. Sac. Kings),
Dec. 28, 1990

11..........David Robinson (vs. Uta. Jazz),
Jan. 12, 1991

11...David Robinson (vs. Por. Blazers),
Feb. 4, 1992

10... Artis Gilmore (vs. G.S. Warriors),
Feb. 4, 1985

10.........David Robinson (vs. L.A. Lakers),
Feb. 20, 1990

10.........David Robinson (vs. Orl. Magic),
Jan. 10, 1991

10...........David Robinson (vs. Mil. Bucks),
Nov. 10, 1992

10...David Robinson (vs. Min. T'Wolves),
Nov. 9, 1993

10.........David Robinson (vs. Det. Pistons),
Feb. 17, 1994

Multiple Triple-Doubles in a Single Season

13..............Dejounte Murray, 2021–22
5..................Johnny Moore, 1984–85
5............... David Robinson, 1993–94
4..............Dejounte Murray, 2020–21
3............... Alvin Robertson, 1985–86
3............... David Robinson, 1989–90
3............... David Robinson, 1990–91
3..............Dejounte Murray, 2021–22
2............... Alvin Robertson, 1987–88
2............... Alvin Robertson, 1988–89
2............... David Robinson, 1991–92

Postseason Play

1968 ABA Western Division Semifinals
vs. Hou. Mavericks, won (3–0)
ABA Western Division Finals
vs. N.O. Buccaneers, lost (4–1)

1969 ABA Western Division Semifinals
vs. N.O. Buccaneers, lost (4–3)

1970 ABA Western Division Semifinals
vs. L.A. Stars, lost (4–2)

1971 ABA Western Division Tiebreaker
vs. Den. Rockets, won
ABA Western Division Semifinals
vs. Uta. Stars, lost (4–0)

1972 ABA Western Division Semifinals
vs. Uta. Stars, lost (4–0)

1974 ABA Western Division Semifinals
vs. Ind. Pacers, lost (4–3)

1975 ABA Western Division Semifinals
vs. Ind. Pacers, lost (4–2)

1976 ABA Semifinals vs. N.Y. Nets,
lost (4–3)

1977 NBA Eastern Conference First
Round vs. Bos. Celtics,
lost (2–0)

1978 Eastern Conference Semifinals
vs. Was. Bullets, lost (4–2)

1979 Eastern Conference Semifinals
vs. Phi. 76ers, won (4–3)
Eastern Conference Finals
vs. Was. Bullets, lost (4–3)

1980 Eastern Conference First Round
vs. Hou. Rockets, lost (2–1)

1981 Western Conference Semifinals
vs. Hou. Rockets, lost (4–3)

1982 Western Conference Semifinals
vs. Sea. Sonics, won (4–1)
Western Conference Finals
vs. L.A. Lakers, lost (4–0)

1983 Western Conference Semifinals
vs. Den. Nuggets, won (4–1)
Western Conference Finals
vs. L.A. Lakers, lost (4–2)

1985 Western Conference First Round
vs. Den. Nuggets, lost (3–2)

1986 Western Conference First Round
vs. L.A. Lakers, lost (3–0)

1988 Western Conference First Round
vs. L.A. Lakers, lost (3–0)

1990 Western Conference First Round
vs. Den. Nuggets, won (3–0)
Western Conference Semifinals
vs. Por. Blazers, lost (4–3)

1991 Western Conference First Round
vs. G.S. Warriors, lost (3–1)

1992 Western Conference First Round
vs. Pho. Suns, lost (3–0)

1993 Western Conference First Round
vs. Por. Blazers, won (3–1)
Western Conference Semifinals
vs. Pho. Suns, lost (4–2)

1994 Western Conference First Round
vs. Uta. Jazz, lost (3–1)

1995 Western Conference First Round
vs. Den. Nuggets, won (3–0)
Western Conference Semifinals
vs. L.A. Lakers, won (4–2)
Western Conference Finals
vs. Hou. Rockets, lost (4–2)

1996 Western Conference First Round
vs. Pho. Suns, won (3–1)
Western Conference Semifinals
vs. Uta. Jazz, lost (4–2)

1998 Western Conference First Round
vs. Pho. Suns, won (3–1)
Western Conference Semifinals
vs. Uta. Jazz, lost (4–1)

1999 Western Conference First Round
vs. Min. T'Wolves, won (3–1)
Western Conference Semifinals
vs. L.A. Lakers, won (4–0)
Western Conference Finals
vs. Por. Blazers, won (4–0)
NBA Finals vs. N.Y. Knicks,
won (4–1)

2000 Western Conference First Round
vs. Pho. Suns, lost (3–1)

2001 Western Conference First Round
vs. Min. T'Wolves, won (3–1)
Western Conference Semifinals
vs. Dal. Mavericks, won (4–1)
Western Conference Finals
vs. L.A. Lakers, lost (4–0)

2002 Western Conference First Round
vs. Sea. Sonics, won (3–2)
Western Conference Semifinals
vs. L.A. Lakers, lost (4–1)

2003 Western Conference First Round
vs. Pho. Suns, won (4–2)
Western Conference Semifinals
vs. L.A. Lakers, won (4–0)
Western Conference Finals
vs. Dal. Mavericks, won (4–2)
NBA Finals vs. N.J. Nets,
won (4–2)

2004 Western Conference First Round
vs. Mem. Grizzlies, won (4–0)
Western Conference Semifinals
vs. L.A. Lakers, lost (4–2)

2005 Western Conference First Round
vs. Den. Nuggets, won (4–1)
Western Conference Semifinals
vs. Sea. Sonics, won (4–2)
Western Conference Finals
vs. Pho. Suns, won (4–1)
NBA Finals vs. Det. Pistons,
won (4–3)

2006 Western Conference First Round
vs. Sac. Kings, won (4–2)
Western Conference Semifinals
vs. Dal. Mavericks, lost (4–3)

2007 Western Conference First Round
vs. Den. Nuggets, won (4–1)
Western Conference Semifinals
vs. Pho. Suns, won (4–2)
Western Conference Finals
vs. Uta. Jazz, won (4–1)
NBA Finals vs. Cle. Cavaliers,
won (4–0)

2008 Western Conference First Round
vs. Pho. Suns, won (4–1)
Western Conference Semifinals
vs. N.O. Hornets, won (4–3)
Western Conference Finals
vs. L.A. Lakers, lost (4–1)

2009 Western Conference First Round
vs. Dal. Mavericks, lost (4–1)

2010 Western Conference First Round
vs. Dal. Mavericks, won (4–2)
Western Conference Semifinals
vs. Pho. Suns, lost (4–0)

2011 Western Conference First Round
vs. Mem. Grizzlies, lost (4–2)

2012 Western Conference First Round
vs. Uta. Jazz, won (4–0)
Western Conference Semifinals
vs. L.A. Clippers, won (4–0)

Western Conference Finals
vs. Ok.C. Thunder, lost (4–2)

2013 Western Conference First Round
vs. L.A. Lakers, won (4–0)
Western Conference Semifinals
vs. G.S. Warriors, won (4–2)
Western Conference Finals
vs. Mem. Grizzlies, won (4–0)
NBA Finals vs. Mia. Heat,
lost (4–3)

2014 Western Conference First Round
vs. Dal. Mavericks, won (4–3)
Western Conference Semifinals
vs. Por. Blazers, won (4–1)
Western Conference Finals
vs. Ok.C. Thunder, won (4–2)
NBA Finals vs. Mia. Heat,
won (4–1)

2015 Western Conference First Round
vs. L.A. Clippers, lost (4–3)

2016 Western Conference First Round
vs. Mem. Grizzlies, won (4–0)
Western Conference Semifinals
vs. Ok.C. Thunder, lost (4–2)

2017 Western Conference First Round
vs. Mem. Grizzlies, won (4–2)
Western Conference Semifinals
vs. Hou. Rockets, won (4–2)
Western Conference Finals
vs. G.S. Warriors, lost (4–0)

2018 Western Conference First Round
vs. G.S. Warriors, lost (4–1)

2019 Western Conference First Round
vs. Den. Nuggets, lost (4–3)

Utah Jazz

Dates of Operation: (as the New Orleans Jazz) 1974–79 (5 seasons)
Overall Record: 161 wins, 249 losses (.393)
Arenas: Municipal Auditorium, 1974–75; Louisiana Superdome, 1975–79

Dates of Operation: (as the Utah Jazz), 1979–present (43 seasons)
Overall Record: 1948 wins, 1510 losses (.563)
Arenas: Salt Palace, 1979–91; Vivint Smart Home Arena (formerly Delta Center, 1991–2006; EnergySolutions Arena, 2006–15), 1991–present (capacity: 18,306)

Year-by-Year Finishes

Year	Finish	Wins	Losses	Percentage	Games Behind	Head Coach	Attendance
				New Orleans Jazz			
				Eastern Conference Central Division			
1974–75	5th	23	59	.280	37.0	Scotty Robertson (1–14), Elgin Baylor (0–1), Butch van Breda Kolff (22–44)	203,141
1975–76	4th	38	44	.463	11.0	Butch van Breda Kolff	513,282
1976–77	5th	35	47	.427	14.0	Butch van Breda Kolff (14–12), Elgin Baylor (21–35)	444,138
1977–78	5th	39	43	.476	13.0	Elgin Baylor	527,351
1978–79	6th	26	56	.317	22.0	Elgin Baylor	364,205
				Utah Jazz			
				Western Conference Midwest Division			
1979–80	5th	24	58	.293	25.0	Tom Nissalke	320,649
1980–81	5th	28	54	.341	24.0	Tom Nissalke	307,835
1981–82	6th	25	57	.305	23.0	Tom Nissalke (8–12), Frank Layden (17–45)	311,779
1982–83	5th	30	52	.366	23.0	Frank Layden	355,219
1983–84	1st	45	37	.549	2.0	Frank Layden	400,065
1984–85	4th (Tie)	41	41	.500	11.0	Frank Layden	371,829
1985–86	4th	42	40	.512	9.0	Frank Layden	477,833
1986–87	2nd	44	38	.537	11.0	Frank Layden	491,382
1987–88	3rd	47	35	.573	7.0	Frank Layden	503,969
1988–89	1st	51	31	.622	+6.0	Frank Layden (11–6), Jerry Sloan (40–25)	509,501
1989–90	2nd	55	27	.671	1.0	Jerry Sloan	517,256
1990–91	2nd	54	28	.659	1.0	Jerry Sloan	514,751
1991–92	1st	55	27	.671	+8.0	Jerry Sloan	806,663
1992–93	3rd	47	35	.573	8.0	Jerry Sloan	815,892
1993–94	3rd	53	29	.646	5.0	Jerry Sloan	814,502
1994–95	2nd	60	22	.732	2.0	Jerry Sloan	811,159
1995–96	2nd	55	27	.671	4.0	Jerry Sloan	813,073
1996–97	1st	64	18	.780	+7.0	Jerry Sloan	811,439
1997–98	1st	62	20	.756	+6.0	Jerry Sloan	815,889
1998–99	1st (Tie)	37	13	.740	—	Jerry Sloan	493,120
1999–00	1st	55	27	.671	+2.0	Jerry Sloan	801,268
2000–01	2nd (Tie)	53	29	.646	5.0	Jerry Sloan	792,196

Year	Finish	Wins	Losses	Percentage	Games Behind	Head Coach	Attendance
2001–02	4th	44	38	.537	14.0	Jerry Sloan	766,108
2002–03	4th	47	35	.573	13.0	Jerry Sloan	786,034
2003–04	7th	42	40	.512	16.0	Jerry Sloan	785,330
				Northwest Division			
2004–05	5th	26	56	.317	26.0	Jerry Sloan	769,014
2005–06	2nd	41	41	.500	3.0	Jerry Sloan	751,621
2006–07	1st	51	31	.622	+6.0	Jerry Sloan	802,214
2007–08	1st	54	28	.659	+4.0	Jerry Sloan	816,211
2008–09	3rd	48	34	.585	6.0	Jerry Sloan	816,042
2009–10	1st (Tie)	53	29	.646	—	Jerry Sloan	794,512
2010–11	4th	39	43	.476	16.0	Jerry Sloan (31–23), Tyrone Corbin (8–20)	799,982
2011–12	3rd	36	30	.545	11.0	Tyrone Corbin	637,124
2012–13	3rd	43	39	.524	17.0	Tyrone Corbin	763,915
2013–14	5th	25	57	.305	34.0	Tyrone Corbin	745,203
2014–15	3rd	38	44	.463	13.0	Quin Snyder	772,059
2015–16	3rd	40	42	.488	15.0	Quin Snyder	791,489
2016–17	1st	51	31	.622	+4.0	Quin Snyder	806,142
2017–18	2nd (Tie)	48	34	.585	1.0	Quin Snyder	734,806
2018–19	3rd	50	32	.610	4.0	Quin Snyder	750,546
2019–20	2nd (Tie)	44	28	.611	1.5	Quin Snyder	567,486
2020–21	1st	52	20	.722	+5.0	Quin Snyder	151,300
2021–22	1st	49	33	.598	+1.0	Quin Snyder	750,546

1998–99: 50-game season.
2011–12: 66-game season.
2019–20: 65-to-75-game season.
2020–21: 72-game season.

Awards

Most Valuable Player
Karl Malone, forward, 1996–97
Karl Malone, forward, 1998–99

Rookie of the Year
Darrell Griffith, guard, 1980–81

Defensive Player of the Year
Mark Eaton, center, 1984–85
Mark Eaton, center, 1988–89
Rudy Gobert, center, 2017–18
Rudy Gobert, center, 2018–19
Rudy Gobert, center, 2020–21

Sixth Man of the Year
Jordan Clarkson, guard, 2020–21

Most Improved Player
none

All-NBA First Team
Pete Maravich, 1975–76 (N.O.)
Pete Maravich, 1976–77 (N.O.)
Truck Robinson, 1977–78 (N.O.)
Karl Malone, 1988–89
Karl Malone, 1989–90
Karl Malone, 1990–91
Karl Malone, 1991–92
Karl Malone, 1992–93
Karl Malone, 1993–94
John Stockton, 1993–94
John Stockton, 1994–95
Karl Malone, 1994–95
Karl Malone, 1995–96
Karl Malone, 1996–97
Karl Malone, 1997–98
Karl Malone, 1998–99

All-Defensive First Team
E.C. Coleman, 1976–77 (N.O.)
Mark Eaton, 1984–85
Mark Eaton, 1985–86
Mark Eaton, 1988–89
Karl Malone, 1996–97
Karl Malone, 1997–98
Karl Malone, 1998–99
Andreis Kirilenko, 2005–06

Rudy Gobert, 2016–17
Rudy Gobert, 2017–18
Rudy Gobert, 2018–19
Rudy Gobert, 2019–20
Rudy Gobert, 2020–21

All-Rookie First Team
Darrell Griffith, 1980–81
Thurl Bailey, 1983–84
Karl Malone, 1986–86
Andrei Kirilenko, 2001–02
Deron Williams, 2005–06
Trey Burke, 2013–14
Donovan Mitchell, 2017–18

Coach of the Year
Frank Layden, 1983–84

Hall of Famers Who Played for the Jazz
Walt Bellamy, center, 1974–75 (N.O.)
Adrian Dantley, forward, 1979–86
Gail Goodrich, guard, 1976–79 (N.O.)

Spencer Haywood, forward, 1978–79 (N.O.)

Bernard King, forward, 1979–80

Karl Malone, forward, 1985–2003

Pete Maravich, guard, 1974–80 (N.O.-Uta.)

John Stockton, guard, 1984–2003

Retired Numbers

HH .... Hot Rod Hundley
1 .... Frank Layden
4 .... Adrian Dantley
7 .... Pete Maravich
9 .... Larry Miller
12 .... John Stockton
14 .... Jeff Hornacek
32 .... Karl Malone
35 .... Darrell Griffith
53 .... Mark Eaton
1223 .... Jerry Sloan

League Leaders, Offense

Points

Pete Maravich, 1976–77 (N.O.) ... 2273
Adrian Dantley, 1980–81 2452
Adrian Dantley, 1983–84 2418

Three Pointers

Darrell Griffith, 1983–84 91
Darrell Griffith, 1984–85 92

Assists

John Stockton, 1987–88 1128
John Stockton, 1988–89 1118
John Stockton, 1989–90 1134
John Stockton, 1990–91 1164
John Stockton, 1991–92 1126
John Stockton, 1992–93 987
John Stockton, 1993–94 1031
John Stockton, 1994–95 1011
John Stockton, 1995–96 916

Scoring Average

Pete Maravich, 1976–77 (N.O.) 31.1
Adrian Dantley, 1980–81 .... 30.7
Adrian Dantley, 1983–84 .... 30.6

Field Goal Percentage

Rudy Gobert, 2018–19 .... .669
Rudy Gobert, 2020–21 .... .675
Rudy Gobert, 2021–22 .... .713

Three Point Percentage

Darrell Griffith, 1983–84 .... .361
Kyle Korver, 2009–10 .... .536

Free Throw Percentage

Jeff Hornacek, 1999–00 .... .950

Assists Average

John Stockton, 1987–88 .... 13.8
John Stockton, 1988–89 .... 13.6
John Stockton, 1989–90 .... 14.5
John Stockton, 1990–91 .... 14.2
John Stockton, 1991–92 .... 13.7
John Stockton, 1992–93 .... 12.0
John Stockton, 1993–94 .... 12.6
John Stockton, 1994–95 .... 12.3
John Stockton, 1995–96 .... 11.2

League Leaders, Defense

Offensive Rebounds

Defensive Rebounds

Truck Robinson, 1977–78 (N.O.) 990
Mark Eaton, 1984–85 720
Karl Malone, 1990–91 731
Karl Malone, 1994–95 715
Rudy Gobert, 2020–21 720

Total Rebounds

Truck Robinson, 1977–78 (N.O.) .. 1288
Rudy Gobert, 2019–20 916
Rudy Gobert, 2020–21 960

Steals

Rickey Green, 1982–83 220
Rickey Green, 1983–84 215
John Stockton, 1988–89 263
John Stockton, 1991–92 244

Blocks

Mark Eaton, 1983–84 351
Mark Eaton, 1984–85 456
Mark Eaton, 1986–87 321
Mark Eaton, 1987–88 304
Andrei Kirilenko, 2005–06 220
Rudy Gobert, 2016–17 214
Rudy Gobert, 2020–21 190

Rebounds Average

Truck Robinson, 1977–78 (N.O.) ... 15.7
Rudy Gobert, 2021–22 .... 14.7

Steals Average

Rickey Green, 1983–84 .... 2.7
John Stockton, 1988–89 .... 3.2
John Stockton, 1991–92 .... 3.0

Blocks Average

Mark Eaton, 1983–84 .... 4.3
Mark Eaton, 1984–85 .... 5.6

Mark Eaton, 1986–87 .... 4.1
Mark Eaton, 1987–88 .... 3.7
Andrei Kirilenko, 2004–05 .... 3.3
Rudy Gobert, 2016–17 .... 2.6

Feats

50-Point Game

68 .... Pete Maravich (vs. N.Y. Knicks), Feb. 25, 1977 (N.O.)
61 .... Karl Malone (vs. Mil. Bucks), Jan. 27, 1990
57 .... Adrian Dantley (vs. Chi. Bulls), Dec. 4, 1982
56 .... Karl Malone (@ G.S. Warriors), Apr. 7, 1998
55 ... Adrian Dantley (vs. Den. Nuggets), Feb. 6, 1981
53 ... Adrian Dantley (vs. Den. Nuggets), Apr. 10, 1982
52 .... Karl Malone (@ Cha. Hornets), Dec. 22, 1989
51 .... Pete Maravich (vs. K.C. Kings), Dec. 14, 1976 (N.O.)
51 .... Pete Maravich (@ Pho. Suns), Mar. 18, 1977 (N.O.)
51 ....Truck Robinson (vs. N.J. Nets), Nov. 21, 1978 (N.O.)
51 ... Adrian Dantley (@ Den. Nuggets), Jan. 7, 1981
51 .... Karl Malone (vs. G.S. Warriors), Dec. 9, 1995
50 .... Pete Maravich (vs. Was. Bullets), Dec. 26, 1976 (N.O.)
50 .... Adrian Dantley (vs. L.A. Lakers), Nov. 27, 1979
50 ... Adrian Dantley (vs. Dal. Mavericks), Oct. 31, 1980

20-Assist Game

28 .... John Stockton (vs. S.A. Spurs), Jan. 15, 1991
27 .... John Stockton (@ N.Y. Knicks), Dec. 19, 1989
26 .... John Stockton (vs. Por. Blazers), Apr. 14, 1988
24 .... John Stockton (@ Hou. Rockets), Jan. 3, 1989
23 .... John Stockton (vs. L.A. Lakers), Apr. 12, 1990
23 .... John Stockton (@ L.A. Clippers), Dec. 8, 1990
23 .... John Stockton (vs. G.S. Warriors), Nov. 29, 1991

23...John Stockton (vs. Min. T'Wolves), Apr. 17, 1992

22..........John Stockton (vs. L.A. Lakers), Jan. 8, 1987

22...John Stockton (vs. Cle. Cavaliers), Dec. 11, 1989

22...........John Stockton (@ Phi. 76ers), Dec. 18, 1992

21......... John Stockton (@ L.A. Clippers), Feb. 19, 1988

21......... John Stockton (vs. L.A. Clippers), Feb. 20, 1988

21.......... John Stockton (vs. Pho. Suns), Mar. 22, 1988

21......... John Stockton (@ L.A. Clippers), Apr. 20, 1988

21...........John Stockton (vs. Pho. Suns), Nov. 19, 1988

21......... John Stockton (vs. Den. Nuggets), Feb. 14, 1989

21.......... John Stockton (vs. Por. Blazers), Mar. 1, 1990

21.......... John Stockton (vs. Pho. Suns), Mar. 13, 1990

21... John Stockton (vs. G.S. Warriors), Dec. 11, 1990

21...........John Stockton (@ S.A. Spurs), Apr. 19, 1992

21...Deron Williams (vs. Mem. Grizzlies), Jan. 24, 2007

20.......... Rickey Green (vs. Atl. Hawks), Feb. 14, 1984

20........ John Stockton (@ Den. Nuggets), Mar. 14, 1988

20........ John Stockton (vs. L.A. Clippers), Apr. 12, 1988

20.......... John Stockton (vs. Was. Bullets), Dec. 7, 1988

20... John Stockton (@ Dal. Mavericks), Apr. 21, 1989

20......... John Stockton (@ L.A. Clippers), Feb. 22, 1990

20......... John Stockton (vs. S.A. Spurs), Mar. 3, 1990

20.......... John Stockton (vs. Sea. Sonics), Mar. 15, 1990

20......... John Stockton (@ L.A. Clippers), Mar. 24, 1990

20.......... John Stockton (vs. Sea. Sonics), Apr. 10, 1990

20.......... John Stockton (@ S.A. Spurs), Mar. 11, 1991

20.....John Stockton (vs. Min. T'Wolves), Dec. 28, 1992

20.............John Stockton (@ Pho. Suns), Mar. 6, 1994

20.............John Stockton (vs. Phi. 76ers), Jan. 7, 1995

20.........Deron Williams (vs. Phi. 76ers), Jan. 2, 2008

20...Deron Williams (vs. Dal. Mavericks), Mar. 3, 2008

20...Deron Williams (@ G.S. Warriors), Mar. 1, 2009

30-Rebound Game

8-Steal Game

9...........Rickey Green (vs. Den. Nuggets), Nov. 10, 1982

9............... Rickey Green (@ Phi. 76ers), Nov. 27, 1982

9..........John Stockton (vs. Hou. Rockets), Feb. 12, 1991

8..........Paul Griffin (@ Den. Nuggets), Nov. 9, 1977 (N.O.)

8.......... Rickey Green (@ G.S. Warriors), Dec. 5, 1982

8.......... Rickey Green (vs. Den. Nuggets), Apr. 12, 1983

8.......... John Stockton (@ L.A. Clippers), Feb. 19, 1988

8...........John Stockton (vs. S.A. Spurs), Mar. 5, 1988

8......... John Stockton (@ Dal. Mavericks), Apr. 21, 1989

8.......... John Stockton (vs. Ind. Pacers), Nov. 17, 1989

8.......... John Stockton (vs. Orl. Magic), Nov. 21, 1990

8......... John Stockton (vs. S.A. Spurs), Jan. 15, 1991

8...........John Stockton (vs. Min. T'Wolves), Dec. 3, 1992

8......... John Stockton (@ Por. Blazers), Mar. 2, 1999

8......... Andrei Kirilenko (@ Hou. Rockets), Dec. 3, 2003

8.......... Paul Millsap (vs. Min. T'Wolves), Mar. 15, 2012

10-Block Game

14...Mark Eaton (vs. Por. Blazers), Jan. 18, 1985

14...Mark Eaton (vs. S.A. Spurs), Feb. 18, 1989

13...Mark Eaton (vs. Por. Blazers), Feb. 18, 1983

12...Mark Eaton (@ Den. Nuggets), Feb. 5, 1983

12...Mark Eaton (vs. Dal. Mavericks), Mar. 17, 1984

12...Mark Eaton (@ Dal. Mavericks), Feb. 26, 1985

12...Mark Eaton (vs. Por. Blazers), Nov. 1, 1986

11...Mark Eaton (vs. Ind. Pacers), Jan. 1, 1985

11... Mark Eaton (vs. G.S. Warriors), Mar. 17, 1987

11...Mark Eaton (vs. Phi. 76ers), Dec. 30, 1988

11...Mark Eaton (vs. S.A. Spurs), Jan. 12, 1989

11...Greg Ostertag (vs. Phi. 76ers), Jan. 6, 1998

10... Joe Meriweather (vs. Pho. Suns), Oct. 28, 1977 (N.O.)

10...Ben Poquette (@ Chi. Bulls), Dec. 12, 1980

10...Mark Eaton (@ S.D. Clippers), Nov. 30, 1983

10... Mark Eaton (@ Chi. Bulls), Feb. 21, 1984

10...Mark Eaton (vs. K.C. Kings), Mar. 27, 1984

10... Mark Eaton (vs. S.A. Spurs), Nov. 7, 1984

10...Mark Eaton (@ Dal. Mavericks), Feb. 1, 1985

10...Mark Eaton (@ Por. Blazers), Feb. 5, 1985

10...Mark Eaton (vs. Pho. Suns), Feb. 22, 1986

10... Andrei Kirilenko (vs. Sac. Kings), Mar. 25, 2006

Multiple Triple-Doubles in a Single Season

5.......... Pete Maravich, 1974–75 (N.O.)

4........................ Mark Eaton, 1984–85

2..................Andrei Kirilenko, 2005–06

Postseason Play

1984   Western Conference First Round vs. Den. Nuggets, won (3–2)

Western Conference Semifinals vs.
Pho. Suns, lost (4–2)

1985 Western Conference First Round
vs. Hou. Rockets, won (3–2)
Western Conference Semifinals
vs. Den. Nuggets, lost (4–1)

1986 Western Conference First Round
vs. Dal. Mavericks, lost (3–1)

1987 Western Conference First Round
vs. G.S. Warriors, lost (3–2)

1988 Western Conference First Round
vs. Por. Blazers, won (3–1)
Western Conference Semifinals
vs. L.A. Lakers, lost (4–3)

1989 Western Conference First Round
vs. G.S. Warriors, lost (3–0)

1990 Western Conference First Round
vs. Pho. Suns, lost (3–2)

1991 Western Conference First Round
vs. Pho. Suns, won (3–1)
Western Conference Semifinals
vs. Por. Blazers, lost (4–1)

1992 Western Conference First Round
vs. L.A. Clippers, won (3–2)
Western Conference Semifinals
vs. Sea. Sonics, won (4–1)
Western Conference Finals
vs. Por. Blazers, lost (4–2)

1993 Western Conference First Round
vs. Sea. Sonics, lost (3–2)

1994 Western Conference First Round
vs. S.A. Spurs, won (3–1)
Western Conference Semifinals
vs. Den. Nuggets, won (4–3)
Western Conference Finals
vs. Hou. Rockets, lost (4–1)

1995 Western Conference First Round

vs. Hou. Rockets, lost (3–2)

1996 Western Conference First Round
vs. Por. Blazers, won (3–2)
Western Conference Semifinals
vs. S.A. Spurs, won (4–2)
Western Conference Finals
vs. Sea. Sonics, lost (4–3)

1997 Western Conference First Round
vs. L.A. Clippers, won (3–0)
Western Conference Semifinals
vs. L.A. Lakers, won (4–1)
Western Conference Finals
vs. Hou. Rockets, won (4–2)
NBA Finals vs. Chi. Bulls,
lost (4–2)

1998 Western Conference First Round
vs. Hou. Rockets, won (3–2)
Western Conference Semifinals
vs. S.A. Spurs, won (4–1)
Western Conference Finals
vs. L.A. Lakers, won (4–0)
NBA Finals vs. Chi. Bulls,
lost (4–2)

1999 Western Conference First Round
vs. Sac. Kings, won (3–2)
Western Conference Semifinals
vs. Por. Blazers, lost (4–2)

2000 Western Conference First Round
vs. Sea. Sonics, won (3–2)
Western Conference Semifinals
vs. Por. Blazers, lost (4–1)

2001 Western Conference First Round
vs. Dal. Mavericks, lost (3–2)

2002 Western Conference First Round
vs. Sac. Kings, lost (3–1)

2003 Western Conference First Round
vs. Sac. Kings, lost (4–1)

2007 Western Conference First Round
vs. Hou. Rockets, won (4–3)
Western Conference Semifinals
vs. G.S. Warriors, won (4–1)
Western Conference Finals
vs. S.A. Spurs, lost (4–1)

2008 Western Conference First Round
vs. Hou. Rockets, won (4–2)
Western Conference Semifinals
vs. L.A. Lakers, lost (4–2)

2009 Western Conference First Round
vs. L.A. Lakers, lost (4–1)

2010 Western Conference First Round
vs. Den. Nuggets, won (4–2)
Western Conference Semifinals
vs. L.A. Lakers, lost (4–0)

2012 Western Conference First Round
vs. S.A. Spurs, lost (4–0)

2017 Western Conference First Round
vs. L.A. Clippers, won (4–3)
Western Conference Semifinals
vs. G.S. Warriors, lost (4–0)

2018 Western Conference First Round
vs. Ok.C. Thunder, won (4–2)
Western Conference Semifinals
vs. Hou. Rockets, lost (4–1)

2019 Western Conference First Round
vs. Hou. Rockets, lost (4–1)

2020 Western Conference First Round
vs. Den. Nuggets, lost (4–3)

2021 Western Conference First Round
vs. Mem. Grizzlies, won (4–1)
Western Conference Semifinals
vs. L.A. Clippers, lost (4–2)

2022 Western Conference First Round
vs. Dal. Mavericks, lost (4–2)

3

AMERICAN BASKETBALL ASSOCIATION (ABA)

Kentucky Colonels

Dates of Operation: 1967–76 (9 seasons)
Overall Record: 448 wins, 296 losses (.602)
Arenas: Louisville Convention Center, 1967–70; Freedom Hall, 1970–76

Year-by-Year Finishes

Year	Finish	Wins	Losses	Percentage	Games Behind	Head Coach	Attendance*
				ABA Eastern Division			
1967–68	4th (Tie)	36	42	.462	18.0	John Givens (5–12), Gene Rhodes (31–30)	N/A
1968–69	3rd	42	36	.538	2.0	Gene Rhodes	162,990
1969–70	2nd	45	39	.536	14.0	Gene Rhodes	174,966
1970–71	2nd	44	40	.524	11.0	Gene Rhodes (10–5), Alex Groza (2–0), Frank Ramsey (32–35)	316,601
1971–72	2nd	68	16	.810	+23.0	Joe Mullaney	369,266
1972–73	2nd	56	28	.667	1.0	Joe Mullaney	298,745
1973–74	2nd	53	31	.631	2.0	Babe McCarthy	344,375
1974–75	1st (Tie)	58	26	.690	—	Hubie Brown	375,279
				American Basketball Association			
1975–76	4th	46	38	.548	+14.0	Hubie Brown	292,821

*Attendance totals are unofficial, and numbers include when listed as home team.

Awards

Most Valuable Player
Artis Gilmore, center, 1971–72

Rookie of the Year
Dan Issel, center, 1970–71*
Artis Gilmore, center, 1971–72
*Tied with Charlie Scott, Vir. Squires.

All-ABA First Team
Dan Issel, 1971–72

All-Defensive First Team
Mike Gale, 1972–73
Artis Gilmore, 1972–73

Mike Gale, 1973–74*
Artis Gilmore, 1973–74
Artis Gilmore, 1974–75
Wil Jones, 1974–75
Artis Gilmore, 1975–76
* 48 games with Ken. Colonels and 32 games with N.Y. Nets.

All-Rookie First Team
Louie Dampier, 1967–68
Gene Moore, 1968–69
Dan Issel, 1970–71
Artis Gilmore, 1971–72

Coach of the Year
Babe McCarthy, 1973–74*
*Tied with Joe Mullaney, Uta. Stars.

Hall of Famers Who Played for the Colonels
Louie Dampier, 1967–76
Artis Gilmore, 1971–76
Dan Issel, 1970–75

League Leaders, Offense
Points
Dan Issel, 1970–71 2480
Dan Issel, 1971–72 2538

Dan Issel, 1972–73 2292

Three Pointers

Louie Dampier, 1968–69 199

Louie Dampier, 1969–70 198

Assists

Scoring Average

Dan Issel, 1970–71 .... 29.9

Field Goal Percentage

Artis Gilmore, 1971–72 .... .598

Artis Gilmore, 1972–73 .... .559

Three Point Percentage

Darel Carrier, 1968–69 .... .379

Darel Carrier, 1969–70 .... .375

Louie Dampier, 1973–74 .... .387

Free Throw Percentage

Darel Carrier, 1969–70 .... .892

Assists Average

League Leaders, Defense

Offensive Rebounds

Artis Gilmore, 1972–73 449

Artis Gilmore, 1973–74 478

Artis Gilmore, 1975–76 402

Defensive Rebounds

Artis Gilmore, 1971–72 1070

Artis Gilmore, 1972–73 1027

Artis Gilmore, 1973–74 1060

Artis Gilmore, 1974–75 934

Artis Gilmore, 1975–76 901

Total Rebounds

Artis Gilmore, 1971–72 1491

Artis Gilmore, 1972–73 1476

Artis Gilmore, 1973–74 1538

Artis Gilmore, 1974–75 1361

Artis Gilmore, 1975–76 1303

Steals

Blocks

Artis Gilmore, 1971–72 422

Artis Gilmore, 1972–73 259

Artis Gilmore, 1974–75 258

Rebounds Average

Artis Gilmore, 1971–72 .... 15.5

Artis Gilmore, 1972–73 .... 18.3

Artis Gilmore, 1973–74 .... 17.6

Artis Gilmore, 1975–76 .... 17.8

Steals Average

Blocks Average

Feats

50-Point Game

55...Louie Dampier (@ Dal. Chaparrals), Mar. 7, 1970

54...Louie Damier (vs. Ind. Pacers), Mar. 22, 1968

53...Darel Carrier (@ Mia. Floridians), Nov. 18, 1968

51...........Dan Issel (vs. Car. Cougars), Mar. 28, 1971

51.................Dan Issel (@ Pit. Condors), Mar. 30, 1971

20-Assist Game

30-Rebound Game

40...Artis Gilmore (@ N.Y. Americans), Feb. 3, 1974

33.......... Artis Gilmore (vs. Ind. Pacers), Jan. 3, 1973

30.......... Artis Gilmore (vs. Vir. Squires), Nov. 17, 1971

30... Artis Gilmore (vs. The Floridians), Feb. 19, 1972

30.......... Artis Gilmore (@ Car. Cougars), Nov. 10, 1972

8-Steal Game

10-Block Game

Multiple Triple-Doubles in a Single Season

Postseason Play

1968   Eastern Division Semifinals vs. Min. Muskies, lost (3–2)

1969   Eastern Division Semifinals vs. Ind. Pacers, lost (4–3)

1970   Eastern Division Semifinals vs. N.Y. Nets, won (4–3)

Eastern Division Finals vs. Ind. Pacers, lost (4–1)

1971   Eastern Division Semifinals vs. The Floridians, won (4–2)

Eastern Division Finals vs. Vir. Squires, won (4–2)

ABA Finals vs. Uta. Stars, lost (4–3)

1972   Eastern Division Semifinals vs. N.Y. Nets, lost (4–2)

1973   Eastern Division Semifinals vs. Vir. Squires, won (4–1)

Eastern Division Finals vs. Car. Cougars, won (4–3)

ABA Finals vs. Ind. Pacers, won (4–3)

1974   Eastern Division Semifinals vs. Car. Cougars, won (4–0)

Eastern Division Finals vs. N.Y. Nets, lost (4–0)

1975   Eastern Division Tiebreaker vs. N.Y. Nets, won (1–0)

Eastern Division Semifinals vs. Mem. Sounds, won (4–1)

Eastern Division Finals vs. Spirits of St.L., won (4–1)

ABA Finals vs. Ind. Pacers, won (4–1)

1976   ABA First Round vs. Ind. Pacers, won (2–1)

ABA Semifinals vs. Den. Nuggets, lost (4–3)

Memphis Sounds

Dates of Operation: (as the New Orleans Buccaneers) 1967–70 (3 seasons)
Overall Record: 136 wins, 104 losses (.567)
Arenas: Loyola Field House, 1967–69; Tulane Gym, 1969–70

Dates of Operation: (as the Memphis Sounds) 1970–75 (5 seasons)
Overall Record: 139 wins, 281 losses (.331)
Arena: Mid-South Coliseum, 1970–75
Other Names: Memphis Pros, 1970–72; Memphis Tams, 1972–74

Year-by-Year Finishes

Year	Finish	Wins	Losses	Percentage	Games Behind	Head Coach	Attendance*
				New Orleans Buccaneers **ABA Western Division**			
1967–68	1st	48	30	.615	+2.0	Babe McCarthy	N/A
1968–69	2nd	48	32	.590	14.0	Babe McCarthy	101,957
1969–70	5th	42	42	.500	9.0	Babe McCarthy	113,775
				Memphis Pros			
1970–71	3rd	41	43	.488	17.0	Babe McCarthy	134,554
1971–72	5th	26	58	.310	34.0	Babe McCarthy	173,232
				Memphis Tams **Eastern Division**			
1972–73	5th	24	60	.286	33.0	Bob Bass	139,461
1973–74	5th	21	63	.250	34.0	Butch van Breda Kolff	97,910
				Memphis Sounds			
1974–75	4th	27	57	.321	31.0	Joe Mullaney	162,919

* Attendance totals are unofficial, and numbers include when listed as home team.

Awards

Most Valuable Player
none

Rookie of the Year
none

All-ABA First Team
Doug Moe, 1967–68 (N.O.)
Jimmy Jones, 1968–69 (N.O.)

All-Defensive First Team
none

All-Rookie First Team
Jimmy Jones, 1967–68 (N.O.)
Wendell Ladner, 1970–71 (Pros)
Johnny Neumann, 1971–72 (Pros)

Coach of the Year
none

Hall of Famers Who Played for the Buccaneers/Pros/Tams/Sounds
Roger Brown, 1974–75
Mel Daniels, 1974–75

League Leaders, Offense

Points
Doug Moe, 1967–68 (N.O.)......... 1884

Three Pointers
none

Assists
Larry Brown, 1967–68 (N.O.) 506
Chuck Williams, 1974–75.............. 576

Field Goal Percantage
Jimmy Jones, 1968–69 (N.O.)........ .535

Three Point Percentage
Billy Shepherd, 1974–75............... .420

Free Throw Percentage
George Lehmann*, 1971–72 (Pros) .880
*.839 with Mem. Pros and .897 with Car. Cougars.

Assists Average
Larry Brown, 1967–68 (N.O.) ... 6.5

League Leaders, Defense

Offensive Rebounds
none

Defensive Rebounds
none

Total Rebounds
none

Steals
none

Blocks

Rebounds Average

Steals Average

Blocks Average

Feats

50-Point Game

51.......... Steve Jones, (vs. Ken. Colonels),
Mar. 29, 1971 (Pros)

20-Assist Game

30-Rebound Game

8-Steal Game

10-Block Game

Multiple Triple-Doubles in a Single Season

Postseason Play

1968   Western Division Semifinals
vs. Den. Rockets, won (3–2)

Western Division Finals
vs. Dal. Chaparrals, won (4–1)
ABA Finals vs. Pit. Pipers,
won (4–3)

1969   Western Division Semifinals
vs. Dal. Chaparrals, won (4–3)
Western Division Finals
vs. Oak. Oaks, lost (4–0)

1971   Western Division Semifinals
vs. Ind. Pacers, lost (4–0)

1975   Eastern Division Semifinals
vs. Ken. Colonels, lost (4–1)

Pittsburgh Condors

Dates of Operation: (as the Pittsburgh Condors) 1967–72 (5 seasons)
Overall Record: 180 wins, 228 losses (.441)
Arenas: Pittsburgh Civic Arena, 1967–68; 1969–72; Metropolitan Sports Center, 1968–69
Other Names: Pittsburgh Pipers (1967–68; 1969–70); Minnesota Pipers (1968–69)

Year-by-Year Finishes

Year	Finish	Wins	Losses	Percentage	Games Behind	Head Coach	Attendance*
			Pittsburgh Pipers				
			ABA Eastern Division				
1967–68	1st	54	24	.692	+4.0	Vince Cazzetta	N/A
			Minnesota Pipers				
1968–69	4th	36	42	.462	8.0	Jim Harding (18–8), Vern Mikkelsen (6–6), Jim Harding (2–5), Verl Young (10–23)	86,394
			Pittsburgh Pipers				
1969–70	5th	29	55	.345	30.0	John Clark (14–25), Buddy Jeannette (15–30)	N/A
			Pittsburgh Condors				
1970–71	5th	36	48	.429	19.0	Jack McMahon	104,682
1971–72	6th	25	59	.298	43.0	Jack McMahon (4–6), Mark Binstein (21–53)	79,192

* Attendance totals are unofficial, and numbers include when listed as home team.

Awards

Most Valuable Player
Connie Hawkins, forward, 1967–68 (Pit.)

Rookie of the Year
none

All-ABA First Team
Connie Hawkins, 1967–68 (Pit.)
Connie Hawkins, 1968–69 (Min.)
Charlie Williams, 1967–68 (Pit.)

All-Defensive First Team
none

All-Rookie First Team
Trooper Washington, 1967–68 (Pit.)
John Brisker, 1969–70 (Pit.)

Coach of the Year
Vince Cazzetta, 1967–68 (Pit.)

Hall of Famers Who Played for the Pipers/Condors
Connie Hawkins, 1967–69 (Pit.)

League Leaders, Offense

Points
none

Three Pointers
none

Assists
none

Scoring Average
Connie Hawkins, 1967–68 (Pit.) 26.8

Field Goal Percantage
Trooper Washington, 1967–68 (Pit.).. .524
Trooper Washington*, 1969–70 (Pit.).. .550
*.536 with Pit. Pipers and .566 with L.A. Stars.

Three Point Percentage
none

Free Throw Percentage
none

Assists Average
none

League Leaders, Defense

Offensive Rebounds
Mike Lewis, 1970–71..................... 435

Defensive Rebounds
none

Total Rebounds
none

Blocks
none

Rebounds Average
none

Blocks Average

Feats

50-Point Game

62...Stew Johnson (vs. The Floridians),
Mar. 6, 1971

57...Connie Hawkins, (@ N.Y. Americans),
Nov. 27, 1968 (Min.)

53... Connie Hawkins, (@ Den. Rockets),
Dec. 5, 1968 (Min.)

53...........John Brisker (vs. Ind. Pacers),
Nov. 12, 1970

52......... John Brisker (@ Car. Cougars),
Feb. 5, 1972

50........ John Brisker (@ Tex. Chaparrals),
Nov. 13, 1970

20-Assist Game

30-Rebound Game

10-Block Game

Multiple Triple-Doubles in a Single Season

Postseason Play

1968 Eastern Division Semifinals vs.
Ind. Pacers, won (3–0)
Eastern Division Finals
vs. Min. Muskies, won (4–1)
ABA Finals vs. N.O. Buccaneers,
won (4–3)

1969 Eastern Division Semifinals
vs. Mia. Floridians, won (4–3)

San Diego Sails

Dates of Operation: (as the San Diego Sails) 1972–76 (4 seasons)
Overall Record: 101 wins, 162 loses (.384)
Arenas: Peterson Gym, 1972–73; Golden Hall, 1973–74; San Diego Sports Arena, 1974–76
Other Name: San Diego Conquistadors, 1972–75

Year-by-Year Finishes

Year	Finish	Wins	Losses	Percentage	Games Behind	Head Coach	Attendance*
				San Diego Conquistadors **ABA Western Division**			
1972–73	4th	30	54	.357	25.0	K.C. Jones	94,372
1973–74	4th (Tie)	37	47	.440	14.0	Wilt Chamberlain	95,470
1974–75	5th	31	53	.369	34.0	Alex Groza (15–23), Beryl Shipley (16–30)	107,399
				San Diego Sails			
1975–76**	N/A	3	8	.273	N/A	Bill Musselman	7,126

* Attendance totals are unofficial, and numbers include when listed as home team.

** Franchise folded after 11 games.

Awards

Most Valuable Player
none

Rookie of the Year
none

All-ABA First Team
none

All-Defensive First Team
none

All-Rookie First Team
Bo Lamar, 1973–74 (S.D.)
Mark Olberding, 1975–76*

* 11 games with S.D. Sails and 70 games with S.A. Spurs.

Coach of the Year
none

Hall of Famers Who Played for the Conquistadors/Sails
none

League Leaders, Offense

Points
none

Three Pointers
Bo Lamar, 1973–74 69

Assists
Chuck Williams, 1972–73 582

Scoring Average
none

Field Goal Percantage
none

Three Point Percentage
Simmie Hill, 1972–73 .... .391

Free Throw Percentage
none

Assists Average
Chuck Williams, 1972–73 .... 7.0

League Leaders, Defense

Offensive Rebounds
none

Defensive Rebounds
none

Total Rebounds
none

Steals
none

Blocks
Caldwell Jones, 1973–74 316

Rebounds Average
none

Steals Average
none

Blocks Average
Caldwell Jones, 1973–74 .... 4.0
Caldwell Jones, 1974–75 .... 3.2

Feats

50-Point Game
50 .... Bo Lamar (vs. Ind. Pacers), Jan. 13, 1974

20-Assist Game
none

30-Rebound Game
none

8-Steal Game
none

10-Block Game
12 ..... Caldwell Jones (vs. Car. Cougars), Jan. 6, 1974

Multiple Triple-Doubles in a Single Season
none

Postseason Play

1973   Western Division Semifinals
           vs. Uta. Stars, lost (4–0)

1974   Western Division Tiebreaker
           vs. Den. Rockets, won
           Western Division Semifinals
           vs. Uta. Stars, lost (4–2)

Spirits of St. Louis

Dates of Operation: (as the Houston Mavericks) 1967–69 (2 seasons)
Overall Record: 52 wins, 104 losses (.333)
Arena: Sam Houston Coliseum, 1967–69

Dates of Operation: (as the Carolina Cougars) 1969–74 (5 seasons)
Overall Record: 215 wins, 205 losses (.512)
Arena: Greensboro Coliseum, 1969–74

Dates of Operation: (as the Spirits of St. Louis) 1974–76 (2 seasons)
Overall Record: 67 wins, 101 losses (.399)
Arena: St. Louis Arena, 1974–76

Year-by-Year Finishes

Year	Finish	Wins	Losses	Percentage	Games Behind	Head Coach	Attendance*
				Houston Mavericks **ABA Western Division**			
1967–68	4th	29	49	.372	19.0	Slater Martin	N/A
1968–69	6th	23	55	.295	37.0	Slater Martin (3–9), Jim Weaver (20–46)	41,394
				Carolina Cougars **Eastern Division**			
1969–70	3rd	42	42	.500	17.0	Bones McKinney	249,614
1970–71	6th	34	50	.405	21.0	Bones McKinney (17–25), Jerry Steele (17–25)	242,263
1971–72	5th	35	49	.417	33.0	Tom Meschery	216,945
1972–73	1st	57	27	.679	+1.0	Larry Brown	287,780
1973–74	3rd	47	37	.560	8.0	Larry Brown	247,349
				Spirits of St. Louis			
1974–75	3rd	32	52	.381	26.0	Bob MacKinnon	193,947
				American Basketball Association			
1975–76	6th	35	49	.417	25.0	Rod Thorn (20–27), Joe Mullaney (15–22)	153,560

* Attendance totals are unofficial, and numbers include when listed as home team.

Awards

Most Valuable Player
Billy Cunningham, forward, 1972–73 (Car.)

Rookie of the Year
Marvin Barnes, forward, 1974–75

All-ABA First Team
Bob Verga, 1969–70 (Car.)
Billy Cunningham, 1972–73 (Car.)
Mack Calvin, 1973–74 (Car.)

All-Defensive First Team
Joe Caldwell, 1972–73 (Car.)

Ted McClain, 1973–74 (Car.)

All-Rookie First Team
Dennis Wuycik, 1972–73 (Car.)
Marvin Barnes, 1974–75
Gus Gerard, 1974–75
M.L. Carr, 1975–76

Coach of the Year
Larry Brown, 1972–73 (Car.)

Hall of Famers Who Played for the Mavericks/Cougars/Spirits
Billy Cunningham, 1972–74 (Car.)
Moses Malone, 1975–76

League Leaders, Offense

Points
none

Three Pointers
George Lehmann, 1970–71 (Car.) .. 154

Assists
none

Scoring Average
none

Field Goal Percantage

Three Point Percentage
George Lehmann, 1970–71 (Car.) . .403

Free Throw Percentage
George Lehmann*, 1971–72 (Car.).. .880
*.897 with Car. Cougars and .839 with Mem.
Pros.

Assists Average
none

League Leaders, Defense
Offensive Rebounds
none

Defensive Rebounds
none

Total Rebounds
none

Steals
Billy Cunningham, 1972–73 (Car.) ... 216
Ted McClain, 1973–74 (Car.)......... 250

Blocks
none

Rebounds Average
none

Steals Average
Ted McClain, 1973–74 (Car.)........ 2.98

Blocks Average
none

Feats
50-Point Game
67.............. Larry Miller (vs. Mem. Pros),
    Mar. 18, 1972
56... Joe Caldwell, (vs. Ken. Colonels),
    Feb. 5, 1971 (Car.)
54... Marvin Barnes (vs. Mem. Sounds),
    Mar. 16, 1975

20-Assist Game
none

30-Rebound Game
31... Marvin Barnes, (vs. Mem. Sounds),
    Jan. 8, 1975
30... Marvin Barnes, (vs. S.D. Conquistadors),
    Oct. 29, 1974

8-Steal Game
12... Ted McClain, (vs. N.Y. Americans),
    Dec. 26, 1973 (Car.)

10...Joe Caldwell, (vs. S.D. Conquistadors),
    Dec. 16, 1972 (Car.)
8... Billy Cunningham, (@ Dal. Chaparrals),
    Dec. 4, 1972 (Car.)

10-Block Game
none

Multiple Triple-Doubles in a Single Season
5...... Billy Cunningham, 1972–73 (Car.)

Postseason Play
1968   Western Division Semifinals
            vs. Dal. Chaparrals, lost (3–0)
1970   Eastern Division Semifinals
            vs. Ind. Pacers, lost (4–0)
1973   Eastern Division Semifinals
            vs. N.Y. Nets, won (4–1)
        Eastern Division Finals
            vs. Ken. Colonels, lost (4–3)
1974   Eastern Division Semifinals
            vs. Ken. Colonels, lost (4–0)
1975   Eastern Division Semifinals
            vs. N.Y. Nets, won (4–1)
        Eastern Division Finals
            vs. Ken. Colonels, lost (4–1)

The Floridians

Dates of Operation: (as the Minnesota Muskies) 1967–68 (1 season)
Overall Record: 50 wins, 28 losses (.641)
Arena: Metropolitan Sports Center, 1967–68

Dates of Operation: (as The Floridians) 1968–72 (4 seasons)
Overall Record: 139 wins, 191 losses (.421)
Arena: Miami Beach Convention Hall, 1968–72
Other Name: Miami Floridians, 1968–70

Year-by-Year Finishes

Year	Finish	Wins	Losses	Percentage	Games Behind	Head Coach	Attendance*
Minnesota Muskies							
ABA Eastern Division							
1967–68	2nd	50	28	.641	4.0	Jim Pollard	N/A
Miami Floridians							
1968–69	2nd	43	35	.551	1.0	Jim Pollard	120,908
1969–70	6th	23	61	.274	36.0	Jim Pollard (5–15), Harold Blitman (18–46)	114,129
The Floridians							
1970–71	4th	37	47	.440	18.0	Harold Blitman (18–30), Bob Bass (19–17)	185,075
1971–72	4th	36	48	.429	32.0	Bob Bass (36–48)	88,003

* Attendance totals are unofficial, and numbers include when listed as home team.

Awards

Most Valuable Player
none

Rookie of the Year
Mel Daniels, center, 1967–68 (Min.)

All-ABA First Team
Mel Daniels, 1967–68 (Min.)
Mack Calvin, 1970–71

All-Defensive First Team
none

All-Rookie First Team
Mel Daniels, 1967–68 (Min.)
Samuel Robinson, 1970–71

Coach of the Year
none

Hall of Famers Who Played for the Muskies/The Floridians
Mel Daniels, 1967–68 (Min.)

League Leaders, Offense
Points
none

Three Pointers
none

Assists
none

Scoring Average
none

Field Goal Percentage
none

Three Point Percentage
none

Free Throw Percentage
none

Assists Average
none

League Leaders, Defense
Offensive Rebounds
Mel Daniels, 1967–68 (Min.).......... 502
Skip Thoren, 1968–69 (Mia.).......... 391

Defensive Rebounds
Mel Daniels, 1967–68 (Min.).......... 711

Total Rebounds
Mel Daniels, 1967–68 (Min.)........ 1213

Steals
none

Blocks
none

Rebounds Average
Mel Daniels, 1967–68 (Min.)......... 15.6

Blocks Average
none

Feats
50-Point Game
none

20-Assist Game
none

30-Rebound Game
none

10-Block Game

Multiple Triple-Doubles in a Single Season

Postseason Play

1968 Eastern Division Semifinals
      vs. Ken. Colonels, won (3–2)

Eastern Division Finals
      vs. Pit. Pipers, lost (4–1)

1969 Eastern Division Semifinals
      vs. Min. Pipers, won (4–3)

Eastern Division Finals
      vs. Ind. Pacers, lost (4–1)

1971 Eastern Division Semifinals
      vs. Ken. Colonels, lost (4–2)

1972 Eastern Division Semifinals
      vs. Vir. Squires, lost (4–0)

Utah Stars

Dates of Operation: (as the Anaheim Amigos) 1967–68 (1 season)
Overall Record: 25 wins, 53 losses (.321)
Arena: Anaheim Convention Center, 1967–68

Dates of Operation: (as the Los Angeles Stars) 1968–70 (2 seasons)
Overall Record: 76 wins, 86 losses (.469)
Arena: Los Angeles Memorial Sports Arena, 1968–70

Dates of Operation: (as the Utah Stars) 1970–76 (6 seasons)
Overall Record: 265 wins, 171 losses (.608)
Arena: Salt Palace, 1970–76

Year-by-Year Finishes

Year	Finish	Wins	Losses	Percentage	Games Behind	Head Coach	Attendance*
				Anaheim Amigos **ABA Western Division**			
1967–68	5th	25	53	.321	23.0	Al Brightman (12–24), Harry Dinnel (13–29)	N/A
				Los Angeles Stars			
1968–69	5th	33	45	.423	27.0	Bill Sharman	90,312
1969–70	4th	43	41	.512	8.0	Bill Sharman	68,543
				Utah Stars			
1970–71	2nd	57	27	.679	1.0	Bill Sharman	258,801
1971–72	1st	60	24	.714	+13.0	LaDell Andersen	327,932
1972–73	1st	55	29	.655	+4.0	LaDell Andersen	303,559
1973–74	1st	51	33	.607	+5.0	Joe Mullaney	286,434
1974–75	4th	38	46	.452	27.0	Bucky Buckwalter (24–32), Tom Nissalke (14–14)	313,299
				American Basketball Association			
1975–76**	N/A	4	12	.250	N/A	Tom Nissalke	54,876

* Attendance totals are unofficial, and numbers include when listed as home team.
** Franchise folded after 16 games.

Awards

Most Valuable Player
none

Rookie of the Year
none

All-ABA First Team
Jimmy Jones, 1972–73
Jimmy Jones, 1973–74
Ron Boone, 1974–75

All-Defensive First Team
Willie Wise, 1972–73
Willie Wise, 1973–74

All-Rookie First Team
Larry Miller, 1968–69 (L.A.)
Mack Calvin, 1969–70 (L.A.)
Willie Wise, 1969–70 (L.A.)
Moses Malone, 1974–75

Coach of the Year
Bill Sharman, 1969–70* (L.A.)
Joe Mullaney, 1973–74**
*Tied with Joe Belmont, Den. Rockets.
**Tied with Babe McCarthy, Ken. Colonels.

Hall of Famers Who Played for the Amigos/Stars
Zelmo Beaty, 1970–74
Roger Brown, 1974–75

Moses Malone, 1974–75

League Leaders, Offense
Points
none

Three Pointers
Lester Selvage, 1967–68 (Ana.)...... 147
Glen Combs, 1971–72.................. 103

Assists
none

Scoring Average

Field Goal Percentage

Trooper Washington*, 1969–70
(L.A.) .... .550
Zelmo Beaty, 1970–71 .... .555
*.566 with L.A. Stars and .536 with Pit. Pipers.

Three Point Percentage

Red Robbins, 1971–72 .... .409

Free Throw Percentage

Mike Butler, 1970–71 .... .911
Jimmy Jones, 1973–74 .... .884

Assists Average

League Leaders, Defense

Offensive Rebounds

Moses Malone, 1974–75 455

Defensive Rebounds

Total Rebounds

Steals

Blocks

Rebounds Average

Steals Average

Blocks Average

Feats

50-Point Game

63 .... Zelmo Beaty (vs. Pit. Condors),
Feb. 21, 1972
50 .... Willie Wise (vs. Ken. Colonels),
Feb. 23, 1972

20-Assist Game

22 ... Stephen Chubin (vs. Dal. Chaparrals),
Jan. 14, 1968 (Ana.)

30-Rebound Game

8-Steal Game

10-Block Game

Multiple Triple-Doubles in a Single Season

Postseason Play

1970 Western Division Semifinals
vs. Dal. Chaparrals, won (4–2)
Western Division Finals
vs. Den. Rockets, won (4–1)
ABA Finals vs. Ind. Pacers,
lost (4–2)

1971 Western Division Semifinals
vs. Tex. Chaparrals, won (4–0)
Western Division Finals
vs. Ind. Pacers, won (4–3)
ABA Finals vs. Ken. Colonels,
won (4–3)

1972 Western Division Semifinals
vs. Dal. Chaparrals, won (4–0)
Western Division Finals
vs. Ind. Pacers, lost (4–3)

1973 Western Division Semifinals
vs. S.D. Conquistadors, won (4–0)
Western Division Finals
vs. Ind. Pacers, lost (4–2)

1974 Western Division Semifinals
vs. S.D. Conquistadors, won (4–2)
Western Division Finals
vs. Ind. Pacers, won (4–3)
ABA Finals vs. N.Y. Nets,
lost (4–1)

1975 Western Division Semifinals
vs. Den. Nuggets, lost (4–2)

Virginia Squires

Dates of Operation: (as the Oakland Oaks) 1967–69 (2 seasons)
Overall Record: 82 wins, 74 losses (.526)
Arena: Oakland-Alameda County Coliseum Arena, 1967–69

Dates of Operation: (as the Washington Capitols) 1969–70 (1 season)
Overall Record: 44 wins, 40 losses (.524)
Arena: Uline Arena, 1969–70

Dates of Operation: (as the Virginia Squires) 1970–76 (6 seasons)
Overall Record: 200 wins, 303 losses (.398)
Arenas: Old Dominion University Fieldhouse, 1970–71; Norfolk Scope, 1971–76

Year-by-Year Finishes

Year	Finish	Wins	Losses	Percentage	Games Behind	Head Coach	Attendance*
				Oakland Oaks **ABA Western Division**			
1967–68	6th	22	56	.282	26.0	Bruce Hale	N/A
1968–69	1st	60	18	.769	+14.0	Alex Hannum	111,793
				Washington Capitols			
1969–70	3rd	44	40	.524	7.0	Al Bianchi	87,547
				Virginia Squires **Eastern Division**			
1970–71	1st	55	29	.655	+11.0	Al Bianchi	178,479
1971–72	2nd	45	39	.536	23.0	Al Bianchi	251,093
1972–73	3rd	42	42	.500	15.0	Al Bianchi	261,024
1973–74	4th	28	56	.333	2.0	Al Bianchi	131,808
1974–75	5th	15	69	.179	43.0	Al Bianchi	190,871
				American Basketball Association			
1975–76	7th	15	68	.181	44.5	Al Bianchi (1–6), Mack Calvin (0–6), Bill Musselman (4–22), Jack Ankerson (1–1), Zelmo Beaty (9–33)	194,677

* Attendance totals are unofficial, and numbers include when listed as home team.

Awards

Most Valuable Player
none

Rookie of the Year
Warren Jabali, guard, 1968–69 (Oak.)
Charlie Scott, guard, 1970–71*
Swen Nater**, center , 1973–74
*Tied with Dan Issel, Ken. Colonels.
**17 games with Vir. Squires and 62 games with S.A. Spurs.

All-ABA First Team
Rick Barry, 1968–69 (Oak.)

Rick Barry, 1969–70 (Was.)
Charlie Scott, 1970–71
Julius Erving, 1972–73

All-Defensive First Team
Fatty Taylor, 1972–73
Fatty Taylor, 1973–74

All-Rookie First Team
Warren Jabali, 1968–69 (Oak.)
Mike Barrett, 1969–70 (Was.)
Charlie Scott, 1970–71
Julius Erving, 1971–72
Swen Nater, 1973–74*

Ticky Burden, 1975–76
* 17 games with Vir. Squires and 62 games with S.A. Spurs.

Coach of the Year
Alex Hannum, 1968–69 (Oak.)
Al Bianchi, 1970–71

Hall of Famers Who Played for the Oaks/Capitols/Squires
Rick Barry, 1968–70 (Oak.-Was.)
Julius Erving, 1971–73
George Gervin, 1972–74
Charlie Scott, 1970–72

League Leaders, Offense

Points

Three Pointers

Assists

Larry Brown, 1968–69 (Oak.)......... 544
Larry Brown, 1969–70 (Was.) 580

Scoring Average

Charlie Scott, 1971–72................. 34.6
Julius Erving, 1972–73 .... 31.9

Field Goal Percentage

Swen Nater*, 1973–74.................. .552

* .556 with Vir. Squires and .551 with S.A.
Spurs.

Three Point Percentage

Steve Jones, 1967–68 (Oak.)......... .426

Free Throw Percentage

Rick Barry, 1968–69 (Oak.) .... .888
Mack Calvin, 1975–76 .... .888

Assists Average

Larry Brown, 1968–69 (Oak.).......... 7.1
Larry Brown, 1969–70 (Was.) 7.1

League Leaders, Defense

Offensive Rebounds

Julius Erving, 1971–72 476

Defensive Rebounds

Total Rebounds

Steals

Blocks

Rebounds Average

Steals Average

Blocks Average

Feats

50-Point Game

58... Julius Erving (vs. N.Y. Americans),
Feb. 8, 1973
55........... Rick Barry, (vs. Den. Rockets),
Mar. 1, 1970 (Was.)
50..........Charlie Scott (@ Car. Cougars),
Dec. 29, 1971
50..........Charlie Scott (@ Den. Rockets),
Jan. 23, 1972

20-Assist Game

30-Rebound Game

32...............Ira Harge, (vs. Pit. Pipers),
Feb. 9, 1968 (Oak.)

8-Steal Game

10-Block Game

Multiple Triple-Doubles in a Single Season

2....................... Julius Erving, 1972–73

Postseason Play

1969   Western Division Semifinals
vs. Den. Rockets, won (4–3)
Western Division Finals
vs. N.O. Buccaneers, won (4–0)
ABA Finals vs. Ind. Pacers,
won (4–1)
1970   Western Division Semifinals
vs. Den. Rockets, lost (4–3)
1971   Eastern Division Semifinals
vs. N.Y. Nets, lost (4–2)
Eastern Division Finals
vs. Ken. Colonels, lost (4–2)
1972   Eastern Division Semifinals
vs. The Floridians, won (4–0)
Eastern Division Finals
vs. N.Y. Nets, lost (4–3)
1973   Eastern Division Semifinals
vs. Ken. Colonels, lost (4–1)
1974   Eastern Division Semifinals
vs. N.Y. Nets, lost (4–1)

4

FRANCHISES NO LONGER IN EXISTENCE

Anderson Packers

Dates of Operation: 1949–50 (1 season)
Overall Record: 37 wins, 27 losses (.578)
Arena: Anderson High School Wigwam, 1949–50

Year-by-Year Finishes

Year	Finish	Wins	Losses	Percentage	Games Behind	Head Coach	Attendance
				BAA Western Division			
1949–50	2nd	37	27	.578	2.0	Howie Schultz (21–14), Ike Duffey (1–2), Doxie Moore (15–11)	N/A

Awards

Most Valuable Player
none

Rookie of the Year
none

All-BAA First Team
none

Coach of the Year
none

Hall of Famers Who Played for the Packers
none

League Leaders

Points
none

Assists
none

Scoring Average
none

Field Goal Percantage
none

Free Throw Percentage
none

Assists Average
none

Feats

50-Point Game
none

20-Assist Game
none

Postseason Play

1950   Western Division Semifinals vs. Tri-Cities Blackhawks, won (2–1)
Western Division Finals vs. Ind. Olympians, won (2–1)
NBA Semifinals vs. Min. Lakers, lost (2–0)

Baltimore Bullets

Dates of Operation: 1947–54 (8 seasons)
Overall Record: 158 wins, 292 losses (.351)
Arena: Baltimore Coliseum, 1947–54

Year-by-Year Finishes

Year	Finish	Wins	Losses	Percentage	Games Behind	Head Coach	Attendance
				BAA Western Division			
1947–48	2nd (Tie)	28	20	.583	1.0	Buddy Jeannette	N/A
				Eastern Division			
1948–49	3rd	29	31	.483	9.0	Buddy Jeannette	N/A
				NBA Eastern Division			
1949–50	5th	25	43	.368	28.0	Buddy Jeannette	N/A
1950–51	5th	24	42	.364	16.0	Buddy Jeannette (14–23), Walt Budko (10–19)	N/A
1951–52	5th	20	46	.303	20.0	Fred Scolari (12–27), Chick Reiser (8–19)	N/A
1952–53	4th	16	54	.229	31.0	Chick Reiser (0–3), Clair Bee (16–51)	N/A
1953–54	5th	16	56	.222	28.0	Clair Bee	N/A
1954–55*	-	-	-	-	-	-	-

*Franchise disbanded on November 27, 1954, with a 3–11 record. Official records do not include these games.

Awards

Most Valuable Player
none

Rookie of the Year
Paul Hoffman, guard-forward, 1947–48
Ray Felix, center, 1953–54

All-NBA First Team
none

Coach of the Year
none

Hall of Famers Who Played for the Bullets
Buddy Jeannette, guard, 1947–50
Bob Houbregs, forward-center, 1953–55

League Leaders, Offense

Points
none

Assists
none

Scoring Average
none

Field Goal Percentage
Buddy Jeannette, 1947–48 .... .349

Free Throw Percentage
none

Assists Average
none

League Leaders, Defense

Offensive Rebounds
none

Defensive Rebounds
none

Total Rebounds
none

Feats

50-Point Game
none

20-Assist Game
none

30-Rebound Game
30 .... Ray Felix (@ N.Y. Knicks), Feb. 6, 1954

Postseason Play

1948 BAA Western Division Tiebreaker
vs. Chi. Stags, won
BAA Quarterfinals
vs. N.Y. Knicks, won (2–1)
BAA Semifinals vs. Chi. Stags, won (2–0)
BAA Finals vs. Phi. Warriors, won (4–2)

1949 BAA Eastern Division Semifinals
vs. N.Y. Knicks, lost (2–1)

1953 NBA Eastern Division Semifinals
vs. N.Y. Knicks, lost (2–0)

Chicago Stags

Dates of Operation: 1946–50 (4 seasons)
Overall Record: 145 wins, 92 losses (.612)
Arena: Chicago Stadium, 1946–50

Year-by-Year Finishes

Year	Finish	Wins	Losses	Percentage	Games Behind	Head Coach	Attendance
BAA Western Division							
1946–47	1st	39	22	.639	+1.0	Harold Olsen	N/A
1947–48	2nd (Tie)	28	20	.583	1.0	Harold Olsen	N/A
1948–49	3rd	38	22	.633	7.0	Harold Olsen (28–21), Philip Brownstein (10–1)	N/A
NBA Central Division							
1949–50	3rd (Tie)	40	28	.588	11.0	Philip Brownstein	N/A

Awards

Most Valuable Player
none

Rookie of the Year
none

All-NBA First Team
Max Zaslofsky, 1946–47
Max Zaslofsky, 1947–48
Max Zaslofsky, 1948–49
Max Zaslofsky, 1949–50

Coach of the Year
none

Hall of Famers Who Played for the Stags
Andy Phillip, guard, 1947–50

League Leaders

Points
Max Zaslofsky, 1947–48............. 1007

Assists
none

Scoring Average
none

Field Goal Percantage
none

Free Throw Percentage
Max Zaslofsky, 1949–50............... .843

Assists Average
Andy Phillip, 1949–50.................... 5.8

Feats

50-Point Game
none

20-Assist Game
none

Postseason Play

1947 BAA Semifinals vs. Was. Capitols, won (4–2)
BAA Finals vs. Phi. Warriors, lost (4–1)

1948 BAA Western Division Tiebreaker vs. Bal. Bullets, lost
BAA Western Division Tiebreaker vs. Was. Capitols, won
BAA Quarterfinals vs. Bos. Celtics, won (2–1)
BAA Semifinals vs. Bal. Bullets, lost (2–0)

1949 BAA Western Division Semifinals vs. Min. Lakers, lost (2–0)

1950 NBA Central Division Third Place Tiebreaker vs. Ft.W. Pistons, lost
NBA Central Division Semifinals vs. Min. Lakers, lost (2–0)

Cleveland Rebels

Dates of Operation: 1946–47 (1 season)
Overall Record: 30 wins, 30 losses (.500)
Arena: Cleveland Arena, 1946–47

Year-by-Year Finishes

Year	Finish	Wins	Losses	Percentage	Games Behind	Head Coach	Attendance
				BAA Western Division			
1946–47	3rd	30	30	.500	8.5	Dutch Dehnert (17–20), Roy Clifford (13–10)	N/A

Awards

Most Valuable Player
none

Rookie of the Year
none

All-BAA First Team
none

Coach of the Year
none

Hall of Famers Who Played for the Rebels
none

League Leaders

Points
none

Assists
none

Scoring Average
none

Field Goal Percentage
none

Free Throw Percentage
none

Assists Average
none

Feats

50-Point Game
none

20-Assist Game
none

Postseason Play

1947   BAA Quarterfinals vs. N.Y. Knicks, lost (2–1)

Denver Nuggets

Dates of Operation: 1949–50 (1 season)
Overall Record: 11 wins, 51 losses (.177)
Arena: Denver Auditorium Arena, 1949–50

Year-by-Year Finishes

Year	Finish	Wins	Losses	Percentage	Games Behind	Head Coach	Attendance
				BAA Western Division			
1949–50	6th	11	51	.177	27.0	Jimmy Darden	N/A

Awards

Most Valuable Player
none

Rookie of the Year
none

All-BAA First Team
none

Coach of the Year
none

Hall of Famers Who Played for the Nuggets
none

League Leaders

Points
none

Assists
none

Scoring Average
none

Field Goal Percentage
none

Free Throw Percentage
none

Assists Average
none

Feats

50-Point Game
none

20-Assist Game
none

Postseason Play

Detroit Falcons

Dates of Operation: 1946–47 (1 season)
Overall Record: 20 wins, 40 losses (.333)
Arena: Detroit Olympia, 1946–47

Year-by-Year Finishes

Year	Finish	Wins	Losses	Percentage	Games Behind	Head Coach	Attendance
				BAA Western Division			
1946–47	4th	20	40	.333	18.5	Glenn Curtis (12–22), Philip Sachs (8–18)	N/A

Awards

Most Valuable Player
none

Rookie of the Year
none

All-BAA First Team
Stan Miasek, 1946–47

Coach of the Year
none

Hall of Famers Who Played for the Falcons
none

League Leaders

Points
none

Assists
none

Scoring Average
none

Field Goal Percantage
none

Free Throw Percentage
none

Assists Average
none

Feats

50-Point Game
none

20-Assist Game
none

Postseason Play

Indianapolis Jets

Dates of Operation: 1948–49 (1 season)
Overall Record: 18 wins, 42 losses (.300)
Arena: Hinkle Fieldhouse, 1948–49

Year-by-Year Finishes

Year	Finish	Wins	Losses	Percentage	Games Behind	Head Coach	Attendance
					BAA Western Division		
1948–49	6th	18	42	.300	27.0	Bruce Hale (4–13), Burl Friddle (14–29)	N/A

Awards

Most Valuable Player
none

Rookie of the Year
none

All-BAA First Team
none

Coach of the Year
none

Hall of Famers Who Played for the Jets
none

League Leaders

Points
none

Assists
none

Scoring Average
none

Field Goal Percantage
none

Free Throw Percentage
none

Assists Average
none

Feats

50-Point Game
none

20-Assist Game
none

Postseason Play

Indianapolis Olympians

Dates of Operation: 1949–53 (4 years)
Overall Record: 132 wins, 137 losses (.491)
Arena: Hinkle Fieldhouse, 1949–53

Year-by-Year Finishes

Year	Finish	Wins	Losses	Percentage	Games Behind	Head Coach	Attendance
				NBA Western Division			
1949–50	1st	39	25	.609	+2.0	Cliff Barker	N/A
1950–51	4th	31	37	.456	13.0	Cliff Barker (24–32), Wah Wah Jones (7–5)	N/A
1951–52	3rd	34	32	.515	7.0	Herm Schaefer	N/A
1952–53	4th	28	43	.394	20.5	Herm Schaefer	N/A

Awards

All-NBA First Team
Alex Groza, 1950–51
Ralph Beard, 1951–52

Coach of the Year
none

Hall of Famers Who Played for the Olympians
none

League Leaders, Offense

Points
none

Assists
none

Scoring Average
none

Field Goal Percentage
Alex Groza, 1949–50.................... .478
Alex Groza, 1950–51.................... .474

Free Throw Percentage
none

Assists Average
none

League Leaders, Defense

Offensive Rebounds
none

Defensive Rebounds
none

Total Rebounds
none

Steals
none

Blocks
none

Rebounds Average
none

Steals Average
none

Blocks Average
none

Feats

50-Point Game
none

20-Assist Game
none

30-Rebound Game
none

8-Steal Game
none

10-Block Game
none

Multiple Triple-Doubles in a Single Season
none

Postseason Play

1950   Western Division Semifinals vs. Sheboygan Red Skins, won (2–1)
      Western Division Finals vs. And. Packers, lost (2–1)
1951   Western Division Semifinals vs. Min. Lakers, lost (2–1)
1952   Western Division Semifinals vs. Min. Lakers, lost (2–0)
1953   Western Division Semifinals vs. Min. Lakers, lost (2–0)

Pittsburgh Ironmen

Dates of Operation: 1946–47 (1 season)
Overall Record: 15 wins, 45 losses (.250)
Arena: Duquesne Gardens, 1946–47

Year-by-Year Finishes

Year	Finish	Wins	Losses	Percentage	Games Behind	Head Coach	Attendance
				BAA Western Division			
1946–47	5th	15 wins	45 losses	.250	23.5	Paul Birch	N/A

Awards

Most Valuable Player
none

Rookie of the Year
none

All-BAA First Team
none

Coach of the Year
none

Hall of Famers Who Played for the Ironmen
none

League Leaders

Points
none

Assists
none

Scoring Average
none

Field Goal Percantage
none

Free Throw Percentage
none

Assists Average
none

Feats

50-Point Game
none

20-Assist Game
none

Postseason Play

534

Providence Steamrollers

Dates of Operation: 1946–49 (3 seasons)
Overall Record: 46 wins, 122 losses (.274)
Arena: Rhode Island Auditorium, 1946–49

Year-by-Year Finishes

Year	Finish	Wins	Losses	Percentage	Games Behind	Head Coach	Attendance
				BAA Eastern Division			
1946–47	4th	28	32	.467	21.0	Robert Morris	N/A
1947–48	4th	6	42	.125	21.0	Albert Soar (2–17), Nat Hickey (4–25)	N/A
1948–49	6th	12	48	.200	26.0	Ken Loeffler	N/A

Awards

Most Valuable Player
none

Rookie of the Year
Howie Shannon, guard-forward, 1948–49

All-BAA First Team

Coach of the Year
none

Hall of Famers Who Played for the Steamrollers
none

League Leaders

Points
none

Assists
Ernie Calverley, 1946–47 202

Scoring Average
none

Field Goal Percantage
none

Free Throw Percentage
none

Assists Average
Ernie Calverley, 1946–47 .... 3.4
Ernie Calverley, 1947–48 .... 2.5

Feats

50-Point Game
none

20-Assist Game
none

Postseason Play

Sheboygan Red Skins

Dates of Operation: 1949–50 (1 season)
Overall Record: 22 wins, 40 losses (.355)
Arena: Sheboygan Municipal Auditorium and Armory, 1949–50
Other Name: Redskins

Year-by-Year Finishes

Year	Finish	Wins	Losses	Percentage	Games Behind	Head Coach	Attendance
				NBA Western Division			
1949–50	4th	22	40	.355	16.0	Ken Suesens	N/A

Awards

Most Valuable Player
none

Rookie of the Year
none

All-NBA First Team
none

Coach of the Year
none

Hall of Famers Who Played for the Red Skins
none

League Leaders

Points
none

Assists
none

Scoring Average
none

Field Goal Percantage
none

Free Throw Percentage
none

Assists Average
none

Feats

50-Point Game
none

20-Assist Game
none

Postseason Play

1950   NBA Western Division Semifinals
vs. Ind. Olympians, lost (2–1)

St. Louis Bombers

Dates of Operation: 1946–50 (4 seasons)
Overall Record: 122 wins, 115 losses (.515)
Arena: St. Louis Arena, 1946–50

Year-by-Year Finishes

Year	Finish	Wins	Losses	Percentage	Games Behind	Head Coach	Attendance
BAA Western Division							
1946–47	2nd	38	23	.623	1.0	Ken Loeffler	N/A
1947–48	1st	29	19	.604	+1.0	Ken Loeffler	N/A
1948–49	4th	29	31	.483	16.0	Grady Lewis	N/A
NBA Central Division							
1949–50	5th	26	42	.382	25.0	Grady Lewis	N/A

Awards

Most Valuable Player
none

Rookie of the Year
none

All-NBA First Team
none

Coach of the Year
none

Hall of Famers Who Played for the Bombers
Ed Macauley, center, 1949–50

League Leaders

Points
none

Assists
none

Scoring Average
none

Field Goal Percentage
none

Free Throw Percentage
none

Assists Average
none

Feats

50-Point Game
none

20-Assist Game
none

Postseason Play

1947 BAA Quarterfinals
vs. Phi. Warriors, lost (2–1)

1948 BAA Semifinals vs. Phi. Warriors,
lost (4–3)

1949 BAA Western Division Semifinals
vs. Roc. Royals, lost (2–0)

Toronto Huskies

Dates of Operation: 1946–47 (1 season)
Overall Record: 22 wins, 38 losses (.367)
Arena: Maple Leaf Gardens, 1946–47

Year-by-Year Finishes

Year	Finish	Wins	Losses	Percentage	Games Behind	Head Coach	Attendance
				BAA Eastern Division			
1946–47	5th (Tie)	22	38	.367	27.0	Ed Sadowski (3–9), Lew Hayman (0–1), Dick Fitzgerald (2–1), Robert Rolfe (17–27)	N/A

Awards

Most Valuable Player
none

Rookie of the Year
none

All-BAA First Team
none

Coach of the Year
none

Hall of Famers Who Played for the Huskies
none

League Leaders

Points
none

Assists
none

Scoring Average
none

Field Goal Percantage
none

Free Throw Percentage
none

Assists Average
none

Feats

50-Point Game
none

20-Assist Game
none

Postseason Play

Washington Capitols

Dates of Operation: 1946–51 (5 seasons)
Overall Record: 157 wins, 114 losses (.579)
Arena: Uline Arena, 1946–51

Year-by-Year Finishes

Year	Finish	Wins	Losses	Percentage	Games Behind	Head Coach	Attendance
				BAA Eastern Division			
1946–47	1st	49	11	.817	+14.0	Red Auerbach	N/A
				Western Division			
1947–48	2nd (Tie)	28	20	.583	1.0	Red Auerbach	N/A
				Eastern Division			
1948–49	1st	38	22	.633	+6.0	Red Auerbach	N/A
				NBA Eastern Division			
1949–50	3rd	32	36	.471	21.0	Bob Feerick (32–36)	N/A
1950–51	6th	10	25	.286	14.5	Bones McKinney (10–25)	N/A

Awards

Most Valuable Player
none

Rookie of the Year
none

All-NBA First Team
Bob Feerick, 1946–47
Bones McKinney, 1946–47
Bob Feerick, 1947–48

Coach of the Year
none

Hall of Famers Who Played for the Capitols
Earl Lloyd, forward, 1950–51
Bill Sharman, guard, 1950–51

League Leaders, Offense

Points
none

Assists
none

Scoring Average
none

Field Goal Percentage
Bob Feerick, 1946–47 .... .401

Free Throw Percentage
Fred Scolari, 1946–47 .... .811
Bob Feerick, 1947–48 .... .788
Bob Feerick, 1948–49 .... .859

Assists Average
none

League Leaders, Defense

Offensive Rebounds
none

Defensive Rebounds
none

Total Rebounds
none

Rebounds Average
none

Feats

50-Point Game
none

20-Assist Game
none

30-Rebound Game
none

Multiple Triple-Doubles in a Single Season
none

Postseason Play

1947 BAA Semifinals vs. Chi. Stags, lost (4–2)
1948 BAA Western Division Tiebreaker vs. Chi. Stags, lost
1949 BAA Eastern Division Semifinals vs. Phi. Warriors, won (2–0)
BAA Eastern Division Finals vs. N.Y. Knicks, won (2–1)
BAA Finals vs. Min. Lakers, lost (4–2)
1950 NBA Eastern Division Semifinals vs. N.Y. Knicks, lost (2–0)

Waterloo Hawks

Dates of Operation: 1949–50 (1 season)
Overall Record: 19 wins, 43 losses (.306)
Arena: McElroy Auditorium, 1949–50

Year-by-Year Finishes

Year	Finish	Wins	Losses	Percentage	Games Behind	Head Coach	Attendance
					NBA Western Division		
1949–50	5th	19	43	.306	19.0	Charley Shipp (8.27), Jack Smiley (11–16)	N/A

Awards

Most Valuable Player
none

Rookie of the Year
none

All-NBA First Team
none

Coach of the Year
none

Hall of Famers Who Played for the Hawks
none

League Leaders

Points
none

Assists
none

Scoring Average
none

Field Goal Percantage
none

Free Throw Percentage
none

Assists Average
none

Feats

50-Point Game
none

20-Assist Game
none

Postseason Play

ACKNOWLEDGMENTS

Below are several of the people who were instrumental in helping make *The Basketball Maniac's Almanac* come to fruition.

Bert Randolph Sugar. The original editor and compiler of *The Baseball Maniac's Almanac* and a multi-time Hall of Famer, his spirit and sly grin were always at the forefront of this project. Although he passed away away in 2012, we hope that he would be proud of this work.

Mark Weinstin. The original in-house editor of *The Baseball Maniac's Almanac* and longtime book editor, Mark's guidance and advice over the years—from before a single category was comiled to the very end stages—helped make this project into a reality.

Ken Samelson. The editor of *The Macmillan Baseball Encylopedia* and longtime book editor, Ken not only offered guidance during the early stages of this project, but also handled the proofreading and fact checking responsibilities. A sports savant, he was instrumental in helping with the minutia of this project, from the small details to overall formatting. Without his keen eye and insight, this would be a shell of the book that you currently hold in your hands.

Tony Lyons. The president and publisher of Skyhorse Publishing, Mr. Lyons had unwavering faith in this project, and offered immense patience in the time and effort that went into this work, spanning almost two years. His continual support of the Sports Publishing imprint has helped it grow exponentially, offering authors and athletes alike the opportuinity to share their incredible lives and stories.

Julie Ganz. Editorial director for Sports Publishing, Julie, with her calm demeanor and support, helped during the long days and nights that it took to finish this tome.

Kirsten Dalley. Senior production editor for Skyhorse Publishing, Kirsten was responsible for facilitating between the editorial and production ends of this project. Her time and patience helped make sure that this book was successful in matching its original vision, while not letting any small detail fall through the cracks.

Todd Radom and Chris Creamer. Authors of *Fabric of the Game*, Radom (writer, sports historian, graphic designer, and sports branding expert) and Creamer (writer, sports historian, and editor of sportslogos.net) were able to offer feedback and ideas during the early stages of this project. They may also be the only two people who are able to have a rousing conversation about the Indianapolis Olympians.

Additional acknowledgment goes out to the many people who offered advice and assistance throughout the process, including Dean Notte and Daniel Flancraich, to name a few.

The Katzman family (Barry, Harriet, Stushey, Jordan, and Mia) and Sauli family (George, Barbara, Matthew, Samantha, Dominick, and Giuliana), as well as Michelle Sauli-Katzman. Family, friends, and duprass, their continued support—especially throughout the several years that it took to create and finish this project—helped during the long nights and struggles to compile the necessary data included herein. None of this would have been possible if not for them.

—Jason Katzman, Senior Editor, Sports Publishing

OTHER GREAT BASKETBALL TRIVIA BOOKS
FROM SPORTS PUBLISHING

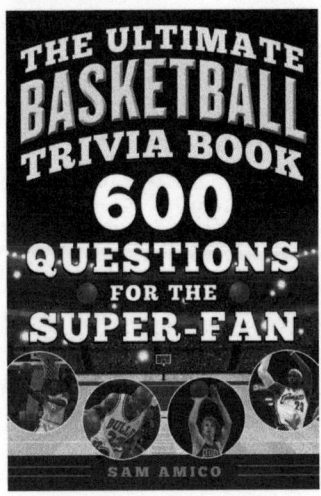

The Ultimate Basketball Trivia Book
600 Questions for the Super-Fan
by Sam Amico

In this collection of 600 questions, Sam Amico tests your level of expertise on all things basketball. Every era of basketball history is represented, from Bob Cousy to Chris Paul, Moses Malone to Joel Embiid, Michael Jordan to LeBron James, Wilt Chamberlain to Shaquille O'Neal, and everyone in between. Some of the many questions that Amico poses include:

- Who was the inventor of the game of basketball (called "Basket Ball") and how many original rules were written by the game's founder?
- What player scored the most points in an NCAA Tournament Game?
- Who was the first international player to be inducted into the Hall of Fame?
- Can you name the four ABA teams that joined the NBA in 1976?

From the Celtics dynasty to the most exciting Final Four games of all time, from Magic Johnson and Larry Bird to Stephen Curry and James Harden, here is the definitive test for knowledgeable basketball fans!

$14.99 Paperback · ISBN 978-1-68358-308-0

OTHER GREAT BASKETBALL TRIVIA BOOKS FROM SPORTS PUBLISHING

You're the Basketball Ref
Mind-Boggling Questions to Test Your Basketball Knowledge
by Wayne Stewart

Do you think you know basketball? Do you think you know it well enough to take the court as an NBA or NCAA referee and accurately make the really tough calls? Well, here's your chance to prove how much you really know about the history and rules of one of the world's most popular sports.

You're the Basketball Ref, newly updated with a dozen fresh scenarios, is designed to inform, challenge, and entertain basketball fans. A brief introduction to the history of basketball is followed by an overview of NBA and NCAA matters. Topics range from situations that typically come up in games—traveling and shot clock violations, for example—to rules that are just a bit more unusual or, for the casual fan, more obscure. Then quiz yourself on what call you would make in each scenario!

$12.99 Paperback · ISBN 978-1-5107-4333-5